MW00967549

THE McGRAW-HILL
DIRECTORY OF MANAGEMENT FACULTY
1994–1995

COMPILED BY

JAMES R. HASSELBACK

Florida State University

McGRAW-HILL, INC.

New York   St. Louis   San Francisco   Auckland   Bogotá   Caracas   Lisbon
London   Madrid   Mexico City   Milan   Montreal   New Delhi
San Juan   Singapore   Sydney   Tokyo   Toronto

The McGraw-Hill Directory of Management Faculty, 1994–1995

1 2 3 4 5 6 7 8 9 0   DOC/DOC   9 0 9 8 7 6 5 4

ISBN 0-07-027018-X

The editor was Lynn Richardson;
the production supervisor was Louise Karam.
R. R. Donnelley & Sons Company was printer and binder.

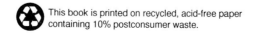

JAMES R. HASSELBACK

James R. Hasselback is a Professor of Taxation at Florida State University and has previously taught at Eastern Michigan University, the University of Florida, and Texas A&M University. He received his PhD in Accounting from Michigan State University. A member of the American Accounting Association and the American Taxation Association, he has published over 120 papers in professional and academic journals, including THE ACCOUNTING REVIEW, THE TAX ADVISER, FINANCIAL MANAGMENT, JOURNAL OF REAL ESTATE TAXATION, and the AMERICAN BUSINESS LAW JOURNAL.

Dr. Hasselback has presented papers at numerous national and regional professional meetings, and served as chairman at tax sessions of professional conferences. He regularly presents continuing education seminars for Certified Public Accountants. He is co-author on a two-volume introductory taxation textbook published by Commerce Clearing House, serving as technical editor on the second volume. Jim teaches in Florida State University's CPA Review Course.

Jim Hasselback has compiled an Accounting Faculty Directory published by Prentice Hall for the past twenty years. The ACCOUNTING FACULTY DIRECTORY may be the most cited reference in the Accounting field. In addition to the McGraw-Hill Directory of Management Faculty, other Directories in the business field include: a Directory of Finance Faculty, a Directory of Marketing Faculty, a Directory of Economics Faculty, and a Directory of Business Law Faculty. An Engineering Faculty Directory, published in November 1992, was his first venture in preparing a Directory outside of the business area. A Directory of Computer Science Faculty was published in March 1994. Work has begun on directories in other fields including Biology, Chemistry, Physics, Criminal Justice, and Nursing.

Welcome to the fourth annual edition of the McGraw-Hill Directory of Management Faculty. As our best-selling texts serve you and your students in the classroom, this directory of management faculty at four-year schools is especially designed to give you easier access to your colleagues across the country and to serve as your one central reference to the entire McGraw-Hill management list. This edition includes a separate section on Foreign Management Faculty from Great Britain, Australia, New Zealand, Japan, and Israel.

Our thanks to James R. Hasselback, Florida State University, for joining the McGraw-Hill team to compile this directory. It is published as a free annual edition. Over 800 domestic and international schools were polled by mail and phone. Please send any corrections, additions, and deletions directly to Professor Hasselback whose mailing information is on the first page of the directory following the catalog of McGraw-Hill management titles.

As that catalog reveals, McGraw-Hill is committed to creating a broad spectrum of educational materials to meet the needs of today's and tomorrow's students. McGraw-Hill has been at the forefront of the publishing industry for more than a century, and we will continue to set the standard for innovation and customer satisfaction for the 1990s and the next century.

To that end, McGraw-Hill is proud to maintain a vibrant cross-publishing venture with the Harvard Business Press. In addition, we are leading the industry in the customization of course materials with Primis, our electronic just-in-time publishing system. With Primis, you can construct the perfect text for your classes from our vast collection of text and case material in HRM, P/OM, strategic management, principles of management and, beginning in 1995, organizational behavior. Other current content options include articles from Business Week and The Harvard Business Review, and cases from the NACRA Case Research Journal, and Pinnacle, McGraw-Hill's strategic management case study database.

We hope you will make good use of this directory and that through your classroom feedback on our texts, manuscript ideas shared with us, and adoption of McGraw-Hill textbooks, you will continue to be part of our growth. For your reference the last page of this directory supplies you with a punch-out Rolodex card with McGraw-Hill Customer Service, Editorial, and Marketing Department addresses and phone numbers.

Lynn Richardson
Senior Management Editor
San Francisco, CA

Daniel M. Loch
Senior Marketing Manager
New York, NY

CATALOG TABLE OF CONTENTS

MANAGEMENT FACULTY DIRECTORY TABLE OF CONTENTS

BUILD YOUR
OWN IDEAL
ORGANIZATION!

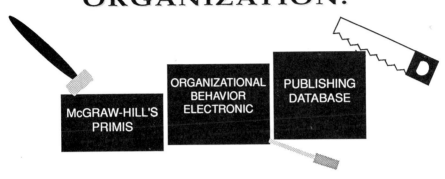

Coming to your OB classroom in 1995 will be McGraw-Hill's Primis electronic publishing database of organizational behavior text modules, case studies, exercises, <u>Business Week</u> and <u>Harvard Business Review</u> articles, and other teaching materials. McGraw-Hill is the industry leader in maximizing the customization option for your classroom.

Beginning in 1995 you will be able to build a textbook specific to each class you teach. Create your own ideal organizational behavior text-just the way you want it organized. With Primis you determine the length, coverage, and sequence of topics, and your students no longer need to buy materials they do not use in your course. With an initial database of more than 100 cases, articles, and text chapters, and the continuous addition of material, you will have an abundance of material to which to choose. Just-in-Time manufacturing techniques assure you of rapid, dependable delivery and text availability because there are no minimum order requirements, no out-of-stocks and no out-of-prints.

OB on

Pinnacle Management Case Studies on Primis

■ **THE MOST POPULAR CASES FROM BEST SELLING STRATEGY & POLICY TEXTBOOKS** Selected by a blue ribbon panel led by Marilyn Taylor of the University of Kansas, an authority in Case Methods. New cases are added on a continuous basis.

■ **THE BEST-SELLING HARVARD BUSINESS SCHOOL CASES**
Vividly capturing the realities of business and encouraging students to play an active role in the learning process.

■ **CASES FROM THE NORTH AMERICAN CASE RESEARCH ASSOCIATION (NACRA)** Cases are available on an ongoing basis. Some of the cases are from the quarterly **CASE RESEARCH JOURNAL** which is printed and distributed by Primis.

■ **HARVARD BUSINESS REVIEW ARTICLES**
Blending research with practice on a wide variety of business topics and challenging conventional wisdom with fresh approaches to business problems as seen from the perspective of the general manager.

■ **CHAPTERS AND CASES FROM *STRATEGIC MANAGEMENT* BY DESS MILLER, 1993** "Executive Interviews" allow students to experience first-hand, the real world issues and challenges faced by executives. These interviews are in addition to a sound treatment of all the basics and in-depth integrated coverage encouraged by the AACSB, such as global competition, social responsibility, and entrepreneurship.

■ **TEACHING NOTES OF THE HIGHEST QUALITY**
Offering extensive and elaborate analysis of each case, including: a listing of the issues involved; teaching tips based on actual classroom experience; suggestions for student preparation; outside reading selections, and notes on more advanced topics related to the case for use in challenging your students.

TITLE: PC CASE, 2/e

AUTHOR: Dan **Baugher** (Pace University)/Andrew **Varonelli** (Pace University)

◆ 841249-8 (IBM, 5.25")	◆ Student Disk & 96 pp. Manual	◆ Publication: 02/15/95
◆ 841250-1 (IBM, 3.50")	◆ Student Disk & 96 pp. Manual	◆ Publication: 02/15/95

■ **DESCRIPTION**

Designed to provide a unique, comprehensive, experiential learning exercise for the student, this user-friendly software program with accompanying manual updates the popular three case studies from the first edition while adding a new behaviorally-oriented case. Students take on the role of decision maker in a variety of general business settings. The software program has been rewritten to exploit color and graphics, enhancing its attractiveness for students.

■ **DISTINCTIONS**

◆ Within **four interactive cases** students are empowered with the role of decision maker.

◆ Cases support a specific set of **learning objectives**.

◆ Designed for the introduction to business or principles of management markets, it will especially appeal to those who want a stronger **experiential flavor** in their course.

◆ Each case is supported by a theoretical introduction to the issues as well as a brief **summary of the issues** facing the firm under consideration.

■ **NEW TO THIS EDITION**

◆ Programs have been **rewritten to exploit color and graphics** as well as to become more user-friendly for both students and faculty.

◆ First edition cases changed so that **prior answers are no longer correct** and previous adopters can use the cases with no concern students already have the answers. Instructors also now have the **option to change each program's parameters** so case answers can vary from semester to semester.

TITLE: **PC CASE, 2/e**

AUTHOR: Dan **Baugher** (Pace University)/Andrew **Varonelli** (Pace University)

CASE LIST:
1. THE VISTA COMPANY-- Evaluating industry attractiveness and business strengths and weakne
2. KRIL INDUSTRIES-- Organizing using the life-cycle theory of leadership.
3. RIVERSIDE MANUFACTURING COMPANY-- "What if" sensitivity analysis.
4. MOTIVATION/HUMAN RESOURCE CASE-- Using equity theory to make compensation deci

■ **SUPPLEMENTS**
   Instructor's Solutions Manual (841251-X)

TITLE: QUALITY: FROM CUSTOMER NEEDS TO CUSTOMER SATISFACTION

AUTHOR: Bo **Bergman** (Linkoping University, Sweeden)/Bengt **Klefsjo** (Lulea University, Sweeden)

♦ 709016-0   ♦ Softcover   ♦ 478 pages   ♦ Publication: 09/30/94

■ **DESCRIPTION**

Aimed at teaching TQM in Business and Engineering Schools and in private industry courses, this new text shows how to use the quality improvement process during all steps of a product life cycle, from customer needs to customer satisfaction, as well as in the support processes of an organization. The authors describe philosophies as well as methods and techniques, the history as well as the future, planning and development as well as manufacturing, and quality for services as well as for goods.

■ **DISTINCTIONS**

♦ **Comprehensive:** Up-to-date, comprehensive review of Total Quality Management philosophies and techniques.

♦ **Up-to-date treatment of current industry topics:** quality in the supply process, service quality, customer satisfaction (formation, measurement, commitment), and leadership for quality (improvement programs, company assessments, quality awards, learning organizations, etc.)

♦ **Links quality** with the market, productivity, logistics, and investments in a win-win strategy.

♦ **Reviews the history of TQM:** Shewhart, WW II, statistical quality control, Deming, Juran, Japan, etc.

♦ **Student-friendly format:** All material presented in an easy-to-read style.

♦ **Twelve chapter treatment of the quantitative aspects of quality:** reliability analysis, design of experiments, robust design and Taguchi's philosophy, statistical process control, control charts, etc.

♦ **Appendix of Basic Statistics:** Appendix A, "Basic Concepts in Statistics," provides a handy refresher on the basics of statistics (random variation and probability) for students.

■ TITLE: QUALITY: FROM CUSTOMER NEEDS TO CUSTOMER SATISFACTION

■ AUTHOR: Bo Bergman (Linkoping University, Sweeden)/Bengt Klefsjo (Lulea
University, Sweeden)

TABLE OF CONTENTS:

■ SUPPLEMENTS: None

TITLE: CORRELATION AND REGRESSION: PRINCIPLES AND
APPLICATIONS IN INDUSTRIAL/ORGANIZATIONAL
PSYCHOLOGY AND MANAGEMENT

AUTHOR: Philip **Bobko** (Rutgers University)

♦ 006223-4   ♦ Cloth   ♦ 448 pages   ♦ Publication: 09/16/94

■ DESCRIPTION

Intended for a second statistics course taken by advanced undergraduates or by masters and doctoral students in business administration and the social sciences, this new text makes correlation and regression accessible to the student. The goal is practical, the style is conversational, the technique is common-sensical, and the underlying philosophy recognizes that the application of correlation and regression techniques is often messy and not necessarily straightforward. A wealth of applied real-world examples from a variety of fields explains how statistical techniques work and demonstrate under what circumstances some creativity and critical-thinking is necessary.

■ DISTINCTIONS

♦ **Spiraling structure:** Each chapter begins with some basic concepts in statistical technique, then continuously builds upon those concepts in increasing detail.

♦ **Conversational,** informal writing style: Difficult concepts are presented accessibly without loss of precision or statistical rigor.

♦ **Chapter-length applications of statistical techniques:** Ch. 4 on applying Correlations to measurement and Ch. 7 on utility analysis, regression to the mean, and partial correlation

♦ Focuses on **critical thinking** as techniques are applied through the use of examples and applications drawn from research and real-world experience.

♦ Expanded explanations of **interactions in regression** (ch. 9) and the **effects of range restriction** (ch. 5), two important topics not usually covered in regression texts.

♦ Discusses **unexpected idiosyncrasies, problems, and pitfalls** that may occur when statistical techniques are applied in social science research; for example, properties of the correlation coefficient in ch. 2 and validity shrinkage in ch. 10.

♦ **Fully worked-out examples and exercises** throughout text

♦ **Numerous problems** and thought-provoking questions are included which test students' understanding of not only the concepts, but how to apply them.

■ TITLE: CORRELATION AND REGRESSION: PRINCIPLES AND APPLICATIONS IN INDUSTRIAL/ORGANIZATIONAL PSYCHOLOGY AND MANAGEMENT

■ AUTHOR: Philip Bobko (Rutgers University)

TABLE OF CONTENTS:

■ SUPPLEMENTS:
Instructor's Manual (006244-2)

TITLE: BUSINESS COMMUNICATION TODAY, 4/e

AUTHOR: Courtland L. **Bovee** (Grossmont College)/John V. **Thill** (President, Communication
   Specialists of America)

♦ 006876-3   ♦ Cloth   ♦ 768 pages   ♦ Publication: 08/05/94

■ **DESCRIPTION**
   Business Communication Today has become the number-one selling text in the field because it
   emphasizes real-life business situations and employs a lively, conversational style to
   capture the dynamics of business communication. It teaches business communication skills,
   and carefully examines communication techniques. Its chapter openers feature real
   companies, and its real-world examples, real-company cases, and involving writing style,
   all bring the subject to life. In the fourth edition the technology and intercultural
   chapters have been heavily revised and brought forward to the start of the book, two-thirds
   of the chapter opening vignettes are new, and greater emphasis is placed on the writing
   process and audience-centered messages   Half of the memo- and letter writing cases are new
   and each is now categorized by academic discipline (e.g., finance, management, accounting,
   etc.) and by the focus of the exercise to emphasize writing across the curriculum.

■ **DISTINCTIONS**
   ♦ "Communication Close-Ups" begin and "Communication Challenges" end each chapter and apply
      the chapter concepts to common business situations and give the students "on the job"
      practice.

   ♦ **39 special boxed features** are strategically placed within each chapter to extend the
      chapter material. Boxes center on four themes: Sharpen Your Skills, Business
      Communication Notebook, Focus on Ethics and Law, and International Outlook.

   ♦ **Exercises (199) and cases (151)** are based on **real companies** such as Xerox, Yamaha, and
      Haagen-Dazs to provide assignments like those that students will most often face at work.

■ **NEW TO THIS EDITION**
   ♦ **Intercultural Communication, now chapter 3,** allows the early introduction of major
      concepts to build on in later chapters, and expands coverage of cultural diversity in the
      U.S. work force.

   ♦ **Communicating Through Technology, now chapter 4,** has been completely rewritten and
      emphasizes how technology affects communication.

   ♦ **NEW: Two-thirds of the chapter opening vignettes** are new, spotlighting companies such as
      Turner Broadcasting, The Nature Company, and Eastman/Kodak.

   ♦ **NEW: 50% of the memo- and letter-writing cases** are new. Each is now categorized by
      academic discipline (e.g., finance, management, accounting, etc.) and by the focus of the
      exercise to emphasize writing across the curriculum.

   ♦ Greater emphasis on **the writing process and audience-centered messages.**

■ TITLE: BUSINESS COMMUNICATION TODAY, 4/e

■ AUTHOR: Courtland L. Bovee (Grossmont College)/John V. Thill (Communication Specialists of America)

TABLE OF CONTENTS:

SUPPLEMENTS:
  Student Study Guide
  Instructor's Manual (006877-1)
  Test Bank (006878-X)
  Computerized Test Bank, IBM, 5-1/4" (840734-6)
  Computerized Test Bank, IBM, 3-1/2" (840735-4)
  Computerized Test Bank MAC
  Report Card Classroom Management Software, IBM, 5-1/4" (553991-8)
  Toll-Free Customized Test Service (1-800/888-EXAM, or FAX 1-404/373-4110)
  Overhead Transparencies (074761-X)
  Video Exercises (911737-6)
  Activities in Business Communication, 2e Software, IBM, 5-1/4" (835417-X)

TITLE: MANAGING HUMAN RESOURCES: Productivity, Quality of
Life, Profits, 4/e

AUTHOR: Wayne Cascio (University of Colorado, Denver)

♦ 011154-5   ♦ Cloth   ♦ 704 pages   ♦ Publication: 10/28/94

■ **DESCRIPTION**
   In his new fourth edition Cascio addresses the latest HRM challenges and trends with the
   addition of an new chapter on workplace diversity, and increased attention to total quality
   management. One of the first books to direct itself to a broad audience of general
   management students, this edition retains a conceptual framework based on three outcome
   variables: productivity, quality of work life, and profits. The book interweaves theory
   and research with practical business applications. A key competitive advantage of the book
   is its attention to the costs and benefits of HRM activities and decisions, covered in both
   a full chapter and in examples throughout the text. The author, a leading HRM scholar, has
   thoroughly integrated the latest theoretical developments and research throughout the book.

■ **DISTINCTIONS**
   ♦ **Approach:** comprehensive, in-depth coverage of all major HRM topics geared to the general
     management student (vs the HRM specialist); emphasizes the strategic use of the human
     resource management function with an emphasis on cost/benefit aspects of HR practice
     unprecedented in any other text.

   ♦ **Current Examples:** a broad range of current examples, focusing upon real people in real
     organizations (both large and small).

   ♦ **Critical-Thinking:** A different **split-sequential case,** called "Human Resource Management
     in Action," starts each chapter. Events lead to a climax, the case stops, and the reader
     is asked to predict the outcome and impact; conclusions are presented at chapter end.

   ♦ **Explicit Applications:** "Questions That This Chapter Will Help Managers Answer" sections
     provide links to actual managerial practice and "Implications for Management Practice"
     sections provide concrete, no-nonsense advice on how to manage the issues.

■ **NEW TO THIS EDITION**
   ♦ **NEW CHAPTER:** a full, early chapter on **workplace diversity** (ch. 3) with examples from
     Xerox, Pacific Bell, J.C. Penny and other companies.

   ♦ **NEW** coverage of legal environment: thoroughly updated to include changes in laws, court
     rulings, and implications for HR practice, such as job analysis under the Americans with
     Disabilities Act.

   ♦ **NEW "Ethical Dilemma" sections** in each chapter require students to choose a course of
     action and defend their reasons for so choosing.

   ♦ **NEW** topics include: new organizational forms, Total Quality Management, downsizing,
     corporate culture, firm performance, strategic partnership, diversity-oriented
     recruiting, job search strategies, impact of organizational strategy and culture on
     staffing, training trends, TQM and performance appraisal, meaning of career success in
     the 1990s, dual-career couples, mentoring, plateaued workers, "at risk" forms of pay,
     market-based pay, skill/knowledge-based pay, strategic use of severance pay, controlling
     workers' compensation and health care costs, employee voice systems, final-offer
     arbitration, fair information practices, violence at work, updated treatment of AIDS,
     globalization as a growth strategy, implications of NAFTA for HR practices, cultural
     differences among IBMers worldwide, and pros and cons of working for a foreign-owned
     company in the U.S.

■ TITLE: MANAGING HUMAN RESOURCES: Productivity, Quality of Work
Life, Profits, 4/e

■ AUTHOR: Wayne Cascio (University of Colorado, Denver)

TABLE OF CONTENTS:

SUPPLEMENTS:
Instructor's Manual/Test Bank (011156-1)
Student Study Guide with Additional Cases
Computerized Test Bank, IBM, 5-1/4" (840929-2)
Computerized Test Bank, IBM, 3-1/2" (840930-6)
Overhead Transparency Acetates (074772-5)
Video Series and Video Guide, 1 VHS videocassette (911791-0)
Annual McGraw-Hill HRM Update (011153-3)

TITLE: THE MCGRAW-HILL DIRECTORY OF MANAGEMENT FACULTY,
1994-1995 EDITION

AUTHOR: James R. Hasselback (Florida State University)

♦ 027018-X   ♦ Paperback   ♦ 352 pages   ♦ Publication: 07/30/94

■ DESCRIPTION

Compiled and updated by James R. Hasselback, the fourth annual *McGraw-Hill Directory of Management Faculty* is the only complete listing of all four-year college and university management faculty in the United States and Canada. The directory lists more than 10,000 individuals representing more than 800 schools. Many countries outside of North America are also represented, including Great Britain, Australia, New Zealand, Japan, and Israel. The directory, published as a free service to the management field, is an invaluable resource for all professors of management. The first 40 pages of the directory feature a complete catalog of all management textbooks available from McGraw-Hill.

■ DISTINCTIONS

♦ Free annual edition appearing in early August of all management faculty.

♦ 96% response rate from survey done by mail and phone of over 800 four-year school management departments in the US and Canada.

♦ First 40 pages are a catalog of all management titles available from McGraw-Hill.

♦ Organized by school, then alphabetically by last name; gives for each professor: title, degree, start year at school, research area, teaching area.

♦ Corrections, additions, deletions are to be sent directly to Professor Hasselback, College of Business R-53A, Florida State University, Tallahassee, FL 32306-1042, Phone/Fax/Recorder 904/644-7884.

■ NEW TO THIS EDITION

♦ Some faculty from outside North America are represented, including individuals from Great Britain, Australia, New Zealand, Japan, and Israel.

TITLE: **THE MCGRAW-HILL DIRECTORY OF MANAGEMENT FACULTY, 1994-1995 EDITION**

AUTHOR: James R. Hasselback (Florida State University)

TABLE OF CONTENTS

Catalog of McGraw-Hill Management Titles
1. 1995 Titles in Management
2. Backlist Titles in Management

Management Faculty Directory
1. Explanation of Directory Abbreviations
2. Listing of Schools Represented
3. USA Management Faculty Directory (alphabetical by school)
4. Canadian Management Faculty (alphabetical by school)
5. Other Foreign Management Faculty (alphabetical by school)
6. All Management Faculty (alphabetical by individual)
7. McGraw-Hill College Publishing Customer Service Rolodex Card

SUPPLEMENTS: None

TITLE: ORGANIZATIONAL BEHAVIOR, 7/e

AUTHOR: Fred Luthans (University of Nebraska)

♦ 039180-7   ♦ Cloth   ♦ 656 pages   ♦ Publication: 08/26/94

■ **DESCRIPTION**

Featuring comprehensive coverage of the most important modern topics in organizational behavior, this classic text is distinguished by a strong conceptual framework and detailed research base. It presents solid coverage of organizational behavior theories always followed by applications. For this seventh edition the author, an internationally renowned researcher and scholar, has incorporated the latest research findings and cutting-edge topics, including all new chapters on diversity, ethics, and emerging organizations.

■ **DISTINCTIONS**

♦ **Scholarship:** the solid research base includes the most current studies and theoretical developments.

♦ **Coverage:** comprehensive, in-depth treatment of micro and macro topics.

♦ **Pedagogy:** applications such as cases (brief chapter-ending and integrative part-ending), and boxes (international, total quality management, diversity, and general topics) help bring important concepts to life; strong graphics program, discussion questions, and learning objectives reinforce student mastery of content.

♦ **Author Reputation:** author is highly regarded by the academic community as a researcher, writer, and educator.

■ **NEW TO THIS EDITION**

♦ **New Paradigm:** recognizes that we are now in a new paradigm and integrates international, diversity, and total quality application examples throughout.

♦ **NEW chapters** on Diversity and Ethics (ch. 3), and on Information Technology, Total Quality, and Organizational Learning (ch. 2)

♦ **Increased emphasis** on teams (ch. 9) and on real world examples and skills throughout (for example, negotiation skills in ch. 10 and leadership skills in ch. 14).

♦ **NEW topics** include the information superhighway (ch. 15), network, virtual, and horizontal organizational designs (ch. 17), knowledge organizations, nature of paradigm shifts, reengineering, agency theory, realistic group conflict theory, benchmarking, empowerment, nature of diversity, managing diversity, impression management tactics, "big five" personality traits, three component commitment, communication technology, radical humanism, chaos theory, cross cultural research, and transnational competencies.

♦ **NEW boxed inserts** on Total Quality in Action and on Diversity in Action in every chapter

■ TITLE: ORGANIZATIONAL BEHAVIOR, 7/e

■ AUTHOR: Fred Luthans (University of Nebraska)

TABLE OF CONTENTS:

SUPPLEMENTS:
    Instructor's Manual with Test Bank (039181-5)
    Computerized Test Bank 5-1/4 (840927-6)
    Computerized Test Bank 3-1/2 (840928-4)
    Overhead Transparency Acetates (074548-X)
    Video Series (911790-2)

TITLE: OPERATIONS MANAGEMENT EXPERT

AUTHOR: Hamid Noori (Wilford Laurier University, Canada)

♦ 832595-1 (IBM, 5.25")   ♦ Student Software & 192 pp. Manual   ♦ Publication: 02/14/95
♦ 832599-4 (IBM, 3.50)   ♦ Student Software & 192 pp. Manual   ♦ Publication: 02/14/95

■ DESCRIPTION

A stand-alone, professional quality, interactive, user-friendly software package designed to solve many of the problem sets in any introductory production and operations management text, OPERATIONS MANAGEMENT EXPERT features powerful abilities and a unique graphic interface so that students can see problem results not only in tabular, but also in graphics format. OM EXPERT has 32 widely-used operations management models or tools grouped into 12 modules.

■ DISTINCTIONS

♦ Powerful computational engine that solves all typical production and operations management problems.

♦ Consists of 32 programs grouped into 12 modules.

♦ Graphical interface, superior to all competing software, allows student to graphically see and print results and permits graphic simulation of selected production and operations management tools. See, for example, the modules on Queueing Simulation, Project Management, or Inventory Control.

♦ Extensive student manual includes problems to solve.

♦ Class tested for four years at author's schoool.

♦ Requires IBM DOS 2.1 or higher and 480K; can be used with either color or monochrome monitors.

■ TITLE: OPERATIONS MANAGEMENT EXPERT

■ AUTHOR: Hamid Noori (Wilford Laurier University, Canada)

TABLE OF CONTENTS:

SUPPLEMENTS:
Instructor's Manual (832602-8)

TITLE: PRODUCTION AND OPERATIONS MANAGEMENT: Total Quality
and Responsiveness

AUTHOR: Hamid Noori (Wilfrid Laurier University)/Russell Radford (University of Manitoba)

♦ 046923-7   ♦ Cloth   ♦ 752 pages   ♦ Publication: 11/18/94

■ DESCRIPTION
This exciting new entry into the Operations Management arena stresses the need for
businesses to implement strategically the principles of quality management and fast
response in order to compete in the global marketplace. With a solid quantitative as well
as qualitative presentation, the authors have a balanced approach to problem solving and
decision making. The accompanying free student workbook is a value-added supplement that
provides timely, realistic case vignettes as well as additional quantitative tools.

■ DISTINCTIONS
♦ Undergraduate first P/OM course text with a modern, cutting-edge global foundation and a
more quantitative orientation

♦ Unique, current coverage of state-of-the-art topics such as fast response, continuous
improvement, customer focus, quality management, and strategic competitive advantage in
the global marketplace.

♦ Opens with 6 plant tours of manufacturing and service companies throughout North America
to set the stage for the text presentation.

♦ Packaged with a free student workbook that offers additional short, realistic, managerial
case studies, a wealth of additional advanced quantitative tools, and various student
study aids to assist learning both the managerial and quantitative text material.

♦ End of chapter problems include those that can be conveniently solved using Noori's OM
EXPERT software package (or any competing package).

■ TITLE: PRODUCTION AND OPERATIONS MANAGEMENT: Total Quality
and Responsiveness

■ AUTHOR: Hamid Noori (Wilfrid Laurier University)/Russell Radford
(University of Manitoba)

TABLE OF CONTENTS:

SUPPLEMENTS:
Instructor's Manual/Test Bank (004917-3)
Student Workbook (packaged free with textbook)
Computerized Test Bank, IBM, 5-1/4"
Computerized Test Bank, IBM, 3-1/2"
Video Program with Video Guide

TITLE: CONTEMPORARY SUPERVISION: Managing People and
Technology, 2/e

AUTHOR: Betty Roper **Ricks** (Old Dominion University)/Mary Lea **Ginn** (Private
business/editorial consultant)/Anne Scott **Daughtrey** (Old Dominion University)

♦ 052648-6   ♦ Softcover   ♦ 640 pages   ♦ Publication: 08/26/94

■ DESCRIPTION

This revision updates the respected Daughtrey-Ricks first edition with new or expanded
coverage of critical topics such as quality management, ethics, decision-making, safety and
health, organizational change and supervising a culturally diverse work force. The authors
have continued to focus on competencies throughout the book, presented at chapter openings,
at appropriate learning points within the chapters, and in competency reviews at the end of
each chapter. Other strong pedagogical elements designed to help the supervisor translate
theory into practice include numerous self-quizzes and questionnaires, forms, exercises,
applications, real-company case studies, and "What the Supervisor Can Do" sections
throughout.

■ DISTINCTIONS

♦ **Comprehensive and highly readable,** covering all of the functional areas of management
from the supervisor's perspective.

♦ Continues to **focus on competencies** with competency lists, checks, and reviews within each
chapter, plus many activities and suggestions to aid the supervisor in translating theory
into practice. "What the Supervisor Can Do" sections are used throughout.

♦ Provides a wealth of other **learning aids** such as self-quizzes and questionnaires, forms,
exercises, applications, and short realistic case studies.

♦ Detailed, full-chapter coverage of **decision making, delegation, health and safety, and
total quality management** with special attention paid to managing diversity and change,
non-discriminatory staffing, managing stress, and participatory management.

♦ Two short **real-world case studies** at the end of each chapter plus an additional 1 to 2 in
each chapter of the Instructor's Manual, and 2 in each chapter of the Student Study
Guide.

■ NEW TO THIS EDITION

♦ Now in **softcover** and reorganized from 18 to 16 chapters

♦ **NEW chapters** on organizational change and diversity (ch. 8), quality management (ch. 15),
and motivation (ch. 11)

♦ Includes **latest legislation** such as the Americans with Disabilities Act and its 1992
amendments, no-smoking legislation, and new OSHA guidelines

♦ More examples using **white collar workers** or office situations while maintaining examples
of blue collar situations

♦ More attention to **participatory management, teams, ethics, and literacy in the workplace**

♦ **NEW appendix on careers** in supervision

■ TITLE: CONTEMPORARY SUPERVISION: Managing People and Technology, 2/e

■ AUTHOR: Betty Roper Ricks (Old Dominion University)/Mary Lea Ginn (Private business/editorial consultant)/Anne Scott Daughtrey (Old Dominion University)

TABLE OF CONTENTS:

SUPPLEMENTS:
> Instructor's Manual/Test Bank/Transparency Masters (052649-4)
> Student Study and Activity Guide (052650-8)
> Computerized Test Bank, IBM, 5-1/4" (834040-3)
> Computerized Test Bank, IBM, 3-1/2" (834041-1)

TITLE: INTERNATIONAL BUSINESS: A Strategic Management Approach

AUTHOR: Alan M. **Rugman** (University of Toronto)/Richard M. **Hodgetts** (Florida International University)

◆ 054915-X   ◆ Cloth   ◆ 736 pages   ◆ Publication: 09/16/94

■ **DESCRIPTION**

Written by a distinguished author team, this distinctive, new, full-color text integrates state of the art theory and solid practical content through the use of a unique strategic management framework. The three elements --theoretical foundation, relevance, and strategic synthesis-- reinforce each other and provide the student with the opportunity to gain a deep and lasting understanding of international business. Students will appreciate the book's numerous pedagogical advantages, including a strong selection of cases and text examples which provide important insights into real-world global business practice.

■ **DISTINCTIONS**

◆ **Theory:** text incorporates the latest theoretical advances in a manner easily comprehensible to university and college students, for example: Porter's diamond theory of international competitiveness, current work on the Multinational Enterprise, and new research on organizational learning within corporations.

◆ **Strategic Synthesis:** first text with a strategic management focus for teaching introductory international business-- helps students choose from the extraordinarily broad menu of events in the international environment by building confidence in understanding which ones are useful for strategic management analysis at the firm level.

◆ **Accessibility:** excessive technical and mechanistic details have been deemphasized to promote student understanding of the material. For example, international finance and economics are examined primarily for their relevance to managers of multinationals in formulating and implementing strategy-- in recognition of the fact that, increasingly, professors of management (especially general management) as well as professors of economics and finance teach the international business course.

◆ **Applications:** strong selection of case examples (5 per chapter, 100 total) based on real world personalities and organizations. In addition, a real-life "Active Learning Case" opens and continues through each chapter and two "International Business Strategy in Action" boxes in each chapter provide specific strategy applications of the chapter material.

◆ **Design:** effective four-color design, including an extensive, first class, full-color map program (22 maps, including endpapers).

◆ **Regional Coverage:** unique coverage of doing business in important geographical regions of the world, especially the triad of North America, the European Community, and Japan.

◆ **Text Package:** a detailed, extensive Instructor's Manual with Test Bank (600 pages), Overhead Transparency Acetates, and a Video Series.

■ TITLE: INTERNATIONAL BUSINESS: A Strategic Management Approach

■ AUTHOR: Alan M. Rugman (University of Toronto)/Richard M. Hodgetts (Florida International University)

TABLE OF CONTENTS:

SUPPLEMENTS:
Instructor's Manual/Test Bank (054916-8)
Video Series (054917-6)
Overhead Transparency Acetates (074558-7)
Transparency Masters (074559-5)
Computerized Test Bank, IBM 5-1/4" (833608-2)
Computerized Test Bank, IBM 3-1/2" (833609-0)

TITLE: STATISTICS: A First Course, 5/e

AUTHOR: Donald H. **Sanders** (Education Consultant)

♦ 054900-1 ♦ Cloth ♦ 736 Pages ♦ Publication: 10/28/94

■ DESCRIPTION

Written in an informal style without omitting the more difficult concepts, this text uses an intuitive presentation and encourages students to take a commonsense approach to data analysis. Over 2,100 problems are in the text, drawn from health care, business and economics, the social and physical sciences, engineering, education, and leisure activities. Numerous examples throughout the text show how computer statistical software packages are used to eliminate computational drudgery and to support analysis and decision-making. A Computer Exercise section at the end of each chapter gives students practice in using statistical software.

In the fifth edition new minicases, "Statistics in Action," frequently appear in the text margins as examples of "real world" statistical applications that can stimulate class discussions. The material on probability has been extensively revised and updated and a timely chapter 10 on quality control has been added. More than 50% of the exercise problems are new.

■ DISTINCTIONS

♦ **Informal and clear presentation:** Sanders' light and sometimes humorous approach helps students grasp material that otherwise can be intimidating to the novice.

♦ **Familiar and comfortable computational and decision making framework:** seven-step hypothesis testing procedure introduced in ch 8 is used throughout the remaining seven chapters.

♦ **Logic flowcharts** graphically outline procedural steps.

♦ **"Looking Ahead"** section opens and previews each chapter. At the end of each chapter a "Looking Back" section (keyed to the learning objectives) summarizes and reviews the main points.

■ NEW TO THIS EDITION

♦ **A new open, full-color design;** important terms are boldface typed and placed in color-shaded boxes; formulas are boxed and numbered.

♦ **"Statistics in Action"** minicases in the text margins show students how statistical concepts are used in the real world. Each is identified with an icon for Engineering & Physical Sciences, Business, Health, Social Sciences, or Leisure Activities.

♦ **Exercises extensively revised and updated** to include "real" data; more than **50% of the problems are new.**

♦ **New Chapter 3** condenses and combines two previous chapters on measures of central tendency and dispersion.

♦ **Two new chapters (4 & 5) on probability** and probability distributions

♦ **New chapter on quality control (ch. 10)** introduces several industrially-important types of quality control procedures and charts

♦ **New computer exercises in each chapter,** keyed to concepts in the chapter, take advantage of available commercial statistical packages.

■ TITLE: **STATISTICS: A First Course, 5/e**

■ AUTHOR: Donald H. **Sanders** (Education Consultant)

TABLE OF CONTENTS:

SUPPLEMENTS:
Instructor's Resource Guide (054944-3)
Student Study Guide (054942-7)
Student Solutions Manual (054943-5)
MYSTAT Software, IBM, 5-1/4"
MYSTAT Software, IBM, 3-1/2"
MYSTAT Software, MAC
"Against All Odds" Video Series

TITLE: **A SYSTEMS APPROACH TO SMALL GROUP INTERACTION, 5/e**

AUTHOR: Stewart L. **Tubbs** (Eastern Michigan University)

♦ 065512-X   ♦ Cloth   ♦ 432 Pages   ♦ Publication: 10/07/94

■ **DESCRIPTION**

A Systems Approach to Small Group Interaction is the only textbook to integrate all the important small group topics into a single comprehensive model. This systems model is Tubbs' own framework borrowed from the social sciences and developed for junior level group communication/teamwork courses. The fifth edition has been extensively revised and updated, and its unique combination of readings, cases and exercises offers students the opportunity to view important concepts in practice. In addition, the book includes extensive coverage of leadership, teamwork and conflict management.

■ **DISTINCTIONS**

♦ Pioneered the "systems approach" to Small Group Communication.

♦ Written for the introductory course, it explains and integrates **all major small group/team theories**, giving students the unique opportunity to fully understand theories that are usually found only in advanced texts.

♦ Every chapter opens with a **case study** to draw students into the concepts and provide a context for learning.

♦ Addresses the importance and benefits of working in **teams and team building** throughout the text.

♦ Offers a wide range of **experiential exercises** and end-of-the-chapter readings.

■ **NEW TO THIS EDITION**

♦ Features new case studies including one on drinking on campus and a group supported murder in Africa and new and revised reading selections including one on "Groups" as it relates to the challenger shuttle disaster, and one discussing the reasons people joins groups.

♦ Includes extensive coverage of leadership and its role in small groups (ch. 4) including a new case study on doctor-assisted suicide.

♦ Provides thorough coverage of negotiation and conflict management (ch. 6) with tips for effective negotiating and a new case study on gun control.

♦ Broader applications of group dynamics as it relates to real life settings, such as health as influenced by one's job and romantic situations within groups, continue to illustrate the books strong integration of research and theory with life and career.

■ TITLE: A SYSTEMS APPROACH TO SMALL GROUP INTERACTION, 5E

■ AUTHOR: Stewart L. Tubbs (Eastern Michigan University)

TABLE OF CONTENTS:

SUPPLEMENTS:
Instructor's Manual/Test Bank (065513-8)

PRINCIPLES OF MANAGEMENT

1994   BARTOL

Kathryn M. Bartol, University of Maryland
David C. Martin, American University
MANAGEMENT, Second Edition
The first edition of Management met with
widespread acclaim for its authoritative coverage,
solid pedagogy, and effective use of case material.
The new edition retains these strengths, but in a
more effective, streamlined presentation. In addition,
the book now offers special features on such vital
issues as workplace diversity, quality, and ethics.
Thoroughly updated, with a superior array of
teaching and learning supplements (including a new
video package with video cases for each chapter),
Bartol/Martin, 2/e offers unparalleled preparation
for managerial challenges into the next century. The
complete text is available on McGraw-Hill's PRIMIS
electronic custom publishing system.
Contents: PART ONE: INTRODUCTION. 1. The
Challenge of Management. 2. Pioneering Ideas in
Management. 3. Understanding External and Internal
Environments. 4. Social Responsibility and ethics.
PART TWO: PLANNING AND DECISION
MAKING. 5. Establishing Organizational Goals and
Plans. 6. Strategic Management. 7. Managing
Innovation and Change. 8. Managerial Decision
Making. PART THREE: ORGANINZING. 9. Basic
Elements of Organization Structure. 10. Strategic
Organization Design. 11. Human Resource
Management. PART FOUR: LEADING. 12.
Motivation. 13. Leadership. 14. Managerial
Communication. 15. Managing Groups. PART FIVE:
CONTROLLING. 16. Controlling the Organization.
17. Managerial Control Methods. 18. Operations
Management. 19. Information Systems for
Management. PART SIX: ACROSS ALL
FUNCTIONS. 20. International Management. 21.
Entrepreneurship and Small Business.
-pp.800
005078-3

STUDY GUIDE
005116-X
INSTRUCTOR'S MANUAL
005080-5
TEST BANK OF 2,500 ITEMS
005082-1
COMPUTERIZED TEST BANK - IBM PC 5 1/4"
833736-4
COMPUTERIZED TEST BANK - IBM PC 3 1/2"
833737-2
119 TRANSPARENCY MASTERS
074642-7
150 OVERHEAD TRANSPARENCIES
074641-9
NEWSLETTER OF CASE UPDATES
005079-1
21 VIDEO CASES
911487-3

1993   BOVEE

Courtland L. Bovee, Grossmont College
John V. Thill, Communication Specialists of America
(President)
Marion Burke Wood, Strategic Management Services
George P. Dovel, Dovel Group
MANAGEMENT
This new management principles text combines solid
coverage of management theory and practice with
innovative pedagogical aids. Each chapter includes a

"Management Challenge"—a unique case and
simulation feature which challenges the student to
apply important chapter concepts to real-world
managerial dilemmas. In addition, such pedagogical
features as boxes on social responsibility/ethics and
global management, hands-on assignments including
"Keeping Current in Management" (research) and
"Sharpen Your Management Skills" (decision-
making and communication), and chapter video
exercises help distinguish this text from its
competitors. Along with a full chapter on global
management featured early on in the text,
MANAGEMENT is filled with a range of well-chosen
international examples. Another unique aspect of
coverage is a full chapter on productivity, quality,
and customer satisfaction.
Contents: PART ONE: UNDERSTANDING
MANAGEMENT TODAY. 1. The Foundations of
Management. 2. Management Theories and
Perspectives. 3. The Complex Organizational
Management Environment. 4. Social Responsibility
and Ethics. 5. Management and the Global
Organization. PART TWO: PLANNING. 6. Decision
Making 7. Organizational Goals and Planning. 8.
Strategic Management and Implementation. PART
THREE: ORGANIZING. 9. Foundations of
Organizational Structure. 10. Organization Design.
11. Organizational Change and Creativity. 12.
Organizing New Ventures. 13. Human Resource
Management. PART FOUR: LEADING. 14.
Management and Motivation. 15. Leadearship in
Organizations. 16. Group Dynamics in
Organizations. PART FIVE: MANAGEMENT
CONTROL. 18. Information Resource Management.
19. Foundations of Management Control. 20.
Operations Management. 21. Quality, Productivity,
and Customer Satisfaction.
-pp.848
006831-3

STUDY GUIDE
006836-4
INSTRUCTOR'S MANUAL/VIDEO GUIDE
006832-1
TEST BANK
006833-X
COMPUTERIZED TEST BANK—IBM 5 1/4"
831683-9
COMPUTERIZED TEST BANK—IBM 3 1/2"
833953-7
100 4-COLOR OVERHEAD TRANSPARENCIES
006835-6
TRANSPARENCY MASTERS
074529-3
VIDEO SERIES (21 PROGRAMS ON 2 VHS)
911519-5

1993   WEIHRICH

Heinz Weihrich, University of San Francisco
Harold Koontz (deceased), formerly of UCLA
MANAGEMENT: A Global Perspective,
Tenth Edition
A revision of one of the classic management
textbooks, the tenth edition features a new
pronounced emphasis on global management. The
research and examples have been thoroughly
updated to reflect he most current developments in
the field. MANAGEMENT continues to offer a five-
functions approach, an integrative systems model,
and a wealth of provocative cases, including a new
part-ending case on the global automotive industry.
-pp.784
069170-3

STUDY GUIDE
069174-6
INSTRUCTOR'S MANUAL
069171-1
TEST BANK
069172-X

COMPUTERIZED TEST BANK—IBM 5 1/4"
832496-3
COMPUTERIZED TEST BANK—IBM 3 1/2"
833950-2
OVERHEAD TRANSPARENCIES
074547-1
VIDEO SERIES PLUS GUIDE
911518-7

1992   BOONE

Louis E. Boone, University of South Alabama
David L. Kurtz, University of Arkansas
MANAGEMENT, Fourth Edition
In addition to solid coverage of the basic functions of
planning, organizing, influencing, and controlling,
this fourth edition provides substantial (full-chapter)
treatment of such frequently neglected areas as
international management, M.I.S., operations
management, and ethics. MANAGEMENT continues
to reinforce the reputation of past editions for
unparalleled readability and pedagogical value while
adding a new full-color design and new part-ending
video cases.
Contents: PART ONE: INTRODUCTION: 1. The
Nature of Management. 3. The Development of
Management Thought. PART TWO: THE SETTING
MANAGEMENT ENVIRONMENT: 3. The Setting
and Environment for Management. 4. Social
Responsibility and Management Ethics. 5.
International and Comparative Management. PART
THREE: PLANNING AND DECISION MAKING: 6.
Fundamentals of Planning. 7. Strategic Planning and
Organizational Objectives. 8. Decision Making.
APPENDIX: Quantitative Techniques. PART FOUR:
ORGANIZING, STAFFING, AND
COMMUNICATING. 9. Fundamentals of
Organizing. 10. Organizational Design and Job
Design. 11. Staffing the Organization. 12.
Communication. PART FIVE: INFLUENCING: 13.
Motivation. 14. Managing Groups. 15. Leadership.
16. Managing Organizational Change and
Development. PART SIX: CONTROLLING: 17.
Fundamentals of Controlling. 18. Control
Techniques. 19. Management Information Systems.
20. Production/Operations Management.
APPENDIX: Careers in Management. Company
Index. Name Index. Subject Index.
-pp.704
540964-X

STUDY GUIDE
006577-2
INSTRUCTOR'S MANUAL
006574-8
TEST BANK
006575-6
COMPUTERIZED TEST BANK, IBM 5 1/4"
831874-2
COMPUTERIZED TEST BANK, IBM 3 1/2"
832497-1
TRANSPARENCY MASTERS
074532-3
100 COLOR ACETATE TRANSPARENCIES
074531-5
PC CASE, IBM 5 1/4"
555795-9
PC CASE INSTRUCTOR'S MANUAL
553738-9
THRESHOLD SIMULATION, STUDENT SET, IBM 5
1/4"
557296-6
THRESHOLD ADOPTER'S DESK SET, IBM 5 1/4"
557172-2
SIX VIDEO CASES
911262-5
CHAPTER VIDEOS WITH GUIDE
911373-7
PHONE-IN TEST SERVICE (1-800-888-EXAM) OR
FAX 1-404-373-4110

<u>1990</u>   **KOONTZ**

Harold Koontz, deceased
Heinz Weihrich, University of San Francisco
**ESSENTIALS OF MANAGEMENT,
Fifth Edition**
This revision of the core introduction to management
text based on the ninth edition of the parent text
features Perspectives to illustrate real-world
applications and Exercises/Action Steps. New
material includes social responsibility and ethics,
planning premises, electronic media in
communication, POM, and an updated section on
international management.
Contents: PART ONE: THE BASIS OF
MANAGEMENT THEORY AND SCIENCE:
Management: Science, Theory, and Practice.
Management and Society: Social Responsibility and
Ethics. PART TWO: PLANNING: The Nature and
Purpose of Planning. Objectives. Strategies, Policies,
and Planning Premises. Decision Making. PART
THREE: ORGANIZING: The Nature and Purpose of
Organizing. Basic Departmentation. Line/Staff
Authority and Decentralization. Effective Organizing
and Organizational Culture. PART FOUR:
STAFFING: Human Resource Management and
Selection. Performance Appraisal and Career
Strategy. Manager and Organization Development.
PART FIVE: LEADING: Managing and Human
Factor. Motivation. Leadership. Communication.
PART SIX: CONTROLLING: The System and Process
of Controlling. Control Techniques and Information
Technology. Productivity and Operations
Management. Overall and Preventive Control. PART
SEVEN: INTERNATIONAL MANAGEMENT AND
THE FUTURE: International Management—Toward
a Unified, Global Management Theory.
-pp.560
035605-X

INSTRUCTOR'S MANUAL by Halff
035611-4
TEST BANK
035612-2
COMPUTERIZED TEST BANK, DIPLOMA—IBM 5
1/4"
COMPUTERIZED TEST BANK, DIPLOMA—IBM 3
1/2"
COMPUTERIZED TEST BANK, DIPLOMA—APPLE

PRINCIPLES OF MANAGEMENT
SOFTWARE

<u>1989</u>   **ANDERSON**

Philip Anderson, St. Thomas College
David Hofmeister, Mankato State University
Timothy Scott, Mankato State University
Michael Thompson, Mankato State University
**THRESHOLD: A Management
Simulation**
Threshold is a computer-based simulation designed
for management principles students to approximate
decisions and problems they would face as managers
of a small manufacturing company. It helps them
understand concepts and develop the skills
associated with the management functions of
planning, organizing, staffing, directing, and
controlling. Threshold provides a common
experience to strengthen students' understanding of
issues presented in the introduction to management
course. Threshold also provides insights into how

other disciplines of business, such as finance and
marketing, fit into the area of management. In
operating the interactive program, students work in
teams in competition with each other, not the
computer. A built-in forecasting model allows for
"what-if" analysis, while moral/ethical "dilemmas"
allow students to analyze qualitative as well as
quantitative decisions. The menu-driven program is
designed to be operated by a novice computer user,
and requires no programming skills.
THRESHOLD: A MANAGEMENT SIMULATION
(ADOPTER'S DESK SET—IBM PC, 5 1/4")
557172-2

THRESHOLD: A MANAGEMENT SIMULATION
(STUDENT SET—IBM PC 5 1/4")
557296-6

PRINCIPLES:
SUPPLEMENTARY

<u>1993</u>   **DLABAY**

Les R. Dlabay, Lake Forest College
**PLANNING YOUR CAREER IN
BUSINESS TODAY, Second Edition**
This practical, results-oriented tool offers students
advice on career trends, self-assessment, career
planning, educational requirements, resume and
interview techniques, and how to achieve job success.
Hands-on, step-by-step exercises in each chapter
match student skills and abilities to career
opportunities.
Contents: 1. The Job Market and You. 2. Your Career
Plan—A Ticket to Success. 3. Packaging and
Presenting the Product—You. 4. Your Career Now—
And in the Future. Appendix: Sources of Further
Information.
-pp.52
006858-5

<u>1987</u>   **BOONE**

Louis E. Boone, University of South Alabama
Donald D. Bowen, University of Tulsa
**GREAT WRITINGS IN
MANAGEMENT AND
ORGANIZATIONAL BEHAVIOR,
Second Edition**
With articles chosen by a poll of management
scholars, this readings text features a collection of
classic writings in management and organizational
behavior appropriate for students at all levels.
Presented in a comprehensive teaching-learning
format, each article includes an outline preview, a
learning review, and retrospective comments. Eight
articles have been added to this edition. An
alternative table of contents organized by managerial
functions is also included.
-pp.446
555030-X

ORGANIZATIONAL
BEHAVIOR AND HUMAN
RELATIONS

<u>1993</u>   **NEWSTROM**

John W. Newstrom, University of Minnesota—
Duluth
Keith Davis, Arizona State University
**ORGANIZATIONAL BEHAVIOR:
Human Behavior at Work, Ninth
Edition**
This thorough revision of a leading text includes
many new topics, model, and concepts from
contemporary organizational behavior literature and
actual practice. In addition to maintaining the highly
readable style and innovative pedagogy of past
editions, the inclusion of many new real company
examples further enlivens the presentation.
International topics are treated in a full chapter near
the beginning of the book and illustrated in
numerous examples throughout the text. New
chapters on individual behavior and interpersonal
relations have also been included.
Contents: 1. Working with People. 2. Models of
Organizational Behavior. 3. Social Systems and
Organizational Culture. 4. International Dimensions
of Organizational Behavior. 5. Managing
Communications. 6. Motivational Basics. 7.
Motivational Applications. 8. Appraising and
Rewarding Performance. 9. Employee Attitudes. 10.
Leadership. 11. Empowerment and Participation. 12.
Managing Change. 13. Organization Development.
14. Structure, Technology, and People. 15. Quality of
Work Life and Sociotechnical Systems. 16. Issues
Between Organizations and Individuals. 17.
Interpersonal Behavior. 18. Group Dynamics. 19.
Informal Organizations. 20. Stress and Counseling.
21. Organizational Behavior in Perspective. Case
Problems. Glossary.
-pp.672
015603-4

STUDY GUIDE
015632-8
INSTRUCTOR'S MANUAL
015621-2
TEST BANK
015646-8
COMPUTERIZED TEST BANK—IBM 5 1/4"
832212-X
COMPUTERIZED TEST BANK—IBM 3 1/2"
833956-1
OVERHEAD TRANSPARENCIES
074548-X
VIDEO SERIES PLUS GUIDE
911521-7

<u>1993</u>   **PLOUS**

Scott Plous, Wesleyan University
**THE PSYCHOLOGY OF JUDGMENT
AND DECISIONS MAKING**
050477-6

INSTRUCTOR'S MANUAL
015833-9

1992 Harvard   GABARRO

John J. Gabarro, Harvard Business School

MANAGING PEOPLE AND ORGANIZATIONS

Designed for a senior-level or first-year MBA course on organizational behavior and human resource management, this new softcover text covers basic concepts and emerging issues through readings by leading academics and practitioners. The text offers readings that focus on important contemporary concerns, including women and minorities in the work force, family and career, and drugs in the workplace. It also provides thorough coverage of the basics, including leadership and managing individual, group, and organizational effectiveness as well as organizational change. Organized like a conventional textbook, the readings provide a practice-oriented grounding that can function alone or be orchestrated and interwoven with cases, exercises, and other materials. The book is also available as a PRIMIS CUSTOM PUBLICATION.
Contents: PART ONE: MANAGING AND LEADING IN ORGANIZATIONS. SECTION A: Managing People. SECTION B: Leading an Organization. PART TWO: Managing Individuals and Groups. SECTION A: Motivating and Managing Individuals. SECTION B: Managing Group Effectiveness. PART THREE: MANAGING ORGANIZATIONAL EFFECTIVENESS. SECTION A: Designing Organizations for Effectiveness. SECTION B: Managing Organizational Change. PART FOUR: MANAGING THE HUMAN RESOURCE.
-pp.572
022668-7

1992   MINER

John B. Miner, S.U.N.Y. Buffalo

INDUSTRIAL/ORGANIZATIONAL PSYCHOLOGY
042440-3

1992 HARVARD   PFEFFER

Jeffrey Pfeffer, Stanford University

MANAGING WITH POWER: Politics and Influence in Organizations

Jeffrey Pfeffer provides an in-depth look at the role of power and influence in organizations. He identifies the sources of power, and shows how power is used, the conditions under which power and influence are important, and how to manage the political dynamics at work in every organization. MANAGING WITH POWER will be the standard text for MBA courses in power and influence.
Contents: PART ONE: POWER IN ORGANIZATIONS: 1. Decisions and Implementations. 2. When Is Power Used? 3. Diagnosing Power and Dependence. PART TWO: Sources of Power: 4. Where Does Power Come From? 5. Resources, Allies, and the New Golden Rule. 6. Location in the Communication Network. 7. Formal Authority, Reputation, and Performance. 8. The Importance of Being in the Right Unit. 9. Individual Attributes as Sources of Power. PART THREE: STRATEGIES AND TACTICS FOR EMPLOYING POWER EFFECTIVELY: 10. Framing: How We Look at Things Affects how They Look. 11. Interpersonal Influence. 12. Timing is (Almost) Everything. 13. The Politics of Information and Analysis. 14. Changing the Structure to Consolidate Power. 15. Symbolic Action: Language, Ceremonies, and Settings. PART FOUR: POWER DYNAMICS: HOW POWER IS LOST AN HOW ORGANIZATIONS CHANGE: 16. Even

the Might Fall: How Power is Lost. 17. Managing Political Dynamics Productively. 18. Managing with Power. Notes. Bibliography. Index.
-pp.400
103360-2

1991   STEERS

Richard M. Steers, University of Oregon
Lyman W. Porter, University of California - Irvine

MOTIVATION AND WORK BEHAVIOR, Fifth Edition

A reader/text for upper-level Organizational Behavior courses (offered in management and psychology departments), with a unique focus on motivation. The authors have retained their basic approach of past editions, organizing the readings by chapter, with each chapter containing introductory text material. 36 articles are featured in this edition, 24 of which are new.
Contents: PART ONE: INITIAL CONSIDERATIONS. 1. The Role of Motivation in Organizations. PART TWO: THEORETICAL APPROACHES TO MOTIVATION. 2. The "Person" in Motivation. 3. The "Environment" in Motivation. 4. The "Person-Environment Interaction" in Motivation. PART THREE: CENTRAL ISSUES IN MOTIVATION AT WORK. 5. Social Influences on Motivation. 6. Job Attitudes and Performance. 7. Employee Attachment to Organizations. 8. Cross-Cultural Influences on Motivation. PART FOUR: TECHNIQUES OF MOTIVATION. 9. Goal-Setting and Self-Management. 10. Work Design. 11. Reward Systems. 12. Communication, Feedback and Motivation. PART FIVE: MOTIVATION THEORY IN PERSPECTIVE. 13. Work and Motivation: Some Concluding Observations.
-pp.640
060956-X

1989   NEWSTROM

John W. Newstrom, Ph.D., University of Minnesota
Keith A. Davis, Ph.D., Arizona State University

ORGANIZATIONAL BEHAVIOR: Readings and Exercises, Eighth Edition

SEE: Management and Organization—Organizational Behavior (Supplementary)
015519-4

1989   SAYLES

Leonard R. Sayles, Ph.D., Columbia University

LEADERSHIP: Managing in Real Organizations, Second Edition

SEE: Management and Organization—Special Topics. Ancillaries are available.
055018-2

1988   MINER

John B. Miner, State University of New York, Buffalo

ORGANIZATIONAL BEHAVIOR: Performance and Productivity

This primary text, by a well-known and respected author, combines a thorough treatment of research and theory in organizational behavior with a unique practical focus on the problems of performance and productivity that plague society today. Through numerous examples, cases, and specific action guidelines, it helps students learn basic theory while showing them how higher performance levels and greater productivity can be achieved. Its comprehensive coverage gives students a full picture of the field at individual, group, and organizational levels, including material drawn from the author's

well-known Theories of Organizational Behavior as well as up-to-date discussions of corporate culture, power, creativity, ethics, and other topics.
-pp.768
554742-2

INSTRUCTOR'S MANUAL
553900-4
TEST BANK
553902-0
COMPUTERIZED TEST BANK, IBM 5 1/4"
556252-9

1987   HIGGINS

James M. Higgins, Roy Crummer School of Business, Rollins College

HUMAN RELATIONS: Behavior at Work, Second Edition

With its unique focus on both concepts and skills, this well-written text provides in-depth coverage of all the traditional topics in human relations as well as current topics such as quality of work life, managing stress and time, and creative problem solving, which reflect an increased concern for culture, creativity, and individual values. Focusing on real-life examples, this revised edition includes more cases, experiential exercises, and "test yourself" quizzes, giving students an opportunity to practice and improve their human relations skills.
-pp.528
554886-0

INSTRUCTOR'S MANUAL/TEST BANK
555079-2

1987   MITCHELL

Terrence R. Mitchell, University of Washington
James R. Larson, Jr., University of Illinois

PEOPLE IN ORGANIZATIONS: An Introduction to Organizational Behavior, Third Edition

This is a revision of a comprehensive introduction to organizational behavior covering both micro and macro approaches. Known for its readability and logical organization, the Third Edition also features a new chapter on stress, and additional material on Japanese management, women, minorities, and older workers in management, and covers the effect of computers in the workplace.
-pp.608
042534-5

INSTRUCTOR'S MANUAL
042535-3
COMPUTERIZED TEST BANK, MICROEXAMINER—IBM
COMPUTERIZED TEST BANK, MICROEXAMINER—APPLE

1986   ARNOLD

Hugh J. Arnold, University of Toronto
Daniel C. Feldman, University of South Carolina

ORGANIZATIONAL BEHAVIOR
-pp.640
002300-X

INSTRUCTOR'S MANUAL AND TEST BANK
002313-1
COMPUTERIZED TEST BANK, MICROEXAMINER—IBM
COMPUTERIZED TEST BANK, MICROEXAMINER—APPLE

1986 Harvard   COHEN

Michael D. Cohen, University of Michigan, Ann Arbor
James G. March, Stanford University
LEADERSHIP AND AMBIGUITY, Second Edition
Leadership and Ambiguity is both a thorough and witty discussion of the role of the college president and a broadly applicable analysis of the problems facing all managers of what the authors call "organized anarchies." The authors identify three symptoms of the organization: a lack of clearly defined goals, no understanding by its members of the organization's processes, and little or no participant attachment to the enterprise as a whole. Given these factors, how can anyone effectively lead an institution or company deep in the throes of organized anarchy? The authors' recommendations range from a reexamination of the functions of management decision making to the modification of traditional views of planning and evaluation. The second edition of Leadership and Ambiguity features a new preface and appendices that update this classic work. Here is a valuable book for managers of all collegial organizations, as well as would-be leaders of "organized anarchies."
-pp.290
103224-X

1986 Harvard   LAWRENCE

Paul R. Lawrence, Harvard Business School
Jay W. Lorsch, Harvard Business School
ORGANIZATION AND ENVIRONMENT: Managing Differentiation and Integration
Breaking with the traditional theory that there is one form of organization that is "best" for all companies at all times, this classic study was the first to make a connection between a company's outside influences (technological, market, and economic) and its pattern of organization and administration. Organization and Environment has practical implications for those concerned with the planning and design of an effective organizational mode. Named "Best Book of the Year" by the Academy of Management, winner of the American College of Hospital Administrators Award, and voted one of the Best Books in Management by the Economist.
-pp.296
103246-0

1985   MCGREGOR

Douglas McGregor, deceased
THE HUMAN SIDE OF ENTERPRISE: 25th Anniversary Printing
-pp.256
045098-6

1983   FELDMAN

Daniel C. Feldman, University of Florida
Hugh J. Arnold, University of Toronto
MANAGING INDIVIDUAL AND GROUP BEHAVIOR IN ORGANIZATIONS
-pp.613
020386-5

INSTRUCTOR'S MANUAL
020389-X

1983   SCHLESINGER

Leonard Schlesinger, Harvard University
Robert G. Eccles, Harvard University
John J. Gabarro, Harvard University
MANAGING BEHAVIOR IN ORGANIZATIONS: Text, Cases, Readings
-pp.684
055332-7

INSTRUCTOR'S MANUAL
055333-5

1982   MYERS

Michele Tolela Myers, Bryn Mawr College
Gail E. Myers, Trinity University
MANAGING BY COMMUNICATION: An Organizational Approach
044235-5

ORGANIZATIONAL BEHAVIOR (SUPPLEMENTARY)

1992 Harvard   BENNIS

Warren Bennis, University of Southern California
LEADERS ON LEADERSHIP
In many companies and organizations in the United States and abroad, leaders are meeting challenges and achieving tangible results. They set agendas for change and innovation, gain commitment, and ensure that real work is done. They aren't getting results by issuing paper calls to action from the corporate suite, but are rolling up their sleeves and doing the hands-on work that needs to be done—wherever it needs to be done. This collection brings together HARVARD BUSINESS REVIEW interviews with prominent business leaders—Jack Welch of General Electric, John Reed of Citicorp, Raymond Smith of Bell Atlantic, Paul Cook of Raychem, Robert Haas of Levi Strauss, Rod Canion of Compaq, Yoshihisa Tabuchi of Nomura Securities, Red Auerbach of the Boston Celtics, and others. The visions, concerns, and instincts they reveal illuminate both the range of abilities that contribute to leadership in different industries and the constants that work regardless of industry, company size, or available resources.
Contents: PART ONE: An Overview. PART TWO: The Importance of Value. PART THREE: Global Leadership. PART FOUR: Perspectives on Changes. PART FIVE: The Politics of Leadership.
-pp.275
103318-1

1989 Harvard   BADARACCO

Joseph L. Badaracco, Jr., Harvard Business School
Richard R. Ellsworth, Claremont Graduate School
LEADERSHIP AND THE QUEST FOR INTEGRITY
In many recent books on leadership, managers have answered the central question "What do you do?" with "It all depends," the phrase that has almost become conventional wisdom. A common given of this view is that a manager's style should depend on the situation. Joseph L. Badaracco, Jr. and Richard R.

Ellsworth take a different stance. They argue that leaders are not consummate stylists. Instead, the best leaders act in a consistent, unadorned way that reflects their personalities, fundamental beliefs and judgments. Through extensive interviews with executives, the authors describe three basic philosophies of leadership and reveal how leaders who hold certain prejudices or predispositions can resolve five critical dilemmas of management. The executives interviewed included the current or former chief executive officers of Citicorp, Colgate-Palmolive, Conoco, Du Pont, Johnson and Johnson, Teradyne, and Time, Inc. The lesson for leaders in Leadership and the Quest For Integrity is broad and vital. The modern world is complex and painful tradeoffs need to be made. With integrity of purpose, however, managers can make the tradeoff in ways that more often than not lead to outstanding performance.
Contents: PART ONE: LEADERSHIP PHILOSOPHIES: 1. Political Leadership. 2. Directive Leadership. 3. Values-Driven Leadership. PART TWO: INTEGRITY AND THE DILEMMAS OF LEADERSHIP: 4. Clarity and Precision versus Flexibility. 5. Top-Down versus Bottom-Up Influence. 6. Substance versus Process. 7. Confrontation versus Compromise. 8. Tangibles versus Intangibles. 9. Integrity in Action.
-pp.236
103207-X

1989   NEWSTROM

John W. Newstrom, Ph.D., University of Minnesota
Keith A. Davis, Ph.D., Arizona State University
ORGANIZATIONAL BEHAVIOR: Readings and Exercises, Eighth Edition
This very successful reader is appropriate for use with any organizational behavior main text. The experiential nature of the exercises continues to appeal to a large segment of the market. This edition includes updated and new readings, cases, and exercises dealing with traditional and modern approaches.
Contents: Organizational Behavior Frameworks. Historical Foundations of Organizational Behavior. Understanding Individual Behavior in Organizations. Individual Outcomes: Loyalty, Commitment, Turnover and Productivity. Interpersonal Relations. Interpersonal Conflict and Its Resolution. Power, Politics, and Performance Appraisal. Groups. Motivation. Reward Systems. Leadership. Participative Management. Quality of Work Life and Sociotechnical Systems. Organizational Culture. Organizational Communications. Stress and Burnout. Labor Relations. Social Issues. International Issues. Emerging Organizational Behavior.
-pp.597
015519-4

1989   SAYLES

Leonard R. Sayles, Ph.D., Columbia University
LEADERSHIP: Managing in Real Organizations, Second Edition
SEE: Management and Organization—Special Topics. Ancillaries are available.
055018-2

1988   TUBBS

Stewart L. Tubbs, Eastern Michigan University
A SYSTEMS APPROACH TO SMALL GROUP INTERACTION, Third Edition
Ancillaries are available.
555073-3

1987   **BOONE**

Louis E. Boone, University of South Alabama
Donald D. Bowen, University of Tulsa
GREAT WRITINGS IN MANAGEMENT AND ORGANIZATIONAL BEHAVIOR, Second Edition
SEE: Management and Organization—Principles
Supplementary
555030-X

1986 Harvard   **COHEN**

Michael D. Cohen, University of Michigan, Ann Arbor
James G. March, Stanford University
LEADERSHIP AND AMBIGUITY, Second Edition
SEE: Management and Organization—Organizational Behavior and Human Relations.
103224-X

1986   **KOPELMAN**

Richard E. Kopelman, Baruch College
MANAGING PRODUCTIVITY IN ORGANIZATIONS
-pp.288
035329-8

1986   **PERROW**

Charles Perrow, Yale University
COMPLEX ORGANIZATIONS: A Critical Essay, Third Edition
554799-6

1986   **PRUITT-ADD**

Dean G. Pruitt, State University of New York, Buffalo
Jeffrey Z. Rubin, Tufts University
SOCIAL CONFLICTS: Escalation, Stalemate, and Settlement
-pp.288
554906-9

1985   **WEIHRICH**

Heinz Weihrich, University of San Francisco
MANAGEMENT EXCELLENCE: Productivity Through MBO
-pp.252
069002-2

1984   **QUICK**

James C. Quick, Ph.D., University of Texas at Arlington
Jonathan D. Quick, Ph.D., Duke University Medical Center
ORGANIZATIONAL STRESS AND PREVENTIVE MANAGEMENT
-pp.368
051070-9

1983   **HACKMAN**

J. Richard Hackman, Yale University
Edward E. Lawler III, University of Southern California
Lyman W. Porter, University of California, Irvine

PERSPECTIVES ON BEHAVIOR IN ORGANIZATIONS, Second Edition
-pp.608
025414-1

1981   **LUTHANS**

Fred Luthans, University of Nebraska
Ken Thompson, Norte Dame
CONTEMPORARY READINGS IN ORGANIZATIONAL BEHAVIOR, Third Edition
-pp.400
039148-3

INDUSTRIAL PSYCHOLOGY

1991   **STEERS**

Richard M. Steers, University of Oregon
Lyman W. Porter, University of California
MOTIVATION AND WORK BEHAVIOR, Fifth Edition
SEE: Management and Organization—Organizational Behavior and Human Relations
060956-X

1987   **MITCHELL**

Terence R. Mitchell, University of Washington
James R. Larson, Jr., University of Illinois
PEOPLE IN ORGANIZATIONS: An Introduction to Organizational Behavior, Third Edition
SEE: Management and Organization—Organizational Behavior and Human Relations.
Ancillaries are available.
042534-5

1986   **ARNOLD**

Hugh J. Arnold, University of Toronto
Daniel C. Feldman, University of South Carolina
ORGANIZATIONAL BEHAVIOR
SEE: Organizational Behavior and Human Relations.
Ancillaries are available.
002300-X

1986   **KOPELMAN**

Richard E. Kopelman, Baruch College
MANAGING PRODUCTIVITY IN ORGANIZATIONS
SEE: Management and Organization: Organizational Behavior (Supplementary)
035329-8

1983   **FELDMAN**

Daniel C. Feldman, University of Florida
Hugh J. Arnold, University of Toronto
MANAGING INDIVIDUAL AND GROUP BEHAVIOR IN ORGANIZATIONS
-pp.613
020386-5

INSTRUCTOR'S MANUAL

020389-X

1983   **HACKMAN**

J. Richard Hackman, Yale University
Edward E. Lawler III, University of Southern California
Lyman W. Porter, University of California, Irvine
PERSPECTIVES ON BEHAVIOR IN ORGANIZATIONS, Second Edition
-pp.608
025414-1

1983   **SCHLESINGER**

Leonard Schlesinger, Harvard University
Robert G. Eccles, Harvard University
John J. Gabarro, Harvard University
MANAGING BEHAVIOR IN ORGANIZATIONS: Text, Cases, Readings
-pp.684
055332-7

INSTRUCTOR'S MANUAL
055333-5

PERSONNEL/HUMAN RESOURCE MANAGEMENT

1993   **BERNARDIN**

H. John Bernardin, Florida Atlantic University
Joyce E.A. Russell, University of Tennessee, Knoxville
HUMAN RESOURCE MANAGEMENT: An Experiential Approach
A combined human resources management text with original experiential exercises, this unique offering is directly compatible with the recent AACSB emphasis on developing student skills and competencies. The text covers all core areas of the HRM curriculum and includes a minimum of two experiential exercises per chapter. These class-tested exercises are designed to encourage students to address current challenges and issues in various organizational settings as they seek to improve HRM practices in each of the areas covered by the course.
Contents: 1. Human Resource Management in a Changing Environment. 2. Competitive Advantage Through Human Resources. 3. Equal Employment Opportunity. 4. Job Analysis. 5. Planning & Recruitment. 6. Personnel Selection 7. Employment Interviewing. 8. Training and Development. 9. Career Development. 10. Performance Appraisal. 11. Direct and Indirect Compensation. 12. Pay for Performance. 13. Strategies for Improving Productivity, Quality, QWL. 14. Labor Relations. 15. Collective Bargaining. 16. Health & Safety. Appendix: Measurement Issues.
SOFTCOVER; AVAAILABLE ON PRIMIS
-pp.752
004916-5

INSTRUCTOR'S MANUAL WITH TEST BANK
004917-3

1993   WERTHER, W.

William B. Werther, Jr., University of Miami
Keith A. Davis, Professor Emeritus, Arizona State
University
HUMAN RESOURCES AND PERSONNEL MANAGEMENT, Fourth Edition

The fourth edition of HUMAN RESOURCES AND
PERSONNEL MANAGEMENT builds upon the
major pedagogical strengths of previous editions
while thoroughly incorporating the most current
developments and trends in this dynamic field. The
book continues to be strikingly readable with a
multitude of real-life vignettes designed to bring
conceptual material to life. This edition is further
distinguished by its inclusion of vital contemporary
issues such as cultural diversity, ethics, globalization,
and the impact of HRM on corporate strategy.
Coverage of legal issues has been thoroughly
updated to reflect significant developments of the
early nineties.
-pp.704
069551-2

STUDY GUIDE
069563-6

INSTRUCTOR'S MANUAL/TEST BANK
069552-0

COMPUTERIZED TEST BANK IBM 5 1/4"
833954-5

COMPUTERIZED TEST BANK IBM 3 1/2"
833955-3

OVERHEAD TRANSPARENCIES
074528-5

VIDEO SERIES PLUS GUIDE
911520-9

1992   WALKER

James W. Walker, The Walker Group
HUMAN RESOURCE STRATEGY

Walker's 1980 McGraw-Hill title, Human Resource
Planning, encompassed the most significant trends in
human resource management of the 1980's; in a
similar manner, this new offering is destined to
become the forward-looking text of the '90's, and
potentially will influence the way human resource
management is taught in many institutions. The shift
from a traditional planning to strategic emphasis,
and special attention to human resource issues are in
line with the most current thinking. Walker's
examples include some of the world's most
innovative, flexible organizations.
Contents: 1. Introduction. 2. Focusing on Human
Resource Issues. 3. Developing Human Resource
Strategies. 4. Shaping Expectations. 5. Designing the
Future Organization. 6. Strategic Staffing. 7.
Developing Employee Talent. 8. Developing
Management Talent for the Future. 9. Providing
Resources for Performance. 10. Evaluating
Performance. 11. Recognizing and Rewarding
Performance. 12. Managing the Human Resource
Function. 13. Evaluating Results in Managing
Human Resources.
-pp.448
067846-4

INSTRUCTOR'S MANUAL/TEST BANK
067847-2

1989   STONEBRAKER

Peter W. Stonebraker, Northeastern Illinois
University
EXERCISES AND PROBLEMS IN HUMAN RESOURCE MANAGEMENT: Using the Microcomputer

SEE: Management and Organization: Personnel/
Human Resource Management (Supplementary)
STUDENT MANUAL AND DISK, IBM 5 1/4"
909169-5

PERSONNEL/HUMAN RESOURCE MANAGEMENT (SUPPLEMENTARY)

1992   Harvard   HILL

Linda A. Hill, Harvard Business School
BECOMING A MANAGER: Mastery of a New Identity

Linda Hill traces the experiences of nineteen new
managers over the course of their first year in a
managerial capacity. She reveals the complexity of
the transition and analyzes the expectations of the
managers, their subordinates, and their superiors.
The new managers describe how they reframed their
understanding of their roles and responsibilities, how
they learned to build effective work relationships,
how and when they used individual and
organizational resources, and how they learned to
cope with the inevitable stresses of the
transformation. Above all, they describe what it was
like to take on a new identity. It is must reading for
human resource professionals and others responsible
for management development, as well as for the
manager struggling to take on a new identity.
Contents: Preface. Introduction. PART ONE:
LEARNING WHAT IT MEANS TO BE A
MANAGER: 1. Setting the Stage. 2. Reconciling
Expectations. 3. Moving toward a Managerial
Identity. PART TWO: DEVELOPING
INTERPERSONAL JUDGMENT: 4. Exercising
Authority. 5. Managing Subordinate Performance.
PART THREE: WORKING ON ONESELF AND
LEARNING ABOUT ONESELF: 6. Discovering the
Self. 7. Coping with the Stress and Emotions of
Transformation. PART FOUR: MANAGING THE
TRANSFORMATION: 8. Critical Resources for the
First Year. 9. Easing the Transition.
-pp.331
103313-0

1989   STONEBRAKER

Peter W. Stonebraker, Northeastern Illinois
University
EXERCISES AND PROBLEMS IN HUMAN RESOURCE MANAGEMENT: Using the Microcomputer

This is a computerized workbook to accompany
Human Resources Management texts. The exercises
provide skill-building and quantitative problems
situations for both the beginning level and the
computer literate student.
Contents: Personnel Management and the Personal
Computer. The Structure of an Organization. The
Functions of Human Resource Management. Equal
Employment Opportunity. Staff Planning Activities.

Progression and Replacement Considerations. Job
Analysis. Recruitment and Selection. Orientation and
Placement, Training and Development. Career
Planning. Performance Appraisal. Factor
Comparison Method. Point System Method.
Incentives and Gainsharing. Employee Benefits and
Services. Employee Safety. Diagnosis of Employee
Relations Issues. Labor Bargaining Based on Cost
Analysis. Personnel Audits.
STUDENT MANUAL AND DISK, IBM, 5 1/4"
909169-5

INSTRUCTOR'S MANUAL
834617-7

LABOR MANAGEMENT AND COLLECTIVE BARGAINING

1994   MILLS

Dr. D. Quinn Mills, Harvard University
LABOR MANAGEMENT RELATIONS, Fifth Edition

The revision of this classic labor relations text,
written by a respected scholar, emphasizes the rapid
social, demographic, and economic changes now
affecting the workplace. To this end, new chapters on
workplace diversity and new work systems have
been added. In addition, all material has been
thoroughly updated, including important recent
court decisions. The text continues to be
distinguished by its comprehensive coverage and
solid research base.
Contents: 1. The Industrial Relations System. 2.
History and Philosophy of American Unions. 3.
Membership and Structure in the American Labor
Movement. 4. Unions, Management, and the New
Workplace. 5. Human Diversity in the Workplace. 6.
Nonunion and Union. 7. Statutory and Judicial
Regulation. 8. The NLRB and Unfair Labor Practices.
9. Union Organization and Representation Elections.
10. Different Patterns of Relations in the Public
Sector. 11. Labor - Management Relations in the
Public Sector. 12. Industrial Relations Abroad. 13.
The Negotiations Process. 14. Union Organization for
Bargaining. 15. Management Preparations for
Negotiations. 16. Strikes and Dispute Settlement. 17.
Rights of Employees, Unions and Management. 18.
Wages: Theory and Practice. 19. Benefits. 20.
Grievances and Arbitration. 21. Quality, Productivity
and Employment Security. 22. The Consequences of
Collective Bargaining.
-pp.704
042512-4

INSTRUCTOR'S MANUAL/TEST BANK
042513-2

1992   KATZ

Harry Charles Katz, Cornell University
Thomas A. Kochan, Massachusetts Institute of
Technology
INTRODUCTION TO COLLECTIVE BARGAINING AND INDUSTRIAL RELATIONS

Authored by a well-respected team in labor relations,
this text covers key topics in industrial relations and
collective bargaining using a unique conceptual
framework based on the three levels of industrial
relations activity (strategic, functional, and

workplace). Formerly a graduate-level book, it has been completely rewritten for undergraduates. Two extensive, class-tested mock-bargaining exercises are included. International and comparative labor relations are both integrated throughout and receive full chapter treatment. The text extensively discusses recent reorganizations in the process and outcome of bargaining, including detailed treatment of the participatory process.
Contents: PART ONE: INTRODUCTION: 1. A Framework for Analyzing Industrial Relations and Collective Bargaining. 2. The Historical Evolution of the U.S. Industrial Relations System. 3. The Legal Regulation of Unions and Collective Bargaining. 4. The Role of the Environment. PART TWO: THE STRATEGIC LEVEL OF INDUSTRIAL RELATIONS: 5. Management Strategies and Structures for Collective Bargaining. 6. Union Strategies and Structures for Representing Workers. PART THREE: THE FUNCTIONAL (MIDDLE) LEVEL OF INDUSTRIAL RELATIONS: 7. Union Organization and Bargaining Structures. 8. The Negotiations Process and Strikes. 9. Impasse Resolution Procedures. 10. Contract Terms and Job Outcomes. PART FOUR: THE WORKPLACE LEVEL OF INDUSTRIAL RELATIONS: 11. Administering the Employment Relationship. 12. Participatory Processes. PART FIVE. SPECIAL TOPICS: 13. Collective Bargaining in the Public Sector. 14. International and Comparative Industrial Relations. 15. The Future of U.S. Labor Policy and Industrial Relations. Mock Bargaining: D.G. Barnhouse. Mock Bargaining: Police Case. Grievance Arbitration Exercises. Glossary.
-pp.640
033645-8

INSTRUCTOR'S MANUAL/TEST BANK
033646-6
COMPUTERIZED TEST BANK, IBM, 5 1/4"
832495-5
MOCK BARGAINING EXERCISE SOFTWARE, IBM 5 1/4"
832051-6

1985   CHAMBERLAIN

Neil W. Chamberlain, Columbia University
James W. Kuhn, Columbia University
COLLECTIVE BARGAINING, Third Edition
010441-7

BUSINESS POLICY AND STRATEGIC MANAGEMENT

1993   DESS

Gregory G. Dess, University of Texas
Alex Miller, University of Tennessee
STRATEGIC MANAGEMENT
This innovative text with cases features solid coverage of core concepts in strategic management. The text portion offers fully integrated treatment of business ethics, small business and entrepreneurship topics, as well as full-chapter coverage of global strategic management. Theories and concepts are brought to life via numerous current examples from a variety of organizations. This emphasis on actual business practice is further supported by such pedagogical features as "Executive Interviews" (commissioned exclusively for use in this book and

linked directly to chapter coverage) and "Strategic Management Applications" boxes. STRATEGIC MANAGEMENT's collection of 36 class-tested cases includes a mix of original author-written cases and additional classic and contemporary cases based on a variety of industries and organization types.
Contents: PART ONE: STRATEGIC ANALYSIS. 1. A Mandate for Strategic Management. 2. The External Environment: Identifying Opportunities and Threats. 3. Assessing the Internal Environment: Determining Strengths and Weaknesses. PART TWO: STRATEGY FORMULATION. 4. Strategic Management at the Business Level: Managing for Competitive Advantage. 5. Strategic Management at the Functional Level: Managing for Customer Value. 6. Strategic Management at the Corporate Level: Diversification for Stockholder Value. 7. Strategic Management at the International Level: Managing for Global Success. PART THREE: STRATEGY IMPLEMENTATION. 8. Translating Strategy into Action and Achieving Integration. 9. Strategy Implementation: The Role of Organizational Structure. 10. Implementing Strategy: Ensuring Strategic Control. 11. Leadership, Culture, and Ethics. PART FOUR: CASE ANALYSIS: 12. Analyzing Strategic Situations and Cases. CASES: SMALL-BUSINESS CASES: 1. United Products, Inc. 2. Brithinee Electric, Inc. 3. Wall Drug Store; Facing the 90's. 4. Brookout Technology, Inc. 5. The Battle of the Superpremium Ice Creams. THE U.S. ATHLETIC SHOE INDUSTRY: 6. A Brief History of Athletic Shoes. 7. Nike and Reebok: One on One. 8. The Sneaker Wars. 9. L.A. Gear. 10. Nike and the Inner-City Youth Market. THE PC SOFTWARE CONNECTION. 11. A Brief History of the PC Software Industry. 12. Lotus Development Corporation. THE SOFT DRINK INDUSTRY. 13. The Seven-Up Co., Division of Philip Morris Incorporated. 14. New Coke: Coca-Cola's Response to the Pepsi Challenge. THE U.S. PHARMACEUTICAL INDUSTRY: 15. A Brief History of the U.S. Pharmaceutical Industry. 16. Eastman Kodak's Acquisition of Sterling Drug. THE PHOTOCOPIER INDUSTRY: 17. Xerox Corporation: 1960-1980. 18. Xerox Corporation: 1980-1983. 19. Xerox Corporation: 1983-1989. CASES EMPHASIZING STRATEGY FORMULATION: 20. American Greetings Looks to the 90's. 21. Federal Express Corporation. 22. The Swatch. 23. Foodplus. 24. From Airline to Empire: United Airlines Under. 25. Northrop Corporation: Dilemma of the Tigershark (Revised). 26. Maytag Corporation. 27. Proctor & Gamble Europe: Vizir Launch. CASES EMPHASIZING IMPLEMENTATION ISSUES: 28. The Lincoln Electric Company. 29. Nucor. 30. J & M AirFrames. 31. Management Wins a Round Against Wall Street? The Santa Fe Southern Pacific Case. 32. Oklahoma Meets Wall Street. 33. The Fallon McElligott Advertising Agency: Image Making by Image Makers. 34. Arco Solar, Inc. 35. Arthur D. Little, Inc. and the Toxic Alert. 36. The GM Acquisition of EDS: A Clash of Organizational Cultures.
-pp.944
016569-6

VOL. 1 INSTRUCTOR'S MANUAL/TEST BANK/VIDEO GUIDE
016570-X
VOL. 2 INSTRUCTOR'S MANUAL: CASE ANALYSIS
016571-8
SAMPLER OF 2 IM VOL 1 & 2 CHAPTERS
016587-4
106 2-C OVERHEAD TRANSPARENCIES
074432-7
SPREADSHEET SOFTWARE—IBM 3 1/2"
835213-4
SPREADSHEET SOFTWARE—IBM 5 1/4"
835217-7
VIDEO SERIES (8 PROGRAMS) 1 VHS

016623-4

1992 Harvard   BOWER

Joseph L. Bower, Harvard Business School
THE CRAFT OF GENERAL MANAGEMENT
Designed for a senior-level or first-year MBA course on general management, this new softcover text covers basic concepts and emerging issues in the field. The text deals with vital issues for the 1990s, including ethical aspects of general management, managing business-government relations, and analyzing the competitive environment. Strategy and leadership are highlighted. The readings provide a practice-oriented grounding that can function alone or be orchestrated and interwoven with cases, exercises, and other materials. The book is also available as a PRIMIS CUSTOM PUBLICATION.
Contents: PART ONE: The Work of General Management. PART TWO: Making Strategy. PART THREE: Building the Organization. PART FOUR: Managing Complexity. PART FIVE: Leadership.
-pp.400
006762-7

1991   THAVIKULWAT

Precha Thavikulwat, Towson State University
CEO STRATEGIC MANAGEMENT SIMULATION
CEO is a new simulation in which students practice strategic management decision-making. Students work in teams on analysis, mission objectives, strategy formulation, implementation, and control. Students scan the business environment, perceive threats and opportunities, note trends, and make forecasts. Class-tested for three years, CEO also includes Lotus templates for linear programming for strategy formulation.
Contents: 1. The CEO Simulation in Strategic Management. 2. Environmental Analysis. 3. Missions and Objectives. 4. Strategy Formulation. 5. Strategy Implementation. 6. Strategic Control
CEO STUDENT SET, IBM 5 1/4"
-pp.128
834713-0

CEO STUDENT SET, IBM 3 1/2"
834710-6
CEO ADOPTER'S DESK SET, IBM 5 1/4"
834708-4
CEO ADOPTER'S DESK SET, IBM 3 1/2"
834704-1
INSTRUCTOR'S MANUAL
010449-2

1989   RUE

Leslie W. Rue, Ph.D., Georgia State University
Phyllis G. Holland, Ph.D., Valdosta State College
STRATEGIC MANAGEMENT: Concepts and Experiences, Second Edition
Designed for the capstone business policy/strategy course, the second edition's emphasis is on practical examples. Extensive support material includes industry notes to accompany 32 cases (12 new) which are now separated out of the text and located in the back. Case data for spreadsheet analysis available on disk (text with software, or text alone).
Contents: The Role of Strategic Management. The Strategic Management Process. Generic Strategy Alternatives. Identifying Mission and Strategy. The

Decision Environment and the Establishment of Objectives. Assessing the Environment. Internal Analysis: Action Capabilities and Corporate Culture. Generating, Evaluating, and Choosing Strategic Alternatives. Implementing Strategy: Communication and Tactical Issues. Implementing Strategy: Leadership, Systems, and Structure. Strategic Control and Evaluation. International Strategy and Global Strategies.
-pp.897
054308-9

INSTRUCTOR'S MANUAL
054309-7
TEXT WITH CASE ANALYST SOFTWARE, IBM, 5 1/4"
909167-9
INSTRUCTOR'S MANUAL FOR CASE ANALYST SOFTWARE
026867-3

1989 Harvard   WALTON

Richard E. Walton, Harvard Business School
UP AND RUNNING: Integrating Information Technology and the Organization
Using the experiences of diverse organizations such as IBM, GE, Mrs. Fields Inc., the IRS, and 14 others, Up and Running illustrates the many ways in which IT and organizational dynamics can affect each other positively and negatively. Walton takes the reader through each step of the implementation process, from creating a context, to design, and through the introduction and diffusion phases. The book provides a practical framework that helps organizations get the most out of their information systems.
Contents: Introduction and Overview. PART ONE: WHY IT IMPLEMENTATION MUST INCLUDE ORGANIZATIONAL CHANGE: 1. The Relationships Between IT and Organization—Crucial, Complex, and Manageable. 2. Relating IT and Organization—A Case in Point. PART TWO: PHASE ONE: CREATING THE CONTEXT: 3. Creating a Strategic Vision. 4. Promoting Organization Commitment and Competence. 5. Ensuring Broad and Informed Political Support. PART THREE: PHASE TWO: DESIGNING AN IT SYSTEM. 6. Choosing Design Concepts. 7. Managing Design Processes. Part FOUR: Phase Three: Putting the It System into Practice. 8. Introducing IT Systems. 9. Diffusing IT Systems. 10. Conclusion—Key Implementation Issues.
-pp.231
103275-4

1986 Harvard   TEDLOW

Richard S. Tedlow
Richard R. John, Jr.
MANAGING BIG BUSINESS: Essays from the Business History Review
-pp.400
103272-X

1985   SHARPLIN

Arthur D. Sharplin, Northeast Louisiana University
STRATEGIC MANAGEMENT
-pp.604
056513-9

INSTRUCTOR'S MANUAL
056514-7

BUSINESS POLICY AND STRATEGIC MANAGEMENT SOFTWARE

1991   RUSSO

Joseph A. Russo, Pace University
Melvyn Fisher, Pace University
DECISION-MAKING TOOLKIT FOR STRATEGIC MANAGEMENT, Second Edition
The Decision-Making Toolkit for Strategic Management gives the student experience in quantitative and qualitative methods in the strategic management decision-making process. As decision maker of a firm, the student enters quantitative data, arrives at a numerical answer, and then makes qualitative decisions. The program represents a significant advance over software currently used in undergraduate strategic management courses. It starts with the general and proceeds to the specific providing students with an approach to decision making that can be used in a variety of circumstances rather than with fixed information to be used only once.

LOTUS TOOLKIT, IBM, 5 1/4"
837209-7
LOTUS TOOLKIT, IBM, 3 1/2"
837210-0
STARCALC TOOLKIT, IBM 5 1/4"
831848-3
INSTRUCTOR'S MANUAL
832189-1

1991   THAVIKULWAT

Precha Thavikulwat, Towson State University
CEO STRATEGIC MANAGEMENT SIMULATION
CEO STUDENT SET, IBM 5 1/4"
SEE: Management and Organization—Business Policy and Strategic Management
-pp.128
834713-0

BUSINESS POLICY (SUPPLEMENTARY)

1991 Harvard   JACOBS

Michael T. Jacobs
SHORT-TERM AMERICA: The Causes and Cures of Our Business Myopia
Americans have a growing conviction that we are losing economic ground to rivals in Europe and Asia. From store shelves to parking lots, the evidence of this competitive decline is abundantly visible. Less apparent are its causes and cures. Pundits point to everything from inadequate public schools to drug abuse as sources of our economic malaise, but savvy business leaders and thoughtful scholars concur that short-term thinking and short-sighted behavior by both corporate managers and investors are at the heart of the problem. We cannot develop the technologies, penetrate the markets, or manufacture

the products necessary to compete on a global basis if our businesses focus on quarterly results and this week's stock prices. Business myopia is undermining the long-term viability of American companies and, in some cases, entire industries
Contents: 1. Business Myopia and U.S. Competitiveness. 2. The Commoditization of Corporate Ownership. 3. How Corporations Are Really Governed. 4. The Truth about Takeovers. 5. The Demise of Relationship Banking. 6. The Cost of Capital Enigma. 7. Management Compensation Plans—Panacea or Placebo? 8. A Cure for Myopia. Notes. Index.
-pp.268
103310-6

1991 Harvard   MONTGOMERY

Cynthia A. Montgomery, Harvard Business School
Michael E. Porter, Harvard Business School
STRATEGY: Seeking and Securing Competitive Advantage
This collection of HARVARD BUSINESS REVIEW articles provides the best thinking available on how to make the critical decisions that determine business success. Montgomery and Porter's introduction places the field of strategy in its historical perspective, tracing the evolution of business strategy from its beginnings in the early 1960s to the present. They elucidate how business organization and environment have affected strategy and, in turn, been affected by it. What makes up an effective strategy? This volume offers insight and practical advice form the leaders in the field: Michael Porter, Kenichi Ohmae, Steven Wheelwright, Gary Hamel, and C.K. Parhalad, among others. Special emphasis is placed on strategy as an integrating device which brings together and balances the key resources of a firm and positions the firm advantageously in its competitive environment.
Contents: PART ONE: Business and Strategy. PART TWO: Linking Competitive Strategy and Functional Strategy. PART THREE: Evolving Nature of International Competition. PART FOUR: Corporate Strategy and Firm Scope. PART FIVE: The Process of Making Strategy. PART SIX: Corporate Governance. Index.
-pp.475
103295-9

1988   REALITY TECH

Reality Technologies
BUSINESS WEEK'S ADVANTAGE
Developed by Reality Technologies, Inc., in conjunction with "Business Week," this user-friendly yet professional software utilities expert offers insight, tutorial, consultant, and analysis modes to create the most exciting software for the strategy area. Undergraduates and graduates alike will find this simulation challenging and find themselves able to make better and more reasoned strategic decisions. It is designed for the IBM PC and compatibles with 386/x, DOS 2.0 or higher and two disk drives. Printer and color monitor are optional. Students receive a user's manual and disk with four simulations. Professors receive an instructor's manual and two copyable system "engine" disks.
834519-7

EXPERT DISK
834521-9
SYSTEM DISK
834520-0
INSTRUCTOR'S MANUAL, EXPERT DISK, SYSTEM DISK
051302-3

BUSINESS AND SOCIETY AND ETHICS

1994 STEINER

George A. Steiner, University of California, Los Angeles
John F. Steiner, California State University at Los Angeles

BUSINESS, GOVERNMENT AND SOCIETY: A MANAGERIAL PERSPECTIVE, Seventh Edition

The revision of this highly regarded text continues to build upon the strengths of past editions, including thorough, in-depth coverage and strong, comprehensive cases. The text has been significantly revised to reflect important current issues and events, although (as always) the historical perspective is treated with respect. This edition emphasizes coverage of developing legal precedent about issues of corporate social responsibility and ethics. In addition, there is increased attention to international business issues. Both authors are respected scholars; the senior author is considered one of the pioneers in the field of business, government, and society.
Contents: PART ONE: A FRAMEWORK FOR STUDYING BUSINESS, GOVERNMENT & SOCIETY. 1. Introduction to the Field. 2. The Business Environment. CASE: Asbestos Litigation "Bankrupts" Manville. 3. Corporate Power and Legitimacy. CASE: Construction of the Central Pacific. 4. Critics of Business. CASE: Time Warner & the "Cop Killer" Controversy. PART TWO: BUSINESS SOCIAL RESPONSIBILITIES. 5. The Social Responsibilities of Business. CASE: War Toys. 6. Institutionalizing Social Concerns in Business. CASE: The Union Carbide Corporation & Bhopal. PART THREE: BUSINESS ETHICS. 7. Ethics in the Business System. CASE: A.H. Robbins and the Palkon Shield. 8. Making Ethical Decisions in Business. CASE: Dow Corning & Breast Implants. PART FOUR: BUSINESS & GOVERNMENT. 9. The Government-Business Relationship: An Overview. CASE: The Savings and Loan Bailout. 10. Reforming the Regulatory System. CASE: Airline Deregulation. 11. Business & the Political Process. CASE: PANPAC & the Senate Candidate. PART FIVE: GLOBAL MANAGEMENT ISSUES. 12. Multinational Corporations & Government Relationships. CASE: NAFTA. 13. Corporate Global Competitiveness. CASE: Caterpillar, Inc. PART SIX: POLLUTION & THE ENVIRONMENT. 14. Assessing and Managing Pollution Risks. CASE: Owls, Loggers, & the Old Growth Forests. 15. Environmental Policy Issues. CASE: The Exxon Valdez Oil Spill. PART SEVEN: BUSINESS & THE CONSUMER. 16. Consumerism. CASE: Restrictions on Alcohol & Tobacco Advertising. PART EIGHT: HUMAN RESOURCES. 17. The Changing Internal Face of Organizational Life. CASE: Drug Testing of Employees. 18. Minorities, Women, & Antidiscrimination Law CASES: A New Plant Manager, Martin v. Wilks, Cotton Springfield. PART NINE: CORPORATE GOVERNANCE. 19. Reforming Corporate Governance. CASE: Pension Funds & Corporate Governance.
-pp.688
061226-9

INSTRUCTOR'S MANUAL/TEST BANK
061227-7
COMPUTERIZED TEST BANK, IBM 3.5"
833737-2

COMPUTERIZED TEST BANK - IBM PC 5 1/4"
833617-1
VIDEO PROGRAM
911744-0

1992 FREDERICK

William C. Frederick, University of Pittsburgh
James E. Post, Boston University
Keith Davis, Arizona State University

BUSINESS & SOCIETY: Corporate Strategy, Public Policy, Ethics, Seventh Edition

The seventh edition of this classic business and society text has a greater global focus and significantly increased emphasis on ethics. The topics of social and ethical responsiveness, the global outlook for multinational corporations, knowledge of geopolitical trends in policies and attitudes, responsiveness to stakeholders, and the social issues in management have all been revitalized in this edition. Ten cases bring to life issues of responsible corporate social policy in areas such as product recalls, international and intercultural business, industrial accidents and disasters, environmental hazards, community activism, ethical dilemmas, and others.
Contents: PART ONE: THE CORPORATION IN SOCIETY: 1. The Corporation and Its Stakeholders. 2. Corporate Social Responsibility. 3. Ethical Dilemmas in Business. 4. Improving Ethical Performance in Business. 5. Socially Responsive Management. PART TWO: THE CORPORATION IN A GLOBAL SOCIETY: 6. Corporate Social Strategy: Global Challenges. 7. Managing in Diverse Social Systems. 8. The Multinational Corporation. PART THREE: THE CORPORATION AND PUBLIC POLICY: 9. Public Policy and the Political Environment. 10. The Government-Business Interface: Regulation, Deregulation, and Collaboration. 11. Competition, Antitrust, and Global Business. PART FOUR: RESPONDING TO CORPORATE STAKEHOLDERS: 12. Stockholders and Corporate Governance. 13. Employees: The Human Factor in the Workplace. 14. Consumer Protection. 15. The Community and the Corporation. PART FIVE: SOCIAL ISSUES IN MANAGEMENT: 16. Women, Men and the Family: Workplace Issues. 17. Business and Media Relations. 18. Science, Technology, and Business. 19. Ecology and Environmental Policy.
-pp.640
015613-1

INSTRUCTOR'S MANUAL/TESTBANK
015614-X
TRANSPARENCY MASTERS
074687-7

1991 MATTHEWS

John B. Matthews Jr., Harvard Business School
Kenneth E. Goodpaster, Harvard Business School
Laura L. Nash, Harvard Business School

POLICIES AND PERSONS: A Casebook in Business Ethics, Second Edition

Ancillaries are available.
040999-4

1991 STEINER

John F. Steiner, California State University, Los Angeles

INDUSTRY, SOCIETY, AND CHANGE: A Casebook

This new book includes 13 well-researched, high quality cases for business and society. The book is compatible with any business and society textbook, or can be used as a stand-alone. The author, a well-respected case writer, has focused on lively and interesting examples, organized around the major topical areas of business and society.
Contents: 1. John D. Rockefeller And The Standard Oil Trust. 2. Every Man A King: The Populism of Huey Long. 3. Deregulation of the Airline Industry. 4. Factory Farming. 5. The Global Threat of Warming. 6. Earth First! The Battle for Old Growth Timber. 7. The Fight for the Road Dispatcher's Job (Johnson v. Transportation Agency). 8. Honesty Testing. 9. The Saturday Night Special Case: Kelly v. R.G. Industries. 10. Selling Tobacco. 11. The KKR-RJR Nabisco Blockbuster Leveraged Buyout. 12. Unrest Over Corporate Involvement In South Africa. 13. Union Carbide And The Bhopal Plant Gas Leak.
-pp.348
061174-2

INSTRUCTOR'S MANUAL
061177-7

1989 Harvard ANDREWS

Kenneth R. Andrews, Harvard Business School

ETHICS IN PRACTICE: Managing the Moral Corporation

What is it about organizational structure that fails to communicate ethical and moral standards to everyone from the CEO to the office clerk? This study looks at the problem from a business point of view, tracing the growth of ethical awareness in corporate life and offering pragmatic suggestions for executive action to produce an ethical environment.
Contents: Introduction. PART ONE: THE EXECUTIVE AS A MORAL INDIVIDUAL. 1. Why "Good" Managers Make Bad Ethical Choices. 2. Can an Executive Afford a Conscience? 3 Moral Hazards of an Executive. 4. Personal Values and Business Decisions. 5. "Skyhooks." 6. Ethical Managers Make Their Own Rules. 7. Storytellers' Ethics. PART TWO: THE CORPORATION AS MORAL ENVIRONMENT. 1. Note on the Corporation as Moral Environment. 2. Is Business Bluffing Ethical? 3. Showdown on "Business Bluffing." 4. Is the Ethics of Business Changing? 5. The Ethical Roots of the Business System. 6. Can a Corporation Have a Conscience? 7. Moral Mazes: Bureaucracy and Managerial Work. 8. Why Do Companies Succumb to Price Fixing? 9. The Parable of the Sadhu. PART THREE: EXECUTIVE ACTION FOR MORAL OUTCOMES. 1. Ethical Imperatives and Corporate Leadership. 2. Case of the Rogue Division. 3. Ethics Without the Sermon. 4. Can the Best Corporations Be Made Moral? 5. Business Leadership and a Creative Society. Epilogue.
-pp.294
103200-2

1989 HOFFMAN

Michael W. Hoffman, Ph.D., Bentley College
Jennifer Mills Moore, Ph.D., University of Delaware

BUSINESS ETHICS: Readings and Cases in Corporate Morality, Second Edition

Ancillaries are available.
029328-7

INTERNATIONAL BUSINESS

1994   HODGETTS

Richard M. Hodgetts, Florida International University
Fred Luthans, University of Nebraska
INTERNATIONAL MANAGEMENT, Second Edition
Thoroughly updated to reflect the critical world developments of the nineties, International Management is the first international text to offer a true managerial orientation. The text features in-depth coverage of both the strategic and behavioral dimensions of international management in a highly accessible style. Written by an experienced author team, International Management offers unparalleled pedagogy including numerous cases, boxed vignettes, review/discussion questions, exercises, and generous tables, charts and exhibits.
Contents: PART ONE: OVERALL PERSPECTIVE OF INTERNATIONAL MANAGEMENT. 1. Worldwide Developements. 2. Foundations for International Management. 3. Cultural Context for International Management. 4. Managing Across Cultures. Case: Protectionism - Pro and Con. Case: The Road to Hell. PART TWO: STRATEGIES & FUNCTIONS OF MANAGING INTERNATIONAL ORGANIZATIONS. 5. Strategic Planning. 6. Managing Political Risk and Negotiations. 7. Organizing International Operations. 8. Decision Making and Controlling. Case: Iridium - Motorola's Global Venture. Case: Pebble Beach Golf Links. PART THREE: FUNCTIONS OF INTERNATIONAL HUMAN RESOURCE MANAGEMENT. 9. Personnel Selection and Repatriation. 10. Training and Organization Development. 11. Labor Relations and Industrial Democracy. Case: Dover Apparel Company. PART FOUR: MANAGING PEOPLE IN INTERNATIONAL ORGANIZATIONS. 12. Communication. 13. Motivating Human Resources. 14. Leading Human Resources. Case: A True Adventure in Mexico. PART FIVE: INTERNATIONAL MANAGEMENT HORIZONS. 15. Ethics and Social Responsibility. 16. Future of International Management. GLOSSARY. REFERENCES. INDEX.
-pp.608
029222-1

INSTRUCTOR'S MANUAL/TEST BANK
029223-X
COMPUTERIZED TEST BANK - IBM PC 5 1/4"
833594-9
VIDEO PROGRAM
911773-2
COMPUTERIZED TEST BANK, IBM 3.5"
841497-0

1994   TRIANDIS

Harry C. Triandis, University of Illinois
CULTURE AND SOCIAL BEHAVIOR, First Edition
SEE: Psychology—Social Psychology—Attitudes and Behavior. Ancillaries are available.
065110-8

1994   YOFFIE

David B. Yoffie, Harvard University
Benjamin Gomes-Casseres, Harvard University

INTERNATIONAL TRADE AND COMPETITION, Second Edition

Through a collection of case studies from the Harvard Business School, this text develops a conceptual framework for students of management that will improve their ability to compete internationally. Its cross-disciplinary approach integrates coverage of international economics, business strategy, government policy, global politics, economic theory, and industrial policy in order to provide a practical yet sophisticated framework for managing international competition. This text explores the chief sources of international competitive advantage available to firms — country environments, government policies, and firm capabilities — and provides students with an understanding of key institutions and regulations of international commerce, such as the GATT and U.S. trade law.
Contents: PART ONE: THEORIES OF INTERNATIONAL TRADE. 1. Note on Comparative Advantage. 2. Note on Sources of Comparative Advantage. 3. "New" Theories of International Trade. PART TWO: COMPARATIVE ADVANTAGE & INDUSTRY STRUCTURE. 4. The Japanese Facsimile Industry in 1990. 5. The Global Semiconductor Industry, 1987. 6. The Global Computer Industry. PART THREE: COMPARATIVE ADVANTAGE & CORPORATE STRATEGY. 7. B-W Footwear. 8. Lotus Development Corporation: Entering International Markets. 9. Hoechst and the German Chemical Industry. 10. Hoechst in the U.S. PART FOUR: INTERMEDIATION IN INTERNATIONAL TRADE. 11. Japan's Sogoshosha. 12. General Electric Trading Company, 1985. 13. Note on Trade Finance. PART FIVE: ALLIANCES IN INTERNATIONAL COMPETITION. 14. Swissair's Alliances. 15. Xerox and Fuji Xerox. 16. Mips Computer Systems. 17. The FS-X Project. PART SIX: THE POLITICAL ECONOMY OF TRADE POLICY. 18. Textiles & the Multi-Fiber Arrangement. 19. Note on Free Trade and Protectionism. 20. Europe 1992. 21. North American Free Trade Agreement: Free for Whom? 22. The General Agreement on Tariffs and Trade. PART SEVEN: TRADE POLICY & CORPORATE STRATEGY. 23. Searching for Trade Remedies: The U.S. Machine Tool Industry, 1983. 24. United States Trade Law. 25. The Semiconductor Industry Association and the Trade Dispute with Japan. 26. Canada Packers and the Canada-U.S. Free Trade Agreement. PART EIGHT: INDUSTRIAL POLICY AND INTERNATIONAL COMPETITION. 27. Motorola and Japan. 28. Collision Course in Commercial Aircraft: Boeing-Airbus-McDonnell Douglas, 1991. 29. Zenith and High Definition Television, 1990. Fusion Systems Corporation in Japan.
-pp.512
072300-1

INSTRUCTOR'S MANUAL/CASE NOTES
072301-X

1992 Harvard   BARTLETT

Christopher A. Bartlett, Harvard Business School
Sumantra Ghoshal, INSEAD
MANAGING ACROSS BORDERS: The Transnational Solution
Bartlett and Ghoshal show how the nature of the competitive game has fundamentally changed, requiring companies to capture global-scale efficiency, respond to national market needs, and develop a worldwide learning capability that drives continuous innovation. They explain why companies that operated on the traditional multinational, international, or global management models built only one or perhaps two of these strategic capabilities. What is required is a new organizational form—the transnational. The authors not only describe the characteristics of the emerging transnational organization, they also provide specific guidance on how companies can develop them.
Contents: PART ONE: THE TRANSNATIONAL CHALLENGE: 1. Organizational Capability: The Next Battleground. 2. New Organizational Challenge: Beyond Structural Fit. 3. Administrative Heritage: Organizational Asset and Constraint. 4. The Transnational: The Emerging Model. PART TWO: CHARACTERISTICS OF THE TRANSNATIONAL: 5. Building Competitiveness: The Integrated Network. 6. Developing Flexibility: Specialized Roles and Responsibilities. 7. Facilitating Learning: Multiple Innovation Processes. PART THREE: BUILDING AND MANAGING THE TRANSNATIONAL: 8. Legitimizing Diversity: Balancing Multiple Perspectives. 9. Managing Complexity: Developing Flexible Coordination. 10. Building Commitment: Creating a Matrix in Managers' Minds. 11. The Transnational Solution. Appendix: Research Methodology.
-pp.288
103314-9

1990 Harvard   LAWRENCE

Paul R. Lawrence, Harvard Business School
Charalambos Vlachoutsicos, Harvard Business School
BEHIND THE FACTORY WALLS: Decision Making in Soviet and U.S. Enterprises
A detailed comparative study of management techniques in the United States and the Soviet Union. Documents the first time that American and Soviet management scholars have conducted in-depth field research in both countries. Shows how managers in each country develop business plans, hire and fire personnel, make capital investment decisions, and introduce new products into the marketplace. Will help pave the way for future joint ventures.
Contents: SECTION ONE: THEORY AND CONTEXT: 1. A Comparative Study of Soviet and American Management Systems. 2. US and USSR Cultural Characteristics. 3. History of US and Soviet Economic Institutions. 4. US and Soviet Contemporary Management Theory. SECTION TWO: FIELD RESEARCH ON DECISION MAKING: 5. Field Sites and Managerial Practices. 6. Planning. 7. Hiring and Firing Managers. 8. Capital Investment Decisions. 9. New Product Introduction. SECTION THREE: COMPARATIVE DECISION-MAKING PATTERNS: 10. Managerial Patterns: Differences and Commonalities. 11. Trends and Conclusions. SECTION FOUR: APPENDICES: APPENDIX A: A Description of Soviet Laws and Policies. APPENDIX B: Aspects of Forming Joint Ventures in the USSR.
-pp.350
103247-9

1990 Harvard   LODGE

George C. Lodge, Harvard Business School
PERESTROIKA FOR AMERICA: Restructuring Business-Government Relations for World Competitiveness

Outlines the history of business-government relations in the U.S., explaining why the laissez-faire doctrine has appealed to Americans. Argues that the government must now encourage collaboration among companies for competitive survival. Discusses the case of Sematech—a semiconductor consortium working in cooperation with the Dept. of Defense.
Contents: Introduction: Restructuring America. 1. Roles and Relationships of Business and Government. 2. Industrial Policy Comes to America. 3. Power and Control: Who's in Charge? 4. Organizing the Interface. 5. Governmental Affairs Managers: Masters of the Fine Line. 6. Recovery. Appendix One: Japan Versus America. Appendix Two: Some Government Policies Affecting Business.
-pp.225
103250-9

1989   DAVIDSON

William H. Davidson, University of Southern California
Jose de la Torre, University of California
MANAGING THE GLOBAL CORPORATION: Case Studies in Strategy and Management
Drs. Davidson and de la Torre have collated both their own cases and the cases of other leading internationalists to produce the first casebook for international business. Each of the authors, both Harvard DBA's, are known for their casework and teaching of cases. This casebook of 35 cases is organized around the areas of strategy, organization, joint venture, and alliances. An extensive instructor's manual with teaching notes is available to adopters.
-pp.678
015593-3

INSTRUCTOR'S MANUAL
015594-1

1988 Harvard   MCCRAW

Thomas K. McCraw, Harvard Business School
AMERICA VERSUS JAPAN: A Comparative Study Why the United States and Japan May Be on a Collision Course for World Economic Leadership
Now, more than ever before, the message of America Versus Japan remains a major issue for everyone who is concerned about the future of the world's economic system. These in-depth essays—ranging from trade and investment competition to energy, the environment, fiscal policy, agriculture, capital markets, and deindustrialization—present thought provoking issues that every manager, leader, and concerned citizen will need to address in months and years ahead.
103254-1

1987 Harvard   LODGE

George C. Lodge
Ezra F. Vogel
IDEOLOGY AND NATIONAL COMPETITIVENESS
A country's ideology—the framework of ideas it uses to make values explicit and its institutions legitimate— shapes the manner in which corporations and managers live and act. If not properly understood, it can blind a manager to problems he cannot avoid; if properly understood, it can alert managers to issues that help them in dealing with government agencies, the public, their workers, and in developing their own business

strategy. In this probing study, Harvard Business School professor George C. Lodge and Harvard University sociologist Ezra F. Vogel have combined their expertise to examine ideology as a useful tool for understanding national communities—how and why they have evolved, the tensions that exist within them, and the differences between them. They and their contributors compare the ideologies of nine countries—Japan, the United States, Taiwan, Korea, Germany, France, the United Kingdom, Brazil, and Mexico— and reveal the gap between the prevailing ideology and what institutions in these countries actually do. Ideology and National Competitiveness does not attempt to describe the "ideal society." Rather, it suggests that successful communities are those that are effective at managing ideological change and achieving goals. Perhaps its most important message to business people and policymakers is that effective managers must understand the ideological implications of their actions. From ideological strength comes competitive advantage.
-pp.350
103251-7

1986   IMAI

Masaaki Imai
KAIZEN: The Key to Japan's Competitive Success
For the professional manager or student of management, a comprehensive handbook of 16 Kaizen management practices that can be put to work. KAIZEN uses more than 100 examples in action and contains 15 corporate case studies.
-pp.260
554332-X

1986 Harvard   PORTER

Michael E. Porter, Harvard Business School
COMPETITION IN GLOBAL INDUSTRIES
This book provides a framework for understanding the nature of international competition in industries and its strategic implications for firms. It documents the historical transformation of international competition and shows how global competition changes the way marketing, production, government relations, and finance should be managed. It analyzes the strategic rationale and risks behind forming coalitions with other companies to compete globally. The book also addresses the organizational challenges involved in implementing global strategies. In-depth case studies illustrate the interplay of these factors in particular industries chosen to illuminate the issues facing today's managers. The conclusions of Competition in Global Industries affect every facet of contemporary corporate management. Old approaches to international strategy are no longer sufficient to meet today's international competition. Those companies that can formulate and implement truly global strategies will be tomorrow's winners.
-pp.582
103262-2

BUSINESS COMMUNICATION

1993   THILL

John V. Thill, Communication Specialists of America
Courtland L. Bovee, Grossmont College

EXCELLENCE IN BUSINESS COMMUNICATION, Second Edition
The revision brings to date the highly successful Excellence in Business Communication. With this edition, the authors have kept in place the basic ingredients of their original text, including the book's primary emphasis on "real-world," "slice of life" snapshots of the American business community. Improvements and changes to the latest edition include: new chapter opening vignettes and chapter closing simulations, all new cases, as well as renovated "Behind the Scenes" boxes.
Contents: PART ONE: FOUNDATIONS OF BUSINESS COMMUNICATION. 1. Understanding Business Communication. 2. Communicating Successfully in an Organization. PART TWO: THE WRITING PROCESS. 3. Planning Business Messages. 4. Organizing and Composing Business Messages. 5. Revising Business Messages. PART THREE: LETTERS, MEMOS, AND OTHER BRIEF MESSAGES. 6. Writing Direct Requests. 7. Writing Routine, Good-News, and Goodwill Messages. 8. Writing Bad-News Messages. 9. Writing Persuasive Messages. PART FOUR: REPORTS AND PROPOSALS. 10. Writing Short Reports. 11. Planning Long Reports. 12. Writing Long Reports. PART FIVE: EMPLOYMENT MESSAGES. 13. Writing Resumes and Application Letters. 14. Interviewing for Employment and Following Up. PART SIX: ORAL COMMUNICATION. 15. Listening, Interviewing, and Conducting Meetings. 16. Giving Speeches and Oral Presentations. PART SEVEN: SPECIAL TYPES OF BUSINESS COMMUNICATION. 18. Giving Speeches and Oral Presentations. APPENDIX. A: Fundamentals of Grammar and Usage. B: Format and Layout of Business Documents. C: Documentation of Report Sources. D: Correction Symbols.
-pp.576
006867-4

STUDY GUIDE
006871-2
INSTRUCTOR'S MANUAL
006868-2
TEST BANK
006869-0
COMPUTERIZED TEST BANK—IBM 5 1/4"
834113-2
COMPUTERIZED TEST BANK—IBM 3 1/2"
834144-0
COMPUTERIZED TEST BANK—MAC
834115-9
ACETATES (150 B&W)
074317-7
7 VIDEO EXERCISES
911361-3

1992   TUBBS

Stewart L. Tubbs, Eastern Michigan University
A SYSTEMS APPROACH TO SMALL GROUP INTERACTION, Fourth Edition
065407-7

1991   HANNA

Michael S. Hanna, University of South Alabama
Gerald L. Wilson, University of South Alabama
COMMUNICATING IN BUSINESS AND PROFESSIONAL SETTINGS
Ancillaries are available.
026019-2

1991   MURPHY

Herta A. Murphy, University of Washington, Emeritus
Herbert W. Hildebrandt, University of Michigan
**EFFECTIVE BUSINESS
COMMUNICATION, Sixth Edition**
Solid revision of one of the leading texts for the business communication course. Changes include (in this edition): new international examples, updating of all discussions, examples, and exercises throughout the text.
Contents: Prologue. PART ONE: BACKGROUND FOR COMMUNICATING. 1. Importance of Effective Communications in Business. 2. The Process of Communication and Miscommunication. 3. Business Communication Principles I. 4. Business Communication Principles II. 5. Legal Aspects of Business Communication. 6. The Process of Preparing Effective Business Messages. PART TWO: MAJOR PLANS FOR LETTERS AND MEMOS. 7. Direct Requests. 8. Good-News and Neutral Messages. 9. Bad-News Messages. 10. Persuasive Requests. PART THREE: SPECIAL MESSAGES. 11. Sales Letters. 12. The Written Job Presentation Self Assessment: Evaluating Your Achievements. 13. Other Job Application Messages. 14. Collection Messages—Written and Oral. 15. Goodwill Messages. PART FOUR: REPORTS. 16. Business Reports: Types, Preparation, Organization, Presentation. 17. Short Reports. 18. Formal (Long) Reports. 19. Proposals. PART FIVE: ORAL COMMUNICATION. 20. Successful Oral Presentations and Successful Listening. 21. Successful Informative Speaking. 22. Successful Persuasive Speaking. 23. Successful Business Meetings. 24. Successful Interpersonal and Other Oral Communications. 25. International and Intercultural Communication. APPENDIXES: A: Mechanics and Style. B: Format and Uses of Business Messages. C: Symbols for Marking Letters, Memos, and Reports. Index. Checklists.
-pp.838
044157-X

INSTRUCTOR'S MANUAL
044158-8
TEST BANK
044159-6
COMPUTERIZED TEST BANK RH TEST, IBM, 5 1/4"
837680-7
COMPUTERIZED TEST BANK RH TEST, IBM PC, 3 1/2"
837679-3
COMPUTERIZED TEST BANK MICROTEST 3, MAC, 3 1/2"
837678-5
50 OVERHEAD TRANSPARENCIES
074510-2
ACTIVITIES IN BUSINESS COMMUNICATION SOFTWARE 2/E, IBM, 5 1/4"
835417-X
PROSE WRITING INSTRUCTION SOFTWARE, MAC
834493-X
PROSE INSTRUCTOR'S VERSION, MAC
834600-2
EDIT STYLECHECKER SOFTWARE, IBM, 5 1/4"
557111-0

1989   ADLER

Ronald B. Adler, Santa Barbara City College
COMMUNICATING AT WORK:
Principles and Practices for Business and Professions, Third Edition
557938-3

1987   MAKI

Peggy Maki, Beaver College
Carol Schilling, Beaver College
WRITING FOR ORGANIZATIONS:
Purposes, Strategies and Processes
030361-4

1985   ROBBINS

Larry M. Robbins, University of Pennsylvania
THE BUSINESS OF WRITING AND SPEAKING: A Managerial Communication Manual
-pp.223
053089-0

1984   OLSON

Gary A. Olson, University of North Carolina, Wilmington
James DeGeorge, Indiana University of Pennsylvania
Richard E. Ray, Indiana University of Pennsylvania
STYLE AND READABILITY IN BUSINESS WRITING
554379-6

BUSINESS COMMUNICATION SOFTWARE

1990   LEARNING DESIGN, INC.

Learning Design, Inc.
ACTIVITIES IN BUSINESS COMMUNICATION, Second Edition
Activities in Business Communication, 2/e, is a series of three modules designed to give students interactive practice in the areas of business writing style, interviewing and career activities, and business word skills. All modules are interactive learning tools, offering hours of tutorial guidance, exercises, and activities. The modules included are: Concepts in Business Style, which covers six concepts of business writing; Calendar: Exercises in Career Skills, which takes students through the job-seeking process; and Business Word Skills: Exercises for Building a Strong Vocabulary for College and Career, which presents ten sections that test students' knowledge of specific vocabulary words. Students are continually reinforced by word and sound, and reviews and HELP screens are provided throughout.

1989   DAVIS

Stuart Davis, Cornell University
Nancy Kaplan, Cornell University
Joseph Martin, Cornell University

PROSE (PROMPTED REVISION OF STUDENT ESSAYS) MACINTOSH VERSION 2.0
834493-X

1989   MCRAE

Pamela McRae, Western Washington University
Ronald Johnson, Western Washington University
RANDOM HOUSE COLLEGIATE WRITER
557110-2

1986   BYRD

David Byrd, University of South Carolina
Paula Feldman, University of South Carolina
Phyllis Fleischel, University of South Carolina
THE MICROCOMPUTER AND BUSINESS WRITING, WORDSTAR VERSION
The Microcomputer and Business Writing takes advantage of the power of word processing for composing, revising, and editing documents for the business world. As students revise and edit the documents on the disk, they replicate the writing tasks they will encounter in the business world. The program has been used with many students for several years at the University of South Carolina, as well as with professionals in training seminars. The 94 exercises cover the following key areas of business writing: mechanics and style, memo revision, letter revision, problem situations, resumes and

information sheets, policies and procedures, proposals, and reports.
556187-5

INSTRUCTOR'S MANUAL
554893-3

SMALL BUSINESS MANAGEMENT

1993   KURILOFF

Arthur H. Kuriloff, formerly of UCLA
John M. Hemphill, Jr., Bob Frick Management
Douglas Cloud, Pepperdine University
STARTING AND MANAGING THE SMALL BUSINESS, Third Edition
This highly readable text provides students with extensive knowledge of the steps needed to start and run a small business. The primary focus of the text is on the creation of a business plan. The solid coverage of past editions has been reinforced with the addition of two important new chapters: "Managing Customer Relations," and "Managing International Trade." The text continues to offer strong entrepreneurial case studies, including three "epilogues" to cases featured in the second edition.
Contents: 1. The Need for Balanced Business Experience. 2. Personal Factors in Starting A Business. 3. Finding a Sound Idea for a Business. 4. Your Small Business As a Marketing System. 5. Analyzing Your Market and Consumer Behavior. 6. Reaching Your Customer. 7. Managing Customer Relations. 8. Controlling Your Retail Operations. 9. Marketing the Service Business. 10. Managing International Trade. 11. Controlling Your

Manufacturing Operations. 12: Raising Money for Your Business. 13. Managing Your Financial Requirements. 14. Management Information and Computers. 15. Buying a Going Business. 16. Is Franchising the Way to Go? 17. Deciding On some Key Legal Matters. 18. Managing Business Risk. 19. Managing Your Personnel Function. 20. Surviving: Managing for Productivity and Growth.
-pp.736
035825-7

INSTRUCTOR'S RESOURCE KIT—INSTRUCTOR'S MANUAL, TEST BANK, AND 5 1/4" IBM DISK
911458-X
VIDEO SERIES PLUS GUIDE
911517-9

1993   STEINHOFF

Dan Steinhoff, (deceased) formerly of University of Miami
John Burgess, Concordia College
SMALL BUSINESS MANAGEMENT FUNDAMENTALS, Sixth Edition
This straightforward guide to establishing, managing and owning a small business has been thoroughly updated and revised while preserving the readability and practical flavor that distinguished past editions. New pedagogical features designed to strengthen the accessibility of the text include a continuing (chapter-by-chapter) exercise called "Developing A Business Plan," new case studies (two per chapter), many of which are computer integrated, and lively real-world vignettes opening each chapter. All new chapters on organizational ethics and social responsibility, development of the business plan, and operations management and production have been added. Finally, an all-new design including the introduction of color to this edition will add visual appeal and help enliven the presentation.
Contents: PART ONE: SMALL BUSINESS, ENTREPRENEURSHIP, AND ORGANIZING FOR SUCCESS. 1. Small Business is Big Business. 2. Ethics and Social Responsibility for Small Business. 3. Entrepreneurship and Small Business Success. 4. Strategic Plans for Small Business. 5. Old Business, New Business, or Franchise? 6. Developing the Business Plan. 7. Legal Forms of Business Ownership. PART TWO: FINANCIAL PLANNING. 8. Financial Statements and Business Ratios. 9. The Desired Income Approach to Planning. 10. Planning the Pro Forma Balance Sheet. 11. Finding the Funds to Finance a Business. PART THREE: MARKETING PLANNING AND DEVELOPMENT. 12. Marketing Strategy and Marketplace Research. 13. Picking the Right Location. 14. Personal Selling, Advertising, Promotion Planning. 15. Product Classes, Life Cycles, and Trends. 16. Consumer Behavior and Layout Planning. 17. Pricing for Profits. 18. Getting Products/Services to the Customers. PART FOUR: PEOPLE AND ORGANIZATIONAL PRODUCTIVITY. 19. Managing Human Resources. 20. Production and Operations Management. 21. Purchasing and Inventory Control. 22. Effective Control and Break Even Analysis. 23. Computers and Information Systems for Management Decisions. PART FIVE: ACCOUNTING AND FINANCIAL CONTROLS. 24. Consumer and Business to Business Credit. 25. User Friendly Accounting and Financial Records. 26. Worksheets, Formal Statements and Cash Flow Statements. 27. Taxes and Depreciation. PART SIX: SPECIAL SMALL BUSINESS ISSUES AND OPPORTUNITIES. 28. International Business for Small Business. 29. Risk Management and Insurance. 30. Business Law, Bankruptcy, and Harvesting the Winner. SOFTCOVER
-pp.608
061221-8

INSTRUCTOR'S RESOURCE KIT—INSTRUCTOR'S MANUAL, TEST BANK AND 5 1/4" IBM DISK

911459-8
VIDEO SERIES PLUS GUIDE
911517-9

1992 Harvard   STEVENSON

Howard H. Stevenson
William A. Sahlman
THE ENTREPRENEURIAL VENTURE
Designed for a senior-level or first-year MBA course on entrepreneurship, this new softcover text covers basic concepts and emerging issues through readings by leading academics and practitioners. Emphasizing that new venture creation requires planning and skill as well as inspiration, these readings portray the entrepreneur as the ultimate general manager, responsible for orchestrating the relationships among all parts of the enterprise. To help readers develop the versatility needed to succeed in this role, the text covers every phase of the entrepreneurial start-up, from self-assessment and idea generation to harvesting. Profiles and case examples challenge sterotypes and show readers the diverse, imaginative ways in which entrepreneurs think and act. Organized like a conventional textbook, the readings provide a practice-oriented grounding that can be interwoven with cases, exercises, and other materials. The book is also available as a PRIMIS CUSTOM PUBLICATION.
Contents: PART ONE: THE ENTREPRENEUR. PART TWO: LAUNCHING THE NEW VENTURE. Section A: Assessing. Section B: Planning. Section C: Financing. PART THREE: MANAGING VENTURE GROWTH. Section A: Building an Effective Organization. Section B: Financial Strategy for the Growing Venture.
-pp.430
054568-5

SUPERVISION

1990 P&R   BITTEL

L. R. Bittel
J. Newstrom
WHAT EVERY SUPERVISIOR SHOULD KNOW, Sixth Edition, Trade Edition
Through five editions since its first release in 1959, WHAT EVERY SUPERVISOR SHOULD KNOW has effectively responded to the changing needs of supervisors, and it remains the standard in the field of supervision. Now in a new edition, this classic guide to handling the day-to-day problems that supervisors face is: more current than ever—two chapters cover the environment and innovation, this latest edition also treats such timely issues as computer surveillance and job competency guidelines; more personalized than ever—the Personal Development Portfolio offers convenient checklists and sound guidelines on planning careers, managing time and coping with stress; leaner, meaner, and easier to use—the format is modular, chapter-end reviews, and lots of easily referenced lists, tables, and charts. It's the best reference available for supervisors just starting out as well as for seasoned managers who need to freshen up on the basics or update their skills.
Contents: PART ONE: SUPERVISORY MANAGEMENT. The Supervisor's Role in Management. Coping With Your Unique Environment. Supervision and the Management Process. PART TWO: PLANNING AND CONTROL. Making Plans and Carrying Out Policy. Exercising Control of People and Processes. Managing

Information and Solving Problems. PART THREE: Organizing, Staffing, and Training. Organizing an Effective Department. Staffing With Human Resources. Appraisal of Employee Performance. Training and Developing Employees. PART FOUR: ACTIVATING THE WORK FORCE. Motivating People at Work. The Art and Science of Leadership. Effective Employee Communications. PART FIVE: MANAGING PROBLEM PERFORMANCE. Counseling Problem Performers. Converting Complaints and Conflict Into Cooperation. How and When to Discipline. PART SIX: IMPROVING DEPARTMENTAL PRODUCTIVITY. Improving Productivity and Innovation. Building a Higher Quality of Performance. Controlling Costs and Budgets. PART SEVEN: LEGAL CONCERNS OF SUPERVISION. Equal Opportunity Under the Law. Employee Safety and Health and OSHA. The Supervisor's Role in Labor Relations. PART EIGHT: PERSONAL DEVELOPMENT PORTFOLIO. Toward Mastery of Your Job. File 1. Taking Charge of Your Career (How to Prepare a Career Development Plan). File 2. Managing Job-Related Time (How to Get the Most of Your Time). File 3. Coping With Stress (How to Keep from Burning Out). File 4. Upward in Your Organization (How to get Along With Your Boss, Network Effectively, and Handle Organizational Politics). PART NINE: BOOTSTRAPPING YOUR CAREER IN SUPERVISION AND MANAGEMENT. PART TEN: APPENDICES: A. Checklist for Planning the Days's Work. B. Supervisory Responsibility Check Chart. C. Checklist for Accepting the Assignment of a New Department or for Turning Over Your Present Department to a New Supervisor.
-pp.640
005583-1

1984   BOYD

Bradford B. Boyd, University of Wisconsin—Extension
MANAGEMENT-MINDED SUPERVISION, Third Edition
-pp.368
006946-8

INSTRUCTOR'S MANUAL AND KEY
006947-6

TOTAL QUALITY MANAGEMENT

1994   BOUNDS

Greg Bounds, University of Tennessee, Knoxville
Lyle Yorks, Eastern Connecticut State University
Mel Adams, University of Alabama, Huntsville
Gipsie Ranney, University of Tennessee, Knoxville
BEYOND TOTAL QUALITY MANAGEMENT: Toward the Emerging Paradigm
Beyond Total Quality Management, the first and only college textbook devoted entirely to TQM, is comprised of 12 conceptual chapters and a collection of chapter-length case studies. The conceptual

chapters introduce students to the philosophies, methods and tools of TQM and suggest a new paradigm for management which goes beyond TQM as it is commonly viewed today. The case studies exemplify the concepts in practice and give students a context for discussing the practical applications of TQM. While maintaining a strong customer value orientation throughout, this text addresses the entire spectrum of issues related to TQM — from human resources management and organizational culture to customer value measurement and statistical quality control. This well-balanced approach is based on sound research and consistently reinforces the crucial link between TQM and business strategy.
Contents: PART ONE: THE NEED FOR A PARADIGM SHIFT. 1. Global Competitiveness and Change. 2. Review of the Field: Foundations of the Emerging Paradigm. 3. Understanding Organizational Culture. 4. Focusing Managerial Roles. PART TWO: THE CORE CONCEPTS OF THE EMERGING PARADIGM. 5. Customer Value Concepts. 6. Strategic Management and Continuous Improvement. 7. Customer Value Measurement. 8. Understanding and Improving Systems for Customer Value. 9. Variation: Source of Confusion and Information for Learning. 10. Variation: Managing the System of Causes. PART THREE: MAKING THE PARADIGM SHIFT. 11. The Strategic Linkage of Operations through Employee Involvement. 12. Culture Change and Organizational Learning. CASES: IBM Rochester, Pt. I: The Seasons of Culture Change. IBM Rochester, Pt. II: Implementing Market Driven Quality. Toyota, Part I: The Standardization of Culture. Toyota, Part II: Customer Satisfaction Measurement. Xerox, Part I: Preparing for Global Optimization. Xerox, Part II: The Integrated Supply Chain. Federal Express: A CEO's Dream. Hewlett Packard: John Young, Champion of Change. St. Mary's Hospital: Continuous Improvement
-pp.832
006678-7

INSTRUCTOR'S MANUAL/TEST BANK
006679-5
COMPUTERIZED TEST BANK - IBM PC 5 1/4"
839788-X
COMPUTERIZED TEST BANK - IBM PC 3 1/2"
839789-8
VIDEO PROGRAM
911775-9

PRODUCTION/ OPERATIONS MANAGEMENT

| 1993 | DILWORTH |

James B. Dilworth, University of Alabama, Birmingham
PRODUCTION AND OPERATIONS MANAGEMENT, Fifth Edition
This leading text for P/OM shows how managers plan and control operations to achieve optimum productivity, top quality, and customer satisfaction. The first text to stress management of on-going systems in both manufacturing and service industries, the fifth edition covers both descriptive and quantitative methods throughout. This revision has been updated to reflect such current issues as JIT, service industries, international operations, and changing technologies. In addition, the problem material has been extensively revised.
Contents: PART ONE: FOUNDATION MATERIAL. 1. Zeroing in on Operations. 2. Operations Strategy.

3. Forecasting Demand. PART TWO: PLANNING AND CONTROLLING OPERATIONS. 4. Planning for Operations and Capacity. 5. Overview of Materials Management. 6. Managing Independent-Demand Inventory. 7. Managing Dependent\Demand Items and Capacity. 8. Scheduling and Controlling Manufacturing. 9. Just-In-Time Manufacturing or Manufacturing Excellence. 10. The Nature and Scheduling of Services. 11: Scheduling and Controlling Projects. 12. Total Quality Management. 13. Statistical Quality Control. PART THREE: DESIGN OF OPERATIONS SYSTEMS. 14. Facility Location. 15. Layout of Facilities. 16. Design and Manage for Technological Advantage. 17. Job Design. 18. Work Measurement and Compensation. 19. The Future: Global Competition and Continuous Improvement.
-pp.784
016987-X

STUDY GUIDE
016989-6
INSTRUCTOR'S MANUAL/TEST BANK
016991-8
COMPUTERIZED TEST BANK—IBM 5 1/4"
833352-0
COMPUTERIZED TEST BANK—IBM 3 1/2"
833353-9
OVERHEAD TRANSPARENCIES
074588-9
SOLUTIONS MANUAL
016992-6
VIDEO PLANT TOURS PLUS GUIDE
911523-3
DISCOUNTED SALES PREPACK: 5/E TEXT WITH TERPENING, TOOLS FOR OPNS MGT, IBM 5 1/4"
833958-8
DISCOUNTED SALES PREPACK: 5/E TEXT WITH TERPENING, TOOLS FOR OPNS MGT, IBM 3 1/2"
833959-6
DISCOUNTED SALES PREPACK: 5/E TEXT WITH GARDNER, SPREADSHEET OPNS MGR. IBM 5 1/4"
833960-X
DISCOUNTED SALES PREPACK: 5/E TEXT WITH GARDNER, SPREADSHEET OPNS MGR. IBM 3 1/2"
833961-8
DISCOUNTED SALES PREPACK: 5/E TEXT WITH SAVAGE, FAST P/OM IBM 5 1/4"
833962-6
DISCOUNTED SALES PREPACK: 5/E TEXT WITH SAVAGE, FAST P/OM, IBM 3 1/2"
833963-4

| 1994 | SAVAGE |

Sam L. Savage, University of Chicago
FAST P/OM: FUNDAMENTAL ANALYTICAL SPREADSHEET TOOLS FOR P/OM
These visual, powerful, professional quality Lotus 1-2-3 templates include add-in's such as WHAT'S BEST, the best-selling professional Lotus-based linear programming software.
Contents: 1. Forecasting. 2. Facility Location. 3. Learning Curves. 4. Aggregate Planning. 5. Inventory Management. 6. Materials Requirement Planing. 7. Scheduling. 8. Quality Assurance. 9. Monte Carlo Simulation. 10. Mathematical Optimization.
-pp.192

STUDENT SET, MANUAL AND 5 1/4" DISK
839553-4
STUDENT SET, MANUAL AND 3 1/2" DISK
839541-0

| 1993 | SCHROEDER |

Roger G. Schroeder, University of Minnesota
OPERATIONS MANAGEMENT: Decision Making in the Operations Function, Fourth Edition
This leading text, renowned for its decision-making approach to operations management, includes realistic case studies (now integrated throughout) in addition to many industry examples. This revision adds demonstration problems that utilize a solutions methodology to help provide students with a solid quantitative foundation. The coverage of quality has been highlighted and placed earlier in the text. There is an all new photo program and full color insert.
-pp.864

4/E TEXT WITH IBM 5 1/4" TEMPLATE DISK
911437-7
4/E TEXT WITH IBM 3 1/2" TEMPLATE DISK
911644-2
STUDY GUIDE
056148-6
INSTRUCTOR'S MANUAL
056147-8
TEST BANK
056145-1
COMPUTERIZED TEST BANK—IBM 5 1/4"
832789-X
COMPUTERIZED TEST BANK—IBM 3 1/2"
833949-9
OVERHEAD TRANSPARENCIES (133, 2-COLOR)
074588-9
VIDEO PLANT TOURS PLUS GUIDE
911523-3

| 1993 | TERPENING |

Willbann D. Terpening, Gonzaga University
SOFTWARE TOOLS FOR OPERATIONS MANAGEMENT
The package can be used by Students to solve problems in their regular text, or the problems at the end of each chapter can be used for homework assignments. The programs also allow for the solution of more complex problems than are usually found in most textbooks, so that they can be used with larger "case" problems. The instructor also has the choice of allowing students to perform all data entry to the programs, or for larger problems, the instructor may create and save a file using the programs and then distribute that file to the students. This may be especially appropriate for modules, such as material requirements planning, that require extensive data entry.
IBM 5 1/4"
Contents: 1. Getting Started. 2. Using Software Tools for Operations Management. 3. Forecasting. 4. Resource Requirements Planing. 5. Aggregate Production Planning. 6. Linear Programming. 7. Transportation Method. 8. Inventory Models. 9. Materials Requirements Planning. 10. Job Shop Scheduling. 11. Queuing. 12. Project Scheduling. 13. Quality Control. 14. Facility Layout. 15. Line Balancing.
-pp.128

STUDENT SET, IBM 5 1/4" AND 128 PP MANUAL
832579-X
STUDENT SET, IBM 3 1/2" AND 128 PP MANUAL
832584-6

1992 Harvard   CLARK

Kim B. Clark, Harvard Business School
Takahiro Fujimoto, Harvard Business School

PRODUCT DEVELOPMENT PERFORMANCE: Strategy, Organization, and Management in the World Auto Industry

This book is the culmination of six years research on how different manufacturing firms around the world approach the development of new products. Its principal focus is on the impact of strategy, organization, and management on this critical component of business strategy. It concentrates on case studies from the world auto industry. Drawing on extensive research on twenty companies in Europe, North America, and Japan, the authors identify the strategies, practices, and capabilities that create superior performance in lead time, engineering productivity, a and total product quality. The authors make the general applications of their findings clear to other industries.
Contents: 1. Introduction. 2. The Framework: An Information Paradigm. 3. Competition and Product Development in the World Auto Industry. 4. Performance of Product Development. 5. Process and Organization in Product Development. 6. Project Strategy: Managing Complexity. 7. Manufacturing Capability in Product Development. 8. Integrating Problem Solving Cycles. 9. Realizing Product Concepts in Product Design. 10. Overall Patterns of Effective Product Development. 11. The Future of Product Development in the Auto Industry. 12. General Management Implications in Product Development.
-pp.409
103300-9

1992   DENTON

D. Keith Denton

MANAGING SERVICES: Improving Services Through Operaitons Management

Managing Service provides the information needed to become more knowledgeable about how to manage services and also provides a source for how to handle real life service situations. Characterized by an appealing writing style and full of real-life vignettes and realistic situations, the book also includes a substantial list of source for those who would like to explore service management further. Managing Service can also be used as a game or simulation. A manual is designed to help players do well in the simulation, and in the process learn more abut how to deliver and manage services. The manual is divided into three sections. Each section reviews a knowledge area needed to be able to manage services. These areas include information on: (1) Strategic and Managerial Issues, (2) Techniques for Improving Services and (3) Employee Involvement and Participative Management approaches used to enhance service. It is accompanied by a game board (similar to a monopoly board) that permits its use in a game of simulation.
Contents: SECTION ONE: STRATEGIC AND MANAGERIAL ISSUES: Cost of Poor Quality. Define Service. Rising Expectations. Road Blocks to Improved Services. Managerial Guidelines. Strategic Niche. Understanding the Business. Commitment to Quality. Customer Perspective. NOAC. Innovation. Appropriate Technology. Operationally Sound. Motivation and Standards. Incentives. SECTION TWO: TECHNIQUES FOR IMPROVING SERVICES:

Assessing Service. Discovering Customer Expectations/Perceptions. QFD. Problem Solving Techniques. Focusing on the Problem. Resolving the Problem. Value Analysis. SPC. Control Charts. SECTION THREE: EMPLOYEE INVOLVEMENT AND PARTICIPATIVE MANAGEMENT: Low Moral. Employee Attitudes. Group Communication Techniques. One-On-One Communication. Diagnosis. Enhancing or Limiting. Summary. Sources of Additional Readings.
-pp.192
016414-2

INSTRUCTOR'S MANUAL
016415-0

1992   DILWORTH

James B. Dilworth, The University of Alabama at Birmingham

OPERATIONS MANAGMENT: Design, Planning, and Control for Manufacturing and Services

An alternate version of our leading text for P/OM shows students how managers design, plan, and control operations to achieve quality productivity. The first text to stress management of ongoing systems in both manufacturing of service industries, it covers both descriptive and quantitative methods throughout. The new version is substantially revised to reflect current issues, such as expanded coverage of JIT, an increased emphasis on services, international operations, and new material on changing technologies. Problem materials have been revised and expanded.
Contents: PART ONE: FOUNDATION MATERIAL: 1. Zeroing in on Operations. Tour of a Continuous Production Plant: Nissan Motor Manufacturing Corporation, U.S.A. Tour of a Job Shop: Teledyne Brown Engineering Fabrication and Assembly Plant I. Tour of a Service Operation: Wal-Mart's Distribution System. Historical Perspective: Progress in Operations Management. 2. Operations Strategy. Decision Making. 3. Forecasting Demand. PART TWO: DESIGN OF OPERATIONS SYSTEMS: 4. Facility Location. 5. Layout of Facilities. 6. Design and Manage for Technological Advantage. 7. Job Design. 8. Productivity, Work Measurement and Compensation. PART THREE: PLANNING AND CONTROLLING OPERATIONS: 9. Aggregate Capacity Planning. 10. Overview of Materials Management. 11. Managing Independent-Demand Inventory. 12. Managing Dependent-Demand Inventory. 13. Scheduling and Controlling Manufacturing. 14. Just-In-Time Manufacturing. 15. The Nature and Scheduling of Services. Sup F Simulation. 16. Scheduling and Controlling Projects. Sup G Maintenance. 17. Total Quality Management. 18. Statistical Quality Control. 19. Global Competition and Continuous Improvement. Sup H Linear Programming.
-pp.876
016988-8

STUDENT STUDY GUIDE
016956-X
INSTRUCTOR'S MANUAL/TEST BANK
017016-9
COMPUTERIZED TEST BANK, IBM 5 1/4"
832945-0
COMPUTERIZED TEST BANK, IBM 3 1/2"
832946-9

OVERHEAD TRANSPARENCIES
074568-4
SOLUTIONS MANUAL
017019-3
DISCOUNTED SALES PREPACK: DILWORTH PLUS TERPENING TOOLS FOR OPNS MGT, IBM 5 1/4"
832929-9
DISCOUNTED SALES PREPACK: DILWORTH PLUS TERPENING TOOLS FOR OPNS MGT., IBM 3 1/2"
832932-9
DISCOUNTED SALES PREPACK: DILWORTH PLUS GARDNER SPREADSHEET OPNS MGR, IBM 5 1/4"
832917-5
DISCOUNTED SALES PREPACK: DILWORTH PLUS GARDNER, SPREADSHET OPNS MGR IBM 3 1/2"
832920-5
6 VIDEO PLANT TOURS PLUS GUIDE
911448-2

1992   GARDNER

Everette S. Gardner, Jr., University of Houston

THE SPREADSHEET OPERATIONS MANAGER

This collection of 55 template models for Lotus 1-2-3 by one of the leading authorities in forecasting automates all important quantitative analysis in the 1992 Dilworth text. Each model is documented with a complete analysis of a sample problem from Dilworth, including instructions for input, interpretation of output, modifications to enlarge the amount of date the model can handle, and suggestions for what-if analysis.
Contents: Demand Forecasting. Inventory Control (Independent Demand). Inventory Control (Dependent Demand). Quality Control. Scheduling.
5 1/4" STUDENT SET
832569-2

3 1/2" STUDENT SET
832574-9

1989   THAVIKULWAT

Precha Thavikulwat, Towson State University

MANAGEMENT 500: A Production and Operations Management Simulation

This standalone software simulation can supplement any P/OM text. Students learn to apply production and operations concepts and see how P/OM issues affect the entire enterprise. The simulation's parameters can be set by the instructor. This allows the instructor to the program to be more or less difficult and longer or shorter.
Contents: Simple Forecasting. Time Series Decomposition. Capacity Planning. Resource Allocation. Transportation. Inventory Management. Financial Planning. Material Management. Pricing.
STUDENT SET, IBM, 5 1/4" ONLY
-pp.128
834733-5

ADOPTER'S DESK SET, IBM, 5 1/4" ONLY
834728-9

1987   MONKS

Joseph G. Monks, Gonzaga University
OPERATIONS MANAGEMENT:
Theory and Problems, Third Edition
This successful production/operations management
text is known for its applied decision-making
approach. There are two chapters on service
operations, "Computer-Oriented Problems" in every
chapter, additional coverage of MRP II, productivity,
and robotics. This edition also features two-color.
The accompanying MICROSOM software contains 12
models for problem solving.
-pp.800
042727-5

STUDY GUIDE
042729-1
INSTRUCTOR'S MANUAL
042728-3
MICROSOM I by Terpening, IBM, 5 1/4"
834448-4

1985   DELMAR

Donald DelMar, University of Idaho
OPERATIONS AND INDUSTRIAL
MANAGEMENT: Designing for
Productivity
-pp.736
016287-5

INSTRUCTOR'S MANUAL
016288-3

1985   MONKS

Joseph G. Monks, Ph.D., Gonzaga University
SCHAUM'S OUTLINE OF
OPERATIONS MANAGEMENT
042726-7

SERVICE MANAGEMENT

1994   FITZSIMMONS

James A. Fitzsimmons, University of Texas, Austin
Mona J. Fitzsimmons, President, Institute for Service
Entrepreneurship
SERVICE MANAGEMENT FOR
COMPETITIVE ADVANTAGE
James Fitzsimmons' 1982 McGraw-Hill text, Service
Operations Management, was the first book on the
topic, and defined the field of service operations
management. Fitzsimmons is now senior author of
an all new 1994 service management text which
promises to become the paradigm for the '90s. This
text is distinguished by its unique focus on service
management for competitive advantage, and its
integration of the authors' first-hand experiences and
research with numerous service firms. Its highly
readable presentation will appeal even to students
with little business experience.
Contents: PART ONE: SERVICES AND THE
ECONOMY. 1: The Role of Service in an Economy. 2:
The Nature of Services. CASE: Village Volvo. PART
TWO: DESIGNING THE SERVICE ENTERPRISE.
COMPETITIVE STRATEGY. 3: Service Strategy and
Market Position. CASE: America West Airlines. 4:
Strategic Role of the Information Resource. CASE:
Mrs. Fields Cookies. PART THREE: STRUCTURING

THE SERVICE ENTERPRISE. 5: The Service Delivery
System. CASE: 100 Yen Sushi House. 6: Service
Facility Design and Layout. CASES: HMO's, Esquire
Department Store. 7: Service Facility Location.
CASES: HMO, Athol Furniture. PART FOUR:
MANAGING SERVICE OPERATIONS. 8: The
Service Encounter. CASE: Amy's Ice Cream. 9:
Service Quality. CASES: Clean Sweep, Inc., The
Complaint Letter. 10: Managing Supply and
Demand. CASES: River City National Bank, Gateway
International Airport. 11: Managing Queues. CASES:
Thrifty Rent-A-Car, Eye'll Be Seeing You. PART
FIVE: TOWARD WORLD CLASS SERVICE. 12:
Productivity and Quality Improvement. CASE: Mega
Bytes Restaurants 13: Growth and Expansion. CASE:
Federal Express. 14: Forecasting Demand for
Services. CASES: Oak Hollow Evaluation Center,
Gnomial Functions, Inc. 15: Queuing Models and
Capacity Planning. CASES: Freedom Express, Cedar
Valley Comm. Coll., Pronto Pizza. 16: Linear
Programming Models in Services. CASES: Munich
Delicatessen, Sequoia Airlines.
-pp.480
021217-1

INSTRUCTOR'S MANUAL/TEST BANK
021218-X

QUANTITATIVE METHODS, SYSTEMS, MANAGEMENT SCIENCE

1994   GAYNOR

Patricia E. Gaynor, Appalachian State University
Rickey C. Kirkpatrick, Appalahian State University
AN INTRODUCTION TO TIME
SERIES MODELING AND
FORECASTING FOR BUSINESS AND
ECONOMICS
This new entry offers comprehensive coverage of
time-series modeling and forecasting in a unique,
user-friendly style. The book is appropriate for
students with minimal math backgrounds (basis
statistics and algebra) and can be effectively used at
both the graduate and undergraduate levels. The
book's readability is complemented by its inclusion
of numerous visual aids (graphs, tables, fully-worked
examples). An ongoing case based on actual
company data illustrates the use of important
procedures described in each chapter.
Contents: 1. Introduction to Forecasting and Time-
Series Analysis. 2. Building Tools for Time-Series
Analysis: Describing and Transforming Data. 3.
Modeling Trend Using Regression Analysis. 4.
Exponential Smoothing; Updated Regression-Based
Trend Models 5. The Decomposition Method. 6.
Updating Seasonal Models with Winters'
Exponential Smoothing. 7. The Box Jenkins
Methodology - Nonseasonal Models. 8. The Box
Jenkins Methodology - Seasonal Models. 9. Multiple
Regression in Time-Series Analysis: The Causal
Model. 10. Combining Forecast Methodologies and
Fine-Tuning the Forecast: Judgmental Factors in
Forecasting.
-pp.656
034913-4

INSTRUCTOR'S MANUAL/TEST BANK/IBM 5.25"
DATA DISK
911319-2
INSTRUCTOR'S MANUAL/TEST BANK/IBM 3,5"
DATA DISK
911835-8

1993   GARDNER

Everette S. Gardner, University of Houston
THE SPREADSHEET FORECASTER
THE SPREADSHEET FORECASTER (TSF) is a toolkit
containing 23 ready-to-use, practical models for
quantitative analysis in business forecasting. The
models are templates that work with Lotus 1-2-3
(release 2.01 or later) and compatible software. To
assist in choosing a forecasting model, TSF provides
five data-analysis models to classify and determine
the strength of trends, identify the current phase of
the business cycle, and compute the amount of
"noise" or randomness present in the data. Four
additional models are available to perform seasonal
adjustment prior to forecasting. The user has a choice
of additive or multiplicative seasonal-adjustment
models for either monthly or quarterly data. Three
categories of forecasting models are available:
regression, growth curves, and exponential
smoothing. The regression models feature automatic
computation of test statistics and prediction intervals.
Each model is documented with a complete case
study and analysis of a sample business problem
including instructions for input, interpretation of
output, and suggestions for what-if-analysis.
Contents: Introduction. The Target User. Worksheet
Tips. SEASONAL ADJUSTMENT MODELS.
Multiplicative Seasonal Adjustment, Monthly Data.
Multiplicative Seasonal Adjustment, Quarterly Data.
Additive Seasonal Adjustment, Monthly Data.
Additive Seasonal Adjustment, Quarterly Data.
REGRESSION ANALYSIS. Causal Regression, 1
Independent Variable. Causal Regression, 2
Independent Variables. Discounted Regression.
Prediction Intervals. Autoregression, 1 Lagged
Variable. Autoregression, 2 Lagged Variable.
GROWTH CURVES. Logistic Growth Curve. Linear Growth
Model. Exponential Growth Model. EXPONENTIAL
SMOOTHING MODELS. Short-range Forecasting.
Analysis of Weights on Past Data. Smoothing a
Linear Trend. Smoothing an Exponential or Damped
Trend. DATA ANALYSIS FOR FORECASTING.
Classification of Trend. Business Cycle Analysis.
Analysis of Variance, Monthly Data. Analysis of
Variance, Quarterly Data. Conversion of Monthly to
Quarterly Data.

STUDENT SET IBM 5 1/4" AND 128 PP. MANUAL
833698-8
STUDENT SET IBM 3 1/2" AND 128 PP. MANUAL
833701-1

1993   SAVAGE

Sam L. Savage, University of Chicago
FAST QM: FUNDAMENTAL
ANALYTICAL SPREADSHEET TOOLS
FOR QUANTITATIVE
MANAGEMENT
These visual, powerful professional Lotus 1-2-3
templates include add-in's such as WHAT'S BEST,
the best-selling professional Lotus-based linear
programming software.
Contents: 1. Equation Solving, Goal Seeking. 2.
Mathematical Optimization. 3. Network Models. 4.
Project Management. 5. Decision Trees. 6. Simulation.
7. Queuing Models.
-pp.192

5 1/4" IBM STUDENT SET (192 PP. MANUAL &
DISK)
839548-8
3 1/2" IBM STUDENT SET (192 PP. MANUAL &
DISK)
839543-7

1993   **TERPENING**

Willbann D. Terpening, Gonzaga University
SOFTWARE TOOLS FOR QUANTITATIVE METHODS AND MANAGEMENT SCIENCE
The package can be used by students to solve problems in their regular text, or the problems at the end of each chapter can be used for homework assignments. The programs also allow for the solution of more complex problems than are usually found in most textbooks, so that they can be used with larger "case" problems. The instructor also has the choice of allowing students to perform all data entry to the programs, or for larger problems, the instructor may create and save a file using the programs and then distributed that file to the students.
Contents: 1. Getting Started. 2. Using Software Tools for Quantitative Methods and Management Science. 3. Forecasting. 4. Inventory Models. 5. Linear Programming. 6. Transportation Method. 7. Assignment Method. 8. Network Models. 9. Integer Programming. 10. Branch and Bound. 11. Goal Programming. 12. Queuing Methods. 13. Markov Models.
-pp.128

STUDENT SET-IBM 5 1/4" AND 128 PP MANUAL
832587-0
STUDENT SET-IBM 3 1/2" AND 128 PP. MANUAL
832592-7

1992   **LEVIN**

Richard I. Levin, University of North Carolina at Chapel Hill
David S. Rubin, University of North Carolina at Chapel Hill
Joel P. Stinson, Syracuse University
Everett S. Gardner, Jr., University of Houston
QUANTITATIVE APPROACHES TO MANAGEMENT, Eighth Edition
This revision of one of the best-selling quantitative methods text uses less mathematical jargon and far fewer symbols than most books of its kind so students can learn from it on their own. The text presents material from the point of view of the operating manager, which allows readers to see how a manager applies techniques presented in the book to real world problems. It also covers linear programming in depth, showing readers how to solve problems, how to work applications on the computer, and how to make linear programming work in actual practice. This edition includes new sections on using print-outs on using Lotus 1-2-3 to solve MS/OR problems as well as a disk containing Lotus templates. The text also features a new continuing case for "real-world" applications in end-of-chapter material.
Contents: 1. Introduction. 2. A Review of Probability Concepts. 3. Forecasting. 4. Decision Making Using Probabilities I. 5. Decision Making Using Probabilities II. 6. Inventor I. 7. Inventor II. Linear Programming I: Solutions Methods. 9. Linear Programming II: The Simplex Methods. 10. Linear Programming III: Building LP Models and Interpreting Solutions. 11. Specially Structured LInear Programs. 12. Networks. 13. Extensions of LInear Programming. 14. Waiting LInes. 15. Simulation. 16. Markov Analysis. 17. MS/OR: Past, Present,and Future. Appendixes. Answers to the Chapter Concepts Quizzes. Bibliography. Index.
-pp.896
832454-8

STUDY GUIDE

037579-8
INSTRUCTOR'S MANUAL
037558-5
TEST BANK
037559-3
IBM 3 1/2" LOTUS TEMPLATES
832456-4
COMPUTERIZED TEST BANK, IBM 5 1/4"
832452-1
COMPUTERIZED TEST BANK, IBM 3 1/2"
832453-X

1988   **GRAY**

Paul Gray, Ph.D., The Claremont Graduate School
GUIDE TO IFPS/PERSONAL: The Interactive Financial Planning System for Personal Computers, IBM PC Version
831426-7

1987   **GRAY**

Paul Gray, Ph.D., The Claremont Graduate School
GUIDE TO IFPS: Interactive Financial Planning System, Second Edition
024394-8

1985   **COOKE**

William P. Cooke, Ph.D., University of Wyoming
QUANTITATIVE METHODS FOR MANAGEMENT DECISIONS
Ancillaries are available.
012518-X

INDUSTRIAL MANAGEMENT

1992   **KATZ**

Harry Charles Katz, Cornell University
Thomas A. Kochan, Massachusetts Institute of Technology
INTRODUCTION TO COLLECTIVE BARGAINING AND INDUSTRIAL RELATIONS
SEE: Management and Organization—Labor Management and Collective Bargaining. Ancillaries are available.
033645-8

1985   **DELMAR**

Donald DelMar, University of Idaho
OPERATIONS AND INDUSTRIAL MANAGEMENT: Designing for Productivity
SEE: Management and Organization: Production/ Operations Management. Ancillaries are available.
016287-5

1983   **CLELAND**

David I. Cleland, University of Pittsburgh
William R. King, University of Pittsburgh

SYSTEMS ANALYSIS AND PROJECT MANAGEMENT, Third Edition
011311-4

1982   **OHMAE**

Kenichi Ohmae, McKinsey & Company, Inc.
THE MIND OF THE STRATEGIST: The Art of Japanese Business
-pp.320
047595-4

QUALITY CONTROL

1993   **GARDNER**

Everette S. Gardner, University of Houston
THE SPREADSHEET QUALITY MANAGER
THE SPREADSHEET QUALITY MANAGER (SQM) is a toolkit containing 16 ready-to-use, practical models for quality analysis, control, and improvement. The models are templates that work with Lotus 1-2-3 (Release 2.01 or later) and compatible software. SQM contains three types of models: control charts, sampling models, and probability distribution models. Each model is documented with a complete case study and analysis of a sample business problem including instructions for input, interpretation of output, and suggestions for what-if-analysis. The sample problems are the result of the author's experience in consulting with manufacturing firms in a variety of industries: pharmaceuticals, petrochemicals, oilfield equipment, machine tools, processed foods, computers, computer components, and automobile parts.
Contents: The Target User. How to Choose a Quality Model. Control Charts for Variables. Control Charts for Attributes. Acceptance Sampling. Sample-Size Models. Confidence-Interval Models. Probability Distributions.
STUDENT SET IBM 5 1/4" AND 128 PP MANUAL
833703-8

STUENT SET IBM 3 1/2" VERSION AND 128 PP. MANUAL
833706-2

1993   **JURAN**

J.M. Juran, The Juran Institute
Frank M. Gryna Jr., University of Tampa
QUALITY PLANNING AND ANALYSIS, Third Edition
ANCILLARIES AVAILABLE.
033183-9

1989   **TAGUCHI**

Genichi Taguchi, Ph.D., International Consultant
Elsayed A. Elsayed, Ph.D., Rutgers University
Thomas Hsiang, Ph.D., Universal Foods Corporation
QUALITY ENGINEERING IN PRODUCTION SYSTEMS
Ancillaries are available.
062830-0

1988   GRANT

Eugene L. Grant, Emeritus, Stanford University
Richard S. Leavenworth, University of Florida
STATISTICAL QUALITY CONTROL,
Sixth Edition
Ancillaries are available.
024117-1

PURCHASING AND
MATERIALS HANDLIING

1990   DOBLER

Donald W. Dobler
David N. Burt, University of San Diego
PURCHASING AND MATERIALS
MANAGEMENT: Text and Cases, Fifth
Edition
This thorough revision reflects the changing role of
Purchasing in industrial operations. New concerns
explored include: Sourcing, the manufacturing of
quality; Supplier management (integrated
throughout); Earlier development of material
specification; and JIT (just-in-time).
Contents: The Functions of Purchasing and
Materials Management. The Generation of
Requirements. Fundamentals of Purchasing. Special
Purchases. Contract Administration. Fundamentals

of Materials Management. General Management
Responsibilities. Institutional and Government
Purchasing.
-pp.864
037047-8

INSTRUCTOR'S MANUAL/TESTBANK
037083-4

SPECIAL TOPICS

1994   HASSELBACK

James R. Hasselback, Florida State University
THE MCGRAW-HILL DIRECTORY OF
MANAGEMENT FACULTY, 1993-1994,
Third Edition
Compiled and updated by James R. Hasselback of
Florida State University, the third annual McGraw-
Hill Directory of Management Faculty is a complete
listing of all four-year college and university faculty
in the USA and Canada. The directory lists more than
10,000 individuals representing more than 800
schools. Many countries outside of North America
are also represented, including Great Britain,
Australia, New Zealand, Japan and Israel. The
directory, published as a free service to the
management field, is an invaluable resource for all
professors of management. It also features a
complete catalog of all management textbooks
available from McGraw-Hill.
Contents: Catalog of McGraw-Hill Management
Textbooks. 1. 1994 Titles in Management. 2. 1993 and
Prior Titles in Management. Management Faculty
Directory. 3. US Management Faculty (alphabetical
by school). 4. Canadian Management Faculty

(alphabetical by school). 5. Other Foreign
Management Faculty (alphabetical by school). 6. ALL
Management Faculty (alphabetical by individual).
-pp.352
027017-1

1992   MCCRAW

Thomas K. McCraw, Harvard Business School
THE ESSENTIAL ALFRED
CHANDLER: Essays Toward a
Historical Theory of Big Business
Now available in paperback, this collection reveals
the evolution of Chandler's theory of big business
and the enormous contribution that he has made to
the field. Included are sixteen essays, as well as the
table of contents and introductions to his three major
books on business history: Strategy and Structure,
The Visible Hand, and Scale and Scope. McCraw
provides a capsule intellectual biography of
Chandler, as well as an introduction to each essay.
Contents: Introduction: The Intellectual Odyssey of
Alfred D. Chandler Jr. by Thomas K. McCraw. Henry
Varnum Poor: Business Analyst. The Beginnings of
"Big Business" in American Industry. Development,
Diversification, and Decentralization. Recent
Developments in American Business Administration
and their Conceptualization. Introduction to Strategy
and Structure. The Railroads: Pioneers in Modern
Corporate Management. The Organization of
Manufacturing and Transportation. The Lare
Industrial Corporation and the Making of the
Modern American Economy. The Structure of
American Industry in the Twentieth Century: A
Historical Overview. Comment [on the New
Economic History]. Business History as Institutional
History. Anthracite Coal and the Beginnings of the
Industrial Revolution in the United States. Decision
Making and Institutional Change. The Development
of Modern Management Structure in the US and UK.
Introduction to The Visible Hand. Administrative
Coordination, Allocation and Monitoring: Concepts
and Comparisons. Government Versus Business: An
American Phenomenon. Markets and Hierarchies: A
Discussion. Introduction to Scale and Scope.
Acknowledgments. A List of Chandler's
Publications. Index.
-pp.560
103317-3

1991 Harvard   CHRISTENSEN

C. Roland Christensen, Harvard Business School
David A. Garvin, Harvard Business School
Ann Sweet, Harvard Business School
EDUCATION FOR JUDGMENT: The
Artistry of Discussion Leadership
Discussion teaching is a powerful tool for developing
skills as well as conveying knowledge. In the give
and take of discussion, students are confronted with
the same kind of ambiguous, many-sided problems
they will face in their professional lives. This
collection of essays describes the building blocks of
successful group leadership, as well as broader, more
philosophical issues. First-person accounts of
discussion leaders' experiences provide useful
insights into the joys and pitfalls of teaching by the
discussion method.
Contents: PART ONE: Learning and Teaching.
PART TWO: Personal Odysseys. PART THREE:
Building Blocks. PART FOUR: Critical Challenges.
PART FIVE: Education for Judgment.
-pp.312
103307-6

1991 Harvard   KEEN

Peter G. W. Keen, International Center for
Information Technologies
EVERY MANAGER'S GUIDE TO
INFORMATION TECHNOLOGY: A
Glossary of Key Terms and Concepts
for Today's Business Leader
Designed for anyone who wants to understand how
information technology is used in business today,
this book is a selective guide to the key terms and
concepts that are reshaping every industry. It
provides a vocabulary of 150 core IT terms needed to
achieve computer fluency, and also explains their
relevance to students and managers in easily
understood language. Keen includes an introductory
essay that gives an excellent overview of information
technology in the organization.
Contents: Introduction. Glossary. Index.
-pp.180
103312-2

1991 Harvard   KEEN

Peter G. W. Keen, International Center for
Information Technologies
SHAPING THE FUTURE: Business
Design through Information
Technology
Keen describes the competitive, organizational,
economic, and technical aspects of using information
technology for business design. He highlights key
management policy decisions, business
opportunities, and potential problems in seven areas.
SHAPING THE FUTURE is the first book to provide
managers with comprehensive and practical advice
on their role in managing information technology as
a business resource.
Contents: Introduction. 1. Management
Responsibility in the 1990s. 2. Competitive
Positioning through Information Technology. 3.
Geographic Positioning through Information
Technology. 4. Redesigning the Organization
through Information Technology. 5. Redeploying
Human Capital. 6. Managing the Economics of
Information Capital. 7. Positioning the IT Platform. 8.
Aligning Business and Technology. Index.
-pp.264
103289-4

1991   MATTHEWS

John B. Matthews, Harvard University
Kenneth E. Goodpaster, College of Saint Thomas
Laura L. Nash, Harvard University
POLICIES AND PERSONS: A
CASEBOOK IN ETHICS, Second
Edition
040999-4

1991   PEGDEN

C. Dennis Pegden, Systems Modeling Corp.
Randall P. Sadowski, Systems Modeling Corp.
Robert E. Shannon, Texas A & M University
INTRODUCTION TO SIMULATION
USING SIMAN
049217-4

THE 1994-95 McGRAW-HILL
DIRECTORY OF MANAGEMENT FACULTY

Compiled by
James R. Hasselback
Professor of Taxation
Florida State University
Tallahassee, Florida 32306-1042
904-644-7884 Phone/Recorder
904-644-5265 Fax

This is the fourth DIRECTORY OF MANAGEMENT FACULTY published by McGraw-Hill, Inc. The Directory includes a listing of the Dean, Department Chairperson, and full-time Management Faculty from over 800 schools. It is compiled from information provided by the respective schools. At least two requests went to any school not responding. Only that information received by May 27, 1994, is included in the Directory. Some missing information was filled in from other sources.

The Directory covers the academic year 1994-95. United States schools are followed by Canadian and then other foreign schools in the school listing.

The years in the right-hand column of each school line are the AACSB Bachelors and Masters accreditation dates. The telephone area code is in parenthesis. The school's e-mail address follows the area code. At the end of the second line are the programs and degrees offered by the school. The college/department fax is included in the second line for each school. The department/area phone number is included in the department line. The department/area fax number follows the department/area phone number.

The columns are as follows:
Name   Rank   School-Phone   Electronic-Mail   Teaching   Research   Degree   Start
$ next to a Dean or Chairperson indicates "Acting"

For the Chairperson, the title and rank are:
C   Chairperson   D   Director   H   Head
Pr   Professor   Ac   Associate   As   Assistant

The degree column represents the highest earned degree or "all but dissertation," date received, and school.

The start column is for the month/year of beginning full-time employment at that school.

The teaching and research columns are as follows:

1 General Management/Public Administration	A. Public Administration B. Management History C. Health for Management D. Innovative Management &. Communications
2 Organizational Behavior/Organization Theory	E. Organizational Behavior F. Organizational Development G. Stress Management H. Organization Theory
3 Strategic Management/Business Policy/Planning	I. Strategic Mgt/Bus Policy
4 Business and Society/Ethics/Legal Environment	J. Ethics K. Legal Environment L. Business & Society M. Environmental Management
5 Personnel/HRM/Labor/Industrial Relations	N. HRM/Personnel O. Career Management P. Training & Development Q. Labor/Industrial Relations R. Women in Management
6 Small Business/Entrepreneurship	S. Small Business T. Entrepreneurship
7 POM/Quantitative Methods/Management Science	U. Production/Operations Mgt V. Quant Methods/Mgt Science W. Purchasing/Materials Mgt X. Research Design
8 International/Multinational	Y. International/Multinational
9 Management Information Systems	Z. MIS

Any mistakes in the Directory are my responsibility. However, some of the misinformation belongs to schools not providing complete information.

Any corrections, additional information, and new schools should be sent directly to me. If your school is not included, send me your listing in a format similar to that in the Directory.

James R. Hasselback

ALABAMA
University of Alabama
U of Alabama at Birmingham
U of Alabama in Huntsville
Alabama A&M University
Alabama State University
Athens State College
Auburn University
Auburn U at Montgomery
Birmingham-Southern College
Jacksonville State Univ
Livingston University
University of Montevallo
University of North Alabama
Samford University
University of South Alabama
Troy State University
Tuskegee University
ALASKA
Univ of Alaska, Anchorage
Univ of Alaska - Fairbanks
Univ of Alaska - Southeast
ARIZONA
Ameridan Grad Sch Intl Mgt
University of Arizona
Arizona State University
Arizona St U - West Campus
Northern Arizona University
ARKANSAS
Arkansas College
University of Arkansas
U of Arkansas at Little Rock
U of Arkansas at Monticello
U of Arkansas at Pine Bluff
Arkansas State University
Arkansas Tech University
Univ of Central Arkansas
Harding University
Henderson State University
Southern Arkansas Univ
CALIFORNIA
Azusa Pacific University
U of California-Berkeley
Univ of California-Davis
Univ of Calif-Irvine
Univ of Calif, Los Angeles
Univ of Calif, Riverside
U of Calif, Santa Barbara
Calif Polytechnic State U
Calif State Poly U-Pomona
Calif State U., Bakersfield
Calif State Univ, Chico
Calif St U-Dominguez Hills
Calif State Univ-Fresno
Calif State Univ, Fullerton
Calif State Univ, Hayward
Calif State Univ - Humboldt
Calif State Univ, Long Beach
Calif State U-Los Angeles
Calif State Univ, Northridge
Calif State Univ-Sacramento
Calif St U-San Bernardino
Calif State U - San Marcos
Calif State U, Stanislaus
Chapman College
Claremont McKenna College
Claremont Graduate School
John F. Kennedy University
LaSierra University
Loyola Marymount Univ
Mount St. Mary's College
Naval Postgraduate School
University of the Pacific
Pacific Union College
Pepperdine Univ-Los Angeles
Pepperdine Univ-Malibu
University of Redlands
Saint Mary's College
University of San Diego
San Diego State University
University of San Francisco
San Francisco State Univ
San Jose State University
Santa Clara University
Sonoma State University
Univ of Southern California
Stanford University
United States Intl Univ
Woodbury University
COLORADO
Univ of Colorado at Boulder
U of Colorado at Co Springs
Univ of Colorado at Denver
Colorado State University
University of Denver
Fort Lewis College
Mesa State College
Metropolitan State College
Univ of Northern Colorado
Univ of Southern Colorado
U.S. Air Force Academy
Western State College of CO

CONNECTICUT
University of Bridgeport
Central Connecticut St Univ
University of Connecticut
Eastern Conn State Univ
Fairfield Universiy
University of Hartford
University of New Haven
Quinnipiac College
Southern Connecticut St Un
Teikyo Post University
Western Conn State Univ
Yale University
DELAWARE
University of Delaware
Delaware State College
Wesley College
FLORIDA
Barry University
Bethune-Cookman College
Embry-Riddle Aeronautical U
Univ of Central Florida
University of Florida
Florida A&M University
Florida Atlantic Univ
Florida International Univ
Florida Southern College
Florida State University
Jacksonville University
University of Miami
University of North Florida
Rollins College
St. Thomas University-FL
University of South Florida
Stetson University
University of Tampa
Warner Southern College
University of West Florida
GEORGIA
Albany State College
Augusta College
Berry College
Clark Atlanta University
Clayton State College
Columbus College
Emory University
Fort Valley State College
Georgia College
University of Georgia
Georgia Institute Tech
Georgia Southern University
Georgia Southwestern College
Georgia State University
Kennesaw College
Mercer Univ-Atlanta
Mercer Univ-Macon
Morehouse College
Morris Brown College
North Georgia College
Oglethorpe University
Piedmont College
Savannah State College
Valdosta State University
Wesleyan College
West Georgia College
HAWAII
Brigham Young Univ-Hawaii
Chaminade University
University of Hawaii at Hilo
Univ of Hawaii at Manoa
Hawaii Pacific University
IDAHO
Boise State University
University of Idaho
Idaho State University
ILLINOIS
Augustana College
Aurora University
Bradley University
University of Chicago
Chicago State University
DePaul University
Eastern Illinois Univ
Elmhurst College
Governors State University
University of Illinois
Univ of Illinois at Chicago
Illinois Benedictine College
Illinois Institute of Tech
Illinois State University
Illinois Wesleyan University
Loyola University of Chicago
Millikin University
Northeastern Illinois Univ
Northern Illinois Univ
Northwestern University
Roosevelt University
Saint Xavier University
Sangamon State University
Southern Illinois Univ
So Illinois, Edwardsville
Western Illinois University

INDIANA
Ball State University
Butler University
University of Evansville
DePauw University
Goshen College
Indiana University
Indiana Univ - Purdue Univ
Indiana Univ at Kokomo
Indiana Univ at South Bend
Indiana Univ Northwest
Indiana Univ Southeast
Indiana State University
University of Indianapolis
Marian College
University of Notre Dame
Purdue University
Saint Marys College
Univ of Southern Indiana
Tri State University
Valparaiso University
IOWA
Buena Vista College
Drake University
University of Iowa
Iowa State University
Loras College
Luther College
University of Northern Iowa
St. Ambrose University
Teikyo Marycrest University
KANSAS
Emporia State University
Fort Hays State University
University of Kansas
Kansas State University
MidAmerica Nazarene College
Pittsburg State University
Washburn Univ of Topeka
Wichita State University
KENTUCKY
Bellarmine College
Brescia College
Cumberland College
Eastern Kentucky University
University of Kentucky
Kentucky State University
University of Louisville
Morehead State University
Murray State University
Northern Kentucky Univ
Transylvania University
Western Kentucky University
LOUISIANA
Dillard University
Grambling State University
Louisiana State University
Louisiana St in Shreveport
Louisiana Tech University
Loyola Univ-New Orleans
Mc Neese State University
University of New Orleans
Nicholls State University
Northeast Louisiana Univ
Northwestern State U of LA
Southeastern Louisiana Univ
Southern University
U of Southwestern Louisiana
Tulane University
MAINE
Univ of Maine at Orono
Univ of Southern Maine
MARYLAND
University of Baltimore
Frostburg State University
Loyola College in Maryland
University of Maryland
Morgan State University
Mount Saint Mary's College
Salisbury State University
Towson State University
MASSACHUSETTS
American International Coll
Assumption College
Babson College
Bentley College
Boston College
Boston University
Clark University
Fitchburg State College
Harvard University
College of the Holy Cross
University of Massachusetts
U Massachusetts at Boston
U Massachusetts at Dartmouth
U Massachusetts at Lowell
Massachusetts Inst of Tech
Merrimack College
Nichols College
North Adams State College
Northeastern University
Pine Manor College

Salem State College
Simmons College
Stonehill College
Suffolk University
Western New England Coll
Westfield State College
Worcester Polytechnic Inst
MICHIGAN
Adrian College
Albion College
Alma College
Andrews University
Aquinas College
Calvin College
Central Michigan University
University of Detroit Mercy
Eastern Michigan University
Ferris State University
GMI Engineering & Mgt Ins
Grand Valley State Univ
Hillsdale College
Hope College
Lake Superior State Univ
Lawrence Technological Un
University of Michigan
Univ of Michigan-Dearborn
Univ of Michigan-Flint
Michigan State University
Michigan Technological Un
Northern Michigan Univ
Northwood Institute
Oakland University
Olivet College
Saginaw Valley State Univ
Wayne State University
Western Michigan Universit
MINNESOTA
Bemidji State University
Concordia College MN
Gustavus Adolphus College
Mankato State University
University of Minnesota
U of Minnesota - Duluth
Moorhead State University
St. Cloud State University
College of St. Scholastica
University of St. Thomas-M
Southwest State University
Winona State University
MISSISSIPPI
Belhaven College
Delta State University
Jackson State University
Millsaps College
Mississippi College
University of Mississippi
Mississippi State Univ
Mississippi Valley St Univ
U of Southern Mississippi
MISSOURI
Central Missouri State Univ
Drury College
U of Missouri at Columbia
U Missouri--Kansas City
U Missouri--St. Louis
Missouri Southern St Col
Missouri Western St Colleg
Northeast Missouri State U
Northwest Missouri St Univ
Rockhurst College
Saint Louis University
Southeast Missouri St Univ
Southwest Baptist Univ
Southwest Missouri St Univ
Washington University
Webster University
William Jewell College
MONTANA
Eastern Montana College
University of Montana
Montana State University
NEBRASKA
Bellevue College
Creighton University
University of Nebraska
Univ of Nebraksa at Kearne
Univ of Nebraska at Omaha
Nebraksa Wesleyan Univ
Wayne State College
NEVADA
Univ of Nevada, Las Vegas
University of Nevada, Reno
NEW HAMPSHIRE
Dartmouth College
Keene State College
New Hampshire College
University of New Hampshi
Plymouth State College

NEW JERSEY
  Centenary College
  Fairleigh Dickinson-Madison
  Jersey City State College
  Monmouth College
  Montclair State College
  New Jersey Ins of Technology
  Ramapo College of New Jersey
  Rider College
  Rowan College of New Jersey
  Rutgers University-Camden
  Rutgers University-Newark
  Rutgers Univ-New Brunswick
  Saint Peter's College
  Seton Hall University
  Trenton State College
  Upsala College
NEW MEXICO
  Eastern New Mexico Univ
  University of New Mexico
  New Mexico Highlands Univ
  New Mexico State Univ
NEW YORK
  Adelphi University
  Alfred University
  Canisius College
  CUNY-Baruch College
  CUNY-Brooklyn College
  CUNY-Hunter College
  CUNY-Queens College
  CUNY-Staten Island
  Clarkson University
  Columbia University
  Cornell University
  Fordham University
  Hofstra University
  Houghton College
  Iona College
  Ithaca College
  LeMoyne College
  Long Isl U, Brooklyn Campus
  Long Island U.C.W. Post
  Manhattan College
  Marist College
  New York University
  New York University-Grad
  New York Institute of Tech
  Niagara University
  Pace University
  Pace University-Westchester
  Polytechnic University
  Rensselaer Poly Institute
  University of Rochester
  Rochester Inst of Technology
  Russell Sage College
  Saint Bonaventure Univ
  St. Francis College
  St. John Fisher College
  St. John's University
  College of St. Rose
  Siena College
  Skidmore College
  SUNY College at Fredonia
  State Un College at Geneseo
  SUNY at Albany
  SUNY at Binghamton
  SUNY at Buffalo
  SUNY at New Paltz
  SUNY at Old Westbury
  SUNY at Oswego
  SUNY at Plattsburgh
  SUNY at Stony Brook
  Syracuse University
  Union College
  Utica College
  Wagner College
  Yeshiva University
NORTH CAROLINA
  Appalachian State Univ
  Barton College
  Campbell University
  Catawba College
  Duke University
  East Carolina University
  Elon College
  Fayetteville State Univ
  Gardner-Webb University
  Greenboro College
  Guilford College
  Lees-McRae College
  Mars Hill College
  Meredith College
  North Carolina at Ashville
  University of North Carolina
  North Carolina at Charlotte
  North Carolina at Greensboro
  North Carolina at Wilmington
  North Carolina A&T State Un
  North Carolina Central Univ
  North Carolina State Univ
  Pfeiffer College
  Wake Forest University

Wake Forest University-Grad
Western Carolina University
Winston-Salem State Univ
NORTH DAKOTA
  Dickinson State University
  Jamestown College
  University of Mary
  Minot State University
  University of North Dakota
  North Dakota State Univ
OHIO
  Air Force Institute of Tech
  University of Akron
  Ashland University
  Baldwin-Wallace College
  Bowling Green State Univ
  Capital University
  Case Western Reserve Univ
  Cedarville College
  Central State Univ-Ohio
  University of Cincinnati
  Cleveland State University
  University of Dayton
  Franklin University
  Heidelberg College
  John Carroll University
  Kent State University
  Marietta College
  Miami University
  Ohio University
  Ohio Northern University
  Ohio State University
  Ohio Wesleyan University
  Otterbein College
  University of Rio Grande
  University of Toledo
  Wittenberg University
  Wright State University
  Xavier University
  Youngstown State University
OKLAHOMA
  Cameron University
  Univ of Central Oklahoma
  East Central University
  Northeastern State Univ
  University of Oklahoma
  Oklahoma Baptist University
  Oklahoma Christian U Sci/Art
  Oklahoma City University
  Oklahoma State University
  Oral Roberts University
  Southeastern Oklahoma State
  Southern Nazarene University
  Southwestern Oklahoma St Un
  University of Tulsa
OREGON
  Linfield College
  University of Oregon
  Oregon State University
  University of Portland
  Portland State University
  Southern Oregon St College
  Willamette University
PENNSYLVANIA
  Albright College
  Beaver College
  Bloomsburg University
  Bucknell University
  California Univ of Penn
  Carnegie Mellon University
  Cheyney University
  Clarion University
  Drexel University
  Duquesne University
  Elizabethtown College
  Franklin and Marshall Coll
  Gannon University
  Geneva College
  Gettysburg College
  Indiana U of Pennsylvania
  LaSalle University
  Lehigh University
  Lock Haven University
  Lycoming College
  Marywood College
  Millersville Univ of PA
  Mulhenberg College
  University of Pennsylvania
  Penn State University
  Penn State Univ-Erie
  Penn State Univ-Harrisburg
  University of Pittsburgh
  U of Pittsburgh at Johnstown
  Robert Morris College
  Saint Francis College
  Saint Joseph's University
  Saint Vincent College
  University of Scranton
  Shippensburg University
  Slippery Rock University
  Susquehanna University
  Temple University

Villanova University
West Chester University
Widener University
Wilkes University
York College of Pennsylvania
RHODE ISLAND
  Bryant College
  University of Rhode Island
SOUTH CAROLINA
  Benedict College
  College of Charleston
  The Citadel
  Clemson University
  Francis Marion College
  Furman University
  Lander College
  Livingstone College
  Univ So Carolina at Aiken
  South Carolina-Coastal Carol
  Univ of South Carolina
  U South Carolina at Spartanb
  South Carolina St College
  Winthrop College
  Wofford College
SOUTH DAKOTA
  Augustana College SD
  Northern State University
  University of South Dakota
TENNESSEE
  Austin Peay State University
  Belmont University
  Carson-Newman College
  Christian Brothers College
  David Lipscomb University
  East Tennessee State Univ
  Fisk University
  Freed Hardeman University
  Memphis State University
  Middle Tennessee State Univ
  Rhodes College
  Southern Col of 7th Day Adv
  University of Tennessee
  Tennessee at Chattanooga
  Univ of Tennessee at Martin
  Tennessee State University
  Tennessee Technological Un
  Vanderbilt University
TEXAS
  Abilene Christian Univ
  Amber University
  Angelo State University
  Baylor University
  University of Dallas
  Dallas Baptist University
  East Texas State Univ
  Hardin-Simmons University
  University of Houston
  Univ of Houston-Clear Lake
  Univ of Houston-Downtown
  Houston Baptist University
  Lamar University
  Univ of Mary Hardin-Baylor
  Midwestern State University
  University of North Texas
  Prairie View A&M University
  Rice University
  St. Edward's University
  St. Mary's University
  University of St. Thomas-TX
  Sam Houston State Univ
  Southern Methodist Univ
  Southwest Texas State Univ
  Southwestern University
  Stephen F. Austin St Univ
  Tarleton State University
  U of Texas at Arlington
  Univ of Texas at Austin
  Univ of Texas at Brownsville
  Univ of Texas at Dallas
  Univ of Texas at El Paso
  Univ of Texas-Pan American
  U of Texas of Permian Basin
  Un of Texas at San Antonio
  Univ of Texas at Tyler
  Texas A&M University
  Texas A&M Univ-Corpus Chr
  Texas A&M Univ-Kingsville
  Texas A&M International Univ
  Texas Christian University
  Texas Lutheran College
  Texas Southern University
  Texas Tech University
  Texas Wesleyan University
  Texas Woman's University
  Trinity University
  West Texas State Univ
UTAH
  Brigham Young University
  University of Utah
  Utah State University
  Weber State University

VERMONT
  Lyndon State College
  Norwich University
  University of Vermont
VIRGINIA
  Averett College
  Christopher Newport College
  Emory and Henry College
  George Mason University
  Hampton University
  James Madison University
  Liberty University
  Longwood College
  Lynchburg College
  Mary Baldwin College
  Mary Washington College
  Marymount University
  Norfolk State University
  Old Dominion University
  Radford University
  Regent University
  University of Richmond
  Roanoke College
  St. Paul's College
  Shenandoah College
  University of Virginia
  University of Virginia-Grad
  Virginia Commonwealth Univ
  Virginia Poly Inst & St Un
  Virginia State University
  Virginia Union University
  Washington and Lee Univ
  College of William & Mary
WASHINGTON
  Central Washington Univ
  Eastern Washington Univ
  Gonzaga University
  Northwest College
  Pacific Lutheran University
  University of Puget Sound
  Saint Martin's College
  Seattle University
  Seattle Pacific University
  University of Washington
  Washington State University
  Western Washington Univ
WASHINGTON DC
  The American University
  Catholic Univ of America
  Univ of District of Columbia
  George Washington Univ
  Georgetown University
  Howard University
  Southeastern University
WEST VIRGINIA
  Alderson-Broadus College
  Shephard College
  Marshall University
  West Virginia University
WISCONSIN
  Carroll College
  Carthage College
  Marquette University
  St. Norbert College
  U of Wisconsin-Eau Claire
  U of Wisconsin-Green Bay
  U of Wisconsin-La Crosse
  Univ of Wisconsin-Madison
  Univ of Wisconsin-Milwaukee
  Univ of Wisconsin-Oshkosh
  Univ of Wisconsin-Parkside
  U of Wisconsin-Platteville
  U of Wisconsin-River Falls
  U of Wisconsin-Stevens Point
  Univ of Wisconsin-Superior
  U of Wisconsin-Whitewater
WYOMING
  University of Wyoming

1994-95 DIRECTORY OF MANAGEMENT FACULTY
ALPHABETICAL BY SCHOOL

NAME	RANK	PHONE	E-MAIL	TCH	RESR	DEGREE		START
Abilene Christian Univ	Abilene, TX	79699-0001	(915)				BA,BBA	
College of Business Adm	1600 Campus Court		FAX=674-2564					
Griggs, Jack	Dean	674-2245			Mgt	PHD	71 Texas	1-91
−Dept Management Sciences	Phone	674-2565	Fax 674-2564					
Reid, Brad	C-Pr	674-2053				JD	73 Texas	1975
Reinsch, N. L. Jr.	Prof		reinsch	15	JND	PHD	73 Kansas	1984
on leave to Georgetown								
Brister, Jozell	Assoc	674-2560				MED	73 Abilene	1980
Associate Dean								
Jackson, Don	Assoc	674-2634				DBA	Geo Wash	1987
Lynn, Monty L.	Assoc	674-2593		2	BEHQ	PHD	85 Brig Yg	1985
Pope, Terry	Assoc	674-2570				PHD	69 So Meth	1992
Small, Charles	Assoc	674-2070				PHD	78 Tx A&M	1977
William, R. Don	Assoc	674-2569				PHD	Tx A&M	1992
Bartee, Jim	Asst	674-2077		78	UY	MA	88 Tx-Dallas	1991
Coco, Malcolm	Asst	674-2429				PHD	Nova	1990
Lytle, Richard	Asst	674-2052				ABD	Ariz St	1991
Bolin, Michael	Inst					ABD	North Tx	1991
Adelphi University	Garden City, NY	11530	(516) ADLIDV.ADELPHI.EDU					
School of Business Adm	South Avenue		FAX=877-3347				BBA,MBA,MS	
Weinstein, Arnold K.	Dean	877-4690	weinstei	81	YD	PHD	73 Columbia	1992
−Dept of Admin Sci & Mgt	Phone	877-4679	Fax 877-4607					
Ashley, Allan	C-Pr	877-4640		7	IUVX	PHD	71 Poly-Brk	1967
Geiss, Gunther	Prof	877-4635	geiss	91	ZD	PHD	64 Poly-Brk	1972
Gutman, Gregory	Prof	877-4628	gutman	26	EFT	MBA	66 Penn	1967
Latham, Jefferson M.	Assoc	877-4644	latham	79	VZ	PHD	75 Hofstra	1978
Ruocco, Joseph	Assoc	877-4631	ruocco	52	NPEF	PHD	62 Fordham	1981
Elenkov Detelin	Asst	877-4636		38	IUY	PHD	92 MIT	1993
Goldstein, Jeffrey	Asst	877-4637	goldstei	21	EFHD	PHD	80 Temple	1989
Gupta, Rakesh C.	Asst	877-4629		27	IUV	MBA	75 CUNY-Bar	1978
Huang, Zhimin	Asst	877-4633	huang	97	ZUVX	PHD	91 Texas	1991
Jolt, Harvey	Asst	877-4642	jolt	12	CAE	PHD	74 NYU	1988
Li, Susan	Asst	877-4613	li	97	ZUVX	PHD	92 Texas	1992
Mather, Rachel	Asst	877-4647		14	DLRY	DA	93 St Johns	1980
Adrian College	Adrian, MI	49221-2575	(517)				BBA	
Dept of Atg & Bus Adm	110 South Madison Street		FAX=					
Bachman, William	C-Pr	265-5161		35	LNQ	ABD	73 Kentucky	8-81
−Management Faculty	Phone							
Theis, Ann	Asst	265-5161		17	IUZ	MBA	86 Michigan	8-89
Air Force Institute of Tech	Wright-Patter OH	45433	(513) AFIT.AF.MIL				MS	
Sch of Log & Acquis Mgt	2950 P Street		FAX=255-8458					
phone 255-7777								
Schuppe, Tom F.	Dean	255-7777	tschuppe			PHD	Ohio St	9-92
−Dept of Grad Mgt Systems	Phone	Ext 3345						
Weaver, Robert B.	H-Ac	Ext 3343	rweaver			PHD	Renssela	7-90
Steel, Robert P.	Prof	Ext 3348	rpsteel	25	EFHN	PHD	Tenn	6-81
Shane, Guy S.	Assoc	Ext 3347	gshane	25	ENXZ	PHD	Geo Wash	N-81
Shoukat, Michael M.	Asst	Ext 3351	mshoukat	9	IZ	PHD	Mo-Rolla	9-92
Stone, Wayne E.	Asst	Ext 3346	wstone	23	EHIZ	DBA	S Illin	8-90
Teal, Steven L.	Inst	Ext 3352	steal	9	IZ	ABD	Car Mel	9-92
VanScotter, James R.				25	EHNZ		Florida	9-94
University of Akron	Akron, OH	44325-4801	(216) AKRONVM				1966,1976	
College of Business Adm	259 S. Broadway		FAX=972-6588				BS,MBA,MS	
−Dept of Management	Phone		Fax 972-6588					
Meek, Gary E.	H-Pr	972-6636	r1gem	7	VUX	PHD	70 Case Wes	9-71
Aupperle, Kenneth E.	Prof	972-6850	r1kea	32	IJE	PHD	82 Georgia	9-86
Dunning, Kenneth A.	Prof	972-7039	r1kad	79	UVZ	PHD	72 Pitt	9-73
Hebert, John E.	Prof	972-6300	r1jeh	79	UVZ	PHD	75 Purdue	9-80
Klafehn, Keith A.	Prof	972-6429	r1kak	7	VCU	DBA	73 Kent St	9-70
Krigline, Alan G.	Prof	972-7037	r1agk	73	IDY	PHD	77 Geo St	9-73
Kuzdrall, Paul J.	Prof	972-6095	r1pjk	79	UZV	PHD	77 St Louis	9-85
Latona, Joseph C.	Prof	972-7337		36	IST	DBA	70 Kent St	9-71
Patankar, Jay G.	Prof	972-7354	r1jgp	7	VXU	PHD	78 Clemson	9-78
Rakich, Jonathon S.	Prof	972-6301		3	CIL	PHD	70 St Louis	9-72
Shilliff, Karl A.	Prof	972-7950		13	IUS	PHD	71 Penn St	9-67
Divoky, James J.	Prof	972-6900	r1jjd	9	ZVU	DBA	84 Kent St	8-83
Figler, Robert A.	Assoc	972-5437		5	QNH	PHD	84 W Virg	9-85

Name	Rank	Phone	Code							
Hanlon, Susan C.	Assoc	972-7685	r1sch	12	DFE	DBA	82	Memphis	1-90
Johnson, Avis L.	Assoc	972-6683		25	ERF	PHD	86	Nebraska	1-84
Meyer, David G.	Assoc	972-6430	r1dgm	5	QDN	PHD	86	Michigan	8-89
Rothermel, Mary Anne	Assoc	972-5440	r1mar	7	VXP	PHD	81	Ohio St	9-84
Simmons, Franklin B.	Assoc	972-6979	r1fbs	36	IJK	PHD	81	Cinn	1-82
Taylor, Richard W.	Assoc	972-5441	r1rwt	7	VUX	PHD	83	Ga Tech	8-89
Vijayaraman, Bindiganavale S	Assoc	972-5442	r1bsv	9	ZUV	PHD	87	Geo St	8-89
Osyk, Barbara A.	Asst	972-5439	r1bao	7	VUD	ABD	88	Kent St	8-89
West, Clifford T.	Asst	972-5443	r1ctw	31	ILD	ABD	89	Indiana	8-90

University of Alabama — Tuscaloosa, AL 35487-0225 (205) UA1VM 1929,1963
College Comm & Bus Adm — FAX=348-2951 — BS,MA,PHD

Name	Rank	Phone								
Mason, J. Barry	Dean	348-7443			Mktg	PHD	67	Alabama	1967

Russell Professsor of Business Administration
—**Dept of Management & Mktg** Phone — Fax 348-2951

Name	Rank	Phone								
Dulek, Ronald E.	H-Pr	348-8930			JMY&	PHD	77	Purdue	1977
Bain, Trevor	Prof	348-8939		58	QY	PHD	64	Berkeley	1974
John R. Miller Professor of Management									
Cashman, James F.	Prof	348-8940		12	DEY	PHD	75	Illinois	1984
Foster, Lawrence W.	Prof	348-8922		38	IY	PHD	73	Texas	1984
Hill, John	Prof	348-6103		8	IY	PHD	80	Georgia	1985
Odewahn, Charles A.	Prof	348-8925		15	ANOQ	PHD	70	Kentucky	1978
Petty, Mickey M.	Prof	348-8926		25	DN	PHD	72	Tenn	1978
Prewitt, Lena B.	Prof	348-8920		45	GNR	EDD	61	Indiana	1975
Strickland, A. J. (Lonnie)	Prof	348-8924		3	I	PHD	69	Geo St	1982
Scott, Clyde J.	Assoc	348-8942		5	AN	PHD	82	Minn	1981
Seers, Anson	Assoc	348-8931		2	E	PHD	81	Cinn	1980
Weaver, K. Mark	Assoc	348-8947		68	LSTY	PHD	74	LSU	1976
Crown, Deborah F.	Asst	348-4631		24	EJX	PHD	90	Colorado	1990
Hilton, Chadwick	Asst	348-9432			EJ&	PHD	83	Tenn	1986

U of Alabama at Birmingham — Birmingham, AL 35294-4460 (205) UABDPO.DPO.UAB.EDU1973,1977
School of Business — 1150 Tenth Avenue South — FAX= — BS,MAC,MBA
* Joint Appt with Dept of Public Health

Name	Rank	Phone	Code						
Newport, M. Gene	Dean	934-8810			Mgt	PHD	63	Illinois	1971

—**Department of Management** Phone 934-8840 Fax 975-6234

Name	Rank	Phone	Code						
McAlister, M. Khris	C-As	934-8840	busf009	91	Z	PHD	76	Iowa	1975
Dilworth, James B.	Prof	934-8840		7	U	PHD	70	Okla St	1970
Duncan, W. Jack	Prof	934-8880		3	CI	PHD	69	LSU	
Fottler, Myron D.	* Prof	934-3113	busf023	15		PHD	70	Columbia	1970
Chairman PhD Program									
Ginter, Peter M.	Prof	934-8840		3	CI	PHD	77	North Tx	1987
Heacock, Marian V.	Prof	934-8840	busf031	4	JL	PHD	67	Alabama	1967
Munchus, George M.	Prof	934-8840	busf021	5	NQ	PHD	76	North Tx	1976
Beeland, James L.	Assoc	934-8840		16		DBA	76	Geo St	1971
McGee, Gail W.	* Assoc	934-8840	shrp060	2	E	PHD	83	Alabama	1983
Scott, Robert A.	Assoc	934-8840		1	A	PHD	78	Geo St	1976
Burnett, Jennifer G.	Asst	934-8840	busf045	25	EN	PHD	93	Florida	1993
Draman, Rexford	Asst	934-8840		73	U	ABD		Georgia	1994
Richardson, Woody	Asst	934-8891		3	JI	PHD	86	Arkansas	1987
Rivera, C. Julio	Asst	934-8840	busf029	9	Z	DBA	92	S Miss	1988
Singh, Sanjay K.	Asst	934-8840	busf044	9	Z	PHD	93	Georiga	1993

U of Alabama in Huntsville — Huntsville, AL 35899 (205)
College of Adm Science — FAX=895-6328 — BS,MAS

Name	Rank	Phone							
Billings, C. David	Dean	895-6735			Econ	PHD	69	Missouri	1981

—**Dept of Management & Mktg** Phone — Fax 895-6328

Name	Rank	Phone							
Sherman, J. Daniel	C-Pr	895-6680		12	DEHX	PHD	81	Alabama	1981
McCollum, James K.	Prof	895-6902		25	BHQN	PHD	79	Va Tech	1984
Gramm, Cynthia L.	Assoc	895-6913		45	QKN	PHD	83	Illinois	1990
Jackson, Conrad N.	Assoc	895-6927		25	EFP	PHD	81	Purdue	1989
Olsen, Eugene	Assoc	895-6906		12	AEFP	PHD	68	NYU	1973
Adams, Melville W.	Asst	895-6908		36	ITD	PHD	91	Tenn	1989
Spann, Mary S.	Asst	895-6944		63	IST	PHD	91	Tenn	1989

—**Dept Mgt Info Sci & Mgt Sci** Phone 895-6590 Fax 895-6328

Name	Rank	Phone							
Paul, Chris	C-Pr	895-6590		4	K	PHD		Tx A&M	1979
Stafford, Edward F.	Prof	895-6565		7	UV	PHD		Penn St	1984
Zant, Robert F.	Prof	895-6857		9	Z	PHD		Florida	1988
Trueblood, Robert	Assoc	895-6826		9	Z	PHD		Va Tech	1991
Tseng, Fan-Tsong	Assoc	895-6804		7	UV	PHD		Texas	1984
Floyd, Steve	Asst	895-6833		9	Z	PHD		Georgia	1984
Lai, Vincent	Asst	895-6878		9	Z	PHD		Texas	1993

3

Alabama A&M University Normal, AL 35762 (205)
School of Business FAX=851-5839 BS,BA,MBA
Did Not Respond-1993 Listing; Department Phone 851-5495
Scott, Stanley V. Dean 851-5485 Mktg PHD 8-93
−**Business Adm Dept** Phone 851-5495 Fax 851-5839
Mixon, Herman C-Pr Ext-235 JD Alabama
Rice, Horace Prof Ext-238 JD Toledo
Jackson, Joe Assoc Ext-239 MBA Alab A&M
Ogburia, Sylvanus S. Assoc Ext-240 PHD LSU
Stewart, Roosevelt Assoc 851-5389 MBA Atlanta
Cnyinda, Chris Asst
on leave to Univ of Tennessee
Han, Sang J. Asst Ext-241 MBA Alab A&M
Hossein, Jamshidi Asst Ext-230
McDaniel, Larry Asst Ext-237 MBA Sanford
on leave
Steele, Thaddeus Asst 851-5685
Sullivan, James Asst Ext 237
Burrus, Robert Inst
Dike, Augustine Inst 851-5389 MBA Alab A&M
Torabinejad, Majid Inst 7 V

Alabama State University Montgomery, AL 36101-0271 (205)
College of Business Adm 915 South Jackson Street FAX=265-9144 BS
Vaughn, Percy J. Jr. Dean 293-4124 Mktg DBA Tx Tech 1074
−**Dept of Business Adm** Phone 293-4142 Fax 265 0014
Yeh, Chious Nan C-Pr 293-4142 Econ PHD Mass 1974
Lim, Yet Mee Asst 293-4119 2 PHD 93 Alabama 8-91
Self, Robin Asst 293-6961 5 N PHD Georgia 8-91

Univ of Alaska Anchorage Anchorage, AK 99508 (907) ACAD2.ALASKA.EDU
School of Business 3211 Providence Drive FAX= BBA,MBA
Blachman, William L. Dean 786-4125 3 Econ PHD 63 Wiscon 1988
−**Department of Business Adm** Phone 786-4127 Fax 786-4119
Srivastava, Sureshma C-Ac 786-4148 PHD 88 Maryland 1987
Geistauts, George A. Prof 786-4154 38 IY PHD 70 Renssel 1974
Hauck, Vern E. Prof 786-4156 53 QNI PHD 74 Iowa 1975
Jordan, Paul C. Prof 786-4147 7 UV PHD 81 N Car St 1984
Marx, Don Prof 786-4152 7 V PHD 74 Houston 1981
Selk, Gary Assoc 786-4150 61 ST MBA 77 Alaska 1981
Choudhury, Askar Asst 786-4161 97 VUZ PHD 90 Ariz St 1990
Uhl-Bien, Mary Asst 786-4162 2 EFH PHD 91 Cinn 1991

Univ of Alaska Fairbanks Fairbanks, AK 99775-6080 (907) ALASKA 1988,1988
School of Management FAX=474-5219 BBA
Porter, David O. Dean 474-7461 1 PHD 70 Syracuse 1994
−**Dept of Business Adm** Phone 474-7253 Fax 474-5219
Lehman, John A. Prof 9 Z PHD 82 Michigan 1987
Director University Computer Network
Taylor, John N. Prof 474-6534 ffjnt 5 N DBA 76 Utah 1982
Collins, James Asst 474-6524 ffjmc 3 I PHD 91 Texas 1991
Joseph, Jacob Asst 474-6532 ffjj 5 N ABD 1990
Warbelow, Art Asst 474-6529 9 Z PHD 91 Harvard 1990
Marshall, Dianne L. Inst 474-5534 9 Z MBA 86 Alaska 1987

Univ of Alaska Southeast Juneau, AK 99801 (907) ALASKA
School Bus & Public Adm 11120 Glacier Highway FAX= BBA,MBA,MPA
Wilson, L. A. II Dean 465-6340 7 X PHD 76 Oregon 1990
−**Management Faculty** Phone 465-6402 Fax 465-6383
Gallagher, Tom Prof 465-6357 24 DJM PHD 77 Michigan 1991
King, Mary Assoc 465-6349 13 DM PHD 83 U Wash 1993
Roberts, Wayne Assoc 465-6350 16 DS PHD 89 Ariz St 1975

Albany State College Albany, GA 31705 (912)
School of Business Adm 504 College Drive FAX=430-5119
Did Not Respond-1993 Listing
Burgess, Walter J. Dean 430-4772 Atg PHD 72 Geo St
−**Dept of Business Adm** Phone Fax 430-5119
Kooti, Ghanbar Assoc 430-4771 PHD Mich St
Okpara-Bush, Rosa Assoc 430-4780 PHD Geo St
Elliard, Maurice Asst 430-4776 MBA Auburn
Fazekas, Alex Asst 430-4781 MBA Albany S
Hazel, Delores Asst 430-4777 MBA Valdosta
Ojemakinde, Abiodun Asst 430-4784 PHD LSU
Rogers, Michael Asst 430-4774 PHD
Shah, Umanglal G. Asst 430-4779 MA Houston

Albion College
Dept of Economics & Mgt
McCarley, James F.
—Management Faculty
Bedient, John
Saltzman, Gregory M.

Albion, MI		49224-1899	(517) ALBION				
616 East Michigan			FAX=629-0509				BA
C-Pr	629-0294		Econ	PHD	70	Mich St	1965
Phone	629-0419	Fax 629-0428					
Assoc	629-0343	jbedient		MBA	79	Indiana	1984
Assoc	629-0422		QN	PHD	82	Wiscon	1986

Albright College
Dept of Business & Econ
Moyer, James T.
—Management Faculty
Lever, Jacqueline

Reading, PA		19612-5234	(215) JOE.ALB.EDU				
13th & Exets Sts			FAX=				BS,BA
C-Pr	921-7781		Econ	PHD	76	Lehigh	9-68
Phone	921-7538	Fax 921-7883					
Asst	921-7704	jacquel	36 IST	PHD	82	Pitt	9-90

Alderson-Broaddus College
Dept of Bus Adm & Econ
phone: 457-1700
Heck, Charles R.
—Mangement Faculty

Philippi, WV		26416	(304)		
			FAX=		BA
C-Ac	Ext 259		79	EDD	8-93
Phone	457-6259	Fax 457-6239			

Alfred University
College of Bus & Adm
Did Not Respond-1993 Listing
Szczerbacki, David
—Dept of Business Adm
Oksoy, Dolun

Alfred, NY		14802	(607) CERAMICS			1987
			FAX=871-2114			
Dean	871-2124	busdean		PHD	SUNY-Buf	1981
Phone		Fax 871-2114				
Prof	871-2294		13 Al	PHD	Union	1985

Alma College
Business Adm Dept
Did Not Respond-1993 Listing
Gazmararian, George
  Charles A. Dana Professor of Business Administration
—Management Faculty
Cameron, Elizabeth A.

Alma, MI		48801	(517)			
614 West Superior Street			FAX=463-7277			BA
C-Pr	463-7184		Fnce	MBA	Detroit	1966
Phone		Fax 463-7277				
Asst	463-7226			MBA	Saginaw	1988

The American University
Kogod College of Bus Ad
Tuggle, Francis D. (Doug)
—Department of Management
Holmberg, Stevan R.
Alexander, Elmore R.
  Associate Dean
DiBacco, Tom
Martin, David C.
O'Connor, Thomas
Bird, Barbara
DeLone, William
Jacobs, David
Selman, Victor
Volkema, Roger
Wasil, Ed
Carmel, Erran
Getz, Kathleen
Kirkpatrick, Shelley
Lane, Larry
Linowes, Richard
Smelcer, John

Washington, DC		20016-8044	(202) AUVM			1991,1991	
4400 Massachusetts Ave NW			FAX=885-1992		BS,MSA,MST,MBA		
Dean	885-1986	ftuggle	23 IZ	PHD	71	Car Mel	1990
Phone	885-1915	Fax 885-1916					
C-Pr	855-1921		36 IST	DBA	71	Indiana	1977
Prof	885-1987	alexand	25 EHNZ	PHD	78	Georgia	1989
Prof	885-1950		4 BL	PHD	65	American	1965
Prof	855-1922	dmartin	25 N	PHD	84	Maryland	1981
Prof	885-1919		7 V	PHD		Stanford	1989
Assoc	885-1924	bbird	26 ET	PHD		S Calif	1991
Assoc	885-1959		9 SZ	PHD	83	UCLA	1986
Assoc	885-1923	djacobs	45 LQ	PHD		Cornell	1984
Assoc	885-1903	vselman	7 UV	DSCI	69	Geo Wash	1976
Assoc	885-6193	volkema	2 EIZ	PHD		Wiscon	1987
Assoc	885-1966	ewasil	7 V	PHD		Maryland	1985
Asst	885-1928	ecarmel	9 Z	PHD	91	Arizona	1991
Asst	885-1998	kgetz	48 JLY	PHD	91	Pitt	1991
Asst	885-1956	skirkpa	25 NE	PHD	92	Maryland	1993
Asst	885-1927			PHD			
Asst	885-1990		23 IYT	DBA		Harvard	1986
Asst	885-1958	smelcer	9 Z	PHD		Michigan	1989

American Grad Sch Intl Mgt
Business
Herberger, A. Roy Jr.
—Management Faculty
Mathis, F. John
Barrett, Edgar
  Vice President for Executive Education
O'Connell, John
Black, Stewart
Johnson, Paul R.
Morrison, Allen
Murray, Alan
Schweizer, Jason
Siehl, Caren Joy

Glendale, AZ		85306-3399	(602)				
15249 N 59th Avenue			FAX=978-8238				MIM
Dean				DBA	71	Colorado	
Phone		Fax 843-6143					
C							
Prof	978-7280		31 IUM	PHD	71	Stanford	
Prof	978-7171		28 EFH	PHD	75	Ohio St	
Assoc	978-7606			DBA	88	Ca-Irvine	1994
Assoc	978-7150		68 TSY	PHD	68	Stanford	8-82
Assoc	978-7824			PHD	89	S Carol	
Assoc	978-7918			PHD			
Assoc	978-7174		52 NEY	PHD	79	Nebraska	
Assoc	978-7215		38 IYH	PHD	84	Stanford	

American International Coll | Springfield, MA | 01109-3189 | (413) | | |
School of Business Adm | 1000 State Street | | FAX=737-2803 | | BS
  Did Not Respond-1993 Listing
Maher, Charles F. | Dean | 747-6230 | | EDD | 79 | Mass
–**Management Faculty** | Phone | | Fax 737-2803
Sparks, Richard E. | Asst | 747-6360 | | 37 | FIU | PHD | 89 | Manchest | 1991

Andrews University	Berrien Spr, MI	49104	(616) ANDREWS.EDU					
School of Business			FAX=471-9751				BS,MBA	
Phillips, Harold	Dean	471-3102	phillips	3		PHD		Florida	1990
–**Department of Management**	Phone	471-3339	Fax 471-6158					
Stembridge, Allen	C-Pr	471-3584	stemb	28	PDE	EDD		Andrews	1988
McBride, Duane	Prof	471-3576	mcbride	1	C	PHD		Kentucky	1986
Oosterwal, Gottfried	Prof	471-6160	ooster	8	YQ	PHD		Utrecht	1990
Schwab, Robert	Prof	471-6859	schwab	2	E	PHD		Oregon	1993
Webster, Neville	Assoc	471-3118	webster	8		DBA		U of SA	1990
Pichot, Kimberly	Asst	471-3116	pichot	8	Y	MBA		Monterey	1990

Angelo State University	San Angelo, TX	76909	(915)					
Dept of Business Adm	2601 W. Ave N		FAX=942-2038				BBA,MBA	
Hegglund, Robert K.	Dean	942-2337		Mgt	PHD	72	Arkansas	1972
–**Management Faculty**	Phone		Fax 942-2038					
Smith, William O.	H Pr	942-2383		Mktg	PHD		Minn	
Alexander, F. David	Prof	942-2305			PHD		Oklahoma	
Bruha, Harlan	Inst	942-2305			MED		Kent St	
Maddox, Ann	Inst	942-2214			MBA		Tx Tech	
Miller, Alan A.	Inst	942-2305			MBA		AngeloSt	
Richardson, James A.	Inst	942-2304			MBA		AngeloSt	
Tomlin, Sharyn	Inst	942-2119			ABD		North Tx	

Appalachian State Univ	Boone, NC	28608	(704) APPSTATE					
Walker College of Bus			FAX=262-2094				1976,1981	
Peacock, Kenneth E.	Dean	262-2058		Atg	PHD	79	LSU	BS,MS 1983
–**Department of Management**	Phone	262-2163	Fax 262-2094					
Lyne, George E. Jr.	C-Ac	262-3174		23	EHI	PHD	74	N Carol	1973
Evans, Michael R.	Assoc	262-6222		1	I	PHD		Tenn	1991
Fox, Jeremy B.	Assoc	262-6225		5	NQ	PHD		Va Tech	1988
Goddard, Robert D. III	Assoc	262-6230		28	EPY	PHD	81	S Carol	1978
Hindman, Hugh D.	Assoc	262-2638		5	NQ	PHD		Ohio St	1988
Minton, John W.	Assoc	262-6227	minton	25	EFJP	PHD	88	Duke	1993
Peterson, Alden	Assoc	262-6224		3	SI	DBA		Kent St	1979
Ray, John W.	Assoc	262-6236		36	STI	PHD	82	S Carol	1980
Reeder, A. John	Assoc	262-6228		38	HIY	PHD		SUNY-Buf	1979
Anderson, Stella	Asst	262-6229		2	EH	PHD		Purdue	1992
Clark, J. Dana	Asst	262-6237		1	HW	PHD		Va Tech	1991
Daly, Joseph P.	Asst	262-6218		2	E	PHD		Northwes	1989
Johnson, Roy	Asst	262-6196		34	IJLQ	PHD	91	N Carol	1989
Villanova, Peter	Asst	262-6220		25	NEX	PHD		Va Tech	1993
–**Dept of Decision Sciences**	Phone	262-2034	Fax 262-2094					
Fitzpatarick, Kathy E.	C-Pr	262-2034	fitzpke	7	UV	PHD		Clemson	1983
Dave, Dinesh S.	Prof	262-2034	daveds	7	UVZ	PHD		Gujarat	1988
Roy, Melvin	Prof	262-2034		9	Z	PHD		N Colo	1973
Burwell, Timothy H.	Assoc	262-2034		7	UV	PHD		Clemson	1986
Crandall, Richard E.	Assoc	262-2034		7	UV	PHD	93	S Carol	1985
Harris, Albert L.	Assoc	262-2034		9	Z	PHD		Geo St	1989
May, Douglas	Assoc	262-2034	maydb	9	Z	PHD		N Colo	1982
Perry, Timothy	Assoc	262-2034		9	Z	PHD		Miss	1986
Tillman, Gerald J.	Assoc	262-2034		9	Z	PHD		Georgia	1985
McCracken, Melody J.	Asst	262-2034		7	UV	PHD		Geo St	1989
Wilkinson, R. Stanley Jr.	Asst	262-2034		9	Z	MA		Appal St	1975
Medlin, Dawn	Lect	262-2034	medlinbd	9	Z	MA		Appal St	1988
Weaver, Amy B.	Lect	262-2034	burgessas	9	Z	MBA		Appal St	1991

Aquinas College	Grand Rapids, MI 49506		(616)					
Bus Adm & Atg Dept	1607 Robinson Road SE		FAX=					
phone 459-8281								
VanGelderen, Cynthia G.	C	Ext 3607		3	I	MBA	84	W Mich	1980
–**Management Faculty**	Phone	Ext 3607						
Hoover, Harwood Jr.	Prof	Ext 3615		48	IJXY	PHD	84	Mich St	1978
McNally, Joyce E.	Prof	Ext 3614		12	BDHR	DBA	87	Intl Gr	1982
Griffin, Charlene J.	Assoc	Ext 3633		23	EHIZ	ABD		Mich St	1980
Kieff, Allene	Assoc	Ext 3642		25	DENP	MA	71	Sam Hou	1986
Neqvi, Syed	Assoc	Ext 3638		25	EFNP	MBA	67	Cen Mich	1977
Tychsen, Norman E.	Assoc	Ext 3601		3	I	MBA	67	Chicago	1974
Heinz, Kristel	Asst	Ext 3643		16	DOSR	MM	80	Aquinas	1991
Kieff, Gary	Asst	Ext 3640		12	BDH	MED	73	Houston	1987

Name	Rank	Phone	Email/Fax		Code	Deg		Inst	Year
University of Arizona	Tucson, AZ	85721	(602) ARIZRVAX					1948,1966	
College of Bus & Pub Ad	McClelland Hall		FAX=621-7483					BA,MBA,PHD	
Smith, Kenneth R.	Dean	621-2165			Econ	PHD	68	Northwes	1980
–Dept Management & Policy	Phone	621-1053	Fax 621-4171						
Gutek, Barbara A.	H-Pr	621-7632	bgutek	2	EXR	PHD	75	Michigan	1989
Beach, Lee Roy	Prof	621-3901	lbeach	3	EI	PHD		Colorado	1990
Connolly, Terry	Prof	621-5937	connolly	2	EHX	PHD	72	Northwes	1983
Gottfredson, Michael R.	Prof	621-1053	gottfred	4	LK	PHD	76	SUNY-Alb	1985
Northcraft, Gregory	Prof	621-3178							
Rapoport, Amnon	Prof	621-1035		7	V	PHD	65	N Carol	1965
Fortman, Marvin	Assoc	621-3891							
Tansik, David M.	Assoc	621-1710	tansik	23	EHN	PHD	69	Northwes	1970
Tindall, Robert M.	Assoc	621-3787		38	IYT	PHD		London	1963
Burns, Lawton R.	Asst	621-1950		2	CH	PHD	81	Chicago	1984
Griffith, Terri L.	Asst	621-5857	griffith	25	EZN	PHD	88	Car Mel	1989
Ordonez, Lisa	Asst	621-7474							
Arizona State University	Tempe, AZ	85287-4006	(602) ASUACAD					1962,1964	
College of Business			FAX=965-8314					BS,MAC,PHD	
Penley, Larry E.	Dean	965-5516	iaclep	25	Mgt	PHD	76	Georgia	1985
–Department of Management	Phone	965-3431	Fax 965-8314						
Gomez-Mejia, Luis	C-Pr	965-7586		5	N	PHD	81	Minn	1989
Bohlander, George	Prof	965-2286		21	KNQ	PHD	78	UCLA	1977
Cardy, Robert L.	Prof	965-6445		5	N	PHD	82	Virginia	1988
Hom, Peter	Prof	965-6466		25	EN	PHD		Illinois	1984
Pastin, Mark J.	Prof	965-2710		4	J	PHD	73	Harvard	1980
on leave									
Reif, William	Prof	965-3431				PHD	66	Iowa	1970
Bassford, Gerald	Assoc	965-4612		24	EL	DBA	70	Indiana	1969
Brenenstuhl, Daniel C.	Assoc	965-5031		38	ITY	DBA	75	Indiana	1978
Cook, Suzanne	Assoc	965-7204		25	GKNR	DBA	73	Tx Tech	1974
Keats, Barbara W.	Assoc	965-2233		3	I	PHD		Okla St	1984
Associate Dean									
Keller, Thomas	Assoc	965-8679		39	DIUZ	EDD		Toledo	1980
Kinicki, Angelo J.	Assoc	965-7717		25	EGNX	DBA		Kent St	1982
Manz, Charles	Assoc	965-8212		25	EGNP	PHD	81	Penn St	1988
Moorhead, Gregory	Assoc	965-4566		12	EFH	PHD	79	Houston	1978
Olivas, Louis	Assoc	965-4996				EDD		Ariz St	1979
Roberson, Loriann	Assoc	965-7571		5		PHD			
VanHook, Barry	Assoc	965-1217		63	ST	EDD	76	N Illin	1976
Blancero, Donna	Asst	965-7118		5		PHD	92	Cornell	8-93
Gooding, Richard	Asst	965-4530		34	EHI	PHD		Michigan	1988
Jacobson, Carol	Asst	965-7482		38	CILY	PHD	88	Minn	1988
Reger, Rhonda Kay	Asst	965-1347		3	I	PHD	88	Illinois	1988
Wiseman, Robert	Asst	965-6135		23	I	ABD			1991
Doran, George	SLect	965-7411		6		PHD			
Kreitner, Robert	SLect	965-6216				PHD			
Lea, John	Lect	965-3729				MBA			
–Dept of Decision & Info Sys	Phone	965-6350	Fax 965-5539						
Smith-Daniels, Vicki L.	C-Ac	965-5439				PHD		Ohio St	1987
Burdick, Richard K.	Prof	965-6473				PHD		Tx A&M	1976
Eck, Roger D.	Prof	965-6097				PHD		Tulane	1970
Hershauer, James C.	Prof	965-5478				DBA		Indiana	1969
Kazmier, Leonard J.	Prof	965-5353				PHD		Ohio St	1965
Kirkwood, Craig W.	Prof					PHD		MIT	1983
Mayer, Lawrence S.	Prof	965-6528				PHD		Ohio St	1983
Philippakis, Andrew S.	Prof	965-5134				PHD		Wiscon	1967
Director Computer Resources Office									
Ruch, William A.	Prof	965-3218		7	U	DBA		Indiana	1968
Wood, Steven D.	Prof	965-1468				PHD		Wiscon	1973
Brooks, Daniel G.	Assoc	965-6184				PHD		Indiana	1977
Callarman, Thomas E.	Assoc	965-3888		7	U	PHD		Purdue	1980
Goul, K. Michael	Assoc	965-5482				PHD		Oregon	1985
Keefer, Donald L.	Assoc	965-5501				PHD		Michigan	1987
Keim, Robert T.	Assoc	965-4445		9	Z	PHD		Pitt	1979
O'Leary, Timothy J.	Assoc	965-2613				DBA		Kent St	1978
Reiser, Mark	Assoc	965-5486				PHD		Chicago	1988
Roy, Asim	Assoc	965-6324				PHD		Texas	1983
Smith-Daniels, Dwight F.	Assoc	965-3814				PHD		Arizona	1987
St. Louis, Robert D.	Assoc	965-1440				PHD		Purdue	1982
Verdini, William A.	Assoc	965-4330				DBA		Kent St	1976
Wilson, Jeffrey R.	Assoc	965-5628				PHD		Iowa St	1985
Carroll, Steven	Asst	965-5481				PHD		Oregon	1985
Ching, Chee	Asst	965-6955		9	Z	PHD		Purdue	1989
Kiang, Melody	Asst	965-0724		9	Z				
Kulkarni, Uday R.	Asst	965-6191				MBA		India In	
Siferd, Sue P.	Asst	965-2232		7	U	PHD		Ohio St	1989

Arizona St U - West Phoenix, AZ 85069-7100 (602) ASUACAD
Business Prog Box 37100 4701 West Thunderbird Rd FAX=543-6220 BS,MBA

Name	Rank	Phone	Code	#	Fld	Deg	#	School	Yr
Silberman, Jonathan	Dean	543-6100	ihjxs		Econ	PHD	73	Fla St	9-92
–Management Faculty	Phone	543-6100	Fax 543-6221						
VanFleet, David	Prof	543-6104	icddv	12	EBHP	PHD	69	Tenn	1989
Bowen, David	Assoc	543-6229		25	EHP	PHD	83	Mich St	1991
Carey, Jane M.	Assoc	543-6216	atjmc	9	ZR	PHD	84	Miss	1988
Hutt, Roger	Assoc	543-6205	icrwh	16	STED	PHD	75	Mich St	1975
Malekzadeh, Ali R.	Assoc	993-0759	icarm	23	IHTY	PHD	82	Utah	1987
McWilliams, Thomas P.	Assoc	543-6222	attpm	7	UV	PHD	79	Stanford	1990
Nahavandi, Afsaneh	Assoc	543-6206	atayn	25	EIST	PHD	83	Utah	1988
Atwater, Leanne	Asst	534-6114		25	EFHN	PHD	85	Claremont	1993
McWilliams, Abagail	Asst			34	IK	PHD	87	Ohio St	1993
Youngdahl, William	Asst	543-6121	icwey	7	UW	PHD	92	S Calif	1992
Graef, David	Lect	543-6105	icdxg	14	LJC	PHD	71	Ariz St	1988

Arkansas College Batesville, AK 72501 (501)
Business Division 2300 Highland Drive FAX=

Name	Rank	Phone	#	Fld	Deg	School	Yr
Cooper, Thomas E.	C-Pr	698-4364		Econ	PHD	Princeton	1987
Anne J. Stewart Professor Economics							
–Management Faculty	Phone	698-4258	Fax 698-4622				
Mitra, Atul	Asst	698-4239	25	EN	DBA	Arkansas	1991

University of Arkansas Fayetteville, AR 72701 (501) 1931,1963
College of Business Adm FAX=575-7687 BS,MS,PHD
Bitnet: Administrative #UAFSYSA; Academic #UAFSYSB

Name	Rank	Phone	#	Fld	Deg	#	School	Yr
Williams, Doyle Z.	Dean	575-5949		Atg	PHD	65	LSU	1993
–Department of Management	Phone		Fax 575-7687					
White, Donald D.	H-Pr	575-6229	2	EHG	PHD	71	Nebraska	1971
Bednar, David A.	Prof	575-2851	2	E	PHD	80	Purdue	1980
Ganster, Daniel C.	Prof	575-6216	25	ENG	PHD	78	Purdue	1990
Raymond F. Orr Chair in General Management								
Todd, John T.	Prof	575-4059	26	EST	DBA	72	Harvard	1972
Gupta, Nina	Assoc	575-6233	2	E	PHD	75	Michigan	1984
Jenkins, G. Douglas Jr.	Assoc	575-6227	2	EN	PHD	77	Michigan	1984
Dass, Parshotam	Asst	575-6232	32	IH	PHD	93	Mich St	1992
Delery, John	Asst	575-6230	25	En	PHD	92	Tx A&M	1992
Doty, D. Harold	Asst	575-6221	32	IH	PHD	90	Texas	1990
Reeves, Carol A.	Asst	575-6220	36	IT	PHD	88	Georgia	1990

U of Arkansas at Little Rock Little Rock, AR 72204-1099 (501) UALR 1976,1982
College of Business 2801 South University FAX=569-8915 BS
Vibhakar, Ashzin Dean 569-3356 Fnce PHD Arkansas

Name	Rank	Phone	Code	#	Fld	Deg	#	School	Yr
–Department of Management	Phone		Fax 569-8915						
Kellogg, Calvin	C-Pr	569-3353	cekellogg	25	NE	PHD	85	Arkansas	1991
Blevins, David E.	Prof	569-8853				PHD		Illinois	1990
Crawford, Marian C.	Prof	569-8854				PHD		Miss	1981
LeBlanc, Louis Anthony	Prof	569-8895				PHD		Tx A&M	1990
Mitchell, Robert B.	Prof	569-8859				DBA		La Tech	1989
Neal, Rodney D.	Prof	569-8850				PHD	72	Northwes	1970
Hall, Frank D.	Assoc	569-8852				PHD		Arkansas	
Madden, Regan B.	Assoc	569-8858				PHD		Va Tech	
Tarwater, Ben B.	Assoc	569-8851				PHD	72	Missouri	
Collins, Judy	Asst	569-8849				PHD	91	Iowa	1991
Wood, Erma	Asst	569-8860				EDD		Arkansas	

U of Arkansas at Monticello Monticello, AR 71655 (501)
Sch of Bus & Info Sys FAX=

Name	Rank	Phone	Deg	#	School
Medlin, Bobby	Dean	460-1241	DBA	93	La Tech
–Management Faculty	Phone	460-1041	Fax 460-1922		
Guy, Baylor	Inst	460-1673			

U of Arkansas at Pine Bluff Pine Bluff, AR 71601 (501)
School of Bus & Mgt University Drive FAX=534-1012 BS
Did Not Respond-1993 Listing

Name	Rank	Phone	Fld	Deg	School	Yr
Fluker, John E.	Dean$	543-8575	Quan	PHD	Houston	1989
–Department of Management	Phone	543-8575	Fax 543-8032			
McMurray, V. F.	C-Pr			EDD	Arkansas	1992
VanWright, Evelyn D.	Prof			EDD	Columbia	
Rucker, William A. III	Asst			MS	US Naval	

Arkansas State University

State Univ, AR 72467-0059 (501) 1979,1985
College of Business — Carroway Road — FAX=972-3868 — BS,MBA
–Dept of Mktg & Management — Phone — Fax 972-3868

Name	Title	Phone		Field	Degree	Yr	School	Yr
Roderick, Roger	Dean	972-3035	24	EGJO	PHD	70	Illinois	1993
Ford, Charles	C-Pr	972-3430		Mktg	PHD	70	Miss St	1969
Hoyt, Daniel R.	Prof	972-3430	5	NPQ	PHD	76	Nebraska	1976
McFarland, C. K.	Prof	972-3430	5	NQ	PHD	65	Arizona	1971
Replogle, Steven	Prof	972-3430	7	UV	PHD	71	Arkansas	1970
Olson, William	Assoc	972-3430	3	I	PHD	78	Texas	1984
Keller, Tiffany	Asst	972-3430	25	EF	PHD	94	SUNY-Buf	1994
Moeeni, Farhad	Asst	972-3430	7	UV	ABD	91	Arizona	1991
Yauger, Charles	Asst	972-3430	32	EI	PHD	90	Miss	1977
Carr, Rececca	Inst	972-3430	7	V	MS	86	Illinois	1986

Arkansas Tech University

Russellville, AR 72801-2222 (501)
School of Business — FAX=968-0677 — BS
–Dept of Business & Econ — Phone — Fax 968-0677

Name	Title	Phone		Field	Degree	Yr	School	Yr
Jones, Royce D.	Dean	968-0490		Atg	MBA	71	E Tx St	1973
Edwards, Robert R.	Assoc	968-0673	36	INS	PHD	88	Arkansas	8-89
McGaughey, Ron	Assoc	968-0495	79	UZ	PHD	91	Auburn	
Roach, Dave	Assoc	968-0613	67	ENF	PHD	91	Arkansas	8-83
Black, Gene M.	Asst	968-0608	25	E	PHD	91	Ga Tech	8-91
Wood, James	Asst	968-0824	9	Z	MBA	83	Houst Bp	8-92

Ashland University

Ashland, OH 44805 (419)
School of Bus Adm, Econ — 401 College Avenue — FAX=289-5333 — BS
–Department of Business Adm — Phone — Fax 289-5333

Name	Title	Phone	Field	Degree	Yr	School	Yr
Rafeld, Frederick J.	Dean	289-5733	Econ	PHD	68	Ohio St	9-70
Shockney, Thomas D.	C-Pr	289-5231	ABCH	PHD	71	Ohio St	9-64
Anderson, Douglas R.	Prof	289-5224	DF	PHD	86	Bowl Gr	9-25
Heimann, Beverly	Assoc	289-5231	IE	DBA		Kent St	1991
Jacobs, Raymond A.	Assoc	289-5931	UV	PHD	85	N Carol	9-90
Pittenger, Khushwant K.	Assoc	289-5219	&ERY	PHD		Cinncinn	9-87
Symons, Richard	Assoc	289-5189	UV	DBA		Tenn	1992
Pool, Steven W.	Asst	289-5239	ST	ABD		Akron	9-86

Assumption College

Worcester, MA 01615-0005 (508) EVE.ASSUMPTION.EDU
Dept Business Studies — 500 Salisbury Street — FAX=756-1780 — BA,MBA
phone 752-5615
–Management Faculty — Phone — Fax 756-1780

Name	Title	Phone		Field	Degree	Yr	School	Yr
Foley, Joseph T.	C-Ac	Ext 456		Atg	MS	73	Northeas	1979
Bennardo, James V.	Assoc	Ext 250	57		MBA	75	Berkeley	1985
Bromberg, Herbert	Assoc	Ext 253	38		MBA	59	New York	1984
Harvey, Carol	Assoc	Ext 459	25	LRHF	EDD	91	Mass	1990
Mohaghegh, Saeed	Assoc	Ext 462	79		MA	86	Clark	1982
Diodati, Egidio A.	Asst	Ext 254	57		MBA	71	Suffolk	1987
Hunter, Jeffrey G.	Asst	Ext 246	38		MBA	77	Wstrn NE	1987
Sadd, William C.	Asst	Ext 256	34	IL	MBA	63	Dartmout	1986

Athens State College

Athens, AL 35611 (205)
School of Business — 300 North Beaty Street — FAX=233-8164
–Management Faculty — Phone — Fax 233-8164

Name	Title	Phone		Field	Degree	Yr	School	Yr
Haynes, James F.	Dean	233-8116		Econ	PHD		Vanderbt	1980
Joiner, Harry	Prof	233-8291	8	AY	PHD		Kentucky	1970
McCain, Wayne	Assoc	233-8501	7	V	PHD		Alabama	1993
Anderson, Mark	Asst	233-8148	4	JK	JD		Alabama	1989
Burton, Von	Asst	233-8123	7	V	DS		SE Inst	1986
Campbell, Oscar S.	Asst	233-8119	9	Z	MBA		Alabama	1978
Kennedy, Bryan	Asst	233-8259	2	ENP	EDD		Vanderbt	1987
Mingo, Dan	Asst	233-8161	9	UZ	MS		Arkansas	1981
Newton, Dahlia	Asst	233-8175	1	&	MBA		W Carol	1987
Nye, David	Asst	233-8180	1	BN	PHD		Auburn	1986
Shonesy, Linda B.	Asst	233-8174	3	I	EDD		Alabama	1985

Auburn University

Auburn, AL 36849-5241 (205) BUSINESS.AUBURN.EDU 1976,1980
College of Business — FAX=844-4016 — BS,MMIS,MBA,PHD
–Department of Management — Phone 844-4071 — Fax 844-4016

Name	Title	Phone	Email		Field	Degree	Yr	School	Yr
Alderman, C. Wayne	Dean	844-4030	walderman		Atg	DBA	77	Tenn	4-77
Snyder, Charles A.	H-Pr	844-6515	snyder	9	Z	PHD	78	Nebraska	9-78
Armenakis, Achilles A.	Prof	844-6506	archille	12	HF	DBA	71	Miss St	6-73
Torchma Professor									
Boulton, William	Prof	844-6529	boulton	38	I	DBA	77	Harvard	9-90
Olan-Mills Professor									
Boyles, Wiley	Prof	844-6502	boyles	12	EN	PHD	63	Tenn	9-84

Carr, Houston H.	Prof	844-6522	hcarr	9	Z	PHD	84	Texas	6-89
Alumni Professor									
Feild, Hubert S. Jr.	Prof	844-6518	junior	32	ENX	PHD	73	Georgia	9-73
Lowder Professor									
Giles, William F.	Prof	844-6528	giles	52	EN	PHD	74	Tenn	9-74
Holley, William H.	Prof	844-6532	holley	5	Q	PHD	70	Alabama	9-69
Lowder Professor									
Mitra, Amit	Prof	844-6530	mitra	7	UV	PHD	77	Clemson	9-79
Acting Associate Dean									
Byrd, Terry A.	Assoc	844-6543	tbyrd	9	Z	PHD	88	S Carol	9-92
Davis, Kermit R.	Assoc	844-6510	davis	32	EN	PHD	77	Georgia	9-79
Gardiner, Lorraine	Assoc	844-6513	lgardine	7	UV	PHD	89	Georgia	3-88
Gibson, Michael	Assoc	844-6525	mlgibson	9	Z	DBA	84	Kentucky	9-88
Harris, Stanley	Assoc	844-6519	stan	52	EN	PHD	88	Michigan	9-86
Niebuhr, Robert E.	Assoc	844-6520	niebuhr	15	EI	PHD	77	Ohio St	9-77
Norris, Dwight R.	Assoc	844-6526	norris	32	EN	PHD	79	Georgia	9-77
Oswald, Sharon	Assoc	844-6508	soswald	3	I	PHD	88	Alabama	9-87
Rainer, R. Kelly Jr.	Assoc	844-6527	rainer	9	Z	PHD	81	Georgia	9-88
Sankar, Chetan	Assoc	844-6504	chetan	9	Z	PHD	81	Penn	9-89
Sutton, Charlotte D.	Assoc	844-6517	sutton	15	EN	PHD	86	Tx A&M	9-86
Assistant Dean									
Swamidass, Paul M.	Assoc	844-1680	swamidas	7	U	PHD	83	U Wash	6-92
Wolters, Roger	Assoc	844-6521	wolters	5	Q	PHD	81	Illinios	9-80
Ford, F. Nelson	Asst	844-6603	ford	9	Z	PHD	82	Alabama	9-82
Gardiner, Stanley	Asst	844-6516	sgardine	7	U	PHD	87	Georgia	9-87
Marshall, Thomas E.	Asst	844-6509	marshall	9	Z	PHD	91	North Tx	9-91
Uzumeri, Mustafa V.	Asst	844-6531	uzumeri	73	U	PHD	91	Renssela	9-91

Auburn U at Montgomery	Montgomery, AL	36193-0401	(205)					1988,1988
School of Business	7300 University Drive		FAX=244-3762					BSBA,MBA
Budden, Michael C.	Dean	244-3478		Mktg	PHD	82	Arkansas	1988
–Department of Management	Phone		Fax 244-3762					
Calvasina, Eugene	H-Pr	244-3520		37	U	PHD	74	Miss	1984
Goodson, Jane R.	Assoc	244-3518		2	E	PHD	86	Alabama	1985
White, Randy	Assoc	244-3517		3	I	PHD	78	Arkansas	1983
Arnold, Ed	Asst	244-3460		5	N	PHD	90	Alabama	1989
Duarte, Neville	Asst	244-3308		2	E	PHD	88	Florida	1989

Augusta College	Augusta, GA	30910	(706) ADMIN.AC.EDU					
School of Business Adm	2500 Walton Way		FAX=737-1773					BBA,MBA
Farmer, Martha K.	Dean	737-1418		Atg	PHD	77	S Carol	1970
–Dept Mgt, Mktg & Info Sys	Phone		Fax 667-4064					
Brannen, Dalton E.	C-Pr	737-1418		5	NPQ	PHD	76	Miss	1990
Rutsohn, Phil	Prof	737-1562		14	ACK	DPH	76	Texas	1976
Bramblett, Richard	Assoc	737-1562		79	Z	PHD	73	Ga Tech	1987
Ibrahim, Nabil A.	Assoc	737-1562		37	IX	PHD	78	Emory	1987
Schultz, Todd A.	Assoc	737-1562		79	UVZ	PHD	87	J Hopkin	1987
Birdseye, Meg G.	Asst	737-1562		75	EN	PHD	90	Alabama	1991
Grayson, James	Asst	737-1562		79	UV	PHD	90	North Tx	1992

Augustana College IL	Rock Island, IL	61201-2296	(309) AUGUSTANA.EDU					
Dept of Business Adm	820 38th Street		FAX=794-7431					BA
Selbyg, Arne	Dean	794-7311	adcas		PHD	75	Chicago	9-88
–Management Faculty	Phone	794-7470	Fax 794-7431					
Lonergan, Janis	C	794-7472	alonergan	38		PHD	78	S Illin	9-76
Strauss, Judy P.	Prof	794-7334	bastrauss	23		PHD	93	Iowa	9-93
Donnelly, John	Assoc	794-7268	baddonnelly	39		PHD	73	Iowa	9-76

Augustana College SD	Sioux Falls, SD	57197	(605) INST.AUGIE.EDU					
Dept of Bus Adm & Econ	29th and Summitt		FAX=336-5477					BA,MASS
Oppegard, Anne M.	C-As	336-5220	oppegard		Atg	MACC	84	N Dakota	1988
–Management Faculty	Phone	336-5226	Fax 336-5229					

Aurora University	Aurora, IL	60506-4892	(708)					
Sch Bus & Prof Studies	1330 Marseillaise Avenue		FAX=					BA
Popper, Edward T.	Dean	844-5529		DBA	78	Harvard	1991
–Bus, Atg, & Econ Division	Phone		Fax 844-5163					
Etheredge, Forest	C-Pr	844-5401		PHD		Layola-C	1991
Madden, Lynne K.	Asst	844-4893		MBA	84	N Illin	1984

Austin Peay State University — Clarksville, TN 37044 — (615) FAX=
College of Business
–Dept of Mgt,Mktg, & Gen Bus — Phone 648-7788 — Fax 648-6267

Name	Title	Phone						
Reagan, Carmen	Dean	648-7675			Mktg	DBA	85	Miss St 1988
Taylor, A. J.	C-Pr	648-7578			Mktg	DBA		La Tech 1984
Nussbaumer, Chris	Prof	648-7575	23	E		PHD		Indiana 1964
Newport, Stephanie	Assoc	648-6363				PHD	90	Texas 1993
Grimmett, David	Asst	648-7560	7	UV		PHD		St Louis 1983

Averett College — Danville, VA 24541 — (804) FAX=
Business — 420 West Main St
–Management Faculty — Phone 791-5600 — Fax 791-5637

Name	Title	Phone					
Bolton, Alfred A.	Prof	791-5605	15	B	DBA	85	Nova

Azusa Pacific University — Azusa, CA 91702-7000 — (818) FAX=969-7180
School of Bus & Mgt — 901 East Alosta Ave
–Department of Management — Phone 812-3090 — Fax 815-3802

Lewis, Phillip V.	Dean 812-3090	34	IJ	EDD	70	Houston	9-92
Bezjian, Ilene	Assoc		TY	DBA		USIU	1-93
Butz, Clarance	Asst	14	BE	MBA		Claremont	9-89
Coop, Lind	Asst	13	IZ	MBA		National	9-89
Gara, Kim	Inst	25	EN	MED		Cent St	9-90

Babson College — Babson Park, MA 02157-0310 — (617) BABSON — 1980,1981 BS,MBA
School of Management — FAX=239-5230
–Division of Management — Phone 239-4390 — Fax 239-5272

Name	Title	Phone						
Cohen, Allan R.	Dean	239-4316			DBA	67	Harvard	
Nemitz, William C.	C-Ac	239-5419			PHD		Boston C	
Allen, Stephen A.	Prof	239-4413			DBA		Harvard	
Gray, Daniel H.	VProf	239-4414			PHD		MIT	
Kassarjian, J. Barkev	Prof	239-4435	3	I	DBA	67	Harvard	
Morgan, Ivor P.	VProf	239-5015			DBA	80	Harvard	
Stamm, John H.	Prof	239-4415			DBA	69	Harvard	
Timmons, Jeffry A.	Prof	239-4448			DBA		Harvard	
Frederic C. Hamilton Professor for Free Enterprise								
Bygrave, William D.	Assoc	239-4567			PHD		Oxford	
Donnellon, Anne	Assoc	239-4314	25	EN	PHD		Penn St	
Ellis, R. Jeffery	Assoc	239-4539			PHD		Cranfield	
Rafii, Farshad	Assoc	239-4334			DBA		Harvard	
Taylor, Natalie T.	Assoc	239-4513			DBA		Harvard	
Thornberry, Neal E.	Assoc	239-4359			PHD		Bowl Gr	
Weintraub, Joseph R.	Assoc	239-4356			PHD	73	Bowl Gr	
Brews, Peter J.	Asst	239-5597			PHD		Witwater	
Chakraborty, Kishore	Asst	239-4521			DED		Harvard	
Engelkemeyer, Susan W.	Asst	239-5071			PHD		Clemson	1991
Handler, Wendy C.	Asst	239-5022			DBA		Boston U	
Landry, Elaine	Asst	239-5131			EDM		Harvard	
Langowitz, Nan S.	Asst	239-4496			DBA	86	Harvard	
Rangan, U. Srinivasa	Asst	239-4237			DBA	88	Harvard	
Rosansky, Lynne N. H.	Asst	239-4525			PHD		Boston U	
Schlesinger, Phyllis F.	Asst	239-4591			DED		Boston U	
Newman, John W.	SLect	239-5014			MBA		Harvard	
Stengrevics, John M.	Lect	239-4306			DBA		Harvard	

Baldwin-Wallace College — Berea, OH 44017 — (216) FAX=826-2329 — BA
Div of Business Adm — 275 Eastland Road
–Management Faculty — Phone — Fax 826-2329

Name	Title	Phone						
Ehresman, Ronald	C-Pr	826-2392					Case Wes	
Bury, Harry	Prof	826-2392	2	N	PHD		Case Wes	
Kerzner, Harold	Prof	826-2392	3	UX	PHD		Illinois	
Barker, Cheryl	Assoc	832-2392	2	GP	PHD		Case Wes	
Blair, Glenn M. Jr.	Assoc	826-2392	5	NO	JD		Illinois	
Krueger, David	Assoc	826-2392	4	J	PHD		Chicago	
Melcher, Bonita	Assoc	826-2392		I	DBA	83	Kent St	1991
Packwood, Gary	Assoc	826-2392	34	MC	MBA		Bald Wal	
Pickler, Lee	Assoc	826-2392	69	XZ	PHD		Nova	
Sears, Paul	Assoc	826-2392	6	ST	PHD		Case Wes	
Winterscheid, Beverly	Assoc	826-2392	8		PHD		Case Wes	
David, Pierre	Asst	826-2392	7	UV	MBA		Pitt	

Ball State University — Muncie, IN 47306-0350 — (317) BSUVC.BSU.EDU — 1978,1984 BS,MS
College of Business — 2000 University Avenue — FAX=285-8024
–Department of Management — Phone 285-5399 — Fax 285-8024

Name	Title	Phone					
Palomba, Neil A.	Dean	285-8192		Econ	PHD	66	Minn 1984
Gupta, Jatinder N. D.	C-Pr	285-5301	00jngupta	7		PHD	Tx Tech 1985

Name	Rank	Phone	Code	Area	Letters	Degree	Yr	School	Year
Ahmed, Nazim U.	Prof	285-5302	7			PHD		Tx A&M	1983
Kuratko, Donald F.	Prof	285-5327	6			DBA		Nova	1983
LaFollette, William R.	Prof	285-5311	1			DBA	73	Indiana	1977
Montagno, Ray V.	Prof	285-5313	2			PHD		Purdue	1980
Walters, James E.	Prof	285-5319	7			DBA		Kent St	1976
Baird, Inga S.	Assoc	285-5314	3			PHD		Illinois	1978
Harris, Thomas M.	Assoc	285-5322	9			DBA		Colorado	1978
Hornsby, Jeffrey S.	Assoc	285-5306	2			PHD		Auburn	1987
Naffziger, Douglas W.	Assoc	285-5312	6			DBA		Colorado	1990
Tunc, Enar A.	Assoc	285-5317	7			PHD		Clemson	1987
Ramnarayanan, Renu	Asst	285-5303	7			PHD		Miss	1991
Ravichandran, R.	Asst	285-5320	9			PHD		Indiana	1988
Smith, Brien N.	Asst	285-5300	5			PHD		Auburn	1989
Wachter, Renee	Asst	285-5305	9			PHD		Indiana	1993
Draguo, John	Inst	285-5315	17			MBA		Indiana	1988
Reigle, Pam	Inst	285-5323	15			MBA		Ball St	1986

University of Baltimore — Baltimore, MD 21201-5779 — (410) UBE.UB.UMD.EDU — 1983,1989
Merrick Sch of Business — 1420 North Charles Street — FAX=752-2821 — BS,MST,MBA

Name	Rank	Phone	Email	Code	Letters	Degree	Yr	School	Year
Costello, Daniel E.	Dean	837-4955	daoa costell	Comm		PHD	68	Mich St	6-90
—Department of Management	Phone							Fax 837-4899	
Zacur, Susan Rawson	C-Pr	837-4977	easgzac	25	ENQ	DBA	79	Maryland	8-76
Adlakha, Veena	Prof	837-4969	radaadl	7	TU	PHD	79	NC-Charl	8-84
Bowers, Mollie	Prof	837-4973	easgbow	58	NQWY	PHD	74	Cornell	9-83
Cuba, Richard	Prof	837-4992	easgcuba	16	BDHR	DBA	71	Geo Wash	0 70
Luchsinger, V. P.	Prof	837-5031	ravjvpl	38	DISW	PHD	62	Tx Tech	8-81
Milbourn, Eugene	Prof	837-4966	eaogene	23	EFI	PHD		North Tx	8-75
Randolph, W. Alan	Prof	837-4984	easgwar	28	DEFW	PHD	75	Mass	8-88
Singhal, Kalyan	Prof	837-4976	radakal	7	T	PHD	72	Kent St	9-83
Cook, Deborah Smith	Assoc	837-4962	easgdsc	38	IWSN	DBA	82	Indiana	8-89
Kemery, Edward	Assoc	837-5064	easgerk	25	EGVN	PHD	83	Auburn	8-87
Mersha, Tigineh	Assoc	837-4965	easgmer	78	TW	PHD	82	Cinn	8-84
Moily, Jaya	Assoc	837-5065	easgjaya	78	TWY	PHD	82	Wiscon	8-89
O'Brien, William	Assoc	837-4979	easgb6y	17	TYW	PHD	71	Ohio St	8-79
Trotter, Richard	Assoc	837-5063	easgtrot	45	KLNQ	PHD	70	Penn	9-79
Bento, Regina	Asst	837-5073			NQ	PHD		MIT	1991
Herron, Lanny	Asst	837-5069	easclan	36	SDIJ	PHD	90	S Carol	9-89
Todd, Wayne	Asst	837-5072	easgtodd	37	DIUX	BA	76	Emory	8-90

Barry University — Miami Shores, FL 33161-6695 — (305) BARRYU
Andreas School of Bus — 11300 Northeast Second Ave — FAX=892-6412 — BS,MBA,MPA

Name	Rank	Phone	Email	Code	Letters	Degree	Yr	School	Year
Lash, Lewis W.	Dean$	899-3500	lash	13	IN	DBA	81	Nova	9-87
—Management Faculty	Phone							Fax 892-6412	
Gallagher, Charles	Prof	899-3513	gallaghe	79	UVZ	DBA	71	Fla St	9-85
Blanco, R. Ivan	Assoc	899-3500		13	ENY	PHD	87	Okla St	9-93
Nickerson, Inge	Assoc	899-3517	nickers		ET&	DBA	77	La Tech	9-89
Scarborough, Jack W.	Assoc	899-3520	jwscarb	38	IYE	PHD	88	Maryland	8-89
Fiedler, Anne M.	Asst		fiedler	13	EN	PHD	93	Fla Intl	9-94

Barton College — Wilson, NC 27893 — (919)
Dept of Business Prog — 600 West Lee Street — FAX=237-4957

Name	Rank	Phone	Code	Letters	Degree	School	Year
Davis, Mark	Dean	399-6343			PHD	Duke	8-78
—Management Faculty	Phone	399-6418	Fax 237-4957				
Eggers, Ronald	C-As	199-6417	3		MBA	E Carol	1978
Stanton, H. T.	Assoc	399-6420	2		EDD	N Carol	1976
Jolly, Geraldine	Asst	399-6427	5		MA	Cen Mich	1988

Baylor University — Waco, TX 76798-8006 — (817) BAYLOR.EDU — 1950,1969
Hankamer Sch Business — 5th and Speight Street — FAX=755-2421 — BBA,MBA,MIM

Name	Rank	Phone	Email	Code	Letters	Degree	Yr	School	Year
Scott, Richard C.	Dean	755-1211		6	Mgt	DBA	68	Indiana	1968
—Department of Management	Phone							Fax 755-2421	
Edwards, Donald Raymond	C-Pr	755-2261		7	U	PHD		Ariz St	1981
Allen, A. Dale Jr.	Prof	755-2261		2	E	DBA		Colorado	1978
Bagby, D. Ray	Prof	755-2265	ray_bagby	6	T	PHD	83	S Carol	1988

  Robert & Louise Rogers Professor of Entrepreneurship

Name	Rank	Phone	Code	Letters	Degree	Yr	School	Year
Chewning, Richard C.	Prof	755-2261	4	J	PHD	63	U Wash	1985

  Harry & Hazel Chavanne Professor of Christian Ethics in Business

Name	Rank	Phone	Code	Letters	Degree	Yr	School	Year
Cox, Joe Allen	Prof	755-2261	5	N	PHD		Okla St	1977
Ireland, R. Duane	Prof	755-2261	63	IT	PHD		Tx Tech	1983

  Associate Dean, Curtis Hankamer Professor of Entrepreuneurship

Name	Rank	Phone	Code	Letters	Degree	Yr	School	Year
Read, Raymond L.	Prof	755-2261	2	EH	PHD	69	Texas	1974
Umble, M. Michael	Prof	755-2261	7	U	PHD		LSU	1977
VanAuken, Philip Mark	Prof	755-2261	3	I	PHD		Tx Tech	1978
Gray, Van D.	Assoc	755-2261	7	U	PHD		North Tx	1986
Jennings, Daniel F.	Assoc	755-2261	32	HI	PHD		Tx A&M	1984

  Mrs. W.A. (Agnes) Mays Professor of Entrepreneurship & Strategic Mgt

Name	Title	Phone			Degree		School	Year
Carini, Gary	Asst	755-2261			PHD		Penn	1991
Livingstone, Linda	Asst	755-2261	25	EN	PHD		Okla St	1991
Miller, C. Chet	Asst	755-2261	23	EHI	PHD		Texas	1989
Munn, Joseph R.	Asst	755-2261	7	U	PHD		Tx A&M	1988
Palich, Leslie	Asst	755-2261	38	I	PHD		Ariz St	1991
Upton, Nancy	Asst	755-2265	6	T	PHD		Baylor	1983
Ben H. Williams Professor in Entrepreneurship								
Boyd, John H.	Lect	755-2261	2	E	MA		W Texas	1985
Vardaman, Betsy	Lect	755-2261			MA		Baylor	1981
Wilmer, Jack	Lect	755-2261			MBA		Baylor	1977
—Dept of Info Mgt Systems	Phone	755-2258	Fax 755-2421					
Willis, G. W. Ketchel	C-Pr	755-2258	gw.willis	Z	PHD	77	Tx A&M	1983
Hart, Maxine Barton	Prof			Z	EDD		Houston	1971
Ligon, Helen H.	Prof			Z	PHD		Tx A&M	1958
Moore, Kris K.	Prof			V	PHD	74	Tx A&M	1970
Ramsower, Reagan Mays	Prof			Z	PHD		Minn	1976
Associate Dean for Teaching & Administrative Systems								
Young, Dean Max	Prof			V	PHD		Tx-Dallas	1980
Ben H. Williams Professor of Information Systems								
Dorsett, Dovalee	Assoc			V	PHD		So Meth	1987
Milligan, Patricia Mayer	Assoc			Z	PHD		North Tx	1983
Seaman, John W. Jr.	Assoc			V	PHD		Tx-Dallas	1989
Randall W. & Sandra Ferguson Professor of Information Systems								
Seaman, Samuel L.	Assoc			V	PHD		Florida	1987
Vaughn, Randal L.	Assoc			Z	PHD		Tx-Arlin	1982
Fuller, Mark A.	Asst			Z	PHD		Arizona	1992
Leidner, Dorothy E.	Asst			Z	PHD		Texas	1992
Trower, Jonathan	Asst			Z	PHD		Minn	1983
Hulme, Fred Sterling Jr.	Lect			VZ	MS		Tx A&M	1975
Ketcham, Emily M.	Lect			Z	MBA		Baylor	1991
Monroe, Carolyn	Lect			VZ	MBA		Baylor	1983
Morris, Brenda K.	Lect			Z	MBA		Baylor	1989
Associate Dean for Undergraduate Program								
Williams, Jane Gray	Lect			VZ	MSED	70	Baylor	1972

Beaver College — Glenside, PA 19038-3295 (215) FAX=572-0240 — BS,BA
Dept of Bus Adm & Econ

Name	Title	Phone			Degree		School	Year
Biggs, William D.	C-Pr	572-2937	32	Atg	PHD	74	Penn St	8-80
—Management Faculty	Phone	572-2937	Fax 572-2126					
Halpin, Annette L.	Asst	572-2900	36	IL	ABD		Drexel	9-84
Hejazi, Sassan	Asst	572-2900	97	UZ	MBA		LaSalle	9-89

Belhaven College — Jackson, MS 39202 (601) FAX= — BS
Div of Business Adm, 1500 Peachtree Street

Name	Title	Phone			Degree		School	Year
Park, James W.	C-Pr	968-5965	7	Atg	PHD	74	Alabama	1977
—Management Faculty	Phone		Fax 968-9998					
Penn, William M.	Prof	968-5966	7	J	PHD	81	Duke	1981
Letourneau, Richard H.	Assoc	968-8722	1	D	PHD	70	Okla St	1993

Bellarmine College — Louisville, KY 40205-0671 (502) FAX=
Rubel Sch- 2001 Newburg, 2001 Newburg Road

Name	Title	Phone			Degree		School	Year
Byrd, John T. III	Dean	452-8240			PHD		Ohio St	1982
—Dept of Bus Adm & Econ	Phone	452-8240	Fax 452-8288					
Trummer, Judith C.	C	452-8240						
Elbert, Norbert F.	Prof	452-8240			DBA		Kentucky	
Feibes, Walter	Prof	452-8240			PHD		SUNY-Buf	
Spalding, James B. Jr.	Prof				PHD		Illinois	
Thiemann, Bernard F.	Prof	452-8240			JD		Louisvil	
Koch, Harold	Assoc				PHD		Clev St	
Stein, Herman	Assoc	452-8240	7	U	PHD		Columbia	
Mattei, Michael D.	Inst	452-8240			MBA		Indiana	

Bellevue College — Bellevue, NE 68005-3098 (402) FAX= — BS,BA,BTS
Faculty of Business Adm, Galvin Rd at Harvell Dr
Did Not Respond-1993 Listing

Name	Title	Phone			Degree		School	Year
Polson, Houston H.	C-As	293-3741	47	K	JD	89	Creighto	8-85
—Management Faculty	Phone		Fax 293-2020					
Hamilton, Harold T.	Asst	293-3750	6		MBA	64		8-81
Janisch, Glenn		293-3739						

Belmont College — Nashville, TN 37212-3757 (615) FAX=385-6455 — BS,MBA
Massey School of Bus, 1900 Belmont Blvd

Name	Title	Phone			Degree		School	Year
Eubanks, Clifford L.	Dean	386-4522	32	I	PHD	67	Arkansas	1992
—Management Faculty	Phone		Fax 385-6455					
Cotham, James C. III	Prof	385-6482	34		DBA	67	Indiana	1986

Name	Rank	Phone			Degree	Yr	School	Year
Lewis, Edward	Prof	385-6480	97	Z	PHD	78	SUNY	1982
Sellick, Jay P.	Prof	385-6427	72	U	PHD	76	Vanderbt	1976
Edwards, Lorena B.	Assoc	386-4525	45	Q	EDS	75	Vanderbt	1982
Hollis, Harry	Assoc	385-6480			PHD		Vanderbt	1975
Lindsley, William B.	Assoc	386-4565	3	I	PHD	87	MIT	1993

Bemidji State University   Bemidji, MN   56601   (218)
College of Prof Studies   1500 Birchmont Drive NE   FAX=

Name	Rank	Phone			Degree		School	Year
Norris, Gerald	Dean	755-3732			EDD		Ill St	1987
—Management Faculty	Phone							
Kyryluk, Robert	C-Ac	755-2758		NR	MBA		Mankato	1978
Scheela, William	Prof	755-3714		ITY	PHD		Minn	1980
Leif, Doug			9	Z				
Phukan, Sanjiev			9	Z				
Thommas, Maureen			9	Z				

Benedict College   Columbia, SC   29204   (803)
Business   1600 Harden Street   FAX=

Name	Rank	Phone			Degree		School	Year
								BS
Scott, Robert L.	C-Pr	253-5187		Mgt	EDD		S Carol	
—Management Faculty	Phone							
Kinley, David	Assoc	253-5189						
Washington, Charles	Assoc	253-5185						

Bentley College   Waltham, MA   02154-4705   (617) BENTI FY   1989,1989
College of Business   175 Forest Street   FAX=891-2819   BS,MBA,MS

Name	Rank	Phone			Degree	Yr	School	Year
Schlorff, H. Lee	Dean	891-2113	hschlorf	Atg	PHD	73	Missouri	1978
—Department of Management	Phone	891-2112	Fax 891-2819					
Buono, Anthony F.	C-Pr	891-2529	abuono	24 FHL	PHD	81	Boston C	1979
Bartolome, Fernando	Prof	891-2530	fbartolo	2 E	DBA	72	Harvard	1982
Byrnes, Joseph	Prof	891-2912	jbyrnes	5 NQ	PHD	74	Northwes	1980
Dolinsky, Larry	Prof	891-2209	ldolinsk	7 UV	DBA	86	Boston U	1969
Epelman, Michael	Prof	891-2553	mepelman	7 UV	PHD	75	Israel	1978
Konoylis, Nickolas	Prof	891-2157	nkonoyli	7 UV	PHD	74	Syracuse	1973
Missirian, Agnes	Prof	891-2528	amissiri	38 IY	PHD	80	Mass	1980
Nurick, Aaron	Prof	891-2526	anurick	2 E	PHD	78	Tenn	1979
O'Connell, Jerimiah	Prof	891-2468	joconnel	28 IY	PHD	66	Columbia	1978
Seeger, John	Prof	891-2532	jseeger	34 I	DBA	78	Harvard	1982
Wondoloski, Edward	Prof	891-2534	ewondolo	1 AE	MBA	65	Northeas	1962
Congram, Carole	Assoc	891-2568	ccongram	7 UW	PHD	69	Wiscon	1990
Crary, Marcy	Assoc	891-2502	mcrary	2 ER	PHD	82	Case Wes	1981
Davis, Mark	Assoc	891-2739	mdavis	7 UV	DBA	86	Boston U	1986
Eshghi, Golpira	Assoc	891-2181	geshigi	38 Y	PHD	84	Illinois	1986
Glidden, Priscilla	VAsoc	891-2527	pglidden	2 F	PHD	83	MIT	1990
Hoffman, Alan	Assoc	891-2287	ahoffman	23 HI	DBA	82	Indiana	1987
Kamm, Judith	Assoc	891-2535	jkamm	23 DT	DBA	80	Harvard	1979
Associate Director, Center for Business Ethics								
Kellogg, Diane	Assoc	891-2531	dkellogg	2 ER	EDD	79	Harvard	1980
Shuman, Jeffrey	Assoc	891-2533	jshuman	36 T	PHD	72	Renssel	1982
Spelman, Duncan	Assoc	891-2217	dspelman	2 ER	PHD	80	Case Wes	1981
Thamhain, Hans	Assoc	891-2189	hthamhai	1 D	PHD	72	Syracuse	1986
Weiss, Joseph	Assoc	891-2215	jweiss	24 HJY	PHD	84	Wiscon	1982
Chin, Louis	Asst	891-2758	lchin	7 UV	DBA	86	Boston U	1988
LaFarge, Vicki	Asst	891-2089	vlafarge	2 E	PHD	88	Yale	1987
Lesko, John	VAsst	891-2572	jlesko	24 ER	PHD	92	Boston C	1994
Rosen, Mark	Asst	891-2693	mrosen	5 N	PHD	90	Wiscon	1989
Rock, Marie	VInst	891-2118	mrock	23 I	MBA	86	Bentley	1990

Berry College   Rome, GA   30149   (706)
Dept of Business & Econ   5024 Mount Berry Station   FAX=

Name	Rank	Phone			Degree		School	Year
								BS,MBA
Mathis, Doyle	Dean$	236-2216			PHD			8-75
—Management Faculty	Phone							
Newton, Lucy A.	Asst	232-5374	35	NQSX	PHD			8-89
Smith, Patricia L.	Asst	232-5374	56	LNSR	PHD			8-90

Bethune-Cookman College   Daytona Bch, FL   32015   (904)
Division of Business   640 Second Avenue   FAX=
Did Not Respond-1993 Listing; Phone 255-1401

Name	Rank	Phone			Degree		School	Year
Long, Aubrey E.	C	Ext 355			PHD		Ohio St	1988
—Management Faculty	Phone							
Patel, Ranjna K.	C-Ac	Ext 413			DBA		Kent St	1985
Beckles, Gina Wilson	Asst	Ext 395						
Barnes, Clifford	Inst	Ext 258						

Biola University
School of Business — LaMirada, CA 90639 — (310) FAX=

Name	Title	Phone	Fax				Degree	School	Year
Strand, Larry	Dean$	903-4770		3	I		MBA	S Calif	1986
—Management Faculty	Phone	903-4770	Fax 903-4748						
Buegler, Paul W.	Assoc	903-4770		35	IN	JD		Wm Mitch	1978
Dill, Glenn V.	Assoc	903-4770		6	S	MBA		Pepperdi	1990
Smith, Virgil O	Assoc	903-4770		39	IZ	ABD		Tx Tech	1994
Wong, Kenman L.	Asst	903-4770		49	JZ	ABD		S Calif	1989
Cooper, Ronald L.	Assoc	903-4770		7	V	PHD		Berkeley	1994

Birmingham-Southern College
Div of Econ & Bus Adm — Birmingham, AL 35254 — 900 Ardadelphia Road — (205) FAX=226-4627

Name	Title	Phone	Fax				Degree	School	Year
									BS
Gunter, Marjorie E.	C-Pr	226-4818			Atg	MBA	71	Samford	1978
—Management Faculty	Phone	226-4820	Fax 226-4843						
Chew, E. Byron	Prof	226-4809		67	I	PHD	71	Alabama	1974
Drewry, L. Aubrey	Prof	226-4816		8	LY	PHD	60	Virginia	1977
Adair, Conrad	Assoc	226-4821		15	LQUY	PHD	86	Alabama	1980

Bloomsburg University
College of Business — Bloomsburg, PA 17815 — (717) BLOOMU.EDU — FAX=389-3892

Name	Title	Phone	Fax/email			Degree		School	Year
Olivo, John	Dean	389-4019							BS,MBA
—Department of Management	Phone		Fax 389-3892						
Larson, Mark D.	C-Ac	389-4763		5		PHD		Ohio St	8-91
Amin, Ruhul	Prof			17		PHD		Akron	8-86
Gallagher, Francis J.	Prof			5		MBA	71	Temple	1-72
Venuto, Peter	Prof			12		PHD		Santa Cl	8-80
Afza, Mainuddin	Assoc			63	U	PHD		USSR	8-89
Chapman, Charles M.	Assoc			1		MA		NYU	
Kinslinger, Howard J.	Assoc	389-4397		15		PHD		Purdue	8-82
Markell, Steve	Assoc			23		PHD		N Carol	8-90
Ozkarahan, Irem	Assoc			7		PHD		ASU	8-92
Tehran, Minoo	Assoc			38		PHD		Ariz St	8-90
Wynn, Pamela	Assoc			46		PHD		Tx-Arlin	8-89
—Dept Computer & Info Sys	Phone	389-4752	Fax 389-3892						
Dutt, James S.	C-Ac		dutt@mercury	9	Z	PHD		Penn St	
Davis, Frank S.	Prof		fsd@cob5.	9	Z	PHD		Pitt	
Chimi, Carl J.	Assoc		cchimi@cob5.	9	Z	PHD		Mass	
Frey, Harold K.	Assoc		frey@husky.	9	Z	MS		Elmira	
Gordon, Gene	Assoc		gg@mc3b2.	9	Z	EDD		Mass	
Hoppel, Charles J.	Assoc		hopp@husky.	9	Z	PHD		Syracuse	
Boyne, Patricia M.	Asst		pboyne@mc3b2	9	Z	MS			
Penn St									

Boise State University
College of Business — Boise, ID 83725 — 1910 University Drive — (208) COBFAC.IDBUS.EDU 1979,1985 — FAX=385-3779 BS,BA,MBA

Name	Title	Phone	email/Fax			Degree		School	Year
Ruud, William N.	Dean	385-1125	aburuud	21		PHD		Nebraska	9-93
—Department of Management	Phone	385-1313	Fax 385-1857						
Wines, William A.	C-Pr	385-3393	rmgwines	4	JK	JD	74	Michigan	1985
Bigelow, J.	Prof	385-1267	rmgbigel	2	EF	PHD	78	Case Wes	1982
Bixby, M.	Prof	385-3675	rmgbixby	4	KM	JD	68	Michigan	1981
Napier, Nancy K.	Prof	385-1314	rmgnapie	38	IY	PHD	81	Ohio St	1986
Wilterding, Jim	Prof	385-1542		5	P	PHD	70	Tx Tech	1976
Glen, Roy	Assoc	385-4258	rmgglen	2	EGD	PHD	78	Case Wes	1982
Kaupins, Gundars	Assoc	385-4014	rmgkaupi	5	PY	PHD	86	Iowa	1986
Waldorf, Larry	Assoc	385-1333	rmgwaldo	2		PHD	71	Colo St	1970
Fronmueller, Michael	Asst	385-1888	rmgfronm	3	I	PHD	91	Wash St	1990
Gough, Newell	Asst	385-4012	rmggough	36	IT	PHD	90	Utah	1989
Shim, Won	Asst	385-1887	rmgshim	28	EY	PHD	91	Oregon	1991
Sleeper, Brad	Asst	385-4013				JD	76	Minn	1994

Boston College
W.E. Carroll Sch of Mgt — Chestnut Hl, MA 02167-3808 — 140 Commonwealth Avenue — (617) BCVMS 1956,1975 — FAX=552-8828 BS,MBA

Name	Title	Phone	email/Fax			Degree		School	Year
Neuhauser, John J.	Dean	552-0460	neuhaujo	9	Sys	PHD	68	Renssele	1969
—Dept Organizational Studies	Phone	552-0450	Fax 552-0433						
Bartunek, Jean	C-Pr	552-0455	bartunek	2	EHF	PHD	76	Ill-Chic	9-77
Torbert, William R.	Prof	552-0459	torbert	2	DEF	PHD	71	Yale	9-78
Fisher, Dalmar	Assoc	552-0453	fisher	23	EFO	DBA	68	Harvard	9-68
Gordon, Judith	Assoc	552-0454	gordonj	25	EOSR	PHD	77	MIT	9-77
Lewis, John W. III	Assoc	552-4013	lewis	25	GFNT	PHD	70	Case Wes	9-70
Neilsen, Richard P.	Assoc	552-0456	nielsen	24	JFEN	PHD	72	Syracuse	9-80
Stevenson, William B.	Assoc	552-0458	stevenw	2	EHX	PHD	80	Calif	9-88
Clair, Judith	Asst	552-0451	clairju	1	EMR	PHD	93	USC	9-93
Creed, W. E. Douglas	Asst	552-0492		2	HJ	PHD	94	Berkeley	9-94
DiBella, Anthony J.	VAsst	552-0452	dibella	1	EHFY	PHD	92	MIT	9-92
Jones, Candace	Asst	552-0457		2	HO	PHD	93	Utah	9-94

–Operations & Strategic Mgt	Phone	552-0460	Fax 552-0433						
Ringuest, Jeffrey L.	C-Pr	552-0460	ringuest	7	VU	PHD	81	Clemson	9-86
Dunn, Thomas W.	VProf	552-0460	dunn	36	BIST	DBA	68	Harvard	9-63
Raelin, Joseph A.	Prof	552-4060	raelin	24	ELNP	PHD	77	SUNY-Buf	8-76
Ritzman, Larry P.	Prof	552-4060	ritzman	7	UV	DBA	68	Mich St	9-91
Galligan Chair									
Graves, Samual B.	Assoc	552-4060	graves	7	VU	DBA	85	Geo Wash	9-86
McClellan, Hassell H.	Assoc	552-4060	mcclella	83	IY	DBA	78	Harvard	9-84
Murphy, David C.	Assoc	552-4060	murphyd	73	UVI	DBA	70	Indiana	1970
Waddock, Sandra A.	Assoc	552-4060	waddock	43	LMHI	DBA	85	Boston U	9-86
Case, Randolph H.	Asst	552-4060	caser	3	IT	PHD	93	Penn	9-93
Downing, Charles E.	Asst	552-0460		97	ZV	PHD	94	Northwes	9-94
Lerme, Catherine S.	Asst	552-4060	lerme	7	UV	PHD	91	Massachu	9-91
Mallick, Debasish N.	Asst	552-4060	mallickd	7	UV	PHD	93	Texas	9-93
Safizadeh, Hossein M.	Asst	552-4060	safizade	7	UV	PHD	80	Okla St	9-89
Segars, Albert H.	Asst	552-4060		93	ZI	PHD	94	S Carol	9-94
Halpern, Larry	Lect	552-4060	halpern	36	JT	MBA	58	Columbia	9-90
McKenna, David R.	Lect	552-4060	mckenna	7	VU	MBA	70	Boston C	9-84

Boston University	Boston, MA	02215		(617) ACS.BU.EDU				1921,1965	
School of Management	621 Comm Ave			FAX=353-6667				BS,MBA,DBA	
Lataif, Louis E.	Dean	353-2668		Mgt	MBA			Harvard	9-91
–Dept of Org Behavior	Phone	353-4405	Fax 353-5244						
Johnson, Leonard	C-Ac	353-4153	ljohnson			PHD		Boston U	
Baird, Lloyd	Prof	353-4168	tbaird	5	NP	PHD		Michigan	
Brown, L. David	Prof	353-4159	janecovey	24	EFHL	PHD		Yale	
Hall, Douglas T.	Prof	353-4166	dhall	25	EFG	PHD		MIT	
Director, Graduate Program									
Labovitz, George H.	Prof	353-4165		21	ECFH	PHD		Ohio St	
Leader, Gerald C.	Assoc	353-4284	gleader	2	EFGH	DBA		Harvard	
Louis, Meryl R.	Assoc	353-4656	mlouis	2	E	PHD		UCLA	
Kahn, William A.	Asst	353-2680	wkahn	2	EH	PHD		Yale	
Kram, Kathy E.	Asst	353-4269	kekram	2	EFGH	PHD		Yale	
McCollom, Marion	Asst	353-4287	mccollom	2	EFG	PHD		Yale	
Yan, Aimin	Asst	353-9199	aimin			PHD	93	Penn St	
–Dept of Operations Mgt	Phone								
Shwartz, Michael	C-Ac	353-2677		17	CU	PHD		Michigan	
Chang, Yu Sang	Prof	353-2656		78	UY	DBA		Wash U	
Leone, Robert A.	Prof	353-2664		7	U	PHD		Yale	
Director of Research									
Miller, J. G.	Prof	353-3458		7	UY	PHD		Purdue	
Rosenthal, Stephen R.	Prof	353-4288		17	U	PHD		Berkeley	
Arnold, Peter M.	Assoc	353-3360		73	UI	PHD		Indiana	
Director Undergraduate Program									
Restuccia, Joseph D.	Assoc	353-4243		17	CU	DPH		Berkeley	
Dixon, J. Robb	Asst	353-5243		7	DU	PHD		Virginia	
Forker, Laura B.	Asst					PHD		Ariz St	1994
Heineke, Janelle	Asst	353-2919		71	CU	DBA		Boston U	
Khurana, Anil	Asst	353-2287						Michigan	
Kim, Jay S.	Asst	353-9749	jkimr	37	IUY	PHD		Ohio St	
Klimberg, Ronald K.	Asst	353-4918		71	UVX	PHD		J Hopkin	
–Dept of Management Policy	Phone	353-2654	Fax 353-2564						
Foulkes, Fred K.	C-Pr	353-4281		5	N	DBA		Harvard	
Post, James E.	Prof	353-4162		34	ILM	PHD	75	SUNY-Buf	1974
Russell, John R.	Prof	353-4156		34	ILQ	DBA		Harvard	
Schwartz, Jules J.	Prof	353-4163		37	IVX	DBA		Harvard	
Davidson, Stephen M.	Assoc	353-2654		1	C	PHD		Chicago	
Dickie, Robert B.	Assoc	353-2658		4	K	JD		Yale	
Hatten, Kenneth J.	Assoc	353-4291		3	I	PHD		Purdue	
Mahon, John F.	Assoc	353-4152		1	DH	DBA		Boston	
Murray, Edwin A. Jr.	Assoc	353-4410		38	IY	DBA		Harvard	
Scott, Frederick C.	Assoc	353-5979		36	LT	MBA		Harvard	
Brush, Candida	Asst	353-3146		36	RT	DBA	93	Boston U	
Kohn, Thomas O.	Asst	353-4298		31	IDY	DBA		Harvard	
Samuelson, Susan S.	Asst	353-2033		4	K	JD		Harvard	
Smith, Clifton	Asst	353-6164		6	ST	MBA		Dartmout	
Stone, Melissa M.	Asst	353-4286		2	E	PHD		Yale	
Vachani, Sushil	Asst	353-4406		38	IY	DBA		Harvard	
Vanderwerf, Pieter	Asst	353-2032		59	QZ	PHD		MIT	
Beatty, Jeffery	Adj	353-2657		4	K	JD		Boston U	
Rothstein, Steven Maze	Adj	353-4576		83	YI	MBA		Northeas	
–Dept of Mgt & Info Systems	Phone								
Sproull, Lee S.	C-Pr	353-2523		29	ZEH	PHD		Stanford	
Henderson, John C.	Prof	353-6142		9	Z	PHD		Texas	
Lawson, Michael E.	Assoc	353-3742		9	Z	PHD		Iowa	
Lenard, Melanie L.	Assoc	353-2678		7	UVX	SCD		Columbia	
Venkatraman, N.	Assoc			39	IZ	PHD		Pitt	
Goldstein, David	Asst	353-4402		9	Z	PHD		MIT	
Guinan, Patricia J.	Asst	353-4500		9	Z	PHD		Indiana	

Name	Rank	Phone				Degree		School	Year
Iacono, Suzanne	Asst	353-4605		9	Z	PHD		Arizona	
Klein, David	Asst	353-4155		9	Z	PHD		Penn	
Lee, Soonchul	Asst	353-4510		9	Z	PHD		MIT	
Strong, Diane	Asst	354-9773		9	Z	PHD		Car Mel	
Davenport, Thomas		353-4161		9	Z	PHD		Harvard	
McKinnon, Richard A.		353-4510				MBA		Harvard	

Bowling Green State Univ — Bowling Gr, OH 43403-0270 (419) BGSUOPIE 1954,1966

Name	Rank	Phone				Degree		School	Year
College of Business Adm	East Worster Street		FAX=372-2875					BS,MAC,MBA	
Williams, Fred E.	Dean	372-2747		7	MgtS	PHD	70	Purdue	1990
—Department of Management	Phone	372-2946	Fax 372-2875						
Bragg, Daniel	C-As	372-8210		7	U	PHD	84	Ohio St	1980
Behling, O. C.	Prof	372-8260		1	EF	PHD	61	Wiscon	1981
Hahn, Chan K.	Prof	372-8220		7	UW	PHD	70	Ohio St	1970
Lunde, Harold I.	Prof	372-2669		3	I	PHD	66	Minn	1980
McFillen, James	Prof	372-2946		25	E	DBA	76	Indiana	1983
Pinto, Peter	Prof	372-2947		7	U	PHD	75	N Carol	1976
Varney, G. H.	Prof	352-7782		2	F	PHD	71	Case Wes	1970
Vogt, Karl	Prof	372-6064		23	I	PHD	61	Syracuse	1967
Darrow, Arthur L.	Assoc	372-2986		2	FH	PHD	82	Iowa	1980
Penlesky, Richard	Assoc	372-6071		7	U	DBA	83	Indiana	1990
Sullivan, Sherry	Assoc	372-2366				PHD	88	Ohio St	1933
Tonnesen, Edwin	Assoc	372-2946		32	I	PHD	70	Syracuse	1971
Ward, R. J.	Assoc	372-2948		35	IN	DBA	72	Colorado	1969
Watts, Charles A.	Assoc	372-8757		7	UW	DBA	87	Indiana	1987
Choi, Thomas	Asst	372-2388		17	EU	PHD	92	Michigan	1993
Duplaga, Ed	Asst	372-8649		7	U	PHD	90	Iowa	1992
Jones, Gwen	Asst	372-2806				PHD	92	SUNY-Alb	1993

Bradley University — Peoria, IL 61625 (309) BRADLEY.BRADLEY.EDU 1978,1983

Name	Rank	Phone				Degree		School	Year
College of Business Adm			FAX=677-3374					BS,BA	
Sullenberger, A. Gale	Dean	677-2255	ags	9	Z	PHD	71	Oklahoma	6-86
—Dept of Bus Mgt & Adm	Phone	677-2306	Fax 677-3374						
Fry, Fred L.	C-Pr	677-2306	ffry	26	TS	PHD	72	Okla St	1976
Alber, Antone F.	Prof	677-2285	jalber	9	Z	PHD	77	Penn St	1975
Cornwell, Larry	Prof	677-2314	larryc	9	Z	PHD	72	Mo-Rolla	1980
Goitein, Bernard	Prof	677-2278	bjg	4	MX	PHD	82	Michigan	1981
Hartman, Richard I.	Prof	677-2308		2	NR	DBA	61	Indiana	1961
Modianos, Doan	Prof	677-2253	dmod	1	U	PHD	73	Tx Tech	1981
Assistant Dean									
Stoner, Charles R.	Prof	677-2311		23	EGTR	DBA	79	Fla St	1980
Teeven, Kevin	Prof	677-2272		4	K	JD	71	Illinois	1974
Perry, Sandra	Assoc	677-2267		4	K	JD	79	S Illin	1984
Buchko, Aaron	Asst	677-2273		3	I	PHD	90	Mich St	1989
Fink, Ross L.	Asst	677-2271	rf	7	UV	PHD	89	Alabama	1991
Lane, Peggy	Asst	677-2279	pll	9	Z	PHD	92	Arkansas	1991
Weinzimmer, Larry	Asst	677-3478	lgw	3	IT	PHD	93	Wiscon	1993

Brescia College — Owensboro, KY 42301 (502) BS

Name	Rank	Phone				Degree		School	Year
Division of Business	717 Frederica Street		FAX=						
Did Not Respond-1993 Listing									
Minks, L. C.	C-Pr	686-4209				EDD	80	N Colo	1988
—Management Faculty	Phone	686-4217	Fax 686-4266						
Bourne, S. Graham	Inst	686-4274				MBA	89	Radford	1989

University of Bridgeport — Bridgeport, CT 06601-2449 (203) 1970,1982

Name	Rank	Phone				Degree		School	Year
Col of Bus & Public Mgt	126 Park Drive		FAX=576-4941					BS,MBA	
Moriya, Frank E.	Dean	576-4384			Mktg	DBA	67	Geo Wash	1967
—Department of Management	Phone	576-4376	Fax 576-4941						
Bassett, Glenn	C-Pr	576-4376		37	IU	PHD	78	Yale	9-79
Brady, Gene F.	Prof	576-4369		35	I	PHD	71	Oregon	9-82
Tong, Vincent	Asst	576-4793		2	EFH	PHD	91	Yale	9-93

Brigham Young University — Provo, UT 84602 (801) BYUVAX 1963,1971

Name	Rank	Phone				Degree		School	Year
Marriott School of Mgt			FAX=378-4501					BS,MAC,MBA,MOB	
Skousen, K. Fred	Dean	378-4122			Atg	PHD	68	Illinois	9-70
KPMG Peat Marwick Professor									
—Dept of Organizational Beh	Phone	378-2664	Fax 378-8098						
Dyer, Gibb	C-Ac	378-2666		26	STOE	PHD	84	MIT	1984
Cherrington, David J.	Prof	378-6828		25	JNVE	DBA	70	Indiana	1970
Pace, R. Wayne	Prof	378-5020		25	&GPX	PHD	60	Purdue	1978
Peterson, Brent	Prof	378-6820		16	FTP	PHD	70	Ohio U	1972
Ritchie, J. Bonner	Prof	378-6832		12	HYQ	PHD	68	Berkeley	1973
Stephan, Eric	Prof	378-3478		25	G&N	PHD	66	Utah	1968
Wilkins, Alan L.	Prof	378-3567	callo	13	DEIP	PHD	79	Stanford	1978

Woodworth, Warner	Prof	378-6834		48	FJLS	PHD	74	Michigan	1976
Kirkham, Kate	Assoc	378-6829		12	RNE	PHD	77	Union	1978
Meek, Christopher B.	Assoc	378-6827		59	YQBL	PHD	83	Cornell	1984
Gregersen, Hal B.	Asst	378-2902		28	FINY	PHD	89	Berkeley	1992
—Inst Business Management	Phone	378-4367	Fax 378-5984						
Rinne, Heikki	C	378-4367				PHD			
Adolphson, Donald L.	Prof	378-2433		7	UV	PHD	73	U Wash	1980
Daines, Robert H.	Prof	378-2447		3	I	PHD	66	Indiana	1959
Giauque, William C.	Prof	378-2409		7	U	DBA	77	Harvard	1977
Smith, Scott	Prof	378-5569		8	Y	PHD	79	Penn St	1981
Jackson, W. Burke	Assoc	378-2394		3	I	PHD	78	Stanford	1973
Lee, Terry Nels	Assoc	378-4810		7	U	PHD	73	U Wash	1970
Plenert, Gerhard J.	Assoc	378-7338		7	U	PHD	89	Co-Mines	1990
Rhoads, Gary	Assoc	378-2198							
Sawaya, William J.	Assoc	378-2417		7	U	PHD	71	Arizona	1978
Wilson, Brent D.	Assoc	378-4867		3	I	PHD	79	Harvard	1982
Merrill, Craig	Asst	378-4563							
Seawright, Kristie	Asst	378-4563		73	UIVL	PHD	93	Utah	1993
Whitlark, David B.	Asst	378-4563		7	U	PHD	88	Virginia	1989
on leave to Virginia									
Murray, Robert B.	Inst	378-2454							
Pearce, Wayne E.	Inst	378-4579							

Brigham Young Univ-Hawaii	Laie, HI	96762-1294	(808) BUYH.EDU						
School of Business	55-220 Kulauni Street		FAX=293-3322						BS
Neal, William G.	Dean	293-3580		9	Z	EDD	77	Va Tech	1984
—Business Management	Phone	293-3580	Fax 293-3582						
Kimzey, Bruce	C-Pr	293-3585		1		PHD	70	Wash St	1989
Bradshaw, James R.	Prof	293-3580		8	Y	EDD	74	Brig Yg	1969
Smith, Gary R.	Prof	293-3586		34	BEJT	EDD	70	Idaho	8-84
Ellis, Bret	Asst	293-3580		9	Z	PHD	89	Brig Yg	1986
Keliiliki, Dale K.	Asst	293-3590		7	V	MS	71	Brig Yg	9-72
McKenzie, Roger I.	Asst	293-3595		38	BILY	MBA	67	Harvard	8-82

Bryant College	Smithfield, RI	02917-1284	(401) RESEARCH1.BRYANT.EDU						
College of Business	1150 Douglas Pike		FAX=232-6319						BS,MBA,MST
Anderson, Roger L.	Dean	232-6088		5	FNQ	PHD	85	Oregon	7-88
—Department of Management	Phone	232-6464	Fax 232-6319						
Chittipeddi, Kumar	C-Ac	232-6438	kchittip	3	ITN	PHD	86	Penn St	6-81
Pollard, Hinda	Prof	232-6367		5	NQ	JD	64	Berkeley	8-79
Bougon, Michel	Assoc	232-6029		3	IHE	PHD	80	Cornell	8-88
DiBattisa, Ronald	Assoc	232-6258		25	EJN	PHD	79	Ariz St	1-85
Powell, Thomas	Assoc	232-6439		3	ITN	PHD	89	NYU	6-91
Coakley, Lori	Asst	232-6735		2	ENY	PHD	93	Mass	8-93
Conti, Robert	Asst	232-6464		71	DUY	PHD	90	Lehigh	8-91
Dent, Anne	Asst	232-6729		8	YI	PHD	91	Nice	8-92
Luthar, Harsh	Asst	232-6388		5	EN	PHD	93	Va Tech	8-93
Ma, Hao	Asst	232-6000		18	IN	PHD	94	Texas	8-94
Noble, Margaret	Asst	232-6313		7	IUWX	PHD	92	Indiana	8-92
Segovis, James	Asst	232-6382		2	EGH	PHD	90	Texas	8-92
Wilson, Shirley	Asst	232-6444		2	E	PHD	92	Case Wes	8-92

Bucknell University	Lewisburg, PA	17837	(717)						
Dept of Management			FAX=524-3760						BS,MS
—Management Faculty	Phone	524-1306	Fax 524-1338						
Zappe, Christopher	C-As	524-3495		7	U	PHD	88	Indiana	9-93
Miller, John A.	Prof	524-1303		2	GH	PHD	74	Rochest	9-78
Shrivastava, Paul	Prof	524-1821		34	IM	PHD	81	Pitt	9-89
Gilbert, Daniel R.	Assoc	524-3161		43	IJ	PHD	87	Minn	9-87
McGoun, Elton G.	Assoc	524-3732		8	Y	PHD	87	Indiana	9-87
Weida, Nancy C.	Assoc	524-1399		7	U	PHD	88	Delaware	9-87
Felan, Joe E. III	Asst	524-1365		7	V	ABD		S Carol	9-93
Hiller, Tammy	Asst	524-1306		25	EN	ABD		N Carol	9-94

Buena Vista College	Storm Lake, IA	50588	(712) BVC.EDU						
School of Business	610 West Fourth Street		FAX=749-2037						BS
Russell, Paul	Dean	749-2422			Bus	EDD	65	N Colo	9-76
—Management Faculty	Phone		Fax 749-2037						
Camburn, Art	Assoc	749-2416		23	EHIL	PHD	88	Florida	8-91

Butler University	Indianapolis, IN	46208	(317) BUTLER.EDU						
College of Business	4600 Sunset Avenue		FAX=283-9930						BSBA,MBA
Dahringer, Lee D.	Dean	283-9221			Mktg	DBA	75	Colorado	1993
—Department of Management	Phone		Fax 283-9930						
Swenson, H. Raymond	H-Pr	283-9221		79	UZ	PHD	63	Chicago	1961

Hicks, Harry E.	Prof	283-9221		4	J	JD	79	Indiana	1974
Nichols, Archie	Prof	283-9221		6	S	PHD	61	Penn	1957
Orris, J. B.	Prof	283-9221		97	ZU	PHD	72	Illinois	1971
King, Barry	Assoc	283-9221		79	UZ	PHD	79	Indiana	1991
Lad, Larry	Assoc	283-9221		3	I	DBA	85	Boston	1991
Roering, William D.	Assoc	283-9221		3	I	PHD	89	Minn	1993
Bennett, Robert B.	Asst	283-9221		4	J	JD	80	Georgia	1991
Fernandez, Eugenia	Asst	283-9221		9	Z	PHD	88	Purdue	1990
Fountain, Gwen	Asst	283-9221		1	A	PHD	72	Michigan	1986
Luechauer, David L.	Asst	283-9221		2	EF	PHD	90	Cinn	1992
Padgett, Margaret	Asst	283-9221		2	E	PHD	88	Mich St	1989
Fox, Marianne	Lect	283-9221		9	Z	MBA	81	Indiana	1988
Jerden, Jonathan	Lect	283-9221		19	AZ	MBA	90	Butler	1986

Calif Univ of Pennsylvania	California, PA	15419-1394		(412)					
Business & Econ Dept	250 University Avenue			FAX=					BS
Hart, Richard	Dean	938-4169				PHD		Minn	1978
–Management Faculty	Phone	938-4371							
Chawdry, Arshad	C-Pr	938-4371				PHD		Illinois	1976
Hashemi, Ali	Prof	938-5727		2	E	PHD		Northwes	1982
Brown, Burrell	Asst	938-5992		5	NQ	JD		Pitt	1989
Clingerman, Debra	Asst	938-5715		15	N	MBA		W Virg	1984
Serafin, Louise	Asst	938-5994		5	FHI	ABD		Pitt	1989
Zderkowski, Jerzy	Asst	938-5992		8		ABD		Pitt	1992

U of California-Berkeley	Berkeley, CA	94720		(510)	HAAS.BERKELEY.EDU		1916,1963		
Haas School of Business				FAX=642-2826				BS,MBA,PHD	
Hasler, William A.	Dean	642-1425				MBA	67	Harvard	1991
–Org Beh & Indus Relations	Phone		Fax 642-2826						
Staw, Barry M.	C-Pr	642-6357		25	EQI	PHD		Northwes	1980
Lorrinae Tyson Mitchell Professor in Leadership and Communication									
Carroll, Glenn R.	Prof	642-0829		25	EHOP	PHD		Stanford	1982
Paul J. Cortese Professor of Management									
Lincoln, James R.	Prof	642-3657		25	EQ	PHD		Wiscon	1988
on sabbatical									
Roberts, Karlene A.	Prof	642-5221		25	EQY	PHD	67	Berkeley	1968
Leonard, Jonathan S.	Assoc	642-7048		25	EQ	PHD		Harvard	1982
Harold Furst Associate Professor of Management Philosophy and Values									
Peterson, Trond	Assoc	642-6423		25	EQO	PHD		Wiscon	1988
Chatman, Jennifer	Asst			2	E	PHD	87	Berkeley	
Levine, David	Asst	642-1697		25	EQ	PHD		Harvard	
on leave									
–Manfacturing & Inform Tech	Phone		Fax 643-6659						
Shogan, Andrew W.	C-Ac$	642-5371	shogan	7	V	PHD		Stanford	1974
Hochbaum, Dorit S.	Prof	642-4952	hochbaum	7	V	PHD		Penn	1981
Marschak, Thomas A.	Prof	642-4726	marschak	7	V	PHD		Stanford	1959
Shanthikumar, J. George	Prof	642-2571	shanthik	7	U	PHD		Toronto	1984
Segev, Arie	Assoc	642-4731	segev	9	Z	PHD		Rochest	1983
Srikanth, Rajan	Asst	643-9994	srikanth	9	Z	PHD		NYU	1990
Beckman, Sara L.	Lect	642-1058	beckman	7	U	PHD		Stanford	1988
–Business & Public Policy	Phone		Fax 642-2826						
VanLoo, Fran	C-Ac	642-4722		1	A	PHD		Berkeley	1981
Teece, David	Prof	642-1075		38	IY	PHD		Penn	1984
Director of Center for Research and Management									
Tyson, Laura	Prof	642-6083		48	Y	PHD		MIT	1978
on leave									
Vogel, David J.	Prof	642-5294		38	IY	PHD	74	Princeton	1974
Williamson, Oliver	Prof	642-8697		34	I	PHD		Minn	1989
Harris, Robert G.	Assoc	642-0961		43	IL	PHD		Berkeley	1977
Mowery, David	Assoc	643-9992		38	YD	PHD		Stanford	1989
Rosen, Christine	Assoc	642-8965		14	BM	PHD		Harvard	1983

Univ of California-Davis	Davis, CA	95616-8609		(916)	UCDAVIS.UCDAVIS.EDU		1992		
Graduate School of Mgt				FAX=752-2924				MBA	
Smiley, Robert H.	Dean	752-7366	rhsmiley		MgtS	PHD	73	Stanford	1989
–Management Faculty	Phone	752-7361	Fax 752-2924						
Biggart, Nicole W.	Prof	752-7362	nwbiggart	2	EFHY	PHD		Berkeley	
Dorf, Richard C.	Prof	752-7395	rcdorf	1	D	PHD		Navy Pos	
Rocke, David M.	Prof	752-7368	dmrocke	79	VXZ	PHD		Illinois	
Topkis, Donald M.	Prof	752-7396	dmtopkis	9	Z	PHD		Stanford	
Bittlingmayer, George	Assoc	752-2277	gnbittlingma	57	QUVX	PHD		Chicago	
Bunch, David S.	Assoc	752-2248	dsbunch	79	VXZ	PHD		Rice	
Palmer, Donald A.	Assoc	752-8566	dapalmer	2	FH	PHD		SUNY-SBr	
Woodruff, David L.	Asst	752-0515	dlwoodruff	7	U	PHD		Northwes	
Suran, Jerome	SLect	752-7397	jjsuran			BSEE		Columbia	

Univ of Calif, Irvine

Graduate School of Mgt — Irvine, CA 92717 — (714) UCI — FAX=856-8469 — 1987 — MBA,PHD

Name	Title	Phone	Email						
Aigner, Dennis J.	Dean	824-6855	djaigner		Econ	PHD	63	Berkeley	7-88
—Department of Management	Phone	824-6855	Fax 824-8469						
Feldstein, Paul J.	Prof	824-8156	pfeldste			PHD	61	Chicago	1987
Kraemer, Kenneth L.	Prof	824-5246	kkraemer	9	AEYZ	PHD	67	S Calif	1967
Margulies, Newton	Prof	824-4948	nmarguli	2	E	PHD	65	UCLA	1969
McKenzie, Richard B.	Prof	824-2604	rbmckez			PHD	72	Va Tech	1991
Porter, Lyman W.	Prof	824-5335	lwporter	25	EPY	PHD	56	Yale	1967
Scott, Carlton H.	Prof	824-5336	chscott	7	UV	PHD	71	NS Wales	1982
Earley, P. Christopher	Asoc	824-6921	cpearley	2	E	PHD	84	Illinios	1992
Gurbaxani, Vijay	Assoc	824-5215	vgurbaxa	9	Z	PHD	87	Rochest	1985
Keller, L. Robin	Assoc	824-6348	lrkeller	7	UV	PHD	82	UCLA	1989
Navarro, Peter	Assoc	824-6225	pnavarro	5	JL	PHD	86	Harvard	1988
Pearce, Jone L.	Assoc	824-6505	jlpearce	25	ENY	PHD	78	Yale	1979
Tsui, Anne	Assoc	824-4062	astsui	25	EHNR	PHD	81	UCLA	1988
Bakos, Yannis	Asst	824-8211	ybakos	9	Z	PHD	87	Mass	1987
Brahm, Richard A.	Asst	824-8795	rabrahm	38	HIY	PHD	89	Penn	1988
Buchmueller, Thomas	Asst	824-5247	tcbuchmu			PHD	92	Wiscon	1992
Nault, Barrie	Asst	824-6855		9	Z	PHD	90	Brit Col	1994
Olk, Paul	Asst	824-2044	polk	2	HYI	PHD	91	Penn	1991
So, Kut C. (Rick)	Asst	824-5054	rso	7	UV	PHD	85	Stanford	1989
Song, Jeanette	Asst	824-2482	jsong	7	UV	PHD	91	Columbia	1991
Wiersema, Margarethe F.	Asst	824-5839	mfwierse	3	I	PHD	85	Michigan	1987
Rosener, Judy B.	SLect	824-5409	jbrosene	1	AR	PHD	79	Claremont	1978

Univ of Calif, Los Angeles

Anderson Grad Sch Mgt — Los Angeles, CA 90024-1481 — (310) AGSM.UCLA.EDU — FAX=206-2002 — 1939 — MBA,PHD

Name	Title	Phone	Email						
Pierskalla, William P.	Dean	825-7982			MgtS	PHD	65	Stanford	1993
—Management Faculty	Phone	825-4461	Fax 206-2002						
Mamer, John W.	C-Ac	825-4461	jmamer	7	V	PHD	82	Berkeley	1981
Buffa, Elwood S.	Prof	825-2247	ebuffa	7	U	PHD	57	UCLA	1952
Culbert, Samuel A.	Prof	825-7784	sculbert	5	N	PHD	66	UCLA	1969
DeLaTorre, Jose'	Prof	825-4507	jdelator	3	I	DBA	71	Harvard	1987
Erlenkotter, Donald	Prof	825-1644	derlenko	7	V	PHD	70	Stanford	1969
Flamholtz, Eric G.	Prof	825-4956	eflamhol	5	N	PHD	69	Michigan	1973
Geoffrion, Arthur M.	Prof	825-1113	ageoffri	7	V	PHD	65	Stanford	1965
Greenberger, Martin	Prof	825-7770	mgreenbe	9	Z	PHD	58	Harvard	1982
Jacoby, Sanford M.	Prof	825-2505	sjacoby			PHD	81	Berkeley	1980
Kleingartner, Archie	Prof	825-2527	akleinga	5	N	PHD	65	Wiscon	1964
Lewin, David	Prof	206-7666	dlewin	5	N	PHD	71	UCLA	1990
Lientz, Bennet P.	Prof	825-1648	blientz	9	Z	PHD	68	U Wash	1974
Lippman, Steven A.	Prof	825-3649	slippman	7	V	PHD	68	Stanford	1967
MacQueen, James B.	Prof	825-3926	jmacquee	7	V	PHD	58	Oregon	1962
Massarik, Fred	Prof	825-7797	fmassari	5	N	PHD	57	UCLA	1950
McDonough, John J.	Prof	825-1454	jmcdonou	2	E	DBA	69	Harvard	1968
McKelvey, William W.	Prof	825-2506	wmckelve	3	I	PHD	67	MIT	1967
Mitchell, Daniel J. B.	Prof	825-1504	dmitchel	5	N	PHD	68	MIT	1968
Ouchi, William G.	Prof	825-5848	wquchi	3	I	PHD	72	Chicago	1979
Rumelt, Richard P.	Prof	825-2592	rrumelt	3	I	DBA	72	Harvard	1976
Sarin, Rakesh K.	Prof	825-3930	rsarin	7	U	PHD	75	UCLA	1979
Swanson, E. Burton	Prof	825-3654	bswanson	9	Z	PHD	71	Berkeley	1974
Wilson, James Q.	Prof	825-2840	jwilson	3	I	PHD	59	Chicago	1984
Gersick, Connie J. G.	Assoc	825-9764	cgersick	5	N	PHD	85	Yale	1984
Goodman, Richard A.	Assoc	825-1219	rgoodman	3	I	DBA	66	Wash U	1966
Lawrence, Barbara S.	Assoc	825-1252	blawrenc	3	I	PHD	83	MIT	1983
Lieberman, Marvin B.	Assoc	206-7665	mlieberm	3	I	PHD	82	Harvard	1990
Osborne, Alfred E. Jr.	Assoc	825-2985	aosborne	6	T	PHD	74	Stanford	1972
Schollhammer, Hans	Assoc	825-3045	hschollh	3	I	DBA	67	Indiana	1967
Tang, Siu S. (Christopher)	Assoc	825-4203	stang	7	V	PHD	85	Yale	1985
Ahmadi, Reza H.	Asst	825-4728	rahmadi	7	U	PHD	88	Texas	1988
Dasu, Sriram	Asst	825-1651	sdasu	7	U	PHD	88	MIT	1988
Erickson, Christopher L.	Asst	825-1697	cerickso	5	N	PHD	90	MIT	1991
Frand, Jason L.	Asst	825-2725	jfrand	9	Z	PHD	76	UCLA	1979
Pentland, Brian T.	Asst	825-8494	bpentlan	9	Z	PHD	91	MIT	1992
Postrel, Steven R.	Asst	825-5292	spostrel	3	I	PHD	88	MIT	1986
Shirley, Gordon V.	Asst	825-5681	gshirley	7	U	DBA	87	Harvard	1987
Stephenson, Karen A.	Asst	825-5826	kstephen	5	N	PHD	90	Harvard	1990
Forman, Janis S.	Adj	206-8086	jforman	1	&	PHD	80	Rutgers	1982
Geis, George T.	Adj	825-2987	ggeis	96	ZT	PHD	77	S Calif	1985
Yost, S. William	Adj	825-6749	syost	3	I	DBA	68	Harvard	1990

Univ of Calif, Riverside

Graduate School of Mgt — Riverside, CA 92521-0203 — (909) — FAX=787-3970

Name	Title	Phone							
Granfield, Michael E.	Dean	787-4237				PHD			9-94
—Management Faculty	Phone		Fax 787-3970						
Hanson, E. Mark	Prof	787-6329		25	EQ	PHD		New Mex	1970
Schaible, Siegfried	Prof	787-4495		7	U	PHD		Hab Koln	1987

Name	Rank	Phone	Email/Fax	Area	Code	Deg	Yr	School	Year
Chung, Peter Y.	Assoc	787-3906							
Dodin, Bajis M.	Assoc	787-4284							
Erevelles, Sunil	Assoc	787-3779		7	U	PHD		N Carol	1984
Zahn, G. Lawrence	Assoc	787-3727							
Fondas, Nanette	Asst	787-6447		25	EQ	PHD	71	Yale	1970
Kim, Michael W.	Asst	787-4557		25	EQ	DBA		Harvard	
Masuda, Yasushi	Asst	787-4493		9	Z	PHD		Stanford	1990
Montgomery, Kathleen	Asst	787-7319		9	Z	PHD		Rochest	1987
Rolland, Erik	Asst	787-6448		25	EQ	PHD		NYU	1990
Sassalos, Susan	Asst	787-3694		9	Z				

U of Calif, Santa Barbara
Department of Economics — Santa Barbara CA 93106
(805) ECON.UCSB.EDU
FAX=961-8830

Name	Rank	Phone	Email/Fax	Area	Code	Deg	Yr	School	Year
Frech, H. E. III	C-Pr	893-3569	frech		Econ	PHD	74	UCLA	BA 1973
—**Management Faculty**	Phone		Fax 893-8830						
Shapiro, Perry	Prof		pxshap			PHD	68	Berkeley	1987

Calif Polytechnic State U
College of Business — S Luis Obispo CA 93407
(805) CYMBAL.CALPOLY.EDU 1981,1987
FAX=756-1473 — BS,MBA

Name	Rank	Phone	Email/Fax	Area	Code	Deg	Yr	School	Year
Haile, Allen C.	Dean	756-2704			PAdm	PHD	71	S Calif	7-93
—**Department of Management**	Phone	756-1301	Fax 756-1473						
Shani, A. B. (Rami)	H-Pr	756-1756		2	EFH	PHD	81	Case Wes	1981
Biggs, Joseph	Prof	756-2955		7	U	PHD	75	Ohio St	1988
Ellis, Rebecca A.	Prof	756-2629		5	NO	PHD	84	Wiscon	1987
Peach, David A.	Prof	756-7187		5	NQ	DBA	69	Harvard	1987
Rogers, Rolf E.	Prof	756-1413		38	IY	PHD	70	U Wash	1975
Sena, James	Prof	756-2680		9	Z	DBA	72	Kentucky	1987
Stebbins, Michael W.	Prof	756-1416		2	EFH	PHD	73	Berkeley	1982
Bird, Allan W.	Assoc	756=1301		23	IYE	PHD	88	Oregon	1994
Floyd, Barry D.	Assoc	756-2032		9	Z	PHD	82	Michigan	1990
Frayne, Colette	Assoc	756-1754	cfrayne	25	ENPY	PHD	86	U Wash	1992
Geringer, Michael	Assoc	756-1755	mgeringe	38	ILTY	PHD	86	U Wash	1992
Haynes, Ray M.	Assoc	756-1418		7	U	PHD	88	Ariz St	1989
Levejhagej, Michael J.	Assoc	576-1301		38	IYT	PHD	93	Illinois	1994
Li, Eldon	Assoc	756-2964		9	Z	PHD	81	Tx Tech	1982

Calif State Poly U-Pomona
College of Business Adm — Pomona, CA 91768-4083
3801 West Temple Avenue
(909) CSUPOMONA.EDU
FAX= — BS,MS,MBA

Name	Rank	Phone	Email/Fax	Area	Code	Deg	Yr	School	Year
Eaves, Ronald W.	Dean	869-2400		9	Z	PHD	76	UCLA	1968
—**Management & Human Res**	Phone	869-2414	Fax 869-6799						
Snyder, Peggy J.	C-Ac	869-2412		2	EPX	PHD	90	Claremont	1981
Abraham, Stanley C.	Prof	869-2420		3	ILY	PHD	76	UCLA	1991
Iman, Stephen	Prof	869-2413		2	E	PHD	72	Michigan	1985
Patten, Thomas H.	Prof	869-2423		5	KQ	PHD	59	Cornell	1984
Pekar, Peter P.	Prof	869-2421		3	IL	PHD	74	Ill Tech	1991
Relf, William B.	Prof	869-2424		6	ST	PHD	71	Clarmont	1976
Sabo, R. Richard	Prof	869-2426		5	N	MBA	65	San Jose	1967
Sakamoto, Shiori	Prof	869-2427		5	N	DBA	75	S Calif	1972
Sethia, Nirmal K.	Prof	869-4152		9	Y	PHD	80	IndianIn	1991
Waters, Gail R.	Prof	869-2359		16	BITY	PHD	82	Arkansas	1992
Weber, Warren C.	Prof	869-2433		5	NP	EDD	69	Ariz St	1969
Allen, Robert W.	Assoc	869-2416		5	B				
Hanson, Lady A.	Assoc	869-2418		2	EF	PHD	78	Clarmont	1986
Jones, Carol Larson	Assoc	869-2428		1	Z	EDD	80	N Colo	1987
Rogers, Percy G.	Assoc	869-2425		6	T	DPA	73	S Calif	1982
Bassett, James C.	Asst	869-2419				PHD	91	Ohio St	1991
Brazeal, Deborah	Asst	869-2338		6	ST				
Lin, Lianlian	Asst	869-2422		8	Y	PHD	92	Texas	1992
Poulson, Christian F.	Asst	869-2415		2	EF	PHD	89	Yale	1991
Sharif-Zadeh, Mansour	Asst	869-2430		3	I	PHD	79	North Tx	1988
Srinivas, Shanthi	Asst	869-2433		7	V	PHD	79	Penn St	1987
—**Operations Management**	Phone	869-2453	Fax 869-2466						
Miller, Ralph H.	C-Pr	869-2452	rhmiller	7	VX	PHD	79	Claremont	1979
Cosgrove, William J.	Prof	869-2461	wcosgrov	73	UVI	PHD	89	Nebraska	1989
El Agizy, Mostafa	Prof	869-2455	meagizy	7	UV	PHD	65	Berkeley	1983
Halati, Abolhassan	Prof	869-2468	ahalati	7	UVM	PHD	85	S Calif	1986
Kupsh, Joyce	Prof	869-2457	jkupsh	94	ZJ	EDD	75	Ariz St	1978
Pinkus, Charles E.	Prof	869-2458	cpinkus	71	UVA	DSC	71	Geo Wash	1980
Ramalingam, Panchatcharam	Prof	869-2459	rramalin	7	UVW	PHD	73	Oregon	1970
Rhodes, Rhonda L.	Prof	869-2362	rrhodes	93	ZI	PHD	83	Ariz St	1985
Director of Graduate Studies									
Ross, Leonard E.	Prof	869-2462	lross	7	Z	PHD	64	Berkeley	1982
Salvate, James M.	Prof	869-2463	jsalvate	73	UWI	PHD	70	Columbia	1985
Knox, John E.	Assoc	869-2457	knox	7	VZ	PHD	89	Colorado	1989
—**Computer Info Systems Dept**	Phone	869-3235	Fax 869-4353						
Klosky, J. Michael	C-Pr	869-3247	jmklosky	9	Z	PHD	75	Clemson	1989
Athey, Thomas H.	Prof	869-3242	thathey	93	DIZ	DBA	76	S Calif	1970

Name	Rank	Phone	Email		Code	Degree	Yr	University	Year
Bell, Donald L.	Prof	869-3862	dlbell	98	STYZ	PHD	77	Claremont	1972
Interim Assoc Vice Pres for Technology & Academic Resources									
Crawford, John B.	Prof	869-3251	jbcrawfo	9	Z	PHD	86	CA-Irvin	1984
Isshiki, Koichiro R.	Prof	869-3240	krisshik	9	Z	PHD	71	UCLA	1971
Mason, Ida	Prof	869-3250	iwmason	9	Z	PHD	84	Ariz St	1980
Stumpf, Robert V.	Prof	869-3245	rvstumpf	9	Z	PHD	75	Claremont	1968
Teague, Lavette C. Jr.	Prof	869-3246	lcteague	9	ZJ	PHD	68	MIT	1980
Testerman, Ward D.	Prof	869-3236	wdtester	9	Z	DBA	75	S Calif	1971
Wagner, Gerald E.	Prof	869-3238	gewagner	9	OZ	EDD	73	UCLA	1966
Wilkins, Susan J.	Prof	869-3249	sjwilkin	9	Z	PHD	85	Nebraska	1985
Deokar, Vijay D.	Assoc	869-4450	vdeokar	9	Z	PHD	68	CSU-LA	1989
Manson, Daniel P.	Assoc	869-3244	dpmanson	9	Z	MSBA	85	CS-Pomon	1992
Powell, Steven R.	Assoc	869-3831	srpowell	93	IVZ	PHD	73	S Calif	1990
Curl, Steven S.	Asst	869-4244	scurl	9	Z	MS	88	Claremont	1990
Olson, Patrick	Asst	869-3959	polson	9	Z	MS	85	S Calif	1987
Preiser-Houy, Larisa	Asst	869-3243	lpreiser	9	Z	MBA	90	Claremont	1992

Calif State U., Bakersfield — Bakersfield, CA 93311-1099 — (805) CALSTATE — 1975,1982
Sch of Bus & Public Adm — 9001 Stockdale Highway — FAX=664-3194 — BS,MBA

Name	Rank	Phone	Email		Code	Degree	Yr	University	Year
Unni, V. K.	Dean	664-2157				DBA			8-93
—Management Faculty	Phone		Fax 664-2438						
Hulpke, John	C-Pr	664-2175		46		PHD			1989
Attaran, Mohsen	Prof	664-2310		7	UVZ	PHD			1984
Bidgoli, Hossein	Prof	664-2331		9		PHD			1983
Bowin, Robert B.	Prof	664-2333		14	GP	PHD	70	Oregon	1984
Flanagan, Michael F.	Prof	664-2313		25	EHNX	PHD			1986
Harvey, Donald	Prof	664-2388		31	S	PHD			1991
McNamara, Brian	Prof	664-2340	hbdsmcn	69	CPSZ	PHD			1986
Stiles, Curt	Prof	664-3087		3		PHD			1988
Tarjan, John	Prof	664-2321	tarjan	29	HZ	PHD			1986
Vigen, James W.	Prof	664-2332	vigen	7	SUV	PHD	65	Ohio St	1971
Ortega, Tony	Asst	664-2284		36	ISTE	PHD			1990

Calif State Univ, Chico — Chico, CA 95929-0031 — (916) — 1972,1976
College of Business — FAX=898-6824 — BS,MBA

Name	Rank	Phone	Email		Code	Degree	Yr	University	Year
Rethans, Arno J.	Dean	898-6271			Mktg	PHD	79	Oregon	8-87
—Dept of Management	Phone		Fax 898-4584						
Morgan, James	C-Pr	898-5663				JD		Ca-Davis	1983
Cambridge, Charles	Prof	898-5302				PHD		Minn	1978
Cotton, Chester C.	Prof	898-4827				PHD	74	Oregon	1972
Gardner, Susan	Prof								
Gomes, Glen	Prof	898-6289				PHD		S Calif	1985
Indvik, Julie	Prof	898-6189				PHD		Wiscon	1983
Levine, Mark	Prof	898-4337				PHD		UCLA	1978
Lewis, Kathryn	Prof	898-6826				PHD		Ariz St	1978
McDonald, Tracy	Prof	898-5888				PHD		Ohio St	1983
McKenna, Jack	Prof	898-4735				PHD		Irvine	1977
Sibary, Scott	Prof	898-5747				JD		Berkeley	1983
Sikula, Andrew	Prof	898-5880				PHD		Mich St	1980
Carraher, Shawn	Assoc	898-5663				PHD		Oklahoma	1994
Daumer, Claudia	Assoc	898-6477				PHD		Ariz St	1983
Johnson, Pam	Assoc	898-6415				PHD		Wiscon	1984
Owens, James	Assoc	898-5193		4	L	JD		Western	1979
Siegall, Marc	Assoc	898-5421				PHD		Northwes	1986

Calif St U-Dominguez Hills — Carson, CA 90747 — (310) CSUDH.CALSTATE.EDU — BS,MBA
School of Management — 1000 East Victoria Street — FAX=516-3664
  Dept of CIS Did Not Respond-1993 Listing

Name	Rank	Phone	Email		Code	Degree	Yr	University	Year
Neumann, Yoram	Dean	516-3548		2	E	PHD	76	Cornell	1990
—Department of Management	Phone	516-3551	Fax 516-3664						
Mills, R. Bryant	C-Pr	516-3551		5	N	PHD	72	Iowa	1983
Associate Dean									
Chirspin, Barbara	Prof	516-3584		52	NE	PHD	71	UCLA	1973
Dowling, Robert	Prof	516-3719		6	S	DBA	77	S Calif	1973
Jenner, Stephen	Prof	516-3551		3	Y	PHD		Sussez	1991
Nehrbass, Richard G.	Prof	516-3602		25	EN	PHD	75	S Calif	1975
—Dept of Computer Info Sys	Phone	516-3579	Fax 474-8053						
Freeman, Raoul J.	C	516-3579		9	Z	PHD		MIT	1984

Calif State Univ-Fresno — Fresno, CA 93740-0007 — (209) CSUFRESNO.EDU — 1959,1977
Sid Craig Sch Business — 5245 N. Backer Avenue — FAX=278-4911 — BS,MBA,MS,MSA

Name	Rank	Phone	Email		Code	Degree	Yr	University	Year
Simis, Peter	Dean$	278-2482			InSy	DBA	78	Ariz St	8-70
—Dept of Management	Phone	278-2851	Fax 278-4911						
Jones, Gerald L.	C-Pr	278-2851		7	U	DBA		Colorado	1979
Anderson, David C.	Prof	278-4988		27	EHU	DBA	70	Geo St	1966
Bertken, Kay	Prof	278-2577		7	U	PHD		Stanford	1991

Name	Title	Phone						
Bowerman, Karen Dill	Prof	278-2626	2	EH	PHD		Tx A&M	1979
Burch-Konda, Regina	Prof	278-4973	25	EN	PHD		Colorado	1993
Calingo, Luis	Prof	278-4012	3	I	PHD		Pitt	1983
Coe, L. Charlene	Prof	278-4979	7	U	MBA		CS-Fresn	1988
Gilbertson, Diana L.	Prof	278-4969	3	I	PHD		North Tx	1988
Halfhill, Susan M.	Prof	278-4953	2	EH	PHD		Bradford	1982
Harris, Harry G.	Prof	278-4965	23	BEIY	PHD		Harvard	1980
Houts, Lisa	Prof	278-4980	27	EU	MBA		CS-Fresn	1990
Johnson, Dewey E.	Prof	278-2496	62	SEI	PHD		Minn	1977
Keppler, Mark J.	Prof	278-4959	45	NJK	JD		Wiscon	1987
Moghaddam, John M.	Prof	278-2915	7	U	PHD		North Tx	1979
Olson, Julie B.	Prof	278-4952	5	N	PHD		Illinois	1992
Panico, Victor G.	Prof	278-3997	2	EH	EDD	71	Ariz St	1970
Penbera, Joseph John	Prof	278-4962	28	EY	PHD	70	American	8-85
Simpson, Douglas B.	Prof	278-2841	2	EH	PHD	71	U Wash	1971
Tellier, Richard D.	Prof	278-2228	7	U	DBA	73	Fla St	1973
Thakur, Manab N.	Prof	278-4970	3	I	PHD		Brunel	1988
Wang, Jia	Prof	278-4977	3	I	PHD	91	Tenn	1991
Young, Debbie	Prof	278-4983	2	EF	MBA		Pitt St	1989

Calif State Univ, Fullerton — Fullerton, CA — 92634-9480 — (714) CALSTATE — 1965,1972
School of Bus Adm & Ec — FAX=449-7101 — BS,MBA,MS,MST

Name	Title	Phone						
Smith, Ephraim P.	Dean	773-2592		Atg	PHD	68	Illinois	8-90
—Dept Management Bx 34080	Phone	773-2251	Fax 773-2645					
Abdelwahed, Farouk H.	C-Ac	773-2251	34	Y	PHD	73	UCLA	8-73
Ames, Michael	Prof	773-3930	67	S	PHD	71	Clarmont	8-76
Apke, Thomas	Prof	773-3945			JD	69	Marquett	
Bickner, Mel Liang	Prof	773-3825	25	Q	PHD	68	UCLA	8-74
Gunawardane, Gamini	Prof	773-3075	37	UV	PHD	77	Chicago	8-82
Johnson, Thomas	Prof	773-3445	25	EN	PHD	72	Illinois	8-81
Kleiner, Brian	Prof	773-3843	2	E	PHD	77	UCLA	8-77
Kushell, Elliot	Prof	773-3171	2	E	PHD	78	Hawaii	8-77
Manoochehri, Ghasem H.	Prof	773-3073	7	U	PHD	78	LSU	8-81
Mayes, Bronston T.	Prof	773-2435	2	EF	PHD	88	Irvine	8-84
Oh, Tai K.	Prof	773-2251	25	NY	PHD	70	Wiscon	8-73
Chan, Peng S.	Assoc	773-3944	3	ISY	PHD	86	Texas	8-89
Dumond, Ellen	Assoc	773-3071	17	U	PHD	86	Indiana	2-91
Erdner, Carolyn	Assoc		31		PHD	90	Inidana	8-91
Kim, Eonsoo	Assoc	773-3936			PHD			1994
Tavakolian, Hamid	Assoc	773-3941	9	Z	PHD	87	Geo St	8-89
Vargas, Gustavo	Assoc	773-3936	7	U	PHD	77	Penn St	8-86
Hefni, Omar	Lect	773-3410			PHD			
Lang, William	Lect	449-7118						
Nour, James	Lect	773-3790			PHD			

Calif State Univ, Hayward — Hayward, CA — 94542-3069 — (510) CSUHAYWARD.EDU — 1973,1981
Sch of Business & Econ — FAX=727-2039 — BS,MBA,MSBA

Name	Title	Phone						
Tontz, Jay L.	Dean	881-3291		Econ	PHD	66	N Carol	9-69
—Dept/ Management & Finance	Phone		Fax 727-2039					
Wort, Donald R.	C-Pr	881-3322	dwort	Fnce	PHD	73	Mich St	1984
Aviel, S. David	Prof	881-3320	87	Y	PHD	80	Gold Gt	1974
Breuning, Loretta	Prof	881-4277	8	Y	PHD	83	Tufts	1983
Doctors, Samuel I.	Prof	881-3316	34	IJLM	DBA	69	Harvard	1983
Director of Center for Business Environmental Studies								
Economides, Spyros	Prof	881-3328	7	V	PHD	74	Texas	1973
Gotcher, J. William	Prof	881-3302	7	U	PHD	72	Berkeley	1968
Kilgour, John G.	Prof	881-4007	5	Q	PHD	72	Cornell	1972
Miller, Stephen H.	Prof	881-3321	25	E	PHD	69	Purdue	1971
Moore, William L.	Prof	881-3924	25	Q	PHD	79	Berkeley	1975
Ozernoy, Vladimir M.	Prof	881-3099	7	V	PHD	75	Moscow	1983
Partridge, Scott H.	Prof	881-3343	34	I	DBA	70	Harvard	1970
Schaefer, Susan	Prof	881-3933	52	NX	PHD	73	Stanford	1970
Schuh, Allen J.	Prof	881-3329	2	E	PHD	73	Ohio St	1971
Staudohar, Paul	Prof	881-3080	5	Q	PHD	69	S Calif	1969
Villarreal, John J.	Prof	881-3376	3	I	PHD	72	CUNY	1971
Waters, Harry Jr.	Prof	881-3531	2	EP	PHD	86	Oregon	1986
Whisler, William D.	Prof	881-3934	7	V	PHD	65	Berkeley	1972
Wiley, Donna	Prof	881-3964	5	NPR	PHD	83	Tenn	1983
Director of Graduate Programs								
Goldberg, Alan	Assoc	881-3304	7	V	PHD	77	Mass	1979
Radovilsky, Zinovy	Assoc	881-3825	7	UVWX	PHD	84	Moscow	1991

Calif State Univ - Humboldt — Arcata, CA — 95521-8299 — (707) CALSTATE
Sch of Business & Econ — 1 Harpst Street — FAX=826-5555 — BS,MBA

Name	Title	Phone						
Hines, Robert L.	C-Pr	826-3762	hinesr	Atg	PHD	78	Ariz St	1973
—Management Faculty	Phone	826-3224	Fax 826-6666					
Bond, Kenneth M.	Prof	826-4277	47	JLVX	PHD	75	Nebraska	1988
Fults, Gail J.	Prof	826-6026	12	FU	PHD	85	Claremont	1986
Mullery, Colleen	Asst	826-6022	34	IK	PHD	91	Port St	1986

Calif State Univ, Long Beach
Sch of Business Adm 092
Walter, C. J.
–Dept Mgt/Human Res Mgt

Long Beach, CA 90840-8502 (310) 1971,1977
1250 Bellflower Blvd FAX=985-7586 BS
Dean 985-5306
Phone Fax 985-4557

Name	Rank	Phone						
Herrmann, John F.	C-Pr	985-4740	17	IU	DBA	77	S Calif	1980
Bates, Donald	Prof	985-8604	31	HIL	PHD	73	Arkansas	1974
Chong, Philip	Prof	985-5756	97	UXZV	PHD	77	Mass	1986
Filemon, Campo-Flores	Prof	985-4579	6	JRTY	PHD	68	UCLA	1972
Hamburger, Charles	Prof	985-5516	24	EOLI	PHD	65	S Calif	1965
Kakalis, Sal	Prof	985-4749	13	HI	PHD	85	Arizona	1986
Lewis, Ralph	Prof	788-8997	12	EOP	PHD	74	UCLA	1972
area code 818								
Monat, Jonathan S.	Prof	985-4757	2	ENOQ	PHD	72	Minn	1978
Quinn, Michel Thomas	Prof	985-5664	2	EOPN	PHD	67	Ohio St	1970
Stanton, Roger	Prof	985-5406	13	AIL	DBA	76	S Calif	1966
Stone, Herbert	Prof	985-7553	13	IOV	DBA	65	UCLA	1958
Abramis, David	Assoc	985-5360	25	DEFH	PHD	85	Michigan	1985
Ford, Gerald	Assoc	985-4561	36	DJKS	DBA	76	S Calif	1969
Madison, Dan	Assoc	985-4749	13	IBH	PHD	81	Irvine	1983
Hansen, Eric	Asst	985-4358	6	DTIY	PHD	89	Tenn	1989

Calif State U-Los Angeles
School of Bus & Econ
Lemos, Ronald S.
–Department of Management

Los Angeles, CA 90032-8126 (213) 1960,1964
5151 State University Dr FAX=343-2890 BS,MBA,MS,MSHCM
Dean 343-2800 Bis PHD 77 UCLA 6-93
Phone Fax 343-2890

Name	Rank	Phone						
Steiner, John F.	C-Pr	343-2891	4	I	PHD	73	Arizona	1973
Alsh, A. M. A.	Prof	343-2903	14	L	PHD	69	UCLA	1966
Ala, Mohammad	Prof	343-2891	7	U	DBA	83	La Tech	1985
Baker, William G.	Prof	343-2903	12	CE	PHD	70	Oklahoma	1972
Blunt, Keith R.	Prof	343-2898	14	Q	PHD	58	Iowa	1967
Hechler, Peter	Prof	343-2900	1	N	PHD	73	Case Wes	1973
Hill, Lawrence	Prof	343-2901	7	U	PHD	68	S Calif	1969
Khan, Rauf-Ur	Prof	343-2901	18	Y	DBA	71	S Calif	1968
Kwong, Kwok Keung	Prof	343-2899	67	U	PHD	86	Geo St	1986
McEnrue, Mary Pat	Prof	343-2900	1	RE	PHD	80	Wayne St	1981
Rosser, James M.	Prof	343-2890	1	C	PHD	69	S Illin	1979
Washburn, Paul V.	Prof	343-2895	12	EIC	PHD	74	Ohio St	1974
Bagot, Gordon	Asst	343-2897	7	U	PHD	74	UCLA	1988
Cordeiro, William	Asst	343-2902	12	LY	PHD	90	Claremont	1990
Li, Cheng	Asst	343-2902	7	U	PHD	89	Indiana	1988
Whitcomb, Laura	Asst	343-2896	34	ILY	PHD	91	Indiana	1989
Yates, Valerie	Asst	343-2896	45	N	PHD	92	Tx A&M	1990

Calif State Univ, Northridge
Sch of Bus Adm & Econ
Hosek, William R.
–Department of Management
Rossy, Gerard L.
Dayal, Sahab
Associate Dean

Northridge, CA 91330-8245 (818) 1977,1982
18111 Nordhoff Street FAX=885-4903 BS,MBA,MS
Dean 885-2455 PHD 67 CA-SnBar 1988
Phone 885-2457 Fax 885-4903

Name	Rank	Phone						
Rossy, Gerard L.	C-Ac	885-2457	34	DIMP	PHD	79	UCLA	1977
Dayal, Sahab	Prof	885-2466	58	NQY	PHD	73	Cornell	1989
Glassman, Alan M.	Prof	885-2457	12	DEPQ	PHD	70	SUNY-Buf	1971
Hanna, Robert W.	Prof	885-2457	23	EFP	PHD	75	UCLA	1975
Mandell, Myra P.	Prof	885-2457	12	ADHL	PHD	81	S Calif	1980
Mitchell, Rex E.	Prof	885-2457	23	EFI	PHD	69	UCLA	1982
Blumenthal, Judith F.	Assoc	885-2457	38	FHIY	PHD	88	S Calif	1987
Dahl, Joan G.	Assoc	885-2457	25	AFNQ	PHD	86	U Wash	1986
Davidson, Naomi Berger	Assoc	885-2457	45	JKNQ	PHD	81	UCLA	1983
Teeter, Shirley L.	Assoc	885-2457	13	EGIN	PHD	75	UCLA	1969
Klein, Johnathan I.	Asst	885-2457	21	EHXF	PHD	87	S Calif	1991
Li, Mingfang	Asst	885-2457	23	DHIX	PHD	90	Va Tech	1990
Hickman, Charles C.	Lect	885-2457	23	DEIO	ABD		Ohio St	1991

Calif State Univ-Sacramento
School of Bus Admin
Dept of Org Beh & Envir Did Not Respond-1993 Listing
Moorehead, Josef D.
–Department of Management

Sacramento, CA 95819-6088 (916) CSUS.EDU 1963,1970
6000 J Street FAX=278-5437 BS,MBA,MS

Dean 278-6578 moorehead REst PHD 71 S Calif 1974
Phone 278-6459 Fax 278-5437

Name	Rank	Phone	Email					
Blake, Herbert Jr.	C	278-6459	blakeh	37	IUV	PHD	85	Santa Cl	1979
Best, Thomas D.	Prof	278-6901	besttd	7	UV	DENG	79	Berkeley	1980
Karagozoglu, Necmi	Prof	278-7389	karagozo	23	HIT	PHD	84	Oregon	1984
Knowles, Joel B.	Prof	278-6895	knowlesj	37	IUV	PHD	76	Oregon	1980
Merchant, John E.	Prof	278-6966	merchant	36	BIST	PHD	73	Denver	1983
Namiki, Nobuaki	Prof	278-6303	namikin	38	IY	PHD	84	Tx-Dallas	1984
Tully, Paul F.	Prof	278-6419	tullypf	37	HIUV	PHD	80	Houston	1983
VanGigch, John P.	Emer	278-6545	vangiegcj	37	IUVX	PHD	68	Oreg St	1968
Wang, Chiang	Prof	278-6001	wangc	37	HIUX	PHD	79	Iowa	1984
Wang, Ruth	Prof	278-6227	wangrl	78	UVY	PHD	79	Iowa	1984
Hatton, Lindle	Assoc	278-6503	hattonlg	36	HIT	PHD	88	Kentucky	1990

—Dept of Org Beh & Environ

Name	Rank	Phone			Deg		School	Year
Sparks, P. Michael	C	278-6463	25	EFP	PHD	74	S Calif	1976
Anderson, A. Janell	Prof	278-7054	24	EL	PHD	77	Ca-Davis	1975
Cowden, Anne C.	Prof	278-7055	25	EPR	DPA	80	S Calif	1979
Goodfellow, Reginald A.	Prof	278-7072	25	EN	PHD	73	Bowl Gr	1976
Harriman, Ann S.	Prof	278-7037	25	ENR	DPA	80	S Calif	1973
Hillsman, Rovena L.	Prof	278-6781	2	E	EDD	78	Ariz St	1978
Koehler, Cortus T.	Prof	278-6022	2	E	PHD	72	Claremont	1973
Putt, Allen D.	Prof	278-7056	2	E	PHD	75	Kansas	1976
Raza, M. Ali	Prof	278-7005	2	ENQ	PHD	62	Oregon	1968
Rehfuss, John A.	Prof	278-6621	24	EL	DPA	65	S Calif	1978
Stockman, John W.	Prof	278-6948	25	ENP	PHD	69	U Wash	1970
Cleek, Margaret A.	Assoc	278-6969	25	EHNO	PHD	81	Wayne St	1990

Calif St U-San Bernardino
S Bernardino, CA 92407-2397 (909) GALLIUM.CSUSB.EDU
Sch of Bus & Public Adm — 5500 University Parkway — FAX= — BS,MBA

Name	Rank	Phone			Deg		School	Year
Lewis, Eldon C.	Dean$	880-5700		Atg	PHD	67	Missouri	1987

—Department of Management
Phone 880-5731

Name	Rank	Phone			Deg		School	Year
Chaney, John S.	C-Pr	880-5731	3	I	PHD	71	Texas	1972
Bassiry, Gabriel R.	Prof	880-5732	38	IY	PHD	77	SUNY-Bin	1987
Bockman, Sheldon	Prof	880-5733	2	E	PHD	68	Indiana	1973
Derakhshan, Foad	Prof	880-5734	83	YI	PHD	79	LSU	1985
Greenfeld, Susan T.	Prof	880-5737	3	I	DBA	78	S Calif	1987
Kritzberg, Joan H.	Prof	880-5714	4	K	JD	84	Brig Yg	1987
Levy, Steven M.	Prof	880-5737	3	E	PHD	78	Geo Wash	1983
McInturff, Patrick S. Jr.	Prof	880-5741	4	K	PHD	79	Ca-River	1978
Molstad, Clark	Prof	880-5742	35	EQ	PHD	89	UCLA	1984
Rogers, James G.	Prof	880-5746	3	E	PHD	74	UCLA	1974
Ryland, Elisabeth K.	Prof	880-5748	3	E	PHD	86	N Carol	1986
Drost, Donald A.	Assoc	880-5735	35	IN	PHD	84	Va Tech	1987
King, Jeanne	Assoc	880-5779	36	EHS	PHD	92	Claremont	1990
Loutzenhiser, Janice	Assoc	880-5739	4	K	JD	75	Virginia	1976
Reza, Ernesto M.	Assoc	880-5745	3	E	PHD	93	Michigan	1987
Hanson, Lee	Asst	880-5736	3	I	PHD	92	Ca-Irvine	1991
Patterson, Gary D.	Asst	880-5743	4	K	JD	83	Wstrn St	1987
Peake, Lloyd	Asst	880-5766	3	E	JD	74	Southwes	1990
Eller, Cherrlyn	Lect	880-5782			MA	88	CS-SnBar	1991
Lovell, Joseph B.	Lect	880-5740	62	SE	MBA	66	Creighto	1981
Reed, Patricia D.	Lect	880-5744	3	E	MA	86	CS-SnBer	1988

—Dept of Info & Decision Sci
Phone 880-5723 — Fax 880-5994

Name	Rank	Phone				Deg		School	Year
Rohm, Tapie C. E. Jr.	C-Pr	880-5786	trohm	9	Z	PHD	77	Ohio	1983
D'Souza, Patricia V.	Prof	880-5726		9	Z	PHD	85	Ohio St	1986
McDonnell, John F.	Prof	880-5701		7	U	PHD	74	Claremont	1969
Sirotnik, Barbara	Prof	880-5729		7	V	PHD	80	Ca-River	1980
Stewart, Walter T. Jr.	Prof	880-5728		9	Z	PHD	84	Ohio	1984
Varzandeh, Javad	Prof	880-5730		7	U	PHD	81	Oklah St	1987
Dyck, Harold	Assoc	880-5765		7	U	PHD	82	Purdue	1989
Farahbod, Kamvar	Assoc	880-5788		7	U	PHD	86	Okla St	2991
Karant, Yasha	Assoc	880-5372		9	Z	PHD	81	Berkeley	1989
Wilson, Robert	Assoc	880-5702		9	Z	PHD	77	Ca-River	1991
Abdol, John	Asst	880-5776		7	U	PHD	89	Tx-Arlin	1992
Bhatia, Anand	Asst	880-5724		7	V	DBA	75	S Calif	1972
Lin, Frank	Asst	880-5787		9	Z	PHD	92	SUNY-Buf	1992
Tegarden, David P.	Asst	880-5792	tegarden	9	Z	PHD	91	Colorado	1993
Pettit, Bryan L.	Lect	880-5727		9	Z	EDD	94	Pepperdi	1988
Shayo, Conrad	Lect	880-5723	cshayo	9	Z	PHD	94	Claremont	1994

—Dept of Public Adm
Phone

Name	Rank	Phone				Deg		School	Year
Bellis, David J.	D-Pr$	880-5759	pfyoung	1	A	PHD	77	S Calif	1985
Young, Clifford	C-Pr	880-5717		1	A	DPA	88	S Calif	1989
Christie, C. Charles Jr.	Prof	880-5760		1	A	PHD	74	S Calif	1972
Clarke, K. Michael	Prof	880-5759		1	A	PHD	75	Georgia	1976
Kress, Guenther G.	Prof	880-5762		1	A	PHD	72	Ca-Davis	1987
Watts, James Brian	Assoc	880-5752		1	A	PHD		Vanderbt	1989

Calif State U - San Marcos
San Marcos, CA 92096-0001 (619)
800 W. Los Vallecitos — 820 West Los Vallecitos — FAX= — BS

—Management Faculty
Phone

Name	Rank	Phone			Deg		School	Year
Diehr, George E.	Prof	752-4242	7	V	PHD	69	UCLA	1990
Hinton, Bernard L.	Prof	752-4043	2	E	PHD	66	Stanford	1989
Lou, Sheldon	Prof		7	U	PHD	85	MIT	1993
Montanari, John R.	Prof	752-4255	3	I	DBA	76	Colorado	1-91
Jessup, Leonard	Assoc		9	Z	PHD	89	Arizona	1990
on leave								
Watson, Kathleen	Assoc	752-4257	2	3	PHD	78	Utah	1-92
Eisenbach, Regina	Asst	752-4253	2	E	PHD	92	U Miami	9-91
Jankowski, David J.	Asst		9	Z	PHD	94	Arizona	1992
Jorjani, Soheila	Asst		7	U	PHD	88	Ca-Irvine	1-92
Leu, Yow-Yuk (Jack)	Asst		7	U	PHD	91	Va Tech	1991
Tan, J. Justin	Asst				PHD	93	Va Tech	9-94

Calif State U, Stanislaus — Turlock, CA 95380 — (209) — FAX=667-3333 — BS,MBA
School of Business Adm — 801 W Monte Vista Avenue
  Did Not Respond-1993 Listing
Chern Kari, H. Rao — Dean$ 667-3071 — PHD 72 N Carol 1970
—Dept of Management — Phone — Fax 667-3333

Name	Title	Phone			Degree		School	Date
Lundquist, Ronald W.	C-Pr	667-3019	2	HBK	PHD	72	Oregon	9-87
Chan, Marjorie	Assoc	667-3229	38	Y	PHD	81	UCLA	9-90
Brown, Randall B.	Asst	667-3064	25	E	PHD	90	Mass	1-89
Gnepa, Tahi J.	Asst	667-3766	85		PHD	89	Wiscon	9-90
Erhler, Richard	Inst				MS		CS-Stani	9-87
Miller, Edwar	Inst				PHD		Gold Gt	9-90

Calvin College — Grand Rapids, MI 49546 — (616) — FAX=957-8551 — BS,BA
Division of Social Sci — 3201 Burton Street SE
Roberts, Frank C. — Dean 957-6203 — PHD 73 Vanderbt 1965
—Dept of Economics & Bus — Phone — Fax 957-8551

Name	Title	Phone	Degree		School	Date
Roels, Shirley	C-Ac	957-6479	PHD	93	Mich St	1979
VandeGuchte, Peter	Prof	957-6094	EDD	73	W Mich	1991
Karppinen, Richard T.	Assoc	957-6492	ABD		Pitt	1987
Porter, Brian	Assoc	957-7191	PHD	94	Indiana	1994

Cameron University — Lawton, OK 73505-6377 — (405) — FAX= — BS
School of Business — 2800 W. Gore Blvd
McClung, Jacquetta J. — Dean 581-2267 — Mktg PHD Oklahoma 8 00
—Dept of Adm Sciences — Phone

Name	Title	Phone			Degree		School	Date
Amyx, Jack	Prof	581-2821			EDD		Okla St	
Stevens, C. Wanda	Assoc	581-2366	9	Z	PHD	87	Oklahoma	1981
Caporaletti, Louis	Asst	581-2371			ABD		Miss	
Chester, Jim		581-2368						

Campbell University — Buies Creek, NC 27506 — (910) — FAX=
Lundy-Fetterman Sch Bus
  Did Not Respond-1993 Listing; Phone 893-1380
Folwell, Thomas Harold Jr. — Dean Ext 1380 — MA Duke 1963
—Department of Management — Phone 893-1380 — Fax 893-1424

Canisius College — Buffalo, NY 14208-1098 — (716) CANISIUS — FAX=888-2525 — 1977,1982 BS,MBA
Wehle School of Bus — 2001 Main Street
Shick, Richard A. — Dean 888-2160 — shick — PHD 73 SUNY-Buf 1978
—Dept of Management & Mktg — Phone 888-2640 — Fax 888-3215

Name	Title	Phone	Email			Degree		School	Date
Snodgrass, Coral R.	C-Pr	888-2607	snodgras	38	YR	PHD	84	Pitt	1988
Vegso, Raymond W.	Prof	888-2643		34	LY	PHD	75	Cinn	1970
Weinstein, Alan G.	Prof	888-2644	agw	26	STE	PHD	69	Wayne St	1976
Farkash, Alexander	Assoc	888-2637		12	IH	PHD	77	Minn	1978
Gent, Michael J.	Assoc	888-2638	gent	25	EPQ	PHD	78	Tx Chr	1978
Glynn, Joseph	Assoc	888-2606	glynn	7	UV	PHD	77	Ohio St	1978
Fish, Lynn	Asst	888-2642	fishl	7	UV	PHD	93	SUNY-Buf	1993
Molloy, Stephen	Asst	888-2635		36	IH	PHD	90	Indiana	1990
Rosenfelder, Gerald	Asst	888-2609	rosenfel	34	IH	PHD	89	SUNY-Buf	1982
Shambu, Girish	Asst	888-2796	shambu	7	UV	PHD	93	SUNY-Buf	1989

—Dept of Mgt Info Sys — Phone 888-2215 — Fax 888-2525

Name	Title	Phone	Email			Degree		School	Date
Duchan, Alan I.	C-Ac	888-2217	duchan	9	Z	PHD	72	Wiscon	1973
Szewczak, Edward J.	Assoc	888-2239	szewczak	9	Z	PHD	88	SUNY-Buf	1988
Garrity, Edward J.	Asst	888-2267	garrity	9	Z	PHD	85	Pitt	1990
Volonino, Linda A.	Asst	888-2219	volonino	9	Z	PHD	88	SUNY-Buf	1987
Cain, Jean A.	Inst					BS		SUNY-Buf	

Capital University — Columbus, OH 43209 — (614) — FAX=
College of Arts & Sci — 2199 East Main Street
McGary, Daina — Dean 239-6204 — PHD Union Gr 1979
—Dept Business & Adm Econ — Phone 236-5552 — Fax 236-6540
Schwab, Richard D. — C-Pr 236-6132 — JD Ohio St 1956
  George H. Moor Professor of Business Administration & Economics
Nicastro, M. L. — Asst 236-6134 — PHD Ohio St 1989
Walsh, J. T. — Asst 236-6523 — MBA Ohio St 1987

Carnegie Mellon University — Pittsburgh, PA 15213-3890 — (412) ANDREW.CMU.EDU — FAX=268-6837 — 1982,1957 BS,MS,PHD
Grad School of Ind Adm
Sullivan, Robert S. — Dean 268-2265 — rss — 7 U PHD 76 Penn St 1991
—Management Faculty — Phone 268-2268 — Fax 268-6837

Name	Title	Phone	Email			Degree		School	Date
Baybars, Ilker	C-Pr	268-2271	ib01	7	U	PHD	79	Car Mel	1979
Balas, Egon	Prof	268-2285		7	V	PHD		Paris	1968
Cornuejols, Gerard P.	Prof	268-2284	cg0v	7	V	PHD	78	Cornell	1978
Goodman, Paul	Prof	268-2288		5	P	PHD	66	Cornell	1966

Hooker, John	Prof	268-7589		7	V	PHD		Vanderbt	1984
Kraut, Robert	Prof	268-7694		9	Z	PHD		Yale	1993
Kriebel, Charles H.	Prof	268-2287		79	VZ	PHD	64	MIT	1964
McKern, Bruce	Prof	268-7346		8	Y	PHD		Harvard	1993
Morton, Thomas	Prof	268-2306		7	U	PHD		Chicago	1969
Sirbu, Marvin A.	Prof	268-3436	sirbu	9	ZL	SCD	73	MIT	1985
Sunder, Shyam	Prof	268-2103		89	YZ	PHD	74	Car Mel	1988

Richard M. Cyert Professor of Management & Economics

Thorne, John R.	Prof	268-2263	thorne	6	T	MSIA	52	Car Mel	

David T. & Lindsay J. Morgenthaler Professor of Enterpreneurship

Williams, Jeffrey	Prof	268-3589		3	I	PHD		Michigan	1977
Fichman, Mark	Assoc	268-3699		2	E	PHD	82	Michigan	1980
Kekre, Sunder	Assoc	268-3586		7	U	PHD		Rochest	1984
Lerch, Javier	Assoc	268-5042		9	Z	PHD		Michigan	1986
Mukhopadyyay, Tridas	Assoc	268-2307		9	Z	PHD		Michigan	1986
Shaw, Kathryn	Assoc	268-7586		5	Q	PHD	81	Harvard	1981
Tayur, Sridhar	Assoc	268-3584		7	U	PHD		Cornell	1991
Trick, Michael	Assoc	268-3697		7	V	PHD		Ga Tech	1988
Flor, N.	Asst			9	Z	PHD		San Dgo	1994
Giridharan, P.	Asst	268-3683		9	Z	PHD		Rochest	1990
Ingram, Paul	Asst			2	EH	PHD		Cornell	1994
Rao, Uday	Asst			7	U	PHD		Cornell	1994
Straus, Susan	Asst	268-8839		52	E	PHD	92	Illinois	1991
Weingart, Laurie R.	Asst	268-7585		25	EQ	PHD	89	Northwes	1989
Shyam, Manjula	Lect	268-7055		8	Y	PHD	75	Pitt	1988
Young, Richard O.	Lect	268-7578		3	&	PHD	89	Car Mel	1985

Carroll College — Waukesha, WI 53186 — (414) CARROLL1.CC.EDU

College of Business	North Benton Avenue		FAX=				BS
Olsen, Gary L.	C-Ac	524-7171	golsen	Agt	PHD	Marquett	9-75
–Department of Management	Phone						
Inveiss, Uldis E.	Prof	782-4094			MBA	Wiscon	1963
Dwinell, Merlene							

Carson-Newman College — Jefferson Cy, TN 37760 — (615)

Division of Bus & Econ	1646 Russel Avenue		FAX=471-3317				BS
Russell, C. W. Jr.	C-Ac	471-3441		45	KNPQ	JD	Tenn	1991
–Department of Management	Phone	471-3316	Fax 471-3502				
Clark, Donald W.	Assoc	471-3417		73	DIVX	MBA	Memphis	1981
Coppock, James Allen	Assoc	471-3418		23	EFNP	MS	Tenn	1962

Carthage College — Kenosha, WI 53140 — (414) CNS.CARTHAGE.EDU

Dept of Mgt & Bus Adm	2001 Alford Drive		FAX=				BA
Custin, Richard E.	C	551-5848	rc	49	JD	84	Drake	9-90
–Management Faculty	Phone		Fax 551-6208				
Dittus, Robert	Prof	551-6200			MBA	Northwes	1989
Jankovich, William S.	Prof	551-5832		8	MBA	Marquett	1977
Johnson, Donald	Prof	551-5882		72	MBA	Mich St	1970
Brunn, David	Asst	551-591			MBA	Northwes	1993
Dawson, Julie	Asst	551-5967			MA	Wiscon	1993
Gottschalk, Donald	Asst	551-5836		5	BS	Marquett	1990
Grant, Robert	Asst	551-5716			MBA	Marquett	1990

Case Western Reserve Univ — Cleveland, OH 44106 — (216) PO.CWRU.EDU 1979,1958

Weatherhead Sch of Mgt	10900 Euclid Avenue		FAX=368-4776			BS,MBA,MA,PHD		
Cowen, Scott S.	Dean	368-2046			Atg	DBA	75	Geo Wash	9-76
–Dept of Org Behavior	Phone	368-2055	Fax 368-4785					
Neilsen, Eric H.	C-Pr	368-2055		2	E	PHD	70	Harvard	1974
Boyatzis, Richard E.	Prof	368-2053		2	E	PHD		Harvard	
Kolb, David A.	Prof	368-2050		2	E	PHD		Harvard	
Pasmore, William A.	Prof	368-2138		2	E	PHD		Purdue	
Srivastva, Suresh	Prof	368-2055		2	E	PHD	60	Michigan	1970
Wolfe, Donald M.	Prof	368-2068		2	E	PHD	60	Michigan	1963
Cooperrider, David L.	Assoc	368-2121		2	E	PHD		Case Wes	
Fry, Ronald	Assoc	368-2060		2	E	PHD		MIT	
Berlinger, Lisa	Asst	368-6135		2	E	PHD	90	Texas	1-91
Bilimoria, Diana	Asst	368-2115		2	E	PHD	90	Michigan	1989
Case, Susan S.	Asst	368-5018		2	E	PHD		SUNY-Buf	1989
–Dept Mktg & Policy Studies	Phone	368-5239	Fax 368-4785					
Salipante, Paul F. Jr.	C-Pr	368-2077		5	QNY	PHD	75	Chicago	1975
on sabbatical Spring 1995								
Alfred, Theodore	Prof	368-2033		3	I	PHD	63	MIT	
Aram, John D.	Prof					PHD	68	MIT	
Hisrich, Robert D.	Prof	368-5354				PHD	71	Cinn	
Chatterjee, Sayan	Assoc	368-5373				DBA		Michigan	
Cort, Stanton G.	Assoc	368-2064		86	YI	DBA	72	Harvard	

Feldman, Steven P.	Assoc	368-5102		3		PHD	Penn	
Gerhart, Paul F.	Assoc	368-2045	pf62	51	QN	PHD	Chicago	1977
Lynn, Leonard H.	Assoc	368-6048		8	Y	PHD	Michigan	
Ramanujam, Vasudevan	Assoc	368-5100		3	I	PHD	Pitt	
Reddy, Mohan	Assoc	368-2038		4	L	PHD	Case Wes	
Andrews, Jonlee	Asst	368-5971						
Freeman, Everette	Asst	368-2154		5		EDD	83 Rutgers	1992
Sirdeshmulch, Deepak	Asst	368-2117				PHD	Ohio St	1994
Teplensky, Jill D.	Asst	368-5005		3	ICD	PHD	90 Penn	1991
–Dept of Mgt Info Systems	Phone	368-2144	Fax 368-4776					
Ginzberg, Michael J.	C-Pr	368-5353		9	Z	PHD	75 MIT	9-85
email: ginzberg@pyrite.som.cwru.edu								
Boland, Richard	Prof	368-6022				PHD	76 Case Wes	1990
email: boland@spider.cwru.edu								
Mason, Robert H.	Prof	368-4777				PHD	73 Ga Tech	9-87
email rmm3@pyrite.som.cwr.edu								
Kennedy, Miles H.	Assoc	368-2094				PHD	71 London	7-69
email: kennedy@ccmail.som.cwru.edu								
Collopy, Fred	Asst	368-2048	flc2			PHD	90 Penn	7-90
Te'eni, Dov	Asst	368-3914				PHD	86 Tel Aviv	7-86
email: teenid@pyrite.som.cwru.edu								
Vandenbosch, Betty	Asst	386-2120				PHD	93 W Ontar	7-93
email bmv@pyrite.som.cwru.edu								
–Dept Operations Research	Phone		Fax 368-4776					
Emmons, Hamilton	C-Pr	368-3841				PHD	68 J Hopkin	
Ballou, Ronald H.	Prof	368-3808				PHD	65 Ohio St	1060
Reisman, Arnold	Prof	368-3854				PHD	03 UCLA	
Ritchken, Peter	Prof	368-3849				PHD	81 Case Wes	
Salkin, Harvey	Prof	368-3859				PHD	69 Renssela	1969
Flowers, A. Dale	Assoc	368-3825				DBA	72 Indiana	
Mathur, Kamlesh	Assoc	368-3857				PHD	80 Case Wes	
Solow, Daniel	Assoc	368-3837				PHD	78 Stanford	
Burnetas, Apostolos N.	Asst	386-4778				PHD	93 Rutgers	1994
Gilbert, Stephen	Asst	368-3811				PHD	91 MIT	1991
Love, Thomas E.	Asst	368-4797				PHD	94 Penn	1994
Nambimadom, Ramakrishnan	Asst	368-5215				PHD	94 Rochest	1993

Catawba College   Salisbury, NC   28144-2488   (704)

Ketner School of Bus		2300 West Innes Street		FAX=637-4304				BA
–Management Faculty	Phone	637-4405	Fax 637-4422					
Carter, J. Alvin	C	637-4406				MBA	Geo St	
Hiatt, Stephen R.	Prof	637-4103		15		PHD	83 Ariz St	1987
Tsengg, S. C.	Prof	637-4407				PHD	Oklahoma	
Oldenburg, Erik	Assoc	637-4104				PHD	Etudes	
Trenchard, Wm. H.	Assoc	637-4483				MS	Va Comm	
Baker, Ben	Asst	637-4488				MA	S Carol	1992
Moscoso, Pedro F.	Asst	637-4105		15	NPS	MS	68 N Carol	1984
Thompson, Pamela L.	Asst	637-4323				MBA	Jms Mad	

Catholic University   Washington, DC   20064   (202)

Dept of Econ & Business		620 Michigan Avenue NE		FAX=				BA,MA,PHD
Zampelli, Ernest M.	C-Ac	319-5236		Econ		PHD		
–Management Faculty	Phone	319-5236	Fax 319-4456					
Karake, Zeinab	Assoc	319-5236		FHIT		PHD		1989

Cedarville College   Cedarville, OH   45314-0601   (513)   CEDARVILLE.EDU

Business Adm Department		251 North Main Street		FAX=766-2760				BA
Johnson, Sharon G.	C-Ac	766-7922	johns	3	I	DBA	78 Fla St	1993
–Management Faculty	Phone	766-7910	Fax 766-2760					
Baldwin, Richard	Prof	766-7915	baldwinr	48	YKL	PHD	87 Ohio St	1975
Fawcett, Clifford	Prof	766-7916	fawcett	23	EIU	DBA	76 Geo Wash	1983
Walker, Ronald J.	Prof	766-7911	walkerr	7	V	DBA	86 Kent St	1978
Hoffmann, Walter	Asst	766-7925		65	QN	MBA	73 SUNY	1990

Centenary College   Hackettstown, NJ   07840-9989   (908)

Business		400 Jefferson Street		FAX=				
Quade, Robert	C-Ac			Mktg		MBA	Iowa	8-86
–Management Faculty	Phone							
Dungam, Heather	Assoc					MBA	Rutgers	1-84
Lewthwaite, Barbara Jayne	Assoc			25	EPR	MBA	St Johns	8-87
Nicholls, Grant	Inst			46	KSTY	BS	LebanonV	1-92

Univ of Central Arkansas — Conway, AR 72032 — (501) FAX=327-9938 — 1984,1990 BBA,MBA
College of Business Adm — Donaghey Street
-Dept of Management & Mktg — Phone — Fax 450-5302

Name	Rank	Phone						
Lorenzi, Peter	Dean	450-3106	23	EFI	PHD	78	Penn St	6-92
Bounds, William T. Jr.	C	450-3149	37	IJN	PHD	86	Miss	8-75
Grider, Douglas T. Jr.	Assoc	450-3149	25	EFI	PHD	72	Geo St	8-90
Moore, Herff L. Jr.	Assoc	450-3149	25	ENP	PHD	80	Tx-Arlin	8-85
Griffin, Kenneth M.	Prof		9	Z	DBA		La Tech	
Bailey, Therold	Prof		9	Z	EDD		Okla St	
Malley, John Corbin	Assoc		9	Z	DBA		Fla St	
Painter, Sidney G.	Inst		9	Z	BBA		Arkansas	

Central Connecticut St Univ — New Britain, CT 06050 — (203) FAX=832-2522 — BS
School of Business — 1615 Stanley Street
-Dept of Management & Org — Phone

Name	Rank	Phone						
Short, Larry E.	Dean	short		Mgt	DBA	71	Colorado	
Dethy, Ray	C-Pr	832-3277	dethyr	13	AI	PHD	63	Ohio St	1973
Baughman, Rowland	Prof	832-3284	baughman	25	DENQ	DBA	75	Geo Wash	1983
Fearon, David S.	Prof	832-3280	fearon	12	DPEH	PHD	73	Conn	1986
Cavaleri, Steven	Assoc	832-3283	cavaleri	23	HUPZ	PHD	88	Renssel	1980
Ferguson, William	Assoc	832-3276	ferguson	38	ISY	DPS	87	Pace	1980
Baten, Eugene	Asst	832-3246	baten	24	BFLP	DED	91	Harvard	1988

International Business Department

Name	Rank	Phone						
Lee, Wonsick	Asst							1994
Logozzo, Richard	Asst	832-3281	logozzo	25	EHN	PHD	89	Mass	1989
Miller, Daniel J.	Asst	832-3286	miller	23	ABFH	PHD	94	Texas	1991
Mitchell, Margaret	Asst	832-3287	mitchellme			PHD	85	Penn	1993

Univ of Central Florida — Orlando, FL 32816-0991 — (407) UCF1VM FAX=823-5741 — 1975,1979 BA,MBA
College of Business Adm — 4000 Central Florida Blvd
-Department of Management — Phone

Name	Rank	Phone						
Huseman, Richard C.	Dean	823-2181	12	&	PHD	65	Illinois	7-90
Lewis, Pamela	C-Ac	823-5685	38	ITY	PHD	88	Tenn	1986
Hatfield John	Prof	823-5053	12	E	PHD	76	Purdue	1990
Associate Dean								
Jones, Halsey R. Jr.	Prof	823-2925	21	EF	PHD		Penn St	1982
Bogumil, Walter A.	Assoc	823-5708	5	NQ	PHD	72	Georgia	1972
Callarman, William G.	Assoc	823-2447	32	EFI	PHD	72	Ariz St	1972
Fernald, Lloyd W.	Assoc	823-5725	25	DEF	DBA	81	Geo Wash	1983
Goodman, Stephen	Assoc	823-2675	7	UWV	PHD	72	Penn St	1984
Harrison, Jeffrey S.	Assoc	823-2916	3	I	PHD	85	Utah	1993
Leigh, William E.	Assoc	823-2923	97	Z	PHD	84	Cinn	1987
Martin, Raymond L.	Assoc	823-2685	7	U	PHD	68	American	1971
Rosenkrantz, Stuart A.	Assoc	823-5683	12	EH	PHD	84	Nebraska	1984
Jones, Foard	Asst	823-5101	23	EFHI	PHD	90	Georgia	1991
Purvis, Russel	Asst	823-5684	9	Z	PHD	94	Fla St	1994
Abramowitz, Benjamin	Inst	823-2924	41		MBA	71	Geo Wash	1983
Burnette, Charles	Inst	823-5682	12		MBA	77	NW Mo St	1977
Pullin, James	Inst	823-5673	7		MBA	77	NW Mo St	1987

Central Michigan University — Mt. Pleasant, MI 48859 — (517) FAX=774-2372 — 1983 1989 BS
College of Business Adm
-Department of Management — Phone 774-3450 — Fax 774-2372

Name	Rank	Phone						
Arndt, Terry L.	Dean	774-3337		Atg	PHD	73	Arkansas	1993
Sprague, David	C-Pr	774-5091	7	U	PHD	75	Iowa	1990
Arben, Philip D.	Prof	774-3363	13		PHD	60	Harvard	1980
Bandyopadhyay, Jayanta	Prof	774-3085	7	U	PHD	73	Tx Tech	1979
Bishop, Ronald C.	Prof	774-7419	25	REP	PHD	69	S Illin	1986
Croll, Robert F.	Prof	774-3907	7	U	DBA	69	Indiana	1970
Jenicke, Lawrence	Prof	774-6965	7	U	PHD	67	Mich St	1977
Love, Kevin G.	Prof	774-3431	25	EFNP	PHD	79	S Fla	1979
Moursi, Mahmoud A.	Prof	774-3667	3	I	PHD	70	NYU	1970
Palaniswami, Shanthakumar	Prof	774-3379	7	UV	PHD	85	IIT	1984
Prasad, S. B.	Prof	774-3927	38	IY	PHD	63	Wiscon	1981
Shahabuddin, Syed	Prof	774-3008	7	U	PHD	76	Missouri	1980
Bahaee, S. Mahmood	Assoc	774-3747	3	STI	PHD	87	Ariz St	1985
Beaulieu, Ronald P.	Assoc	774-3409	25	EFP	DBA	76	Indiana	1979
Knowlton, Stuart L.	Assoc	774-3732	35		PHD	50	MIT	1980
Lichtman, Robert Jay	Assoc	774-7811	25	EN	PHD	77	LSU	1983
Smith, Susan Kay	Assoc	774-6525	15	NQ	PHD	86	Mich St	1981
Utecht, Kathleen	Assoc	774-3394	12	EN	PHD	85	Mich St	1980
Theeke, Herman	Asst	774-3844	15	Q	PHD	86	Minn	1989

Central Missouri State Univ | Warrensburg, MO | 64093-5071 | (816)
College of Bus & Econ | East South Street | | FAX=543-4026 | | | | BSBA,MBA
Shaffer, Paul | Dean | 543-4560 | | 35 | Mgt | PHD | 74 | Oklahoma | 1986
—Department of Management | Phone | 543-4026 | Fax 543-8885
Stephens, Ron | C-Pr | 543-4247 | | 51 | NR | EDD | 76 | Missouri | 1972
Nelson, Wayne | Prof | 543-8598 | | 15 | YD | PHD | 78 | Arkansas | 1984
Mullin, Ralph F. | Assoc | 543-4818 | | 3 | HJ | PHD | 87 | Florida | 1986
Sherman, Rodney | Assoc | 543-8604 | | 56 | LE | PHD | 72 | Geo St | 1986
Lummus, Rhonda | Asst | 543-8595 | | 7 | UW | PHD | 92 | Iowa | 1992
Poole, Rob | Asst | 543-8600 | | 7 | UVW | ABD | | Texas | 1993
Popejoy, Steven | Asst | 543-8603 | | 5 | KQ | ABD | | Iowa | 1993
Vazzana, Gary | Asst | 543-8569 | | 3 | LZ | PHD | 87 | Missouri | 1990
Edwards, Sandra | Inst | 543-8575 | | 1 | | MBA | 88 | Cen Mo | 1991

Univ of Central Oklahoma | Edmond, OK | 73034-0115 | (405)
College of Business Adm | 100 North University Drive | | FAX=341-4964 | | | | BS,MBA,BBA
Wert, Frank S. | Dean | 341-2980 | | | Econ | PHD | 72 | Colo St | 8-72
—Department of Management | Phone | | Fax 341-4964
Fortenberry, Ed | C | 341-2980 | | | | EDD | 70 | Oklahoma | 8-62
Allen, Doug | Prof | 341-2980 | | | | PHD | 80 | Okla St | 1975
Brewster, Jim | Prof | 341-2980 | | | | EDD | 72 | Geo Wash | 1982
Samaras, John | Prof | 341-2980 | | | | PHD | 82 | Oklahoma | 1975
Jennings, Sandra | Assoc | 341-2980 | | | | PHD | 84 | Oklahoma | 1988
Bergman, Tom | Asst | 341-2980 | | | | PHD | 93 | Oklahoma | 1989
Blythe, Steve | Asst | 341-2980 | | | | PHD | 70 | Arkansas | 1992
Rickman, Charles | Asst | 341-2980 | | | | PHD | 90 | Oklahoma | 1989
Farr, Blair | Inst | 341-2980 | | | | ABD | 93 | North Tx | 1993

Central State Univ-Ohio | Wilberforce, OH | 45384 | (513)
College of Business | | | FAX=376-6652 | | | | BSBA
Showell, Charles H. Jr. | Dean | 376-6441 | | | BAdm | PHD | | Ohio St | 9-88
—Department of Business Adm | Phone | | Fax 376-6652
Davison, Edwin | Asst | 376-6436 | | 46 | KLST | JD | | Wiscon | 4-86
Ghauvmi, Firooz | Asst | 376-6615 | | 7 | UV | MBA | | Dayton | 9-83
Harvey, Santhi | Asst | 376-6152 | | 12 | Z | MBA | | WrightSt | 9-89

Central Washington Univ | Ellensburg, WA | 98926 | (509) CWU.EDU
School of Bus & Econ | | | FAX=963-3042
* Faculty located in Seattle (206)
Dauwalder, David P. | Dean | 963-1955 | dauwalde | | | PHD | 83 | Ariz St | 1993
—Department of Business Adm | Phone | 963-3339 | Fax 963-3042
Esbeck, Edward S. | * Prof | 640-1569 | | | | PHD | 72 | Case Wes | 1978
Gulezian, Allen K. | Prof | 963-3560 | | | | PHD | 71 | Oregon | 1973
Mueller, Leslie C. | Prof | 963-2032 | | | | DBA | 78 | S Calif | 1979
Nimnicht, James L. | Prof | 963-2455 | | | | PHD | 90 | Nebraska | 1988
Nixon, Don R. | * Prof | 764-5573 | | | | PHD | 82 | Geo St | 1986
Parson, Gary I. | Asst | 963-1458 | | | | ABD | 69 | Wiscon | 1975
Silvers, Robert C. | * Asst | 640-1311 | | | | PHD | 92 | Stanford | 1993

Chaminade University | Honolulu, HI | 96816-1578 | (808)
School of Business | | | FAX=735-4734 | | | | BA,MBA,BBA,MSJB
Murray, Peter W. | Dean | 735-4744 | | 13 | | MBA | | Penn | 1966
—Management Faculty | Phone | 735-4744 | Fax 735-4734
Hutter, Dean | H | 735-4744 | | 13 | BDKQ | PHD | | Bath Eng | 1979
Murray, William | Prof | 735-4744 | | 13 | | EDD | | S Calif | 1982
Steelquist, John A. | Prof | 735-4744 | | 13 | | PHD | | Tx A&M | 1984

Chapman University | Orange, CA | 92666-1032 | (714) NEXUS.CHAPMAN.EDU
School of Bus & Econ | 333 North Glassell Street | | FAX=532-6081 | | | | BS,BA,MBA
McDowell, Richard L. | Dean | 997-6684 | mcdowell | | Adm | PHD | 74 | Tufts | 1991
—Management Faculty | Phone | 997-6684 | Fax 532-6081
Shukla, Pradip K. | Assoc | 997-6817 | shukla | | IEY | PHD | | UCLA | 1985
Turk, Thomas | Assoc | 997-6664 | turk | | IN | PHD | | Ca-Irvine | 1992
Slocomb, Thomas | Asst | 997-6705 | slocomb | | EFT | PHD | | Missouri | 1991
Sterling, Charles | Asst | 997-7094 | sterling | | NPO | PHD | | Ohio St | 1992

College of Charleston | Charleston, SC | 29424 | (803) | | | | 1988
Sch of Bus Adm & Econ | 66 George Street | | FAX=
Rudd, Howard F. | Dean | 953-8110 | | | | PHD | 73 | Tx Tech | 1984
—Dept of Management & Mktg | Phone | 953-7835 | Fax 953-5697
Mack, Rhonda | C-Pr | 953-8037 | | | | PHD | 83 | Georgia | 1994
Anderson, Robert L. | Prof | 953-8108 | | | | PHD | | Texas | 1979
Nelson, Paul T. | Prof | 953-8037 | | | | PHD | 70 | Mich St | 1970
Snyder, James F. | Prof | 953-8192 | | | | PHD | 70 | Georgia | 1975

Name	Rank	Phone			Degree		School	Year
Aziz, Abdul	Assoc	953-8109			PHD		Delhi	1983
Benich, Joseph J.	Assoc	953-8193			DBA		Kent St	1972
Hartley, Mark F.	Asst	953-5955			DBA		La Tech	1985
Hawkes, James S.	Asst	953-8102			PHD		Clemson	1977
Bohn, Gerhard	Exec	953-5953						1990
Neilsen, Eric H.	Exec	953-5953						1989

Cheyney University — Cheyney, PA 19319 (215) FAX=
Business Adm Department
Did Not Respond-1993 Listing

Name	Rank	Phone	Codes	Field	Degree		School	Year
Williams, Edward E.	C-Pr	399-2368		Mgt	PHD		Drexel	1972
—Management Faculty	Phone							
Shelton, Deanna	Asst	399-2205	12 E	MPA		68	American	1977

University of Chicago — Chicago, IL 60637-1561 (312) GSBACD.UCHICAGO.EDU 1916
Graduate School of Bus — 1101 East 58th Street — FAX=702-0458 — MS,PHD

Name	Rank	Phone	Email	Codes	Field	Degree	Yr	School	Year
Hamada, Robert S.	Dean	702-1680			Fnce	PHD	69	MIT	1966

Edward Eagle Brown Distinguished Service Professor of Finance
—Management Faculty — Phone 702-7743 Fax 702-0458

Name	Rank	Phone	Email	Codes		Degree	Yr	School	Year
Aliber, Robert Z.	Prof	702-7401				PHD	62	Yale	1965

Director, Center for Studies in International Finance

Ashenhurst, Robert L.	Prof	702-7454				PHD	56	Harvard	1957
Becker, Selwyn W.	Prof	702-7301		2	EH	PHD	58	Penn St	1959
Bradburn, Norman M.	Prof	702-1066				PHD	60	Harvard	1960

Tiffany & Margaret Blake Distinguished Service Professor of Beh Science

Camerer, Colin F.	Prof	702-3675		37	IUVY	PHD	81	Chicago	7-85

on leave to Calif Inst of Tech 1994-95

Davis, Harry L.	Prof	702-9637				PHD	70	Northwes	1963

Roger L. & Rachel M. Goetz Professor of Creative Management

Eppen, Gary D.	Prof	702-3272		78	UVY	PHD	64	Cornell	1964

Robert Law Professor of Industrial Adm; email: gary.eppen@gsbv

Fogel, Robert W.	Prof	702-7709		4	JL	PHD	63	JHopkins	1963

Charles R. Walgreen Professor of American Institutions

Graves, Robert L.	Prof	702-9316	rlgg@uchicag	7	UV	PHD	52	Harvard	1958
Hogarth, Robin M.	Prof	702-7271	fac_horarth	2	E	PHD	72	Chicago	1979

Wallace W. Booth Professor of Behavior Sci; Deputy Dean for MBA Programs

Huizinga, John	Prof	702-7272				PHD	80	MIT	1980

Deputy Dean for the Faculty

Klayman, Joshua	Prof	702-7273				PHD	82	Minn	1980
Madansky, Albert	Prof	702-7288		7	V	PHD	58	Chicago	1974
Martin, R. Kipp	Prof	702-7456		37	IV	PHD	80	Cinn	1980
Murphy, Kevin M.	Prof	702-7280		37	IV	PHD	86	Chicago	1976
Mussa, Michael	Prof					PHD	74	Chicago	1976

William H. Abbott Professor of International Business; on leave

Schrage, Linus E.	Prof	702-7449	fac_schrage	79	UVZ	PHD	66	Cornell	1967
Topel, Robert H.	Prof	702-7524				PHD	80	UCLA	1983

Isidore Brown & Gladys J. Brown Professor of Urban & Labor Economics

Zangwill, Williard I.	Prof	702-7289		7	V	PHD	65	Stanford	1978
Zonis, Marvin	Prof	702-8753		38	IJY	PHD	68	MIT	1989

email: marvin.zonis@gsb

Baker, Wayne E.	Assoc	702-6403		23	HDIL	PHD	81	Northwes	1987
Gertner, Robert	Assoc	702-7203				PHD	86	MIT	1986
Griffin, Abbie	Assoc	702-3657	fac_ajg	71	U	PHD	89	MIT	1989
Iyer, Ananth V.	Assoc	702-4514	fac_al	7	UV	PHD	87	Ga Tech	1987
Kashyap, Anil	Assoc	702-7260	miakk00	8	Y	PHD	89	MIT	1991
Lalonde, Robert J.	Assoc	702-3429	lalonde	5	QP	PHD	85	Princeton	1985
Mannix, Elizabeth A.	Assoc	702-4508	fac_mannix	2	E	PHD	89	Chicago	1989
Weber, Elke U.	Assoc	702-0459	fac_eweber			PHD	84	Harvard	1988
Eisenstein, Donald D.	Asst	702-2576		7	UW	PHD	92	Ga Tech	1992
Heath, F. R. (Chip)	Asst	702-9677		2	EHN	PHD	90	Stanford	1990
Helsen, Kristiaan	Asst	702-7292				PHD	90	Penn	1990
Hsee, Christopher K.	Asst	702-7728				PHD	93	Yale	1993
Irwin, Douglas A.	Asst	702-6348		8	Y	PHD	88	Columbia	1991
Kenz, Marc	Asst	702-9297				PHD	92	Penn	1991
Kroszner, Randall S.	Asst	702-8779				PHD	90	Harvard	1990
Larrick, Richard P.	Asst	702-3549	rick.larrick	2	E	PHD	91	Michigan	1993
Mondino, Guillermo	Asst	702-9478				PHD	91	Yale	1991
Prendergast, Canice	Asst	702-9159				PHD	89	Yale	1990
Rodriguez, Andres	Asst	702-8867				ABD	94	Stanford	1994
White, Sally Blount	Asst	702-4438				PHD	92	Northwes	1992
Barbeau, J. Bradley	SLect	702-7560	brad.barbeau	23	FHPI	PHD	87	Michigan	
Bateman, George	SLect	702-7174				MBA	67	Chicago	
Ginzel, Linda	SLect	702-7889	fac_ginzel	2	E	PHD	89	Princeton	1992
Kleinman, David C.	SLect	702-7458		3	I	PHD	77	Chicago	1971
Schrager, James E.	SLect	702-1045				PHD	93	Chicago	

Chicago State University	Chicago, IL	60628-1598	(312)					
College of Bus & Adm	9501 S. King Drive		FAX=					BS
Roper, Barbara E.	Dean$ 995-3976			Atg	MST	82	DePaul	1988
—Dept Mgt, Mktg & Info Sys	Phone 995-3978	Fax 995-2269						
Sanders, Eddie Jr.	C-Ac 995-3978		5	N	PHD		Cal Coas	1973
Kpo, Wolanyo	Prof 995-3978		5	N	PHD		Ill Tech	1985
Bibb, Stephanie	Assoc 995-3978							
Freeman, Eldridge T. Jr.	Assoc 995-3978				PHD		Cal Coas	1973
Orange, Warren	Assoc 995-3978							
Alwan, Suad	Asst 995-3978		9	Z	DBA		Miss St	1988
Boundaoui, Necar	Asst 995-4525		9		PHD		IL Tech	1992
Collier, Millicient	Asst 995-3978		52	E	MS			
Harris, George	Asst 993-3978				MBA		Roosevlt	1986
Kim, Jin	Asst 995-3978				MBA		Fordham	1989
Mousa, Haidar	995-3857		9		PHD		Ill Tech	1992

Christian Brothers Univ	Memphis, TN	38104-5581	(901)					
School of Business	650 East Parkway South		FAX=					BS,MBA
House, Ray S.	Dean 722-0316			Mktg	PHD	66	Miss	1985
—Dept of Management & Mktg	Phone	Fax 722-0494						
Doddridge, Benjamin	C-Ac				MBA		Mich St	
Megley, John E.	Prof				PHD	70	Memphis	
Marion, Frank M.	Assoc				DBA		Memphis	
Peyton, Reginald	Assoc				DBA	91	Memphis	
Rhodes, James T.	Assoc				MBA		Memphis	

Christopher Newport Univ	Newport News VA	23606-2988	(804) POWHATAN.CC.CNU.EDU					
College of Bus & Econ	50 Shoe Lane		FAX=					BS
McCallister, Linda	Dean 594-7184	mccall	28	EOPY	PHD	81	Purdue	1993
—Dept of Management & Mktg	Phone	Fax 594-7808						
McCubbin, Kathryn O.	C-As 594-7215	mccubbin			MS	60	Marquett	1983
Anderson, John E. Jr.	Prof				PHD		Ohio St	1963
Coker, Robert C.	Prof				PHD		Illinois	1977
Boyd, Edwin C.	Assoc				MBA		Penn	1972
Hunter, Richard L.	Assoc				MBA		New York	1982
Mathews, Mayes D.	Assoc 594-7215				PHD	89	Va Comm	1991
Mills, Lawrence L.	Asst				MBA		Ohio St	1984
Spiller, Lisa D.	Asst				PHD	90	Missouri	1991

University of Cincinnati	Cincinnati, OH	45221-0211	(513)					1919,1966
College of Business Adm			FAX=556-4891					BA,MBA,MAT,PHD
—Department of Management	Phone 556-7120	Fax 556-4891						
Angle, Harold L.	H-Pr 556-7120							
Gore, George J.	Prof 556-7120		3	I	PHD	61	Michigan	1959
Graen, George B.	Prof 556-7120		2	F	PHD	76	U Wash	
Barton, Sidney L.	Assoc 556-7120		3	I	PHD	85	Indiana	
Boyer, Caroline K.	Assoc 556-7120		2	F	PHD	66	Case Wes	1968
Dean, James W.	Assoc 556-7118							
Gales, Lawrence M.	Assoc 556-7120		2	E	PHD	87	N Carol	
Katerberg, Ralph Jr.	Assoc 556-7002		2	H	PHD	78	Illinois	
Associate Dean								
Welsh, M. Ann	Assoc 556-7120		2	F	PHD	82	Missouri	
Kamath, Rajan R.	Asst 556-7120							
Matthews, Charles H.	Asst 556-7120							
Zirger, B. J.	Asst 556-7148							
Vidal, Robert	Adj 556-7154							
Horwitz, Lawrence H.	Adj 556-7120							
Lawrence, Clark	Adj 556-7120							

The Citadel	Charleston, SC	29409-0215	(803) CITADEL.EDU					
Dept of Business Adm			FAX=953-7084					BBA,MBA
Did Not Respond-1993 Listing								
Bebensee, Mark A.	H-Ac 953-5056				PHD	77	Duke	8-77
—Management Faculty	Phone 953-5056	Fax 953-7084						
Moore, Dorothy Perrin	Prof 953-5056	moored	25	ENR	PHD	81	S Carol	
Pokryfka, Richard T.	Prof 953-5153		79	VZ	PHD		Pitt	
Simmons, Susan A.	Prof 953-5165		7	UVX	PHD	76	Miss	
Vozikis, George S.	Prof 953-7089		38	IET	PHD		Georgia	
Zigli, Ron M.	Prof 953-6945		39	YZ	PHD		Geo St	
Alford, J. Michael	Assoc 953-5170		36	IT	PHD		Georgia	
Craig, Jerry W.	Assoc 953-6946		4	K	JD		NC Cen	
Sharbrough, William C.	Assoc 953-5164		52	E&	PHD		LSU	
Strauch, A. Bruce	Assoc 953-6957		4	KJ	JD		N Carol	
Moody, Janette W.	Asst 953-6947		9	Z	ABD		S Fla	

CUNY-Baruch College

CUNY-Baruch College	New York, NY 10010	(212) CUNYVM					1933,1981
Sch of Bus & Public Adm	17 Lexington Avenue	FAX=447-3364					BS,MBA,PHD
Connelly, Francis J.	Dean 447-3280	7	V	DBA	72	Indiana	1972
–Department of Management	Phone 447-3550 Fax 447-3574						
Dannenbring, David G.	C-Pr 447-3280	7	U	PHD		Columbia	1973
Chanin, Michael N.	Prof 447-3571	3	I	PHD		CUNY	1980
Kopelman, Richard E.	Prof 447-3565	1	A	PHD	74	Harvard	1974
Korman, Abraham K.	Prof 447-3573	2	Psy	PHD		Minn	1962
Kraut, A.	Prof 447-3557	5	N	PHD		Michigan	1965
Lirtzman, S.	Prof 447-3581	2	E	PHD		Columbia	1973
Loomba, Narendra P.	Prof 447-3559	1	B	PHD	59	Wiscon	1968
Puryear, A.	Prof 447-3562	7	V	PHD		Columbia	1970
Rosen, Henry M.	Prof 447-3408	1	C	PHD		Cornell	1973
Savas, E. S.	Prof 447-3550	1	A	PHD		Columbia	1960
Sethi, S. Prakash	Prof 447-3395	8	Z	PHD		Columbia	1968
Shapiro, Harris J.	Prof 447-3395	1	A	PHD	73	CUNY	1973
Sphicas, Georghios P.	Prof 447-3562	7	X	PHD	73	Columbia	1973
Vredenburgh, Donald	Prof 447-3325	2	E	PHD		SUNY-Buf	
Chien, William	Assoc 447-3580	7	U	PHD		Purude	1987
Das, T. K.	Assoc 447-3575	3	I	PHD		UCLA	1984
Hsu, L. F.	Assoc 447-3573	7	U	PHD		Case Wes	1987
Rothstein, H.	Assoc 447-3576	5	P	PHD		Maryland	1980
Schneller, G.	Assoc 447-3558	1	B	PHD		Lehigh	1977
Stern, Louis W.	Assoc 447-3560	9	Z	PHD	70	Lehigh	1970
Bamundo, P.	Asst 447-3568	1	I	PHD		CUNY	
Banai, Moshe	Asst 447-3555	5	Q	PHD		London	1985
Job, Tony	Asst 447-3566	3	IS	PHD		Claremont	1993
Kabaliswaran, M.	Asst 447-3565	2	H	PHD		NYU	1991
McCutchen, William Jr.	Asst 447-3567	1	A	PHD		Indiana	1988
Mohan, R.	Asst 447-3564	7	U	PHD		Ohio St	1991
Mulkowsky, G.	Asst 447-3561	1	A	PHD		NYU	1977
Rogoff, Edward	Asst 447-3566	6	ST	PHD		Columbia	1993
Son, Y. K.	Asst 447-3561	1	B	PHD		Auburn	1987
Thompson, Cynthia A.	Asst 447-3581	5	N	PHD		Tenn	1985
Veral, E.	Asst 447-3576	1	B	PHD		Clemson	1986
Booke, A.	Inst 447-3557	3		MBA		CUNY	
Holsinger, Alden	Inst 447-3565	4	Y	MS		Lehigh	
Kalman, Elias	Inst 447-3564	1	B	MBA	62	Baruch	1965

CUNY-Brooklyn College

CUNY-Brooklyn College	Brooklyn, NY 11210	(718)					
Department of Economics	Bedford Ave at Avenue H	FAX=951-6885					BS,MA
–Management Faculty	Phone 951-4867 Fax 951-6885						
Zelcer, Moishe	C-Ac 780-5658		Atg	PHD	91	Baruch	2-77
Bell, Robert	Prof 780-5686	13	A	PHD			1986
Friedman, Hershey H.	Prof 780-5119	14	L	PHD			1986
Mobilia, Pam	Asst 780-5569	5	P	PHD			1991

CUNY-Hunter College

CUNY-Hunter College	New York, NY 10021	(212)				
Div of Social Science	695 Park Avenue	FAX=				BS
Only Offers One Management Course						
Lees, Susan	Dean$ 772-5400		PHD		Michigan	
–Department of Economics	Phone 772-5400 Fax 772-5398					
Honig, Marjorie	C-Pr 772-5401		PHD		Columbia	9-81
Smith, Ronald	Prof 772-5431		DBA		Louisian	

CUNY-Queens College

CUNY-Queens College	Flushing, NY 11367-0904	(718)		
Business	65-30 Kissena Boulevard	FAX=		BA
No Full-Time Management Faculty				
Smith, Charles	Dean 997-5210		PHD	

CUNY-Coll of Staten Island

CUNY-Coll of Staten Island	Staten Isl, NY 10314	(718)					
Dept of Business Bld 3N	2800 Victory Blvd	FAX=					AAS,BS
Affron, Mirella	Dean 982-2315			PHD		Yale	1969
–Management Faculty	Phone 982-2936 Fax 982-2965						
Nigro, Peter D.	C-Pr 982-2936			PHD	68	NYU	1962
DiPaolo, Gordon	Assoc 982-2936	23	JLST	PHD		NYU	1971
Garaventa, Eugene	Assoc 982-2936	12	AEL	PHD		NYU	1980
Lang, Dorothy	Assoc 982-2936	15	EGOV	PHD		CUNY	1988
O'Donoghue, Joseph	Assoc 982-2936	38	GISY	PHD		Catholic	1990
Schwarz, Samuel	Assoc 982-2936	7	UV	PHD		Columbia	1986
Meltzer, Yale	Asst 982-2936	78	VYUZ	MBA		NYU	1979
Klein, Esther	Inst 982-2936	79	LSVZ	ABD		CUNY	1990
Barcus, Gilbert M.	Lect 982-2936			PHD		NYU	1971
Osakue, John	Lect 982-2936			PHD		Nebraska	1990
Stern, George A. Jr.	Lect 982-2936	25	DEFP	MBA		Pace	1968

Claremont McKenna College Claremont, CA 91711-6184 (909) CLAREMONT.EDU
Department of Economics 890 Columbia Avenue FAX=621-8249 BA
no Management Faculty; only Accounting within an Economics Dept
Fucaloro, Anthony Dean$ 621-8117 PHD 69 Arizona 1974

Claremont Graduate School Claremont, CA 91711-6186 (909) CLARGRAD
Claremont Graduate Sch 925 N. Dartmouth FAX=
Harris, Sidney E. Dean 621-8216 harriss 17 DUVY PHD Cornell 1987
–Drucker Grad Mgt Center Phone 621-8216 Fax 621-8009
Cooper, Robin Prof 621-8073 cooperr 9 ZDUY DBA Harvard 1992
Drucker, Peter F. Prof 621-8073 12 DRJU Frankfur 1971
  Clarke Professor of Social Science & Management
Farquhar, Peter H. Prof 621-8647 farquhap 38 IYV PHD Cornell 1992
Gold, Bela Prof 621-8073 37 IUVY PHD Columbia 1983
  Fletcher Jones Professor of Technology & Management
Gold, Sonia Prof 621-8073 13 DDIJ PHD Pitt 1983
Gray, Paul Prof grayp 9 ZIV PHD Stanford 1982
Griesinger, Donald W. Prof 621-8193 griesind 12 DEFH PHD Ca-SnBar 1982
Hollerman, Leon Prof hollerml 8 LY PHD Berkeley 1990
Lipman-Blumen, Jean Prof 621-8083 lipmanj 12 ADEF PHD Harvard
  Bradshaw Professor of Public Policy & Organizational Behavior
Maciariello, Joseph Prof 621-8073 maciarij 13 DI PHD 72 NYU 1979
  Horton Professor of Business Administration
Myers, James H. Prof 621-8073 myersj 1 D PHD S Calif
Sathe, Vijay Prof 621-8073 sathev 12 DEFH PHD Ohio St 1987
Ellsworth, Richard R. Assoc 621-8073 ellsworr 13 DHI,I DBA Harvard
Markus, M. Lynne Assoc markusm 9 Z&X PHD 79 Case Wes 1992
Olfman, Lorne Assoc olfmanl 9 ZPVX PHD Indiana 1987

Clarion University Clarion, PA 16214 (814) UAXA.CLARION.EDU
College of Business Wood Street FAX=226-1910 BS,MBA
Grunenwald, Joseph P. Dean 226-2600 DBA 81 Kent St 8-78
–Department of Adm Sciences Phone Fax 226-1910
Pesek, James G. C-Pr 226-2626 57 NQ PHD 84 Pitt 8-80
Ackerman, Leonard Prof 226-2613 25 EGOP EDD 67 Geo Wash 8-81
Fulmer, William E. Prof 226-2624 75 NQU MBA 76 Clarion 8-76
Reed, John H. Prof 226-2611 73 AUV PHD 72 American 8-71
Anderson, Carole Assoc 226-1893 57 NQR ABD Kent St 8-90
Johns, T. Reid Assoc 226-2104 79 UVW PHD 92 Fla St 8-92
Roth, Kevin J. Assoc 226-2055 36 I ABD Pitt 8-90

Clark University Worcester, MA 01610-1477 (508) 1986,1986
Grad School of Mgt 950 Main Street FAX=793-8890
Ullrich, Robert A. Dean 793-7670 2 EH DBA 68 Wash U 7-88
–Management Faculty Phone Fax 793-8890
Chaison, Gary N. Prof 793-7134 5 Q PHD 72 SUNY-Buf
Bradbury, Robert Assoc 793-7669 1 C PHD 75 Ohio
Arndt, Margarete Asst 793-7668 1 C DBA 91 Boston U
Bigelow, Barbara Asst 793-7103 3 I PHD 87 MIT
Elsass, Priscilla Asst 793-7633 2 EF PHD 92 Conn
Graves, Laura M. Asst 793-7466 2 EFG PHD 82 Conn
Ottensmeyer, Edward J. Asst 793-7463 43 IJ PHD 83 Indiana
Sundarraj, R. P. Asst 793-7648 9 Z PHD 90 Tenn
Xue, Jue Asst 793-7659 7 U PHD 91 Car Mel

Clark Atlanta University Atlanta, GA 30314-4391 (404) 1974
School of Business Adm FAX=880-8458
  Dept of Decision Sciences Did Not Respond-1993 Listing
Irons, Edward D. Dean 880-8454 Fnce DBA 60 Harvard 9-90
–Dept of Business Adm Phone Fax 880-8462
Welch, H. Oliver C PHD Geo St 1992
Byars, Lloyd Prof 35 IQ PHD 70 Geo St
Neil, Thomas C. Assoc PHD Florida
Brown, William H. Asst MBA Geo St 1979
Conn, Jennie Asst JD Geotown 1984
Hill, Andrew Asst
–Dept of Decision Sciences Phone Fax 880-8458
Davis, Edward C-Pr 880-8461 PHD N Car St
Singh, Ranjit Prof PHD S Illin
Kim, Young Hwa Assoc PHD Geo St

Clarkson University Potsdam, NY 13699-5790 (315) CLARKSON.EDU 1977,1982
School of Management FAX=268-3810 BS,MS,MBA
Pease, Victor P. Dean 268-2300 PHD 70 Arizona

–Department of Management   Phone 268-3977   Fax 268-3810

Name	Rank	Phone		field		Degree	yr	School	
O'Neil, Brian F.	C-Pr	268-3977		7	U	PHD	71	Purdue	
Bommer, Michael	Prof	268-6456		7	V	PHD	71	Penn	
Janaro, Ralph E.	Assoc	268-3830		7	V	DBA	82	Fla St	
Martin, Gene	Assoc	268-6431		7		PHD		Wash U	
Mosier, Charles T.	Assoc	268-7719		7	V	PHD	83	N Carol	
Mahmoodi, Farzad	Asst	268-4281		1		PHD		Minn	
Raynis, Susan A.	Asst	268-6437		5		PHD		Colo St	
Throop, Gary	Asst	268-3814				PHD		Mass	

Clayton State College	Morrow, GA	30260		(404)					
School of Business				FAX=961-3700					BS
Oglesby, Norman	Dean	961-3410		4	Mgt	PHD	77	Georgia	1991
–Dept of Management & Mktg	Phone	961-3410	Fax 961-3700						
Hubbard, Charles	C	961-3410				PHD	70	Arkansas	1989
Arjomand, H. Lari	Prof	961-3729		7		PHD	80	Oklahoma	1975
Phillips, Joseph Donald	Prof	961-3418		37		PHD	66	Alabama	1989
Feathers, John E.	Assoc	961-3476		8		MBA		Alabama	1975
Foster, Howard	Asst$	961-3451		2		MBA		Geo St	1989
Haberland, Chris	Asst$	961-3451		1		MBA		Geo St	1989

Clemson University	Clemson, SC	29634-1305		(803) CLEMSON				1977,1983	
Coll of Commerce & Ind				FAX=656-2015				BS,MS,PHD	
Trapnell, Jerry E.	Dean	656-3177		Atg	PHD	77	Georgia	1986	
–Department of Management	Phone		Fax 656-2015						
Hendrix, William H.	H-Pr	656-2011	whhendr	2	CEGX	PHD	74	Purdue	1982
Butler, John K.	Prof	656-3751	jkbtl	2	EH	DBA	77	Florida	1977
Crino, Michael D.	Prof	656-3753	crino	2	EH	PHD	78	Florida	1984
Grigsby, David W.	Prof	656-3755	grigsby	3	I	PHD	77	N Carol	1980
Kanet, Jack	Prof	656-3754	kanet	7	UV	PHD	79	Penn St	1986
LaForge, R. Lawrence	Prof	656-3758	rllafg	7	UV	PHD	76	Georgia	1984
Leap, Terry	Prof	656-3759	tleap	2	EH	PHD	78	Iowa	1985
McKnew, Mark	Prof	656-3761	mamckn	7	UV	PHD	78	MIT	1978
Cantrell, R. Stephen	Assoc	656-3752	rscnt	7	UV	PHD	82	N Car St	1980
Davis, J. Steven	Assoc	656-3768	davis	9	Z	PHD	84	Ga Tech	1985
Patterson, J. Wayne	Assoc	656-3765	jwptt	7	UV	PHD	77	Arkansas	1982
Roth, Phillip L.	Assoc	656-1039	rothp	2	EH	PHD	88	Houston	1991
Sridharan, V.	Assoc	656-2624	suhas	7	UV	PHD	87	Iowa	1987
Summers, Timothy P.	Assoc	656-3767	summers	2	EH	PHD	86	S Carol	1987
Swanson, David M.	Assoc	656-3771	sdavid	8	Y	PHD	72	N Carol	1970
Clarke, Richard L.	Asst	656-3755	clarker	1	A	PHD	88	Texas	1988
Fiet, James O.	Asst	656-3764	fietj			PHD		Tx A&M	1992
Fredendall, Lawrence	Asst	656-2016	flawren	7	UV	PHD	90	Michigan	1990
Lipp, Astrid	Asst	656-3770	lastrid	9	Z	PHD	84	Georgia	1989
Miller, Janis	Asst	656-3757	janism	7	UV	PHD	90	Missouri	1990
Pouder, Richard W.	Asst	656-1042	pouder	3	I	PHD	93	Conn	1993
Robbins, Tina	Asst	656-3756	rtina	2	EH	PHD	91	S Carol	1990
Soroush, Hossein	Asst	656-3769	shossei	7	UV	PHD	84	Renssel	1988
St. John, Caron H.	Asst	656-3760	scaron	3	I	PHD	88	Geo St	1988
Ellis, Steve	Lect	656-2625	brizig	7	UV	DSC	68	Wash U	
Huneycutt, T. B.	Lect	656-1333	tben	7	UV	MSC	73	Air Forc	1993
Assistant Head									
Newkirk, Gary L.	Lect	656-1582	ngary	7	UV	EDD	93	Clemson	1993

Cleveland State University	Cleveland, OH	44115		(216) CSUOHIO				1974,1978	
Nance Col of Bus Adm				FAX=687-9354				BA,MBA,DBA,MLRH	
–Dept of Management & Labor	Phone	687-4754	Fax 687-9354						
Martin, Harry J.	C-Ac	687-3790	r0426	12	FEN	PHD		S Illin	1980
Brooks, Charles H.	Prof	687-4759		1	C	PHD		Michigan	1984
Davis, Tim R. V.	Prof	687-3785		15	DN	PHD		Nebraska	1979
Graham, Harry E.	Prof	687-3781		5	QK	PHD		Wiscon	1978
Klein, Stuart M.	Prof	687-3789		23	UV	PHD	63	Cornell	1972
Muczyk, Jan P.	Prof	687-5056		25	EFQ	DBA		Maryland	1973
Reimann, Bernard C.	Prof	687-4754		23	DH	DBA	72	Kent St	1976
Walker, Larry R.	Prof	687-3835		1	C	PHD		Temple	1988
Wiener, Yoash	Prof	687-3791		5	NP	PHD	69	Ohio St	1975
Alemi, Farrokh	Assoc	687-4749		7	C	PHD		Wiscon	1989
Dunegan, Kenneth J.	Assoc	687-4735		2	EF	PHD		Cinn	1987
Erenburg, Mark	Assoc	687-4750		5	NQ	PHD		Wiscon	1987
Heshizer, Brian P.	Assoc	687-4748		35	PQ	PHD	79	Wiscon	1979
Nelson, Nels E.	Assoc	687-4742		47	Q	PHD		Conn	1977
Susbauer, Jeffery C.	Assoc	687-4747		36	STI	PHD		Texas	1970
Vardi, Yoav	Assoc	687-4782		23	EH	PHD		Cornell	1989
Lado, Augustine A.	Asst	687-4731		3	I	PHD		Memphis	1992
Marshall, Brenda S.	Asst	687-7232		1	C	PHD		Michigan	1991
Wilson, Mary C.	Asst	687-5058		5	NPR	PHD		Tenn	1991

Univ of Colorado at Boulder   Boulder, CO   80309-0419   (303) CUBLDR.COLORADO.EDU 1938,1967
College of Bus & Adm   FAX=492-5962   BS,MBA,MS,PHD

Singell, Larry	Dean	492-1809			Econ	PHD	65	Wayne St 1993
–Strategy & Org Mgt Div	Phone	492-4479	Fax 492-7676					
Meyer, G. Dale	C-Pr	492-2376				PHD	70	Iowa 1970
Boss, R. Wayne	Prof	464-3189				DPA	73	Georgia 1973
Huff, Anne	Prof	492-8410		3	IX	PHD	74	Northwes 1991
Morrison, Edward J.	Prof	492-3254				DBA	59	Indiana 1959
Sorenson, Ralph Z.	Prof	492-1809		3	I	DBA	67	Harvard 1992
Ambrose, Maureen	Assoc	492-8966				PHD	86	Illinois 1991
Balkin, David B.	Assoc	492-5780				PHD	81	Minn 1988
Koberg, Christine S.	Assoc	492-8677				PHD	81	Oregon 1982
Lawless, Michael W.	Assoc	492-8366				PHD	80	UCLA 1982
Rosse, Joseph G.	Assoc	492-6254				PHD	83	Illinois 1984
Bumpus, Minnette	Asst	492-4741	bumpus_m			PHD	92	S Carol 1991
DeCastro, Julio O.	Asst	492-4312	decastro_j			PHD	90	S Carol 1989
Nicholls-Nixon, Charlene	Asst	492-6323				PHD	93	Purdue 1992
Garnand, John J.	Inst	492-2340				PHD	76	Colorado 1984
–Operations Mgt & Transport	Phone		Fax 492-5962					
Gordon, Ken	H-Ac	492-4235		78	UVMY	PHD	73	Northwes 1977
Glover, Fred W.	Prof	492-8589		7	VX	PHD	65	Car Mel 1970
US West Chair in System Science & Information Systems								
Foster, Jerry	Assoc	492-6166		7	W	PHD	73	Syrcuse 1973
Spinetto, Richard D.	Assoc	492-7213		7	UVX	PHD	71	Cornell 1971
Kelly, James	Asst	492-4689		7	UVWX	PHD	90	Maryland 1990
Laguna, Manuel	Asst	492-6368		7	UVWX	PHD	90	Texas 1991
Lawrence, Stephen R.	Asst	492-4351		78	UIMY	PHD	88	Car Mel 1993

U of Colorado at Co Springs   Colorado Spr, CO 80933-7150   (719) COLOSPGS   1991,1991
College of Bus & Adm   1420 Austin Bluffs Parkway   FAX=593-3362   BS,BA,MBA

Discenza, Richard X.	Dean$	593-3113	rxdiscenza	7	U	PHD	74	Oklahoma 8-82
–Management & Org Beh Dp	Phone		Fax 593-3362					
Gardner, Donald G.	C-Pr	593-3356	dggardner	5	NE	PHD	81	Purdue 1-81
Couger, J. Daniel	Prof	593-3403	jdcouger	9	Z	DBA	64	Colorado 5-65
Distinguished Professor of Management Science								
Knapp, Robert W.	Prof	593-3404	rwknapp	3	T	PHD		Michigan 8-67
McFadden, Fred R.	Prof	593-3409	frmcfadd	9	Z	PHD	68	Stanford 8-70
Opperman, Edward B.	Prof	593-3411	ebopperm	7	V	PHD	65	Indiana 8-74
Warrick, Donald D.	Prof	593-3407	ddwarrick	2	EFGH	DBA	72	S Calif 1-71
Zawacki, Robert A.	Prof	593-3420	razawacki	2	EF	PHD	73	U Wash 8-75
Atwater, J. Brian	Asst	593-3676	batwater	7	U	PHD	92	Georgia 8-92
Milliman, John F.	Asst	593-3116	jfmilliman	5	N	PHD	92	S Calif 1-92

Univ of Colorado at Denver   Denver, CO   80204-5300   (303) CUDNVR   1986,1986
College of Bus & Adm   FAX=628-1299   MBA,MS

Gupta, Yash P.	Dean	628-1205		79	IUVZ	PHD	76	Bradford 1992
–Department of Management	Phone	628-1293	Fax 628-1299					
Zammuto, Raymond	C-Pr	628-1293		2	EH	PHD	80	Illinois 1984
Cascio, Wayne	Prof	628-1230		5	NPQ	PHD	72	Rochest 1981
O'Connor, Edward J.	Prof	628-1247		2	EF	PHD	72	Akron 1988
Ruhnka, John C.	Prof	628-1242				LLM	91	Cambridg
Cho, Kang Rae	Assoc	628-1280		8	Y	PHD	82	U Wash 1989
Conry, Edward J.	Assoc	628-1295		4	J	JD		Ca-Davis
Bettenhausen, Kenneth	Asst	628-1237		2	EFH	PHD	87	Illinois 1991
Boerstler, Heidi	Asst	628-1256				JD	90	Denver
Fiol, C. Marlene	Asst	628-1212		23	HIT	PHD	86	Illinois 1991
Gifford, Blair	Asst	628-1286				PHD	93	Chicago
Kovoor, Sarah	Asst	628-1241		24	EFGM	PHD	91	S Calif 1991
Serapio, Manuel	Asst	628-1232		28	HY	PHD	88	Illinois 1989
Giese, Cary	Inst	628-1294				LLM	92	San Diego
Patinka, Paul J.	Inst	628-1207				PHD	59	Purdue
Rice, Charles A.	Inst	628-1253				MBA	75	Denver

Colorado State University   Fort Collins, CO   80523   (303) VINES.COLOSTATE.EDU 970,1976
College of Business   FAX=491-0596   BS,MBA,MS

Heird, James	Dean$	491-6471				AgSc	PHD	78 Tx Tech 1986
–Department of Management	Phone	491-5323	Fax 491-0596					
Bolander, Steve	C-Pr	491-5636	sbolande	79	U	PHD	72	Kent St 1972
Benton, Doug	Prof	491-5507	dbenton	5	JLMN	PHD	69	Ariz St 1968
Francis, G. James	Prof	491-5323	gfrancis	23	EFHI	PHD	71	Nebraska 1970
Hogler, Raymond Lewis	Prof	491-5221	rhogler	45	BKQ	PHD	72	Colorado 1989
Middlemist, Dennis	Prof	491-6742	dmiddlem	12	EJN	PHD	73	U Wash 1981
Pegnetter, Richard	Prof	491-6471		5	Q	PHD	71	Cornell 1986
Roselius, Ted	Prof	491-6886	troseliu	36	IST	PHD	67	Colorado 1964
Thornton, Billy	Prof	491-7397	bthornto	27	HUZ	PHD	72	Tx A&M 1981
Hivner, Walter	Assoc	491-1023	whivner			PHD	71	Calif 1993
Hopkins, Willie E.	Assoc	491-5323	whopkins	3	IJNY	PHD	84	Colorado 1983

Name	Rank	Phone	Email		Area	Deg	Yr	School	Year
Kaman, Vicki	Assoc	491-6368	vkaman	5	NPRE	PHD	80	Colo St	1981
King-Miller, Elaine	Assoc	491-7154	eking	15	HJNY	PHD	80	Michigan	1990
Jankovich, Jackie	Asst	491-5559	jjankovi	15	P&	MS	80	Kan St	1987
Mallette, Paul	Asst	423-2631	pmallett	3	DIL	PHD	88	Nebraska	1988
McCambridge, James A.	Asst	491-7633	jmccambr	1	EFNA	PHD	76	Colo St	1982
Nie, Winter	Asst	491-2205	wnie			PHD	93	Utah	
Spagnola, Robert G.	Asst	491-5323	rspagnol			PHD	89	Nebraska	1991
Sterkel-Powell, Karen	Asst	491-5321		15	NPR&	PHD	87	N Colo	1976
Tucker, Mary L.	Asst	491-6842		21	E&				

Columbia University	New York, NY	10027	(212)						1916
Graduate School of Bus			FAX=864-4857						MBA,PHD
Feldberg, Meyer	Dean	854-6083		28	EY	PHD	69	Capetown	1989
−Mgt/ Organizations Faculty	Phone		Fax 932-0545						
Warren, E. Kirby	C-Pr	854-4429		35	FIN	PHD	61	Columbia	1961
Brockner, Joel	Prof	854-4435		25	EN	PHD	77	Tufts	1984
Ference, Tom	Prof	854-2211		35	IO	PHD	67	Car Mel	1966
Hambrick, Donald	Prof	854-4421		23	HI	PHD	79	Penn St	1979
Harrigan, Kathryn	Prof	854-3494		23	EI	DBA	79	Harvard	1981
Horton, Ray	Prof	854-4425		15	AQ	PHD	71	Columbia	1970
Ichniowski, Casey	Prof	854-4433		5	NQ	PHD	83	MIT	1984
Kuhn, James	Prof	854-4424		45	JQ	PHD	54	Yale	1955
Patrick, Hugh	Prof	854-3497		8	Y	PHD	60	Michigan	1984
Tushman, Michael	Prof	854-4271		19	DFZ	PHD	76	MIT	1975
Whitney, John	Prof	854-5767		23	HI	AB	48	Tulsa	1987
Beechler, Schon	Assoc	854-4416		58	IYN	PHD	90	Michigan	1989
Bontempo, Robert	Assoc	854-4479		58	NY	PHD	89	Illinois	1989
Abrahamson, Eric	Asst	854-4432		32	IH	PHD	90	NYU	1989
Boeker, Warren	Asst	854-2009		36	IT	PHD	86	Berkeley	1987
Chen, Ming-Jer	Asst	854-4431		3	I	PHD	88	Maryland	1988
Low, Murray	Asst	854-4403		6	ST	PHD	90	Penn	1990
Wageman, Ruth	Asst	854-4427		2	E	PHD	92	Harvard	1992

Columbus College	Columbus, GA	31907-5645	(706) USCN.BITNET						
Abbott Turner Sch Bus	4225 University Avenue		FAX=568-2084						BBA
Johnson, Robert S.	Dean	568-2044				PHD		Virginia	1993
−Dept of Business Adm	Phone	568-2284	Fax 568-2184						
Embry, Olice H.	C-Pr	568-2284	embryo	23	EI	PHD		Geo St	1973
Fleck, Robert A. Jr.	Prof			9	Z	PHD	71	Illinois	1986
Foundation Distinguished Professor									
Hamilton, William C.	Prof			7	V	DBA		La Tech	1973
Klein, Ronald D.	Prof	568-2044		9	Z	PHD		Geo St	1974
Director MBA Program									
Loughman, Thomas P.	Asst			1	E	PHD		Auburn	1975
Stephens, Charlotte	Asst			79	Z	PHD		Auburn	1990

Concordia College	Moorhead, MN	56562	(218)						
Dept of Econ & Bus Adm	901 South 8th Street		FAX=299-3947						BA
Harrison, Cliff	C-Pr	299-3476		15	JN	EDD		Fairl Di	1986
−Management Faculty	Phone		Fax 299-3947						
Heimarck, Theodore	Prof	299-3477		1	C	JD			
Anderson, Daniel	Asst	299-4411		1	C	MBA			

University of Connecticut	Storrs, CT	06269-2041	(203) UCONNVM						1958,1971
School of Business Adm	28 North Eagleville Road		FAX=486-6415						BS,MBA,PHD
Gutteridge, Thomas G.	Dean	486-2317		5	QNO	PHD	71	Purdue	9-92
−Department of Managment	Phone	486-3638	Fax 486-6415						
Veiga, John F.	H-Pr	486-3638		2	E	DBA	71	Kent St	1972
Powell, Gary N.	Prof	486-3862		2	E	PHD	74	Mass	1976
Yanouzas, John N.	Prof	486-3085		2	E	PHD	63	Penn St	1970
Floyd, Steven W.	Assoc	486-3389		3	I	PHD	81	Colorado	1986
Huffmire, Donald W.	Assoc	486-4309		3	I	DBA	71	Geo St	1971
Lubatkin, Michael	Assoc	486-3482		3	I	DBA	82	Tenn	1982
Ralston, David A.	Assoc	486-3640		2	E	DBA	81	Fla St	1981
Shore, Harvey H.	Assoc	486-2390		5	N	DBA	66	Harvard	1966
Thompson, John Clair	Assoc	486-2588		3	I	PHD	61	Illinois	1966
Buchholtz, Ann K.	Asst	486-6417	buchholt	3	I	PHD	91	New York	1991
Dechant, Kathleen	Asst	322-1673		3	I	PHD	82	Columbia	1988
Mulvey, Paul W.	Asst	486-6418		5	N	PHD	91	Ohio St	1991
Palmer, David D.	Asst	486-3096				PHD	75	SUNY-Buf	1976
Schulze, W.	Asst				I	PHD	94	Colorado	1994
−Dept Operations & Info Mgt	Phone	486-5295	Fax 486-4839						
Marsden, James R.	H-Pr	486-4065				PHD	70	Purdue	8-93
Garfinkle, Robert S.	Prof	486-4431		79	UZ	PHD	68	J Hopkin	
Director of PHD program									
Scott, George M.	Prof	486-4176		79	UZ	DBA	68	U Wash	9-81

Spirer, Herbert F.	Emer	322-1673		79	UZ	PHD	70	NYU	
Campbell, Gerard M.	Assoc	486-3639		79	UZ	PHD	88	Indiana	9-88
Diaby, Moustopha	Assoc			7	U	PHD	87	SUNY-Buf	9-94
Nair, Suresh K.	Assoc	486-3641		79	UZ	PHD	89	Northwes	9-88
Thakur, Lakshman S.	Assoc	486-2581		79	UZ	SCD	71	Columbia	9-87
Buzby, Bruce K.	Asst	322-1673		97	UZ	PHD	60	Indiana	9-87
Goes, Paulo	Asst	486-2379		79	UZ	PHD	91	Rochest	9-90
Gopal, Ram	Asst	486-2408				PHD	93	SUNY-Buf	
Webb, Ian R.	Asst	486-6416		79	UZ	PHD	89	MIT	9-89

Cornell University	Ithaca, NY		14853-4201	(607)					1950
Johnson Grad Sch of Mgt	410 Thurston Avenue			FAX=254-4590					MBA,PHD
Merten, Alan G.	Dean	255-6418	merten	9	Z	PHD	70	Wiscon	8-89
The Anne & Elmer Lindseth Dean									
–Management Faculty	Phone		Fax 254-4590						
BenDaniel, David	Prof	255-4220	davidb	6	T	PHD		MIT	1-85
Don and Margi Berens Professor of Entrepreneurship									
Conway, Richard W.	Prof	255-7207	conway	9	Z	PHD		Cornell	7-84
Emerson Electric Company Professor of Manufacturing Management									
Lind, Robert C.	Prof	255-4252	lind	1	A	PHD	66	Stanford	8-74
McClain, John O.	Prof	255-4022	mcclain	7	V	PHD	70	Yale	2-70
Thaler, Richard H.	Prof	255-5002	thaler	2	H	PHD	74	Rochest	7-78
Henrietta Johnson Louis Professor of Management									
Thomas, L. Joseph	Prof	255-4854	jthomas	7	UV	PHD	68	Yale	9-67
Nicholas H. Noyes Professor of Manufacturing									
Orman, Levent	Assoc	255-4728	levent	9	Z	PHD		Northwes	
Robinson, Lawrence W.	Assoc	255-4721	robinson	7	U				
Kumar, Akhil	Asst	255-4186	akhil	9	Z	PHD		Berkeley	7-88
Malik, Kavindra	Asst	255-2354	malik	7	V	PHD		Penn	7-88
–Sch Hotel Adminstration	Phone	255-3673	Fax 255-4179						
Dittman, David A.	Dean	255-5107			Atg	PHD	73	Ohio St	1990
Berger, Florence	Prof	255-8362		25	ENP	PHD	79	Cornell	9-79
Cullen, Thoms	Prof	255-4611		23	EIY	PHD	82	Cornell	8-85
Lundberg, Craig	Prof	255-8361		2	EF	PHD	66	Cornell	1-87
Blanchard Professor of Human Resources Management									
Sherry, John E. H.	Prof	255-3847		4	JK	JD	69	Columbia	7-72
Eng, Cathy	Assoc	255-8841		2	EH	PHD	85	Ohio St	7-90
Moore, Richard	Assoc	255-7257		9	Z	MBA	70	Cornell	1970
Brownell, Judi	Asst	255-8863		56	&HNP	PHD	78	Syracuse	8-86
Fulford, Mark	Asst	255-8140		25	ENP	PHD	92	Indiana	9-91
Hinkin, Timothy	Asst	255-2938		15	OB	PHD	85	Florida	1992
Jameson, Daphne	Asst	255-8372		18	YD	PHD	79	Illinois	8078
Kimes, Sheryl	Asst	255-8302		7	UV	PHD	87	Texas	8-88
Alvarez, Roy	Lect	255-8358		9	Z	MED		Cornell	1-82
Huettman, Elizabeth	Lect	255-8374		1	D	PHD	90	Purdue	8-86
Katz, Norman	Lect	255-9806		1	E	EDD	85	Harvard	8-92
Kiner, Susan	Lect	255-9017		1	&D	ABD		Illinois	8-88
Lumley, Jane	Lect	255-8375		1	D	MA	76	Penn St	1979

Creighton University	Omaha, NE		68178-0130	(402) CREIGHTON.EDU					1949,1981
College of Business Adm	California Street at 24th			FAX=280-2172					BSBA
Reznicek, Bernard	Dean	280-2852				MBA	79	Nebraska	7-94
–Dept of Mgt, Mktg & Systems	Phone	280-2617	Fax 280-2172						
Hutchens, Stephen P.	C-Ac	280-2091	hutchens		Mktg	PHD	81	Arkansas	8-81
Brannen, Kathleen C.	Assoc	280-2129	kbrannen	26	EST	PHD	79	Nebraska	8-79
Donahue, Eugene L.	Assoc	280-2931	edonahue	4	JL	PHD	68	St Louis	8-71
Hoh, Andrew K.	Assoc	280-2621	ahoh	13	EFI	PHD	76	Minn	8-76
Schminke, Marshall J.	Assoc	280-2613	mschminke	23	IHJB	PHD	86	Car Mel	8-89
Karcher, Beverly J.	Asst	280-2061	bkarcher	4	JL	PHD	91	Nebraska	8-90
McNary, George W.	Asst	280-2623	gmcnary	4	K	JD	80	Creightn	8-83
Wells, Deborah L.	Asst	280-2841	dwells	5	NR	PHD	87	Iowa St	8-87

Cumberland College	Williamsburg, KY		40769-7056	(606)					
Business Adm Department	820 Walnut Street			FAX=					BS
Hubbard, Harold F.	C-Pr	549-2200			Atg	MBA	60	Kentucky	1960
–Management Faculty	Phone								
Tan, Chinteck		549-2200				MBA	88	Tenn Tec	1988

University of Dallas	Irving, TX		75062-4799	(214) ACAD.UDALLAS.EDU					
Graduate School of Mgmt	1845 East Northgate Drive			FAX=721-5254					MBA,MM
Perry, Charles E.	Dean	721-5008				CPH	72	Michigan	5-93
–Management Faculty	Phone		Fax 721-5254						
Gellerman, Saul W.	Prof	721-5185		2	E	PHD	56	Penn	8-84
Hughes, Paula Ann	Prof	721-5086		52	QG	PHD	78	North Tx	8-79
Dunikoski, Robert H.	Assoc	721-5352	dunikosk	9	Z	PHD	84	Tx Tech	8-85
Evans, Bruce D.	Assoc	721-5360		32	I	MBA	58	Michigan	1-70

Name	Rank	Phone	Email			Degree	Yr	School	Date
Gordon, David	Assoc	721-5354		72		DENG	69	Oklahoma	8-69
Hammons, Charles B.	Assoc	721-5032	hammons	9	ZVX	PHD	79	Rice	8-92
Higgins, David P.	Assoc	721-5304		3	I	PHD	79	Texas	5-86
Kusewitt, John B.	Assoc	721-5230		17		PHD	79	Tx-Arlin	8-81
Lynch, Robert G.	Assoc	721-5326		13	BI	MBA	66	Ohio St	6-66
Peregoy, Richard P.	Assoc	721-5046		13	I	DPS	78	Pace	8-91
Cunningham, Bernard J.	Asst	721-5034		3		PHD	81	Tx-Dallas	8-81
Kottukapalli, Joseph A.	Asst	721-5097		8		PHD	66	Montreal	8-87
Kroder, Stanley L.	Asst	721-5080		3		MS	59	Case Wes	5-89
Nash, Bernard A.	Asst	721-5068		8		PHD	80	North Tx	8-90
Oberstein, Samuel G.	Asst	721-5173		3		PHD	88	Minn	8-92
Strouble, Dennis D.	Asst	721-5396	strouble	94	ZKN	PHD	84	Tx Tech	5-92

Dallas Baptist University	Dallas, TX	75211-9299	(214)	DBU.EDU					
College of Business	3000 Mountain Creek Parkway		FAX=						
Linamen, Larry H.	Dean	333-5244	larry	26		EDD		Ball St	1991
—**Management Faculty**	Phone		Fax 333-5193						
Nelson, MaryJane	Prof	333-5244	maryjane	2	EG	PHD		Oklahoma	1992
Smiles, Ronald	Prof	333-5253	rons	13		PHD		Tx-Arlin	1987
Thompson, William J.	Prof	333-5292	billt	79		PHD		Geo St	1991
Underwood, Jim D.	Assoc	333-5403	jimu	31		DBA		US Intl	1989
Arnett, David	Asst	333-5203	davea	38		PHD		Texas	1994
Arnott, Dave	Asst	333-5203		38		PHD		Tx-Arlin	1994
Byniem, Karen	Asst	333-5244	karen	9		PHD		Tx A&M	1994
Bynum, Karen	Asst	333-5244		9		PHD		Tx A&M	1994
Park, Jinsop	Asst	333-5296	jwsop	1		PHD		Berkeley	1993
Sims, Dale B.	Asst	333-5249	dale	9		MS		Houst Bp	1990
Weintraub, Rick	Asst	333-5239	rickw	7		MS		SnDgo St	1992
Willis, Donald E.	Asst	333-5257	donald	7		MDS		Geo St	1978
Kaloki, Philip K.	Inst	333-5218		18		ABD		Dal Bapt	1991

Dartmouth College	Hanover, NH	03755-1798	(603)	DARTMOUTH.EDU					1916
Amos Tuck Sch of Bus Ad			FAX=646-1308						MBA
Fox, Edward A.	Dean	646-2460				MBA	60	NYU	1990
—**Management Faculty**	Phone	646-2460	Fax 646-1308						
Assmus, Gert	Prof	646-2830				PHD	71	Berkeley	1970
Baker, Kenneth R.	Prof	646-2064				PHD	69	Cornell	1979
Blaydon, Colin C.	Prof	646-3160				PHD	66	Harvard	1983
Deshpande, Rohit	Prof	646-3981				DBA	79	Pitt	1986
Govindarajan, Vijay	Prof	643-6477				DBA	78	Harvard	1986
Greenhalgh, Leonard	Prof	646-2181				PHD	79	Cornell	1978
Hansen, Robert	Prof	646-2079				PHD	84	UCLA	1983
Joyce, William F.	Prof	646-2082				PHD	77	Penn St	1983
Loque, Dennis E.	Prof	646-2801				PHD	71	Cornell	1974
McGee, Victor E.	Prof	646-2517				PHD	62	Princeton	1969
Neslin, Scott A.	Prof	646-2841				PHD	78	MIT	1978
Rogalski, Richard J.	Prof	646-2512				PHD	74	Michigan	1976
Schoonhoven, Claudia B.	Prof	646-2515	kaye.schoonh	26	HTD	PHD	76	Stanford	1993
Shank, John K.	Prof	646-3827				PHD	69	Ohio St	1984
Stickney, Clyde P.	Prof	646-2640				DBA	70	Fla St	1977
Webster, Frederick E.	Prof	646-3134				PHD	64	Stanford	1965
Williamson, J. Peter	Prof	646-2842				DBA	61	Harvard	1961
Anderson, Philip C.	Assoc	646-2460				PHD	88	Columbia	1993
D'Aveni, Richard	Assoc	646-2921				PHD	87	Columbia	1988
Finkelstein, Sydney	Assoc	646-2460		3	IQ	PHD	88	Columbia	1994
Maloney, Kevin J.	Assoc	646-2691				PHD	83	U Wash	1983
Powell, Stephen G.	Assoc	646-2844				PHD	83	Stanford	1987
Pyke, David M.	Assoc	646-2136				PHD	87	Penn	1987
Seward, James M.	Assoc	646-3423				PHD	87	Wiscon	1987
Singh, Medini R.	Assoc	646-2460				PHD	89	Car Mel	1994
Sundaram, Anant K.	Assoc	646-3415				PHD	87	Yale	1986
Aggarwal, Rajesh	Asst	646-3954				PHD	94	Harvard	1994
Ailawadi, Kusum L.	Asst	646-2460				PHD	91	Virginia	1993
Bourland, Karla E.	Asst	646-3579				PHD	91	Michigan	1989
Cooper, Joseph E.	Asst	646-2460				PHD	92	Harvard	1993
Davidson, Martin N.	Asst	646-3611				PHD	88	Stanford	1992
Emmons, William M. III	Asst	646-2667				PHD	92	Northwes	1992
Soybel, Virginia E.	Asst	646-3612				PHD	89	Columbia	1988
Wansink, Brian C.	Asst	646-1336				ABD		Stanford	1990
Womack, Kent L.	Asst	646-3954				PHD	94	Cornell	1994
Argenti, Paul A.	Adj	646-2983				MBA	81	Columbia	1981
Henderson, Caroline M.	Adj	646-3710				DBA	83	Harvard	1984
Munter, Mary F.	Adj	646-2290				MA	75	Stanford	1983

David Lipscomb University Nashville, TN   37204-3951   (615) DLU.EDU
Dept of Business Adm   Granny White Pike   FAX=269-1796   BS,BA
  phone 269-1000

Name	Rank	Phone		Dept	Degree	Yr	School	Date
Boulware, George W.	C-Pr	Ext 2406		4 L	PHD	76	S Carol	9-79
–Management Faculty	Phone		Fax 269-1796					
Fulks, L. Gerald	H-Pr	Ext 2232		18 BISY	DA		Mid Tenn	9-78
Curmody, Seth	Prof	Ext 2508		79 VZ	PHD		Missouri	9-85
Daniel, Hugh Jr.	Assoc	Ext 2225		7 VU	PHD		Miss	9-86
Boulware, Jeanna	Inst	Ext 2406		25 BEN	MBA		Gold Gt	9-79
Houghton, Jeff	Inst	Ext 2225		25 EL	MBA		W Virg	9-93
Groom, Steve	Lect	Ext 2225		4 K	JD		Tenn	9-89

University of Dayton Dayton, OH   45469-2235   (513) DAYTON   1983,1988
School of Business Adm   300 College Park   FAX=229-4000   BS,MBA

Name	Rank	Phone		Dept	Degree	Yr	School	Date
Gould, Sam	Dean	229-3731		2 EH	PHD	75	Mich St	1985
–Management/Mktg Depts	Phone		Fax 229-3788					
Sekely, William	C-Ac	229-3744		Mktg	DBA	75	Kent St	1976
Lee, David	Assoc	229-2021		13 BI	PHD	72	Purdue	8-82
Schenk, Joseph	Assoc	229-3116		38 IO	DBA	76	Kent St	8-80
Berger, Robert	Asst	229-3706		4	JD	70	Chase	8-64
Bickford, Deborah J.	Asst	229-3516	bickford	3 IU	PHD	80	Mass	8-88
Dehler, Gordon	Asst	229-2025		2 EH	PHD	90	Cinn	8-88
Miller, Van V.	Asst	229-2027		38 Y	PHD	81	New Mex	1988
Stillwell, C. Dean	Asst	229-3556		25 ENO	PHDA	93	Geo Tech	8-90
–Dept MIS & Decision Science	Phone		Fax 229-3301					
Dunne, James	C-Pr	229-2938		79 VZ	PHD	73	Illinois	1982
De, Prabuddha	Prof	229-2292		9 UVZ	PHD	79	Car Mel	1987
Standard Register-Sherman Distinguished Professor								
Ferratt, Thomas	Prof	229-2728		9 PZ	PHD	74	Ohio St	1986
Vlahos, George	Prof	229-3520		7 VYZ	PHD	74	N Colo	1978
Wells, Charles	Prof	229-3332		7 UV	PHD	82	Cinn	1984
Agarwal, Ritu	Assoc	229-2249		9 Z	PHD	88	Syracuse	1988
Amsden, Robert	Assoc	229-2217		7 U	PHD	69	Rutgers	1978
Bohlen, George	Assoc	229-2226		79 UZ	PHD	73	Purdue	1980
Young, Saul	Assoc	229-2969		7 UV	PHD	75	Stanford	1983
Casey, Anthony	Asst	229-2024		7 U	MS	75	Dayton	1969
Popken, Douglas	VAsst	229-3912		7 UV	PHD	88	Berkeley	1991
Prasad, Jayesh	Asst	229-2286		9 Z	ABD		Pitt	1990
Sinha, Atish	Asst	229-2247		9 Z	PHD	93	Pitt	1991
Davis, Thomas	Lect	229-2408		79	MS	70	Air FIT	1990

University of Delaware Newark, DE   19716   (302) UDELVM   1966,1982
College of Bus & Econ   South College Avenue   FAX=831-6750   BS,MS

Name	Rank	Phone		Dept	Degree	Yr	School	Date
Biederman, Kenneth R.	Dean	831-2551		Econ	PHD		Purdue	
–Dept of Business Adm	Phone	831-2554	Fax 831-6750					
Garland, Howard	C-Pr	831-2554			PHD	72	Cornell	
Billon, S. Alexander	Prof	831-1764			PHD	60	Mich St	1965
Sloane, Arthur A.	Prof	831-1784			DBA	63	Harvard	1966
Conlon, Donald E.	Assoc	831-2081			PHD	88	Illinois	1988
Ferry, Diane	Assoc	831-1769			PHD	78	Penn	1979
Kernan, Mary C.	Assoc	831-1016			PHD	85	Akron	1989
Kmetz, John L.	Assoc	831-1773			DBA	75	Maryland	1977
Pohlen, Michael F.	Assoc	831-1777		U	PHD	67	Ohio St	1973
Preble, John F.	Assoc	831-1778			PHD	81	Mass	1982
Weiss, Richard M.	Assoc	831-1785			PHD	81	Cornell	1980
Gopinath, C.	Asst	831-2516			PHD	90	Mass	1990
Sawyer, John E.	Asst	831-1787			PHD	87	Illinois	1991
Sullivan, Daniel	Asst	831-4566			PHD	88	S Carol	1993
Weaver, Gary	Asst				PHD	94	Penn St	1994

Delaware State University Dover, DE   19901-4932   (302)
Dept of Econ & Bus Adm   1200 North DuPont Highway   FAX=   BS

Name	Rank	Phone	Dept	Degree	Yr	School	Date
Awadzi, Winston	Dean$	739-3521	Mktg	PHD			
–Management Faculty	Phone						
Grandfield, Raymond J.	C-Pr	739-3516		EDD			1968
Sadoughi, Mohammad	Assoc	739-3515		EDD			1990
Deeney, John	Asst	739-5247		MBA			1972
Panda, Dandeson	Asst	739-5181		PHD			1989
Sheth, Kishor	Asst	739-2704		MBA			1971

Delta State University Cleveland, MS   38733   (601)
School of Business   FAX=   BBA,MBA

Name	Rank	Phone	Dept	Degree	Yr	School	Date
Moore, Roy N.	Dean	846-4200	15 Q	PHD	71	Alabama	8-88
–Div of Management & Mktg	Phone	846-4198					
Wilder, Kathy H.	C-As	846-4237	13 FIXZ	ABD	94	Memphis	8-91
Crook, Leo V.	Prof	846-4193	57 QV	DBA	78	Miss St	8-79

Long, Albert W.	Prof	846-4213		28	EIY	DBA	83	US Intl	8-83
Dale, Cheryl F.	Asst	846-4194		17	UVW	ABD	91	Alabama	8-92
Johnson, B. Cooper	Asst	846-4192		57	ENUV	ABD	90	Miss	8-83
Starkey, Paul L.	Asst	846-4204		25	EJP	MBA	85	Miss	8-86
Fleming, Robert F.	Inst	846-4203		13	I	MBA	87	S Miss	8-92

University of Denver — Denver, CO 80208-0233 — (303) DU.EDU — 1923,1966

College of Business	2020 S. Race Street						FAX=871-2156			BS,MBA,MA,MIM
Hanbery, Glyn	Dean	871-2019				Atg	PHD	71	Ariz St	
–Department of Management	Phone	871-2489	Fax 871-2294							
Fukami, Cynthia	C-Ac	871-2193	cfukami	2	E		PHD		Northwes	9-83
Johnston, Van R.	Prof	871-2231		2	L		PHD		S Calif	9-76
Sampson, Nancy S.	Prof	871-2195	nsampson	1	Z		DBA	71	Oklahoma	1-72
Sotiriou, Constantine E.	Prof	871-2199		3	D		DBA	70	Colorado	9-70
VonStroh, Gordon E.	Prof	871-3435		3	O		PHD	67	Oklahoma	9-67
Watkins, Thomas L.	Prof	871-3444		5	Q		PHD	71	Cinn	9-74
Associate Dean of Graduate Studies										
Hopkins, David M.	Assoc	871-2210		8	Y		PHD		Syracuse	9-79
McGowan, Robert P.	Assoc	871-4399	rmcgowan	3	I		PHD		Syracuse	9-83
Allen, Douglas B.	Asst	871-2428	dallen	5	Y		PHD	91	Michigan	9-89
Narapareddy, V.	Asst	871-2198		8	Y		PHD	87	Illinois	9-93
Silver, William	Asst	871-2248	wsilver	5	N		PHD		Nebraska	9-90
Stewart, Kim A.	Asst	871-2194	kistewar	3	I		PHD		Houston	9-89
Winn, Joan	Asst	871-2192	jwinn	3	I		PHD		Georgia	9-88
Wittmer, Dennis	Asst	871-2489		1	J		PHD		Syracuse	9-91

DePaul University — Chicago, IL 60604-2287 — (312) — 1957,1963

College of Commerce	25 East Jackson Boulevard						FAX=362-5322			BS,MA,MB,MS,MST
Patten, Ronald J.	Dean	362-6783				Atg	PHD	63	Alabama	1989
–Department of Management	Phone	362-6783	Fax 362-6973							
Coye, Ray W.	C-Ac	362-8710					PHD		Oregon	
Almaney, Adnan J.	Prof	362-6785					PHD	67	Indiana	
Alwan, A. J.	Prof	362-8787					PHD	67	Chicago	
LaVan, Helen N.	Prof	362-8364					PHD		Loyola	
Mathys, Nicholas J.	Prof	362-8778					PHD		Ill Tech	
Murray, Michael A.	Prof	362-8749					JD		Illinois	
Ryan CSV, Leo V.	Prof	362-8846					PHD		St Louis	
Welsch, Harold P.	Prof	362-8471					PHD	75	Northwes	
Belohlav, James A.	Assoc	362-8382					PHD		Cinn	
Briggs, Steven	Assoc	362-6131					PHD		UCLA	
Devience, Alexander	Assoc	362-6298					JD		Loyola	
Drehmer, David E.	Assoc	362-8406					PHD		Ill Tech	
Grossman, Jack H.	Assoc	362-8493					PHD		Loyola	
Koys, Daniel J.	Assoc	362-8307					PHD		Cornell	
Succari, Owais R.	Assoc	362-8797					PHD		Louvain	
Thompson, Kenneth R.	Assoc	362-8783					PHD		Nebraska	
Young, Earl C.	Assoc	362-8750					PHD		Northwes	
Brusco, Michael J.	Asst	362-8113					PHD	90	Fla St	
Garber, Samuel B.	Asst	362-6788					JD		Illinois	
Gundry, Lisa K.	Asst	362-8075					PHD		Northwes	
Head, Thomas C.	Asst	362-8422					PHD		Tx A&M	
Heyl, Jeff	Asst	362-6145					PHD		Ariz St	
Pincus, Laura	Asst	362-6569					JD		Chicago	
Plaschka, Gerhard	Asst	362-5451					PHD		Vienna	
Staruck, James E.	Asst	362-6783					JD		Chi-Kent	
Venkataraman, Ramanathan	Asst	362-6786					PHD		Ill Tech	

DePauw University — Greencastle, IN 46135 — (317)

Dept of Econ & Business	313 South Locust Street						FAX=658-4177			
Dilillo, Leonard	Prov									
–Management Faculty	Phone	658-4882	Fax 658-4878							
Lemon, Gary Dale	C-Ac						PHD	82	Kansas	
Catanese, Margaret	Assoc	658-4161	mcantes				MBA	78	Mich St	8-79
Gray, Ralph							PHD			

University of Detroit Mercy — Detroit, MI 48219-0900 — (313) — 1949,1963

College of Business Adm	4001 West McNichols Road						FAX=993-1052			BS,MBA
Ulferts, Gregory W.	Dean	993-1204		7	U		DBA	75	La Tech	1983
–Management Prog Box 19900	Phone		Fax 993-1052							
Mawhinney, Thomas	C-Pr	993-1084					PHD	76	Ohio St	1987
Dempsey, Richard	Prof	993-1923					PHD	58	Wiscon	1958
Weber, Leonard	Prof	993-3355					PHD	74	McMaster	
Whitty, Michael	Prof	993-3357					PHD	69	Syracuse	1967
Bossman, Larry	Assoc	993-1195					PHD	67	Wiscon	1971
Dreifus, Suzanne	Assoc	993-1189					JD	86	Detroit	1986
Fish, Bob	Asst	993-3319					MA	82	Wayne St	1986

Name	Rank	Phone				Field	Degree	Year	School	Grad
Hazen, Mary Ann	Asst	993-3356					PHD	84	Case Wes	1989
Walton, Alice	Asst	993-1084					PHD	88	Iowa St	1990
Zeff, Lawrence	Asst	993-1179					PHD	80	Pitt	1973

Dickinson State University — Dickinson, ND 58601 — (701)
School of Bus & Adm — 291 Campus Drive — FAX=227-2006 — BS,BA
Did Not Respond-1993 Listing

Name	Rank	Phone				Field	Degree	Year	School	Grad
Goetz, William G.	Dean	227-2333					MA	67	N Dakota	9-67
Vice President of Development										
–Management Faculty	Phone		Fax 227-2006							
Dragseth, Deborah M.	Asst	227-2696		13			MBA	89	S Dakota	9-89
Director, Center for Management & Leadership										
Elton, Mark	Inst	227-2309		27			MBA	90	Brig Yg	9-90

Dillard University — New Orleans, LA 70122 — (504)
Division of Business — FAX=
Did Not Respond-1993 Listing

Name	Rank	Phone				Field	Degree	Year	School	Grad
Chase, Edgar L. III	C-Pr	286-4697			Atg		JD		Loyola	
–Management Faculty	Phone		Fax 286-4851							
Igwike, Richard	Asst	286-4698								
Sanders, Charles	Asst	286-4698								

Univ of District of Columbia — Washington, DC 20008 — (202)
Col of Bus & Public Mgt — 4200 Connecticut Ave NW — FAX=727-1907 — RPA,BDA,MBA,MPA

Name	Rank	Phone				Field	Degree	Year	School	Grad
Hahn, Worden W.	Dean	282-3701					JD	78	Illinois	1992
–Dept of Management MB1900	Phone	282-3719	Fax 282-3706							
Makhlouf, Hany H.	C-Pr	282-3718		15	IY		PHD	70	American	1971
Ashe, Amnon Vincent	Prof	282-3718		12	E		PHD	74	Claremont	1989
Attaway, John D.	Prof	282-3718		13	N		DBA	79	Geo Wash	1986
Azani, Hossein	Prof	282-3718		7	EUV		DSC	84	Geo Wash	1986
Bachman, Paul	Prof	282-3718		13	N		DBA	78	Geo Wash	1971
Choi, Yearn H.	Prof	282-3718		1	A		PHD	74	Indiana	1985
Hughes, Carlyle D.	Prof	282-3718		13	I		PHD	66	U Wash	1974
Nowell, Antonia Hall	Prof	282-3718		12	AE		PHD	78	Wayne St	1980
Poag, Lois A.	Prof	282-3718		2	GR		PHD	81	Howard	1986
Alsaaty, Falih	Assoc	282-3718		38	Y		PHD	73	NYU	1990
Ramey, Judith	Asst	282-3718		1	A		MPA	72	Pitt	1973

Drake University — Des Moines, IA 50311-4505 — (515) DRAKE — 1949,1973
Col of Bus & Pub Adm — 2507 University Avenue — FAX=271-2001 — BS,MBA

Name	Rank	Phone				Field	Degree	Year	School	Grad
Weinbrenner, Hugh	Dean	271-2871		1	A		PHD	73	Colorado	1979
–Department of Management	Phone		Fax 271-4518							
Moore, Willie M.	C-As	271-3159		52	QN		PHD	87	Ohio St	1987
Dailey, Robert	Prof	271-2008		12	EFCN		DBA	77	Colorado	1989
Kemp, Robert	Prof	271-2807		38	JTY		PHD	79	Ariz St	1982
Kirk, Delaney	Assoc	271-3724		57	JKSR		PHD	88	North Tx	1989
Reed, Diana	Assoc	271-3143		15	EHYR		PHD	77	Wiscon	1981
Clapham, Stephen	Asst	271-2579	sc8701r	32	IFH		PHD	93	Indiana	1990
Meyer, Bradley	Asst	271-2490	bm4111r	7	JUV		PHD	89	Iowa St	1989

Drexel University — Philadelphia, PA 19104 — (215) DUVM — 1967,1978
College of Bus & Adm — 32nd and Chestnut Streets — FAX=895-2891 — BS,MBA,MTA,PHD

Name	Rank	Phone				Field	Degree	Year	School	Grad
Baer, Art	Dean	895-2110					MBA		Columbia	1993
–Department of Management	Phone	895-2143	Fax 895-2891							
Silver, Milton	H-Pr	895-2150		12	FDPT		PHD	62	Columbia	1965
Banerjee, Avijit	Prof	895-1449	banerjea	7	UVW		PHD	77	Ohio St	1977
Burton, Jonathan S.	Prof	895-1799	burton		U		PHD	77	Tx Tech	1971
Chung, An-Min	Emer	895-2148					PHD	53	Penn	1957
Greenhaus, Jeffrey	Prof	895-2139		2	EGOR		PHD	70	NYU	1981
Hess, Sidney W.	Prof	895-1794	hessw	37	JVUX		PHD	60	Case Wes	1987
Igbaria, Magid	Prof	895-2142	magid	9	Z		PHD	87	Tel Aviv	1987
Laessig, Robert E.	Prof	895-2110		37	MAVU		PHD	71	Cornell	1970
Parasuraman, Saroj	Prof	895-1796		2	EG		PHD	77	SUNY Buf	1983
Arinze, Orakwue Bay	Assoc	895-1798	arinze		VZ		PHD	87	London	1988
Jarrell, Donald W.	Assoc	895-2151		5	HRPL		PHD	58	Penn	1958
Siegel, Sidney R.	Assoc	895-6933		27	EFHU		PHD	72	Drexel	
Weiner, Joan	Assoc	895-1797		42	DEFJ		PHD	81	Penn	1981
Banerjee, Snehamay	Asst	895-2121	banerjes		VZ		PHD	89	Maryland	1988
Kim, Seung-Lae	Asst	895-2181			UV		PHD	90	Penn St	1989
Partovi, Fariborz Y.	Asst	895-6611		7	UV		PHD	88	Penn	1988
Subbanarasimha, P. N.	Asst	895-6763	subbanpn	3	IT		PHD	90	NYU	1989
Wormley, Wayne M.	Asst	895-1733		25	EHNO		PHD	78	Stanford	1984
White, Daniel L.	Inst	895-1792		35	GT		MBA	69	Mich St	1979

Drury College Springfield, MO 65802 (417)
Breech Sch of Bus Adm FAX =
Did Not Respond-1993 Listing

Strube, W. Curtis	D-Pr	865-8731				PHD	72	Arkansas
Burlington Northern Chair in Business Administration								
–Management Faculty	Phone		Fax 865-3138					
Barefield, Robert								

Duke University Durham, NC 27708-0120 (919) DUKEFSB 1979
Fuqua School of Bus 2138 Campus Drive FAX = 684-2818 MBA,PHD

Keller, Thomas F.	Dean	660-7725	keller		Atg	PHD	60	Michigan 1959
R. J. Reynolds Professor of Business Administration								
–Operations Management Area	Phone		Fax 684-2818					
Mazzola, Joseph B.	C-Ac	660-7856				PHD		Car Mel
Kouvelis, Panagiotis	Assoc	660-7833		7	UV	PHD	88	Stanford 1992
Rummel, Jeff	Assoc	660-7858				PHD		Rochest
Nandakumar, P.	Asst	660-7853				PHD		Car Mel
–Organizational Behavior	Phone		Fax 684-8742					
Payne, John W.	C-Pr	660-7850	payne	27	EVZ	PHD	73	Ca-Irvine 1977
Baligh, Helmy H.	Prof	660-7761	baligh	38	YHZ	PHD	63	Berkeley 1967
Burton, Richard M.	Prof	660-7847	burton	28	HIY	DBA	67	Illinois 1970
DeSunctis, Geraldine	Prof			9	Z	PHD	82	Tx Tech 1994
Fischer, Gregory	Prof	660-7834	fischer	2	CEI	PHD	72	Michigan 1990
Lewin, Arie Y.	Prof	660-7832	lewin	4	HJ	PHD	68	Car Mel 1974
Sheppard, Blair	Prof	660-7845	sheppard	23	EQ	PHD	80	Illinois 1986
Sotkin, S. B.	Prof			2	E	PHD	86	Stanford 1994
Belliveau, Marua A.	Asst			25	EN	ABD		Berkeley 1994
Salk, Jane E.	Asst	660-7843	salk	8	EH	PHD		MIT 1991
Sondak, Harris	Asst	660-7821	sondak	54	Q	PHD	90	Northwes 1990

Duquesne University Pittsburgh, PA 15282-0104 (412) 1961,1963
School of Bus & Adm 600 Forbes Avenue FAX = 642-9106 BS,MBA

Murrin, Thomas J.	Dean			DMS		Duquesne 1991
–Department of Management	Phone		Fax 642-9106			
Kurke, Lance B.	C-Ac		23	PHD		Cornell 1989
Burnham, James	Prof		38	PHD		Wash U 1990
Matejka, J. Kenneth	Prof		23	PHD		Arkansas 1987
South, John	Prof		25	PHD		Arkansas 1965
Abboushi, Suhail	Assoc		38	PHD		Pitt 1986
Liebowitz, Jay	Assoc			PHD		Tenn 1984
Presutti, William D. Jr.	Assoc		17	PHD		Carn Mel 1985
Associate Dean						

East Carolina University Greenville, NC 27858-4353 (919) ECUVM1 1967,1976
School of Business East Fifth Street FAX = 757-6836 BS,MBA

Uhr, Ernest B.	Dean	757-6966			Mktg	PHD	69	Renssel 1983
–Department of Management	Phone	757-6836	Fax 757-6664					
Tomkiewicz, Joseph M.	C-Pr	757-6026	mgtomkie	25	EFNR	PHD	78	Temple 8-81
Hill, Joseph A.	Prof	757-6354	sbhill	82	YEIT	PHD	66	Florida 8-65
Hughes, R. Eugene	Prof	757-6836	mghughes	25	EFNP	DBA	75	Kentucky 8-85
Eckstein, Louis W. Jr.	Assoc	757-6363		18	FHY	PHD	79	Georgia 8-79
Hunt, Judith R.	Assoc	757-6590		35	BRIY	PHD	87	Tenn 8-88
Smith, James O. Jr.	Assoc	757-6559	sbsmith	25	FER	PHD	80	Miss 8-78
Adeyemi-Bello, Tope	Asst	757-4856	mgbello	83	IYXD	PHD	92	Arkansas 6-90
Bass, Kenneth Ernest	Asst	757-6384	mgbass	31	IEJL	DBA	91	La Tech 8-92
Hebert, Frederic J.	Asst	757-6582	mghebert	36	IT	DBA	90	La Tech 8-90
Simerly, Roy L.	Asst	757-6632	mgsimerl	13	IJ	PHD	90	Va Tech 8-90
Boldt, Donald B.	DLect	757-6970		36		MBA	62	Harvard 8-81
Hart, Pamela M.	Lect	757-6063		56		MBA	86	E Carol 8-86
–Dept of Decision Sciences	Phone							
Schellenberger, Robert E.	C-Pr			7	V	PHD	73	N Carol 8-81
Collins, William H. Jr.	Prof	757-6569			V	PHD		S Illin 1970
Gulati, Umest C.	Prof	757-6565			Y	PHD		Virginia 9-67
Kerns, Richard L.	Prof	757-6350			Z	PHD		Virginia 1975
Thornton, Jack W. Jr.	Prof	757-6364			Z	PHD		Missouri 1968
Zincone, Louis H. Jr.	Prof	757-6970	sbzicon		V	PHD		Virginia 1966
Associate Dean								
Capen, Margaret M.	Assoc	757-6570			X	PHD		S Carol 8-81
Hsu, Yuan-Hsi	Assoc	757-6572			V	PHD		LSU 1980
Killingsworth, Brenda Lou	Assoc	757-6235			Z	PHD	87	S Carol 1987
McLeod, Michael E.	Assoc	757-6588			Z	PHD		Georgia 8-82
Bradley, John	Asst	757-6801			Z	PHD		UTA 8-90
Coffin, Mark	Asst	757-6370			U	PHD		Va Tech 8-92
Dellana, Scott	Asst	757-4893			U	PHD		Mo-Rolla 8-93
Gupta, Uma	Asst	757-6796			Z	PHD	91	Cen Fla 8-93
Hauser, Richard D. Jr.	Asst	757-6410			Z	PHD	91	Fla St 8-90
MacLeod, Kenneth R.	Asst	757-6637			V	PHD	90	S Carol 1989
Menneck, G.	Asst	757-6599			Z	PHD		Indiana 8-93

East Central University

Ada, OK 74820-6899 (405)

School of Business — 12th Street — Phone 332-8000 — FAX=

BS

Name	Rank	Ext		#	Code	Degree	Yr	School	Year
Brown, William J.	Dean	Ext 649			Fnce	PHD	67	NYU	1993
–Management Faculty									
Bardin, Carl	Asst	Ext 530		9	Z	MS	70	Okla St	1970
Jones, Charlie C.	Asst	Ext 605		34	INKQ	JD	86	Oklahoma	8-86
Rundle, Jaclyn	Asst	Ext 561		23	EFHJ	PHD	92	Utah	8-93
Smith, Weldon	Asst	Ext 531		7	UVWX	MBA	72	Oklahoma	1980
Fountain, Patrick	Inst	Ext 273		1		MS	88		1988

East Tennessee State Univ

Johnson City, TN 37614-0002 (615) ETSU

FAX=929-5274

College of Business — 1987,1987 BS,MBA

Name	Rank	Phone	Email	#	Code	Degree	Yr	School	Year
Spritzer, Allan D.	Dean	929-5489	i64sprit		Mgt	PHD	71	Cornell	1981
–Dept of Management & Mktg	Phone		Fax 929-5274						
Riecken, W. Glen	C-Pr	929-4422	raxglen		Mktg	PHD	79	Va Tech	1982
Frierson, James G.	Prof	929-5384		4	KLN	JD	65	Arkansas	1973
Perlaki, Ivan	VProf	929-5299		25	EFHN	PHD	76	Czechosl	1988
Stead, W. Edward	Prof	929-5399	iaxwalt	3	EFMP	PHD	76	LSU	1982
Zimmerer, Thomas W.	Prof	929-6486		3	I	PHD	71	Arkansas	1993
Allen & Ruth Harris Chair of Excellance									
Quigley, John V.	Assoc	929-5397	raxquig	9	Z	PHD	79	Geo St	1984
Stead, Jean Garner	Assoc	929-5398	1axjean	3	IM	PHD	83	LSU	1982
Green, Ronald F.	Asst	929-5099	raxgreen	37	IVY	PHD	86	Clemson	1986
Miller, Phillip E.	Asst			7	U	PHD	85	N Carol	1994
Rockmore, B. Wayne	Asst	929-5389	raxrcky	53	NQI	PHD	91	Georgia	1990
Small, Michael	Asst			7	UV	PHD	93	Cleve St	1994
Smith, Allen E.	Asst	929-5854	raxallen	79	UZ	PhD	90	S Carol	1987
Swinehart, Kerry D.	Asst	929-5395	raxkerry	7	U	PHD	89	Georgia	1990
Tarnoff, Karen	Asst			5	N	PHD	94	Va Tech	1994
Yasin, Mahmoud M.	Asst	929-5877	iaxyusin	79	UVXY	PHD	86	Clemson	1988
Bartoll, Nancy O.	Inst	929-5586		1		MA	78	Northwes	1989
Dumstorf, Theodore A.	Inst	929-5199		1		MA	51	Louisvil	1985
Pollock, Eugenia	Inst	929-5592		4		JD	77	Tennesse	1988

East Texas State Univ

Commerce, TX 75429-3011 (903)

FAX=886-5650

College of Business — 2600 Neal Street — 1975,1982 BBA

Name	Rank	Phone	Fax	#	Code	Degree	Yr	School	Year
Pressley, Trezzie A.	Dean	886-5189			Mgt	PHD	66	Arkansas	1965
–Dept Mktg & Management	Phone	886-5703	Fax 886-5702						
Noe, Robert M.	H-Pr	886-5695		25	N	EDD	72	North Tx	1965
Caruth, Donald L.	Prof	886-5697		35	P	PHD	70	North Tx	1982
Odom, Randall Y.	Assoc	886-5700		37	I	PHD	84	Miss	1985
Seay, Robert M.	Asst	886-5190		27	U	DBA	85	La Tech	1982

Eastern Conn State Univ

Willimantic, CT 06226-2295 (203)

FAX=456-2231

School of Prof Studies — 83 Windham Street

Name	Rank	Phone	Fax	Code	Degree	School	Year
Comer, Kelvie C.	Dean	456-5293			EDD	Temple	
–Dept of Econ & Mgt Sciences	Phone		Fax 456-2231				
Lowy, Ronald	C-Ac	456-5254			PHD	Kent St	1989
Yorks, Lyle	Prof	456-5210			ABD	Columbia	1978
St. Onge, John	Assoc	456-5321			MBA	Harvard	1980

Eastern Illinois Univ

Charleston, IL 61920-3099 (217)

FAX=581-6247

Lumpkin College of Bus — 600 Lincoln Avenue — BS,MBA

Name	Rank	Phone	Fax	Code	Degree	Yr	School	Year
Ivarie, Theordore W.	Dean	581-3526		BusE	EDD	68	Ariz St	1979
–Dept Management & Mktg	Phone	581-2020	Fax 581-6247					
Arnold, Aline	C-Pr	581-2020		IH	PHD		North Tx	1988
Elmuti, Dean	Prof	581-6920		IY	PHD		North Tx	1987
Marlow, Edward K.	Prof	581-3019		E	PHD	75	Illinois	1984
Payne, Stephen L.	Prof	581-6635		JL	PHD		Ariz St	1989
Prasad, Jyoti	Assoc	581-6922			PHD			1989
Rinefort, Foster C.	Assoc	581-6923		I	PHD		Tx A&M	1981
Kemmerer, Barbara	Asst	581-6904		EQ	PHD		Nebraska	1990
Oglesby, Marilyn S.	Asst	581-6921		D	MSED		E Illin	1969
Wayland, Robert	Asst	581-2925		NQI	PHD		North Tx	1991

Eastern Kentucky University

Richmond, KY 40475-3111 (606) EKU

FAX=622-2359

College of Business — BA,MBA

Name	Rank	Phone	Fax/Email	#	Code	Degree	Yr	School	Year
Patrick, Alfred	Dean	622-1409							
–Dept of Business Adm	Phone	622-1377	Fax 622-2359						
Hilton, Charles L.	C-Pr	622-1377	cbohilto		Mktg	PHD	73	Mich St	1979
Brewer, Peggy D.	Prof	622-4970		35	DPR	DBA	82	La Tech	1980
Brown, Stephen M.	Prof	622-4986		63	STU	PHD	74	Georgia	1988
Roberson, Michael T.	Prof	622-4984		5	NPQ	PHD	86	Tenn	1987
Wright, J. Ward	Prof	622-2353		45	KLJ	DPA	78	S Calif	1983
Davig, William A.	Assoc	622-4971		36	ST	PHD	74	Northwes	1984

Engle, Allen	Assoc	622-1121		18	EBH	DBA	89	Kentucky	1989
McGlone, Teresa	Assoc	622-1121		7	U	DBA	90	Kentucky	1989
Friel, Terri	Asst	622-4931		7	UV	PHD	92	So Meth	1991
Tabibzadeh, Kambiz	Asst	622-4974		7	ZQ	PHD	85	Houston	1985

Eastern Michigan University — Ypsilanti, MI 48197 — (313)
College of Business — 300 W. Michigan, Suite 466 — FAX=487-7099 — 1973,1982 BBA,MSA

Tubbs, Stewart L.	Dean	487-4140		2	E	PHD	69	Kansas	1986

—**Department of Management** — Phone 487-3240 — Fax 487-4100

Andrews, Fraya W.	Prof	487-1215		1		DBA		Memphis	1982
Blanchard, P. Nick	Prof	487-3446		2		MA		Sn Dgo S	1979
Camp, Richaurd	Prof	487-0453		2		MA		Wayne St	1979
Conley, James H.	Prof	487-2169		1		PHD	69	Mich St	1969
Hendrickson, Lorraine	Prof	487-1722		2		PHD		Michigan	1981
Hermon, Mary E.	Prof	487-2468		1		PHD		Michigan	1977
Hill, Raymond	Prof	487-3240		25		PHD	70	Purdue	1989
Hoyer, Denise Tanguay	Prof	487-0468		3		PHD		Michigan	1986
Huszczo, Gregory E.	Prof	487-2253		2		PHD		Mich St	1978
McEnery, Jean	Prof	487-0224		2		PHD		Wayne St	1980
Patrick, Floyd A.	Prof	487-0227		5		PHD	62	Iowa	1970
Waltman, John L.	Prof	487-0323		1		PHD		Texas	1985
Chowdhry, Pradeep	Assoc	487-0113		3		PHD		Arkansas	1980
Crowner, Robert P.	Assoc	487-2215		3		MS		Butler	1976
Danak, Jagdish T.	Assoc	487-3447		1		PHD	70	Oklahoma	1969
Victor, David A.	Assoc	487-0105		1		PHD		Michigan	1985
Bush-Bacelis, Jean	Asst	487-3445				PHD	93	Wayne St	1984
Ettington, Debbie	Asst	487-0160		3		PHD	92	Michigan	1992
Nightingale, John P.	Asst	487-0157		1		MA		N Dakota	1980

Eastern New Mexico Univ — Portales, NM 88130 — (505) EMAIL.EMU.EDU
College of Business — FAX=562-4331 — BS,BBA,MBA

Martin, Dolores	Dean	562-2343			Econ	PHD	76	Va Tech	1993

—**Department of Management** — Phone — Fax 562-4331

Huybregts, Gerry	C-Ac	562-2737		38	IOY	PHD	88	UCLA	1988
Davis, Dale N.	Prof	562-2772			BEFH	DBA	80	Geo St	1982
DeWitt, Calvin	Asst	562-2704		79	UVZ	PHD	93	Houston	1987
Johns, Roger	Asst	562-2332		4	JKL	LLM	88	Boston	1988
Sanchez, Victoria D.	Asst	562-2352		52	ENR	PHD	86	Ariz St	1972
Morrison, Beth	Inst	562-2360		89	DRYZ	MBA	90	E N Mex	1992
Nix, Timothy W.	Inst	562-2358		23	CFHI	ABD	94	Tx Tech	1992

Eastern Washington Univ — Cheney, WA 99004-2490 — (509)
College of Business Adm — FAX=359-6649 — 1975,1981 BA,MBA
Both Departments Did Not Respond-1993 Listing

—**Department of Management** — Phone — Fax 359-6649

Brown, Charles	C-Pr	359-6381							
Hasan, Syed M. Jameel	Prof	359-6645		28	EYL	ABD	64	S Carol	1969
McGinty, Robert L.	Prof	359-2873		35	NIP	PHD	79	Denver	1980
Simpson, Leo R.	Prof	359-2474		67	STU	DBA	75	Colorado	1977
Christensen, Sandra L.	Asst	359-2801		48	LKY	PHD	89	U Wash	1990
Eager, Wendy M.	Asst	359-4248		52	NPE	PHD	90	Penn St	1989
Nemetz-Mills, Patricia L.	Asst	359-6920		37	UI	PHD	89	U Wash	1989
Pooley, John M.	Asst	359-6647		7	UVX	PHD	89	Penn St	1989
Welsh, Dianne	Asst	359-2258		25	ENQP	PHD	88	Nebraska	1988

—**Dept of Mgt Info Systems** — Phone — Fax 359-6649

Zurenko, John	C-Pr	359-2250							
Burnham, Kent T.	Prof	359-6632		9	Z	PHD	71	Iowa	1967
Palmer, Kermit G.	Prof	359-6631		9	Z	EDD	67	S Carol	1968
Reitsch, Arthur G.	Prof	359-7980		3	IV	PHD	73	Oregon	1969
Ford, John P.	Assoc	359-7977		9	ZV	MS	65	Wash St	1970
Kuo, Chin	Asst	359-6548		9	ZV	PHD	88	Ariz St	1989
Stewart, Morag I.	Asst	359-6641		9	ZY	PHD	88	Ariz St	1988

Elizabethtown College — Elizabethtown PA 17022-2298 — (717)
Department of Business — 1 Alpha Drive — FAX=367-7567 — BS

Trostle, Randolph	C-Ac	361-1270				PHD	83	Lehigh	9-72

—**Management Faculty** — Phone 361-1270 — Fax 361-1487

Buffenmyer, Jay	Prof	Ext 1413		58	YN	PHD	76	Pitt	9-76
Stone, Richard G.	Assoc	Ext 1284		37	IU	PHD	88	Temple	9-87
Muston, Donald	Asst	Ext 1278		23	EQ	BIM	77	Thunderb	9-77

Elmhurst College — Elmhurst, IL 60126-3296 — (708)
Center for Bus & Econ — 190 Prospect — FAX=
Did Not Respond Again-1992 Listing — BS,BA

Bohnert, John E.	Dean	617-3123				PHD		S Illin	1967

Name	Rank	Phone	Email			Degree		School	Year
–Management Faculty	Phone		Fax 617-3282						
Heiney, Joseph N.	Dir	617-3123				Econ PHD		Chicago	
Carroll, Lawrence B.	Asst					MBA		Roosevel	1974

Elon College — Elon College, NC 27244-2020 — (919) VAX1.ELON.EDU
Love School of Business — Haggard Avenue — FAX=584-2575 — BS,BA,MBA

Name	Rank	Phone				Degree	Yr	School	Year
–Management Faculty	Phone	584-2566	Fax 538-2735						
Weavil, Linda	Prof	584-2236		1		EDD	85	NC-Green	1973
Baxter, Robert	Assoc	584-2365		4		JD	59	Duke	1959
McClellan, Robie	Assoc	584-2710		51		EDD	79	NC-Green	1980
Guffey, W. Robert	Asst	584-2110				PHD	92	Va Tech	1992
O'Mara, Kevin	Asst	584-2494		35		PHD	91	N Carol	1988
Peterson, Charles	Asst	584-2238		7		MBA	75	American	1988
Strempek, R. Barth	Asst	538-2697		39	Y	DBA	89	Miss St	1994

Embry-Riddle Aeronautical U — Daytona Bch, FL 32114-3900 — (904) BART.DB.ERAU.EDU
Aviation Bus Adm — 600 Clyde Morris Boulevard — FAX=226-6459

Name	Rank	Phone	Email			Degree	Yr	School	Year
Harraf, Abe	C-Pr	226-6694	harraf			Econ PHD	84	Utah St	1984
–Management Faculty	Phone	226-6694	Fax 226-6696						
Chadbourne, Bruce	Prof	226-6730	chadbourne			EDD	85	Fla Atl	1973
Pope, John L.	Prof	226-6723	pope	25		PHD	75	Stetson	1981
Chamberlin, William	Assoc	226-6704	chamberlin			MBA	69	Stetson	1979
James, Dean F.	Assoc	226-6684	james	9		MS	71	UCLA	1981
Knabe, Rudy	Assoc	226-6731	knabe			MBA	76	Mid Tenn	1976
Longshore, John	Assoc	226-6730	longshore			PHD	88	Nova	1992
Maulden, Hoyt	Assoc	226-6702	maulden			MBA	68	Geo Wash	1980
Swanson, James	Assoc	226-6693	swanson	9	Z	PHD	70	Fla St	1986
Tacker, Tom	Assoc	226-6701	tacker			PHD	87	N Carol	1988
Trnavskis, Doris	Assoc	226-6705	trnavskis	37		PHD	74	Calgary	1986
Vasigh, Bijan	Assoc	226-6722	vasigh	7		PHD	84	SUNY	1990
Weatherford, Philip A.	Assoc	226-6721	weatherford	31		EDD	83	Fla Atl	1973
Wilson, Katherine	Assoc	226-6670	wilson			MBA	77	Stetson	1984
Bulmer, Gail T.	Asst	226-6246	bulmer	1		MA	76	Ball St	1986
Fedorovich, Shirely M.	Asst	226-6685	fedorovich	9		MSM	78	Rollins	1976
McQuillen, Charles	Asst	226-6703	mcquillen			PHD	69	Florida	1993
Obi, Joseph E.	Asst	226-6700	obi	13		MBAA	79	Embry-Ri	1980
Rollins, John	Asst	226-6247	rollins			MBA	73	Embry-Ri	1993
Thamer, Theresa	Asst	226-6732	thamer			MBA	81	Geo St	1990

Emory University — Atlanta, GA 30322 — (404) EMUBUS.BUS.EMORY.EDU — 1949,1963
Emory Business School — FAX=727-6313 — BBA,MBA

Name	Rank	Phone	Email			Degree	Yr	School	Year
Frank, Ronald E.	Dean	727-6377	squalls			Mktg PHD	60	Chicago	1989
Asa Griggs Candler Professor of Marketing									
–Organization & Management	Phone	727-6369	Fax 727-6663						
Miles, Robert H.	C-Pr	727-6369	dleach	2	HI	PHD	74	N Carol	1987
Isaac Stiles Hopkins Professor of Organization & Management									
Sonnenfeld, Jeffrey A.	Prof	727-2752	jsonnenf	5	NO	DBA	80	Harvard	1989
Director Center of Leadership and Career Change									
Drazin, Robert	Assoc	727-6337	rdrazin	2	H	PHD	82	Penn	1988
Glynn, Mary Ann	Assoc	727-0798		2	E	PHD	88	Columbia	1993
Gresov, Christopher G.	Assoc	727-0526		6	H	PHD	88	Columbia	1993
Kazanjian, Robert K.	Assoc	727-6359	rkazanji	3	I	PHD	83	Penn	1988
Thomas, Lacy Glenn	Assoc	727-0539	lthomas	3	I	PHD	79	Duke	1991
Barr, Pamela S.	Asst	727-4967		3	I	PHD	91	Illinois	1990
Elsbach, Kimberly	Asst	727-0527		2	H	PHD	93	Stanford	1993
Golden-Biddle, Karen A.	Asst	727-7823	kgolden	5	N	PHD	88	Case Wes	1988
Rao, M. V. Hayagreeva	Asst	727-2753	hrao	2	H	PHD	89	Case Wes	1989
Waring, Goeffry	Asst	727-0809		3	I	PHD	93	UCLA	1993
–Decision & Information Anal	Phone	727-6698	Fax 727-0868						
Konsynski, Benn	C-Pr		bkonsyns	9	Z	PHD		Purdue	
George S. Craft Professor of Business Administration									
Jensen, Ronald L.	Prof		rjensen	9	Z	DBA	64	Wash U	
Bharadwiaj, Anandhi	Asst		abharadw	7		PHD		Tx A&M	
Chambers, Robert J.	VAsst		rchamber	7	U	PHD		Purdue	
Elofson, Gregg	Asst		geloffso			PHD		Arizona	
Stuk, Stephen P.	Asst		sstuk	7	U	PHD		Ga Tech	
Vargas, Vince	Asst								
Wurst, John C.	Asst		jwurst	7	V	PHD		Georgia	

Emory and Henry College — Emory, VA 24327-0947 — (703) FAX=944-4438
Dept of Econ & Business

Name	Rank	Phone				Degree	Yr	School	Year
–Management Faculty	Phone		Fax 994-4438						
Cumbo, James	C	944-4121		12	EHJS	PHD	81	Va Tech	1975
Russell, Robert	Asst	944-4121		37	IU	MBA	84	Virginia	1984

Emporia State University

Name	Title	Phone	Email/Fax			Degree	Yr	School	Yr
Emporia State University		Emporia, KS	66801-5087	(316)					
School of Business				FAX=341-5997					BS
Hashmi, Sajjad A.	Dean	341-5274				PHD	66	Penn	8-83
–Div of Mgt,Mktg,Fin & Econ	Phone	341-5347	Fax 341-5418						
Titus, Varkey	C-Ac	341-5347				PHD	80	Wash St	8-79
DeVito, Raffaele	Prof	341-5384		13	Y	EDD	82	Northeas	8-82
Miller, Donald	Prof	341-5456		35		EDD	72	Okla St	8-66
Director of MBA Program									
Finney, Bartlett	Assoc	341-5308		25		PHD	80	Kan St	8-79
Crosby, Leon	Asst	341-5306				PHD	94	Miss St	8-92
Smith, William	Asst	341-5729				MBA	74	Drake	8-94
Nichols, Joan	Inst	341-5227		6		MA	91	Webster	8-88

University of Evansville

Name	Title	Phone	Email/Fax			Degree	Yr	School	Yr
University of Evansville		Evansville, IN	47722	(812) EVANSVILLE.EDU					
School of Business Adm		1800 Lincoln Avenue		FAX=479-2320					BS
Mullins, Terry W.	Dean	479-2851	mullins	2	E	PHD	78	Houston	1993
–Department of Management	Phone	479-2851	Fax 471-6995						
Faust, Ronald	Prof	479-2867		5	NQE	PHD	72	Iowa	1964
Hockstra, Dale J.	Prof	479-2865	dh3	7	UV	PHD	74	Stanford	1976
Holmes, Barbara	Asst	479-2854	bh9	25	ENO	PHD	88	LSU	1988
Steenberg, Laurence	Asst	479-2387		36	IJ	MBA	70	Chicago	1989

Fairfield University

Name	Title	Phone	Email/Fax			Degree	Yr	School	Yr
Fairfield Universiy		Fairfield, CT	06430-7524	(203) FAIR1					
School of Business		North Benson Road		FAX=254-4105					BS
phone 254-4000									
Boisjoly, Russell C.	Dean$	Ext 4070				DBA	78	Indiana	1989
–Management Faculty	Phone		Fax 254-4105						
Tyler, Richard F.	C-As	Ext 2831	tyler	15	EQP	MBA	66	New York	1977
Katz, Lucy V.	Assoc	Ext 2822	lvkatz	45	KLR	JD	68	New York	1983
Mainiero, Lisa A.	Assoc	Ext 2820	lamainie	23	FGEI	PHD	83	Yale	1983
Ryba, Walter G. Jr.	Assoc	Ext 2819	wrryba	43	JILY	JD	75	Conn	1982
Cavanaugh, J. Michael	Asst	Ext 2820		23	DHI	PHD	91	Mass	1990
McEvoy, Sharlene A.	Asst	Ext 2836	samcevoy	34	JLKI	PHD	85	UCLA	1986
Tromley, Cheryl L.	Asst	Ext 2814	cltromle	24	EFLH	PHD	84	Yale	1987

Fairleigh Dickinson Univ

Name	Title	Phone	Email/Fax			Degree	Yr	School	Yr
Fairleigh Dickinson Univ		Madison, NJ	07940	(201)					
Silberman Col of Bus Ad		285 Madison Avenue		FAX=593-8804					
Lerman, Paul	Dean	460-5346				PHD	74	NYU	
–Department of Management	Phone		Fax 593-8804						
Ottaway, Rich	C-Pr	593-8858		45	GIJN	PHD	79	Manchest	1983
Beaven, Mary	Prof	692-2157		2		PHD		Northwes	
Budish, Bernard	Prof			13		PHD		NYU	
Butler, Thomas	Prof					PHD			
Lucas, Ann F.	Prof	692-2312		2		PHD		Fordham	
Scotti, Dennis J.	Prof	692-2157		1		PHD		Temple	
Twomey, Dan	Prof	593-8802		56	NTM	DBA		Kent St	1987
Taylor, Stuart	Assoc			15	NTM	DBA		Indiana	1992
Harmon, Joel I.	Asst	648-5468		12	DEZ	PHD		SUNY-Alb	1993
O'Brien, John F.	Asst	692-2157		1		PHD		NYU	
–Info Systems & Sciences De	Phone	460-5462	Fax 593-8804						
Naadimuthu, G.	C-Pr	460-5345				PHD		KSU	
Bronson, Gary	Prof	593-8871				PHD		Stevens	
Gnanadesikan, Mrudulla	Prof	593-8873				PHD		Purdue	
Panicucci, Richard	Prof	692-2135				MBA		Fairl Di	
Soles, Stanley	Prof	593-5423				PHD		Stanford	
Walker, William F. Jr.	Prof					PHD		Rutgers	
Yoon, K. Paul	Prof	460-5417				PHD		KSU	
Fask, Alan	Assoc	593-8872				PHD		NYU	
Mendoza, Gaston	Assoc	460-5418		7	V	PHD		Temple	
Gambhir, Dinesh	Asst	593-8875				PHD		Polytech	
Gupta, Vandna	Asst	460-5310				MS		Carleton	
Kim, Yongeom	Asst	593-8856				PHD		NYU	
Piccoli, Michael	Asst	692-2519				BS		Fairl Di	
Director									
Stawicki, Robert	Asst	593-8879				PHD		Rutgers	
Wang, Zhaobo	Asst	460-5425				PHD		Rutgers	
Kim, Youngjin	Inst	460-5312				MS		NJ Tech	
Giordano, Daniel	Lect	460-5309				MA		Manhatan	

Fayetteville State Univ

Name	Title	Phone	Email/Fax			Dept	Degree	Yr	School	Yr
Fayetteville State Univ		Fayetteville, NC	28301-4298	(919)						
Sch of Business & Econ		1200 Murchison Road		FAX=						
Davis, Charles	Dean	486-1267				Mktg	DBA	81	Tenn	1993
–Dept of Management & Mktg	Phone	486-1595								
Wlaker, Moses	C-Pr$	486-1595					PHD	83	Iowa	1987
Constas, Kimon	Prof	486-1198					PHD			
Robinson, Patricia	Prof	486-1310					PHD			
Tavakoli, Assad	Prof	486-1267					PHD	76	England	1983

Griffin, Barry	Assoc	486-1698			PHD			
Bajwa, Deepinder	Asst	486-1067			PHD			
Brenan, Ian	Asst	486-1487			PHD			
Goodwin, Chester	Asst	486-1764			PHD			
Lee, Jonathan	Asst	486-1736			ABD			
Holt, Joseph	Inst	486-1698			MBA			
Johnson, Walter II	Inst				MBA			

Ferris State University — Big Rapids, MI 49307-2284 (616)
College of Business — 901 South State Street — FAX=592-2990 — BS,MACC

Hansen, Richard C.	Dean	592-2422		3	PHD	71	Wiscon	1983
—**Management Department**	Phone	592-2427	Fax 592-3521					
Rallo, Joseph C.	H-Pr	592-2427		8	PHD	80	Syracuse	1992
Borseth, Earl	Prof	592-2450		2	MBA		Indiana	1983
Pomnichowski, Alex S.	Prof	592-2467		5	PHD		Mich St	1967
Smith, Wanda V.	Prof	592-2972		3	PHD		Mich St	1979
Swartz, Rose Ann	Prof	592-2465		2	PHD		Mich St	1978
Valas, John	Prof	592-2473		2	MA		Michigan	1982
Balcerzak, Raymond F. Jr.	Assoc	592-2478		7	MBA		SUNY-Buf	1985
LaBarre, Richard E.	Assoc	592-2459		6	MBA		Central	1978
Lunden, John H.	Assoc	592-2462		3	MBA		Michigan	1980
Perdue, John	Assoc	592-2471		5	MBA		Detroit	1983
Wozniak, Douglas R.	Assoc	592-2475		2	MBA		Bowl Gr	1978
Bell, Sharon E.	Asst	592-2450		2	MBA		Wrght St	1980
Hartman, Karen	Asst	592-2462		8	JD	79	Michigan	1993
Kelson, David	Asst	592-2466		8	MIM		Amr Grad	1990

Fisk University — Nashville, TN 37208-3051 (615)
Div of Business Adm — 1000 17th Avenue North — FAX=329-8715

Smith, Solomon	D-Pr	329-8573		37	UVY	PHD	S Illin	1988
—**Management Faculty**	Phone		Fax 329-8758					
Ponder, Eunice	Prof	329-8763		26	REN	PHD	S Carol	1993
Shackelford, James	Assoc	329-8696		7	UVX	PHD	Vanderbt	1992
Cambronero, Alfredo	Asst	329-8698		78	UVY	PHD	Vanderbt	1992

Fitchburg State College — Fitchburg, MA 01420-2697 (508)
Dept of Business Adm — 160 Pearl Street — FAX=343-8603
Did Not Respond-1993 Listing; phone 345-2151

Noonan, James	C-As	Ext 3378			MBA		Suffolk	1981
—**Management Faculty**	Phone		Fax 343-8603					
Boursy, John J.	Prof	Ext 3378		4	GJ	MBA	Clark	1964
Caggiano, Diane P.	Asst	Ext 3378		2	EHLR	MBA	Babson	1983

University of Florida — Gainesville, FL 32611-2017 (904) NERVM.NERDC.UFL.EDU929,1963
College of Business Adm — FAX=392-2398 — BSA,MBA,MAC,PHD

Kraft, John	Dean	392-2397		Econ	PHD	71	Pitt	1990
—**Dept Management & B Law**	Phone		Fax 392-6020					
Ray, J. B. Jr.	C-Pr	392-0163		BLaw	JD	63	Florida	1962
Champion, John M.	Prof	392-0277		34	EIJN	PHD	58	Purdue	1964
Tosi, Henry L. Jr.	Prof	392-6147		12	E	PHD	64	Ohio St	1978
McGriff Professor								
James, John H.	Assoc	392-0108		23	IJ	DBA	61	Indiana	1961
Motowidlo, Stephan J.	Assoc	392-3190		25	EGNR	PHD	76	Minn	
Young, Jerald W.	Assoc	392-0102		12	DEFP	PHD	74	Yale	1974
Hall, H. John	Asst	392-9639		13	IJLT	PHD	89	Georgia	1989
Schmit, Mark	Asst	392-0163		36	ITQ	PHD	94	Bowl Gr	1994
Scully, Judity	Asst	392-0163		25	ENQ	PHD	94	Maryland	1994
Plater, Michael	Lect	392-5815		36	IT	PHD	93	Wm&Mary	1993
Wyman, John	Lect	392-8793		3	I	DPS	89	Pace	1988
—**Dept Decision & Info Sci**	Phone	392-9600	Fax 392-5438					
Erenguc, S. Selcuk	C-Pr	392-4633	erenguc		PHD	80	Indiana	1982
Benson, Harold P.	Prof	392-0134	benson		PHD	76	Northwes	1979
Elnicki, Richard A.	Prof	392-6640	dicke		DBA	67	Harvard	1971
Horowitz, Ira	Prof	392-9600	rohari		PHD	59	MIT	1972
Koehler, Gary J.	Prof	392-8110	koehler	9	Z	PHD	73	Purdue	1987
on leave to Purdue University								
Majthay, Antael	Assoc	392-0117	majthay		PHD	61	Szeged	1972
Hurd, Joanne	Asst	392-7300	hurd		PHD	92	Tx Tech	1993
Piramuthu, Selwyn	Asst	392-9600	selwyn		PHD	92	Illinois	1991
Thompson, Patrick	Asst	392-9731	pthomp		PHD	84	Wiscon	1989
Vakharia, Asoo	Asst	392-9600			PHD	87	Wiscon	1994

Florida A&M University

Tallahassee, FL 32307 (904)
Sch of Bus & Industry — South Adams Street — FAX=599-3533
—Management Faculty — Phone 599-3170 — Fax 599-3533

Name	Rank	Phone			Degree	Yr	School	Year
Mobley, Sybil C.	Dean	599-3565		Atg	PHD	64	Illinois	BS,MBA 1963
Carpenter, Vivian L.	D-Ac	599-3170		Atg	PHD	86	Michigan	1992
Evans, Charles	Prof	561-2329	9		PHD		Syracuse	
Bradford, Amos	Assoc	561-2380	2		PHD		Michigan	
Clark, George	Assoc	561-2373	29		PHD		Illinois	
Davis, Bobby	Assoc	561-2328	25		PHD		Wiscon	
Lester, Wanda	Asst				ABD		Fla St	8-92
Lockamy, Archie	Asst	764-6174	7	U	PHD	91	Georgia	1993
Major, Don	Asst	561-2327	83		ABD		Miami	
Neely, George	Asst	561-2322	12		PHD		Michigan	
Nkansah, Paul	Asst	561-2333	7		PHD		Iowa St	
Ridley, Dennis	Asst	561-2335	7		PHD		Clemson	

Florida Atlantic Univ

Boca Raton, FL 33431-0991 (407) FAUVAX 1977,1977
College of Business — 500 Northwest 20th Street — FAX=367-3978 — BS,MBA,PHD
—Dept/Management & Intl Bus — Phone 367-3654 — Fax 367-3978

Name	Rank	Phone	email			Degree	Yr	School	Year
Hille, Stanley J.	Dean	367-3630	hille			PHD	66	Minn	1988
Unwalla, Darab B.	C-Pr	367-3655	unwalla	32	STL	PHD	57	Bombay	1969
Abbott, Jarold G.	Prof	367-3658	abbott	25	EFN	PHD	60	MIT	1971
Bernardin, H. John	Prof	367-3634	bernardi	5	NV	PHD	76	BG	8-83
Keon, Tom	Prof	355-5216	afauvax-keon	32	HIS	PHD		MSU	8-90
Klatt, Lawrence A.	Prof	367-3656	klatt	56	NST	PHD	57	Missouri	1972
Kossack, Edgar	Prof	355-3662	kossack			PHD		Georgia	1977
Landrum, Fred	VProf	355-2675				MBA		Fla Atl	1974
Moor, R. Carl	Prof	355-3663	moor	83		PHD	71	Geo St	1971
Murdick, Robert G.	Prof	367-3660	murdick	3	I	PHD	72	Florida	9-68
Nicewander, Dennis	Prof	355-2637		12	D	EDD	77	Fla Atl	8-67
Schuster, Fred E.	Prof	367-3672	schuster	25	NEFL	DBA	69	Harvard	1969
Ryan, William	Assoc	367-3659	wmtryan	23	HIY	DBA	66	Indiana	8-67
Becker, Thomas	Asst	367-2769	tbecker			PHD	86	New Mex	1991
Cooke, Donna K.	Asst	355-5252	cooke	25	EN	PHD	89	Mia	8-88
Golden, Peggy A.	Asst	369-3654	golden			PHD	89	Kentucky	9-91
Guglielmino, Paul	Asst	367-3177	guglielm	89	NPZY	EDD	78	Georgia	1978
Smith, Jerald R.	Asst	367-3654	jrsmith	38	FTY	PHD	78	Louisvil	9-91

Florida International Univ

Miami, FL 33199 (305) SERVAX 1983,1986
College of Business Adm — Primera Casa #140 — FAX=348-3278 — BBA,MA,MST
—Dept/ Management & Intl Bus — Phone 348-2791 — Fax 348-3278

Name	Rank	Phone			Degree	Yr	School	Year
Wyman, Harold E.	Dean	348-2754		Atg	PHD	67	Stanford	1990
Dessler, Gary	C-Pr	348-2791		END	PHD	73	CUNY	1971
Farrow, Dana L.	Prof	348-2751		NEP	PHD	75	Rochest	1978
Associate Dean								
Hodgetts, Richard M.	Prof	448-4788		IEB	PHD	68	Oklahoma	1976
Jerome, William T.	Prof	348-2791		E	DSC	52	Harvard	1963
Distinguished University Professor								
Luytjes, Jan B.	Prof	348-2791		TY	PHD	62	Penn	1971
Maidique, Modesto A.	Prof	348-2111		TD	PHD	70	MIT	
President of University								
Rodriguez, Leonardo	Prof	348-2101		ES	DBA	75	Fla St	1973
Vice President								
Taggart, William M.	Prof	348-2791		DGZ	PHD	71	Penn	1972
Valenzi, Enzo R.	Prof	348-2791		NEV	PHD	70	Bowl Gr	1975
Associate Dean								
Bates, Constance S.	Assoc	348-2791		IY	DBA	79	Indiana	1983
Dorsett, Herman W.	Assoc	348-2791		EN	EDD	69	Columbia	1972
Gilbert, Ronald	Assoc	348-2791		EFHP	PHD	73	S Calif	1977
Kroeck, K. Galen	Assoc	348-2675		NEX	PHD	82	Akron	1982
Magnusen, Karl O.	Assoc	348-2791		QH	PHD	70	Wiscon	1974
Director Ph.D. Program								
Silverblatt, Ronnie	Assoc	940-5870		QN	PHD	82	Geo St	1983
Specter, Christine	Assoc	348-2791		VM	DBA	86	Geo Wash	1986
on leave								
Sutija, George	Assoc	348-2791		Y	MBA	61	Columbia	1973
Friday, Earnest	Asst	348-2791		EIF	PHD	80	U Miami	1972
Moss, Sherry E.	Asst	348-2791		HE	PHD	91	Fla St	1990
Ramaswamy, Kannan	Asst	348-2791		I	PHD	90	Va Tech	1990
Thomas, Anisya	Asst	348-2791		I	PHD	90	Va Tech	1990
Ahlers, Richard	Inst	348-2781		EN	MBA	72	Detroit	1989
Jordan, Williabeth	Inst	348-4236		E	MPA	78	Fla Intl	1979
Mann, Phillip	Inst	348-4200		E	EDD	67	Virginia	1991
Polster, Eleanor	Inst	348-2781		T	MBA	81	Fla Intl	1981
Pradas, Antonio	Inst	348-2791		Y	MS	70	MIT	1991

Florida Southern College — Lakeland, FL 33801-5698 (813)
Dept of Business & Econ — 111 Lake Hollingsworth Drive — FAX=680-4126 — BS,BA,MBA

Name	Rank	Phone	email		code	Degree	yr	School	year
Hopkins, Duane L.	C-As	680-4280			Mktg	MBA		Harvard	1982
—Management Faculty	Phone		Fax 680-4126						
Larsen, Allen F.	Assoc	680-4284				PHC		Indiana	1982
Britton, George H.	Asst	680-4286				MBA		W Fla	1988
Coleman, Walter J.	Asst	680-4283				MBA		Nova	1988
Wiley, C. Jeffrey	Asst	680-4276				MBA		Indiana	1976

Florida State University — Tallahassee, FL 32306-1042 (904) COB.FSU.EDU — 1962,1964
College of Business — FAX=644-0915 — BS,MBA,PHD

Name	Rank	Phone	email		code	Degree	yr	School	year
Stith, Melvin T.	Dean	644-3090	mstith		Mktg	PHD	77	Syracuse	8-85
—Department of Management	Phone	644-5505	Fax 644-7843						
Perrewe, Pamela L.	C-Ac	644-7848	pperrew	25	EGNR	PHD	85	Nebraska	1-84
Anthony, William P.	Prof	644-7844	banthon	32	IHN	PHD	71	Ohio St	1970
Fiorito, Jack T.	Prof	644-7852	jfiorit	57	QHN	PHD	80	Illinois	8-90
Hodge, B. J.	Prof	644-9754			I	PHD	61	LSU	8-67
Martinko, Mark J.	Prof	644-7846		2	EX	PHD	77	Nebraska	9-78
Voich, Dan Jr.	Prof	644-7835	dvoich	38	IBLY	PHD	65	Illinois	1964
Wilkens, Paul L.	Prof	644-7851		23	BP	PHD	71	Ohio St	1970
Hoffman, James J.	Assoc	644-7845	jhoffma	3	IY	PHD	88	Nebraska	6-88
Kuhn, David G.	Assoc	644-7855	dkuhn	23	EFI	PHD	71	Penn St	1971
Lamont, Bruce T.	Assoc	644-9846	blamont	3	HIJY	PHD	89	N Carol	8-89
Matherly, Timothy A.	Assoc	644-7854		34	DEI	DBA	83	Indiana	9-80
Steen, Jack E.	Assoc	644-7853		5	Q	PHD	05	Alabama	1964
teaching Fall semesters only									
Stepina, Lee P.	Assoc	644-7847		25	EN	PHD	81	Illinois	8-81
Kacmar, Miki	Asst	644-7881	mkacmar	25	EN	PHD	90	Tx A&M	8-92
—Dept Info & Mgt Sciences	Phone	644-5508	Fax 644-8225						
Clark, Thomas D. Jr.	C-Pr	644-5508	tclark	97	ZVX	DBA	77	Fla St	8-84
Showalter, Michael J.	Prof	644-8230	mshowal	7	U	PHD	76	Ohio St	8-81
Shrode, William A.	Prof	644-8228	wshrode	97	ZV	DBA	68	Oregon	9-69
Stair, Ralph M. Jr.	Prof	644-8232	rstair	97	ZV	PHD	74	Oregon	9-78
Zmud, Robert W.	Prof	644-4713	bzmud	9	ZX	PHD	73	Arizona	8-87
Thomas L. Williams Jr. Eminent Scholar in Management Information Systems									
George, Joey	Assoc	644-8213	jgeorge	9	Z	PHD	86	Ca-Irvine	8-93
Larsen, John E.	Asst	644-5508	jlarsen	7	UV	PHD	89	Texas	8-91
Sambamurthy, V.	Asst	644-7449	vsambam	9	Z	PHD	89	Minn	8-89
Sampson, Scott	Asst	644-2047	ssampso	7	U	DBA		Virginia	8-93
West, Larry	Asst	644-7890	lwest	97	ZV	PHD	91	Tx A&M	8-90
Couch, Darryl V.	Lect	644-8227	dcouch	9	Z	MA	62	Fla St	8-85
Ooten, Homer A.	Lect	644-2090		97	ZV	DBA	73	Fla St	9-73

Fordham University — New York, NY 10023 (212) FORDHULC — 1939,1982
School of Business Adm — 113 West 60th Street — FAX=765-5573 — BS,MBA

Name	Rank	Phone	email		code	Degree	yr	School	year
Scalberg, Ernest	Dean	636-6111			EU	PHD		UCLA	1994
—Management Area	Phone		Fax 765-5573						
Wharton, Robert M.	C-Pr	636-6154		7	UV	PHD		Temple	1981
Ramsey, Patricia P.	Prof	636-6130		7	UV	PHD		Hofstra	1981
Stoner, James A. F.	Prof	636-6178		2	EH	PHD	67	MIT	1975
Zeleny, Milan	Prof	636-6175		7	UV	PHD	72	Rochest	1981
Belding, Eser U.	Assoc	636-6179		28	EY	PHD		Michigan	1988
Egelhoff, William G.	Assoc	636-6206		23	EIY	PHD		Columbia	1989
Georgantzas, Nicholas C.	Assoc	636-6216		37	IU	PHD		CUNY	1987
Hessel, Marek P.	Assoc	636-6214		7	UV	PHD		NYU	1980
Mooney, Marta W.	Assoc	636-6221		2	EH	PHD		UCLA	1976
Orsini, Joyce N.	Assoc	636-6219		27	EUV	PHD		NYU	1986
Rackow, Paul	Assoc	636-6207		7	UV	PHD		NYU	1973
Sen, Falguni K.	Assoc	636-6160		13	DEI	PHD		Northwes	1986
Solomon, Esther E.	Assoc	636-6187		2	EH	PHD		Jerusale	1984
Klotz, Dorothy	Asst	636-6189		7	UV	PHD		Penn St	1990
Yang, Zhuang	Asst	636-6191		25	EINY	PHD		Columbia	1990

Fort Hays State University — Hays, KS 67601-4099 (913) FHSUVM.FHSU.EDU
College of Business — FAX=628-4096 — BBA,MBA

Name	Rank	Phone	email		code	Degree	yr	School	year
McCullick, Jack J.	Dean	628-5339			Econ	PHD	70	Kan St	1966
—Department of Business Adm	Phone	628-4201	Fax 628-4096						
Masters, Robert	C-Pr	628-4201				PHD	75	Purdue	1980
Griffith, Tom	Assoc	628-5877		3	U	PHD	79	Indiana	1992
King, William	Assoc	628-4102		2	E	PHD		Colo St	1987
McKemey Dale	Assoc	628-5803		2	H	PHD		Indiana	1990

Fort Lewis College — Durango, CO 81301-3999 (303) FLC — 1974
School of Business Adm — 1000 Rim Drive — FAX=247-7310 — BA
phone 247-7010

Name	Rank	Phone	email		code	Degree	yr	School	year
Cave, John E. Jr.	Dean	247-7294		23	EI	PHD	67	Minn	1990

–Department of Management	Phone	247-7294	Fax 247-7623						
Coleman, Jeremy J.	Prof	247-7392		37	IUV	DBA	74	Geo Wash	1983
Hale, John F.	Prof	247-7319		25	EGNO	PHD	63	Car Mel	1970
Perry, O. D.	Prof	247-7162		19	DTZ	DBA	86	US Inter	1972
Associate Dean									
Podlesnik, Richard A.	Prof	247-7296		17	SU	PHD	77	Northwes	1979
Corman, Lawrence S.	Assoc	247-7402		19	DZ	PHD	89	North Tx	1982
Blue, Thomas Ralph	Asst	247-7317		28	EFSY	PHD	86	Case Wes	1990
Cook, Roy Allen	Asst	247-7550		23	BINS	DBA	89	Miss St	1989
Tustin, Charles O.	Asst	247-7209		17	JUV	PHD	92	Ariz St	1986
Fort Valley State College	Fort Valley, GA		31030	(912)					
Sch of Arts & Sciences				FAX=825-6394					BBA
Did Not Respond-1993 Listing									
Dallis, Charles	Dean$	825-6454			Art	EDD			
–Dept Business Adm & Econ	Phone	825-6270	Fax 825-6319						
Wilson, Richard	H-Pr	825-6270			Econ	PHD	82	Missouri	9-91
Givens, Norma	Prof	825-6270		35		EED	77	Georgia	8-79
Hatchett, Paul	Asst	825-6270		4		JD	93	Widner	9-92
Francis Marion University	Florence, SC		29501-0547	(803)					
School of Business				FAX=661-1165				BBA,MBA,BA,BS	
Fenton, James W. Jr.	Dean$	661-1422		56	N	PHD	81	Iowa	1-89
Forrest Williams Professor of Entrepreneuship & Human Resources									
–Management Faculty	Phone	661-1419	Fax 661-1165						
David, Fred R.	Prof	661-1431		3	I	PHD	81	S Carol	8-88
TranSouth Professor of Strategic Management									
Kelley, Donald E.	Prof	661-1421		2	E	PHD	78	S Carol	8-81
Barrett, Robert	Assoc	661-1435		7	U	PHD	84	Va Tech	6-89
Pugh, Robert	Assoc	661-1414		7	U	PHD	75	American	8-90
Franklin University	Columbus, OH		43215-5399	(614)					
Col of Business & Tech	201 South Grant Avenue			FAX=221-7723					BS
Schiavo, Richard	Dean	341-6388				MBA		Rochest	1993
–Department of Management	Phone	341-6391	Fax 221-7723						
Vaughan, Jerry	D	341-6315		23	EFHI	MBA		Capital	
Hartley, Lorraine	AsDn	341-6384		12	EFGH	DBA	92	Nova	1-94
Franklin and Marshall Coll	Lancaster, PA		17604-3003	(717) ACAD.FANDM.EUD					
Dept of Busines Adm	College Avenue			FAX=291-4329					AB
Glazer, Alan S.	C-Pr	291-4069	a_glazer		Atg	PHD	77	Penn	7-75
–Management Faculty	Phone	291-4069	Fax 291-4329						
Kasperson, Conrad J.	Prof	291-3935	c_kasper	23	HY	PHD	76	Renessla	7-76
Wagner, Samuel	Prof	291-3922		27	B	PHD	71	Penn	7-82
Clair R. McCullough Professor of Business Administration									
Steffy, Brian D.	Assoc	291-3891		23	NC	PHD	84	Georgia	7-88
Freed Hardeman University	Henderson, TN		38340-2399	(901)					
School of Business	158 East Main Street			FAX=					
Wilson, Dwayne	Dean	989-6091		36	IST	PHD	91	Miss	8-75
–Management Faculty	Phone	989-6091	Fax 989-6065						
Bush, Bobby	Prof	989-6094		25	ENPQ	EDD	77	Miss St	8-76
Willis, David	Inst	989-6053		35	IP	MA	87	Webster	8-93
Frostburg State University	Frostburg, MD		21532-1099	(301)					
School of Business				FAX=689-4737				BS,BA,MBA	
Wilkinson, Steven P.	D-Pr	689-4089				PHD	77	S Illin	8-87
–Department of Business Adm	Phone	689-4297	Fax 689-4737						
Poorsoltan, Keramat	C-Ac	689-4297				PHD	77	Georgia	8-86
Concordia, Louis R.	Prof	689-4011				PHD		N Colo	
Sterrett, Charles R.	Prof	689-4392				PHD		American	
Pesta, Richard E.	Assoc	689-4735				MSBA		Bucknell	
Rahman, M. Shakil-Ur	Asst	689-4189				PHD	89	Iowa St	8-89
Shah, Amit J.	Asst	689-4408				DBA		US Intl	8-89
Tootoonchi, Ahmad	Asst	689-4740				PHD		US Intl	8-89
Gulve, Salil	Inst	689-7270				MS		Conn St	8-88
–MBA Department	Phone	685-4375	Fax 689-4380						
Hawk, Thomas F.	C-Ac	689-4485		3	FI	PHD	91	Pitt	8-72
Donnelly, Robert S.	Prof	689-4009		5	OP	EDD	77	Mass	8-76
Leonard, Marion S.	Prof	689-4010		1	&	MBA		Drexel	8-78
Lyons, Paul R.	Prof	689-4179		2	EK	PHD		Florida	8-84
Busey, Barbara H.	Assoc	689-4375				MBA		Frostbur	8-88
Dulz, Thomas H.	Assoc	689-4486		7	U	PHD		Mich St	8-90
Ashley-Cotleur, Catherine	Asst	689-4375		3	IJ	PHD		Geo Wash	8-84

Name	Rank	Phone		Num	Code	Deg	Yr	School	Year
Lewis, Suanne M.	Asst	689-4417		12	&E	EDD		W Virg	8-93
McClive, Marthe A.	Asst	689-4376		25	FN	PHD		USC	8-89
Ross, Ronald L.	Asst	689-4375		7	V	MBA		Frostbur	8-82

Furman University — Greenville, SC 29613 — (803)
Dept of Econ & Bus Adm — 3300 Pointsett Highway — FAX= — BA

Name	Rank	Phone		Num	Code	Deg	Yr	School	Year
Roe, R. David	C-Pr	294-3320			Econ	PHD	78	Duke	1977
—Management Faculty	Phone	294-2132	Fax 294-3001						
Alford, Charles L.	Prof	294-3309		6	XT	PHD	71	Alabama	1971
Belote, Arthur	Prof	294-3312		3	NEI	PHD	62	Florida	1965
James C. Self Professor of Business Administration									
Holmes, Judy	Asst	294-3338		9	Z	PHD	88	Clemson	1990
Patterson, Cheryl	Asst	294-3311		23	EHUI	PHD	87	Clemson	1984

Gannon University — Erie, PA 16541 — (814) CLUSTER.GANNON.EDU
Dahlkemper Sch Bus Adm — West 6th and Peach Streets — FAX= — BS,MBA

Name	Rank	Phone		Num	Code	Deg	Yr	School	Year
Licata, Betty Jo	Dean	871-7582		5	NP	PHD		Renssel	
—Department of Management	Phone	871-7577	Fax 871-7210						
Eichelsdorfer, David	C	871-7577		17	HV	MBA		SUNY-Buf	
Frew, David R.	Prof	871-7579		2	EG	PHD		Kent St	
Fuller, Lee	Assoc	871-7575		45	Q	JD		Clev St	
Kliorys, Constantine	Assoc	871-7571		7	V	PHD		Kent St	
Bargielski, Mary	Asst	871-7578		24	EL	MBA		Gannon	

Gardner-Webb University — Boiling Spr, NC 28017 — (704)
Broyhill Sch of Mgt — FAX= — BS,MBA

Name	Rank	Phone		Num	Code	Deg	Yr	School	Year
Griggs, F. Keith	C-Pr	434-4382		68	SY	EDD	86	Va Tech	1965
—Management Faculty	Phone		Fax 434-6246						
Bottoms, I. Glenn	Prof	434-4377		97	ZUV	PHD	81	Geo St	1983
Camp, Sue	Prof	434-4378		1	DR	EDD	87	Tenn	1975
Smedlay, Stanley	Prof	434-4622		23	ELY	PHD	80	Penn St	1981
Carpenter, Wallace R.	Assoc	434-4379		93	ZIL	EDS	80	W Carol	1964
Negbenebor, Anthony	Assoc	434-4385		8	Y	PHD	88	Miss St	1989
Hardin, Russell	Asst	434-4375		67		ABD		Miss	1985
Hartman, Jim Jr.	Asst	434-4383		73	UP	ABD		Clemson	1983
Honts, Arlen K.	Asst	434-4630		25	EQN	ABD		Vanderbt	1993

GMI Engineering & Mgt Inst — Flint, MI 48504-4898 — (810)
Management Department — 1700 West Third Avenue — FAX=762-9807 — BS,MS

Name	Rank	Phone		Num	Code	Deg	Yr	School	Year
Kangas, J. Eugene	H	762-7959		17	DIUY	PHD	65	Cinn	1990
—Management Faculty	Phone	762-7952	Fax 762-9944						
Greenwood, Ronald	Prof	762-7966		12	BEIL	PHD	71	Oklahoma	1983
F. James McDonald Professor of Industrial Management									
Thornton, Carl L.	Prof	762-7983		25	EHNP	PHD	74	Akron	1989
Zima, Joseph P.	Prof	762-7981		12	EFDP	PHD	68	Purdue	1970
Baumgartner, Samuel R.	Assoc	762-7954		19	EPW	MA	58	Ball St	1964
Dombrowski, Norman J.	Assoc	762-7974		78	UWY	MBA	63	Detroit	1960
Rogers, Donald B.	Assoc	762-7975		45	KQ	JD	71	Detr Law	1968
White, Charles W.	Assoc	762-7956		39	IJVZ	PHD	71	Tx A&M	1989
Bauermeister, Larry A.	Lect	762-9774		9	Z	MSEE	62	Illinois	1990

Geneva College — Beaver Falls, PA 15010-3599 — (412)
Dept of Business — 3200 College Avenue — FAX=847-6687 — BSBA

Name	Rank	Phone		Num	Code	Deg	Yr	School	Year
Nutter, J. Randall	C-Ac	847-6613		53	NQIE	DSC	91	Nova	1992
—Management Faculty	Phone		Fax 847-6687						
Jordan, David A.	Assoc	847-6718		75	UX	MBA	85	Gold Gt	1980
Raver, Daniel H.	Asst	847-6618		13	I	MBA	85	Pitt	1980

George Mason University — Fairfax, VA 22030-4444 — (703) GMUVAX — 1989,1989
School of Business Adm — 4400 University Drive — FAX=993-1809 — BS,MBA,MS

Name	Rank	Phone	Email	Num	Code	Deg	Yr	School	Year
Fulmer, William E.	Dean$	993-1802	wfulmer	3	I	PHD	74	Penn	1993
—Department of Management	Phone	993-1820	Fax 993-1809						
Schulte Jr., William D.	Dir	993-1823	bschulte	16	IDTY	MS	86	LSU	1988
English, Jon	Prof	993-1628	jenglish	23	EFPT	PHD	72	Florida	1975
Fagenson, Ellen A.	Prof	993-1815	fagenson	2	EFOR	PHD	81	Princeton	1987
Kovach, Kenneth	Prof	993-1826	kkovach	5	QNBP	PHD	75	Maryland	1975
Pearce, John A. II	Prof	993-1618	jpearce	3	IT	PHD	76	Penn St	1986
Fink, Laurence	Asst	993-1614	lfink	52	N	PHD	90	Purdue	1988
Robbins, D. Keith	Asst	993-1816	krobbins	31	ITLF	PHD	89	S Carol	1987

George Washington Univ	Washington, DC	20052		(202) GWUVM			1977,1982
Sch of Bus & Public Mgt	2121 I Street NW			FAX=994-6382			BACCT,MAC,PHD
Fowler, F. David	Dean	994-6380			BSC		Missouri 7-92
—Department of Management	Phone		Fax 994-6382				
Askari, Hossein	C-Pr	994-6880		8 Y	PHD	70	MIT
Burdetsky, Ben	Prof	994-7067		5 N	PHD	68	American 1962
Catron, Bayard	Prof	994-6295		1 A	PHD	75	Berkeley
Chitwood, Stephen	Prof	994-6295		1 A	PHD	66	S Calif
Eldridge, Rodney	Prof	994-6880		8 Y	PHD	66	Columbia
Ghadar, Fariborz	Prof	994-6880		8 Y	DBA	75	Harvard
Harmon, Michael	Prof	994-6516		1 A	PHD	68	S Calif
Harvey, Jerry	Prof	994-7375		2 H	PHD	63	Texas
Lobuts, John	Prof	994-7375		2 E	EDD	70	Geo Wash
Newcomer, Kathryn	Prof	994-6295		1 A	PHD	78	Iowa
Park, Yoon	Prof	994-6880		8 Y	DBA	70	Harvard
Tolchin, Susan	Prof	994-6295		1 A	PHD	68	New York
Kasle, Jill	Assoc	994-6295		1 A	JD	72	Boston
Kee, James	Assoc	994-6295		1 A	JD	69	New York
Lenn, D. Jeffrey	Assoc	994-4988		4 J	PHD	81	Boston C
Robles, Fernando	Assoc	994-6880		8 Y	PHD	79	Penn St
Visudtibhan, Kanoknart	Asst	994-6880		8 Y	PHD	88	Penn
—Dept of Management Science	Phone		Fax 994-6382				
Winslow, Erik K.	C-Pr	994-6447		5 N	PHD	67	Case Wes
Artz, John	Prof	994-4931		9 Z			
Carson, John	Prof	994-8246		9 Z	PHD	76	Lehigh
Forman, Ernest	Prof	994-6204		7 V	DSC	75	Geo Wash
Frame, David	Prof	994-5818		9 Z			
Halal, William	Prof	994-5975		1 D			
Liebowitz, Jay	Prof	994-6969		9 Z	DSC	85	Geo Wash
Lobutz, John	Prof	994-6918		2 E			
Sanchez, Pedro	Prof	994-6852		7 V			
Swiercz, Paul M.	Prof	994-0399		5 N	PHD	84	Virg St
Vaill, Peter	Prof	994-7597		2 E	DBA	64	Harvard
Wirtz, Philip	Prof	994-6369		7 V	PHD	83	Geo Wash
Zalkind, David	Prof	994-5735		7 V			
Zvi, Covaliu	Prof	994-6969		7 V			
Cohen, Debra	Assoc	994-7055		5 N	PHD	87	Ohio St
Coyne, John	Assoc	994-5819		9 Z	PHD	70	Lehigh
Donnelly, Richard	Assoc	994-7155		1 D			
Granger, Mary	Assoc	994-7159		9 Z			
Malone, Paul B. III	Assoc	994-4933		5 N	DBA	73	Geo Wash
Nagy, Thomas	Assoc	994-7090		9 Z	PHD	74	Texas
Prasad, Srinivas	Assoc	994-2078		9 Z			
Soyer, Refik	Assoc	994-6445		5 N			
Toftoy, Charles	Assoc	994-4935		6 S	DBA	85	Nova
Umpleby, Stuart	Assoc	994-7530		2 H			
Wells, William	Assoc	994-6678		8 Y			

Georgetown University	Washington, DC	20057		(202) GUVAX			1983,1988
School of Business Adm	57th and O Streets NW			FAX=687-4031			BSBA,MBA,MS
Parker, Robert S.	Dean	687-3877		Fnce	PHD	69	Penn 1986
—Management Faculty	Phone		Fax 687-4031				
Byron, William SJ	Prof	678-4476		4 JL	PHD	69	Maryland 1993
Donaldson, Thomas J.	Prof	687-4062		43 JLM	PHD	76	Kansas 1989
Ferdows, Kasra	Prof	687-3814		7 UYI	PHD	72	Wiscon 1990
Grant, Robert	VProf	687-3844		36 IT	PHD	83	London 1993
McCabe, Douglas M.	Prof	687-3778		52 QNE	PHD	77	Cornell 1976
Nollen, Stanley D.	Prof	687-3826		85 YPN	PHD	74	Chicago 1974
Onto, John G.	Prof	687-6977		8 IY	PHD	74	Ariz St 1987
Shelby, Annette	Prof	687-3804		1 BD	PHD	73	LSU 1980
Bies, Robert J.	Assoc	687-5406		2 EJHK	PHD	82	Stanford 1990
Culnan, Mary J.	Assoc	687-3802	mculnan	9 ZJLI	PHD	80	UCLA 1988
Gaertner, Karen Newman	Assoc	687-3769		2 EOHJ	PHD	78	Chicago 1984
Gartner, William B.	Assoc	687-3828		6 T	PHD	82	U Wash 1989
McHenry, William K.	Assoc	687-3808	mchenry	9 YZ	PHD	85	Arizona 1985
Quinn, Dennis P.	Assoc	687-1027		48 LYQK	PHD	84	Columbia 1984
Reinsch, N. L. Jr.	VAsoc	687-5125		1 SD	PHD	73	Kansas 1992
visiting from Abilene Christian							
Romanelli, Elaine F.	VAsoc	687-4188		3 FI	PHD	85	Columbia 1992
visiting from Duke							
Woolley, John T.	VAsso	687-3904		34 IJ	PHD	80	Wiscon 1992
Cohen, Deborah	VAsst	678-3816		2 EFH	PHD	92	Columbia 1993
Ernst, Ricardo	Asst	687-3816		7 UW	PHD	87	Penn 1987
Hasnas, John	Asst	687-5398		4 JKL	PHD	88	Duke 1991
Langlois, Catherine	Asst	687-5404		73 DIJY	PHD	83	Berkeley 1991
Salorio, Eugene M.	Asst	687-5407		83 YIL	PHD	91	Harvard 9-89
Smith, H. Jeff	Asst	687-3824		93 ZIJL	DBA	90	Harvard 1991
Armstrong, Pamela K.	Inst	687-3035		7 U	PHD	93	Penn 1992

University of Georgia — Athens, GA — 30602 — (706) UGA.CC.UGA.EDU — 1926,1964
Terry College of Bus — FAX=542-3743 — BBA,MBA,MA,PHD

Name	Rank	Phone	Email			Deg		School	
Niemi, Albert W. Jr.	Dean	542-8100		Econ		PHD	69	Conn	1968
—Dept of Management	Phone	542-1294	Fax 542-3743						
Gatewood, Robert D.	C-Ac	542-3700	gatewood	5	NP	PHD	71	Purdue	1971
Blackstone, John H. Jr.	Prof	542-3718	jblackstone	7	UW	PHD	79	Tx A&M	1983
Bostrom, Robert P.	Prof	542-3559	bostrom	9	DZ	PHD	78	Minn	1988
Carroll, Archie B.	Prof	542-3748	acarroll	34	IJL	DBA	72	Fla St	1972
Robert W. Scherer Chair of Management & Corporate Public Affairs									
Cox, James F. III	Prof	542-3747	jcox	7	U	PHD	75	Clemson	1983
Davis, K. Roscoe	Prof	542-3580		7	VW	PHD		North Tx	1972
Hofer, Charles W.	Prof	542-3724	chofer	36	IST	DBA	69	Harvard	1981
UGA Regents Professor									
Kefalas, Asterios G.	Prof	542-3731	akefalas	89	IMYZ	PHD	71	Iowa	1971
Ledvinka, James D.	Prof	542-3745	ledvinka	52	NQ	PHD	69	Michigan	1970
McKeown, Patrick G.	Prof	542-3587	pmckeown	79	VZ	PHD	73	N Carol	1976
Watson, Hugh J.	Prof	542-3744	hwatson	9	Z	DBA	69	Fla St	1970
C. Herman & Mary Virginia Terry Chair of Business Administration									
Aronson, Jay E.	Assoc	542-0991	aronson@phoe	79	VZ	PHD	80	Car Mel	1987
Dowling, Michael J.	Assoc	542-3702	dowling	36	ITY	PHD	88	Texas	1988
Gilbert, James P.	Assoc	542-3701	jgilbert	7	UW	PHD	84	Nebraska	1984
Lahiff, James M.	Assoc	542-3750	jlahiff	15	DEP	PHD	69	Penn St	1972
Stam, Antonie	Assoc	542-3589	astam	79	VZ	PHD	86	Kansas	1986
Vandenberg, Robert J.	Assoc	542-3720	vberg	25	EFHX	PHD	82	Georgia	1993
Watson, Richard T.	Assoc	542-3706	rwatson	9	DZ	PHD	87	Minn	1989
Wilson, E. Walter	Assoc	542-3742	wwilson	67	SU	PHD	74	Georgia	1964
Brown, Robert D.	Asst	542-3594	bbrown	9	Z	MA	57	Alabama	1967
Dennis, Alan R.	Asst	542-3902	adennis	9	DZ	PHD	91	Arizona	1991
Ryan, Lori V.	Asst	542-3749		34	HIJL	PHD	94	Wash	1994
Satzinger, John W.	Asst	542-3746	jsatzing	9	Z	PHD	91	Claremont	1991
Horton, Gerald T.	Lect	542-9465		36	IJS	AB	56	Harvard	1987
—Dept Insur, Legal St, MgtSc	Phone		Fax 542-3835						
Gustavson, Sandra G.	H-Pr	542-4290			RIEs	PHD		Illinois	
Steuer, Ralph E.	Prof	542-3782		7	V	PHD	73	N Carol	
Whitten, Betty J.	Prof	542-3588		7	V	PHD		Georgia	
Seila, Andrew F.	Assoc	542-3586		7	V	PHD		N Carol	

Georgia College — Milledgeville GA — 31061 — (912) GCVAX.GAC.PEACHNET.EDU
School of Business — Hancock Street — FAX=453-5249 — BBA,MBA

Name	Rank	Phone	Email			Deg		School	
Jones, Jo Ann	Dean	453-5497	jones			PHD	77	La Tech	1976
—Department of Management	Phone	453-4324	Fax 453-5249						
Carpenter, James B.	C-Pr	453-4324	carpenter	57	ENU	PHD	69	Purdue	1987
Brumfield, Bruce	Prof	471-2847	bbrumfi	7	A	DBA	72	Miss	1978
Coleman, Lucretia	Prof	453-4324	coleman	25	ENR	EED	76	Tenn	1977
Craft, Robert	Prof	471-2990	craft	7	HL	DBA	77	Indiana	1988
Harlow, Howard R.	Prof	453-4324	harlow	38	IL	PHD	73	Nebraska	1984
Yehle, Arthur L.	Prof	453-5772	yehle	6	FNS	PHD	67	U Miami	1984
Phillips, Steve	Assoc	453-4324	phillips	39	VZ	PHD	74	Illinois	1990
Burgar, Paul	Asst	453-4324	burgar	37	HIP	PHD	80	Memphis	1990
Dent-Crews, Marie	Asst	453-4324	demtcrews	13	CI	PHD	91	Georgia	1991
Frankenberger, John	Asst	453-4324	frankenb	17	GN	PHD	90	North Tx	1986
Krilowicz, Thomas J.	Asst	453-4324	krilowicz	45	GJP	DBA	75	Florida	1988
Wahlers, James	Asst	453-4324	wahlers	57	NQU	PHD	93	Georgia	1989

Georgia Institute Tech — Atlanta, GA — 30332-0520 — (404) — 1969,1969
School of Management — 225 North Avenue NW — FAX=894-6030 — BS,MS,PHD

Name	Rank	Phone	Email			Deg		School	
Kraft, Arthur	Dean	894-8713		Econ		PHD	70	SUNY	1993
—Management Faculty	Phone		Fax 894-6030						
Covin, Jeffrey	C-Ac	894-4372	covin#m#	13	IT	PHD	85	Pitt	1986
Adler, Philip	Prof	894-4371	adler#m#	13	CHN	PHD	66	Ohio St	1962
Blum, Terry	Prof	894-4924	blum#m#	2	CH	PHD	82	Columbia	1986
Gaimon, Cheryl	Prof	894-4934	gaimon#m	7	UV	PHD	81	Car Mel	1988
Herold, David M.	Prof	894-4920	herold#m	2	EFN	PHD	74	Yale	1973
Parsons, Charles K.	Prof	894-4921	parsons#	2	ENP	PHD	80	Illinois	1979
Director Graduate Program									
Chang, Yih-Long	Assoc	894-4334	chang#m#	7	UV	PHD	85	Texas	1989
Fedor, Donald B.	Assoc	894-4925	fedor#m#	2	E	PHD	87	Illinois	1988
McDougall, Patricia P.	Assoc	894-4373		3	IR	PHD	87	S Carol	1991
McIntyre, John R.	Assoc	894-4379	mcintyre	8	Y	PHD	81	Georgia	1981
Higa, Kunihiko	Asst	894-4365	higa#m#	9	Z	PHD	88	Arizona	1989
Shane, Scott	Asst	894-3979		68	TY	PHD	92	Penn	1993
Singhal, Vinod	Asst	894-4908	singhal#	7	U	PHD	88	Rochest	1989
Wing, Kevin	Asst	853-2995		7	U				
Mackey, Gerald	SrRes	894-2611	mackey#m	39	IZ	PHD	83	Geo St	1979

Georgia Southern University — Statesboro, GA 30460-8152 — (912) USCN — 1977,1982
College of Bus Admin — Rosenwald Boulevard — FAX=681-0292 — BBA
Gooding, Carl W. — Dean 681-5106 — Phone 681-5216 — Fax 681-0292

Name	Rank	Phone	Email		Code	Deg		School	Year
Gooding, Carl W.	Dean	681-5106		7	UV	PHD	76	Georgia	1986
–Dept of Management LB 8152	Phone	681-5216	Fax 681-0292						
McCartney, William W.	C-Pr	681-5775		23	EIZ	PHD		LSU	8-91
Carper, William	Prof	681-0103		3	I	PHD	79	Va Tech	1987
Carter, Harrison	Prof	681-5258		79	VZ	PHD	74	Georgia	1975
VPAA									
Case, Thomas L.	Prof	681-5205	tcase	19	ZEF	PHD	82	Georgia	1981
Knotts, Ulysses S. Jr.	Prof	681-5087		37	CIU	PHD	71	Nebraska	1977
McDonald, James Michael	Prof	681-5321		32	EDF	PHD	76	Georgia	1987
Parrish, Leo	Prof	681-5579		7	UV	PHD	74	Ga Tech	1990
Pickett, John R.	Prof	681-5746		79	ZV	PHD	79	Georgia	1979
Stapleton, Richard J.	Prof	681-5799		36	STI	PHD	69	Tx Tech	1970
Bleicken, Linda A.	Assoc	681-5526		25	ONE	PHD	90	Geo St	1990
Burns, O. Maxie Jr.	Assoc	681-5652	burnsm	79	UZ	PHD	87	Geo St	1983
Dosier, Lloyd N.	Assoc	681-5086		5	NQ	MBA	66	Geo St	1968
Gutknecht, John	Assoc	681-5483		37	I	MBA	65	LSU	1986
Kent, Russell L.	Assoc	681-5700		25	EN	PHD	91	Fla St	1990
Murkison, Eugene C.	Assoc	681-5931		15	QENP	PHD	86	Missouri	1984
Stone, Robert W.	Assoc	681-5217		79	ZV	PHD	83	Purdue	1983
Wells, Robert A.	Assoc	681-5837		79	ZV	EDD	73	Georgia	1975
Campbell, Constance	Asst	681-0757		25	ENXG	PHD	92	Fla St	1-92
Henry, John	Asst	681-0755		29	EZV	PHD	92	Fla St	8-91
McClurg, Timothy	Asst	681-5435		7	U	PHD	93	Purdue	1993
Randall, Cindy House	Asst	681-5582		79	ZV	MBA	81	Memphis	1982
Rebstack, Susan	Asst	681-5216		79	Z	ABD		Okla St	1994
Russell, Gregory R.	Asst	681-0759		7	U	PHD	93	S Carol	1992
Turner, Charles F. III	Asst	681-0379		79	Z	PHD		Georgia	1989
Evans, Cheri	Inst	681-5811		7	UVZ	MBA	89	Pitt	1990
Smith, Larry	Inst	681-0586		9	Z	MBA	81	So Meth	1989

Georgia Southwestern College — Americus, GA 31709 — (912)
Division of Bus Adm — 800 Wheatley Street — FAX=
phone 928-1347

Name	Rank	Phone			Code	Deg		School	Year
Henry, John F.	C-Pr	928-1340		57		PHD		Alabama	
–Management Faculty	Phone	928-1340	Fax 928-1630						
Bohleber, Michael	Assoc	928-1340		34	I	PHD		Wiscon	
Stephens, Robert L.	Assoc	928-1340		56	US	PHD		Miss St	
Wilson, Mary E.	Asst	928-1340		15	DIN	PHD		Alabama	

Georgia State University — Atlanta, GA 30303-3083 — (404) GSUVM1.GSU.EDU — 1960,1963
College of Bus Adm — 33 Gilmer Street SE — FAX=651-2804 — BA,MP,MB,MT,PHD

Name	Rank	Phone	Email		Code	Deg		School	Year
Hogan, John D.	Dean	651-2604		Econ		PHD	52	Syracuse	6-91
–Department of Management	Phone	651-3400	Fax 651-2804						
Deane, Richard H.	C-Pr	651-3400		7	U	PHD	71	Purdue	1981
Alexandrides, Costas G.	Prof	651-3400		8	Y	PHD	61	New York	1967
Athanasiades, John C.	Prof	651-3400		2	EJ	PHD	70	New York	1971
Burden, Charles Albert	Prof	651-3400		28	ELY	DBA	70	Geo St	1970
Clark, Thomas B.	Prof	651-2600		7	UZL	PHD		Geo St	1978
Griffieth, Roger	Prof	651-3400							
Jedel, Michael Jay	Prof	651-3400		5	NQ	DBA	72	Harvard	1971
Jones, William A. Jr.	Prof	651-3400		13	HIL	DPA	72	Georgia	1981
Rue, Leslie W.	Prof	651-3400		13	I	PHD	73	Geo St	1974
Scarpello, Vida	Prof	651-3400		25	EFIN	PHD	80	Minn	1992
Smits, Stanley J.	Prof	651-3400		25	E	PHD	64	Missouri	1969
Williams, D. Ervin	Prof	651-3400		6	ST	PHD	65	Ohio St	1968
Zahra, Shaker A.	Prof	651-3400	szahra	3	IDTY	PHD	82	Miss	1992
Missick, Judith	Assoc	491-2656	jmessick			PHD	82	Ca-SnBar	1992
Riggs, Walter E.	Assoc	651-3400		7	U	PHD	81	S Carol	1985
Shore, Lynn M.	Assoc	651-3400		25	EN	PHD	85	Colo St	1986
Bogner, William	Asst	651-3400		3	I	PHD	90	Illinois	1991
Houghton, Susan	Asst	651-3400				PHD	93	N Carol	1993
Lee, Michael B.	Asst	651-3400		5	NQ	PHD	88	Minn	1991
Miles, Edward W.	Asst	651-3400		2	EX	PHD	88	Georgia	1989
Oviatt, Benjamin M.	Asst	651-3400		3	HIQ	PHD	85	S Carol	1988
Ragan, James W.	Asst	651-3400		5	ENQ	PHD	88	Houston	1988
–Dept of Computer Info Sys	Phone	651-3880	Fax 651-2804						
Welke, Richard J.	C-Pr	651-3880	cisrjw	9	Z	PHD		SUNY-Buf	
Cotterman, William W.	Prof		ciswwc	9	Z	PHD		Geo St	
Greene, Myron T.	Prof		cismtg	9	Z	PHD		Geo St	
McLean, Ephraim R. III	Prof		ciserm	9	Z	PHD		MIT	

George E. Smith Eminent Scholar Chair in Computer Information Systems

Name	Rank	Phone	Email		Code	Deg		School	Year
Nevins, Arthur J.	Prof		cisajn	9	Z	PHD		Rochest	
Senn, James A.	Prof		cisjas	9	Z	PHD		Minn	
Vaishnavi, Vijay K.	Prof		cisvkv	9	Z	PHD		Indian T	
Williams, Charles M.	Prof		ciscmw	9	Z	PHD		Texas	
Brown, James F.	Assoc		cisjfb	9	Z	PHD		Geo St	

Name	Rank		Code			Degree		School
Howell, Gordon C.	Assoc		cisgch	9	Z	PHD		Geo St
Kumar, Kuldeep	Assoc		ciskuk	9	Z	PHD		McMaster
Straub, Detmar W. Jr.	Assoc		cisdws	9	Z	PHD		Indiana
Young, Carol E.	Assoc		ciscey	9	Z	PHD		Ohio St
Beranek, Margaret M.	Asst		cismmb	9	Z	PHD		Arizona
Chatterjee, Samir	Asst		cisssc	9	Z	PHD		Cen Fla
Hong, Shugang	Asst		cisssh	9	Z	PHD		Conn
Keil, Mark	Asst		cismmk	9	Z	PHD		Harvard
Purao, Sandeep	Asst		cisssp	9	Z	PHD		Wi-Milwa
Robinson, William N.	Asst		ciswnr	9	Z	PHD		Oreg St
Swartzmeyer, Elmer G.	Asst	cisdpt		9	Z	PHD		Geo St
Truex, Duane P. III	Asst		cisdpt	9	Z	PHD		SUNY-Bin
Wells, Connie E.	Asst		ciscew	9	Z	PHD		Minn
Haase, Milton R.	Inst		cismrh	9	Z	BS		Hofstra
Hopkins, Byron K.	Inst		cisbkh	9	Z	MBA		Geo St

–Dept of Decision Sciences   Phone 651-4000   Fax 681-2804

Name	Rank	Phone				Degree		School
Tabor, Charles Dwight Jr.	C-Pr	651-4011				PHD		Geo St
Berhold, Marvin	Prof	651-4062		7	V	PHD		UCLA
Brightman, Harvey J.	Prof	651-4061		7	V	PHD		Mass
Regents' Professor of Decision Sciences								
Churchill, Geoffrey	Prof	651-4063		7	V	PHD	66	N Carol
El-Sheshai, Kamal M.	Prof	651-4068		7	V	PHD		Indiana
Elliott, Merwyn Lee	Prof	651-4066		7	V	PHD		S Carol
Garcha, Bikramjit Singh	Prof	651-4015		7	V	PHD		Ohio St
Schneider, Howard Charles	Prof	651-4090		7	V	PHD		Virginia
Schott, Brain Mark	Prof	651-4070		7	V	PHD		Geo St
Whalen, Thomas H.	Prof	651-4080		7	V	PHD		Mich St
Elrod, Robert H.	Assoc	651-4067		7	V	PHD		Clemson
Fazlollahi, Bijan	Assoc	651-4064		7	V	PHD		Syracuse
Katz, Joseph L.	Assoc	651-4072		7	V	PHD		LSU
Loch, Karen D.	Assoc	651-4095		7	V	PHD		Nebraska
Mize, Jan Lee	Assoc	651-1532		9	Z	PHD		Geo St
Srivastava, Alok	Assoc	651-4093		7	V	PHD		Clemson
Thachenkary, Cherian S.	Assoc	651-4078		7	V	PHD		Waterloo

Gettysburg College   Gettysburg, PA   17325-1486   (717)   FAX=337-6251   BA
Dept of Management

Name	Rank	Phone	Code			Degree		School	Year
Schein, Virgina E.	C-Pr	337-6653	vschein	52	EI	PHD	69	NYU	1986
–Management Faculty	Phone	337-6640	Fax 337-6251						
Pitts, Robert A.	Prof	337-6651	pitts	23	YI	PHD	72	Harvard	1986
Rosenbach, William E.	Prof	337-6648	wrosenba	2	E	PHD	77	Colorado	1984
Evans Professor of Eisenhower Leadership Studies									
Walton, H. Charles	Assoc	337-6988	cwalton	9	Z	PHD	81	Fla St	1989
Star, Harold	Asst	337-6655	hstar	34	I	PHD		Concordi	1989
Tracy, Kay	Asst	337-6968	ktracy	2		PHD	92	Maryland	1990
Walton, Spring	Asst	337-6646	swalton	4	K	JD	90	Maryland	1990

Gonzaga University   Spokane, WA   99258-0001   (509) GONZAGA   FAX=   1990,1990
School of Business Adm   East 502 Boone Avenue   BBA,MBA
  Did Not Respond-1993 Listing

Name	Rank	Phone	Code			Degree		School	Year
Barnes, Clarence H.	Dean	328-4220			Econ	PHD	73	Tenn	9-73
–Div of Mgt, Mktg & Oper	Phone								
Buller, Paul	Prof	328-4220	buller	13	IN	PHD	82	U Wash	1989
Anderson, Kenneth	Assoc	328-4220	anderson	12	HE	PHD	88	Nebraska	9-86
Elloy, David F.	Assoc	328-4220	elloy	25	EFD	PHD	84	S Carol	1985
Kohls, John	Assoc	328-4220	kohls	42	JL	PHD	83	U Wash	9-80
Hedin, Scott R.	Asst	328-4220		7	U	PHD	93	S Carol	

Goshen College   Goshen, IN   46526   (219) GOSHEN.EDU   FAX=535-7660   BA
Dept of Atg, Bus & Econ   1700 South Main Street

Name	Rank	Phone	Code			Degree		School	Year
Nyce, John D.	Dean$				Math	MATM		Detroit	1966
–Management Faculty	Phone		Fax 535-7660						
Good, Delmar	C-Pr	535-7452		14	LJ	PHD		Illinois	2-67
Eby, John	Prof	535-7503	delgg	12	AD	PHD		Cornell	8-89
Geiser, Leonard	Prof	535-7451		36	IS	MBA		Chicago	8-81

Governors State University   Univ Park, IL   60466-0975   (708) UIUCVMD   FAX=534-0054
College Bus & Pub Adm
  Did Not Respond-1993 Listing

Name	Rank	Phone				Degree		School
Allen, Esthel B.	Dean	534-4932			Law	JD		
–Div of Mgt/Adm Sciences	Phone		Fax 534-8457					
Howes, Mary E.	C-Pr	534-4935				PHD	81	Kansas
Isaac, Akkanad M.	Prof	534-4951		9	Z	PHD	69	Lehigh
Katz, Marsha	Prof	534-4952				PHD	78	Mich St
Malik, Zafar	Prof	534-4953				PHD		Renessel
Olson, Charles L.	Prof	534-4954				MBA	72	Chicago
Shaaban, Farouk	Prof	534-4955				PHD	72	Illinois
Tsolakides, Jordan A.	Prof	534-4956				PHD	68	Mich St

Grambling State University — Grambling, LA 71245 — (318) — FAX=274-2191 — BS
College of Business — 100 Main Street

Name	Rank	Phone	#	Fields	Degree	Natl	School	Year
Dhanani, Karim	Dean	274-2275		Atg	DBA	86	La Tech	9-77
—Department of Management	Phone	Fax 274-2191						
Udeh, Igwe	H	274-2884	38	SYTH	PHD	87	St Louis	1989
Emmanuel, Tsegai	Prof	274-2468			PHD	78	Missouri	8-80
Vinson, Earl	Prof	274-2371	15	Q	PHD		U Wash	1977
Al-Dwairi, Musa	Asst	274-2467	12	AY	PHD	90	North Tx	1991
Ensley, Lillie	Asst	274-2465	14		MBA	70	La Tech	1970
Haile, Semere	Asst	274-2462	58	Y	PHD	81	Cinn	1987
Hayajneh, Abdalla	Asst	274-2463	23	ENRY	PHD	90	North Tx	1990
Oko, Okechukwu	Asst	274-3850	4	JKLM	JSD	92	Yale	1992
Rollins, Harris	Asst	274-2192	14		MBA	51	Michigan	1960
Vaicys, Remigijus	Asst	274-2371	27	N	DBA	90	La Tech	1981
White, Donald	Inst	274-2462	7		MBA	87	Gramblin	1989

Grand Valley State Univ — Allendale, MI 49401 — (616) GVSU.EDU — FAX=895-3106 — MBA,MST
Seidman Sch Bus & Adm — 1 Campus Drive

Name	Rank	Phone		Fields	Degree	Natl	School	Year
Pitman, Glenn A.	Dean	895-2163		Mktg	PHD	77	Penn St	1990
—Department of Management	Phone	Fax 895-3286						
Larson, Lars L.	C	895-2381			PHD	71	Illinois	1994
Castro, Barry	Prof	895-3060			PHD		NYU	1973
Harper, Earl	Prof	771-6684			PHD		Tx Tech	1971
Hodge, John	Prof	771-6682			EDD		W Mich	1977
IsHak, Samir	Prof	771-6653			PHD		Indiana	1968
Margulis, Stephen	Prof	771-6744			PHD		Minn	1986
Mishra, Jitendra M. (Jim)	Prof	895-3460			PHD		Lucknow	1972
Hall, Richard	Assoc	895-2498			PHD		Cinn	1983
Vrancken, Robert	Assoc	771-6741			MBA	84	Notre Dm	1982
Cheng, Chen Hung	Asst	771-6703			PHD	90	Iowa	1993
Jiang, James J.	Asst				PHD	92	Cinn	1994
Kumar, Ashok	Asst	771-6522			PHD	90	Purdue	1992
McKendall, Marie A.	Asst	895-3368			PHD	90	Mich St	1988
Motwani, J. D.	Asst	771-6743			PHD	90	North Tx	1990
Subramanian, Ram	Asst	895-3533			PHD	90	North Tx	1990

Greensboro College — Greensboro, NC 27401-1875 — (910) — FAX= — BA,BS
Div of Business Adm — 815 West Market Street
Did Not Respond-1993 Listing

Name	Rank	Phone	Degree	Natl	School	Year
Jones, Thomas O. Jr.	C-Pr	271-2289	DBA	72	Geo Wash	1986
Fred L. Proctor Sr. Professor						
—Management Faculty	Phone	Fax 271-2237				
Branan, Carson	Assoc	271-2234	MS		N Car St	1958
Hanson, Cynthia	Asst	272-7102	PHD	93	Maryland	1993

Guilford College — Greensboro, NC 27410 — (910) RASCAL.GUILFORD.EDU — FAX= — BS,BAS
College of Business — 5800 West Friendley Avenue

Name	Rank	Phone	Email	#	Fields	Degree	Natl	School	Year
—Department of Management	Phone								
Turner, Betty	C-As	316-2242		4	K	JD		Vanderbt	1991
Bobko, Peter B.	Assoc	316-2243	bobkopb	7	U	DBA	83	Indiana	
on leave to USAF Academy									
Stevens, William F.	Assoc	316-2202		2	E	PHD	77	Mich St	1982

Gustavus Adolphus College — Saint Peter, MN 56082-9989 — (507) — FAX=
Econ & Management Dept — 800 College Avenue

Name	Rank	Phone	#	Fields	Degree	Natl	School	Year
—Management Faculty	Phone	933-7414		Fax 933-7041				
Johnson, Bruce H.	C-Ac	933-7011	28		PHD	79	Houston	1986
Jones, Ellis	Prof	933-7420	9	Z	EDD	65	N Dakota	1958
McRostie, Clair	Prof	933-7407	38		PHD	64	Wiscon	1957
Bungum, John	Assoc	933-7406	37		PHD	77	Nebraska	1979

Hampton University — Hampton, VA 23668 — (804) UNIXVAX.HAMPTONV.EDU — FAX=727-5048 — BS
School of Business
Did Not Respond-1993 Listing

Name	Rank	Phone	Email	#	Fields	Degree	School	Year
Carter, Alphonse H.	Dean	727-5361		23	P	PHD	Cinn	8-88
—Department of Management	Phone	Fax 727-5048						
Miller, Lois S.	C	727-5858		9	PYZ	EDD	N Illin	9-64
Beaty, David	Assoc	727-5866		2	8	PHD	P Eliz	1989
D'Souza, Kelwyn	Assoc	727-5505		7	Uvxz	PHD	S Fla	1991
Razavi, Mehdi B.	Assoc	727-5035		7	DIUV	PHD	Nebraska	8-89
Anyiwo, David E.	Asst	727-5867		7	DUVZ	PHD	Virginia	8-88
Brassil, James P.	Asst	727-5036		1	P	MBA	Geo Wash	8-88
Ekure, Ebuta E.	Asst	727-5605		35	IJN	PHD	Oklahoma	8-88
Hickey, John	Asst	727-5763		4	JKLM	JD	Geo Wash	8-87
Maheshwari, Sharad	Asst	727-5605	sharad		UVZX	PHD	S Fla	8-91

Muse, Andrew	Asst	727-5361	3	I	JD		Lincoln	1-91
Assistant Dean								
Rice, John J.	Asst	727-5760	4	KM	JD	73	Marsh-Wy	8-73
Volard, Sam	Asst	727-5763	8		PHD		Queensln	8-91
Zapatero, Enrique G.	Asst	727-5505	79	UV	ABD		Hampton	8-84
Zhao, Xiande	Asst	727-5882	7	U	PHD		Utah	8-90
Havird, Lloyd B.	Inst	727-5763	58		MBA		Gold Gt	8-82

Hardin-Simmons University	Abilene, TX	79698		(915)				
School of Business	2200 Hickory Street			FAX=670-1572			BBA,BS,MA,MBA	
Presley, Ronald W.	Dean	670-1356		Econ	PHD	75	Oklahoma	1988
–Dept of General Business	Phone	670-1363	Fax 670-1523					
Hebron, Arthur E.	H-Pr	670-1363		15	ELNQ	PHD	73	Missouri	1979
Myers, James	Prof	670-1360		25	DENP	PHD	84	North Tx	1981
White, Charles	Prof	670-1313						
Moritz, Thomas	Asst	670-1361						

Harding University	Searcy, AR	72149-0001		(501)	ACS.HARDING.EDU			
Sch of Business Box 774	900 East Center			FAX=			BBA,MS	
Tucker, David S.	Dean	279-4240		Econ	PHD	87	Arkansas	1980
–Management Faculty	Phone		Fax 279-4665					
McLeod, Randall J.	D-As	279-4201			JD	74	Memphis	
Associate Dean								
Reely, Robert H. Jr.	Prof	279-4497			EDD	76	Auburn	
Carter, Lavon	Assoc	279-4368			ABD		Memphis	
Hebert, Budd	Assoc	270 4552			PHD			
Hemphill, Bill	Asst	279-4075			MA			

University of Hartford	W Hartford, CT	06117-0395		(203)	HARTFORD			
Barney Sch Bus & P Adm	200 Bloomfield Avenue			FAX=243-4198			BS,MBA,MS	
Did Not Respond-1993 Listing								
Libassi, Peter	Dean	243-4243						
–Department of Management	Phone							
Stork, Diana	C-Ac	243-4566	stork	2	EH	PHD	88	Columbia
Decker, Philip	Assoc	243-4566		5	N	PHD	79	Ohio St
Fairfield-Sonn, James	Assoc	243-4566	fairfiel	25	EN	PHD	85	Yale
Miles, Wilford G.	Assoc	243-4566	wmiles	3	I	PHD	68	Arkansas
Moschella, Paul	Assoc	243-4566	mosch	3	I	PHD	73	Mass
Ogilvie, John R.	Assoc	243-4195	ogilvie	25	EN	PHD	78	Mich St
Charalambedies, Leo C.	Asst	243-4566	charalam	3	I	PHD	78	S Carol
Herniter, Bruce	Asst	243-4566	herniter	9	Z	PHD	90	Arizona
London, Anne	Asst	243-4566	london	2	E	PHD	91	Case Wes
Morgan, Sandra	Asst	243-4566	morgan	2	EF	PHD	83	MIT
Motiwalla, Luvai	Asst	243-4566	motiwall	9	Z	PHD	89	Arizona

Harvard University	Boston, MA	02163		(617)	HARVBUS1			1916
Grad School of Bus Adm	Soldiers Field Road			FAX=495-6001			MBA,DBA,PHD	
Did Not Respond-1993 Listing								
McArthur, John H.	Dean	495-6550		Fnce	DBA		Harvard	1959
–General Management Area	Phone		Fax 495-6001					
Yoshino, Michael Y.	C-Pr	495-6305		25	EN			
Herman C. Krannert Professor of Business Administration								
Aguilar, Francis J.	Prof	495-6494		1				
Argyris, Chris	Prof	495-6650				PHD	51	Cornell
Austin, James E.	Prof	495-6497		4	L			
Richard P. Chapman Professor of Business Administation								
Barnes, Louis B.	Prof	495-6658		25	EN			
Bartlett, Christopher A.	Prof	495-6308		1				
Beer, Michael	Prof	495-6655		25	EN			
Berg, Norman A.	Prof	495-6251		1				
Bowen, Kent	Prof	495-6567		7	U			
Bower, Joseph L.	Prof	495-6282		1				
Donald Kirk David Professor of Business Administration								
Bradley, Stephen P.	Prof	495-6344		4	L			
William Ziegler Professor of Business Administration								
Caves, Richard E.	Prof	495-6429		4	L			
George Gund Professor of Economics and Business Administration								
Clark, Kim B.	Prof	495-6288		7	U			
Harry E. Figgle, Jr. Professor of Business Administration								
Eccles, Robert G. Jr.	Prof	495-6250		25	EN			
Gabarro, John J.	Prof	495-6635		25	EN			
The UPS Foundation Professor of Human Resources								
Garvin, David A.	Prof	495-6280		7	U			
Robert & Jane Cizik Professor of Business Administration								
Ghemawat, Pankaj	Prof	495-6270		4	L	PHD		Harvard
Hackman, J. Richard	Prof	495-6467		25	EN			
Cahners-Rabb Professor of Social & Organizational Psychology								

Name	Rank	Phone						
Hayes, Robert H.	Prof	495-6330	7	U				
Philip Caldwell Professor of Business Administration								
Heskett, James L.	Prof	495-6340	7	U				
The UPS Foundation Professor of Business Logistics								
Hinsey, Joseph IV	Prof	495-6369	1					
Class of 1957 Professor of Business Administration								
Jaikumar, Ramchandran	Prof	495-6303	7	U				
Jensen, Michael C.	Prof	495-6058	25	EN				
Edsel Bryant Ford Professor of Business Administation								
Kanter, Rosabeth M.	Prof	495-6053	1					
Class of 1960 Professor of Business Administration								
Kotter, John P.	Prof	495-6529	25	EN				
Konosuke Matsushita Professor of Leadership								
Lorsch, Jay W.	Prof	495-6413	25	En				
Louis E. Kirstein Professor of Human Relations; Senior Associate Dean								
McCraw, Thomas K.	Prof	495-6364	4	L				
Isidor Straus Professor of Business History; Chairmam Executive Education								
Mills, D. Quinn	Prof	495-6206	25	EN				
Alfred J. Weatherhead Jr. Professor of Business Administration								
Montgomery, Cynthia A.	Prof	495-6991	4	L				
Pearson, Andrall	Prof	495-6371						
Poorvu, William J.	Prof	495-6609	1					
MBA Class of 1961 Adjunct Professor in Entrepreneurship								
Porter, Michael E.	Prof	495-6309	4	L	PHD	73	Harvard	
C. Roland Christensen Professor of Business Administation								
Rosenbloom, Richard S.	Prof	495-6295	4	L				
David Sarnoff Professor of Business Administration								
Sahlman, William A.	Prof	495-6593	1					
Dimitri V. Arbeloff MBA Class of 1955 Professor of Business Administration								
Salter, Malcolm S.	Prof	495-6623	1					
MBA Class of 1952 Professor of Business Administration								
Sasser, W. Earl Jr.	Prof	495-6439	7	U				
The UPS Foundation Professor of Service Management								
Shapiro, Roy D.	Prof	495-6638	7	U				
Sloane, Carl S.	Prof	495-6984	1					
Stevenson, Howard H.	Prof	495-6339	1		DBA	69	Harvard	1971
Sarofim-Rock Professor Business Administration								
Stobaugh, Robert B.	Prof	495-6296	7	U				
Charles E. Wilson Professor of Business Administration								
Uyterhoeven, Hugo E. R.	Prof	493-6622	1					
Timken Professor of Business Administration								
Vietor, Richard H. K.	Prof	495-6460	4	L				
Walton, Richard E.	Prof	495-6279	25	EN				
Wallace Brett Donham Professor of Business Administration								
Wells, Louis T. Jr.	Prof	495-6107	4	L				
Herbert F. Johnson Professor of International Business Management								
Wheelwright, Steven C.	Prof	495-6054	7	U				
MBA Class of 1949 Professor of Business Administration								
Yoffie, David B.	Prof	495-6363	4	L				
Zuboff, Shoshana	Prof	495-6662	25	EN				
Casseres-Gomes, Benjamin	Assoc	495-6387	4	L				
Chew, W. Bruce	Assoc	495-6543	7	U				
Collis, David J.	Assoc	495-6331	4	L				
Dees, J. Gregory	Assoc	495-6574	1					
Encarnation, Dennis J. III	Assoc	495-6284	4	L				
Goodman, John B.	Assoc	495-6287	4	L				
Hammond, Janice H.	Assoc	495-6620	7	U				
Hill, Linda	Assoc	496-6696	25	EN				
Jick, Todd D.	Assoc	495-6654	25	EN				
Kao, John J.	Assoc	495-6660	25	EN				
Leonard-Barton, Dorothy	Assoc	495-6637	7	U				
Murphy, Kevin J.	Assoc	495-6121	25	EN				
O'Brien, Patricia A.	Assoc	495-6328	1					
Paine, Lynn	Assoc	495-6781						
Schlesinger, Leonard A.	Assoc	495-6489						
Simons, Robert	Assoc	495-6757						
Bhide, Amarnath V.	Asst	495-6190	1					
Christensen, Clayton	Asst	495-6723						
Enright, Michael J.	Asst	495-6568	4	L				
Friedman, Raymond A.	Asst	495-6484	25	EN				
Gibbs, Michael J.	Asst	495-6148	25	EN				
Hohma, Nitin	Asst	495-6653	25	EN				
Iansiti, Marco	Asst	495-6643	7	U				
Ibarra, Herminia M.	Asst	495-6485	25	EN				
Koehn, Nancy F.	Asst	495-6483	4	L				
Loveman, Gary W.	Asst	495-6652	25	EN				
McGahan, Anita M.	Asst	495-6896	4	L				
Mishina, Kazahiro	Asst	495-6268	7	U				
Pisano, Gary P.	Asst	495-6562	7	U				
Reinhardt, Forest L.	Asst	495-6610	4	L				

Roberts, Michael J.	Asst	495-6871	1	
Robinson, Robert J.	Asst	495-6068	25	EN
Rosenzweig, Philip M.	Asst	495-6692	1	
Shapiro, Helen	Asst	495-6322	4	L
Teisberg, Elizabeth Olmsted	Asst	495-6607	4	L
Thomas, David A.	Asst	495-6327	25	EN
Upton, David M.	Asst	495-6636	7	U
Brown, Donald	SLect	495-6608	1	
Jones, Thomas O.	SLect	495-6898		
Badaracco, Joseph L. Jr.	Lect	495-6333	1	
Hafrey, Leigh	Lect	495-6738	1	&
Hattersley, Michael	Lect	495-6735	1	&
Herman, Ellen D.	Lect	495-6737	1	&
Kent, Robert W.	Lect	495-6731	1	&
Livesey, Sharon M.	Lect	495-6733	1	&
Yanowitz, Richard B.	Lect	495-6736	1	&

University of Hawaii at Hilo	Hilo, HI	96720-4091	(808)	UHCCVM				BBA
Coll of Arts & Sciences			FAX=933-3685					
–Div of Bus Adm & Econ	Dean	933-3300			PHD	74	Stanford	1992
Boneparth, Ellen	Phone		Fax 933-3685					
Stack, Robert T.	H	933-3432	6	S	PHD	78	Mich St	1984
Hora, Stephen C.	Prof	933-3457	7	V	PHD	73	S Calif	1986
Hennessey, Harry W. Jr.	Assoc	933-3554	harryh	25	EIN	PHD	80	Georgia	8-90
Calton, Jerry	Asst		3		PHD			

Univ of Hawaii at Manoa	Honolulu, HI	96822	(808)	UHCCVM			1967,1972
College of Business Adm	2530 Dole Street		FAX=956-3766				BBA,MACC
Did Not Respond-1993 Listing							
Bess, H. David	Dean	956-8377	cbaodbe	Tran	PHD	67	UCLA
–Department of Management	Phone		Fax 956-3766				
Folk, Hugh	C-Pr	956-6999		PHD	60	Duke
Cotlar, Morton	Prof	956-8732		PHD	69	Georgia
Doktor, Robert H.	Prof	956-8740		PHD	70	Stanford
Edge, Alfred	Prof	956-7648		PHD	72	Arkansas
El-Ramly, Nobel	Prof	956-8731	7	B	PHD	70	UCLA
Kelley, Lane	Prof	956-7610		PHD	70	North Tx
Panko, Raymond R.	Prof	956-7626	7	B	PHD	75	Stanford
Peterson, W. Wesley	Prof	956-7563	9	Z	PHD	64	Michigan
Remus, William F.	Prof	956-7608	7	B	PHD	74	Mich St
Sprague, Ralph H.	Prof	956-7082	7	B	DBA	64	Indiana
Miyataki, Glenn K.	Assoc	956-9617		DBA	77	Colorado
Shenkar, Oded	Assoc	956-6684		PHD	81	Columbia
Suyderhould, Jack P.	Assoc	956-7446	7	B	PHD	78	Purdue
Hill, Timothy R.	Asst	956-6657	7	B	PHD	88	Indiana
Bailey, Elaine K.	Inst	956-7397		MA	78	Cen Mich

Hawaii Pacific University	Honolulu, HI	96813	(808)				
Business Administration	1188 Fort Street Mall		FAX=544-0243				BA,MBA,MS,MA
Romig, Rodney	Dean	544-0279		Econ	PHD	75	Nebraska	8-87
–Management Faculty	Phone	544-178	Fax 544-0280				
Davis, Frederick G.	Prof	544-1175	9	Z	PHD	68	Mich St	8-91
Ghosh, Stanley	Prof	544-0227	14	BL	PHD	50	Indiana	8-82
Glover, Gerald	Prof	544-1183	25	EFN	PHD	81	Florida	1-89
Lohmann, David	Prof	544-1157	79	BHN	PHD	73	Ariz St	8-86
Ward, Richard T.	Prof	544-0236	57	BHN	EDD	86	S Calif	8-86
Wee, Warren	Prof	544-9325	7	X	PHD	82	U Wash	8-88
Kanekoa, S. Meilani	Assoc	544-1118	8	Y	PHD	86	U Miami	1-90
Mardfin, Ward	Assoc	233-3213	17	STVY	PHD	79	Hi-Manoa	8-93
Hines, D. Spencer	Asst	544-1115	23	HIL	MBA	82	Pepperdi	1-89
Pavelle, James R.	Inst	544-1177	35	ANIL	MBA	91	HI Pacif	6-91
Wiletzky, Les	Inst	544-1177	15	AFNP	MPA	78	Penn St	8-91

Heidelberg College	Tiffin, OH	44883	(419)				
Dept of Bus Adm & Econ	310 East Market Street		FAX=448-2124				
Wickham, Wm. T.	C-Pr	448-2280	15	EN	PHD	56	Case Wes	1977
–Management Faculty	Phone		Fax 448-2124				
Kirklin, W. Wayne	Assoc	448-2280	14	Y	MS	61	NYU	1978
Brickner, Laura	Asst	448-2280	57	U	MBA	86	Bowl Grn	1989

Henderson State University	Arkadelphia, AR	71923	(501)				
School of Business	1100 Henderson Street		FAX=246-3199				
Did Not Respond-1993 Listing							
Fisher, Robert C.	Dean	246-5511		PHD	75	Arkansas	1986

-Dept of Adm Sciences — Phone — Fax 246-3199

Name	Rank		Degree		Yr	School
Akin, Ramona	Prof		EDD			
Tatum, James C.	Prof		DBA	76		Miss St
Meadows, Jack E. Jr.	Assoc		MBA			Arkansas
Wright, Alan	Asst		ABD			Memphis

Hillsdale College — Hillsdale, MI — 49242 — (517) FAX=
Dept of Econ, Bus & Atg

Name	Rank		Field	Degree	Yr	School	Year
VanEaton, Charles	C-Pr	Ext 2412	Econ	PHD	74	Tulane	1978

-Management Faculty — Phone — Fax 437-7341

Hofstra University — Hempstead, NY — 11550 — (516) HOFSTRA.EDU — 1968,1982
School of Business — 1000 Fulton Avenue — FAX=564-4296 — BS,MBA,MTA

Name	Rank	Phone	Email	Code	Field	Degree	Yr	School	Date
Haynes, Ulric	Dean	463-5015	bizush	34		JD		Yale	9-91
-Department of Management	Phone	564-5726	Fax 564-4296						
Blonder, Mauritz D.	C-Ac	463-5730		23	HLY	PHD	76	CUNY	9-78
Greenbaum, Howard	Emer	463-5364	mgbhzg	2	DEX	PHD	52	Columbia	9-77
Lazarus, Harold	Prof	463-5734	mgbhzl	2	EFP	PHD	63	Columbia	9-61
Mel Weitz Distinguished Professor									
Montana, Patrick J.	Prof	463-5136		25	AOP	PHD	66	NYU	9-80
Roukis, George S.	Prof	463-5736		5	KQY	PHD	73	NYU	9-78
Sonfield, Matthew C.	Prof	463-5728	mgbmcs	36	ST	PHD	75	NYU	9-75
Charnov, Bruce H.	Assoc	463-5326		12	KR	PHD	76	US Intl	9-80
Flynn, David M.	Assoc	463-5930	mgbdmf	34	YIT	PHD	79	Mass	9-87
Smith, Charles H.	Assoc	463-5731	mcbchs	23	DHJ	PHD	85	Syracuse	7-86
Wahba, Mahammed	Assoc	463-5727	mgmaw	1	EI	PHD	80	Penn St	9-81
Buda, Richard	Asst	463-5732	mgbrzb	15	NP	PHD	84	Stevens	9-93
Comer, Debra R.	Asst	463-5201	mgbdrc	25	EGR	PHD	86	Yale	9-87
Davidson, Anthony R.	Asst	463-6763	mgbard	79	UVZ	MBA	85	Baruch	9-93
Elsayed, Sayed M.	Asst	463-5729		79	UZ	PHD	90	Baruch	9-88
Farid, Mamdouh I.	Asst	463-5735	mgbmif	38	TY	PHD	88	Baruch	9-85
Gao, Li-Lian	Asst	463-5729	mgblzg	79	UVZ	PHD	88	Indiana	9-88
Lee, Yoon R.	Asst	463-5201	mgbyrl	79	UVZ	PHD	86	Kansas	9-87
Gordon, Roy H.	SpAst	463-5733		13	IY	MME	54	Polytech	2-84
Merolla, C. R.	SpAst	463-5735		13	AI	MBA	62	NYU	9-89

College of the Holy Cross — Worcester, MA — 01610 — (508) FAX=793-2677 — BS
Dept of Economics — 1 College Street
Offers No Business Curriculum

Name	Rank	Phone	Field	Degree	Yr	School	Year
Kosicki, George	C-Ac	793-2689	Econ	PHD	85	Cornell	1985

Hope College — Holland, MI — 49423-3698 — (616) FAX=394-7922 — BA,BS
Econ & Business Adm — 69 East 10th Street

Name	Rank	Phone	Email	Code	Field	Degree	Yr	School	Year
Heisler, James B.	C-Pr	394-7915			Econ	PHD	75	Nebraska	1981
-Management Faculty	Phone	394-7580	Fax 394-7506						
Gibson, C. Kendrick	Prof	394-7580		35	INT	PHD	78	Arkansas	1986
Muiderman, Anthony	Assoc	394-7580		16		MBA	77	Grd Vall	1977

Houghton College — Houghton, NY — 14744-0128 — (716) FAX= — BS
Dept of Business & Econ — One Willard Ave

Name	Rank	Phone	Code	Field	Degree	Yr	School	Year
Halberg, Richard A.	C-Ac	567-9447	46	SJ	MBA	76	Akron	1975
-Management Faculty	Phone	Fax 567-9570						
Bates, Kenneth J.	Assoc	567-9448	13	ID	MBA	81	Loyola	1989
Frasier, David W.	Assoc	567-9450	18	YJ	ABD		Nova	1979

University of Houston — Houston, TX — 77204-6283 — (713) UHUPVM1.UH.EDU — 1964,1967
College of Business Adm — FAX=749-6896 — BBA,MBA,MAC,PHD

Name	Rank	Phone	Email	Code	Field	Degree	Yr	School	Date
Ivancevich, John M.	Dean	743-4603	mana6hz	25	GCEN	DBA	68	Maryland	1974
-Department of Management	Phone	743-4646	Fax 743-4652						
Matteson, Michael	C-Pr	743-4646		2	GE	PHD	69	Houston	8-68
Freedman, Sara M.	Prof	743-4609	mana3bx	2	ER	PHD	76	N Carol	8-76
Associate Dean									
Keller, Robert	Prof	743-4676		28	HDYE	PHD	72	Penn St	8-72
McMahon, Timothy	Prof	743-4651		28	EFHY	DBA	72	Kentucky	8-72
Phillips, James	Prof	743-4660	mana3bu	25	ENYR	PHD	81	Akron	8-80
Pratt, Joseph	Prof	743-4659		48	BILY	PHD	81	J Hopkin	8-86
Szilagyi, Andrew	Prof	743-4655		36	DEIT	PHD	73	Indiana	8-73
Blakeney, Roger N.	Assoc	743-4803	mana6hy	28	YJRE	PHD	69	Houston	1968
Defrank, Richard	Assoc	743-4678	mana7wr	26	ETYG	PHD	80	Rochest	8-89
Rechner, Paula	Assoc	743-4674	mana7wu	34	ILRJ	PHD	86	Indiana	8-90
Rude, Dale E.	Assoc	743-4673	mana7wq	2	EX	PHD	84	Iowa	8-84
Arch, Gail	Asst	743-4663		58	NQY	PHD	91	Ohio St	9-91
Busenitz, Lowell	Asst	743-4665		35	IST	PHD	92	Tx A&M	9-92
Hill, Robert	Asst	743-4679	mana7wv	36	ITDH	PHD	86	Tx A&M	8-90

Neupert, Kent	Asst			38	IY	PHD	93	W Ontar	1-94
Ones, Deniz	Asst			58	NQY	PHD	93	Iowa	9-93
Seth, Anju	Asst	743-4656	mana7qy	38	IYXL	PHD	88	Michigan	8-87
Werner, Steve	Asst			58	NQY	PHD	93	Florida	9-93
—Dept of Decision & Info Sci	Phone	743-4747	Fax 743-4940						
Gardner, Everette S. Jr.	C-Pr	743-4720		7	U	PHD	78	N Carol	1-87
Hirschheim, Rudolf A.	Prof	743-4692	rudy	9	Z	PHD	85	London	9-88
Khumawala, Basheer A.	Prof	743-4721	bkhumawala	7	U	PHD	70	Purdue	9-78
Ostrofsky, Benjamin	Prof	743-4739		7	U	PHD	68	UCLA	9-69
Scamell, Richard W.	Prof	743-4733	manag	9	Z	PHD	72	Texas	1972
Adams, Dennis	Assoc	743-4730	adams	9	Z	PHD	88	Tx Tech	9-87
Cooper, Randolph B.	Assoc	743-4732	rcooper	9	Z	PHD	83	UCLA	8-90
Mitchell, Alfred Cameron	Assoc	743-4726		9	Z	PHD	72	Texas	1972
Parks, Michael S.	Assoc	743-4729	parks	9	Z	PHD	73	Georgia	1973
Anderson, Elizabeth A.	Asst	743-4740	anderson		U	PHD	92	Houston	9-91
email: anderson@ricsi.cba.uh.edu									
Bregman, Robert L.	Asst	743-4722		7	U	PHD	88	Ohio St	9-93
Cossick, Kathy L.	Asst	743-4727	kathy	9	Z	PHD	92	Fla St	8-91
Green, Carolyn W.	Asst	743-4728	cgreen	9	Z	PHD	93	Houston	9-93
Kadipasaogul, Sukran	Asst	743-4707		7	U	PHD	93	Clemson	9-93
email: disc5g1jetson									
Robichaux, Barry	Asst	743-4731	barry	9	Z	PHD	90	Georgia	8-90

Univ of Houston-Clear Lake	Houston, TX	77058-1098		(713)	UHCL				1981,1986
Sch of Bus & Public Adm	2700 Bay Area Boulevard			FAX=					BA,BS,BA,MS,MBA
Staples, William A.	Dean	283-3100			Mktg	PHD	68	Houston	9-79
—Management Faculty	Phone	283-3235	Fax 283-3951						
Allison, Richard C.	C-Pr	283-3251		4	AM	PHD		Tx A&M	8-75
Elden, J. Maxwell	Prof	283-3258	eldel	12	DEFQ	PHD		UCLA	1-90
McGlashan, Robert	Prof	283-3246		3	I	PHD	68	Texas	8-74
Starling, G.	Prof	283-3256		4	AHL	PHD		Texas	8-74
White, Louis P.	Prof	283-6769		12	EF	PHD		S Fla	8-76
Black, Kenneth U.	Assoc	283-3239		7	UV	PHD		North Tx	9-79
Tombaugh, Jay R.	Assoc	283-3244		24	DE	PHD		Bowl Gr	8-84
Wolfe, Michael N.	Assoc	283-3243		53	NQI	PHD		Mass	8-74
Lam, Long W.	Asst	283-3125		14		PHD		Oregon	9-94
Muir, Nan	Asst	283-3241		38	IYHD	PHD		Tx-Arlin	8-90
Sherman, Mark R.	Asst	283-3242	sherman	45	KNQY	PHD		NS Wales	8-89
Wooten, Kevin C.	Asst	283-3257		52	JPNO	PHD		Tulane	9-92

Univ of Houston-Downtown	Houston, TX	77002-1001		(713)					
College of Business	One Main Street			FAX=221-8064					BS
Bizzell, Bobby G.	Dean	221-8179		38	IY	PHD	71	Texas	1989
—Bus Mgt & Adm Services Dpt	Phone	221-8017	Fax 221-8632						
Jackson, Gary	C-Pr$	221-8905							
Evans, Gail S. M.	Prof	221-8017		4	JKL	JD	72	Texas	1-80
Interim Associate Dean									
Efraty, David	Assoc	221-8964		25	EFOP	PHD	75	Case Wes	9-88
Johnson, Madeline	Assoc	221-8067							
Ruthstrom, Carl R.	Assoc	221-8962		67	SUVW	PHD	86	Texas	9-90
Ashe, Carolyn	Asst	221-8051							
Aven, Forrest F. Jr.	Asst	221-8593		25	EFNR	PHD	88	Colorado	9-90
Bullard, A. Davant	Asst	221-8671				PHD	87	Geo St	
Shipley, Margaret F.	Asst	221-8571		27	UVS	PHD	86	Pitt	9-86
Wallman, Kenneth		221-8525		68	QSTY	MBA	70	New Eng	9-76

Houston Baptist University	Houston, TX	77074-3298		(713)					
College of Bus & Econ	7502 Fondren Road			FAX=995-3408					BS,BA,BBA,MA
Garrison, R. Bruce	Dean	995-3325				PHD	75	N Colo	1983
—Management Faculty	Phone		Fax 995-3408						
Franklin, Carter L. II	Prof	995-3325		78	UVYZ	PHD	68	Purdue	1974
Associate Dean									
Mahoney, Frank	VProf	995-3325							
Barbee, Cliff	Assoc	995-3325		39	IMT	PHD	72	American	1989

Howard University	Washington, DC	20059		(202)					1976,1980
School of Business	2400 Sixth Street NW			FAX=797-6393					BA
Did Not Respond-1993 Listing									
Johnson, Lawrence	Dean				Mktg	PHD	70	Stanford	
—Dept of Management	Phone		Fax 797-6393						
Lacy, Gywynette	C	806-1537		5	N	PHD			
McKinney, T. Charles	Prof	806-1539		2	E	PHD			
Murphy, Charles	Prof	806-1540		3	I	PHD			
Nowell, Gadis	Prof	806-1538		2	E	PHD			
Ofong, Chigbo	Prof	806-1330		5	N	PHD			
Howard, Cecil G.	Assoc	806-1541		3	I	PHD			
Robertson-Sanders, Pat	Assoc	806-1534		1	E	PHD			

University of Idaho — Moscow, ID — 83844-3178 — (208) UIDAHO.EDU

College of Bus & Econ — FAX=885-8939 — BS

Name	Rank	Phone	Email		Field	Deg		School	Year
Dangerfield, Byron	Dean	885-6478	cbedean	79	UVXZ	PHD	85	U Wash	1981
--Department of Business	Phone	885-6295	Fax 885-8939						
Byers, C. Randall	C-Ac	885-7341	rbyers	97	Z	PHD	73	Minn	1973
Dacey, Raymond	Prof	885-7345		87	VY	PHD	70	Purdue	1984
Dinoto, Michael J.	Prof	885-7148		5	Q	PHD	73	SUNY	1970
Dept of Economics									
Gieger, Joseph J.	Prof	885-7154	joeg	36	SIAB	EDD	77	Colorado	1988
Hallaq, John	Prof	885-7340		8	YL	PHD	72	U Wash	1970
Olson, Philip D.	Prof	885-7153		62	TSI	PHD	72	Oregon	1973
Morris, John S.	Assoc	885-6820	jmorris	73	UV	PHD	88	Oklahoma	1973
Pendegraft, Norman	Assoc	885-7157	norman	79	VZ	PHD	78	UCLA	1983
Reyes, Mario	Assoc	885-7146	mgcreyes	8	Y	PHD	87	Arkansas	1965
Wegman, Jerry	Assoc	885-7342	wegman	4	K	JD	70	Columbia	1977
Bailey, Jeffrey	Asst	885-7156	jbailey	5	JNP	PHD	91	Akron	1991
Lawrence, John	Asst	885-5821	jjl	7	UD	PHD	93	Penn St	1993
Stover, Dana L.	Asst	885-7140		25	REHD	PHD	90	Wash St	1990
Toelle, Richard A.	Asst	885-6938		7	UVW	PHD	86	Oklahoma	1986
VanOver, David	Asst	885-5794	dvanover	9	Z	PHD	88	Houston	1991

Idaho State University — Pocatello, ID — 83209-8020 — (208) SDSC.ISU.EDU — 1975,1980

College of Business — FAX=236-4367 — BA,MBA
CIS Dept Did Not Respond-1993 Listing

Name	Rank	Phone			Field	Deg		School	Year
Fannin, William R.	Dean	236-3585			Mgt	PHD	80	Tx A&M	1988
--Management Department	Phone		Fax 236-4367						
Stratton, William E.	C-Pr	236-3535			EH	PHD	74	Case Wes	1974
Gallagher, Michael C.	Prof	236-2362			E	PHD	75	Tx A&M	1987
Vice President for Academic Affairs									
Gantt, Garnewell	Prof	236-2580			K	DJ	72	Texas	1987
Johnson, George A.	Prof	236-2966			U	PHD	70	Oregon	1973
MBA Director									
Jolly, James P.	Assoc	236-3455			N	PHD	85	Tx-Dallas	1988
Kilpatrick, John A.	Prof	236-3920			IY	PHD	78	Iowa	1977
Pawar, Sheelwant B.	Prof	236-3585			Q	PHD	67	Utah	1967
Johnson, Mark A.	Assoc	236-2155			N	PHD	88	Iowa	1987
Dunn, Steven	Asst	236-3708			UW	PHD	92	Penn St	1993
Salazar, Ron	Asst	236-3597			I	PHD	90	Texas	1993
--CIS Department	Phone	236-3040	Fax 233-4939						
Schou, Corey D.	C-Pr	236-3040	shou	9	Z	PHD	75	Fla St	1985
Director Simplot Group Decision Support Center									
deRaadt, J. D. R.	Assoc		deraadt	9	Z	PHD	86	LaTrobe	1987
Watts, Robert T.	Assoc		watts	9	Z	PHD	71	New Mex	1978
Aytes, Krai G.	Asst		aytes	9	Z	PHD	93	Arizona	1993
Frost, James	Asst		frost	9	Z	ABD		FSU	1993
Ramana, Sheela	Asst		ramana	6	Z	PHD	91	Kan St	1991

University of Illinois — Champaign, IL — 61820 — (217) UIUCVMD — 1924,1963

College Comm & Bus Adm — FAX=244-7969 — BS,MS,MBA,PHD

Name	Rank	Phone			Field	Deg		School	Year
Thomas, Howard	Dean	333-2747		3	IX	PHD	70	Edinburg	1981
--Dept of Business Adm	Phone	333-4240	Fax 244-7969						
Monroe, Kent	H-Pr	333-4240				PHD	68	Illinois	1991
Blair, Charles	Prof	333-2471		7	V	PHD	75	Car Mel	1980
Engelbrecht-Wiggans, Richard	Prof	333-1088		7	V	PHD	78	Cornell	1982
Evans, Richard	Prof	333-4240		7	V	DR	59	J Hopkin	1969
Kindt, John	Prof	333-6018		4	KY	JD		Georgia	1978
Lansing, Paul	Prof	333-8141		4	KY	JD	71	Illinois	1990
Leblebici, Huseyin	Prof	333-4512		2	EFH	PHD	75	Illinois	1982
Oldham, Greg R.	Prof	333-6340		2	DEFH	PHD	74	Yale	1973
Roberts, Donald	Prof	333-4554		7	UV	PHD	59	Stanford	1959
Black, Robert	Assoc	333-4592		4	K	JD	55	Illinois	1955
Cohen, Susan	Assoc	333-1337		7	V	PHD	77	Northwes	1986
Hennart, Jean-Francois	Assoc	333-4597		8	Y	PHD	77	Maryland	1990
Kulik, Carol T.	Assoc	244-0208		2	EFH	PHD	87	Illinois	1990
Monahan, George	Assoc	333-8270		7	UV	PHD	77	Northwes	1986
Porao, Joseph F.	Assoc	333-4515		2	DEFH	PHD	79	Rochest	1978
Ritz, Zvi	Assoc	333-7966		7	V	PHD	81	Northwes	1979
Roszkowski, Mark	Assoc	333-0886		4	KL	JD	75	Illinois	1975
Shaw, Michael	Assoc	333-5159		79	VZ	PHD	84	Purdue	1984
Smunt, Timothy L.	Assoc	333-4519		7	UV	PHD	81	Indiana	1990
Tang, Ming-Je	Assoc	333-2504		3	IY	PHD	85	MIT	1985
Chhajed, Dilip	Asst	333-3778		7	UV	PHD	89	Purdue	1989
Farjoun, Moshe	Asst	333-2652		7	UV	PHD	90	Northwes	1990
Jourden, Forest	Asst	244-8051		2	EFH	PHD	91	Stanford	1991
Liu, Ben S.	Asst	333-9003				PHD		SUNY-Buf	
Mahoney, Joseph	Asst	244-8257		3	I	PHD	88	Penn	1988
Raman, Narayan	Asst	333-5255		7	UV	PHD	88	Michigan	1987
Roehl, Thomas	Asst	333-0147		8	Y	PHD		Wash	1992

Name	Title	Phone	ID	#	Fields	Degree	Yr	School	Year
Rosa, Jose A.	Asst					PHD		Michigan	1992
Sanchez, Ronald	Asst	333-2963		3	I	PHD	91	MIT	1991
Wade, James	Asst	333-4556		2	EFH	PHD	92	Berkeley	1992
Willard, Gary	Asst	333-9344		36	IT	PHD	82	Purdue	1991

Univ of Illinois at Chicago — Chicago, IL 60607-7122 (312) UICVM.EDU 1971,1981
College of Bus Adm 240 — 601 South Morgan Street — FAX=996-0773

Name	Title	Phone	ID	#	Fields	Degree	Yr	School	Year
Uselding, Paul J.	Dean	996-2671	u59382		DecS	PHD	70	Northwes	1992
—Department of Management	Phone	996-2739	Fax 996-0773						
Salancik, Gerald R.	H-Pr	996-5764	u27770	2	BECH	PHD	71	Yale	8-93
Barnum, Darold	Prof	996-3073	u48433	53	NIQ	PHD	73	Penn	1-85
Burack, Elmer	Prof	996-7404	u18848	25	NEOI	PHD	64	Northwes	7-78
Heckmann, Irvin	Emer	996-2523			1991	PHD	54	Wiscon	6-68
Huneryager, S. G.	Emer	996-2925	u31314	23	NEI	PHD	64	Illinois	6-66
Albrecht, Maryann	Assoc	996-4480	u09909	25	EFH	PHD	75	Emory	9-72
Bartlett, Hale C.	Assoc	996-5552	u19995	34	IL	PHD	65	Michigan	9-67
Cooke, Robert	Assoc	996-3794		25	E	PHD	73	Northwes	9-81
Elwert, Bert	Assoc	996-3568		4	HILK	PHD	65	Indiana	9-64
Liden, Robert C.	Assoc	996-4481	u42026	25	EN	PHD	81	Cinn	8-91
McLimore, Fred	Assoc	996-0529	u31319	45	NLJG	PHD	71	Purdue	1-81
Pagano, Anthony	Assoc	996-8063	u14876	34	ILN	PHD	78	Penn St	9-78
Suntrup, Edward	Assoc	413-0180	u31324	85	QNKY	PHD	75	Minn	9-76
Torres, David	Assoc	996-8285	u20247	24	HQTS	PHD	83	Northwes	1-91
Wayne, Sandra L.	Assoc	996-2799	u23430	5	NE	PHD	87	Tx A&M	9-87
Hybles, Ralph C.	Asst	996-2739				PHD	04	Cornell	8-94
Shelton, Lois	Asst	410-0237	u28993		I	PHD	85	Harvard	8-93

Illinois Benedictine College — Lisle, IL 60532-0900 (708)
Business Economic Dept — 5700 College Road — FAX=
phone: 960-1500

Name	Title	Phone	ID	#	Fields	Degree	Yr	School	Year
Kittel, Phyllis	Dean	960-1500							
—Management Faculty	Phone	Ext 7000	Fax 960-1126						
Lee, Soyun	C-Pr	Ext 7003			Econ	PHD	77	N Illin	1974
Madura, Jeffrey	Prof					MBA	72	Northwes	1971
Quick, Larry	Prof					PHD	84	Northwes	1984
Eschbacm, Doris	Asst					ABD		St Louis	1993

Illinois Institute of Tech — Chicago, IL 60661-3691 (312) IITVAX
Stuart School Business — 10 West 33rd Street — FAX=567-9360 — BBA,BS,MBA,PHD

Name	Title	Phone	#	Fields	Degree	Yr	School	Year
Hassan, M. Zia	Dean	906-6516	7	V	PHD	65	Ill Tech	1960
—Management Faculty	Phone	906-6500	Fax 906-6549					
Chung, Joseph	Prof	906-6542			PHD	64	Wayne St	1964
Goldhar, Joel	Prof	906-6526			PHD	71	Geo Wash	1983
Smith, Spencer	Prof	906-6535			PHD	58	Columbia	1966
Thomopoulos, Nick	Prof	906-6536	7	V	PHD	66	Ill Tech	1968
Bariff, Martin	Assoc	906-6522			PHD	73	Illinois	1983
Calero, Thomas M.	Assoc	906-6523	5	N	PHD	68	Northwes	1968
Ginn, Martin E.	Assoc	906-6525			PHD	83	Northwes	1983
Hall, W. Clayton	Assoc	906-6527			PHD	64	Illinois	1966
Knowles, Thomas	Assoc	906-6530			PHD	70	Chicago	1969
Kraft, George	Assoc	906-6531			PHD		Case Wes	1968
Tourk, Khairy	Assoc	906-6537			PHD	71	Calif	1971
Flanagan, Michael	Asst	906-6539						1993
Hamilton, Charles	Asst	906-6528			PHD		Illinois	1991
Imam, Syed	Asst	906-6504						
Makhija, Indra	Asst	906-6532			PHD		Chicago	1986
Myma, Peter	Asst	906-6529						1993
Prabhaker, Paul	Asst	906-6533			PHD			1992
Twombly, John	Asst	906-6538			PHD		Chicago	1992
Hampson, Jane	Lect	906-6529						1993
Rausch, Bernard	Lect	906-6534						1986

Illinois State University — Normal, IL 61761-6901 (309) 1981,1986
College of Business — 2200 North & School Streets — FAX=438-5510 — BS,MS

Name	Title	Phone	#	Fields	Degree	Yr	School	Year
Jefferson, Robert M.	Dean	438-2251		Mktg	PHD	69	Iowa	1989
—Dept of Mgt & Quant Methods	Phone		Fax 438-5510					
Nielsen, Warren R.	C-Pr	438-5703	25		PHD	73	Illinois	
Chitgopekar, Sharad	Prof	438-7993	7		PHD		Fla St	
Couch, Peter D.	Prof	438-3022	5		PHD	65	Wiscon	1970
Dumler, Michael P.	Prof	438-5701	32		PHD		Kentucky	1982
Graeff, Claude	Prof	438-7580	23		PHD		Illinois	1977
Graf, Lee A.	Prof	438-7878	25		PHD		Miss St	1976
Hemmasi, Masoud	Prof	438-8765	32		PHD		LSU	1983
Newgren, Kenneth E.	Prof	438-2395	35		PHD	76	Georgia	8-84
Radhakrishnan, Ramaswamy	Prof	438-5658	7		PHD		Car Mel	
Ross, Jerry	Prof	438-7577	2		PHD	79	Northwes	1979

Fazel, Farzaneh	Assoc	438-3883	7		PHD		Illinois	
Park, Paul	Assoc	438-5306	7		PHD		Oregon	1988
Robinson, Don R.	Assoc	438-2760	7		PHD		La St	
Devinatz, Victor	Asst	438-3403	5		PHD		Minn	1990
Fitzgibbons, Dale E.	Asst	438-5093	2		PHD		Illinois	1988
Lust, John	Asst	438-8764	51		PHD		Kentucky	1989
Nicholson, Joel D.	Asst	438-2995	83		PHD	91	Fla St	1991
Ringer, Richard	Asst	438-2995	12		PHD	93	Colorado	1993
Russ, Gail	Asst	438-8772	32		PHD		Tx A&M	1990
Salegna, Gary	Asst	438-3466	7		PHD		Tx Tech	1991
Stewart-Belle, Sue	Asst	438-2954	52		PHD	92	Houston	1991
Strong, Kelly	Asst	438-2467	34		PHD	92	Colorado	1992

Illinois Wesleyan University — Bloomington, IL 61702-2900 (309)

Dept of Business Adm		1312 North Park Steet			FAX=556-3411			BA,BS
Gardner, Mona J.	Dir	556-3171			Fnce	PHD	80 Cinn	9-88
Adlai H. Rust Professor of Finance/Insurance								
—Management Faculty	Phone	556-3171	Fax 556-3411					
Ling, Cyril	Prof	556-3490		34 IJLN	DBA		Indiana	9-90
Telling Chair of Business Administration								
Walsh, William	Asst	556-3488		15 NQ	PHD		Indiana	9-90

Indiana University — Bloomington, IN 47405-1701 (812) INDIANA.EDU 1921,1963

School of Business		300 North Jordan Avenue			FAX=855-8679			BS,MBA,PHD
274- phone # have (317) area code & INDYVAX bitnet node								
Rau, John	Dean	855-8489	jrau		MBA	72	Harvard	1993
—Department of Management	Phone	855-9200	Fax 855-8679					
Near, Janet P.	C-Pr	855-9200	near	4 L	PHD	77	SUNY-Buf	1979
Bunke, Harvey C.	Prof	855-9209	bunke	4 L	PHD	51	Illinois	1967
Dalton, Dan R.	Prof	855-9209	dalton	5 Q	PHD	79	Ca-Irvine	1979
Daniels, John D.	Prof	855-9200	daniels	8 Y	PHD	69	Michigan	1987
Dreher, George F.	Prof	855-8529	dreher	5 N	PHD	77	Houston	1987
Hegarty, W. Harvey	Prof	855-0221	hegarty	3 I	PHD	72	N Carol	1974
Lenz, R. Thomas	Prof	274-2481	tlenz	3 I	DBA	78	Indiana	1977
Associate Dean								
Marer, Paul	Prof	855-0221	marer	8 Y	PHD	68	Penn	1967
Organ, Dennis W.	Prof	855-9209	organ	2 E	PHD	70	N Carol	1970
Podsakoff, Philip M.	Prof	855-9200	podsakof	5 N	DBA	80	Indiana	1982
Schwenk, Charles R.	Prof	855-9200	schwenk	3 I	DBA	80	Indiana	1986
Waldman, Joseph M.	Prof	855-2614	waldman	6 S	DBA	66	Indiana	1963
Wood, Donald A.	Prof	855-8529		5 N	PHD	68	Purdue	1968
Childers, Victor E.	Assoc	274-3585	vchilders	8 Y	DBA	67	Indiana	1966
Lyles, Marjorie A.	Assoc	274-2558	mlayles	8 Y	PHD	77	Pitt	1990
Mills, Peter K.	Assoc	855-9209	pkmills	2 H	PHD	80	Ca-Irvine	1989
Novit, Mitchell S.	Assoc	855-8529	novit	5 NQ	PHD	66	Michigan	1966
Weldon, Elizabeth	Assoc	855-9209	ivaxweldon	2 E	PHD	82	Ohio St	1991
Baldwin, Timothy T.	Asst	855-9209	baldwint	5 NP	PHD	87	Mich St	1987
Dollinger, Marc J.	Asst	855-9200	dollinge	3 IT	PHD	83	Lehigh	1987
Grover, Steven L.	Asst	855-0221	groversl	4 J	PHD	89	Columbia	1988
Magjuka, Richard J.	Asst	274-0874		2 H	PHD	86	Chicago	1988
McCarthy, Anne M.	Asst	855-0221	ammccarth	6 ST	PHD	92	Purdue	1990
Parkhe, Arvind	Asst	855-0221	aparkhe		PHD	89	Temple	1989
Tyler, Beverly Baker	Asst	855-9209	btyler	3 I	PHD	92	Tx A&M	1991
Wimbush, James	Asst	855-8529	jwimbush	5 N	PHD	91	Va Tech	1991

Indiana-Purdue/Ft Wayne — Fort Wayne, IN 46805-1499 (219) 1987,1987

School of Bus & Mgt Sci		2101 Coliseum Blvd Neff 330			FAX=481-6880			BS
—Dept of Management & Mktg	Phone	481-6470	Fax 481-6083					
Karim, Ahmad R.	C-Ac	481-6473		35 QN	PHD	81	Iowa	8-85
Leonard, Edwin C. Jr.	Prof	481-6489		24 EJNP	PHD	70	Purdue	8-66
Lingaraj, Bangalore P.	Prof	481-6479		7 W	PHD	73	Pitt	8-83
Hockemeyer, Sherrill	Assoc	481-6491		4 L	MS	67	Ind St	8-67
Moore, James S.	Assoc	481-6488		97 VZ	PHD	74	Purdue	8-80
Sriram, Ramaier	Asst	481-6007		97 VZ	PHD	90	Tenn	8-91
Turnipseed, David L. Jr.	Asst	481-6476		23 EYV	PHD	87	Alabama	8-92

Indiana Univ at Kokomo — Kokomo, IN 46904-9003 (317)

Div of Business & Econ					FAX=			BS
Von der Embse, Thomas J.	Dean	455-9446		34 FIJP	PHD	68	Ohio St	1990
—Management Faculty	Phone		Fax 455-9475					
Vaden, Richard	Prof	455-9471		25 AEFP	PHD	70	Tx Tech	1992
Amba-Rao, S. C.	Assoc	455-9318		25 YFNS	PHD	67	Purdue	1978

Indiana Univ South Bend
Div of Business & Econ
Joray, Paul A.
–**Management Faculty**

Indiana Univ South Bend	South Bend, IN	46634	(219)	IUSB				1989,1989
Div of Business & Econ	1700 Mishawaka Avenue		FAX=237-4599					BS,MBA
Joray, Paul A.	Dean	237-4227			PHD			
–Management Faculty	Phone	237-4138	Fax 237-4866					
Swanda, John R. Jr.	D-Pr	237-4294		24	EJ	PHD	68	Illinois	9-68
Norton, Steven D.	Assoc	237-4418		25	EN	PHD	70	Case Wes	8-83
Vollrath, David A.	Assoc	237-4365		24	EJ	PHD	84	Illinoia	8-88
Frankforter, Steven A.	Asst	237-4283		3		PHD	90	U Wash	8-91
Sutton, Cynthia	Asst	237-4884				PHD	93	Ariz St	8-92

Indiana Univ Northwest	Gary, IN	46408	(219)					1986,1986
Div of Business & Econ	3400 Broadway		FAX=980-6579					BS,MBA
Vasquez, Marilyn	Dean	980-6633		Law	JD	88	Valparis	1979
–Management Faculty	Phone		Fax 980-6579					
Pati, Gopal C.	Prof	980-6910		45	FLN	PHD	70	Ill Tech	1972
Gupta, Omprakash K.	Assoc	980-6901		7	UVW	PHD	80	Purdue	1990
Hobson, Charles J.	Assoc	980-6903		12	CE	PHD	81	Purdue	1981
Scott, Cuthbert L. III	Assoc	980-6912		23	FHI	PHD	75	Oregon	1982
Shreve, Richard R.	Assoc	980-6915		39	IZ	PHD	78	Ill Tech	1991
Kini, Ranjan B.	Asst	980-6906		79	UVZ	PHD	85	Tx Tech	1990

Indiana Univ Southeast	New Albany, IN	47150	(812)	IUSMAIL.IUS.INDIANA.EDU				990
Div of Business & Econ	4201 Grant Line Road		FAX=941-2672					BA,MBA
Greckel, Fay E.	Dean	941-2362		R	PHD	69	Indiana	1967
–Management Faculty	Phone	941-2362	Fax 941-2672					
Wheat, Jerry	C-Pr	941-2362		48	JY	DBA	73	Indiana	1977
Rriscoe, John	Prof	941-2362		7	U	PHD	77	Louisvil	1978
Ramsey, Gerald D.	Assoc	941-2362		1		PHD	75	Purdue	1980
Ernstberger, Kathy	Asst	941-2362		9	Z	PHD	91	Indiana	1991
Hufft, Edward M.	Asst	941-2362		3	I	DBA	91	Kentucky	1990
Keefe, Thomas	Asst	941-2362		25	ENQ	PHD	89	SUNY-Buf	1989
Kuzmicki, Jana	Asst	941-2362		3	I	PHD	93	Alabama	1993
Pittman, Paul	Asst	941-2362		7	UV	PHD	93	Georgia	1993
Beckman, Eugene	Lect	941-2362		1		MBA	75	Louisvil	1987
Griffth, Miriam	Lect	941-2362		5	O	MED	76	Louisvil	1991
Scinta, Kate	Lect	941-2362		1	&	MA	80	Boston C	1993

Indiana U of Pennsylvania	Indiana, PA	15705-1071	(412)	IUP				
College of Business			FAX=357-5743					BS,MBA,MS
Did Not Respond-1993 Listing								
Camp, Robert C.	Dean	357-2520		Econ	PHD	75	Miss	1988
–Dept of Management	Phone		Fax 357-5743					
Chaubey, Manmohan	C	357-2535	mchaubey	56	NSTI	PHD	82	Iowa	1985
Ali, Abbas J.	Prof	357-5759	aaai	38	EIJY	PHD	82	W Virg	1989
Falcone, Thomas	Prof	357-2535	yunzubb	16	DIST	DBA	80	Kent St	1980
Gibbs, Manton	Prof	357-2535	mgibbs	37	ISUY	PHD	75	Mich St	1989
Ashamalla, Mari	Assoc	357-2535		23	EY	PHD	87	Univ Cen	1992
Orife, John N.	Assoc	357-2535	jorife	56	EN	PHD	74	Mich St	1989
Osborne, Stephen	Assoc	357-2535		32	HI	MBA	85	Pitt	1989
Ryan, John	Assoc	357-2535	john-rya	12	EZ	PHD	92	Pitt	1987
Soni, Ramesh	Assoc	357-2535	rgsoni	7	UV	PHD	88	Tx-Arlin	1988
Anderson, Fred	Asst	357-2535	anderson	23	HIT	ABD	84	Pitt	1976
Ryan, Grace Ann	Asst	357-2535		23	DEFH	PHD	82	Pitt	1981

Indiana State University	Terre Haute, IN	47809	(812)	INDST				1980,1983
School of Business	217 North 6th Street		FAX=237-7675					BS
Ross, Herbert L.	Dean	237-2000		Mktg	PHD	68	Illinois	9-67
–Dept of Management & Fin	Phone	237-2086	Fax 237-7631					
Davis, Tammy J.	C-Ac$	237-2087		21	NO	PHD		Georgia	8-90
Douglas, Max E.	Prof	237-2104		26	S	EDD		Indiana	8-68
Scott, William C.	Prof	237-2090		13	I	PHD		Iowa	8-77
Chait, Herschel N.	Assoc	237-2000		15	N	PHD		Indiana	8-81
Acting Associate Dean								
Budd, Jim L.	Asst	237-2110		13	I	PHD		Waynesbg	8-92
Hand, Barry M.	Asst	237-2108		31	I	ABD		Kentucky	8-91
Wong, Yim Yu	Asst	237-2094		13	I	PHD		Nebraska	8-91

University of Indianapolis	Indianapolis, IN	46227-3697	(317)	GANDLF.UINDY.EDU				
School of Business	1400 East Hanna Avenue		FAX=					BBA,BA,MBA
Livesay, Robin R.	Dean	788-3370			PHD		Ohio St	1978
–Management Faculty	Phone		Fax 788-3275					

Iona College — New Rochelle, NY 10801-1890 — (914) IONA.BITNET
Hagan School of Bus — 715 North Avenue — FAX= — BBA
O'Donnell, Charles F. — Dean 633-2256 — Econ PHD — 9-61
–Department of Management — Phone 633-2588 — Fax 633-2012

Name	Rank	Phone							
Andersson, Marie Louise	C $	633-2588		8	YEHI	PHD	88	CUNY	1980
Grunewald, Donald	Prof	633-2588		2	EIL	DBA	62	Harvard	1986
Schwartz, Theodore M.	Prof	633-2588		2	EF	PHD	65	New York	1963
Doyle, Stephen X.	Assoc	633-2588		2	EFHN	DBA	76	Harvard	1990
Duffy, Charles	Assoc	633-2588		25	EQYI	EDD	80	Columbia	1972
Eberle, Robert	Assoc	633-2588		1	DEH	MBA		NYU	1987
Halpern, David	Assoc	633-2588		5	QE	PHD	79	NYU	1985
Wittig-Berman, Ursula	Assoc	633-2588		2	EHI	PHD	85	CUNY	1985

University of Iowa — Iowa City, IA 52242-1000 — (319) UIOWA.EDU — 1923,1963
College of Business Adm — FAX=335-1956 — BBA,MA,PHD
–Dept Mgt & Organizations — Phone 335-0927 — Fax 335-1956

Name	Rank	Phone							
Christensen-Szalanski, Jay	Prof	335-0927		79	V	PHD	78	U Wash	1986
Delaney, John T.	Prof	335-0893		45	Q	PHD	83	Illinois	1989
Klasson, Charles	Prof	335-0887		3	FI	PHD	60	Indiana	9-75
Lopes, Lola	Prof	335-0960		2	E	PHD	74	Ca-SnDgo	1990
Pomerantz Professor									
Mount, Michael K.	Prof	335-0953		5	N	PHD	77	Iowa St	1986
Rose, Gerald L.	Prof	335-0884		2	E	PHD	69	Berkeley	1967
Rynes, Sara	Prof	335-0838		5	N	PHD	81	Wiscon	1990
Schmidt, Frank L.	Prof	335-0949		7	N	PHD	70	Purdue	1985
Ralph L. Sheets Professor									
Schoderbek, Peter P.	Prof	335-0950		3	I	PHD	64	Michigan	1964
Thompson, Duane E.	Prof	335-1037		5	N	PHD	69	Iowa	1965
Bretz Jr., Robert D.	Assoc			5	NP	PHD	88	Kansas	1994
Gilroy, Thomas P.	Assoc	335-0958		5	Q	MILR	58	Cornell	1980
Hauserman, Nancy R.	Assoc	335-0643		4	K	JD	76	Iowa	7-83
McLeod, Poppy L.	Assoc	335-0954		2	E	PHD	85	Harvard	1992
West, Jude P.	Assoc	335-1021		5	GNQ	PHD	69	Iowa	1965
Barrick, Murray R.	Asst	335-0924		5	NP	PHD	88	Akron	1988
Boles, Terry L.	Asst	335-0947		2	E	PHD	91	Ca-SnBar	1993
Schwochau, Susan	Asst	335-0839		5	Q	PHD	86	Illinois	1990
–Dept Management Sciences	Phone	335-0858	Fax 335-1956						
Kortanek, Ken	C-Pr	335-0922	ken-kort	7	V	PHD	64	Northwes	1986
Anstreicher, Kurt	Prof	335-0890	kurt-ans	7	V	PHD	83	Stanford	1991
Bell, Colin E.	Prof	335-0865	colin-be	97	ZV	PHD	69	Yale	1980
Boe, Warren J.	Prof	335-0889	warren-b	7	UZ	PHD	70	Purdue	1970
Daughety, Andy	Prof	335-0857	andy-dau	7	U	PHD	72	Case Wes	1981
Fethke, Gary C.	Prof	335-0865	gary-fet	7	U	PHD	68	Iowa	1975
Jagannathan, Raj	Prof	335-0957	raj-jaga	7	U	PHD	69	Car Mel	1975
Jones, Philip C.	Prof	335-0858	philip-j	7	U	PHD	77	Brekeley	1994
Ledolter, Johannes	Prof	335-0822	johannes	7	V	PHD	75	Wisconsi	1978
Lowe, Tim	Prof	335-0963	tim-lowe	7	U	PHD	73	Northwes	1989
Reinganum, Jennifer	Prof	335-0841	jennifer	7	V	PHD	79	Northwes	1987
Ye, Yinyu	Prof	335-1947	yinyu-ye	7	V	PHD	87	Stanford	1988
Srinivasan, Padmini	Assoc	335-5715	padmini-	9	Z	PHD	85	Syracuse	1989
DeMatta, Renato	Asst	335-0956	renato-d	7	U	PHD	89	Penn	1990
Morrison, Joline	Asst	335-0894	joline-m	9	Z	PHD	92	Arizona	1992
Morrison, Mike	Asst	335-3812	mike-mor	9	Z	PHD	92	Arizona	1992
Park, June	Asst	335-2087	june-par	9	Z	PHD	88	Ohio	1989
Traub, Rodney	Asst	335-0943	rodney-t	7	U	PHD	94	Purdue	1993

Iowa State University — Ames, IA 50011-2065 — (515) ISUMVS — 1991,1991
College of Business — FAX=294-6060 — BBA,BS,MS,MBA
Shrock, David L. — Dean 294-6060 — Tran DBA — 74 Indiana 1989
–Department of Management — Phone 292-8116 — Fax 294-6060

Name	Rank	Phone							
McElroy, James C.	C-Pr	294-8116		21	EN	PHD	79	Okla St	1979
Chacko, Thomas I.	Prof	294-2422		51	EN	PHD	77	Iowa	1980
Hunger, J. David	Prof	294-8463		31	IS	PHD	73	Ohio St	1982
Morrow, Paula C.	Prof	294-8109		2	EON	PHD	78	Iowa St	1978
Wacker, J.	Prof	294-8111		7	U	PHD	75	Wayne St	1983
Wortman, Max S.	Prof	294-3657		6	IT	PHD	62	Minn	
Pioneer Chair of Agricultural Business									
Aitchison, Gary L.	Assoc	294-8107		36		PHD	72	Iowa St	1965
Blackburn, V.	Assoc	294-3084		3	I	DBA	87	Kentucky	1986
Chu, Chao	Assoc	294-9693		7	UZ	PHD	84	Penn St	1986
Flynn, Barbara B.	Assoc	294-8108		7	U	DBA	84	Indiana	1987
Flynn, E. James	Assoc	294-8100		31	I	PHD	85	Indiana	1987
Johnson, R.	Assoc	294-8267		5	N	PHD	86	Bowl Gr	1992
Nilakanta, Sree	Assoc	294-8113		9	Z	PHD	85	Houston	1986
Shrader, Charles B.	Assoc	292-3050		34	IHLJ	PHD	84	Indiana	1984
Moser, K.	Asst	294-2839		9	Z	PHD	91	Ariz St	1991
Premkumar, G.	Asst	294-1833		9	Z	PHD	89	Pitt	1989
Ramirez, R.	Asst	294-8116		9	Z	PHD	87	Tx A&M	1991

Ithaca College — Ithaca, NY 14850 — (607) ITHACA.EDU

School of Business — FAX=274-1137 — BS

Name	Title	Phone				Degree		School	
Long, David K.	Dean	274-3341		2	E	PHD	74	Kent	8-73
—Department of Management	Phone	274-3117	Fax 274-1137						
Kelly, Eileen P.	C-Ac	274-3117	kelly	54	QJB	PHD	82	Cinn	8-93
Barken, Marlene E.	Assoc	274-3946		4		PHD	81	Harvard	8-84
on leave									
Lifton, Donald E.	Assoc	274-3234		32	ADE	PHD	88	Cornell	8-82
Markowitz, James R.	Assoc	274-3943		5	Q	JD	70	Yale	8-73
Rosenthal, Susan P. S.	Assoc	274-3312	roses	2	EFZ	PHD	90	Syracuse	8-86
Seaquist, Gwen	Assoc	274-3944		4		JD	78	Miss	8-79
Congden, Steven W.	Asst	274-1552		3	I	PHD	91	Mass	8-90
Dickson, Warren L.	Asst	274-1327		9	Z	ABD	91	Oklahoma	8-90
Rabin, Bonnie R.	Asst	274-3661		5	N	PHD	87	Cornell	8-89
Tunwall, Craig A.	Asst	274-3278		53	IN	PHD	91	Iowa	8-89
Youssef, Mohamed A.	Asst	274-1127		7	UI	PHD	91	CUNY	8-91

Jackson State University — Jackson, MS 39217-0560 — (601) JSUMS.EDU

School of Business — 1400 John R. Lynch Street — FAX=968-2358 — BS,BBA,MBA

Name	Title	Phone				Degree		School	
Swinton, David H.	Dean	968-2411		Econ		PHD	75	Harvard	1987
—Dept of Management & Mktg	Phone	968-2534	Fax 968-2690						
Semko, Elizabeth A.	C	968-2536		N		PHD		Wayne St	1981
Cooley, William	Prof	973-3313				DBA		Miss St	1984
Karp, Robert	Prof	973-3325				EDD		Illinois	1985
Smith, J. R.	Prof	968-2982				DBA		Tenn	1971
Gray, Kenneth	Assoc	986-2974				PHD		Walden	1992
Iyengar, Jagannathan	Assoc	968-2979				PHD		Geo St	1993
Marshall, Kimball P.	Assoc	968-2426		DILZ		PHD	75	Florida	9-92
Rana, Dharam	Assoc	968-2973				PHD		Georgia	1980
Robinson, Bettye	Assoc	968-2979				EDD		Miss St	1992
Belay, Leul	Asst	968-2981				PHD		Missouri	1972

Jacksonville University — Jacksonville, FL 32211 — (904)

College of Business — FAX=744-0101 — BS,BA

Name	Title	Phone				Degree		School	
Pordeli, Hassan	Dean$	Ext 9431		Econ		PHD	83	Nebraska	1983
—Management Faculty	Phone		Fax 744-0101						
Hooper, Donald B.	Prof	744-3950		23	EIY	PHD	68	Ohio St	1976
Morgan, Catherine L.	Prof	744-3950		7	SVUE	PHD	75	S Carol	1975
Jones, Douglas E.	Assoc	744-3950		15	KLNQ	EDD	86	Florida	1980
Sepehri, Mohamad	Assoc	744-3950		38	DIYZ	PHD	82	Indiana	1989
Arbogast, Gordon	VAsst	744-3950				PHD	86	Clemson	1993
McFarland, Tom	Asst	744-3950		23	EHI	PHD	88	Florida	1990

Jacksonville State Univ — Jacksonville, AL 36265 — (205)

College Comm & Bus Adm — 700 Pelham Road North — FAX=782-5312 — BS,MBA

Name	Title	Phone				Degree		School	
O'Brien, J. Patrick	Dean	782-5773		Econ		PHD	77	Okla St	1991
—Dept of Management & Mktg	Phone	782-5787	Fax 782-5312						
McCormick, Micheal B.	H-Pr	782-5770		27	EF	PHD	75	Missouri	1984
Granger, Sue C.	Prof	782-5273		12	D	EDD	76	Arkansas	1969
Loftin, William E.	Prof	782-5763		12		DBA	72	Miss St	1978
Yunker, Gary W.	Prof	782-5779		25	EN	PHD	73	S Illin	1980
Butler, Grady	Assoc	782-5298		45	NQ	DBA	82	Oklahoma	1990
Gulbro, Robert	Assoc	782-5794		36	SL	DBA	91	Miss St	1983
Cobb, Richard	Asst	782-5503		37	ZUV	PHD	90	Alabama	1975
Hearn, W. Mark	Asst	782-5756		28	EY	PHD	92	Arkansas	1989
Marker, Michael	Asst	782-5789		12	JM	PHD	84	Alabama	1978
Borstorff, Patricia C.	Inst	782-5748		12	NOQ	MBA	89	Jackv St	1989
Davis, George C.	Inst	782-5272		45	NJ	MBA	80	W N Eng	1981

James Madison University — Harrisonburg, VA 22807 — (703) VAX1.ACS.JMU.EDU — 1982,1985

College of Business — FAX=568-3299 — BBA,MBA

Name	Title	Phone				Degree		School	
Holmes, Robert E.	Dean	568-3252	fac rholmes	31	I	PHD	71	Arkansas	9-83
—Department of Management	Phone	568-3232	Fax 568-3299						
Gallagher, Daniel G.	H	568-3232	fac dgallagh	5	NQ	PHD	77	Illinois	9-87
Brenner, Otto C.	Prof	568-3239	fac brenner	23	I	PHD	77	Stevens	9-77
Holt, David H.	Prof	568-3232	fac holt	16	ST	PHD	78	Strathcl	9-81
Pringle, Charles D.	Prof	568-3257	fac cpringle	12	EI	PHD	76	Kentucky	9-86
Ramsey, Jackson Eugene	Prof	568-3258	fac jramsey	3	I	PHD	75	SUNY-Buf	9-73
Veglahn, Peter A.	Prof	568-3237	fac veghlahn	5	QN	PHD	74	Iowa	9-83
Christoph, Rick	Assoc	568-3038	fac rchristo	3	I	PHD	85	Clemson	9-92
Dubose, Phillip B.	Assoc	568-3235	fac dubose	12	E	PHD	83	N Carol	9-83
Ford, Roger H.	Assoc	568-3238	fac ford	36	ST	PHD	86	Syracuse	9-85
Patzig, William	Assoc	568-3236	fac dpatzig	13	IE	PHD	73	Texas	9-80
Zimmerman, D. Kent	Assoc	568-3234	fac kzimmerm	24	E	PHD	79	SUNY-Buf	9-75
Schoenfeld, Gerald	Asst	568-3095	fac gschoenf	51	NQ	ABD		Pitt	9-92
Tansky, Judith	Asst	568-3047	fac jtansky	52	NP	PHD	92	Ohio St	9-92
White, Marion	Asst	568-3231	fac mowyar	18	EY	PHD	90	Houston	9-90
Stone, Ron	Inst	568-3025	fac rstone	13	IE	PHD	90	Nova	9-93

Jamestown College

Jamestown College — Jamestown, ND 58401-3405 (701) FAX=253-4318
Bus Adm Dept Box 6009
phone 252-3467

Name	Rank	Phone						
Klaudt, William J.	C-Ac	Ext 2552		68	STY	MED	64	Black Hl	1967
—Management Faculty	Phone	252-3467	Fax 253-4318					
Dick, James	Asst	Ext 2553		34	IJKN	MBA	88	Moorhead	1984
Dilocker, Tom	Asst	Ext 2474		15	DQS	MBA	89	S Dakota	1989

Jersey City State College

Jersey City State College — Jersey City, NJ 07305-1597 (201) FAX=
Dept of Business Adm — 2039 Kennedy Boulevard

Name	Rank	Phone				
Means, Fred	Dean	200-3321			EDD	Rutgers
—Management Faculty	Phone	200-3353				
Ettinger, Marilyn	C-As	200-3353			MBA	NYU
Egan, John	Prof	200-3353	15		PHD	NYU
Fabris, Richard H.	Prof	200-3353	23		PHD	Illinois
Kinory, Shimshon	Assoc	200-3353	7		PHD	Sc SocRs
O'Neil, Barbara	Asst	200-3353	8		MBA	Rutgers
Stern, Joseph	Asst	200-3353	8		PHD	NYU
Young, Roslyn	Asst	200-3353	4		JD	Brooklyn

John Carroll University

John Carroll University — Cleveland, OH 44118 (216) FAX=397-4256   1988,1988
School of Business — 20700 North Park Boulevard   BS,MBA
Did Not Respond-1993 Listing; Department Phone 397-4386

Name	Rank	Phone						
Navratil, Frank J.	Dean	397-4521		Econ	PHD	74	Notre Dm	1973
—Department of Management	Phone		Fax 397-4256					
Bockanic, William N.	C-Pr	397-1606			JD		Clev St	1978
Domm, Donald R.	Prof	397-4419			PHD		Ohio St	1987
Extejt, Marian M.	Prof	397-4618			PHD		Purdue	1985
Forbes, J. Benjamin	Prof	397-4608			PHD		Akron	1975
Smith, Jonathan E.	Assoc	397-4605			PHD		Georgia	1985
Treleven, Mark D.	Assoc	397-3035			PHD	82	N Carol	1989
James S. Reid Professor								
Hayes, Thomas L.	Asst	397-4535			MA		J Carrol	1969
Hiemstra, Kathleen	VAsst	397-3037			PHD		Pitt	1990
Lynn, Marc P.	Asst	397-1640			PHD		Clev St	1987
Brown, Marvin	VInst	397-4385			MA		Morehead	1989

John F. Kennedy University

John F. Kennedy University — Walnut Creek, CA 94596 (510) FAX=295-0604   MSBA,MBA,MACDV
School of Management — 12 Altarinda Road
Did Not Respond-1993 Listing

Name	Rank	Phone						
Carroll, Frank	Dean			3	I	MBA		St Marys	1-85
—Management Faculty	Phone	295-0600	Fax 295-0604					
Aiken, Susan	Lect	295-0600		5	P	MA	82	JFKenned	9-90
Aleva, David				16	&	MBA		Harvard	3-93
Brown, Gillian		295-0600		52	F	ABD		Felding	9-89
Garrett, Suzanne		295-0643		7	VR	MBA		JFKenned	9-88

University of Kansas

University of Kansas — Lawrence, KS 66045-2003 (913) UKANVM FAX=864-5328   1925,1970
School of Business   BS,MS,PHD

Name	Rank	Phone						
Bauman, L. Joseph	Dean	864-7575		7	U	BS	61	Kansas	1990
—Management Faculty	Phone		Fax 864-5325					
Ash, Ronald A.	Prof	864-7550		5	N	PHD		S Fla	1981
Cogger, Kenneth O.	Prof	864-7554		7	V	PHD	71	Michigan	1971
Fitch, H. Gordon	Prof	864-7545		3	L	PHD	69	Purdue	1967
Hillmer, Steven C	Prof	864-7549		7	V	PHD		Wiscon	1977
Karney, Dennis F.	Prof	864-7569		7	V	PHD		Illinois	1984
MacKenzie, Kenneth D.	Prof	864-7502		2	EH	PHD	64	Berkeley	1972
Narayanan, V. K.	Prof	864-7561		3	I	PHD		Pitt	1978
Redwood, Anthony L.	Prof	864-3700		5	N	PHD		Illinois	1972
Reitz, Joe	Prof	864-7580		2	VJ	PHD		MIT	1988
Shenoy, Prakash	Prof	864-7551		7	U	PHD		Cornell	1978
Sherr, Lawrence A.	Prof	864-7531		7	U	PHD	66	Michigan	1965
Taylor, Marilyn L.	Prof	864-7518		3	I	DBA		Harvard	1977
Yu, Po-lung	Prof	864-7565		7	V	PHD		J Hopkin	1977
Carl A. Scupin Distinguished Professor of Business								
Datta, Deepka K.	Assoc	864-7520		3	I	PHD		Pitt	1986
Garland, John S.	Assoc	864-7512		8	Y	DBA		Indiana	1980
Mai-Dalton, Renate R.	Assoc	864-7566		2	E	PHD		U Wash	1979
Schwoerer, Catherine	Assoc	864-7502		2	EO	PHD	90	N Carol	1989
Spencer, Daniel G.	Assoc	864-7527		2	E	PHD		Orgeon	1979
Guthrie, James P.	Asst	864-7546		5	N	PHD		Maryland	1988

Kansas State University

Manhattan, KS 66506-0507 (913) KSUVM.KSU.EDU 1973,1980
College of Business FAX=532-7024 BS,MAC

Name	Rank	Phone	ID			Deg		Univ	Date
Short, Daniel G.	Dean	532-7227	dshort			PHD	77	Michigan	6-92
—Department of Management	Phone	532-6296	Fax 532-7024						
Townsend, James B.	H-Pr	532-6296	jimtown	3	AIKY	DBA	76	Geo Wash	9-77
Ebadi, Yar M.	Prof	532-7351	ebadi	7	UV	DBA	77	Indiana	1-83
Paul, Robert J.	Prof	532-4360		25	ENPR	PHD	66	Arkansas	9-78
Elsea, Stanley W.	Assoc	532-4353	selsea	15	ENQ	DBA	84	Indiana	1-85
McCahon, Cynthia S.	Assoc	532-4358	cmccahon	7	UV	PHD	87	Knsas St	1-89
Niehoff, Brian P.	Assoc	532-4359	niehoff	23	EFP	PHD	88	Indiana	8-88
Babbar, Sunil	Asst	532-4351	babbar	7	DIUY	PHD	88	Kent St	8-90
Bunch, John	Asst	532-4352	bunch	24	EJNP	PHD	90	N Carol	8-90
Hagmann, Constanza	Asst	532-4354	hagmann2	9	Z	PHD	88	Kan St	9-76
Henricks, Tom	Asst	532-4366	henricks	38	EHIX	PHD	91	Nebraska	8-90
Hightower, Ross	Asst	532-4356	rth	9	Z	PHD	91	Geo St	8-91
Pearson, John M.	Asst	532-4361	jmpearsn	9	SYZ	DBA	91	Miss St	8-89
Sheu, Chwen	Asst	532-4363	csheu	7	UVWY	PHD	90	Ohio St	8-90

Keene State College

Keene, NH 03431-4183 (603)
Dept of Management 229 Main Street FAX= BS
Did Not Respond-1993 Listing

Name	Rank	Phone	ID			Deg		Univ	Date
Pruchansky, Neal R.	C-Ac	358-2624		Mgt		PHD		Mass	1985
—Management Faculty	Phone								
Curran, A. Ranger	Prof	358-2616				DBA	77	Georgia	1982
Charkey, Barbara	Assoc	358-2621				MBA		Mass	1987
King, Stephen C.	Assoc	358-2617				PHD		Kentucky	1986
Hawes, Beth	Asst	050-2018				EDD		Mass	1987
Herman, Susan	Asst	358-2623				EDD	91	Massachu	1987
Martin, Roger	Asst	358-2614				MBA		Hartford	1986
Pappalardo, John	Asst	358-2622				PHD		Va Comm	1990
Rosenberg, Victor	Asst	358-2608				PHD		Boston U	1991

Kennesaw College

Marietta, GA 30061-0444 (404) USCH.USC
School of Business Adm 3455 Steve Frey Road FAX=423-6539 BBA,MBA

Name	Rank	Phone				Deg		Univ	Date
Mescon, Timothy S.	Dean	423-6342				PHD	79	Georgia	1990
—Dept Management & Entrepr	Phone	423-6552	Fax 423-6539						
Covin, Teresa J.	C-Ac	423-6406		25	FNR	PHD	87	Pitt	1987
Aronoff, Craig E.	Prof	423-6045		46	FL	PHD	75	Texas	1983
Lasher, Harry J.	Prof	423-6041		15	DFNP	PHD	70	Syracuse	1984
Adams, Janet S.	Assoc	423-6089		12	EJOR	PHD	88	Arkansas	1985
Astrachan, Joseph	Assoc	423-6621		2	F	PHD	89	Yale	1989
Brawley, Dorothy	Assoc	423-6478		36	DIST	PHD	82	Geo St	1989
Brush, Christina C.	Assoc	423-6321		25	EFOP	PHD	83	Geo St	1984
Desman, Robert	Assoc	423-6326		48	BDH	PHD	83	Ariz St	1987
Kolenko, Tom	Assoc	423-6079		15	EFNO	PHD	86	Wiscon	1990
Roberts, Gary B.	Assoc	423-6078		36	BIST	PHD	82	Geo St	1985
Roebuck, Deborah M.	Assoc	423-6364		1	DEFP	PHD	90	Geo St	1984
Fitzgerald, Elizabeth	Asst	423-6588		2	F	PHD	92	Syracuse	1992
Prochaska, Nancy	Asst	423-6055		1		MBA			1989
Roller, Robert	Asst	423-6446		36	IST	PHD	93	Okla St	1993
Shore, Ted H.	Asst	423-6097		25	EN	PHD	85	Colo St	1986
Sightler, Kevin	Asst	423-6549		25	ENVX	PHD			1990

Kent State University

Kent, OH 44242-0001 (216) KENTVM 1964,1965
College of Business Adm FAX=672-2448 BS,MBA,MS,PHD
phone: 672-2750

Name	Rank	Phone				Deg		Univ	Date
Upton, Charles W.	Dean	672-2772		Econ		PHD	69	Car Mel	8-89
—Dept of Adm Sciences	Phone	672-2750	Fax 672-2448						
Weinroth, Jay	C-Ac	672-2750				PHD		Union	1976
Brown, J. Randall	Prof	672-2750				PHD	70	MIT	1970
Hung, Ming	Prof	672-2750				DBA		Kent St	1970
Mehrez, Abraham	Prof	672-2750				PHD		J Hopkin	1977
Smith, Robert D.	Prof	672-2750				PHD	66	Penn St	1966
Acar, William	Assoc	Ext 305		23	HI	PHD		Penn	1983
Booth, David	Assoc	672-2750				PHD		N Carol	1984
Faley, Robert H.	Assoc	672-2750				PHD		Tenn	1980
Howard, Geoffrey	Assoc	672-2750				DBA		Kent St	1984
Madey, Gregory	Assoc	672-2750				PHD		Case Wes	1984
Mendelow, Aubrey L.	Assoc	672-2750		23	HI	PHD		S Africa	1982
Offodile, O. Felix	Assoc	672-2750				PHD		Tx Tech	1984
Bakes, Catherine	Asst	672-2750				PHD		Penn St	1982
Dubois, Cathy L. Z.	Asst	672-2750				PHD		Minn	1992
Patuwo, B. Eddy	Asst	672-2750				PHD		Va Tech	1988
Shanker, Murali	Asst	672-2750				PHD		Minn	1990
Steinberg, Geoffrey	Asst	672-2750				PHD		Penn	1991
Winfrey, Frank	Asst	672-2750		23	HI	PHD	91	S Carol	1990

University of Kentucky — Lexington, KY 40506-0034 (606) UKCC.UKY 1926,1963
College of Bus & Econ — FAX=257-8938 — BS,MS,PHD
Furst, Richard W. — Dean 257-8939 — Fnce DBA 68 Wash 1981
—Department of Management — Phone 257-2962 Fax 257-3577

Name	Rank	Phone						
Gibson, James L.	Prof		21	HD	PHD	62	Kentucky	1966
Grimes, Andrew J.	Prof	257-1784	2	H	PHD	64	Minn	1967
Provan, Keith G.	Prof	257-2768	2	HCA	PHD	78	SUNY-Buf	1985
Amburgey, Terry	Assoc	257-2962	36	HT	PHD	82	Stanford	1992
Davis, Mark Alan	Assoc	257-2962	5	NEC	PHD	84	Va Tech	1987
Freeman, James	Assoc	257-2962	4	K	LLM	81	Harvard	1984
Johnson, Nancy Brown	Assoc	257-2976	5	QNR	PHD	87	Kansas	1986
Folta, Timothy	Asst	257-2962	36	IST	PHD	94	Purdue	1994
Shaffer, Brian	Asst	257-2962	3	L	PHD	92	Calif	1991
Sunduramurthy, C.	Asst	257-2962	3	I	PHD	92	Illinois	1991
Tepper, Bennett J.	Asst	257-2962	2	E	PHD	91	U Miami	1990

Kentucky State University — Frankfort, KY 40601 (502)
School of Business — East Main Street — FAX= — BA
Lee, Dae Sung — Dean 227-6708 — ECON PHD 69 Mass 1969
—Management Faculty — Phone Fax 564-5068

Name	Rank	Phone						
Close, Jay G.	Assoc		35	ZO	DBA		US Intl	1984
Yoon, Shinil	Asst	227-6919	93	UZ	DBA		Miss St	1993

Lake Superior State Univ — Sault S Marie MI 49783-1699 (906)
School of Business — 1000 College Drive — FAX=635-2193 — BS
Harger, Bruce T. — Dean 635-2421 — Econ PHD 91 Mich St 9-67
—Management Faculty — Phone 635-2426 Fax 635-2193

Name	Rank	Phone						
Erkkila, John	C-Ac	635-2108		Econ	PHD		W Ontar	9-90
Marinoni, Ann	Prof	635-2320	23	DEJP	PHD		Mich St	9-76
Saluja, Madan	Prof	635-2740	15	KNQR	PHD		Minn	9-69
Adams, Mary	Assoc	635-2424	7	IV	PHD		Mich St	9-84
Lundin, Jean	Assoc	786-5802	23	EIJL	PHD		Wiscon	9-91
Meiser, Charles	Assoc	635-2473	67	DTUV	ABD		Purdue	9-68

Lamar University — Beaumont, TX 77710 (409) 1980,1986
College of Business — 4400 Martin Luther King Pkwy — FAX=880-8088 — BBA,MBA
Swerdlow, Robert A. — Dean$ 880-8604 — Mktg PHD 76 Arkansas 1978
—Dept of Management & Mktg — Phone 880-8622 Fax 880-8088

Name	Rank	Phone						
Godkin, R. Lynn	C-Pr	880-8624			PHD	81	North Tx	1981
Howard, Jack	Asst	880-8659		Mgt	PHD	92	Illinois	9-92
Lee, Huei	Asst	880-8629			PHD	91	Geo St	1991
Steirert, Alfred	Asst	880-2204			MBA	59	Florida	9-66

Lander University — Greenwood, SC 29649 (803)
School of Business Adm — Stanley Avenue — FAX=229-8890 — BS
Molander, J. Dale — Dean 229-8232 — Mktg PHD 66 U Wash 1989
—Management Faculty — Phone Fax 229-8890

Name	Rank	Phone						
Chang, Chan S.	Prof	229-8401	18	YO	PHD	74	American	1974
Pinckney, Richard P.	Prof	229-8356	79	V	PHD	75	Clemson	1980
Shurden, Michael C.	Asst	299-8703	7	UV	DBA	87	La Tech	1987
Smith, Stephanie C.	Asst	229-8753	35	ID	DBA	88	Memphis	1986

LaSalle University — Philadelphia, PA 19141 (215) LASALLE.EDU
School of Business — 20th and Olney Avenue — FAX=951-1892 — BS,MBA
Kane, Joseph A. — Dean 951-1040 — Econ PHD Temple 1961
—Department of Management — Phone 951-1007 Fax 951-1892

Name	Rank	Phone						
Tavana, Madjid	C-As	951-1007 tavana	9	Z	MBA		LaSalle	1984
Jogkelar, Prafulla	Prof	951-1007	7	U	PHD		Penn	1972
Miller, Lynn E.	Prof	951-1007 miller	2	E	PHD		N Illin	1981
Seltzer, Joseph	Prof	951-1007 seltzer	2	E	PHD		Pitt	1976
Smither, James	Assoc	951-1007	5	N	PHD		Stevens	1992
Troxell, Joseph R.	Assoc	951-1007 troxell	9	Z	PHD		Rutgers	1971
Vanbuskirk, William	Assoc	951-1007	2	E	PHD		Case Wes	1987
Bohl, Alan	Asst	951-1007	7	V	PHD		Temple	
Chung, Q.	Asst	951-1007 clung	9	Z	PHD		Renssel	1993
Gauss, Marianne S.	Asst	951-1007	7	V	MBA		LaSalle	1987
Kruger, Evonne J.	Asst	951-1007	3	I	PHD		Temple	1991
Lee, Patrick S.	Asst	951-1007	7	U	PHD		Car Mel	1989
Meisel, Steven Ian	Asst	951-1364 meisel	2	E	PHD		Temple	1981
Rappaport, Jack M.	Asst	951-1007	7	U	MS		NYU	1979
Szabat, Kathryn A.	Asst	951-1007	3	I	PHD		Penn	1981

LaSierra University — Riverside, CA 92515-8247 — (909) PLARIS.LASIERRA.EDU
School of Bus & Mgt — 4700 Pierce Street — FAX = 785-2901 — BA,BBA,MBA

Name	Title	Phone	Email			Deg	Yr	School	Dates
Yacoub, Ignatius I.	Dean	785-2064	iyacoub	25	EHN	PHD	76	Claremont	7-84
–Management Faculty	Phone	Fax 785-2700							
Selivanoff, George A.	Prof	785-2313		8	Y	PHD	64	American	7-84
McClymont, Trevor L.	Assoc	785-2314				DBA	88	Intl Grd	7-91
Rocha, Joseph R.	Assoc	785-2315		12	ACEK	PHD	75	Claremont	7-83
Leeper, Jeffrey C.	Asst	785-2161		5		MAC	89	Auburn	9-89
Thomas, Johnny	Asst	785-2058		16	ST	MBA	88	Loma Lin	9-89
Willis, Harry W. Jr.	Asst	785-2507		3	I	MBA	68	Geo St	7-84

Lawrence Technological Univ — Southfield, MI 48075-1058 — (313) LTUVAX
College of Management — 21000 West Ten Mile Road — FAX = EXT 3005 — BSBA,BSIM,MBA
phone 356-0200

Name	Title	Phone	Email			Deg	Yr	School	Dates
Hopson, James F.	Dean	Ext 3050		Atg		JD	73	So Meth	1993
–Department of Management	Phone		Fax Ext 3005						
Buck, Cleophas M.	Prof	356-0200	buck	7		MBA			1957
DeGennaro, Louis A.	Prof	356-0200	degennar	4		JD			1975
Hoffner, Vernon	Prof	356-0200	hoffner			PHD			1987
Lahr, Leland A.	Prof	356-0200	lahr	37		PHD	81	Mich St	1964
Maier, Ernest L.	Prof	356-0200	ernie	1		MBA	61	Detroit	1972
Condit, Donald F.	Assoc	356-0200	condit	37		MBA	62	Michigan	1985
Harris, Stanley F.	Assoc	356-0200	stan	2		PHD			1968
Koch, Douglass V.	Assoc	356-0200	koch	5		MBA	70	Nevada	1980
Matika, Lawrence	Assoc	356-0200				PHD			1994
Mumford, Larry G.	Assoc	356-0200	mumford	19		MBA	77	Wayne St	1983
Sheehy, William J.	Assoc	356-0200	sheehy	4		LLM	72	NYU	1984
Stevens, Flumo Y.	Assoc	356-0200	stevens	78		PHD	74	Nebraska	1987
Woznick, Jan	Assoc	356-0200	woznick			PHD			1993
Kouskoulas, Barbara	Asst	356-0200	kouskoulas			PHD			1993
McKenna, Thomas J.	Asst	356-0200	mckenna	14		LLM	60	Wayne St	1986
Raghavan, Srikant	Asst	356-0200	raghavan	7		PHD	78	Houston	1987

Lees-McRae College — Banner Elk, NC 28604 — (704)
Div Math Scie & Bus Adm — 3 Main Street — FAX = 898-4310 — BS
Did Not Respond-1993 Listing

Name	Title	Phone	Email		Deg	Yr	School	Dates
Sheffield, Susie E.	C-Ac	898-8770		Atg	MS	85	Appal St	8-89
–Management Faculty	Phone		Fax 898-8311					
Fuller, Floyd	Assoc	898-8796						
Burton, Samuel A.	Asst	898-8780	56					

Lehigh University — Bethlehem, PA 18015-3117 — (610) LEHIGH
College of Bus & Econ — 621 Taylor Street — FAX = 758-4499 — 1938,1963 — BS,MBA,PHD

Name	Title	Phone		Deg	Yr	School	Dates
Schmotter, James W.	Dean	758-3402		PHD		Northwes	1992
–Management Faculty	Phone	Fax 758-4499					
Bainbridge, D. Raymond	C-Ac	758-4453	Atg	PHD	78	Lehigh	9-72
Barsness, Richard W.	Prof	758-4355		PHD	63	Minn	1978
Bean, Alden S.	Prof	758-3427		PHD	69	Northwes	1983
Kenan Professor of Management and Technology							
Bonge, John W.	Prof	758-3980		PHD	68	Northwes	1972
Kolchin, Michael G.	Prof	758-3421		DBA	80	Indiana	1979
Litt, Benjamin	Prof	758-3444		PHD	70	NYU	1970
Stevens, John E.	Prof	758-4961		PHD	75	Cinn	1975
Poole, Peter	Assoc	758-3419		PHD	86	Penn St	1988
Schlie, Theodore W.	Assoc	758-5341		PHD	73	Northwes	1989
Sherer, Susan A.	Assoc	758-3424		PHD	88	Penn	1987
Trent, Robert J.	Assoc	758-4952		PHD	93	Mich St	1993
Moesel, Douglas	Inst	758-4953		MS		Oklahoma	1993

LeMoyne College — Syracuse, NY 13214-1399 — (315) LEMOYNE
Business — LeMoyne Heights — FAX = 445-4540 — BS

Name	Title	Phone			Deg	Yr	School	Dates
Barnett, William R.	Dean$	445-4310	Rel		PHD		Chicago	1977
–Department of Business Adm	Phone	Fax 445-4540						
Elmer, Wally	C-Pr	445-4433			PHD	80	Syracuse	1979
Arogyaswawy, Bernard	Prof	445-4431	36	I	PHD	88	Kent St	1988
Lepak, Gregory	Assoc	445-4335	7	VX	PHD	85	SUNY-Alb	1987
O'Conner, Dennis	Assoc	445-4483	2	EF	PHD	85	Case Wes	1988
Orne, Daniel	Assoc	445-4478	34	FJ	PHD	83	RPI	1990
Wright, Ronald	Assoc	445-4370	7	UV	PHD	76	Kentucky	1977
Ammar, Salwa	Asst	445-4348	7	UV	PHD	87	Florida	1988
Clifton, Thomas	Asst	445-4340	5	NQ	PHD	90	Minn	1990
Grabowski, Martha	Asst	445-4427	9	Z	PHD	87	RPI	1989
Kulick, George	Asst	445-4485	7	V	PHD	88	Syracuse	1989
Sugumaran, Vijay	Asst	445-4163	9	Z	PHD	93	G Mason	1993

Liberty University
School of Bus & Gov
Did Not Respond-1993 Listing
Lynchburg, VA 24506-8001
3765 Candler's Mountain Road
(804) FAX=
BS

Name	Title	Phone		Degree		Year School Year
Adkins, Robert	Dean	582-2480	Mktg	PHD	77	Arkansas 1991
—Department of Management	Phone	582-2470	Fax 582-7677			
George, John	C	582-2340		PHD		
Livesay, Corinne	Asst	582-2341	5	MBA		Oakland 8-86
Torrence, Nancy	Asst	582-2319	2	MBA		Lynchbur 8-88
Sloan, Carla L.	Inst	582-2341	1	MS		Twsn St 8-84

Linfield College
Dept of Economics & Bus
McMinnville, OR 97128-6894
450 Linfield Avenue
(503) FAX=472-3198

Name	Title	Phone		Degree		Year School Year
Emery, Richard F.	C-Ac	434-2298	Tax	MBA	71	E N Mex 1986
—Management Faculty	Phone		Fax 472-3198			
Bell, Eugene C.	Prof	434-2243	2	PHD	74	Houston 1992
Kiehl, Sandra	Assoc	434-2252	3	PHD	88	Port St 1988

Livingston University
College of Bus & Comm
phone: 652-9661
Livingston, AL 35470
Highway 11
(205) FAX=
BS

Name	Title	Phone		Degree		Year School Year
Hudnall, Jarrett	Dean	652-9661	Mktg	PHD	66	Alabama 9-92
—Management Faculty	Phone	Ext 260	Fax 652-9318			
Cook, Charlie T.	Asst	652-9661	23 GP	ABD	93	Alabama 9-92
Turner, Gregory	Asst	652-9661	48	ABD	93	Miss St 1-94

Livingstone College
Div Soc Behav Sci & Bus
Salisbury, SC 28144
701 W. Monroe St
(704) FAX=

Name	Title	Phone		Degree		Year School Year
Ahmed, Hasseb	C-As	638-5604	13 BSVY	ABD		Miss 8-92
—Management Faculty	Phone	638-5640	Fax 638-5522			
Anekwu, Daniel	C-In	638-5640	71	MBA	89	Jack St 8-90
Osakwe, Lawrence	Asst	638-5635	37 IU	PHD	90	SE Tech 8-92

Lock Haven University
Dept Cpt Sc, Mgt & Atg
Lock Haven, PA 17745
(717) FAX=893-2600
BS

Name	Title	Phone		Degree		Year School Year
Berry, Nancy W.	C-Ac	893-2492	8 Y	MBA	78	Penn St 9-84
—Management Faculty	Phone	893-2235	Fax 893-2600			
Seyfarth, Robert	Prof	893-2273	25 UIN	EDD		Nev-Reno 9-81
Robertson, Bruce D.	Asst	893-2274	83 YI	MAS		Illinois 9-90

Long Isl U, Brooklyn Campus
Sch Bus, Adm & Info Sci
Brooklyn, NY 11201-5372
Flatbush & DeKalb Avenues
(718) EAGLE.LIUNET.EDU
FAX=852-3447
BS,MBA,MS

Name	Title	Phone		Degree		Year School Year
Petrello, George	Dean	488-1160		PHD	69	NYU
—Department of Management	Phone		Fax 852-3447			
Gadgil, Shashi	C-Pr	488-1158	Mktg	PHD		New York
Teitelbaum, Israel	Prof	488-1147		PHD	69	NYU
Silber, Harriet	Assoc	488-1151		MBA		Lg Islnd
Stucke, Harry	Assoc	488-1148		MBA		New York
Carbonell, Dora	Asst	488-1142		EDD		Columbia
Canavan, Thomas		488-1162				
Madden, Ronald		488-1159		PHD		Iowa
Markovich, Michael		488-1150				
McKenna, Dorothy		488-1136				
McMeen, Albert		488-1143				
Paulas, John		488-1144				
Rochlin, Robert		488-1139				
St. John, August		488-1128				

Long Island U.-C.W. Post
College of Management
Brookville, NY 11548-0570
(516) FAX=299-2361
BS,MS,MBA

Name	Title	Phone		Degree		School
—Management Faculty	Phone		Fax 299-2361			
Cillis, Dan	C-As			PHD		NYU
Fiore, Mike	Assoc			PHD		NYU
Freeley, James	Assoc			PHD		Fordham
Lobert, Beata	Asst			PHD		Baruch
Spiegel, Ruth	Inst			MBA		Long Isl
Akel, Anthony				PHD		
Caoncelliere, Frank				PHD		

Longwood College
School of Bus & Econ
Farmville, VA 23901
High Street
(804) LWCVM1.LWC.EDU
FAX=395-2203
BS

Name	Title	Phone		Degree		Year School Year
Farmer, Berkwood M.	Dean	395-2045	Econ	PHD	70	N Car St 1991
—Dept of Management & Mktg	Phone	395-4042	Fax 395-2203			
Dukes, Thomas A.	C-Pr	395-2368	18 EY	DBA	83	La Tech 1990

Humphreys, Neil J.	Prof	395-2778	36	JOST	PHD	70	Penn	1992
Hott, David D.	Assoc	395-2384	7	JUVX	PHD	77	Lehigh	1991
Fowlkes, Melinda J.	Asst	395-2379	12	D	MBA	90	Va Comm	1976
Qiu, Man Ying	Asst	395-2042	78	UVXY	PHD	93	Clemson	1994
Wood, Cynthia	Asst	395-2383	12	EFH	PHD	75	Virginia	1992

Loras College — Dubuque, IA 52004-0178 (319) ICA1.LORAS.EDU

Dept Accounting & Bus		1450 Alta Vista		FAX=588-7964				BA
Cosgrove, Margaret Mary	C-Ac	588-7765		Atg	MBA	80	Iowa	1987
—Management Faculty	Phone	588-7695	Fax 588-7964					
Burnett, Derek	Assoc	588-7379	27	AV	ABD		Newcastl	1984
Graham, Gerald H. Jr.	Asst	588-7518	37	DTUV	MBA	87	Wichita	1987
Steidinger, Gene L.	Asst	588-7626	25	N	MBA	85	Wiscon	1989

Louisiana State University — Baton Rouge, LA 70803-6312 (504) LSUVM 1931,1963

College of Business Adm				FAX=388-6140				BA,MS,PHD
—Department of Management	Phone		Fax 388-6140					
Bedeian, Arthur G.	C-Pr	388-6141	mgbede	12	BE	DBA	73	Miss St	5-85
Justis, Robert T.	Prof	388-6645		IST	DBA	72	Indiana	8-86
Marin, Daniel B.	Prof	388-5257	4	L	PHD	72	Iowa	8-84
Associate Dean								
Mossholder, Kevin	Prof	388-5187	mgmoss	2	NO	PHD	78	Tenn	8-91
Farh, Jiing-Lih	Assoc	388-6129	mgfarh	25	NEX	PHD	83	Indiana	1-84
Russell, Craig	Assoc	388-6177	mgruss	5	PN	PHD	02	Iowa	8-91
Werbel, James D.	Assoc	388-6156	mgwerb	2	FNO	PHD	80	Northwes	8-84
Adkins, Cheryl L.	Asst	388-6146	mgadki	2	N	PHD	90	S Carol	8-89
Bennett, Nathan	Asst	388-6160	mgbenn	2	NE	PHD	89	Ga Tech	8-89
Chandler, Tim	Asot	388-6113	mgchan	5	QL	PHD	90	Illinois	8-90
Keels, J. Kay	Asst	388-6110	mgkeel	3	I	PHD	89	S Carol	1-89
Ketchen, David	Asst	388-5187	mgketc	3	I	PHD	94	Penn St	8-93
Palmer, Timothy	Asst	388-6101	mgpalm	3	I	PHD	94	Ariz St	8-94
Chaney, Courtland	Inst	388-6151		5	N	PHD	80	LSU	8-83

Louisiana St in Shreveport — Shreveport, LA 71115 (318) 1992,1992

College of Business		One University Place		FAX=797-5156				BS
Clark, Lawrence S.	Dean	797-5383		Law	LLM	78	DePaul	8-81
—Dept of Management & Mktg	Phone	797-5017	Fax 797-5208					
Martin, Christopher	C	797-5028	25	E	PHD	87	Ga Tech	1-88
Vassar, John	Prof	797-5020	35	CN	PHD	81	North Tx	8-80
Hatcher, Jerome M.	Assoc	797-5187	7	U	PHD		Arkansas	8-85
Krajewski, Lorraine	Assoc	797-5019	81	D	PHD		Ariz St	8-83
Lin, Binshan	Assoc	797-5186	79	VZ	PHD		LSU	8-88
Pace, Larry	Assoc	797-5276	2	FH	PHD	77	Georgia	8-90
Kidwell, Roland	Asst	797-5146	3	I	PHD	94	LSU	8-93
Mitchell, Donna	Asst	797-5185	79	Z	DBA		La St Sh	1987
Smith, Gwendolyn N.	Asst	797-5024	1	D	MS		E Tx St	8-78

Louisiana Tech University — Ruston, LA 71272-0046 (318) 1955,1979

College of Adm & Bus				FAX=				BS,MBA,MPA,DBA
Owens, Bob R.	Dean	257-4526	3	IT	PHD	65	Arkansas	1965
—Dept of Management & Mktg	Phone							
Hester, James L.	H-Pr	257-4012	36	INST	PHD	65	Arkansas	1966
Jurkus, Anthony F.	Prof	257-2112	38	HINY	PHD	74	Geo St	1975
White, Michael C.	Prof	257-2509	23	EHIM	PHD	78	Georgia	1991
Balloun, Joseph L.	Assoc	257-3522	57	ENVX	PHD	71	Berkeley	1988
Busch, Frank M.	Assoc	257-2467	18	JSTY	PHD	66	Indiana	1966
Willis, T. Hillman	Assoc	257-2389	71	ISUV	PHD	72	LSU	1979
Barnett, Timothy R.	Asst	257-3871	25	EHJN	DBA	89	Miss St	1991
Inman, Ray Anthony	Asst	257-3522	7	UV	DBA	88	Memphis	1989
Long, Rebecca	Asst	257-2809	23	ONIQ	PHD	92	LSU	1992

University of Louisville — Louisville, KY 40292 (502) ULKYVM 1982,1987

Cl Business & Public Ad		2211 South Brook Street		FAX=588-7557				BS,MBA
Taylor, Robert L.	Dean	852-6443	rltayl01	3	FIP	DBA	72	Indiana	8-84
—Department of Management	Phone	852-7830	Fax 852-7557					
Shiffler, Ronald E.	C-Pr	852-7830	reshif01	7	VOP	PHD	80	Florida	7-82
Adams, Arthur J.	Prof	852-7830	ajadam01	7	V	PHD	78	Iowa	1979
Bracker, Jeffrey S.	Prof	852-7830	jsbrac01	36	ISTY	PHD	82	Geo St	7-91
Brown & Williamson Professor of Entrepreneurship								
Kuzmits, Frank E.	Prof	852-7830	fekuzm01	5	NOP	PHD	75	Geo St	8-78
Mears, Peter M.	Prof	852-7830	pmmear01	4	AU	DBA	72	Miss St	8-71
Sussman, Lyle	Prof	852-7830	l0suss01	2	EF	PHD	73	Purdue	1973
Clouse, Van G. H.	Assoc	852-7830	vgclou01	36	ISTZ	PHD	86	Clemson	8-86
Hancock, Terence	Assoc	852-7830	t0hanc01	79	UVXZ	PHD	87	Indiana	1-87
Herden, Richard P.	Assoc	852-7830	rpherd01	12	EF	PHD	79	Pitt	1978

Kemelgor, Bruce H.	Assoc	852-7830	bhkeme01	26	EFST	PHD	72	Illinois	1979
Myers, Robert C.	Assoc	852-7830	rcmyer01	7	UV	MS	64	Richmond	1966
Bruce, Reginald A.	Asst	852-7830	rabruc01	12	DEOX	PHD	89	Michigan	7-93
Gupta, Mahesh C.	Asst	852-7830	mcgupt01	78	UVY	PHD	90	Louisvil	8-90
Magill, Sharon L.	Asst	852-7830	slmagi01	32	HIYZ	PHD	92	Indiana	8-92
Newkirk-Moore, Susan E.	Asst	852-7830	senewk01	34	DLPR	EDD	85	Tenn	8-92
Saxton, Todd	Asst	852-7830	t0saxt01	38	ITY	BA	85	Virginia	8-94
−Computer Info Sys Dept	Phone	852-7830	Fax 852-7557						
Chandra, Satish	Assoc	852-7830	s0chan01	9	USYZ	PHD	75	Cinn	7-78
DosSantos, Brain	Assoc	852-4787	bldoss01	9	Z	PHD	82	Case Wes	8-93
Raho, Louis E.	Assoc	852-4798	leraho01	9	ZJM	PHD	80	Fla St	8-79
Srinivasan, S.	Assoc	852-4681	s0srini01	9	Z	PHD	81	Pitt	8-87
Barker, Robert M.	Asst	852-4779	rmbark01	9	ZEY	PHD	91	Syracuse	1-92
Fabbri, Anthony J.	Asst	852-7830	a0fabb01	9	Z	MS	67	ISU	1-88
Guan, Jian	Asst	852-7830	j0guan01	9	Z	PHD	92	Louisvil	9-86
Ifeacho, Peter	Asst	852-4791	pcifea01	9	ZKMT	PHD	91	Kan St	8-93
Strickland, Ted	Asst	852-4940	tjstri01	9	Z	PHD	89	Arizona	8-89
Zurada, Jozef	Asst	852-7830	jmzura01	9	Z	MS	73	Gdansk	5-87
Grove, Ralph F. Jr.	VInst	852-7830	rfgrov01	9	Z	MS	74	Louisvil	9-93

Loyola College in Maryland	Baltimore, MD	21210-2699	(410) LOYOLA.EDU				1988,1988		
The Sellinger School	4501 North Charles Street		FAX=323-2768				BBA,MBA		
phone 617-2000									
Anton SJ, Ronald J.	Dean	617-2301		2	J	PHD		Northwes	1989
−Dept of Management	Phone	617-2691	Fax 617-2117						
Desai, Harsha B.	C-Pr	617 2395	desai	36	IST	PHD	70	Penn St	1982
Franke, Richard H.	Prof	617-2751		38	IY	PHD	74	Rochest	1984
Gilroy, Faith D.	Prof	617-2332	fdg	2	R	PHD		St Louis	
Mento, Anthony J.	Prof	617-2754		2	E	PHD		Maryland	1984
Sagafi-Nejad, Tagi	Prof	617-2450	sagafine	8	Y	PHD		Penn	1985
DeVader, Christy L.	Assoc	617-2609		1	En	PHD		Akron	1987
Ergler, Paul C.	Assoc	617-2322		3	H	DBA	69	Geo Wash	1967
Jones, Raymond M.	Asst	617-2377		3	IY	PHD		Maryland	1990
Kashlak, Roger	Asst	617-2163		83	Y	ABD	93	Temple	1993
Liang, Neng	Asst	617-2453	nl	8	Y	PHD		Indiana	1990
Lyles, Carole	Asst	617-2616		2	EN	ABD	94	Geo Wash	1993
−Dept of IS & Dec Sci	Phone	617-2934	Fax 617-2117						
DeHaemer, Michael	C-Ac	617-2669	deh	9	Z	PHD		Renssel	
Margenthaler, C. Robert	Prof	617-2097	crm	9	Z	PHD	72	Illinois	1981
Simmons, LeRoy	Prof	617-2892		7	V	PHD		Tenn	
Burbridge, John J. Jr.	Assoc	617-2457		9	Z	PHD		Lehigh	1985
Harris, William	Assoc	617-2848		7	V	DSC		J Hopkin	
Sharkey, C. B.	Assoc	617-2396		7		PHD		JHopkins	
Sherman, Kimbrough	Assoc	617-2460	kim	7	V	PHD		Maryland	1975
Simmons, Laurette P.	Assoc	617-2597		9	Z	PHD		North Tx	
Hoadley, Ellen D.	Asst	617-2756	ehoadley	9	Z	PHD		Indiana	
McFadden, John	Asst	617-2727		3		MSA		Geo Wash	
Thompson, John	Asst	617-2812		2		MBA		Temple	
Wright, George	Asst	617-2749	geo	9	Z	DBA		Geo Wash	

Loyola University of Chicago	Chicago, IL	60611	(312) LUCCPUA				1955,1980		
School of Business Adm	820 North Michigan Avenue		FAX=915-6619				BBA,MBA		
Meyer, Donald G.	Dean	915-6113			Mktg	PHD	65	Northwes	9-61
−Department of Management	Phone	915-6541	Fax 915-6619						
Keeley, Michael	C-Pr	915-6539				PHD		Northwes	
Petersen, Donald J.	Prof	915-6542				PHD	70	Ill Tech	
Ward, John L.	Prof	915-6544				PHD	73	Stanford	
Barney, Joseph A.	Assoc	915-6657		2	N	PHD	74	Loyola-C	7-76
Jensen, Eunice	Assoc	915-6545				DBA		Harvard	
Massengill, Douglas	Assoc	915-6538				PHD		Tenn	
Dienesch, Richard M.	Asst	915-6543		25	EUN	PHD	87	Ga Tech	8-88
Graham, Jill W.	Asst	915-6540		2	E	PHD	83	Northwes	
Harris, Dawn	Asst	915-6537				PHD		Northwes	
Reilly, Anne	Asst	915-6536				PHD		Northwes	
−Dept of Management Science	Phone		Fax 915-6432						
Ramenofsky, Samuel D.	C-Ac					PHD		Oklahoma	1973
Nicholas, John	Prof					PHD		Northwes	1977
Venta, Enrique R.	Prof					PHD		Northwes	1979
Forst, Frank	Assoc					PHD		Illinois	1986
Guder, Faruk	Assoc					PHD		Wiscon	1983
Nourie, Francis J.	Assoc					PHD		Chicago	1972
Salchenberger, Linda M.	Assoc					PHD		Northwes	1985
Zydiak, James Lee	Assoc					PHD		Northwes	1988
Kizior, Ronald J.	Asst					PHD		Not Dame	1969
Malliaris, Mary	Asst					PHD		Chicago	1990
Olson, Rick T.	Asst					PHD		Illinois	1989
Pellissier, James M.	Asst					PHD		Northwes	1990
VanBuer, Michael	Asst					PHD		Northwes	1991
Vijayalakshmi, Viji B.	Asst					PHD		IIM	1992

Loyola Univ-New Orleans	New Orleans, LA	70118	(504)				1950,1974
College of Business Adm	6363 Saint Charles Avenue		FAX=865-3496				BBA,MBA
Dauterive, Jerry W.	Dean	865-3545		Econ	PHD	76 Tx Tech	1979
—Dept Mgt,Mktg & Legal Stde	Phone	865-3544	Fax 865-3496				
Fok, Wing M.	C-Ac	865-3691	6	UV	DBA	91 Geo St	1988
Buchholz, Rogene	Prof	865-2789	4	JM	PHD	74 Pitt	1989
Ganitsky, Joseph	Prof	865-2779			PHD	74 Harvard	
Arnold, Karen	Assoc	865-3549	1	DI	PHD	84 LSU	1986
Paranilam, Margaret A.	Assoc	865-2100	15	NP	PHD	67 Nebraska	1970
Weymann, Elizabeth (Betsy)	Assoc	865-2115	2	GHE	PHD	87 Tulane	1979

Loyola Marymount Univ	Los Angeles, CA	90045	(310)				1981,1987
College of Business Adm	7101 West 80th Street		FAX=338-5187				BS,MBA
Wholihan, John T.	Dean	338-7504	13	Mgt	PHD	73 American	1984
—Department of Management	Phone		Fax 338-5187				
Mathison, David L.	C-Pr	338-5143	48	ELYR	PHD	78 Bowl Gr	1983
Boje, David M.	Prof	338-7415	12	EFH	PHD	79 Illinois	1989
Gale, Jeffrey	Prof	338-7406	13	ILY	PHD	76 UCLA	1985
Gray, Edmund R.	Prof	338-7408	14	BIL	PHD	66 UCLA	1986
Hess, George L.	Prof	338-7661	16	STU	DBA	74 Ariz St	1975
Kiesner, W. Frederick	Prof	338-4569	16	ST	PHD	84 Claremont	1977
Ring, Peter	Prof	338-7411	34	IJN	PHD	Irvine	1990
Stage, H. Daniel	Prof	338-2848	12	DY	DBA	75 S Calif	1973
Vance, Charles M.	Prof	338-4508	25	FNO	PHD	81 Syracuse	1985
Paik, Youngsun	Asst	338-7402	4	L	PHD	91 U Washin	1991
White, Judith	Asst	338-5162	2	R	PHD	92 Case Wes	1992
Zhupler, Antoly	Asst	338-7414	8	TY	PHD	81 Moscow	1992

Luther College	Decorah, IA	52101-1045	(319)				
Dept of Econ & Business	700 College Drive		FAX=387-1657				BA
Kaschins, Edward A.	H-Pr	387-1130	48	LY	PHD	73 Iowa	1965
—Management Faculty	Phone	387-1340	Fax 387-1088				
Berg, Warren	Prof	387-1279	13	BI	PHD	60 Iowa	1948
Evensen, Donald	Prof	387-1189	56	NT	MBA	48 Northwes	1985
Lund, Mark	Prof	387-1275	48	LY	PHD	75 Iowa St	1978
Nelson, John	Prof	387-1568	37	IU	MBA	65 Iowa	1987
Royksund, Conrad	Prof	387-1274	49	LZ	PHD	70 Chicago	1969
Rudolf, Uwe	Prof	387-1295	18	DY	MBA	78 S Calif	1971
Heltne, Mari	Assoc	387-1338	9	Z	PHD	88 Arizona	1975
Leake, Richard	Assoc	387-1812	56	NS	ABD	75 Ohio U	1975
Moorcroft, Christina	Assoc	387-1035	15	CR	MBA	85 Wi-LaCro	1978
Schweizer, Timothy	Assoc	387-1131	25	EQ	PHD	88 Arkansas	1987
Christianson, Charles	Asst	387-1187	13	DI	MBA	75 S Dakota	1988
Gomersall, Nicholas	Asst	387-1133	47	LVM	PHD	90 Cornell	1991
Nelson, Ramona	Asst	387-1569	16	DS	MBT	85 Minn	1990

Lycoming College	Williamsport, PA	17701	(717)				
Dept of Business Adm			FAX=				BA
—Management Faculty	Phone	321-4005	Fax 321-4090				
Weaver, H. Bruce	Prof	321-4168			JD		
Sterngold, Arthur	Asst	321-4169			PHD		
Cannon, James	Inst	321-4170			MS		1992
Henninger, Edward	Inst	321-4167			MS		1988

Lynchburg College	Lynchburg, VA	24501-3199	(804) CAVAX.LYNCHBURG.EDU				
School of Business	1501 Lakeside Drive		FAX=				
Husted, Stewart	Dean	522-8261	husted	56 JPSY	PHD	77 Mich St	9-89
—Management Faculty	Phone	522-8417	Fax 522-0658				
Abouzeid, Kamal	Prof	522-8257	3	I	PHD		9-78
Johnson, Donald W.	Assoc	522-8255	52	NQ	MA	67 Geo Wash	7-75
Whitehouse, Frank Jr.	Assoc	522-8264	27	EGL	ABD	87	7-80
Sosdian, Allen E.	Asst	522-8389	16	JS	MED		9-90

Lyndon State College	Lyndonville, VT	05851	(802) QUEEN.LSC.VSC.EDU				
Business Adm Department			FAX=626-9770				BS,BA,MS
Myers, Rex	Dean	626-9371		Hst	PHD	72 Montana	9-91
—Management Faculty	Phone		Fax 626-9770				
Mitchell, Linda M.	C-As	626-9371		Mktg	MBA	Columbia	1989
Bradley, David B.	Assoc	626-9371			MBA	Plymouth	1981
Ingraham, Henry	Assoc	626-9371			MBA	McGill	9-83
email sealer@home.attica.gov							
Loseby, Paul	Asst	626-9371	losebyp		OB	DPS	90 Pace	1992
Siegel, Rachel	Asst	626-9371	siegelr			MPPM	Yale	1990

Univ of Maine

Orono, ME 04469-5723 (207) 1974,1982
College of Business Adm — FAX=581-1930 — BS,MBA
-Management Faculty

Name	Rank	Phone		Field	Deg	Yr	School	Yr
Devino, W. Stanley	Dean	581-1968		Econ	PHD	59	Mich St	1960
	Phone		Fax 581-1956					
Alpander, Guvenc G.	Prof	581-1984			PHD	66	Mich St	1965
Forsgren, Roderick A.	Prof	581-1973			DBA	65	Colorado	1965
Gilmore, Carol	Prof	581-1977		Q	PHD	79	Mass	1977
Pinto, Jeffrey K.	Asst	942-5709			PHD	86	Pitt	1988

Manhattan College

Riverdale, NY 10471 (718) MANVAX
School of Business — FAX=884-0255 — BS,MBA
-Dept of Management & Mktg

Name	Rank	Phone			Field	Deg	Yr	School	Yr
Suarez, James M.	Dean	920-0440				PHD	72	Columbia	1984
	Phone		Fax 884-0255						
Manduley, Alfredo R.	C-As	0469			Mktg	MBA	60	NYU	
Huggins, Lawrence P.	Prof	920-0470	12	HIU		PHD	72	Penn	1979
O'Sullivan, Br. Malcolm	VProf	920-0460	4	M					
Czander, William	Assoc	920-0437	25	EOR		PHD	75	NYU	1981
Fitzpatrick, Richard C.	Assoc	920-0221	24	NL		PHD	84	SUNY-Alb	1984
Greene, Frederick D.	Assoc	920-0455	36	IST		PHD	74	SUNY-Buf	1974
Spiegelglas, Stephen	Emer	920-0460	48	MY		PHD	54	Wiscon	1978
Weil, Jeffrey	Assoc	920-0468	57	NOPQ		PHD	80	CUNY	1980
Khelfaoui, Salah	Asst	920-0181	7						
Rovenpor, Janet	Asst	920-0181	34	DI					

Mankato State University

Mankato, MN 56001-8400 (507) FAX=
College of Business
-Dept Management & Ind Rel

Name	Rank	Phone		Deg	Yr	School	Yr
Abouelenein, Gaber A.	Dean	389-5420		PHD	69	Illinois	1968
	Phone	389-2966	Fax 389-5497				
Kalinowski, Jon G.	C-Pr	389-1194		PHD	87	Iowa	1984
Klocke, Ronald A.	Prof	389-5346		PHD	73	Wash St	1966
Miller, Howard	Prof	389-5400		PHD	81	Illinois	1986
Mulford, Oliver J.	Prof	389-1606		EDD	71	Illinois	1962
Paulson, C. Richard	Prof	389-5174		PHD	73	Florida	1968
Pettman, Philip J.	Prof	389-5343		PHD	76	Minn	1980
Schoennauer, Alfred W.	Prof	389-5403		PHD	62	UCLA	1975
Scott, Timothy	Prof	389-2478		PHD	74	Minn	1974
Smayling, Miles	Prof	389-2324		PHD	87	Minn	1982
Stanford, Melvin J.	Prof	389-6097		PHD	68	Illinois	1982
Chown, David	Assoc	389-5304		PHD	91	Iowa	1985
Schumann, Paul	Assoc	389-5349		PHD	83	Cornell	1987
Shin, Dooyoung	Assoc	389-5333		PHD	87	Iowa	1987
Fox, Marilyn	Asst	389-5247		PHD	90	Nebraska	1990
Kaliski, John	Asst	389-5337		PHD	92	Iowa	1993
Kawatra, Rakesh	Asst	389-1826		PHD	91	Iowa	1990
Kim, Eyong	Asst	389-5089		PHD	90	Nebraska	1990
Pragman, Claudia	Asst	389-5304		PHD	93	Nebraska	1991
Roychoudhury, Buddhadev	Asst	389-1287		PHD	91	Indiana	1990

Marian College

Indianapolis, IN 46222-1997 (317)
Department of Business — 3200 Cold Spring Road — FAX=929-0263
Did Not Respond-1992 Listing
-Management Faculty

Name	Rank	Phone		Field	Deg	Yr	School	Yr
Alin, Timothy R.	C-Pr	929-0221		Atg	MBA	73	Xavier	1975
	Phone		Fax 929-0263					
Hoogerwerf, Richard	Asst	929-0279			MS	77	Butler	1988
Schuttler, Robert	Inst	929-0269			MBA	80	Evansvil	

Marietta College

Marietta, OH 45750-3031 (614)
College of Business — 215 Fifth Street — FAX=374-4763 — BA
-Dept of Econ, Mgt & Acctg

Name	Rank	Phone			Field	Deg	Yr	School	Yr
MacHaffie, Fraser G.	C-Ac	376-4629	7	U		MBA	82	Clev St	1982
	Phone	376-4633	Fax 376-7501						
Osborne, Edward H.	Prof	376-4632	6	S		MBA	65	Indiana	1971
Potash, Sidney	Prof	376-4623	25	EHN		PHD	73	SUNY	1974
Taylor, Michael B.	Prof	376-4633	48	BJY		PHD	76	Harvard	9-77
Johnson, Grace F.	Asst	376-4631	9	Z		MACC	88	So Fla	1989

Marist College

Poughkeepsie, NY 12601-1387 (914)
Division of Mgt Studies — 290 North Road — FAX=575-3225 — BS,MBA,MPA
-Management Faculty

Name	Rank	Phone			Deg	School	Yr
Kelly, John C.	Dean	575-3225			PHD	Boston C	1962
	Phone	575-3225	Fax 575-3640				
Melan, Eugene H.	Prof	575-3000	37	UV	MS	Union C	1988
Prenting, Theodore O.	Prof	575-3000	53	QU	MBA	Chicago	1968
Calista, Donald J.	Assoc	575-3000	12	KL	EDD	Sarasota	1977
Grossman, Robert	Assoc	575-3000	4	KL	LLM	NYU	1984
Rider, Caroline V.	Assoc	575-3000	45	K	JD	New York	1984
Barker, Richard	Asst	575-3000	23	EF	EDD	Ca-SnDgo	1991

Name	Rank	Phone				Degree		School	Year
Gauch, Ronald	Asst	575-3000	17	AV		PHD		NYU	1990
Jessen, Diane	Asst	575-3000				PHD		Renssel	1994
Murray, Vernon	Asst	575-3999				PHD		Alabama	1993
Ng, Billy	Asst	575-3000				PHD		Ariz St	1993
Sacino, Joseph J.	Asst	575-3000	34	EIL		EDD		Seton Hl	1988
Sherman, Herbert	Asst	575-3000	34	EIL		PHD		Union	1988

Marquette University — Milwaukee, WI 53233 — (414) MUCSD — 1928,1963 — FAX=288-1660 — BS,MBA
Straz College of Bus Ad — 1217 West Wisconsin Avenue
Giacomino, Don E. — Dean$ 288-5669 — Atg — DBA 78 Kentucky 1977
—Department of Management — Phone — Fax 288-1660

Name	Rank	Phone			Degree		School	Year
Keaveny, Timothy J.	C-Pr	288-3643	5	NQ	PHD	71	Minn	1986
Bausch, Thomas A.	Prof	288-7141	4	L	DBA	69	Indiana	1978
Reynolds, Paul	Prof	288-5578	6	T	PHD	69	Stanford	1990
Carter, Nancy	Assoc	288-5100	3	HIT	PHD	81	Nebraska	1987
Cotton, John L.	Assoc	288-7558	2	E	PHD	79	Iowa	1987
Heintz, Timothy	Assoc	288-1634	9	Z	DBA	72	Indiana	1972
Inderrieden, Edward J.	Assoc	288-3365	2	E	DBA	83	Colorado	1979
Kaiser, Kate	Assoc	288-7338	9	Z	PHD	79	Pitt	1988
McFarlin, Dean B.	Assoc	288-3549	2	E	PHD	86	SUNY-Buf	1986
Rotondi, Thomas	Assoc	288-3545	3	I	DBA	72	Colorado	1973
Cass, Kimberly	Asst	288-7339	9	Z	PHD	88	Arizona	1989
Foo, Suan Tong	Asst	288-5462	7	UV	PHD	90	Wiscon	1990
Healy, Howard T.	Asst	288-7180	4		MBA	54	Harvard	1947
Hosseini, Jamshid	Asst	288-7534	7	V	PHD	87	Port St	1987
Kim, DaeSoo	Asst	288-7146	7	II	PHD	91	Indiana	1991
Maranto, Cheryl L.	Asst	288-1441	5	NQ	PHD	82	Mich St	1989
Ragins, Bello Rose	Asst	288-1447	25	EOR	PHD	87	Tenn	1987
Rehbein, Kathleen	Asst	288-1446	48	JL	PHD	85	Wash U	1987
Srivastava, Baharatendu	Asst	288-3408	7	UV	PHD	92	Wash St	1992
Stearns, Timothy M.	Asst	288-5101	3	HIT	DBA	83	Indiana	1988
Sweeney, Paul	Asst	288-7337	27	EY	PHD	83	Pitt	1987

Mars Hill College — Mars Hill, NC 28754 — (704) FAX=
Div of Bus Adm & Econ
Goose, Jack N. — C-Pr 689-1179 — 34 — DBA 74 Miss St 1964
—Management Faculty — Phone — Fax 689-1474
Pendleton, Barbara A. — Assoc 689-1205 — 15 — EDD 76 Va Tech 1988

Marshall University — Huntington, WV 25755 — (304) FAX=696-6565 — BBA,BS,MBA,MS
College of Business — 400 Hal Greer Boulevard
—Department of Management — Phone 696-5423 — Fax 696-4344

Name	Rank	Phone			Degree		School	Year
Kim, Chong W.	C-Pr	696-2682	2	H	PHD	76	Ohio St	1976
Alexander, Robert P.	Prof	696-2614	5	NI	PHD	69	Ohio U	1969
Bolling, W. Blaker	Prof	696-2679	3	I	DBA	79	Virginia	1979
Damewood, Earl	Assoc	696-2676	7	V	PHD	81	W Virg	
McInerney, Marjorie L.	Assoc	696-2675	4	RQ	PHD	83	Ohio St	1983
Wallace, John	Assoc	696-2680	6	ST	PHD	68	Florida	1968
Blankenship, Ray	Asst	696-2678	9	Z	ABD		Miss	1992
Ha, Daesung	Asst	696-2681	7	V	PHD	91	Penn St	1991
Weible, Ray	Asst	696-2673	9	Z	DBA	93	Miss St	1993
Cooper, Juett	Inst	696-2672	3	I	ABD		Kentucky	1993

University of Mary — Bismarck, ND 58501-9652 — (701) FAX= — BA,BS
Division of Business — 7500 University Drive
phone 255-7500
Borgelt, Marvin — C-Ac Ext 439 — 34 — MBA 82 Maryland 9-82
—Management Faculty — Phone
Brown, Larry — Assoc Ext 434 — 15 — MBA 82 Temple 9-82

Mary Baldwin College — Staunton, VA 24401 — (703) FAX= — BA
Business Administration — Frederick & New Streets
—Management Faculty — Phone 887-7067 — Fax 886-5561
Hammock, Gordon L. — H-Ac 887-7067 — 18 EN — MS — Pace 1987

Univ of Mary Hardin-Baylor — Belton, TX 76513 — (817) FAX=939-4535 — BBA
School of Business
Baldwin, Lee E. — Dean 939-4644 — 23 — PHD 80 North Ex 1992
—Management Faculty — Phone 939-4644 — Fax 939-4535
Deckard, Noble — C-Pr 939-4656 — 23 — PHD — U Wash 1990
Meredith, John W. — Prof 939-4654 — 78 UVYZ — PHD 75 North Tx 1-88
Chandler, Pamela Sue — Asst 939-4653 — 14 — MBA 79 SW Texas 1987
Horton, Howard — Asst 939-4647 — 1 — MBA 75 SW Texas

Mary Washington College

FredericksburgVA 22401-5358 (703)   BS
Dept of Business Adm — 1301 College Avenue — FAX=899-4373

Name	Rank	Phone	Fax	N	Code	Degree	Yr	School
Evans, Gano S.	C-Pr	899-4099		32	DEFH	PHD	69	U Wash
—Management Faculty	Phone	899-4786	Fax 899-4373					
Davidson, Frederick	Prof	899-4467		76	PTVF	PHD		Pitt
Penwell, Larry W.	Asst	899-4595		25	FEGP	PHD		Cinn
Skinker, Harry J.	SLect	899-4063		13		MBA		Alabama
Whitman, Fred T.	SLect	899-4067		13		MBA		Alabama

University of Maryland

College Park, MD 20742 (301) UMDD   1940,1964
College of Bus & Mgt — FAX=314-9157 — BS,MBA,PHD

Name	Rank	Phone	Fax	N	Code	Degree	Yr	School	Yr
Mayer, William	Dean	405-2308				MBA	67	Maryland	1992
—Faculty of Mgt & Org	Phone		Fax 314-9157						
Locke, Edwin A.	C-Pr	405-2238		2	E	PHD	64	Cornell	1967
Bartol, Kathryn M.	Prof	405-2249		5	NR	PHD	72	Mich St	1977
Carroll, Stephen J. Jr.	Prof	405-2239		25	E	PHD	64	Minn	1964
Gannon, Martin J.	Prof	405-2234		23	Y	PHD	69	Columbia	1969
Gupta, Anil	Prof	405-2221		38	IY	PHD	80	Harvard	1986
Levine, Marvin J.	Prof	405-2264		5	Q	PHD	64	Wiscon	1967
Sims, Henry P.	Prof	405-2258		2	E	PHD	71	Mich St	1989
Smith, Ken G.	Prof	405-2250		36	IT	PHD	83	Washingt	1983
Olian, Judy	Assoc	405-2237		5	NG	PHD	80	Wiscon	1981
Taylor, M. Susan	Assoc	405-2240		5	FNO	PHD	78	Purdue	1983
Stevens, Cindy	Asst	405-2233		5	N	PHD	91	Wash	1990
Wally, Stefan	Asst	405-2135		23	HI	PHD	91	New York	1990

Marymount University

Arlington, VA 22207-4299 (703)   BBA,MBA
School of Business Adm — 2807 North Glebe Road — FAX=527-3865

Name	Rank	Phone	Fax	N	Code	Degree	School	Yr
Sigethy, Robert	Dean	284-5110		13	IAY	PHD	American	1983
—Management Faculty	Phone		Fax 527-3830					
O'Sullivan, Hanora	H-Pr	284-5936		30	ENY	PHD	Michigan	1987
Bailey, Edward	Prof	284-5929				PHD	Iowa	1986
Fiebelkorn, George	Prof	284-5939				PHD	Geo St	1986
Hassanein, Saad	Prof	284-5938				PHD	Catholic	1988
Hess, Carl	Prof	284-5943				PHD	Michigan	1984
Hurst, Charles	Prof	284-5925				PHD	Wayne St	1991
Kaitz, Edward	Prof	284-5937		38	IY	DBA	Harvard	1987
Kenneally, Teresa	Prof	284-5918				PHD	Iowa St	1981
Knode, Steve	Prof	284-5944				PHD	Syracuse	1985
Lavanty, Donald	Prof	284-5917				JD	Geo Wash	1979
Spirer, Janet	Prof	284-5924		13	INPZ	PHD	Ohio St	1984
Vest, Carl	Prof	284-5927				PHD	American	1976
Feeney, Joan	Assoc	284-5922				MA	NYU	1974
Herd, Ann M.	Assoc	284-5934		2	E	PHD	Tenn	1992
Ibrahim, Hassan	Assoc	284-5930				DSC	Geo Wash	1992
Jacobson, Carolyn	Assoc	284-5931		9	Z	PHD	Ohio U	1992
Landson, Barry	Assoc	284-5920				PHD	Syracuse	1985
Marshall, Louise	Assoc	284-5932				PHD	Maryland	1976
Meiners, Arthur	Assoc	284-5921		14	JUBD	DBA	Geo Wash	1988
Associate Dean								
Miller, Charles	Assoc	284-5928				MBA	Geo Wash	1985
Ryeson, James	Assoc	284-5926				MBA	Clarkson	1982
Ubelhoer, Jane	Assoc	284-5933				PHD	Missouri	1992
Cahill, Patrick Joseph Sr.	Asst	284-5916				MBA	Duquesne	1970
Carleton, Joseph	Asst	284-5940				MA	Catholic	1987
St. John, Anne	Asst	284-5935				JD	Geo Wash	1991
Wyvill, Maribeth	Asst	284-5912		5	NP	MA	Marymoun	1987
Assistant Dean								
Behrs, David		284-5901						
Assistant Dean								

Marywood College

Scranton, PA 18509-1598 (717)   BS,MBA,MS/MIS
Bus & Mgr Science Prog — 2300 Adams Avenue — FAX=348-1817

Name	Rank	Phone	Fax	Code	Degree	Yr	School
Dagher, Sam P.	Dir	348-6274		Fnce	PHD	74	Ohio St
—Management Faculty	Phone		Fax 348-1817				
Adams, David C.	Assoc	348-6274			PHD		Syracuse
Galante, Joseph	Asst	348-6274		K	JD		Cooley

University of Massachusetts

Amherst, MA 01003 (413) MGMT.UMASS.EDU 1958,1963
School of Management — FAX=545-3858 — BBA,MS,PHD

Name	Rank	Phone	Email/Fax	N	Code	Degree	Yr	School	Yr
O'Brien, Thomas	Dean	545-5581				PHD	69	Cornell	1987
—Department of Management	Phone	545-5675	Fax 545-3858						
Butterfield, D. Anthony	C-Pr	545-5678	dabutter	2	ER	PHD	68	Michigan	1972
Smircich, Linda	Prof	545-5693		2	ERBJ	PHD	78	Syracuse	1982
Spiro, George	Prof	545-5584	spiro	4	KJQ	JD	74	Syracuse	1981
Calas, Marta	Assoc	545-5679	marta	28	ERBY	PHD	87	Mass	1986

Grady, Susan	Assoc	545-5684		4	K	JD	77	W Nw Eng	1978
Greenfield, Patricia	Assoc	545-2884		5	QN	PHD	86	Cornell	1986
Karren, Ronald J.	Assoc	545-5688	ronkarren	5	NO	PHD	78	Maryland	1982
Marx, Robert D.	Assoc	545-5691	marx	2	EP	PHD	71	Illinois	1982
Wooldridge, William	Assoc	545-5697		34	I	DBA	84	Colorado	1985
Zacharias, Lawrence	Assoc	545-5699		4	KLB	JD	73	Columbia	1982
Barringer, Melissa	Asst	545-5628		5	QN	PHD	92	Cornell	1992
Giacobbe, Jane	Asst	545-5692		5	NOE	PHD	86	Cornell	1989
Mangaliso, Mzamo	Asst	545-5616	mangaliso	34	YI	PHD	88	Mass	1989
Sharma, Anurag	Asst	545-5682		3	I	PHD	93	N Carol	1993
Theroux, James	VAsst	545-5677		16		EDD		Mass	1990
Hopley, Robert	VLect	545-5699		63		MBA		Mass	

U Massachusetts Boston	Boston, MA	02125-3393	(617) UMB.SKY						BS,MBA
College of Management			FAX=287-7725						
Hayden, Eric W.	Dean	287-7700				PHD	75	JHopkins	1993
–Management Faculty	Phone	287-7850	Fax 265-7173						
Boroschek, Gunther	C-Pr	287-7855	boroschek	8	Y	PHD	70	Harvard	1975
DeSouza, Glenn	VProf	287-7853		3	I	PHD	76	Fordham	1989
Shimshak, Daniel	Prof	287-7700		7	V	PHD	76	CUNY	1978
Goldsmith, Art	Assoc	287-7854		3	I	PHD	81	Cornell	1980
MBA Director									
Novak, Michael	Assoc	287-7861		2	E	PHD	84		1981
Quaglieri, Phillip	Assoc	287-7862		5	N	PHD	82	Stevens	1080
Schmidt, Vivien	Assoc	287-7863		3	L	PHD	81	Chicago	1977
Tonn, Joan C.	Assoc	287-7864		2	E	PHD	73	Michigan	1975
Wilkie, Pat	Assoc	287-7865		2	E	PHD	73	Wayne St	1973
Greenberg, Ellen	Asst	287-7700		2	E	PHD	85	Columbia	1983
Ives, Jane	Asst	287-7857		6	T	PHD	85	London	1989
Lindamood, Robert	Lect	287-7858		4	JH	PHD	75	Ohio St	1987

U Massachusetts-Dartmouth	No Dartmouth MA	02747	(508)						
College of Bus & Indus	Old Westport Road		FAX=999-8776						
McNeil, Ronald	Dean	999-8432		2	DFP	PHD	82	Memphis	9-92
–Department of Management	Phone		Fax 999-8776						
Golen, Richard F.	C-Ac	999-8425				JD	83	Suffolk	1984
Dorris, James	Prof	999-8430				PHD	75	S Illin	1983
Gilmore, Harold L.	Prof	999-8435				PHD	70	Syracuse	1987
Higginson, Thomas J.	Prof	999-8429				EDD	79	Boston U	1963
Legault, Richard D.	Prof	999-8428				PHD	79	Boston U	1973
Ward, Richard J.	Prof	999-8439				PHD	58	Michigan	1974
Allen, William	Assoc	999-8435				PHD	88	Union	1989
Einstein, Walter O.	Assoc	999-8326				PHD	81	Syracuse	1985
Kobu, Bulent	Assoc	999-8741				PHD	71	Istanbul	1987
Tirtiroglu, Ercan	Assoc	999-8433				PHD	75	Florida	1992
Hodges, Peter B.	VLect	999-8326				MBA	76	Northeas	1982

U of Massachusetts at Lowell	Lowell, MA	01854	(508)						1987,1987
College of Management	1 University Avenue		FAX=934-3011						BS,MBA,MMS
Kahalas, Harvey	Dean	Ext 2845				Mgt	PHD	71	Mass
–Dept Management & Finance	Phone	934-2801	Fax 934-3035						
Hinchey, Braxton	C	934-2801							
Freedman, Stuart	Prof	Ext 2776		2	E	PHD	77	Cornell	
Kainen, Timm	Prof	Ext 2766		2	EH	PHD	79	Mass	
Curtis, Ellen Foster	Assoc	Ext 2770		3	IJ	DBA	79	Indiana	
Moser, Martin	Assoc	Ext 2768		32	JF	PHD	83	Mass	
Hargareaves-Heald, Brooke	Asst	Ext 2769		5	QN	JD	74	Northeas	
Suchon, Kathleen	Asst	Ext 2753		3	IN	PHD	90	SUNY-Alb	

Massachusetts Inst of Tech	Cambridge, MA	02142-1347	(617) SLOAN.MIT.EDU						1957,1963
Sloan School of Mgt	50 Memorial Drive		FAX=258-6617						MS,PHD
email: @1=mit.edu; @2=Mltvma.mit.edu									
Urban, Glen L.	Dean	253-6615	urban			PHD		Northwes	
Dai-Ichi Kangyo Bank Professor of Management									
–Management Sciences Dept	Phone		Fax 258-7579						
Barnett, Arnold I.	Prof	253-2670		7	U	PHD			
Bitran, Gabriel R.	Prof	253-2652		7	U	PHD			
The Nippon Telegraph & Telephone Professor of Management									
Eppinger, D. Steven	Prof	253-0468		7	U	SCD			
Freund, Robert M.	Prof	253-8997	rfreund@1	7	V	PHD	83	Stanford	
Elisha Gray II Career Development Associate Professor of Management Science									
Hauser, John R.	Prof	253-2929	jhauser			SCD	75	MIT	
Kaufman, Gordan M.	Prof	253-2651		7	U	DBA			
Little, John D. C.	Prof	253-3738	jlittle@2	7	V	PHD	55	MIT	
Madnick, Stuart E.	Prof	253-6671	smadnick@1	9	Z	PHD	72	MIT	
Leaders for Manufacturing Professor of Mgt Sci & John Norris Maguire Prof									

Name	Rank	Phone	Email			Degree			
Magnanti, Thomas L.	Prof	253-6604	magnanti@1	7	UV	PHD	72	Stanford	
George Eastman Professor of Management Science									
Malone, Thomas W.	Prof	253-6843	malone@1	9	Z	PHD			
Patrick J. McGovern Professor of Information Systems									
Orlin, James B.	Prof	253-6606	jorlin@1	7	V	PHD	79	Stanford	
Shapiro, Jeremy F.	Prof	253-7980	jshapiro	7	UV	PHD			
Wein, Lawrence M.	Prof	253-6697		7	U	PHD			
Welsch, Roy E.	Prof	253-6601		7	X	PHD	69	Stanford	
Leaders for Manufacturing Professor									
Wernerfelt, Birger	Prof	253-7192	bwerner@1	7	V	DBA	77	Harvard	
Balakrishnan, Anantaram	Assoc	253-0467		7	U	PHD		MIT	
Bertsimas, Dimitris	Assoc	253-4223	dbertsmim@1	7	UV	PHD	88	MIT	
Fine, Charles H.	Assoc	253-3632		7	U	PHD			
Kemerer, Chris F.	Assoc	253-2971	ckemerer@1	9	Z	PHD			
Douglas Drane Career Development Assistant Professor of Management Science									
Orlikowski, Wanda J.	Assoc	253-0443	wanda@1	9	Z	PHD			
Prelec, Drazen	Assoc	253-2833	dprelec@1	7	V	PHD	83	Harvard	
Ulrich, Karl T.	Assoc	253-0487		7	U	SCD			
Ford International Career Development Associate Professor									
Wang, Y. Richard	Assoc	253-0442	rwang@1	9	Z	PHD			
Brooke, Geoffrey	Asst	253-8353	gbrooke	9	Z				
Brynjolfsson, Eric	Asst	253-4319	brynjolffso	9	Z				
Leclerc, France	Asst	253-7174	fleclerc	7	V	PHD	91	Cornell	
Nguyen, Vien	Asst	253-0486	vien@1	7	U	PHD	90	Stanford	
Qualls, William J.	Asst	253-0492	wqualls	3	I	DBA	82	Indiana	
Resnick, Paul	Asst	253-8694	presnick@1	9	Z	PHD	92	MIT	
Zhou, Bin	Asst	253-5140		7	V				
Bund, Barbara	SLect	258-5095		3	IZ	PHD		Harvard	
MacKinnon, Richard	SLect	253-9413		9	Z				
Meldman, Jeffrey A.	SLect	253-4932	jmeldman@1	9	Z	PHD			
Rockart, John F.	SLect	253-6608	jrockart	9	Z	PHD	68	MIT	1966
Rosenfield, Don	SLect	253-1065		7	U				
—Behavioral & Policy Sci Dpt	Phone		Fax 258-2660						
Allen, Thomas J.	Prof	253-6651				PHD		MIT	1966
Gordon Billard Fund Professor of Management									
Ancona, Deborah G.	Prof	253-0568		2	H	PHD			
Bailyn, Lotte L.	Prof	253-6674		2	H	PHD			
Carroll, John S.	Prof	253-2617		2	H	PHD			
Hax, Arnoldo C.	Prof	253-4930		3	I	PHD	67	Berkeley	1972
Alfred P. Sloan Professor of Management									
Kochan, Thomas A.	Prof	253-6689		5	NQ	PHD			
George Maverick Bunker Professor of Management									
Lessard, Donald R.	Prof	253-6688		3	I	PHD	70	Stanford	1974
McKersie, Robert B.	Prof	253-2671		5	Q	DBA			
Leaders for Manufacturing Professor									
Nyhart, J. Dan	Prof	253-1582		3	I	JD			
Osterman, Paul	Prof	253-2667		5	QN	PHD			
Piore, Michael J.	Prof	253-3377		5	NQ	PHD			
Pounds, William F.	Prof	253-2611		3	I	PHD	62	Case Wes	1961
Roberts, Edward B.	Prof	253-4934				PHD			
David Sarnoff Professor of Management of Technology									
Schein, Edgar J.	Prof	253-3636		2	H	PHD			
Sloan Fellows Professor of Management									
Scott Morton, Michael S.	Prof	253-7175		3	I	DBA	67	Harvard	1966
Jay W. Forrester Professor of Management									
Siegel, Abraham J.	Prof	253-7158		5	NQ	PHD	61	Berkeley	
Howard W. Johnson Professor of Management									
Utterback, Jim	Prof	253-2661							
VanMaanen, John E.	Prof	253-3610		2	H	PHD			
Edwin H. Schell Professor of Organizational Studies									
vonHippel, Eric A.	Prof	253-7155				PHD			
Westney, D. Eleanor	Prof	253-7998		35	IN	PHD			
Lachman, Judith A.	Assoc	253-0901				PHD			
Lynch, Lisa	Assoc	253-0803		5	QN	PHD			
Sterman, John	Assoc	253-1951		9	Z	PHD			
Thomas, Robert J.	Assoc	253-7376		5	N	PHD			
Leaders for Manufactuirng Associate Professor									
Cusumano, Michael A.	Asst	253-2574		3	I	PHD			
Mitsubishi Career Development Assistant Professor of Management									
Henderson, Rebecca M.	Asst	253-6618		3	I	PHD			
Locke, Richard M.	Asst	253-2610		5	Q	PHD			
I.R.I. Careeer Development Assistant Professor of Mgt & Political Science									
Rappa, Michael A.	Asst	253-3627				PHD			
Rebitzer, James B.	Asst	253-7782		35	IN	PHD			
Schrader, Stephan	Asst	253-5219				PHD			
Tyre, Marcie J.	Asst	253-6679				PHD			
Yates, JoAnne	Asst	253-7157				PHD			
Ziegler, J. Nicholas	Asst	253-6437		8	Y	AM			
Ephlin, Don	SLect	253-3659		5	QN				
Segall, Maurice	SLect	253-3408		3	I				

Name	Rank	Phone	email		Deg		School	
Rowe, Mary P.	Adj	253-5921		5	QN			
Guillen, Mauro		253-4417		3	I			
Ocasio, William		253-8412		3	I			
Scully, Maureen		253-5070		5	QN			

McNeese State University — Lake Charles, LA 70609-1415 (318) FAX=475-5010 — 1989,1989
College of Business — BS
Mondy, R. Wayne — Dean 475-5514 — DBA 74 La Tech 1986
−Dept of Management & Mktg — Phone — Fax 475-5010

Name	Rank	Phone		Deg		School	
Phelps, Lonnie D.	H-Pr	475-5520		DBA		La Tech	
Bettinger, Charles O.	Prof	475-5542		PHD	69	Texas	
Premeaux, Shane	Prof	475-5576		PHD		Arkansas	
Sharpin, Arthur	Prof	475-5531		PHD		LSU	
Distinguished Professor of Management							
Comish, C. Ray	Assoc	475-5540		DBA		La Tech	
Newmiller, Clyde E.	Assoc	475-5541		PHD		Tx A&M	
Cabell, David W.	Asst	475-5538		DBA		Kent St	
Durrett, Virginia	Asst	475-5539					
Mondy, Judy B.	Asst	475-5535		MS		La Tech	
Daboval, Jeanne	Inst	475-5544					
Premeaux, Sonya A.	Inst	475-5517		MBA		McNeese	

University of Memphis — Memphis, TN 38152 (901) MSUVX1.MEMPHIS.EDU1970,1971
Fogelman Col Bus & Econ — FAX=678-4282 — BBA,MBA,MS,PHD
Ferrell, O. C. — Dean$ 678-2432 — Mktg PHD 72 LSU 1989
−Department of Management — Phone 678-2466 Fax 670-4990

Name	Rank	Phone	email			Deg		School	
Miller, Thomas R.	O-Pr	678-2466	millerth	12	BN	PHD	72	Ohio St	1971
Raskin, Otis W.	Prof	678-2038		1	D	PHD	75	Texas	1991
Bhagat, Rabi S.	Prof	678-3436		28	EGY	PHD	77	Illinois	1990
Duhaime, Irene M.	Prof	678-2431	duhaimei	3	I	PHD	81	Pitt	1991
Hodgetts, James C.	Prof	678-4659		5	N	PHD	54	N Dakoka	1965
Jones, Coy A.	Prof	678-4649	jonesca	25	EFN	PHD	82	Oklahoma	1981
Kedia, Banwari L.	Prof	678-4044		38	IY	PHD	76	Case Wes	1988
Oliphant, Van	Prof	678-2991		25	ND	DBA	69	Miss St	1969
Rosser, Leonard	Prof	678-4454		26	St	DBA	70	Miss St	1967
Wright, Peter	Prof	678-2434	pwright	38	IY	PHD	75	LSU	1988
Davis, Peter S.	Assoc	678-2084	davisps	3	I	PHD	88	S Carol	1989
Gilmore, J. Barry	Assoc	678-3568		36	IT	PHD	71	Oklahoma	1971
Taylor, Robert R.	Assoc	678-4551		2	EP	PHD	79	LSU	1983
Barksdale, Kevin	Asst	678-2466		25	ENQ	ABD	94	Geo St	1994
Danehower, V. Carol	Asst	678-4656	danehowervc	25	EN	DBA	87	Kentucky	1987
Krug, Jeffrey	Asst	678-2466		38	IY	PHD	93	Indiana	1994
Renn, Robert W.	Asst	678-2886	rennrw	12	EN	PHD	89	Geo St	1989
Tu, Howard	Asst	678-4317		38	IY	PHD	88	Mass	1988

Mercer University-Atlanta — Atlanta, GA 30341 (404) FAX=986-3337 — BBA,MBA,MSHCA
Stetson Sch of Bus & Ec — 3001 Mercer University Drive
Joiner, W. Carl — Dean 986-3235 — 16 CDT PHD 78 Alabama 1974
−Management Faculty — Phone 986-3199 Fax 986-3337

Name	Rank	Phone			Deg		School	
McNay, William Rose	Prof	986-3171		35	IN	PHD		Penn	1981
Johnson, Victoria	Assoc	986-3235		14	ACNO	DPA		Georgia	1986
Associate Dean									
Southern, Lloyd J. F.	Assoc	986-3234		13	TZ	PHD		Ga Tech	1989
Corey, Sharon	Asst	986-3303		97	Z	ABD		Florida	1992
Juett, Samuel	Asst	986-3167		48	AEJN	ABD		Georgia	1989

Mercer University-Macon — Macon, GA 31207-0001 (912) FAX=752-2635 — BBA,MBA
Stetson Sch Bus & Econ — 1400 Coleman Avenue
email ACADMN.MERCER.PEACHNET.EDU
Joiner, W. Carl — Dean 752-2832 — 16 CDT PHD 78 Alabama 1974
−Management Faculty — Phone — Fax 752-2635

Name	Rank	Phone	email			Deg		School	
Austin, Walter W.	Assoc	752-2861				PHD	88	Georgia	1989
Deile, Andrew J.	Assoc	752-2843		23	HI	PHD	74	Illinois	1986
Vaughan, Mary Jo	Asst	752-5313	vaughan_mj	25	ENP	ABD		Florida	1993

Meredith College — Raleigh, NC 27607-5298 (919) FAX=829-2828 — BS,MBA
Dept of Business & Econ — 3800 Hillsborough Street
Spanton, Donald L. — H-Pr 829-8470 — 18 JL PHD American 1983
−Management Faculty — Phone 829-8470 Fax 829-2828

Name	Rank	Phone			Deg		School	
Oatsvall, Rebecca S.	Prof	829-8484		2	R	PHD	78	S Carol	1984
Bledsoe, Maynard T.	Assoc	829-8476		15	TPR	EDD		NC-Green	1982
Crew, James	Assoc	829-8471		23	EI	PHD		N Car St	1990

Merrimack College North Andover MA 01845 (508) MERRIMACK.EDU
Division Business Adm 300 Turnpike Road FAX=831-5013 BS,BA
DelGaudio, Richard Dean 837-5000 MBA 70 Northeas 1977
–Department of Management Phone Fax 831-5013

Name	Rank	Phone	Email		Deg		School	Year
Kapelner, David I.	Assoc	837-5000			JD		Suffolk	
Koziell, John	Assoc	837-5000			MBA		Conn	
Pariseau, Susan E.	Assoc	837-5417	spariseau	U	PHD	94	Mass	
Stevens, Kathy	Assoc	837-5000		Z	PHD	80	Purdue	1987
Stewart, James E.	Assoc	837-5000			MBA		Gold Gt	
Han, S. Bruce	Asst	837-5000		U	MBA		Michigan	
Momen, Abdul	Asst	837-5000			PHD		Northeas	
Sendall, Patricia	Asst	837-5000		ZOR	MBA		St Joe	1990

Mesa State College Grand JunctionCO 81502 (303)
Sch of Professional Std FAX=248-1903 BBA
Blair, Kenneth W. Dean 248-1969 Mktg PHD 76 Ariz St 1986
–Department of Business Adm Phone Fax 248-1730

Name	Rank	Phone			Deg		School	Year
Dickson, Dale L.	Prof	248-1213	16	S	EDD		N Colo	1969
Zimmerer, Mary E.	Assoc	248-1719	1		PHD		Colo St	1988
Kappenberger, John	Asst	248-1724	12	E&	PHD		Colorado	1992
Mallory, Elgin	Asst	248-1727	17		PHD		Colo St	1990
Mayer, Robert W.	Asst	248-1728	1	OP	MBA		N Colo	1987
McIntire, Harold B.	Asst	248-1725	1		MBA		E Nw Mex	1987
Ralser, Thomas	Asst	248-1731	1		MS		Utah	1987
Slauson, Mike	Asst	248-1944	1	OP	MBA		S Colo	1990

Metropolitan St Col Denver Denver, CO 80217-3362 (303) ZENO.MSCD.EDU
School of Business FAX=556-4429 BS
Geisler, Jerry L. Dean 556-3245 3 PHD 75 Missouri 9-93
–Department of Management Phone Fax 556-4429

Name	Rank	Phone	Email			Deg		School	Year
Khandekar, Rajendra	C-Ac	556-3242	khandekr	32	IHES	PHD	83	Kansas	8-89
Breitenbach, Robert	Prof	556-2765		47	KWY	PHD	67	Ohio St	1982
Lucas, Robert	Prof	556-3248		67	STUW	DBA	71	Colorado	1976
Patrone, Ferdinand	Prof	556-3061		13	IST	PHD	71	Syracuse	1975
Price, Courtney	Prof	556-3917		65	TCDN	DPA	81	Colorado	1982
Taylor, Ronald	Prof	556-3125		4	JKL	JD	75		1980
Faurer, Judson	Assoc	556-8569		12	DEHS	PHD	72	Denver	1983
Foegen, George	Assoc	556-4682		16	DSZ	DBA	71	Geo Wash	1986
Frederick, Elizabeth	Assoc	556-3004		25	EJNQ	PHD	85	Maryland	1987
Hanson, Roberta	Assoc	556-3955		54	JLPR	DBA	79	Colorado	1987
Knights, Ronald	Assoc	556-4641		25	DEFH	PHD	76	New Mex	1982
Odden, Arthur	Assoc	556-3064		4	KLY	JD	62	Denver	1976
Scott, C. Richard	Assoc	556-4337		35	YIN	DBA	88	La Tech	1991
Holloway, Madison	Asst	556-2804		25	DGNQ	PHD	77	Colorado	1990

University of Miami Coral Gables, FL 33124-9145 (305) UMIAMI 1957,1963
School of Business Adm 1252 Memorial Drive FAX=284-3655 BBA,MBA,MS,PHD
Sugrue, Paul K. Dean 284-4643 Mas PHD 77 Mass 1977
–Department of Management Phone 284-5846 Fax 284-3655

Name	Rank	Phone	Email			Deg		School	Year
Neider, Linda L.	C-Pr	284-6123	lneider	25	EFNT	PHD	79	SUNY-Buf	1979
Berkman, Harold W.	Prof	284-2510		2	ESTR	PHD	71	St Johns	1977
Associate Dean									
Fedor, Kenneth J.	Prof	284-5846		38	IY	PHD	66	Tenn	1990
Glaskowsky, Nicholas A. Jr.	Prof	284-5846		37	BIUK	PHD	60	Stanford	1974
Grosse, Robert E.	Prof	284-5846		8	Y	PHD	77	N Carol	1980
Kujawa, Duane A.	Prof	284-5846		38	Y	PHD	70	Michigan	1980
McKenry, Carl E. B.	Prof	284-5846		56	YTNK	LLM	65	NYU	1956
Natiello, Thomas A.	Prof	284-5846		23	CDHI	PHD	66	Mich St	1966
Schriesheim, Chester A.	Prof	284-5846	cschries	25	ENVX	PHD	78	Ohio St	1986
Strauss, Harold	Prof	284-5846		28	BNOP	PHD	52	Geneva	1968
Ullmann, Steven G.	Prof	284-2002		14	CDJL	PHD	80	Michigan	1979
Vice Provost									
Werther, William B.	Prof	284-5846		35	INOP	PHD	71	Florida	1985
Bradford, John W.	Assoc	284-5846		7	UV	PHD	86	Columbia	1986
Hudson, Donald R.	Assoc	284-5846		13	I	PHD	74	Geo St	1974
Kerr, Jeffrey L.	Assoc	284-5846		38	IN	PHD	77	Penn St	1989
Scandura, Terri A.	Assoc	284-5846	scandura	28	EOYR	PHD	88	Cinn	1990
Medsker, Gina J.	Asst	284-5846		25	ENY	PHD	93	Purdue	1993
Pillai, Rajnandini K.	Asst	284-5846		2	E	PHD	93	SUNY-Buf	1993
Schweitzer, Maurice E.	Asst	284-5846		17	CVX	PHD	93	Penn	1994
Shafer, Scott M.	Asst	284-5846	sshafer	79	IUVZ	PHD	89	Cinn	1988
Trevino, Len J.	Asst	284-5846	ltrevino	83	IY	PHD	91	Indiana	1990

Miami University — Oxford, OH 45056 — (513) MIAMIU — 1932,1963
School of Business Adm — FAX=529-6992 — BS,MBA,MACC

Name	Title	Phone	Email		Area	Degree	Yr	School	Dates
Cumming, John	Dean$	529-6212			Atg	PHD	73	Illinois	8-77
--**Department of Management**	Phone	529-4215	Fax 529-6992						
Crain, Charles R.	C-Pr	529-4215	crcrain	37	U	PHD	71	Missouri	8-71
Altman, John W.	Prof	529-5409		16	ST	MA	88	Fuller	8-92
Bolon, Donald S.	Prof	529-4217		5	JN	PHD	71	Ohio St	8-76
Douglas, John	Prof	529-6643		1	Y	PHD	60	Cornell	8-73
Twotress, Kaylynn	VProf	529-4746		8	Y	MS	88	Drake	1-92
Watson, Charles E.	Prof	529-4241		23	LP	PHD	70	Illinios	8-74
Cowan, David S.	Assoc	529-3689	dc62mgtf	2	EFG	PHD	84	Kansas	8-88
Finch, Byron J.	Assoc	529-3159		7	U	PHD	86	Georgia	8-86
King, Wesley C.	Assoc	529-4231		2	EFH	PHD	88	Georgia	8-87
Luebbe, Richard L.	Assoc	529-4229		7	U	PHD	85	Nebraska	8-84
Newman, William E.	Assoc	529-4219	weneman	7	U	PHD	88	Iowa	8-87
Schwarz, Joshua L.	Assoc	529-1653	jschwarz	5	KL	PHD	85	Cornell	8-89
Snavely, B. Kay	Assoc	529-4238	ks51mfrd	2	EFHR	PHD	87	Cinn	8-80
Snavely, William B.	Assoc	529-7258	wsnavely	2	EFH	PHD	77	Nebraska	8-84
Hanna, Mark D.	Asst	529-4745	mhanna	7	U	PHD	89	Clemson	8-89
Hinson, Thomas D.	Asst	529-1651	tdhinson	3	I	PHD	91	Georgia	8-89
Johnson, Pamela	Asst	529-4215		1	EH	PHD	93	Case Wes	8-93
Leonard, Joseph W.	Asst	529-4239	jleonard	38	IY	PHD	83	Arkansas	8-82
Luzadis, Rebecca A.	Asst	529-1654	rluzadis	5	NX	PHD	86	Cornell	8-89
Maffei, Mary Jo	Asst	529-1673		7	U	PHD	91	Cinn	1-91
McNeill, John D.	Asst	529-4230	fmbumgtf	23	EFI	DBA	79	Kentucky	8-75
Walsh, David	Asst	529-4215		25	EQ	PHD	91	Cornell	8 01
Wesolowski, Mark	Asst	529-1652	mwesolow	25	EN	PHD	91	Auburn	1-90
Barille, Judy A.	Inst	529-6643		10	5I	MBA	81	Miami U	8-81
Brant, Clyde L.	VInst	529 1220		7	U	MBA	90	Miami U	8-90
Harp, Robert M.	Inst	529-4232		1	L	MA	62	Naval Po	8-79
Irwin, W. Graham	Inst	529-1818		13	I	MBA	81	Miami U	1-82
Madison, William J.	Inst	529-4236		15	L	MPA	74	Cinn	1-87

University of Michigan — Ann Arbor, MI 48109-1234 — (313) — 1919,1963
School of Business Adm — 701 Tappan Street — FAX=763-5688 — BBA,MAC,MBA,PHD

Name	Title	Phone		Area	Degree	Yr	School	Year
White, B. Joseph	Dean	764-1361	2	E	PHD	75	Michigan	1987
--**Dept of Operations Mgt**	Phone		Fax 763-5688					
Talbot, F. Brian	C-Pr	764-6842	7	U	PHD	76	Penn St	1977
Lovejoy, William	Prof	763-1391	7	U	PHD	83	Delaware	1994
Reece, James S.	Prof	764-1395	3	I	DBA	70	Harvard	1975
Ettlie, John E.	Assoc	936-2835	7	U	PHD	75	Northwes	1987
Haessler, Robert W.	Assoc	764-2314	7	U	PHD	68	Michigan	1975
Stecke, Kathryn E.	Assoc	763-0485	7	U	PHD	81	Purdue	1981
Sethuraman, Kannan	Asst	764-0199	7	U	PHD	93	Penn	1992
Svaan, Eric	Asst	763-3298		U	PHD	93	Car Mel	1991
Sweeney, Paul E.	Asst	764-0275	7	U	PHD	88	Michigan	1987
--**Org Behavior & Hum Res Mgt**	Phone	764-1376	Fax 763-5688					
Dutton, Jane E.	C-Pr	764-1376	2	E	PHD	83	Northwes	1989
Cameron, Kim S.	Prof	763-1179	5	Q	PHD	78	Yale	1984
Danielson, Lee E.	Emer	764-1387	5	N	PHD	56	Michigan	1955
Miller, Edwin L.	Prof	764-1408			PHD	64	Berkeley	1964
Quinn, Robert E.	Prof	763-9310	2	E	PHD	75	Cinn	1988
Tichy, Noel M.	Prof	764-1289	2	E	PHD	72	Columbia	1980
Weick, Karl E.	Prof	763-1339	2	E	PHD	62	Ohio St	1988
Rensis Likert College Professor of Org Behavior & Psychology								
Weiss, Janet A.	Prof	764-1309	2	E	PHD	77	Harvard	1983
Associate Dean								
Ashford, Susan	Assoc			E	PHD	83	Northwes	1991
Cox, Taylor Jr.	Assoc	764-6120	3	E	PHD	81	Arizona	1988
Denison, Daniel R.	Assoc	763-4717	2	E	PHD	82	Michigan	1983
Sandelands, Lance E.	Assoc	764-3128	2	E	PHD	82	Penn	1989
Walsh, James P.	Assoc	936-2768		E	PHD	85	Northwes	1991
Brannen, Mary Yoko	Asst	747-3292			PHD		UCLA	1985
Brockbank, Joseph W.	Asst	764-6105	35	EN	PHD	90	Yale	
Caproni, Paula J.	Asst	763-1010	3	E	PHD	90	Yale	
Meyerson, Debra E.	Asst	763-5808	2	E	PHD	89	Stanford	
Ulrich, David O.	Adj	763-9781	2	E	PHD	82	UCLA	1982
--**Dept of Corporate Strategy**	Phone		Fax 763-5688					
Karnani, Aneel G.	C-Ac	764-0276	38	IY	PHD	81	Harvard	1980
Hosmer, LaRue Tone	Prof	764-2325	46	IJT	DBA	71	Harvard	1971
Prahalad, C. K.	Prof	763-5573	38	IY	DBA	75	Harvard	1978
Mitchell, William G.	Assoc	764-1230	3	IY	PHD	88	Berkeley	1988
Conner, Kathleen R.	Asst		3	I	PHD	86	UCLA	1991
Hart, Stuart L.	Asst	763-6820	3	IMH	PHD	83	Michigan	1986
Majumdar, S. K.	Asst	763-4610			PHD	90	Minn	1990
Methe, David T.	Asst		3	IY	PHD	85	Ca-Irvine	1991
Swaminathan, Anand	Asst		3	IH	PHD	91	Berkeley	1991

Univ of Michigan-Dearborn

Dearborn, MI 48128-1491 (313)
School of Management 4901 Evergreen Road FAX=593-5436 BBA,MBA
* Info Sys/Dec Sci/Op Mgt Dept; # Education Faculty

Name	Rank	Phone	Email	Fax		Field	Deg		School	Year
Brucker, Eric	Dean	593-5248				Fnce	PHD	66	Duke	1992
–Management Faculty	Phone	593-5469		Fax 593-5636						
Martin, William R. D.	C-Pr	593-5106			12	EIPS	MBA	58	Chicago	1976
Krachenberg, A. Richard	Emer	593-5578			23	HIY	PHD	63	Michigan	1968
Lev, Benjamin	* Prof	593-5124			7	UV	PHD	70	Case Wes	9-90
Lyons, Thomas F.	Prof	593-5106			12	EFHP	PHD	67	Michigan	1974
Streeter, Victor J.	* Assoc	593-5084			9	Z	PHD	69	Michigan	1963
Callahan, Thomas J.	Asst	593-5109			23	HIN	PHD	90	Mich St	1987
Choi, JaeHwa	Asst	593-5578			9	Z	PHD	91	Maryland	9-91
Green, Brian	Asst	593-5301								
McCraken, Gail K.	Asst	593-5476	gmccrack		4	JK	JD	83	Wayne St	1987
Rossin, Donald F.	* Asst	593-5475			7	TU	PHD	85	UCLA	1994
Waissi, Gary	* Asst	593-5102			7	V	PHD	85	Michigan	1986
McWilliam, Dave	VLect	436-9140								
Kampfner, Roberto A.	Adj	593-5239			97	HUVZ	PHD	81	Michigan	1987

Univ of Michigan-Flint

Flint, MI 48502-2186 (810) UMICHUB 1982,1986
School of Management 303 East Kearsley FAX=762-3687 BBA,MBA

Name	Rank	Phone		Fax		Field	Deg		School	Year
Hallam, Stephen F.	Dean	762-3164			9	Z	PHD	73	Iowa	
–Management Faculty	Phone	763-3160		Fax 762-3282						
Chastain, Clark E.	Prof	762-3160			3	E	PHD	58	Michigan	1968
Ellis, Dennis F.	Prof	762-3160			7	V	PHD	72	Wayne St	9-70
Fesmire, Walker	Prof	762-3160			1	A	PHD	82	Miss	1982
Kartha, C. P.	Prof	762-3160			7	UVX	PHD	73	Wiscon	7-79
Larson, John A.	Prof	762-3160			43	LJ	PHD	56	Northwes	1976
Moon, I. Doug	Prof	762-3160			7	UV	PHD	76	Va Tech	9-89
Widgery, Robin N.	Prof	762-3160			2	EF	PHD	71	Mich St	7-88
Bokemeier, L. Charles	Assoc	762-3160			1	AGR	DBA	83	Kentucky	9-90
Davis, Dale A.	Assoc	762-3160			13	AYZ	PHD	78	Michigan	9-72
Lotfi, Vahid	Assoc	762-3160			7	UV	PHD	81	SUNY-Buf	8-90
Marquardt, John D.	Assoc	762-3160			1	A	PHD	75	Illinois	1980
Angur, Madhukar	Asst	762-3160			6	S	PHD			
Asquith, JoAnn	Asst	762-3160			6	S	PHD	90	Claremont	9-89
Carayannopoulos, Peter	Asst	762-3160			1		PHD			
Kretovich, Duncan J.	Asst	762-3160			1		PHD	85	Mich St	1988
Ludwick, Mark H.	Asst	762-3160			52	NPF	PHD	87	Wayne St	9-91
Mensah, Samuel	Asst	762-3160			1		PHD		Toronto	1991
Skivington, Kristen D.	Asst	762-3160			2	H	PHD	87	Tx A&M	8-86
Taghaboni, Fataneh	Asst	762-3160			7	UV	PHD	89	Purdue	9-90
Velthouse, Betty A.	Asst	762-3160			28	EJY	PHD	90	Pitt	9-88
Cheslow, David	Lect	762-3160			9	Z	ABD			
McGaugh, Jack D.	Lect	762-3160			23	PS	PHD	74	US Intl	9-85

Michigan State University

East Lansing, MI 48824-1121 (517) MSU.EDU 1953,1963
Grad School of Bus Adm FAX=336-1111 BA,MBA,PHD

Name	Rank	Phone	Code	Fax		Field	Deg		School	Year
Carter, Phillip L.	Dean$	355-8378	plcarter		7	U	DBA	70	Indiana	1970
–Department of Management	Phone	353-5415		Fax 336-1111						
Moch, Michael K.	C-Pr	355-1878	21751mkm		3	H	PHD	73	Cornell	8-84
Hollenbeck, John R.	Prof	355-2413	22019mgr		2	E	PHD	84	New York	9-84
Ilgen, Daniel R.	Prof	336-3513	11535drl		2	E	PHD	69	Illinois	9-83
Hannah Professor										
Melnyk, Steven A.	Prof	336-3506	16513sam		7	U	PHD	80	W Ontar	9-80
Monczka, Robert M.	Prof	336-3503	21482rmm		7	W	PHD	70	Mich St	1974
NAPM Professor										
Narasimhan, Ram	Prof	336-3517	16754RN		7	UV	PHD	76	Minn	9-77
Schmitt, Neal	Prof	355-8305	10259NWS		5	N	PHD	72	Purdue	1974
Chao, Georgia T.	Assoc	353-5418	19922gtc		5	O	PHD	82	Penn St	9-85
Coleman, Bruce P.	Assoc	336-3523			3	O	DBA	67	Indiana	9-65
Ghosh, Soumen	Assoc	336-3505	20517sng		7	UV	PHD	87	Ohio St	8-86
Ragatz, Gary L.	Assoc	336-3504	19393glr		7	U	PHD	85	Indiana	9-84
Rubin, Paul A.	Assoc	336-3509	15552par		7	U	PHD	80	Mich St	1-80
Vickery, Shawnee K.	Assoc	336-3511	22645skv		7	UV	PHD	83	S Carol	1-84
Wagner, John A. III	Assoc	353-5419	23272mgr		2	H	PHD	82	Illinois	9-81
Barber, Alison E.	Asst	336-3522	aebarber		2	Q	PHD	90	Wiscon	9-90
Forker, Laura B.	Asst	336-3507	forker		7	W	PHD	93	Arizona	8-92
Handfield, Robert B.	Asst	336-3514	23073mgr		7	W	PHD	90	N Carol	8-92
Pommerenka, Pamela	Asst				5	O	PHD		Stanford	8-94
Stimpert, J. Larry	Asst	336-3518	22764mgr		3	M	PHD	91	Illinois	9-91
VanDyne, Linn	Asst	336-3512	23251mgr		2	E	PHD	93	Minn	8-93

Michigan Technological Univ — Houghton, MI 49931-1295 (906) MTUS5

School of Bus & Eng Adm — 1400 Townsend Drive — FAX=487-2944 — BS,MS
—Department of Management — Phone 487-2669 — Fax 487-2944

Name	Rank	Phone	email			Deg		School	Year
Monson, Terry D.	Dean	487-2669	tdmonson	8	YP	PHD	72	Minn	1977
Nelson, Paul A.	C	487-2809	pnelson	17	HU	PHD	74	Wiscon	1972
Jambekar, Anil B.	Prof	487-2285	abjambek	7	UV	PHD	71	U Wash	1971
Pelc, Karol I.	Prof	487-2663	kipelc	78	DIY	PHD	68	Poland	1985
Brokaw, Alan J.	Assoc	487-2885	ajbrokaw	6	IST	PHD	76	Michigan	1976
Dorweiler, Vernon P.	Assoc	487-2180	vdorweil	34	IKMY	PHD	59	Iowa	1985
McCoy, Walter D.	Assoc	487-2181	wmccoy	5	Q	PHD	80	Texas	1989
Walck, Christa L.	Assoc	487-2205	cwalck	28	EFYR	PHD	80	Harvard	1986
Aytug, Haldun	Asst	487-2514	haytug	9	Z	PHD	93	Florida	1994
Dogan, Can	Asst	487-2251	cdogan	7	UV	PHD	89	Clemson	1989
Frendewey, Jim O.	Asst	487-2139	jimf	7	UVPH	PHD	83	Colorado	1989
Rahali, Boubekeur	Asst	487-2679	borahali	7	UV	PHD	84	Oklahoma	1989
Vician, Chelley	Asst			9	Z	PHD	94	Minn	1994
Aho, Paul E.	Lect	487-2587	peaho	9	Z	MBA	83	DePaul	1983
Chapel, William B.	Lect	487-2767	wbchapel	6	&T	MS	90	Mi Tech	1985

MidAmerica Nazarene Coll — Olathe, KS 66061-1776 (913)

Div of Business Adm — FAX=791-3290 — BA
Did Not Respond-1992 Listing; Phone 782-3750
—Management Faculty — Phone — Fax 791-3290

Name	Rank	Phone			Deg		School	Year
McGee, Corlis	C	Ext 170			DA	87	M Tenn	
Jones, Mary	Asst	Ext 177	41	L&				
Ford, Mark	Inst	Ext 173	56	NS	,ID			1991

Middle Tennessee State Univ — Murfreesboro, TN 37132 (615) 1977,1983

College of Business — FAX=898-5538 — BS,MBA,MS
—Management & Mktg Dept — Phone 898-2736 — Fax 898-5538

Name	Rank	Phone			Deg		School	Year
Haskew, Barbara S.	Dean	898-2764		Econ	PHD	69	Tenn	1988
Peters, Michael	Prof	898-5917	7	U	DBA	71	Indiana	1990
Singer, Marc G.	Prof	898-2736	25	ENQ	PHD	73	Tenn	1990
Thomas, Joe G.	Prof	898-2736	31	I	PHD	83	Texas	1989
Wilson, Glenn T.	Prof	898-2341	7	U	PHD	65	Penn	1989
Austin, M. Jill	Assoc	898-2438	34	IJ	DBA	86	Miss St	1985
Desai, Kiran J.	Assoc	898-2340	7	U	PHD	72	Penn St	1972
Hart, William S.	Assoc	898-2780	35	IQ	PHD	69	Florida	1986
Jacobs, George W.	Assoc	898-2433	2	EH	PHD	79	Georgia	1979
Sokoya, S. Kim	Assoc	898-2352	38	IY	DBA	85	Miss St	1989
Tang, Thomas	Assoc	898-2005	25	EFN	PHD	81	Case Wes	1983
Tillery, Kenneth R.	Assoc	898-2342	38	IY	PHD	85	Georgia	1988
Horton, Veronica	Asst	898-5126	3	I	PHD	92	Ohio St	1992
Lyman, Steve	Asst	898-2736	7	U	PHD	93	Mich St	1994
Parnell, John	Asst	898-5125	38	IY	DBA	92	Memphis	1992

Midwestern State University — Wichita Falls TX 76308-2099 (817)

Div of Business Adm — 3400 Taft Boulevard — FAX= — BBA
phone 689-4360
—Department of Management — Phone — Fax 689-4280

Name	Rank	Phone			Deg		School	Year
McCullough, Charles	Dean	689-4360		Mktg	PHD		Tx Tech	
Patterson, Mike C.	Prof	689-4710	7	UVQ	PHD	78	North Tx	9-78
Ramser, Charles D.	Prof	689-4362	25	ENST	PHD	69	North Tx	9-69
Dailey, Mike	Asst	689-4289	25	ENST	DBA	78	La Tech	9-92

Millersville Univ of PA — Millersville, PA 17551 (717)

Dept of Business Adm — North George Street — FAX=
Brady, Donald — C-Pr 872-3566 — Mktg PHD 78 Alabama 1985
—Management Faculty — Phone 872-3566 — Fax 871-2203

Name	Rank	Phone			Deg		School	Year
Molz, Ferdinand L.	Prof	872-3857	36	AT	PHD	68	Catholic	1970
Nakhai, Behnam	Prof	872-3753	78	UWY	PHD	82	Claremnt	1987
Ghoreishi, Minoo	Assoc	871-2206	23	REPY	PHD	87	Arkansas	1988
Heckert, Richard J.	Asst	872-3757	59	EFMP	MA	76	St Franc	1979
Lo, Amber	Asst	872-3757	79	IVYZ	ABD	91	Tx A&M	1993

Millikin University — Decatur, IL 62522 (217)

Tabor School Bus & Eng — 1184 West Main Street — FAX=424-3993 — BS
Did Not Respond-1992 Listing
Mannweiler, Richard A. — Dean 424-6284 — MSIR Purdue 1979
—Dept of Business Adm — Phone — Fax 424-3993

Name	Rank	Phone			Deg		School	Year
Decker, C. Richard	Prof	424-6382	3	I	EDD	68	Indiana	1974
Williams, William Lee	Prof	424-6289	7	ZU	EDD		Illin St	
Dahl, James G.	Asst	424-6232	2	EG	MS		St Louis	

Millsaps College

Jackson, MS 39210-0001 (601) OKRA.MILLSAPS.EDU 1990,1990
1701 North State Street FAX=974-1260 BBA,MBA

Name		Phone					Degree	Yr	School	Year
Else School of Mgt										
Parker, Hugh J.	Dean	974-1250			Atg	PHD	82	Okla St	1987
—Management Faculty	Phone	974-1250	Fax 974-1260						
Brooking, Carl G.	Prof	974-1261		7	V	PHD	74	Penn	1981
Hailey, William A.	Prof	974-1262		79	UVZ	DBA	78	Kentucky	1987
Whitt, Jerry D.	Prof	974-1250		84	YL	PHD	73	Arkansas	1980
Grubbs, M. Ray	Assoc	974-1265		35	IN	PHD	87	Miss	1986
Aggarwal, Ajay	Asst	974-1270		79	UVZ	PHD	91	Va Tech	1989

University of Minnesota

Minneapolis, MN 55455-0413 (612) CSOM.UMN.EDU 1920,1963
271 19th Avenue South FAX=624-2873 BS,MBA,MBT,PHD

Name		Phone					Degree	Yr	School	Year
Carlson School of Mgt										
Kidwell, David	Dean	625-0027			Fnce	PHD	75	Oregon	1991
—Dept Strategic Mgt & Org	Phone	624-5232	Fax 625-2873						
Bowie, Norman E.	C-Pr	626-7430	nbowie	4	JKLM	PHD	68	Rochest	1989
Cummings, Larry L.	Prof	624-3582	lcummings	2	EH	DBA	64	Indiana	1984
Erickson, W. Bruce	Prof	624-4531	werickson	4	LS	PHD	65	Mich St	1966
Galaskiewicz, Joseph	Prof	624-7548	jgalaskiewic	2	H	PHD	76	Chicago	1976
Marcus, Alfred A.	Prof	624-2812	amarcus	4	IJ	PHD	77	Harvard	1984
VanDeVen, Andrew H.	Prof	624-1864	avandeven	2	DH	PHD	72	Wiscon	1983
Willis, Raymond E.	Prof	624-2303	rwillis	3	BDI	PHD	61	MIT	1959
Albert, Stuart	Assoc	624-5739	salbert	2	EFG	PHD	68	Ohio St	1982
Balakrishnan, S. (Cheenu)	Assoc	624-0575	cbalakrishna	3	I	PHD	83	Michigan	1989
Bromiley, Philip	Assoc	624-5746	pbromiley	3	I	PHD	81	Car Mel	1985
Chakravarthy, Balaji S.	Assoc	624-5232	bchakravarth	3	I	DBA	78	Harvard	1986
Lenway, Stephanie A.	Assoc	624-1343	slenway	4	LY	PHD	82	Berkeley	1984
Maitland, Ian H.	Assoc	624-2091	imaitland	4	LJ	PHD	79	Columbia	1979
Mauriel, John J.	Assoc	624-5845	jmauriel	3	ADP	DBA	64	Harvard	1965
Murtha, Thomas	Assoc	624-5232		3	LY	PHD	89	NYU	1994
Nichols, Mary L.	Assoc	625-2583	mnichols	2	EF	PHD	74	Kansas	1981
Bruderer, Erhard	Asst	625-0583	ebruderer	3	I	PHD	93	Michigan	1993
Liang, Diane Wei	Asst	624-5232		2	EH	PHD	94	Car Mel	1994
Shah, Pri P.	Asst	624-5232		2	E	PHD	94	Northwes	1994
Sutcliffe, Kathleen	Asst	625-3548	ksutcliffe	2	EH	PHD	91	Texas	1991
Zaheer, Akbar	Asst	626-8389	azaheer	3	I	PHD	91	MIT	1991
Zaheer, Srilata	Asst	624-5590	szaheer	4	IM	PHD	91	MIT	1991
—Industrial Relations Center	Phone	624-2500	Fax 624-8360						
Bognanno, Mario F.	D-Pr	624-1090	mbognanno	5	Q	PHD	69	Iowa	
Ahlburg, Dennis	Prof	624-0260	dahlburg	57	QV	PHD	79	Penn	
Arvey, Richard	Prof	624-1063	rarvey	5	NP	PHD	70	Minn	
Avner, Ben-Ner	Prof	624-0867	abenner	2	EHF	PHY	81	SUNY-SBr	
Fossum, John A.	Prof	624-2500	jfossum	5	N	PHD	75	Mich St	
Sackett, Paul	Prof	624-9842	psackett	5	NP	PHD	79	Ohio St	
Scoville, James	Prof	624-1579	jscoville	5	Q	PHD	65	Harvard	
Zaidi, Mahmood	Prof	625-0578	mzaidi	5	Q	PHD	65	Berkeley	
Azevedo, Ross	Assoc	624-1098	razevedo	5	QN	PHD		Cornell	
Keane, Michael	Assoc	624-0840	mkeane	57	QV	PHD	90	Brown	
Noe, Raymond	Assoc	624-0233	rnoe	57	PN	PHD	85	Mich St	
Ostross, Cheri	Assoc	624-4804	costroff	5	NP	PHD	87	Mich St	
Budd, John	Asst	624-0357	jbudd	57	Q	PHD	91	Princeton	
McCall, Brian	Asst	624-4804	bmccall	57	QV	PHD	88	Princeton	
McLean Parks, Judi	Asst	624-9013	jparks	2	EFHN	PHD	90	Iowa	
Wang, Yijiang	Asst	624-6814	ywang	2	HE	PHD	91	Harvard	

U of Minnesota - Duluth

Duluth, MN 55812-2496 (218) UMDDUL
10 University Drive FAX=726-6388 BA,BAC,MBA

Name		Phone					Degree	Yr	School	Year
School of Bus & Econ										
Duff, Thomas B.	Dean	726-8759	tduffua.	9	Z	PHD	76	Minn	1974
—Dept of Management Studies	Phone		Fax 726-6388						
Pierce, Jon L.	H-Pr	726-7929		12	EFH	PHD	77	Wiscon	1968
Boyer, John W. Jr.	Prof	726-7254		5	NQ	PHD	70	Minn	1970
Castleberry, Stephen B.	Prof					PHD	83	Alabama	1993
Grehu, Joyce	Prof					PHD	79	Minn	
Newstrom, John W.	Prof	726-8762		15	FNP	PHD	71	Minn	1967
Rubenfeld, Stephen A.	Prof	726-6107		5	NOPQ	PHD	77	Wiscon	1973
Kindsers, Kjell R.	Assoc					PHD	73	Minn	1980
Parry, Linda	Asst	726-8988		24	HIRL	PHD	90	SUNY-Alb	1983
Rockford, Linda	Asst					PHD	89	Minn	1993
Vaidyanathers, Rajiv	Asst					PHD	93	Wash St	1993
Warton, Robert	Asst	726-8553		23	DHIY	PHD	88	Rutgers	1979

Minot State University

Minot, ND 58702-5002 (701) FAX=857-3111 BA,BS
Business Administration
Did Not Respond-1993 Listing

Name		Phone					Degree	Yr	School	Year
Robinson, Earl J.	Dean	857-3110				PHD	77	Georgia	1991
—Department of Management	Phone		Fax 857-3111						
Witwer, Keith L.	C-As	857-3313				MBA		Michigan	1982
Darrow, Orien	Asst	857-3866				PHD		Denver	1987

Ross, Gary	Asst	857-3219			MBA	N Dakota	1984
Lower, Robert	Inst	857-3825			MA	Cen Mich	1986
Herreid, Todd J.		857-3124					
Walizer, Ottis		857-3295					

Mississippi College — Clinton, MS — 39058 — (601) — BS
School of Business Adm — 200 South Capital Street — FAX=925-3804
Did Not Respond-1993 Listing

Lee, Gerald D.	Dean	925-3220			Econ	PHD	73	Miss	
–Management Faculty	Phone		Fax 925-3804						
Roberts, Lloyd	Prof	925-3419				PHD	74	Miss	1983

University of Mississippi — University, MS — 38677 — (601) UMSVM — 1944,1972
School of Business Adm — — — FAX=232-7010 — BBA,MBA,PHD

Boxx, Randy	Dean	232-5820		12	IM	PHD	71	Arkansas	1971
–Dept of Management & Mktg	Phone	232-7102	Fax 232-5821						
Paolillo, Joseph G. P.	C-Pr	232-7493	mgjoseph	3	HI	PHD	77	Oregon	1986
Terpstra, David E.	Prof	232-5827		5	NP	PHD	78	Tenn	1990
Wiebe, Frank A.	Assoc	232-5471		26	ET	PHD	75	Kansas	1978
Canty, Ann L.	Asst	232-5498		2	RS	PHD	85	Miss	1990
Gardner, William L.	Asst	232-7555		12	EP	PHD	84	Fla St	1989
Gillenwater, Edward L.	Asst	232-5829		7	UV	PHD	88	Kentucky	1989
McKenney, William A.	Asst	232-5839		7	UV	PHD	87	Tenn	1990
Robinson, Robert K.	Asst	232-7635		35	NQ	PHD	88	North Tx	1990
Seydel, John F.	Asst	232-5466		7	UV	PHD	90	Tx A&M	1990

Mississippi State Univ — Miss St, MS — 39762 C004 — (601) MSSTATE — 1960,1964
College of Bus & Indus — — — FAX=325-2410 — BBA,MBA,MSBADBA

Lewis, Harvey S.	Dean	325-2580			Fnce	PHD	66	Arkansas	
–Dept of Mgt & Info Systems	Phone	325-3928	Fax 325-8651						
Smith, Garry D.	C-Pr	325-3928		3	I	DBA	76	La Tech	1980
Cochran, Daniel S.	Prof	325-3928		12	EG	PHD	78	Arkansas	1980
Litecky, Charles R.	Prof	325-3928		9	XZ	PHD	74	Minnesot	1991
Newsom, Walter Burton	Prof	325-3928		7		PHD	74	Missouri	1974
Shim, Jung P.	Prof	325-3928		79	VXZ	PHD	83	Nebraska	1983
Arnett, Kirk P.	Assoc	325-3928		9	XZ	DBA	84	Miss St	1985
Banks, McRae C.	Assoc	325-3928		12	IST	PHD	87	Va Tech	1987
Giallourakis, Michael	Assoc	325-3928		1	&Y	PHD	75	Indiana	1982
Lehman, Carol	Assoc	325-3928		1	&	EDD	84	Arkansas	1984
Pearson, Rodney	Assoc	325-3928		9	Z	DBA	84	Harvard	1987
Spencer, Barbara A.	Assoc	325-3928		23	HIR	PHD	85	Va Tech	1987
Taylor, Stephen	Assoc	325-3928		5	NP	PHD	85	Va Tech	1987
Amason, Allen C.	Asst	325-3928		5	N	PHD	93	S Carol	1993
Harrison, Allison W.	Asst	325-3928		5	N	PHD	93	Clemson	1993
Hochwarter, Wayne	Asst	325-3928		5	N	PHD	93	Fla St	1-94
Jones, Mary C.	Asst	325-3928		6	UVX	PHD	90	Oklahoma	1990

Mississippi Valley St Univ — Itta Bena, MS — 38941 — (601)
Business Adm Department — — — FAX=
phone 254-9041

Williams, Cliff F.	C-Pr	254-9041			BEd	EDD		Houston	1960
–Management Faculty	Phone	Ext 6562							
Kim, Juho	Prof	Ext 6567				PHD		Oklahoma	1973
Chowdhury, Farhad	Asst	Ext 6570				PHD		Miss St	1993
Warner, Ricky	Inst	Ext 6572				MBA		Atlanta	1988

U of Missouri at Columbia — Columbia, MO — 65211 — (314) BPA.MISSOURI.EDU — 1926,1964
College Bus & Pub Adm — — — FAX=882-0365 — BSBA,MBA,PHD

Walker, Bruce J.	Dean	882-6688			Mktg	DBA	71	Colorado	
–Department of Management	Phone	882-7374	Fax 882-0365						
Jago, Arthur G.	C-Pr	882-7374	jago	2	E	PHD	77	Yale	1994
Adam, Everett E. Jr.	Prof	882-4271	adam	7	U	DBA	70	Indiana	1971
Cecil, Earl	Prof	882-2773	cecil	5	N	PHD	67	W Virg	1967
Dougherty, Thomas W.	Prof	882-4412	dougherty	25	EN	PHD	81	Houston	1979
Ebert, Ronald J.	Prof	882-4533	ebert	7	U	DBA	69	Indiana	1974
Franz, Lori S.	Prof	882-8372	franzl	7	V	PHD	80	Nebraska	1985
Associate Dean									
Slusher, E. Allen	Prof	882-7472	slusher	29	HZ	PHD	73	Iowa	1975
Wall, James A. Jr.	Prof	882-4561	wall	2	E	PHD	72	N Carol	1978
Bluedorn, Allen C.	Assoc	882-3089	bluedorn	2	E	PHD	76	Iowa	1981
Franz, Charles	Assoc	882-7637	franzc	9	Z	PHD	79	Nebraska	1985
Penfield, Robert	Assoc	882-4562	penfield	5	Q	PHD	66	Cornell	1972
Associate Dean									
Greening, Daniel W.	Asst	882-1932	greening	3	I	PHD	91	Penn St	1991
Johnson, Richard A.	Asst	882-1933	johnson	3	I	PHD	92	Tx A&M	1991
Macy, Granger	Asst	882-5470	macy	3	I	PHD	91	Indiana	1990
Turban, Daniel B.	Asst	882-0305	turban	52	NE	PHD	89	Houston	1989

U Missouri--Kansas City

Bloch School of Bus — Kansas City, MO 64110-2499 — (816) — 1969,1971

FAX=235-2312 — BS,MS

Name	Rank	Phone				Deg		School	Year
Eddy, William B.	Dean	235-2204		2	E	PHD	65	Mich St	1965
—Department of Management	Phone	235-2201	Fax 235-2312						
Bolman, Lee	Prof	235-2201		2	HJ	PHD		Yale	1994
Elison, Nolen	Prof	235-2201		1	AD	PHD	71	Mich St	1992
Heimovics, Richard D.	Prof	235-2201		2	E	PHD		Kansas	1973
Herman, Robert D.	Prof	235-2201		2	E	PHD		Cornell	1972
Jesaitis, Patrick	Prof	235-2201		2	E	DBA	69	Harvard	1968
Johnson, Karl	Prof	235-2201		1	AD	PHD	70	Oregon	1972
Robertson, Leon	Prof	235-2201		3	I	PHD	68	Geo St	1990
Sarachek, Bernard	Prof	235-2201		8	Y	PHD	62	Illinois	1970
Singer, Joe	Prof	235-2201		6	ST	PHD	71	Arkansas	1975
Smilor, Raymond W.	Prof	235-2201		6	ST	PHD	78	Texas	1992
Ashley, David Warren	Assoc	235-2201		7	V	PHD		Cinn	1974
Cain, Rita	Assoc	235-2201		4	JK	JD	83	Kansas	1987
Crossland, Philip	Assoc	235-2201		3	I	PHD	87	Nebraska	1988
Delurgio, Stephen A.	Assoc	235-2201		7	U	PHD		St Louis	1976
Peroff, Nicholas	Assoc	235-2201		1	AD	PHD	77	Wiscon	1974
Picle, Roger	Assoc	235-2201		9	Z	PHD		Purdue	1994
Roy, Prober	Assoc	235-2201		7	V	PHD		Cinn	1983
Williams, Art	Assoc	235-2201		1	AC	PHD	81	Cornell	1989
Booth, Francis Dean	Asst	235-2201		7	U	PHD		Okla St	1987
Day, Nancy	Asst	235-2201		5	NQ	PHD	87	Kansas	1990

U Missouri--St. Louis

School of Business Adm — St. Louis, MO 63121-4499 — (314) UMSLVMA — 1970,1973

FAX=553-5268 — BS,MBA,MAC

Name	Rank	Phone				Deg		School	Year
Nauss, Robert M.	Dean	553-5886				PHD		UCLA	
—Management Area	Phone		Fax 553-5268						
Breaugh, James A.	C-Ac	553-6287		5	N	PHD	77	Ohio St	1977
Thumin, Frederick J.	Prof	553-6286		25	EN	PHD	66	Wash U	1966
Dossett, Dennis L.	Assoc	553-6277	c1960	25	EN	PHD	78	U Wash	1982
Harris, Michael M.	Assoc	553-6280		5	N	PHD	84	Ill-Chic	1988
Kuehl, Charles R.	Assoc	553-6289	scrkueh	36	IS	PHD	71	Iowa	1971
Warlick, Steven	Assoc	553-6297	sswarti	34		PHD	79	U Wash	1990
Johnson, Julius	Asst	553-5309		34		PHD	91	Geo Wash	1991
Maher, Karen	Asst	553-6374	skmaher	25	EN	PHD	91	Akron	1991

Missouri Southern St Col

School of Business — Joplin, MO 64801-1595 — (417)

FAX=625-3121 — BSBA

Name	Rank	Phone				Deg		School	Year
Gray, James M.	Dean	625-9601				MBA	69	Arkansas	1969
—Dept of Management & Mktg	Phone		Fax 625-3121						
Johnson, Bernard A.	Assoc	625-9339				MBA	72	C Mo St	1974
Rozell, Elizabeth	Asst					PHD	93	Miss	1992
Stevens, William R.	Asst	625-9518				PHD	85	Arkansas	1988
Vernon, Alex	Asst					MBA	88	Miss	

Missouri Western St College

Div of Professional Std — Saint Joseph, MO 64507-2294 — (816) ACAD.MWSC.EDU

FAX= — BSBA

Name	Rank	Phone				Deg		School	Year
Perkins, Charles A.	Dean	271-4338	perkins		UW	PHD		Geo Wash	1991
—Management Faculty	Phone	271-4338							
Lawson, Larry	C-Ac	271-4338	lawson		Fnce	PHD		Colorado	
Dick, Richard J.	Asst	271-4459	dick		NW	MA		N Colo	1985
Jenner, Paul F.	Asst	271-4278	jenner		SY	MA		Drury	1986
Krueger, Dale	Asst	271-4459	krueger		EFH	PHD		Mo-KC	1984
Pritchett, Jeannette	Asst	271-4338	pritche		V	MA		Mo-KC	1991
Wang, JinChang	Asst	271-4347	wang		ZUV	PHD		Ga Tech	1990

Monmouth College

School of Business Adm — W Lg Branch NJ 07764 — (201)

FAX=571-3523 — BS

Name	Rank	Phone				Deg		School	Year
Dempsey, William A.	Dean	571-3423				DBA	73	Maryland	1-89
—Management Department	Phone		Fax 571-3523						
Nersesian, Roy L.	C-Ac	571-3654		7	UV	MBA	71	Harvard	9-85
Oakes, Guy	Prof	571-3651		4	JE	PHD	68	Cornell	9-68
Mosca, Joseph	Assoc	571-3495		13	DFNI	DED	83	NYU	9-87
Simko, Gene	Assoc	571-3646		3	I	PHD	91	CUNY	9-79
Bays, Marianne	Asst			93	FZ	PHD	93	CUNY	8-92
Bierly, Paul	Asst			3	I	PHD	94	Rutgers	9-94
Boronico, Jess	Asst	571-3434		7	V	PHD	92	Penn	9-93
Kuei, Chu-Hua	Asst	571-4961		79	UZ	PHD	90	CUNY	9-90
Mahmoud, Watad	Asst			9	Z	PHD	91	NYU	9-94

University of Montana

Missoula, MT 59812-1216 (406) FAX=243-2086 — 1949,1982
School of Business Adm — BS,MBA,MACCT

Name	Rank	Phone						
Gianchetta, Larry D.	Dean	243-4831	7	V	PHD	75	Tx A&M	1969
—Department of Management	Phone	243-2273	Fax 243-2086					
Evans, Gerald	C-Ac	243-2273	97	ZVXS	PHD	85	Clairmon	1988
Andreason, Aaron	Prof	243-4473	18		PHD	75	Brig Yg	1975
Campbell, Mary Ellen	Prof	243-6790	48	CDZ	MA	69	Illinois	1973
Cleveland, Gary	Prof	243-5954	37	IUX	PHD	86	Minn	1985
Connole, Robert	Prof	243-2069	3	DI	PHD	68	Iowa	1969
Dailey, Richard T.	Prof	243-6644	46	IJSY	PHD	68	Penn St	1981
Fleming, Maureen J.	Prof	243-6681	25	YEFN	PHD	69	S Illin	1971
Hollmann, Robert W.	Prof	243-4663	51	NP	PHD	73	U Wash	1980
Kirkpatrick, Thomas	Prof	243-2273	13	INSX	PHD	67	Ohio St	1967
Morton, Jack	Prof	243-6717	4	K	JD	71	Montana	1971
Polzin, Paul	Prof	243-5113	7	V	PHD	68	Mich St	1968
Shooshtari, Nader	Prof	243-2728			PHD	83	Ariz St	1991
Steele, Thomas	Prof	243-2415			PHD	74	Penn St	1987
Tangedahl, Lee	Prof	243-6687	79	V	PHD	76	Colorado	1976
Withycombe, Richard	Prof	243-4983	7	UV	PHD	72	Oregon	1972
Furniss, Jerry	Assoc	243-2062	5	KP	JD	80	Idaho	1987
Keegan, Charles	Assoc	243-5113						
Johnson, Bradley	Asst	243-5880			PHD	89	St Louis	1992
Larson, Paul	Asst	243-6840	36	ISTD	PHD	84	Utah	1985
Smith, C. A. P.	Asst	243-2098	9	Z	PHD	90	Arizona	1990
Swanson, Larry	Asst	243-5113	37	LVMX	PHD	80	Nebraska	1988

Montana State University

Bozeman, MT 59717-0306 (406) MSU:: FAX=994-6206 — 1981
College of Business — BS

Name	Rank	Phone	Email					
Owen, Mike	Dean	994-4423			MS	63	MIT	9-89
—Management Faculty	Phone		Fax 994-6206					
Lee, James B.	Prof	994-1776	gemini::ibmj	3	PHD	74	Arizona	9-87
Vinton, Karen	Prof	994-6187	zdb7004	26	PHD	83	Utah	1-83
Muhs, Bill	Assoc	994-6199		3	PHD	76	Tx Tech	9-82
Swinth, Robert L.	Assoc	994-6191	msu::ubmrs	4	PHD	64	Stanford	9-79
Benham, Harry	Asst	994-6196	zdb7008	9	PHD	78	Berkeley	9-90
Dodd, Nancy	Asst	994-6195	ubmnd	56	PHD	87	Nebraska	9-89
McClelland, Douglas	Asst	994-6198		4	JD	71	Berkeley	9-78
Raymond, Bruce	Asst	994-4322	ibmbr	7	PHD	87	Utah	8-90
Taylor, Shannon	Asst	994-6197	zdb7007	92	PHD	76	Colorado	9-79
Crawford, Pam	Adj	994-2093		12	MSHR	86	Gold Gt	9-88
Kyle, William Jr.	Adj	994-4692		48	MSSC	91	Maccau	9-89
Reichman, Deborah	Adj	994-6203		4	JD	83	Texas	9-88

Montana State Univ-Billings

Billings, MT 59101-0298 (406) FAX=657-2051 — BSBA
School Business & Econ — 1500 North 30th Street

Name	Rank	Phone						
Kerby, Joe Kent	Dean	657-2295		Mktg	PHD	66	Columbia	1993
—Dept Management & Econ	Phone	657-2812	Fax 657-2051					
Graham, Reg	C-Pr	657-1610		Mktg	PHD	70	Case Wes	1991
Harris, R. Scott	Assoc	657-1653		Econ	PHD	85	Calif	1988
Hinthorne, Thomas D.	Assoc	657-2099	3		PHD	72	Oregon	1993
Mendenhall, J. Stanley	Assoc	657-2907	63		PHD	75	Wiscon	1986
Lynch, Dan	Asst	657-2035	1		MPA	77	Boulder	1989
McNally, Mary	Asst	657-1650	12		PHD	91	Chicago	1987
Metheny, William	Asst	657-1609	75		PHD	90	North Tx	1990
Holman, Pat	Inst	657-2914	1		MS	82	Utah	1992

Montclair State College

U Montclair, NJ 07043 (201) FAX=
School of Business

Name	Rank	Phone						
—Department of Management	Phone		Fax 655-5312					
Min, Byung K.	C-Ac	655-7465	59	EHNZ	PHD		Penn St	1973
Turner, John H.	Prof	655-4281	2	EFH	PHD	72	CUNY	1972
Bewayo, Edward D.	Assoc	655-7419	16	ANST	DPA		SUNY-Alb	1981
Jayaraman, L.	Assoc	655-7288	37	ILUV	PHD			1988
Kaplan, Eileen	Assoc	655-7469	25	NOPR	PHD		Rutgers	1981
Rodrigues, Carl A.	Assoc	655-7455	18	EHY	DPA		Nova	1982
Zey, M.	Asst	655-4425	15	ENOP	PHD			1990
—Dept of Info & Decision Sci	Phone		Fax 655-5312					
Blumberg, Harvey	Prof	655-7515			PHD		CUNY	1978
Chen, Chuan Yu	Prof	655-4253			PHD		NYU	1971
Oppenheim, Alan J.	Prof	655-4284			PHD	74	NYU	1973
Sora, S.	Assoc	655-7521					Pace	1992
Kumar, L.	Asst	655-7518					Va Tech	1988
Shim, Sung J.	Asst	655-7470		RPI	ABD		Renssela	1993
Wang, J.	Asst	655-7519					Temple	1992

University of Montevallo — Montevallo, AL 35115-6540 (205) 1987
College of Business FAX=665-6003 BBA

Name	Rank	Phone						
Word, William R.	Dean	665-6540		Econ	PHD	70	Tenn	1979
–Management Faculty	Phone		Fax 665-6560					
Forbes, Jessie L.	Assoc	665-6533	2		MBE		Monteval	1981
Hamilton, Harold C.	Assoc	665-6543	3		DBA		La Tech	1981
Mikan, Kurt W.	Assoc	665-6543	6		PHD		Alabama	1980
Bartolich, Eugene	Asst	665-6532	7		PHD		Va Comm	1988
McMinn, Nathan E.	Asst	665-6537	9		MBA		W Carol	1978

Moorhead State University — Moorhead, MN 56560 (218) MHD1.MOORHEAD.MSUS.EDU
Did Not Respond-1993 Listing

Name	Rank	Phone						
Bus, Ind & Applied Prog		1104 11th Avenue South		FAX=				BS,MBA
Crockett, David J.	Dean	236-2076		Fnce	PHD		Iowa	1993
–Business Adm Department	Phone		Fax 236-2168					
Geib, Peter	Prof	236-4657	83	YI	PHD		Michigan	1982
Hoops, Linda	Prof	236-4654	1		PHD		SUNY-Buf	1980
Swenson, James K.	Prof	236-4663	2	EH	PHD	71	N Dakota	1972
Moore, Molly	Assoc	236-4648	9	Z	PHD		N Dakota	1975
Pearce, Thomas	Assoc	236-4660	25	NEQ	PHD		U Wash	1988
Roy, Sam	Assoc	236-4647	97	VZ	MBA		LSU	1978
Walker, James	Assoc	236-4658	63	IS	PHD		North Tx	1989
Wilson, Carol	Assoc	236-4653	1		PHD		Missouri	1988
Peschke, Richard	Asst			7	UV	PHD	Houston	1993

Morehead State University — Morehead, KY 40351-1689 (606) MOREKYVM
Sch of Business & Econ 214 University Boulevard FAX=783-5025 BBA,MBA

Name	Rank	Phone						
McCormick, Beverly	Dean	783-5156	4	JL	JD	85	Louisvil	1985
–Dept of Management & Mktg	Phone	783-2174	Fax 783-5025					
Harford, Michael	Prof	783-2756	54	JL	JD	88	Wake For	1983
Carlson, Rodger	Prof	783-2543	7	U	PHD	83	Claremont	1983
Meadows, Robert	Assoc	783-2475	72	EP	PHD	82	Kent St	1982
Brown, Sheryl	Asst	783-2723			PHD	93	Kentucky	1992
Grier, Wilson C.	Asst	783-2752	65	RXIQ	MBA	83	Kentucky	1983
Caudill, C. Dale	Inst	783-2912	15	C	MBA	80	Morehead	1983
Ferguson, Janet	Inst	783-2390			MBA	92	Morehead	1992
–Dept of Information Sciences	Phone	783-2163	Fax 783-5025					
Albin, Marvin	C	783-2730	9	Z				
Berry, Herbert	Prof	783-2749	9	Z				
Hicks, Charles	Prof	783-2744	9	Z				
Aminilari, Mansoor	Assoc	783-2770	9	Z				
Tesch, Robert	Assoc	783-2747	9	Z				
Tesch, Deborah	Asst	783-2745	9	Z				
Bailey, Bonnie	Inst	783-2742	9	Z				

Morehouse College — Atlanta, GA 30314 (404)
Dept of Econ & Bus Adm 830 Westview Drive SW FAX=681-2650 BA

Name	Rank	Phone						
Sheftall, Willis B. Jr.	C	215-2618		Econ	PHD		Geo St	1986
Charles E. Merrill Professor of Economics								
–Management Faculty	Phone	215-2618	Fax 681-2650					
Williams, Anderson	Prof				PHD		Geo St	1982
Sillah, Marion	Assoc				PHD		S Carol	1987
Carr, T. Franklin	Asst				MBA		NYU	1983
Dadzie, Evelyn	Asst				MBA			
Goldin, Elizabeth C.	Asst				MA		Boston C	1983

Morgan State University — Baltimore, MD 21239 (410)
School of Bus & Mgt Cold Spring Lane & Hillen Rd FAX= BS
Did Not Respond-1993 Listing

Name	Rank	Phone						
Thomas, Otis A.	Dean	319-3160		QMth	PHD	71	American	1972
–Department of Business Adm	Phone		Fax 319-3358					
Boghossian, Fikru H.	C-Pr	319-3434			PHD	79	Arkansas	
Alford, Howard	Prof	319-3439			PHD		Stanford	
Adams, Marjorie	Asst	319-3439			PHD			
Edlund, Timothy W.	Asst	319-3641	twe	63	ILS	DBA		Boston U	
Gatewood, Wallace C.	Asst	319-3434			PHD	75	Illinois	
Sealy, Hyacinth	Lect	319-3608						

Morris Brown College — Atlanta, GA 30314 (404)
Business Administration 643 Martin Luther King Jr Dr FAX=688-5985 BS

Name	Rank	Phone						
Heyliger, Wilton	C	220-0233			PHD	81	Indiana	
–Management Faculty	Phone	220-0233	Fax 220-3794					
Das, Krishna K.	Prof				DCS	56	Harvard	
Paisley, Clyde A.	Assoc				MBA	69	Calif St	1981
Butts, Hector	Asst	220-0157			MA	84	E Anglia	1992
Jacobson, Jeffrey	Asst	220-2040			MTX	84	Geo St	1992
Sharma, Sat Pal	Asst				MBA	67	Atlanta	1968
Johnson, Guy	Inst	220-0238			MTX		CAU	1992
Strickland, Ben	Inst	220-0241			MBA	76	CAU	1992

Mount St. Mary's College Los Angeles, CA 90049-1599 (310)
Management 12001 Chalon Road FAX=
Geranios, John W. C 471-9517 PHD S Calif
—Management Faculty Phone 471-9517 Fax 440-3268
Leese, David Prof PHD Brandeis
Whitman, Katherine Assoc MA UCLA
Alhanati, Mark S. Asst MBA LoyolaMr
Hamington, Maurice Asst PHD S Calif
Malone, Elizabeth Anne Asst MA UCLA
Antoniou, Peter Lect PHD US Intl
Colivas, Kynthia Lect JD Santa Cl
Klugman, Ellen Lect JD UCLA
Paz, Armando Lect PHD US Intrl
Randolph, Janice Lect MBA Florida
Vessal, Ahmad Lect PHD Clark

Muhlenberg College Allentown, PA 18104-5586 (610)
Dept of Business & Atg 2400 Chew Street FAX=
Frary, Paul E. H-Pr 821-3478 15 PHD Arkansas 9-90
—Management Faculty Phone
Miller, Holmes 821-3279 79 PHD Northwes 9-91
Norling, Fred 821-3292 12 PHD Yale 9-88

Murray State University Murray, KY 42071-3304 (502) 1976,1981
Coll Bus & Public Affrs FAX=762-3482 BS,MBA
Thompson, John A. Dean 762-4181 Atg PHD 74 Arkansas 1987
—Dept of Management & Mktg Phone 762-6196
Brockway, Gary R. C-Pr 762 6190 Mktg PHD Arkansas 1976
Clement, Ronald W. Prof 762-6570 25 EFHP PHD 78 Mich St 1982
Schoenteldt, Roger Prof 762-6208 37 BIUY PHD 73 Arkansas 1968
Barton, R. B. Assoc 762-6200 68 IMST PHD 68 Arkansas 1968
Jeanquart, Sandy Ann Asst 762-6203 25 ENOQ DBA 91 S Illin 1991
Lanier, Michael T. Asst 762-6207 37 DIUW DBA 91 S Illin 1990
McNeely, Bonnie Asst 762-3009 25 DEGR PHD 91 S Carol 1987

Naval Postgraduate School Monterey, CA 93943-5104 (408) NAVPGS
Systems Management Dept FAX=646-3407 MS
* Members of Defense Resources Management Institute
Whippple, David R. C-Pr 656-2161 7 D PHD 71 Kansas 8-71
—Management Faculty Phone 656-2161 Fax 656-3407
Blandin, James S. * Prof 656-2306 23 AQHI PHD 71 Oregon 6-74
Dawson, John E. * Prof 656-2349 13 ABI PHD 71 Syracuse 1966
Evered, Roger D. Prof 656-2646 32 IFHD PHD 73 UCLA 1970
Frederikson, Peter C. * Prof 656-2661 78 VY PHD 74 Wash St 1974
Harris, Reuben T. Prof 656-2471 23 FHIY PHD 75 Stanford 7-78
Jones, Lawrence R. Prof 656-2482 34 AIL PHD 77 Berkeley 9-87
McCaffery, Jerry L. Prof 656-2554 4013p 13 ADIJ PHD 72 Wiscon 8084
McMasters, Alan W. Prof 656-2678 0935p 7 VU PHD 66 Berkeley 9-65
Morris, James H. * Prof 656-2992 2 EFH PHD 76 Oregon 1982
Schneidewind, Norman F. Prof 656-2719 0442p 9 ZV DBA 66 S Calif 3-71
Thomas, Kenneth W. Prof 656-2776 12 EG PHD 71 Purdue 1-87
VonPagenhart, Robert * Prof 656-2320 38 AIYF PHD 71 Stanford 7-67
Wall, Kent D. * Prof 656-2158 79 VZ PHD 71 Minn 8-85
Abdel-Hamid, Tek K. Assoc 656-3686 3991p 9 ZV PHD 84 MIT 7-86
Boyton, Robert E. * Assoc 656-2310 25 EFPQ PHD 68 Stanford 1970
Bui, Tung X. Assoc 656-2630 3867p 93 ZV PHD 84 NYU 9-84
Dolk, Daniel R. Assoc 656-2260 0541p 9 ZV PHD 82 Arizona 8-82
Doyle, Richard B. Assoc 656-3302 1 A PHD 84 U Wash 1-90
Eitelberg, Mark J. Assoc 656-3160 15 AN PHD 79 NYU 9-82
Kamel, Magdi N. Assoc 656-2494 5036p 9 Z PHD 88 Penn 8-88
LaCivita, Charles J. * Assoc 656-2445 78 VY PHD 81 Ca-SnBar 1985
Melese, Francois * Assoc 656-2009 78 VY PHD 82 Catholic 6-87
Roberts, Benjamin Assoc 656-2792 25 EFMP PHD 77 Penn St 9-85
Roberts, Nancy C. Assoc 656-2742 32 DFIH PHD 83 Stanford 1-86
Suchan, James Assoc 656-2905 12 DEZ PHD 80 Illinois 1-86
Thomas, Gail Fann Assoc 656-2756 5120p 12 EFHT EDD 86 Ariz St 6-86
Weitzman, Ronald A. Assoc 656-2694 72 EPJ PHD 59 Princeton 9-71
Whitt, Darnell * Assoc 656-2367 13 IY PHD 77 JHopkins 1988
Barrett, Frank Asst 656-2328 21 DFHX PHD 89 Case Wes 8-91
Bhargava, Hemant Asst 656-2264 5186p 79 VZ PHD 90 Penn 1-90
Chermak, Janie M. * Asst 656-2389 7 UV PHD 91 Colorado 1992
Keller, Christopher M. * Asst 656-2457 79 VZ PHD 91 Indiana 1991
Sengupta, Kishore Asst 656-3212 5162p 9 VX PHD 90 Case Wes 9-89
Suh, Myung W. Asst 656-2637 5084p 9 VZU PHD 90 Rochest 1-89
Webb, Natalie J. * Asst 656-2013 7 UV PHD 92 Duke 1992
Zviran, Moshe Asst 656-2489 5046p 9 Z PHD 88 Tel Aviv 8-88
Sessions, Sterling Inst 656-3544
Barrios-Choplin, John R. Adj 656-3121 12 DEFH ABD Texas 7-91

Name	Rank	Phone							
Crawford, Alice M.	Adj	656-2481		25	DEFP	MA	73	S Dgo St	4-88
Haga, William	Adj	656-3094	5080p	92	ZVXH	PHD	72	Illinois	4-88
Hocevar, Susan Page	Adj	656-2249	5292p	12	DEFL	PHD	89	S Calif	9-90
Kang, Keebom	Adj	656-3130	5030p	79	UZV	PHD	84	Purdue	7-88
Keller, John E.	* Adj	656-2376		13	APVE	BA	57	Harvard	9-90

Univ of Nebraska-Lincoln	Lincoln, NE	68588-0491		(402)	UNLVM			1916,1963	
College of Business Adm	14th & R Streets			FAX=472-5855				BS,MBA,MS,PHD	
Schwendiman, Gary	Dean	472-9500			BCom	PHD	71	Brig Yg	1973
—Department of Management	Phone	472-3915	Fax 472-5855						
Lee, Sang M.	C-Pr	472-3915		79	DPUV	PHD	68	Georgia	1975
University Eminent Scholar									
Digman, Lester A.	Prof	472-3364		37	IPV	PHD	70	Iowa	1987
Metropolitan Federal Charter Professor									
Luthans, Fred	Prof	472-2324		28	EGLY	PHD	65	Iowa	1967
George Holmes Professor									
Schniederjans, Marc	Prof	472-6732		7	UVN	PHD	78	St Louis	1982
Torrence, William D.	Emer	472-3915		5	Q	PHD	62	Nebraska	1957
Happold Professor									
Schaubroeck, John	Assoc	472-3179		24	FHJ	PHD	88	Purdue	8-88
Thorp, Cary D.	Assoc	472-3361		5	N	PHD	70	Missouri	9-70
Davis, Sidney M.	Asst	472-3001		9	VXZ	PHD	89	Indiana	8-89
Hall, Phillip D.	Asst	472-3362		38	IY	PHD	88	Nebraska	1987
Kim, Bonn Oh	Asst	472-2317		9	Z	PHD	90	Minn	8-89
May, Douglas	Asst	472-8885		2	E	PHD	92	Illinois	8-89
Meyer, Jennifer	Asst	472-3078		79	V	PHD	89	Stanford	8-88
Sebora, Terrence C.	Asst	472-3368		3	I	PHD	92	N Carol	8-89
Sommer, Steve	Asst	472-2314		2	H	PHD	89	Ca-Irvine	8-89
Swenseth, Scott	Asst	472-3308		7	UVX	PHD	88	Tx A&M	8-87
Anderson, Robin	Lect	472-3353		6	TYS	EDD	84	Nebraska	1987
Cox, Larry	Lect	472-3358		6	ST	MA	90	Nebraska	8-90

Univ of Nebraska at Kearney	Kearney, NE	68849-0518		(308)					
Col of Business & Tech				FAX=234-8669				BS,BA,MBA	
Hadley, Galen	Dean	234-8342			Atg	PHD	75	Nebraska	1991
—Dept of Management & Mktg	Phone	234-8515	Fax 234-8669						
Nemecek, Barbara	C-Ac	234-8515		53	ENO	PHD	87	Minn	1993
Lebsack, Richard	Prof	234-8515		19	DENZ	PHD	76	N Colo	1976
Reno, Sam C.	Prof	234-8050		34	IJL	EDD	72	Nebraska	1967
Theye, Larry D.	Prof	234-8515		25	E	PHD	77	Nebraska	1977
Cooper, James	Assoc	234-8574		6	ST	PHD	81	Michigan	1992
Landstrom, Ronald L.	Assoc	234-8342		24	EFGN	MBA	59	Denver	1958
Assistant Dean									
Nelson, Jon	Assoc	234-8515		13	JI	ABD	67	Nebraska	1967
Ridgley, Jerry	Assoc	234-8515		13	ES	PHD	77	Denver	1984
Schmitz, Ruth	Assoc	234-8347		9	RZ	MS	71	Cen Mo	1972
Carstenson, Larry	Asst	234-8570		34	IK	JD		Nebraska	1991
Hodge, Kay	Asst	234-8515		35	NQI	PHD	88	Nebraska	1984
Konecny, Ron	Asst	234-8366		7	UV	PHD		Nebraska	1988
Sehadri, Srivatsa	Asst	234-8515		87	XYVI	PHD	93	Arkansas	1993
Sluti, Donald	Asst	234-8869		17	UW	PHD	92	N Zealan	1992
Lebsack, Sandra	Lect	234-8515		7	VX	MAC		Mankato	1977
Moffett, Dave	Lect	234-8478		9	Z	MBA		Nebraska	1989
Ridgley, Diane	Lect	234-8622		9	Z	MBA	92	Nebraska	1992
Zimmerman, Ken	Lect	234-8482		12	F	MBA	85	Nebraska	1985

Univ of Nebraska at Omaha	Omaha, NE	68182-0048		(402)	UNOMA1			1965,1981	
College of Business Adm	60th & Dodge Streets			FAX=554-3363				BS,MPA	
Carrell, Michael R.	Dean	554-2599		15	CNPQ	DBA	76	Kentucky	1992
—Department of Management	Phone		Fax 554-3363						
Martin, Thomas	C-Pr	554-3655		12	EFH	PHD	77	Iowa	1989
Mathis, Robert L.	Prof	554-2825				DBA	72	Colorado	1974
Specht, Pam	Prof	554-2599				PHD		Nebraska	
Anstey, John R.	Assoc	554-2534				PHD	74	Arkansas	1969
Ottemann, Robert L.	Assoc	554-2782				PHD	74	Nebraska	1973
Harland, Lynn	Asst	554-2808				PHD	91	Iowa	1989
McGee, Jeff	Asst	554-3156				PHD	92	Georgia	1992
Morris, Rebecca	Asst	554-3542				PHD	88	Nebraska	1983
Oliphant, Rebecca	Asst	554-3158				PHD	94	Fla St	1992
Smart, Dennis	Asst	554-3163				PHD	93	Tx A&M	1993

Nebraska Wesleyan Univ	Lincoln, NE	68504-2796		(402)					
Business Adm & Econ	5000 Saint Paul Avenue			FAX=				BA,BS	
Rudell, LaVerne	C-Pr	465-2201		45		PHD	82	Nebraska	1971
—Management Faculty	Phone	465-2213	Fax 465-2179						
Hruska, James	Asst	465-2207		9		MS	76	Nebraska	1984

Hudson, Thomas	Asst	465-2205	31		PHD	91	Nebraska	1989
Jackman, Thomas	Asst	465-2191	18		MBA	86	DePaul	1991
Spero, Stuart	Asst	465-2200	12		MBA	85	Nebraska	1990

Univ of Nevada, Las Vegas	Las Vegas, NV	89154-6009	(702)	UNSVAX			1991,1991
College of Bus & Econ	4505 Maryland Parkway		FAX=739-3606				BS,MS,MBA
Pohl, Norval F.	Dean	895-3362		QT	PHD	73	Ariz St	1986
—Department of Mangagement	Phone		Fax 895-4370				
Kohl, John	C-Pr	895-3960	45	JLNR	PHD	82	Penn St	1988
Corney, William J.	Prof	895-3195	78	UVYZ	PHD	76	Ariz St	1976
Miller, Alan N.	Prof	895-3814	23	INE	PHD	81	CUNY	1978
Moore, Robert	Prof	895-3365	38	LOY	PHD	77	Claremont	1971
Richman, Eugene	Prof	895-3841	17	DIUY	PHD	50	NYU	1989
Yantis, Betty	Prof	895-3842	34	DI	PHD	72	Arkansas	1975
Brock, Floyd	Assoc	895-3086	79	MUVX	PHD	86	Port St	1987
Erickson, Ranel	Assoc	895-3843	79	IUVZ	PHD	78	Stanford	1980
Hames, David S.	Assoc	895-3675	5	NQ	PHD	85	N Carol	1989
McAllister, Dan	Assoc	895-3211	23	EFIP	PHD	78	U Wash	1982
Newman, William	Assoc	895-3287	39	DTXP	PHD	86	Canterbu	
Richards, Clinton	Assoc	895-3654	23	EJNP	PHD	78	Kansas	1977
Ball, Gail	Asst	895-3873	24	ELJ	PHD	91	Penn St	1990
Gilbert, Joseph	Asst	895-3798	23	HIJ	PHD	91	S Calif	1990
Hicks, Richard	Asst	895-3343	9	Z	PHD	91	Texas	1991
Thomsen, Wayne	Asst	895-3054	9	JPZ	PHD	91	Ariz Ot	1991
Wisner, Joel	Asst	895-3385	7		PHD	91	Ariz Ot	1991
Wendt, Steve	Lect	895-0944	69	TUR	MBA	87	Nev-LV	1985
Flueck, John	Visit				PHD		Chicago	1992
Tilton, Rita	Visit	895-3673	4	GR	PHD	67	Minn	1987

University of Nevada, Reno	Reno, NV	89557-0016	(702)	UNSSUH			1961,1971
Col of Bus Adm Stop 028			FAX=784-1769				BS,MBA
Reed, Michael	Dean	784-4912			PHD	74	Utah	1992
—Dept of Management Sciences	Phone	784-4028	Fax 784-1769				
Stedham, Yvonne	C-As	784-4699	52	NE	PHD	90	Kansas	1988
Larwood, Laurie G.	Prof	784-6962	larwood	23	ERJI	PHD	74	Tulane	1990
Spraggins, H. Barry	Assoc	784-6885	7	UV	PHD	76	Minerto	1987
Winne, Donald W.	Assoc		4	JKL	LLD			
Beekun, Rafik I.	Asst	784-6824	beekun	2	EI	PHD	88	Texas	1989
Doherty, Elizabeth	Asst	784-6425	25	EFNH	PHD	88	U Wash	1990
Rogers, Dale	Asst	784-6814	mickey	7	UM	PHD	90	Michigan	1990
Wright, Thomas	Asst	784-6011	25	EGHN	PHD		Berkeley	1990

University of New Hampshire	Durham, NH	03824-3593	(603)	UNHH			
Whittemore Sch Bus & Ec	15 College Road		FAX=862-4468				BA,MBA
Goodridge, Lyndon E.	Dean	862-1983		Econ	PHD	71	Purdue	1990
—Department of Management	Phone		Fax 862-4468				
Kaufman, Allen	C-Ac	862-4535	3	I	PHD	80	Rutgers	1983
Fink, Stephen L.	Prof	862-3361	2	E	PHD	59	West Res	1968
Boccialetti, Gene	Assoc	862-3346	2	EFQ	PHD	82	Case Wes	1983
Gittell, Ross	Assoc	862-3340	4	J	PHD	89	Harvard	1991
Hall, Francine	Assoc	862-3360	2	EFQ	PHD	75	Toronto	1980
Merenda, Michael	Assoc	862-3352	3	I	PHD	78	Mass	1977
Naumes, Williams	Assoc	862-2618	3	I	PHD	71	Stanford	1989
Weathersby, Rita	Assoc	862-3358	2	EFQ	DED	77	Harvard	1978
Barnett, Carole	Asst		2	E	ABD	94	Michigan	9-94

New Hampshire College	Manchester, NH	03106-1045	(603)			
Undergraduate School	2500 North River Road		FAX=645-9603			BS,MBA,MS
—Business Adm Faculty	Phone 645-9691	Fax 645-9603				
Bradley, Martin	C-In	668-2211	24	E	MED		Notre Dm
Grace, James L. Jr.	Prof	668-2211	48	K	EDD		Penn
Evans, John K.	Assoc	668-2211	15	Q	EDD		Boston C
Losik, Robert	Assoc	668-2211	23	I	EDD		Vanderbt
Bean, William	Asst	668-2211	12	F	ABD		Vanderbt
Nieuwejaar, C. Erik	Asst	668-2211	67	V	MS		Minn

University of New Haven	West Haven, CT	06516-1999	(203)			
School of Business	315 Turnpike Street		FAX=933-2036			BS,MBA,MS,PHD
McLaughlin, Marilou	Dean	932-7115	36	D	PHD		Wisconsi	9-77
—Department of Management	Phone	932-7126	Fax 933-2036			
Nadim, Abbas	C-Pr	932-7122	36	DIT	PHD		Penn
Ellis, Lynn	Prof	932-7105	37		PHD		Pace
Pan, William S. V.	Prof	932-7351	7	VX	PHD		Columbia
Sack, Allen	Prof	932-7090	1	BD	PHD		Penn St

Name	Rank	Phone			Degree		School	
Smith, Warren	Prof	932-7350	7	V	MBA		Northeas	
Bockley, William	Assoc	932-7123	12	EH	PHD		Boston C	
Mensz, Pawel	Assoc	932-7370	7	UV	PHD		Polish A	
Mottola, Louis F.	Assoc	932-7354	79	VZ	PHD	72	N Colo	
Neal, Judith A.	Assoc	932-7370	54	FJR	PHD		Yale	
Nodoushani, Omid	Assoc	932-7126	48	IJY	PHD		Penn	
Gersony, Neal	Asst	932-7094	36	ITY	PHD		Renssel	9-93
Goldberg, Steve	Asst	932-7093	63	STI	PHD		Mass	
Torello, Robert	Asst	932-7354	7	V	MBA		SCSU	

New Jersey Institute of Tech — Newark, NJ 07102 (201)
Sch of Industrial Mgt — 323 Martin Luther King Blvd — FAX=
Did Not Respond-1993 Listing

Name	Rank	Phone			Degree		School	
Chakrabarti, Alok	Dean	592-3256			PHD	72	Northwes	1989

Distinguished Professor and Sponsored Chair
—**Management Faculty** Phone

Name	Rank	Phone			Degree		School	
Bagchi, Amitava	VProf	596-3252	9	Z	SCD	72	MIT	1991
Hawk, David	Prof		82	YE	PHD	79	Penn	1981
Helfgott, Roy	Prof	596-3257	5	N	PHD	68	New Sch	1957
Distinguished Professor								
Kirchhoff, Bruce	Prof	596-5658	3	I	PHD	71	Utah	1992
Lawrence, Kenneth	Prof	596-6425	7	U	EDD	79	Rutgers	1992
Murray, Thomas	Prof	596-8568	9	Z	PHD	73	Mass	1992
Rotter, Naomi	Prof	596-3290	52	NE	PHD	74	NYU	1974
Schachter, Hindy L.	Prof	596-3251	92	ZE	PHD	79	Columbia	1979
Stochaj, John	Prof	596-3255	9	Z	PHD	63	NYU	1963
Subramanian, S. K.	Prof	596-4009	8	Y	PHD	60	Bingham	1993
Distinguished Professor								
Turoff, Murray	Prof	596-3399	9	Z	PHD	65	Brandeis	1973
Goldberg, Henry	Assoc	596-6418	7	U	PHD	76	Cornell	1990
Kahng, Anthony	Assoc	596-3260	5	N	JSD	64	NYU Law	1981
Sylla, Cheickna	Assoc	596-3260	79	UZ	PHD	83	SUNY-Buf	1989
Chang, Tung-Lung	Asst	596-3020	8	Y	PHD	90	Geo Wash	1990
Cordero, Rene	Asst	596-6417	75	UNE	PHD	85	Rutgers	1990
Sen, Anup	VAsst	596-8569	9	Z	PHD	90	Calcutta	1992
Somers, Mark	Asst	596-3279	92	ZE	PHD	87	Cty C NY	1986
Pulhamus, Aaron	Lect	596-3254	5	N	EDD	84	Rutgers	1984
Director, Undergraduate Program								
Worrell, Malcolm	Lect	596-3262	9	Z	MBA	66	Mich St	1990
Director, Graduate Program								

University of New Mexico — Albuquerque, NM 87131-1221 (505) UNM.EDU — 1975,1975
R O Anderson Sch of Mgt — FAX=277-7108 — BBA,MBA,MA

Name	Rank	Phone				Degree		School	
Walters, Kenneth D.	Dean	277-6471			Mgt	PHD	72	Berkeley	1990
—**Human Resources Mgt**	Phone		Fax 277-7108						
Muller, Helen Juliette	C-Pr	277-7133			N	PHD	82	S Calif	
Champoux, Joseph E.	Prof	277-3237			N	PHD	74	Ca-Irvine	1973
Rehder, Robert R.	Prof	277-4631			N	PHD	61	Stanford	
Hood, Jacqueline	Asst	277-7279			N	PHD	89	Colorado	
Miners, Ian	Asst	277-5230			N	PHD	84	Mich St	
—**Policy and Planning**	Phone	277-6471	Fax 277-7108						
Logsdon, Jeanne M.	C-As	277-8352		4	JL	PHD	83	Berkeley	
Coes, Donald V.	Prof	277-8871		8	V	PHD	78	Princeton	
Parkman, Allen M.	Prof	277-5222				PHD	73	UCLA	
Radosevich, Raymond	Prof	277-5928		3	I	PHD	69	Carnegie	
Smith, Howard L.	Prof	277-5710		3	IL	PHD	76	U Wash	
DeGouvea, Raul	Assoc	277-8448		8	Y	PHD	88	Illinois	
Porter, James L.	Assoc	277-3618		4	K	JD	75	Temple	
Young, John E.	Assoc	277-4702		6	T	PHD	80	Kansas	
Banbury, Catherine	Asst	277-0332		3	IT	PHD	94	Michigan	
Thompson, Judith K.	Asst	277-8880		4	JL	PHD	87	Berkeley	
Dry, Eddie	Lect	277-3403				PHD	75	Tx A&M	
—**Operations Mgt & Mgt Inf Sy**	Phone	277-6471	Fax 277-7108						
Burd, Stephen D.	C-Ac	277-6418		9	Z	PHD	83	Purdue	1984
Bullers, William I.	Prof	277-4901		9	Z	PHD	80	Purdue	1980
Kassicieh, Suleiman	Prof	277-8881		9	ZUV	PHD	78	Iowa	1980
Reid, Richard A.	Prof	277-3011		7	UV	PHD	70	Ohio St	1971
Schultz, Carl R.	Prof	277-6250		7	UV	PHD	79	N Carol	1981
Ravinder, H. V.	Assoc	277-5996		7	UV	PHD	86	Texas	1986
Bose, Ranjit	Asst	277-7097		9	Z	PHD	89	Texas	1989
Rattner, Laurie	Asst	277-4961		9	ZU	PHD	90	Renssela	1992
Yourstone, Steven	Asst	277-3248		7	U	PHD	88	U Wash	1987

New Mexico Highlands Univ — Las Vegas, NM 87701-4211 (505)
School of Prof Studies — University Avenue — FAX=454-0026 — BA,MBA

Name	Rank	Phone		Degree		School	
Sanchez, Lorenzo	C-As	454-3522	Fnce	MBA	77	North Tx	1991

-Department of Business   Phone   Fax 454-0026

Name	Rank	Phone						
Feeran, Manuel A.	Assoc	454-3575	36	ISTV	PHD	69	Oklahoma	1993
Kellerman, Marcus E.	Asst	454-3173	19	DUVZ	MBB	68	New Mex	1992
Maestas, Ronald W.		454-3584	24	Z	EDD			1972

New Mexico State Univ   Las Cruces, NM   88003-8001   (505) NMSUVM1   1973,1981
College Bus Adm & Econ   University Avenue   FAX=646-6155   BA,MA,MBA,PHD
Arnold, Danny   Dean 646-2821   DBA 76 La Tech 7-94
-Department of Management   Phone 646-1201   Fax 646-6155

Name	Rank	Phone						
Wieters, C. David	C-Ac$	646-5684	7	UVW	PHD	76	Ariz St	1985
Blum, Albert A.	Prof	646-5162	25	BQY	PHD	53	Columbia	1985
Costley, Dan L.	Prof	646-1303	25	EFPD	PHD	64	Mich St	1972
Dorfman, Peter W.	Prof	646-1294	52	ENY	PHD	72	Maryland	1978

Robert O. Anderson Distinguished Professor

Name	Rank	Phone						
Howell, Jon P.	Prof	646-4900	2	ENY	PHD	73	Ca-Irvine	1978
Loveland, John P.	Prof	646-1201	23	EIJM	PHD	70	Ariz St	1972
Whatley, Arthur A.	Prof	646-4137	58	FNPY	PHD	71	North Tx	1970
Benson, Joseph E.	Assoc	646-5164	35	NQ	PHD	85	Okla St	1981
Benson, Philip G.	Assoc	646-5695	25	NPM	PHD	82	Colo St	1987
Manning, Michael R.	Assoc	646-2532	25	EFN	PHD	79	Purdue	1989
Clark, Marian F.	Asst	646-1001	23	CI	PHD	83	Ariz St	1983
Daily, Bonnie	Asst	646-2105	79	UVZ	PHD	91	Missouri	1991
Jun, Minjoon	Asst	646-4987	37	IUVW	PHD	89	Geo St	1988
Santana-Melgoza, Carmen	Asst	646-1503	24	EIR	PHD	90	Ariz St	1984
Teich, Jeffrey E.	Asst	646-3703	79	VXZ	PHD	91	SUNY-Buf	1990

University of New Orleans   New Orleans, LA   70148   (504) UNO   1969,1975
College of Business Adm   Lake Front   FAX=286-6958   BS,MBA,MS,MS-TX
Ryan, Timothy P.   Dean 286-6241   Econ PHD   Ohio St
Hibernai Professor of Economics
-Department of Management   Phone   Fax 286-6958

Name	Rank	Phone						
Lundberg, Olof H. Jr.	C-Pr	286-6481	32	IH	PHD	71	Penn St	8-71
Baroni, Barry J.	Prof	286-6481	17	LE	LLM	74	Tulane	1-67
Cone, Randolph E.	Prof	286-6481	21		PHD	71	LSU	8-76
Galle, William P. Jr.	Prof	286-6481	21	E	PHD	72	Arkansas	8-85
Hartman, Sandra J.	Prof	286-6481	12	E	PHD	85	LSU	8-81
Lacho, Kenneth J.	Prof	286-6481	27		DBA	69	Wash U	8-64
Mahesh, Sathiadev	Prof	286-6481	79	Z	PHD	84	Purdue	8-84
Nelson, Beverly H.	Prof	286-6481	19	BC	PHD	82	LSU	8-78
Villere, Maurice F.	Prof	286-6481	2	NE	PHD	71	Illinois	8-71
Im, Jin H.	Assoc	286-6481	5	Z	PHD	86	Nebraska	8-86
Koen, Clifford M.	Assoc	286-6481	5		JD	84	Memphis	8-86
Yrle, Augusta C.	Assoc	286-6481	59	BC	EDD	78	New Orl	8-72
Crow, Steve M.	Asst	286-6481	53	NE	PHD	89	North Tx	8-89
Fok, Yee Man L.	Asst	286-6481	2	Z	BSC	86	Hong Kon	8-89
Hammond, Don H.	Asst	286-6481	2	DT	PHD	89	Fla St	8-89
Logan, James W. Jr.	Asst	286-6481	13	I	PHD	90	LSU	8-88
Payne, Dinah M.	Asst	286-6481	5	KJ	JD	87	Loyola	8-88
White, Ellen E.	Asst	286-6481	9		PHD	85	Fla St	6-85
Cheek, Ronald G.	Inst	286-6481	4	M	MBA	90	New Orl	9-89

New York University   New York, NY   10012-1126   (212) STERN.NYU.EDU   1916,1916
Stern School of Bus   44 West 4th Street   FAX=995-4000   BS,MBA,MS,PHD
Daly, George   Dean 998-0222   Econ PHD 67 Northwes 1993
-Dept of Mgt & Org Behavior   Phone 998-0200   Fax 995-4234

Name	Rank	Phone						
Rogers, David	C-Pr	998-0222			PHD	60	Harvard	
Bedrosian, Hrach	Prof	998-0252			PHD	62	Columbia	
Dutton, John M.	Prof	998-0251			MBA	57	Harvard	
Fombrun, Charles	Prof	998-0211			PHD	80	Columbia	
Freedman, Richard D.	Prof	998-0260			PHD	67	NYU	
Gladwin, Thomas N.	Prof	998-0426	8	Y	PHD	75	Michigan	
Guth, William D.	Prof	998-0214	6	T	DBA	60	Harvard	

Harold Price Professor of Mgt; Director Center for Entrepreneurial Studies

Name	Rank	Phone						
Howell, Robert A.	Prof	998-0031			DBA	66	Harvard	
Lamb, Robert	Prof	998-0231			PHD		LondonEc	
Schuler, Randall S.	Prof	998-0245			PHD	73	Mich St	

Research Professor

Name	Rank	Phone						
Shapiro, Zur	Prof	998-0225			PHD	76	Rochest	
Starbuck, William H.	Prof	998-0232			PHD	64	Car Mel	

ITT Professor Of Creative Management; Director of Doctoral Program

Name	Rank	Phone						
Zand, Dale E.	Prof	998-0249			PHD	54	NYU	
Dunbar, Roger	Assoc	998-0246			PHD	70	Cornell	
Ginsberg, Ari	Assoc	998-0233			PHD	85	Pitt	
Milliken, Frances	Assoc	998-0227			PHD	85	CUNY	
Moses, Michael A.	Assoc	998-0290			PHD	67	Northwes	
Baum, Joel	Asst	998-0228			PHD	89	Toronto	
Borucki, Chester	Asst	998-0256			PHD	87	Columbia	

Garud, Raghu	Asst	998-0255				MBA		
King, Andrew	Asst	998-0288				PHD	93	MIT
Kotha, Suresh	Asst	998-0285				PHD	88	Renssela
Lampel, Joseph	Asst	998-0247				MS		
Lant, Theresa K.	Asst	998-0226				PHD	87	Stanford
Mezias, Stephen	Asst	998-0229		2	E	PHD		Stanford
Morrison, Elizabeth	Asst	998-0230				PHD	91	Northwes
Nayyar, Praveen	Asst	998-0286				PHD	88	Michigan
Robinson, Sandra	Asst	998-0244				PHD	92	Northwes
Shamsie, Jamal	Asst	998-0248				PHD	92	McGill
Sirower, Mark	Asst	998-0200				PHD	93	Columbia
Fox, William	Inst	998-0235				MBA		
Shaver, Myles	Inst	998-0400				ABD		Michigan
Weisenfeld, Batia	Inst	998-0200				ABD		Columbia
Barker, Jane	Adj	998-0200				JD	75	Wiscon
Boice, Craig K.	Adj	998-0200				MPHL	77	Yale
Chernoff, Harry	Adj	998-0280		7	U	PHD	85	NYU
DiPietro, Ralph A.	Adj	998-0252				PHD	71	NYU
Engelhardt, Herbert	Adj	998-0238				MBA	51	Harvard
Mullen, Thomas	Adj	998-0200				PHD	86	NYU
–Dept Information Systems	Phone	998-0800	Fax 995-4228					
Stohr, Edward	C-Pr	998-0846	estohr			PHD	73	Berkeley
Laudon, Kenneth C.	Prof	998-0815	klaudon	9	Z	PHD	72	Stanford
Lucas, Henry C. Jr.	Prof	998-0814	hlucas	9	Z	PHD	70	MIT
Research Professor								
Uretsky, Myron	Prof	998-0844	muretsky	9	Z	PHD	65	Ohio St
Director of the Management Decision Laboratory								
Baroudi, Jack J.	Assoc	998-0804	jbaroudi	9	Z	PHD	84	NY Univ
Director, Undergraduate Information Systems Program								
Clifford, James	Assoc	998-0808	jcliffor	9	Z	PHD	82	SUNY-SBr
Director, M.S. in Information Systems								
Dhar, Vasant	Assoc	998-0816	vdhar	9	Z	PHD	84	Pitt
Coordinator, Info Syst Graduate Prgm								
Kauffman, Robert J.	Assoc	998-0824	rkauffma	9	Z	PHD	88	Car Mel
Director M. S. in Information Science								
Turner, Jon A.	Assoc	998-0805	jturner	9	Z	PHD	80	Columbia
Director, Center for Research on Information Systems								
White, Norman H.	Assoc	998-0842	nwhite	9	Z	PHD	74	NYU
Isakowitz, Tomas	Asst	998-0833	tisakowi	9	Z	PHD	89	Penn
Kambil, Ajit	Asst	998-0843	akambil	9	Z	PHD	92	MIT
Schocken, Shimon	Asst	998-0841	sschocke	9	Z	PHD	87	Penn
Silver, Mark S.	Asst	998-0800	msilver	9	Z	PHD	86	Penn
Slade, Stephen	Asst	998-0818	sslade	9	Z	PHD	91	Yale
Tuzhilin, Alexander	Asst	998-0832	atuzhili	9	Z	PHD	89	NYU
Weber, Bruce W.	Asst	998-0806	bweber	9	Z	PHD	92	Penn

New York University-Grad	New York, NY	10003	(212)			MSM,MPA,DPA,PHD
738 Tisch 40 W 4th St			FAX = 995-4162			
Did Not Respond-1993 Listing						
Newman, Howard	Dean	998-7410		Law	JD	70 Temple 1988
–Wagner Grad Sch Public Serv	Phone		Fax 995-4162			
Boise, William	Prof	998-7464	12		PHD	Penn
Kovner, Tony	Prof	998-7444	12		PHD	
Kropf, Roger	Assoc	998-7458	12		PHD	
Sparrow, Roy	Assoc	998-7505	12		PHD	

New York Institute of Tech	New York, NY	11568	(516)			BS,MS,MBA
School of Management			FAX =			
Did Not Respond-1993 Listing; 399- phone numbers have 212 area code						
Poczter, Abram	Dean	686-7554		Mktg	PHD	Columbia
–Management Faculty	Phone					
Gray, Irwin	Prof	686-7554	73		PHD	
Kleinstein, Arnold	Prof	686-7554	79		PHD	
Tibrewala, Raj	Prof	686-7554	73		PHD	
Amundsen, Robert	Assoc	686-7554	14		PHD	
Bochanan, Richard	Assoc	686-7554	52		PHD	
Dibble, Richard	Assoc	686-7722	15		PHD	
Fried, Theodore	Assoc	686-7554	7		MA	
Hartman, Stephen	Assoc	348-3061	12		PHD	
Lee, Nag	Assoc	686-7554	97		PHD	
Omidi, A. C.	Assoc	399-8328	97		DBA	
Ozelli, Tunc	Assoc	399-8330	61		PHD	
Wachspress, David	Assoc	686-7838			PHD	
Capela, John	Asst	686-7554	18		MBA	

Niagara University
College of Business — Niagara Univ, NY 14109 — (716) FAX= — BA,BS,BBA
Did Not Respond-1993 Listing

Name	Rank	Phone		Field	Degree	Yr	School	Year
Kalogares, Constantine	Dean	286-8052		Fnce	PHD	74	Baruch	1992
—Department of Commerce	Phone							
Pikas, Bodhans	C-Pr	286-8166		Mktg	PHD		SUNY-Buf	1981
Libby, Barbara	Prof	286-8178						
Eastwood, Karen	Asst	286-8180						
Smith, Chuck	Asst	286-8179						

Nicholls State University
College of Business — Thibodaux, LA 70310 — (504) CENAC.NICH.EDU 1983,1989 — FAX=448-4922

Name	Rank	Phone			Field	Degree	Yr	School	Year
Gros, Ridley J. Jr.	Dean	448-4170				PHD		LSU	1971
—Dept of Management & Mktg	Phone	448-4175	Fax 448-4922						
Pizzolatto, Allayne	C-Ac	448-4174		24	EJLN	PHD	88	LSU	1981
Balsmeier, Philip W.	Prof	448-4190				PHD	73	Arkansas	1980
Fry, Elaine Hobbs	Prof	448-4179		45	NKJL	DBA	78	Miss St	1978
Shell, L. Wayne	Prof	448-4178		79	UZ	PHD	77	LSU	1971
Caillouet, Aaron	Asst	448-4242		3	I	DBA	87	Nova	1973
Frey, Len	Asst	448-4211							
Roger, Craig	Asst	448-4202		97	Z	MBA	77	NicholSt	1971
Dalrymple, Gerald	Inst	448-4236		12		MBA	65	Loyola	1979

Nichols College
Div of Business & Econ — Dudley, MA 01570-5000 — Center Road — (508) FAX=EXT 102 — BS
Did Not Respond 1993 Listing; phone 943-1560

Name	Rank	Phone		Degree	Yr	School	Year
Warren, Edward G.	Dean	Ext 201		PHD	79	Brown	1974
—Dept of Business Management	Phone		Fax Ext 102				
Pfeiffer, Frank K. Jr.	C-Pr	943-1560		PHD	74	Mass	1973
Concoran, Jeffrey	Asst			MBA		Nichols	
Downs, Larry	Asst			MBA		Mich St	
Farrell, Charles	Asst			MBA		Penn	
Hilliard, Richard Lee	Asst	987-1741		MBA		Trinity	
Hannah, Gregg							
Lelon, Tom							
Oden, Howard							
Smelewicz, Jean	Adj						
Winston, Rudy	Adj						

Norfolk State University
School of Business — Norfolk, VA 23504 — 2401 Corprew Avenue — (804) FAX=683-2506 — 1990 — BS

Name	Rank	Phone			Field	Degree	Yr	School	Year
Boyd, Joseph L.	Dean	683-8920			Atg	PHD	77	S Carol	7-83
—Department of Management	Phone	683-8955	Fax 683-2506						
Sawyer, Granville	H-Ac	683-2564			T	PHD		Tenn	7-92
Abussi, Sami	Prof	683-8320			IN	PHD		Miss St	7-92
Maanavi, Noureddin	Prof	683-8351		37	U	PHD	76	Penn	1983
Williams, Edgar	Prof	683-2505		3	I	PHD	76	Utah	7-84
Assistant Dean									
Chen, Jim	Assoc	683-8739		79	VZ	PHD	82	North Tx	7-84
Mohanty, Bidhu B.	Assoc	683-8005			U	PHD		Case Wes	7-92
Belhadjali, Moncef	Asst	683-2494		9	Z	PHD	90	Penn	7-90
Cherikh, Moula	Asst	683-2490			U	PHD		Case Wes	7-92
Dondeti, Reddy	Asst	683-8009		7	V	PHD		Case Wes	7-90
Liu, Lai	Asst	683-2587		9	Z	PHD		Miss St	7-90
Quaye, Ago	Asst	683-2489			Z	PHD	90	S Carol	7-92
Whaley, Gary	Asst	683-8009		24	EJ	PHD	83	SUNY	7-84
Yballe, Leodones	Asst	683-2536		24	EJ	PHD	91	Case Wes	7-90

North Adams State College
Business Adm/Econ Dept — North Adams, MA 01247 — 21 Highland Avenue — (413) FAX=
Did Not Respond Again-1992 Listing

Name	Rank	Phone		Degree	School
Markou, Peter J.	D-Pr			MSBA	Suffolk
Director Small Business Institute					
—Management Faculty	Phone		Fax 663-3033		
Croteau, Barbara A.	C-As			MBA	Providen
Grant, Stephen	Prof			PHD	Clark
Kendall, Elizabeth	Prof			MLS	Mass
O'Conner, Gregory P.	Prof			BA	Boston C
Kahn, Ben Abraham	Assoc				
Moriarty, James	Assoc			MBA	Am Intl
Dodge, Sheryl	Asst				
Hovaizi, Fraidoon	Asst				
Miano, Edward	Asst			MBA	Pace

University of North Alabama
School of Business
Stewart, William — Dean 760-4261
—**Management Faculty** Phone

		Phone							

Florence, AL 35632-0001 (205)
Wesleyan Avenue FAX=760-4234 BS
Dean 760-4261 PHD 77 Miss 1960
Phone Fax 760-4811

Name	Rank	Phone		Deg	Yr	School	Yr
Gatlin, Kerry P.	C-Pr	760-4401		PHD	82	Oklahoma	1980
Lester, Rick A.	Prof	760-4405		PHD	85	Miss	1984
Thorne, Neil	Assoc	760-4399		DBA	92	Memphis	1993
Borah, Santano	Asst	760-4605		PHD	93	Illinois	1992
Smith, Bud	Asst	760-4465		MBA	72	Harvard	1977
Williams, Robert	Asst	760-4148		PHD	93	Fla St	1993

North Carolina at Asheville Asheville, NC 28804-3329 (704) UNCA
Dept of Management One University Heights FAX=251-6142 BS
Lisnerski, Donald D. — C-Ac 251-6842 lisnerski 14 HAdm DPH 74 N Carol 8-82
—**Management Faculty** Phone 251-6554

Name	Rank	Phone				Deg	Yr	School	Yr
Green, Bill	Assoc	251-6843	green	27	&W	PHD	85	North Tx	8-92
Kauffman, Nancy	Asst	251-6846	kauffman	5	NQ	PHD	89	North Tx	8-88
Yates, George	Asst	251-6853	yates	5	I	PHD	91	North Tx	8-91
Yearout, Robert D.	Asst	251-6854	yearout	7	MUV	PHD	87	Kan St	8-87

University of North Carolina Chapel Hill, NC 27599-3490 (919) 1923,1963
School of Business FAX=962-0054 BS,MBA,MAC,PHD
Fulton, Paul Dean 962-3232 4 JKL 1-94
Zeithaml, Carl P. Dean$ 962-3165 3 IH DBA 80 Maryland 1986
—**Management Faculty - CB3490** Phone Fax 962-0054

Name	Rank	Phone				Deg	Yr	School	Yr
Rosen, Benson	C-Pr	962-3166		25	NEXO	PHD	69	Wayne St	1969
Hanes Professor									
Aldrich, Howard E.	Prof	962-5044		2	HSR	PHD	69	Michigan	1982
Anderson, Carl R.	Prof	962-3163		3	IHE	PHD	74	Penn St	1979
Bateman, Thomas S.	Prof	962-3128		2	EGO	DBA	80	Indiana	1986
Behrman, Jack N.	Emer	962-3149		8	JLW	PHD	52	Princeton	1964
Luther Hodges Distingushed Professor Emeritus									
Bettis, Richard A.	Prof	962-3165		3	IH	PHD	79	Michigan	1992
Luther Hodges Professor									
Bigoness, William J.	Prof	962-3144		25	QEH	PHD	74	Mich St	1976
Director - Center For Managment Studies - Dean MBA Program									
Kalleberg, Arne L.	Prof	962-1007		2	EFHQ	PHD	75	Wiscon	1992
Kasarda, John D.	Prof	962-8201		3	WHM	PHD	71	N Carol	1976
Director - Kenan Institute of Private Enterprise									
Lee, J. Finley	Prof	962-3191		4	Z	PHD	65	Penn	1970
Julian Price Professor									
Levin, Richard I.	Prof	962-3117		36	LISU	PHD	59	N Carol	1959
Phillip Hettleman Professor									
Mann, Richard A.	Prof	962-3220		4	JKL	JD	73	Yale	1974
Roberts, Barry S.	Prof	962-3152		4	JKL	LLM	76	Harvard	1976
Rondinelli, Dennis	Prof	962-8201		28	WHM	PHD	69	Cornell	1990
Director International Private Enterprise Research Center									
Adler, Robert	Assoc	962-3156		4	JKL	JD	69	Michigan	1987
Blackburn, Richard S.	Assoc	962-3162		25	EHNV	PHD	80	N Carol	1979
Kesner, Idalene F.	Assoc	962-3140	u21258	3	ILE	PHD	83	Indiana	1983
O'Neill, Hugh M.	Assoc			3	IH	PHD	80	Mass	1993
Peirce, Ellen R.	Assoc	962-3208		4	JKLQ	JD	76	Duke	1980
Undergraduate Faculty Chair									
Shapiro, Debra L.	Assoc	962-3224	usunny	2	E	PHD	86	Northwes	1986
Victor, Bart Irwin	Assoc	962-3159	ubartv	34	HEJD	PHD	85	N Carol	1988
Pearson, Christine	Asst			25	EN	PHD	88	S Calif	1993
Black, Sylvia	Inst			3	IH				
Miguel, Mabel	Inst	962-3141		25	EN	PHD	93	N Carol	
Baunach, Warren	Adj	962-0327		25	EHN	PHD		N Carol	
Associate Dean Executive Education									
Bell, Gerald D.	Adj	962-3164		2	EFG	PHD	64	Yale	1963
Berry, Mike	Adj/Ac	541-4172		3	I	PHD		N Carol	1992
Johnson, James	Adj	962-0116		4	J	PHD	80	Mich St	1992
E. Maynard Adams Professor									
Stanford, Donald M.	Adj	962-3142		4	K				
Stodt, Martha	Adj	962-3142		2	EC				

North Carolina at Charlotte Charlotte, NC 28223 (704) UNCCVM.UNCC.EDU 1983,1985
College of Business Adm FAX=547-4888
Mazze, Edward M. — Dean 547-2165 Mktg PHD 66 Penn St 1993
—**Department of Management** Phone 547-2062 Fax 547-3123

Name	Rank	Phone		Deg	Yr	School	Yr
Curran, Kent E.	C-Ac	547-2062		DBA		LSU	1984
Geurin, Virginia S.	Prof	574-2076		PHD		Arkansas	1972
Nkomo, Stella M.	Prof	547-4412		PHD		Mass	1983
Kohut, Gary F.	Assoc	547-4420		PHD		S Illin	1983
Sage, Earl R.	Assoc	547-4417		PHD	73	Ohio St	1973

Name	Rank	Phone	Email			Degree		School	Year
Beggs, Joyce M.	Asst	547-2736				PHD		Tenn	1989
Booth, Rose Mary	Asst	547-3245				PHD		Kentucky	
Calvasina, Gerald E.	Asst	547-4422				PHD		Miss	1982
Carpano, Claudio	Asst	547-2167	fba00cc1			PHD	91	S Carol	1990
Jernigan, I. Edward	Asst	547-4302				DBA		Memphis	1989
Kerr, Daryl L.	Asst	547-2548				PHD		Fla St	1988
Klich, Nancy R.	Asst	547-4411				PHD		Florida	
Smith, Teresa L.	Asst	547-2005				PHD		Va Tech	1989
Baxter, Carol M.	Lect	547-4334				MA		Ball St	1978
Carriher, Susan	Lect	547-4426				PHD		N Car St	
–MIS/Operations Mgt Dept	Phone	547-2064	Fax 547-3123						
Cooper, W. Douglas	C-Ac	547-2064				PHD		N Car St	1985
Barnes, Frank C.	Prof	547-4424				PHD		Geo St	1075
Conrad, Robert B.	Prof	547-4421				PHD		N Carol	1970
Hogue, Jack T.	Assoc	547-4131				PHD		Georgia	1984
Robbins, Stephanie S.	Assoc	547-4410				PHD		LSU	1981
Saydam, Cem A.	Assoc	547-2047				PHD		Clemson	1986
Crook, Connie	Asst	547-3360	fba00cwc	9	Z	PHD	92	S Carol	
Gorman, Kevin J.	Asst	547-2049				MBA		Cal St	1988
Jeffries, Carol J.	Asst	547-4429				PHD		Tx-Arlin	1989
Khouja, Moutaz	Asst	547-3242							
Repede, John	Asst	547-2701							
Stylianou, Anthony C.	Asst	547-2006				PHD		Kent St	1990
Lindsay, Alice J.	Lect	574-2046				MS		Winthrop	1988

North Carolina at Greensboro	Greensboro, NC	27412-5001	(910) UNCG						1982,1982
Bryan Sch of Bus & Econ	1000 Spring Garden Street		FAX=334-5580						BS,MSA,MBA
Weeks, James K.	Dean	334-5338	weeksjk	7	U	PHD	74	S Carol	1976
–Dept of Management & Mktg	Phone	334-5691	Fax 334-5580						
Miles, Benton E.	H-Pr	334-5691				Mktg	PHD	71 Ohio St	1971
Muchinsky, Paul	Prof	334-5691		25	EFN	PHD	73	Purdue	1993
Bryan Distinguished Professor of Business									
Kane, Jeffrey S.	Assoc	334-5691		25	NVXA	PHD	77	Michigan	8-90
Land, Frank P.	Assoc	334-5691		48	JYNL	JD	66	Colorado	8-79
Tullar, William L.	Assoc	334-5691		25	EHNY	PHD	75	Rochest	8-73
Buttner, E. Holly	Asst	334-5691		23	TGR	PHD	86	N Carol	8-85
Gryskiewicz, Nur	Asst	334-5691		25	NPRY	PHD	79	London	1-86
Paradise-Tornow, Carol	Asst	334-5691		23	IDFN	PHD	86	Minn	8-93
Rathburn, Jodi	Asst	334-5691		23	HIJY	ABD		Ariz St	8-93
Hassell, Eloise M.	Lect	334-5691		4	JK	JD	83	Wake For	9-89
–Dept Info Sys & Oper Mgt	Phone	334-5666	Fax 334-5580						
Hershey, Gerald L.	H-Pr	334-5666	hershey	9	Z	PHD		Indiana	1976
Grill, George P.	Prof	334-5666	grillgp	9	Z	EDD		N Dakota	1963
Eatman, John L.	Assoc	334-5666	eatmanj	9	UZ	PHD	72	S Carol	1981
Ehrhardt, Richard A.	Assoc	334-5666	ehrhardt	7	UV	PHD		Yale	1982
Taube, Larry R.	Assoc	334-5666	taube	7	U	PHD	84	N Carol	1982
Amoako-gyampah, Kwasi	Asst	334-5666	amoakogy	7	UV	PHD		Cinn	1990
Balthazard, Pierre	Asst	334-5666	balthazp	9	Z	PHD		Arizona	1993
Gargeya, Vidyaranya	Asst	334-5666	gargeya	9	U	PHD	91	Geo St	1993
Herschel, Richard	Asst	334-5666	herschel	9	Z	PHD		Indiana	1991
Koh, Chang	Asst	334-5666	kohcxx	9	Z	PHD		Georgia	1990
Steiger, David	Asst	334-5580	steigerd	9	Z	PHD		Okla St	1993
Cantrell, Joyce	Lect	334-5666	cantrela	9	Z	MBA		NC-Green	1993

North Carolina at Wilmington	Wilmington, NC	28403-3297	(910) VXC.OCIS.UNCWIL.EDU						
Cameron Sch of Bus Adm	601 South College Road		FAX=395-3815						BS,MBA
Rockness, Howard O.	Dean	395-3501	rockness			Atg	PHD	73 U Wash	1993
–Department of Management	Phone	395-3424	Fax 395-3815						
Howe, Vince	C-Ac	395-3882	howe			Mktg	PHD	85 Georgia	1988
Harper, Steve	Prof	395-3517	harpers	36	DIST	PHD	75	Ariz St	1976
Adams, Shelia A.	Assoc	395-3745	adamss	23	EH	PHD	79	U Wash	1984
Engdahl, Richard A.	Assoc	395-3779	engdahlr	25	EFN	PHD	86	U Wash	1986
Galbraith, Craig	Assoc	395-3775	galbraithc	36	DITU	PHD	81	Purdue	8-92
Hunt, Tammy G.	Assoc	395-3684	huntt	31	I	PHD	88	Fla St	1990
Keating, Robert	Assoc	395-3069	keatingr	38	DIY	DBA	87	Kent St	1985
Latham, Donald	Assoc	395-3880	lathamd	23	EI	PHD	78	Arkansas	1988
Porterfield, Rebecca	Asst	395-3514	porterfieldr	37	UYI	PHD	86	Clemson	8-91
–Dept of Production & Dec Sc	Phone	395-3068	Fax 395-3815						
Schell, George P.	C-Ac	395-3068		9	Z	PHD		Purdue	
Anderson, John Michael	Prof	395-3807		9	Z	PHD		N Car St	
Badarinathi, Ravija	Assoc	395-3518		7	Z	PHD		Georgia	
Garris, John M.	Assoc	395-3739		7	V	PHD		Clemson	
Gowan, Jack A. Jr.	Assoc	395-3676		9	Z	PHD		Clemson	
Markham, In	Asst	350-4150		7	V	PHD		Va Tech	
Mathieu, Richard	Asst	350-4077		9	Z	PHD		Virginia	
Rosen, L. Drew	Asst	395-3677		7	U	PHD	90	S Carol	
Wray, Barry	Asst	395-3515		7	V	PHD		Va Tech	

North Carolina A&T State Un

Greensboro, NC 27411 (910) ATSUVAX1.BITNET 1979
School Business & Econ — 1601 East Market Street — FAX=334-7093 — BS

Name	Rank	Phone	Email/Fax		Field	Degree	Yr	School	Date
Craig, Quiester	Dean	334-7632			Atg	PHD	71	Missouri	8-72
–Dept of Business Adm	Phone	334-7656	Fax 334-7093						
Johnson, Melvin	C-Pr	334-7526	mjohnson		S&Ls	DBA		Indiana	8-90
Sen, Tapan	Prof	334-7656		7		DBA	80	Tx Tech	8-92
Anyansi-Archibong, Chi	Assoc	334-7216		3		PHD		Kansas	1-86
Lind, Mary R.	Assoc	334-7656		9	Z	PHD	88	N Carol	8-86
Pogue, Danny H.	Assoc	334-7526		5		PHD	73	Ohio St	1-73
Assistant Dean									
Ross, Novella	Assoc	334-7526		5		PHD		Ohio St	8-88
Harris, James R.	Asst	334-7656		5		PHD	90	Fla St	8-90
Perez, Jorge	Asst			9	Z	ABD		Fla St	1-93
Sulek, Joanne M.	Asst	334-7635		7		PHD	89	N Carol	8-86
Udoka, Sylanus	Asst	334-7656		5		PHD		Okla St	8-92
Ugboro, Isaiah O.	Asst	334-7656		3		PHD		North Tx	1-89
Walton, Steve	Asst	334-7656				PHD		N Carol	1993
White, Sharon	Asst			9	Z	ABD		Fla St	8-92
Perry, Laura L.	Inst	334-7656		3		MBA		NC-Green	1-88

North Carolina Central Univ

Durham, NC 27707 (919)
School of Business — Lawson Street — FAX=560-6413

Name	Rank	Phone	Email/Fax		Field	Degree	Yr	School	Date
Fleming, Sundar W.	Dean	560-6458			Mktg	PHD	77	Duke	1987
–Department of Management	Phone		Fax 560-6413						
Kuklah, Hooshang	C-Pr	560-6015		38	EGIY	DPA	74	SUNY-Alb	9-80
Harris, Claudia	Assoc	560-6148		24	ELRY	PHD	84	Utah	9-92
Kargar, Javad	Asst	560-6146		36	IS	PHD	81	Clarmont	9-90
Reitz, Frank	Asst	560-6373		25	BQS	ABD		Duke	9-89

North Carolina State Univ

Raleigh, NC 27695-7229 (919) NCSU.EDU
College of Management — FAX=737-7873 — BA,MSM

Name	Rank	Phone	Email/Fax		Field	Degree	Yr	School	Date
Lewis, Richard J.	Dean	515-5560			Mktg	DBA	64	Mich St	1993
–Dept of Business Management	Phone	515-5567	Fax 515-5564						
Wilson, Jack W.	H-Pr	515-5567	jack_wil	7	V	PHD	66	Oklahoma	1965
Allen, Steven G.	Prof	515-6941	steve_al	5	NPQ	PHD	78	Harvard	1978
Director MSM Program									
Clark, Robert L.	Prof	515-5567	robert_c	5	NQ	PHD	74	Duke	1975
Holthausen, Duncan M.	Prof	515-5567	duncan_h	7	V	PHD	74	Northwes	1976
Baumer, David L.	Assoc	515-6950	dave-bau	4	K	PHD	80	Virginia	1979
Dutton, John C.	Assoc	515-6948	john_dut	8	Y	PHD	78	Duke	1989
McDermed, Ann	Assoc	515-6946	ann_mcde	7	QV	PHD	83	N Car St	1983
Bozarth, Cecil	Asst	515-4511	cecil_bo	7	U	PHD	92	N Carol	1992
Chapman, Stephen N.	Asst	515-4512	stephen	73	UWI	PHD	86	Mich St	1992
Davis, K. Shannon	Asst	515-3349	shannon	52	NOPF	PHD	92	Maryland	1992
Markham, Stephen K.	Asst	515-5592	stephen_	23	EDHI	PHD	93	Purdue	1992
Mitchell, Victoria	Asst	515-5567		93	ZI	PHD	93	Fla St	1993
Tang, Y. Edwin	Asst	515-6954	edwin_ta	13	DIV	PHD	89	Tx-Dall	1988
Young, Greggry S.	Asst	515-5567		36	IZYS	PHD	93	Maryland	1993
Bostic, Pam		515-5587						Duke	
Assistant Director MSM Program									

University of North Dakota

Grand Forks, ND 58202 (701) NDSUVM1 1984,1990
Box 8097, Univ Station — Centennial Drive — FAX=777-5099 — BS,MBA
Did Not Respond-1993 Listing; 777-3631 Office Phone

Name	Rank	Phone	Email/Fax		Field	Degree	Yr	School	Date
Lawrence, W. Fred	Dean	777-2135			Mgt	PHD	80	Geo St	8-76
–Dept of Business & Mgt	Phone		Fax 777-5099						
Eberhardt, Bruce J.	C-Pr	777-3632		25	ENR	PHD	79	Iowa St	8-81
Kassner, Marcia	Assoc	777-3228		12	OP	PHD	85	Illinois	8-84
Park, Jaesun	Assoc	777-2317		7	DUV	PHD	85	Northwes	8-84
Porter, Donald E.	Assoc	777-4148		36	T	PHD	61	Stanford	8-82
Vitton, John J.	Assoc	777-3229		35	IN	PHD	82	Nebraska	8-88
Chong, K.S. John	Asst	777-3990		38	IY	DBA	88	Miss St	8-88
Moser, Steven B.	Asst	777-4695		25	ENS	PHD	90	Cinn	8-90
Westby, Kenneth L.	Asst	777-4697		35		MS	67	Geo Wash	8-77
Yang, Jiagin	Asst	777-3223		7	UV	PHD	90	Geo St	8-90
Jones, Kathleen	Lect	777-4093		15		MBA	88	N Dakota	8-88
Vistad, Jeffrey S.	Lect	777-4092		17		MBA	91	N Dakota	8-90

North Dakota State Univ

Fargo, ND 58105-5137 (701) NDSUVM1
College of Business Adm — FAX=237-7050 — BS,MBA

Name	Rank	Phone	Email/Fax		Field	Degree	Yr	School	Date
McCaul, Harriette S.	Dean	237-7503	nuoso568	25	EN	PHD	86	Nebraska	1983
–Department of Management	Phone	237-7503							
Bahrami, Bahman	Assoc	237-8293		59	QZ	PHD	83	Nebraska	1983
Froelich, Karen	Asst	237-8808		23	HI	ABD		Minn	1990
Jacobson, Sarah	Asst			25	EN	ABD		Mass	1991
Moreno, Abel	Asst	237-7061		78	U	PHD	90	N Dak St	1989

University of North Florida — Jacksonville, FL 32216-6699 (904) 1976,1981
College of Business Adm — 4567 St John's Bluff Road So — FAX=646-2594 — BS,MBA,MAC

Name	Rank	Phone		Fields	Degree		School	Year
Traynham, Earle	Dean$	646-2590		Econ	PHD	73	S Carol	1973
—Dept of Mgt,Mktg & Logistic	Phone			Fax 646-2594				
Pickhandt, Robert C.	C-Pr	646-2780	7	UV	DBA	69	Indiana	1973
Coltrin, Sally Ann	Prof	646-2780	25	EHN	PHD		Missouri	
Horn, Kevin H.	Prof	646-2780	7	U	PHD		Penn St	
Jennings, Kenneth M.	Prof	646-2780	5	NQ	PHD	73	Illinois	1973
Johnson, Edward A.	Prof	646-2590	25		PHD	68	Mich St	1989
McLaughlin, Frank S.	Prof	646-2590	7	UV	PHD	67	Florida	1971
Associate Dean								
Paulson, Steven K.	Prof	646-2780	24	EHLX	PHD		Iowa St	
Vaghefi, M. Reza	Prof	646-2780	38	IY	PHD		Mich St	
Harms, Craig G.	Assoc	646-2780	7	UV	PHD		Ohio St	
Tomlinson, William H.	Assoc	646-2780	35	INY	PHD	74	American	1972
Williamson, Steven A.	Assoc	646-2780	12	EFHP	DBA		Memphis	
Baker, Huel E. III	Asst	646-2780	12	EFH	PHD		Florida	1989
Coleman, B. Jay	Asst	646-2780	7	UVW	PHD	88	Clemson	1988
Fortado, Bruce	Asst	646-2780	5	NQ	PHD	86	Case Wes	1986
Kavan, C. Bruce	Asst	646-2780	9	ZUV	PHD	91	Georgia	1991
Webster, William F.	VAsst	646-2780	37	UV	PHD		Texas	1993

North Georgia College — Dahlonega, GA 30597 (706) FAX=
Dept of Business Adm — BBA

Name	Rank	Phone		Fields	Degree		School	Year
Dennis, H. Lawrence	H-Pr	864-1610		Atg	DBA	76	Kentucky	
—Management Faculty	Phone	864-1607	Fax 864-1562					
Piper, William	Prof	864-1610			PHD	93	Am Londn	1985
Singleton, Timothy	Prof	864-1610			PHD	89	Geo St	

University of North Texas — Denton, TX 76203-6677 (817) COBAF.UNT.EDU 1961,1966
College of Business Adm — FAX=565-6540 — BS,MS,MBA,PHD

Name	Rank	Phone			Fields	Degree		School	Year
Singleton, J. Clay	Dean	565-3037	singleto		Fnce	PHD	79	Missouri	1991
—Department of Management	Phone	565-3140	Fax 565-4394						
Taylor, Lewis A. III	C-Pr	565-3140	taylor	23	EFIX	DBA	84	India U	1992
Adams, R. Sexton	Prof	565-3156	adams	3	IK	PHD	65	LSU	1968
Pettit, John D. Jr.	Prof	565-4332	pettit	25	EHNX	PHD	69	LSU	1969
Powell, J. Don	Prof	565-3153	powell	3	ILM	PHD	77	LSU	1977
Rachel, Frank M.	Prof	565-3150	rachel	25	FNPE	DBA	62	Illinios	1962
Stephens, Elvis C.	Prof	565-3159	stephens	5	NQ	DBA	66	Indiana	1963
Williams, Fredrik P.	Prof	565-2236	williams	7	U	PHD	68	Texas	1968
Bimmerle, Charles F.	Assoc	565-3145	bimmerle	7	UIPW	PHD	77	Cinn	1976
Ebrahimi, Bahman	Assoc	565-3483	ebrahimi	38	IJLY	PHD	84	Geo St	1981
Johnson, J. Lynn	Assoc	565-3147	johnsonl	12	EJ	PHD	76	Arkansas	1979
Ledgerwood, Donna E.	Assoc	565-3157	ledgerwo	45	KMNQ	PHD	80	Oklahoma	1978
Rosenfeldt, Martin	Assoc	565-4333	rosenfel	78	MUY	PHD	75	Texas	1975
Swanson, Carl L.	Assoc	565-3160	swanson	3	IKL	PHD	82	Tx-Dallas	1982
Thibodeaux, Mary S.	Assoc	565-3086	thibodea	76	HIYR	PHD	76	North Tx	1976
Watson, Warren E.	Assoc	565-3277	watson	2	EFGH	PHD	74	Chicago	1983
Boyd, Nancy	Asst	565-3158	boyd	5	EN	PHD	91	Memphis	1991
Dsouza, Derrick	Asst	565-3168	dsouza	38	ISUY	PHD	90	Geo St	1989
Goodwin, Vicki	Asst	565-4766	goodwin	2	E	PHD	91	Tx-Arlin	1991
Hassell, Barbara L.	Asst	565-4334	hassell	25	ENC	PHD	91	Fla St	8-89
Insley, Robert	Asst	565-4331	insley	1	D	EDD	88	N Illino	1988
Knotts, Rose	Asst	565-4486	knotts	36	IRY	PHD	72	Tx A&M	1982
Ponthieu, Louis	Asst	565-3155	ponthieu	3	ST	PHD	68	Arkansas	1988
Ryan, Mike	Asst	565-4710	ryan	3	ILM	PHD	85	Tx-Dallas	1991
White, Richard	Asst	565-4487	white	37	IU	PHD	90	Ariz St	1990

Northeast Louisiana Univ — Monroe, LA 71209-0140 (318) MERLIN.NLU.EDU 1972,1977
College of Business Adm — 700 University Avenue — FAX=342-5161 — BBA,MBA

Name	Rank	Phone			Fields	Degree		School	Year
Dunn, J. Paul	Dean	342-1100	mmdunn	6	IST	PHD	70	Arkansas	1968
Distinguished Professor of Entrepreneurship & Small Business									
—Dept of Management & Mktg	Phone	342-1185	Fax 342-5161						
Loudon, David L.	H-Pr	342-1185	mmloudon		Mktg	PHD	71	LSU	1980
Bethke, Art L.	Prof	342-1100	mmbethke	5	N	PHD	72	Nebraska	1974
Harris, O. Jeff Jr.	Prof	342-1191	mmharris	2	EN	PHD	66	Texas	1986
Jauch, Lawrence R.	Prof	342-1210	mmjauch	3	I	PHD	73	Missouri	1987
Biedenharn Professor									
McGraw, Van C.	Prof	342-1202	mmmcgraw	1	EN	PHD	66	LSU	1959
Wall, Jerry L.	Prof	342-1215	mmwall	5	I	PHD	74	Missouri	1983
Clinton, Roy	Assoc	342-1199	mmclinto	7	UVW	DBA	88	S Illin	1986
Martin, Robert G.	Assoc	342-1100	mmmartin	36	IST	PHD	80	Texas	1983
Chachere, Greg	Asst	342-1193	mmchache	25	EJNQ	PHD	89	Tx A&M	1988
McBeth, James M.	Asst	342-1196	mmmcbeth	12	EN	DBA	84	La Tech	1969
Orwig, Robert A.	Asst	342-1194	mmorwig	57	BSNU	DBA	94	Miss St	1991
Williamson, Stan	Asst	342-1195	mmwillia	23	EJ	PHD	90	North Tx	1990
Greenlaw, James A.	Inst	342-1189	mmgreenl	57	N	MS	67	AFIT	1984

Northeast Missouri State U   Kirksville, MO   63501   (816) NEMOUS
Div of Business & Accty   FAX=EXT 4366   BS,MA

Name	Title	Phone	Office	#	Code	Deg	School	Year
Dager, Robert A.	H-Pr	Ext 4346	bu15	25	NP	EDD	74 Ball St	1974
—Management Faculty	Phone	7875-434	Fax 785-7471					
Jones, Bryce	Prof	Ext 4351	bu27	4	JKL	PHD	79 Wiscon	1977
Vittetoe, Jerry	Prof	Ext 4361	bu12	9	Z	EDD	73 N Illin	1966
Gilchrist, Neil	Assoc	Ext 4370	bu38	23	IS	PHD	91 Nebraska	1984
Giovanni, Mary	Assoc	Ext 4365	bu20	59	RZ	PHD	80 Missouri	1975
Han, Pyung	Assoc	Ext 4364	bu57	28	EY	EDD	75 S Calif	1980
Alghalith, Nabil	Asst	Ext 4378	bu63	97	ZU	PHD	93 Missouri	1988
Allen, Stephen	Asst	Ext 4373	bu03	7	UV	PHD	89 Mo-Rolla	1989
Blum, Michael	Asst	Ext 4368	bu23	25	Q	PHD	93 Missouri	1984
Ellebracht, Pat	Asst	Ext 4373	bu17	1	T	MBA	54 Tx Tech	1967
Ho, Johnny C.	Asst	Ext 4332	bu65	79	UV	PHD	91 Ga Tech	1991
Smith, Steve	Asst	Ext 4304	bu47	4	JKL	JD	85 Texas	1986
Poyner, Catherine	Inst	Ext 4352	bu37	9	Z	MBA	90 LSU	1990

Northeastern University   Boston, MA   02115   (617)
College of Business Adm   360 Huntington Avenue   FAX=437-2056   1962,1974   BS,MS,MBA

Name	Title	Phone		#	Code	Deg	School	Year
Boyd, David P.	Dean	437-3239		5	N	PHD	Oxford	9-78
—General Management Dept	Phone		Fax 437-2056					
Molloy, James F. Jr.	C-Ac	437-4812		68	STY	PHD	MIT	9-81
Atherton, Roger M. Jr.	Prof	437-3719		32	I	PHD	Michigan	7-85
Associate Dean								
Baker, Charles D.	Prof	437-4712		31	Ai	MBA	Harvard	9-85
Lieb, Robert C.	Prof	437-4813				DBA	Maryland	9-70
McCarthy, Daniel J.	Prof	437-3255		3	IY	DBA	Harvard	9-62
Sarathy, Ravi	Prof	437-4806		8	IZY	PHD	Michigan	9-80
Vernon-Wortzel, Heidi	Prof	437-4756		8	Y	PHD	Boston U	9-80
Crittenden, William F.	Assoc	437-4757		13	I	PHD	Arkansas	9-84
Kinnunen, Raymond M.	Assoc	437-4736		3	I	DBA	LSU	9-74
Meyer, Marc H.	Assoc	437-5948		6	TZ	PHD	MIT	9-86
Patrick F. & Helen C. Walsh Research Professor								
Ramamurti, Ravi	Assoc	437-4760		3	YI	DBA	Harvard	9-81
Wint, Alvin	Asst	437-5239		18	YI	DBA	Harvard	9-88
Berkowitz, Stanley R.	Lect	437-4811		4		JD	Boston	9-85
Cook, James S.	Lect	437-4759		3		AB	Brown	4-87
Costello, Mary F.	Lect	437-4805		4		JD	Boston	1-85
Goldberg, Robert	Lect	437-4737		3		MBA	Boston	9-89
Olsen, Richard	Lect	437-4638		6		DBA	Harvard	9-90
Stuart, Robert W.	Lect	437-5206		6	TO	PHD	Renssela	9-87
Tilles, Seymour	Lect	437-5138		3	I	DBA	Harvard	9-87
—Human Resources Dept	Phone	373-3251	Fax 437-2056					
Bannister, Brendan D.	C-Ac	437-2503		25	EN&	DBA	Kent St	9-83
Katz, Ralph	Prof	437-4724		2	D	PHD	Penn	9-82
Andre, Rae	Assoc	437-4731		82	NE	PHD	Michigan	9-82
Begley, Thomas M.	Assoc	437-4723		26	E	PHD	Cornell	9-80
Lee, Cynthia K.	Assoc	437-5146		25	EG	PHD	Maryland	9-87
McDonough, Edward F. III	Assoc	437-4726		2	D	PHD	Mass	9-79
Spector, Bert A.	Assoc	437-2504		25	EFN	PHD	Missouri	9-86
Spital, Frank C.	Assoc	437-4722		23	D	PHD	MIT	9-76
Wertheim, Edward G.	Assoc	437-4725		25	N	PHD	Yeshiva	9-77
Puffer, Sheila M.	Asst	437-5249		25	YE	PHD	Berkeley	9-88
—Management Science Group	Phone	373-4764	Fax 437-8628					
Maggard, Michael	C-Pr	373-4750				PHD	UCLA	
Chatterjee, Sangit	Prof	373-4785				PHD	NYU	
Millen, Robert A.	Prof	373-4754				PHD	UCLA	
Balachandra, R.	Assoc	373-4755				PHD	Columbia	
Curley, Kathleen Foley	Assoc	373-5052				DBA	Harvard	
Godin, Victor B.	Assoc	373-4801				DBA	Harvard	
Parsons, Robert	Assoc	373-4749					Boston C	
Platt, Marjorie	Assoc	373-4748				PHD	Michigan	
Solomon, Marius	Assoc	373-5050				PHD	Penn	
Trauth, Eileen M.	Assoc	373-2759				PHD	Pitt	
Yilmaz, Mustafa R.	Assoc	373-4753				PHD	JHopkins	
Carrera, Maria-Cecilla	Asst	373-5252				PHD	Car Mel	
Collins, Stephanie J.	Asst	373-5259				PHD	Wis-Milw	
Zack, Michael	Asst	373-4734				DBA	Harvard	
Sorenson, Erl	Lect	373-4777				PHD	Syracuse	

Northeastern Illinois Univ   Chicago, IL   60625-4699   (312)
College Business & Mgt   5500 North St. Louis Avenue   FAX=794-6288   BS,MBA

Name	Title	Phone		#	Code	Deg	School	Year
Falk, Charles F.	Dean	794-2646		16	PSTW	EDD	75 N Illin	7-92
—Department of Management	Phone		Fax 794-6288					
Afifi, Rasoul	C-Pr	583-4050		7	U	PHD	North Tx	9-86
Hoffer, Durward	Prof	794-2652		21	FH	PHD	Northwes	9-79
Akbari, Hamid	Assoc	794-2896		32	TH	PHD	Ohio St	9-86
Macey, William	Assoc	794-2656		52	E	PHD	Loyala	5-82

Shub, Allen	Assoc	794-2650		26	EP	PHD	Loyola	9-85
Stonebraker, Peter W.	Assoc	794-2642		7	U	PHD	Ariz St	9-90
Chen, Mei-lung	Asst	583-4050		7	U	PHD	Florida	9-87
Dunphy, Steve	Asst	794-2583		36	IY	PHD	Indiana	9-91

Northeastern State Univ	Tahlequah, OK	74464-2399		(918)				
College of Business				FAX=				
Williams, Earl R.	Dean	456-5511			Econ	PHD	68 Tenn	1968
–Department of Management	Phone	458-2091	Fax 458-2193					
Holmes, Juanita	Prof	456-5511		2	E	EDD	77 Arkansas	
Migliore, R. Henry	Prof	456-5511		3	I	PHD	75 Arkansas	1987
Underhill, George	Prof	456-5511		3	I	PHD	84 Arkansas	1985
Davey, Anne	Asst	456-5511		7	UV	PHD	93 Tx A&M	1993
Slattery, Jeff	Asst	456-5511		3	I	PHD	93 Arkansas	1993
Jacob, Ronald	Inst	456-5511		6	S	MBA	71 Tulsa	1989

Northern Arizona University	Flagstaff, AZ	86011-5066		(602)	NAUVM			1969,1977
College of Business Adm				FAX=523-7331				BS,MBA
Walka, Joseph J.	Dean	523-3657			Econ	PHD	69 Harvard	1986
–Department of Management	Phone		Fax 523-7331					
Ozmun, Jon	C-Pr	523-7380		73	IU	PHD	75 Oklahoma	
Dustman, Jack	Prof	523-7374		5	NQ	DBA	70 S Calif	
Helmer, Ted	Prof	523-7373		13	C	PHD	69 Pitt	
Jacobs, Nell W.	Prof	523-7382		2	IZ	PHD	78 Santa Cl	
Kemper, Robert	Prof	523-7361		3	EI	PHD	67 U Wash	
Raynolds, Peter	Prof	523-7350		2	ED	PHD	69 UCLA	
Winfield, Fairlee	Prof	523-7384		18	RY	PHD	78 New Mex	
McKnight, Mel	Assoc	523-7367		2	M	PHD	79 UCLA	
Anderson, Joe	Asst	523-1389		86	EY	DBA	93 Ariz St	
Lockwood, Chris	Asst	523-7401		13	IN	PHD	91 Ariz St	

Univ of Northern Colorado	Greeley, CO	80639		(303)	SLINKY.UNIVNORTHCO.EDU			1992
College of Business Adm				FAX=351-2500				BS
Duff, William L. Jr.	Dean	351-2764				PHD	69 UCLA	1971
–Department of Management	Phone	351-2088	Fax 351-1097					
Clinebell, Sharon	C-Ac	351-1217		25		DBA	88 S Illin	
Clinton, James W.	Prof	351-1219		43		PHD	73 St Louis	
Fowler, Karen L.	Assoc	351-1221		3		PHD	85 Nebraska	
Hoffman, D. Lynn	Assoc	351-1224		56		PHD	81 Iowa	
Rowley, Daniel James	Assoc	352-9047		23		PHD	87 Colorado	

Northern Illinois Univ	Dekalb, IL	60115-2854		(815)				1969,1977
College of Business				FAX=753-8515				BS,MAS
800-323-8714								
Graf, David K.	Dean	753-6176			Z	PHD	N Dakota	
–Department of Management	Phone	753-1124	Fax 753-6198					
Catalanello, Ralph F.	C-Ac	753-6305		38	EF	PHD	71 Wiscon	1975
Wunsch, Daniel R.	C-Ac	753-6303		1	D	PHD	UCLA	
Hill, Marvin F. Jr.	Prof	753-6308		45	Q	PHD	Iowa	
King, Albert S.	Prof	753-6315		35	HIP	DBA	69 Tx Tech	1975
Rouse, Joanne	Prof	753-1403				MS	N Illin	
Director Small Business Development Center								
Yaney, Joseph P.	Prof	753-6310		25	EQ	PHD	69 Michigan	
Behrens, Curtiss	Assoc	753-6304		5	Q	LLM	DePaul	
Bishop, Terrence R.	Assoc	753-6316		5	N	PHD	Iowa	
Flores, Luis G.	Assoc	753-6307		38	IY	PHD	Tx Tech	
Gowen, Charles R.	Assoc	753-6306		3	I	PHD	Ohio St	
Neeley, C. Lynn	Assoc	753-6314		36	RS	PHD	Tenn	
Pender, Albert R.	Assoc	753-6188		1	D	PHD	67 N Dakota	
Scheck, Christine L.	Assoc	753-6311		2	EFG	PHD	Ariz St	
Schroeder, Betty L.	Assoc	753-6191				PHD	Mich St	
Scriven, Jolene D.	Assoc	753-6192		1	D	EDD	N Illin	
Simpson, Bertrand Jr.	Asst	753-6190		4	K	JD	Wiscon	
Wade, David	Asst	753-6160		4	K	JD	Iowa	
Lemanski, Daniel V.	Inst	753-0779				MBA	N Illin	
Director Small Business Institute								
–Operations Mgt & Info Sys	Phone	753-1286	Fax 753-7460					
Tallon, William J.	C-As	753-1185			U	PHD	Iowa	1987
Basti, Abdul Z.	Prof	753-1328			V	PHD	68 Colorado	1967
Chang, Wei-Chien	Prof	753-6376			V	PHD	71 Wiscon	1971
Lauer, Joachim A.	Prof	753-6373			Z	PHD	Ill Tech	
Rifai, Ahmed K.	Prof	753-6381			V	PHD	70 Syracuse	1970
Born, Richard G.	Assoc	753-6380			Z	PHD	Ill Tech	
Galvin, Thomas M.	Assoc	753-6375			U	PHD	Ill Tech	
Jacobs, Larry W.	Assoc	753-6301			U	PHD	89 Fla St	
Kim, Gyu Chan	Assoc	753-0554			U	PHD	Nebraska	

Albrecht, Wayne L.	Asst	753-1325		U	MS	59	Illinois	1962
Assistant Dean								
Mann, Thomas	Asst	753-6298		V	PHD		Iowa St	1973
Marchewka, Jack	Asst	753-1286			PHD		Geo St	1994
McFadden, Kathleen	Asst	753-6374			PHD		Texas	1993
Russo, Nancy	Asst	753-1287		Z				
Towell, Elizabeth	Asst	753-6377			PHD		Wiscon	1993
Goad, Susan	Inst			V				

University of Northern Iowa	Cedar Falls, IA	50614-0125	(319) UNI.EDU				1993,1993
College of Business Adm			FAX=273-2922				BA
Minter, Robert L.	Dean	273-6240	minter		PHD	69 Purdue	1990
—Dept of Management	Phone	273-6202	Fax 273-2922				
Power, Daniel J.	H-Pr	273-2750	power	3 I	PHD	82 Wiscon	8-89
Das, Chandra	Prof	273-6224	das		PHD	71 Case Wes	1-86
Goulet, Peter G.	Prof	273-2556	gouletp		PHD	70 Ohio St	1974
Jedlicka, Allen D.	Prof	273-2396			PHD	73 Northwes	9-73
McAdams, Tony N.	Prof	273-6020	mcadams		JD	69 Iowa	6-82
Waller, Robert J.	Prof	273-6202			DBA	68 Indiana	9-68
on leave							
Ashbaugh, Donald L.	Assoc	273-6022	ashbaugh		DBA	88 Kentucky	2-81
Forintos, Bruce M.	Assoc	273-5851	forintos		PHD	87 Michigan	2-93
Frost, Taggart Ford	Assoc	273-6110	frost		PHD	81 Brig Yg	8-78
Moussavi, Farzad	Assoc	273-2310	moussavi		PHD	85 Arkansas	8-85
Rueschhoff, M. Susan	Assoc	273-2166	rueschhoff		PHD	86 Nebraska	8-85
Abraham, Steven E.	Asst	273-6202	abrahams		PHD	92 Wiscon	8-94
Kaparthi, Shashidhar	Asst	273-2958	kaparthi		PHD	92 SUNY-Buf	8-92
Karsten, Rex A.	Asst	273-6202	karsten		PHD	94 Nebraska	8-94
Kirk, Carey H.	Asst	273-2108	kirk		PHD	72 Vanderbt	8-83
Loomba, Arvinder P.S.	Asst	273-6143	loomba		PHD	93 USC	8-93
Roth, Roberta M.	Asst	273-6896	roth		PHD	90 Iowa	8-80
Spencer, Michael S.	Asst	273-6793	spencer		PHD	92 Georgia	8-92
Timpany, Gordon A.	Asst	273-2831	timpany		MA	67 Minn	9-67
Wilson, Leslie K.	Asst	273-2964	wilson		PHD	92 Iowa	8-87
Wood, William C.	Asst	273-6278	woodw		PHD	84 Virginia	8-87
Frye, Crissie M.	Inst	273-2352	frye		MBA	89 N Iowa	8-89
Goulet, Lynda L.	Inst	273-2556	gouletl		MBA	77 N Iowa	1-78

Northern Kentucky Univ	Highland Hght KY	41099-0506	(606)				
College of Business			FAX=572-5566				BS,MBA
Comte, Thomas E.	Dean	572-5551		I	PHD	78 Missouri	7-91
—Dept of Management & Mktg	Phone	572-6559	Fax 572-6177				
Snyder, Robert A.	C-Pr	572-6367		25 EN	PHD	76 Maryland	1-81
Allyn, Compton	Prof	572-5150		34 B	PHD	73 Cinn	8-73
Lindsay, William M.	Prof	572-5157		17 DU	PHD	75 Geo St	8-72
Serey, Timothy T.	Prof	572-6310		28 EY	PHD	81 Cinn	8-80
Holloway, William L.	Assoc	572-5159		34 I	EDD	78 Cinn	8-76
Verderber, Kathleen S.	Assoc	572-6409		27 ER	PHD	84 Cinn	8-82
Ball, Rebecca W.	Asst	572-5161		36 I	PHD	94 Va Tech	8-93
Lawson, Marian B.	Asst	572-6334		34 EH	PHD	89 Minn	1-90
Kent, Daniel	Inst	572-5719		15	MBA	86 Cinn	8-87
Wilmer, James A.	Inst	572-6582		17	MBA	62 Xavier	8-90

Northern Michigan Univ	Marquette, MI	49855	(906) NMUMUS				
Walker L. Cisler Sch Bs			FAX=227-2930				BS
Gnauck, Brian G.	Dean	227-2947	fabg	Econ	PHD	68 Minn	1963
—Department of Management	Phone	227-2605	Fax 227-2930				
Carnahan, George R.	Prof	227-2605	fagc		PHD	67 Ohio St	1987
Sherany,	Prof				PHD			
Allen, David E.	Assoc	227-1244	fada		PHD	74 Utah	1987
Drosen, James W.	Assoc	227-1247	fajd		PHD	83 Northwes	
Miller, Robert J.	Assoc	227-1241	famr		PHD	78 U Wash	1978

Northern State University	Aberdeen, SD	57401-7198	(605)				
School of Bus & Industr	1200 South Jay Street		FAX=622-3022				BA,BS
Arnold, Clyde	Dean	622-2400	naca01	7 V	PHD	82 Oklahoma	1988
—Department of Management	Phone		Fax 622-3022				
Ohmer, Douglas	Asst			1 EIY	ABD	Kentucky	
Smith, James	Asst	622-2639		3 AHE	DPA	92 Alabama	8-91

Northwest College	Kirkland, WA	98083-0579	(206)				
Divion of Business Adm	5520 108th Ave NE		FAX=				BS,BA
McMillin, John G.	C-Pr	889-5331		38 IY	PHD	74 U Wash	1991
—Management Faculty	Phone	889-5331	Fax 889-5321				
Stoops, David L.	Asst	889-5324		56 T	MBA	91 Phoenix	1993

Northwest Missouri St Univ — Maryville, MO — 64468-6001 — (816) NORTHWEST.MISSOURI.EDU

Coll Bus, Gov & Cpt Sci — FAX=562-1900 — BS,MBA

Name	Rank	Phone	Code		Degree	Yr	School	Year
DeYoung, Ron C.	Dean	582-7682	0700037	BEd	EDD	71	N Illin	1984
–Dept of Management & Mktg	Phone	562-1837	Fax 562-1484					
Ballantyne, Edwin J. Jr.	C-As	562-1756	0100166		PHD	89	Mo-Rolla	1989
Browning, Sharon	Prof	562-1282	0100051		PHD	73	Missouri	1964
Kramer, Gerald H.	Assoc	562-1859	0100253		PHD		Iowa	1988
Moss, Martha	Asst	562-1283	0100343		MSED		Missouri	1958
Nothstine, Don	Asst	562-1758	0100363		MBA		Missouri	1970
Stanley, Sande Richards	Asst	562-1858	0100537		ABD		S Illin	1991
Knappp, Jeff	Inst	562-1652	0100373		MBA	91	NW Mo St	1992
Northup, Russell	Inst	562-1751	0100157		MBA	90	NW Mo St	1990
White, Sandra	Inst	562-1857			MBA	89	NW Mo St	1989

on education leave

Northwestern University — Evanston, IL — 60208-2001 — (708) ACNS.NWU.EDU — 1916

Kellogg Grad Sch of Mgt — 1801 Hinman Avenue — FAX=491-5071

email: @1 = casbah.acns.nwu.edu; @2 = merle.acns.nwu.edu; @3 = nuacvm.acns.nwu.edu

Name	Rank	Phone	Email	c1	c2	Field	Degree	Yr	School	Year
Jacobs, Donald P.	Dean	491-2838				Fnce	PHD	57	Columbia	1957
–Organization Behavior	Phone	491-3470	Fax 491-8896							
Moag, Joseph S.	C-Pr	491-8071					PHD	64	Northwes	1960
Bazerman, Max H.	Prof	491-8077	mbazer@1	2			PHD	79	Car Mel	1985

J. Jay Gerber Distinguished Professor of Dispute Resolution & Organizations

Brett, Jeanne M.	Prof	491-8075	jmbrett@1	5	N		PHD	72	Illinois	1070

DeWitt W. Buchanon, Jr. Professor of Dispute Resolution & Organization

Duncan, Robert B.	Prof	491-4954		3	I		PHD	71	Yale	1970

J. L. Kellogg Distinguished Professor of Strategy & Organization Behavior

Hirsch, Paul M.	Prof	491-8069					PHD	73	Michigan	1989

James L. Allen Distinguished Professor of Strategy & Organization Behavior

Messick, David	Prof	491-8074	dmessick@1				PHD	65	N Carol	1991

Alice and Morris Kaplan Professor of Ethics & Decision in Management

Neale, M. A.	Prof	491-8274	mneal@1	2	E		PHD	82	Texas	1987

J. L. & Helen Kellogg Distinguished Prof of Dispute Resolution & Organization

Radnor, Michael	Prof	491-5617		2	E		PHD	64	Northwes	1964
Rousseau, Denise M.	Prof	491-8076		2	E		PHD	77	Berkeley	1981
Shortell, Stephen M.	Prof	491-2688					PHD	72	Chicago	1982

A.C. Buehler Professor of Hospital & Health Services Management

Dewar, Robert D.	Assoc	491-8070		2	E		PHD	76	Wiscon	1974
Messick, Judith	Assoc	491-2656	jmessick@1				PHD	82	Ca-SnBar	1992

Clinical Associate Professor of Communication

Zajac, Edward	Assoc	491-8272	ezblo585@3	2	E		PHD	86	Penn	1986

James F. Bere Professor of Organization Behavior

Gruenfeld, Deb	Asst	491-8286	dgruen@2				PHD	93	Illinois	1993
Gulati, Ranjay	Asst	491-2685					PHD	93	Harvard	1993

email ran@merle.nwu.edu

Stoller, Martin	Asst	491-3470					PHD	89	Northwes	1991
Straub, Paul	VAsst	467-2366	pstaub@2				PHD	93	Illinois	1993
Uzzi, Brian	Asst	491-8072	buzzi@3				PHD	93	SUNY-SBr	1993
VanCamp, Karen	Asst	467-2366					ABD		Northwes	1990
–Dept Management & Strategy	Phone		Fax 467-1777							
Besanko, David	C-Pr	491-7753		37	IU		PHD	82	Northwes	

Michael L. Nemmers Distinguished Professor; email: besanko@merle.acns.nwu.edu

Alexis, Marcus	Prof	467-1318		31	IQ		PHD	69	Minn	

Board of Trustees Professor of Economics

Benishay, Haskel	Prof	491-5131		37	IU		PHD	60	Chicago	1967
Juris, Hervey A.	Prof	491-8684		5	NPQ		PHD	67	Chicago	1970
Lavengood, Lawrence G.	Prof	491-8687		4	JKL		PHD	53	Chicago	
Manheim, Marvin L.	Prof	491-8676		39	IZ		PHD	64	MIT	

William A. Patterson Distinguished Professor of Transportation

Neuschel, Robert	Prof	491-8674		18	DY		MBA	47	Harvard	
Roomkin, Myron J.	Prof	491-8673		58	NQY		PHD	71	Wiscon	
Satterwaite, Mark A.	Prof	491-5482		37	IUV		PHD	73	Wiscon	

Earl Dean Howard Professor of Managerial Economics

Scott, Walter D.	Prof	491-2686		18	DY		MS	58	Columbia	
Spulber, Daniel	Prof	491-8675		37	IV		PHD	79	Northwes	

Thomas G. Ayers Professor of Energy Resource Management

Christensen, H. Kurt	Assoc	491-8678		3	I		PHD	77	Columbia	
Dana, James	Assoc	491-3465		3	I		PHD	88	MIT	
Dranove, David	Assoc	491-8682		17	CU		PHD	83	Stanford	
Isenman, Albert W.	Assoc	491-3177		13	IJ		PHD	82	Northwes	
Meyer, Stuart	Assoc	491-8688		6	ST		PHD	62	Princeton	
Shanley, Mark T.	Assoc	491-8683		32	IE		PHD	86	Penn	1991
Spier, Kathryn	Assoc	491-3465		34	IK		PHD	89	MIT	
Cech, Paula-Ann	Asst	491-8672		3	I		PHD	89	Arizona	
Peteraf, Margaret	VAsst	491-8698		3	I		PHD	87	Yale	
Prokop, Jacek	Asst	467-1896		78	UY		PHD		Va Tech	
Regibeau, Pierre	Asst	491-4271		78	UY		PHD	87	Berkeley	
Rockett, Katharine	Asst	491-4270		3	HI		PHD	88	Berkeley	
Adams, Laurel	Lect	491-8677		8	IY		PHD	93	Penn	

Northwestern State U of LA
Natchitoches, LA 71497 (318)

Division of Business — FAX= — BS

Name	Rank	Phone			Deg		School	
Smiley, Barry A.	D-Pr				DBA	75	La Tech	
—Management Faculty	Phone 357-5161	Fax 357-5990						
Fusilier, Marcelline R.	Assoc	357-5264			PHD		Purdue	
Worley, Joel K.	Assoc	357-4538			PHD		Va Tech	
Creighton, Walter H.	Asst	357-5704			PHD		Colo St	
Durlabhji, Subhash	Asst	357-5708			PHD		Mich St	
White, Susan C.	Inst				PHD		Tx A&M	8-94
on sabbatical leave to Texas A&M University								
Wilkerson, Mary Lynn	Inst	357-5611			MBA		Northwes	
Dir. S.B.D.C.								
Williams, John G.	Inst	357-5722			JD		Tulane	

Northwood University
Midland, MI 48640-2398 (517)

College of Business — 3225 Cook Road — FAX=832-9590 — BBA,MBA

Name	Rank	Phone			Deg		School	Year
Nash, Timothy G.	Dean$ 837-4371				MA	87		1981
—Business Division	Phone 837-4371	Fax 832-9590						
Firenze, Louis J.	D-Pr	837-4240	35	BDEN	PHD	82	Mich St	1974
Haywood, Dale	Prof	837-4291	3	I	PHD		Texas	1970
Nehil, Tom	Assoc	837-4295	8	Y	BA		Oberlin	1981
Schell, Richard	Asst	837-4257			MBA		Cen Mich	1989

Norwich University
Northfield, VT 05663 (802)

Div of Business & Mgt — FAX=485-2580 — BS

Name	Rank	Phone			Deg		School	
Vanecek, Frank T.	H	485-2212	9		DBA			
—Management Faculty	Phone 485-2210	Fax 485-2580						
Buckley, Harry A.	C-Pr	485-2226	25		PHD			
Kennedy, Patricia	Prof	485-2225	15		EDD			
Macdonald, Jean L	Prof	485-2223	16		PHD			
Kilgore, Jeffrey	Assoc	485-2219	36		JD			
Susmann, Philip	Assoc	485-2227	79		MBA			
Eitel, Douglas	Asst	485-2222	34		JD			
Thibault, Christopher	Asst	485-2214	9		MBA			

University of Notre Dame
Notre Dame, IN 46556 (219) IRISHMVS 1962,1972

College of Business Adm — FAX=239-5255 — BBA,MBA

Name	Rank	Phone			Deg		School	Year
Keane, John G.	Dean	631-7992	3	I	PHD	65	Pitt	1989
—Department of Management	Phone 631-6183	Fax 631-5255						
Conlon, Edward J.	C-Pr	631-7685 econlon	2	EH	PHD	78	Car Mel	1992
Houck, John W.	Prof	631-6685	4	KL	LLM	63	Harvard	1957
Sexton, William P.	Prof	631-6122	12	EF	PHD	66	Ohio St	
Vecchio, Robert P.	Prof	631-6073	12	EFH	PHD		Illinois	1976
Franklin D. Schurz Professor of Management								
Chang, Yu-Chi	Assoc	631-5215	7	V	PHD	72	Wiscon	1971
Cho, Byung T.	Assoc	631-7562	7		PHD	63	Illinois	1966
Ghiaseddin, Nasir	Assoc	631-5184	9	Z	PHD		Purdue	1982
Hartvigsen, David	Assoc	631-9470	7		PHD	85	Car Mel	1993
Matta, Khalil F.	Assoc	631-6333	79	UZ	PHD	82	Notre Dm	1982
Sinha, Diptendu	Assoc	631-6078	7	UV	PHD	85	Wiscon	1985
Wei, Che-Yung	Assoc	631-5460	7	UV	PHD	87	Tx A&M	1987
Williams CSC, Oliver F.	Assoc	631-6858	4	KLM	PHD		Vanderbt	
Chen, Houn-Gee	Asst	631-5833	79	UZ	PHD	88	Wiscon	1987
Crant, J. Michael	Asst	631-6765	12	EFH	PHD	90	N Carol	1990
Davis, James	Asst	631-8614	13		PHD	91	Iowa	1991
Giannantonio, Cristina	Asst	631-6139	15	NOPR	PHD	88	Maryland	1988
Goltz, Sonia M.	Asst	631-5104	12	EFHR	PHD	87	Purdue	1987
Huguenard, Brian	Asst	631-9467	9	Z	PHD	93	Car Mel	1993
Mayer, Roger C.	Asst	631-6764	25	EFHN	PHD	89	Purdue	1988
Patterson, Dennis	Asst	631-8435	13	I	PHD	92	Illinois	1990
Seibert, Scott	Asst	631-6128	15		PHD	93	Cornell	1991
Simon, John T.	Asst	631-5074	7	UV	PHD	89	Northwes	1989
Tama, Joseph M.	Asst	631-5057	7		PHD	90	Car Mel	1991
Michel, John	Inst	631-9469	3		ABD		Columbia	1993

Oakland University
Rochester, MI 48309-4401 (313) ARGO.ACS.OAKLAND.EDU 1988,1988

School of Bus Adm — FAX=370-4275 — BS,MBA

Name	Rank	Phone			Deg		School	Year
Stevens, George E.	Dean	370-3286 stevens	45	NJLR	DBA	79	Kent St	1-91
—Dept of Management & Mktg	Phone	Fax 370-4274						
York, Kenneth M.	C-Ac	370-3272 york	52	N	PHD	86	Bowl Gr	1986
Braunstein, Daniel N.	Prof	370-3298 braunste	52	N	PHD	64	Purdue	1971
Gregory, Karl	Prof	370-3295 gregory	36	IST	PHD	62	Michigan	1968
Schwartz, Howard S.	Prof	370-2212 schwartz	2	HJ	PHD	80	Cornell	1978
Barclay, Lizabeth A.	Assoc	370-3293 barclay	52	N	PHD	81	Wayne St	8-80
VanSell, Mary P.	Assoc	370-2213 vansell	2	RG	PHD	81	Iowa	1985
Willoughby, Floyd G.	Assoc	370-3290 willough	3	I	PHD	84	Mich St	1983
Mayer, Donald O.	Asst	370-3238 mayer	4	KJ	LLM	85	Geotown	8-90

–Decision & Info Sciences		Phone	370-3285	Fax 370-4275						
Lederer, Albert L.	C-Pr	370-4281	lederer		9	Z	PHD	83	Ohio St	1989
Doane, David P.	Prof	370-4002	doane		79	VZ	PHD	69	Purdue	1969
Hough, Robbin R.	Prof	370-4089	hough		97	ZV	PHD	62	MIT	1962
Lauer, Thomas M.	Assoc	370-3278	lauer		9	Z	PHD	86	Indiana	1985
Tower, John E.	Assoc	370-3280	tower		9	Z	PHD	68	SUNY-Buf	1968
Wharton, T. J.	Assoc	370-4284	wharton		7	UV	PHD	85	Minn	1990
Hormozi, Amir M.	Asst	370-4093	hormozi		7	U	PHD	87	Houston	1986
Jacobs, Sheila M.	Asst	370-4088	jacobs		9	Z	PHD	87	Ariz St	1987
Mathieson, Kieran	Asst	370-3507	mathieso		9	Z	PHD	87	Indiana	1991

Oglethorpe University		Atlanta, GA		30319-2797	(404)					BBA
Div of Business & Econ		4484 Peachtree Road NE			FAX=					
Tucker, Dean	C-Ac	261-1441			13	IM	PHD	79	Mich St	1-88
Rikard Chaired Professor										
–Management Faculty		Phone		Fax 364-8500						
Shropshire, William O.	Prof	261-1441				Econ	PHD	63	Duke	1979
Calloway Professor										
Straley, William	Assoc	261-1441			78	UXAT	PHD	79	Auburn	8-90
Schulz, William	Asst	261-1441			36	TIYD	PHD	93	Georgia	8-92

Ohio University		Athens, OH		45701-2979	(614) OUVAXA.CATS.OHIOU.EDU			50,1969		
College of Business Adm					FAX=593-1388					BA
Kelley, C. Aaron	Dean	593-2000			3	IFES	PHD	79	North Tx	8-93
–Dept Management Systems		Phone	593-2061	Fax 593-0319						
Marinolli, Arthur	C-Pr	600 2003			4	Law	JD		Ohio St	
Boland, Thomas	Prof	593-2082			7		PHD	66	Chicago	
Day, William A.	Prof	593-2000			13		DBA	67	Harvard	1965
Fuller, Stephen	Prof	593-0484			12					
Manjulika, Koshal	Prof	593-2076			7	U	PHD	64	Patna	
Schermerhorn, John R.	Prof	593-1788			12		PHD	74	Northwes	
O'Bleness Professor										
Spataro, Lucian P.	Prof	593-2008			25		PHD	65	Illinois	
Stinson, John E.	Prof	593-2073			23		PHD	70	Ohio St	1964
Tracy, Lane N.	Prof	593-2006			25		PHD	71	U Wash	
Carvalho, Gerry	Assoc	593-1988			3		PHD	68	Michigan	
Cutright, Ken	Assoc	593-2081			8		PHD	90	W Virg	
Fuller, Frances	Assoc	593-0484			2					
Gunn, Patricia	Assoc	592-1983			4		JD	74	Boston C	
Keifer, Mary	Assoc	593-2069			4		JD	71	Virginia	
Martin, Clarence	Assoc	593-2079			7		PHD	79	Car Mel	
Milter, Richard G.	Assoc	593-2072			29		PHD	86	SUNY-Alb	
Perotti, Valerie	Assoc	593-2068			12		PHD	87	Ohio U	
Roberson, Jessie	Assoc	593-2066			4		JD	80	Michigan	
Yost, Edward B.	Assoc	593-2085			25		PHD	87	Ohio St	
Bridges, Carl	Asst	593-0026			25		PHD	92	N Illin	
Coombs, Garth	Asst	592-1987			12		PHD	94	Colorado	
Thacker, Rebecca A.	Asst	593-2060			5	KNQ	PHD	87	Tx A&M	
Boger, Pamela A.	Inst	593-2071			7		PHD	84	Ohio U	
Woolley, Virginia	Inst	593-2071			1		MA	61	Wiscon	
Gray, Michael	Lect				4		JD	75	Wiscon	
Assistant to the Dean of Cultural Div										
Miller, Peggy	Lect	593-2077			12		PHD	87	Ohio U	
Scamehorn, Richard	Lect	593-2025			38		MBA	67	Indiana	
–Dept of Mgt Info Systems		Phone	593-0646	Fax 593-0319						
Day, John	C-Pr	593-2065	dayj				PHD		Ohio U	
Luce, Thomas G.	Prof	593-2058	luce				PHD		Purdue	
McClanahan, Anne H.	Prof	593-2089	mcclanahan				PHD		Ohio U	
Perotti, James	Prof	593-2059	perotti				PHD		Duquesne	
Sutherland, David	Assoc	593-1801	sutherland				PHD		Kansas	
Holden, Ellsworth	Asst	593-2074	holden				MA		Harvard	
Brown, Corrine	Lect	593-0656	brownc				MBA		Ohio U	

Ohio Northern University		Ada, OH		45810	(419) ONU.EDU					BSBA
College of Business Adm					FAX=772-1932					
Maris, Terry L.	Dean	772-2070	t maris			Mgt	PHD	79	Nebraska	1990
–Management Faculty		Phone		Fax 772-1932						
Cooper, Ken	Prof	772-2235	k_cooper		3	IJ	PHD	84	Minn	6-86
Savino, David M.	Assoc	772-2070	d_savino		52	QNE	MBA	79	Young St	6-86

Ohio State University		Columbus, OH		43210-1399	(614)			1916,1963		
College of Business		1775 College Road			FAX=292-1651			BS,MBA,MAC,PHD		
Alutto, Joseph A.	Dean	292-2666			2	E	PHD	68	Cornell	1991
–Dept Mgt & Human Resources		Phone	292-5028	Fax 292-7062						
Mangum, Stephen	C-Ac	292-3834			5	NQ	PHD	84	Geo Wash	1983

Name	Rank	Phone		Codes		Degree	Yr	School	Yr
Greenberg, Jerald	Prof	292-9829		2	EJN	PHD	75	Wayne St	1981
Lewicki, Roy	Prof	292-0258		3	I	PHD	74	Wiscon	1974
Miceli, Marcia P.	Prof	292-2668		5	N	DBA	82	Indiana	1981
Associate Dean for Academic Programs									
Sandver, Marcus H.	Prof	292-4586		5	Q	PHD	76	Wiscon	1976
Sexton, Don	Prof	292-5707		3	IT	PHD	72	Ohio St	1986
Wanous, John P.	Prof	292-4591		2	E	PHD	72	Yale	1983
Campagna, Anthony F.	Assoc	292-2833		5	Q	PHD	71	UCLA	1970
Cheng, Joseph L. C.	Assoc	292-8692		8	Y	PHD	77	Michigan	1992
Ford, Jeffrey D.	Assoc	292-4563		2	EH	PHD	75	Ohio St	1983
Greenberger, David B.	Assoc	292-5291		2	E	PHD	81	Wiscon	1982
Heneman, Robert L.	Assoc	292-4587		5	N	PHD	84	Mich St	1984
Hills, Stephen M.	Assoc	292-2158		5	Q	PHD	75	Wiscon	1977
Kim, Jay	Assoc	292-3045		2	E	PHD	75	Mich St	1980
Klein, Howard	Assoc	292-0719		5	P	PHD	87	Mich St	1987
Reichers, Arnon E.	Assoc	292-0737		2	E	PHD	83	Mich St	1982
Todor, William D.	Assoc	292-4588		2	E	PHD	79	Ca-Irvine	1979
Daily, Catherine M.	Asst	292-4588		3	I	PHD	91	Indiana	1992
—Dept of Management Science	Phone	292-1275	Fax 292-1272						
Schilling, David A.	C-Pr	292-1275		7	V	PHD	76	J Hopkin	1978
Benton, W. C.	Prof	292-8868		7	U	PHD	81	Indiana	1982
Berry, William	Prof	292-3173		7	U	DBA	69	Harvard	1992
Krajewski, LeRoy J.	Prof	292-9218		7	U	PHD	69	Wiscon	1969
Milligan, Glenn W.	Prof	292-6318		7	V	PHD	78	Ohio St	1979
Nutt, Paul C.	Prof	292-4605		3	I	PHD	74	Wiscon	1974
Rhee, Wansoo T.	Prof	292-5297		7	V	PHD	79	Kent St	1981
Collier, David A.	Assoc	292-8305				PHD	78	Ohio St	1986
Current, John R.	Assoc	292-3766		7	V	PHD	82	J Hopkin	1982
Hall, Nicholas G.	Assoc	292-9216		7	V	PHD		Berkeley	
Storbeck, James E.	Assoc	292-3081		7	V	PHD	80	Texas	1980
Vohra, Rakesh V.	Assoc	292-4600		7	V	PHD	85	Maryland	1985
Cheng, Richard	Asst	292-4136		7	Y	PHD	92	Minn	1992
Ward, Peter T.	Asst	292-5294		7	U	PHD	88	Boston U	1988

Ohio Wesleyan University   Delaware, OH   43015   (614) OWUCOMCN
Department of Economics   FAX=369-0810   BA

Name	Rank	Phone		Codes		Degree	Yr	School	Yr
Cook, Clifford G.	C-Ac	368-3539		9	Z	MBA		Drexel	1984
—Management Faculty	Phone		Fax 369-0810						
Gharrity, Norman J.	Prof	368-3543		8	Y	PHD		J Hopkin	1962
Gitter, Robert J.	Prof	368-3536		5	OQ	PHD	78	Wiscon	1976
Leavy, Richard L.	Prof	368-3807		2	FL	PHD		Mass	1980
Murchland, Bernard	Prof	368-3793		4	J	PHD		SUNY Buf	1967
Smith, Jan	Prof	368-3838		28	EHY	PHD		Princeton	1977
Woltemade, Uwe J.	Prof	368-3547		4	J	PHD		Texas	1965
Boos, John D.	Assoc	368-3546		34	IJT	JD		Geo Wash	1983
Harvey, Joann P.	Assoc	368-3541		9	Z	MBA	82	Ohio St	1981
Simon, Alice E.	Assoc	368-3540		5	Q	PHD		Ohio St	1985
Alexander, Peter	Asst	386-3538							
Dorrian, Anne M.	Asst	368-3547		3		MBA	82	Ohio St	1992

University of Oklahoma   Norman, OK   73019-0450   (405) CBAFAC.UOKNOR.EDU 1926,1963
College of Business Adm   307 W. Brooks, Rm 206A   FAX=325-7688   BAC,BBA,MBA,PHD

Name	Rank	Phone	Email	Codes		Degree	Yr	School	Yr
Cosier, Richard A.	Dean	325-3611			Mgt	PHD	76	Iowa	1-93
Fred E. Brown Professor; email: rjc@cbadeans.uoknor.edu									
—Division of Management	Phone	375-2651	Fax 325-1957						
Schwarzkopf, A. B.	D-Ac	325-5703	aschwar	97	ZVU	PHD	68	Virginia	9-70
Alonso, Ramon C.	Prof	325-2653	ralonso	38	IY	PHD	70	SUNY	9-74
Driver, Russell W.	Prof	325-2697	rdriver	25	&ENK	PHD	79	Georgia	1-79
Associate Dean									
Evans, Rodney E.	Prof	325-2656	revans	38	IST	PHD	66	Mich St	1970
Harvey, Michael G.	Prof	325-3376	mharvey	38	ISTY	PHD	76	Arizona	8-92
Puterbaugh Chair of American Free Enterprise									
Michaelsen, Larry K.	Prof	325-5692	lmichael	23	EGD	PHD	73	Michigan	1974
David Ross Boyd Professor									
Scanlan, Bert K.	Prof	325-2651	bscanlan	12	DEX	PHD	64	Nebraska	6-69
David Ross Boyd Professor									
Tersine, Richard J.	Prof	325-5698	rtersine	7	UV	DBA	69	Fla St	8-80
Baldwin Professor									
VanHorn, Richard	Prof	325-0900							
Weitzel, William	Prof	325-5732	wweitzel	25	EHNP	PHD	66	Wayne St	8-78
Whitely, William T.	Prof	325-5733	wwhitely	25	OY	PHD	76	Minn	8-80
Wren, Daniel A.	Prof	325-5699	dwren	13	BI	PHD	64	Illinois	1973
David Ross Boyd Prof; McCasland Prof of Am Free Entrpr; Curator Bass Collectn									
Barman, Samir	Assoc	325-5717	sbarman	7	UV	PHD	87	Clemson	8-87
Buckley, Michael R.	Assoc	325-5729	mbuckley	25	ENXP	PHD	85	Auburn	8-87
Price, R. Leon	Assoc	325-5739	rprice	9	Z	DBA	78	Oklahoma	9-79
Sethi, Vijay	Assoc	325-2594		9	Z	PHD	88	Pitt	9-91
Dejoie, Roy	Asst	325-5724	rdejoie	9	Z	PHD	91	Tx A&M	8-92

Name	Rank	Phone	email			Degree	Yr	School	Date
Pinkston, T. S.	Asst	325-5943	tpinksto	38	IJ	PHD	91	Georgia	8-91
Sharfman, Mark P.	Asst	325-5689		38	IJY	PHD	85	Arizona	8-90
Tersine, Michele G.	Inst	325-5719	mtersin	7	U	MBA	79	Old Dom	8-80

Oklahoma Baptist University — Shawnee, OK 74801-2590 (405) FAX=878-2069 — BBA
School of Business — 500 West University
phone 878-2115

Name	Rank	Phone				Degree	Yr	School	Date
Babb, Robert M.	Dean	Ext 2115		92	ZPF	EDD			8-89
—**Management Faculty**	Phone		Fax 878-2069						
Adair, Manoj	Prof	Ext 3285				MBE			8-55
Cragin, John P.	Prof	Ext 2157		38	DITY	PHD			8-90
Willis, J. Clay	Asst	Ext 2121		18	DHNP	MBA			8-86

Oklahoma Christian Univ — Oklahoma City OK 73136-1100 (405) FAX=425-5149
College of Business — 2501 East Memorial

Name	Rank	Phone				Degree	Yr	School	Date
Skaggs, W. Jack	Dean	425-5567				EDD	87	Okla St	1-81
—**Management Faculty**	Phone	425-5560	Fax 425-5574						
Goad, Bill	Assoc	425-5565		9		EDD	86	Okla St	8-82
Smith, Robert	Assoc	425-5566		15		ABD			
Snyman, Johannes	Assoc	425-5563		23	I	ABD		N Mex St	

Oklahoma City University — Oklahoma City OK 73106 (405) FAX=521-5098
Meinders School of Bus — 2501 North Blackwelder — D3,MBA

Name	Rank	Phone				Degree	Yr	School	Date
Brown, Thomas L.	Dean	521-5276				PHD		Okla St	8-90
C. R. Anthony Chair of Competitive Enterprises									
—**Management Faculty**	Phone		Fax 521-5098						
Cawthon, David L.	C-Pr	521-5056		23	E	EDD		Okla St	8-88
Shafa, Hossein	Prof	521-5126		8	Y	PHD		Texas	8-88
Frew, Michael	Assoc	521-5143		12	O	ABD		Oklahoma	8-82
Smith, Clayton G.	Assoc	521-5276		3	I	PHD		Purdue	8-93
Krueger, David	Asst	521-5827		3	I	ABD		Purdue	8-92
McCain, Barbara	Asst	521-5268		1	R	PHD		Oklahoma	8-89
Middleton, Karen	Asst	521-5276		2	E	PHD		Houston	8-93

Oklahoma State University — Stillwater, OK 74078-0555 (405) OSUCC FAX=744-5180 — 1958,1964 BS,MS,PHD
College of Business Adm

Name	Rank	Phone	email			Degree	Yr	School	Date
Sandmeyer, Robert L.	Dean	744-5064		Econ		PHD	62	Okla St	1962
—**Department of Management**	Phone	744-5201	Fax 744-5180						
Meinhart, Wayne A.	H-Pr	744-5201	mgmtwam	32	H	PHD	64	Illinois	1962
Aukerman, Richard A.	Prof	744-5117	mgmtraa	9	Z	PHD	75	N Dakota	1980
Ho, David C.	Prof	744-8634	mgmtdch	7	UV	PHD	85	Mich St	1983
Ireland, Timothy C.	Prof	744-8642	mgmttci	7	UV	PHD	78	Okla St	1981
Kletke, Marilyn G.	Prof	744-5111	mgmtmgk	9	Z	PHD	81	Okla St	9-81
Lau, Hon-Shiang	Prof	744-5105	mgmthsl	7	V	PHD	73	N Carol	1984
Regents Professor									
Nord, G. Daryl	Prof	744-8632	mgmtgdn	9	Z	PHD	76	N Dakota	1977
Sharda, Ramesh	Prof	744-8638	mgmtrs	7	V	PHD	81	Wiscon	9-80
Stone, Thomas H.	Prof	744-8641	mgmtths	5	NQ	PHD	69	Minn	1-89
Turner, J. Scott	Prof	744-5107	mgmtjst	7	V	PHD	70	So Meth	1982
Barr, Steven H.	Assoc	744-5202	mgmtshb	2	E	PHD	86	Iowa	1-82
Fried, Vance H.	Assoc	744-8633	mgmtvhf	3	IT	JD	76	Michigan	1-87
Labig, Chalmer E.	Assoc	744-8635	mgmtcel	5	NQP	PHD	84	Texas	1984
Nelson, Debra L.	Assoc	744-5106	mgmtdln	2	EG	PHD	85	Texas	8-85
Nord, Jeretta H.	Assoc	744-5090	mgmtjhn	9	Z	EDD	82	Okla St	1985
White, Margaret A.	Assoc	744-8645	mgmtmaw	23	I	PHD	89	Tx A&M	8-86
Basu, Raja	Asst	744-5118	mgmtrxb	2	E	PHD	91	Purdue	8-91
Bogert, James D.	Asst	744-8647	mgmtjdb	3	I	ABD		Tx A&M	8-91
Dalal, Nikunj	Asst	744-5089	mgmtnd	9	Z	PHD	90	Tx Tech	8-90
Eastman, Kenneth K.	Asst	744-8646	mgmtkke	2	E	PHD	89	Nebraska	8-89
Ramanathan, Jayaram	Asst	744-7546	mgmtjr	9	Z	ABD		Pitt	1-91
Smith, Faye L.	Asst	744-5083	mgmtfls	3	I	PHD	89	Iowa	8-89
Wilson, Rick L.	Asst	744-5084	mgmtrlw	9	Z	PHD	90	Nebraska	8-90

Old Dominion University — Norfolk, VA 23529-0223 (804) ODUVM FAX=683-5155 — 1974,1980 BS,MBA,DBA
College of Bus & Pub Ad
Did Not Respond-1993 Listing

Name	Rank	Phone				Degree	Yr	School	Date
Wallace, William H.	Dean	683-3521		Econ		PHD	62	Illinois	
—**Department of Management**	Phone	683-3544	Fax 683-5155						
Chung, Kae H.	C-Pr	683-3547				PHD	68	LSU	
Chadwin, Mark L.	Prof	683-4598							
McAfee, R. Bruce	Prof	683-3539				PHD	79	Wayne St	
Anderson, Claire June	Assoc	683-4715				PHD	76	Mass	
Chapagne, Paul J.	Assoc	683-3505				PHD	77	Mass	
Greene, G. Robert	Assoc	683-3561				PHD	83	Geo St	
Simmonds, Paul G.	Assoc	683-4224		38	ISY	PHD	87	Temple	1992

Zahrly, Janice H.	Assoc	683-3566				PHD	84	Florida	
Archer, Richard W.	Asst	683-3548				PHD	91	Georgia	
Boyd, Brian K.	Asst	683-3564	bkb100f	3	I	PHD	89	S Calif	8-92
Morris, Sara A.	Asst	683-3406				PHD	87	Texas	
Quarstein, Vernon A.	Asst	683-3506				PHD	87	Va Comm	

Olivet College Olivet, MI 49076 (616)
Dept of Business & Econ FAX=749-7650

Kiebala, Susan	C-As	749-7610		18		MBA	77	W Mich	1989
—**Management Faculty**	Phone		Fax 749-7650						
Butler, G. Robert	Prof	749-7664		6		MBA	56	Chicago	1992

Oral Roberts University Tulsa, OK 74171 (918)
School of Business 7777 South Lewis Avenue FAX=495-6033 BS,MBA

Swearingen, Eugene	Dean	495-7040		46	TJ	PHD	55	Stanford	8-82
—**Management Faculty**	Phone		Fax 495-6500						
Dyson, David	Prof	495-6112		38	IY	PHD	88	Arkansas	8-85
Assistant Dean									
Lewandowski, Mark	Inst	495-6562		1	H	MBA	92	Oral Rob	8-92
Winslow, Rob	Inst	495-6560		3	I	MBA	90	Oral Rob	8-94

University of Oregon Eugene, OR 97403-1208 (503) OREGON 1923,1963
College of Business Adm FAX=346-3341 BS,BA,PHD

Reinmuth, James E.	Dean	346-3300	ier		Quan	PHD	69	Oreg St	
—**Dept of Management**	Phone	346-3339	Fax 346-3341						
Brown, Warren B.	H-Pr	346-3363		36	IT	PHD	62	Car Mel	1967
Meyer, Alan D.	Prof	346-5178		2	HE	PHD	78	Berkeley	1984
E. E. & J. W. Cone Professor of Management									
Mowday, Richard T.	Prof	346-3307		2	EH	PHD	75	Ca-Irvine	1977
Gerald B. Bashaw Professor of Management									
Steers, Richard M.	Prof	346-3318		2	HEY	PHD	73	Ca-Irvine	1975
Kazumitsu Shiome Professor of Management									
Terborg, James R.	Prof	346-3354		2	E	PHD	75	Purdue	1980
Carolyn S. Chambers Professor of Management									
Hundley, Greg S.	Assoc	346-3347		5	Q	PHD	81	Minn	1983
Ungson, Gerardo R.	Assoc	346-5137		3	IY	PHD	78	Penn St	
Koch, Marianne J.	Asst	346-3338		5	N	PHD	88	Columbia	1988
Russo, Michael V.	Asst	346-5182		34	IL	PHD	89	Berkeley	1989
Steckler, Nicole	Asst	346-2691		2	E	PHD	90	Harvard	1990
Dusseau, David t.	VInst	346-3398		28	EY	PHD	92	Oregon	1992
Lytle, Donald E.	SInst	346-3329		1		MBA	76	Oregon	1976
Director of Undergraduate Programs									
Swangard, Randy	AdjIn	346-3349		6		MBA	71	Wash	1987

Oregon State University Corvallis, OR 97331-2603 (503) 1960,1970
College of Business FAX=737-4890 BS

Parker, Donald F.	Dean	737-6025			Mgt	PHD	75	Cornell	1991
—**Dept of Management & Mktg**	Phone	737-3520	Fax 737-4890						
Miller, Ronald L.	C-Pr	737-3520		5	Q	PHD	69	Penn	1987
Bloomfield, Stefan David	Prof	737-6056		7	V	PHD	72	Stanford	1971
Gobeli, David	Prof	737-6007		1	D	PHD	82	Minn	1982
Drexler, John A. Jr.	Assoc	737-2727		2	E	PHD	75	Michigan	1980
King, Jonathan	Assoc	737-4601		4	J	PHD	80	U Wash	1980
Larson, Erik	Assoc	737-6054		2	E	PHD	82	SUNY-Buf	1980
Lawton, Stephen J.	Assoc	737-2158		8	Y	MBA	75	Cornell	1980
Paschke, Paul Edward	Assoc	737-2363		7	V	DBA	70	Indiana	1969
Shane, Barry	Assoc	737-6063		3	I	PHD	73	Mass	1972
Fiegener, Mark	Asst	737-6058		3	I	PHD	90	Penn	1990
Gonzalez, Manolete	Asst	737-6061		3	I	PHD	85	S Calif	1985
Browne, Beverly	Inst	737-4461							
Dowling, Tom	Inst	737-3520		2	E				
Milosevic, Dragan	Inst	737-3529							
Schwallie, Ed	Inst	737-3520		7	U				

Otterbein College Westerville, OH 43081 (614)
Dept of Bus, Atg & Econ Grove & College Streets FAX=898-1200 BA,BS

Prindle, Allen M.	C	823-1481				PHD			
—**Management Faculty**	Phone	823-1361	Fax 823-1304						
Brown, Gerald C.	Assoc	823-1468		37	IJ	PHD	67	Ohio St	1988
Abdallah, Kamel	Asst	823-1892		38	YLID	PHD	92	Ohio St	1990
Eskew, Don	Asst	823-1212		15		PHD	93	Ohio St	1993
Mafi, Shirine	Asst	823-1796		7	U	MBA	78	Marshall	1987

Pace University	New York, NY	10038-1502	(212) PACEVM						
Lubin Sch of Business	Bedford Road		FAX=346-1613				BBA,MBA,MS,DPS		
442 exchange are at White Plains NY and have 914 area code									
Centonze, Arthur L.	Dean	346-1962			Adm	PHD	83	New York	1991
–Dept of Management/Mgt Sci	Phone	346-1214	Fax 346-1573						
Varanelli, Andrew Jr.	C-Pr	346-1214		37	IUV	DED	71	Rutgers	1968
Allan, Peter	Prof	346-1988		25		PHD		NYU	
Baugher, Daniel	Prof	346-1880		23	DNV	PHD	76	Rutgers	7-78
Bhandari, Narendra C.	Prof	346-1877		68	STY	PHD	72	Georgia	1978
Camgemi, Robert	Prof	442-4194				PHD	72	NYU	
Carter, John	Prof	442-4151		7		PHD	75	Columbia	
Dwyer, Hubert	Prof	442-4154		7		PHD	71	NYU	
El-Adawy, Zaki	Prof	346-1853				PHD		Illinois	
Hoefer, Peter	Prof	346-1990		7	F	PHD		Baruch	
Madu, Christian	Prof	346-1919		7	F	PHD		Baruch	
Russo, Joseph A.	Prof	346-1220				PHD	93	Rutgers	
Silverman, Fred	Prof	442-4186		7		PHD	74	Columbia	
Welty, William	Prof	346-1939		3		PHD		NYU	
Yurkiewicz, Jack	Prof	346-1908		7	F	PHD		Yale	
Bridwell, Larry	Assoc	346-1937		8		PHD		CUNY	
Dory, John	Assoc	346-1936		3		DBA		Harvard	
Francesco, Anne Marie	Assoc	346-1932	francesc	82	YERN	PHD	77	Ohio St	6-90
Gold, Barry A.	Assoc	346-1877		5		PHD	78	Columbia	
Hall, James C.	Assoc	346-1668		25	PE	PHD		Chicago	5-79
Keck, Sara	Assoc	346-1946		3	F	PHD	90	Columbia	9-93
Mangum, Wiley	Assoc	346-1884		37	EOUV	PHD	85	Fordham	1980
Morrow, Ira	Assoc	346-1846		25		PHD		NYU	
Russell, James W.	Assoc	346-1884		37	IVY	PHD	86	New York	1-76
Bhat, Vasanthakumar	Asst	346-1873			F	PHD		Yale	

Pace University-Westchester	Pleasantville NY	10570-2799	(914)						
Lubin School of Bus Adm			FAX=773-3785				BBA,MBA		
Centonze, Arthur L.	Dean	773-3715			Adm	PHD	83	NYU	1972
–Department of Management	Phone	773-3795	Fax 773-3785						
Dennehy, Robert F.	C-Pr	773-3519		2		PHD		NYU	1978
Cahn, E. S.	Prof	773-3686		7		PHD	80	Columbia	1985
Isaak, Robert A.	Prof	773-3686		8		PHD	71	NYU	1977
Pastore, Joseph Jr.	Prof	773-3620				PHD	69	St Louis	1976
Reitman, Frieda	Prof	773-3516		4		PHD		NYU	1982
Associate Dean									
Seldin, Peter	Prof	773-3305		2		PHD	74	Fordham	1979
Distinguished Professor									
Streever, Donald C.	Prof	773-3305		3		PHD	57	Illinois	1981
Cozzolino, John	Assoc	773-3517		7		PHD	67	MIT	1989
Schor, Susan	Assoc	773-3520				PHD	89	Mass	1993
Weisbord, Ellyn S.	Assoc	773-3520				PHD	90	NYU	1993
Anakwe, Uzo	Asst	773-3520		5		PHD	93	Drexel	1994
LeMoult, William D.	Asst	773-3493		5		JD	62	Fordham	1984
Lyew, Peter A.	Asst	773-3686		7		DBA	85	La Tech	1981

University of the Pacific	Stockton, CA	95211	(209) VMSI.UOP.EDU				1983		
School of Bus & Pub Adm	3601 Pacific Avenue		FAX=946-2586					BS	
Plovnick, Mark S.	Dean	946-2476	mplovnic	21	EFQ	PHD	75	MIT	3-89
–Management Faculty	Phone		Fax 946-2586						
Ballot, Michael H.	Prof	946-2623	mballot	57	QUV	PHD	73	Stanford	9-71
Banner, David K.	Prof	946-0263	dbanner	24	DHTE	PHD	73	Northwes	1-87
Buntz, C. Gregory	Prof	946-2476	gbuntlz	12	AD	PHD	73	Ohio St	7-78
Peery, Newman S.	Prof	946-2637	npeery	46	JLTI	PHD	74	U Wash	8-82
Blasingame, John W.	Assoc	946-2476	jblasing	23	IE	PHD	75	Houston	8-82
Kulisch, William A.	Assoc	946-2635	tkulisch	25	DENP	PHD	76	Colorado	8-81

Pacific Lutheran University	Tacoma, WA	98447	(206)				1971,1976		
School of Business			FAX=535-8723				BBA,MBA		
McCann, Joseph E.	Dean	535-7251		13	DINS	PHD	80	Penn	1992
–Management Faculty	Phone	535-7244	Fax 535-8723						
Barndt, Stephen E.	Prof	535-7255		13	IU	PHD	71	Ohio St	1978
Barnowe, J. Thad	Prof	535-7300		58	FGOY	PHD	73	Michigan	1977
Sepic, F. Thomas	Prof	535-7307		25	EFNP	PHD	79	U Wash	1979
Berniker, Eli	Assoc	535-7289		7	EFN	PHD	85	UCLA	1982
MacDonald, Diane	Assoc	535-7257		4	KLPS	JD	80	J Marsh	1987
Yager, William F.	Assoc	535-8722		35	IY	PHD	91	Oregon	1987
Ahna, Barbara	Asst	535-7253		4	IJLM	JD	78	UPS	1987
Gibson, Linda	Asst	535-7254		25	ENOR	PHD	89	Missouri	1989
Kibbey, Richard	Asst	535-8718		9	LVYZ	PHD	93	Port St	1988

Pacific Union College   Angwin, CA   94508-9797   (707)
Dept of Bus Adm & Econ   FAX=965-6237   BBA,BA,BS
Voth, Richard   Dean   965-6238   32 IE   PHD   73 Ariz St   1968
–**Management Faculty**   Phone   Fax 965-6237
Neergrand, Keith   Assoc 965-6238   7 U   PHD   Ca-Irvine   1994
Taylor, Lary   Assoc 965-6238   8 Y   MBA   Maryland   1978

University of Pennsylvania   Philadelphia, PA 19104-6370 (610) WMGTFAC.WHARTON.UPENN1916,1963
Wharton Sch 2000 SH-DH   34th & Spruce Street   FAX=898-0401   BSE,MBA,PHD
Decision Sci Dept & Public Policy Dept Did Not Respond-1993 Listing
Gerrity, Thomas P.   Dean   898-4851   gerrity   ZI   PHD   70 MIT   1990
   Reliance Professor of Management & Private Enterprise
–**Department of Management**   Phone 898-7722   Fax 898-1001
Webber, Ross A.   C-Pr   898-9368   webber   25 EOPR   PHD   66 Columbia   7-64
Bowman, Edward H.   Prof   898-1094   bowman   3 IMYL   PHD   54 Ohio St   7-83
   Reginald H. Jones Professor of Corporate Management
Cappelli, Peter   Prof   898-2722   cappelli   5 QN   DPHI   83 Oxford   7-85
   Co-Director Center for Human Resources
Hamilton, William F.   Prof   898-4145   36 DIT   PHD   67 London   7-67
   Landau Professor of Management and Technology; Director, Mgt & Tech Program
House, Robert J.   Prof   898-2278   house   2 EH   PHD   60 Ohio St   7-88
   Joseph Frank Bernstein Professor of Organizational Studies
Kimberly, John R.   Prof   898-7937   kimberly   2 DHX   PHD   70 Cornell   7-82
   Henry Bower Professor of Entrepreneurial Studies
Kobrin, Stephen J.   Prof   898-7732   kobrin   8 YI   PHD   75 Michigan   7-82
   William H. Worster Professor of Multinational Mgt;Director Wurster Center
MacMillan, Ian C.   Prof   898-9472   macmillan   36 IT   DBA   75 S Africa   7-86
   George W. Taylor Professor of Entrepreneurinal Studies;Dir Sol C Snider Er
Merrifield, D. Bruce   VProf   898-2231   merrifield   36 ADIT   PHD   50 Chicago   7-89
   Walter C. Bladstrom Visiting Executive Professor of Management
Meyer, Marshall W.   Prof   898-6992   meyer   2 HA   PHD   67 Chicago   7-87
   Anheuser-Busch Professor of Management
Perlmutter, Howard V.   Prof   898-7707   8 PHD   PHD   52 Kansas   7-68
Rowan, Richard L.   Prof   898-7906   rowan   5 NQY   PHD   61 N Carol   7-61
   Co-Director, Center for Human Resources;Chairperson Labor Relations Council
Stern, Paul G.   VProf   898-0487   stern   PHD   Manchest   7-93
Winter, Sidney G.   Prof   898-4140   winter   3 I   PHD   64 Yale   7-93
   Deloitte and Touche Porfessor of Management
Hrebiniak, Lawrence G.   Assoc 898-8254   hrebiniak   23 I   PHD   71 SUNY-Buf 7-76
Kogut, Bruce M.   Assoc 898-1093   kogut   8 Y   PHD   83 MIT   7-83
Levinthal, Daniel A.   Assoc 898-6826   levinthal   3 IHD   PHD   85 Stanford   7-85
   May Department Stores Term Associate Professor
Pennings, Johannes M.   Assoc 898-7755   pennings   23 HD   PHD   73 Michigan   7-83
Perry, Charles R.   Assoc 898-9129   perry   5 NQ   PHD   68 Chicago   7-68
Sherer, Peter D.   Assoc 898-6485   sherer   5 NQEP   PHD   85 Wiscon   7-89
   N. Richard Kalikow Term Associate Professor of Management
Singh, Harbir   Assoc 898-6752   singhh   38 IYD   PHD   84 Michigan   7-84
Singh, Jitendra V.   Assoc 898-6605   singhj   34 BIKY   PHD   83 Stanford   7-87
Tschoegl, Adrian   VAsso 898-0619   tschoegl   8 Y   PHD   80 MIT   7-93
Weigelt, Keith   Assoc 898-6369   weigelt   3 I   PHD   86 Northwes   7-88
Brooks, Geoffrey   Asst   898-7731   brooks   32 HI   PHD   91 Oregon   7-91
   Anheuser-Busch Term Assistant Professor
Burkhardt, Marlene E.   Asst   898-2526   burkhardt   2 EH   PHD   90 Penn St   7-90
   Anheuser-Busch Term Professor of Management
Day, Diana L.   Asst   898-3022   day   3 I   PHD   86 Columbia   7-85
   Ehrenkranz/Greenwall Term Assistant Professor of Management
Dyer, Jeffrey H.   Asst   898-9371   dyer   38 YI   PHD   93 UCLA   7-93
   Stanley Goldstein Term Assistant Professor of Management
Harder, Joseph W.   Asst   898-7519   harder   25 ENQ   PHD   89 Stanford   7-89
   Anheuser-Busch Term Assistant Professor
Helfat, Constance E.   Asst   898-2723   helfat   3 I   PHD   85 Yale   7-91
   Charter Banks/Jerry E. Finger Term Assistant Professor of Management
Hunter, Larry   Asst   898-5739   hunter   5 NQ   PHD   92 MIT   7-92
   Joseph Wharton Term Assistant Professor of Management
Jehn, Karen   Asst   898-0525   jehn   2 E   PHD   92 Northwes   7-92
   May Dept Stores Term Asstistant Professor of Management
Krickx, Guido A.   Asst   898-3031   krickx   34 IDHB   PHD   88 UCLA   7-87
MacDuffie, John Paul   Asst   898-2588   macduffi   2 EJ   PHD   90 MIT   7-90
   Roger Stone Term Assistant Professor of Management
Malnight, Thomas W.   Asst   898-8735   malnight   83 YI   DBA   92 Harvard   7-92
   Roger Stone Assistant Professor of Management
Mylonadis, Yiorgas   Asst   898-9372   mylonadis   34 IM   PHD   93 MIT   7-92
   Douglas Vickers Lecturer in Management
Nishiguchi, Toshihiro   Asst   898-9367   nishiguchi   8 DPHL   DPHI   90 Oxford   7-91
   Anheuser-Busch Term Assistant Professor of Management
Rosenkopf, Lori   Asst   898-0525   rosenkopf   6 T   PHD   Columbia   7-93
Thomas, Louis A.   Asst   898-2488   thomas   3 I   PHD   91 Harvard   7-92
   Whitney M. Young, Jr. Term Assistant Professor of Management

Name	Rank	Phone	Email			Degree		School	
Udayagiri, Naren D.	Asst	898-7818	udayagiri	38	I	PHD	92	Minn	7-92
John Sculley Lecturer in Management									
Venkataraman, S.	Asst	898-7734	venkat	63	ITSD	PHD	89	Minn	7-89
Paul M. Yeakel Term Assistant Professor of Management									
–**Decision Sciences Dept**	Phone		Fax 898-4851						
Cohen, Morris A.	C-Pr					PHD	74	Northwes	1974
Matsushita Professor of Manufacturing and Logistics									
Emery, James C.	Prof					PHD	65	MIT	1965
Fisher, Marshall L.	Prof					PHD	70	MIT	1975
Stephen J. Heyman Professor									
Guignard-Spielberg, Monique	Prof					DOCT	80	DeLille	1972
Harker, Patrick T.	Prof					PHD	83	Penn	1984
UPS Trnsportation Professor for the Private Sector									
Hershey, John C.	Prof					PHD	70	Stanford	1976
Senior Fellow, Leonard Davis Institute of Health Economics									
Katsenelinboigen, Aron	Prof					DSE	66	Moscow	1977
Kleindorfer, Paul R.	Prof					PHD	70	Car Mel	1973
Universal Furniture Professor									
Kunreuther, Howard	Prof					PHD	65	MIT	1972
Meshulam Riklis Professor in Practice of Creative Management									
Laing, James D.	Prof					PHD	67	Stanford	1976
Clemons, Eric K.	Assoc	898-7747	clemons	39	IYZ	PHD	76	Cornell	1976
Hurst, E. Gerald Jr.	Assoc					PHD	67	MIT	1969
Kimbrough, Steven Orla	Assoc					PHD	82	Wiscon	1984
Ross, Keith W.	Assoc					PHD	85	Michigan	1985
Zenios, Stavros A.	Assoc					PHD	86	Princeton	1986
Jain, Anjani	Asst					PHD	87	UCLA	1986
Atlantic Richfield Foundation Term Assistant Professor									
Lohse, Gerald	Asst					PHD	91	Michigan	1991
Nelson Peltz Term Assistant Professor									
Tzur, Michal	Asst					PHD	92	Columbia	1991
Anheuser-Busch Lecturer									
Zheng, Yu-Sheng	Asst					PHD	87	Columbia	1987
Milken Family Foundation Term Assistant Professor									
Donohue, Karen L.	Lect					MS		Northwes	1992
–**Public Policy & Mgt Dept**	Phone		Fax 898-9635						
Pack, Janet Rothenberg	C-Pr	898-5851				PHD	65	Berkeley	1970
Allen, W. Bruce	Prof	898-7896				PHD	69	Northwes	1974
Bailey, Elizabeth E.	Prof	898-0926				PHD	72	Princeton	1991
John C. Hower Professor									
Diver, Colin S.	Prof	898-7061							
Bernard G. Segal Professor of Law; Dean Law School									
Faulhaber, Gerald R.	Prof	898-7860		3		PHD	75	Princeton	7-89
Pack, Howard	Prof	898-9053							
Postlewaite, Andrew	Prof	898-7350							
Schinnar, Arie P.	Assoc	898-81				PHD	76	Car Mel	1976
Yao, Dennis A.	Assoc	898-3019		34	AIL	PHD	84	Stanford	7-83
Ingberman, Daniel Evan	Asst	898-3013				PHD	86	Car Mel	1985
Lott Jr., John R.	Asst	898-8920				PHD	84	UCLA	1991
Carl D. Covitz Term Assistant Professor									

Penn State University	Univ Park, PA	16802-1914	(814) PSUVM					1957,1963	
College of Business Adm			FAX = 863-7261					BS,MBA,MS,PHD	
Hammond, J. D.	Dean	863-0448			Insu	PHD	61	Penn	1961
–**Dept of Management & Org**	Phone	863-7261	Fax 863-7261						
Susman, Gerald I.	C-Pr	863-2382	upn	3	DFU	PHD	68	UCLA	1969
Gioia, Dennis A.	Prof	865-6370	dag4	2	EF	DBA	79	Fla St	
Gray, Barbara	Prof	865-3822	b9g	2	HLMY	PHD		Case Wes	1979
Greenlaw, Paul S.	Prof	865-2732		5	AKNQ	PHD	55	Syracuse	1960
Snow, Charles C.	Prof	865-2463	ccs4	3	HIY	PHD	72	Berkeley	1974
Brass, Daniel J.	Assoc	865-1522	d4	2	EH	PHD		Illinois	1979
Cochran, Philip L.	Assoc	865-1576	plc	4	JLM	PHD		Wash	
Thomas, James B.	Assoc	865-2193	j2t	23	HI	PHD		Texas	1987
Bergh, Donald D.	Asst	863-0740	ddb2	3	BI	ABD		Colorado	1990
DeWitt, Rocki-Lee	Asst	865-0381	rld10	3	BIN	ABD		Columbia	1989
Geletkanycz, Marta	Asst	865-0385	mag9	3	I	ABD		Columbia	1992
Kilduff, Martin	Asst	865-9822	mxk6	28	EHY	PHD	88	Cornell	1990
Mishra, Aneil	Asst	863-0642	akm6	25	EFP	PHD	92	Michigan	1992
Rands, Gordon	Asst	863-0430	gpr3	4	JLM	ABD		Minn	1992
Snell, Scott A.	Asst	865-2195	ukn	35	IN	PHD		Mich St	1987
–**Dept of Mgt Sci & Info Sys**	Phone	865-0073	Fax 863-2381						
Kleindorfer, George B.	C-Pr	865-0073	gbk	7	V	PHD		Car Mel	
Chatterjee, Kalyan	Prof	863-2643	k1c	7	V	DBA		Harvard	
Director Center for Research in Conflict & Negotiation									
Hayya, Jack S.	Prof	865-1461	jch	7	V	PHD		UCLA	
Koot, Ronald S.	Prof	865-3126	rsk4	7	V	PHD		Oregon	
Associate Dean for Undergraduate Programs									
Lilien, Gary L.	Prof	863-2782	g5l	7	V	DES		Columbia	
Research Professor of Management Science									

Ord, J. Keith	Prof	865-1206	jko	7	V		PHD		London
David H. McKinley Professor of Business Administration									
Rigby, Paul	Prof	863-0449	phr	7	V		PHD		Texas
Associate Dean for Research & Graduate Programs									
Christy, David P.	Assoc	863-4175	cti	7	V		PHD		Georgia
Davis, Samuel G.	Assoc	863-2645	sgd	7	V		PHD		Syracuse
Fong, Duncan	Assoc	863-3541	12v	7	V		PHD		Purdue
Harrison, Terry P.	Assoc	863-3357	hbx	7	V		PHD		Tenn
Hottenstein, Michael	Assoc	863-3229	m7h	7	V		PHD		Indiana
Nti, Kofi O.	Assoc	863-2484	kon	7	V		PHD		Yale
Reutzel, Edward T.	Assoc	863-2644	etr	7	V		PHD		Penn St
Twark, Richard D.	Assoc	863-0751	rdt	7	V		PHD		Penn St
Vessey, Iris	Assoc	865-5234	ixv1	9	Z		PHD		Queensld
Xu, Susan H.	Assoc	863-0531	shx	7	V		PHD		Rennsela
Bolton, Gary E.	Asst	865-0611	geb3	7	V		PHD		Car Mel
Dasgupta, Aniruddha	Asst	865-2189	axd7	7	V		PHD		Princeton
Lewis, Holly S.	Asst	863-3797	hsl2	7	V		PHD	89	S Carol

Penn State Univ-Erie — Erie, PA — 16563-1400 — (814) PSUVM
FAX=898-6233 — BS,MBA
School of Business

Magenau, John M.	Dir	898-6173	owc	25	EQ	PHD	88	SUNY-Buf	1985
—**Management Faculty**	Phone	898-6107	Fax 898-6233						
Govekar, Michele	Asst	898-6435		38	I	PHD	93	Minn	1993
Lee, Wonsick	Asst	898-6432		25	EH	PHD	90	SUNY-Buf	1990
Palmer, Todd	Asst	898-6107		43	IK	PHD	94	Georgia	1994
Pinto, Jeffrey K.	Asst	898-6107		2	H	PHD	86	Pitt	1994
Thoms, Margaret	Asst	898-6107		25	EN	PHD	94	Ohio St	1994
Bestoso, Mark	Lect	898-6258		15		MBA	85	Penn St	1991

Penn State Univ-Harrisburg — Middleton, PA — 17057-4898 — (717) PSUVM
School of Business — 777 W. Harrisburg Pike — FAX= — BS,MBA

Dhir, Krishna S.	Dir	948-6141	ksd3	3	IV	PHD	75	Colorado	1991
—**Management Faculty**	Phone	948-6141	Fax 948-6456						
Blumberg, Melvin	Prof	948-6165	mqb1	2	EFH	PHD	77	Penn St	1985
Dexter, Carolyn R.	Prof	948-6163	gbl	2	ERY	PHD	67	Columbia	1969
Culpan, Refik	Assoc	948-6166	rc5	8	Y	PHD	73	NYU	1981
Parkum, Kurt	Assoc	948-6144	khp	1	D	PHD	69	Wiscon	1981
Brown, Karen	Asst	948-6148	klb12	7	V	PHD	93	La Tech	1993
Culpan, Oya	Asst	948-6149	oqc	4	LR	PHD	74	Hacettep	1984
Kuo, Ching-Chung	Asst	948-6172	cck1	7	U	PHD	89	Northwes	1989
Morand, David	Asst	948-6158	dam9	5	Q	PHD	91	Cornell	1990
Russell, Robert D.	Asst	948-6159	rdr	6	ST	PHD	90	Pitt	1991
Schappe, Stephen	Asst	948-6150	sxs28	5	NQ	PHD	93	Ohio St	1991

Pepperdine Univ-Los Angeles — Culver City, CA — 90230 — (310)
School of Bus & Mgt — 400 Corporate Point — FAX=568-5727 — BS,MBA

Wilburn, James R.	Dean	568-5500			Econ	PHD	71	UCLA	1970
—**Management Faculty**	Phone	568-5545	Fax 568-5727						
Snow, Sheldon C.	C-Ac	568-5545				PHD	76	S Calif	1968
Kaehler, Richard C.	Prof	568-5500		3	I	PHD	60	S Calif	1975
Motamedi, Kurt K.	Prof	568-5545				PHD	74	UCLA	1982
Wright, Robert G.	Prof	568-5545				DBA	67	S Calif	1976
Julian A. Virtue Distinguished Fellowship									
Darden, Clifford E.	Assoc	568-5545				DBA	82	Harvard	1984
Parsinia, Alex	Assoc	568-5545				PHD	76	LSU	1982

Pepperdine Univ-Malibu — Malibu, CA — 90263 — (310) PEPVAX
Seaver College — 24255 Pacific Coast Highway — FAX=456-4758 — BS

Wilson, John	Dean	456-4281	jwilson		Rel	PHD	67	Iowa	1983
—**Management Faculty**	Phone		Fax 456-4758						
Yates, Jere E.	C-Pr	456-4237	jyates	14	GJLP	PHD	68	Boston	1969
Mallinger, Mark A.	Prof	456-4538	emalling	2	EFGP	PHD	80	S Calif	1980
Summers, Michael R.	Prof	456-4536	msummers	7	UV	PHD	78	Illinois	1980
Seshan, Venkatachalam	Assoc	456-4240	vseshan	38	ILMY	PHD	65	Lehigh	1986
Whitney, L. Keith	Assoc	456-4545	kwhitney	4	K	JD	77	Tx Tech	1990

Pfeiffer College — Misenheimer, NC — 28109 — (704)
Div of Business & Econ — FAX=463-2046 — AB,BS,MBA,MCE

Bleau, Barbara Lee	H-Pr	463-1360		7	UV	PHD	80	Penn St	8-86
Jefferson-Pilot Professor of Management Science									
—**Management Faculty**	Phone		Fax 463-2046						
Morton, James R.	Prof	463-1360		31	IV	DBA	74	S Calif	5-89
MBA Coordinator									
Jozsa, Frank P. Jr.	Assoc	463-1360		18		PHD	77	Geo St	7-91
Poplin, Toby L.	Assoc	463-1360		1		MA	68	Appal St	8-76
Carpenter, Gerald E.	Asst	463-1360		12		MBA	76	Appal St	8-84

Piedmont College — Demorest, GA 30535-0010 (706) FAX=
Division of Business — 165 Central Avenue
Carmack, Ed — C 778-3000
–Management Faculty — Phone 778-8000 Fax 776-2811
Bryan, Norman — Asst 778-3000 — 12 EHNO PHD Geo St 8-93

Pine Manor College — Chestnut Hill MA 02167 (617) FAX=731-7199
Business — 400 Heath Street
Pascal, Laurie — C-Ac 731-7051 — 34 IE MBA Northwes 1982
David & Barbara Gray Professor of Management
–Management Faculty — Phone 731-7051 Fax 731-7199
Abdullah, Siddiq — Assoc 731-7168 — 7 UV PHD Boston U 1982
Bergman, Ruthann — Assoc 731-7050 — MBA Penn 1983
Grossman, Amy — Assoc 731-7169 — 9 TS MBA Northeas 1981

Pittsburg State University — Pittsburg, KS 66762 (316) FAX=232-2430 BS,MBA
Kelce School Bus & Econ — 1701 South Broadway
Mendenhall, Terry L. — Dean 235-4598 — 56 NSTY PHD 81 Kans St 1964
–Dept of Management & Mktg — Phone 235-4588 Fax 232-7515
Crouch, Henry L. — C-Pr 235-4588 — 78 SUVY PHD 77 S Carol 1975
Kash, Toby J. — Prof 235-4588 — 28 LTYI PHD 78 Mich St 1982
Baack, Donald — Assoc 235-4588 — 23 EH PHD 87 Nebraska 1988
Fischer, Arthur K. — Assoc 235-4588 — 25 CEHN PHD 84 Missouri 1988
Fogliasso, Christine — Assoc 235-4588 — 4 JKLR JD 79 Kansas 1984
Lee, Choong — Assoc 235-4588 — 7 UVZ PHD 88 Iowa St 1989
Box, Thomas M. — Asst 235-4588 — 36 IST PHD 91 Okla St 1990

University of Pittsburgh — Pittsburgh, PA 15260 (412) PITTVMS 1979,1916
Katz Grad School of Bus — FAX=648-1693 MBA,PHD
Zoffer, H. J. — Dean 648-1561 — PHD 56 Pitt 1953
–Management Faculty — Phone — Fax 648-1552
Blair, Andrew — Prof 648-1570 — 8 PHD Fordham
Director, International Business Center
Camillus, John C. — Prof 648-1599 — 3 DBA 72 Harvard
Donald Beall Chair in Strategic Management
Craft, James A. — Prof 648-1680 — 5 PHD 68 Berkeley 1972
Director, Exec;utive MBA Program
Fogel, Daniel — Prof 648-1642 — 2 PHD Wiscon
Director, Center for Intl Enterprise Development & Associate Dean
Gal-Or, Esther — Prof 648-1722 — PHD 80 Northwes
Grant, John H. — Prof 648-1707 — 3 DBA 72 Harvard
Robert Kirby Chair in Strategic Management
Kilmann, Ralph H. — Prof 648-1530 — 2 PHD 72 UCLA
George H. Love Chair in Orgnization & Management
King, William R. — Prof 648-1587 — 9 PHD 64 Case Wes 1967
University Professor
May, Jerrold H. — Prof 648-1549 — 7 PHD Yale
Olson, Josephine — Prof 648-1715 — 8 PHD Brown
Saaty, Thomas L. — Prof 648-1539 — 7 PHD 53 Yale
University Professor
Slevin, Dennis P. — Prof 648-1553 — 2 PHD 69 Stanford
Spiro, Michael — Prof 648-1720 — PHD 65 MIT
Sussna, Edward — Prof 648-1697 — 8 PHD Illinois
Wendell, Richard E. — Prof 648-1630 — 7 PHD Northwes
Galletta, Dennis — Assoc 648-1699 — 9 PHD Minn
Hegde, Gajanan G. — Assoc 648-1698 — 7 PHD Rochest
Leana, Carrie R. — Assoc 648-1674 — 2 PHD Houston
Masters, Marick F. — Assoc 648-1643 — 5 PHD Illinois
Mitnick, Barry M. — Assoc 648-1555 — 3 PHD Penn
Nath, Raghu — Assoc 648-1684 — 2 PHD MIT
Prescott, John — Assoc 648-1573 — 3 PHD Penn St
Tadikamalla, Pandu R. — Assoc 648-1596 — 7 PHD Iowa
Vargus, Luis G. — Assoc 648-1575 — 7 PHD Penn
Wood, Donna J. — Assoc 648-1547 — 3 PHD Vanderbt
Florkowski, Gary W. — Asst 648-1626 — 5 PHD Syracuse
Kim, Young-Gul — Asst 648-1678 — 9 PHD Minn
King, Ruth C. — Asst 648-1634 — 9 PHD Texas
Makhija, Mona — Asst 648-1534 — 8 PHD Wiscon
Mirchandani, Prakash — Asst 648-1652 — 7 PHD MIT
Murrell, Audrey J. — Asst 648-1651 — 7 PHD Delaware
Shang, Shiou-Chen — Asst 648-1681 — 7 PHD Texas
Agle, Bradley — Lect 648-1571 — 3 ABD U Wash
Choudhury, Vivek — Lect 648-1614 — 9 PHD UCLA
Kirby, Daria — Lect 648-1567 — 2 ABD Michigan
Kirsch, Laurie — Lect 648-7672 — 9 ABD Minn
Parham, James — Lect 648-1725 — 3 ABD Michigan
Stewart, Alice C. — Lect 648-1716 — 3 PHD 90 N Carol

U of Pittsburgh at Johnstown — Johnstown, PA 15904 (814)
Dept of Business Econ — FAX=
–Management Faculty

Name	Rank	Phone		Deg		School	Year
Vickroy, Ronald	C-Ac	269-2965	12	MS	80	Car Mel	1985
McCarty, Donald	Asst (Phone)		23	MA		USC	1989
McGrath, John	Inst		13	MA		Northwes	1994

Plymouth State College — Plymouth, NH 03264 (603)
Department of Business — Highland Street — FAX=   BS,MBA
Did Not Respond-1993 Listing
–Management Faculty

Name	Rank	Phone		Deg		School	Year
Boggess, Trent	Dean	535-2414	Econ	PHD	80	Kansas	
Kent, David	Prof			JD	71	Boston	
Bechard, Bonnie	Assoc			EDD	87	Ariz St	
Leuser, David	Assoc			PHD	79	N Hamp	
Shlager, Julian M.	Assoc			PHD	72	Boston	
Benoit, William	Asst			MS	80	S Calif	
Murphy, Terence M.	Asst			MBA	69	Suffolk	
Harding, Edward	Inst			MBA	77	Dartmout	
Abelmann, Arthur							
Babin, Jane							
Moore, Daniel							

Polytechnic University — Brooklyn, NY 11201 (718)
Division of Managment — 333 Jay Street — FAX=   MS
–Management Department — Phone 260-3760   Fax 260-3874

Name	Rank	Phone	Deg	School
Weindling, Ralph E.	H-Pr	260-3983	MBA	Harvard
Kaufman, Harold G.	Prof		PHD	NYU
Schillinger, A. George	Prof		SCD	Columbia
Sabavala, Darius	Assoc		PHD	Columbia
Blecherman, Barry	Asst		PHD	Penn
Dufner, Donna	Asst		PHD	Rutgers

University of Portland — Portland, OR 97203-5798 (503) 1977,1981
School of Business Adm — 5000 N. Willamette Blvd — FAX=283-7399   BBA,MBA
–Management Faculty — Phone   Fax 283-7399

Name	Rank	Phone			Deg	Yr	School	Year
Robertson, James W.	Dean	283-7224		Atg	PHD	63	U Wash	1988
Freed, Ned	Prof	283-7280	7	U	PHD	78	Colorado	
Drake, Bruce H.	Assoc	283-7289	2	H	PHD	76	U Wash	1987
Feldman, Howard D.	Assoc	283-7270			PHD	76	Geo St	1991
Kondrasuk, John N.	Assoc	283-7278			PHD	72	Minn	1975
Springer, Donald M.	Assoc	283-7283	9	Z	PHD	74	Colo St	1975
Davalos, Sergio	Asst	283-7467	9	Z	PHD	92	Arizona	1991
Osland, Joyce	Asst	283-7421	2	E	PHD	89	Case Wes	1989

Portland State University — Portland, OR 97207-0751 (503) SBAMAIL.SBA.PDX.EDU 1970,1982
School of Business Adm — 724 Southwest Harrison — FAX=725-4882   BS,BA,MT,MBA
–Department of Management — Phone   Fax 725-5850

Name	Rank	Phone			Deg	Yr	School	Year
Ahlbrandt, Roger	Dean	725-3721			PHD			1993
Brenner, Steven N.	Prof	725-4768	4	JL	PHD	72	Harvard	1971
Goslin, Lewis	Prof	725-3760	3	DTI	PHD	64	U Wash	1968
Manning, William A.	Prof	725-3787	97	Z	PHD	70	Oregon	1969
Molander, Earl A.	Prof	725-3766	4	L	PHD	72	Berkeley	1975
Raedels, Alan R.	Prof	725-3728	7	UW	PHD	77	Purdue	1980
White, Sam E.	Prof	725-3700	3	I	PHD	76	U Wash	1983
Cabelly, Alan	Assoc	725-3789	5	N	PHD	80	U Wash	1980
Gerbing, David	Assoc	725-4767	7	V	PHD	79	Mich St	1987
Murphy, Jerry	Assoc	725-3777	7	UZ	ABD	70	Wash St	
Buddress, Leland	Asst	725-4769	7	UYW	ABD		Mich St	1990
Crockett, Henry D.	Asst	725-3709	9	Z	PHD	90	Tx-Arlin	1989
Owens, Heidi	Asst	725-3770	9	Z	PHD	92	Ariz St	1992
Taylor, Mary S.	Asst	725-3761	85	YN	PHD	89	U Wash	1990
Tierney, Pam	Asst	725-5486	2	EQ	PHD	92	Cinn	1992
West, Ellen L.	Asst	725-3706	2	EP	PHD	81	Oreg St	1986

Prairie View A&M University — Prairie View, TX 77446 (409)
College of Bus Box 638 — FAX=857-2797   BBA,MBA
–Dept of Management & Mktg — Phone 857-2797   Fax 857-2787

Name	Rank	Phone			Deg	Yr	School	Year
Jones, Barbara A. P.	Dean	857-4310		Econ	PHD	73	Geo St	1987
Bryant, Milton R.	Prof	857-4310	79	VZSU	PHD	73	Tx A&M	1985
Distinguished Professor of Management								
Debnath, Sukumar C.	Asst	857-4010	23	EHIN	DBA	89	Miss St	1987
Nelson Jr., George W.	Asst	857-4010	13	EHJX	PHD	88	North Tx	1988
MBA Program Coordinator for the College of Business								
Selladurai, Raja S.	Inst	857-4010	25	EHNY	ABD	89	Tx A&M	1986
Moran, Thomas M.	Lect	857-4010	38	KLY	MBA	51	Michigan	1990

University of Puget Sound — Tacoma, WA 98416-0121 (206) UPS.EDU
School of Bus & Pub Adm — 1500 North Warner Street — FAX=756-3500 — BA

Name	Title	Phone	Email		Field	Degree	Yr	School	Yr
Waldo, Robert D.	Dean	756-3496	waldo			PHD	72	Claremnt	1974
–Department of Management	Phone	756-3153	Fax 756-3500						
Baarsma, William H.	Assoc	756-3393	wbaarsma	A		DPA	72	Geo Wash	1970
Bernhart, Michael	Assoc	756-3557	mbernhart	C		PHD	77	MIT	1986

Purdue University — W Lafayette, IN 47907-1310 (317) MGMT.PURDUE.EDU 1967,1969
Krannert School of Mgt — FAX=494-9658 — BS,MS,PHD

Name	Title	Phone	Email		Field	Degree	Yr	School	Yr
Weidenaar, Dennis J.	Dean	494-4366	weidend	1	Mgt	PHD	69	Purdue	1966
–Management Faculty	Phone	494-9700	Fax 494-4360						
Dworkin, James B.	C-Pr	494-4364	jdworkin	2	Q	PHD	77	Minn	1976
Associate Dean									
Campion, Michael A.	Prof	494-5909	campionm	2	E	PHD	82	N Car St	1986
Chand, Suresh	Prof	494-4530	suresh	7	U	PHD	79	Car Mel	1979
Cooper, Arnold C.	Prof	494-4401	coopera	3	T	DBA	62	Harvard	1963
Green, Stephen	Prof	494-6852	green	2	E	PHD	76	U Wash	1987
Koehler, Gary J.	Prof	494-9013	koehler	9	Z	PHD	73	Purdue	1994
Moskowitz, Herbert	Prof	494-4421	herbm	7	V	PHD	70	UCLA	1970
Plante, Robert	Prof	494-4464	bob	7	V	PHD	80	Georgia	1980
Scaletta, Phillip J.	Prof	494-4479	scaletta	4	K	JD	50	Iowa	1966
Schendel, Dan E.	Prof	494-8485	schendel	3	I	PHD	63	Stanford	1965
Schwarz, Leroy	Prof	494-4510	lee	7	U	PHD	71	Chicago	1977
Woo, Carolyn Y.	Prof	494-4403	woo	3	I	PHD	79	Purdue	1981
Wright, Gordon P.	Prof	494-4429	gordy	7	V	PHD	67	Case Wes	1970
Altinkemer, Kemal	Assoc	494-9009	kemal	9	Z	PHD	87	Rochest	1986
Berger, Chris J.	Assoc	494-4423	cjb	2	E	PHD	78	Wiscon	1978
Chaturvedi, Alok	Assoc	494-9048	alok	9	Z	PHD	89	Wiscon	1988
Dada, Macqhool	Assoc	494-4490	dada	7	U	PHD	84	MIT	1992
Schoorman, David	Assoc	494-4391	schoor	2	E	PHD	83	Car Mel	1986
Strausbaugh, Rolland L.	Assoc	494-4472	strausb	4	K	JD	63	Indiana	1970
Tang, Jen	Assoc	494-4497	jtang	7	V	PHD	82	Bowl Gr	1991
Ward, James	Assoc	494-4509	jw7402	7	U	PHD	80	Car Mel	1981
Williams, Larry	Assoc	494-4491	larryw	2	E	PHD	88	Indiana	1987
Arthur, Jeffrey	Asst	494-4408	jarthur	2	Q	PHD	90	Cornell	1990
Brush, Thomas H.	Asst	494-4441	brusht	3	I	PHD	90	Michigan	1992
Eppel, Thomas	Asst	494-4432	eppelt	7	V	PHD	90	S Calif	1989
Hannon, John	Asst	494-5871	hannon	2	N	PHD	91	Cornell	1991
Kraay, David	Asst	494-0320	dkraay	9	Z	ABD	91	Penn	1991
Miller, Kent	Asst	494-5903	kmiller	3	I	PHD	91	Minn	1991
Sinha, Deepak	Asst	494-4439	dsinha	3	I	PHD	90	MIT	1990
Smith, Stuart	Asst	494-4531	shsmith	7	V	PHD	90	Texas	1991
Srinivasan, Ashok	Asst	494-4514	ashok	7	U	PHD	89	Car Mel	1989
Williams, Margaret	Asst	494-6564	pegw	2	N	PHD	89	Indiana	1989

Quinnipiac College — Hamden, CT 06518-0569 (203)
School of Business — Mount Carmel Avenue — FAX=281-8664 — BS,MBA
Faculty Phone 288-5251

Name	Title	Phone		Field	Degree	Yr	School	Yr
Strang, Roger	Dean	281-8720	3	ISY	DBA		Harvard	
–Department of Management	Phone		Fax 281-8664					
Sawhney, Shiv	C	281-8789	13	BDI	PHD		NYU	
Dearden, Marlin	Prof	Ext 8503	2	CEF	PHD		Yale	
Bellizzi, Frank	Assoc	Ext 8469	26	EGJT	PHD		Mass	
Cadden, David	Assoc	Ext 8502	37		PHD		CUNY	
DeVivo, Rosemarie	Assoc	Ext 8342	12		PHD		Minn	
Hedrick, Travis	Assoc	Ext 8743	5	BQ	PHD		Brown	
McMullen, Ronald	Assoc	Ext 8784	25	FHNP	EDD		Mass	
Miller, Keith T.	Assoc	Ext 8755	5	Q	PHD		Arizona	
Associate Dean								
Halliday, Robert M.	Asst	Ext 8572	2	FHO	MA	69	Fairfiel	1974

Radford University — Radford, VA 24142-6954 (703) RUACAD 1992,1992
College of Bus & Econ — FAX=831-6103 — BBA,MBA

Name	Title	Phone		Field	Degree	Yr	School	Yr
–Department of Management	Phone	831-5481	Fax 831-6261					
Bures, Allen L.	C-Pr	831-5481	21	EY	PHD	80	Nebraska	8-81
Beheshti, Hooshang M.	Prof	831-5380	79	UZ	PHD	77	Okla St	8-79
Green, Forrest B.	Prof	831-5080	7	ZUV	PHD	82	Va Tech	8-87
Kroeber, Donald W.	Prof	831-5481	79	UVZ	PHD	76	Georgia	8-85
McNichols, Charles W.	Prof	831-5358	9	Z	PHD	73	Stanford	8-90
Holder of Dalton Chair								
White, Clarence D.	Prof	831-5328	12	E	PHD	82	Ohio St	8-82
Champion, Donald L.	Assoc	831-5384	7	UVX	DBA	79	Fla St	8-82
Kopf, Jerry	Assoc	831-5075	36	IST	PHD	89	Arkansas	8-92
Mendleson, Jack L.	Assoc	831-5086	25	NPQ	DBA	67	Mich St	8-91
Oseghale, Braimoh D.	Assoc	831-5457	38	IY	PHD	89	Temple	8-88
Smith, Albert C. Jr.	Assoc	831-5139	25	GN	EDD	81	Va Tech	8-80
Herring, Robert A. III	Asst	831-5076	25	EFN	PHD	87	Fla St	8-91

Name	Rank	Phone			Degree		School	Year
Markham, Frank B.	Asst	831-5072	23	I	ABD		La Tech	8-91
Mayfield, Jacqueline R.	Asst	831-5082	12	DE	PHD	93	Alabama	8-92
McLaughlin, Josetta	Asst	831-5192	34	IJL	PHD	93	Va Tech	8-91
Spillman, Robert D.	Asst	831-5306	9	Z	PHD	83	Ohio St	8-84
Rasnake, Lee R.	Inst	831-5759	7	U	MBA	90	Va Tech	8-80
Skelton, Bonnie M.	Inst	831-5085	9	Z	MS	86	Radford	8-89

Ramapo Coll of New Jersey — Mahwah, NJ 07430-1680 (201)
School of Adm & Bus — 505 Ramapo Valley Road — FAX=529-7508 — BS

Name	Rank	Phone			Degree		School	Year
Raciti, Sebastian J.	Dir	529-7377			PHD	68	Fordham	1971
—Management Faculty	Phone	529-7378	Fax 529-6728					
Champlin, Frederic	Asst	529-6736	5	NQ	PHD	82	Minn	1990
Zbib, Imad	Asst	529-7388	71	UV	PHD	90	North Tx	1993

University of Redlands — Redland, CA 92373-0999 (909)
College of Arts & Sci — 1200 East Colton Avenue — FAX= — BS,BA

Name	Rank	Phone			Degree		School	Year
Marvasti, Frank	C-Ac	793-2121	79	VZ	PHD			
—Dept of Business Adm & Atg	Phone	793-2121						
Barnes, A. Keith	Prof	793-2121	23	HLJI	EDD			
Hunsaker Professor of Management								
Pavelchak, Mark	Asst	793-2121	27	EX	PHD			
Winick, Mara	Asst	793-2121	15	EKNQ	PHD			

Regent University — Virginia Bch, VA 23464-5041 (804) BEACON.REGENT.EDU
School of Business — FAX=424-7051 — MBA,MA
phone 523-7421

Name	Rank	Phone			Degree		School	Year
Mulford, John E.	Dean	523-7421		Econ	PHD		Cornell	1982
—Management Faculty	Phone	523-7421	Fax 523-7932					
Hunt, Carle M.	Prof	Ext 4273		I	DBA		S Calif	1986
Redmer, Timothy	Prof	Ext 4360			PHD	88	Va Comm	1982
Chamberlin, Daniel P.	Assoc	Ext 4359	23	EI	MBA	57	Harvard	1985
Miller, Ralph A.	Asst	Ext 4411			MA		Regent	
Winston, Bruce	Asst	Ext 4274	57	UVN	MBA		Regent	1991

Rensselaer Poly Institute — Troy, NY 12180-3590 (518) RPITSMTS 1977,1983
School of Management — Sage & Eaton Streets — FAX=276-8661

Name	Rank	Phone			Degree		School	Year
Morone, Joseph	Dean	276-8710	3	I	PHD		Yale	1988
—Managerial Policy & Org Dpt	Phone		Fax 276-8661					
Baron, Robert A.	C-Pr	276-2864	32	EFGH	PHD		Iowa	
Abetti, Pier A.	Prof	276-6834	32	EFGH	PHD		Ill Tech	
Berg, Daniel	Prof	276-2895	3	I	PHD		Penn	
Northworthy, J. R.	Prof	276-6808						
Reitman, Walter	Prof	276-2955						
Durgee, Jeffrey F.	Assoc	276-6588			PHD		Pitt	1982
Leifer, Richard P.	Assoc	276-6831	92	EZ	PHD		Wiscon	
LeMay, Richard P.	Assoc	276-6583			PHD		Iowa	1970
Lynch, Jeanne M.	Assoc	276-6833	3	I	DBA		Harvard	
Wellington Professor								
Miccio, Ralph	Assoc	276-8635	4	K	JD		Albany L	
Peters, Lois S.	Assoc	276-6836			PHD		NYU	1986
Piasecki, Bruce	Assoc	76-2705	4	M	PHD		Cornell	
Sanderson, Susan	Assoc	276-2933	8	Y	PHD		Pitt	
Schneider, Donald P.	Assoc	276-6851	1	C	PHD	73	Florida	1974
Bessler, Woolfgang	Asst	276-2996						
Boylan, Robert L.	Asst	276-2956			PHD		Duke	1987
McDermott, Christopher	Asst	276-6587	3	I	PHD		N Carol	1994
O'Connor, Gina	Asst	276-6842			PHD		NYU	1989
Paulson, Albert	Asst	276-6850						
Silvester, Katherine	Asst	276-6818						
Veryzer, Robert	Asst	276-8634			PHD		Florida	1993
Bigelow, David	SLect	276-2961	38	IY	MBA		Chicago	
St. John, William	SLect	276-2961			PHD		Renssela	1990

University of Rhode Island — Kingston, RI 02881-0801 (401) URIMVS 1969,1973
College of Business — FAX=792-4312 — BS,MBA,MS,PHD

Name	Rank	Phone			Degree		School	Year
Stern, Sydney V.	Dean	792-2337	3	Engr	PHD	62	Ga Tech	1990
—Department of Management	Phone		Fax 792-4312					
Sink, Clay V.	C-Pr	792-4354	16	PSE&	PHD	68	Ohio St	1969
Coates, Norman	Prof	792-2068	38	IYH	PHD	67	Cornell	1971
De Lodzia, George	Prof	792-2068	24	EFH	PHD	69	Syracuse	1970
Overton, Craig	Prof	792-4208	5	QN	PHD	71	Mass	1969
Schmidt, Charles	Prof	792-4329	5	Q	PHD	68	Mich St	1968
Scholl, Richard W.	Prof	792-4347	25	EFHN	PHD	79	Ca-Irvine	1979
Beauvais, Laura Lynn	Assoc	792-4341	12	EFHR	PHD	87	Tenn	1984
Cooper, Elizabeth	Assoc	295-4211	25	EFNX	PHD	85	Akron	1985

Name	Rank	Phone		Code	Field	Deg		Yr	School	Year
Disney, Diane	Assoc	792-4348		53	CIQN	PHD		88	Brandeis	1988
Dugal, Sanjiv	Asst	792-4326		34	IYJ	PHD		91	Mass	1989
Randall, Linda	Asst	792-2068		38	YI	PHD		93	Mass	1993

Rhodes College
Dept of Econ & Bus Adm — Memphis, TN 38112 — (901) FAX=
Did Not Respond-1993 Listing — 2000 North Parkway

Name	Rank	Phone		Code	Field	Deg		Yr	School	Year
Planchon, John M.	C-Ac	726-3978			Mktg	PHD			Alabama	
—**Management Faculty**	Phone									
Birnbaum, Dee	Assoc	726-3853		2	E	PHD				

Rice University
Jones Grad Sch of Adm — Houston, TX 77251 — (713) RICE FAX=285-5251 — MAC,MBA,PHD
6100 South Main Street

Name	Rank	Phone		Code	Field	Deg		Yr	School	Year
Bailar, Benjamin F.	Dean	527-4838			Adm	MBA		59	Harvard	1987
—**Management Faculty**	Phone	527-4838	Fax 285-5251							
Taylor, Ronald	Prof	285-5380		23	EI	PHD		70	Minn	1983
Chaired Professor										
Von der Mehden, Fred	Prof	527-4848		8	Y	PHD		57	Berkeley	1980
Chaired Professor										
Wilkinson, Harry	VProf	527-6060		23	AEI	DBA		60	Harvard	1990
Windsor, Oliver Duane	Prof	285-5372		34	AIJL	PHD		78	Harvard	1977
Chaired Professor										
Schuler, Douglas	Asst	285-5472		4	K	PHD		91	Minn	1991
Flatt, Robert	Adj	527-8101		7	U	MBA		73	Harvard	1988
Hannan, John	Adj	527-8101		48	KY	BA		75	Rice	1990
Hewitt, Charles	Adj	527-8101		7	U	PHD		56	Michigan	1987

University of Richmond
E. C. Robins Sch of Bus — Richmond, VA 23173 — (804) URVAX FAX=289-8878 — 1965,1981 BSBA,BS

Name	Rank	Phone		Code	Field	Deg		Yr	School	Year
New, J. Randolph	Dean	289-8550		13	D	PHD		78	Ariz St	1994
—**Dept of Management Systems**	Phone		Fax 289-8878							
Litteral, Lewis A.	C-Ac	289-8576		7	UV	PHD		82	Clemson	1982
Ashworth, D. Neil	Prof	289-8550		25	ENH	PHD		79	S Carol	1981
Goodwin, James C. Jr.	Prof	289-8574		73	IJU	PHD		74	N Carol	8-76
Rose, John S.	Prof	289-8579		7	V	PHD		71	Northwes	1977
Giacalone, Robert A.	Assoc	289-8678	giacalon	24	EJNY	PHD		84	SUNY-Alb	1988
Beard, Jon W.	Asst	289-8571	beard	29	EFPZ	PHD		91	Tx A&M	8-90
Brown, Michelle	Asst					ABD			York	1994
Eylon, Dafna	Asst	289-8625			DZ	PHD		93	Brit Col	1994
Gray, Sam	Asst	289-8598			VY	PHD		93	Tx A&M	1993

Rider University
College of Business Adm — Lawrenceville NJ 08648-3099 — (609) RIDER FAX=896-5304 — BSBA,MBA
phone 896-5000 — 2083 Lawrenceville Road

Name	Rank	Phone		Code	Field	Deg		Yr	School	Year
Ruch, Richard S.	Dean	896-5152		32	DFNQ	PHD		76	Rennesl	1982
—**Dept Mgt & Human Resources**	Phone	895-5275	Fax 896-5304							
Klein, Gerald D.	Assoc	895-5561		12	DELN	PHD		77	Case Wes	1977
Lentz, Christine	Assoc	895-5552		18	YR	PHD		81	Northwes	1984
Ruble, Thomas L.	Assoc	896-5134		12	E	PHD		73	UCLA	1981
Sandberg, Mark E.	Assoc	896-5127		2	P	PHD		71	Cornell	1970
Associate Dean										
Schneer, Joy	Assoc	895-5549		25	ROE	PHD		85	CUNY	1990
Schwartz, Stanley J.	Assoc	895-5557		15	Q	EDD			Temple	1978
Stander, Norman E.	Assoc	895-5560		2	E	PHD		60	Ohio St	1970
Watson, Carol D.	Assoc	896-5069		12	ER	PHD			Columbia	1989
Cook, Ronald	Asst	895-5522		16	ST	PHD		93	Syracuse	1993
—**Dept of Bus Policy & Envir**	Phone		Fax 896-5304							
Sprotzer, Ira B.	C-Ac	896-5280		4	K	JD			Boston C	1979
Chaganti, Radha	Assoc	895-5529				PHD			SUNY-Buf	1986
Haydel, Belmont F.	Assoc	896-5051		38	IY	PHD		83	North Tx	1979
Smeltz, Wayne J.	Assoc	895-5548				PHD			Houston	1979
White, Thomas	Assoc	895-5471		4	JR	PHD		74	Columbia	1989
Denbo, Susan	Asst	895-5466		4	JKLM	JD		77	Villanov	1989
Goldberg, Ilene	Asst	895-5469				JD			Temple	
Nesteruk, Jeffrey	Asst	896-5124		4	JKL	JD		84	Penn	1990

University of Rio Grande
College of Business Mgt — Rio Grande, OH 45674 — (614) FAX=245-9220 — BS
phone: 245-5353 — Ridge Avenue

Name	Rank	Phone		Code	Field	Deg		Yr	School	Year
Kool, Krishna L.	Dean$	245-7268			Econ	PHD		76	Tenn	1978
—**Management Faculty**	Phone	245-7267	Fax 245-7123							
Vardhau, Harsh	Prof	Ext 388		38	IY	MBA		78	Ohio St	9-85
Ickinger, William	Assoc	Ext 292		12	BEFH	PHD		82	Yale	9-92
Clark, Catherine	Asst	Ext 291		2	EFHN	PHD		90	Tenn	9-90

Roanoke College — Salem, VA 24153-3794 — (703) ACC.ROANOKE.EDU
Business — 221 College Lane — FAX=375-2426 — BBA,BS,BA
Garren, Kenneth — Dean 375-2203 — PHD 68 Va Tech 1967
—**Management Faculty** — Phone 375-2426 Fax 375-2205
Lynch, Larry A. — C-Pr 375-2413 — 3 PHD 87 Va Tech 1978
McCart, Christina D. — Asst 375-2414 — 79 Z PHD 1990
McKee, Gaile H. — Asst 375-2427 — 52 NG PHD Va Tech 1986

Robert Morris College — Coraopolis, PA 15108-1189 — (412) ROBERT-MORRIS.EDU
School of Management — Narrows Run Road — FAX=391-3329 — BS,MS,MBA
Biles, George E. — Dean 262-8452 — 5 BPN PHD 69 Ohio St 8-92
—**Management Faculty** — Phone 262-8294 Fax 262-8494
Hartley, Nell T. — H-Ac 262-8294 hartley — 21 DEH PHD 80 Vanderbt 9-81
Gomolka, Eugene G. — Prof 262-8398 — 4 I PHD 74 SUNY-Buf 9-93
Nicholson, Edward A. — Prof 262-8322 — 35 IJ PHD 70 Ohio St 9-89
Page, David A. — Assoc 227-6889 — 3 AIX PHD 65 Harvard 9-85
Paper, Lawrence N. — Assoc 227-6843 — 4 KL JD 71 Duquesne 9-67
Guiler, Jeffrey — Asst 262-8316 — 5 BNQ MBA 87 Ind-PA 9-90
Repack, William — Asst 262-4065 — 56 PS MS 74 Loyola 8-86
Swartz, Louis B. — Asst 262-8249 — 4 JK JD 69 Duquesne 9-83
Thiel, Glenn R. — Asst 227-6891 — 57 NPQW MBA 77 Duquesne 9-83
Waldman, Joel A. — Asst 227-6842 — 4 K JD 74 U Miami 9-81
Yahr, Michael A. — Asst 227-6842 — 12 BEDY MBA 75 Pitt 9-87

University of Rochester — Rochester, NY 14627 — (716) — 1964
Simon Grad Sch of BusAd — Intercampus Drive — FAX=271-8752 — MBA,PHD
Plosser, Charles I. — Dean 275-3316 — Econ PHD 76 Chicago 1978
John M. Olin Distinguished Professor of Economics & Public Policy
—**Management Faculty** — Phone 275-2771 Fax 271-8752
Schweitzer, Paul J. — Prof 275-4297 — 7 U SCD MIT
Dobson, Gregory — Assoc 275-2670 — 7 U PHD Stanford
Groenevelt, Henri — Assoc 275-2825 — 7 U PHD Columbia
Lederer, Phillip J. — Assoc 275-3368 — 7 U PHD Northwes
Seidmann, Abraham — Assoc 275-5694 — 97 ZU PHD Tx Tech
Sumita, Ushio — Assoc 275-3102 — 79 UZ PHD Rochest
Dewan, Rajiv — Asst — 9 Z PHD 86 Rochest 1994
Storey, Veda — Asst 275-5468 — 9 Z PHD Brit Col

Rochester Inst of Technology — Rochester, NY 14623-0887 — (716) RITVAX — 1988,1988
College of Business — 108 Lomb Memorial Drive — FAX=475-7055 — BS,MBA
Rosett, Richard N. — Dean 475-6915 rnrbbu — Econ PHD 57 Yale 7-90
—**Dept of Management & Mktg** — Phone — Fax 475-5989
Dubrin, Andrew J. — Prof 475-2298 ajdbbu — PHD 60 Mich St 1970
Nowlin, William A. — Prof 475-2319 wanbbu — PHD 86 SUNY-Buf 1981
  Associate Dean
Pearse, Robert — Prof 475-6010 rfpbbu1 — PHD Chicago
Barbato, Robert J. — Assoc 475-2350 rjbbbu1 — PHD 79 Mich St 1979
Barnard, Janet C. — Asst 475-6032 jabbbu — EDD 78 Rochest 1983
Wilson, Donald O. — Asst 475-6798 dowbbu — PHD 88 Calif 1987
Gehani, Ramesh — 475-6072 — PHD 81 Tokoy In 1990
McCanna, Walter F. — 475-6479 wfmbbuu — PHD 69 Wiscon 1982

Rockhurst College — Kansas City, MO 64110-2508 — (816)
School of Management — 1100 Rockhurst Road — FAX=926-4666 — BSBA,MBA
Clark, Robert M. — Dean 926-4200 — PHD 88 Syracuse 1991
—**Management Faculty** — Phone — Fax 926-4693
Frey, Merle E. — Prof 926-4095 — 32 EFHI PHD 77 NYU 1981
Newman, Richard — Prof 926-4563 — 71 VUI DBA 90 Indiana 1990
Arthur S.J., E. Eugene — Assoc 926-4085 — 4 JKL DBA 76 Indiana 1968
Hope, Jon W. — Assoc 926-4002 — 39 IEDZ PHD 86 Kansas 1983
Hunt, Richard E. — Assoc 926-4086 — 62 STEN PHD 77 Cornell 1978
Miller, Patricia A. — Asst 926-4093 — 42 ERLM PHD 83 Texas 1984
Myles, Keith — Asst 926-4152 — 83 YISE PHD 90 Kansas 1989
Schwering, Randolph — Asst 926-4510 — 91 APZF PHD 87 Kansas 1989

Rollins College — Winter Park, FL 32789-4499 — (407) ROLLINS — 1985
Crummer Grad Sch of Bus — 1000 Holt Avenue — FAX=646-1550 — MBA
Nagle, Allan R. — Dean$ 646-2405 — MBA Harvard 1993
—**Faculty of Management** — Phone — Fax 646-1550
Certo, Samuel C. — Prof 646-2249 scerto — 23 PHD 73 Ohio U 1986
Herbert, Theodore T. — Prof 646-2530 therbert — 23 DBA 71 Geo St 1985
Higgins, James — Prof 646-2678 jhiggins — 23 PHD 74 Geo St 1980
Plane, Donald — Prof 646-2288 dplane — 7 V DBA 65 Indiana 1984
Render, Barry — Prof 646-2657 brender — 79 UVZ PHD 75 Cinn 1989
  Harwood Chair Professor
Schatz, Martin — Prof 646-1505 mschatz — 3 I PHD 72 NYU 1979

Roosevelt University — Chicago, IL 60605-1394 (312)
Heller College Bus Adm — 430 South Michigan Avenue — FAX=341-3827 — BS,MBA,MS
–Department of Management — Phone 341-3828 — Fax 341-3827

Name	Rank	Phone			Degree		School	Year
Cooley, John W.	Prof	341-3820			PHD	76	Okla St	1992
Ghez, Gilbert R.	Prof	341-3939			PHD		Columbia	
Hedegard, James M.	Prof	341-3816	2	F	PHD		Michigan	
Noty, Charles	Prof	341-3840	25	FN	PHD		Loyola	
Ahsmann, Leroy L.	Assoc	341-3840	25		PHD		Ill Tech	
Bernstein, Donald S.	Assoc	341-3714	25	EN	PHD		Ill Tech	
Kratzec, Thomas	Assoc	341-3833	7	U				
Wagner, Jennifer	Assoc	341-3831	9	Z	PHD		Northwes	
Bradley, Steven A.	VAsst	437-9200	3	I	PHD		Northwes	
Area code (208)								

Rowan College of New Jersey — Glassboro, NJ 08028-1748 (609) ELAN.ROWAN.EDU
School of Business Adm — FAX=863-6553 — BS,MBA
Fleming, Robert — Dean$ 863-6025 — flem0785 — 39 IJNZ EDD 86 Temple 1989
–Dept of Mgt & Mgt Info Sys — Phone 863-6026 — Fax 863-6167

Name	Rank	Phone	email			Degree		School	Year
Hamilton, Diane M.	C	863-6411	hami2927	97	Z	PHD	94	Temple	1983
Lynch, Robert D.	Prof	863-6033	lync4226	37	I	PHD	55	Car Mel	1973
Byrd, Kimble A.	Assoc	863-6037	byrd9710	45	JKLN	JD	76	Penn	1984
Enslin, William L.	Assoc	863-6412	enslin16	42	FOP	EDD	80	Rutgers	1974
Frankl, Razelle	Assoc	863-6339	fran7845	25	FHR	PHD	84	Bryn Maw	1983
Lee, Jooh	Assoc	863-6037	lee0315	7	IUY	PHD	88	Miss	1988
Michael, Thomas A.	Assoc	863-6157	mich4852	23	EFIO	PHD	73	Drexel	1972
Cuthbertson, Harry	Asst	863-6464	cuth5708	14		MBA	87	LaSalle	1982
Davis, Daniel	Asst	863-6031	davi6520	9		MBA	84	Drexel	1984

Russell Sage College — Troy, NY 12180-4115 (518)
Econ & Business Dept — 51 First Street — FAX=271-4545
Brandt, Frederick — D-Ac 445-1763 — 23 EY PHD — Ariz St 1982
–Management Faculty — Phone 270-2245 — Fax 271-4545

Name	Rank	Phone			Degree	School	Year
Dalton, Robert	C-As	270-2378	34	IJ	MBA	Syracuse	1984
Biggs, Monica	Asst	270-2050	52	PR	MHR	Geo Wash	1990
Menard, Kirk	Asst	445-1763	52	NP	MBA	SUNY-Buf	1990

Rutgers University-Camden — Camden, NJ 08102 (609)
School of Business — FAX=225-6231 — BA,BS
Leontiades, Milton — Dean 225-6217 — Mgt PHD 66 American 1974
–Management Faculty — Phone 225-6217 — Fax 225-6231

Name	Rank	Phone			Degree		School
Coleman, Charles J.	Prof	225-6216			PHD		
Kendall, Kenneth L.	Prof	225-6216			PHD		
Mascarenhas, Briance	Prof	225-6216	8	Y	PHD	80	Berkeley
Weissenberg, Peter	Prof	225-6216			PHD		
Kendall, Julie E.	Assoc	225-6216			PHD		
Rabinowitz, Samuel	Assoc	225-6216			PHD		
Assistant Dean							
Baveja, Alok	Asst	225-621			PHD		
Jamil, Mamnoon	Asst	225-6216			PHD		
Peffers, Kenneth G.	Asst	225-6216			PHD		
Porter, Gayle	Asst	225-6216			PHD		
Sambharya, Rakesh	Asst	225-6216			PHD		

Rutgers University-Newark — Newark, NJ 07102-1895 (201) DRACO.RUTGERS.EDU 1983,1941
Grad School of Mgt — 92 New Street — FAX=648-5889 — MS,MBA,PHD
email: @1=gsmack.rutgers.edu
Benson, P. George — Dean 648-5129 — PHD 77 Florida 7-93
–Organization Mgt Dept — Phone — Fax 648-1459

Name	Rank	Phone	email			Degree		School	Year
DiTomaso, Nancy	C-Pr	648-5984	ditomaso	2	HORY	PHD	77	Wiscon	1983
Farris, George F.	Prof	648-5982	farris@1	23	DENO	PHD	66	Michigan	1980
Hoffman, L. Richard	Prof	648-5120	lhoffman	2	ENS	PHD	57	Michigan	
Spender, J.C.	Prof	648-5533	spender	23	BHIT	PHD	80	Manchest	1991
Damanpour, Fariborz	Assoc	648-5050	damanpo	12	DHI	PHD	83	Penn	1985
McCabe, Donald L.	Assoc	648-5308	mccabe	34	HIJ	PHD	85	New York	1988
Bailey, James	Asst	648-5983	bailey	27	EXZ	PHD	91	Wash U	1991
Chen, Chao C.	Asst	648-5425	ccchen	28	EHTY	PHD	92	SUNY-Buf	1992
Ford, Cameron M.	Asst	648-1062	cford	23	DEI	PHD	90	Penn St	1989
Greene, Patricia	Asst	648-1152	pggreene	6	TSH	PHD	93	Texas	1993
Hooijberg, Robert	Asst	648-1066	rhooijbe@1	2	E	PHD	92	Michigan	1993
Ogilvie, D. T.	Asst		dogilvie@1	38	IY	ABD		Texas	1994
Rothberg, Helen	Asst	648-1065	hrothberg	23	EIA	PHD	90	Baruch	1989
–International Business	Phone 648-1651		Fax 648-1273						
Rosenberg, Jerry M.	C-Pr	648-5812		8	Y	PHD		NYU	1980
Contractor, Farok	Prof	648-5348		8	Y	PHD		Penn	1980
Dunning, John	Prof	648-5885		8	Y	PHD		SHampton	1988
Roth, Allan	Prof	648-5027		8	Y	JD		Harvard	1969

Gilad, Benjamin	Assoc	648-5168	8	Y		PHD	82	NYU	1981
Hartman, Ed	Assoc	648-5987				PHD		Princeto	1984
Hetzner, Candace	Assoc	648-5121	8	Y		PHD		Chicago	1989
Beldona, Sam	Asst	648-1063	8	Y		PHD		Temple	1993
Eastman, Wayne	Asst	648-1001	8	Y		JD		Harvard	1991
Raghunathan, Sankaran P.	Asst	648-5734	8	Y		PHD		Temple	1991

Rutgers Univ-New Brunswick	New BrunswickNJ 08903		(908)						1991
School of Business			FAX=932-5647						BS
–Department of Management	Phone	932-3560	Fax 932-5647						
Gordon, Michael E.	C-Pr	932-3560			QEN	PHD	69	Berkeley	1989
Bobko, Phil	Prof	932-3279			EN	PHD	76	Cornell	1988
Kovach, Barbara E.	Prof	932-5756			EO	PHD	73	Maryland	1984
Colella, Adrienne	Asst	932-5648			ENR	PHD	89	Ohio St	1989
Gedajlovic, Eric R.	Asst	932-5273			IY	PHD	93	Concordi	1993
Park, Seung Ho	Asst	932-4458			IY	PHD	92	Oregon	1992

Saginaw Valley State Univ	Univ Center, MI	48710	(517)						
College of Bus & Mgt			FAX=790-1314						BBA,MBA
Carlson, Severin C.	Dean	790-4064			Fnce	DBA	79	Indiana	1994
–Dept of Management & Mktg	Phone	790-4235	Fax 790-7656						
Bishop, Deborah R.	C-Ac	790-4476	25	EHN		PHD	86	Mass	1987
Cheek, Robert E.	Assoc	790-4016	32	IF		EDD	70	Wayne St	1984
Ofori-Dankwa, Joseph	Assoc	790-4181	58	NQY		PHD	87	Mich St	1987
Reddy, Surender C.	Assoc	790-4099	78	UVXY		PHD	91	Case Wes	1989
Sype, Gail E.	Asst	790-5606	28	EHY		PHD	93	Mich St	1990

St. Ambrose University	Davenport, IA	52803	(319)						
College of Business	518 West Locust Street		FAX=383-8942					BA,BS,MBA,MACC
Did Not Respond-1993 Listing									
Jensen, James O.	Dean	383-8759	12	BEH		PHD	69	Iowa	1980
–Dept Economics & Bus Adm	Phone	383-8950	Fax 383-8942						
Harris, Ralph	C-Pr	383-8962		Stat		PHD	73	Iowa	1994
Begin, Floyd C.	Prof	383-8701	18	DY		PHD	74	Iowa	1985
Bereskin, J. Gregory	Prof	383-8764	79	UZ		PHD	76	Cinn	1991
Brown, Linda K.	Prof	383-8708	19	AZ		MBA	84	St Ambro	1987
Chohan, Ray V.	Prof	383-8738	79	UZ		PHD	75	Port St	1978
Collis, John W.	Prof	383-8899	24	HK		PHD	85	Iowa	1984
Kabis, Zeinhom M.	Prof	383-8739	79	VZ		PHD	68	Illinois	1973
Mullins, James E.	Prof	383-8714	79	UZ		MA	65	Marquett	1969
Shovlain, Ray	Prof	383-8773	19	AZ		MBA	80	St Ambro	1982
VanSpeybroeck, James O.	Prof	383-8736	79	VZ		MS	80	W Illin	1983
Vogel, Joseph P.	Prof	383-8968	79	VZ		MA	60	Arizona	1989
Borst, Frank	Assoc	383-8872	37	IU		EDD	82	Memphis	1990
Lindemann, Bonnie	Assoc	383-8708	25	EN		PHD	93	Iowa	1993
Jacobson, Robert	Asst	794-9887	74	V		MA	79	Webster	1991
Morgan, David T.	Asst	383-8962	27	EU		MS	76	Fla Inst	1992
Shoemaker, Craig	Asst	383-8904	17	DU		MBA	83	Keller	1992
Sztager, George	Asst	383-8968	17	DU		MBA	79	Iowa	1993
Christopherson, Reid	Inst	383-8896	19	AZ		MBA	90	St Ambro	1990

Saint Bonaventure Univ	S Bonaventure NY 14778		(716) SBU.EDU						
School of Business	Route 417		FAX=375-2005					BBA,MBA
Burns, John	Dean	375-2200	jburns			Fnce	PHD	70	Mich St	1991
–Dept of Management Science	Phone	375-2076	Fax 375-2191						
Korukonda, A. Rao	C-Pr	375-2076	akorukonda	2		PHD		Tx Tech	1986
Diminnie, Carol B.	Prof	375-2359	cdiminnie	7		PHD		St Louis	1977
Khairullah, Zahid Y.	Prof	375-2093	zkhairullah	79	UVZ	PHD		SUNY-Buf	1976
Watson, John G.	Prof	375-2203	jwatson	23		PHD		St Louis	1975
Murphy, Kathleen M.	Assoc	375-2192	kmurphy	24		PHD		Denver	1986
Pohl, Stuart M.	Asst	375-2096	spohl	5		JD		SUNY-Buf	1987

St. Cloud State University	Saint Cloud, MN	56301-4498	(612) MSUS1					1976,1982
College of Business			FAX=255-3986					BS,MBA,MS
Kelly, James M.	Dean	255-3213	3	I		DBA	67	Colorado	1987
–Dept of Management & Fin	Phone	255-3225	Fax 255-3986						
Tallent, Dwaine	C-Pr	255-3226	36	IS		PHD	70	Nebraska	1979
Saraph, Jayant	Prof	255-3231	73	UV		PHD	87	Minn	1985
Sebastian, Richard J.	Prof	255-3006	2	GE		PHD	74	Wiscon	1983
Thomas, Dave	Prof	255-2247	36	ST		PHD	79	Nebraska	1980
Vora, Jay	Prof	255-3911	38	UY		PHD	69	Renssela	1978
Davis, Elaine	Assoc	255-4951	21	EF		PHD	92	Nebraska	1990
Eagle, Bruce	Assoc	654-5444				ABD		Georgia	1993
Haugen, Dyan	Assoc	255-3006	7	UV		PHD	93	Minn	1991
King, Paula	Assoc	255-3243	34	AFN		PHD	89	Minn	1990

Pesch, Michael J.	Assoc	255-4990	7	UV	PHD	90	Minn	1987
Polley, Doug	Assoc	255-4830	3	IJ	PHD	91	Minn	1991
Rhee, Yinsog	Assoc	255-3225	5	NQ	PHD	85	Minn	1988
Ribbens, Barbara	Assoc	654-5443			ABD		Conn	1993
Roth, Larry	Assoc	654-5144	51	NPQ	PHD	71	Tulane	1990
Skalbeck, Bruce	Assoc	255-3200	7	UV	PHD	75	N Colo	1977
Ward, Ed	Assoc	654-5143	25	EJNS	PHD	86	Nebraska	1990

St. Edward's University — Austin, TX 78704 (512) BBA,MBA
School of Business Adm — 3001 South Congress Avenue FAX=488-8492
Myers, Lewis A. Jr. — Dean$ 448-8696

—**Management Faculty**	Phone	448-8696	Fax 416-8192					
Krafka, Frank	Prof	448-8601	27	UV	PHD	81	Texas	1978
Poulos, Mark S.	Assoc	778-8608	36	IS	PHD	84	Texas	1985
Dailey, John G.	Asst	448-8644	14	JL	MBA	78	Geo Wash	1991
Hallock, Daniel	Asst	448-8647			PHD	92	Tenn	1993
Loucks, John	Asst	448-8605			PHD			1993
Simon, Bernard	Asst	448-8602	25	EPUX	MBA	76	St Edwar	1991

St. Francis College — Brooklyn Hght NY 11201 (718) BS
Business Division — 180 Remsen Street FAX=522-1274
Gomori, Peter — C-Ac 522-2300 PHD CUNY

—**Management Faculty**	Phone	522-2300	Fax 522-1274			
Barcun, Seymour	Prof	522-2300	7	PHD	New York
Goldberg, Robert I.	Assoc	522-2300	16	MA	Columbia
Petrucelli, Ernest Jr.	Assoc	522-2300		MBA	New York
Morse, Gail	Inst	522-2300	25	MBA	Baruch

Saint Francis College — Loretto, PA 15940 (814) BS
Dept of Business Adm — FAX=472-3044
Owens, Kathleen — Dean 472-3004 PHD 1992

—**Management Faculty**	Phone	472-3087	Fax 472-3044					
Frye, Randy L.	C-Pr	472-3087	5	MBA	80	Ind-PA	1980
McIlnay, Dennis	Assoc	472-3095	2	MBA			
Elwell, Bruce	Asst	472-3071	7	DBA	USC		1991
Thomas, Sebastian	Asst	472-3072		MBA			

St. John Fisher College — Rochester, NY 14618 (716) SJFC.EDU
Grad School of Mgt — 3690 East Avenue FAX=385-8094
*Area Code (315)

Ilter, Selim	C-Pr	385-8079	ilter		PHD	Geo St
--**Department of Management**	Phone	385-8079	Fax 385-8094			
Deligonul, Seyda	Prof	337-9083	18	PHD	Haccette
Kozan, Kamil	Prof	425-2639	12	PHD	UCLA
Sen, Asim	Prof	385-8079	79	PHD	Rutgers
Berman, Jason	Assoc	473-0461	12	PHD	UR
Mamaghani, Farrokh	Assoc	586-3689	7	DSD	Geo Wash
Costigan, Robert	Asst	223-5421	25	PHD	Missouri
Jackson, LaMarr	Asst	877-4143	4	JD	Buffalo
Luxmore, Stephen	Asst	377-0334	38	PHD	Toronto

St. John's University — Jamaica, NY 11439 (718) SJUVM 1968,1982
College of Business — Grand Central & Utopia Prkwy FAX=591-8784 BSMGT,MBA
Did Not Respond-1993 Listing; Dept Phone 990-6161 Queens; 390-4545 Staten Isl
Mauer, Laurence J. — Dean 990-6477 Econ PHD 67 Tenn 1983

—**Department of Management**	Phone		Fax 591-8784				
Carey, Justin	C	990-6495		PHD	51	Columbia	1951
Kavanagh, Michael J.	Prof	990-7405		PHD	61	Fordham	
Maasarani, Aly	Prof	990-7409		PHD	62	Texas	
Mockler, Robert J.	Prof	990-7416		PHD	61	Columbia	1963
Pagano, LeRoy	Prof	390-4545		PHD	74	American	
Distinguished Professor							
Stanton, Erwin S.	Prof	990-7420		PHD	58	Columbia	
Lyons, Patrick	Assoc	990-7404		PHD	73	Adelphi	
Magee-Egan, Pauline	Assoc	990-7406		PHD	63	Fordham	
Persek, Stephen	Assoc	990-7414		PHD	76	NYU	
Wankel, Charles	Assoc	990-7401		PHD	89	NYU	
Wirth, Itzhak	Assoc	990-7423		PHD	76	Berkeley	
Abraham, Thomas	Asst	990-7412		PHD	90	Mass	
Angelidis, John	Asst	990-7413		PHD	88	Geo St	
Boone, Larry	Asst	990-5523		PHD	87	Pitt	
Director of Business Research Institute							
Chao, Chiang-Nan	Asst	990-7401		PHD	89	Ariz St	
Cusack, Gerald P.	Asst	990-7403		PHD	76	NYU	
Goeller, Thomas	Asst	390-4545		DBA	89	Miss St	

Massetti, Brenda	Asst	390-4545			PHD	91	Fla St	
McGowen, Raymond D.	Asst	990-7407			PHD	70	St Johns	
Ruhnke, Henry O.	Asst	990-7418			MBA	64	Baruch	
Director Executive in Residence Program								
Hollingsworth, John	Inst	390-4545			MBA		Wheeling	
Meyer, Harry	Inst	990-7415			MIE		NYU	

Saint Joseph's University	Philadelphia, PA	19131-1395		(215) SJUPHIL				
College of Bus & Adm	5600 City Avenue			FAX=660-1625				
Bowditch, James L.	Dean				PHD	69	Purdue	1993
–Dept of Mgt & Info Systems	Phone	660-1630	Fax 660-1649					
Davis, Elizabeth	C-As	660-1644	edavis*	23 EIJY	PHD	84	Penn	1988
Robak, Nicholas J.	Prof	660-1635	nrobak	9 PSXZ	PHD	72	Penn	1972
Delaney, Michael M.	Assoc	660-1167	mdelaney	9 YZ	PHD	76	Penn	1992
Dell'Orno, Gregory G.	Assoc	660-1629	gdellomo	25 NPQ	PHD	87	Wiscon	1991
Associate Dean								
McDevitt, William J.	Asst	600-1634		4 KLQ	JD	75	Villanov	1987
McNally, Vincent	Asst	660-1641	vmcnally	1 AGMP	PHD	79	Temple	1976
Monteverde, Kirk A.	Asst	660-1626	kmonteve	39 FIVZ	PHD	81	Stanford	1992
Paul, Allison A.	Asst	660-1621	apaul	23 ENPR	PHD	91	Temple	1990
Porth, Stephen J.	Asst	660-1639	sporth	38 EIY	PHD	88	Temple	1984
Vaughan, Thomas P.	Asst	660-1631	tvaughan	79 CUVW	PHD	81	Michigan	1994
Yermish, Ira	Asst	660-1636	iyermish	79 ISUZ	PHD	75	Penn	1984
Gaitley, Normandic J. SSJ	Inst	660-1630		12 ECLR	ABD		Drexel	1994
Joshi, Mahesh P.	Inst	660-1630		38 EIY	ABD		Temple	1994

Saint Louis University	St. Louis, MO	63108		(314) SLUVCA				1948,1978
School of Bus & Adm	221 North Grand Boulevard			FAX=658-3874				BS,MPA,PHD
Seitz, Neil E.	Dean	658-3833		Fnce	PHD	73	Ohio St	1975
–Dept of Mgt & Dec Science	Phone		Fax 658-3878					
Kwon, Ik-Whan	C-Pr	658-3878			PHD	68	Georgia	1968
Brockhaus, Robert H.	Prof	658-3826			PHD		Wash U	
Drebes, Charles B.	Prof	658-3829			DSC	69	Wash U	
Kwak, NoKyoon	Prof	658-3867			PHD	64	S Calif	1985
Levary, Reuven R.	Prof	658-3804			PHD		Case Wes	
Parker, Gerald E.	Prof	658-3843			PHD	72	St Louis	1972
Stoeberl, Phillip A.	Prof	658-3841			PHD	72	St Louis	
Favilla, Edward	Assoc	658-3867			PHD		North Tx	
Katz, Jerome A.	Assoc	658-3864			PHD		Michigan	
Shaner, Michael C.	Assoc	658-3870			PHD	74	S Carol	
Debusk, Susan	Asst	658-3860			PHD		Texas	1992
Ferris, Mark	Asst	658-3851			PHD		Illinois	
Hardway, Donald E.	Asst	658-3840			PHD		Houston	
Harshman, Ellen	Asst	658-2476			PHD		St Louis	1993
Huston, Terry	Asst	658-7158			PHD		Pitt	1993
Jones, Lawrence	Asst	658-3818			PHD		St Louis	
Rudin, Joel	Asst	658-7155			PHD		Cornell	

Saint Martin's College	Lacey, WA	98503		(206)				
Business Division	5300 Pacific Avenue SE			FAX=				BS
Knutson, Jerry L.	Dean	438-4511			MBA	83	Puget Sd	
–Department of Management	Phone	438-4326	Fax 438-4124					
Wilson, Haldon D. Jr.	C-As	438-4326		35	MBA		Puget So	
Wallace, William D.	Asst	438-4329		24	PHD		U Wash	

Saint Mary's College	Moraga, CA	94575		(510) GALILEO.SYMARYS-CA.EDU				
Sch of Econ & Bus Adm	1928 St. Mary's Road			FAX=376-5625				BS
Edpstein, Edwin	Dean	631-4607		Law	LLD		Berkeley	1994
–Management Faculty	Phone	631-4607	Fax 376-5625					
Thompson, John	C	631-4599		Fnce	MBA		Chicago	1985
Bowen, David J.	Prof	631-4582		25 FQE	PHD	76	Berkeley	1983
Bedford, Norman	Assoc			7 V	PHD		Gold Gt	1992
Wu, Diana	Assoc	631-4582		2 EHR	PHD	80	Wright I	1981

Saint Marys College	Notre Dame, IN	46556-5001		(219)				
Dept of Bus Adm & Econ				FAX=284-4716				BBA,BA
Vance, Susan M.	C-Ac	284-4501			JD		Cooley	
–Management Faculty	Phone		Fax 284-4716					
Ruhe, John A.	Assoc	284-4510		34 J	PHD	73	Florida	8-78
Strach, Lauren K.	Asst	284-4509		15 R	PHD	90	Mich St	8-89

St. Mary's University-Tx	San Antonio, TX 78228		(210) STMARYTX				
School of Bus & Adm	1 Camino Santa Maria		FAX=431-2115				
Manuel, David P.	Dean			Econ	PHD	75	Miss
—Department of Management	Phone	Fax 431-2115					
Preismeyer, Richard	C	431-2041			PHD	84	Arkansas
Ferguson, R. Wayne	Prof				PHD	72	North Tx
Myra Stafford Pryor Professor of Free Enterprise							
Goelz, Paul C.	Prof	436-3124			PHD	54	Northwes 1946
Langford, Margaret	Prof				PHD	92	Houston
Martinez, Zaida L.	Prof	431-2115			PHD	87	S Carol
Menger, Richard	Prof				PHD	92	Tx A&M
Merrell, Ronald D.	Prof	431-6761			PHD	75	Oklahoma
Szecsy, Richard E.	Prof				PHD	73	Illinois
Toyne, Brian	Prof				PHD	75	Geo St
Howe, Robert C.	Assoc		7	V	MBA	64	Tx Chr
Davis, J. Jackson	Asst				PHD	71	Tx Tech
Litherland, David	Asst						
Mattox, Charles	Asst						
Mehta, Kamlesh	Asst				DBA	90	US Intl
—Dept of Finance & Quant	Phone 436-3705	Fax 431-2115					
Todd, Jerry	C-Pr 431-2043				PHD	68	Wiscon
Charles E. Cheever Professor of Risk Management							
Weaver, Charles N.	Prof 431-2039		27	IVX	PHD	67	Texas 1965
Emil C. E. Jurica Professor of Quantitative Management							
Anderson, Wendell	Asst 431-2035		79	UVZ	MBA	69	Harvard 1985
Reeves, E. Thomas	Asst 431-2025		79	UVZ	PHD		1992
Welch, O. James	Asst 431-1127		79	UVZ	ABD		1993
St. Norbert College	DePere, WI 54115-2099		(414) SNCAC.SNC.EDU				
Dept of Business Adm	100 Grant Street		FAX=337-4073				BBA
Ritter, Jeffrey D.	D-As 337-3234	rittjd		Atg	MBA	74	Miami U 1983
—Management Faculty	Phone 337-3113	Fax 337-4098					
Elfner, Eliot S.	Prof 337-3233	elfnes	17	OUY	PHD	69	Wiscon 1971
Shihadeh, Emile	Prof 337-3154	shihes	23	EINY	PHD	65	Cornell 1985
Saint Paul's College	Lawrenceville VA 23868		(804)				
Dept Business Adm & Ed	406 Windsor Ave		FAX=				
phone 848-4008;848-3111							
Oshunkentan, Samson	C-Ac Ext 210		12	EINY	PHD		1991
—Management Faculty	Phone Ext 120	Fax 848-0403					
Rainey, Bessye C.	Prof Ext 263		9	Z	EDD		1969
Ford, Kenneth C.	Asst Ext 257		9	Z	MBA		1991
Summiel, Laverne S.	Asst Ext 259		9	Z	MBA		1973
Johnson, David W.	Inst Ext 257		69	SZ	ABD		1989
Jones, Hester B.	Inst Ext 277		1	D	ABD		1985
Luthar, Vipan K.	Inst Ext 257		23	FIY	MBA		1989
Wilson, Keathen A.	Inst Ext 258		7	UW	MA		1984
Saint Peter's College	Jersey City, NJ 07306		(201)				
College of Business	2641 Kennedy Boulevard		FAX=435-3662				
Rosenbluth, Martin H.	C 915-9278				MBA		Rutgers 1968
—Dept of Management & Mktg	Phone 915-9278	Fax 451-0036					
Cross, Jeffrey	Assoc				DBA		Nova 1985
Talbot, Irwin N.	Assoc 915-9283	talbot		ESTH	PHD		NYU 9-79
Caccamise, Richard	Asst				EDD		Temple 1990
Henson, Joyce M.	Asst				PHD		Fordham 1982
Lawson, James W.	Asst 915-9284	jlawson			DBA	88	Nova 9-88
Lieberman, Herman	Asst				MS		Michigan 1978
Abrams, Bernard	Inst				MBA		Geo Wash 1989
College of Saint Rose	Albany, NY 12203		(518)				
School of Business	1001 Madison Avenue		FAX=438-3293				BS,MS,MBA
Feingold, Paul	Dean 454-5272				PHD	76	Purdue 1992
—Management Faculty	Phone 454-5272	Fax 458-5493					
DeCastro, Sister Ida	Assoc 454-5233		25		MSBA	70	Notre Dm 1973
Stevens, Dixon	Assoc 454-5202		3	FIDE	PHD	76	SUNY-Alb 1978
Billet, Martin	Asst 454-5151		9	Z	PHD	91	Warsaw T 1985
Hurley, Michael	Asst 458-5465		25	NQVX	PHD	87	Renssela 1986
Sung, Simona	Asst 454-5269		7	V	PHD	90	Renssela 1990
College of St Scholastica	Duluth, MN 55811		(218)				
Management Department			FAX=723-6290				
Jenner, Jessica R.	C-Pr 723-6150				PHD		Columbia
—Management Faculty	Phone 723-6415	Fax 723-6290					
Barrett, Anthony	Prof				PHD		Geo Wash 1990

Kotamraju, P.	Assoc				PHD		1991
Anstett, David	Asst				MBA	Minn-Dul	1985
Fenton, Howard	Asst				MBA	Geo Maso	1989
Gregoria, Gary	Asst				MBA	Mich St	1982
Mogg, Melanie	Asst				MBA	Minn	1988
Smith, George	Asst				MBA	CorpusCh	1986
Omar, H. M.					PHD		1993
Swenson, David					PHD		1992

St. Thomas University-FL	Miami, FL	33054		(305)			
Business Administration	16400 Northwest 32nd Avenue			FAX=628-6510			
–Management Faculty	Phone		Fax 628-6504				
Bradley, John H.	C-Pr	628-6598		19		DCS	78 Georgia	1978
Diehl, Pidge L.	Prof	628-6780		27 FGPX	EDD		1983
Amann, Robert J.	Asst	628-6629		35 IQST	PHD	Va Tech	1991
Axx, John R.	Asst	628-6625		38	MBA		1983
Flax, Stanley	Asst	628-6635		38	MBA		1986
Kory, Delores	Asst	628-6628		12	DPA		1984
Kulzick, Raymond S.	Asst	628-6624		39 IZS	DBA		1977
Tapia, Daniel	Asst	628-6621		48	LLM		1985

University of St. Thomas-MN	St. Paul, MN	55105-1096	(612)				BA
Bus Adm Mail MCN 6063	32 South Finn		FAX=647-5897				
–Department of Management	Phone	Fax 962-5093					
Buckeye, Jeanne	C-Ac	962-5137					
Anderson, Philip H.	Prof	962-5136	3 I	PHD	75 Minn	8-77
Power, Sally J.	Prof	962-4303				
Trostel, Al	Prof	962-5098				
Johnson, Stanley	Assoc	962-5139				
Kennedy, Robert	Assoc	962-5140				
Mason, Thomas	Assoc	962-5143				
McNamara, Daniel	Assoc	962-5144				
Militello, Jack	Assoc	962-5146				
Woodhouse, Robert	Assoc	962-5099				
Elm, Dawn	Asst	962-5138				
Helberg, Patricia	Asst	962-4305				
Meyer, Jan	Asst	962-5145				
Raffield, William	Asst	962-5148				
Sheppeck, Michael	Asst	962-5485				
Gorski, Barbara	Lect	962-5513				
Owens, Ernest	Lect	962-5141				

University of St. Thomas-TX	Houston, TX	77006-4696	(713)				BA,BBA,MBA
Cameron School of Bus	3905 Yoakum		FAX=				
Ho, Yhi-Min	Dean	522-7911			PHD	Vanderbt
–Management Faculty	Phone	525-2100	Fax 525-2110			
Burke, Antaro R.	Assoc	525-2122		25 EFHP	PHD	62 Boston	8-91
Davis, Anne	Asst	525-2124		25 ENY	PHD	90 Ohio St	1992

Saint Vincent College	Latrobe, PA	15650-2690	(412)				BA,BS
Business Adm Department	301 Fraser Purchase Rd		FAX=				
DePasquale, Robert J.	C-Pr	537-4589		Atg	PHD	92 Pitt	1978
–Management Faculty,	Phone	537-4589	Fax 537-4554			
Hisker, William J.	Prof	539-9761		23	PHD	Pitt	1974
Rand, Shirley M.	Asst	539-9761		45	JD	Missouri	1987

Saint Xavier University	Chicago, IL	60655	(312) SXU.EDU				BA,MBA
Graham School of Mgt	3825 West 103rd Street		FAX=799-9073				
Fremgen, Bonnie	Dean$	298-3600		12 CE	PHD	88 Illinois	1993
–Management Faculty	Phone	298-3600	Fax 298-3610			
Weeks, Benjamin	D-Ac	298-3627		34 JLD	PHD	Miss	1986
Clott, Christopher	Assoc	298-3612		81 Y	MBA	St Xavie	1989
Mohammadi, Hamid	Assoc	298-3621		7 UV	PHD	Ill Tech	1988
Novak, Henry	Assoc	298-3622		59 QZ	ABD	Ill Tech	1981
Lanser, Kris	Asst	298-3625		23 EFI	PHD	Miss	
Lindman, Frank	Asst	298-3619		7 UV	PHD	Arizona	1988
McKenna, Brian	Asst	298-3620		4 K	JD	J Marsha	1989
Shanabruch, Chuck	Asst	298-3624		3 IJ	PHD	Chicago	1988
McCabe, Jim	AsDn	298-3605		69 TZ	MBA	Gov St	1981

Salem State College	Salem, MA	01970-4589	(508)			
School of Bus & Econ	352 Lafayette Street		FAX=			
Burton, Wayne	Dean	741-6640		EDD	91 Vanderbt

–Management Department

Name	Title	Phone			Degree	School
		Phone 741-6608	Fax 741-6027			
Hansen, Theodore L.	C	741-6627	5	N	MBA	Stanford
Farahbakhsh, Massoud	Prof		8		DBA	Nova
LaPorte, Arthur J. Jr.	Prof		1		MBA	Arizona
Mack, John E.	Prof		1		PHD	St Louis
Barry, David F.	Assoc		46		JD	Suffolk
Berman, Jeffrey A.	Assoc	741-6000	25		PHD	New York
Kenney, John R.	Assoc		4		JD	Boston C
Little, Lillian O.	Assoc		2		PHD	Syracuse

Salisbury State University

Salisbury, MD 21801-6860 (410) SAE.TOWSON.EDU

Franklin Perdue Sch Bus FAX=543-6068 BS,MBA

Name	Title	Phone	Email	Fld	Code	Degree	Yr	School	Date
Bebee, Richard F.	Dean	543-6316	rfbebee		Atg	DBA	71	Colorado	7-91
–Dept of Management & Mktg	Phone	543-6315	Fax 548-2908						
Decker, Wayne H.	C-Pr	543-6094	whdecker	27	EJO	PHD	72	Pitt	8-86
Shipper, Frank M.	Prof	543-6333	fmshipper	23	EFIL	PHD	78	Utah	8-91
Hoffman, Richard C. IV	Assoc	548-5398	rchoffman	38	IY	PHD	83	Indiana	9-93
Rubenson, George	Assoc	543-6187	gcrubenson	35	INT	PHD	89	Maryland	8-87
Associate Dean									
Hanebury, Jean M.	Asst	543-6212	jmhanebury	54	INOP	PHD	90	Geo St	8-88
–Dept Info & Decision Sci	Phone	543-6315	Fax 543-2908						
Kottermann, Jeffrey	C-Pr	543-6315				PHD	84	Arizona	8-94
Ramakrishna, Hindupur	Assoc	543-6507		79	Z	PHD	83	Geo St	8-92
Dillon, Thomas	Asst	543-6419		9	Z	ABD		UMBC	1-93
Harrison, Benjamin	Asst	543-6319		7	UV	PHD	90	Geo St	0-88
Kuilboer, Jean-Pierre	Asst	543-6207		9	Z	PHD	92	Tx-Arlin	8-91
Lee, Choong	Asst	548-5390		9	Z	PHD	93	S Carol	
Salimian, Fatollah	Asst	543-6321		7	UV	ABD		Kent St	8-82
Fagan, Mary Helen	Inst	543-6315				ABD		Texas	8-94

Sam Houston State Univ

Huntsville, TX 77341 (409)

College of Business Adm 2000 Sam Houston Avenue FAX=294-3612

Name	Title	Phone		Fld	Degree	Yr	School	Date
Gilmore, James E.	Dean	294-1254		Fnce	EDD	69	Houston	1956
–Dept of Management & Mktg	Phone	294-1256	Fax 294-3612					
Abshire, Roger D.	C-Ac	294-1255		Mktg	DBA	90	La Tech	1989
Kilbourne, William	Prof	294-1234			PHD	73	Houston	1982
Lewis, R. Dean	Prof	294-1246			PHD	72	Arkansas	1987
Lovell, Ross	Prof	294-1312			PHD	62	Texas	1972
Thornton, Nelson L. Jr.	Prof	294-1275			PHD	73	North Tx	1970
Earl, Ronald	Assoc	294-1273			PHD	78	Tx A&M	1971
Reed, Paul	Assoc	294-1281			DBA	82	Miss St	1983
Capps, Charles	Asst	294-1895			DBA	88	La Tech	1988
Duffy, Jo Ann	Asst	294-1518			PHD	87	Texas	1988
Sower, Victor	Asst	294-1272			PHD	90	North Tx	1990
Walker, George H.	Asst	294-1296			PHD	67	Texas	1990
Gentry, Paul	Inst	294-1274			MBA	69	N Carol	1982
Blasick, James	Lect	294-1270			MBA	90	Sam Hous	1990
Richardson, Gary	Lect	294-1842			PHD	70	North Tx	1987
Stewart, Wayne	Lect	294-1236			MBA	88	W Carol	1993

BBA,MBA,MS

Samford University

Birmingham, AL 35229 (205) FAX=870-2464

School of Business
 Did Not Respond-1993 Listing

Name	Title	Phone		Fld	Degree	School	Date
David, Robert T.	Dean	870-2308			MBA	Harvard	1988
–Department of Management	Phone		Fax 870-2464				
Ruchs, Andy	Prof	870-2888		7 U			
Associate Dean							
Marshall, Jennings B.	Assoc	870-2539			PHD	Kentucky	1986
Reed, Marlene M.	Assoc	870-2542			DBA	La Tech	1981
Steckler, Mel	Asst	870-2172		7 U			

University of San Diego

San Diego, CA 92110 (619) ACUSD 1980,1981

School of Business Adm Alcala Park FAX=260-4891 BS,MS,MBA,MIB

Name	Title	Phone	Email	Fld	Code	Degree	Yr	School	Date
Burns, James M.	Dean	260-4886		3	I	DBA	68	Harvard	1974
–Management Faculty	Phone		Fax 260-4891						
Briscoe, Dennis R.	Prof	260-4862		58	NOQY	PHD	77	Mich St	1978
Hunsaker, Phillip L.	Prof	260-4870		2	EFG	DBA	70	S Calif	1977
Pavett, Cynthia	Prof	260-4851	pavett	28	CGY	PHD	78	Utah	1978
Hunsaker, Johanna S.	Assoc	260-4858		2	GHR	PHD	77	Wisc	1977
Rothman, Miriam	Assoc	260-4856		25	NQY	PHD	84	U Wash	1984
Whitney, Gary	Assoc	260-4859	gwhitney	3	EI	PHD	76	U Wash	1980
Kunkel, Scott W.	Asst	260-4830	kuncel	32	IT	PHD	91	Georgia	1992
Morris, Tom	Asst	260-4885	tmorris	38	IY	PHD	89	Denver	1988
Pienta, Darlene A.	Asst	260-4869	pienta	38	JY	PHD	87	S Calif	1985

San Diego State University
College of Business Adm — San Diego, CA 92182-0096 — 5300 Campanile Drive — (619) SCIENCES.SBSU.EDU 1959,1963 — FAX=594-1573 BS,MS,MBA

Name	Title	Phone	email	#	code	Deg	#	School	Year
Bailey, Allan R.	Dean	594-5259			Atg	PHD	69	UCLA	1968
–Department of Management	Phone	549-5306	Fax 594-1573						
Hergert, Michael L.	C-Pr	594-5314	mhergert	38	IY	PHD	83	Harvard	1985
Belasco, James A.	Prof	296-5918	jbelasco	2	EH	PHD	66	Cornell	1971
Butler, Mark C.	Prof	594-4790	mbutler	28	EFGY	PHD	77	Tx Chr	1981
DeNoble, Alex F.	Prof	594-4890	adenoble	36	IT	PHD	83	Va Tech	1983
Ghorpade, Jaisingh V.	Prof	594-6848	jghorpade	5	N	PHD	68	UCLA	1965
Hampton, David R.	Prof	594-4309	dhampton	2	E	PHD	64	Columbia	1964
Marino, Kenneth E.	Prof	594-5339	kmarino	3	I	PHD	78	Mass	1986
Wright, Penny L.	Prof	594-6839	pwright	2	EH	PHD	80	Ca-Irvine	1972
Ehrlich, Sanford B.	Assoc	594-4892	sehrlich	2	EH	PHD	87	SUNY-Buf	1986
Hatch, Mary Jo	Assoc	594-5322	mhatch	2	EH	PHD	85	Stanford	1987
Rhyne, Larry C.	Assoc	594-5905	lrhyne	3	I	PHD	81	Northwes	1987
Teagarden, Mary	Assoc	594-5739	mteagarden	83	YI	PHD	89	S Calif	1986
Dunn, Craig P.	Asst	594 5783	cdunn	4	LM	PHD	92	Indiana	1991

University of San Francisco
McLaren Sch of Business — San Francisco CA 94117-1080 — 2130 Fulton Street — (415) ALM.ADMIN.USFCA.EDU 1953,1982 — FAX=666-2502 BS

Name	Title	Phone	email	#	code	Deg	#	School	Year
Williams, Gary G.	Dean	666-6384			Mktg	PHD	66	Stanford	7-78
–Management Faculty	Phone		Fax 666-2502						
Babcock, Richard D.	Prof	666-6483				PHD	70	UCLA	1977
Efendioglu, Alev M.	Prof	666-6389		19	AZ	PHD	78	LSU	1977
Harari, Oren	Prof	666-6277				PHD'	78	Calif	1977
Imparato, Nicholas I.	Prof	666-6740				PHD	70	Bowl Gr	1970
Matsuura, Nanshi	Prof	666-6785		78	JMQY	PHD	78	Inidana	1981
Muscat, Eugene	Prof	666-2526		79	VZ	EDD	74	S Calif	1973
Weihrich, Heinz	Prof	666-6780				PHD	73	UCLA	1980
Barsky, Jonathan	Assoc	666-6219	barsky	13	CDPX	PHD	92	Gold Gt	1985
Becker, W. Michael	Assoc	666-6125				PHD	75	Brig Yg	1975
Bell, Arthur	Assoc	666-6264		12	DGJU	PHD	73	Harvard	1993
Kane, Kathy	Assoc	666-6865		12	DERY	PHD	92	Clarmont	1991
Rodgers, William	Assoc	666-6272		3	I	MBA	52	S Calif	1990
Smith, Dayle	Assoc	666-6696		25	GP	PHD	86	S Calif	1993

San Francisco State Univ
School of Business — San Francisco CA 94132 — 1600 Holloway Avenue — (415) SFSUVAX1.SFSU.EDU 1963,1975 — FAX=338-6237 BS,MBA

Name	Title	Phone	email	#	code	Deg	#	School	Year
Wallace, Arthur	Dean	338-2665			AgEc	PHD	64	Okla St	1993
–Dept of Management	Phone	338-2201	Fax 338-6237						
Albert, Michael	Prof	338-1353		12	FHNP	PHD	77	Geo St	1977
Carr-Ruffino, Norma J.	Prof	338-7473		14	EGR	PHD	72	North Tx	1973
Castaldi, Richard M.	Prof	338-2829		13	ITYM	PHD	82	Va Tech	1988
Dopp, John A.	Prof	338-1703		12	EHDF	DA	78	Lehigh	1979
Ericson, H. Edward	Prof	338-2665	ericson	14	ADJL	PHD	75	Stanford	1975
Gappa, Joseph A.	Prof	338-7486		7	VY	PHD	76	Utah	1984
Glenn, James R. Jr.	Prof	338-1235	jglenn	24	EHJL	PHD	75	Stanford	1983
Harrison, Frank	Prof	338-1321	efh	1		PHD	70	U Wash	1984
Jenner, Richard A.	Prof	338-2042	rjenner	6		PHD	64	Colorado	1984
Kowalczyk, Stan J.	Prof	338-7484	sjk	34	IL	PHD	76	Berkeley	1973
Silverman, Murray I.	Prof	338-7489		3	I	PHD	72	Stanford	1986
Spier, Leo	Prof	338-2130			IJLY	PHD	62	U Wash	1980
Staley, Tom	Prof	338-7471		1	K	PHD	74	Texas	1975
Sullivan, John	Prof	338-1817		5	NQ	PHD	78	Florida	1978
Baack, Jane	Assoc	338-1268		2	ENRL	PHD	83	Nebraska	1984
Kuhn, Arthur J.	Assoc	338-2667		23	BHI	PHD	72	Berkeley	1987
MacColl, Michael	Assoc	338-2763		23	HIY	PHD	92	Toronto	1989
Yeung, Arthur	Assoc	338-2255		2	HINY	PHD	90	Michigan	1992
Fox-Wolfgramm, Susan	Asst	338-1953	sfox	23	AHIT	PHD	91	Tx Tech	1991
Pelletier, Monique A.		338-7482	map	23	HI	PHD	77	Ill St	1986

San Jose State University
College of Business — San Jose, CA 95192-0070 — One Washington Square — (408) CALSTATE 1967,1973 — FAX=924-3419 BS,MBA

Name	Title	Phone	email	#	code	Deg	#	School	Year
Burak, Marshall J.	Dean	924-3400			Fnce	DBA	68	S Calif	1981
–Dept of Organization & Mgt	Phone	924-3550	Fax 924-3419						
Dean, Burton V.	C-Pr	924-3551		7	U	PHD	52	Illinois	1985
Bean, Marshall	Prof	924-3570		4	K	JD	57	Santa Cl	1957
Boschken, Herman	Prof	942-3563		31	AHI	PHD	72	Wash U	1982
Boyacigiller, Nakiye	Prof	924-3579	nakiye	84	YNEH	PHD	86	Berkeley	1-86
Cook, Curtis	Prof	924-3400		32	EFHI	DBA	74	S Calif	1982
Associate Dean									
Edfelt, Ralph B.	Prof	924-3582	rbedfelt	8	Y	PHD	75	UCLA	1976
El-Shaieb, Abdel	Prof	924-3571	abdel	37	IUVY	DENG	68	Berkeley	1966
Jankovich, Leslie	Prof	924-3581		38	YIJT	DSC	72	Brussels	1979
Norwood, Scott	Prof	924-3418		38	YI	MBA	51	Harvard	1955
Oddou, Gary	Prof	924-3515		52	YENO	PHD	83	Brig Yg	1983

Dept of Marketing & Quantitative Studies

Name	Rank	Phone	Email			Deg		School	Year
Oestreich, Herbert	Prof	924-3565		51	NQP	PHD	67	Cornell	1968
teaching fall semesters only									
Probasco, Preston	Prof	924-3577		21	EFGJ	PHD	69	Wiscon	1967
Stross, Randall	Prof	924-3566		84	Y	PHD	82	Stanford	1986
Wells, Stuart Jay	Prof	924-3584		13	DFIT	PHD	74	Stanford	1976
Whaley, George	Prof	924-3564		52	NEPV	PHD	74	Colorado	1979
Williams, Patrick	Prof	924-3583		21	F	PHD	66	UCLA	1964
Bolton, Michele	Assoc	924-3578		36	DI	PHD	90	UCLA	1-89
Cohen, Isaac	Assoc	924-3567		41	LBQY	PHD	81	Ca-Davis	1985
Crews, Kenneth D.	Assoc	924-3542		4	KJ	PHD	90	UCLA	1990
Denzler, Dave	Assoc	924-3562	drdsob	73	U	DBA	67	Wash U	1987
Farber, Bonnie M.	Assoc	924-3575		52	FGPY	PHD	88	Cornell	1991
Jiang, William Y.	Assoc	924-3572	jiang	5	NQY	PHD	92	Columbia	1991
Lawrence, Anne T.	Assoc	924-3586		25	HNQL	PHD	85	Berkeley	1-88
Park, Taeho	Assoc	942-3561	parkth	7	U	PHD	87	Wiscon	1988
Salstrom, Roger	Assoc	924-1343		7	UV	PHD	89	Berkeley	1989
Turner, Marlene E.	Assoc	924-3585		21	E	PHD	88	Car Mel	1987
Zachary, William B.	Assoc	924-3559		27	UE	PHD	78	Berkeley	1978

Sangamon State University	Springfield, IL	62794-9243	(217)						
School of Bus & Mgt			FAX=786-7188						BA,MA
Nosari, John S.	Dean	786-6533				PHD	84	St Louis	1978
–Department of Management	Phone	786-7612	Fax 786-7188						
Arkley, Alfred S.	C-Pr	786-6712		12	AEFP	PHD		Mich St	1977
Vanover, Donald	Prof	786-6712		13	IF	PHD		3 Illln	1981
Leatherwood, Marya	Assoo	700-0712		12	EF	PHD		Iowa	1991
Miller, Tim R.	Assoc	786-6712		12	AEF	PHD		Utah	1987
Wilkins, C. Joseph	Assoc	786-6712		13	IY	MA		S Illin	1978
Benson, Joy	Asst	786-6712		12	EJ	ABD		S Illin	1993
Dinges, Rodney	Asst	786-6712		12	EFJD	PHD		S Illin	1989
Ettinger, Judy	Asst	786-6712		12	EFPD	PHD		Ariz St	1993
Ferk, Dyanne	Asst	786-6712		12	EFN	MBA		S Illin	1993
Newman, Laurel	Asst	786-6712		15	HN	MBA		Lake For	1993
O'Neal, Donald	Asst	786-6712		13	IJ	MBA		Illinois	1993

Santa Clara University	Santa Clara, CA	95053	(408) SCU						1953,1963
Leavey School Bus & Adm	500 El Camino Real		FAX=554-4571						BS,MBA
Koch, James L.	Dean	554-4523		Mgt		PHD	72	UCLA	1990
–Org Analysis & Mgt	Phone	544-4469	Fax 554-5206						
Hall, James L.	C-Pr	554-4503				PHD	71	U Wash	1970
Caldwell, David F.	Prof	554-4114				PHD	78	UCLA	1978
Delacroix, Jacques	Prof	554-4685				PHD	74	Stanford	1983
Delbecq, Andre L.	Prof	554-4629				DBA	63	Indiana	1979
Moberg, Dennis J.	Prof	554-4713				DBA	74	S Calif	1975
Posner, Barry Z.	Prof	554-4634				PHD	79	Mass	1976
Velasquez, Manuel G.	Prof	554-4848				PHD	75	Calif	
Leidecker, Joel K.	Assoc	554-4671				PHD	69	U Wash	1968
Levitt, Barbara	Asst	554-4623				PHD	88	Stanford	1990
Palmer, David	SLect	554-4052				PHD	83	Calif	1980

Savannah State College	Savannah, GA	31404	(912)						
School of Business			FAX=						BBA
Honeycutt, Andrew E.	Dean	356-2816		Mktg		DBA	75	Harvard	1991
–Management, Mktg & Inf Sys	Phone		Fax 356-2837						
Stevenson, Charlease	C-Pr	356-2831		12	AEL	DPA	91	Georgia	1973
Alemayehu, Tsehai	Prof	356-2830		84	Y	PHD	79	Kentucky	1985
Bart, Barbara	Prof	356-2861		64		PHD	80	Georgia	1982
Eason, Thomas	Prof	356-2835		6		PHD	68	Miss	1979
Harven, Jeraline	Prof	356-2828		17	P	EDD	64	Indiana	1975
Philbrick, Jane H.	Prof	356-2856		27	EGV	PHD	76	S Carol	1984
Traxler, Ralph	Prof	356-2834		13	BI	PHD	53	Chicago	1982
Alban, Edward	Assoc	356-2858		7	V	PHD	73	Georgia	1979
Hahn, William	Assoc	356-2836		26	EGQ	PHD	80	Geo St	1982
Jankowski, Jan	Assoc	356-2846		4	K	JD	74	Emory	1979
Lamb, Mary Lou	Assoc	356-2819		17	P	EDD	69	Indiana	1979
Ayadi, O. Felix	Asst	356-2826				PHD			
Conlin, George	Asst	356-2847		14	EK	JD	78	JMarshal	1979
Davis, Carl	Inst	356-2821		79	UZ	MBA	80	Sav St	1983
Coordinator of Marketing/Information Systems									
Tapp, Carol	Inst	356-2820		17	PV	MED	83	Armst St	1983

University of Scranton	Scranton, PA	18510-4602	(717) LION.UOFS.EDU						
School of Management			FAX=941-4201						BS,MBA
Horton, Joseph J.	Dean	941-4208	hortonj1	Econ		PHD	68	So Meth	1986
–Department of Management	Phone	941-7612	Fax 941-4201						
Biberman, Gerald	C-Ac	941-7707	bibermang1	2	DE	PHD	78	Temple	1981

Chowdhury, Jafor	Assoc	941-7631	chowdhuryj1	8	Y	PHD	89	Temple	1987
McGowan, Richard A.	Assoc	941-7520	mcgowanr1	4	L	PHD	88	Boston U	1993
Brumagim, Alan	Asst	941-7480	brumagima1	3	I	PHD	91	Temple	1990
Goll, Irene	Asst	941-4044	golli1	35	Q	PHD	87	Temple	1988
Hewitt, Eileen B.	Asst	941-7642	hewitte1	2	ER	MA	76	Hartford	1982
McKeage, R. L.	Asst	941-7703	mckeager1	2	E	EDD	91	Temple	1974
Tischler, Len	Asst	941-7782	tischlerl1	23	ED	PHD	90	Maryland	1990
Wormuth, Frank	Asst	941-7752	wormuthf1	4	K	JD	72	Duquesne	1979

Seattle University	Seattle, WA	98122-4460				(206) SEATTLE.EDU			1965,1980
Albers School of Bus	Broadway & Madison					FAX=461-5795			BA
Viscione, Jerry A.	Dean	296-5700				Econ	PHD	73	Boston U	1988
–Dept of Administration	Phone	296-2550	Fax 296-5795						
Fleenor, C. Patrick	C-Pr	296-2550		23	IY	PHD	75	U Wash	1973
Brown, Karen A.	Prof	296-5712		7	U	PHD		U Wash	
Stephenson, Harriet B.	Prof	296-5702		26	IS	PHD	66	U Wash	1967
Toh, Rex	Prof	296-6007		7	X	PHD		Minn	
Callahan, Robert E.	Assoc	296-5738		25	EN	PHD		Case Wes	
Grimm S.J., Robert B.	Assoc	296-5738		45	JNOD	PHD		Colorado	
Lobel, Sharon A.	Assoc	296-6486	lobel	25	ENOR	PHD	84	Harvard	8-91
Lockwood, Diane	Assoc	296-5687		9	Z	PHD		U Wash	
Ansari, Al	Asst	296-5718		79	UZ	PHD		Nebraska	
Bird, Shawn	Asst			9	Z	PHD		Tx Tech	
Magnan, Gregory	Asst			7	U	ABD		Mich St	
Parker, Barbara	Asst	296-5703		38	IY	PHD	89	Colorado	8-91
Prussia, Gregory	Asst			5	N	PHD		Ariz St	
Willis, Geoff	Asst			7	V	PHD		Tx Tech	
Culbertson, John	Inst	296-5747		23	IE	DBA		Harvard	

Seattle Pacific University	Seattle, WA	98119				(206) SPU.EDU			
School of Bus & Econ	3rd Ave West at W Nickerson					FAX=281-2500			BA,MBA
Knight, Kenneth E.	Dean	281-2992	kknight	36	DITZ	PHD	63	Carnegie	9-89
–Management Faculty	Phone	281-2992	Fax 281-2733						
Hill, Alexander	Assoc	281-2087	adhill	14	KJA	JD	80	U Wash	9-79
Joseph C. Hope Professor of Leadership and Ethics									
Steinke, Gerhard	Assoc	281-2377	gsteinke	49	JLZ	PHD	92	Passau	9-92
Diddams, Margaret	Asst	281-2870	mdiddams	57	NOPQ	PHD	94	NYU	9-93
Franz, Ranoal	Asst	281-2729	r franz	24	HEFD	PHD	91	Stanford	9-91
Olsen, Cyrus	Asst	281-2088	colsen	39	FHIX	PHD	91	Northwes	9-92
Rand, James	Exec	281-2960		57	NOPU	PHD	76	Cal West	9-93

Seton Hall University	South Orange, NJ	07079-2692		(201)			1978,1984
Stillman Sch Business				FAX=761-9217			BS,MBA,MST
Beutell, Nicholas	Dean$	761-9220			PHD	79	Stevens
–Management Faculty	Phone	761-9013	Fax 761-9151				
Coll, Joan	C-Ac	761-9151			PHD	81	Fordham
Amar, Amar D.	Prof	761-9684			PHD	80	CUNY
Stoever, William	Prof	761-9241			PHD	78	NYU
Endowed Chair							
Alexander, Paula	Assoc	761-5235			PHD	79	Rutgers
Stelzer, Leigh	Assoc	761-9218			PHD	71	Michigan
Boroff, Karen	Asst	761-9151			PHD	90	Columbia
Forbes, Paul	Asst	761-9229			BS	49	Fordham
Mason, Phyllis	Asst	761-9256			PHD	86	Columbia
Parthasarthy, Raghavan	Asst	761-9133			PHD	91	CUNY
Yin, Jason ZS	Asst	761-9360			PHD	89	New York

Shenandoah College	Winchester, VA	22601-5195		(703)			BBA,MBA
Byrd School of Business	1460 University Drive			FAX=665-4508			
Pavsek, Daniel A.	Dean	665-4526		Econ	PHD	81	Case Wes	1992
–Management Faculty	Phone	665-4572	Fax 665-5437				
Collins, Verne	Prof	665-4503			EDD		Michigan	1958
Proe, John D.	Prof	665-3492			PHD		Iowa	1990
Sample, Travis	Prof	777-7413			DPA		USC	1987
Thies, Clifford F.	Prof	665-5450			PHD		Boston C	1992
Durell Professor of Money, Banking & Finance							
Tyree, L. Mark	Prof	665-4616			EDD		Wm&Mary	1987
Samuel, Phillips	Assoc	665-4615			PHD		Houston	1993
Jackson, Giles A.	Asst	665-4617			PHD		Va Techf	1992
Howard, Michelle E.	Inst	665-4577			MA		G Mason	1992

Shepherd College	Shepherdstwn WV	25443-1569	(304)			
Division of Bus Adm	King Street		FAX=			BS
Costello, John	Dean			EDD		1991

–Management Faculty | Phone
Rath, G. Norris	C-Pr	876-2511	35	EOQ	MS	W Virg	1963
Beard, Barbara E.	Prof	876-2511	1	D	PHD	Maryland	1976
Juul, Kenneth A.	Asst	876-2511	17	BX	MS	Auburn	1975
Moison, G. Lawrence	Asst	876-2511	26	SD	MS	Southeas	1989
Scales, Cinda	Asst	876-2511	4	K	LLD	Maryland	1984

Shippensburg University — Shippensburg, PA 17257-2299 — (717) — 1981
Grove Coll of Business — FAX=532-1273 — BS

Pope, James A.	Dean	532-1435	7	V	PHD	78 N Carol	
–Dept Management & Mktg	Phone	Fax 532-1273					
Hollon, Charles J.	C-Pr	532-1439			PHD	74 Syracuse	1974
Bright, Thomas	Prof	532-1606			JD	Maryland	
Cole, George S.	Prof	532-1632			PHD	Mich St	
Holoviak, Stephen J.	Prof	532-1430			PHD	West Va	
Senn, Robert	Prof	532-1610			JD	Syracuse	
Verney, Thomas P.	Prof	532-1677			PHD	Bowl Gr	
Weigle, Jerry	Prof	532-1610					
Hatfield, Louise	Assoc	532-1623			MBA		
Frideger, Marcia	Asst	532-1691			MA	81 Birg Yg	
–Mgt Science & Info Sys Dp	Phone	532-1434	Fax 530-4003				
Armstrong, Ruth D.	C-Pr	532-1434	9	Z	DED	67 Penn St	1967
Armstrong, Gary R.	Prof	532-1725	9	Z	DED	Temple	
Bassin, William M.	Prof	532-1587	7	V	DBA	70 Geo Wash	1970
Hocking, Ralph T.	Prof	532-1757	7	V	DBA	72 Kent St	1972
Kohn, Johnathan W.	Prof	532-1775	7	V	PHD	NY Univ	
Mottilla, Donna T.	Prof	532-1173	7	V	DBA	Kent St	
Rollins, Robert D.	Prof	532-1670	9	Z	DED	Penn St	
Hou, Margaretha M.	Assoc	532-1422	7	V	PHD	Va Tech	
Stepp, Randy	Assoc	532-1178			PHD	Georgia	
Marsh, Michael	Asst	532-1766	7	V	PHD	Ohio St	

Siena College — Loundonville, NY 12211-1462 — (518) SIENA
Division of Business — 515 Loudon Road — FAX=783-4293

Sanders, Patricia	Dean$	783-2321	sanders	28 FY	PHD	Conn	9-93
–Management Faculty	Phone	783-4133	Fax 783-4293				
Curran, Terence P.	C-Pr	783-4133	curran	34 M	PHD	SUNY-Alb	9-88
Johnson, Richard	Prof			14	EDD	SUNY-Alb	
Baker, Bonni Perrott	Assoc	783-4274	baker	15 NY	MBA	Ohio St	9-87
Ballinger, Robert M.	Asst	783-4253	ballinge	18 LMY	ABD	SUNY-Alb	9-81
Brookins, Gilbert M.	Asst	783-4273	brookins	12 DEST	ABD	SUNY-Alb	9-85
Mahaffey, Thomas R.	Asst	783-4281	mahaffey	18	MBA	Chicago	9-86
Wheeler, Patricia A.	Asst	783-2928	wheeler	1 DIST	PHD	90 Renssel	9-91

Simmons College — Boston, MA 02115-5898 — (617)
Dept of Management — 300 The Fenway — FAX=738-2099 — BA

–Management Faculty	Phone	521-2400	Fax 521-3199				
Warren, Bruce W.	C-Pr	521-2396			JD	76 Suffolk	
Betters-Reed, Bonita L.	Assoc	521-2398			PHD	83 Boston C	
Bevacqua, Katherine	Assoc	521-2390			MED	68 Boston U	
Gillis, Marlyn	Assoc	521-2392			MBA	75 Babson	1975
Moore, Lynda L.	Assoc	521-2391	2	R	EDD	83 Mass	
Considine, Caroline	Asst	521-2393	6	T	MBAM	83 Boston C	
Robinson, Alan	Exec	521-2397	38	Y	MBA	60 Columbia	

Skidmore College — Saratoga Sprg NY 12866-1632 — (518)
Department of Business — North Broadway — FAX=584-3023 — BS

Balevic, Betty V.	C-Ac	Ext 2330	3		MS	SUNY-Alb	9-69
–Management Faculty	Phone	584-5000	Fax 584-3023				
Canavan, Martin J.	Assoc	584-5000	16		MS	SUNY-Alb	1979

Slippery Rock University — Slippery Rock PA 16057-1326 — (412) SRUVM.SRU.EDU
Business Administration — FAX=738-2098 — BSBA

Mastrianna, Frank V.	Dean	738-2008		Econ	PHD	68 Cinn	3-87
–Dept of Management & Mktg	Phone	738-2060	Fax 738-2959				
Lorentz, Royce A.	C-Ac	738-2592	ral	79 UTRS	ABD	Colorado	8-75
Alkhafaji, Abbass F.	Prof	738-2588	afa	38 ILW	PHD	84 Texas	8-87
Guhde, Lynn	Assoc	738-2591		25 ENPQ	PHD	91 Kent St	8-92
Manocha, Dineshnandini	Assoc	738-2586	dnm	79 UT	DBA	86 Kent St	8-86
Tompkins, Donald	Assoc	738-2590		25 EW	PHD	72 Ohio St	8-82
Azad, Abbas	Asst	738-2584	ana	97 UTVY	PHD	88 Texas	8-88
Calhoun, Kenneth J.	Asst	738-2583	kjc	13 D	PHD	91 Pitt	8-87
Mukherjee, Pracheta	Asst	738-2347	pxm	23 EHY	PHD	92 Kansas	1989

Sonoma State University
School Business & Econ
Clark, Lawrence
–Management Faculty
Dove, Duane
Girling, Robert K.
Johnson, George C.
Liddell, Wingham
McGough, Philip
Seward, Samuel
Wright, Judy
Anderson, Sherri C.
Munshi, Jamal
Lowry, Wally
Oakley, Joyce

Rohnert Park, CA 94928
1801 East Cotati Avenue
Dean 644-2220
Phone   Fax 664-4009
C-Pr 664-2954
Prof 664-2228
Prof 664-2532
Prof 664-2548
Prof 664-2647
Prof 664-2626
Prof 664-2462
Assoc 664-2377
Assoc 664-2121

(707)
FAX=664-4009   BA,MBA

5	QH	PHD	71	Fla St	9-86
28	Y	PHD	74	Stanford	9-76
7	UV	PHD	72	Berkeley	9-73
23	EH	PHD	69	Berkeley	9-71
4	KL	PHD	72	Berkeley	9-88
7	UV	DBA	76	Colorado	9-89
		PHD	73	Indiana	9-73
	SD	MBA	83	Sn Frn S	1980
9	Z	PHD	91	Arkansas	2-91

University of South Alabama
Col Bus & Mgt Studies
Moore, Carl C.
–Department of Management
Harrison, Edward
Beatty, Warren A.
Flynn, Warren R.
  Associate Dean
Ford, Terrell F.
Mosley, Donald C.
Pietri, Paul
Zimmerman, Steve
Shearer, Robert
Slagle, Michelle L.
Maes, Jeanne
Jeffery, Arthur
Weldy, Teresa

Mobile, AL 36688
307 University Boulevard
Dean 460-6418
Phone 460-6411   Fax 460-6529
C-Pr 460-6715
Prof 460-6717
Prof 460-6418
Prof 460-6718
Prof 460-6719
Prof 460-6130
Prof 460-6720
Assoc 460-6723
Assoc 460-6721
Asst 460-6737
Inst 460-7228
Inst 460-6707

(205)
FAX=460-6529   1976,1980
                      BS,MACC,MBA

7	FDJ	PHD	71	Alabama	1973
25	FNPQ	PHD	75	North Tx	1974
79	UVXZ	PHD	86	Fla St	1980
23	EFGI	PHD	73	Colorado	1988
23	IH	PHD	69	Miss	1970
23	EFGH	PHD	65	Alabama	1973
12	EFP	DBA	69	Miss St	1975
79	UVXZ	PHD	70	Arkansas	1971
45	JKNQ	JD	81	Stetson	1986
23	DFIL	DPA	83	Geo Wash	1986
12	DEFT	PHD	94	S Miss	1994
79	UV	MBA	90	Kansas	1991
12	DFH	MBA	92	S Alab	

Univ So Carolina at Aiken
School Bus Adm & Econ
Hargrove, C. LaFaye
–Management Faculty
McGrath, Leanne C.
Mitcham, Don
Rogers, Dennis

Aiken, SC 29801
171 University Parkway
H 648-6851   hargrve
Phone   Fax 641-3445
Prof 648-6851
Prof 648-6851
Prof 648-6851

(803) UNIUSCVM
FAX=641-3302   BS

25	EFPR	PHD		Geo Col	1987
13	CQ	PHD	83	S Carol	1989
12	SI	PHD		E Tenn	1975
14	T	ABD		Michigan	1987

South Carolina-Coastal Carol
Wall School of Bus Adm
Barr, Peter B.
–Dept of Business Adm
Nale, Robert D.
  Assistant Dean
Katsioloudes, Marios I.
Levsen, Virginia
Wathen, Samuel

Conway, SC 29526
Dean 349-2640
Phone 349-2640   Fax 349-2455
Prof 347-3161
Assoc 347-3161
Asst 347-3161
Asst 347-3161

(803)
FAX=349-2455   BS

7	U	DBA	85	LTU	1986
5	E	PHD	84	Miss	1985
3	I	PHD	90	Penn	1990
25	HZ	PHD	92	Wash	1992
7	U	PHD	88	Minn	1993

Univ of South Carolina
College of Bus Adm
VanHuss, Susie H.
–Department of Management
Bauerschmidt, Alan D.
Feldman, Daniel Charles
Meglino, Bruce M.
Robinson, Richard
Schweiger, David M.
Ullman, Joseph C.
Wheeler, Hoyt
Kuiper, Shirley
Logan, John E.
Ravlin, Elizabeth C.
Sandberg, William R.
Klaas, Brian S.
Korsgaard, M. Audrey
Werner, Jon
Clamp, Carl
Halkyard, Edwin M.

Columbia, SC 29208
Dean$ 777-3176
Phone 777-5969   Fax 777-6876
Prof 777-5977
Prof 777-5971
Prof 777-5970   fmubruce
Prof 777-6961
Prof 777-5955
Prof 777-5986
Prof 777-5959
Assoc 777-5974
Assoc 777-5973
Assoc 777-5964
Assoc 777-5980
Asst 777-4901
Asst 777-5967
Asst 777-5979
DisLe 777-5978
DisLe 777-5976

(803) BAGAMCOK
FAX=777-6876   1962,1964
                      BS,MAC,MTX,PHD

	PHD	69	Indiana	
	PHD	68	Florida	
	PHD	76	Yale	8-89
25	ENHX PHD	75	Mass	8-73
	DBA	80	Maryland	
	PHD	65	Chicago	
	PHD	74	Wiscon	
	EDD	79	Indiana	
	PHD	69	Columbia	
	PHD	86	Car Mel	
	PHD	84	Georgia	
	PHD	87	Wiscon	
	PHD	90	NYU	
	PHD	92	Mich St	

U South Carolina/Spartanburg	Spartanburg, SC	29303	(803)					BSBA
School of Bus Adm & Eco	800 University Way		FAX=599-2598					
Bennett, Jerome V.	Dean	599-2593		Atg	PHD	76	S Carol	1986
–Management Faculty	Phone	599-2581	Fax 599-2598					
Berry, Steven	Assoc	599-2557		21	EVUF	PHD	82	Georgia	1988
Hastings, Barbara	Assoc	599-2531		25	EFIN	PHD	77	North Tx	1985
Lancaster, Lilly	Assoc	599-2597		71	UVDH	PHD	86	Mass	
Pauley, Robert	Lect	599-2503		43	JIST	MBA	65	Howard	1985

South Carolina St University	Orangeburg, SC	29117	(803)					
School of Business			FAX=536-8066					
Wright, Karl S.	Dean	536-7994		AgBs	PHD			1985
–Dept of Bus Administration	Phone	536-7138	Fax 536-8066					
Singh, Ashok K.	C-Pr	536-8443		Mktg	PHD	71	Oreg St	1979
Beraho, Enoch Karobe	Assoc	536-7135		7	U	PHD			1982
Salama, Ibrahim M.	Assoc	536-8455		2	E	MS	65	Colo St	1973
He, Xin	Asst	536-8454		7	U	PHD			1991
Robinson, Marion	Asst	536-8451		9	Z	PHD			1988

University of South Dakota	Vermillion, SD	57069-2390	(605) SDNET				1949,1965
School of Business	414 East Clark		FAX=677-5427				BS,MPA,MBA
Johnson, Jerry W.	Dean	677-5455		Econ	PHD	71	Iowa St	1967
–Management Faculty	Phone	677-5455	Fax 677-5427					
Oppedahl, Richard A.	C-Pr			Fnce	PHD	67	Wash	
Kaufman, Charles	Prof	677-5355		25	AENF	DBA	65	Indiana	1961
Dean of Graduate School								
Roegiers, Charles	Prof	677-5670		2	EP	PHD	72	Kansas	1980
Arogyaswamy, Kamala	Asst	677-5694		32	IH	PHD	92	Wi-Milwa	1988
Card, Mike	Asst	677-5559		32	IH	PHD	92	Ohio St	1992
Gillian, Allen	Asst	677-6319		5	EN	PHD	92	Illinois	1993

University of South Florida	Tampa, FL	33620-5500	(813) CFRVM				1969,1980
College of Business Adm	4202 East Fowler Avenue		FAX=974-3030				BA,MBA,MACC,PHD
Pappas, James L.	Dean	974-4281		Fnce	PHD	56	UCLA	1968
–Department of Management	Phone	974-4155	Fax 974-3030					
Anderson, Robert	C $							
Barlett, Alton C.	Prof	974-4155		24	FCQE	PHD	64	Wiscon	1967
Cohen, Cynthia	Prof	974-4155		5	QKNR	PHD	80	Geo St	1982
Dutton, Richard E.	Prof	974-4155		28	YE	PHD	63	LSU	1963
Jermier, John M.	Prof	974-4155	jermier	2	EH	PHD	79	Ohio St	1983
Karlins, Marvin	Prof	974-4155		12	E	PHD	66	Princeton	1974
Nord, Walter	Prof	974-4155		2	HE	PHD	67	Wash U	1989
Schilit, W. Keith	Prof	974-4155		36	TIS	PHD	82	Maryland	1985
VanVoorhis, Kenneth	Prof	974-4155		36	STI	DBA	71	LSU	1970
Wheelen, Thomas L.	Prof	974-4155		3	I	DBA	69	Geo Wash	1983
Balfour, G. Alan	Assoc	974-4155		45	QKLJ	PHD	75	Mich St	1980
Knippen, Jay T.	Assoc	974-4155		13	PI	DBA	70	Fla St	1970
Koehler, J. W.	Assoc	974-4155		26	F	DED	68	Penn St	1985
McIntosh, Nancy J.	Assoc	893-9588		21	EH	PHD	84	Florida	1984
Michaels, Charles E. Jr.	Assoc	359-4274		25	NE	PHD	83	S Fla	1984
Miljus, Robert	Assoc	432-5523		23	NQ	PHD	83	Wiscon	1991
Nixon, Robert L.	Assoc	974-4155		2	E	PHD	76	Cornell	1977
Gaines, Jeannie	Asst	893-9154		52	EHN	PHD	84	Florida	1989
Hargis, Edyth	Inst	974-4155		25	EN	MS	80	S Fla	1980

Southeast Missouri St Univ	C Girardeau, MO	63701-4799	(314) SEMOVMSE				BS,MBA
Harrison Col of Bus	One University Plaza		FAX=651-2909				
McDougall, Gerald S.	Dean	651-2112		Econ	PHD	74	Claremont	1993
–Department of Management	Phone	651-2121	Fax 651-2909					
Stough, Stanley	C-Pr	651-2568	c849bum	13	IY	PHD	75	Arkansas	1987
Buckenmyer, James	Prof	651-2902		15	E	DBA	70	Wash U	1982
Eom, Sean	Prof	651-2615		9		PHD	85	Nebraska	
Farris, Roy	Prof	651-2903		25	EFN	PHD	72	Miss	1974
Karathanos, Demetrius	Prof	651-2901	c255bum	7	VX	PHD	75	N Colo	1979
Kuntz, Ed	Prof	651-2898		38	I	DBA	78	Tx Tech	1977
Pettypool, Diane	Assoc	651-2907	c613bum	7	UVX	DBA	90	S Illin	1984
Somarajan, Chellappa	Assoc	651-2900	c822bum	79	UV	PHD	89	Okla St	1988
Ehie, Ike	Asst	651-2905		7	UVY	PHD	89	Mo-Rolla	1989
Byrd, Steve	Inst	651-2851		56	S	MS	75	St Marys	1985

Southeastern University	Washington, DC	20024	(202)			BS,MS,MBA
School of Business	501 I Street SW		FAX=488-8093			
Did Not Respond-1993 Listing; phone 488-8162						
Agbonyitor, Florence	Dean	488-8162			EDD	

−Dept of Business Mgt & Mkt Phone Fax 488-8093

Name	Rank	Phone				Degree	School	Year
Garmat, John	H-Pr	488-8162				MBA	Conn	
Abbey, Robert						PHD	UCLA	
Adams, Andrew						PHD	S Calif	
Adigun, Isaac						PHD	U Kent	
Allen, James	Adj					MPA	Geo Wash	
Bajwa, Shaid						LLB		
Cochran, Charles	Adj					PHD	Tufts	
Cooper, Colin	Adj					PHD	Maryland	
Durrani, M. A.						MBA		
Garcia, Thomas	Adj					PHD	Mass	
Hasan, Naila						MBA		
Hechler, Hans	Adj					MA	American	
Howell, John	Adj					PHD	Columbia	
Joseph, Marks	Adj					PHD	Mich St	
Khalid, Amin						FCMA		
Koyuncu, Ibrahim						PHD	Toronto	
Langer, Manfred						PHD	Enlargen	
Lucchetti, Lynn	Adj					MA	San Fran	
Marks, Joseph	Adj					MADM	SEastern	
Saenz, Francisco R.	Adj					PHD	Columbia	
Smith, Peter	Adj					PHD	Penn St	
Stern, Stephen	Adj					MBA	Penn	
Stokes, George	Adj					MA	NC Cen	
Suphi, Djan						MBA	Boston U	
Swain, Donald	Adj					PHD	Stanford	
Tisone, Albert Sr.	Adj					DBA	Geo Wash	
Wallace, Clarence S.	Adj					MA	Dist Col	
Walsh, Malcomb						PHD	Bradford	
Wilson, Ronald	Adj					MBA	SEastern	
Zaidi, S. A. Askari						MBA		

−Dept of Comp Sci & Info Sys Phone Fax 488-8093

Name	Rank	Phone				Degree	School	Year
Ho, Daniel	H-Pr	488-8162				PHD		
Bednorz, John	Adj		9	Z		MPA		
Cheng, Roger	Adj		9	Z		MS		
Darling, Paul						PHD		
Liu, You Jen	Adj					MBA		
Omade, Yunuse						MBA		
Sheehan, Thomas						PHD		

Southeastern Louisiana Univ Hammond, LA 70402 (504) SELU.EDU 1987,1987
College of Business FAX = 549-5038 BS,MBA

Name	Rank	Phone				Degree		School	Year
Miller, Joseph H.	Dean	549-2258		Adv	PHD	77	Miss	9-76
−Dept of Management Box 530	Phone		Fax 549-5038					
Cappel, Samuel	H-Ac	549-2051	23	EHIK	DBA	90	Memphis	8-91
Yeargain, John W.	Prof	549-2298	48	JKQY	JD	76	Loyola	8-79
Blalock, Mary	Assoc	549-2298	53	NOPR	PHD	73	LSU	9-70
Hotard, Daniel G.	Assoc	549-2167	7	UV	PHD	76	Miss St	1985
Waikar, Avinash	Assoc	549-2167	7	UV	PHD	84	Oklahoma	8-91
Barbera, Fran	Asst	549-2065			ABD			8-92
Chen, Edward	Asst	549-5930			ABD			8-92
Cope, Rachelle F.	Asst	549-2051		ZI	ABD			
Jamal, A. M. M.	Asst	549-3736	79	UVZ	PHD	79	Tx A&M	1986
Morris, Joella W.	Asst	549-2051			MBA			
Phillips, Antoinette	Asst	549-2167	12	EN	PHD	91	LSU	8-90
Phillips, Carl	Asst	549-2304	52	NOEB	PHD	91	LSU	8-90
Wayman, Shari	Asst	549-2051			MBA			
Danos, Barbara	Inst	549-2298	48	JKLY	JD	73	N Carol	8-85

Southeastern Oklahoma State Durant, OK 74701-0609 (405)
School of Business FAX = 924-7313 BS
phone: 924-0121

Name	Rank	Phone				Degree		School	Year
−Dept of Management & Mktg	Phone	924-0121	Fax 924-7313					
Whitlock, David	C-As	Ext 2683	61	TPS	MAS	85	SE OK St	8-95
Oliver, Robert	Assoc	Ext 2685	37	V	PHD	74	Colo St	8-84
Campbell, Kitty	Asst	Ext 2586	51	NS	MAS		SE Okla	8-93
Jose, Anita	Asst	Ext 2233		JY	MBA	93	Dallas	8-93
Testerman, Jack	Asst	Ext 2234			PHD	70	Texas	8-86

Southern Col of 7th Day Adv Collegedale, TN 37315-0370 (615)
Dept of Bus & Office Ad Taylor Circle FAX = BBA

Name	Rank	Phone				Degree		School	Year
Vandevere, Wayne E.	C-Pr	238-2750		Atg	PHD	67	Mich St	1956
−Management Faculty	Phone	238-2751	Fax 238-3151					
Erickson, Richard J.	Assoc	238-2755	16	EIS	MBA	82	Aust Pea	1984
Segar, James	Assoc	238-2752	15	ABI	MA	68	Cen Mich	1994
Haley, David	Asst	238-2756	7	V	MBA	89	Tenn Tec	1989
Olson, Cliff	Asst	238-2757		D	MBA	88	Colo St	1989

Southern University	Baton Rouge, LA	70813-2064	(504)					
College of Business			FAX=771-2495					BS,MPA
Birkett, Brenda S.	Dean	771-5641		Atg	PHD	80	LSU	8-80
—Department of Management	Phone		Fax 771-5262					
LeBlanc, Audrey	C-Ac$	771-5643		4	JK	JD	58	Southern	1962
Brown, Harold	Prof	771-5643		2	GS	PHD	75	Wiscon	1964
Adewuyi, Joseph	Asst	771-5643		5	EHMU	PHD	75	North Tx	1990
Clark, Albert	Asst	771-5643		45	KLJQ	JD	75	Southern	1975
Harris, Walter	Asst	771-5643		13	GI	MBA	69	Atlanta	1973
Marcelle, Earl	Asst	771-5643		16	ENST	MBA	70	Texas	1980
Thomas, Lula	Asst	771-5463		15	GSK	MED	71	Southern	1972
Julian, Scott	Inst	771-5643				ABD	94	LSU	1993
Miller, Pamela	Inst	771-5643				ABD	94	LSU	1993

Southern Arkansas Univ	Magnolia, AR	71753	(501)					
School of Business Adm	McNeil Highway		FAX=235-5005					BBA
Rankin, David	Dean	235-4300			PHD			1967
—Dept of Management & Mktg	Phone	235-5005						
Trexler, Anna	C	235-4300						
Kolb, Harry	Assoc	235-4300			MS		Arkansas	1983
Funderburg, Dianna	Asst	235-4311			MED			1992
Tabor, Patty	Inst	235-4318			MBA		La Tech	1988
Wise, Timothy		235-5159			MBA			1993

Univ of Southern California	Los Angeles, CA	90089-1421	(213) USCVM					1922,1963
School of Business Adm			FAX=749-0541				BS,MBA,MACC,PHD
—Dept of Management & Org	Phone	740-0728	Fax 749-0541					
Coffey, Robert E.	C-Pr$	740-0738		2	EFH	PHD		Illinois	1963
Bennis, Warren	Prof	740-0766		2	EFH	PHD		MIT	1980
Birnbaum-More, Phillip	Prof	740-0744		3	IUY	PHD		U Wash	9-86
Cummings, Thomas G.	Prof	740-0733		2	EFH	PHD		UCLA	1976
Driver, Michael J.	Prof	740-0757		2	EFH	PHD		Princeton	1968
Greiner, Larry	Prof	740-0765		2	EFH	DBA		Harvard	1973
Lawler, Edward	Prof	740-3929		2	EFH	PHD		Berkeley	1978
Mitroff, Ian	Prof	740-0154		3	GI	PHD		Berkeley	1980
Adler, Paul	Assoc	740-0748		23	HI	PHD		Picardie	1991
Bhambri, Arvind	Assoc	740-0730		3	IL	DBA		Harvard	9-83
Davidson, William	Assoc	740-0745		8	Y	DBA		Harvard	9-86
Patz, Alan L.	Assoc	740-0761		3	I	PHD	67	Car Mel	1972
Reardon, Kathleen	Assoc	740-0175		1	D	PHD		Mass	1990
Argyres, Nicholas	Asst	740-5552		3	I	PHD		Berkeley	1993
Hariharan, Sam	Asst	740-0742		3	I	PHD		Michigan	9-90
Kurland, Nancy	Asst	740-6647		4	JLKM	PHD		Pitt	1993
Liebeskind, Julia	Asst	740-0749		3	I	PHD		UCLA	1991
Mahoney, Joan	Asst	740-7481		2	E	PHD		SUNY-Buf	1-92
Pelled, Lisa	Asst	740-6382		2	E	PHD		Stanford	1993
Rajagopalan, Nandini	Asst	740-0750		3	I	PHD		Pitt	9-88
Spreitzer, Gretchen	Asst	740-9419		2	E	PHD		Michigan	1992

Univ of Southern Colorado	Pueblo, CO	81001-4901	(719)					
School of Business	2200 Bonforte Boulevard		FAX=					BSBA
Askwig, William J.	Dean	549-2142			Bus	PHD	69	Tx Tech
—Dept Business Adm & Econ	Phone	549-2108	Fax 549-2909					
Billington, Peter	C-Pr	549-2880		7	U	PHD		Cornell	1989
Ahmadian, Ahmad	Assoc	549-2154		3	I	PHD		North Tx	1986
Browne, James	Assoc	549-2186		5	N	PHD		Illinois	1991
Eisenbeis, Richard	Assoc	549-2105		2	E	PHD		Arizona	1988
Watkins, Donna	Assoc	549-2317		6	S	PHD		New Mex	1988
Zeis, Charles	Assoc	549-2157		7	V	PHD		Tx A&M	1987
Chandler, William D.	Asst	549-2653		34	ZI	PHD		Arkansas	1982
Hanks, Sue	Asst	549-2882		1	&	EDD		Arkansas	1992
Warnock, Stuart	Asst	549-2567		73	IUV	PHD		North Tx	1994

Southern Connecticut St Un	New Haven, CT	06515-1355	(203) SCSUD.CTSTATEU.EDU					
School of Business	501 Crescent Street		FAX=397-4207					BSBA,MS
Leader, Alan H.	Dean	397-4461	leader		DBA	63	Indiana
—Dept of Management	Phone	397-4775	Fax 397-4198					
Kidney, James A.	C-Ac	397-4465	kidney	38	ITY	PHD	86	UCLA	1989
Frank, Ellen J.	Prof	397-7049	frank	52	NRX	PHD	73	Purdue	1983
Whelan, Frank E.	Prof	397-4463	whelanf	79	UVZ	EDD	75	Nova	1979
Cottrill, Melville T.	Assoc	397-4782	cottrill	36	KLS	PHD	91	Conn	1990
Javian, Setrak	Assoc	397-4515	javian	26	EFST	PHD	74	Case Wes	1991
Nangia, Madan M.	Assoc	397-4147	nangia	15	BEIN	PHD	73	NYU	1986
Prasad, Durga	Assoc	397-7049	prasad	48	JKL	JSD	82	Yale	1982
Durnin, Ellen	Asst	397-4515	durnin	25	EQR	ABD	92	CUNY	1990
Mullen, Robert	Asst	397-4463	mullen	79	UZ	SCD	92	NewHaven	1992

Southern Illinois Univ — Carbondale, IL 62901-4631 — (618) SIUCVMB — 1962,1972
College of Bus & Adm — FAX=453-7961 — BS,MBA,MA,PHD

Name	Rank	Phone	Code			Deg		School	
Mathur, Iqbal	Dean$	453-3328	ga3810		Fnce	PHD	74	Cinn	1977
–Department of Management	Phone	453-3307	Fax 453-7835						
Melcher, Arlyn J.	C-Pr	453-3307	ga4012	23	DHYW	PHD	64	Chicago	8-89
Bateman, David N.	Prof	453-3307	ga4233	12	EF	PHD	70	S Illin	1-65
Ramaprasad, Arkalgud	Prof	453-3307	ga0708	39	IHY	PHD	80	Pitt	8-80
Troutt, Marvin	Prof	453-3307	gao435	79	UTY	PHD	75	Ill-Chic	6-80
McKinley, William	Assoc	453-3307	ga3964	28	HIW	PHD	83	Columbia	8-90
Nelson, Reed	Assoc	453-3307	ga4095	28	EFW	PHD	83	Cornell	8-91
Stubbart, Charles I.	Assoc	453-3307	ga4192	38	IW	PHD	83	Pitt	6-91
White, Greg	Assoc	453-3328	ga2607	7	UT	PHD	76	Cinn	8-78
Bhattacharyya, Sid	Asst	453-3307	sbhatta	9	Z	PHD	93	Florida	5-93
Ponce-De-Leon, Jesus	Asst	453-3307	ga3574	38	ITYW	PHD	89	Indiana	8-87
Rai, Arun	Asst	453-3307	ga3984	79	DUTY	PHD	90	Kent St	8-90
Tadisina, Suresh	Asst	453-3307	ga3491	79	UVTY	PHD	87	Cinn	8-86

So Illinois, Edwardsville — Edwardsville, IL 62026-1100 — (618) SIUEMUS — 1975,1980
School of Business — FAX=692-3979 — BS,BSA,MBA,MMR

Name	Rank	Phone			Deg		School	
Ault, David E.	Dean	692-3823		Econ	PHD	69	Illinois	1969
–Department of Management	Phone	692-2750	Fax 692-3979					
Strickland, Donald E.	C-Ac	692-2750	2	EFH	PHD	77	Tulane	1985
Harrick, Edward J.	Prof	692-2750	5	NQ	PHD	74	St Louis	1974
Steffen, Hans	Prof	692-2750	28	Y	PHD	60	Nebraska	1969
Virgo, John M.	Prof	692-2750	45	LQY	PHD	72	Claremont	1974
McKinney, Richard	Assoc	692-2750	2	DEF	PHD	69	St Louis	1966
Sullivan, George	Assoc	692-2750	4	KL	JD	71	Seton HI	1987
Joplin, Janice	Asst	692-2750	2	E	ABD		Tx-Arlin	1994
Martell, Kathryn	Asst	692-2750	38	INY	PHD	89	Maryland	8-91
Michlitsch, Joseph	Asst	692-2750	23	IH	PHD	80	Minn	1979
Schoenecker, Timothy	Asst	692-2750	36	IT	PHD	93	Purdue	1992
Swanson, Laura	Asst	692-2750	7	U	ABD		Purdue	1994

Univ of Southern Indiana — Evansville, IN 47712 — (812) SMTP.USI.EDU
Business — 8600 University Boulevard — FAX=464-1960

Name	Rank	Phone			Deg		School	
Fisher, Phil	Dean	464-1718	23	IH	PHD	79	Stanford	1991
–Management Faculty	Phone		Fax 464-1960					
Jermakowicz, Walter	Prof	464-1718	18	IS	PHD	74	Warsaw T	1985
Forough, Abbas	Assoc	465-1667	9	Z	PHD	90	Indiana	1983
Gillard, Sharlett	Assoc	464-1732	9	Z	EDD	78	North Tx	1986
Hemaida, Ramadan	Assoc	464-1975	7	V	PHD	90	St Louis	1988
Wafa, Marvin	Assoc	464-1944	7	U	PHD	86	Clemson	1986
Hall, Ernest H. Jr.	Asst	465-7038	36	I	PHD	88	Miss	1992
Partridge, Dane M.	Asst	465-7147	5	Q	PHD	91	Cornell	1993
Pelechette, Joy V.	Asst	464-1803	12	E	PHD	91	S Illin	1991
Williams, Jennifer	Asst	465-7012	9	Z	PHD	94	S Illin	1992

Univ of Southern Maine — Portland, ME 04103-4899 — (207) USM.MAINE.EDU
Sch of Bus, Econ, & Mgt — 96 Falmouth Street — FAX=780-4662 — BS

Name	Rank	Phone	Code			Deg		School	
–Management Faculty	Phone	780-4020	Fax 780-4662						
Parsons, Henry	C-Ac	780-4328	hparsons	7	UV	PHD	83	Oregon	1974
Clarey, Richard J.	Assoc	780-4605	rclarey	6	ST	PHD	68	Cornell	1979
Grover, Richard A.	Assoc	780-4407	rgrover	2	EFC	PHD	84	Ohio St	1988
Lombardo, Gary A. Associate Dean	Assoc	780-4189	lombardo	3	IY	PHD	86	Oregon	1987
Voyer, John J.	Assoc	780-4597	jvoyer	3	I	PHD	86	Mass	1987

Southern Methodist Univ — Dallas, TX 75275-0333 — (214) SMUVM1 — 1925,1979
Cox School of Business — 6425 Boaz Street — FAX=692-4099 — BBA,MBA,EMBA
  Internet Address 120.119.64.2

Name	Rank	Phone			Deg		School	
Blake, David H.	Dean	768-3011			PHD	68	Rutgers	1-90
–Dept Org Beh & Bus Policy	Phone	768-2513	Fax 768-4099					
McGill, Michael E.	C-Pr	768-3337			PHD	71	S Calif	1971
Slocum, John W.	Prof	768-3157			PHD	67	U Wash	1979
Jackofsky, Ellen F.	Assoc	768-3181			PHD	82	Texas	1982
Walker, Gordon	Assoc	768-2191	3	HIX	PHD	82	Penn	1993
Wooton, L. Michael	Assoc	768-2717			PHD	72	S Calif	1972
Brett, Joan	Asst	768-3630			PHD	92	NYU	1990
Hurry, DiLeep	Asst	768-2104			PHD	90	Penn	1990
Lei, David	Asst	768-3005			PHD	85	Columbia	1990
Parayre, Roch	Asst	768-3587			PHD	91	Brit Col	1990
Pinkley, Robin L.	Asst	768-3172			PHD	88	N Carol	1989
Rasberry, Robert W.	Asst	768-3514			PHD	77	Kansas	1974
–Dept of Mgt Info Sciences	Phone	768-4108	Fax 768-4099					
Ives, Blake	C-Pr	768-4108			PHD	78	Minn	
Mason, Richard O.	Prof	768-3145			PHD	68	Calif	

Sobol, Marion G.	Prof	768-3171				PHD	61	Michigan	1974
Apte, Uday	Assoc	768-4102				PHD	82	Penn	
Beath, Cynthia	Assoc	768-2547				PHD	86	UCLA	
Grout, John	Asst	768-2597				PHD	92	Penn St	
Smith, Gordon	Asst	768-3185				PHD	91	Car Mel	
Collins, James	Inst	768-2636				MSIE	65	So Meth	
Downs, Brian	Inst	768-3638				PHD	91	Cinn	

U of Southern Mississippi	Hattiesburg, MS	39406-5077	(601) USMCD6					1976,1980	
College of Business			FAX=266-4630					BSBA,MBA	
Black, Tyrone	Dean	266-4659			Econ	PHD	70	Tulane	1978
–Department of Management	Phone	266-4920	Fax 266-4630						
Bushardt, Step	C-Pr	266-4677		2	EH	DBA	81	Miss St	1980
Brooking, Stan	Prof	266-4678		79	IUVZ	PHD	73	Tx A&M	1975
Hunt, David Marshall	Prof	266-4033		38	EFIY	PHD	80	Houston	1987
Allen, Billie	Assoc	266-4513		25	KNPY	PHD	86	North Tx	1974
Boothe, Robert	Assoc	266-4674		17	SU	DBA	84	Fla St	1988
Davis, James	Assoc	266-4676		36	FIST	ABD	61	LSU	1965
Duhon, David	Assoc	266-4827		36	ISTY	PHD	81	LSU	1988
Vest, Michael	Assoc	266-4030		52	ENQ	PHD	88	Va Tech	1989
Wolfe, Douglas	Assoc	266-5817		23	DEFH	PHD	69	Case Wes	1980
Topping, Sharon	Asst	266-5345		13	I	PHD		Al-Birm	1990
Vest, Jusanne	Asst	266-4675		25	NOQR	PHD	89	Va Tech	1989

Southern Nazarene University	Bethany, OK	73008	(405)						
School of Business	6729 NW 39th Expressway		FAX–						
Mills, Larry	C-Pr	491-6392		23		PHD	78	Oklahoma	1969
–Department of Management	Phone	491-6359	Fax 491-6384						
Dennard, Lou	Assoc	491-6358		23		EDD	81	Okla St	1991
Sloan, B. H.	Assoc	491-6358		79		PHD	91	Oklahoma	1980
Gaddis, Richard	Asst	664-4100		14		EDD	84	Arkansas	1992
Seyfert, Jeff	Asst	789-6400		25		MBA	89	Tulsa	1990

Southern Oregon St College	Ashland, OR	97520-5022	(503)						
School of Business	1250 Siskiyou Boulevard		FAX=482-6429					BS,BA,MSBA	
Did Not Respond-1993 Listing									
Carney, Keith T.	Dean	482-6483			Atg	PHD	76	N Colo	1965
–Management Faculty	Phone	552-6484	Fax 552-6715						
Laughlin, John	C-Ac	552-6718		15	AFN	PHD	90	S Calif	1984
Cottle, Richard	Prof	552-6710		4	K	JD	70	Washburn	1982
Farrimond, George F.	Prof	552-6712		79	DUZ	PHD	89	Portland	1976
Houghton, Edward L.	Prof	552-6715		1	B	EDD		Oreg St	1980
Varin, Dennis L.	Prof	552-6724		37	IV	PHD	75	Oreg St	1970
Gaston, Terry L.	Assoc	552-6713		26	EFNS	DBA	83	Geo Wash	1984
Jones, Thomas E.	Assoc	552-6716		15	FJL	MBA	64	Santa Cl	1965
Bacon, Curtis J.	Asst	552-6487		1	Z	MBA	81	N Dakota	1987
Jackson, William	Asst	552-6725		79	DVZ	PHD	73	N Colo	1991
Ordonez, Rene	Asst	552-6720		79	UV	MBA	87	Dayton	1989

Southwest Baptist Univ	Bolivar, MO	65613-2496	(417)						
College of Business	1601 South Springfield St		FAX=326-1652					BS	
Middleton, Ken	Dean	326-1752		52		PHD			1991
–Department of Management	Phone		Fax 326-1887						
Clark, W.	Asst	326-5281		36		MBA		SMSU	1991
Credille, Ronda	Asst	326-1750		16		MBA		Drury	1990
DeBauche, Susan D.	Asst	326-1759		79		EDD		Arkansas	1985

Southwest Missouri St Univ	Springfield, MO	65804-0094	(417) SMSVMA					1992,1992	
College of Business Adm	901 South National		FAX=836-6337					BS,MACC	
Bottin, Ronald R.	Dean	836-5646			Atg	PHD	74	Missouri	8-90
–Department of Management	Phone	836-5415	Fax 836-6337						
Wisdom, Barry L.	C-Pr$	836-5082	blw355f	27	E	PHD	81	Arkansas	1987
Abraham, Yohannan T.	Prof	836-5562	yta614f	85	N	PHD	76	Oklahoma	1969
Denton, Keith	Prof	836-5573		7	U	PHD	82	S Illin	1984
Trewatha, Robert L.	Prof	836-5415	rlt020f	38	YN	PHD	63	Arkansas	1968
Vaught, Bobby C.	Prof	836-5077	bcv415f	52	QN	PHD	79	North Tx	1979
Williams, Ralph W.	Prof	836-5647	rww614f	21	Y	PHD	66	Oregon	1980
Boyd, Charles W.	Assoc	836-5556	cwb758f	63	L	PHD	80	Kan St	1983
Coulter, Mary K.	Assoc	836-5572	mkc164f	52	QN	PHD	84	Arkansas	1983
Kopp, Daniel G.	Assoc	836-5414	dgk986f	3	I	PHD	77	Va Tech	1981
Richardson, Peter E.	Assoc	836-5576	per300f	2	CG	PHD	79	Houston	1979
Feltes, Patricia E.	Asst	836-6342	pef760f	3	Y	PHD	88	Nebraska	1988
Karuppan, Corinne	Asst	836-6671		7	UV	PHD	90	Nebraska	1991
Thomas, Steve L.	Asst	836-5077	slt600f	52	QN	PHD	89	Kansas	1990

Southwest State University — Marshall, MN 56258 (507)
Business — 1501 State Street — FAX=537-7154 — BS
Did Not Respond-1993 Listing

Name	Rank	Phone				Degree		School	Year
Ramos, Melba	Dean	537-6218				PHD		Mass	1993
—Department of Management	Phone		Fax 537-7154						
Mitchell, George	C	537-6223		79	UZ	ABD			
Babcock, James	Prof	537-6223		3	I				
Buerkley, Deborah	Assoc	537-6223		5	N				
Goodenow, Mark	Assoc	537-6223		1					

Southwest Texas State Univ — San Marcos, TX 78666-4616 (512)
School of Business — 429 North Guadalupe Street — FAX=245-3089 — BBA,MBA

Name	Rank	Phone				Degree		School	Year
Gowens, Paul R.	Dean	245-2311			Econ	PHD	73	Miss	1980
—Dept of Management & Mktg	Phone		Fax 245-3089						
Ross, John K.	C-Ac	245-2571		3	IJY	PHD	80	North Tx	1980
Abrahamson, Royce	Prof	245-3186		2	EFH	PHD	67	Texas	1965
Bell, James D.	Prof	245-2311		1	DEF	PHD		Akron	1985
Chiodo, Beverly A.	Prof	245-3238		1	OP	PHD	80	Tx A&M	1968
Halatin, Theodore J.	Prof	245-2571		4	JLS	PHD	73	Tx Tech	1976
Hunnicutt, Garland	Prof	245-3193		37	U	PHD	77	Arkansas	1973
Middlebrook, Bill	Prof	245-3180		3	I	PHD	80	North Tx	1983
Olney, Robert J.	Prof	245-2311		1	D	PHD	80	Oklahoma	1982
Piersol, Darrell	Prof	245-2311		5	NO	PHD	55	Purdue	1982
Roach, Ed D.	VProf	245-3196		3	I	PHD		Texas	1993
Keeffe, Michael J.	Assoc	245-2571		3	I	PHD	86	Arkansas	1986
Minifie, Janet R.	Assoc	245-3176		7	U	PHD	83	S Carol	1988
Roderick, Joan C.	Assoc	245-3236		1	DY	EDD	85	Okla St	1985
Pompian, Richard O.	VAsst	245-3309		1	D	PHD	92	Texas	1993
Temponi, Cecilia	Asst	245-3189		7	U	PHD	92	Tx-Arlin	1990
Mollenkopf, Douglas	Inst	245-3191		2	F	MBA	77	SW Texas	1984
Zigrossi, Sam J.	Inst	245-2606		5	N	MBA	80	Gold Gt	1983
Dietert, Judy	Lect	245-2614		6	S	MBA	80	SW Tx St	1984
Hinkson, Diana W.	Lect	245-3314		1	D	MBA	77	Tarleton	1985
Scow, Roger	Lect	245-3183		6	S	MBA	83	SW Tx St	1983
Till, Lee	Lect	245-3189		5	N	MS	67	Chicago	1987

Southwestern University — Georgetown, TX 78627-0770 (512) RALPH.TXSWU.EDU
Dept of Econ & Bus Adm — University at Maple — FAX=863-5788 — BA

Name	Rank	Phone				Degree		School	Year
Rosenthal, Michael R. M.	Dean	863-1567	rosenthm		Chem	PHD		Illinois	1989
Sellers, Fred E.	C-Ac$	863-1996	sellersf		Atg	PHD	84	Kansas	1987
—Management Faculty	Phone	863-1996	Fax 863-5788						
Parks, Don M.	Assoc	863-1996		38	IY	PHD	88	Tx A&M	1994
Brightwell, George A.	Asst	863-1951				MBA		Northwes	1978

U of Southwestern Louisiana — Lafayette, LA 70504-3570 (318) USL.EDU
Col of Bus Adm Box43570 — FAX=231-5898 — BS

Name	Rank	Phone				Degree		School	Year
Duggar, Jan W.	Dean	231-6491			Econ	PHD	67	Fla St	1989
—Dept of Management & QM	Phone		Fax 231-5898						
Roe, C. William	H-Pr	231-6087	cwr0406	25	ENOR	DBA	76	Miss St	1990
Knouse, Stephen	Prof	231-6387	sbk4151	25	EJN	PHD	77	Ohio St	1986
Scheuermann, Larry	Prof	231-5378	les2097	97	VUZ	DBA	74	Miss St	1985
Tanner, John	Prof	231-6149	jrt4671	7	ZRO	PHD	73	Arkansas	1990
Wallin, Jerry	Prof	231-6160		26	ENT	PHD	74	Nebraska	1986
Meredith, Mary	Assoc	231-5762		79	VRZ	DBA	81	Indiana	1983
Meredith, Paul	Assoc	231-5753	phm8871	39	DIR	DBA	81	Indiana	1983
Smith, Mark	Assoc	231-6262		3	IZT	MBA	77	Howard	1985
Carson, Kerry	Asst	231-6866		21	BCEP	PHD	91	LSU	1992
Carson, Paula	Asst	231-5386		5	NPE	PHD	92	LSU	1991
Hamilton, James	Asst	231-6247		42	JLME	PHD	72	Emory	1990
Heady, Ron	Asst	231-6865		7	UVX	PHD	69	MIT	1989
Langford, Hal	Asst	231-5745		76	STUV	PHD	86	Geo St	1981
Zhu, Zhiwei	Asst	231-6867		7	UVX	PHD	88	Clemson	1989
Boudreaux, Phil	Inst	231-5390	pab4153	7	VI	ABD		LSU	1976
Toma, Al	Inst	231-6061		81	YST	MBA	70	American	1983

Southwestern Oklahoma St Un — Weatherford, OK 73096-3098 (405)
School of Business — 100 Campus Drive — FAX=772-5447 — BA,MBA

Name	Rank	Phone				Degree		School	Year
Kaufman, Jerry M.	Dean	774-3282			Atg	PHD	74	Okla St	1992
—Dept Econ & Business Adm	Phone		Fax 772-5447						
Gabriel, Albert H.	C-Pr	774-3049		5	M	PHD	65	Mich St	1956
Reeder, Robert	Prof	774-3048		78	QS	PHD	81	Arizona	1982
Jawahar, Jim	Asst	774-3045				PHD	93	Okla St	1994
Long, James	Inst	774-3045		1	S	MBA	88	Utah	1992
White, Max	Inst	774-3051		9	Z	MBA	83	Southwes	1983
Wright, David	Inst	774-3046		1	E	MBA	90	Texas-PB	1992

Stanford University   Stanford, CA   94305-5015   (415)   1926
Graduate School of Bus   FAX=725-7979   MBA,PHD

Name	Rank	Phone		Areas	Deg	Yr	School	Year
Spence, A. Michael	Dean			Econ	PHD	72	Harvard	1990
Philip H. Knight Professor of Economics & Management								
–Management Faculty	Phone		Fax 725-6125					
Baron, James N.	Prof	723-4832	2	E	PHD	82	Ca-SnBar	1982
Walter Kenneth Kilpatrick Professor of Organizational Behavior & Human Res								
Bonini, Charles P.	Prof	723-2830	7	V	PHD	62	Carnegie	1959
William R. Timken Professor of Management Science								
Harrison, J. Michael	Prof	723-4727	7	U	PHD	70	Stanford	1970
Gregor C. Peterson Professor of Operations Management								
Hausman, Warren H.	Prof	723-9279	6	UM	PHD	66	MIT	1977
Holloway, Charles A.	Prof	723-2142	47	UVX	PHD	69	UCLA	1968
Herbert Hoover Professor of Public and Private Management								
Howard, Ronald A.	Prof	723-4176	37	IVXU	SCD	58	MIT	1965
Leavitt, Harold J.	Prof	723-2080	2	E	PHD	49	MIT	1966
Walter Kenneth Kilpatrick Prof of Organizational Behavior & Psy, Emeritus								
March, James G.	Prof	723-2105	2	H	PHD	53	Copenhag	
Fred H. Merrill Professor of Managment								
Mendelson, Haim	Prof	725-8927	9	Z	PHD	79	Rochest	1989
James Irvin Miller Professor of Information Systems								
Miller, William F.	Prof	723-3219	3	I	PHD	56	Purdue	1965
Montgomery, David	Prof							
Sebastian S. Kresge Professor of Marketing Strategy								
O'Reilly, Charles A.	Prof	725-2110	25	EFHN	PHD	75	Berkeley	1993
Parker, George G. C.	Prof	723-9117			PHD	67	Stanford	1973
Co-Director of the Financial Management Program								
Pfeffer, Jeffrey	Prof	723-2915	2	E	PHD	72	Stanford	1979
Thomas D. Dee II Professor of Organizational Behavior								
Porras, Jerry I	Prof	723-2850	2	EH	PHD	74	UCLA	1972
Fred H. Merrill Professor of Organizational Behavior and Change								
Saloner, Garth	Prof		3	I				
Robert A. Magowan Professor of Economics and Strategic Management								
Scott, W. Richard	Prof	723-3959	2	EFGH	PHD	61	Chicago	1960
Webb, Eugene J.	Prof	723-2834	2	E	PHD	56	Chicago	1968
Lane Professor of Organizational Behavior								
Burgelman, Robert A.	Assoc	723-4488	3	I	PHD	80	Columbia	1981
Kramer, Roderick M.	Assoc	723-2158	2	E	PHD	85	UCLA	1985
Martin, Joanne	Assoc	723-4791	2	E	PHD	77	Harvard	1977
Augsburger, Robert	Lect	725-7358			JD	50	Case Wes	1971
Bagley, Constance E.	Lect	725-3044	8	Y	JD	77	Harvard	1985
Bradford, David	Lect	723-4918	2	E	PHD	66	Michigan	1969
Grousbeck, H. Irving	Lect	723-0709	6	ST	MBA	60	Harvard	1985
LeDuc, Robert W.	Lect	723-8536	2	E	PHD	75	Stanford	1988
Moore, Jeffrey H.	Lect	723-4058	9	Z	PHD	73	Berkeley	1972
Rohan, Dennis M.	Lect	723-3480	8	Y	PHD	62	Yale	1973

SUNY College at Fredonia   Fredonia, NY   14063-1198   (716)
Dept of Business Adm   178 Central Avenue   FAX=673-3397   BS
Did Not Respond-1993 Listing

Name	Rank	Phone		Areas	Deg	Yr	School	Year
Bankosh, John J.	C-As	673-3402		Atg	MBA	80	Lehigh	1981
–Management Faculty	Phone		Fax 673-3397					
Telly, Charles S.	Prof	673-3404	13	BI	PHD		U Wash	1985
Aghazadeh, Seyed M.	Assoc	673-3503	79	VZ	PHD		Nebraska	1983
Hartley, William B.	Assoc	673-3504	53	NI	PHD		Wiscon	1977
Borycki, Christine	Asst	673-3404	37	IF	MBA		SW La	1990
Manley, Douglas	Adj	673-3404	35					

SUNY College at Geneseo   Geneseo, NY   14454-1401   (716)
Jones Sch of Business   1 College Circle   FAX=245-5005   BA,BS

Name	Rank	Phone		Areas	Deg	Yr	School	Year
Moore, Gary	H-Pr	245-5367	45	KQ	PHD	74	Nebraska	9-74
–Department of Management	Phone	245-5367	Fax 245-5467					
Strang, Daniel	Prof	245-5365	7	V	PHD	75	Cornell	9-72
Zaremba, Joseph	Prof	245-5363	7	UV	PHD	68	Harvard	9-70
Markulis, Peter	Assoc	245-5365	39	IZ	PHD	80	SUNY-Buf	9-81
Cook, Jack	Asst	245-5466	79	UZ	PHD	93	Wash St	9-93
Malik, S. Dolly	Asst	245-5358	35	EN	PHD	89	Mich St	9-88
Morse, Kenneth	Asst	245-4364	8	Y	PHD	91	Denver	9-91
Sciarrino, Alfred	Asst	245-5366	4	K	LLM	84	Wiscon	9-90

SUNY Coll at Old Westbury   Old Westbury, NY   11568-0210   (516) SNYOLDVA
Business Division   223 Storehill Road   FAX=876-3209   BS,BPS

Name	Rank	Phone		Areas	Deg	Yr	School	Year
Armandi, Barry R.	C-Pr	876-3318	23	EHPT	PHD	77	St Johns	1985
–Management Faculty	Phone		Fax 876-3209					
Podell, Lawrence	Prof	876-3313	48	JLMY	PHD	54	Cornell	1992
Crocitto, Madeline	Asst	876-3313	25	EFNR	PHD	89	CUNY	1988
Walsh, Lynn	Asst	876-3318	16	LSTR	PHD	80	NYU	1987

SUNY College at Oswego　　Oswego, NY　　13126　　(315) SNYOSWVA
Business Adm Department　　　　　　　　　　　　FAX=341-3154　　　　　BS,MSM
　Did Not Respond-1993 Listing

Karns, Lanny	C-Pr	341-2272		37	DIJV	PHD	78	Syracuse	1976
–**Management Faculty**	Phone		Fax 341-5440						
Herring, Donald	Prof	341-2535		5	FHNG				
Mena, Manuel	Prof	341-2769		28	FPY	PHD	75	Cornell	1974
Ingram, Thomas	Asst	341-2527		35	EKNG	ABD		Cornell	
Jalife, Paloma	Asst	341-2493		38	DIUY	MBA	88	Syracuse	1990
Maher, Larry	Asst	341-2525		25	EFNP				
Mian, Sarfraz	Asst	341-2498		36	ISTD	PHD	91	Geo Wash	1992

SUNY @ Stony Brook　　Stony Brook, NY　11794-3775　(516) FAC.HAR.SUNYSB.EDU
Harriman School Mgt　　　　　　　　　　　　　　FAX=632-7176　　　　　　BS,MS

Sobel, Matthew	Dean	632-7175	msobel	74	UVM	PHD	79	Stanford	1986
–**Management Faculty**	Phone	632-7180	Fax 632-9412						
Feinberg, Eugene	Prof	632-7189	efeinber	7	V	PHD	79	Vilnius	1990
London, Manuel	Prof	632-7159	mlondon	25	ENOP	PHD	74	Ohio St	1989
Pidot, George	Prof	632-7173	george	19	Z	PHD	66	Harvard	1987
Associate Dean									
Wolf, Gerrit	Prof	632-7744	gwolf	26	ESTX	PHD	67	Cornell	1985
Altman, Stanley M.	Assoc	632-6265	saltman	13	AF	PHD	67	Brookpol	1970
Carroll, Owen T.	Assoc	632-7993	ocarroll	79	VZ	PHD	68	Cornell	1967
Preston, Anne E.	Assoc	632-7177	apreston	5	OR	PHD	83	Harvard	1986
Sexton, Thomas R.	Assoc	632-7181	tsexton	7	CV	PHD	79	SUNY-SBr	1979
Skorin-Kapov, Jadranka	Assoc	632-7426	jskorin	79	VZ	PHD	87	Brit Col	1988
Weiner, Harry	Assoc	632-7184	hweiner	1	ABLJ	MS	70	MIT	1973
Yago, Glenn	Assoc	632-7188	gyago	3	HI	PHD	80	Wiscon	1980
Casey, Jeff	Asst	632-7179	jcasey	25	E	PHD	86	Wiscon	1986
Chatterjee, Subimal	Asst		schatter	17	&V	PHD	93	Pitt	1993
Deshmukh, Abhijit	Asst		adeshmuk	17	UV	PHD	93	Purdue	1993
Hurley, Amy	Asst		ahurley	15	QR	PHD	93	NYU	1993
Paulson, Kathy	Asst		kpaulson	15	PQ	MS	91	Purdue	1993
Robinson, Laura	Asst		lrobinso	46	LJ	PHD	93	Columbia	1993
Siegel, Donald	Asst	632-7163	dseigel	34	IL	PHD	88	Columbia	1990
Skorin-Kapov, Darko	Asst	632-7478	dskorin	79	VZ	PHD	89	Brit Col	1989
Slotnick, Susan	Asst		sslotnic	79	UVZ	PHD	93	Car Mel	1993
Procelli, M.	Lect	632-7770		5	NQ	MBA	53	Hofstra	1985
Robbins, M.	Lect	632-7172	mrobbins	3	I	MBA	80	Harvard	1988

SUNY-Univ at Albany　　Albany, NY　　12222　　(518) ALBNYVM1　　　　1974,1974
School of Business　　　　1400 Washington Avenue　FAX=442-3944　　BS,MBA,MS,PHD

Hughs, Richard	Dean	442-4910		3	IT	PHD	62	Purdue	1991
–**Management Department**	Phone	442-4966	Fax 442-4765						
Gueutal, Hal G.	C-Ac	442-4941		59	NZVR	PHD	80	Purdue	1985
Kavanagh, Michael J.	Prof	442-4956		52	NXEF	PHD	69	Iowa St	1982
Taber, Thomas D.	Prof	442-4937		25	EN	PHD	72	Illinios	1979
Yukl, Gary	Prof	442-4932		25	EN	PHD	67	Berkeley	1977
Dandridge, Thomas C.	Assoc	442-4914		64	STL	PHD	75	UCLA	1975
Falbe, Cecilia M.	Assoc	442-4958	cmf08	34	HIT	PHD	80	Columbia	1986
Miesing, Paul	Assoc	442-4992		34	IL	DBA	77	Colorado	1979
Stone, Dianna L.	Assoc	442-4911		25	NEJ	PHD	81	Purdue	1990
Tannenbaum, Scott I.	Assoc	442-4957		5	NPZ	PHD	86	Old Dom	1985
Castaneda, Maria	Asst	442-4176		25	NEX	PHD	88	Wiscon	1991
Seymour, William E.	Asst	442-4940		3	IP	MBA	58	Cornell	1958

SUNY at Binghamton　　Binghamton, NY　13902-6000　(607) BINGVMA　　　1991,1991
School of Management　　　　　　　　　　　　　　FAX=777-4422　　　　　　BA,MBA
　email: @m=BINGSOM; @b=BINGVMB

Norgaard, Corine T.	Dean	777-2314			Atg	PHD	65	Texas	8-93
–**Department of Management**	Phone	777-2314	Fax 777-4422						
Avolio, Bruce J.	Prof	777-2544	lead5	25	EFHN	PHD	82	Akron	1981
Bass, Bernard M.	Prof	777-3007	bg1584	25	EFHN	PHD	49	Ohio St	1977
Distinguished Professor Emeritus									
Chatterji, Manas	Prof	777-2475	bg0141@a	1	C	PHD	63	Penn	1969
Agnihothri, Saligrama	Assoc	777-2125	bg5029	7	UVX	PHD	85	Rochest	1984
Klein, Heinz K.	Assoc	777-6854	hklein@b	9	Z	DBA	68	Munich	1984
Schulman, Martin	Assoc	777-2630	mschul@m	1	A	PHD	83	Fla St	1986
Spangler, William D.	Assoc	777-2563	spandl@b	2	EFG	PHD	85	Michigan	1986
Steidlmeier, Paul	Assoc	777-2376	psteidl	34	IJL	PHD	75	Stanford	1987
Ullmann, Arieh A.	Assoc	777-6858	bg4229	3	I	PHD	76	St Gall	1982
Westacott, George H.	Assoc	777-6644	geowest	8	Y	PHD	70	Cornell	1971
Yammarino, Francis	Assoc	777-6066	fjyammo	2	EFH	PHD	83	SUNY-Buf	1986
Baskerville, Richard	Asst	777-2337	rbask@a	9	Z	PHD	86	London	1988
Kahai, Surinder	Asst	777-2410	kahai@b	9	Z	PHD	91	Michigan	1991
Lewis, Alfred	Asst	777-6638	alfl	3	I	PHD	89	US Intl	1989
Murry, William D.	Asst				EFHN	PHD	93	Va Tech	1994

Name	Rank	Phone	Email			Degree		School	
Sandbothe, Richard	Asst	777-6761	sandbo@b	7	UVX	PHD	86	Car Mel	1989
Reeves-Ellington, Richard	Lect	777-2733	reeves@b	3	I	PHD	79	City Col	1991
Roodman, Gary M.			groodm@m	7	UVX	DBA	69	Indiana	1977

SUNY at Buffalo — Buffalo, NY 14260 — (716) UBVM — 1930,1972
School of Management — 1300 Elmwood Avenue — FAX=636-5926 — BS,MBA,PHD

Name	Rank	Phone	Email			Degree		School	
Winter, Frederick W.	Dean	645-3221			Mgt	PHD	72	Purdue	5-94
–Dept Org & Hum Resources	Phone	645-3280	Fax 645-2131						
Becker, Brian	C-Pr	645-3235	mgtbeck	5	NQ	PHD	77	Wiscon	9-70
Foster, Howard G.	Prof	645-3247	mgtfoste	5	Q	PHD	69	Cornell	9-69
Meindl, James R.	Prof	645-3244	mgtmei	2	EHJ	PHD	81	Waterloo	9-81
Miner, John B.	Prof	645-3622		26	ENPT	PHD	55	Princeton	9-87
Bunker, Douglas	Assoc	645-3228		2	F	PHD	60	Harvard	9-67
Dansereau, Fred E. Jr.	Assoc	645-3236	mgtdanse	2	EH	PHD	72	Illinios	9-73
Krzystofiak, Frank J.	Assoc	645-3230		5	NP	PHD	78	Minn	1977
Newman, Jerry M.	Assoc	645-3238		5	NP	PHD	74	Minn	9-74
Salamone, Joseph F.	Assoc	645-3237		5	NQ	MBA	73	SUNY-Buf	9-81
Thomas, John M.	Assoc	645-3217	mgtjthom	48	EKY	PHD	60	MIT	9-68
Connelley, Debra	Asst					PHD	92	Cornell	0-94
Goodrick, Elizabeth	Asst	645-3234	mgtgood	2	EHR	DBA	91	Illinios	1991
–Mgt Science & Systems Dept	Phone		Fax 645-2131						
Boot, John	C-Pr	645-3254	mgtboot	7	V	PHD	64	Netherl	1-65
Pegels, C. Carl	Prof	645-3259	mgtpegls	37	IUY	PHD	66	Purdue	9-66
Zionts, Stanley	Prof	645-3260	mgtzio	37	IUVY	PHD	66	Car Mel	9-67
Chatov, Robert	Assoc	645-3226	mgtchat	4	JKL	PHD	73	Berkeley	197?
Frase, Donald W.	Assoc	645-3507		31	IUD	MBA	64	OUNY-Buf	9-88
Lin, Winston T.	Assoc	645-3257	mgtfewtl	7	V	PHD	76	Northwes	9-75
Ramesh, Ramaswamy	Assoc	645-3050	mgtrames	79	UZV	PHD	85	SUNY-Buf	9-84
Sanders, G. Lawrence	Assoc	645-3273	mgtsand	9	Z	PHD	83	Tx Tech	1983
Suresh, Nallan C.	Assoc	645-3279	mgtsure	7	U	PHD	82	Cinn	1986
Kellogg, Stephen	Asst	645-3911	mgtlegal	4	K	JD	66	SUNY-Buf	8-89
Rajagopalan, Srinivasan	Asst	645-3253	mgtrajag	3	IU	DBA	91	Columbia	1990
Rao, H. Rhagav	Asst	645-3425	mgtrao	9	Z	PHD	87	Purdue	8-87

SUNY at New Paltz — New Paltz, NY 12561 — (914) SNYNEWVM — BS
Dept of Business Adm — 75 South Manheim Boulevard — FAX=257-3009

Name	Rank	Phone	Email			Degree		School	
Salavitabar, Hadi	C-Ac		salavith			PHD		SUNY-Bin	
–Management Faculty	Phone	257-2930	Fax 257-2947						
Neuman, Joel H.	Asst	257-2928	neumanj	25	EN	PHD	90	SUNY-Alb	1989

SUNY at Plattsburgh — Plattsburgh, NY 12901-2697 — (518) SNYPLAVA — BS
School of Bus & Econ — Beekman Street — FAX=564-7827

Name	Rank	Phone	Email			Degree		School	
Gandhi, Prem P.	Dean	564-3184	gandhipp		Econ	PHD	73	New Scho	9-66
–Department of Management	Phone	564-3184	Fax 564-3183						
Guydosh, Ray	C	564-4189	guydosrm	57	QUV	PHD	74	Carnegie	1976
Bethlen, Francis	Prof	564-4211	bethlefr	8	Y	PHD		Purdue	1961
Deresky, Helen	Prof	564-3876	dereskhk	38	IY	PHD	84	Concordi	1983
Feldman, Wallace	Prof	564-4214	feldmanw	38	SY	DBA	73	Harvard	1986
Martin, Miles	Prof	564-4221	martinmw	38	IY	PHD		Case	1982
O'Hara, John	Prof	564-4210	oharaje	3	IY	PHD		Columbia	1982
Church, Nancy	Assoc	564-4187	churchnj	56	RSYL	PHD		Concordi	1977
McGrath, T. J.	Assoc	564-4188	mcgrattj	7	UVW	PHD	71	Okla St	1980
Heroux, Lise	Asst	564-4209	herouxla	8	Y	PHD	87	Concordi	1980
Moussa, Faten	Asst	564-4220	moussafm	38	IY	PHD		CUNY-Bar	1989
O'Neill, Kevin	Asst	564-3184	oneillke	32	AFHI	PHD	93	SUNY-Alb	1993
Hobson, R. H.		564-4197	hobsonrh	7	UV	MBA	63	Fair Dic	1976
Assistant Dean									

Stephen F. Austin St Univ — Nacogdoches, TX 75962-9070 — (409) CCSVAX.SFASU.EDU — 1976,1982
School of Business — 1936 North Street — FAX=568-1117 — BBA,MBA

Name	Rank	Phone	Email			Degree		School	
Young, Marlin C.	Dean	568-3101			BEd	EDD	74	Ariz St	1967
–Dept of Management & Mktg	Phone	568-4103	Fax 568-1600						
Franklin, Geralyn M.	C-Ac	568-4103		52	NQRS	PHD	89	North Tx	1988
Fisher, Warren W.	Assoc	568-4103	f_fisherww	7	UV	PHD	83	Texas	1990
Ormsby, Joseph G.	Assoc	568-4103		7	SUV	PHD	80	Arkansas	1981
Watts, Larry R.	Assoc	568-4103		36	ISTE	PHD	87	Ariz St	1987
Behara, Ravi S.	Asst	568-4103		79	UVW	PHD	89	Manchest	1992
Gundersen, David E.	Asst	568-4103		59	NPZE	PHD	92	Miss	1992
Jackson, William T.	Asst	568-4103		36	DIST	DBA	91	Memphis	1991
Scifres, Elton L.	Asst	568-4103		32	I	PHD	94	LSU	1993
Bigoness, Ronald A.	Lect	568-4103		26		MBA	78	S F Aust	1979
Cormany, C. D. (Rip)	Lect	568-4103		78	Y	MBA	83	Lindenwo	1984
Jacobs, Karen L.	Lect	568-4103		12	JGD	MBA	88	S F Aust	1988

Stetson University

Deland, FL 32720-3757 (904) STETSON
Sch of Bus Adm Box 8398
FAX=822-8832 — BBA,MBA,MACC

Name	Rank	Phone	Email	Code	Field	Degree	GradYr	School	Year
Dascher, Paul E.	Dean	822-7405			Atg	PHD	69	Penn St	1993
–Department of Management	Phone	822-7430	Fax 822-8832						
Rosetti, Daniel K.	C-As	822-7438	elh	29	HZ	PHD		Fla St	1983
DeZoort, Frank	Prof	822-7410		78	HUY	PHD		Georgia	1973
Boozer, Robert	Assoc	822-7433	ehi	21	EB	DBA		Miss St	1990
Heine, R. Peter Jr.	Assoc	822-7434	ceep	25	CINE	DBA		Memphis	1987
Maddox, E. Nicholas	Assoc	822-7435	ef6jopx	24	EFGJ	PHD		Fla St	1985
Andrews, William A.	Asst	822-7437		68	STY	PHD		Georgia	1993

Stonehill College

North Easton, MA 02357-1150 (508)
Business Adm Department
320 Washington Street
FAX=238-9253 — BA,BS

Name	Rank	Phone	Email	Code	Field	Degree	School	Year
Burke, William A.	C	230-1398		38		MBA	NYU	1982
–Management Faculty	Phone	230-1463	Fax 238-9253					
Aurelio, Jeanne		230-1349		12		DBA	Geo Wash	1990
Russell, Robert		230-1278		16		MBA	Boston U	1987

Suffolk University

Boston, MA 02108-2770 (617) SUFFOLK.EDU 1989,1989
School of Management
8 Ashburton Place
FAX=573-8704
Did Not Respond-1993 Listing

Name	Rank	Phone	Email	Code	Field	Degree	GradYr	School	Year
Brennan, John F.	Dean	573-8301		3	I	MBA	58	Harvard	1991
–Management Department	Phone		Fax 573-8704						
Sankowsky, Daniel A.	C-Ac	573-8375				PHD		Berkeley	
Arthur, Michael B.	Prof	573-8357				PHD		Cranfield	
Castellano, John	Prof					PHD		SUNY-Buf	
Corman, Joel	Prof					PHD	73	Penn	
Perles, Benjamin M.	Prof					PHD		Boston U	
Sundberg, Ronald E.	Prof	573-8301				EDD		Boston U	
Associate Dean									
Cooper, Clarence A.	Assoc					MPA		Harvard	
Executive in Residence									
Landau, Jacqueline C.	Assoc	865-5665				PHD		Cornell	
Mazen, A. Magid	Assoc					PHD		Purdue	
Ornstein, Suzyn	Assoc					PHD		Ohio St	
Zanzi, Alberto L.	Assoc	573-8358				PHD		S Calif	
Amatucci, Frances Marie	Asst	648-1683				PHD		Pitt	
Clarke, Ruth	Asst					PHD		Mass	
DeFillipi, Robert	Asst					ABD		Yale	
McDaniel, J. R.	Asst					PHD		Mass	
Shelley, Charles J.	Asst					PHD		Mass	
Sutherland, Lee	Asst					EDD		Nova	
Tarimcilar, M. Murat	Asst					PHD		LSU	
–Computer Info Systems Dept	Phone	573-8381	Fax 573-8704						
Briggs, Warren	C-Pr	573-8368	w.briggs	9	Z	PHD	64	MIT	1979
Lee, Denis	Prof	573-8442	d.lee	9	Z	PHD	80	MIT	1989
Frank, Jonathan	Assoc	573-8617	j.frank	9	Z	PHD	78	Strathcl	1983
Kahn, Beverly	Assoc	573-8642	b.kahn	9	Z	PHD	79	Michigan	1985
Carlson, Patricia	Asst	573-8077	p.carlso	9	Z	PHD	92	Minn	1992

Susquehanna University

Selinsgrove, PA 17870-1001 (717) EINSTEIN!
Weis School of Business
514 University Avenue
FAX=372-4310

Name	Rank	Phone	Email	Code	Field	Degree	GradYr	School	Year
Bellas, Carl J.	Dean	372-4455	bellas	31	BLD	PHD	69	Oregon	9-83
–Department of Management	Phone	372-4456	Fax 372-4491						
Dion, Paul	C-Pr	372-4034	dion		W	PHD	86	Toronto	1992
Growney, Wallace	Prof	372-4464	growneyw	9	Z	PHD	70	Oklahoma	1965
Remaley, William	Prof	372-4235	remaley			PHD	71	NYU	1973
Sauer, William	Prof	372-4436	sauer	6		PHD	75	Minn	1989
Ward, William A.	Prof	372-4463	wardw	3	I	PHD	70	Colorado	1986
Alan Warehime Distinguished Professor									
Bussard, David T.	Assoc	372-4307	bussard	3	I	PHD	91	Penn	1978
Cianni, Mary	Asst	372-4459	cianni	5	NR	PHD	86	Penn St	1982
Rishel, Tracy D.	Asst	372-4448	risel	3	I	PHD	91	Penn St	1988
Sauter, Fred	Asst	372-4462	sater	4		MBA	67	Columbia	1967

Syracuse University

Syracuse, NY 13244-2130 (315) SUVM 1920,1963
School of Management
900 S. Crouse Avenue
FAX=443-5389 — BS,MBA,MS,PHD

Name	Rank	Phone	Email	Code	Field	Degree	GradYr	School	Year
Burman, George	Dean	443-3751				PHD	73	Chicago	1990
–Dept of Organization & Mgt	Phone	443-2601	Fax 443-5389						
Chesser, Rodney J.	C-Ac	443-2601		2	E	PHD	71	Mich St	1971
Desalvia, Donald N.	Prof	443-2601		3	F	PHD	65	Syracuse	1965
Oliker, L. Richard	Prof	443-2601		3	I	DBA	65	Indiana	1968
Schuster, Michael	Prof	443-2601		5	N	PHD	79	Syracuse	1980
Doering, Mildred	Assoc	443-2601		5	NP	PHD	78	Minn	1978
Gillen, Dennis	Assoc	443-2601		3	I	PHD	81	Maryland	1980
Rhodes, Susan R.	Assoc	443-3672		5	NE	PHD	78	Oregon	1978

Wesman, Elizabeth	Assoc	443-2601	5	NQR	PHD	82	Cornell	1981
Harrington, Kermith	Asst	443-2601	2	H	PHD	91	Tx A&M	1990
Smith, Kenneth	Asst	443-2601	3	I	PHD	90	Maryland	1990
Smith, Wanda J.	Asst	443-3392	25	CEFR	PHD	91	N Carol	

University of Tampa Tampa, FL 33606-1490 (813)
College of Business 401 West Kennedy Boulevard FAX=251-0016 BA,MBA
phone 253-3333 COB Phone 253-6221

Vaughn, Ronald L.	Dean	253-6221			Mtkg	PHD	75	Georgia	1984
–Department of Management	Phone		Fax 258-7408						
Shirley, Britt M.	C-Ac	Ext 3638	7	UV	PHD	88	Alabama	1992
Stumpf, Stephen A.	Prof	Ext 3840	25	EF	PHD	78	NYU	1993
Director Center for Leadership								
Kraft, Kenneth L.	Assoc	Ext 3353	23	HIT	DBA	82	Maryland	1991
Director Graduate Business Program								
Endres, Al C.	Asst		37	IUV	PHD	77	Ill Tech	1994
director Center for Quality								
Jenzarli, Ali	Asst	Ext 3306	7	UV	ABD	93	Kansas	1993
Puia, George	Asst	Ext 3549	46	IST	PHD	93	Kansas	1992
Director Small Business Institute								
Watson, Mary Anne	Asst	Ext 3431	28	ELY	PHD	88	S Carol	1986
Coordinator International Business								
Young, Corinne	Asst	Ext 3507	38	Y	PHD	93	Tulane	1993
Fogg, Dana T.	Inst	Ext 3384	15	NQ	MS	75	Columbia	1989
Simendinger, Earl A.	V		12	ACE	PHD	81	Case Wes	1994

Tarleton State University Stephenville, TX 76402 (817)
College of Business Adm 1257 West Washington FAX= BBA,MBA

DeHay, Jerry M.	Dean	968-9350			Mktg	PHD	78	North Tx	1985
–Dept of Mgt,Mktg & Info Sci	Phone	968-9098	Fax 968-9329						
Barker, Ruby F.	H								
Chandler, William G.	Prof	968-9275	17	PQVX	PHD	72	North Tx	1973
Mills, R. Lavelle	Prof	968-9050	2	EHP	PHD	81	North Tx	1979
Associate Dean								
Kirkland, B. R.	Assoc	968-9052	18	BE	EDD	78	E Tx St	1979
Freed, Rusty	Asst	968-9335	25	NS	MBA		Tarleton	1993
Hazen, Samuel E.	Asst	968-9033	5	NOPQ	DBA	88	La Tech	1988
Madkins, Jerry B.	Asst	968-9343	45	JLQO	DMIN	80	SBTS	1989

Teikyo Marycrest University Davenport, IA 52804-4096 (319)
Business Admin Dept 1607 W. 12th Street FAX= BA,BIB

–Division of Intl Business	Phone	326-9512	Fax 327-9615						
Thalmann, Gerald	C-Ac	326-9505	18	CY	MBA		Wi-White	8-87
Arshad, Ali	Assoc	326-9372	48	LY	PHD		Conn	8-87
Fisher, Harry E.	Assoc	326-9222	52	DN	MBA	86	Illinois	8-87
Lynn, Billy G.	Assoc	326-9239	46	TM	PHD	91	Illinois	8-87
Hoyt, Brian	Asst	326-9259	37	CI	MBA	85	Bryant	8-91

Teikyo Post University Waterbury, CT 06708-2540 (203)
School of Business Adm 800 Country Club Road FAX= AS,BS

Hartman, Frederic C.	Dean	596-4651			MBA			
–Management Faculty	Phone	596-4652	Fax 575-9691					
Annable, Bryan K.	Assoc	596-4653		MBA			
Wolfe, Helen W.	Asst	596-4664		MBA			

Temple University Philadelphia, PA 19122 (215) TEMPLEVM 1934,1973
School of Bus & Mgt 13th & Montgomery Streets FAX=787-5698 BBA,MBA,MSX,PHD

Dunkelberg, William C.	Dean	204-1062			Econ	PHD	69	Michigan	1987
–General & Strategic Mgt Dpt	Phone	204-1692	Fax 204-5698						
Andrisani, Paul J.	C-Pr	204-8193			PHD	73	Ohio St	1974
Phatak, Arvind V.	Prof	204-8191			PHD	66	UCLA	1966
Changanti, Raj	Assoc	204-5675			PHD	78	SUNY-Buf	1981
Hopkins, Harold D.	Assoc	204-8146			PHD	83	Penn St	1982
Klein, Harold E.	Assoc	204-8883			PHD	73	Columbia	1975
Titus, George J.	Assoc	204-8188			PHD	77	Penn	1977
Deeds, David	Asst	204-6877			PHD	92	U Wash	
Habib, Mohammed	Asst	204-6876						
Hamilton, Robert D. III	Asst	204-6870			PHD	81	Northwes	1981
Meszaros, Jacqueline	Asst	204-5828			PHD	88	Penn	1991
Tirney, Thomas	Asst	204-8192			PHD	71	Penn	1989
–MSOM Department	Phone	204-8170	Fax 204-5698						
Gershon, Mark	C-Pr	204-8130	7	UVY	PHD	81	Arizona	1983
Murphy, Frederic	Prof	204-8189	7	AUV	PHD	71	Yale	1982
Weiss, Howard	Prof	204-6829	7	UVW	PHD	75	Northwes	1976
Milutinovich, Jugoslav V.	Assoc	204-8192	7	UYZ	PHD	70	NYU	1969

Name	Rank	Phone				Deg		School	
Rosenthal, Edward	Assoc	204-8177		7	UV	PHD	85	Northwes	1985
Gunter, Sevket I.	Asst	787-8461		7	UVW	PHD	87	Syracuse	1988
–Human Resource Adm	Phone	204-8099	Fax 204-5698						
Schmidt, Stuart M.	C-Pr	204-1621				PHD		Wiscon	
Blau, Gary J.	Prof	204-6906				PHD		Minn	
Koziara, Karen S.	Prof	204-8138				PHD		Wiscon	
Loewenberg, J. Joseph	Prof	204-8187				DBA		Harvard	
Daymont, Thomas	Assoc	204-8370				PHD		Wiscon	
Deckop, John	Assoc	204-1933				PHD		Minn	
Hochner, Arthur	Assoc	204-8133				PHD		Harvard	
Johannesson, Russell E.	Assoc	204-6904				PHD		Bowl Gr	
Konrad, Alison M.	Assoc	204-6807				PHD		Claremnt	
Portwood, James	Assoc	204-6905				PHD		Michigan	
Zeitz, Gerald	Assoc	204-6871				PHD		Wiscon	
Geddes, Deanna	Asst	204-8195				PHD		Purdue	
Mangel, Robert	Asst	204-8184				PHD		Penn	
McClendon, John	Asst	204-1910				PHD	89	S Carol	

University of Tennessee	Knoxville, TN	37996-0545	(615) UTK.UTKVX.EDU						1941,1971
College of Business Adm			FAX=974-3100					BS,MBA,MA,PHD	
Neel, C. Warren	Dean	974-5061		3	IL	PHD	69	Alabama	9-69
–Department of Management	Phone		Fax 974-3163						
Fowler, Oscar S.	H-Ac	974-3161	fms	78	U	PHD	72	Georgia	9-71
Dewhirst, H. Dudley	Prof	974-3161		23	DEIH	PHD	69	Texas	6-69
Dobbins, Greg H.	Prof	974-3161	pall4308	25	ENP	PHD	83	Va Tech	9-87
William B. Stokely Chair									
James, Lawrence R.	Prof	974-3161		25	ENX	PHD	70	Utah	8-88
Pilot Oil Chair									
Rush, Michael C.	Prof	974-3161		25	ENP	PHD	78	Akron	9-78
Stahl, Michael	Prof	974-5061		3	EHI	PHD	75	Renssel	8-89
Associate Dean									
Fryxell, Gerald E.	Assoc	974-3161	pa105478	34	ILX	PHD	86	Indiana	9-86
Gilbert, Kenneth C.	Assoc	974-4116	gilbert	79	UV	PHD	76	Tenn	9-80
Ladd, Robert T.	Assoc	974-3161	pa75268	25	ENX	PHD	80	Georgia	9-80
Maddox, Robert C.	Assoc	974-3161	rmaddox	18	Y	PHD	68	Texas	9-72
Miller, Alex	Assoc	974-3161	pa125918	36	ITX	PHD	83	Wash	9-84
Noon, Charles E.	Assoc	974-4116	noon	79	UV	PHD	88	Michigan	9-87
Russell, Joyce E. A.	Assoc	974-3161		25	ENP	PHD	82	Akron	9-82
Srinivasan, M. M.	Assoc	974-4116	srini	79	UVZ	PHD	85	Northwes	8-92
Bowers, Melissa R.	Asst	974-4116	pa126378	79	UV	PHD	89	Clemson	1-89
Clelland, Iain	Asst	974-3161		43	MIZ	PHD	93	S Calif	8-93
Dean, Thomas	Asst	974-3161	tdean	36	IT	ABD		Colorado	8-91
Endirsinge, Chanaka	Asst	974-4116		79	UVZ	PHD	91	Brit Col	8-91
Judge, William Q.	Asst	974-3161	pa132008	34	ILJ	PHD	89	N Carol	8-89

Tennessee at Chattanooga	Chattanooga, TN	37403-2598	(615) UTCVM						1982,1988
School of Business Adm	615 McCallie Avenue		FAX=755-5255					BS,MBA	
Fletcher, Linda Pickthorne	Dean	755-4333				Fnce PHD	64	Penn	7-91
–Department of Management	Phone		Fax 755-5255						
Ettkin, Lawrence P.	H-Pr	755-4403		7	UVW	PHD	68	Nebraska	9-76
White Professor									
Ahmadi, Mohammad	Prof	755-4410	mfma	7	VX	PHD	76	North Tx	1979
Hart Professor									
Kleiman, Lawrence S.	Prof	755-4451		5	NPL	PHD	78	Tenn	1979
Nixon, Judy C.	Prof	755-4160		1	D	PHD	75	Geo St	1975
Raiszadeh, Mohammad E.	Prof	755-4146		7	UVW	PHD	82	LSU	1981
West, Judy F.	Prof	755-4162		1	D	PHD	76	Geo St	1981
White, Charles Stephen	Prof	755-4686		21	EH	DBA	81	Arizona	1981
UC Foundation Professor									
Dileepan, Pathasarati	Assoc	755-4675	mfpd	79	UVX	PHD	84	Houston	1985
UC Foundation Professor									
Helms, Marilyn M.	Assoc	755-4412		3	I	DBA	87	Memphis	1987
UC Foundation Associate Professor									
Jih, W. J. Kenny	Assoc	755-5318		9	Z	PHD	85	North Tx	1988
Macomber, James Howard	Assoc	755-4417		7	UVX	DBA	79	Kent St	1978
Mendenhall, Mark E.	Assoc	755-4417		28	EX	PHD	83	Brig Yg	1989
Frierson Chair of Excellence									
Wiley, Carolyn	Assoc	755-4158		51	NE	PHD	82	UCLA	1990
Brabston, Mary	Asst			9	Z	ABD		Fla St	8-93

Univ of Tennessee at Martin	Martin, TN	38238-5015	(901) UTKVM1						
School of Business Adm			FAX=						
Young, Gary F.	Dean	587-7225				PHD	77	La Tech	
–Dept of Management & Mktg	Phone	587-7306							
Noble, Thomas A.	C-Pr	587-7231		35	IP	PHD	76	Alabama	9-76
Kemp, B. Wayne	Prof	587-7303		3	I	DBA	72	Miss St	9-71
Knight, John E.	Prof	587-7351		7	V	PHD	71	Ga Tech	9-71

Name	Rank	Phone	Email	#	Code	Degree	Yr	School	Year
Cates, Tommy A.	Assoc	587-7307		36	D	DBA	83	Memphis	9-74
Olorunniwo, Festus	Assoc	587-7350		7	V	PHD	87	Texas	8-90
Overby, John D.	Assoc	587-7268		25	EHN	DBA	85	La Tech	9-81
Ramarapu, Nariender	Asst	587-7325		79	UVZ	DBA	93	Memphis	8-93

Tennessee State University Nashville, TN 37203-3401 (615) BS,MBA
School of Business 3500 John A. Merritt Blvd FAX=320-3114
Did Not Respond-1993 Listing

Name	Rank	Phone		#	Code	Degree	Yr	School	Year
Curry, Tilden J.	Dean	251-1505			Plan	PHD	78	Fla St	1976
–Dept of Business Adm	Phone		Fax 251-1129						
Reynolds, John E.	H-Pr					PHD	72	Okla St	1961
Miller, Louis	Prof					PHD	60	Rochest	1973
Richard, Donald W.	Prof					PHD			
Tucker, Bernard	Prof					PHD			
Lownes, Millicent G.	Assoc					PHD			

Tennessee Technological Un Cookeville, TN 38505 (615) TNTECH 1978,1981
College of Business Adm FAX=372-6112 BS

Name	Rank	Phone		#	Code	Degree	Yr	School	Year
Bell, Robert R.	Dean	372-3372	rrb6250	24	EHUI	PHD	70	Florida	1976
–Dept of Management & Mktg	Phone		Fax 372-6249						
Pickett, Gary C.	C $								
Bonner, William H.	Prof	372-3861		1	O	PHD	61	Ohio St	1962
Henshall, Joy L.	Prof	372-3371		1	EFO	PHD	71	North Tx	1975
Associate Dean									
Phifer, Clifford C.	Assoc	372-3784		25	E	MC	64	Richmond	1970
Phillips, Stanley J.	Assoc	372-3793		5	N	MA	57	Delhi	1965
Lernor, Linda D.	Asst	372-3994		23	IR	PHD	91	Tenn	1991
Miller, Christine	Asst	372-6251		2	EY	PHD	93	Houston	1993
Pineda, Rodley C.	Asst	372-6253		38	IY	PHD	93	Tx Tech	1993

U of Texas at Arlington Arlington, TX 76019-0467 (817) WILLARD.UTA.EDU 1969,1973
College of Business Adm 800 South Cooper Street FAX=273-3145 BBA,MBA,MS,PHD

Name	Rank	Phone		#	Code	Degree	Yr	School	Year
Petersen, Russell J.	Dean	273-2881			Atg	PHD	71	U Wash	8-94
–Dept of Management	Phone	273-3166	Fax 273-3122						
Worrell, Dan L.	C	273-3166	dano	34	IJL	PHD	78	LSU	1993
Dess, Gregory G.	Prof	273-3857		3	I	PHD	80	U Wash	1987
Gerloff, Edwin A.	Prof	273-3864		2	H	PHD	71	Texas	1970
Quick, James C.	Prof	273-3869	jquick	2	GE	PHD	77	Houston	1977
Wofford, Jerry C.	Prof	273-3855		2	E	PHD	62	Baylor	1966
Ayres, Ray M.	Assoc	273-3868		6	PS	PHD	74	Maryland	1981
Gray, David A.	Assoc	273-3166		5	QN	PHD	74	Mass	1973
Harrison, David A.	Assoc	273-3854		2	ENX	PHD	88	Illinois	1989
Price, Kenneth H.	Assoc	273-3863		2	E	PHD	73	Mich St	1973
Rasheed, Abdul	Assoc	273-3867	b028msmr	3	IN	PHD	88	Pitt	1988
Walker, Burley	Assoc	273-3870		7	U	MBA	60	Oklahoma	1960
Wheeler, Kenneth	Assoc	273-3866		5	N	PHD	78	Minn	1979
Farnsworth, Regena	Asst	273-3860	regena	5	ENR	PHD	93	Tx A&M	1993
Priem, Richard L.	Asst	273-3865		3	I	PHD	90	Tx-Arlin	1990

Univ of Texas at Austin Austin, TX 78712-1172 (512) 1916,1963
College of Business Adm Red River & M.L. King Blvd FAX=471-3937 BBA,MBA,MPA,PHD

Name	Rank	Phone		#	Code	Degree	Yr	School	Year
Witt, Robert E.	Dean	471-5921			Mktg	PHD	68	Penn	9-68
Centennial Chair in Business Education Leadership									
–Department of Management	Phone	471-3676	Fax 471-3937						
Jemison, David B.	C-Pr	471-3676		3	IHY	PHD	78	U Wash	1988
Arnold, Victor L.	Prof	471-3676		34	MAI	PHD	71	Wiscon	1983
Bagchi, Uttarayan	Prof	471-3676		7	UV	PHD	82	Penn St	1982
Beyer, Janice M.	Prof	471-3676		2	EH	PHD	73	Cornell	1988
Brandt, Floyd S.	Prof	471-3676		34	IJL	DBA	60	Harvard	1963
Cooper, William W.	Prof	471-3676		37	IUVX	DSC	70	Ohio St	1980
Dyer, James S.	Prof	471-3676		7	UV	PHD	69	UCLA	1978
Fitzsimmons, James A.	Prof	471-3676		7	UV	PHD	70	UCLA	1971
Graham-Moore, Brian E.	Prof	471-3676		25	EN	PHD	70	Wash U	1972
Huber, George P.	Prof	471-3676		2	EHI	PHD	66	Purdue	1983
Kozmetsky, George	Prof	471-3676		38	DITY	DCS	57	Harvard	1966
McDaniel, Reuben R.	Prof	471-3676		3	IACH	EDD	71	Indiana	1972
Ruefli, Timothy W.	Prof	471-3676		3	IV	PHD	69	Car Mel	1968
Chammah, Albert M.	Assoc	471-3676		28	EY	PHD	69	Michigan	1969
Davis-Blake, Alison	Assoc	471-3676		25	EHNO	PHD	86	Stanford	1990
Dukerich, Janet M.	Assoc	471-3676		2	EHJ	PHD	85	Minn	1989
Fredrickson, James W.	Assoc	471-3676		3	IH	PHD	80	U Wash	1990
Glick, William H.	Assoc	471-3676		2	EHX	PHD	81	Berkeley	1981
Matsuo, Hirofumi	Assoc	471-3676		7	UV	PHD	84	MIT	1984
Schkade, David A.	Assoc	471-3676		29	EVZ	PHD	85	Car Mel	1984
Tirupati, Devanath	Assoc	471-3676		7	UV	PHD	87	MIT	1986
Breund, Britt	Asst	471-3676		7	UV	PHD	94	Cornell	1994

Name	Rank	Phone						
Golden, Brian R.	Asst	471-3676	3	IH	PHD	89	Northwes	1989
Gutierrez, Genaro J.	Asst	471-3676	7	UV	PHD	88	Stanford	1988
Krishnan, Vish	Asst	471-3575	7	UV	PHD	93	MIT	1993
Mang, Paul	Asst	471-3676	3	I	PHD	93	Harvard	1993
Polzer, Jeffrey	Asst	471-3676	2	E	PHD	94	Northwes	1994
Ramdas, Kamalini	Asst	471-3676	7	UV	PHD	94	Penn	1994

—Dept of Mgt Sci & Info Sys   Phone 471-3322   Fax 471-0587

Name	Rank	Phone						
Dyer, James S.	C-Pr	471-5278	7	UV	PHD	69	Texas	1978
George, Edward	Prof	471-5253	7	V	PHD	81	Stanford	1992
Lasdon, Leon S.	Prof	471-9433	7	UV	PHD	64	Case Wes	1977

David Bruton Jr. Centennial Chair in Business Decision Support Systems

Name	Rank	Phone						
Whinston, Andrew	Prof	471-8879	9	Z	PHD	62	Car Mel	1989
Jaillet, Patrick	Assoc	471-9447	7	UV	PHD	85	MIT	1991
Jordan, Eleanor W.	Assoc	471-5240	9	Z	PHD	78	Texas	1977
Mote, John R.	Assoc	471-9436	7	UV	PHD	79	Texas	1985
Sager, Thomas W.	Assoc	471-5232	7	V	PHD	73	Iowa	1979
Stokes, S. Lynne	Assoc	471-5216	7	V	PHD	79	N Carol	1985
Barua, Anitesh	Asst	471-7895	9	Z	PHD	90	Car Mel	1990
Cooprider, Jay	Asst	471-7868	9	Z	PHD	90	MIT	1990
Delquie, Philippe	Asst	471-1650	7	UV	PHD	89	MIT	1989
Greenberg, Betsy S.	Asst	471-1756	7	V	PHD	85	Berkeley	1986
Jarvenpaa, Sirkka L.	Asst	471-1751	9	Z	PHD	86	Minn	1986
Kumar, Rachna	Asst	471-4766	9	Z	PHD	93	NYU	1993
Morrice, Douglas	Asst	471-7857	7	V	PHD	90	Cornell	1990
Nielsen, Soren	Asst	471-5252	7	UV	PHD	92	Penn	1992
Pearlson, Keri	Asst	471-5214	9	Z	PHD	92	Harvard	1992
Shively, Thomas S.	Asst	471-1753	7	V	PHD	86	Chicago	1986
Yu, Gang	Asst	471-1677	7	UV	PHD	89	Penn	1989

Univ Texas at Brownsville   Brownsville, TX   78520   (210)
School of Business   FAX=

Name	Rank	Phone						
Boze, Betsy V.	Dean	982-0231		Mktg	PHD	84	Arkansas	1994

—Business Adm Department

Name	Rank	Phone						
Florey, Randall	C-Ac	982-0230		Mktg	PHD	82	North Tx	1992
Vaughn, William	Prof	982-0234			PHD	72	North Tx	1975
Permenter, Vivian	Assoc	982-0150			MS	70	Oklahoma	1974
Hollier, Gerald	Asst	544-8856			MBA	86	Pan Am-B	1982
Maldonado, Leo	Asst	544-8859			MBA	84	Pan Am-B	1973
Tala, Jasmine	Asst	548-670			PHD	93	Syracuse	1993

Univ of Texas at Dallas   Richardson, TX   75083-0688   (214)
School of Management   2601 North Floyd Road   FAX=690-2799

Name	Rank	Phone						
Kroncke, Charles O.	Dean	690-2705		Fnce	PHD	68	Minn	1988

—Management Faculty   Phone 690-2705   Fax 690-2799

Name	Rank	Phone						
Bass, Frank M.	C-Pr	690-2744		Mktg	PHD	54	Illinois	1982

Eugene McDermott University of Texas System Chair

Name	Rank	Phone						
Chandrasekaran, R.	Prof	690-2032	7	V				
Ford, David L. Jr.	Prof	690-2015	2	E	PHD	72	Wiscon	1975
Gaddis, Paul O.	Prof	690-2714	3	I	MS	61	MIT	1979
Guisinger, Stephen E.	Prof	690-2715	9	Y	PHD	70	Harvard	1976
Lutz, Raymond	Prof	690-2239	7	U				
Niu, Shun Chen	Prof	690-2707	7	V				
Harrison, J. Richard	Assoc	690-2569	2	E	PHD	86	Stanford	1985
Brittain, Jack W.	Asst	690-2708	2	E	PHD	89	Berkeley	1989
McKendrick, David	Asst	690-2548		Y				
Nehrt, Chad	Asst	690-2103		E				
Neustadter, Laurel	Asst	690-2152	7	V				
Ryu, Young	Asst	690-2146	7	V				
Stout, Suzanne K.	Asst	690-2726		E	PHD	91	Stanford	
Yang, Ping	Asst	690-2785	7	Z				

Univ of Texas at El Paso   El Paso, TX   79968-0544   (915)   1989,1989
College of Business Adm   FAX=747-5147   BA,BBA,MBA

Name	Rank	Phone						
Hoy, Frank	Dean	747-7719	6	FIST	PHD	79	Tx A&M	9-91

Texas Commerce Bank Professor of Business Administration

—Dept of Mktg & Management   Phone 747-5185   Fax 747-5348

Name	Rank	Phone						
Sullivan, Gary L.	C-Pr	747-5185		Mktg	PHD	78	Florida	1985

Betty M. MacGuire Professor of Business Administration

Name	Rank	Phone						
Ibarreche, Santiago	Assoc	747-7756	37	IY	DBA	79	Colorado	1983
Trevino, Melanie	Assoc	747-7749	3	IY	DBA	87	Geo Wash	1987
Gowan, Mary	Asst	747-7751	5	N		92	Georgia	1992
Stevens, Michael	Asst	747-7770	2	E	PHD	93	Purdue	1993
Wilhelm, Paul G.	Asst	747-7765	53	NPQ	PHD	82	Iowa	1988
Frederickson, E. Wayne	Lect	747-5185	3	I	PHD	70	Baylor	1994

—Dept Info & Decision Sci   Phone 747-5496   Fax 747-5126

Name	Rank	Phone						
Torkzadeh, G.	C-Pr	747-5496	9	ZV	PHD	83	Lanc UK	1993
Mahmood, Mo Adam	Assoc	747-5496	9	Z	PHD	82	Tx Tech	1987

Martin, William B.	Assoc	747-5496			PHD	72	North Tx	1975
Gemoets, Leopaldo A.	Asst	747-5496	9	Z	PHD	83	xan Luci	1987
Pettingell, Karen J.	Asst	747-5496	9	Z	PHD	91	North Tx	1990
Starner, John W.	Asst	747-5496	9	Z	PHD	76	New Mex	1990
McCrae, Ralph S.	Inst	747-5496	9	Z	MS	86	Drake U	1988

Univ of Texas-Pan American — Edinburg, TX   78539-2999   (210)   1979,1985
School of Business Adm   FAX=381-2354   BBA,MBA

Prock, Jerry	Dean	381-3311			Fnce PHD	70	Ariz St	
–Dept of Mgt & Cpt Info Sys	Phone			Fax 381-2354				
Crews, R. Michael	C-Ac	381-3388			PHD		Utah St	1982
Lee, Daniel	Prof	381-3367	9	Z	PHD		Florida	1977
Strong, Charles R.	Prof	381-3358	5	Q	PHD	73	Alabama	1972
Greene, Walter E.	Assoc	381-3355			PHD		Arkansas	1976
Thorn, Ron	Assoc	381-3397	7	U	PHD	73	Tx Tech	1988
Wilson, James M.	Assoc	381-3338	1		PHD	71	Arkansas	1971
Allison, Margaret	Asst	381-3360	9	Z	MED		Houston	1976
Hawang, Mark I.	Asst	381-3558	9	Z	PHD		Texas	1990
Nasif, Ercan	Asst	381-3336	1	EH	PHD	88	North Tx	1988
Brough, Charles	Lect	381-3337	9	Z	MBA		Tx-Pan A	1983
Smith, James	Lect	381-3386	9	Z	MBA			
Hodges, DeWayne		381-3348	79	VZ	PHD			
Rydl, Les		381-3366	79	VZ	PHD			
Vincent, Vern		381-3311	7	V	PHD			

U of Texas of Permian Basin — Odessa, TX   79762-8301   (915) UTPB
Div of Business Adm   4901 East University   FAX=367-2115   BBA,MBA

Watts, William A.	Dean				Fnce PHD	66	Iowa
–Dept of Mktg & Management	Phone 367-2162	Fax 367-2115					
Tinney, Cathie	C	367-2238			PHD	81	Minn
Griffin, Waylon D.	Prof				PHD	72	Texas
Schaefer, Thomas E.	Asst				PHD	63	Geotown
Kyungdoo, Nam	Asst	367-2160			PHD		North Tx
Scarborough, David	Asst	367-2265			ABD		North Tx

Un of Texas at San Antonio — San Antonio, TX   78285-0632   (210) UTSAVM1   1980,1980
College of Business   6900 North Loop 1604 West   FAX=691-4308   BBA,MPA
Did Not Respond-1993 Listing; * Members of Division of Accounting & Info Syst

Gaertner, James F.	Dean	691-4313			Atg PHD	77	Tx A&M	1983
–Dept of Management & Mktg	Phone			Fax 691-4308				
Bodensteiner, Wayne D.	D-Pr	691-4311						
Flannery, William T.	Assoc	691-5372			PHD	74	Houston	
Heller, Vic	Assoc	691-5778						
Coordinator of Tourism Management Program								
Lengel, Robert	Assoc	691-5376						
Preston, Paul	Assoc	691-5378			DBA	72	Colorado	
Raffaele, Gary C.	Assoc	691-5379			DBA	73	Harvard	
Wadsworth, Richard B.	Assoc	691-5382			PHD	69	Arizona	1973
Ashmos, Donde	Asst	691-5377						
Dietrick, Glenn	* Asst	691-5354	9	Z	PHD			
Duchon, Dennis J.	Asst	691-5373						
Gonzalez, Juan J.	Asst	691-5374			PHD	83	S Carol	
Howorka, Gary V.	* Asst	691-4320	9	Z	ABD		Arizona	8-93
McCray, John	Asst	691-5834						
Minghe, Sun	Asst	691-5777						
Tullous, Raydel	Asst	691-5381						
Walz, Diane	* Asst	691-5246	9	Z	PHD			
Williams, Karen	* Asst	691-5784	9	Z	PHD	92	Fla St	8-92
Wynekoop, Judy	* Asst	691-5244	9	Z	PHD			
Drinka, Dennis E.	Lect	691-5388						
Galloway, Robert D.	Lect	691-5775						
Holmgreen, John	Lect	691-5375						
McDonald, George	Lect	691-5389						
Spruce, William	Lect	691-5241						
Welch, Jane	Lect	691-5370						
Valdez, Jude	Adj	691-4313						
Buchanan, Ellis	TAsoc	691-5391						

Univ of Texas at Tyler — Tyler, TX   75701-6699   (903)   BBA,MBA
School of Business Adm   3900 University Blvd   FAX=566-7365

Kroll, Mark J.	Dean$	566-7346	3	I	DBA	87	Miss St	5-87
–Dept of Management & Mktg	Phone 566-7363	Fax 566-7211						
Toombs, Leslie A.	C-As	566-7217	3	I	DBA	89	La Tech	1989
Gullett, C. Ray	Prof	566-7213	5	Q	PHD	70	LSU	1978
Young, Marilyn	Prof	566-7437	2	S	PHD	74	Arkansas	1974

Texas A&M University — Coll Station, TX — 77843-4217 — (409) TAMVM1 — 1972,1972
College of Business Adm — FAX=845-9641 — BS,MS,PHD

Name	Rank	Phone	email	Code	Deg	Yr	School	Year
Cocanougher, A. Benton	Dean	845-4711		Mktg	PHD	69	Texas	7-87
–Department of Management	Phone 845-4851	Fax 845-9641						
Woodman, Richard W.	C-Pr	845-2310		FED	PHD	78	Purdue	1978
Clayton Professor of Business Administration								
Albanese, Robert	Prof	845-3132		EN	PHD	62	Ohio St	1971
Baysinger, Barry D.	Prof	845-4045		ITY	PHD	78	Va Tech	1979
Griffin, Ricky W.	Prof	845-3134		EN	PHD	78	Houston	1981
Lawrence E. Fouraker Professor of Business Administration								
Hellriegel, Don	Prof	845-4573		IEH	PHD	69	U Wash	1975
Bennett Chair in of Business Administration								
Hitt, Michael A.	Prof	845-5577		ITY	PHD	74	Colorado	1985
Paul M. and Rosalie Robertson Chair in Business Administration								
Keim, Gerald D.	Prof	845-1445		LYK	PHD	75	Va Tech	1974
Pustay, Michael W.	Prof	845-4254		LYK	PHD	73	Yale	1980
Schoenfeldt, Lyle F.	Prof	845-4801		NOP	PHD	66	Purdue	1981
Ernest and Dorothy Niederer Professor of Business Administration								
Zardkoohi, Ashghar	Prof	845-2043			PHD	77	Va Tech	1981
T. J. Barlow Professor of Business Administration								
Abelson, Michael A.	Assoc	845-3686		EC	PHD	81	Penn St	1980
Barney, Jay B.	Assoc	845-1405		IY	PHD	82	Yale	1986
Bierman, Leonard	Assoc	845-3233		KOY	MA	80	UCLA	1982
Chamberlain, Howard E.	Assoc	845-2825		IT	PHD	73	U Wash	1970
George, Jennifer M.	Assoc	845-3905		E	PHD	87	New York	1987
Hoskisson, Robert E.	Assoc	845-1041		ITY	PHD	82	Ca-Irvine	1983
Jones, Gareth R.	Assoc	845-0330		HI	PHD	78	Lancaste	1982
Cannella, Albert A. Jr.	Asst	845-0329		ITY	PHD	89	Columbia	1989
Dacin, M. Tina	Asst	845-4882		HI	PHD	93	Toronto	1992
Gely, Rafael	Asst	845-3883		QK	PHD	91	Illinois	1990
Gimeno, F. Javier	Asst	845-3881		IT	PHD	93	Purdue	1993
Kilbourne, Lynda M.	Asst	845-3133		NE	PHD	90	Texas	1990
O'Leary-Kelly, Anne M.	Asst	845-8813		ENR	PHD	90	Mich St	1990
Paetzold, Ramona L.	Asst	845-5429		XR	DBA	79	Indiana	1990
Wright, Patrick M.	Asst	845-4892		NE	PHD	88	Mich St	1989
Welch, Ben D,	SLect	845-6127		EN	PHD	90	Tx A&M	1990
Braneff, Ann	Lect	845-3882		K	JD	88	Houston	1992
Elmore, O. E.	Lect	845-3882		K	JD	76	Texas	1982
Glasgow, Douglas K.	Lect	845-1045		KL	JD	79	Miami	1980
Larson, Frederick A.	Lect	845-3883		KL	JD	78	S Calif	1989
Rowland, Sam E.	Lect	845-1456		St	JD	69	So Meth	1985
Swim, Keith D. Jr.	Lect	845-0328			JD	80	Tx Tech	1989
–Dept Bus Analysis & Resr	Phone 845-0361	Fax 845-5653						
Buffa, Frank P.	C-Pr	845-1616	buffa	V	PHD	71	LSU	1970
Courtney, James F. Jr.	Prof		c111jc	Z	PHD	74	Texas	1986
Tenneco Professorship in Business Administration								
Dinkel, John J.	Prof		k184jd	V	PHD	75	Northwes	1980
Flores, Benito E.	Prof		flores	U	PHD	69	Houston	1984
Sheppard, Sallie	Prof			Z	PHD	77	Pitt	1992
Wichern, Dean W.	Prof		h010dw	V	PHD	69	Wiscon	1984
John E. Pearson Professorship in Business Administration								
Anthony, Ted F.	Assoc		anthony	V	DBA	71	Colorado	1976
Choobineh, Joobin	Assoc		j0c1099	Z	PHD	85	Arizona	1985
@tamsigma								
Davis, Robert A.	Assoc	845-0659	davis	U	PHD	82	S Carol	1982
Fowler, George C.	Assoc		fowler	Z	PHD	76	Tx A&M	1979
Fuerst, William Lee	Assoc		bfuerst	Z	PHD	79	Tx Tech	1979
McLeod, Raymond Gregg Jr.	Assoc		mcleod	Z	DBA	75	Colorado	1980
Olson, David L.	Assoc		dolson	V	PHD	81	Nebraska	1981
Sen, Arun	Assoc		sen	Z	PHD	79	Penn St	1986
Shetty, Bala	Assoc		shetty	V	PHD	85	So Meth	1985
Stein, William E.	Assoc		stein	V	PHD	75	N Carol	1982
Tretter, Marietta J.	Assoc		e021mt	V	PHD	73	Wiscon	1981
Arreola-Risa, Antonio	Asst		arreola	V	PHD	89	Stanford	1993
Bretthauer, Kurt	Asst		kmb7223	V	PHD	90	Indiana	1990
Chung, Hyung-Min	Asst		hmchung	Z	PHD	89	UCLA	1989
El-Shinnawy, Maha	Asst		melshin	Z	PHD	93	UCLA	1993
Fleidner, Eugene	Asst		flied	U	DBA	89	Indiana	1988
Paradice, David B.	Asst		twodice	Z	PHD	86	Tx Tech	1986
Robinson, E. Powell	Asst		robinso	U	PHD	85	Texas	1992
Vinze, Ajay	Asst		vinze	Z	PHD	88	Arizona	1988
Darcy, Louise	Lect		darcy	V	MS	74	Tx A&M	1980
Kasiraj, Jothi	Lect		c147jk	V	MA	68	New Mex	1985

Texas A&M - Corpus Christi — Corp Christi, TX — 78412 — (512) — MPACC,MBA
College of Business Adm — 6300 Ocean Drive — FAX=994-2725

Name	Rank	Phone		Code	Deg	Yr	School	Year
Abdelsamad, Moustafa H.	Dean	994-2655		15 Fnce	DBA	70	Geo Wash	1991

–Department of Management

Name	Title	Phone						
Irwin, Charles D.	C-Pr	994-2701		34		EDD	Oklahmoa	
Brown, Aaron H.	Prof	994-2379		7		DBA	Miss St	
Pierce, Milo C.	Prof	994-2480		28		PHD	Illinois	
Barnes, Joyce M.	Assoc	994-2403		1		MBED	E Txs St	
Hanebury, Jean	Assoc			5	N	PHD	Geo St	
Hormozi, Amir	Assoc			7	U	PHD	Houston	
Myers, Elwin	Assoc	994-2492		1		PHD	Ariz St	
Carson, Kerry	Asst			25	N	PHD	LSU	
Carson, Paula	Asst			25	N	PHD	LSU	

Phone / Fax 994-2725

Texas A&M Univ-Kingsville — Kingsville, TX 78363 — (512) TAIVM1 — FAX=595-2143

College of Business Adm — University Boulevard — BBA,MBA

Name	Title	Phone	email					
Bigbee, Dalton L.	Dean	595-3801			Fnce	PHD	81 Tx Tech	1985

–Department of Management — Phone — Fax 595-2143

Name	Title	Phone	email					
Stanford, Jane	C-Ac	595-3938	kfjhs00	38	HIYE	PHD	92 North Tx	1990
Gibson, Donald	Prof	595-3944	kfdrg00		Mktg	PHD	84 Memphis	1988
Ketcham, Allen	Prof	595-2148		6	DUV	PHD	82 Arizona	1983
Taylor, Frank	Assoc	595-2712	kffat00	7	UV	PHD	79 Houston	1979
Wagman, George	Assoc	595-3942	kfgrw00	25	CGNS	PHD	84 Tx A&M	1984

–Dept of Accounting & CIS — Phone 595-2501 — Fax 595-3912

Name	Title	Phone						
VanZante, Neal R.	C-Pr	595-3930			Atg	PHD	76 Okla St	1989
Bonno, John A.	Prof	595-3936		9	Z	PHD	69 Arkansas	1970
Diersing, Robert J.	Assoc	595-3937		9	Z	PHD	91 Tx A&M	1990
Shorter, Jack D.	Asst	595-2130		9	Z	EDD	84 Okla St	1000

Texas A&M International Univ — Laredo, TX 78040-9960 — (210) — FAX=725-3348

Grad Sch Intl Trade/BA — One West End Washington St — BBA,MBA

Name	Title	Phone						
Fatemi, Khosrow	Dean	724-6429		8	Y	PHD	S Calif	8-82

–Management Faculty — Phone — Fax 726-3405

Name	Title	Phone						
Vicmas, Robert	Prof	722-8001				PHD		1994
Giermanski, Jim	Assoc	722-8001		58	Y	DA	U Miami	1989
Parhizgar, Kamal D.	Assoc	722-8001		12	E	PHD	Northwes	1992
Richard, Sandra	Assoc	722-7046		38	Y	PHD	Texas	1981
Willman, Edward	Assoc	722-8001		7	V	PHD	North Tx	1971
Broin, Martin	Asst	722-8001		7	U	PHD	Purdue	1993
Hurtado, Pedro	Asst	722-8001				PHD	Maryland	1993
LeMaster, Jane	Asst	722-8001		28	HY	ABD	North Tx	1992

Texas Christian University — Fort Worth, TX 76129 — (817) TCUAMUS — FAX=921-7227

MJ Neeley School of Bus — 1963,1966 — BS,MBA

Name	Title	Phone						
Downey, H. Kirk	Dean	921-7526	ibo41bu	38	E	PHD	74 Penn St	1983

–Department of Management — Phone 921-7537 — Fax 921-7227

Name	Title	Phone						
MacKay, Jane M.	C-Ac	921-7540		9	Z	PHD	87 Texas	1986
Greer, Charles R.	Prof	921-7565		15	NQ	PHD	75 Kansas	1988
Peters, Lawrence H.	Prof	921-7538		25	EN	PHD	75 Purdue	1985
Steele, Joe L.	Prof	921-7578		13	V	PHD	68 Texas	1965
Youngblood, Stuart A.	Prof	921-7562	sbu0127r			PHD	78 Purdue	1981
Neeley Professor								
Jones, Jack W.	Assoc	921-7558		13		PHD	77 North Tx	1973
Williams, Charles R.	Assoc	921-7216		12	EN	PHD	90 Mich St	1991
Freeman, Elizabeth B.	Asst	921-7122	freeman	36	IT	PHD	88 S Carol	1990
Jain, Virod K.	Asst	921-7537		3	I	PHD	94 Maryland	1994
Stephens, Gregory K.	Asst	921-7578		28	EY	PHD	92 Ca-Irvine	1991
Szajna, Bernadette A.	Asst	921-7217		9	Z	PHD	90 Houston	1990
Clark, Sharon C.	Lect	921-7536		9	Z	PHD	88 Tx-Arlin	1984

Texas Lutheran College — Seguin, TX 78155-5999 — (210) — FAX=

Dept of Business Adm — 1000 W. Court Street — BA

Name	Title	Phone						
Lockard, Nick A.	C-Ac	372-6051		15	EQ	MBA	Trinity	1980

–Management Faculty — Phone 372-6051

Name	Title	Phone						
Heizer, Jay	Prof	372-6056		7	UV	PHD	69 Ariz St	1988
Utecht, Ronald	Prof	372-6052		12	E	PHD	70 Ariz St	1985

Texas Southern University — Houston, TX 77004 — (713) — FAX=527-7701

Jesse H. Jones Sch Bus — 3100 Cleburne Avenue — BBA,MBA

Name	Title	Phone						
Slade, Priscilla D.	Dean	527-7215			Atg	PHD	90 Texas	1991

–Dept of Gen Business & Econ — Phone — Fax 527-7701

Brookins, Terry M.	C-Pr	527-7947		38	IRTY	PHD	68 Texas	1975
Ramsey, V. Jean	Prof	527-7945		23	R	PHD	90 Michigan	1979
Perkins, Carlton	Asst	527-7187		46	JKLT	JD	Tx South	1978

Texas Tech University
Lubbock, TX 79409-4320 (806) TTACS1.TTU.EDU 1958,1981
College of Business Adm — University Avenue & Broadway — FAX=742-2099 — BA,MS,PHD

Name	Rank	Phone	Email	C1	C2	Deg	Yr	School	Yr
Stem, Carl H.	Dean	742-3186			Econ	PHD	69	Harvard	1970
–Department of Management	Phone							Fax 742-2099	
Whitehead, Carlton J.	C-Pr	742-2154	odwhi	28	HYC	PHD	64	LSU	1965
Blair, John D.	Prof	742-2134		31	CIEH	PHD	75	Michigan	1981
Hunt, James G.	Prof	742-3175	odjgh	12	DEHX	PHD	66	Illinois	1981
Macy, Barry A.	Prof	742-1530	odbam	23	XIFH	PHD	75	Ohio St	1980
Peterson, Mark F.	Prof	742-2147	odmfp	28	HXY	PHD	79	Michigan	1985
Phillips, Robert	Prof	742-3420	odrlp	35	INE	PHD	72	Ohio St	1986
Associate Dean									
Boal, Kimberly B.	Assoc	742-2150	odkbb	23	EHI	PHD	80	Wiscon	1989
Krefting, Linda A.	Assoc	742-2157		5	N	PHD	74	Minn	1981
Savage, Grant T.	Assoc	742-3164	odgts	12	CEI	PHD	84	Ohio St	1983
Sorenson, Ritch L.	Assoc	742-1544	odrls	12	EGNP	PHD	79	Purdue	1986
Stewart, Alex	Asst	742-2133	odstw	38	ITY	PHD	87	York U	1990

Texas Wesleyan University
Fort Worth, TX 76105-1536 (817) FAX=531-4814 — BBA
School of Business — 1201 Wesleyan

Name	Rank	Phone	C1	Deg	Yr	School	Yr
Hart, Sandra Hile	Dean$	531-4840		PHD	84	Tx A&M	1985
–Management Faculty	Phone	531-4340				Fax 531-4814	
Dollar, Alta L.	Prof			PHD	81	North Tx	1970
Norwood, Frank G.	Prof	531-4840		EDD	68	Oklahoma	1960
McKenzie, R. Kenneth	Assoc			MBA	66	North Tx	1967
McWilliams, Donald B.	Assoc			PHD	74	North Tx	1982

Texas Woman's University
Denton, TX 76204-1805 (817) TWU.EDU — BBA,BS,BA,MBA
College of Arts & Scien — 1322 Oakland Avenue — FAX=898-3198

Name	Rank	Phone	Email	C1	C2	Deg	Yr	School	Yr
Bulls, Derrell W.	C-Pr	898-2102		14	CG	PHD	71	Tx Tech	1977
–Dept of Bus & Economics	Phone	898-2111						Fax 898-2120	
Griffin, Adelaide	Prof	898-2111	f_griffin	23	HE	PHD	79	North Tx	1979
Gibson, Dana	Asst	898-2111		9	Z	PHD	84	Texas	1993
Newcomer, Julia	Asst	898-2111		56	NQSR	PHD	89	North Tx	1991
Taylor, Sherrie	Inst	898-2903		56	NST	MBA	86	Tx Woman	1993

University of Toledo
Toledo, OH 43606-3390 (419) FAX=537-7744 1955,1963
College of Business Adm — 2801 West Barcroft — BBA,MBA,MS

Name	Rank	Phone	C1	Deg	Yr	School	Yr
Deans, Robert H.	Dean	537-2558	Econ	PHD	66	Pitt	1993
–Department of Management	Phone					Fax 537-7744	
Bhatt, Bhal J.	C-Pr	537-2969	38	PHD		Wiscon	1980
Beeman, Don	Prof	878-7980	38	DBA		Indiana	1976
Doll, William J.	Prof		32	DBA		Kent St	1980
Kassem, Sami M.	Prof		25	PHD		NYU	1967
Nykodym, Nick	Prof	472-5753		PHD		Nebraska	1976
Portaro, Ron M.	Prof		1	JD		Toledo	1982
Simonetti, Jack L.	Prof		25	DBA	72	Kent St	1972
Spirn, Steve	Prof	537-2380		PHD	73	Toledo	1973
Sullivan, Dale B.	Prof		2	DBA		Kent St	1973
Timmins, Sherman A.	Prof		2	PHD		Penn St	1976
Ariss, Sonny S.	Assoc	537-2366	31	PHD		Ohio St	1985
Kim, Ken I.	Assoc	537-2366	23	DBA		Indiana	1985
Longenecker, Clinton O.	Assoc		25	PHD		Penn St	1978
Schwartz, Robert H.	Assoc	255-7578	2	PHD		Michigan	1988
Sharkey, Thomas W.	Assoc		38	PHD		Indiana	1984
Wedding, Donald K.	Assoc			JD		American	1968
Bennet, Rebecca	Asst		2	DBA		Northwes	1991
Dwyer, Deborah J.	Asst	537-4059	2	PHD		Nebraska	1989
Ludwig, Dean C.	Asst		4	PHD		Penn	1988
Post, Frederick R.	Asst			JD		Toledo	1988

Towson State University
Towson, MD 21204-7097 (410) TOWSONVX 1992
School of Bus & Econ — FAX=830-3454 — BS,BA

Name	Rank	Phone	Email	C1	Deg	Yr	School	Yr
Barone, Sam	Dean	830-3342	e730bar		Econ PHD	62	Illinois	1985
–Department of Management	Phone	830-2934					Fax 830-3236	
Basuray, M. Tom	C-Pr	830-3301	d7pcmg1	24	PHD	74	Oklahoma	1986
DeCenzo, David A.	Prof	830-3235	e7b3dec	15	PHD	81	W Virg	1986
Solomon, Janet Stern	Prof	830-4106		5	DBA	83	Geo Wash	1983
Darrow, William P.	Assoc	830-3875		37	PHD	80	Penn St	1984
Nag, Barin N.	Assoc	830-2693	r73bnag	79	PHD	86	Maryland	1987
Smith, William P.	Assoc	830-2900	e7b3wil	45	PHD	82	Arizona	1988
Somers, Trudy L.	Assoc	830-2118	e7b3son	25	PHD	88	Michigan	1988
Thavikulwat, Precha	Assoc	830-3230	e7b3tha	37	PHD	78	Minn	1988
Jain, Bharat	Asst	830-3542		79	PHD	92	Penn St	1992
Ross, Douglas	Asst	830-4071	e7b3dnr	48	PHD	72	Colorado	1990
Sen, Babita	Asst	830-2117		79	PHD		Alabama	1992
Smith, Raymond D.	Asst	830-3028	e7b3smi	13	PHD	88	Maryland	1990

Transylvania University

Lexington, KY 40508 (606) FAX=
Div of Bus Adm & Econ — 300 N. Broadway
-Management Faculty — Phone 233-8104

Name	Rank	Phone			Degree		School	Year
Pepper, Michael R.	C-Pr	233-8249		BA MS			N Hamp	1969
Rarick, Charles A.	Prof	233-8224			PHD		St Louis	1986

Trenton State College

Trenton, NJ 08650-4700 (609) TSCVM.TRENTON.EDU
School of Business — FAX=530-7686 — BS
-Dept of Management & Mktg — Phone 771-3063 — Fax 771-2845

Name	Rank	Phone	email		Degree		School	Year
Robinson, James W.	Dean	771-3050			PHD	67	Duke	1992
Hofmann, Lewis A.	C-As	771-3063	lhofmann		DBA		Intl Grd	1979
Everard, Kenneth	Prof	771-3062			EDD		Indiana	
Neves, Joao M.M. dos Santos	Prof	771-2242			PHD	84	Penn	1987
Vincelette, Joyce P.	Prof	771-2567			DBA		Indiana	
Butler, Roosevelt D.	Assoc	771-2868			PHD		US Intl	
Sanyal, Rajib	Assoc	771-2688			PHD		Geo St	
McGill, John	Asst	771-2900			PHD			1992

Tri State University

Angola, IN 46703-0307 (219) TRISTATE.EDU
Business — 320 South Darling — FAX=665-4830 — BSBA,BS
-Management Faculty — Phone 665-4177 — Fax 665-4830

Name	Rank	Phone	email			Degree		School	Year
Woodin, Norman J.	Dean	665-4177	fwoodinnj			EDD		WMU	1984
Neyman, Aldo R.	Asst	665-4186		27		MBA		Indiana	1986

Trinity University

San Antonio, TX 78212 (210) FAX=736-8134 BS,BA
Dept of Business Adm — 715 Stadium Drive
-Management Faculty — Phone 736-7238 — Fax 736-8134

Name	Rank	Phone		code		Degree		School	Year
Robertson, Kim R.	C	736-7238							
Waldron, Darryl G.	Prof	736-7286	38	IY	PHD	75	Miss	8-80
Kosnik, Rita	Assoc	736-7294	13	DKIL	PHD	86	Northwes	9-89
VanEynde, Donald F.	Assoc	736-7670	12	EFP	PHD	84	Columbia	1-84

Troy State University

Troy, AL 36082 (205) FAX=670-3592 BS
Sorrell College of Bus — University Avenue
-Dept of Mktg, Mgt & Econ — Phone 670-3459 — Fax 670-3599

Name	Rank	Phone	code		Degree		School	Year
Curtis, Wayne C.	Dean$	670-3137		Econ	PHD	71	Miss St	1967
Cain, Fred	Assoc	670-3156	26	ENST	PHD	74	LSU	1974
Turnquist, Philip	Assoc	670-3150	31	IUV	DBA	86	Miss St	1990
Amsler, Gordon	Asst	670-3149	23	EFHP	PHD	91	Alabama	1992
Findley, Hank	Asst	670-3271	25	ENQU	ABD	93	Auburn	1992

Tulane University

New Orleans, LA 70118-5669 (504) TCSVM 1981,1916
Freeman Sch of Business — 6823 Saint Charles Avenue — FAX=865-6751 — BSM,MBA,PHD
-Management Group — Phone — Fax 865-6751

Name	Rank	Phone	code		Degree		School	Year
McFarland, James W.	Dean	865-5407	78	IY	PHD	71	Tx A&M	1988
Barach, Jeffrey A.	Prof	865-5473	34	IJLS	DBA	67	Harvard	1965
Mindak, William	Prof	865-5485			PHD	54	Illinois	1978
Burnett, Walter M.	Assoc	865-5423	13	BIL	PHD	65	Iowa	1968
Long, Hugh W.	Assoc	865-5465	4	AK	PHD	74	Stanford	1969
Watzke, Gerard E.	Assoc	865-5483	28	IY	PHD	72	Stanford	1977

University of Tulsa

Tulsa, OK 74104-3189 (918) VAX1.UTULSA.EDU 1949,1972
College of Business Adm — 6th & Evanston — FAX=631-2142 — BS,MBA,MTX,MAC
-Department of Management — Phone 631-2586 — Fax 631-2142
-Department of Quant Method — Phone 631-2588 — Fax 631-2142

Name	Rank	Phone	email	code		Degree		School	Year
Mabry, Rodney H.	Dean	631-2213			Fnce	PHD	75	N Carol	1994
Bowen, Donald D.	Prof	631-2586		2	E&FO	PHD	71	Yale	8-76
Wolfe, Joseph A.	Prof	631-2428	jwolfe	38	IP	PHD	71	NYU	6-78
Peterson, Tim O.	Assoc	631-2586	mgt_top	2	E	PHD	88	Tx A&M	9-91
Smith, Peggy C.	Assoc	631-2941	psmith	25	DENR	PHD	79	Oklahoma	1982
Bruton, Garry D.	Asst	631-2476	mgt-gdb	3	ITY	PHD	89	Okla St	9-92
Urban, Timothy L.	C-Ac	631-2588	qm_tlu	7	UV	PHD	87	Tx-Arlin	1987
Russell, Robert A.	Prof	631-2588	qm-rar	7	UV	PHD	72	Texas	1973
Rasher, Arthur A.	Assoc	631-2862	mis_aar	9	Z	PHD	82	Mich St	1988
Roberts, C. Richard	Assoc	631-2588	mis-crr	9	Z	PHD	78	Minn	1976
Umanath, N. S.	Assoc	631-2588	mis_uma	9	Z	PHD	87	Houston	1993
Chiang, Wen-C.	Asst	631-2588	qm_wc	7	UV	PHD	91	Texas	1991
Dixon, Angela J.	Asst	631-2588	mis_ajd	9	VZ	PHD	89	Okla St	1978
Shaft, Teresa M.	Asst	631-2588	mis_ts	9	Z	PHD	92	Penn St	1990

Tuskegee University Tuskegee, AL 36088 (205)
School of Business FAX=727-8451
  Did Not Respond-1993 Listing

Newhouse, Benjamin	Dean	727-8286		Atg	PHD	82	Michigan	1-84
–Department of Management	Phone		Fax 727-8451					
Sara, Tejinder	C-Pr	727-8266			PHD	74	Mass	9-73
Upchurch, Leo	Assoc	727-8732						
Moten, Sebrena	Asst	727-8713						
Oluji, Louis	Asst	727-8709						
Pinkney, Willie	Asst	727-8733						
Powell, Catherine	Asst	727-8712						
Thompson, Denise	Asst	727-8972						
Carr, Amelia	Inst							
on leave								
Freeman, Mark	Inst	727-8732						
Kopp, Lori	Inst	727-8775						

Union College Schenectady, NY 12308-2311 (518)
Institute of Adm & Mgt FAX=370-6789 BA,BS,PHD

Strosberg, Martin	D-Ac	388-6299			PHD	77	Syracuse
–Management Faculty	Phone		Fax 388-6686				
Arnold, Donald F.	Prof	388-6302			PHD	72	SUNY-Buf 9-82
Schmee, Josef	Prof	388-6248					
Lambrinos, James	Assoc	388-6253			PHD	79	Rutgers 1979

U.S. Air Force Academy Colorado Spr, CO 80840 (719)
Dept of Management FAX=472-3135 BS

Woody, James R.	H-Pr	472-4130	3	I	PHD	81	Virginia	7-78
–Management Faculty	Phone				Fax 472-3135			
Yoos, Charles J. II	Prof	472-4130	3	I	DBA		Colorado	
Bobko, Peter B.	Assoc	472-4130	7	U	DBA	83	Indiana	
Campbell, Rita A.	Assoc	472-4130	5	NR	PHD		Colorado	
Green, Steve G.	Assoc	472-4130	7	W	PHD			
McKinney, Earl Jr.	Assoc	472-4130	9	Z	PHD		Texas	
Wenger, Michael S.	Assoc	472-4130	3	I	PHD		Oxford	
Abderhalden, Richard	Asst	472-4130	5	I	ABD		N Carol	
Chemielewski, Robert	Asst	472-4130	7	V	ABD		SMU	
Colburn, Tracy W.	Asst	472-4130	3	I	MBA		FIT	
D'Amico, Robert J.	Asst	472-4130	3	I	MGA		Maryland	
Fekula, Michael J.	Asst	472-4130	2	I	ABD		Penn St	
Grant, Charles T.	Asst	472-4130	3	I	PHD		Fla St	
Heppard, Kurt A.	Asst	472-4130	3	I	MBA		UCLA	
Baker, Steven F.	Inst	472-4130	7	V	MS		AFIT	
Burgess, Thornton W.	Inst	472-4130	1	I	MBA		Oklahoma	
Carr, Mary	Inst	472-4130	3	I	MBA		WrightSt	
Dunlevy, John K.	Inst	472-4130	3	I	MBA		RPI	
Robinson, John W. Jr.	Inst	472-4130	1	I	MBA		RPI	
Smith, Wayne A.	Inst	472-4130	9	Z	MBA		E Wash	
Strigel, Stephen	Inst	472-4130	1	I	MS		Arkansas	

United States Intl Univ San Diego, CA 92131 (619)
College of Business Adm 10455 Pomerado Road FAX=693-8562

Stavenga, Mink	Dean$	693-4695		Fnce	DBA		US Intl	1986
–Department of Management	Phone	693-4695	Fax 693-8562					
Ansoff, H. Igor	Prof	693-4615	3	I	PHB		Brown	1986
Distinguished Professor of Strategic Management								
Dow, Fred	Prof	693-4758	8	Y	PHD		Yale	1978
Khalil, Mohamed	Prof	693-4601	8		PHD		UCLA	1972
Korf, Fred	Prof	693-4623			PHD		Columbia	1973
Krishnamoorthy, M.	Assoc	693-4550	7		PHD		Manchest	1989
Sullivan, Patrick H.	Assoc	693-4622			DBA	72	Fla St	1987
Walker, John	Assoc	693-4627			DBA		US Intl	1985
Program Director for Hotel, Restaurant, Tourism Management								
Black, William	Asst	693-4551	9	Z	EDD		N Ariz	1987
Mount, Daniel	Asst	693-4803			MBA		Mich St	1991
Olson, Lois	Asst	693-4694			DBA		US Intl	1994
Salameh, Tamer	Asst	693-4529	9	Z	DBA		US Intl	1989
Sullivan, Jay	Asst	693-4783			PHD		US Intl	1992

Upsala College East Orange, NJ 07091-1186 (201)
Business 308 Propsect Street FAX=266-7000
  Did Not Respond-1993 Listing

Funk, Warren H.	Dean			Reli	PHD		Columbia 1976
–Management Faculty	Phone 266-7822	Fax 266-7000					

University of Utah — College of Business

Salt Lake CY, UT 84112 · (801) UTAHBUS · FAX=581-7214 · 1936,1963 · BA,BS,MHRM,PHD

Name	Rank	Phone	email	code	field	degree	#	school	year
Seybolt, John W.	Dean	581-7347		2	O	PHD	75	Cornell	1974
—Department of Management	Phone	Fax 581-7214							
Young, Scott	C-Ac	581-7415		7	UX	PHD	87	Geo St	1987
Bentley, Joseph C.	Prof	581-5048		2	EFHP	PHD	63	Minn	1967
Derr, C. Brooklyn	Prof	585-3360		2	EFHO	EDD	71	Harvard	1978
Director of Global Business									
Gardner, James H.	Prof	581-4423		38	IY	PHD	51	Harvard	
Herzberg, Frederick I.	Prof	581-6839		52	HEF	PHD	50	Pitt	1972
Mangum, Garth	Prof	581-5574		5	NQ	PHD	60	Harvard	1968
Nelson, Roger H.	Prof	581-7458		6	STYI	EDD	58	Columbia	
Pate, Larry	Prof	585-6924		2	E	PHD			1993
Robson, R. Thayne	Prof	581-7274		5	Q	ABD		Cornell	1967
Watson, Collin	Prof	581-6939		7	V	PHD	76	Utah	1981
Wiest, Jerome	Prof	581-8554		7	V	PHD	63	Car Mel	1958
Chesteen, Susan	Assoc	581-8693		73	V	PHD	78	Utah	1986
Lee, Tien-Sheng	Assoc	581-5079		7	U	PHD	82	Missouri	1985
Seybolt, Patricia	ResAc	581-8019		5	QNP	PHD	86	Utah	1988
Research Associate Professor									
Tallman, Stephen	Assoc	581-8774		38	YI	PHD	88	UCLA	1990
Thompson, Gary M.	Assoc	581-8695		7	UX	PHD	88	Fla St	1987
Fladmoe-Lindquist, Karin	Asst	581-6506		86	YI	PHD	90	Minn	1990
Hesterly, William S.	Asst	581-6378		21	HNI	PHD	89	UCLA	1988
Jansen, Erik	Asst	581-3074		52	EFHO	PHD	87	S Calif	1988
Madhok, Anoop	Asst	585-5719		38	IY	PHD	93	McGill	1000
Wardell, Don G.	VAsst	585-5718		7	VII	PHD	90	Purdue	1992
visiting from Idaho									
Wilkins, Allison M.	VAssl	581-3823		7	U	PHD	93		1993
McConnoll, Renee V.	ClAc	581-4739		2	ED	PHD	88	Utah	1988

Utah State University — College of Business

Logan, UT 84322-3555 · (801) B202.USU.EDU · FAX=750-1091 · 1972,1981 · BS,BA

Name	Rank	Phone	email	code	field	degree	#	school	year
Stephens, David B.	Dean	797-2272		35	IQ	PHD	75	Texas	6-87
—Dept of Mgt & Human Res	Phone	797-2787	Fax 797-1091						
Cragun, John R.	H-Pr	797-2271	jcragun	25	EPN	PHD	66	Purdue	1966
Hansen, Gary	Prof	797-2287	ghansen	5	Q	PHD	71	Cornell	9-67
Kartchner, Allen	Prof	797-2366		7	UV	PHD	68	Utah	9-67
Kartchner, Eugene	Prof	797-2361		7	UV	PHD	65	U Wash	9-65
Lowe, Calvin	Prof	797-2368		6	S	EDD	63	Utah	9-62
McCarrey, Leon	Prof	797-1905	lmccarrey	31	DH	PHD	63	Oregon	9-82
McEvoy, Glenn	Prof	797-2375	gmcevoy	52	EPN	DBA	85	Colorado	9-85
Shetty, Y. K.	Prof	797-2369		31	I	PHD	67	UCLA	1967
Beck-Dudley, Caryn	Assoc	797-2376	cbeck	4	JK	JD	83	Idaho	9-84
Daines, David	Assoc	797-2384	ddaines	4	JK	JD	55	Utah	9-67
Robson, Ross	Assoc	797-2286	rrobson	45	N	PHD	73	Maryland	9-79
Chandler, Gaylen N.	Asst	797-2365	gchandler	56	NTS	PHD	90	Utah	9-93
Hanks, Steven	Asst	797-2373	shanks	63	IST	PHD	90	Utah	9-88
Siebers, Larry	Inst	797-2301		15	IN	PHD			9-93
Tarnutzer, Sharon	Inst	797-3736	starnutzer	12	DE	MBA	86	Utah St	9-90

Utica College — Div of Business Admin

Utica, NY 13502-4892 · 1600 Burrstone Road · (315) · FAX=792-3292 · BS

Name	Rank	Phone	code	field	degree	#	school	year
Rossi, Thomas	D-Ac	792-3085	15	BHIN	MBA			1979
—Management Faculty	Phone	792-3134	Fax 792-3173					
Dimon, Annette	C-Ac			Atg	MBA		Renssel	
Echtermann, Helmut	Assoc	792-3081		FILY	MBA			1978
Hickman, William	Assoc	792-3167	38	ISTY	MBA			1985
Peek, Stephen	Assoc	792-3329	27	FUVW	MBA			1987

Valdosta State University — School of Business Adm

Valdosta, GA 31698 · 1500 North Patterson Street · (912) · FAX=245-6498 · 1990 · BBA

Name	Rank	Phone	code	field	degree	#	school	year
Stanley, Kenneth L.	Dean	333-5991		Fnce	PHD	78	Purdue	1984
—Dept of Management/Info Sys	Phone	245-2233	Fax 245-6498					
Oliver, John E.	H-Pr	245-2236	25	EHIN	PHD	80	Geo St	1985
Ray, Howard N.	Prof	245-2239	9	Z	PHD	86	North Tx	1986
Schnake, Mel	Prof	245-3822	12	E	DBA	82	MSU	1989
Ware, Fred A.	Prof	245-2244	68	PY	PHD	74	Geo St	1971
Holland, Phyllis G.	Assoc	245-3821	3	IS	PHD	81	Georgia	1987
Moore, W. Kent	Assoc	333-5991	7	PZ	PHD	75	Texas	1971
Ostapski, S. Andrew	Assoc	249-2622	4	JKL	LLM	86	Miami	1993
South, John B.	Assoc	245-2245	7	U	PHD	73	Utah	1989
Fredenberger, William B.	Asst	245-2238	9	Z	PHD	90	Georgia	1988
Hogan, Eileen A.	Asst	245-3875	2	EH	PHD	83	Berkeley	1993
Superville, Claude	Asst	249-2621	7	UVWX	ABD	93	Alabama	1993

154

Valparaiso University — Valparaiso, IN 46383 — (219) EXODUS.VALPO.EDU
College of Business — FAX=464-5381 — BS

Name	Rank	Phone	Email		Codes	Degree		School	Year
Miller, John A.	Dean	464-5040	jmiller		Mktg	DBA	72	Indiana	1986
—Management Area	Phone	464-5040	Fax 464-5789						
Mainstone, Lawrence	Prof	464-5308	lmainsto	17	EFV	PHD		Mich St	1991
McCuddy, Michael K.	Prof	464-5046	mmccuddy	25	EF	PHD	77	Purdue	1983
Schlender, William E.	Emer	464-5461	wschlend			PHD	55	Ohio St	1976
Schroeder, David Lee	Assoc	464-5050	dlschrod	9	Z	PHD	90	Okla St	1988
Schroeder, Dean	Assoc	464-5177	dmschrod	3	IU	PHD	85	Minn	1990
Ozgur, Ceyhun	Asst	464-5178	cozgur	7	UV	PHD	90	Kent St	1988
Strasser, Sandra	Asst	464-5406	sstrasse	7	VU	PHD	90	Colorado	1990
Stuck, James Michael	Asst	464-5308	jstuck	38	IYZ	PHD	81	Claremont	1987

Vanderbilt University — Nashville, TN 37203 — (615) VUCTRVAX — 1979
Owen Grad School of Mgt — 401 21th Avenue South — FAX=343-7177 — MBA,PHD

Name	Rank	Phone		Codes	Degree		School	Year
Geisel, Martin S.	Dean	322-2316	7	V	PHD	70	Chicago	7-87
—Management Faculty	Phone	322-2219	Fax 343-7177					
Blackburn, Joseph D.	Prof	322-2995	7	WUVX	PHD	71	Stanford	9-79
Blanning, Robert W.	Prof	322-3593	9	Z	PHD	71	Penn	9-80
Daft, Richard L.	Prof	343-7822	12	DEF	PHD	74	Chicago	9-89
Gavish, Bezalel	Prof	322-3659	9	Z	DSC	75	Technion	9-88
Leblanc, Larry J.	Prof	322-3662	7	VUWX	PHD	73	Northwes	9-80
Mahoney, Thomas A.	Prof	322-3665	5	NOPQ	PHD	56	Minn	9-82
Scheffman, David T.	Prof	343-7570	3	I	PHD	71	MIT	6-89
Scudder, Gary D.	Prof	322-2625	7	UVWX	PHD	81	Stanford	9-90
Ball, Clifford A.	Assoc	322-2909	7	UVWX	PHD	80	N Mexico	9-90
Basu, Amit	Assoc	322-7043	9	Z	PHD	86	Rochest	9-90
Cohen, Mark A.	Assoc	322-6814	4	KLM	PHD	85	Car Mel	9-86
Cooil, Bruce K.	Assoc	322-3336	7	UVXW	PHD	82	Penn	9-82
Hyer, Nancy Lea	Assoc	322-2219	7	UVWX	PHD	82	Inidana	1-92
Arora, Seema	Asst	322-2534	4	KLM	PHD	93	UCLA	9-94
Barry, Bruce	Asst	322-3489	12	DEF	PHD	91	N Carol	9-91
Johnson, M. Eric	Asst	343-7748	7	UVWX	PHD	91	Stanford	9-91
Metters, Richard D.	Asst	322-2389	7	UVWX	PHD	93	N Carol	9-93
Stewart, Greg L.	Asst	322-2642	5	NOPQ	PHD	93	Arizona	9-93

University of Vermont — Burlington, VT 05405-0158 — (802) UVMVM — 1986,1986
School of Business Adm — FAX=656-8279 — BS,MBA

Name	Rank	Phone		Codes	Degree		School	Year
Shirland, Larry E.	Dean$	656-3177	7	U	PHD	72	Oreg St	1976
—Management Faculty	Phone	656-3177	Fax 656-8279					
Brandenburg, Richard G.	Prof	656-3177	31	IU	PHD	64	Cornell	1987
Gurdon, Michael A.	Assoc	656-0513	25	QTDY	PHD	79	Cornell	1980
McIntosh, Barbara R.	Assoc	656-4015	25	ENY	PHD	79	Purdue	1984
Parke, E. Lauck	Assoc	656-0517	13	DJY	PHD	76	Mass	1977

Villanova University — Villanova, PA 19085-1678 — (610) VUVAXCOM — 1975,1985
Coll of Commerce & Fin — FAX=645-7864 — BS,MBA

Name	Rank	Phone		Codes	Degree		School	Year
Clay, Alvin A.	Dean	519-4340		Atg	MBA	57	Drexel	1955
—Department of Management	Phone	519-4390	Fax 519-7864					
Liberatore, Matthew	C-Pr	519-4390	7	DUVZ	PHD	76	Penn	1983
Wolek, Francis W.	Prof	519-4316	27	DI	DBA	67	Harvard	1983
Burke, Donald R.	Assoc	519-6441	15	IN	PHD	70	Penn	1972
Chaudhry, Sohail	Assoc	519-4369	7	UVW	PHD	85	Columbia	1991
El-Najdawi, Mohamad	Assoc	519-4049	7	UZV	PHD	89	Penn	1985
Hopeman, Richard J.	Assoc	519-6440	39	HIZ	PHD	62	U Wash	1979
Nydick, Robert	Assoc	519-6444	7	UV	PHD	85	Temple	1985
Varano, Michael	Assoc	519-7799	79	ZV	PHD	71	Penn	1968
Arvanites, Debra A.	Asst	519-4325	12	KN	PHD	82	Rennsele	1983
Chaudhry, Peggy	Asst	519-6442	8	Y	PHD	92	Wiscon	1991
Fitzpatrick, William	Asst	519-4068	32	EHIZ	PHD	86	Maryland	1983
Klingler, James W.	Asst	519-4352	15	ENOR	PHD	85	Temple	1979
Rusinko, Cathy	Asst	519-6432	32	IFH	PHD	92	Penn St	1991
Shaw, Karyll	Asst	519-6445	21	EHNO	PHD	84	Maryland	1990
Sipior, Janice C.	Asst	519-4347	9	Z	PHD	88	SUNY-Buf	1990
Tymon, Walter G.	Asst	519-4363	23	EFHI	PHD	88	Temple	1990
Wagner, William	Asst	519-6446	9	ZY	PHD	92	Kentucky	1991

University of Virginia — Charlottesvil VA 22903-2493 — (804) — 1925,1981
McIntire Sch Commerce — McCormick Road — FAX=924-7074 — BS,MS

Name	Rank	Phone		Codes	Degree		School	Year
Guiton, Bonnie	Dean	924-3176			EDD	85	Berkeley	7-92
—Dept of Management	Phone		Fax 924-7074					
Whitener, Ellen M.	C-Ac	924-7091			PHD		Mich St	
Scott, Charlotte H.	Prof	924-3040			LLD		Alleghen	
University Professor								
Snyder, Neil	Prof	924-3218			PHD		Georgia	
Ralph A. Beeton Professor of Free Enterprise								

Name	Rank	Phone	Col1	Col2	Degree	Year	School
Akin, Gib	Assoc	977-1302			PHD	75	UCLA
Malone, Stewart C.	Assoc	924-6134			PHD		Temple
Brown, Robert B.	Asst	924-3232			PHD	89	U Wash
Dodd, Diane	Asst	924-3499					
Dowd, James J. Jr.	Asst	924-7089	2	E	DBA	87	Harvard

on leave to Intl Mgt Dev

University of Virginia-Grad — Charlottesvil VA 22906-6550 — (804) VIRGINIA.EDU 1971
Darden Grad Sch Bus Adm — McCormick Road — FAX=924-4859 — MBA,PHD
Higdon, Leo I. Jr. — Dean 924-7481 — MBA 72 Chicago 1993
Charles C. Abbott Professor of Business Administration
—Department of Management — Phone — Fax 924-4859

Name	Rank	Phone	Login	Col1	Col2	Degree	Year	School	Yr2
Werhane, Patricia	C-Pr	924-4840	phw2m	4	J	PHD	69	Northwes	1993
Ruffin Professor of Business Administration									
Bodily, Samuel E.	Prof	924-4813	seb1w	7	V	PHD		MIT	1977
Bourgeois, L. J. III	Prof	924-4833	ljb8f	3	I	PHD		U Wash	1986
Colley, John L. Jr.	Prof	924-4841		7	U	DBA	68	S Calif	1967
Almand R. Coleman Professor of Business Administration									
Davis, Edward W.	Prof	924-4819	ewd	7	U	PHD	67	Yale	1978
Oliver Wight Professor of Business Administration									
Freeland, James R.	Prof	924-4831	jrf8v	7	UVX	PHD	73	Ga Tech	1979
Sponsors Professor of Business Adm									
Freeman, R. Edward	Prof	924-0935	ref8d	3	IJ	PHD		Wash U	1986
Elis and Signe Olsson Professor of Business Administration									
Frey, Sherwood C.	Prof	924-4834		7	V	PHD		Hopkins	1979
Ethyl Corp. Professor of Business Administration									
Horniman, Alexander B.	Prof	924-7246		2	E	DBA	68	Harvard	1968
Landel, Robert D.	Prof	924-4832		3	U	PHD	70	Ga Tech	1969
Henry E. McWane Professor of Business Administration									
MacAvoy, Thomas C.	Prof	924-4817		3	U	PHD		Cinn	1969
Paul M. Hammaker Professor of Business Administration									
Pfeifer, Philip E.	Prof	924-4803		7	V	PHD		Ga Tech	1980
Rosenblum, John W.	Prof	924-7481	jur8j	3	I	DBA	72	Harvard	1979
Charles C. Abbott Professor of Business Administration									
Carraway, Robert L.	Assoc	924-4828	ric69	7	V	PHD		Purdue	1985
Clawson, James G.	Assoc	924-7488	jgc4m	5	O	DBA		Harvard	1981
Isabella, Lynn A.	Assoc	924-4818	jai7m	2	E	DBA		Boston	1990
Liedtka, Jeanne	Assoc	924-1404		3	I	DBA		Boston	1989
Weber, R. Jack	Assoc	924-4844		5	P	PHD		Berkeley	1972
Weiss, Elliott N.	Assoc	924-4815	enw2z	7	U	PHD		Penn	1987
Brodt, Susan E.	Asst	924-4810	seb5m	2	E	PHD		Stanford	1988
Johnson, Robin	Asst			2	E	PHD	94	Harvard	1994
Larson, Andrea	Asst	924-3221	all3w	6	TR	PHD		Harvard	1988

Virginia Commonwealth Univ — Richmond, VA 23284-4000 — (804) 1975,1981
School of Business — 821 West Franklin Street — FAX=367-8884 — BS,MS,MBA,PHD
Neither Info Sys Dept or Dec Sci Dept Responded

Name	Rank	Phone		Col1	Col2	Degree	Year	School	Yr2
Tuckman, Howard P.	Dean	367-1595			Econ	PHD	70	Wiscon	1993
—Department of Management	Phone	367-1623	Fax 367-8884						
Brown, Darrel R.	C-Pr	367-1623		25	EN	PHD	68	Oregon	1970
DeGenaro, Guy J.	Prof	367-7165		2	E	PHD	71	Florida	1970
Hunt, Eugene H.	Prof	367-7171		12	BEJ	EDD	67	Maryland	1968
Lambert, John D.	Prof	367-7138		7	EU	PHD	73	Michigan	1955
Myers, Donald W.	Prof	367-7122		5	FNPQ	DBA	72	Geo St	1982
Rimler, George W.	Prof	367-1487		67	STU	DBA	69	Geo St	1970
Trumble, Robert R.	Prof	367-7483		3	IQ	PHD	71	Minn	1988
Wood, D. Robley	Prof	367-6053		3	DI	DBA	77	Tenn	1979
Ackley, R. Jon	Assoc	367-7106		9	Z&	EDD	80	Utah St	1979
Barker, Randolph T.	Assoc	367-7124		12	&EFP	PHD	76	Fla St	1989
Gray, George R.	Assoc	367-1732		5	NQ	PHD	75	Alabama	1977
Johnston, Wallace R.	Assoc	367-7137		1	EFHN	DBA	72	Geo Wash	1971
Pearce, C. Glenn	Assoc	367-7123		12	&EP	PHD	74	Geo St	1975
Pitts, Michael W.	Assoc	367-7107		36	CIS	DBA	84	Tenn	1981
Sleeth, Randall G.	Assoc	367-1540		2	DE	PHD	77	Mass	1975
Byles, Charles M.	Asst	367-7125		38	CIY	DBA	86	Kent St	1990
Miller, Marianne	Asst	367-7185		25	EHNR	PHD	92	Oregon	1993
—Dept of Information Systems	Phone		Fax 367-8884						
—Dept Decision Sci & Bus Law	Phone		Fax 367-8884						

Virginia Poly Inst & St Un — Blacksburg, VA 24061-0233 — (703) VTVM1 — 1966,1971
Pamplin Col of Business — FAX=231-4487 — BS,MS,PHD
* Northern Virginia Graduate Center

Name	Rank	Phone	Login	Col1		Degree	Year	School	Yr2
Sorensen, Richard E.	Dean	961-6601	sorensen	7	U	PHD	73	NYU	1982
—Department of Management	Phone	231-6653	Fax 231-4487						
Shepard, Jon M.	H-Pr	231-6353	shepard	4		PHD	68	Michigan	1989
Badawy, Michael K.	* Prof	698-6075	badawy	2		PHD	69	NYU	1987
Bonham, T. W.	Prof	231-6595	bonham	2		PHD	69	S Carol	1969

Lang, James R.	Prof	231-6345	jrlang	6		PHD	76	Mass	1990
Charles O. Strickler Professor of Entrepreneurial Studies									
Litschert, Robert J.	Prof	231-6105	litschrt	3		DBA	66	Colorado	1965
Markham, Steve E.	Prof	231-7381	markham	2		PHD	78	SUNY-Buf	1978
Robinson, Jerald F.	Prof	231-6585	jfr	5		PHD	73	Illinois	1970
Wokutch, Richard E.	Prof	231-5084	wokutch	4		PHD	77	Pitt	1977
Alexander, Larry D.	Assoc	231-7382	herman	3		PHD	79	UCLA	1981
Cobb, Anthony T.	Assoc	231-6363	tcobb	2		PHD	77	Ca-Irvine	1978
French, J. Lawrence	* Assoc	698-6072	french	6		PHD	76	Mass	1990
Madigan, Robert M.	Assoc	231-5695	madig	5		PHD	82	Mich St	1980
Murrmann, Kent F.	Assoc	231-5820	murrmann	5		PHD	79	Mich St	1978
Scott, K. Dow	Assoc	231-5021	scott	5		PHD	79	Mich St	1979
Connerley, Mary	Asst			5		PHD	93	Iowa	1993
Hatfield, Donald	Asst			3		PHD	93	UCLA	1993
Lehrman, William G.	Asst	231-4553	lehrman	2		PHD	89	Princeton	1987
Neck, Christopher P.	Asst	231-4559		1		PHD	93	Arizona	1994
Stephens, Carroll	Asst			2		PHD	93	Duke	1993
Teagarden, Linda	Asst	231-5065		3		PHD	92	Colorado	1994

Virginia State University		Petersburg, VA	23803		(804)				
School of Business		20708 Fourth Avenue			FAX=524-6512				BS
Gregory, Sadie R.	Dean	524-5166				Econ	PHD	87	Howard	1-79
—Dept of Mktg & Management	Phone	524-5782	Fax 524-6512						
Jackson, Janice J.	C-Ac	524-5791		31	DER	DBA	90	Memphis	9-92
Amaram, Donatus I.	Prof	524-5791		52	NE	PHD	76	Ohio St	9-84
Brown, Henry	Asst	524-5362		41	JK	JD	75	NC Cent	9-75
McLain, David	Asst	524-5361		21	MH	PHD	91	Wiscon	9-93

Virginia Union University		Richmond, VA	23220		(804)				
S. Lewis Sch of Bus Adm		1500 North Lombardy Street			FAX=				BS
Did Not Respond-1993 Listing									
Altimus, Cyrus A.	Dean	257-5710				BAdm	PHD	71	Penn St	8-87
—Dept of Business Adm	Phone		Fax 257-5753						
Lloyd, Antoinette	C-As					MBA			
Olanrewaju, Larry A.	Asst					MBA			
Simmons, Yvonne M.	Asst					MS			
Wiggins, Bynetta M.	Asst					MED			
Murray, Patricia	Inst					MBA			1991
Odutola, Adelaja	Inst					MS			

Wagner College		Staten Island,NY	10301		(718)				
Business					FAX=				
—Management Faculty	Phone	390-3122							
Olson, W. C.	C-Pr	390-3442		4	D	MBA			9-85
Michael, James	Asst	390-3442		25	EH	PHD		SUNY-Alb	9-92

Wake Forest University		Winston-SalemNC	27109		(910)				1985
Sch Bus & Accountancy		2601 Wake Forest Road			FAX=759-5830				BS
Johnson, Dana J.	Dean	759-5027				Fnce	PHD	76	Kent St	9-92
—Management Faculty	Phone		Fax 759-6133						
Easley, Eddie	Prof	759-5374				PHD		Iowa St	9-84
Akinc, Umit	Assoc	759-5035		79	UVW	PHD	74	N Carol	9-82
Dewasthali, Arun	Assoc	759-5736		7	UV	PHD		Delaware	9-75
Ewing, Stephen	Assoc	759-5731		28	Y	PHD	72	Tx Tech	9-71
Hipp, Clayton	Assoc	759-5306		4	JKL	JD		S Carol	9-91
Deans, Candace	Asst	759-5733		9	YZ	PHD	89	S Carol	9-89
Harrison, Kline	Asst	759-4907		25	EHNP	PHD	87	Maryland	9-90
Thompson, Michael	Asst	759-5734		4	JK	JD		N Carol	1-91
Assistant Dean									
Kelly, Horace	Lect	759-5098		46	ILST	BA		Baylor	9-87

Wake Forest University-MBA		Winston-SalemNC	27109		(910)				1985
Babcock Grad Sch of Mgt		2601 Wake Forest Road			FAX=759-5830				MBA
McKinnon, John B.	Dean	759-5418				Fnce	MBA	61	Harvard	7-89
—Management Faculty	Phone		Fax 759-5830						
Shively, Robert W.	Prof	759-7671		2	E	PHD	72	Cornell	1970
Baliga, B. Ram	Assoc	759-5040		38	DIY	DBA	80	Kent St	1989
Clapper, James M.	Assoc					PHD		Mass	
Associate Dean									
Gagnon, Roger	Assoc	759-5046		7	UV	PHD	82	Cinn	1988
Hayford, Stephen L.	Assoc	761-0707		54	NJ	JD	87	Indiana	1990
Kennedy, Charles R. Jr.	Assoc	759-5034		38	IY	PHD	80	Texas	1989
Director Flow Institute of International Studies									
Makens, James C.	Assoc			8	Y	PHD		Mich St	
Middaugh, J. Kendall II	Assoc	759-5047		3	I	PHD	81	Ohio St	1987

Name	Rank	Phone	email	#	Code	Degree	Yr	School	Yr
Peacock, Peter R.	Assoc			9	Z	PHD		Chicago	
Saladin, Brooke	Assoc	759-5050		7	U	PHD	80	Ohio St	1983
Kane, Kimberly F.	Asst	759-5031		25	EN	PHD	90	Indiana	1990
Kinney, Susan T.	Asst			19	&Z	PHD		Georgia	
Pinder, Jonathan P.	Asst	759-5036		7	UV	PHD	89	Carolina	1990
Ferner, Jack D.	Lect	759-5575		3	I	MBA	55	Harvard	1971
Ptaszynski, James G.	Lect	759-5422		2	F	PHD	89	N Carol	1985

Associate Dean for Administrative & Planning

Warner Southern College — Lake Wales, FL 33853 — (813) FAX= — BA
Department of Business — 5301 U.S. Hwy. 27 South

Name	Rank	Phone		#	Code	Degree	Yr	School	Yr
Satterlee, Brian	C-Ac	638-1426		14	EIJN	EDD	91	Nova	1992
—Department of Business	Phone	638-1426	Fax 638-1472						
Thompson, Lloyd	Prof	629-4471		20	UVWZ	EDD	77	N Colo	1993
Schwarze, John	Assoc	638-1426		5	UZ	MBA	74	St Franc	1989
Wiseman, Timothy	Asst	638-1426		2	K	JD	85	Illinois	1992

Washburn University — Topeka, KS 66621 — (913) ACC.WUACC.EDU — FAX= — BBA
School of Business — 1700 College — phone: 231-1010

Name	Rank	Phone		#	Code	Degree	Yr	School	Yr
McKibbin, Lawrence E.	Dean	Ext 1309			Mgt	PHD	67	Stanford	6-91
—Department of Management	Phone		Fax 231-1063						
Roach, William L.	Prof	Ext 1748	zzroac			PHD	73	Michigan	1983
Cameron, Gary	Assoc	Ext 1247	zzcram			PHD	79	Nebraska	1982
Crumpacker, Martha	Assoc	Ext 1597	zzcrum		Mgt	DBA	80	La Tech	1977
Salinas, Teresita S.	Assoc	Ext 1601	zzsali			PHD	80	Kansas	1982

University of Washington — Seattle, WA 98195 — (206) U.WASHINGTON.EDU 1921,1963
School of Business Adm — 1410 Noreast Campus Parkway — FAX=685-9392 — BA,MBA,MPA,PHD

Name	Rank	Phone	email	#	Code	Degree	Yr	School	Yr
Mueller, Gerhard G.	Dean$	543-4750			Atg	PHD	62	Berkeley	1960
—Dept of Management & Org	Phone		Fax 685-9392						
Bell, Cecil	C-Ac	543-4367		5		PHD	70	Boston	1968
Jones, Thomas M.	Prof	543-6380	rebozo	4	JLK	PHD	77	Berkeley	1977
Knudson, Harry	Prof	543-4460		36		PHD	58	Harvard	1961
Mitchell, Terence R.	Prof	543-6779		5	BFHN	PHD	69	Illinois	1969
Newell, William T.	Prof	543-4898	wtnewell	37	IUVY	PHD	62	Texas	1960
Peterson, Richard	Prof	543-7695		58	NQY	PHD	66	Wiscon	1971
Saxberg, Borje	Prof	543-4470	borjeo	26	DHTY	PHD	58	Illinois	1957
Scott, William G.	Prof	543-7699		12	ABH	DBA	57	Indiana	1966
Vesper, Karl	Prof	543-6737		36		PHD		Stanford	1988
Beard, Donald W.	Assoc	543-4559		3		PHD	75	Nebraska	1975
Buck, Vernon E.	Assoc	543-2165		5	EFG	PHD	63	Cornell	1968
Butler, John E.	Assoc	543-8194		25		PHD	85	NYU	1965
Gist, Marilyn	Assoc	543-1913		57	EPX	PHD	85	Maryland	1987
Hansen, Gary S.	Assoc	543-0784		3	DISY	PHD	87	Michigan	1984
Hill, Charles W. L.	Assoc	543-4867	chill	3		PHD	83	Manchest	1988
Huber, Vandra L.	Assoc	543-5365		5		PHD	82	Indiana	1987
Kienast, Philip	Assoc	543-7141	kienast	25		PHD	72	Mich St	1970
Associate Dean									
Lee, Thomas W.	Assoc	543-4389		25	NQ	PHD	84	Oregon	1983
Moxon, Richard	Assoc	543-4587	moxon	38	IY	DBA	73	Harvard	1976
Woodworth, Robert	Assoc	543-4877		5		PHD	64	Northwes	1966
Collins, Paul	Asst	543-0197	collins	2		PHD	86	Rutgers	1990
Fuller, Sally	Asst	545-1321	srfuller	25		ABD		Wiscon	1992
Schulz, Martin	Asst	543-4777	martinus	27	JH	ABD		Stanford	9-93
Thomas, Tom E.	Asst	543-6849		2		PHD	88	Berkeley	1988
Wicks, Andrew	Asst	543-7913		4	J	PHD	92	Virginia	1992
—Dept Management Science	Phone	543-1043	Fax 685-9392						
Klastorin, Theodore D.	C-Pr			7	U	PHD	73	Texas	1974
Chiu, John S. V.	Prof			7	V	PHD	60	Illinois	1960
Faaland, Bruce H.	Prof			7	V	PHD	71	Stanford	1971
Moinzadeh, Kamran	Prof			7	V	PHD	84	Stanford	1984
Siegel, Andrew F.	Prof			7	V	PHD	77	Stanford	1983
Tamura, Hirokuni	Prof			7	V	PHD	67	Michigan	1967
Prater, George L.	Assoc			9	Z	PHD	63	Stanford	1965
Schmitt, Thomas G.	Assoc			7	U	DBA	79	Indiana	1979
DeCroix, Greg	Asst			7	V	PHD	91	Stanford	1991
Hillier, Mark	Asst					PHD	94	Stanford	1993
Koushik, Murlidhar V.	Asst			9	Z	MBA	72	Calcutta	1986
Langford, Joe	Asst			9	Z	PHD	87	Rochest	1987
Mannino, Michael V.	Asst			9	Z	PHD	83	Arizona	1991
Mookerjee, V.	Asst			9	Z	PHD	91	Purdue	1991
Burrows, William	SLect			9	Z	MBA	72	U Wash	1979
Pilcher, M.	SLect				ZUV	PHD	85	Ga Tech	1987
Lou, Cheri	Lect			9	Z	MBA	84	Wyoming	1990

Washington University — St. Louis, MO 63130-4899 — (314) WUOLIN.WUSTL.EDU 1921,1963
Olin School of Business — One Brookings Drive — FAX=935-6359 — BS,MBA,PHD
Pankoff, Lyn D. — Dean$ 935-6344 — pankoff — PHD 67 Chicago 1967
—Management Faculty — Phone 935-6326 — Fax 935-6359
Baloff, Nicholas — Prof 935-6363 — baloff — 2 EFHU PHD 63 Stanford 1978
Hilgert, Raymond L. — Prof 935-6367 — 45 JNQ DBA 63 Wash U 1964
Kropp, Dean — Prof 935-4563 — kropp — 7 UVW PHD 77 Stanford 1986
  Dan Broida Professor of Operations & Manufacturing Management
Miller, Gary J. — Prof 935-6382 — miller — 2 AHIL PHD 76 Texas 1986
  Ruben C. Taylor Jr., & Anne Carpenter Taylor Professor of Political Econ
Rosenblatt, Meir J. — Prof 935-6769 — rosenblatt — 7 UVW PHD 77 Stanford 1989
  Myron Northrop Professor of Operations and Manufacturing Mgt.
Walsh, John E. Jr. — Prof 935-6365 — walshj — 83 YI DBA 60 Harvard
Bottom, William — Assoc 935-6351 — bottomb — 2 EFGH PHD 89 Illinois 1988
Coff, Russell W. — Asst 935-6342 — coff — 23 IH PHD 93 UCLA 1993
Erlebacher, Steven J. — Asst 935-4528 — erlebacher — 7 UVW PHD 93 Michigan 1993
Eynan, Amit — Asst 935-6090 — eynan — 7 UVW ABD — Wash U 1993
Kim, Ihlyung — VAsst — kimi — 7 UVW ABD — UCLA 1994
Li, Chung-Lun — Asst 935-6323 — lic — 7 UVW ENGD 90 Columbia 1990
Poppo, Laura — Asst 935-6374 — poppo — 32 I PHD 91 Penn 1991
Zenger, Todd R. — Asst 935-6399 — zenger — 32 IH PHD 89 UCLA 1990

Washington and Lee Univ — Lexington, VA 24450 — (703) FS.COMMERCE.WLU.EDU 1927
Sch Comm, Econ, & Pol — FAX=463-8945 — BS
Peppers, Larry C. — Dean 463-8602 — peppers.l.c — Econ PHD Vanderbt 1986
—Management Faculty — Phone 463-8639 — Fax 463-8945
Cline, Philip L. — H 463-8610 — cline.p.l — 79 Z PHD 75 Okla St 1975
Dean, Roger A. — Prof 463-8610 — dean.r.a — 25 JKNO PHD 81 Mich St 1984
DeVogt, John Frederick — Prof 463-8609 — devogt.j — 47 JUV PHD 66 N Carol 1962
Goldsten, Joseph — Prof 463-8619 — goldsten.j — 1 PHD 74 Ohio St 1972
Lamont, Lawrence Michael Jr. — Prof 463-8613 — lamont.l.m — 1 DIX PHD 69 Michigan 1974
Pirkle, Kipling M. — Assoc 463-8719 — pircle.k.m — 36 IST PHD 85 Clemson 1989
Holliday, A. J. — Asst 463-8628 — holliday.a.j — 4 KL JD 76 IL Tech 1976

Washington State University — Pullman, WA 99164-4726 — (509) WSUVM1 1960,1965
Coll of Business & Econ — FAX=335-4275 — BA,MAC,PHD
  phone 335-7580
Markin, Rom J. — Dean 335-3596 — Mktg DBA 61 Indiana 1961
—Dept of Management & Sys — Phone 335-7527 — Fax 335-7736
Randall, Donna — C-Pr — PHD
Baker, Douglas D. — Prof — PHD — Nebraska
Cullen, John — Prof
Morgan, Cyril P. Jr. — Prof 335-7527 — Mgt PHD — Case Wes
Wang, Min-Chiang — Prof — PHD — Wiscon
Fotopoulos, Stergios — Assoc — PHD — Liverpol
Huo, Paul Y. — Assoc — PHD — Calif
Reed, Richard — Assoc
Ahn, Sung — Asst
Chen, B. — Asst
Chen, W-T — Asst
Fox, Isaac — Asst
Goodstein, Jerry — Asst
Han, Bernie — Asst
Lemak, David — Asst
Miskin, Val — Asst
Tripp, Tom — Asst
Tyran, Craig — Asst

Wayne State College — Wayne, NE 68787 — (402)
Division of Business — 200 East 10th Street — FAX= — BS,BA
Benson, Vaughn L. — H-Ac 375-7245 — Atg PHD 85 Nebraska 1974
—Management Faculty — Phone — Fax 375-7574
Kochenash, Tony — Prof 375-7464 — 23 AEN PHD 73 Colo St 1990
Paxton, John — Assoc 375-7022 — 79 VX PHD 88 Nebraska 1992
Nelson, Jeryl — Inst 375-7251 — 32 HI MBA 89 S Dakota 1986

Wayne State University — Detroit, MI 48202 — (313) 1976,1982
School of Business Adm — FAX=577-4515 — BS,BA,MBA
Volz, William H. — Dean 577-4500 — 4 JK MBA 78 Harvard 1978
—Dept Management & Org Sci — Phone 577-4515 — Fax 993-7664
Stulberg, Joseph — C-Ac 577-6043 — 45 KQ PHD 75 Rochest 1989
Doherty, Victor — Prof 577-4841 — 23 C PHD 67 Mich St 1962
Martin, James E. — Prof 577-4485 — 5 NQ PHD 73 Wash 1976
Maurer, John — Prof 577-4517 — 26 UTS PHD 67 Mich St 1965
Osborn, Richard N. — Prof 577-4519 — 28 HIMY DBA 71 Kent St 1985
Fried, Yitzhak — Assoc 577-4509 — 5 EGN PHD 85 Illinois 1985

Krishnan, K. S.	Assoc	577-4556		7	UV	PHD	71	Penn	1981
Naughton, Thomas J.	Assoc	577-6043		24	EGOT	PHD	82	SUNY-Buf	1980
Nussbaum, Harvey	Assoc	577-4484		24	L	PHD	63	Wayne St	1966
Verma, Harish	Assoc	577-4543		7	U	PHD	70	Mich St	1970
Bantel, Karen	Asst	577-4466		23	HI	PHD	87	Michigan	1988
Kirchmeyer, Catherine	Asst	577-6876	kirchmey	25	EN	PHD	88	York	1992
Mudrack, Peter	Asst	577-4581		24	EL	ABD	91	Toronto	1990
Reddy, Sabine	Asst	577-4515				PHD	94	Illinois	1994
Chambers, Brian	Lect	577-2253		34	IT	PHD	91	Michigan	1990

Weber State University — Ogden, UT 84408-3803 (801) FAX=626-7930 1992,1992 BS,MPACC
School of Bus & Econ — 3750 Harrison Boulevard Econ PHD 80 Nebraska 1981

Vaughan, Michael B.	Dean	626-7308						
–Dept of Management	Phone		Fax 626-7423					
Addams, Lon	Prof	626-6111						
Handley, W. Bruce	Prof	626-6729		PHD	72	Ariz St	1971
Harris, Alma F.	Prof	626-7104		PHD	73	Purdue	1973
Storey, Jerry	Prof	626-6078		PHD	72	Utah	1971
Powell, Sandra	Asst	626-6103		PHD	93	Utah	
Schraneveldt, Shone	Asst	626-6083		PHD	92	Toyoko	1992

Webster University — St. Louis, MO 63119-3194 (314) FAX=
School of Bus & Mgt — 470 East Lockwood Avenue

Dittrich, John E.	Dean	968-7474		1		PHD	70	U Wash	1994
–Department of Management	Phone	968-7020	Fax 060-7077						
Brasfield, James M	C-Pr	968-7063		1	AC	PHD	73	Case Wes	1975
DiMarco, Nicholas J.	Assoc	968-7026		2	ENP	PHD	70	Case Wes	1988
Quirk, Thomas	Assoc	968-7015		1		PHD	67	Stanford	1987
Brennan, David J.	Asst	968-7156		8	YD	PHD	92	St Louis	1991
Risker, D. Christopher	Asst	968-7557		1	CA	PHD	92	Colorado	1991

Wesley College — Dover, DE 19901-9912 (302) FAX=736-2301 BA,BS
Division of Business — North State Street

Jacobs, Kathleen C.	C-Pr	736-2519		12		EDD	87	Temple	1988
–Management Faculty	Phone	736-2514	Fax 736-2301						
Murchison, Richard L.	Assoc	736-2451		15		MAS	66	Delaware	1988

Wesleyan College — Macon, GA 31297-4299 (912) FAX=474-7572 AB
Business & Economics — 4760 Forsyth Road
email WESMAIL.WESLEYAN.PEACH NET.EDU phone: 474-7057

Dod, Glenna A.	C-Pr	Ext 282	gdod	83	RY	EDD		S Miss	1975
D. Abbot Turner Professor of Free Enterprise									
–Management Faculty	Phone	477-1110	Fax 477-7572						

West Chester University — West Chester, PA 19383 (610) WCUPA.EDU FAX= BS,MBA
Sch of Bus & Public Afr — 100 West Rosedale Avenue
Did Not Respond-1993 Listing

Fiorentino, Christopher	Dean$	436-2824			PHD	89	Temple	9-85
–Department of Management	Phone		Fax 436-3170					
Selvanathan, Rani G.	C-Ac	436-2409			PHD		Paris	1986
Chu, Hung M.	Prof	436-2649			PHD		LSU	1976
Paden, David L.	Prof	436-1095			DBA		Indiana	1988
McGee, Charles H.	Assoc	436-2261			PHD		Northwes	1987
Snow, Roberta	Assoc	436-2303			PHD		Penn	1989
Hamilton, James W.	Asst	436-2608			MBA		Northeas	1989
Leach, Evan	Asst	436-2261						
Murphy, Anne P.	Asst	436-2296			MBA		Penn	1989
Saddoris, Jane Weston	Inst				MA		Villanov	1971
Vaughan, Thomas		436-2306						

University of West Florida — Pensacola, FL 32514-5752 (904) UWF FAX=474-3131 BS,MBA,MACC
College of Business — 11000 University Parkway

Dimsdale, Parks B.	Dean	474-2349	pdimsdal		Econ	PHD	69	Florida	1978
–Dept of Management/MIS	Phone	474-2309	Fax 474-2716						
Cox, John Lew	C-Pr	474-2313	jcox	79	TUY	PHD	70	Ariz St	1978
Armstrong, Terry R.	Prof	474-2475	tarmstro	74	EFHJ	PHD	73	Union	1983
Murrell, Kenneth L.	Prof	474-2308	kmurrell	28	FHW	DBA	77	Geo Wash	1982
Roberts, Ralph M.	Prof	474-2311	rroberts	34	BI	PHD	69	Alabama	1969
Olsen, Ronald J.	Assoc	678-3727	rolsen7	7		PHD	84	Geo St	1987
Schultz, Marian C.	Assoc	678-3727	mschultz	12	CEGO	PHD	82	S Calif	1989
Wheatley, Walter J.	Assoc	474-2353	wwheatle	39	DIV	PHD	85	Fla St	1985
Baugh, Gayle M.	Asst	474-2206	gbaugh	25	EOX	PHD	92	Cinn	1989
Long, Esther	Asst	474-2039		12	NO	PHD	92	Tenn	1991
Page, Diana	Asst	474-2133	dpage	12	DNX	EDD	86	Fla St	1988

Peach, Brian	Asst	474-2309	bpeach	23	EI	PHD	92	Oklahoma	1991
Platt, Richard G.	Asst	474-2317	rplatt	97	UY	PHD	72	North Tx	1991
Snyder, Stephen	Asst	474-2309	ssnyder	34	IJ	PHD	92	Ariz St	1991
Waring, Craig W.	Asst	474-2314	cwaring	79	TUVY	PHD	92	Fla St	1988
Rasheed, Howard	VInst	474-3087	hrasheed	67	RS	MBA		W Fla	1990

West Georgia College — Carrollton, GA 30118 — (404) — FAX=836-6717 — 1984,1990 BBA,MBA

West Georgia College	Carrollton, GA	30118	(404)						1984,1990
School of Business			FAX=836-6717						BBA,MBA
Hovey, David H. Jr.	Dean	836-6467		1	T	PHD	78	LSU	8-84
—Department of Management	Phone		Fax 836-6774						
Hunsicker, Frank R.	C-Pr	836-6472		3	I	DBA	71	Geo Wash	9-75
Chisholm, Thomas A.	Prof	836-6472		1	B	PHD	75	Auburn	9-85
Padgett, Thomas A.	Prof	836-6472		7	UZ	DBA	75	Fla St	9-82
Ashley, Nancy	Asst	836-6472		9	Z	PHD	93	Arizona	9-93
Beise, C.	Asst	836-6472		9	Z	PBD	89	Geo St	1-89
Carr, James W.	Asst	836-6472		5	N	PHD	82	Geogia	6-79
Inman, J. W.	Asst	836-6472		1		MBA	72	Geo Wash	9-91
Parsa, Farmarz	Asst	836-6472		7	U	PHD	86	Geo St	9-86
Zachary, M. K.	Asst	836-6472		4	JKLM	JD	79	Georgia	9-86

West Texas A&M University	Canyon, TX	79016-0001	(806)						
Pickens Col of Business			FAX=656-2071						BS,MPA
Miller, Jerry	Dean	656-2530			Fnce	PHD	70	LSU	1993
—Dept of Mgt, Mktg & Bus Adm	Phone	656-2500	Fax 656-2927						
Stahlecker, Winston D.	H-Pr	656-2500		6	Mktg	DBA		Ariz St	1986
Dixon, Rolf	Asst	656-2490		13	I	PHD		Tx Tech	1991
Gopalan, Suresh	Asst	656-2497		23		DBA		La Tech	1990
Rivera, Joan	Asst	656-2503		12		PHD		Tx Tech	1993
Summers, David F.	Inst	656-2496		13	EI	MBA		West Tx	1985

West Virginia University	Morgantown, WV	26506-6025	(304)						1954,1963
Coll of Business & Econ	University Avenue & Hough St		FAX=293-7061						BS,MBA
Maust, Robert S.	Dean$	293-7800			Atg	ABD		Michigan	1959
—Department of Management	Phone		Fax 293-7061						
Mansour, Ali	C-Pr	293-7931		7	V	PHD	78	Georgia	1978
Fuller, Jack A.	Prof	293-7935		7	V	PHD	72	Arkansas	1985
Schaupp, Dieter L.	Prof	293-7941		2	E	DBA	73	Kentucky	1972
Blaskovics, Thomas L.	Assoc	293-7933		9	Z	PHD	65	Wiscon	1985
Harpell, John L. Jr.	Assoc	293-7936		7	V	DBA	74	Geo St	1967
Banerji, Kunal	Asst	293-7945		3	I				1990
Blakely, Gerald	Asst	293-7932		2	E	PHD	88	N Carol	1989
Denton, James	Asst	293-7931		7	V				1991
Martinec Ponte, Cindy	Asst	293-7940		3	I	PHD	88	SUNY	1988
Merah, Ajay	Asst					PHD		Mass	1992
Moorman, Robert H.	Asst	293-7944		2	E	PHD	90	Indiana	1990
Perkins, Nichelle	Asst					JD		Iowa	1992
Renard, Monika	Asst	293-4495		2	E				1991
Sayeed, Lutfus	Asst	293-7931		9	Z				1991
Sypolt, Linda T.	Asst	293-7942		4	K	JD	75	W Virg	1975
Wolfe, Michael	Asst	293-7943		9	Z	PHD	88	Texas	1989
Gardner, Richard M.	Lect	293-7801		2	E	MBA	69	W Virg	1989

Western Carolina University	Cullowhee, NC	28723	(704) WCUVAX1						1983,1984
College of Business			FAX=227-7414						BSBA,MBA
McCreary, John	Dean	227-7401		89	JXYZ	EDD	68	Tenn	5-77
—Department of Management	Phone	277-7401	Fax 277-7414						
Kinard, Jerry L.	C-Ac	227-7401			Mgt	DBA	71	Miss St	8-94
Adams, John R.	Prof	227-7401		23	DHIN	PHD	74	Syracuse	8-80
Kane, William D.	Assoc	227-7401		23	DEH	PHD	77	Cornell	8-76
Kinnear, Terry L.	Assoc	227-7401		12	EFH	DBA	81	Kent St	8-79
Mechling, George W.	Assoc	227-7401		17	UVX	PHD	85	Nebraska	8-92
Owens, Stephen D.	Assoc	227-7401		58	NQY	PHD	81	North Tx	8-81
Little, Beverly L.	Asst	227-7401	little	25	EFN	PHD	93	Va Tech	8-93
Pearce, James W.	Asst	227-7401		27	IKUV	JD	73	S Carol	8-91
Smith, Hanson H.	Asst	227-7401		17	UV	MBA	75	W Carol	8-75

Western Conn State Univ	Danbury, CT	06810	(203)						
Ancell School of Bus	181 White Street		FAX=						
Blaylock, Bruce K.	Dean	837-9600			Q	PHD		Geo St	1989
—Department of Management	Phone	837-8651	Fax 837-8339						
Buccini, Eugene	C-Pr	837-8651		25	EFNP	PHD		NYU	1980
Benson, Ronald	Prof	837-8650		72	JSUF	PHD		Iowa	1983
Fox, Douglas M.	Prof	837-8653		14	AFLJ	PHD		Columbia	1978
Tesch, Frederick F.	Prof	837-8654		25	FINP	PHD		Cinn	1976

–Dept of Mgt Info Systems Phone 837-9339 Fax 837-8339

Name	Rank	Phone			Degree	School	Year
DeLoughy, Sara T.	C-Ac	837-9339	7	V	PHD	New Sch	
Fischer, Marla	Prof	837-9340	7	X	PHD	Conn	
Jin, Gregory	Prof	837-9343			DBA	Geo Wash	1976
Montague, Richard A.	Prof	837-9341	9	Z	PHD	Columbia	1985
Goldstein, Joel	Assoc	837-9342	7	Z	PHD	Poly NY	1986
Wright, Marie	Assoc	837-9344			PHD	Mass	1988

Western Illinois University Macomb, IL 61455 (309) ECNCDC 1978,1983
College of Business — Adams Street — FAX=298-2142 — BB,MAC
Walzer, Norman C. — Dean 298-2442 — Econ PHD 70 Illinois 1970
–Department of Management Phone — Fax 298-1039

Name	Rank	Phone			Degree		School	Year
Shane, Hugh	C-Pr	298-1535			PHD	77	Iowa	1977
Axley, Stephen	Prof	298-1395			PHD	81	Purdue	1981
Daniels, John P.	Prof	298-1653			PHD	76	LSU	1976
Knod, Edward M. Jr.	Prof	298-1451			PHD	74	Nebraska	1974
Morey, Russell W.	Prof	298-1440			PHD	73	Nebraska	1973
Sproull, Natalie	Prof	298-1997			PHD	69	Mich St	1969
Krell, Terence	Assoc	792-5330			PHD	84	UCLA	1984
Maakestad, William	Assoc	298-1193			JD	77	Valparai	1977
March, Douglas	Assoc	298-1394			JD	73	Illinois	1973
McCarthy, John J.	Assoc	298-1010			JD	68	Illinois	1968
Meyers, Bruce	Assoc	298-1626			DBA	73	Wash U	1973
Morey, Nancy	Assoc	298-1330			PHD	86	Nebraska	1986
Brakefield, James	Asst	298-1342			PHD	90	Buffalo	1990
Dobson, Joseph	Asst	298-1071			ADD	90	Wash U	1990
Fields, W. Calvin III	Asst	298-1010			PHD	86	Tx-Dallas	1986
Nwachukwu, Osita	Asst	298-1627			PHD	87	Miss	1987
Ashenhuret, Anthony	Inst	298-1453			JD	79	Drake	1979
Buller, Charlotte	Inst	298-1535			MS	77	Fla Tech	1977
Sendry, Jeanett	Inst	298-1535			PHD	77	UCLA	1977
Smith, Fred	Inst	298-1625			MBA	87	W Illin	1987

Western Kentucky University Bowling Green KY 42101 (502) WKYUVM 1982
College of Business — 1526 Russelville Road — FAX= — BS
Brown, J. Michael — Dean 745-3893 — Econ PHD 71 Kentucky 1988
–Department of Management Phone 745-5408 Fax 745-3893

Name	Rank	Phone			Degree		School	Year
Galloway, Rex F.	C-Pr	745-2421	13	DI	DBA	70	Miss St	1991
Busch, Edgar T.	Prof	745-2424	13	DI	PHD	70	Arkansas	1979
Evans, Eugene E.	Prof	745-5408	4	K	PHD	63	Illinois	1965
Ferguson, Wade	Prof	745-2918	7	V	PHD	77	Ohio St	1985
Finley, Lawrence K.	Prof	745-2480	36	ST	PHD	71	Ohio St	1977
Rahim, M. Afzalur	Prof	745-2499	2	EFH	PHD	76	Pitt	1983
Buntzman, Gabriel F.	Assoc	745-5329	13	CDI	PHD	83	N Carol	1983
Reber, Robert A.	Assoc	745-2490	15	NPQ	PHD	82	LSU	1982
Sullivan, Brian	Assoc	745-2522	4	K	JD	72	Kentucky	1976
Mohamed, Zubair	Asst	745-6360	7	U	PHD	91	Kentucky	1989
Graham, Carol	Inst	745-5851	15	N	ABD	94	Vanderbt	1992

Western Michigan University Kalamazoo, MI 49008-3806 (616) GW.WMICH 1970,1981
Haworth College of Bus — FAX=387-5710 — BBA,MS
Vellenga, David — Dean 387-5050 — Mktg
–Department of Management Phone 387-5860 Fax 387-5710

Name	Rank	Phone	code			Degree		School	Year
Golhar, Damodar Y.	C-Pr	387-5966	golhar	7	UV	PHD	83	Michigan	1984
Beam, Henry H.	Prof	387-5986	beam	37	ISB	PHD	75	Michigan	1975
Farrell, Daniel	Prof	387-5956	farrell			PHD		Iowa	1980
Keenan, J. Michael	Prof	387-5928	keenan	12	NORZ	PHD	65	Ohio St	1968
Rizzo, John R.	Prof	387-5951	rizzo	25	EGFP	PHD	64	Ohio St	1969
Stamm, Carol Lee	Prof	387-5826	stamm	7	UV	PHD	74	Wiscon	1981
Alie, Raymond E.	Assoc	387-5981	alie	43	EHJY	EDD	80	W Mich	1979
Carey, Thomas A.	Assoc	387-5969		36	IS	EDD	75	W Mich	1974
Deshpande, Satish	Assoc	387-5998	deshpand	5	NPQS	PHD	90	Iowa	1990
Verser, Gertrude	Assoc	387-5964		32	TSNP	DBA	78	Harvard	1985
Ahire, Sanjay	Asst	387-5423		7	UV	PHD	92	Alabama	1992
Flanagan, David	Asst	387-6051		38	IY	PHD	92	Indiana	1992
Landeros, Robert	Asst	387-5988	landeros	73	UOZ	PHD	88	Mich St	1989
Milman, Claudio	Asst	387-5839		38	IY	PHD	92	Ohio St	1992
Waller, Matthew	Asst	387-5928	waller			PHD	93	Penn St	1993

Western New England College Springfield, MA 01119-2684 (413) WNEC.BITNET
School of Business — 1256 Wilbraham Road — FAX=782-3111 — BS,MBA MS
Kowalski, Stanley Jr. — Dean 782-1224 — Econ PHD 76 Mass 1973
–Department of Management Phone 782-1505 Fax 782-3111

Name	Rank	Phone	code			Degree	School	Year
Schwartz, Ned S.	C-Ac	782-1496	nschwartz	3	I	JD	Emory	1979
Bazan, Henry J.	Prof	782-1254	hbazan	2	FG	MA	Mass	1964
Chelte, Anthony F.	Prof	782-1553	achelte	5	Q	PHD	Mass	1982

Name	Rank	Phone	Email	#	Code	Degree	Yr	School	Year
Fanelli, Russell	Prof	782-1558	rfanelli	2	E	PHD		Renssela	1982
Ferris, William P.	Prof	782-1629	wferris	5	N	PHD		Renssela	1981
Hess, Peter W.	Prof	782-1389	phess	2	E	EDD		Mass	1980
Brown, Fredrick W.	Assoc	782-1280	fbrown	4	LJ	MBA		WNEC	1962
Shrage, Harvey M.	Assoc	782-1719	hshrage	5	QK	JD		Northeas	1988
Siciliano, Julie	Asst	782-1786	jsiciliano	3	I	PHD		Mass	1990

Western State College of CO — Gunnison, CO 81231 — (303) WSC.COLORADO.EDU
Dept of Bus & Acctg — FAX=943-2212 — BS

Name	Rank	Phone	Email	#	Code	Degree	Yr	School	Year
Klingsmith, Phil C.	C-Pr	943-2040		4		JD	79	Calif We	1980
—Management Faculty	Phone		Fax 943-7042						
Drexel, Cynthia	Prof	943-2125		79		PHD	90	Brig Yg	1982
Hahn, F. James	Prof	943-3110		4		JD	66	Wiscon	1969
Pribyl, Frank J.	Prof	943-3000		8		PHD	76	North Tx	1967
Burkhardt, Peter H.	Assoc	943-2095		12		JD	65	Minn	1989
Couch, T. Grantham	Assoc	943-2870		3		PHD	92	Fla St	1992
Haverly, Frederick S.	Assoc	943-2105		13		MBA	66	Syracuse	1977
Herz, Paul	Assoc	943-2299		7		ABD	93	Utah St	1987
Liesz, Thomas J.	Assoc	943-3055		16		PHD	89	Idaho	1990
Newman, Monica J.	Assoc	943-2183		7		PHD	88	Texas	1990
Newman, Scott G.	Assoc	943-2116		7		PHD	86	Texas	1989

Western Washington Univ — Bellingham, WA 98225-5996 — (206) WWU.EDU — 1990,1990
College of Bus & Econ — 516 High Street — FAX=650-4844 — BA

Name	Rank	Phone	Email	#	Code	Degree	Yr	School	Year
Murphy, Dennis R.	Dean	650-3896			Econ	PHD	74	Indiana	1979
—Department of Management	Phone	650-2902	Fax 650-4844						
Wonder, Bruce D.	C-Ac	650-3908		5	NOEL	PHD	71	Wash	9-81
Garcia, Joseph E.	Prof	650-3916	garcia	28	EFA	PHD	83	Utah	9-85
Keleman, Ken S.	Prof	650-4805	keleman	25	EPZ	PHD	76	Utah	9-77
Owens, Eugene	Prof	650-2905		15	DFNQ	PHD	70	UCLA	1975
Plumlee, E. Leroy	Prof	650-4808		41	JLMF	PHD	71	Tx Tech	9-76
Haug, Peter	Assoc	650-4807		78	UY	PHD	78	U Wash	9-86
Petersen, Lois E.	Assoc	650-4809		19	ZR	EDD	76	N Dakota	9-74
Springer, Mark	Assoc	650-4806		7	UX	PHD	88	Vanderbt	9-87
Warner, Daniel	Assoc	650-3390		4	KM	JD	75	U Wash	9-84
Kelley, Patricia C.	Asst	650-3389		43	IJLM	DBA	88	Boston U	1990

Westfield State College — Westfield, MA 01086 — (413) RCN
Dept of Econ & Bus Mgt — FAX=562-3613 — BS

Name	Rank	Phone	Email	#	Code	Degree	Yr	School	Year
Ettman, Philip	C-Ac	572-5695		45		JD		Boston U	1982
—Management Faculty	Phone	572-5590	Fax 562-3613						
Daniel, Cornelia	Asst	572-5696				PHD		Mass	1990
Knipes, Bradford	Asst	572-5574				PHD		Mass	1988
McFarlin, Thomas	Asst	572-5314				MBA		W New En	1978
Sullivan, Kathryn	Asst	572-5592				PHD		Mass	1992

Wichita State University — Wichita, KS 67260-0088 — (316) TWSUVM — 1968,1974
Barton School of Bus — 1845 North Fairmount — FAX=689-3770 — BBA,MBA

Name	Rank	Phone	Email	#	Code	Degree	Yr	School	Year
Graham, Gerald H.	Dean	689-3200		12	EPNT	PHD	67	LSU	9-67
—Department of Management	Phone	689-3214	Fax 689-3845						
Belt, John A.	C-As	689-3214		52	NPEO	PHD	71	Tx Tech	9-71
Desilva, Dharma	Prof	689-3214		84	LYS	PHD	66	Indiana	9-79
Fatehi-Sedeh, Kamal	Prof	689-3214	fatehi	38	IY	PHD	76	LSU	6-83
Lengnick-Hall, Cynthia	Prof	689-3214	clengnic	32	HINT	PHD	81	Texas	9-90
Bereman, Nancy	Assoc	689-3214	bereman	52	NPQK	PHD	83	Minn	1-80
Lengnick-Hall, Mark	Assoc	689-3214	mlengnic	25	ENPR	PHD	88	Purdue	9-90
Duval, Margaret	Asst	689-3214		36	TCEF	ABD		Texas	9-94
Sanders, Martha	Asst	689-3214		25	EFNP	PHD	91	Ohio St	9-91
Wolff, James	Asst	689-3214		32	HIY	ABD		Wash St	9-94

Widener University — Chester, PA 19013-9987 — (610)
School of Management — 14th Street — FAX=876-6598 — BS,MS

Name	Rank	Phone	Email	#	Code	Degree	Yr	School	Year
DiAngelo, Joseph A. Jr.	Dean	499-4301		5	N	EDD	87	Temple	1980
—Department of Management	Phone		Fax 876-6598						
Ozatalay, Savas	H-Pr	499-4319				PHD		Northwes	
Meli, John T.	Prof	499-1175				PHD	71	Penn	
Reilley, Bernard James	Prof	499-4325				PHD		Geo St	
Salam, Ahmad W.	Prof	499-4315				PHD	68	Illinois	
Bender, Douglas	Assoc	499-4325				PHD		Jeff Med	
Kyj, Myroslaw J.	Assoc	499-4368				PHD		Temple	
Laker, Dennis R.	Assoc	499-4512				PHD		Illinois	
Mansur, Iqbal	Assoc	499-4321				PHD		Cinn	
Marshall, Paul S.	Assoc	499-1174				PHD		Bath	
Pal, Surenda	Assoc	499-4312				PHD		Penn	
Saad, Germaine	Assoc	499-1177				PHD		Penn	

Shimko, Barbara	Assoc	499-4288				PHD		Wash	
Vlahovich, Vladimir	Assoc	499-1179				PHD		Penn	
Antonucci, Yvonne	Asst	499-4330				MS		Lehigh	
Tucci, Louis	Asst	499-4510				PHD			
Lacy, Joyce	Inst	499-4368				MBA			

Wilkes University — Wilkes-Barre, PA 18766 — (717) WILKES1.WILKES.EDU
Sch Bus, Society & PPol — 170 South Franklin St — FAX=

Giamartino, Gary A.	Dean	831-4700	gglamar	28	YTE	PHD	79	Vanderbt	7-93
—Business & Economics Dept	Phone	831-4725	Fax 831-4917						
Raspen, Richard G.	C-Ac	831-4702	rraspen	12	&EJL	PHD		Penn	7-67
Taylor, Wagiha A.	Prof	831-4712		8	Y	PHD		Clark	6-69
Batory, Anne H.	Assoc	831-4719		68	RTY	PHD		Maryland	9-87
Engel, Theodore	Assoc	831-4338		7	UV	MA		U Miami	9-66
Liuzzo, Anthony L.	Assoc	831-4709		45	KQ	PHD		NYU	9-90
Peper, Merle J.	Assoc	831-4706	mpeper	12	BHIY	PHD		LSU	9-89
Schwartz, Ronald D.	Assoc	831-4715	rschwar	79	UVXZ	PHD		Akron	9-90
Seeley, Robert D.	Assoc	831-4717		5	Q	PHD		Maryland	9-89
Latzko, David	Asst	831-4718	dlatzko	57	Q	PHD		Maryland	9-93
Loftus, Barbara S.	Asst	831-4703		6	DRT	PHD		Syracuse	9-91

Willamette University — Salem, OR 97301 — (503) WILLAMETTE.EDU
Atkinson Grad Sch Mgt — 900 State Street — FAX=370-3011 — MM

Weight, G. Dale	Dean	370-6440			Fnce	PHD	68	Oregon	1990
—Management Faculty	Phone	370-6440	Fax 370-3011						
Connor, Patrick E.	Prof	370-0440		2	EFGH	PHD	70	U Wash	1982
Gates, Bruce L.	Prof	370-6440		37	ISTV	PHD	71	Pitt	1974
Hand, Michael L.	Prof	370-6440		79	VZ	PHD	78	Iowa St	1979
Maser, Steven M.	Prof	370-6115		14	AJKL	PHD	75	Rochest	1978
Thompson, G. Fred	Prof	370-6440		14	ABJL	PHD	72	Claremont	1986

Grace and Elmer Goudy Professor of Public Management and Policy Analysis

Truitt, J. Frederick	Prof	370-6115		8	Y	DBA	69	Indiana	1991

Helen Simpson Jackson Professor of International Management

Powers, Kathleen J.	Assoc	370-6440		52	JNPQ	PHD	86	Florida	8-89

College of William & Mary — Williamsburg, VA 23185 — (804) — 1972,1974
School of Business Adm — Richmond Road — FAX=221-2937 — BBA,MBA

Page, Alfred N.	Dean	221-2890		8	Y	PHD	64	Chicago	1990
—Department of Management	Phone		Fax 221-2937						
Brown, Charlotte	D	221-2916							

Director of the PRC

Fulmer, Robert	Prof	221-2961		3	EI	PHD	65	UCLA	1991

W. Brooks George Professor of Business Administration

Sims, Ronald R.	Prof	221-2855		2	EFH	PHD	81	Case Wes	1986
Solomon, Robert	Prof	221-2870		5	N	PHD	75	Rochest	1975
Locke, Karen	Asst	221-2889		1	EF	PHD	89	Case Wes	1989

William Jewell College — Liberty, MO 64068-9988 — (816)
Business Department — 500 College Hill — FAX=781-3164 — AB,BS
phone 781-7700

Helsing, J. Eric	C-Pr	781-5698				JD		Rutgers	1988

A. Major & Dorthy Hull Chair of Communication Business & Leadership

—Management Faculty	Phone	Ext 5698	Fax 781-3164						
Miller, Otis	Prof	Ext 5703		37	U	PHD	62	Missouri	1978
Jacobsen, Lowell R. Jr.	Assoc	781-5693		36	T	PHD	86	Edinburg	1981
Colapietro, Vito	Asst	Ext 5674		24	Q	MA	71	Conn	1992
Harris, Kimberly H.	Asst	781-5704		79	U	MBA	78	Kansas	1986
Hoyt, Elizabeth R.	Asst	781-5702		32	IE	MBA	79	Wiscon	1981

Winona State University — Winona, MN 55987 — (507)
College of Business — FAX=457-5697 — BS

Gorman, Ken	Dean	457-5014			BusE	EDD		Illinois	1980
—Dept of Management & Mktg	Phone		Fax 457-5170						
Bjorke, JoEll W.	C-Pr	457-5188				JD	79	Wm Mitch	1981
Foegen, Joseph H.	Prof	457-5190				PHD		Wiscon	1958
Gander, Mary J.	Prof	457-5470				PHD		Wiscon	1987
Schmid, H. Giles	Prof	457-5173				PHD		U of M	1979
Wolfmeyer, Pamela	Prof	457-5189				MA		Wiscon	1969
Dewan, Shashi	Assoc	285-7448				PHD		India	1988
Rasch, Sara B.	Assoc	457-5197				PHD		Kansas	1988
Sinkiewicz, Anthony T.	Assoc	285-7131				DBA		US Intl	1987
McDaniel, James	Asst	457-5682				PHD		Tx Tech	1989

Winston-Salem State Univ — Winston-SalemNC 27110 — (910)
Division of Bus & Econ — 601 Martin Luther King Drive — FAX= — BS

Name	Title	Phone	Fax/email			Deg	Yr	School	Yr
Bailey, Willie H. Sr.	Dir	750-2330		6	T	PHD	74	Illinois	1986
—Department of Management	Phone	750-2338	Fax 750-2335						
Namit, Kal	Assoc	750-2352		7	U	PHD	78	Wiscon	
Taylor, Gregory	Assoc	750-2348							
Khojasteh, Mak	Asst	750-2357				DBA		US Intl	

Winthrop University — Rock Hill, SC 29733 — (803) WINTHROP.EDU — 1979,1983
School of Business Adm — FAX=328-3960 — BS,MBA

Name	Title	Phone	Fax/email			Deg	Yr	School	Yr
Padgett, Jerry H.	Dean	323-2185		13	IP	PHD	68	Purdue	1970
—Department of Management	Phone	323-2186	Fax 328-3690						
Perselay, Gerald	C-Pr	323-2186	perselayg	25	ENQ	DBA	70	Geo Wash	1978
Archer, Earnest R.	Prof	323-2186		23	DE	PHD		Georgia	1970
Kline, Robert S.	Prof	323-2186		12	P	EDD	70	Pitt	1970
Ward, Edna C.	Prof	323-2186		12	NP	EDD		Tenn	1975
Weikle, Roger D.	Prof	323-2186		52	NQ	PHD	85	S Carol	1982
Bradbard, David A.	Assoc	323-2186		9	VZ	EDD		Georgia	1987
Jones, Marilyn S.	Assoc	323-2186		7	UV	PHD		Va Tech	1989
Riddle, Emma Jane	Assoc	323-2186		7	UZYS	PHD		S Carol	1988
Woodruff, Charles K.	Assoc	323-2186		23	EI	PHD		Geo St	1980
Hacker, James O.	Asst	323-2186		1	C	MBA		San Fran	1990

U of Wisconsin-Eau Claire — Eau Claire, WI 54701-4004 — (715) UWEC — 1991
School of Business — 105 Garfield Avenue — FAX=836-2380 — BBA

Name	Title	Phone	Fax/email			Deg	Yr	School	Yr
Dock, V. Thomas	Dean	836-5509	dockv	9	Z	PHD	70	N Colo	7-92
--Department of Business Adm	Phone	836-3677	Fax 836-2944						
Sutton, Robert	C-Ac$	836-3677	suttonr		Mktg	PHD	84	Iowa	8-80
Bergmann, Thomas J.	Prof	836-4427	bergmantj		NQ	PHD		Minn	1975
Associate Dean									
Gunderson, Harvey S.	Prof	836-4107	gunderso		UVW	PHD		Wiscon	1974
Weil, D. Wallace	Prof	836-2962	weild		I	PHD		Wilmette	1971
Close, M. John	Assoc	836-4759			E	PHD		LSU	1975
DeMeuse, Kenneth P.	Assoc	836-2953	demeukp		EFP	PHD		Tenn	1990
Hostager, Todd J.	Assoc	836-2963	hostagtj		EI	PHD		Minn	1988
Lorentz, Richard D.	Assoc	836-5829	lorentrd		STI	PHD		N Colo	1971
Ready, Kathryn J.	Assoc	836-5354	readykj		QRNY	PHD		Iowa	1988
—Mgt Info Systems Dept	Phone	836-4320	Fax 836-4959						
Schillak, John R.	C-Pr	836-5243	schilak	9	Z	PHD	75	Wiscon	1973
Korn, Willard M.	Prof	836-3522	bkorn	9	Z	EDD	68	N Colo	1968
LaBarre, James E.	Prof	836-3416	jlabarre	9	Z	PHD	72	N Dakota	1970
Melrose, John E.	Prof	836-3053	melrose	9	Z	EDD	74	Montana	1970
Johnson, Dale A.	Assoc	836-3839	dajohn	9	Z	PHD		Wi-Milwa	1987
Jung, Jeong-Duk	Asst	836-3155	jungj	9	Z	DBA	93	Miss St	1991
Suh, Yung-Ho	Asst	836-5968	suhy	9	Z	PHD	91	Syracuse	1991

Univ of Wisconsin-Green Bay — Green Bay, WI 54311-7001 — (414) GBUAXA.UWGB.EDU
Business Administration — 2420 Nicolet Drive — FAX=465-2660 — BS,BA,MS

Name	Title	Phone	Fax/email			Deg	Yr	School	Yr
Bauer, Robert	Dean	465-2336							
—Management Faculty	Phone	465-2051	Fax 465-2660						
Zehms, Karl M.	C-Ac	465-2553			Atg	PHD	70	Wiscon	9-70
Harris, John	Assoc	465-2466	harrisj	12	EFGQ	PHD	81	Kentucky	1978
Troyer, Michael D.	Assoc	465-2434	troyerm	34	DIJT	PHD	75	Duke	1971
Sridhar, Sandhya	Asst	465-2004	sridhars	25	EFHN	PHD	88	Ohio St	1989
Arendt, Lucy	Lect	465-2495	arendtl	12	DEGH	MS	90	Wi-GrBay	1990

U of Wisconsin-La Crosse — La Crosse, WI 54601 — (608) — 1982,1987
College of Business — 1725 State Street — FAX= — BS,MBA

Name	Title	Phone	Fax/email			Deg	Yr	School	Yr
Fuller, Rex	Dean	785-8090			Econ	PHD	82	CS-Chico	8-81
—Department of Management	Phone	785-8110	Fax 785-6700						
Betton, John H.	C-Ac	785-8112				PHD	86	S Carol	
Abbey, Augustus	Prof					PHD	81	Arizona	
Keaton, Paul	Assoc	785-6662				PHD	78	Minn	
Kuffel, Thomas	Assoc	785-8699				PHD	79	Iowa	
Redel, Charles	Assoc	785-6669				JD		Wiscon	
Reis, Dayr	Assoc	785-6663				PHD		Mich St	
Ross, William	Assoc	785-8450				PHD		Illinois	
Wehrs, William E.	Assoc	785-8103				PHD	72	Purdue	1972
Willey, Susan	Assoc	785-6668				JD		Indiana	
Lynch, Brian	Asst				Z	PHD		SUNY-Buf	
Pati, Niranjan	Asst	785-8114				PHD		Nowthwes	
Pena, Leticia	Asst	785-6661				ABD		Harvard	
Bast, Karin	Lect	785-6660				MBA		Wis-LaCr	
Bowen, Barbara	Lect	785-6670				MBA		Wis-LaCr	
Petersen, Allan	Lect	785-6667				MBA		Wis-LaCr	

Univ of Wisconsin-Madison

Univ of Wisconsin-Madison	Madison, WI 53706	(608) WISCMACC		1916,1963
School of Business	750 University Avenue	FAX=263-0477		BBA,MBA,MS,PHD
Policano, Andrew J.	Dean 262-1555	PHD	76 Brown	1991
–Dept Management & Human Res	Phone	263-3460 Fax 262-8773		

Name	Rank	Phone	email			Deg		School	Year
Heneman, Herbert	C-Pr	263-3461	hheneman	5	ENQX	PHD	70	Wiscon	1970
Aldag, Ramon J.	Prof	263-3771	raldag	12	EGLX	PHD	74	Mich St	1974
Dunham, Randall	Prof	265-2343	rdunham	25	EGNX	PHD	75	Illinois	1975
Associate Dean									
Filley, Alan C.	Prof	263-1644		26	EHST	PHD	62	Ohio St	
Miller, Richard U.	Prof	263-7979	rumiller	5	NQ	PHD	66	Cornell	1971
Olson, Craig	Prof		colson	5	HINQ	PHD	79	Wiscon	1985
Prieve, E. Arthur	Prof	263-4161		1		DBA	65	Geo Wash	
Schwab, Donald P.	Prof	263-3473	dschwab		ENQX	PHD	68	Minn	
Miner, Anne S.	Assoc	263-4143	aminer	23	HI	PHD	85	Stanford	1985
Goodman, Robert	Asst			34	HIJS	PHD	88	Minn	1991
Haunschild, Pamela	Asst				EH	PHD	92	Car Mel	1992
Jehn, Karen	Asst			24	EHJ	PHD	93	Northwes	1994

Univ of Wisconsin-Milwaukee

Univ of Wisconsin-Milwaukee	Milwaukee, WI 53201	(414)		1970,1971
School of Business Adm	2500 E. Kenwood Blvd	FAX=229-6957		BBA,MS,MAT
Schenker, Eric	Dean 229-4235	PHD	57 Florida	1959
–Management Faculty	Phone Fax 229-6957			

Name	Rank	Phone			Deg		School	Year
Nystrom, Paul C.	Prof	229-4337	2	H	PHD	70	Minn	1969
Weber, C. Edward	Prof	229-6576	3	IJ	PHD	58	Princeton	1966
Yasai, Masoud	Assoc	229-4544	3	I	PHD	79	Cty Lond	1981
Barker, Vincent	Asst	229-6524	3	I	PHD	92	Illinois	1992
Chi, Tailan	Asst	229-5429	8	Y	PHD	90	Wash	1990
Crooker, Karen	Asst	229-4235	2	HE	ABD	94	Indiana	1994
Freeman, Sarah	Asst	229-6824	2	H	PHD	92	Michigan	1992
Mone, Mark A.	Asst	229-4355	2	H	PHD	88	Wash St	
Robbins, Shelley R.	Asst	229-6823	32	IH	PHD	89	Northwes	

Univ of Wisconsin-Oshkosh

Univ of Wisconsin-Oshkosh	Oshkosh, WI 54901-8678	(414) VAXA.CIS.UWOSH.EDU 1970,1978		
College of Business Adm	800 Algoma Boulevard	FAX=424-0010		BBA,MS,MBA
Milam, Robert L.	Dean 424-1424	9 U	PHD	68 N Car St	1984
–Dept of Mktg, Mgt & Hum Res	Phone 424-1437 Fax 424-7413			

Name	Rank	Phone			Deg		School	Year
Sibley, Stan	C	424-1013			PHD	72	Mich St	1972
Hartman, E. Alan	Prof	424-3441	26	ENOT	PHD	72	Mich St	1976
Feinauer, Dale M.	Assoc	442-4152	51	ACNP	PHD	83	Ohio St	1983
Hegedus, David M.	Assoc	424-0186	62	TE	PHD	81	MIT	1985
Tower, Burk	Assoc	424-0351	6	T	DBA	73	Kentucky	
Dedee, J. Kim	Asst	424-7199	3	I	PHD	85	Arkansas	1987
Gudmundson, Donald	Asst	424-7401	32	IHJS	ABD		Kentucky	1991
Hartenian, Linda	Asst	424-1395	5	NQX	PHD	91	Kentucky	1990
Lemke, Dwight	Asst	424-7191	34	IJ	ABD		Iowa	1991
Sridhar, B. S.	Asst	424-0199	23	EHJY	PHD	87	Ohio St	1989

Univ of Wisconsin-Parkside

Univ of Wisconsin-Parkside	Kenosha, WI 53141-2000	(414) CS.UWP.EDU		
School of Business	Wood Road	FAX=		BS,MBA
Brown, Richard D.	Dean 595-2243	Mktg	PHD	67 Illinois	7-93
–Dept of Administration Sci	Phone 595-2280 Fax 595-2680			

Name	Rank	Phone			Deg		School	Year
Rovelstad, James	Asst	595-2105		Mktg	PHD	70	Michigan	8-82
Dudycha, Arthur	Prof	595-2217	7	V	PHD	67	Ohio St	8-77
Hawk, Stephen R.	Assoc	595-2416	9	Z	PHD	87	Wiscon	8-93
Hudson, Roger	Assoc	595-2125	3	I	PHD	90	Minn	8-91
McArthur, Angeline	Assoc	595-2436	2	EH	PHD	88	Oregon	8-88
Rajan, Roby	Assoc	595-2413	7	VU	PHD	83	Va Tech	8-84
Sounderpandian, Jay	Assoc	595-2194	7	UVX	PHD	83	Kent St	8-83
Gee, Michele	Asst	595-2280	3	I	PHD	94	WI-Milwa	7-94
Norton, Sue	Asst	595-2193	5	OPQ	PHD	86	Iowa	8-90
Subramanian, Vankat	Asst	595-2163	9	Z	PHD	90	Kent St	8-87

U of Wisconsin-Platteville

U of Wisconsin-Platteville	Platteville, WI 53818-3099	(608) UWPLATT.EDU		
Coll Bus, Ind, & Comm		FAX=		
–Department of Business Adm	Phone 342-1465 Fax 342-1466			

Name	Rank	Phone	email			Deg		School	Year
White, Scott A.	C-Ac	342-1467	white	4	J	JD	79	Creighto	1980
Fidrych, Robert	Assoc	342-1305		4	J	LLM	79	Mo-KC	1980
Kleisath, Stephen	Assoc	342-1468	kleisath	25	E	DBA		Nova	1980
Schilling, Charles	Assoc	342-1717		1		PHD		St Louis	1980
Karsten, Margaret	Asst	342-1459	karsten	5	N	MBA	81	Wiscon	1981
Schroeder, Machelle	Asst	342-1459	schroeder	5	N	MBA		Wi-White	1990

U of Wisconsin-River Falls — River Falls, WI 54022-5001 (715)

College of Arts & Sci	410 South 3rd Street		FAX=425-3335					BA,BS
Prochnow, Neal	Dean	425-3366			Phys	PHD	Duke	9-64
–Dept of Business Adm	Phone	425-3335	Fax 425-3304					
Potts, Glenn	C							
Kim, Young J.	Prof	425-3335		23		PHD	Oklahoma	9-64
Huffman, Brian	Inst	425-3335				MS		
Kalina, Megan	Inst	425-3335				MS		

U of Wisconsin-Stevens Point — Stevens Point WI 54481-3897 (715)

Col of Letters & Sci			FAX=346-4277					BA,BS
Haine, James	C-Pr	346-2728		49	ZKJ	JD	75 Indiana	8-76
–Division of Business & Econ	Phone	346-2728	Fax 346-4215					
Gillo, Diane	Prof	346-3872		25	JLOR	EDD	82 Michigan	8-83
Judy, Richard B.	Prof	346-3770		3	ST	PHD	84 Indiana	1-85
Witte, Robert	Prof	346-3877		52	EH	PHD	67 Wiscon	8-87
Meyers, Martin	Assoc	346-3866		81	YD	MS	79 DePaul	8-86
Poutinen, Jay	Assoc	346-3160		1	D	MBA	68 Michigan	8-82

Univ of Wisconsin-Superior — Superior, WI 54880-2898 (715) UWSUPER.EDU

Business & Economics	1800 Grand Avenue		FAX=					BS
Did Not Respond-1993 Listing								
Abrahamsson, Bernhard	Dean	394-8209			Econ	PHD	Wiscon	1989
–Management Faculty	Phone		Fax 394-8454					
Williams, Barbara	C-Pr	394-8206				EDD	Utah St	1974
Garsombke, Diane J.	Assoc	394-8547	dgarsomb	23		PHD	83 Tenn	1991

U of Wisconsin-Whitewater — Whitewater, WI 53190-1790 (414)

College of Bus & Econ			FAX=472-4863					1974,1980 BBA,MS,MBA
Domitrz, Joseph	Dean	472-1343			Econ	PHD	71 S Illin	1976
–Department of Management	Phone	472-3964	Fax 472-4863					
Jacobson, Russell E.	C-Pr	472-3965		7	JUV	PHD	76 Mass	1976
Anderson, Peggy	Prof	472-3210		5	NRS	PHD	70 Illinois	1965
Benson, Gary	Prof	472-5680		6	JTY	PHD	77 Ariz St	1990
Geisler, Eliezer	Prof	472-3971		1	DITZ	PHD	79 Northwes	1988
Godiwalla, Yezdi	Prof	472-1958		1	CILY	PHD	77 Oklah St	1977
Gosenpud, Jerry	Prof	472-3956		1	EI	PHD	74 Case Wes	1980
Sauer, Robert	Prof	472-5456		5	ENQY	PHD	69 Wiscon	1965
Scharinger, Dale	Prof	472-3182		5	JNOP	DBA	64 Indiana	1964
Bramorski, Tom	Assoc	472-5444		7	UVWY	PHD	89 Iowa	1989
Goroff, Iza	Assoc	472-1468		9	UVWZ	PHD	68 Penn	1977
Larson, Lars Erik	Assoc	472-3983		1	ABHL	PHD	66 Cornell	1982
Leitheiser, Robert	Assoc	472-5005		9	EHXZ	PHD	88 Minnesot	1991
Madan, Manohar	Assoc	472-5455		7	UVWZ	PHD	88 Tenn	1989
Munro, David	Assoc	472-5004		9	JVZ	PHD	88 Wis-Milw	1989
Pulich, Marcia	Assoc	472-5442		5	NPQ	PHD	79 North Tx	1980
Sargent, George	Assoc	472-5734		9	DZ	PHD	75 Mich St	1987
Beal, Reginald	Asst	472-5445		6	EIST	ABD	93 Wis-Milw	1988
Clements, Christine	Asst	472-5443		2	EFHR	PHD	90 Arkansas	1990
Drago, William	Asst	472-3994		3	HILM	PHD	90 Arkansas	1990
Wagner, Richard	Asst	472-5478		5	FNPQ	PHD	90 Indiana	1990
Washbush, John	Asst	472-3902		1	BEHI	PHD	75 Marquett	1989
Hancock, P. Daniel	Lect	472-3950		7		MBA	72 Wis-Milw	1980
Sisak, James	Lect	472-5441		7	EUW	MBA	78 Wis-Whit	1981
Svanoe, Atlee	Lect	472-5735		9	Z	MBA	72 Wis-Whit	1972

Wittenberg University — Springfield, OH 45501 (513)

Dept of Business Adm	Ward Street at N. Wittenberg		FAX=327-6340					BA
Maurer, Wayne O.	C-Ac	327-7903			Atg	MBA	74 Wright	9-74
–Management Faculty	Phone		Fax 327-6340					
Vrooman, David M.	Prof	327-7905		3	B	PHD	75 Northwes	1974
Lucchesi, Carol Y.	Assoc	327-7932		2	NR	PHD	83 Georgia	1983
Stockstill, Lowell E.	Assoc	327-7903		4	KST	JD	82 Toledo	9-81
Lucchesi, Ronald P.	Asst	327-7911		7	UV	ABD	Georgia	1983

Wofford College — Spartanburg, SC 29303-3663 (803)

Dept of Econ & Atg	429 North Church Street		FAX=582-1816					BA,BS
No Management Faculty								
Stephenson, Matthew A.	C-Pr	597-4570			Econ	PHD	65 Tulane	1970

Woodbury University	Burbank, CA	91510-7846	(818)					
School of Business	7500 Glenoaks Boulevard		FAX=504-9320					
Richman, Marvin	Dean	767-0888				MBA	Chicago	9-93
–Management Faculty	Phone	767-0888	Fax 504-9320					
Dhiman, Satinder	Asst	767-0888		1	H	MBA	W Coast	9-92
Saba, Alexandra	Asst	767-0888		23	E	PHD	81 Stanford	4-93

Worcester Polytechnic Inst	Worcester, MA	01609-2280	(508) WPI.EDU					
Business	100 Institute Road		FAX=				BS,MBA,MS	
–Department of Management	Phone	831-5119	Fax 831-5720					
Vassallo, Helen	H	831-5119	vassallo	12	DEFG	PHD	67 Clark	8-82
Gerstenfeld, Arthur	Prof	831-5471	ag	6	DST	PHD	67 MIT	9-76
O'Connor, John T.	Prof	831-5452	jocoonor	1	C	PHD	70 Notre Dm	9-70
Onorato, Nicholas L.	Prof	831-5208	onorato	13	Y	PHD	59 Clark	9-55
Woods, Douglas W.	Prof	831-5451	dwwoods	1		PHD	70 MIT	9-70
Graubard, Leon S.	Assoc	831-5226	graubard	37	IY	ABD	67 Brown	9-69
Klein, Deiter	Assoc		dklein	14	C&U	PHD	73 Berkeley	9-79
Noonan, Francis	Assoc	831-5290	fnoonan	7	JMUV	PHD	73 Mass	9-78
Wimmergren, Lyle E.	Assoc	831-5450	lew	13	IST	MBA	57 Penn	9-69
Elmes, Michael B.	Asst	831-5182	mbelmes	12	DEFH	PHD	89 Syracuse	7-90
Johnson, Sharon	Asst	831-5183	sharon	7	UV	PHD	89 Cornell	7-88
Kasou, Chickery J.	Asst	831-5548	chick		S	PHD	91 Syracuse	7-90
Ross, Jeanne W.	Asst	831-5626	jross	9	Z	PHD	87 Wiscon	9-89
Ruhleder, Karen	Asst	831-5573	ruhleder	9	Z	PHD	91 Ca-Irvine	8-92

Wright State University	Dayton, OH	45435-0001	(513)				1974,1979	
Coll of Business & Adm	3640 Colonel Glen Highway		FAX=873-3545				BS,MBA	
Kumar, Rishi	Dean	873-3242			Econ	PHD	72 Wayne St	1974
–Department of Management	Phone	872-2290	Fax 873-3545					
Scherer, Robert F.	C-Pr	873-2290		25	EF	PHD	87 Miss	1991
Stickney, Frank A.	Prof	873-2327		3	EFG	PHD	69 Ohio St	1969
Owen, Crystal	Assoc	873-2390		2	EFN	PHD	87 Ohio St	1989
Petrick, Joseph A.	Assoc	873-2428		34	IJY	PHD	72 Penn St	1989
Wagley, Robert E.	Assoc	873-2085		34	AIJ	EDD	74 Cinn	1972
Wendt, Ann C.	Assoc	873-2468		5	QNR	PHD	87 Utah	1988
Baker, Francis	Asst	873-3001				PHD	84 Claremont	1990
Davy, Jeanette	Asst	873-2871		5	N	PHD	86 Arizona	1992
–Mgt Science & Info Systems	Phone	873-2895	Fax 873-3545					
Cox, Myron K.	C-Pr	873-2895		7	V	DSC	64 London	1969
Cleary, Michael J.	Prof	873-2230		7	V	PHD	71 Nebraska	1971
Demmy, W. Steven	Prof	873-2658		7	V	PHD	71 Ohio St	1975
Coleman, Joseph W.	Assoc	873-2648		7	VZ	PHD	82 Ariz St	1988
Constable, Gordon K.	Assoc	873-2719		7	U	PHD	72 Purdue	1971
Hobbs, Jon R.	Assoc	873-2216		7	Z	PHD	72 Stanford	1977
Lai, Andrew W.	Assoc	873-2441		7	V	PHD	74 Ohio St	1967
Polak, George G.	Assoc	873-3489		7	V	PHD	83 Car Mel	1988
Yen, Vincent C.	Assoc	873-3486		9	Z	PHD	75 Ohio St	1980
Denison, Barbara B.	Asst	873-2960		7	Z	MBA	74 Dayton	1976
Koop, Rebecca B.	Asst	873-2748		9	Z	PHD	94 Cinn	1992
Sanders, Nada R.	Asst	873-4079		7	U	PHD	86 Ohio St	1988
Xu, Li D.	Asst	873-3480		7	Z	PHD	86 Port St	1988
Chesen, Alan S.	Inst	873-4597		7	V	MBA	89 Wright	1993
Lumpkin, Joan B.	Inst	873-3304		9	Z	MBA	76 Dayton	1991
Weinstein, Larry	Inst	873-2890		7	Uz	MS	88 GMI	1993

University of Wyoming	Laramie, WY	82071-3275	(307) UWYO				1956,1982	
Coll of Commerce & Ind			FAX=766-5090				BS,MBA	
Forster, Bruce A.	Dean	766-4194			Econ	PHD	74 Australi	1987
–Dept of Management & Mktg	Phone	766-3124	Fax 766-4028					
McGann, Anthony F.	C-Pr	766-3124			Mktg	PHD	Missouri	8-71
Allen, Robert E.	Prof	766-6322		51	JNQD	PHD	SUNY-Buf	8-74
Associate Dean								
Jackson, John H.	Prof	766-5340		51	NPS	DBA	Colorado	8-73
Taylor, Samuel G.	Prof	766-6251		7	UVW	PHD	Ariz St	8-78
Greller, Martin	Assoc	766-3637		12	H	PHD	Yale	8-91
Jacobs, Lester	Assoc	268-2415				PHD		
at Casper Wyoming								
Snook-Luther, David C.	Assoc	766-6140		32	HID	PHD	Okla St	8-84
Varca, Philip E.	Assoc	766-3799		52	EGKY	PHD	LSU	8-89
Lindstrom, Grant L.	Asst	766-6288		31	IST	PHD	Utah	8-90
Lucero, Margaret A.	Asst	766-3263		52	NOE	PHD	Houston	8-90
Parks, Don M.	Asst	766-5260		36	IHTY	PHD	Tx A&M	8-88
Weatherford, Larry		766-3639		7	UVW	ABD	Virginia	8-91

Xavier University — Cincinnati, OH 45207-1096 — (513) XAVIER
College of Business — 3800 Victory Parkway — FAX=745-1954
Did Not Respond-1993 Listing

Name	Rank	Phone		Area	Deg	Yr	School	Yr
Geeding, Daniel W.	Dean	745-3528		Mgt	PHD	72	Cinn	1969
—Department of Management	Phone	745-3236	Fax 745-4383					
Eustis, Andrew C.	C-Ac	745-3429		26 ST	PHD	75	Cornell	1984
Clark, Thomas D.	Prof	745-2025		12 DES	PHD	76	Indiana	1981
Klekamp, Robert C.	Prof	745-3609		27 DU	PHD	77	Cinn	1963
Brodzinski, James D.	Assoc	745-2026		27 MUV	PHD	83	Ohio U	1993
Shriberg, Arthur	Assoc	745-4371		23 DEGS	EDD	72	Columbia	1982
Bycio, Peter	Asst	745-2027		15 EN	PHD	86	Bowl Gr	1987
Krishnan, Hema	Asst	745-3420		34 ILRY	PHD	93	Tenn	1993
Park, Daewoo	Asst	745-2028		23 DEFY	PHD	92	Tx A&M	1992
—Dept of Info & Dec Science	Phone		Fax 745-2929					
Thierauf, Robert J.	Prof	231-0431			PHD	66	Ohio St	1965

Yale University — New Haven, CT 06520-7368 — (203) 1991
Sch Organization & Mgt — 135 Prospect Street — FAX=432-6316 — MPPM,PHD

Name	Rank	Phone		Area	Deg	Yr	School	Yr
MacAvoy, Paul W.	Dean	432-6035		31 I	PHD	60	Yale	1991
Anand, Bharat				1	PHD	94	Princeton	1994
—Management Faculty	Phone	432-6035	Fax 432-5092					
Bracken, Paul	Prof	432-5962		8 Y	PHD	82	Yale	1981
Garstka, Stanley J.	Prof	432-6042		1 IS	PHD	70	Car Mel	1978
Marmor, Theodore R.	Prof	432-3238		1 A	PHD	66	Harvard	1979
Nalebuff, Barry	Prof	432-5968		1 IV	DPHL	83	Oxford	1989
Oster, Sharon M.	Prof	432-5969		1 IM	PHD	74	Harvard	1974
Swersey, Arthur J.	Prof	432-6057		7 UV	DENG	72	Columbia	1976
Vroom, Victor H.	Prof	432-6059		1 EFH	PHD	58	Michigan	1972
Feinstein, Jonathan	Assoc	432-5975		1 IM	PHD	87	MIT	1992
Kaplan, Edward H.	Assoc	432-6031		7 V	PHD	84	MIT	1989
Li, Lode	Assoc	432-5978		7 UV	PHD	84	Northwes	1988
Mason, Mark	Assoc	432-3235		8 Y	PHD	88	Harvard	1990
O'Neill, Barry	Assoc	432-6132		7 V	PHD	76	Michigan	1992
O'Regan, Katherine M.	Assoc	432-6024		1 A	PHD	90	Berkeley	1990
Ha, Albert	Asst	432-6056		7 UV	PHD	92	Stanford	1992
Strauss, Todd	Asst	432-6029		7 V	PHD	92	Berkeley	1992

Yeshiva University — New York, NY 10033-3299 — (212)
Sy Syms School of Bus — 500 West 185th Street — FAX=960-0055 — BS
No full-time Management faculty

Name	Rank	Phone		Area	Deg	Yr	School	Yr
Nierenberg, Harold	Dean	960-0845		Mgt	PHD	71	Columbia	2-92
—Management Faculty	Phone	960-0845	Fax 960-0824					

York College of Pennsylvania — York, PA 17403-3426 — (717) YORKCOL.EDU
Dept of Business Adm — Country Club Road — FAX=
phone 846-7788

Name	Rank	Phone		Area	Deg	Yr	School	Yr
Sherman, Hugh D.	C-As	Ext 497		38	PHD		Temple	1985
—Management Faculty	Phone		Fax 849-1607					
Sauers, Dale G.	Prof	Ext 255		7 UV	MBA		Houston	1978
Briercheck, Glenn F.	Assoc	Ext 4258		7 V	PHD		Conn	1975
Landis, Brook I.	Assoc	Ext 416		5	PHD		Cornell	1977
Craven, Thomas	Asst	Ext 348		5	MBA		Penn St	1982
Kline, Max E.	Asst	Ext 328		3 I	MS		Loyola C	1982
Meisenhelter, Christopher M.	Asst	Ext 404		14 JL	MBA		Baltimor	1987
Meisenhelter, Mary	Asst	Ext 277		5	MBA		Baltimor	1985
Sappington, Sidney	Asst	Ext 248		4 K	JD		Balitmor	

Youngstown State University — Youngstown, OH 44555-0001 — (216) YSUB
Williamson Sch Bus Adm — 410 Wick Avenue — FAX=742-1998 — BS,MBA

Name	Rank	Phone		Area	Deg	Yr	School	Yr
Cicarelli, James	Dean	742-3062		Econ	PHD	68	Conn	7-88
—Management Department	Phone		Fax 742-1998					
Kasuganti, Ram	C-Pr	742-3070		37 IUVX	DBA	76	Kent St	9-77
Arlow, Peter	Prof	742-7180		13 LR	PHD	79	Cinn	3-85
Daly, James	Prof	742-1890		15	MBA	72	Akron	9-72
Guzell, Stanley	Prof	742-3219		58	PHD	80	Pitt	9-79
Hovey, Donald	Prof	742-1855		2	PHD	62	Colorado	9-70
Karpak, Birsen	Prof	742-1892		7 UV	DBA	72	Istanbul	9-85
Katz, Louis	Prof	742-1887		4	JD	74	Clevelan	9-77
Krishnan, Rama	Prof	742-3177		3	PHD	67	American	9-69
McMahon, Anne	Prof	742-7241		13 REF	PHD	70	Mich St	9-83
Psenicka, Clement	Prof	742-1886		7 EUVX	DBA	76	Kent St	9-77
Sellaro, Louise	Prof	742-1893		23 EIN	PHD		Kent St	9-84
Fowler, Aubrey	Assoc	742-3124		57 NQP	PHD	84	Geo St	9-91
Granito, James	Assoc	742-3584		4 J	JD	63	Chicago	1-83
Rakestraw, Thomas L.	Assoc	742-1891		29 EX	PHD		Purdue	9-83
Wolanin, Robert	Assoc	742-1888		12	MA	60	Pitt	9-67
Wong, Bo	Assoc	742-1889		9 Z	PHD	90	Miss St	9-89
Dastoli, Anthony	Asst	742-3271		37	MBA	64	Pitt	9-69

CANADIAN SCHOOLS

University of Alberta — EdmontonCanada AB T6G 2R6 — (403) UALTAMTS — 1968,1973
Faculty of Business — 89 Avenue & 114 Street — FAX=492-3325 — BCOM,MBA,PHD
Did Not Respond-1993 Listing

Schneck, Rodney E.	Dean	492-2456		23	HIL	PHD	65	U Wash	1966
–Dept Organizational Analys	Phone		Fax 492-3325						
Greenwood, Royston	C	492-2797		23	HIS	PHD	76	Birm UK	1982
Brown, John Lewis	Prof	492-5777		23	HI	PHD	71	Cornell	1971
Field, Richard	Prof	492-5921		2	E	PHD	81	Toronto	1985
Gephart, Robert P.	Prof	492-5715		23	HI	PHD	79	Brit Col	1978
Hinings, C. Bob	Prof	492-2801		23	HI	BA	60	Leeds	1982
Nedd, Albert	Prof	492-2333		25	EN	PHD	70	Cornell	1970
Rasmussen, Raymond	Prof	492-2458		2	EM	PHD	70	Berkeley	1970
Cullen, Dallas M.	Assoc	492-5721		2	R	PHD	68	Ohio St	1970
Stratton-Devine, Kay	Assoc	774-9688		5	NQ	PHD	88	Wash St	1988
Townley, Barbara	Assoc	492-5883		5	NR	PHD	82	LSE UK	1990
Pant, Narayan	Asst	492-3949		3	HI	PHD	91	NYU	1991
Parkinson, David	Asst			38	HY			Penn	1993
Ryan, Allan	Asst			43	HI			Cornell	1993
Steier, Lloyd	Asst	492-5176		36	S	PHD	85	Alberta	1991
Usher, John	Asst	492-5721		23	HI	PHD	90	Toronto	1988
Wolfe, Richard A.	Asst	492-5826		23	D	PHD	89	Michigan	1988

Athabasca University — AthabascaCanada AB T0G 2R0 — (403)
Administrative Studies — FAX=676 4222 — BADM,BA,BGS,BN

Winter, George M.	Dean	675-6348		I		PHD	62	Iowa	1993
–Management Faculty	Phone		Fax 675-6338						
Khan, Andy	Prof	675-6195		4	K	MA	71	Keele	1986
Murgatroyd, Stephen	Prof	675-6197		2	EUH	PHD	87	Open	1986
Thomas, Dwight	Prof	675-6482		6	STY	DBA	75	Colorado	1980
Woudstra, Andrew	Prof	675-6188		91	Z	MBA	78	W Ontar	1981
Allan, Randi	Assoc	675-6130		2	&EFH	MBA	76	Toronto	1992
Cunningham, Craig	Assoc	675-6190		91		BCOM	76	Alberta	1979
Mahmoud, Mohamed	Assoc	675-6294		79	UV	PHD	79	Penn	1991
McGuire, Sharon	Assoc	675-6253		2	EFHJ	PHD	88	Alberta	1979
Pasis, Harvey	Assoc	675-6113		1	AI	MA	70	McMaster	1981
Spencer, Bruce	Assoc	675-6347		5	Q	MA	76	Warwick	1990
Annand, David	Asst	675-6193		91		MBA	78	Dalhous	1989
Chowdhury, Duha	Asst	675-6402		3	I	PHD	90	Kentucky	1990
Crocker, Kevin	Asst	675-6191		91		MBA	82	Windsor	1986
Jacobs, Mavis	Asst	675-6356		91		MBA	91	Alberta	1988
Marsden, Richard	Asst	675-6192		5	Q	PHD	94	Warwick	1983
Redpath, Lindsay	Asst	675-6130		2	EFH	PHD	92	Alberta	1992

Bishop's University — Lennoxvil Canada — J1M 1Z7 — (819) BISHOPS.CA
Faculty of Bus Adm — FAX=822-9661 — BBA,BABUS

–Management Faculty	Phone		Fax 822-9661						
Oldland, John	Prof	822-9600		36	ST	MBA		Indiana	1984
McRae, Lissa	Assoc	822-9600		12	E	MBA		St Marys	1987
Robson, Bill	Assoc	822-9600		12	DH	MBA		McMaster	1982
Bowey, Jim	Asst	822-9600		38	Y	MA		Lancastr	1993
Harvey, Steve	Asst	822-9600	sharvey	25	NPQ	PHD		Guelph	1994

Univ of British Columbia — Vancouver Canada — BC V6T 1Z2 (604) COMMERCE.UBC.CA
Faculty Comm & Bus Adm — 2075 Westbrook Mall — FAX=224-8489 — BCO,MBA,MSC,PHD
email: @1=unixg.ubs.ca; otherwise firstname.lastname@commerce.ubc.ca

Goldberg, Michael A.	Dean	822-8555		Y		PHD	68	Berkeley	1968
–Department of Management	Phone	822-8555	Fax 822-8468						
Amit, Raphael	Prof	822-8481		36	TSI	PHD	77	Northwes	1990
Atkins, Derek	Prof	822-9411		7	UV	PHD	72	Warwick	1976
Benbasat, Izak	Prof	822-8396	izak@1	9	Z	PHD	74	Minn	1974
Boardman, Anthony	Prof	822-8474		13	Ai	PHD	75	Car Mel	1979
Brander, James A.	Prof	822-8483		83	IYM	PHD	79	Stanford	1984
Brumelle, Shelby	Prof	822-8386		7	V	PHD	69	Berkeley	1969
deJong, Piet	Prof	822-8371	piet.dejong	7	V	PHD	75	LaTrobe	1982
Franot, Frieda	Prof	822-8376	frieda.grano	7	V	PHD	74	Texas	1975
Frost, Peter J.	Prof	822-8318	frost@1	2	EL	PHD	73	Minn	1975
Granot, Daniel	Prof	822-8432	daniel.grano	7	V	PHD	74	Texas	1978
Heaver, Trevor D.	Prof	822-4510	haver@1			PHD	66	Indiana	1960
MacCrimmon, K. R.	Prof	822-8350	kenneth.macc	3	I	PHD	65	UCLA	1970
Murnighan, J. Keith	Prof	822-8427	keith.murnig	2	EFHX	PHD	74	Purdue	1993
Oum, Tae	Prof	822-8320	tae.oum	Y		PHD	79	Brit Col	1983
Pinder, Craig C.	Prof	822-8374	craig.pender	2	EN	PHD	75	Cornell	1975
Pollay, Richard W.	Prof	822-8338	richard.poll	4		PHD	70	Chicago	1970
Puterman, Martin	Prof	822-8388	martin.puter	7	V	PHD	71	Stanford	1974
Queyranne, Maurice	Prof	822-8429		7	V	PHD	77	Grenoble	1983

Name	Rank	Phone	Email			Degree		Institution	Year
Schwab, Bernhard	Prof	822-8385	bernhard.sch	7	IV	PHD	67	UCLA	1968
Spencer, Barbara	Prof	822-8479	barbara.spen	83	YA	PHD	79	Car Mel	1985
Stanbury, William	Prof	822-8525	william.stan	13	AIL	PHD	72	Berkeley	1970
Thompson, Mark	Prof	822-8375	mark.thompso	5	QY	PHD	66	Cornell	1971
Vertinsky, Ilan	Prof	822-9406		38	AIVY	PHD	68	Berkeley	1970
Wehrung, Donald A.	Prof	822-8557	donald.wehru	37	IV	PHD	75	Stanford	1974
Weinberg, Charles B.	Prof	822-8327	chuck.weinbe	7		PHD	70	Columbia	1979
Ziemba, William	Prof	822-8382	william.ziem	7	V	PHD	69	Berkeley	1968
Ace, Merle	Assoc	822-8379	merle.ace	25	E	PHD	72	Minn	1970
Bemmels, Brian	Assoc	822-8372	brian.bemmel	5	Q	PHD	84	Minn	1992
Chen, Hong	Assoc	822-8360	hchen@1	7	V	PHD	87	Stanford	1989
Dexter, Albert	Assoc	822-9402	aldexter@1	9	Z	PHD	70	Columbia	1971
Frank, Murray	Assoc	822-8480	murry.frank	31	IL	PHD	86	Queen's	1988
Gerlach, Michael L.	Assoc	822-8384	michael.gerl	28	Y	PHD	87	Yale	1993
Goldstein, Robert	Assoc	822-8389	goldstei@1	9	Z	DBA	74	Harvard	
Jennings, P. Devereaux	Assoc	822-8383	dev.jennings	2	HN	PHD	89	Stanford	1988
Knight, Tom	Assoc	822-8370	tom.knight	5	Q	PHD	82	Cornell	1982
McCormick, Thomas	Assoc	822-8426	thomas.mccor	7	V	PHD	83	Stanford	1989
McPhillips, David	Assoc	822-8441	david.mcphil	54	QK	LLM	79	Brit Col	1975
Moore, Larry F.	Assoc	822-8381	larry.moore	2	NYE	DBA	65	Colorado	1965
Nemetz, Peter	Assoc	822-8443	peter.nemetz	34	IM	PHD	73	Harvard	1973
Ross, Thomas	Assoc	822-8478	tross@1	12	ALI	PHD	81	Penn	1992
Tomlinson, William	Assoc	822-8434	william.toml	8	Y	PHD	68	MIT	1970
Tretheway, Michael	Assoc	822-8322	mike.trethew		Y	PHD	81	Wiscon	1983
Tse, David	Assoc			8	Y	PHD	84	Berkeley	1984
Uyeno, Dean H.	Assoc	822-8392	dean.uyeno	7	UV	PHD	71	Northwes	1971
Walter, Gordon A.	Assoc	822-8351	gordon.walte	2	EJH	PHD	71	Berkeley	1970
Wand, Yair	Assoc	822-8395	yair.wand	9	Z	DSC	77	IsraelIn	1986
Waters, W. G. II	Assoc	822-8330	bill.waters			PHD	69	Wiscon	1969
Ansari, Asim	Asst	822-8362	asim.ansari	7		PHD	93	NYU	1993
Cockburn, Iain	Asst	822-8476	iain.cockbur	31	IA	PHD	90	Harvard	1989
Head, Keith	Asst	822-8492	keith.head	81	YA	PHD	91	MIT	1991
Langton, Nancy	Asst	822-8393	nancy.langto	2	HER	PHD	84	Stanford	1988
McCabe, Brendan	Asst	822-8394	brendan.mcca	7	V	PHD	89	Amsterda	1989
Rao, V. Srinivasan	Asst	822-8368	chino.rao	9	Z	PHD	90	Texas	1990
Ries, John	Asst	822-8493	john.ries	81	YA	PHD	90	Michigan	1990
Siddarth, Sivaramakrishnan	Asst	822-8329	sivaramakris	7		PHD	92	UCLA	1992
Tombak, Mihkel	Asst	822-8482		73	UI	PHD	88	Penn	1991
Woo, Carson	Asst	822-8390	woo@1	9	Z	PHD	88	Toronto	1991
Booth, Mary Ann	Lect	822-8495	mary-ann.boo	4	K	LLB	85	Brit Col	1989
Graham, Brian	Lect	822-8435	brian.graham	7		MBA	84	Brit Col	1984
McIntosh, Ellen	Lect	822-8487	ellen.mcinto	4	K	LLM	91	Alberta	1987
Meridith, Deborah J.	Lect	822-8440	deborah.mere	4	K	LLM	87	Brit Col	1980

Brock University	St CatharinesCda	ON L2S 3A1	(905)	SPARTAN.AC.BROCKU.CA					
Faculty of Business	600 Glenridge Avenue		FAX=984-4188				BBA,BACTG,BBE		

Did Not Respond-1993 Listing; phone 688-5550

Name	Rank	Phone	Email			Degree		Institution	Year
Barker, Tansu	Dean	Ext 3921	tbarker	8	Y	DBA		Istanbul	1988
—Department of Management	Phone	Ext 3994	Fax 984-4188						
Whitehead, J. David	C-Ac	Ext 3449	jwhite	25	Q	PHD		Western	1987
Liddell, William W.	Prof	Ext 3901		12	EFHE	PHD		Penn St	1981
Loucks, Kenneth E.	Prof	Ext 3448	keloucks	13	IST	PHD		Western	1986
Austin, Barbara J.	Assoc	Ext 3896		3	BEFI	PHD		Concorda	1983
Kaciak, Eugene	Assoc	Ext 3902	ekaciak	79	UVZ	DECO		Warsaw	1989
Levanoni, Eli	Assoc	Ext 3450	elevanon	25	EFGH	PHD		Toronto	1979
Metcalfe, Brian	Assoc	Ext 3132	bmetcalf	8	Y	PHD		Queens	1981
Mulligan, Thomas M.	Assoc	Ext 3904	tmulliga	49	JZ	PHD		Northwes	1987
Prout, Howard W.	Assoc	Ext 3546	hprout	7	UW	PHD		Western	1984
Sales, Carol A.	Assoc	Ext 3905	csales	25	EFGH	PHD		Waterloo	1979
Thomas, Mark J.	Assoc	Ext 3908		25	ENH	PHD		New York	1983
Yannopoulos, P. Peter	Assoc	Ext 3909	pyannop	7	U	PHD		Toronto	1983
Davis, J. Bradley	Lect	Ext 3899		1		MBA		York	1986
Mason, E. Sharon	Lect	Ext 3903		25	EFLZ	PHD		Toronto	1991

University of Calgary	Calgary, Canada	AB T2N 1N4	(403)	ACS.UCALGARY.CA				1985,1985	
Faculty of Management			FAX=282-0095				BCOM,MBA,PHD		

Name	Rank	Phone	Email			Degree		Institution	Year
Maher, P. Michael	Dean	220-5689	14011		Mgt	PHD	70	Northwes	
—Management Area	Phone	220-5685	Fax 282-0095						
Javidan, Mansour	C-Pr	220-8244	mjavidan	3	I	PHD	83	Minn	1990
Licker, Paul	C-Pr	220-3375	licker	9	Z	PHD	77	Penn	1981
Ponak, Allen	C-Pr	220-7584	ponak	5	Q	PHD	77	Wiscon	1982
Bayer, Max	Prof	220-7163	bayer	7	UVX	PHD	72	Toronto	1968
Cahoon, Allan	Prof	220-7583	cahoon	25	EFNR	PHD	74	Syracuse	1974
Chrisman, James J.	Prof	220-7247		6	T	PHD	86	Georgia	1993
Lane, George	Prof	220-6683		34	ILM	PHD	69	U Wash	1974
McMullan, Ed	Prof	220-7143		6	T	PHD	75	Brit Col	1973
Munro, Malcolm	Prof	220-7147	munro	9	Z	PHD	75	Minn	1974
Newsted, Peter	Prof	220-6883	newsted	9	Z	PHD	71	Car Mel	1977

Robinson, James	Prof	220-7150	jmrobino	13	DI	PHD	65	Ohio St	1967
Rowney, J. I. A.	Prof	220-6592		25	FNR	PHD	75	Calgary	1978
Schulz, Robert	Prof	220-6591	schulz	36	IT	PHD	71	Ohio St	1973
Silver, Edward	Prof	220-6996	esilver	7	UVX	PHD	63	MIT	1981
Azim, Ahmed	Assoc	220-6116		24	EHL	PHD	72	Illinois	1971
Chin, Wynne	Assoc	220-3732	chin	9	Z	PHD	91	Michigan	1990
Conway, H. Allan	Assoc	220-7458		13	ID	DBA	83	Harvard	1986
Dugan, Sloane	Assoc	2207582	dugan	25	FOP	PHD	81	Syracuse	1980
Falkenberg, Loren	Assoc	220-7172		54	QJLR	PHD	81	Illinois	1985
Graham, Jim	Assoc	220-7149		6	ST	PHD	78	W Ontari	1976
Gupta, Ashis	Assoc	220-6723	agupta	38	IY	PHD	78	Boston	1978
Janz, Tom	Assoc	220-7303		5	NP	PHD	76	Minn	1982
Pablo, Amy	Assoc	220-8537	apablo	2	IH	PHD	91	Texas	1991
Prasad, Pushkala	Assoc	220-8803		28	EH	PHD	92	Mass	1993
Robinson, Peter	Assoc	220-6115		6	ST	PHD		Brig Yg	1992
Russell, Randy	Assoc	220-3368		7	U	PHD		Ohio St	1993
Ursacki, Terry	Assoc	220-3358	ursabki	8	Y	PHD	91	Brit Col	1990
Waters, Donald	Assoc	220-7784	cdwaters	7	UVX	PHD	86	Strathcl	1987
Weber, Myron	Assoc	220-7145		25	NQ	PHD	86	Minn	1975
Woiceshyn, Jaana	Assoc	220-7705	jmwoices	34	IJ	PHD	88	Penn	1987
Zerbe, Wilfred J.	Assoc	220-7142	zerbe	25	FN	PHD	88	Brit Col	1987
Balakrishnan, Jaydeep	Asst	220-7844	balakris	7	UV	PHD	91	Indiana	1990
Cottrell, Thomas	Asst	220-5947	cottrell	3	I	ABD		Berkeley	1993
Daellenbach, Urs	Asst	220-8523		3	I	PHD	93	Purdue	1992
Enns, Van	Asst	220-7164		7	U	PHD	91	Minn	1991
Gopal, Abhijit	Asst	220-7432	gopal	9	Z	PHD	91	Georgia	1990
Hayne, Stephen	Asst	220-7161	schayne	9	Z	PHD	90	Arizona	1990
Marcolin, Barbara	Asst	220-6975		9	Z	PHD	93	Western	1993
Martello, Bill	Asst	220-8632	wcimartel	3	I	ABD		Pitt	1993
Pollard, Carol	Asst	220-7477		9	Z	ABD		Pitt	1991
Rohleder, Tom	Asst	220-7159	rohleder	7	U	PHD	91	Minn	1991
Fraser, Michele	Inst	220-7847	mfraser	25	EN	PHD	82	Minn	1990
Murch, Ron	Inst	220-3814	murch	9	Z	MBA		Calgary	1985
Stewart, Carol	Inst	220-6112	conlin	38	IY	MBA		Lancastr	1982

Carleton University Ottawa, Canada ON K1S 5B6 (613) CARLETON.CA
School of Business FAX =
  Did Not Respond-1993 Listing
Thomas, D. Roland D-Ac 788-2384 rolandth Mgt PHD Imperial
—Management Faculty Phone 788-2388 Fax 788-2532

Gerwin, D.	Prof			7	U	PHD	Car Mel
Haines, G.	Prof					PHD	Car Tech
Bailetti, A.	Assoc					PHD	Cinn
Callahan, J.	Assoc					PHD	Toronto
Cray, D.	Assoc			8	Y	PHD	Wiscon
Kersten, G.	Assoc			7	V	PHD	Warsaw
Kiggundu, M.	Assoc			28	EY	PHD	Toronto
Kirk, F.	Assoc			38	IY	PHD	N Carol
Kumar, U.	Assoc			9	Z	PHD	Kanpur
Kumar, V.	Assoc			7	U	PHD	Manitoba
Lawson, W.	Assoc					PHD	York
Michalowski, W.	Assoc					PHD	Warsaw
Papadopoulos, Nick	Assoc			8	Y	DBA	Athens
Weber, W.	Assoc			5	N	PHD	Car Mel
Compeau, D.	Asst			9	Z	PHD	W Ontar
Duxbury, L.	Asst			9	Z	PHD	Waterloo
Hobbs, C.	Asst			79	VZ	PENG	Ontario
Lee, I.	Asst			3	I	PHD	Carleton
Mallory, G.	Asst					PHD	Brandon
Dyke, L.	Lect			2	E	PHD	Queens

Concordia University Montreal, Canada PQ H3G 1M8 (514)
Faculty Commerce & Adm 1455 deMaisonneuve Blvd West FAX = 848-8645 BCOM,MBA,D
Ross, C. A. Dean$ 848-2703 PHD 82 W Ontar 1985
—Department of Management Phone Fax 848-8645

Ibrahim, A. B.	C-Pr	848-2925	gm 503-35	36	IST	PHD	82	Concorda	1982
Appelbaum, S. H.	Prof	848-2906	gm503-01						
Baba, V. V.	Prof	848-2933	gm500-19						
Editor-in-Chief, CJAS									
Crawford, R.	Prof	848-2910	gm503-09						
Jamal, M.	Prof	848-2935	ch233						
Johns, G.	Prof								
Kelly, J.	Prof	848-2912	gm503-15						
Argheyd, K.	Assoc	848-2917	gm503-19						
Ashforth, B.	Assoc		gm503-19						
Brunet, J. P.	Assoc	848-2932	gm407-07						
Director EMBA									

Carney, M.	Assoc	848-2960	gm903-15
Director M.Sc. (Admin)			
Dyer, L.	Assoc	848-2936	gm503-31
Franklin, M.	Assoc	848-2915	gm503-18
Lande, R.	Assoc	848-2780	gm503-25
McGuire, J.	Assoc		
Molz, R.	Assoc	848-2913	gm503-11
Oppenheimer, R.	Assoc	848-2934	ch202-04
Pitsiladis, P. E.	Assoc	848-2908	gm503-07
Prince, J. B.	Assoc	848-2778	gm500-15
Rajan, G. S.	Assoc	848-2918	gm503-21
Sen, J.	Assoc	848-2919	gm500-11
Taylor, W.	Assoc	848-2963	fb811
Director, AMBA			
Waldman, D.	Assoc	848-2988	gm500-13
Hebert, L.	Asst	848-2946	gm503-23
Lituchy, T.	Asst	848-2911	gm503-13
Saks, A.	Asst	848-2909	gm503-03
Sovik, N.	Asst	848-2783	gm503-27

Dalhousie University Halifax, Canada NS B3H 1Z5 (902) EARTH.SBA.DAL.CA
School of Business Adm 6152 Coburg Road FAX=494-1107 MBA
  Human Resource Mgt Dept Did Not Respond

McNiven, James D.	Dean	494-7080			Econ	PHD	Michigan	1988
–Human Resource Mgt	Phone		Fax 494-1107					
Grude, Jan K.	C-As			2	E	PHD	London	
Sankar, Yassin	Prof					PHD	JHopkins	
Duffy, Jack F.	Assoc			2	E	PHD	Iowa St	
Mealiea, Laird W.	Assoc			2	E	PHD	Mass	
Patton, Donald J.	Assoc			8	Y	DBA	Indiana	
Shafai, Yaghoub	Assoc			2	E	PHD	Mich St	1980
–Management & Info Sciences	Phone		Fax 494-1107					
Gassmann, Horand I.	C-Ac			7	V	PHD	Brit Col	
MacLean, Leonard	Prof			9	V	PHD	Dalhousi	1975
Martin, Michael J. C.	Prof			7	V	PHD	Sheffiel	
Archibald, Blyth C.	Assoc			7	V	PHD	Waterloo	
Larsson, Stig O.	Assoc			7	V	PHD	Brit Col	
Sheridan, Donald P.	Assoc			9	Z	PHD	Alberta	
Pinter, Janos				9	Z	PHD	82 MoscowSt	
Ireland, Alice				9	Z	PHD	Dalhous	
–Business Policy	Phone	494-7080	Fax 494-1107					
Blunden, Robert G.	C-Ac	494-7080	blunden	36	IT	PHD	W Ontar	
Klapstein, Raymond E.	Assoc	494-7080	klapstein	3	I	LLM	Osgoode	
Baltazar, Ramon G.	Asst	494-7080	baltazar	23	HI	ABD	W Ontari	

Ecole des Hautes Etudes Com Montreal, Canada PQ H3T 1V6 (514)
School of Business 5255 avenue Decelles FAX=340-5635 BAA,MSC,MBA,PHD
Guertin, Jean Dean DBA

–Dept of Management	Phone		Fax 340-5635					
Seguin, Francine	D-Pr	340-6338		12	H	PHD	Harvard	
Zanibbi, Louis	D-Ac	675-1151				PHD	88 Bradford	7-79
Archambault, Guy	Prof	340-6698		12	DHN	MBE	Harvard	
Chanlat, Alain	Prof	340-6328		12	BFY	DBA	Geo Wash	
Chausse, Raymond	Prof	340-6333		16	DS	LSC	HEC-Mont	
Cote, Marcel	Prof	340-6337		15	CIY	MBA	Chicago	
Hafsi, Taieb	Prof	340-6341		13	AFI	DBA	Harvard	
Aktouf, Omar	Assoc	340-6348		34	DY	PHD	HEC-Mont	
Chanlat, Jean-Francois	Assoc	340-6359		25	CHNR	PHD	Montreal	
Cote, Daniel	Assoc	340-6343		23	I	PHD	LSU	
Desforges, Jean-Guy	Assoc	340-6317		13	IX	PHD	Pitt	
Filion, Louis Jacques	Assoc	340-5619				PHD	Lancastr	
Harel Giasson, Francine	Assoc	340-6309		12	EOR	PHD	HEC-Mont	
Hogue, J. P.	Assoc	340-5600						
Hugron, Pierre	Assoc	340-6330		6	ST	MBA	HEC-Mont	
Lapierre, Laurent	Assoc	340-6352		25	D	PHD	McGill	
Lavoie, Dina	Assoc	340-6358						
Levesque, Delmas	Assoc	340-6331		25	EFQ	MA	Montreal	
Malo, Marie-Claire	Assoc	340-6350		5	Q	D.3	Paris	
Noel, Alain	Assoc	340-6340		58	IY	PHD	McGill	
Provost, Michel	Assoc	340-6329		1	AFJM	MBA	HEC-Mont	
Rondeau, Alain	Assoc	340-6255		5	NQ	DPS	Montreal	
Tremblay, Benoit	Assoc							
on leave								
Ayotte, Gaetan	Asst	340-6356		12	AHIM	MBA	HEC-Mont	
Demers, Christiane	Asst	340-6345		2	I	PHD	HEC-Mont	
Dery, Richard	Asst	340-6344		12	HV	PHD	Laval	
Dupuis, Jean-Pierre	Asst	340-6355		25	FM	MSC	Montreal	

Name	Rank	Phone				Degree	School	Year
Joly, Allain	Asst	340-6357		13	IY	PHD	SaoPaulo	
Ouimet, Gerard	Asst	340-6346		17	DEJR	PHD	Montreal	
Pauchant, Thierry C.	Asst	340-6375		23	DFM	PHD	S Calif	
Dufour, Yvon	Lect	340-6351		35	CDI	PHD	Worwick	
Kisfalvi, Veronika	Lect	340-6360		5	E	MBA	HEC-Mont	
Morin, Estelle M.	Lect	340-6376		12	EN	PHD	Montreal	
Pitcher Johnston, Patricia	Lect	340-6730		1	I	PHD	McGill	
—Production & Operations	Phone	340-6279	Fax 340-5632					
Nollet, Jean	C-Pr			68	TY	PHD	Montreal	
Diorio, Mattio O.	Prof			37	IUVY	MSC	MIT	
Kelada, Joseph	Prof			27	EFUV	MBA	McGill	
Deschamps, Isabelle	Assoc			76	TUV	MBA	Montreal	
Duguay, Cluade R.	Assoc			7	UVX	MPH	Yale	
Etienne, Eisenhower C.	Assoc	340-6277		75	QUI	PHD	W Ontari	
Handfield, Roger	Assoc			79	UVXZ	MS	Cornell	
Jobin, Marie-Helene	Asst					PHD	Quebec	
Landry, Sylvain	Asst					PHD	Montreal	
Pasin, Federico	Asst					PHD	Paris	
—Quant Methods & Info Sys	Phone	340-6472	Fax 340-5643					
Chokron, Michel	CAgre	340-6477	p220	9	ZIC	DEA	Paris	
Barki, Henri	Agreg	340-6482	p102	9	Z	PHD	W Ontari	
Breton, Michele	Agreg	340-6490		7	ITUZ	PHD	U of M	
Chriqui, Claude	Agreg	340-6484		9	Z	PHD	U of M	
Cusson, Rene	Agreg	340-6485	p360	7		CES	Paris	
Dahan, Simon	Agreg	340-6471		7		DEA	Paris	
Desrosiers, Jacques	Prof	340-6505	jacques			PHD	Montreal	
Goyette, Herve	Agreg	340-6479	p440	9	Z	CPHL	IICLA	
Guerard, Jean-Claude	Prof	340-6480		7		MSIA	N Carol	
Hansen, Pierre	Prof	340-6503	pierreh	7		PHD	Bruxelle	
Laporte, Gilbert	Prof	340-6504	gilbert	7		PHD	London	
LaTour, Robert	Agreg	340-6483		7	EGNP	CES	Paris	
Mireault, Paul	Agreg	340-6492	mireault	9	Z	PHD	MIT	
Ouellet, Roch	Agreg	340-6481		7		PHD	Montreal	
Parent, Regis	Agreg	340-6501		7	UVX	MSC	N Ariz	
Picard, Jean-Marc	Agreg	340-6478		7		MSTA	N Carol	
Pilon, Pierre-Paul	Agreg	340-6488		9	Z	MPH	Yale	
Pinsonneault, Alain	Agreg	340-6489	p109	9	Z	PHD	Ca-Irvine	
Rivard, Suzanne	Prof	340-6493		9		PHD	W Ontar	
Archer, Yves	Assoc	340-6487		9	Z	DEA	Grenoble	
Pare, Guy	Assoc	340-6472		9	Z	MSC	Montreal	
Belisle, Jean-Pierre	Adj	340-6486	poo2	9	VXZ	MSC	U of M	
Bernier, Carmen	Adj	340-6495	r162	9	Z	PHD	Montreal	
Chauny, Fabien	Adj	340-6875	fabien	7		PHD	EcolePol	
Talbot, Jean	Adj	340-6494	p033	9		PHD	Montpell	
—Dept of Mgt of Human Resour	Phone	340-6887	Fax 340-5635					
Lemelin, Maurice	Dir	340-6575		5	QN	PHD	UCLA	1969
Leck, Johanne	Prof	340-6717		5	NR	PHD	McGill	1991
Doucet, Rene	Assoc	340-6625		45	KQY	LLM	Montreal	1971
Gerin-Lajoie, Jean	Assoc	340-6354		5	Q	PHD	McGill	1984
Gosselin, Alain	Assoc	340-6353		5	EV	PHD	Maryland	1981
Martin, Roger G.	Assoc	340-6361		5	Q	MA	Montreal	1978
Meloche, Gaston	Assoc	340-6334		48	Y	DES	Ottawa	
Bouteiller, Dominique	Asst	340-6895		5	PQ	PHD	Montreal	1993
Levesque, Christian	Asst	340-6372		5	Q	PHD	Quebec	1993
Pozzebon, Sylvana	Asst	340-6729		15	NQ	MS	Cornell	1990
St-Onge, Sylvie	Asst	340-6381		15	N	PHD	Toronto	1985
Tremblay, Michel	Asst	340-6349		3	O	DEA	Aix-Mars	1989

Lakehead University — Thunder Bay Can — ON P7B 5E1 — (807) CS ACAD LAN.LAKEHEADUC
School of Business Adm — 955 Oliver Road — FAX=343-8023 — BADMIN,HBCOM

Name	Rank	Phone				Degree	School		Year
Isotalo, R. M.	D-Ac	343-8547	fbaisot		Mktg	MBA	York		
—Management Faculty	Phone	343-8386	Fax 343-8443						
Glew, Richard J.	C-As	343-8635	fbaglew	9	Z	MBA	88	Queens	8-89
Archibald, R. W.	Prof	343-8388	fbaarch	34	IL	PHD	76	W Ontari	7-81
Phillips, G. E.	Prof	343-8636	fbaphil	57	Q	MA		Queen's	1968
Cameron, R. A.	Assoc	343-8320	fbacame	25	EFP	MBA		Toronto	1-76
Handford, S. B.	Assoc	343-8217	fbahandf	25	EHNP	MBA		Alberta	7-87
Hartviksen, K.	Assoc	343-8497	fbahart	6	T	MBA		York	
Honey, W. C.	Assoc	343-8543	fbahone	19	BCDZ	MBA		Oregon	7-69
Nelson, R. A.	Assoc	343-8525	fbanel	7	U	MSIA		Purdue	7-70
Cole, S.	Asst	343-8419	fbacole	25	DFNR	MA		Waterloo	7-88
Fine, M. A.	Asst	343-8422	fbafine	9	Z	MBA		Boston C	1-82
Sacchetti, G.	Asst	343-8763	fbasacc	9	Z	MBA	93	Queens	

Laurentian University — Sudbury, Canada — ON P3E 2C6 — (705)
Professional Schools — FAX=673-6518 — BCOMM,BAA,MBA
  Did Not Respond-1993 Listing

Name	Rank	Phone				Degree	School	Year
Ganjavi, Ozhand	D-Ac	675-1151		7	Mgt	PHD	84 W Ontar	7-79
—School Commerce & Admin	Phone	675-1151	Fax 673-6518					

–School Commerce & Admin — Phone 675-1151 — Fax 673-6518

Name	Rank	Phone	Email						
Church, John	Prof	675-1151		7	VZ	PHD	78	W Ontar	7-74
Paul, R. H.	Prof	675-1151		2		PHD		London	
Schell, Bernie	Prof	675-1151		5		PHD	77	Renssela	8-78
Cachon, Jean-Charles	Assoc	675-1151	f2100004	36	PRST	MA	77	Sherbroo	7-83
Cotton, G. B.	Assoc	675-1151		8		MBIM		Bath	
Dodge, John	Assoc	675-1151	jdodge	31		MBA	80	W Ontar	7-90
Hilldrup, David J.	Assoc	675-1151		7		MBA		Hawaii	
on sabbatical									
Shenas, D.	Assoc	675-1151		5		PHD		NTS	
Zanibbi, Louis	Assoc	675-1151		9		PHD	88	Bradford	7-79
Djerdjour, M.	Asst	675-1151		7		PHD		Clevelnd	
Grzeda, M.	Asst	675-1151		5		PHD			
Kivikink, Ron	Asst	675-1151		71		MBA	84	Laurenti	7-82
Ribordy, A.	Asst	675-1151		1		MBA		Laurentn	
Sina, Reza	Asst	675-1151		38		PHD	87	Grenoble	7-88
Durand, L.	Lect	675-1151		5		MBA		Sher	
Lafreniere, Ginette	Lect	675-1151		48	DEJR	MA	87	Sherbroo	7-90
Lebrasseur, Roland	Lect	675-1151		25		MBA		McGill	1-85

Universite Laval — Sainte-Foy, Cand — PQ G1K 7P4 — (418) LAVALVM1 — FAX=656-2624 — BAA,MBA,PHD
Faculte Sciences Adm
Did Not Respond

Name	Rank	Phone	Email						
Khowry, Nabil	Dean	656-2216	khowryn		Fnce	PHD	68	Indiana	

–Department of Management — Phone — Fax 656-2624

University of Lethbridge — Lethbridge Canad — AB T1K 3M4 — (403) GH.ULETH.CA — FAX=329-2038 — BMGT
Faculty of Management — 4401 University Drive

Name	Rank	Phone	Email						
Lermer, George	Dean	329-2633	lermer	1	AK	PHD		McGill	1981

–Management Faculty — Phone 329-2633 — Fax 329-2038

Name	Rank	Phone	Email						
England, Geoffrey	Prof	329-2630	england	54	KG	LLM	74	Dalhouse	1976
Shimazaki, Hiroshi (Tanaka)	Prof	329-2728	shimazak	8	Y	PHD	75	S Fraser	1976
Balderson, Wes	Assoc	329-2648	balderso	6	ST	MBA	73	Alberta	1977
Boudreau, Bob	Assoc	329-2646	boudreau	2	EFGH	PHD	85	Calgary	1983
Elias, Doug	Assoc	329-5180	elias	1	ADHI	PHD		Toronto	1988
Gattiker, Urs	Assoc	329-2169	gattiker	2	DEHO	PHD	85	Claremont	1985
Loo, Bob	Assoc	329-2174	loo	25	EGNP	PHD	78	Calgary	1989
McKenna, Ian	Assoc	329-2349	mckenna	54	QR	LLM		Dundee	1985
Nicol, Ken	Assoc	329-2159	nicol	36	ILU	PHD	73	Iowa St	1984
Schroeder, Hal	Assoc	329-2631	schroede	34	IL	PHD	81	S Calif	1981
Gellatly, Ian	Asst	329-2068	gellatly	25	EN	PHD	91	W Ontar	1993
Hunter, Gordon	Asst		hunterg	9	ZV	PHD	92	Strathcl	1994
Rutland, John	Asst	329-2249	rutland	31	IML	PHD		Wash	1990
Zahir, Sajjad	Asst	329-2054	zahir	79	ZV	PHD	81	Oregon	1989
Brown, Grant	Lect	329-2075	browng	4	JKLX	ABD		Oxford	1990
Hughes, Geoffrey	Lect	329-2151	hughesg	38	IY	MBA	82	Cty Lond	1989
Low, George	Lect					ABD			1988
Chiste, Katherine	AcAs	329-2139	chiste	4	K	PHD	91	Calgary	1992
Davies, Karen	AcAs	329-2007	davies	6	T	MBA	86	Alberta	1988
Elemans, Patricia	AcAs	329-2163	elemans	5	PT	MBA	92	York	1985
Seely, Doug	AcAs	329-2727	seely	9		BED		Lethbrid	1988
Thompson, Mark	AcAs	329-2689	thompson	9		BMGT	92	Lethbrid	1992
Thompson, Mary	AcAs	329-2647	thompson	25		ABD		Calgary	1992

University of Manitoba — Winnipeg, Canada — MB R3T 5V4 — (204) UOFMCC — FAX=275-0181 — BCOM,MBA,MACC
Faculty of Management
Faculty Bitnet MAN23432

Name	Rank	Phone	Email						
Mackness, William	Dean	474-9711			Econ	MA	66	W Ontar	1988

–Faculty of Management — Phone 474-9672 — Fax 275-0181

Name	Rank	Phone	Email						
Bector, C. R.	H-Pr$	474-8445		7	V	PHD	68	Ill Tech	1970
Good, Walter	H-Pr	474-8852		6	St	PHD	69	Michigan	1970
Gray, Jerry L.	D-Pr	474-8483		2	EH	PHD	70	S Carol	1970
Associate Dean									
Starke, Frederick A.	H-Pr	474-8510		12	EH	PHD	74	Ohio St	1968
Atwell, John F.	Prof	474-8430		5	Q	MA	63	Manitoba	1964
Bartell, Marvin	Prof	474-8423		26	EHT	PHD	72	Northwes	1971
Bhatt, Suresh	Prof	474-9231		7	V	PHD	73	Ill Tech	1975
Bruning, Edward	Prof	474-8347		8	Y	PHD	81	Alabama	1990
Bruning, N. Sue	Prof	474-6566		25	EGO	PHD	81	Alabama	1990
Frohlich, Norm	Prof	474-6385		14	LA	PHD	71	Princeton	1979
Hall, Roger	Prof	474-9709		12	EH	PHD	73	U Wash	1970
Hercus, Terry	Prof	474-9662		5	N	MBA	55	Toronto	1967
Mundie, John	Prof	474-9438		13	I	PHD	66	Stanford	1955
Notz, William W.	Prof	474-8425		2	EH	PHD	72	Northwes	1975
Anderson, G. Bruce	Assoc	474-8421		14	L	BA	63	Idaho	1970
Godard, John	Assoc	474-8433		25	Q	PHD	89	Cornell	1991
Nuttall, Gary A.	Assoc	474-9886		5	Q	MA	60	Minn	1966

Cooper, Christine L.	Asst	474-6464	25	EQ	PHD	90	Ohio St	1990
Dobing, Brian	Asst	474-6774	9	Z	PHD	92	Minn	1992
Dyck, Bruno	Asst	474-6385	12	EH	PHD		Alberta	1990
Keefe, Michael	Asst	474-9529	9	Z	ABD	92	North Tx	1991
Lee, Raymond	Asst	474-6745	25	Jne	PHD	89	Wayne St	1991
McLachlin, Ron	Asst	474-9431	7	U	PHD	92	Ontario	1993
Radford, Russell	Asst	474-9170	7	U	DBA	86	Harvard	1990
Rubin, Beth	Asst	474-8437	25	AQR	PHD	90	Michigan	1990
Sickmeier, Marie	Asst	474-8349	25	QE	PHD	89	Ohio St	1991

Mc Gill University — Montreal, Canada PQ H3A 1G5 — (514) MANAGEMENT.MCGILL.CA
Faculty of Management — 1001 Sherbrooke Street West — FAX=398-3876 — BCOM,MBA,PHD
—Management Faculty — Phone 398-4000 — Fax 398-3876

Crowston, Wallace	Dean	398-4001	crowston		PHD		Car Mel	1987
Adler, Nancy J.	Prof	398-4031	adler	2		PHD	UCLA	1980
Brenner, R.	Prof	398-7327	brenner	3		PHD	Jerusale	1978
Detemple, J.	Prof	398-4059	detemple	1		DES	LPasteur	1985
Drury, D.	Prof	398-4057	drury	1		PHD	Northwes	1976
Errunza, V.	Prof	398-4056	errunza	8		PHD	Calif	1976
Friesen, P.	Prof	398-4036	friesen	7		PHD	Stanford	1974
Goffin, J.	Prof	398-4003	goffin	7		PHD	Berkeley	1976
Kanungo, R. N.	Prof	398-4040	kanungo	2		PHD	McGill	1969
Loulou, R.	Prof	398-4013	loulou	7		PHD	Berkeley	1970
Mintzberg, Henry	Prof	398-4017	mintzber	3		PHD	MIT	1968
Morrison, R.	Prof	398-4009	morrison	3		MA	Oxon	1962
Picard, L.	Prof	398-4055	picard	3		DBA	Harvard	1977
Sealey, C. W.	Prof	398-1054	sealey	1		PHD	Georgia	1980
Smith, J. G.	Prof	398-4030	smith	3		PHD	Ohio St	1973
Teitlebaum, A. D.	Prof	398-4665	teitleba	7		PHD	McGill	1968
Whitmore, A.	Prof	398-4049	whitmore	7		PHD	Minn	1969
Wright, R.	Prof	398-4016	wright	8		DBA	Indiana	
Basu, K.	Assoc	398-4022	basu	3		PHD	Florida	1986
Bawa, K.	Assoc	398-4041	bawa	3		PHD	Columbia	1984
Bennett, R.	Assoc	398-4064	bennett	3		DBA	Harvard	1976
Chandra, P.	Assoc	398-4475	chandra	7		PHD	Penn	1988
Conger, Jay Allen	Assoc	398-4032		2		PHD	Harvard	1985
Dougherty, Deborah Jane	Assoc	398-2115	dougbert	3		PHD	87	MIT	1987
Duan, J. C.	Assoc	398-4053	duan	1		PHD	Madison	1986
Duff, A.	Assoc	398-4052	duff	1		MA	Cantab	1968
Etemad, H.	Assoc	398-4018	etemad	8		PHD	Calif	1978
Hardy, Cynthia	Assoc	398-4020	hardy	3		PHD	Calif	1981
Hartwick, J.	Assoc	398-4039	hartwick	2		PHD	Illinois	1980
Howson, H.	Assoc	398-4005	howson	9		PHD	Syracuse	1968
Jaeger, A.	Assoc	398-4067	jaeger	2		PHD	Stanford	1978
Jorgensen, J.	Assoc	398-4027	jorgense	3		PHD	McGill	1980
Keesal, N.	Assoc	398-3971	keesal	3		MBA	Harvard	1984
Lee, Mary Dean	Assoc	398-4034	lee	2		PHD	Yale	1982
Miller, D.	Assoc	398-4029	miller	3		PHD	McGill	1978
Moreau, A.	Assoc	398-4025	moreau	1		PHD	Iowa	1986
Sarigollu, Emine	Assoc	398-4662	sarigoll	3		PHD	Penn	1988
Saunders, David M.	Assoc	398-4028	saunders	2		PHD	W Ont	1986
Thomason, T.	Assoc	398-4509	thomason	5		PHD	Cornell	1988
Westley, F.	Assoc	398-4042	westley	3		PHD	McGill	1983
Yalovsky, M.	Assoc	398-4058	yalovsky	9		PHD	McGill	1974
Bandyopadhyay, S.	Asst	398-1490	bandyopa	3		PHD	Cinn	1992
Choi, B.	Asst	398-4000	choi	1		PHD	94	Iowa	1994
Del Pilar, R.	Asst	398-8950	delpilar	7		PHD	Cornell	1989
Dimnick, T.	Asst	398-4000	dimnick	1		PHS	London	1993
Dimnik, P.	Asst	398-1228	dimnik	1		PHD	Western	1994
Hale, A.	Asst	398-4029	hale	3		PHD	Texas	1992
Hogan, K.	Asst	398-4060	hogan	8		PHD	Arizona	1990
Hung, M. W.	Asst	398-3614	hung	1		PHD	Northwes	1990
Li, S.	Asst	398-2407	li	7		PHD	Texas	1991
Mazumdar, S.	Asst	398-4062	mazumdar	1		PHD	Dallas	1990
McWatters, C.	Asst	398-5851	mcwatters	1		PHD	Queens	1993
Nagarajan, S.	Asst	398-4047	nag	1		PHD	Northwes	1988
Phillips, N.	Asst	398-4000	phillips	3		PHD	Edmonton	1993
Smith, Anne	Asst	398-2075	smitha	3		PHD	93	N Carol	1992
Tan, L. H.	Asst	398-4130	tan	8		PHD	Harvard	1993
Troy, P.	Asst	398-4023	troy	9		PHD	Yale	1990
Wrigley, C.	Asst	398-4661	wrigley	9		PHD	Brit Col	1989
Wybo, M.	Asst	398-2869	wybo	9		PHD	Minn	1992
Yoo, S. M.	Asst	398-1073	yoo	8		PHD	Columbia	1993
Zwerling, H.	Asst	398-4502	zwerling	5		PHD	Wiscon	1988

McMaster University Hamilton, Canada ON L8S 4M4 (905) MCMASTER
DeGroote Sch of Bus 1280 Main Street West FAX=527-0100 BCOM,HONBCO,MBA
phone: 525-9140

Name	Rank	Ext	Fax/email			Deg	Yr	School	Yr
Truscott, William G.	Dean	Ext24431		17	UV	DBA	73	Indiana	7-69
–Hum Resources & Labour Rel	Phone	Ext23598	Fax 521-8995						
Hackett, Rick D.	C-Ac	Ext23958		5	NE	PHD	85	Bowl Gr	
Rose, Joseph B.	C-Pr	Ext23951		5	Q	PHD	71	SUNY-Buf	
Agarwal, Naresh C.	Prof	Ext23953		5	N	PHD	74	Minn	
Jain, Harish C.	Prof	Ext23952		5	NQ	PHD		Wiscon	
Roy, J. Adams	Prof	Ext23963		5	Q	PHD	73	Wiscon	
Basadur, Min S.	Assoc	Ext23954		2	F	PHD		Cinn	
Zeytinoglu, F. Isik	Assoc	Ext23957		5	Q	PHD	85	Penn	
Medcof, John W.	Asst	Ext24648		2	E	PHD	84	Toronto	
Associate Dean									
Wiesner, W.	Asst	Ext23985	wiesner	5	NE	PHD	88	Waterloo	
Pitts, Barbara M. C.	Lect	Ext23956		2	EFNP	MBA		McMaster	
–Mgt Science & Info Sys Ar	Phone	Ext24434	Fax 521-8995						
Miltenburg, John G.	C-Pr		miltenb	17	UV	PHD		Waterloo	
Abad, Prakash L.	Prof		abad	17	UV	PHD		Cinn	
Archer, Norman P.	Prof		archer	19	VZ	PHD		McMaster	
Love, Robert F.	Prof			17	UV	PHD		Stanford	
Parlar, Mahmut	Prof		parlar	71	UV	PHD		Waterloo	
Steiner, George	Prof		steiner	17	UV	PHD		Waterloo	
Wesolowsky, George O.	Prof		wesolows	17	UV	PHD		Wiscon	
Gupta, Diwakar	Assoc		guptad	17	UV	PHD		Waterloo	
Montazemi, Ali R.	Assoc		montazem	9	Z	PHD		Waterloo	
Yuan, Yufei	Assoc		yuanyuf	9	Z	PHD		Michigan	
Salisbury, Tiina	Lect			17	UV	MBA		McMaster	

Memorial U of Newfoundland StJohns, Canada NF A1B 3X5 (709) KEAN.UCS.MUN.CA
Faculty of Business Adm Elizabeth Avenue FAX=737-7680 BCOM,MBA

Name	Rank	Phone	email			Deg	Yr	School	Yr
Blake, R. William	Dean	737-8851	bblake	2	E	PHD	77	Western	1986
–Management Faculty	Phone	737-8851	Fax 737-7680						
Barth, Richard T.	Prof	737-2656		25		PHD	70	Northwes	1986
Roskin, Rick	Prof	737-8854	rroskin	2	E	PHD	77	Bradford	1968
Saha, Sudhir K.	Prof	737-8556	sksaha	25		PHD	72	Brit Col	1980
Sexty, Robert	Prof	737-4514	rsexty	43		PHD	74	Colorado	1968
Gregory, Ann	Assoc	737-8526	agregory	38		PHD	76	Columbia	1982
Gupta, Raj	Assoc	737-8527	rgupta	7		PHD	74	Rochest	1975
Kubiak, Wieslaw	Assoc	737-4412	wkubiak	7		PHD	86	Warsaw	1990
Redlack, Austin R.	Assoc	737-8511	austin	7	V	PHD	73	Warford	1969
Skipton, Michael D.	Assoc	737-8509	mskipton	13	DIPT	PHD	74	Warwick	4-85
Withey, Michael J.	Assoc	737-8513	mwithey	2		PHD	86	Queen'n	1984
Foster, K. Dale	Asst	737-4412	fletcher	79	VZ	PHD	94	Dalhousi	1989
McKay, Kenneth N.	Asst	737-4747	kmckay	9	UZ	PHD	92	Waterloo	1992
Parsons, Jeffrey	Asst	737-4741	jeffrey	9	Z	PHD	92	Brit Col	1993
Tulett, David M.	Asst	737-4097	dtulett	7	V	PHD	86	Queen's	1985

Mount Allison University Sackville Canada NB E0A 3C0 (506) MTA.CA
Commerce Department FAX=364-2625

Name	Rank	Phone	Fax			Deg	Yr	School	Yr
Ralph, Neville W.	Head								
–Management Faculty	Phone	364-2326	Fax 364-2625						
Wehrell, Roger	Assoc	364-2329		26	T	PHD	82	Ottawa	7-83
Fullerton, Gordon	Asst	364-2322		23		MBA	88	Dalhousi	7-88

Mount Saint Vincent Univ Nova Scotia Can NS B3M 2J6 (902) MSVU
Dept of Business Adm 166 Bedford Highway FAX=445-3960 BBA
Did Not Respond-1993 Listing

Name	Rank	Phone	Fax			Deg	Yr	School	Yr
–Management Faculty	Phone	457-6175	Fax 455-3960						
Darling, N.	Asst	457-6328		25	EFNP	MBA	89	Dalhoise	1989
Kelleher, N.	Asst	457-6390		38	BKY	MBA	82	Dalhousi	1986
Thompson, A.	Asst	457-6391		79	UTRZ	MBA	82	Dalhousi	1986
Young, J.	Asst	457-6361		25	POEF	MBA	83	Saint Ms	1987
Farrell, E.		457-6368		16	DRST	MBA		Saint Ms	1991
Fisher, R.		457-6209		29	FBVZ	PHD	92	Bath	1984

University of New Brunswick Fredericton, Can NB E3B 5A3 (506) UNB.CA
Faculty of Adm Box 4400 FAX=453-3561 BBA,MBA

Name	Rank	Phone	email			Deg	Yr	School	Yr
Storey, Ronald L.	Dean	453-4869	faddean	2	E	PHD	74	Mich St	1989
–Management Area	Phone	453-4869	Fax 453-3561						
Askanas, Wictor	Prof	453-4869	askanas	32	Y	PHD		Warsaw	1983
Schaefer, Norbert V.	Prof	453-4869	schaefer	34	XLY	PHD	78	Berkeley	1976
Staber, Udo H.	Prof	453-4869	uhs	2	H	PHD		C'Nell	1985
Tolliver, James	Prof	453-4689	gryphon	2	E	PHD	77	Ohio St	1981
Boothman, Barry Edward	Assoc	453-4869		34	ABIL	PHD	89	York	1986
Coleman, Daniel F.	Assoc	453-4869	dan	2	ENY	PHD		SUNY-Buf	1986
Nasierowski, Wojciech	Assoc	453-4869	nasierow	83	Y	PHD		Warsaw	1990
Mighty, E. Joy	Asst	453-4869	ejmighty	2	E	PHD		York	1992

177

University of Ottawa — Ottawa, Canada ON K1N 6N5 (613)
Faculty of Adm   CANADA — 550 Cumberland Street   FAX=564-5074   BA,MBA
Did Not Respond-1993 Listing

Name	Title	Phone					School	Year
Malouin, Jean-Louis	Dean	564-4918			Atg	PHD	70 UCLA	1992
–Management Faculty	Phone	564-4918	Fax 564-6518					

Queen's University — Kingston Canada ON K7L 3N6 (613) QUCDN
School of Business — 131 Union Street   FAX=545-2013   BCOM,MBA,PHD

Name	Title	Phone					School	Year
Anderson, D.	Dean	545-2305				PHD	75 Queen's	1988
–Management Faculty	Phone		Fax 545-2972					
Downie, Bryan M.	D-Pr	545-2972		5	Q	PHD	70 Chicago	1968
Director, School of Industrial Relations								
Burns, R. N.	Prof	545-2314		7	UV	PHD	70 Waterloo	1981
Gordon, J. R. M.	Prof	545-2375	gordonj	37	IU	PHD	66 MIT	1975
Alcan Chair in Management and Technology								
Nightingale, D. V.	Prof	545-2336		12	DEFH	PHD	71 Michigan	1973
Petersen, E. R.	Prof	545-2349	petersen	7	UV	PHD	67 Stanford	1968
Richardson, P. R.	Prof	545-2339		13	DI	PHD	75 Western	1977
Rutenberg, D. P.	Prof	545-2330	rutenber	38	IY	PHD	67 Berkeley	1977
Willes, J. A.	Prof	545-2343		4	K	LLM	67 Osgoode	1970
Buchan, P. Bruce	Assoc	545-2317	buchanb	13	BI	PHD	69 Michigan	1969
Cassidy, R. G. R.	Assoc	545-2352		17	AV	PHD	71 Dalhousi	1974
Collom, F. D.	Assoc	545-2320		5	PQ	MBA	67 Queen's	1963
Chair, Undergraduate Program in Commerce								
Cooper, W. H.	Assoc	545-2333		2	EHFX	PHD	78 Toronto	1976
Dowling, J. B.	Assoc	545-2330		4	LM	PHD	78 Stanford	1979
Gallupe, R. B.	Assoc	545-2361	gallupeb	9	ZF	PHD	85 Minn	1986
McKeen, Carol A.	Assoc	545-2326			R	MBA	76 Queen's	1982
McKeen, J. D.	Assoc	545-2360	mckeenj	9	Z	PHD	81 Minn	1973
Taylor, A. J.	Assoc	545-2335	tayloraj	7	UV	PHD	76 Stanford	1977
Beatty, C. A.	Asst	545-2318	beattyc	25	EGU	PHD	86 Western	1985
Jackson, R. L.	Asst	545-2321	jacksonr	5	Q	MBA	71 Queen's	1974
McKirdy, J. G. M.	Asst	545-2330	mckirdyj	67	ST	MSC	66 Car Mel	1966
Todd, P.A.	Asst	545-6687		9	Z	PHD	88 Brit Col	1989
Wright, Lorna L.	Asst	545-6296		8	IMY	PHD	90 Western	1986
Cunningham, M. H.	Inst	545-2327		4	J	ABD	91 Tx A&M	1991

University of Regina — Regina, Canada SK S4S OA2 (306)
Faculty of Adm — 3737 Wascana Parkway   FAX=585-4805
Did Not Respond-1993 Listing

Name	Title	Phone					School	Year
Turtle, John P.	Dean$	585-4162			Fnce	PHD	74 Wash	1981
–Management Faculty	Phone	585-4724	Fax 585-4805					
Allan, J. R.	Prof	585-4386		1	A	PHD	Prin	
Barber, L. I.	Prof	585-4696		13	I	PHD	Wash	
Kwon, O. Yul	Prof	585-4722		18	ALY	PHD	McMaster	
McLaren, R. I.	Prof	585-4605		14	ABHL	PHD	Pitt	
Muthuchidambaram, S.	Prof	585-4713		45	JKLQ	PHD	Wiscon	
Sankaran, Sam	Prof	585-4988		47	LUVX	DBA	Indiana	
Shaw, D. E.	Prof			34	ILZ	PHD	Saskatch	
Srinivas, K. M.	Prof	585-4717		25	EFNP	PHD	UCLA	
Chadwick, W. F.	Assoc	585-4989		35	GINY	MSC	Col	
Ito, J. K.	Assoc	585-4714		23	EHIN	PHD	Wash	
Johns, J. G.	Assoc	585-4721		36	IST	MBA	Calif	
Mason, Jim R.	Assoc	585-4727		36	IST	PHD	Wash	
Ricker, H. O.	Assoc	585-4710		79	UVZ	PHD	Waterloo	
Southam, D. N.	Assoc	585-4723		79	UZ	MSC	Saskatch	
Wu, Terry Y. S.	Assoc	585-4040		14	A	PHD	Manitoba	
Bentham, K. J.	Asst	585-4735		5	NQR	MIR	Queens	
Long, Stephen F.	Asst	585-4731		25	FHNP	MBA	Dalhousi	
Rasmussen, Ken A.	Asst	585-4712		12	AHJL	PHD	Toronto	
Epp, L.	Lect	585-4964		36	DISY	MBA	Saskatch	

St. Francis Xavier Univ — Antigonish, Cand NS B2G 1CO (902)
Dept of Bus Adm   CANADA   FAX=867-5153   BBA
Did Not Respond-1992 Listing; *Members of Dept of Mathematics & Computing Sci

Name	Title	Phone					School	Year
Spencer, Ian	C-Ac	863-3300				MBA	73 W Ontar	1973
–Management Faculty	Phone		Fax 867-5153					
MacKinnon, Ronald J.	* Prof	863-3300		9	Z	PHD	Okla St	1961
Gilson, Clive H. J.	Assoc	863-3300		52	Q	PHD	83 Warwick	1984
Young, R. Kent	Assoc	863-3300		2	O	PHD	68 Toronto	1976
Ramadurai, K. S.	* Asst	863-3300		7	V	PHD	W Ontar	1989
Diochon, Monica C.	Lect	863-3300		56	T	MBA	87 Dalhousi	1990

Saint Mary's University
Halifax, Canada NS B3H 3C3 (902) HUSKY1
FAX=420-5561 BCOM,MBA
Faculty of Commerce
Did Not Respond-1993 Listing

Name	Title	Phone	email		Code	Deg		School	Year
Carson, Scott	Dean	420-5421		34	TU	PHD	80	London	1993
—Department of Management	Phone		Fax 420-5561						
Summers, Russell	C-Ac	420-5774		25	ENX	PHD	87	Waterloo	1987
Chamard, John	Prof	420-5769		36	RS	MBA	66	Harvard	1974
Das, Hari	Prof	420-5772		25	HFN	PHD	79	Brit Col	1978
Fitzgerald, Patricia	Prof	420-5771		23	EIX	PHD	74	N Colo	1976
Miner, Rick	Prof	420-5663		25	EFN	PHD	76	Minn	1976
Pendse, Shripad G.	Prof	420-5773		23	DEIH	PHD	73	Stanford	1966
Schwind, Hermann F.	Prof	420-5775		58	NW	PHD	79	Brit Col	1976
Badawi, Jamal	Assoc	420-5776		25	EJNR	PHD	70	Indiana	1970
Stevenson, Lois	Assoc	420-5781		36	ST	MPH	90	Bath	1992
Wagar, Terry H.	Assoc	420-5770		45	KNQ	PHD	91	Va Tech	1985
Carceller, Araceli	Asst	420-5282		2	EN	PHD	83	Madrid	1990
Greer, William	Asst	420-5804		12	CEJL	MBA	75	Boston	1990

Univ of Saskatchewan
SaskatoonCanada SK S7N 0W0 (306) COMMERCE.USASK.CA
FAX=966-8709 BCOM,MSC
College of Commerce
* Dept of Management & Marketing

Name	Title	Phone	email		Code	Deg		School	Year
Brennan, W. John	Dean	966-4786	brennan		Atg	PHD	72	Michigan	1967
—Indust Relations & Org Beh	Phone	966-8450	Fax 966-8709						
Wetzel, Kurt	H-Pr	966-8450	wetzel	5	DQ	PHD	78	Illinois	1976
Long, Richard J.	Prof	966-8398	long	2	DFNH	PHD	77	Cornell	1977
Sass, Robert	Prof	966-8455		5	QC	MS	67	Cornell	1982
Bicknell, Douglas	Assoc	966-4785	bicknell	5	NB	MBA	71	Saskatch	1968
Edmonds, Ron	Assoc	966-8410	edmonds	25	DNOP	PHD	84	Purdue	1985
Haiven, Larry	Assoc	966-8451	haiven	25	NQ	PHD	89	Warwick	1988
Clarke, Louise	Asst	966-8409	clarke	25		PHD	92	York	1991
Mentzer, Marc S.	Asst	966-8458	mentzer	2	HN	PHD	86	Indiana	1989
Venne, Rosemary	Asst	966-8446	venne	25	NO	PHD	93	Toronto	1991

Simon Fraser University
Burnaby, Canada BC V5A 1S6 (604) SFU.CA
FAX=291-4920 BA,MBA
Faculty of Business Adm
Faculty Office Phone 291-3708

Name	Title	Phone	email		Code	Deg		School	Year
Shapiro, Stanley	Dean	291-4183			Mktg	PHD		Penn	9-80
—Management Faculty	Phone		Fax 291-4920						
Eng, Ung Choo	Prof	291-4209	choo	7	V	PHD	80	Brit Col	1982
Holmes, A. Richard	Prof	291-3560	holmes	7	QVX	PHD	60	Indiana	1966
Love, C. Ernest	Prof	291-4746	userinds	37	IUVX	PHD	75	London	1977
Wedley, William C.	Prof	291-4528	wedley	67	SUVY	PHD	71	Columbia	1986
Jones, Christopher V.	Assoc	291-4963	chris-jo	79	UVZ	PHD	85	Cornell	1990
Parker, Drew C.	Assoc	291-3102	userdrew	9	DZ	PHD	86	W Ontari	1984
Warburton, Arthur R.	Assoc	291-3749	artw	79	VZ	PHD	81	Brit Col	1987
Reich, Blaize Horner	Asst	291-5834	blaize_r	93	FHIZ	ABD	93	Brit Col	1991

University of Toronto
Toronto, Canada ON M5S 1V4 (416)
315 Bloor Street West FAX=978-5549 BCOM,MBA
Faculty of Management
Did Not Respond

Wolff, Roger N.	Dean					
—Department of Management	Phone		Fax 978-5549			

University of Victoria
Victoria, Canada BC V8W 2Y2 (604)
FAX=721-6067 BCOM,MBA
School of Business

Name	Title	Phone	email		Code	Deg		School	Year
Boag, David	Dean	721-6060		6	ST	PHD		Toronto	1-91
—Management Faculty	Phone	721-8264	Fax 721-6067						
Beckman, Dale	H	721-6074	dbeckman	8	Y	PHD		Mich St	7-91
Head, International Program									
Dastmalchian, Ali M.	Prof	721-6083	-	2	EFH	PHD	81	Wales	7-91
Head, Graduate Program									
Ng, Ignace	Assoc	721-6073		25	FQY	PHD	86	S Fraser	7-91
Bu, Nailin	Asst	721-6071		2	EY	PHD		Brit Col	7-91
Smith, Brock	Asst	721-6070		1	X	ABD		W Ontar	7-91
Murphy, Peter		721-6072		12	AD	PHD		Ohio St	7-91
Head, Tourism Program									

University of Waterloo
Waterloo, Canada ON N2L 3G1 (519) SAILUWATERLOO.CA
FAX=746-7252 MASC,PHD
Faculty of Engineering
phone 888-4567; email @1=sail

Name	Title	Phone	email		Code	Deg		School	Year
—Dept of Management Science	Phone	Ext 3286	Fax 746-7252						
Fuller, J. D.	C-Ac	855-1211	dfuller@1	7	V	PHD	80	Brit Col	1979
email @mansail1									
Bookbinder, J. H.	Prof	885-4013	jbookbin	7	UV	PHD	69	Calif	1982
Magazine, M. J.	Prof	888-4440	mmagazin	7	UV	PHD	69	Florida	1975

Name	Rank	Phone	Email			Degree		School	Year
Saleh, S. D.	Prof	885-1211		25	DEYH	PHD	63	Case Wes	1967
Vickson, R. G.	Prof	888-4729	rvickson		UV	PHD	69	MIT	1973
Bernhardt, I. B.	Assoc	885-1211	ibernhar		NQSR	PHD	66	Calif	1970
Dilts, D.	Assoc	888-4838	sdilts@1	79	CUYZ	PHD	83	Oregon	1986
Fraser, N.	Assoc	855-1211	nfraser	7	V	PHD	83	Waterloo	1983
Gerchak, Y.	Assoc	855-1211	ygerchak	7	V	PHD	80	Brit Col	1982
Guild, P.	Assoc	855-4802	guild@1	36	DITX	PHD	78	Oxford	1990
Jewkes, E.	Assoc	855-1211	emjewkes	7	UV	PHD	88	Waterloo	1988
Moore, J. B.	Assoc	888-4036	jbmoore	79	UZV	PHD	71	Waterloo	1971
Safayeni, F.	Assoc	885-1211		2	EH	PHD	79	Victoria	1980
Webster, Jane	Assoc	885-1211		25	O	PHD	89	New York	1994
Astebro, T.	Asst	885-1211		2	D	PHD	94	Car Mel	1994
Blake, C.	Asst	885-1211	cblake@1	25	EFHT	PHD	93	Waterloo	1988

Univ of Western Ontario — London, Canada — ON N6A 3K7 — (519) NOVELL.BUSINESS.UWO.CA
School of Business Adm — FAX=661-3485 — BA,MBA,PHD
Did Not Respond

Name	Rank	Phone	Email			Degree		School	Year
Ryans, Adrian B.	Dean	661-3226	aryans			Mktg	PHD	73 Stanford	1973
—Department of Management	Phone		Fax 661-3485						

Wilfrid Laurier University — Waterloo Canada — ON N2L 3C5 — (519) MACH1.WLU.CA
School of Bus & Econ — 75 University Avenue West — FAX=884-0201 — MBA,BBA,AD,DMS
phone 884-1970

Name	Rank	Phone	Email			Degree		School	Year
Murray, J Alex	Dean	Ext 2214	amurray						
—Management Areas	Phone	Ext 2283	Fax 884-0201						
Craig, Ronald G.	D-Ac	Ext-2283	rcraig2	79	SUZ	PHD		Waterloo	1979
Associate Dean of Human Resources									
Baetz, Mark C.	Prof	Ext-2564	mbaetz	34	LIA	PHD		Western	1980
Area Coordinator: Policy									
Carroll, Glenn E.	Prof	Ext-2562	gcarroll	2	E	MBA		Western	1960
Cawsey, Tupper F.	Prof	Ext-2055	tcawsey	2	E	PHD		Western	1972
Area Coordinator: Management & Organizational Behavior									
Haney, Reginald A.	Prof	Ext-2675		4	K	LLM		Osgoode	1974
Keller, Gerald	Prof	Ext-2537	gkeller6	7	V	PHD		Windsor	1974
Noori, A. Hamid	Prof	Ext-6662	hnorri	7	U	PHD		Western	1983
Adamson, Raymond S.	Assoc	Ext-2607		25	QE	PHD		Waterloo	1974
Banks, John C.	Assoc	Ext-2552	jbanks	38	YI	PHD		York	1984
De, Mitali	Assoc	Ext-2532	mde4	7	V	PHD		Waterloo	1988
Deszca, Gene	Assoc	Ext-2560	gdeszca	5	E	PHD		York	1980
Director: MBA Program									
Ellis, Robert J.	Assoc	Ext-2283	bellis	2	E	PHD		Waterloo	1980
Fleisher, Craig	Assoc	Ext 2187	cfleishe	34	I	PHD		Pitt	1993
Fournier, Bruce	Assoc	Ext-2883	bfournie	2	EH	PHD		York	1978
Harling, Kenneth F.	Assoc	Ext-2531	kharling	3	I	PHD		Purdue	1989
Iyogun, Paul O.	Assoc	Ext-2543	piyogun	7	V	PHD		Brit Col	1987
Area Coordinator: Operations & Decision Sciences									
Leonard, Kevin	Assoc	Ext-2489	kleonard	7	V	PHD		Concordi	1990
Harris, C. Ruth	Asst	Ext-2637	rharris	7	UV	PHD		Waterloo	1986
Harvey, Cheryl A.	Asst	Ext-2557	charvey	2	E	PHD		Western	1988
Jha, Shelly	Asst	Ext-2678	sjha	7	U	PHD		Iowa	1990
Mazerolle, Maurice	Asst	Ext-2672	mmazerol		Q	PHD		Toronto	1990
McCutcheon, James R.	Asst	Ext-2058	jmccutch	3	I	MBA		McMaster	1974
Miles, Grant	Asst	Ext-2058	gmiles	3	I	PHD		Penn St	1993
Preece, Stephen	Asst	Ext 2636	spreece	38	IY				
Ramsoomair, H. Franklin	Asst	Ext-2673	framsom	2	P	PHD		Toronto	1989
Currie, Elliott	Lect	Ext-2119	ecurrie	3	I	MBA		McMaster	1992
Hubberstey, Chris	Lect	Ext-2587	chubbers	3	I	MBA		Wilfrid	1992
Morouney, Kim	Lect	Ext 2485	kmoroune	2	EHR	PHD		Alberta	1993

University of Windsor — Windsor, Canada — ON N9B 3P4 — (519) UWINDSOR.CA
Faculty of Business Adm — 401 Sunset Avenue — FAX=973-7073 — BCOM,MBA
phone 253-4232

Name	Rank	Phone	Email			Degree		School	Year
Peterson, Rein	Dean	Ext 5059	rein	36	ISTU	PHD	69	Cornell	1993
—Management Area	Phone		Fax 973-7073						
Andiappan, P.	Prof	Ext 3145	andy	25	NPQR	PHD	77	Iowa	1980
Associate Dean									
Aneja, Y.	Prof	Ext 3110	aneja	79	UVXZ	PHD		JHopkins	1984
Brill, P.	Prof	Ext 3099	brill	79	UVWZ	PHD		Toronto	1984
Crocker, O. L.	Prof	Ext	mx7	25	EFNR	PHD		U Wash	198-
Morgan, A.	Prof	253-4232	ragab	36	ISTU	PHD		American	1969
Solomon, Norman	Prof	Ext 3137	nynorm	25	NPQR	PHD	80	Wiscon	1984
Templer, Andrew	Prof	Ext 3159	andrew	25	NOPQ	PHD	80	Witwater	1984
Thacker, James	Prof	Ext 3144	jwt	25	NOPQ	PHD	84	Wayne St	1982
West, E.	Prof	Ext 3118	enwest	79	UVWY	PHD		Iowa St	1983
Withane, S.	Prof	Ext 3150	ha6	23	FHNY	PHD		SUNY	1987
Cattaneo, R. J.	Assoc	Ext 3146	brc	25	ENPY	PHD		Michigan	1980
Fields, Mitchell	Assoc	Ext 3121	tl0	25	EFNP	PHD	83	Wayne St	1985

Name	Rank	Phone	Email		Field	Degree		School	Year
Forrest, A.	Assoc	Ext 3113		25	PNQR	PHD		Warwick	1986
Punnett, B. J.	Assoc	Ext 3108	bjp	28	EJNY	PHD		NYU	1985
Rieger, F.	Assoc	Ext 3089	fritz	38	HISY	PHD		McGill	1984
Singh, Jang	Assoc	Ext 3141	jang	14	JKLY	PHD		Toronto	1986
Armstrong-Stassen, Marjorie	Asst	Ext 3106	mas	25	EGNP	PHD	89	Ohio St	1989
Chaouch, B.	Asst	Ext 3149	chaouch	79	UVWZ	PHD		Waterloo	1985
Hommel, M.	Asst	Ext 3133		25	ENOR	MBA		Windsor	1993
Kao, D.	Asst	Ext 3123	kao	79	UVWZ	PHD		McMaster	1990
Miller, P.	Asst	Ext 3138	plum	79	UVWZ	MBA		Toronto	1977
Prince, M.	Asst	Ext 3130		36	ISTU	PHD		Bradford	1986
Reavley, Martha	Asst	Ext 3135	r16	25	AENR	PHD	92	Wayne St	1986

York University
Faculty of Adm Studies
  Did Not Respond-1993 Listing

Toronto, Canada ON M3J 1P3 (416)
4700 Keele Street FAX=736-5687 BBA,MBA,MPA,PHD

Name	Rank	Phone		Field	Degree		School	Year
Horvath, Dezso J.	Dean	736-5070	3	IY	PHD		UMEA	
—Management Faculty	Phone	Fax 736-5687						
Burke, Ronald J.	Prof	736-5096	2	EGR	PHD	66	Michigan	
Buzacott, John A.	Prof	736-5074	7	U	PHD	67	Birm Eng	1991
Cook, Wade D.	Prof	736-5074	7	V	PHD		Dalhouis	
Cragg, Wesley A.	Prof	736-5090	4	J	PHD		Oxford	
Cuff, Robert D.	Prof	736-5087	1	AB	PHD		Princeton	
Dermer, Jerry	Prof	736-5089	3	I	PHD		Illinios	
Gillies, James M.	Prof	736-5089	1	A	PHD		Indiana	
Green, Joseph G.	Prof	736-5087	1	I	PHD		Indiana	
Litvak, Isaiah A. (Al)	Prof	736-5089	8	Y	PHD		Columbia	
Macdonald, Ian H.	Prof	736-5088	1	A	PHD		Oxford	
McKellar, James	Prof	736-5967	1	A	MSC		Penn	
Morgan, Gareth	Prof	736-5096	2	H	PHD		Lancast	
Murray, Victor V.	Prof	736-5096	5	N	PHD		Cornell	
Roome, Nigel J.	Prof	736-5809	4	M	PHD		Cambridg	
Tryfos, Peter	Prof	736-5075	7	V	PHD		Berkeley	
Wilson, H. Thomas	Prof	736-5088	4	JR	PHD		Rutgers	
Auster, Ellen R.	Assoc	736-5087	38	FIY	PHD	83	Cornell	
Bradshaw, Patricia	Assoc	736-5093	2	EFR	PHD		York	
Darroch, James L.	Assoc	736-5082	3	I	PHD		York	
Dimick, David E.	Assoc	736-5096	2	E	PHD		Minn	
Irving, Richard H.	Assoc	736-5074	9	Z	PHD		Waterloo	
Johnston, David A.	Assoc	736-5075	7	U	PHD		W Ontari	
Lucas, Robert G.	Assoc	736-5096	5	Q	PHD		Cornell	
McKechnie, Graeme H.	Assoc	736-5096	5	Q	PHD		Wiscon	
McMillan, Charles J.	Assoc	736-5089	8	Y	PHD	75	Bradford	1974
Oliver, Christine	Assoc	736-5095	5	Q	PHD		Toronto	
Peridis, Theodoros	Assoc	736-5089	3	I	PHD		NYU	
Rosin, Hazel M.	Assoc	736-5095	5	NOR	PHD		Yale	
Weiss, Stephen E.	Assoc	736-5087	38	IY	PHD	85	Penn	
Barnett, Steven T.	Asst	736-5096	28	EQY	PHD	93	S Carol	
Karambayya, Rekha	Asst	736-5095	5	N	PHD		Northwes	
McClean, Ronald J.	Asst	736-5075	9	Z	PHD		Waterloo	
Newell, Stephanie	Asst	736-5088	3	I	PHD		Mass	
Phan, Phillip H.	Asst	736-5087	36	ITY	PHD	92	U Wash	1992
Thomassin, Singh Daniele	Asst	736-5074	79	Z	PHD		Case Wes	
Wesson, Thomas	Asst	736-5087	1	A	PHD		Harvard	
Yeomans, J. Scott	Asst	736-5074	79	UZ	PHD		McMaster	

OTHER FOREIGN SCHOOLS

University of Adelaide Adelaide, S Aust 5001 61-
Dept of Commerce   FAX=224-0464   BCO,MBA,MEC,PHD
No Management Faculty
Henderson, M. Scott   Dean 303-5527   Atg   PHD   69 UCLA   1979

University of Auckland Auckland   NewZealand 64-9 ACC.AUKUNI.AC.NZ
Commerce and Economics   FAX=3660891   BCOM,MCOM,PHD
–Department of Management Phone Ext 7216 Fax 373-7477

Inkson, Kerr	H-Pr	Ext 7198	k inkson	12	EO	PHD	80	Otago	9-80
Deeks, John	Assoc	Ext 7961	j deeks	45	LQT	MA	64	Cambridg	9-72
Haworth, Nigel	Assoc	Ext 7256	n hawort	58	QY	PHD	82	Liverpol	5-88
Wilson, Marie	Assoc	Ext 7667	m wilson	52	EFNP	PHD	90	Arizona	7-91
Boxall, Peter F.	SLect	Ext 7355	p boxall	53	NQIB	MCOM	87	Auckland	1-87
Powell, Michael	SLect	Ext 7283	m powell	21	HBL	PHD	82	Chicago	1-89
Barry, David	SLect	Ext 7153	d. barry	28	FEP	PHD	86	Maryland	4-93
Casey, Catherine	Lect	Ext 5905	e casey	58	HLQY	PLH	93	Rochest	5-93
Hughes, Stephen G.	Lect	Ext 7314	s hughes	58	QYE	MA	85	Warwick	7-91
Johnson, E. K.	Lect	Ext 5032	ek johns	25	ENP	PHD	90	Tulane	9-92
Kolb, Darl	Lect	Ext 8928	d Kolb	21	FPXY	PHD	91	Cornell	1-92
Rasmussen, Erling	SLect	Ext 7256	e rassmu	51	QNPA	PHD	86	Florente	3-93
Lamm, Felicity A.	STut	Ext 7201	f-lamm	54	QMKC	MPHI	89	Auckland	1-91
Lindberg, Lynne R.	STut	5700200		25		MA	89		1-91

Australian National Univ CamberraAct0200 Australia (06) FAC.ANU.EDU.AU
Faculty of Econ & Comm   FAX=2495005
–Management Faculty   Phone 249-3664 Fax 249-5005

Craig, Russell J.	H-Pr		14	ABCL	PHD	89	N'cle	1991
Clarke, Roger	Read		9	ILYZ	MCOM	75	NS Wales	1984
Burritt, Roger L.	SLect	294-3664		MF	MPHL	75	Oxon	1989
Hodgson, Allan	SLect		37	HILV	MEC	88	NE	1989
Jubb, Peter	SLect		12	AJY	MA	73	Oxon	1975
Kelly, Gary	SLect			AEHL	MEC	87	NE	1987
Shailer, Gregory	SLect		14	ESIL	MCOM	85	Newcastl	1990
Brehaut, Steven	Lect		9	ZS	BSC	80	LaTrobe	1984
Fink, Dieter	Lect		9	Z	DCOM	91	S Africa	1994
Greinke, Andrew	Lect		4	JKL	BCOM	90	Aust Nat	1992
Haswell, Stephen	Lect		8	Y	MEC	90	Aust Nat	1986
Hooper, Vince	Lect		8	Y	BAHO	90	UofP UK	1994
Jenkins, Sarah	Lect		3	BEFI	GRDI	90	CU	1993
Klumpes, Paul	Lect		4	KY	MCOM	90	NS Wales	1990
Oliver, Barry	Lect		7	VY	MEC	91	Monash	1991
Pedler, Michael	Lect		9	AISZ	MEC	93	NE	1993
Rigby, Elaine	Lect		1	AE	MED	89	Sydney	1992
Tahir, Mohammad	Lect		7	VY	MSC	82	Aust Nat	1990
Tran, Alfred	Lect		4		MSS	88	HongKong	1991

University of Bath Claverton Down BA27AY 0225
School of Management   FAX=826473
–Management Faculty   Phone 82659382 Fax 6473

Mangham, I. L.	H-Pr	2	E	PHD
Baden-Fuller, C.	Prof	3	I	PHD
Bayliss, B. T.	Prof	8	Y	PHD
Ford, I. D.	Prof	6	St	PHD
Lamming, R. C.	Prof	7	W	
IPS Professor of Purchasing and Supply Management				
Targett, D.	Prof	9	Z	PHD
ICL Professor of Information Systems				
Tomkins, C. R.	Prof	1	A	MSC
Butt, Philip A.	Read	8	Y	DPH
Fineman, S.	Read	2	EFG	PHD
Robinson, O.	Read	5	N	PHD
Marshall, J.	SLect	2	E	PHD
Reason, P. W.	SLect	2	E	PHD
Sims, D. B. P.	SLect	2	F	PHD
Arthurs, A. J.	Lect	5	Q	PHD
Bate, S. P.	Lect	5	Q	PHD
Clarke, K.	Lect	3	I	MSC
Doyle, J. R.	Lect	9	Z	DPHL
Edwards, J. P.	Lect	3	I	MA
Director of the Centre for Enterprise Policy Studies				
Gabriel, Y.	Lect	2	E	PHD
Green, R. H.	Lect	79	UZ	PHD
Kinnie, N. J.	Lect	5	QN	PHD
Pye, A.	Lect	2	F	PHD
Staughton, R. V. W.	Lect	7	U	MIPR

Name	Title					Degree		Institution	Year
Brockington, R. B.	Lect			1	A	MSC			
Clegg, J. L.	Lect			8	Y	PHD			
Colville, I. G.	Lect			1	A	PHD			
Cousins, P. D.	Lect			7	W	MBA			
Harris, D. J.	Lect			7	U	MSC			
McAulay, L.	Lect			9	Z	MSC			
Morgan, E. J.	SLect			3	I	MA			
Nicholls, J. R.	Lect			8	Y	MSC			
Pitt, M. R.	Lect			3	I	MSC			
Ray, G. H.	Lect					PHD			
Vass, P.	Lect			1	A	MSC			
Wabe, J. S.	Lect			8	Y	DPH			
Wilson-Ward, J. S.	Lect			4	K	BBA			

Bond University — Gold Coast, Qld — Australia — (075) BU.OZ.AU
School of Business 4229 — FAX=95-1160 — BCOM,MBA,PHD

Name	Title	Phone	email			Degree		Institution	Year
Goldsworthy, Ashley W.	Dean	952202	a_goldsw			MSC	80	Griffith	1991
—Management Faculty	Phone	95-2210	Fax 95-1160						
Crouch, Agd	Prof	952221		23	FI	PHD	82	NS Wales	1989
Fisher, Cynthia D.	Assoc	952215	c_fisher	25	ENY	PHD	78	Purdue	8-90
Gibson, Peter	Assoc	952209	p_gibson	37	I	PHD	84	Leichstr	1994
Shaw, James B.	Assoc	952235	b_shaw	58	ENY	PHD	78	Purdue	8-90
Basch, John A.	Asst	952258	—	23	EHI	MBA	79	Queensld	1989
Hickey, Kristin	SrTch	952233	k_hickey	3	I	MBA	92	Bond	1992
Shepherd, Dean	SrTch	951162	d_shepherd	36	IT	MBA	92	Bond	1992

Bournemouth Polytechnic — Dorset, England — BH12 5BB — 0202
Dept of Finance & Law — FAX=513293 — BA,MA,HRM
Did Not Respond-1992 Listing; School: 0202 524111

Name	Title					Degree		Institution	Year
—Management Faculty	Phone		Fax 513293						
Williams, David	H	Ext 5151			I	MSC			1980
Orper, Chritonie	Read	Ext-5141			EN	PHD			1990
Brown, Ray	SLect	595140		14		MSC	67	Notting	9-63
Haywood, Helen	SLect			8		BA			7-90
Oberoi, Usha	SLect			12	EXZ	PHD			3-90
Perry, Keith	SLect			48	LY				
Prescott, Jean	SLect	5148		52	ON	MSC		Salford	9-71
Swindley, David	Lect	595120		34	IJL	MSC			1-91
Watford, Louise	Asst	595146		12	NH	BA	87		1990
Harris, Christine		595119				MSC			
Harvey, Christine		595118		7	V	MSC		Brunel	9-71
Kilburn, David				8	Y	MBA			
Shiel, Christine		595145		25	NYR	BA			1990

University of Bristol — Bristol BS81TN — 0272 UK.AC.BRISTOL
Department of Economics — FAX=288577 — BSC,MSC,PHD

Name	Title		email			Degree		Institution	Year
—Faculty of Social Sciences	Phone	303030	Fax 288577						
Egginton, D. A.	H-Pr		ecdae	39	L	BSC	60		1963
Ashton, D. J.	Prof		ecda	79	V	PHD	79	Warwick	1989
Forker, J. J.	Lect	ecjjf		78	L	MS	74		1976
Green, Susan	Lect	ecsg		2	HI	PHD			1988
Lyne, S. R.	Lect	ecsrl		2	HI	PHD	90	Bristol	1980
Merriman, A. M.	Lect	ecamm		2	J	BA	56		1969
Shah, A.	Lect	ecas		3	I	PPD	93	LSE	1992

University of Canterbury — Christchurch1 NZ — NewZealand — (03) MANG.CANTERBURY.AC.NZ
Faculty of Commerce — FAX=364-2999 — BCO,MCO,MBA,PHD

Name	Title		email			Degree		Institution	Year
—Department of Management	Phone	364-2606	Fax 364-2020						
George, John A.	H-SLe	364-2886	jag	7	V	PHD	80	Canterbu	1968
Daellenbach, H. G.	Prof	364-2630	hgd	7	V	PHD		Berkeley	1970
Hamilton, R. T.	Prof	364-2467	rth	36	IS	PHD	82	London	1983
Dakin, S. R.	SLect	364-2671	srd	2	EF	PHD	73	Toronto	1973
Lamar, Bruce W.	SLect	364-2941	bwl	7	UV	PHD		MIT	1991
McNickle, Donald	SLect	364-2643	dcm	7	V	PHD	74	Auckland	1977
Paul, H.	SLect	364-2663	hrp	7	Y	DENG	75	Asian Te	1987
Read, E. G.	SLect	364-2885	egr	7	V	PHD	79	Canterbu	1985
Singer, A. E.	SLect	364-2662	aes	34	IJL	PHD	93	Canterbu	1984
Addison, R.	Lect	366-7001	rza	25	Q	MCOM		Canterbu	
Cammock, P. A.	Lect	366-7001	pac	12	E	PHD	91	Canterbu	1983
Fenwick, Graham D.	Lect	364-2670	gdf	14	L	PHD	84	Canterbu	1990
Neal, Derrick J.	Lect	364-2564	djn	3		PHD	80	Canterbu	1987
Nilakant, V.	Lect	364-2672	vnk	25	EH	PHD	84	Case Wes	1988
Lye, A. R.	ALect	364-2654	arl	8	Y	MBA	81	Iowa	1994
Venkateswarlu, P.	Lect	364-2629	pvl	7	UV	PHD	83	IITBomba	1991

Chinese Univ of Hong Kong — Shatin, NT — Hong Kong — (852) @VAX.CSC.CUHK.HK
Faculty of Business Adm — FAX=6035114
–Department of Management — Phone 609-7898 — Fax 603-5104

Name	Title	Phone						
Chow, Irene H.	C-SLe	609-7798		35	NOE	PHD	83	Geo St 8-83
Poon, Wai K.	SLect	609-7799		25	EFNP	PHD	76	Toronto 8-91

City Polytechnic - Hong Kong — Kowloon — Hong Kong — (852) CPHKVX
Faculty of Business — 83 Tat Chee Avenue — FAX=788-7220 — BA,MBA,MPHL,PHD
–Dept Business & Management — Phone 788-7880 — Fax 788-7220

Taylor, Keith	Read	788-7892	bmkeith	2	EFHO	PHD	75	Melbourn 1-91
De Leon, Corinna T.	SLect	788-7969	bmdeleon	28	DEJP	PHD		UK 3-90
McFetridge, Peter R.	SLect	788-7868	bmprmcfe			PHD		8-85
Poblador, N. S.	SLect	788-7937	pmpobl	2	H	PHD	72	Penn 9-89
Snell, Robin S.	Assoc	788-7988	bmsnell	12	JPS	MA	74	UK
Weininger, Michael	SLect	788-7965	bmmaw	38	YIB	PHD	90	Texas 9-91
Associate Head								
Akhtar, Syed	Lect	788-7870	bmsyed	25	EFNP	PHD	83	IITDelhi 1-91
Chan, Andrew	Lect	788-7300	bmandrew	52	BHN	MBA	91	HongKong 3-92
Chan, H. L.	Lect	788-7955	bmhlchan	34	ISTY	MBA	79	HongKong 8-87
Chu, Priscilla P.	Lect	788-7181	bm8301	14	FILR	MSC	86	HongKong 8-86
Ding, Daniel	Lect	788-8667				PHD		
Herndon, Neil	Lect	788-9652				PHD		
Izumi, Hiroaki	Lect	788-7240	bmrockiz	28	EFHY	PHD	92	Tx Tech 9-90
Ko, Anthony C. K.	Lect	788-7976	bmackko	16	HINY	MBA	85	HongKong 8-88
Lau, Agnes T. W.	Lect	788-8953	bmagnes	25	DFOP	MSC	88	UK 3-92
Lau, Pinky M. M.	Lect	788-7881	pmmlau	14	ELP	MA	85	Lancast 9-88
Lee, Jenny S. Y.	Loot	708-7954	bmjenny	19	PZ	MBA	80	St Louis 8-87
Leong, Foo Weng	Lect	788-7877	bmleong	81	INPY	MBA	84	Okla St 9-89
Mak, Simon K. M.	Lect	788-7957	bmsimak	38	ILY	MBA	84	Cty P HK 8-88
Martinsons, Maris G.	Lect	788-7958	bmmaris	39	ITYV	MBA	84	Toronto 8-88
Mondejar, Reuben	Lect	788-7200	bmreuben	14	BHLY	PHD	89	Navarre 9-89
Ng, Judy W. F.	Lect	788-7959	bmjudyng	13	DIPY	MSC	85	Salford 9-90
Ngai Ding yuen, Ernest	Lect	788-7857	bmernest	79	IWZ	MSC	87	Lancast 9-88
Pang, Mary Y. N.	Lect	788-7874	bmpang			PHD		
Tan, Doreen S. K.	Lect	788-7853	bmdoreen	25	ENPQ	MSC	78	London 1-91
Taylor, William	Lect	788-9612	bmwkty	58	MQUY	MA	86	UK 1-93
Tse, Olivia K. M.	Lect	788-7953	bmolivia	35	INGY	MBA		HongKong 9-87
Tseng, C. S.	Lect	788-7956	bmtseng	38	DIY	MSC	70	London 1-89
Wong, May M. L.	Lect	788-8921	samay	25	EN	MSC	85	Tokyo 9-89
Wyatt, Thomas	Lect	788-9631				PHD		
Yu, Eddie J. K.	Lect	788-7879	bmeddie	13	FIT	MSC	84	Durham 9-89
Cheung, Fanny S. L.	ALect	788-7893	bmfanny	14	LR	MA	87	Lancast 9-89
Chow, Esther L. Y.	ALect	788-7875	bm211592	13	DIPY	MBA	87	UK 8-90
Dines, Teck	ALect	788-7858		38	Y	MBA	90	Japan 2-93
Fok, Vincent S. C.	ALect	788-7876	bmfokv	36	ISTY	MBA	91	HongKong 2-93
Tham, Alex K. S.	ALect	788-7851	bmalexth	37	IPSY	MBA	92	UK 9-92
Wong, Helen	ALect	788-8842		25	EHPQ	BA	89	London 9-92
Wong, Ralph L. K.	ALect	788-7850	bm4875	25	NO	MA	85	Hull 9-90
Yeung, Jack K. W.	ALect	788-7852	bmyeung	1	DSZ	MSC	88	London 1990
Brivins, Aelita G.	Demo	788-7871	bmaelita	12	EFGP	BA	85	Canada 9-92

Deakin University-Burwood — Burwood Vic 3125 — Australia — (03) DEAKIN
Bowater School of Mgt — FAX=
–Faculty of Management — Phone 2446170 — Fax 2446967

Smart, John P.	C-Pr	244 6170	smart	35	EN	MBA	68	Melbourn
Mahoney, Darrell	Prof	244 6189		38	I	MADM		Monash
Holden, Alison	Assoc	244 6265		12	AZ	EMD		Melbourn
Auston, John	SLect	244 6512		5		MA		LaTrobe
Shepparat, Barie	SLect	244 6373		14		MA		Monash
Shilbury, David	SLect	244 6164		13	ID	MSC		Mass
Zulian, Flora	SLect	244 6276		19	Z	BCOM		Melbourn
Deane, John	Lect	244 6678		13	BF	MED		Liverpoo
Drennan, Judy	Lect	244 6272		12	SZ	MED		Melbourn
Graetz, Fiona	Lect	244 6296		1	D	GRAD		Camberra
Hagel, Pauline	Lect	244 6934		12	DR	MBA		Deakin
Hoffmann, Terry	Lect	244 6165		5	OP	BA		LaTrobe
Krejcar, Barbara	Lect	244 6329		1	D	MED		Monash
Lawrence, Ann	Lect	244 6904		35	DR	BED		Monash
Sneddon, Margaret	Lect	244 6270		12	P	BED		MSC
Trigg, Marie	Lect	244 6166		38	DR	MBA		Monash

Deakin University — Geelong Vic 3217 — Australia — (052)
Bowater School of Mgt — FAX=41 1542 — BCOM,MCOM,MBA

Name	Title	Phone						
Wolnizer, Peter W.	Dean	271-275				PHD	86	Sydney 1989
Wolnizer, Peter W.	Dean	271-275				PHD	86	Sydney 1989
–Department of Management	Phone	27 1277	Fax 272 151					
Lethbridge, David G.	Prof	271-283		13	I	MSC		London 1979

Buxey, Geoff M.	SLect	271-421		7	U	PHD	82	Reading	1984
McCarthy, Terry E.	SLect	271-564		25	NQ	MA	80	Melbourn	1982
McWilliams, John	SLect	271-360		2	EF	PHD	82	Manchest	1990
Petzall, Stanley B.	SLect	271036		2	EF	PHD		LaTrobe	1986
Robertson, Helen	STut	271-743		25	EFN	BA	75	Monash	1989

Deakin Univ at Warrnambool	Warrnambool 3280			Australia	(055)				
Bowater School of Mgt				FAX=618320					
Wolnizer, Peter W.	Dean	271-275				PHD	86	Sydney	1989
—Faculty of Management	Phone	633 284	Fax 633 320						
Symons, Ian R.	SLect			12	DG	MBA	85	Deakin	1991

University of East Anglia	Norwich, England	NR4 7TJ		0603	UK.AC.UEA.SYS				
School of Info Systems				FAX=507720					
Did Not Respond-1992 Listing									
—Department of Management	Phone		Fax 507720						
Hinings, P. H.	Asst	56161		3	I	FCA			1979
Lawrenson, D.	Asst	56161		2	EH	PHD			1991

University of Essex	Colchester, Eng	CO4 3SQ		0206	UK.AC.ESSEX				
Business Faculty				FAX=873598			BA,MA,MBA		
—Management Faculty	Phone		Fax 873598						
Brown, Reva	Asst	872375	reva	12	BH	PHD	91		1991
King, Ian	Asst	872637	kingi	23	DFP	PHD	90		1990

Flinders U of S Australia	GPO Box2100Ade	AUST 5001		61-08	AFML.LAW.FLINDERS.EDU				
Faculty of Soc Sciences				FAX=201-2566		BCOM,MCOM,MA,PH			
—Sch of Atg, Finance, & Mtg	Phone	201-2226	Fax 201-2644						
Parker, Lee D.	H-Pr	201-2643	parker	13	ABIJ	PHD	83	Montash	5-88
McMahon, Richard G. P.	Assoc	201-2840	mcmahon	6	ST	MBA	80	Adelaide	1978
Forsaith, David M.	LectB	201-2344	forsaith	6	ST	MSC	75	London	7-90
Fuller, Donald E.	LectB	201-2299	fuller	37	AS	PHD	84	Adelaide	1991
Hall, Katherine H.	LectB	201-2729	hall	84	KL	LLB	88	Adelaide	1990
Kandunias, Chris	LectA	201-3839	kandunia	1	S	BCOM	92	Adelaid	3-92
Lewis, Neil R.	LectC	201-2479	lewis	12	HTZI	MBA	87	Montash	7-91
Mangos, Nicholas C.	LectB	201-2361	mangos	34	DJ	MBA	85	Adelaide	7-90
Mathews, Clive M. H.	LectB	201-2728	mathews	19	Z	MBS	90	Massey	1990
O'Brien, Peter W.	LectC	201-2707	obrien	18	NOYR	DED	76	S Africa	1-91
Petrone, Franca	LectB	201-2013	petrone	4	JKM	LLB	88	Adelaide	3-93
Roffey, Bet H.	LectB	201-2195	roffey	35	AFIP	MBA	90	RMIT	1991
Superina, Susan C.	LectA	201-2766	superina	69	ZST	BEC	79	Adelaide	1988
Symes, Christopher S.	LectA	201-3890	symes	4	KS	LLB	89	Adelaide	3-93
Tilt, Carol A.	LectA	201-3892	tilt	1	M	DACC	91	Flinders	3-93
Xydias, Maira	LectA	201-3891	xydias	1	D	BCOM	92	Adelaide	3-93
Stanger, Anthony M. J.	LectB	201-2764	stanger	6	ST	BCOM	85	Tasmania	2-89

Griffith University	Nathan, Brisbane	AUST 4111		61-7	CAD.GU.EDU.AU				
Fac of Commerce & Adm				FAX=875-7750		BA,BCOM,MA,PHD			
Did Not Respond-1993 Listing; Includes only faculty voluntarily listing									
—Management Faculty	Phone		Fax 875-7750						
Limerick, David	Prof	875-7145		23	DEFI	PHD		Witwatnd	7-79
Nguyen, D. T.	Prof	875-7617		38	ILVY	PHD		Austr Na	1-89
Quinlan, Michael	Assoc	875-7582		5	Q	PHD		Sydney U	1-81
Dagwell, Ron	SLect	875-7232		13	AELP	MFM		Queens	2-82
Gardner, Margaret	SLect	875-7725	margaret	5	ANPR	PHD		Sydney	7-82
Glen, William	SLect	875-7609		6	ST	PHD			7-89
McCoy, Elaine	SLect	875-7665		38	AIKL	PHD			9-89
Selvanathan, Saroja	SLect	875-7616		7	VY	PHD	89	W.A.	8-89
Wanna, John	SLect	875-7361		14	AL	PHD		Adelaide	1-85
Bryant, Kay C.	Lect	875-7668		79	VXZ	BCOM	84	Queensld	3-86
Campbell, John	Lect	875-7741		79	VXZ	BCOM		Hons	1-88
Harker, Michael	Lect	875-7696		38	IPT	MA			2-90
Sheehan, Michael J.	Lect	875-7456		25	FJNP	MSC	92	Griffith	2-91
Sheldon, Peter	Lect	875-7659	psheldon	5	BQ	PHD	89	Wollong	2-91
Thornthwaite, Louise	Lect	875-7652		5	BQ	PHD	91	Sydney	7-90

University of Guam	Mangilao, Guam	96923		(671)	UOG.EDU				
College of Bus & Pub Ad				FAX=734-5362		BS			
McGillivray, Robert E.	Dean	734-9225	mcgilliv		Atg	PHD	74	North Tx	1990
—Management Faculty	Phone	734-9247	Fax 734-5362						
Bradberry, William	C-Ac	734-9237	wbrad	83	ULJI	PHD	86	Tx-Dallas	1990
Blaise, Hans	Prof	734-9424	hblaise	28	EYD	PHD	81	Pitt	1981
Kim, Duck Shin	Assoc	734-9418	dkim	28	YE	PHD	77	Geo St	1989
Ko, Kwangsoo	Assoc	734-9428	kwangsoo	79	VZ	PHD	90	Purdue	1991
Sauget, Clyde	Assoc	734-9532	csauget	81	Z	PHD	77	Gold Gt	1993
Featherman, Morris	Inst	734-9417	mfeather	97	Z	MSSM	90	S Calif	1993
McGahey, Stanley	Inst	734-9483	smchahey	1	X	MS	82	W Illin	1993

Hebrew Univ of Jerusalem

Mount Scopus ISR 91905   9722   FAX=322545

BA,MBA,PHD

School of Business Adm

Name	Rank	Phone	Email	Code	University
Meshulach, Avraham	D	88-3235	msavim	DBA	Harvard
–Department of Management	Phone	88-3235	Fax 32-2545		
Galai, Dan	Prof	88-3228		PHD	Chicago
Kornbluth, Jonathan	Prof	88-3102	mskorn	PHD	Imperial
Levy, Haim	Prof	88-3101	mshlevy	PHD	Hebrew
Peles, Yoram	Prof	88-3215	mspeles	PHD	
Sarnat, Marshall	Prof	88-3107		PHD	Northwes
Zuckerman, Dror	Prof	88-3082	msdzuck	PHD	Cornell
Bar-Yosef, Sasson	Assoc	88-3104		PHD	Aston Bm
Barlev, Benzion	Assoc	88-3103	bbarlev	PHD	NYU
Ben-Horin, Moshe	Assoc	88-3235	msmoney	PHD	NYU
Benninga, Simon	Assoc	88-3105	mssimon	PHD	Tel Aviv
Friedman, Avraham	Assoc	88-3108	friedman	PHD	Chicago
Goldman, Arieh	Assoc	88-3114		PHD	Berkeley
Kroll, Yoram	Assoc	88-3084		PHD	Hebrew
Landskroner, Yoram	Assoc	88-3440	msdinah	PHD	Penn
Toren, Nina	Assoc	88-3232	msntoren	PHD	Columbia
Venezia, Itzhak	Assoc	88-3222	msvenez	PHD	Berkeley
Mazursky, David	SLect	88-3217	msmazur	PHD	NYU
Ofir, Chezy	SLect	88-3117k	msofir	PHD	Columbia
Rafaeli, Anat	SLect	88-3073	msrafa	PHD	Ohio
Rafaeli, Sheizaf	SLect	88-3106	sheizaf	PHD	Stanford
Raveh, Adi	SLect	88-3216	msraveh	PHD	Hebrew
Ben-David, Arie	Lect	88-3449	msariebd	PHD	Cas West
Bergman, Yaakov	Lect	88-3116	msyberg	PHD	Berkeley
Ganzach, Yoav	Lect	88-3049	mskbugy	PHD	Columbia
Kluger, Avraham	Lect	88-1009	mskluger	PHD	Stevens
Moshe, Leshno	Lect	88-3227		PHD	Tel Aviv
Mosheiov, Gur	Lect	88-3790	msomer	PHD	Columbia
Spector, Yishay	Lect	88-3226	mspector	PHD	Tel Aviv
Weber, Yaakov	Lect	88-3218	msohad	PHD	S Carol
Yahalom, Raphel	Lect	88-3078	yahalom	PHD	Cambridg

Hitotsubashi University

Kunitachi, Tokyo 186   0425   FAX=74-8992

BA,MA,DBA

Faculty of Commerce   phone (0425) 72-1101

Name	Rank	Phone						
Kataoka, Hiroshi	Dean							
–Management Faculty	Phone		Fax 74-8992					
Komatsu, Akira	Prof	Ext 3574	4	L	MC	72	Hitotsub	1992
Murata, Kazuhiko	Prof	Ext 3466	5	U	DC	78	Hitotsub	1973
Shibakawa, Rinya	Prof	Ext 3559	8	I	DE	80	Hitotsub	1990
Tajima, Moriyuki	Prof	Ext 3563	2	U	DC	74	Hitotsub	1961
Hiraga, Ryuta	Asst	Ext 3495	5	U	MC	90	Hitotsub	1993
Kusunoki, Takeshi	Asst	Ext 3592	7	I	MC	89	Hitotsub	1992

University of Hong Kong

Hong Kong   Hong Kong   (852) HKUCC   FAX=858-5614

BBA,MBA,PHD

Dept of Mgt Studies

Name	Rank	Phone	Fax/Email			Code	Date
–Management Faculty	Phone	859-1020	Fax 858-5614				
Stewart, S. E. A.	C-Ac	859-1010	sstewart	18	M	MA	1-83
Redding, S. G.	Prof	859-2266		23	EIN	PHD	9-82
Tricker, R. I.	Prof	859-1022	tricker	23	IJFD	PHD	9-86
Donleavy, G. D.	Assoc	859-1014	gdon	4	JL	PHD	9-88
Frankenstein, J.	Assoc	859-1004	kfranken	38	IY	PHD	1-91
Ng, S. H.	Assoc	859-1003		52	QN	PHD	1-78
Chiu, E. K. C.	Asst	859-1005		1		BEC	9-79
Lam, S. S.	Asst	859-1008	simonlam	79	VUZ	MSC	9-89
Newton, J.	Asst	859-1012	jnewton	68	SY	MSC	9-81
Pyatt, R.	Asst	859-1026	trpyatt	13	I	MSC	9-90
Reid, D. M.	Asst	859-1025	davereid	3	IX	PHD	1-90
Tam, S. K. W.	Asst	859-1013		26	HT	MSC	1-85
Tao, I. H. H.	Asst	859-1002	ivytao	9	Z	MSC	9-83
Tso, P. S.	Asst	859-1007	hrnmpst	17	Z	PHD	4-79
Whitman, J. D.	Asst	859-1011	whitman	9	Z	MSC	9-86
Wong, D. W. S.	Asst	859-1006	dwongws	1		MBA	9-76
Wong, G. Y. Y.	Asst	859-1016	gilwong	12	EF	MBA	1-81
Wong, M. Y.	Asst	859-7033	mywong	37	IUV	PHD	3-92

University of Humberside

Cottingham, Hull   HU6 7RT   0482   FAX=471345

BA,MHIL,MBA,PHD

ENGLAND   Did Not Respond-1993 Listing

Name	Rank	Phone		Code
Pardoe, Kevin	Dean	440-3066		7
–Humberside Business School	Phone	440550	Fax 471345	
Golding, D.	Read	440-3068		2
Simon, D. S.	Read	440-3080		
Argent, M.	SLect	440-3016		3

Name	Title	Phone	
Caldwell, T.	SLect	440-3088	7
Chadburn, D.	SLect	440-3065	3
Gregory, D.	SLect	440-3805	2
Herbert, R.	SLect	440-3196	7
Hogg, C.	SLect	440-3237	2
Hornsby, C. R.	SLect	440-3006	
Maksymiw, W.	SLect	440-3160	2
Marchant, A.	SLect	440-3139	3
Mason, R.	SLect	440-3185	7
Milsom, B.	SLect	440-3069	2
Varlow, P.	SLect	440-3016	
Watson, J.	SLect	440-3106	7
Agyeman, S.	Lect	440-3349	2
Cagney-Watts, H.	Lect	440-3056	2
Dispenza, V.	Lect	440-3807	2
Barclay, N.	PLect	440-3070	2
Barnes, Ian	PLect	440-3015	3
Associate Dean			
Burnett, P.	PLect	440-3000	
Golding, J.	PLect	440-3055	2
Jones, Rosina	PLect	440-3153	3
Associate Dean			
Pike, C.	PLect	440-3060	2
Currie, D.			2
Desa, D.			2
Dixon, J.			7
Dobson, F.			2
Flynn, J.			7
Gibson, T.			2
Gribbin, S.			3
Grimble, M.			2
Jenkins, M.			2
Jones, M.			
Associate Dean			
Kellie, J.			2
McGivern, F.			2
Murtagh, T.			7
Thompson, C.			3
Thompson, J.			2

Intl Inst for Mgt Develop	Lausanne, Switze	CH-1001	41 21					
Ch Bellerive 23 Box 915			FAX=					
Lorange, Peter	Pres	618-0111	3	I		DBA	72 Harvard	1979
—Management Faculty	Phone	618-0111	Fax 618-0707					
Abell, Derek F.			3	I		DBA	Harvard	
Aykac, Ahmet			7	VX		MPHI	Columbia	
Bidault, Francis			7	U		DE	Montpell	
Boscheck, Ralf			3	I		PHD	St Galln	
Boshyk, Yury			4	L		DPH	Oxford	
Bouvard, Jacques M.			3	I		MBA	Harvard	
Campbell, Terry L.			9	Z		DBA	Indiana	
Casse, Pierre			2	E		PHD	Lille	
Collins, Robert S.			72	U		DBA	Indiana	
Cordon, Carlos			7	UV		PHD	Insead	
Dowd, James J. Jr.			2	E		DBA	87 Harvard	
Ellert, James C.			3	I		PHD	Chicago	
Gilbert, Xavier			3	I		DBA	Harvard	
Greville, Mary Rose			2	E		MPHI	Kent	
Haour, Georges			5	Q		PHD	Toronto	
Jenster, Per V.			3	I		PHD	Pitt	
Jolly, Vijay K.			8	Y		PHD	Harvard	
Kashani, Kamran			38	IY		DBA	Harvard	
Ketelhohn, Werner			35	IQ		PHD	LSU	
Kubes, Z. Jan.			35	IN		MBAA	Harvard	
Lank, Alden G.			56	NS		DBA	Harvard	
Marchand, Don						PHD	UCLA	
Matthews, William H.			13	DI		PHD	MIT	
Neubauer, Franz-Friedrich			38	IY		DR	Wurzburg	
Schar, Kurt			3	I		DBA	Harvard	
Sjoblom, Leif			9	Z		PHD	Stanford	
Strebel, Paul			38	IY		PHD	Princeton	
Taucher, George			3	I		DR	Lausanne	
Turpin, Dominique V.			83	YI		PHD	Sophia	
Vandermerwe, Andre'			83	YI		DCOM	Stellenb	
Vandermerwe, Sandra			38	IY		DBA	Stellenb	
Vollmann, Thomas E.			7	UV		PHD	UCLA	
Wood, Jack D.			2	E		PHD	Yale	

INSEAD 77305	Fontainebleau France	(331) INSEAD.FR			
Business	Boulevard de Constance	FAX=60724242			MBA,PHD

Strategy Dept Did Not Respond-1993 Listing; Phone (33) 1 60724322

Name	Rank	Phone	Fax			Degree		School	
Rameau, Claude	Dean	60724221		7		MBA	62	INSEAD	9-67
Van Der Heyden, Ludo	Dean	60724221		7	V	PHD	79	Yale	9-88
–Strategy Department	Phone		Fax 60724242						
Dyas, Gareth P.	C-Ac	60724000		3	I	DBA	72	Harvard	1-73
Chakravarthy, Balaji S.	Prof	60724349		3	I	DBA	78	Harvard	1-92
Doz, Yves L.	Prof	60724673		8	YI	DBA	76	Harvard	9-80
Ghoshal, Sumantra	Prof	60724000		38	IY	DBA	86	Harvard	9-85
Heau, Dominique	Prof	60724250		3		DBA	76	Harvard	7-73
Lasserre, Phillippe	Prof	60724000		3	I	PHD	75	Texas	5-75
Thanheiser, Heinz T.	Prof	60724000		3	I	DBA	72	Harvard	1-72
Cool, Karel	Assoc	60724000		3	I	PHD	85	Purdue	1-85
Dierickx, Ingemar	Assoc	60724000		3	I	PHD	85	Harvard	9-85
Haspeslagh, Philippe	Assoc	60724000		3	I	DBA	83	Harvard	9-79
Sick, Todd	Assoc	607-2400		25	EF	PHD7	78	Cornell	9-92
Muzyka, Daniel	Asst	60724000		6	I	DBA	89	Harvard	9-90
Overmeer, Willem	Asst	60724000		3	I	PHD	89	MIT	9-90
Verdin, Paul	Asst	60724393		3	I	PHD	89	Harvard	9-91
–Organizational Behavior Dep	Phone	60724000	Fax 60724242						
Brimm, Michael	C-Ac	60724000		25	EF	DBA	75	Harvard	9-78
Evans, Paul	Prof	60724000		25	NY	PHD	74	MIT	8-74
Kets De Vries, Manfred F. R.	Prof	60724000		26	ET	DBA	70	Harvard	1-85
Laurent, Andre	Prof	60724000		28	EY	DOCT	68	Paris	8-72
Thoenig, Jean-Claude	Prof	60224805		?	H	LIC	03	Geneve	9-78
Schneider, Susan	Assoc	00724000		25	H	PHD	76	Adelphi	9-85
Gargiulo, Martin	Asst	60724000		2	EH	PHD	92	Columbia	9-92
Koza, Mitchell P.	Asst	60724000		23	IY	PHD	85	Chicago	1-89
Brimm, Linda	Affil	60724000		25	EP	DOCT	82	Paris	9-83
–Econ & Political Sci Dept	Phone	60724212	Fax 60724242						
Gabel, H. Landis	C-Pr	60724000		4		PHD	77	Penn	9-82
Ayres, Robert	Prof	60724000				PHD		London	
Story, Jonathan	Prof	60724000		8	Y	PHD	73	J Hopkin	7-74
Walter, Ingo	Prof	60724000		8	Y	PHD	66	NYU	9-88
Wyplosz, Charles	Prof	60724000				PHD		Harvard	
Burda, Michael	Assoc	60724000				PHD		Harvard	
Roller, Lars-Hendrik	Assoc	60724000				PHD		Penn	
Cadot, Oliver	Asst	60724000				PHD		Princeton	
Fatas, Antonio	Asst	60724000				PHD		Harvard	
Kende, Michael	Asst	60724000				PHD		MIT	
Webber, Douglas	Asst	60724000		8	Y	PHD	85	Essex	1-91
–Management Inform Systems	Phone		Fax 60724242						
Jelassi, Tawfik	C-Ac	60724000	jelassi	9	Z	PHD	85	NYU	1-89
Angehrn, Albert A.	Asst	60724000	angehrn	9	Z	PHD	89	Eth	9-90
Dutta, Soumitra	Asst	60724000	dutta	9	Z	PHD	89	Berkeley	9-89

Lancaster University	Lancaster, UK LA1 4YX	0524 UK.AC.LANCASTER			
Management School		FAX=381454			BA,BSC,MBA,PHD

1991 Listing; Area Code (0524) - school phone 65201

Name	Rank	Phone	Fax			Degree	School
Ashton, D. J. L.	Dean			25	NOPY	MSC	Bradford
–Management Faculty	Phone		Fax 381454				
Blackler, F. H. M.	Prof			25	EGH	MPHL	London
Burgoyne, J. G.	Prof	52465201		25	NOP	PHD	Manchest
Checkland, P. B.	Prof			13	AEIZ	MA	Oxford
Fildes, R.	Prof			71	UVZ	PHD	Calif
Kingsman, B. G.	Prof			7	UVZ	PHD	Lancaste
Legge, Karen	Prof			25	EHN	DSAS	Oxford
Mercer, A.	Prof			73	AUVZ	PHD	London
Cooper, R. C.	Read			25	EH	PHD	Liverpoo
Crookes, J. G.	SLect			7	UVZ	MSC	Birmingh
Easterby-Smith, M. P. V.	SLect			25	NOPY	PHD	Durham
Eglese, R. W.	SLect			7	AUVZ	MA	Lancaste
Hindle, A.	SLect			47	AUVZ	PHD	Nottingh
Pidd, M.	SLect			47	AUVZ	MSC	Birmingh
Rand, G. K.	SLect			7	UVYZ	BSC	Liverpoo
Reynolds, P. M.	SLect			25	NOP	PHD	Durham
Wilson, B.	SLect			1	AEIZ	PHD	Nottingh
Ackroyd, S. C.	Lect			25	EHQ	MSC	London
Avmitage, S. E.	Lect			25	PZ	MPH	Lancaste
Boot, R. L.	Lect			25	NOP	MSC	City
Brown, C. A.	Lect			25	EGH	PHD	Wales
Brown, D. H.	Lect			39	IYZ	MA	Lancast
Fox, S.	Lect			25	NOP	PHD	Manchest
Hardy, Virginia L.	Lect			25	NOP	MSC	UMIST
Hendry, Linda C.	Lect			7	UVZ	PHD	Lancaste
Hodgson, Vivien E.	Lect			25	NOP	PHD	Surrey
Jex, C. F.	Lect			7	UVZ	MSC	London
Lee, M.	Lect			25	NPY	PHD	

Lees, S.	Lect			25	EHIP	PHD		London
Lewis, P. J.	Lect			9	IZ	PHD		Lancast
Lorbiecki, Anna	Lect			25	NOP	MAP		Lancaste
McConnell, D.	Lect			59	NOP	PHD		Surrey
Reed, M. I.	Lect			25	EHP	PHD		Wales
Singh, R.	Lect			25	EQ	PHD		Leeds
Snell, R. S.	Lect			25	NOPY	MA		Lancastr
Tanton, Morgan	Lect			25	NOPR	CTED		Lancaste
Whitaker, A.	Lect			52	EHNQ	DCOM		Birmingh
Worthington, D. J.	Lect			74	AUVZ	PHD		Reading
Wright, M. B.	Lect			74	AUVZ	MSC		Oxford
Chia, C. H. R.	MTFel			25	PYZ	MA		Lancaste

University of Leeds — Leeds, England — LS2 9JT — 44532 UK.AC.LEEDS.CMS1
Sch of Bus & Econ Studi — FAX=334465 — BA,BSC,MBA,PHD
Listing; Area Code (0532) school phone # 334466

–Management Faculty	Phone		Fax 334465						
Chartres, John A.	C-Pr	44532	334500	1	B	PHD	73	Oxford	1969
Allinson, Christopher	Prof	44532	332637	2	EF	PHD	83	Leeds	1973
Duckworth, Douglas	Prof	44532	332627	2	EF	PHD	76	Leeds	1971
Hayes, John	Prof	44532	332632	2	EF	PHD	70	Leeds	1965
Lynch, James E.	Prof	44532	332626	3	I	PHD	82	Bradford	1991
Nolan, Peter	Prof	44532	334460	5	NQY	MSC	79	London	1990
Pearman, Alan D.	Prof	44532	334489	7	VU	PHD	78	Leeds	1971
Alderson, Siobhan	Assoc	44532	336861	48	JY	MA	86	Dublin	1993
Ansic, David	Assoc	44532	334473	37	IV	DPHI	91	York	1993
Burgess, Thomas F.	Assoc	44532	332615	97	ZU	MBA	81	Bradford	1990
Davies, Stuart	Assoc	44532	332631	13	AI	PHD	82	LSE	1993
Davis, Ann	Assoc	44532	334497	2	EF	BSC	85	Nottingh	1990
Duke, Robert	Assoc	44532	332623	39	I	MBA	85	Bradford	1987
Falshaw, J. Richard	Assoc	44532	334488	79	IZ	BTEC	73	Bradford	1990
Glaister, Keith W.	Assoc	44532	332633	3	IY	MA	77	Lancaste	1990
Grey, Christopher	Assoc	44532	332642	25	EO	PHD	92	Manchest	1993
Gulliford, Richard	Assoc	44532	332611	2	EF	MSC	86	UWIST	1989
Hillard, John	Assoc	44532	332635	5	NQ	BA	67	Durham	1972
Kerfoot, Deborah	Assoc	44532	332636	24	NP	PHD	92	Manchest	1993
Kidd, Callum	Assoc	44532	332634	79	UZ	MSC	92	Salford	1993
King, Stephen	Assoc	44532	334462	79	UZ	MPHI	92	Bradford	1994
Maule, John	Assoc	44532	332622	2	EG	PHD	76	Dundee	1991
Reid, Margaret A.	Assoc	44532	332610	5	P	MA	76	Leeds	1989
Thwaites, Desmond	Assoc	45532	332625	3	DI	PHD	90	Bradford	1989
Walsh, Janet	Assoc	44532	334511	5	QR	PHD	89	Warwick	1991
Wood, Douglas	Assoc	44532	332621	7	V	MA	60	Combridg	1977

University of Limburg — Maastricht6200MD Netherland — 31-43 RULIMBURG.NL
Faculty Econ & Bus Adm — Tongersestraat 53 — FAX=270999
Did Not Respond-1992 Listing

Muysken, Joan	Dean	883 808			Econ	PHD	84	Groning	1984

–Management Faculty Box 616	Phone		Fax 270999						
De Rooij, A. H.	Prof	888 257		18	YD	MS	58	Delft	1990
Den Hertog, Friso	Prof	888 764				PHD	75	Delft	1985
Hofstede, Geert	Prof	888 296	efbedgho	28	ERXY	PHD	67	Groninge	1985
Pennings, Hans	Prof	888 296		32	IXY	PHD	73	Michigan	1987
Schreuder, Hein	Prof	888 802		23	DEFG	PHD	81	Amsterda	1984
Sorge, Arndt	Prof	888 803	efbedsor	25	&HLP	PHD	75	Munster	1988
Vd Grinten, P.M.E.M.	Prof	888 802		23	DIY	PHD	62	Eindhove	1990
V Witteloostuijn, Arjen	Assoc	888 816		23	EHIY	PHD	86	Masstric	1990
Lasker, Jos	Asst	888 112		25	EFHN	MA	90	Nijmegen	1991
Mulder, Maria	Asst	888 806		25	RPT	MA	80	Leiden	1986
Nijhuis, Jan	Asst	888 531	efbedjan	79	OU	MBA	83	Groninge	1987
Olie, Rene	Asst	888 126		28	EHLY	MA	85	Amsterda	1986
Romme, Sjoerd	Asst	888 807	efbedsjd	35	HIN	MA	84	Tilburg	1984
Tolner, Thera	Asst	888 806		23	IEFH	MA	90	Utrecht	1990
V Iterson, Ad	Asst	888 318		42	BHLT	MA	79	Amsterda	1986

Liverpool John Moores Univ — Liverpool — L3 5UZ — 44-51
Business School — FAX=707-0423 — BA
School Phone: 051-231-3406

–Department of Business	Phone	231-3406	Fax 707-0423					
Smith, D.	H	Ext 3406	busdsmith	5	GHIL	MBA		1990

London Business School — London, England NW1 4SA — 447-1 UK.AC.LON.LBS
Grad Sch of Bus Studies — Sussex Place; Regent's Park — FAX=724-7875 — MBA MSC,PHL,PHD
Statecic Dept & Oper Mgt Did Not Respond; Phone number: 262-5050

–Organizational Behavior Phone Fax 724-7875
Nicholson, Nigel C-Pr 262-5050 nnichols 2 EFJO PHD Wales
  Director of Centre for Organisational Research
Hunt, John W. Prof 262-5050 2 EFHO PHD NS Wales
  Plowden Professor of Organisational Behaviour
–Strategic & Intl Mgt Area Phone Fax 724-7875
Stopford, John M. C-Pr 262-5050 38 YI DBA Harvard 1971
Earl, Michael J. Prof 262-5050 39 ZYI MSC Warwick 1991
  Andersen Consulting Professor of Information Management
Eccles, Anthony J. Prof 262-5050 38 FIY BENG Liverpoo 1978
Hamel, Gary Assoc 262-5050 3 I PHD Michigan 1983
Johnson, Rob Assoc 262-5050 6 T MBA Virginia 1990
Morecroft, John Assoc 262-5050 39 IY PHD MIT 1986
Slatter, Stuart St. P. Assoc 262-5050 36 IS PHD London 1972
Davies, Robert Asst 262-5050 13 DEIY PHD Warwick 1991
Hay, Michael Asst 262-5050 36 SI PHD York 1986
Markides, Costas Asst 262-5050 38 DIY DBA Harvard 1990
Sampler, Jeff Asst 262-5050 9 ZDIH PHD 1990
Short, Jim Asst 262-5050 93 ZIHX PHD MIT
Warren, Kim Asst 262-5050 31 MBA London 1991
Williamson, Peter J. Asst 262-5050 38 YI PHD Harvard 1987
–Operations Management Phone Fax 724-7875
Nicholson, Alastair J. C-Pr 262-5050 7 U PHD London
–Decision Science Phone 262-5050 Fax 724-7675
Bunn, Derek W. C-Pr 262-5050 7 V PHD London
Refenes, Paul Assoc
VanAckere, Ann Assoc 262-5050 7 V PHD Stanford
Jackson, Mary Asst 262-5050 7 V MA Oxford
Vlahos, Kiriakos Asst 262-5050 7 V PHD London
–Dept Not Known Phone
Bain, George S. Prof 262-5050 52 QP DPHL Oxford
Chambers, David J. Prof 262-5050 78 YUV PHD Car Mel
Handy, Charles B. VProf 262-5050 52 OLJA MS MIT
Hill, Terry Prof 262-5050 7 U MSC Manchest
Markowitz, H. M. VProf 262-5050 7 V PHD Chicago
Marsh, Paul R. Prof 262-5050 1 PHD London
Mintzberg, Henry VProf 262-5050 23 HIO PHD MIT
Moore, Peter G. VProf 262-5050 7 V PHD London
Shubert, Janelle J. VProf 262-5050 24 LFI PHD Michigan
Voss, Chris Prof 262-5050 7 UI PHD London
Willman, Paul W. Prof 262-5050 52 OZN DPHL Oxford
  Director Sloan Fellowship Programme
Goffee, Rob E. Assoc 262-5050 2 RTOF PHD Kent
Timperley, Stuart R. Assoc 262-5050 23 FHIO PHD Liverpoo
Beaumont, Chris D. VAsst 262-5050 7 V MSC Birmingh
Coughlan, Paul Asst 262-5050 7 U PHD W Ontari
Gratton, Lynda C. Asst 262-5050 2 NOEF PHD Liverpoo
Jones, Gareth L. Asst 262-5050 25 FHOR PHD Kent
Mellon, Elizabeth O. Asst 262-5050 25 AF MBA London
Morris, Tim J. Asst 262-8300 52 QF PHD London
Westbrook, Roy K. Asst 262-5050 7 UZ ABD London
Whitehead, Jo Asst 262-5050 3 I MBA Harvard
DeGeus, Arie VFel 262-5050 38 IY MBA Rotterdm
Lomi, Alessandro PostD 262-5050 2 F PHD Cornell

London Guildhall University London EC2M 6SQ 071
  Faculty of Business FAX=320-1422
  Did Not Respond-1993 Listing; phone 320-1000
Conway, B. Dean 320-1600 59 NY PHD 1-91
–Department of Management Phone Fax 320-1422
Proudfoot, Susan Dir 3 I MBA 4-93

London School of Economics London, England WC2A 2AE 44-1 LSEACUK
  Business FAX=242-0392 BSC,MSC
Abell, Peter Dean 955-7357 abell 26 EMT PHD 1991
–Interdisciplinary Ins Mgt Phone Fax 242-0392
Hodges, Michael SLect 955-7325 hodges 73 IKY PHD Penn 1988
Crouchly, Robert Lect 955-7630 crouchly 79 VXZ PHD 1991
Reyniers, Diane Lect 955-7921 7 V PHD London

Loughborough U Technology Loughborough LE LE11 3TU 0509
  Business School FAX=210232 BSC
  Area Code 0509 phone extension: 3393
Buchanan, David A. D-Pr 5 N PHD Edinburg
–Management Faculty Phone Fax 210232
Finlay, Paul N. Prof 7 V PHD Nottingh
Hill, Malcolm R. Read 7 U PHD Birmingh

King, M.	Prof	7	V	DPHL	Oxford
Lawrence, Peter A.	Prof	8	Y	MA	Essex
Calvert, John R.	SLect	9	Z	PHD	Loughbor
Johnson, David G.	SLect	7	V	BSC	Leeds
Storey, John	SLect	5	N	PHD	Lancast
Wilson, John M.	SLect	7	V	DPHL	Sussex
Clarke, Barbara A.	Lect			BA	Open
Coates, David S.	Lect	7	V	PHD	Newcastl
O'Connor, Michael J.	Lect	5	N	MCOM	NUI
Preston, Diane	Lect	5	N	BA	Lancast
Saker, James M.	Lect	3	I	MSC	Warwick
Walley, Paul	Lect	7	X	MBA	Warwick

Macquarie University   New South Wales 2109 AUST   (02)
Sch of Econ & Fin Stds   FAX=805-8586   BEC,MEC,PHD
   Did Not Respond-1993 Listing; School Phone 805-7111

Carey, Bernard	DSLec	805-8996			
—Department of Management	Phone	905-9010	Fax 805-9022		
More, Elizabeth	D-Pr	805-9000			
Davis, Ed	Prof	805-8999			
Gilmour, Peter	Prof	805-8987			
Murtagh, Bruce	Prof	805-9913			
Spillane, Robert	Prof	805-8995			
Weston, Rae	Prof	805-7807			
Gibson, Donald	Assoc	805-8988			
Glaser, Stanley	Assoc	805-8989			
Halliday, Michael	Assoc	805-9028			
Elliott, Greg C.	SLect	805-8990		MSC	CNAA
Godbee, Graham	Lect	805-8998			
Lamond, David	Lect	805-8984			
Spillane, Lynda	Lect	805-8995			

University of Manchester   Manchester, Engl   M15 6PB   (061)   MBS.UK.AC
Manchester Bus School   FAX=273-7732   BA,MBA,MBS,PHD

Pearson, Alan W.	Dean	275-6455	pearsoaw	12	DIOS	BSC	London	1970
—Faculty of Business Adm	Phone		Fax 273-7732					
Davies, G. J.	Prof	275-6457				PHD	London	1992
Harvey, Brian	Prof	275-6377		14	CM	PHD	Nottingh	1992
Lockett, A. Geoffrey	Prof	275-6421	locketag	79	TUY	MSC	Manchest	1984
Oakey, R. P.	Prof	275-		26		PHD	LSE	1992
Whitley, Richard D.	Prof	275-6336	whitlerd	28	HLW	PHD	Penn	1977
Campbell, Nigel C. G.	SLect	275-6466	campbenc	38	IW	PHD	Manchest	1985
Rickards, Tudor	SLect	275-6468	rickart	2	DEFZ	PHD	Wales	1980
Westwood, John B.	SLect	275-6419	westwojb	37	ITU	PHD	Manchest	1981
Barlow, K. Graham I.	Lect	275-6414	barlowkg	12	EFZ	PHD	Manchest	1975
Barrar, Peter R. N.	Lect	275-6476	barrarp	37	ITY	MSC	Cranfield	1987
Hall, Graham C.	Lect	275-6458	hallg	3	IRS	MSC	City	1981
Holland, Christopher P.	Lect	275-6480	hollanc		YZ	BSC	Warwick	1993
Kiu, Hong	Lect	275-6351	liuh			PHD	Warwick	1992
Mandry, Gordon D.	Lect	275-6479	mandrygd	3	IZ	MA	Oxford	1976
Morgan, G. D.	Lect	275-6388		2	EG	MA	Cambridg	1992
Naude, Peter	Lect	275-6583	naudep	7	IUZ	MSC	Sussex	1990
Pandit, N. R.	Lect	275-6492				MSC	Manchest	1991
Tanner, Ian R.	Lect	275-6483	tannerir	23	EFHT	BSC	Aston	1982
Thomas, Alan B.	Lect	275-6345	thomasa	25	EHZ	PHD	Open	1984
Buttle, F. A.	SFell	275-6426				PHD	UMUT	1992
Carr, Christopher H. C.	SFell	275-6422	carrchc	38	IWZ	PHD	Warwick	1991
Chittenden, Francis C.	SFell	275-6535	chittef	69	KRSY	MBA	Manchest	1989
Henderson, Jeffrey W.	SFell	275-6470	henderjw	23	EHI	PHD	Warick	1990
Byrne, Francis	Fell	275-6356				BA	Liverpol	1993
Carruthers, Neil	Fell	275-6484				MBA	Manchest	1994
Collett, Nick J.	Fell	275-6355	colletnj	4	SZ	BA	London	1988
Cook, Gas	Fell	275-6530				PHD	Manchest	1992
Gaston, Kevin C.	Fell	275-6529	gasronkc	25	F	PHD	Manchest	1988
Hipkin, I. B.	Fell			7	UV	MA	Capetown	1994
Ingleton, Colin C.P.	Fell	275-6497	ingletc	25	EFQZ	BSC	Bradford	1990
Jagiello, Kevin G.	Fell	275-6469	jagielkg	3	FIZ	DPBA	Manchest	1987
Mukhtar, S. M.	Fell	275-6545		6	ST	MPHI	London	1993
Roberts, Hilary J.	Fell	275-6526	roberthj	29	EFHY	PHD	Manchest	1988
Hetherington, Barrie	Tutor	275-6429	hetherbh	9	YZ	MBCS		1974

U Manchester Inst Sci & Tech   Manchester UK   M60 1QD   (061)
School of Management   FAX=200-3505   BSC,MSC,MBA,PHD
   Did Not Respond-1992 Listing; School phone: 061 200 3500

—Management Faculty	Phone	200-3505					
Goodman, John F. B.	C-Pr	200-3481	5	Q	PHD	Nottingh	1975
Cooper, Cary L.	Prof	200-3440	2	G	PHD	Leeds	1975

Hollier, Robert H.	Prof	200-3421	7	T	PHD	Birmingh	1977
Robertson, Ivan T.	Prof	200-3443	2	E	PHD		9-90
Torrington, Derek P.	Prof	200-3414	5	N	MPHI	CNAA	6-90
Knights, David	Read	200-3413	45	H	PHD	Manchest	7-71
Burton, Frederick N.	SLect	200-3482	8	W	BSC	Hull	9-69
Carew, Anthony B.	SLect	200-3411	5	Q	PHD	Sussex	6-76
Coombs, Roderick W.	SLect	200-3435	79	D	PHD	Manchest	9-79
Dale, Barrie G.	SLect	200-3424	7	T	PHD	Nottingh	1981
Davidson, Marilyn J.	SLec	200-3449	2	EX	PHD	Manchest	9-84
Marchington, Michael P.	SLect	200-3415	5	N	PHD	Manchest	1-86
Smith, J. Michael	SLect	200-3448	2	E	PHD	Liverpol	1976
Walsh, Vivien M.	SLect	200-3434	7	T	PHD	Manchest	8-84
Willmott, Hugh C.	SLect	200-3412	5	H	PHD	Mancehst	9-88
Arnold, John M.	Lect	200-3442	2	E	PHD	Sheffiel	6-88
Berridge, John R. K.	Lect	200-3416	58	N	MSC	London	5-80
Bloor, George	Lect	200-3417	5	Q	BA	Liverpol	1963
Boaden, Ruth J.	Lect	200-3436	7	T	PHD	Manchest	9-89
Conrad, Simon A.	Lect	200-3429	79	U	PHD	Manchest	9-72
Cox, Charles J.	Lect	200-3446	2	E	BA	Bristol	1966
Dewhurst, Frank W.	Lect	200-3426	7	U	MSC	Manchest	9-80
Earnshaw, Jill M.	Lect	200-3491	5	K	BLAW		1991
Freeman, James M	Lect	200-3430	7	U	PHD	Salford	9-81
Goodman, Jordan	Lect	200-3436	5	B	PHD	London	9-90
Gotting, David A.	Lect	200-3410	5	L	BA	Strathcl	9-71
Greatorex, Michael	Lect	200-3468	7	U	BCOM	Birmingh	9-69
Green, Kenneth	Lect	200-3432	7	M	ΠID	Manchest	9-88
Gwinnett, E. Anne	Lect	200-3428	79	U	PHD	Manchest	9-84
Makin, Peter J.	Lect	200-3445	2	E	PHD	Bradford	7-81
Murphy, David	Lect	200-3409	45	L	PHD	Manchest	9-74
New, Stephen J.	Lect		7	T	BSC	S Hampto	9-91
Rubery, Jill C.	Lect	200-3406	5	Q	PHD	Cambridg	8-89
Talbot, Reginald J.	Lect	200-3444	2	E	BSC	London	9-76
Walbank, W. Martin	Lect	200-3431	7	T	MSC	London	1-75
Wilkinson, Adrian J.	Lect	200-3420	5	N	PHD	Durham	9-91

Massey Univesity   Palmerston N, NZ 30974   (06) MASSEY
Faculty of Bus Studies   FAX=3505608
–Human Resources Management Phone 3569099   Fax 3505608

Dewe, P. J.	Prof	3569099	pdewe	25	EG	PHD	84	London	1980
Sligo, F. X.	Assoc	3569099	fsligo	25	EZN	PHD	87	Massey	1980
Toulson, P. K.	Assoc	3569099		25	EN	PHD	91	Massey	1985

Murdoch University   Murdoch 6150   W Australi   (09) COMMERCE.MURDOCH.EDUAU
Sch of Econ, Comm   FAX=310 5004   BCOM,MBA,MP,PHD

Davison, Alan G.	Dean	360 2618	davison		Atg	MBA		Queen's	1985
–Commerce Programme	Phone	360-2705	Fax 310 5004						
Bazley, Michael	C-Ac	360-2410	bazley		Atg	MCOM		W Aust	1985
Entrekin, Lanny	Assoc	360-2528	entrekin	25	ENPQ	PHD		W Aust	1989
Krasnostein, John	Assoc	360-6039	krasnostein	38	IY	MBA		Notre Dm	1990
Pearson, Cecil	Assoc	360-6022	pearson	2	EFHU	PHD		W Aust	1992
Duffy, Carol	Asst	360-2264	duffy	5	N	MSC		Manchest	1991
Nash, Allen	Asst	360-2362	nash	39	IZ	MBA		W Aust	1989

Napier University   Edinburgh Scotla   EH10 5BR   (031)
Napier Business Sch   66 Spylaw Road   FAX=346-8553   BA,MBA
  School Phone: 455 5021

McLachlan, Jeffrey E.	Dean	455 3382		3	I	BA		1975
–Dept of Management Studies	Phone		Fax 346-8553					
Stobie, David H.	Head			49	JLW	MSC		1975
Worden, Jack	Assoc			25	ENPT	MA		1985
Fernie, June M.	SLect			17	CUVX	PHD		1989
Macpherson, Neil C.	SLect			38	IY	MSC		1971
Ryan, John	SLect			3	IY	MBA		1976
Stewart, Jean C.	SLect			5	O	BSC		1973
Thomas, Graham	SLect			7	UV	MENG		1980
Thomson, Jim S.	SLect			79	VZ	BSC		1973
Tully, Lindsay B.	SLect			17	CUV	MSC		1980
Wallace, Mary	SLect			5	NPQR	BA		1986
Caldwell, Dan	Lect			13	ABI	DMS		1973
Cemery, Alan	Lect			17	CUV	MBA		1991
Cottam, Angela	Lect			38	IY	BSC		1990
Drummond, Graeme	Lect			37	IYZ	MBA		1985
Ensor, John	Lect			38	IY	MBA		1990
Francis, Helen	Lect			5	FNPQ	BSC		1989
Heavisides, Alan	Lect			5	O	BSC		1983
Henderson, Iain	Lect			25	FNPQ	MBA		1991
Laing, Susan	Lect			38	IY	BA		1989

Name	Rank	Phone	Code	Num	Field	Degree	Yr	School	Year
Low, William T.	Lect			25	EFNP	MPHI			1983
McCormick, Lis	Lect			25	EFNP	MA			1990
Mudie, Peter	Lect			38	IY	MED			1973
Murray, Ian E.	Lect			17	BU	BA			1978
Oldham, Fiona	Lect			25	FNP	BSC			1992
Paxton, Ian	Lect			71	BIV	MBA			1977
Revuelta, John	Lect			38	IY	BA			1990
Shepherd, Jennifer	Lect			5	NPQ	BCOM			1989
Thomson, John R.	Lect			38	IY	MBA			1990
Walker, Ian R. S.	Lect			38	IY	BA			1988
Wilson, Elaine	Lect			5	O	MA			1975

National Taiwan University	Taipei, TAIWAN	10020 ROC		886-2	TWNMOE10				
College of Management				FAX=351-0907				BBA,MBA,PHD	
Lin, Yu-Tsung	Dean	362-2249		Fnce	PHD	76	Minn		1978
–Department of Management	Phone		Fax 351-0907						
Bai, Jan-Erh	C-Pr	362-5008		7	UV	MS	73	Rutgers	1972
Chang, Hong-Chang	C-Pr	362-3857		7	U	PHD	78	Penn	1969
Chen, Shi-Chaug	D-Pr	363-8399		18	Y	MBA	70	Ohio St	1965
Lee, Chng-Kuei	C-Pr	708-4034		25	NEPQ	PHD	65	Pitt	1981
Wu, Hui-Lin	C-Pr	931-1765		5	Q	PHD	84	Nat Taiw	1990
Bian, Yu-Yuan	Prof	363-2708		8	Y	PHD	78	Nat Taiw	1978
Chao, Chieh-Chien	Prof	321-7074		1		PHD	73	Nat Taiw	1969
Hiseh, Ching-Cha	Prof	363-3487		9	Z	PHD	88	Nat ChiT	1975
Ho, Hsien-Chan	Prof	351-9641		8	Y	PHD	85	Texas	1986
Hsu, Mu-Lan	Prof	351-9641		25	EFHD	PHD	78	Ohio St	1986
Huang, Jun-Ying	Prof			7	IV	PHD	74	Iowa	1978
Hung, Wen-Hsing	Prof	363-0785		9	Z	MBA	67	Houston	1970
Hus, Paul Shih-Chun	Prof	362-2249		18	IY	PHD	74	Michigan	1987
Lin, Tsong-Ming	Prof	351-3111		17	U	PHD	77	Clemson	1980
Tang, Foh-Tsrang	Prof	782-2120		3	I	PHD	75	Penn	1975
Wang, Chih-Kang	Prof				I	PHD	78	Tx A&M	1979
Wea, Chi-Lin	Prof	396-1394		8	Y	PHD	81	Paris U	1987
Yang, Chau-Jan	Prof	391-7895		1	L	MBA	68	Rockches	1963
Yang, Chung-Sen	Prof	311-3981		4	K	JSD	72	NYU	1989
Yeh, Hsiaw-Chan	Prof	391-7895		7	V	PHD	83	Calif RS	1984
Chang, Chung-Chau	Assoc	939-8005		10	I	PHD	74	Nat Chen	1983
Chen, Chia-Shen	Assoc	351-9641	a26a8001	25	ENF	PHD	78	Nat Taiw	1984
Chen, Wen-Hsien	Assoc	351-9641		79	UZ	PHD	80	Berkeley	1986
Chen, Yong-Chang	Assoc	351-9641		8	IY	PHD	87	Penn	1987
Chiu, Ching-Po	Assoc	562-1025		1		MBA	76	Berkeley	1984
Don, Raymond Yuming	Assoc	217-2645		4	K	PHD	74	Cambridg	1988
Hong, Min-Chow	Assoc	363-3487		3	IMHT	PHD	89	Illinois	1990
Huang, Chung-Hsing	Assoc	351-9641	p8701002	79	VZU	PHD	87	Texas	1990
Hwang, Peter	Assoc	363-3487		78	VXY	PHD	88	Mich St	1990
Jaw, Yi-Long	Assoc	351-9641		38	YI	PHD	87	Ohio St	1987
Kuo, Cheng-Kun	Assoc	391-7895		1	Y	PHD	86	Texas	1989
Lee, Tsun-Siou	Assoc	391-7895		1		PHD	88	Berkeley	1988
Liao, Jun-Yuan	Assoc	322-5636		8	Y	MS	68	Nat Taiw	1971
Lin, Neng-Pai	Assoc	363-3487	t8701002	79	UZ	PHD	89	Ohio St	1989
Liu, Christina	Assoc	363-3487		8	Y	PHD	86	Chicago	1990
Tsai, Yann-Ching	Assoc	363-3487	ntut157	7	V	PHD	90	UCLA	1990
Weng, James C. M.	Assoc	363-3487		8	DIVY	PHD	90	Mich St	1990
Wu, Ching-Sung	Assoc	391-7895		38	DITY	PHD	88	UCLA	1990
Yen, Ching-Chang	Assoc			4	K	PHD	80	Michigan	1990
Yen, Yueh-Chu	Assoc	391-7895		7	V	BS	69	Nat Taiw	1969
Yu, Chang-Sung	Assoc	362-1327		9	Z	PHD	84	Car Mel	1987
Yu, Sung-Pei	Assoc	362-5008		7	V	MS	73	S Carol	1973

University of Navarra	Barcelona, Spain	21-08034		34-3					
Avenida Person				FAX=					
Did Not Respond-1993 Listing									
Cavalle, Carlos	Dean	204-4000		3	I	PHD		ETSII	O-58
–Intl Grad School of Mgt	Phone	204-4000	Fax 280-1177						
Abadia, Leopoldo	Prof	204-4000		3	I	PHD		ETSII	9-62
Agell, Pere	Prof	204-4000		7	V	PHD		Pol Cata	5-68
Andreu, Rafael	Prof	204-4000		7	VZ	PHD		Pol Cata	4-73
Argandona, Antonio	Prof	204-4000		7	V	PHD		Barcelon	9-63
Ballarin, Eduard	Prof	204-4000		3	IY	DBA		Harvard	9-69
International Business Chair									
Dionis, Lorenzo	Prof	204-4000		7	U			Artiller	7-59
Farran, Juan	Prof	204-4000		7	W	PHD		Complute	9-58
Faus, Josep	Prof	204-4000		7	V	PHD		ETSII	1-60
Font, Vicente	Prof			7	V	PHD		Barcelon	O-76
Gallo, Miguel Angel	Prof	204-4000		3	I	PHD		ETSII	2-66
Nueno, Pedro	Prof	204-4000		6	Z	DBA		Harvard	N-68
Ocariz, Jose	Prof	204-4000		7	V	PHD		ETSIN	9-63
Pereria, Fernando	Prof	204-4000		7	H	PHD		ETSICCP	9-58

Name	Title	Phone			Degree	School	Code
Perez, Juan Antonio	Prof	204-4000	2	E	DBA	Harvard	O-61
Ribera, Jaume	Prof	204-4000	7	V	PHD	Politecn	9-82
Ricart, Joan Enric	Prof	204-4000	3	I	PHD	Politecn	9-84
Riverola, Josep	Prof	204-4000	7	U	PHD	ETSII	9-64
Rodriguez, Jose Maria	Prof	204-4000	2	EN	DBA	Navarra	3-61
Roig, Barto	Prof	204-4000	3	I	PHD	ETSII	9-63
Rosanas, Josep Maria	Prof	204-4000	7	V	PHD	Politecn	7-71
Roure, Juan	Prof	204-4000	7	V	PHD	Stanford	7-81
Suaraez, Jose Luis	Prof	204-4000	7	V	DBA	Navarra	7-82
Sutton, Tim	VProf	204-4000	7	V	PHD	U Wash	7-89
Tapies, Josep	Prof	204-4000	7	V	PHD	Politecn	9-82
Valero, Antonio	Prof	204-4000	3	I	PHD	EEIIT	9-58
Valor, Josep	Prof	204-4000	4	Z	PHD	MIT	9-85
Vazquez-Dodero, Juan Carlos	Prof	204-4000	4	V	DBA	Navarra	8-69
Velilla, Manuel	Prof	204-4000	7	V	DBA	Navarra	7-71
Arino, Miguel Angel	Assoc	204-4000	7	V	PHD	Barcelon	6-87
Canals, Jordi	Assoc	204-4000	3	IY	PHD	Barcelon	3-87
Fernandez, Pablo	Assoc	204-4000	7	V	PHD	Harvard	4-85
Gomez, Sandalio	Assoc	204-4000	5	N		Complute	8-65
Grual, Jordi	Assoc	204-4000	7	VY	PHD	Berkeley	3-87
Huete, Luis Maria	Assoc	204-4000	7	U	PHD	Boston	6-82
Joachimsthaler, Erich A.	Assoc	204-4000	7	V	PHD	Kansas	1-89
Masifern, Esteban	Assoc	204-4000	3	I		ETSII	7-60
Mele, Domenec	Assoc	204-4000	4	J	PHD	Politecn	D-85
Miller, Paddy	Assoc	204-4000	2	F	DBA	Navarra	5-84
Santoma, Javier	Assoc	204-4000	7	V	PHD	Penn	7 81
Alvarez de Mon, Santiago	Asst	204-4000	2	E	MBA	Navarra	D-89
Alvarez, Jose Luis	Asst	204-4000	2	EH	PHD	Harvard	9-84
Arino, Maria Africa	Asst	204-4000	3	I	MBA	Navarra	6-88
Carcia, Carlos	Asst	204-4000	3	I	PHD	MIT	6-87
Cardona, Pablo	Asst	204-4000	2	E	MBA	Navarra	6-90
Chinchilla, Maria Nuria	Asst	204-4000	2	F	MBA	Navarra	O-58
Fontrodona, Juan	Asst	204-4000	2	H	MBA	Navarra	6-90
Fraguas, Rafael	Asst	204-4000	3	I	MBA	Navarra	6-82
Gomez-Llera, German	Asst	204-4000	5	N	PHD	Politecn	5-82
Grandes, Maria Jusus	Asst	204-4000	7	V	MBA	Navarra	N-84
Iniesta, Francisco	Asst	204-4000	7	V	MBA	Navarra	6-90
Martinez, Eduardo	Asst	204-4000	7	V	PHD	Barcelon	9-60
Munoz-Seca, Beatriz	Asst	204-4000	7	V	PHD	Navarra	1-90
Nueno, Jose Luis	Asst	204-4000	7	T	DBA	Harvard	6-85
O'Callaghan, Ramon	Asst	204-4000	4	V	DBA	Harvard	6-84
Palencia, Luis Enrique	Asst	204-4000	7	V	MBA	Navarra	9-72
Penalva, Fernando	Asst	204-4000	7	V		Politecn	9-92
Pin, Jose Ramon	Asst	204-4000	2	V	PHD	Pontific	D-86
Pons, Jose Maria	Asst	204-4000	7	V		Automona	O-83
Director MBA Program							
Pregel, Gert	Asst	204-4000	7	V	MBA	Navarra	6-87
Rahnema, Ahmad	Asst	204-4000	7	V	DBA	Navarra	6-91
Renart, Lluis G.	Asst	204-4000	7	V	MBA	Chicago	9-81
Sabria, Frederic	Asst	204-4000	7	V	PHD	ETSICCP	6-87
Sanchez-Runde, Carlos	Asst	204-4000	5	N	MBA	Navarra	6-90
Segarra, Jose Antonio	Asst	204-4000	7	V	MBA	Navarra	9-80
Sison, Alejo Jose	Asst	204-4000	4	J	PHD	Navarra	9-92
Toro, Juan Manuel de	Asst	204-4000	7	V	MBA	Navarra	6-88
Torres, Maximilian B.	Asst	204-4000	4	J	PHD	Harvard	9-92
Vila, Joaquim	Asst	204-4000	3	I	PHD	Penn	9-90
Weber, Eric	Asst	204-4000	7	V	MBA	Navarra	6-87
Baucells, Manuel	Inst	204-4000	3	I	MBA	Navarra	6-93

University of New England   Armidale 2351   Australia   067
Economic Studies   FAX=711531   BAGECO,MECO,PHD
  Did Not Respond-1992 Listing

Musgrave, W. F.	D-Pr	732-200			PHD	Sydney	
—Dept of Agr Econ & Bus Mgt	Phone		Fax 711531				
Hardaker, J. B.	C-Pr	732-195			PHD	New Engl	
Wright, V. E.	Assoc	732-915	vwright	13 I	PHD	New Engl	1975

Univ of New South Wales   Sydney NS Wales   Australia   (02)
Faculty of Comm & Econ   FAX=662-6130
Layton, Roger   Dean   385-5899
—Department of Management   Phone   Fax 662-6130
Doubell, Jennifer

University of Newcastle   New South Wales   Australia   (049)
Sch of Econ & Info Sys   FAX=216911
  Did Not Respond-1992 Listing; Phone 21-5996

–Department of Management | Phone | | Fax 216911
| | | | | | | | |

Name	Rank	Phone					
Cheek, B. R.	H-SLe	21-5993		9	Z	MACS	
Williams, A. J.	Prof	21-5992		36	GIST	PHD	W Austra
Mernlees, W.	Asst	21-6649		23	DIS	PHD	Toronto
Rappell, J. C.	SLect	21-5012		25	EFNS	MBA	NSWIT
Richins, H.	SLect	21-6847		4	DLS	MBA	Oregon
Starr, G. W.	SLect	62-2077		14	AIL	PHD	West VA
Weiler, B.	SLect	21-6031		4	DLS	PHD	Victoria
Zeffane, R.M.	SLect	21-5014		25	ENYZ	PHD	Wales
Brown, G. V.	Lect	62-2077		4	KY	LLB	NS Wales
Dugas, J.	Lect	21-6609		59	FNP	MED	Middlese
Finlay, A.	Lect	21-6769		45	KLY	BLS	Macquari
Hafey, L.	Lect	21-6015		45	KLQ	DIPL	BAB
Hunt, J.	Lect	21-6850		2	DEFR	MA	Kent
Mankelow, G.	Lect	21-6774		46	DT	BCOM	NS Wales
Miller, D.	Lect	21-6851		25	EFNR	MBA	SAInstTe
Miller, J.	Lect	21-6778		14	AKL	LLB	Sydney
Nuesink, R. F.	Lect			23	I	MBA	Deakin
Polonsky, M. J.	Lect	21-5013		8	MY	MA	Temple
Walker, G. P.	Lect	21-5010		36	ST	MBA	
Waller, D.	Lect	62-2077		8	Y	MCOM	NS Wales
Christie, M.	STut	62-2077		1	AL	MAEC	New Eng
Mayo, G.	STut	21-6848		52	EFNQ	BCOM	
Noble, R.	STut	21-6836		5	FQ	BA	New Engl
Rugimbona, R.	STut	21-6836		8	Y	MBA	

Univ College of North Wales | Bangor, Gwynedd LL57 2DG | 248 UKACBANGOR
Sch Atg,Banking,& Econ | | FAX=370451 | | | | | BA,MA,PHD
Did Not Respond-1993 Listing

–Management Faculty | Phone 382158 | Fax 364760

Name	Rank	Phone					
Gardener, E. P. M.	C-Pr	382158	abs022	13	DHI	PHD	9-75

Director Institute of European Finance

McLeay, S. J.	Prof	382180	abs021	1	D	PHD	1-88

TBS Professor of Treasury

Treble, J. G.	Prof	382165	abs003	5	NPQ	PHD	9-91
Burke, C. M.	SLect	382166	abs026	1	A	MA	9-88
Chakravarty, S. P.	SLect	382171	abs024	13	DI	PHD	8-78
McKay, R. Ross	SLect	382169	abs034	5	QS	MA	6-79

Director of Institute of Econmic Research

Molyneux, P.	SLect	382170	abs005	13	DI	MA	9-86

Deputy Director

Ayling, D. E.	Lect	382174	abs032	3	IM	PHD	9-81
Brown, Z. M.	Lect	382177	abs004	7	V	MSC	9-86
Goddard, John	Lect	382166	abs071	7	V	MSC	1-93
Hodgkinson, L.	Lect	382172	abs007	9	ZM	PHD	9-87
Jones, D. R.	Lect	382164	abs028	5	PQ	PHD	9-85
Lloyd-Williams, M.	Lect	382161	abs002	13	DI	MA	9-90
Morrell, J. B.	Lect	382178	abs006	23	FI	BA	9-75
Lloyd-Williams, J.	Tutor	382089	abs0rr	3	I	MPHL	4-91

Royal Insurance Tutorial Fellow

Norwegian School Econ & Bus | Bergen-Sandviken N-5035 | (55) DEBET.NHH.NO
NORWAY | | FAX= | | | | | MS,PHD
Did Not Respond-1993 Listing; Phone +475 959483; Fax 55 475 256944

–Dept Organization Sciences | Phone 959 483 | Fax 256944

Name	Rank	Phone				
Nordhaug, Odd	C	959489	org_on			DRPH
Colbjornsen, Tom	Prof	959452	org_tc			PHD
Reve, Torger	Prof	959454	org_tr			PHD
Fredriksen, Tor	Assoc	959635	org_tf			ABD
Greve, Avent	Assoc	959453	org_ag			DREC
Grimso, Oddleif	Assoc	959570	org_og			MAGA
Haugland, Sven	Assoc		org_sh			DREC
Haukedal, Wiley	Assoc	959414	org_wh			DREC
Espedal, Bjarne	Asst		org_be			ABD
Falkenberg, Joyce	Asst	959486	org_jf			PHD

Univ of Puerto Rico-Mayaguez | Mayaguez, PR | 00680-5000 | (809) RUMAS.UPR.CLU.EDU
College of Business Adm | | | FAX= | | | | BSBA,MBA

Name	Rank	Phone						
Jetter, Ina	Dean	265-3800				MACC	80	Va Tech 8-78

–Managment Faculty, | Phone | | Fax 832-5320

Name	Rank	Phone					
Asundi, Ramachandra K.	Prof	265-3800		8		PHD	62 Liverpoo 8-79
Colon, Jose F.	Prof	265-3800		7		MS	70 Stevens 7-68
Gandhi, Bodapati	Prof	265-3800		7		PHD	83 Tx A&M 7-87
Lopez-Molina, Radames	Prof	265-3800		9		MBA	71 Inter Am 7-69
Riera, Juan	Prof	265-3800		4		LLB	63 P Rico 8-67
Velez, Jorge I.	Prof	265-3800		78		PHD	78 Florida 8-72
Calderon, Carmen	Assoc	265-3800		7		MS	74 P Rico 8-58

Name	Rank	Phone		Code		Deg	Yr	School	Date
Colon, Marta	Assoc	265-3800		5		MBA	80	U Miami	8-77
Fernandez, Lucyann	Assoc	265-3800		9		MS	80	Tx A&M	1-81
Gonzalez, Candida	Assoc	265-3800		53		MBA	83	Loyola	8-83
Pabon, Jaime	Assoc	265-3800		3		MBA	83	Tx A&M	8-83
Rivera, Fernando	Assoc	265-3800		9		MS	75	Penn St	7-68
Associate Dean									
Romaguera, Jose M.	Assoc	265-3800		6		MBA	80	Conn	8-80
Hamilton, Leonora	Asst	265-3800		3		MA	78	Monterre	1-79
Oliver, Marisol	Asst	265-3800		2		MBA	85	P Rico	2-82
Oronoz, Maria J.	Asst	265-3800		5		MPA	77	Penn St	8-83
Segui, Miguel	Asst	265-3800		7		MBA	92	Catholic	6-86
Valle, Awilda	Asst	265-3800		9		MS	81	Purdue	1-90
Gandhi, Srinivas	Inst	265-3800		7		MPP	91	Harvard	7-88
Larracuente, Maria	Inst	265-3800		9		MS	91	Akron	8-87
Medina, Maria	Inst	265-3800		7		MS	92	P Rico	8-92
Ortiz, Norma I.	Inst	265-3800		3		MBA	84	P Rico	8-85
Pawle, Laura	Inst	265-3800		5		MS	88	Mass	1-90
Puig, Maria	Inst	265-3800		9		MS	92	Wiscon	1-92
Rodriguez, Julissa	Inst	265-3800		3		MBA	91	Loyola	1-92

University of Queensland   Queensland   AUST 4067   (07)   MAILBOX.UQ.OZ.BU
Grad Sch of Management   FAX=365-6988   BCO,MBA,MMN,PHD

Name	Rank	Phone		Code		Deg	Yr	School	Date
Finn, Frank J.	Dean	365-7111			Fnce	PHD	81	Queensld	1969
–Management Faculty	Phone	365-6225	Fax 365-6988						
Grigg, Trevor J.	H-Pr	365-6225	tgrigg	3	IA	PHD	81	Queensld	1983
Callan, Victor J.	Prof	365-6675		2	F	PHD	70	Aust Nat	1990
vc@psych.psy.uq.oz.au									
Kiel, Geoffrey C.	Prof	365-6758		31	I	PHD	77	NS Wales	1977
Tucker, Ken A.	Prof	365-6288		8	Y	PHD		London	1986
Director Australian International Business Center									
Edwards, Clive T.	Read	365-6745		8	Y	PHD	66	Aust Nat	1988
Shulman, Arthur D.	Read	365-6748	ashulman	25	QF	PHD	69	SUNY-Buf	1990
Tamaschke, Rick U.	Read	365-6602		78	Y	PHD		Queensld	1989
McColl-Kennedy, Janet	SLect	365-6673		1	R	PHD	86	Queensld	1985
Williams, Steven C.	SLect	365-6746		8	R	PHD	88	Queensln	1989
Bohle, Phil	Lect			3	E	PHD	94	Griffith	1994
Bramble, Thomas	Lect	365-6233	tbramble	5	Q	PHD	93	La Trobe	1993
Carmichael, Donna	Lect			1		PHD	94	York	1994
Koerner, Richard	Lect	365-6749		3	I	PHD	93	Queensln	1992
Lane, Richard O.D.	Lect	365-6561	lane	7	V	PHD	66	Lancast	1974
Steffans, Paul	Lect			3	I	PHD	94	Monash	1994

University of Stirling   Stirling Scotlan   FK9 4LA   (011)   FAX=786-6300   BS,MS,MBA,PHD
Business Faculty
  No Management Faculty
–Department of Management   Phone 786-6300

University of Strathclyde   Glasgow Scotland G4 OGE   44-41   FAX=552-2501   BA,BS,MBA,MS,PH
Strathclyde Bus School
  School Phone: 553-6000

Name	Rank	Phone	Code		Deg	School	Date
Pitt, D.	Dean		2	E			
–Management Faculty	Phone	Fax 552-6000					
Greensted, Chris	Dir		7	V			
Fletcher, K.	Prof		3		PHD		
Gill, Roger	Prof		2	E			
Gunn, L.	Prof		3		PHD		
Heijden, Kees Van Der	Prof		3	I			
Bothams, J.			2	F			
Cameron, David					PHD		
Clarke, Sandra			9	Z			
Huxham, C.			7	V	PHD		
MacMillan, Ronnie			7	U			
Mullen, Tom			7	U			
Wersun, Alec			8	Y			
Wright, George			7	V			
Deputy Director							

University of Sydney   New South Wales 2006 AUST   61-2   GSB.SU.OZ.AN
Faculty of Economics   FAX=550-8603   MBA,MPP,MTM
  Dept of Mgt Did Not Respond-1993 Listing

Name	Rank	Phone		Code		Deg	School	Date
Wells, Murray C.	Dean	550-8601		9	B	PHD	Sydney	1972
–Department of Management	Phone		Fax 550-8603					
Wood, Jack M.	D-Ac	550-8621		25	DEFN	PHD	Alberta	1990
Adam, Chris	Prof			8	Y	PHD	Harvard	1992
Domberger, Simon	Prof	550-8612		32		PHD	Warwick	1988
Johnson, Les	Prof	550-8627		3	I	PHD	Conn	1992

Name	Rank	Phone	email/fax		Degree		University	Year
Aimond, Tim	Asst	550-8631		VX	BA		Macquari	1990
Brewer, Ann M.	SLect	550-8620		25 ENQH	PHD		NS Wales	1991
Laffin, Martin J.	SLect	550-8617		12 AEH	PHD		Bradford	1989
Walsh, Paul K.	SLect	550-8627		79 UV	PHD		NewCastl	7-91
Johnstone, David J.	Asst	550-8615		17 VXY	PHD		Sydney	6-89
–Inst of Transport Studies	Phone	550-8631	Fax 550-4013					
Hensher, David	D-Pr	550-8631	davidh	17 LVX	PHD		NS Wales	1990
Hooper, Paul	SLect	550-8630	paulh	17 VNX	MS		Tasmania	1991
Smith, Nariida	SLect	550-8631	nariidas	79 VXZ	PHD	72	Monash	1990
Daniels, Rhonda	Asst	550-8631	rhondad	L	BSC		NS Wales	1991
Milthorpe, Frank		550-8631	frankm	VNXZ	BSC		Macquari	1990
Zhu, William	ResFl		williamz	X	AIT		Banglesh	1990

Tel Aviv University	Ramat Aviv Israe	69978		972-3 TAUNIVM				
Faculty of Management				FAX=			BA,MBA,PHD	
Zang, Israel	Dean	640-8720		V	PHD	78	Technion	1978
–Department of Management	Phone	640-9901	Fax 640-9560					
Givoly, Dan	C-Ac	640-9901	givoli	F	PHD	75	New York	1976
Swari, Ifschak	Prof	640-9063		F	PHD	78	Rochest	1989
Aharoni, Joseph	Assoc	640-8517	aharoni	F	PHD	74	Northwes	1980
Dotan, Amihud	Assoc	640-8112		FM	PHD	77	Cornell	1978
Lieber, Zvi	Assoc	640-9959		M	PHD	71	Chicago	1975
Sadan, Simcha	Assoc	640-8512		F	PHD	72	Berkeley	1974
Sarig, Oded	Assoc	640-8216	sarig	F	PHD	83	Berkeley	1987
Talmor, Eli	Assoc	640-8029		M	PHD	81	N Carol	1983
Bachar, Joseph	Asst	640-8016		M	PHD	87	Berkeley	1990

University of Tsukuba	Tsukuba Ibaraki	305 Japan		0298 SHAKO.SK.TSUKUBA.AC.JP				
Inst of Socio-Econ Plan				FAX=55-3849			BS,MS,PHD	
Did Not Respond-1993 Listing								
–Management Faculty	Phone		Fax 55-3849					
Hotaka, Ryosuke	C-Pr$	53-5087	hotaka	19 Z	DR			3-78
Eto, Hajime	Prof	53-5097		37 HX	DENG			4-76
Fujishige, Satoru	Prof	53-5006	fujishig	7 V	DENG	75	Kyota	8-79
Monden, Yasuhiro	Prof	53-5554		37 UI	PHD			3-83
Shiba, Shoji	Prof	53-5171		57 PU	DECO	74	Tokyo	4-76
Suzuki, Shinichi	Prof	53-5167		5 NP	MPOL			4-92
Takayanagi, Satoru	Prof	53-5223		23 HI	MECO	59	Tokyo	4-79
Yamamoto, Yoshitsugu	Prof	53-5001	yamamoto	7 UV	DENG	78	Keio	9-80
Kishimoto, Kazuo	Assoc	53-5085	kishimot	7 V	DENG	80	Tokyo	1-87
Sato, Ryo	Asst	53-5543	rsato	9 Z	PHD	89	Toyko In	4-88
Shirakawa, Hiroshi	Asst	53-5556	sirakawa	7 V	DENG	89	Toyko In	1-92
Takemura, Kazuhisa	Asst	53-5168	takemura	1 EHX	MART	85		4-92
Yoshise, Akiko	Asst	53-5557	yoshise	7 V	DENG	90	Tokyo In	4-91

Victoria University	Wellington		NewZealand	64 4 VUW.AC.NZ				
Commerce & Adm Faculty				FAX=471 2200			BCA,MCA,MBA,PHD	
Mann, Athol W.	Dean	472-1000						
–Management Group	Phone	471-5381	Fax 471-2200					
Davies, John	C-SLe	471 5382	davies	37 HIUV	MA		Lancast	5-80
Director DBA Programme								
Dunford, R.	Prof	495 5015		23 EFHI	PHD		Aust Nat	2-94
Brocklesby, R. John	SLect	495 5136		25 HQ	MSC		London	1-82
Campbell-Hunt, Colin	SLect	495 5066		13 I	PHD		York	5-74
Cavana, R. Y. (Bob)	SLect	495 5137		37 IVX	PHD		Bradford	1-90
Corbett, Lawrie M.	SLect	495 5138	corbett	7 U	MBA		Cranfield	1-85
Gilbertson, Dai W.	SLect	495 5145		56 DFNT	PHD		Victoria	5-73
Mabin, Vicky J.	SLect	495 5140	mabin	7 RUVW	PHD		Lancaste	5-91
McDonald, Paul	SLect	495 5141	mcdonald	25 PHDE	PHD		W Ontari	8-91
McLennan, W. Roy	SLect	495 5143		25 EFNO	MA		Auckland	7-74
Cooper, J.	Lect	495 5025		13 IDT	MBA		Victoria	
Cummings, S.	Lect	Ext 8097			BA		Victoria	
Davenport, Sally J	Lect	495 5144		13 DSMI	PHD	86	Victoria	1-91
Gilbertson, Deb K.	Lect	495 5139		16 DRST	BAGC		Lincoln	9-91
Stockport, G.	Lect	495 5149		36 ISTY	PHD		Cranfield	7093

Univ of the Virgin Islands	St. Thomas, VI	00802		(809)				
Business Adm Division				FAX=			BA	
Did Not Respond Again--1991 Listing								
–Business Adm Division	Phone							
Williams, James D.	C-Ac	776-9200		8 YST	DBA			1988
Corcoran, Wayne A.	Prof	776-9200		7 UV	PHD	66	SUNY-Buf	1990
Bayne, Keith	Assoc	776-9200		73 SZD	MS			1990
Bryan, Magdeline	Assoc	776-9200		25 STLY	MBA			1972
Goldfarb, Jay	Assoc	776-9200		36 ST	MBA			1990
Hill, Valdemar	Assoc	776-9200		36 AFPQ	MBA			1978
Manns, Curtis	Assoc	776-9200		7 DT	PHD			1989

Univ of Western Australia Nedlands, W Aust 6009
Faculty of Econ & Comm FAX=380-1004
  Area Code 0011 691
–Dept of Org & Labour Stds Phone 380-2741 Fax 380-1055

Name	Title		Degree	University
Feus, Ray	H			
Mulvey, C.	Prof		PHD	
Wood, R.	Prof		PHD	Wash
on leave				
Cordery, J. C.	Assoc		PHD	Sheffiel
Lambert, R.	SLect		PHD	Witwater
Walton, E. J.	SLect		PHD	London
Lees, C.	Lect		PHD	Monash
Willoughby, K.	Lect		PHD	Murdoch
Bartey, J.	Lect			
Cant, A. G.	Lect		MIR	W Austra
Mead, R.	Lect		MBA	W Austra
Rosser, D.	Lect		MIR	W Austra
Silve, N.	Lect		BCOM	W Austra
Todd, P.	Lect		MIR	W Austra

University of Wollongong Wollongong, NSW AUST 2500 (042) UOW.EDU.AU
P.O. Box 1144 Australia FAX=272785 BCO,MCO,MBA,PHD
–Department of Management Phone 213707 Fax 2727785

Name	Title	Phone	email			Degree		University	Date
Parry, Thomas	Dean	21 3686	t.parry			PHD			4-94
Palmer, Gill	H-Pr	21 3707	g.palmer			PHD		City UK	1-92
Falt, Greame	Prof	21 4040				MBAM		Melbourn	1-93
Freed, Gerry	Prof	21 3820	g.freed	38	DIY	BSC	58	Manchest	O-91
Greatorex, David	Prof	21 4049				BA		Sydney	4-90
Hough, Michael	Prof	21 3751	m.hough			BA		Macquari	1-89
Linstead, Stephen	Prof		s.linstead			PHD		Sheffiel	9-94
Badham, Richard	Assoc	21 3634	r.badham			PHD		Warrick	D-92
Cheung, Karin	Assoc	21 4145				MCOM		Wollongo	1-92
Fullop, Liz	Assoc	21 3647				PHD		NS Wales	7-94
Patterson, Paul	Assoc	21 3687	p.patterson			PHD		Wollongo	1-89
Romm, Celia	Assoc	21 4043				PHD		Toronto	D-90
Sim, A. B.	Assoc	21 3611	a.sim	38	IY	PHD	75	UCLA	O-87
Cicic, Muris	SLect	21 4053	m.cicic			PHD		Sarajevo	7-91
Couchman, Paul	SLect	21 4681	p.couchman			PHD			4-93
Flanagan, John	SLect	21 4047	j.flanagan			BSC		NS Wales	8-88
Jones, Robert	SLect	21 3754	b.a.jones			PHD			2-94
Naughton, Anthony J.	SLect	21 3611	a.naughton	78	Y	MBA	80	Bradford	2-87
Sewell, Graham	SLect		g.sewell	7	Y	PHD		Wales	9-94
Zanko, Michael	SLect	21 3749	m.zanko	25	HNQ	MBA	80	Bradford	2-87
Atuaheme-Gima, Kwaku	Lect	21 3642	k.atuaheme-g			PHD			1-91
Graham, Gail	Lect	21 4045		82	WJE	PHD	90	Melbourn	2-90
Hill, Constance	Lect	21 3729	c.hill			MBA		UTS	7-90
Kirchmajer, L.	Lect	21 4042	l.kirchmajer	63	TSDI	MBA	88	U Wollon	2-91
Masters, Neil	Lect	21 3753	n.masters	79	RUTA	MSC	77	U Wollon	7-83
Rifkin, Willy	Lect		w.rifkin			PHD		Stanford	9-94
Scott, Philip	Lect	21 3368	p.scott			MBA		Georgia	1-92
White, Lesley	Lect	21 3610	l.white			MCOM		NS Wales	3-93
Horner, Katherine	AcLec	21 4145				MCOM			6-93
Laneyrie, Frances	AcLec	21 4145				BA			D-90

ALPHABETICAL BY INDIVIDUAL

Name	Rank	School		Code	Degree	Yr	Institution	Year
Agyeman, S.	Lect	Humberside	2					
Aharoni, Joseph	Assoc	Tel Aviv Un		F	PHD	74	Northwes	1980
Ahire, Sanjay	Asst	W Michigan	7	UV	PHD	92	Alabama	1992
Ahlburg, Dennis	Prof	Minnesota	57	QV	PHD	79	Penn	
Ahlers, Richard	Inst	Fla Internat		EN	MBA	72	Detroit	1989
Ahmadi, Mohammad	Prof	Tenn-Chattan	7	VX	PHD	76	North Tx	1979
Hart Professor								
Ahmadi, Reza H.	Asst	UCLA	7	U	PHD	88	Texas	1988
Ahmadian, Ahmad	Assoc	So Colorado	3	I	PHD		North Tx	1986
Ahmed, Hasseb	C-As	Livingstone	13	BSVY	ABD		Miss	8-92
Ahmed, Nazim U.	Prof	Ball State	7		PHD		Tx A&M	1983
Ahn, Sung	Asst	Wash State						
Ahna, Barbara	Asst	Pacific Luth	4	IJLM	JD	78	UPS	1987
Aho, Paul E.	Lect	Mich Tech	9	Z	MBA	83	DePaul	1983
Ahsmann, Leroy L.	Assoc	Roosevelt	25		PHD		Ill Tech	
Aiken, Susan	Lect	J.F. Kennedy	5	P	MA	82	JFKenned	9-90
Ailawadi, Kusum L.	Asst	Dartmouth			PHD	91	Virginia	1993
Aimond, Tim	Asst	Univ Sydney		VX	BA		Macquari	1990
Aish, A. M. A.	Prof	CS-L Angeles	14	L	PHD	69	UCLA	1966
Aitchison, Gary L.	Assoc	Iowa State	36		PHD	72	Iowa St	1965
Akbari, Hamid	Assoc	NE Illinois	32	TH	PHD		Ohio St	9-86
Akel, Anthony		Lg Isl-Post			PHD			
Akhtar, Syed	Lect	City Poly HK	25	EFNP	PHD	83	IITDelhi	1-91
Akin, Gib	Assoc	Virginia			PHD	75	UCLA	
Akin, Ramona	Prof	Henderson St			EDD			
Akinc, Umit	Assoc	Wake Forest	79	UVW	PHD	74	N Carol	9-82
Aktouf, Omar	Assoc	HEC-Montreal	34	DY	PHD		HEC-Mont	
Al-Dwairi, Musa	Asst	Grambling St	12	AY	PHD	90	North Tx	1991
Ala, Mohammad	Prof	CS-L Angeles	7	U	DBA	83	La Tech	1985
Alban, Edward	Assoc	Savannah St	7	V	PHD	73	Georgia	1979
Albanese, Robert	Prof	Texas A&M		EN	PHD	62	Ohio St	1971
Alber, Antone F.	Prof	Bradley	9	Z	PHD	77	Penn St	1975
Albert, Michael	Prof	San Fran St	12	FHNP	PHD	77	Geo St	1977
Albert, Stuart	Assoc	Minnesota	2	EFG	PHD	68	Ohio St	1982
Albrecht, Maryann	Assoc	Ill-Chicago	25	EFH	PHD	75	Emory	9-72
Albrecht, Wayne L.	Asst	No Illinois		U	MS	59	Illinois	1962
Aldag, Ramon J.	Prof	Wisconsin	12	EGLX	PHD	74	Mich St	1974
Alderson, Siobhan	Assoc	Univ Leeds	48	JY	MA	86	Dublin	1993
Aldrich, Howard E.	Prof	No Carolina	2	HSR	PHD	69	Michigan	1982
Alemayehu, Tsehai	Prof	Savannah St	84	Y	PHD	79	Kentucky	1985
Alemi, Farrokh	Assoc	Cleveland St	7	C	PHD		Wiscon	1989
Aleva, David		J.F. Kennedy	16	&	MBA		Harvard	3-93
Alexander, Elmore R.	Prof	American U	25	EHNZ	PHD	78	Georgia	1989
Alexander, F. David	Prof	Angelo State			PHD		Oklahoma	
Alexander, Larry D.	Assoc	Virg Tech	3		PHD	79	UCLA	1981
Alexander, Milton J.	Retir	Auburn	13	6-93	DBA	68	Geo St	9-68
Alexander, Paula	Assoc	Seton Hall			PHD	79	Rutgers	
Alexander, Peter	Asst	Ohio Wesley						
Alexander, Robert P.	Prof	Marshall	5	NI	PHD	69	Ohio U	1969
Alexandrides, Costas G.	Prof	Georgia St	8	Y	PHD	61	New York	1967
Alexis, Marcus	Prof	Northwestern	31	IQ	PHD	69	Minn	
Board of Trustees Professor of Economics								
Alford, Charles L.	Prof	Furman	6	XT	PHD	71	Alabama	1971
Alford, Howard	Prof	Morgan State			PHD		Stanford	
Alford, J. Michael	Assoc	Citadel	36	IT	PHD		Georgia	
Alfred, Theodore	Prof	Case Western	3	I	PHD	63	MIT	
Alghalith, Nabil	Asst	NE Missouri	97	ZU	PHD	93	Missouri	1988
Alhanati, Mark S.	Asst	Mt St Mary's			MBA		LoyolaMr	
Ali, Abbas J.	Prof	Ind-Penna	38	EIJY	PHD	82	W Virg	1989
Aliber, Robert Z.	Prof	Chicago			PHD	62	Yale	1965
Alie, Raymond E.	Assoc	W Michigan	43	EHJY	EDD	80	W Mich	1979
Alkhafaji, Abbass F.	Prof	Slippery Roc	38	ILW	PHD	84	Texas	8-87
Allan, J. R.	Prof	Univ Regina	1	A	PHD		Prin	
Allan, Peter	Prof	Pace	25		PHD		NYU	
Allan, Randi	Assoc	Athabasca Un	2	&EFH	MBA	76	Toronto	1992
Allen, A. Dale Jr.	Prof	Baylor	2	E	DBA		Colorado	1978
Allen, Billie	Assoc	So Miss	25	KNPY	PHD	86	North Tx	1974
Allen, David E.	Assoc	No Michigan			PHD	74	Utah	1987
Allen, Doug	Prof	Central Okla			PHD	80	Okla St	1975
Allen, Douglas B.	Asst	Denver	5	Y	PHD	91	Michigan	9-89
Allen, James	Adj	Southeastern			MPA		Geo Wash	
Allen, Robert E.	Prof	Wyoming	51	JNQD	PHD		SUNY-Buf	8-74
Allen, Robert W.	Assoc	CS-Pomona	5	B	PHD			
Allen, Stephen	Asst	NE Missouri	7	UV	PHD	89	Mo-Rolla	1989
Allen, Stephen A.	Prof	Babson			DBA		Harvard	
Allen, Steven G.	Prof	N Carol St	5	NPQ	PHD	78	Harvard	1978
Allen, Thomas J.	Prof	MIT			PHD		MIT	1966
Gordon Billard Fund Professor of Management								
Allen, W. Bruce	Prof	Pennsylvania			PHD	69	Northwes	1974
Allen, William	Assoc	Mass-Dartmou			PHD	88	Union	1989

Name	Rank	School			Degree		School	Year
Allinson, Christopher	Prof	Univ Leeds	2	EF	PHD	83	Leeds	1973
Allison, Margaret	Asst	Tx-Pan Amer	9	Z	MED		Houston	1976
Allison, Richard C.	C-Pr	Houston-C Lk	4	AM	PHD		Tx A&M	8-75
Allyn, Compton	Prof	No Kentucky	34	B	PHD	73	Cinn	8-73
Almaney, Adnan J.	Prof	DePaul			PHD	67	Indiana	
Alonso, Ramon C.	Prof	Oklahoma	38	IY	PHD	70	SUNY	9-74
Alpander, Guvenc G.	Prof	Maine			PHD	66	Mich St	1965
Alsaaty, Falih	Assoc	Univ of D C	38	Y	PHD	73	NYU	1990
Altinkemer, Kemal	Assoc	Purdue	9	Z	PHD	87	Rochest	1986
Altman, John W.	Prof	Miami U-Ohio	16	ST	MA	88	Fuller	8-92
Altman, Stanley M.	Assoc	SUNY-Stony B	13	AF	PHD	67	Brookpol	1970
Alutto, Joseph A.	Dean	Ohio State	2	E	PHD	68	Cornell	1991
Alvarez de Mon, Santiago	Asst	Univ Navarra	2	E	MBA		Navarra	D-89
Alvarez, Jose Luis	Asst	Univ Navarra	2	EH	PHD		Harvard	9-84
Alvarez, Roy	Lect	Cornell	9	Z	MED		Cornell	1-82
Alwan, A. J.	Prof	DePaul			PHD	67	Chicago	
Alwan, Suad	Asst	Chicago St	9	Z	DBA		Miss St	1988
Amann, Robert J.	Asst	St Thomas-FL	35	IQST	PHD		Va Tech	1991
Amar, Amar D.	Prof	Seton Hall			PHD	80	CUNY	
Amaram, Donatus I.	Prof	Virginia St	52	NE	PHD	76	Ohio St	9-84
Amason, Allen C.	Asst	Miss State	5	N	PHD	93	S Carol	1993
Amatucci, Frances Marie	Asst	Suffolk			PHD		Pitt	
Amba-Rao, S. C.	Assoc	Ind-Kokomo	25	YFNS	PHD	67	Purdue	1978
Ambrose, Maureen	Assoc	Colorado			PHD	86	Illinois	1991
Ames, Michael	Prof	CS-Fullerton	67	S	PHD	71	Clarmont	8-76
Amey, L.	Retir	McGill Univ	1		PHD		Nott	1969
Amin, Ruhul	Prof	Bloomsburg	17		PHD		Akron	8-86
Amit, Raphael	Prof	British Colu	36	TSI	PHD	77	Northwes	1990
Ammar, Salwa	Asst	LeMoyne	7	UV	PHD	87	Florida	1988
Amoako-gyampah, Kwasi	Asst	N Car-Greens	7	UV	PHD		Cinn	1990
Amsden, Robert	Assoc	Dayton	7	U	PHD	69	Rutgers	1978
Amsler, Gordon	Asst	Troy St	23	EFHP	PHD	91	Alabama	1992
Amundsen, Robert	Assoc	NY Inst Tech	14		PHD			
Anyx, Jack	Prof	Cameron			EDD		Okla St	
Anakwe, Uzo	Asst	Pace-Westch	5		PHD	93	Drexel	1994
Anand, Bharat		Yale	1		PHD	94	Princeton	1994
Ancona, Deborah G.	Prof	MIT	2	H	PHD			
Anderson, A. Janell	Prof	CS-Sacrament	24	EL	PHD	77	Ca-Davis	1975
Anderson, Carl R.	Prof	No Carolina	3	IHE	PHD	74	Penn St	1979
Anderson, Carole	Assoc	Clarion	57	NQR	ABD		Kent St	8-90
Anderson, Claire June	Assoc	Old Dominion			PHD	76	Mass	
Anderson, Daniel	Asst	Concordia C	1	C	MBA			
Anderson, David C.	Prof	CS-Fresno	27	EHU	DBA	70	Geo St	1966
Anderson, Douglas R.	Prof	Ashland		DF	PHD	86	Bowl Gr	9-25
Anderson, Elizabeth A.	Asst	Houston		U	PHD	92	Houston	9-91
Anderson, Fred	Asst	Ind-Penna	23	HIT	ABD	84	Pitt	1976
Anderson, G. Bruce	Assoc	U Manitoba	14	L	BA	63	Idaho	1970
Anderson, Jerry W. Jr.	Retir	Xavier	12	BEGH	PHD	76	Cinn	1978
Anderson, Joe	Asst	No Arizona	86	EY	DBA	93	Ariz St	
Anderson, John E. Jr.	Prof	Chris Newpor			PHD		Ohio St	1963
Anderson, John Michael	Prof	N Car-Wilmin	9	Z	PHD		N Car St	
Anderson, Kenneth	Assoc	Gonzaga	12	HE	PHD	88	Nebraska	9-86
Anderson, Mark	Asst	Athens State	4	JK	JD		Alabama	1989
Anderson, Peggy	Prof	Wis-Whitewat	5	NRS	PHD	70	Illinois	1965
Anderson, Philip C.	Assoc	Dartmouth			PHD	88	Columbia	1993
Anderson, Philip H.	Prof	St Thomas-MN	3	I	PHD	75	Minn	8-77
Anderson, Robert L.	Prof	Charleston			PHD		Texas	1979
Anderson, Robin	Lect	Nebraska	6	TYS	EDD	84	Nebraska	1987
Anderson, Roger L.	Dean	Bryant	5	FNQ	PHD	85	Oregon	7-88
Anderson, Sherri C.	Assoc	Sonoma State		SD	MBA	83	Sn Frn S	1980
Anderson, Stella	Asst	Appalach St	2	EH	PHD		Purdue	1992
Anderson, Wendell	Asst	St Marys-Txs	79	UVZ	MBA	69	Harvard	1985
Andersson, Marie Louise	C $	Iona	8	YEHI	PHD	88	CUNY	1980
Andiappan, P.	Prof	Univ Windsor	25	NPQR	PHD	77	Iowa	1980
Andre, Rae	Assoc	Northeastern	82	NE	PHD		Michigan	9-82
Andreason, Aaron	Prof	Montana	18		PHD	75	Brig Yg	1975
Andreu, Rafael	Prof	Univ Navarra	7	VZ	PHD		Pol Cata	4-73
Andrews, Fraya W.	Prof	E Michigan	1		DBA		Memphis	1982
Andrews, Jonlee	Asst	Case Western						
Andrews, William A.	Asst	Stetson	68	STY	PHD		Georgia	1993
Andrisani, Paul J.	C-Pr	Temple			PHD	73	Ohio St	1974
Aneja, Y.	Prof	Univ Windsor	79	UVXZ	PHD		JHopkins	1984
Anekwu, Daniel	C-In	Livingstone	71		MBA	89	Jack St	8-90
Angehrn, Albert A.	Asst	INSEAD	9	Z	PHD	89	Eth	9-90
Angelidis, John	Asst	St Johns			PHD	88	Geo St	
Angle, Harold L.	H-Pr	Cincinnati						
Angur, Madhukar	Asst	Mich-Flint	6	S	PHD			
Annable, Bryan K.	Assoc	Teikyo Post			MBA			
Annand, David	Asst	Athabasca Un	91		MBA	78	Dalhous	1989
Ansar, Jasmin	Asst	St Marys-Cal	7	V	PHD		S Hampto	

Name	Rank	School			Degree		Institution	Year
Ansari, Al	Asst	Seattle	79	UZ	PHD		Nebraska	
Ansari, Asim	Asst	British Colu	7		PHD	93	NYU	1993
Ansari, Nazir A.	Retir	Nevada-Reno	3	1994	PHD	63	Illinois	1967
Ansic, David	Assoc	Univ Leeds	37	IV	DPHI	91	York	1993
Ansoff, H. Igor	Prof	US Intl	3	I	PHB		Brown	1986
Distinguished Professor of Strategic Management								
Anstett, David	Asst	St Scholasti			MBA		Minn-Dul	1985
Anstey, John R.	Assoc	Neb-Omaha			PHD	74	Arkansas	1969
Anstreicher, Kurt	Prof	Iowa	7	V	PHD	83	Stanford	1991
Anthony, Ted F.	Assoc	Texas A&M		V	DBA	71	Colorado	1976
Anthony, William P.	Prof	Florida St	32	IHN	PHD	71	Ohio St	1970
Anton SJ, Ronald J.	Dean	Loyola-Maryl	2	J	PHD		Northwes	1989
Antoniou, Peter	Lect	Mt St Mary's			PHD		US Intl	
Antonucci, Yvonne	Asst	Widener			MS		Lehigh	
Anyansi-Archibong, Chi	Assoc	N Carol A&T	3		PHD		Kansas	1-86
Anyiwo, David E.	Asst	Hampton	7	DUVZ	PHD		Virginia	8-88
Apke, Thomas	Prof	CS-Fullerton			JD	69	Marquett	
Appelbaum, S. H.	Prof	Concordia U						
Apte, Uday	Assoc	So Methodist			PHD	82	Penn	
Aram, John D.	Prof	Case Western			PHD	68	MIT	
Arben, Philip D.	Prof	Cen Michigan	13		PHD	60	Harvard	1980
Arbogast, Gordon	VAsst	Jacksonvil U			PHD	86	Clemson	1993
Arch, Gail	Asst	Houston	58	NQY	PHD	91	Ohio St	9-91
Archambault, Guy	Prof	HEC-Montreal	12	DHN	MBE		Harvard	
Archer, Earnest R.	Prof	Winthrop	23	DE	PHD		Georgia	1970
Archer, Norman P.	Prof	McMaster Un	19	VZ	PHD		McMaster	
Archer, Richard W.	Asst	Old Dominion			PHD	91	Georgia	
Archer, Yves	Assoc	HEC-Montreal	9	Z	DEA		Grenoble	
Archibald, Blyth C.	Assoc	Dalhousie U	7	U	PHD		Waterloo	
Archibald, R. W.	Prof	Lakehead U	34	IL	PHD	76	W Ontari	7-81
Arendt, Lucy	Lect	WI-Green Bay	12	DEGH	MS	90	Wi-GrBay	1990
Argandona, Antonio	Prof	Univ Navarra	7	V	PHD		Barcelon	9-63
Argent, M.	SLect	Humberside	3					
Argenti, Paul A.	Adj	Dartmouth			MBA	81	Columbia	1981
Argheyd, K.	Assoc	Concordia U						
Argyres, Nicholas	Asst	So Calif	3	I	PHD		Berkeley	1993
Argyris, Chris	Prof	Harvard			PHD	51	Cornell	
Arino, Maria Africa	Asst	Univ Navarra	3	I	MBA		Navarra	6-88
Arino, Miguel Angel	Assoc	Univ Navarra	7	V	PHD		Barcelon	6-87
Arinze, Orakwue Bay	Assoc	Drexel		VZ	PHD	87	London	1988
Ariss, Sonny S.	Assoc	Toledo	31		PHD		Ohio St	1985
Arjomand, H. Lari	Prof	Clayton St	7		PHD	80	Oklahoma	1975
Arkley, Alfred S.	C-Pr	Sangamon St	12	AEFP	PHD		Mich St	1977
Arlow, Peter	Prof	Youngstown	13	LR	PHD	79	Cinn	3-85
Armandi, Barry R.	C-Pr	SUNY Old Wes	23	EHPT	PHD	77	St Johns	1985
Armenakis, Achilles A.	Prof	Auburn	12	HF	DBA	71	Miss St	6-73
Torchma Professor								
Armstrong, Gary R.	Prof	Shippensburg	9	Z	DED		Temple	
Armstrong, Pamela K.	Inst	Georgetown	7	U	PHD	93	Penn	1992
Armstrong, Ruth D.	C-Pr	Shippensburg	9	Z	DED	67	Penn St	1967
Armstrong, Terry R.	Prof	West Florida	74	EFHJ	PHD	73	Union	1983
Armstrong-Stassen, Marjorie	Asst	Univ Windsor	25	EGNP	PHD	89	Ohio St	1989
Arndt, Margarete	Asst	Clark	1	C	DBA	91	Boston U	
Arnett, David	Asst	Dallas Bapt	38		PHD		Texas	1994
Arnett, Kirk P.	Assoc	Miss State	9	XZ	DBA	84	Miss St	1985
Arnold, Aline	C-Pr	E Illinios		IH	PHD		North Tx	1988
Arnold, Clyde	Dean	Northern St	7	V	PHD	82	Oklahoma	1988
Arnold, Donald F.	Prof	Union			PHD	72	SUNY-Buf	9-82
Arnold, Ed	Asst	Auburn-Montg	5	N	PHD	90	Alabama	1989
Arnold, John M.	Lect	Manches Inst	2	E	PHD		Sheffiel	6-88
Arnold, Karen	Assoc	Loyola-N Orl	1	DI	PHD	84	LSU	1986
Arnold, Peter M.	Assoc	Boston Univ	73	UI	PHD		Indiana	
Arnold, Victor L.	Prof	Texas	34	MAI	PHD	71	Wiscon	1983
Arnott, Dave	Asst	Dallas Bapt	38		PHD		Tx-Arlin	1994
Arogyaswamy, Kamala	Asst	South Dakota	32	IH	PHD	92	Wi-Milwa	1988
Arogyaswawy, Bernard	Prof	LeMoyne	36	I	PHD	88	Kent St	1988
Aronoff, Craig E.	Prof	Kennesaw St	46	FL	PHD	75	Texas	1983
Aronson, Jay E.	Assoc	Georgia	79	VZ	PHD	80	Car Mel	1987
Arora, Seema	Asst	Vanderbilt	4	KLM	PHD	93	UCLA	9-94
Arreola-Risa, Antonio	Asst	Texas A&M		U	PHD	89	Stanford	1993
Arshad, Ali	Assoc	Teikyo Mary	48	LY	PHD		Conn	8-87
Arthur S.J., E. Eugene	Assoc	Rockhurst	4	JKL	DBA	76	Indiana	1968
Arthur, Jeffrey	Asst	Purdue	2	Q	PHD	90	Cornell	1990
Arthur, Michael B.	Prof	Suffolk			PHD		Cranfield	
Arthurs, A. J.	Lect	Univ Bath	5	Q	PHD			
Artz, John	Prof	George Wash	9	Z				
Arvanites, Debra A.	Asst	Villanova	12	KN	PHD	82	Renssele	1983
Arvey, Richard	Prof	Minnesota	5	NP	PHD	70	Minn	
Ash, Ronald A.	Prof	Kansas	5	N	PHD		S Fla	1981
Ashamalla, Mari	Assoc	Indiana-PA	23	EY	PHD	87	Univ Cen	1992

Name	Rank	School			Degree		University	
Badarinathi, Ravija	Assoc	N Car-Wilmin	7		PHD		Georgia	
Badawi, Jamal	Assoc	St Marys-Cnd	25	EJNR	PHD	70	Indiana	1970
Badawy, Michael K.	Prof	Virg Tech	2		PHD	69	NYU	1987
Baden-Fuller, C.	Prof	Univ Bath	3	I	PHD			
Badham, Richard	Assoc	U Wollongong			PHD		Warrick	D-92
Baetz, Mark C.	Prof	Wilfrid Laur	34	LIA	PHD		Western	1980
Bagby, D. Ray	Prof	Baylor	6	T	PHD	83	S Carol	1988
Robert & Louise Rogers Professor of Entrepreneurship								
Bagchi, Amitava	VProf	NJ Inst Tech	9	Z	SCD	72	MIT	1991
Bagchi, Uttarayan	Prof	Texas	7	UV	PHD	82	Penn St	1982
Bagley, Constance E.	Lect	Stanford	8	Y	JD	77	Harvard	1985
Bagot, Gordon	Asst	CS-L Angeles	7	U	PHD	74	UCLA	1988
Bahaee, S. Mahmood	Assoc	Cen Michigan	3	STI	PHD	87	Ariz St	1985
Bahrami, Bahman	Assoc	N Dakota St	59	QZ	PHD	83	Nebraska	1983
Bai, Jan-Erh	C-Pr	Nat Taiwan U	7	UV	MS	73	Rutgers	1972
Bailetti, A.	Assoc	Carleton Un			PHD		Cinn	
Bailey, Edward	Prof	Marymount			PHD		Iowa	1986
Bailey, Elaine K.	Inst	Hawaii-Manoa			MA	78	Cen Mich	
Bailey, Elizabeth E.	Prof	Pennsylvania			PHD	72	Princeton	1991
John C. Hower Professor								
Bailey, James	Asst	Rutgers-Newk	27	EXZ	PHD	91	Wash U	1991
Bailey, Jeffrey	Asst	Idaho	5	JNP	PHD	91	Akron	1991
Bailey, Therold	Prof	Cen Arkansas	9	Z	EDD		Okla St	
Bailey, William A. Jr.					PHD	89	Fla St	
Bailey, Willie H. Sr.	Dir	Winston-Sal	6	T	PHD	74	Illinois	1986
Baillie, Allan S.	Retir	Cal Poly-SLO	32	1993	PHD	78	U Wash	1978
Bailyn, Lotte L.	Prof	MIT	2	H	PHD			
Bain, George S.	Prof	London Bus	52	QP	DPHL		Oxford	
Bain, Trevor	Prof	Alabama	58	QY	PHD	64	Berkeley	1974
John R. Miller Professor of Management								
Baird, Bruce F.			7	V	PHD	67	N Carol	
Baird, Inga S.	Assoc	Ball State	3		PHD		Illinois	1978
Baird, Lloyd	Prof	Boston Univ	5	NP	PHD		Michigan	
Bajwa, Deepinder	Asst	Fayetteville			PHD			
Bajwa, Shaid		Southeastern			LLB			
Baker, Ben	Asst	Catawba			MA		S Carol	1992
Baker, Bonni Perrott	Assoc	Siena Coll	15	NY	MBA		Ohio St	9-87
Baker, Charles D.	Prof	Northeastern	31	AI	MBA		Harvard	9-85
Baker, Douglas D.	Prof	Wash State			PHD		Nebraska	
Baker, Francis	Asst	Wright State			PHD	84	Claremont	1990
Baker, Huel E. III	Asst	North Fla	12	EFH	PHD		Florida	1989
Baker, Kenneth R.	Prof	Dartmouth			PHD	69	Cornell	1979
Baker, Steven F.	Inst	USAF Academy	7	V	MS		AFIT	
Baker, Wayne E.	Assoc	Chicago	23	HDIL	PHD	81	Northwes	1987
Baker, William G.	Prof	CS-L Angeles	12	CE	PHD	70	Oklahoma	1972
Bakes, Catherine	Asst	Kent State			PHD		Penn St	1982
Bakos, Yannis	Asst	Calif-Irvine	9	Z	PHD	87	Mass	1987
Balachandra, R.	Assoc	Northeastern			PHD		Columbia	
Balakrishnan, Anantaram	Assoc	MIT	7	U	PHD		MIT	
Balakrishnan, Jaydeep	Asst	Univ Calgary	7	UV	PHD	91	Indiana	1990
Balakrishnan, S. (Cheenu)	Assoc	Minnesota	3	I	PHD	83	Michigan	1989
Balas, Egon	Prof	Carnegie Mel	7	V	PHD		Paris	1968
Balcerzak, Raymond F. Jr.	Assoc	Ferris State	7		MBA		SUNY-Buf	1985
Balderson, Wes	Assoc	U Lethbridge	6	ST	MBA	73	Alberta	1977
Baldwin, Lee E.	Dean	Mary Hrdn-By	23		PHD	80	North Ex	1992
Baldwin, Richard	Prof	Cedarville	48	YKL	PHD	87	Ohio St	1975
Baldwin, Timothy T.	Asst	Indiana	5	NP	PHD	87	Mich St	1987
Balfour, G. Alan	Assoc	South Fla	45	QKLJ	PHD	75	Mich St	1980
Baliga, B. Ram	Assoc	Wake Fr-MBA	38	DIY	DBA	80	Kent St	1989
Baligh, Helmy H.	Prof	Duke	38	YHZ	PHD	63	Berkeley	1967
Balkin, David B.	Assoc	Colorado			PHD	81	Minn	1988
Ball, Clifford A.	Assoc	Vanderbilt	7	UVWX	PHD	80	N Mexico	9-90
Ball, Gail	Asst	Nev-L Vegas	24	ELJ	PHD	91	Penn St	1990
Ball, Rebecca W.	Asst	No Kentucky	36	I	PHD	94	Va Tech	8-93
Ballantyne, Edwin J. Jr.	C-As	NW Missouri			PHD	89	Mo-Rolla	1989
Ballarin, Eduard	Prof	Univ Navarra	3	IY	DBA		Harvard	9-69
International Business Chair								
Ballinger, Robert M.	Asst	Siena Coll	18	LMY	ABD		SUNY-Alb	9-81
Ballot, Michael H.	Prof	Pacific	57	QUV	PHD	73	Stanford	9-71
Ballou, Ronald H.	Prof	Case Western			PHD	65	Ohio St	1968
Balloun, Joseph L.	Assoc	Louisiana Te	57	ENVX	PHD	71	Berkeley	1988
Baloff, Nicholas	Prof	Wash Univ	2	EFHU	PHD	63	Stanford	1978
Balsmeier, Philip W.	Prof	Nicholls St			PHD	73	Arkansas	1980
Baltazar, Ramon G.	Asst	Dalhousie U	23	HI	ABD		W Ontari	
Balthazard, Pierre	Asst	N Car-Greens	9	Z	PHD		Arizona	1993
Bamundo, P.	Asst	CUNY-Baruch	1	I	PHD		CUNY	
Banai, Moshe	Asst	CUNY-Baruch	5	Q	PHD		London	1985
Banbury, Catherine	Asst	New Mexico	3	IT	PHD	94	Michigan	
Bandyopadhyay, Jayanta	Prof	Cen Michigan	7	U	PHD	73	Tx Tech	1979
Bandyopadhyay, S.	Asst	McGill Univ	3		PHD		Cinn	1992

Name	Rank	School	#	Code	Degree	Yr	Institution	Yr
Banerjee, Avijit	Prof	Drexel	7	UVW	PHD	77	Ohio St	1977
Banerjee, Snehamay	Asst	Drexel		VZ	PHD	89	Maryland	1988
Banerji, Kunal	Asst	W Virginia	3	I				1990
Banetta, Anna	Deces	Portland St	2	1994	PHD	92	U Wash	1992
Banks, John C.	Assoc	Wilfrid Laur	38	YI	PHD		York	1984
Banks, McRae C.	Assoc	Miss State	12	IST	PHD	87	Va Tech	1987
Banner, David K.	Prof	Pacific	24	DHTE	PHD	73	Northwes	1-87
Bannister, Brendan D.	C-Ac	Northeastern	25	EN&	DBA		Kent St	9-83
Bantel, Karen	Asst	Wayne State	23	HI	PHD	87	Michigan	1988
Bar-Yosef, Sasson	Assoc	Hebrew Univ			PHD		Aston Bm	
Barach, Jeffrey A.	Prof	Tulane	34	IJLS	DBA	67	Harvard	1965
Barbato, Robert J.	Assoc	Rochest Tech			PHD	79	Mich St	1979
Barbeau, J. Bradley	SLect	Chicago	23	FHPI	PHD	87	Michigan	
Barbee, Cliff	Assoc	Houston Bapt	39	IMT	PHD	72	American	1989
Barber, Alison E.	Asst	Michigan St	2	Q	PHD	90	Wiscon	9-90
Barber, L. I.	Prof	Univ Regina	13	I	PHD		Wash	
Barbera, Fran	Asst	SE Louisiana			ABD			8-92
Barclay, Lizabeth A.	Assoc	Oakland	52	N	PHD	81	Wayne St	8-80
Barclay, N.	PLect	Humberside	2					
Barcun, Seymour	Prof	St Fran-NY	7		PHD		New York	
Barcus, Gilbert M.	Lect	CUNY-Stn Isl			PHD		NYU	1971
Bardin, Carl	Asst	East Central	9	Z	MS	70	Okla St	1970
Barefield, Robert		Drury						
Bargielski, Mary	Asst	Gannon	24	EL	MBA		Gannon	
Bariff, Martin	Assoc	Illinois Tch			PHD	73	Illinois	1983
Barille, Judy A.	Inst	Miami U-Ohio	16	ST	MBA	81	Miami U	8-81
Barken, Marlene E.	Assoc	Ithaca	4		PHD	81	Harvard	8-84
Barker, Cheryl	Assoc	Baldwin-Wal	2	GP	PHD		Case Wes	
Barker, Jane	Adj	New York U			JD	75	Wiscon	
Barker, Randolph T.	Assoc	Virg Comm	12	&EFP	PHD	76	Fla St	1989
Barker, Richard	Asst	Marist	23	EF	EDD		Ca-SnDgo	1991
Barker, Robert M.	Asst	Louisville	9	ZEY	PHD	91	Syracuse	1-92
Barker, Tansu	Dean	Brock Univ	8	Y	DBA		Istanbul	1988
Barker, Vincent	Asst	Wis-Milwauke	3	I	PHD	92	Illinois	1992
Barki, Henri	Agreg	HEC-Montreal	9	Z	PHD		W Ontari	
Barksdale, Kevin	Asst	Memphis	25	ENQ	ABD	94	Geo St	1994
Barlett, Alton C.	Prof	South Fla	24	FCQE	PHD	64	Wiscon	1967
Barlev, Benzion	Assoc	Hebrew Univ			PHD		NYU	
Barlow, K. Graham I.	Lect	Manchest Bus	12	EFZ	PHD		Manchest	1975
Barman, Samir	Assoc	Oklahama	7	UV	PHD	87	Clemson	8-87
Barnard, Janet C.	Asst	Rochest Tech			EDD	78	Rochest	1983
Barndt, Stephen E.	Prof	Pacific Luth	13	IU	PHD	71	Ohio St	1978
Barnes, A. Keith	Prof	Redlands	23	HLJI	EDD			
Hunsaker Professor of Management								
Barnes, Clifford	Inst	Bethune-Cook						
Barnes, Frank C.	Prof	N Car-Charl			PHD		Geo St	1075
Barnes, Ian	PLect	Humberside	3					
Barnes, Joyce M.	Assoc	Corpus Chris	1		MBED		E Txs St	
Barnes, Louis B.	Prof	Harvard	25	EN				
Barnett, Arnold I.	Prof	MIT	7	U	PHD			
Barnett, Carole	Asst	New Hampshir	2	E	ABD	94	Michigan	9-94
Barnett, John H.	Deces	New Hampshir	4	3-94	DBA	78	Colorado	1983
Barnett, Steven T.	Asst	York Univ	28	EQY	PHD	93	S Carol	
Barnett, Timothy R.	Asst	Louisiana Te	25	EHJN	DBA	89	Miss St	1991
Barney, Jay B.	Assoc	Texas A&M		IY	PHD	82	Yale	1986
Barney, Joseph A.	Assoc	Loyola-Chicg	2	N	PHD	74	Loyola-C	7-76
Barnowe, J. Thad	Prof	Pacific Luth	58	FGOY	PHD	73	Michigan	1977
Barnum, Darold	Prof	Ill-Chicago	53	NIQ	PHD	73	Penn	1-85
Baron, James N.	Prof	Stanford	2	E	PHD	82	Ca-SnBar	1982
Walter Kenneth Kilpatrick Professor of Organizational Behavior & Human Res								
Baron, Robert A.	C-Pr	Rensselaer	32	EFGH	PHD		Iowa	
Baroni, Barry J.	Prof	New Orleans	17	LE	LLM	74	Tulane	1-67
Baroudi, Jack J.	Assoc	New York U	9	Z	PHD	84	NY Univ	
Barr, Pamela S.	Asst	Emory	3	I	PHD	91	Illinois	1990
Barr, Peter B.	Dean	SC-Coastal	7	U	DBA	85	LTU	1986
Barr, Steven H.	Assoc	Oklahoma St	2	E	PHD	86	Iowa	1-82
Barrar, Peter R. N.	Lect	Manchest Bus	37	ITY	MSC		Cranfield	1987
Barrett, Anthony	Prof	St Scholasti			PHD		Geo Wash	1990
Barrett, Edgar	Prof	Am Grad Intl	31	IUM	PHD	71	Stanford	
Barrett, Frank	Asst	Naval Postgr	21	DFHX	PHD	89	Case Wes	8-91
Barrett, Robert	Assoc	Fran Marion	7	U	PHD	84	Va Tech	6-89
Barrick, Murray R.	Asst	Iowa	5	NP	PHD	88	Akron	1988
Barringer, Melissa	Asst	Massachusett	5	QN	PHD	92	Cornell	1992
Barrios-Choplin, John R.	Adj	Naval Postgr	12	DEFH	ABD		Texas	7-91
Barry, Bruce	Asst	Vanderbilt	12	DEF	PHD	91	N Carol	9-91
Barry, David	SLect	U Auckland	28	FEP	PHD	86	Maryland	4-93
Barry, David F.	Assoc	Salem State	46		JD		Suffolk	
Barsky, Jonathan	Assoc	San Francisc	13	CDPX	PHD	92	Gold Gt	1985
Barsness, Richard W.	Prof	Lehigh			PHD	63	Minn	1978
Bart, Barbara	Prof	Savannah St	64		PHD	80	Georgia	1982

Name	Rank	Institution		Code	Degree		School	Year
Bartee, Jim	Asst	Abilene Chr	78	UY	MA	88	Tx-Dallas	1991
Bartell, Marvin	Prof	U Manitoba	26	EHT	PHD	72	Northwes	1971
Bartell, Nancy O.	Inst	East Tenn St	1		MA	78	Northwes	1989
Bartey, J.	Lect	W Australia						
Barth, Richard T.	Prof	Memorial Un	25		PHD	70	Northwes	1986
Bartlett, Christopher A.	Prof	Harvard	1					
Bartlett, Hale C.	Assoc	Ill-Chicago	34	IL	PHD	65	Michigan	9-67
Bartol, Kathryn M.	Prof	Maryland	5	NR	PHD	72	Mich St	1977
Bartolich, Eugene	Asst	Montevallo	7		PHD		Va Comm	1988
Bartolome, Fernando	Prof	Bentley	2	E	DBA	72	Harvard	1982
Barton, R. B.	Assoc	Murray State	68	IMST	PHD	68	Arkansas	1968
Barton, Sidney L.	Assoc	Cincinnati	3	I	PHD	85	Indiana	
Bartunek, Jean	C-Pr	Boston Coll	2	EHF	PHD	76	Ill-Chic	9-77
Barua, Anitesh	Asst	Texas	9	Z	PHD	90	Car Mel	1990
Basadur, Min S.	Assoc	McMaster Un	2	F	PHD		Cinn	
Basch, John A.	Asst	Bond Univ	23	EHI	MBA	79	Queensld	1989
Baskerville, Richard	Asst	SUNY-Bingham	9	Z	PHD	86	London	1988
Baskin, Otis W.	Prof	Memphis	1	D	PHD	75	Texas	1991
Bass, Bernard M.	Prof	SUNY-Bingham	25	EFHN	PHD	49	Ohio St	1977
Distinguished Professor Emeritus								
Bass, Kenneth Ernest	Asst	East Carol	31	IEJL	DBA	91	La Tech	8-92
Bassett, Glenn	C-Pr	Bridgeport	37	IU	PHD	78	Yale	9-79
Bassett, James C.	Asst	CS-Pomona			PHD	91	Ohio St	1991
Bassford, Gerald	Assoc	Arizona St	24	EL	DBA	70	Indiana	1969
Bassin, William M.	Prof	Shippensburg	7	V	DBA	70	Geo Wash	1970
Bassiry, Gabriel R.	Prof	CS-San Bern	38	IY	PHD	77	SUNY-Bin	1987
Bast, Karin	Lect	Wis-La Cross			MBA		Wis-LaCr	
Basti, Abdul Z.	Prof	No Illinois		V	PHD	68	Colorado	1967
Basu, Amit	Assoc	Vanderbilt	9	Z	PHD	86	Rochest	9-90
Basu, K.	Asst	McGill Univ	3		PHD		Florida	1986
Basu, Raja	Asst	Oklahoma St	2	E	PHD	91	Purdue	8-91
Basuray, M. Tom	C-Pr	Towson State	24		PHD	74	Oklahoma	1986
Bate, S. P.	Lect	Univ Bath	5	Q	PHD			
Bateman, David N.	Prof	So Illinois	12	EF	PHD	70	S Illin	1-65
Bateman, George	SLect	Chicago			MBA	67	Chicago	
Bateman, Thomas S.	Prof	No Carolina	2	EGO	DBA	80	Indiana	1986
Baten, Eugene	Asst	Central Conn	24	BFLP	DED	91	Harvard	1988
Bates, Constance S.	Assoc	Fla Internat		IY	DBA	79	Indiana	1983
Bates, Donald	Prof	CS-Long Bch	31	HIL	PHD	73	Arkansas	1974
Bates, Kenneth J.	Assoc	Houghton	13	ID	MBA	81	Loyola	1989
Batory, Anne H.	Assoc	Wilkes	68	RTY	PHD		Maryland	9-87
Baucells, Manuel	Inst	Univ Navarra	3	I	MBA		Navarra	6-93
Bauermeister, Larry A.	Lect	GMI	9	Z	MSEE	62	Illinois	1990
Bauerschmidt, Alan D.	Prof	So Carolina			PHD	68	Florida	
Baugh, Gayle M.	Asst	West Florida	25	EOX	PHD	92	Cinn	1989
Baugher, Daniel	Prof	Pace	23	DNV	PHD	76	Rutgers	7-78
Baughman, Rowland	Prof	Central Conn	25	DENQ	DBA	75	Geo Wash	1983
Baum, Joel	Asst	New York U			PHD	89	Toronto	
Baumer, David L.	Assoc	N Carol St	4	K	PHD	80	Virginia	1979
Baumgartner, Samuel R.	Assoc	GMI	19	EPW	MA	58	Ball St	1964
Baunach, Warren	Adj	No Carolina	25	EHN	PHD		N Carol	
Bausch, Thomas A.	Prof	Marquette	4	L	DBA	69	Indiana	1978
Baveja, Alok	Asst	Rutgers-Camd			PHD			
Bawa, K.	Assoc	McGill Univ	3		PHD		Columbia	1984
Baxter, Carol M.	Lect	N Car-Charl			MA		Ball St	1978
Baxter, Robert	Assoc	Elon	4		JD	59	Duke	1959
Baybars, Ilker	C-Pr	Carnegie Mel	7	U	PHD	79	Car Mel	1979
Bayer, Max	Prof	Univ Calgary	7	UVX	PHD	72	Toronto	1968
Bayliss, B. T.	Prof	Univ Bath	8	Y	PHD			
Bayne, Keith	Assoc	Virgin Islan	73	SZD	MS			1990
Bays, Marianne	Asst	Monmouth	93	FZ	PHD	93	CUNY	8-92
Baysinger, Barry D.	Prof	Texas A&M		ITY	PHD	78	Va Tech	1979
Bazan, Henry J.	Prof	W New Eng	2	FG	MA		Mass	1964
Bazerman, Max H.	Prof	Northwestern	2		PHD	79	Car Mel	1985
J. Jay Gerber Distinguished Professor of Dispute Resolution & Organizations								
Beach, Lee Roy	Prof	Arizona	3	EI	PHD		Colorado	1990
Beal, Reginald	Asst	Wis-Whitewat	6	EIST	ABD	93	Wis-Milw	1988
Beam, Henry H.	Prof	W Michigan	37	ISB	PHD	75	Michigan	1975
Bean, Alden S.	Prof	Lehigh			PHD	69	Northwes	1983
Kenan Professor of Management and Technology								
Bean, Marshall	Prof	San Jose St	4	K	JD	57	Santa Cl	1957
Bean, William	Asst	New Hamp Col	12	F	ABD		Vanderbt	
Beard, Barbara E.	Prof	Shepherd	1	D	PHD		Maryland	1976
Beard, Donald W.	Assoc	U Washington	3		PHD	75	Nebraska	1975
Beard, Jon W.	Asst	Richmond	29	EFPZ	PHD	91	Tx A&M	8-90
Beath, Cynthia	Assoc	So Methodist			PHD	86	UCLA	
Beatty, C. A.	Asst	Queen's Univ	25	EGU	PHD	86	Western	1985
Beatty, Jeffery	Adj	Boston Univ	4	K	JD		Boston U	
Beatty, Warren A.	Prof	So Alabama	79	UVXZ	PHD	86	Fla St	1980
Beaty, David	Assoc	Hampton	2	8	PHD		P Eliz	1989

Name	Rank	School			Degree		Institution	Year
Beaulieu, Ronald P.	Assoc	Cen Michigan	25	EFP	DBA	76	Indiana	1979
Beaumont, Chris D.	VAsst	London Bus	7	V	MSC		Birmingh	
Beauvais, Laura Lynn	Assoc	Rhode Island	12	EFHR	PHD	87	Tenn	1984
Beaven, Mary	Prof	F Dick-Madis	2		PHD		Northwes	
Bechard, Bonnie	Assoc	Plymouth St			EDD	87	Ariz St	
Bechtold, Stephen E.	Deces	Florida St	7	3-94	DBA	77	Indiana	8-74
Beck-Dudley, Caryn	Assoc	Utah State	4	JK	JD	83	Idaho	9-84
Becker, Brian	C-Pr	SUNY-Buffalo	5	NQ	PHD	77	Wiscon	9-70
Becker, Selwyn W.	Prof	Chicago	2	EH	PHD	58	Penn St	1959
Becker, Thomas	Asst	Fla Atlantic			PHD	86	New Mex	1991
Becker, W. Michael	Assoc	San Francisc			PHD	75	Brig Yg	1975
Beckles, Gina Wilson	Asst	Bethune-Cook						
Beckman, Dale	H	Victoria Can	8	Y	PHD		Mich St	7-91
Beckman, Eugene	Lect	Indiana SE	1		MBA	75	Louisvil	1987
Beckman, Sara L.	Lect	Cal-Berkeley	7	U	PHD		Stanford	1988
Bector, C. R.	H-Pr$	U Manitoba	7	V	PHD	68	Ill Tech	1970
Bedeian, Arthur G.	C-Pr	Louisiana St	12	BE	DBA	73	Miss St	5-85
Bedient, John	Assoc	Albion			MBA	79	Indiana	1984
Bednar, David A.	Prof	Arkansas	2	E	PHD	80	Purdue	1980
Bednorz, John	Adj	Southeastern	9	Z	MPA			
Bedrosian, Hrach	Prof	New York U			PHD	62	Columbia	
Beechler, Schon	Assoc	Columbia	58	IYN	PHD	90	Michigan	1989
Beekun, Rafik I.	Asst	Nevada-Reno	2	EI	PHD	88	Texas	1989
Beeland, James L.	Assoc	Alabama-Birm	16		DBA	76	Geo St	1971
Beeman, Don	Prof	Toledo	38		DBA		Indiana	1976
Beer, Michael	Prof	Harvard	25	EN				
Beggs, Joyce M.	Asst	N Car-Charl			PHD		Tenn	1989
Begin, Floyd C.	Prof	St Ambrose	18	DY	PHD	74	Iowa	1985
Begley, Thomas M.	Assoc	Northeastern	26	E	PHD		Cornell	9-80
Behara, Ravi S.	Asst	S F Austin	79	UVW	PHD	89	Manchest	1992
Beheshti, Hooshang M.	Prof	Radford	79	UZ	PHD	77	Okla St	8-79
Behling, O. C.	Prof	Bowling Gr	1	EF	PHD	61	Wiscon	1981
Behrens, Curtiss	Assoc	No Illinois	5	Q	LLM		DePaul	
Behrman, Jack N.	Emer	No Carolina	8	JLW	PHD	52	Princeton	1964
Luther Hodges Distingushed Professor Emeritus								
Behrs, David		Marymount						
Beise, C.	Asst	West Georgia	9	Z	PBD	89	Geo St	1-89
Belasco, James A.	Prof	San Diego St	2	EH	PHD	66	Cornell	1971
Belay, Leul	Asst	Jackson St			PHD		Missouri	1972
Belding, Eser U.	Assoc	Fordham	28	EY	PHD		Michigan	1988
Beldona, Sam	Asst	Rutgers-Newk	8	Y	PHD		Temple	1993
Belhadjali, Moncef	Asst	Norfolk St	9	Z	PHD	90	Penn	7-90
Belisle, Jean-Pierre	Adj	HEC-Montreal	9	VXZ	MSC		U of M	
Bell, Arthur	Assoc	San Francisc	12	DGJU	PHD	73	Harvard	1993
Bell, Cecil	C-Ac	U Washington	5		PHD	70	Boston	1968
Bell, Colin E.	Prof	Iowa	97	ZV	PHD	69	Yale	1980
Bell, Donald L.	Prof	CS-Pomona	98	STYZ	PHD	77	Claremont	1972
Bell, Eugene C.	Prof	Linfield	2		PHD	74	Houston	1992
Bell, Gerald D.	Adj	No Carolina	2	EFG	PHD	64	Yale	1963
Bell, James	Assoc	Cen Arkansas	9	V	EDD		Oklahoma	
Bell, James D.	Prof	SW Texas St	1	DEF	PHD		Akron	1985
Bell, Robert	Prof	CUNY-Brookly	13	A	PHD			1986
Bell, Robert R.	Dean	Tenn Tech	24	EHUI	PHD	70	Florida	1976
Bell, Sharon E.	Asst	Ferris State	2		MBA		Wrght St	1980
Bellas, Carl J.	Dean	Susquehanna	31	BLD	PHD	69	Oregon	9-83
Bellis, David J.	D-Pr$	CS-San Bern	1	A	PHD	77	S Calif	1985
Belliveau, Marua A.	Asst	Duke	25	EN	ABD		Berkeley	1994
Bellizzi, Frank	Assoc	Quinnipiac	26	EGJT	PHD		Mass	
Belohlav, James A.	Assoc	DePaul			PHD		Cinn	
Belote, Arthur	Prof	Furman	3	NEI	PHD	62	Florida	1965
James C. Self Professor of Business Administration								
Belt, John A.	C-As	Wichita St	52	NPEO	PHD	71	Tx Tech	9-71
Beltsos, Nicholas J.	Retir	E Michigan	1	1994	MA	61	Mich St	1962
Bemmels, Brian	Assoc	British Colu	5	Q	PHD	84	Minn	1992
Ben-David, Arie	Lect	Hebrew Univ			PHD		Cas West	
Ben-Horin, Moshe	Assoc	Hebrew Univ			PHD		NYU	
Benbasat, Izak	Prof	British Colu	9	Z	PHD	74	Minn	1974
BenDaniel, David	Prof	Cornell	6	T	PHD		MIT	1-85
Don and Margi Berens Professor of Entrepreneurship								
Bender, Douglas	Assoc	Widener			PHD		Jeff Med	
Benham, Harry	Asst	Montana St	9		PHD	78	Berkeley	9-90
Benich, Joseph J.	Assoc	Charleston			DBA		Kent St	1972
Benishay, Haskel	Prof	Northwestern	37	IU	PHD	60	Chicago	1967
Bennardo, James V.	Assoc	Assumption	57		MBA	75	Berkeley	1985
Bennet, Rebecca	Asst	Toledo	2		DBA		Northwes	1991
Bennett, Nathan	Asst	Louisiana St	2	NE	PHD	89	Ga Tech	8-89
Bennett, R.	Assoc	McGill Univ	3		DBA		Harvard	1976
Bennett, Robert B.	Asst	Butler	4	J	JD	80	Georgia	1991
Benninga, Simon	Assoc	Hebrew Univ			PHD		Tel Aviv	
Bennis, Warren	Prof	So Calif	2	EFH	PHD		MIT	1980

Name	Rank	School			Degree		Institution	Year
Bluedorn, Allen C.	Assoc	Missouri	2	E	PHD	76	Iowa	1981
Blum, Albert A.	Prof	New Mex St	25	BQY	PHD	53	Columbia	1985
Blum, Michael	Asst	NE Missouri	25	Q	PHD	93	Missouri	1984
Blum, Terry	Prof	Georgia Tech	2	CH	PHD	82	Columbia	1986
Blumberg, Harvey	Prof	Montclair St			PHD		CUNY	1978
Blumberg, Melvin	Prof	Penn St-Harr	2	EFH	PHD	77	Penn St	1985
Blumenthal, Judith F.	Assoc	CS-Northrdge	38	FHIY	PHD	88	S Calif	1987
Blunden, Robert G.	C-Ac	Dalhousie U	36	IT	PHD		W Ontar	
Blunt, Keith R.	Prof	CS-L Angeles	14	Q	PHD	58	Iowa	1967
Blythe, Steve	Asst	Central Okla			PHD	79	Arkansas	1992
Boaden, Ruth J.	Lect	Manches Inst	7	T	PHD		Manchest	9-89
Boag, David	Dean	Victoria Can	6	ST	PHD		Toronto	1-91
Boal, Kimberly B.	Assoc	Texas Tech	23	EHI	PHD	80	Wiscon	1989
Boardman, Anthony	Prof	British Colu	13	Ai	PHD	75	Car Mel	1979
Bobbitt, H. Randolph Jr.	Retir	Ohio State	2	7-93	PHD	66	Penn	1966
Bobko, Peter B.	Assoc	Guilford	7	U	DBA	83	Indiana	
on leave to USAF Academy								
Bobko, Phil	Prof	Rutgers-N Br		EN	PHD	76	Cornell	1988
Boccialetti, Gene	Assoc	New Hampshir	2	EFQ	PHD	82	Case Wes	1983
Bochanan, Richard	Assoc	NY Inst Tech	52		PHD			
Bock, Heather E.			3	I	PHD	87	N Carol	
Bockanic, William N.	C-Pr	John Carroll			JD		Clev St	1978
Bockley, William	Assoc	New Haven	12	EH	PHD		Boston C	
Bockman, Sheldon	Prof	CS-San Bern	2	E	PHD	68	Indiana	1973
Bodensteiner, Wayne D.	D-Pr	Tx-S Antonio						
Bodily, Samuel E.	Prof	Virg-Grad	7	V	PHD		MIT	1977
Boe, Warren J.	Prof	Iowa	7	UZ	PHD	70	Purdue	1970
Boeker, Warren	Asst	Columbia	36	IT	PHD	86	Berkeley	1987
Boerstler, Heidi	Asst	Colo-Denver						
Boger, Pamela A.	Inst	Ohio Univ	7		PHD	84	Ohio U	
Bogert, James D.	Asst	Oklahoma St	3	I	ABD		Tx A&M	8-91
Boghossian, Fikru H.	C-Pr	Morgan State			PHD	79	Arkansas	
Bognanno, Mario F.	D-Pr	Minnesota	5	Q	PHD	69	Iowa	
Bogner, William	Asst	Georgia St	3	I	PHD	90	Illinois	1991
Bogumil, Walter A.	Assoc	Cen Florida	5	NQ	PHD	72	Georgia	1972
Bohl, Alan	Asst	LaSalle	7	V	PHD		Temple	
Bohlander, George	Prof	Arizona St	21	KNQ	PHD	78	UCLA	1977
Bohle, Phil	Lect	U Queensland	3	E	PHD	94	Griffith	1994
Bohleber, Michael	Assoc	Georgia SW	34	I	PHD		Wiscon	
Bohlen, George	Assoc	Dayton	79	UZ	PHD	73	Purdue	1980
Bohn, Gerhard	Exec	Charleston						1990
Boice, Craig K.	Adj	New York U			MPHL	77	Yale	
Boise, William	Prof	New York-Gr	12		PHD		Penn	
Boje, David M.	Prof	Loyola Marym	12	EFH	PHD	79	Illinois	1989
Bokemeier, L. Charles	Assoc	Mich-Flint	1	AGR	DBA	83	Kentucky	9-90
Boland, Richard	Prof	Case Western			PHD	76	Case Wes	1990
Boland, Thomas	Prof	Ohio Univ	7		PHD	66	Chicago	
Bolander, Steve	C-Pr	Colorado St	79	U	PHD	72	Kent St	1972
Boldt, Donald B.	DLect	East Carol	36		MBA	62	Harvard	8-81
Boles, Terry L.	Asst	Iowa	2	E	PHD	91	Ca-SnBar	1993
Bolin, Michael	Inst	Abilene Chr			ABD		North Tx	1991
Bolling, W. Blaker	Prof	Marshall	3	I	DBA	79	Virginia	1979
Bolman, Lee	Prof	Mo-Kansas Ct	2	HJ	PHD		Yale	1994
Bolon, Donald S.	Prof	Miami U-Ohio	5	JN	PHD	71	Ohio St	8-76
Bolton, Alfred A.	Prof	Averett	15	B	DBA	85	Nova	
Bolton, Gary E.	Asst	Penn State	7	V	PHD		Car Mel	
Bolton, Michele	Assoc	San Jose St	36	DI	PHD	90	UCLA	1-89
Bommer, Michael	Prof	Clarkson	7	V	PHD	71	Penn	
Bond, Kenneth M.	Prof	CS-Humboldt	47	JLVX	PHD	75	Nebraska	1988
Bonge, John W.	Prof	Lehigh			PHD	68	Northwes	1972
Bonham, T. W.	Prof	Virg Tech	2		PHD	69	S Carol	1969
Bonini, Charles P.	Prof	Stanford	7	V	PHD	62	Carnegie	1959
William R. Timken Professor of Management Science								
Bonner, William H.	Prof	Tenn Tech	1	O	PHD	61	Ohio St	1962
Bonno, John A.	Prof	Tx A&M-Kings	9	Z	PHD	69	Arkansas	1970
Bontempo, Robert	Assoc	Columbia	58	NY	PHD	89	Illinois	1989
Bookbinder, J. H.	Prof	Un Waterloo	7	UV	PHD	69	Calif	1982
Booke, A.	Inst	CUNY-Baruch	3		MBA		CUNY	
Boone, Larry	Asst	St Johns			PHD	87	Pitt	
Boos, John D.	Assoc	Ohio Wesley	34	IJT	JD		Geo Wash	1983
Boot, John	C-Pr	SUNY-Buffalo	7	V	PHD	64	Netherl	1-65
Boot, R. L.	Lect	U Lancaster	25	NOP	MSC		City	
Booth, David	Assoc	Kent State			PHD		N Carol	1984
Booth, Francis Dean	Asst	Mo-Kansas Ct	7	U	PHD	87	Okla St	1987
Booth, Mary Ann	Lect	British Colu	4	K	LLB	85	Brit Col	1989
Booth, Rose Mary	Asst	N Car-Charl			PHD		Kentucky	
Boothe, Robert	Assoc	So Miss	17	SU	DBA	84	Fla St	1988
Boothman, Barry Edward	Assoc	New Brunswic	34	ABIL	PHD	89	York	1986
Boozer, Robert	Assoc	Stetson	21	EB	DBA		Miss St	1990
Borah, Santano	Asst	No Alabama			PHD	93	Illinois	1992

Name	Rank	School			Degree		Institution	
Borgelt, Marvin	C-Ac	Mary	34		MBA	82	Maryland	9-82
Born, Richard G.	Assoc	No Illinois		Z	PHD		Ill Tech	
Boroff, Karen	Asst	Seton Hall			PHD	90	Columbia	
Boronico, Jess	Asst	Monmouth	7	V	PHD	92	Penn	9-93
Boroschek, Gunther	C-Pr	Mass-Boston	8	Y	PHD	70	Harvard	1975
Borseth, Earl	Prof	Ferris State	2		MBA		Indiana	1983
Borst, Frank	Assoc	St Ambrose	37	IU	EDD	82	Memphis	1990
Borstorff, Patricia C.	Inst	Jacksonvl St	12	NOQ	MBA	89	Jackv St	1989
Borucki, Chester	Asst	New York U			PHD	87	Columbia	
Borycki, Christine	Asst	SUNY-Fredon	37	IF	MBA		SW La	1990
Boscheck, Ralf		Intl Mgt Dev	3	I	PHD		St Galln	
Boschken, Herman	Prof	San Jose St	31	AHI	PHD	72	Wash U	1982
Bose, Ranjit	Asst	New Mexico	9	Z	PHD	89	Texas	1989
Boshyk, Yury		Intl Mgt Dev	4	L	DPH		Oxford	
Boss, R. Wayne	Prof	Colorado			DPA	73	Georgia	1973
Bossman, Larry	Assoc	Detroit Merc			PHD	67	Wiscon	1971
Bostic, Pam		N Carol St					Duke	
Bostrom, Robert P.	Prof	Georgia	9	DZ	PHD	78	Minn	1988
Bothams, J.		Strathclyde	2	F				
Bottom, William	Assoc	Wash Univ	2	EFGH	PHD	89	Illinois	1988
Bottoms, I. Glenn	Prof	Gardner-Webb	97	ZUV	PHD	81	Geo St	1983
Boudreau, Bob	Assoc	U Lethbridge	2	EFGH	PHD	85	Calgary	1983
Boudreaux, Phil	Inst	SW Louisiana	7	VI	ABD		LSU	1976
Bougon, Michel	Assoc	Bryant	3	IHE	PHD	80	Cornell	8-88
Boulton, William	Prof	Auburn	38	I	DBA	77	Harvard	9-90
Olan-Mills Professor								
Boulware, George W.	C-Pr	David Lipsc	1	L	PHD	76	S Carol	9-79
Boulware, Jeanna	Inst	David Lipsc	25	BEN	MBA		Gold Gt	9-79
Bourdaoui, Necar	Asst	Chicago St	9		PHD		IL Tech	1992
Bounds, William T. Jr.	C	Cen Arkansas	37	IJN	PHD	86	Miss	8-75
Bourgeois, L. J. III	Prof	Virg-Grad	3	I	PHD		U Wash	1986
Bourland, Karla E.	Asst	Dartmouth			PHD	91	Michigan	1989
Bourne, S. Graham	Inst	Brescia			MBA	89	Radford	1989
Boursy, John J.	Prof	Fitchburg St	4	GJ	MBA		Clark	1964
Bouteiller, Dominique	Asst	HEC-Montreal	5	PQ	PHD		Montreal	1993
Bouvard, Jacques M.		Intl Mgt Dev	3	I	MBA		Harvard	
Bovee, Stephen	Inst	Oral Roberts	3	I	MBA	90	Oral Rob	8-91
Bowditch, James L.	Dean	St Joseph			PHD	69	Purdue	1993
Bowen, Barbara	Lect	Wis-La Cross			MBA		Wis-LaCr	
Bowen, David	Assoc	Ariz St-West	25	EHP	PHD	83	Mich St	1991
Bowen, David J.	C-Pr	St Marys-Cal	25	FQE	PHD	76	Berkeley	1983
Bowen, Donald D.	Prof	Tulsa	2	E&FO	PHD	71	Yale	8-76
Bowen, Kent	Prof	Harvard	7	U				
Bower, Joseph L.	Prof	Harvard	1					
Donald Kirk David Professor of Business Administration								
Bowerman, Karen Dill	Prof	CS-Fresno	2	EH	PHD		Tx A&M	1979
Bowers, Melissa R.	Asst	Tennessee	79	UV	PHD	89	Clemson	1-89
Bowers, Mollie	Prof	Baltimore	58	NQWY	PHD	74	Cornell	9-83
Bowey, Jim	Asst	Bishop's Un	38	Y	MA		Lancastr	1993
Bowie, Norman E.	C-Pr	Minnesota	4	JKLM	PHD	68	Rochest	1989
Bowin, Robert B.	Prof	CS-Bakersf	14	GP	PHD	70	Oregon	1984
Bowman, Edward H.	Prof	Pennsylvania	3	IMYL	PHD	54	Ohio St	7-83
Reginald H. Jones Professor of Corporate Management								
Box, Thomas M.	Asst	Pittsburg St	36	IST	PHD	91	Okla St	1990
Boxall, Peter F.	SLect	U Auckland	53	NQIB	MCOM	87	Auckland	1-87
Boxx, Randy	Dean	Mississippi	12	IM	PHD	71	Arkansas	1971
Boyacigiller, Nakiye	Prof	San Jose St	84	YNEH	PHD	86	Berkeley	1-86
Boyatzis, Richard E.	Prof	Case Western	2	E	PHD		Harvard	
Boyd, Brian K.	Asst	Old Dominion	3	I	PHD	89	S Calif	8-92
Boyd, Charles W.	Assoc	SW Missouri	63	L	PHD	80	Kan St	1983
Boyd, David P.	Dean	Northeastern	5	N	PHD		Oxford	9-78
Boyd, Edwin C.	Assoc	Chris Newpor			MBA		Penn	1972
Boyd, John H.	Lect	Baylor	2	E	MA		W Texas	1985
Boyd, Nancy	Asst	North Texas	5	EN	PHD	91	Memphis	1991
Boyer, Caroline K.	Assoc	Cincinnati	2	F	PHD	66	Case Wes	1968
Boyer, John W. Jr.	Prof	Minn-Duluth	5	NQ	PHD	70	Minn	1970
Boylan, Robert L.	Asst	Rensselaer			PHD		Duke	1987
Boyles, Wiley	Prof	Auburn	12	EN	PHD	63	Tenn	9-84
Boyne, Patricia M.	Asst	Bloomsburg	9	Z	MS		Penn St	
Boyton, Robert E.	Assoc	Naval Postgr	25	EFPQ	PHD	68	Stanford	1970
Bozarth, Cecil	Asst	N Carol St	7	U	PHD	92	N Carol	1992
Boze, Betsy V.	Dean	Tx-Brownsvil			Mktg	84	Arkansas	1994
Brabston, Mary	Asst	Tenn-Chattan	9	Z	ABD		Fla St	8-93
Bracken, Paul	Prof	Yale	8	Y	PHD	82	Yale	1981
Bracker, Jeffrey S.	Prof	Louisville	36	ISTY	PHD	82	Geo St	7-91
Brown & Williamson Professor of Entrepreneurship								
Bradbard, David A.	Assoc	Winthrop	9	VZ	EDD		Georgia	1987
Bradberry, William	C-Ac	Guam	83	ULJI	PHD	86	Tx-Dallas	1990
Bradburn, Norman M.	Prof	Chicago			PHD	60	Harvard	1960
Tiffany & Margaret Blake Distinguished Service Professor of Beh Science								

Name	Rank	School	#	Codes	Degree	Yr	Degree School	Yr
Bradbury, Robert	Assoc	Clark	1	C	PHD	75	Ohio	
Bradford, Amos	Assoc	Florida A&M	2		PHD		Michigan	
Bradford, David	Lect	Stanford	2	E	PHD	66	Michigan	1969
Bradford, John W.	Assoc	U Miami	7	UV	PHD	86	Columbia	1986
Bradley, David B.	Assoc	Lyndon State			MBA		Plymouth	1981
Bradley, John	Asst	East Carol		Z	PHD		UTA	8-90
Bradley, John H.	C-Pr	St Thomas-FL	19		DCS	78	Georgia	1978
Bradley, Martin	C-In	New Hamp Col	24	E	MED		Notre Dm	
Bradley, Stephen P.	Prof	Harvard	4	L				
William Ziegler Professor of Business Administration								
Bradley, Steven A.	VAsst	Roosevelt	3	I	PHD		Northwes	
Bradshaw, James R.	Prof	Brighm Yg-HI	8	Y	EDD	74	Brig Yg	1969
Bradshaw, Patricia	Assoc	York Univ	2	EFR	PHD		York	
Brady, Gene F.	Prof	Bridgeport	35	I	PHD	71	Oregon	9-82
Bragg, Daniel	C-As	Bowling Gr	7	U	PHD	84	Ohio St	1980
Brahm, Richard A.	Asst	Calif-Irvine	38	HIY	PHD	89	Penn	1988
Brakefield, James	Asst	W Illinois			PHD	90	Buffalo	1990
Bramble, Thomas	Lect	U Queensland	5	Q	PHD	93	La Trobe	1993
Bramblett, Richard	Assoc	Augusta	79	Z	PHD	73	Ga Tech	1987
Bramorski, Tom	Assoc	Wis-Whitewat	7	UVWY	PHD	89	Iowa	1989
Branan, Carson	Assoc	Greensboro			MS		N Car St	1958
Brandenburg, Richard G.	Prof	Vermont	31	IU	PHD	64	Cornell	1987
Brander, James A.	Prof	British Colu	83	IYM	PHD	79	Stanford	1984
Brandt, Floyd S.	Prof	Texas	34	IJL	DBA	60	Harvard	1963
Brandt, Frederick	D-Ac	Russell Sage	23	EY	PHD		Ariz St	1982
Braneff, Ann	Lect	Texas A&M		K	JD	88	Houston	1992
Brannen, Dalton E.	C-Pr	Augusta	5	NPQ	PHD	76	Miss	1990
Brannen, Kathleen C.	Assoc	Creighton	26	EST	PHD	79	Nebraska	8-79
Brannen, Mary Yoko	Asst	Michigan						
Brant, Clyde L.	VInst	Miami U-Ohio	7	U	MBA	90	Miami U	8-90
Brasfield, James M.	C-Pr	Webster	1	AC	PHD	73	Case Wes	1975
Brass, Daniel J.	Assoc	Penn State	2	EH	PHD		Illinois	1979
Brassil, James P.	Asst	Hampton	1	P	MBA		Geo Wash	8-88
Braunstein, Daniel N.	Prof	Oakland	52	N	PHD	64	Purdue	1971
Brawley, Dorothy	Assoc	Kennesaw St	36	DIST	PHD	82	Geo St	1989
Brazeal, Deborah	Asst	CS-Pomona	6	ST				
Breaugh, James A.	C-Ac	Mo-St Louis	5	N	PHD	77	Ohio St	1977
Brechtel, Donald L.					DBA	81	Fla St	
Bregman, Robert L.	Asst	Houston	7	U	PHD	88	Ohio St	9-93
Bregman, Robert L.	Retir	Texas A&M		1994	MBA	83	Ohio St	1987
Brehaut, Steven	Lect	Australian N	9	ZS	BSC	80	LaTrobe	1984
Breitenbach, Robert	Prof	Metro State	47	KWY	PHD	67	Ohio St	1982
Brenan, Ian	Asst	Fayetteville			PHD			
Brenenstuhl, Daniel C.	Assoc	Arizona St	38	ITY	DBA	75	Indiana	1978
Brennan, David J.	Asst	Webster	8	YD	PHD	92	St Louis	1991
Brennan, John F.	Dean	Suffolk	3	I	MBA	58	Harvard	1991
Brenner, Otto C.	Prof	Jms Madison	23	I	PHD	77	Stevens	9-77
Brenner, R.	Prof	McGill Univ	3		PHD		Jerusale	1978
Brenner, Steven N.	Prof	Portland St	4	JL	PHD	72	Harvard	1971
Breton, Michele	Agreg	HEC-Montreal	7	ITUZ	PHD		U of M	
Brett, Jeanne M.	Prof	Northwestern	5	N	PHD	72	Illinois	1976
DeWitt W. Buchanon, Jr. Professor of Dispute Resolution & Organization								
Brett, Joan	Asst	So Methodist			PHD	92	NYU	1990
Bretthauer, Kurt	Asst	Texas A&M		V	PHD	90	Indiana	1990
Bretz Jr., Robert D.	Assoc	Iowa	5	NP	PHD	88	Kansas	1994
Breund, Britt	Asst	Texas	7	UV	PHD	94	Cornell	1994
Breuning, Loretta	Prof	CS-Hayward	8	Y	PHD	83	Tufts	1983
Brewer, Ann M.	SLect	Univ Sydney	25	ENQH	PHD		NS Wales	1991
Brewer, Peggy D.	Prof	E Kentucky	35	DPR	DBA	82	La Tech	1980
Brews, Peter J.	Asst	Babson			PHD		Witwater	
Brewster, Jim	Prof	Central Okla			EDD	72	Geo Wash	1982
Briant, P.	Prof	McGill Univ	3		PHD		Michigan	1952
Brickner, Laura	Asst	Heidelberg	57	U	MBA	86	Bowl Grn	1989
Brickner, William	Retir	San Jose St	36	TL	PHD	66	Stanford	1971
Bridges, Carl	Asst	Ohio Univ	25		PHD	92	N Illin	
Bridwell, Larry	Assoc	Pace	8		PHD		CUNY	
Briercheck, Glenn F.	Assoc	York of PA	7	V	PHD		Conn	1975
Briggs, Steven	Assoc	DePaul			PHD		UCLA	
Briggs, Warren	C-Pr	Suffolk	9	Z	PHD	64	MIT	1979
Bright, Frank J.					DBA	82	Fla St	
Bright, Thomas	Prof	Shippensburg			JD		Maryland	
Brightman, Harvey J.	Prof	Georgia St	7	V	PHD		Mass	
Regents' Professor of Decision Sciences								
Brightwell, George A.	Asst	Southwestern			MBA		Northwes	1978
Brill, P.	Prof	Univ Windsor	79	UVWZ	PHD		Toronto	1984
Brimm, Linda	Affil	INSEAD	25	EP	DOCT	82	Paris	9-83
Brimm, Michael	C-Ac	INSEAD	25	EF	DBA	75	Harvard	9-78
Briscoe, Dennis R.	Prof	San Diego	58	NOQY	PHD	77	Mich St	1978
Briscoe, John	Prof	Indiana SE	7	U	PHD	77	Louisvil	1978
Brister, Jozell	Assoc	Abilene Chr			MED	73	Abilene	1980

Name	Rank	School			Degree		Institution	Year
Brittain, Jack W.	Asst	Texas-Dallas	2	E	PHD	89	Berkeley	1989
Britton, George H.	Asst	Fla Southern			MBA		W Fla	1988
Brivins, Aelita G.	Demo	City Poly HK	12	EFGP	BA	85	Canada	9-92
Brock, Floyd	Assoc	Nev-L Vegas	79	MUVX	PHD	86	Port St	1987
Brockbank, Joseph W.	Asst	Michigan	35	EN	PHD		UCLA	1985
Brockhaus, Robert H.	Prof	St Louis			PHD		Wash U	
Brockington, R. B.	Lect	Univ Bath	1	A	MSC			
Brocklesby, R. John	SLect	Victoria NZ	25	HQ	MSC		London	1-82
Brockner, Joel	Prof	Columbia	25	EN	PHD	77	Tufts	1984
Brodt, Susan E.	Asst	Virg-Grad	2	E	PHD		Stanford	1988
Brodzinski, James D.	Assoc	Xavier	27	MUV	PHD	83	Ohio U	1993
Broin, Martin	Asst	Tx A&M Intl	7	U	PHD		Purdue	1993
Brokaw, Alan J.	Assoc	Mich Tech	6	IST	PHD	76	Michigan	1976
Bromberg, Herbert	Assoc	Assumption	38		MBA	59	New York	1984
Bromiley, Philip	Assoc	Minnesota	3	I	PHD	81	Car Mel	1985
Bronson, Gary	Prof	F Dick-Madis			PHD		Stevens	
Brooke, Geoffrey	Asst	MIT	9	Z				
Brooking, Carl G.	Prof	Millsaps	7	V	PHD	74	Penn	1981
Brooking, Stan	Prof	So Miss	79	IUVZ	PHD	73	Tx A&M	1975
Brookins, Gilbert M.	Asst	Siena Coll	12	DEST	ABD		SUNY-Alb	9-85
Brookins, Terry M.	C-Pr	Txs Southern	38	IRTY	PHD	68	Texas	1975
Brooks, Charles H.	Prof	Cleveland St	1	C	PHD		Michigan	1984
Brooks, Daniel G.	Assoc	Arizona St			PHD		Indiana	1977
Brooks, Geoffrey	Asst	Pennsylvania	32	HI	PHD	91	Oregon	7-91
Anheuser-Busch Term Assistant Professor								
Brooks, William W.			2	E	PHD	76	N Carol	
Brough, Charles	Lect	Tx-Pan Amer	9	Z	MRA		Tx-Pan A	1983
Brown, Aaron H.	Prof	Corpus Chris	7		DBA		Miss St	
Brown, Burrell	Asst	Calif U-Penn	5	NQ	JD		Pitt	1989
Brown, C. A.	Lect	U Lancaster	25	EGH	PHD		Wales	
Brown, Charles	C-Pr	Eastern Wash						
Brown, Charlotte	D	Wm & Mary						
Brown, Corrine	Lect	Ohio Univ			MBA		Ohio U	
Brown, D. H.	Lect	U Lancaster	39	IYZ	MA		Lancast	
Brown, Darrel R.	C-Pr	Virg Comm	25	EN	PHD	68	Oregon	1970
Brown, Donald	SLect	Harvard	1					
Brown, Fredrick W.	Assoc	W New Eng	4	LJ	MBA		WNEC	1962
Brown, G. V.	Lect	U Newcastle	4	KY	LLB		NS Wales	
Brown, Gerald C.	Assoc	Otterbein	37	IJ	PHD	67	Ohio St	1988
Brown, Gillian		J.F. Kennedy	52	F	ABD		Felding	9-89
Brown, Grant	Lect	U Lethbridge	4	JKLX	ABD		Oxford	1990
Brown, Harold	Prof	Southern	2	GS	PHD	75	Wiscon	1964
Brown, Henry	Asst	Virginia St	41	JK	JD	75	NC Cent	9-75
Brown, Howard H.	C-Pr	Bradford	12	D	EDD	74	Boston U	8-86
Brown, J. Randall	Prof	Kent State			PHD	70	MIT	1970
Brown, James F.	Assoc	Georgia St	9	Z	PHD		Geo St	
Brown, John Lewis	Prof	Univ Alberta	23	HI	PHD	71	Cornell	1971
Brown, Karen	Asst	Penn St-Harr	7	V	PHD	93	La Tech	1993
Brown, Karen A.	Prof	Seattle	7	U	PHD		U Wash	
Brown, L. David	Prof	Boston Univ	24	EFHL	PHD		Yale	
Brown, Larry	Assoc	Mary	15		MBA	82	Temple	9-82
Brown, Linda K.	Prof	St Ambrose	19	AZ	MBA	84	St Ambro	1987
Brown, Marvin	VInst	John Carroll			MA		Morehead	1989
Brown, Michelle	Asst	Richmond			ABD		York	1994
Brown, Randall B.	Asst	CS-Stanislau	25	E	PHD	90	Mass	1-89
Brown, Ray	SLect	Bournemouth	14		MSC	67	Notting	9-63
Brown, Reva	Asst	Univ Essex	12	BH	PHD	91		1991
Brown, Robert B.	Asst	Virginia			PHD	89	U Wash	
Brown, Robert D.	Asst	Georgia	9	Z	MA	57	Alabama	1967
Brown, Stephen M.	Prof	E Kentucky	63	STU	PHD	74	Georgia	1988
Brown, Warren B.	H-Pr	Oregon	36	IT	PHD	62	Car Mel	1967
Brown, William H.	Asst	Clark Atlant			MBA		Geo St	1979
Brown, Z. M.	Lect	North Wales	7	V	MSC			9-86
Browne, Beverly	Inst	Oregon State						
Browne, James	Assoc	So Colorado	5	N	PHD		Illinois	1991
Brownell, Judi	Asst	Cornell	56	&HNP	PHD	78	Syracuse	8-86
Browning, Sharon	Prof	NW Missouri			PHD	73	Missouri	1964
Bruce, Reginald A.	Asst	Louisville	12	DEOX	PHD	89	Michigan	7-93
Bruderer, Erhard	Asst	Minnesota	3	I	PHD	93	Michigan	1993
Bruha, Harlan	Inst	Angelo State			MED		Kent St	
Brumagim, Alan	Asst	Scranton	3	I	PHD	91	Temple	1990
Brumelle, Shelby	Prof	British Colu	7	V	PHD	69	Berkeley	1969
Brumfield, Bruce	Prof	Georgia Col	7	A	DBA	72	Miss	1978
Brunet, J. P.	Assoc	Concordia U						
Bruning, Edward	Prof	U Manitoba	8	Y	PHD	81	Alabama	1990
Bruning, N. Sue	Prof	U Manitoba	25	EGO	PHD	81	Alabama	1990
Brunn, David	Asst	Carthage			MBA		Northwes	1993
Brusco, Michael J.	Asst	DePaul			PHD	90	Fla St	
Brush, Candida	Asst	Boston Univ	36	RT	DBA	93	Boston U	
Brush, Christina C.	Assoc	Kennesaw St	25	EFOP	PHD	83	Geo St	1984

Name	Rank	School			Degree		Institution	Year
Brush, Thomas H.	Asst	Purdue	3	I	PHD	90	Michigan	1992
Bruton, Garry D.	Asst	Tulsa	3	ITY	PHD	89	Okla St	9-92
Bryan, Magdeline	Assoc	Virgin Islan	25	STLY	MBA			1972
Bryan, Norman	Asst	Piedmont	12	EHNO	PHD		Geo St	8-93
Bryant, Kay C.	Lect	Griffith Un	79	VXZ	BCOM	84	Queensld	3-86
Bryant, Milton R.	Prof	Prairie View	79	VZSU	PHD	73	Tx A&M	1985
Distinguished Professor of Management								
Brynjolfsson, Eric	Asst	MIT	9	Z				
Bu, Nailin	Asst	Victoria Can	2	EY	PHD		Brit Col	7-91
Buccini, Eugene	C-Pr	Western Conn	25	EFNP	PHD		NYU	1980
Buchan, P. Bruce	Assoc	Queen's Univ	13	BI	PHD	69	Michigan	1969
Buchanan, David A.	D-Pr	Loughborough	5	N	PHD		Edinburg	
Buchanan, Ellis	TAsoc	Tx-S Antonio						
Buchholtz, Ann K.	Asst	Connecticut	3	I	PHD	91	New York	1991
Buchholz, Rogene	Prof	Loyola-N Orl	4	JM	PHD	74	Pitt	1989
Buchko, Aaron	Asst	Bradley	3	I	PHD	90	Mich St	1989
Buchmueller, Thomas	Asst	Calif-Irvine			PHD	92	Wiscon	1992
Buck, Cleophas M.	Prof	Lawrence Tec	7		MBA			1957
Buck, Vernon E.	Assoc	U Washington	5	EFG	PHD	63	Cornell	1968
Buckenmyer, James	Prof	SE Missouri	15	E	DBA	70	Wash U	1982
Buckeye, Jeanne	C-Ac	St Thomas-MN						
Buckley, Harry A.	C-Pr	Norwich	25		PHD			
Buckley, Michael R.	Assoc	Oklahoma	25	ENXP	PHD	85	Auburn	8-87
Buda, Richard	Asst	Hofstra	15	NP	PHD	84	Stevens	9-93
Budd, Jim L.	Asst	Indiana St	13	I	PHD		Waynesbg	8-92
Budd, John	Asst	Minnesota	57	Q	PHD	91	Princeton	
Buddress, Leland	Asst	Portland St	7	UYW	ABD		Mich St	1990
Budish, Bernard	Prof	F Dick-Madis	13		PHD		NYU	
Buegler, Paul W.	Assoc	Biola	35	IN	JD		Wm Mitch	1978
Buerkley, Deborah	Assoc	SW State	5	N				
Buffa, Elwood S.	Prof	UCLA	7	U	PHD	57	UCLA	1952
Buffa, Frank P.	C-Pr	Texas A&M		V	PHD	71	LSU	1970
Buffenmyer, Jay	Prof	Elizabethtwn	58	YN	PHD	76	Pitt	9-76
Bui, Tung X.	Assoc	Naval Postgr	93	ZV	PHD	84	NYU	9-84
Bullard, A. Davant	Asst	Houston-Down			PHD	87	Geo St	
Buller, Charlotte	Inst	W Illinois			MS	77	Fla Tech	1977
Buller, Paul	Prof	Gonzaga	13	IN	PHD	82	U Wash	1989
Bullers, William I.	Prof	New Mexico	9	Z	PHD	80	Purdue	1980
Bulls, Derrell W.	C-Pr	Txs Woman's	14	CG	PHD	71	Tx Tech	1977
Bulmer, Gail T.	Asst	Embry-Riddle	1		MA	76	Ball St	1986
Bumpus, Minnette	Asst	Colorado			PHD	92	S Carol	1991
Bunch, David S.	Assoc	Cal-Davis	79	VXZ	PHD		Rice	
Bunch, John	Asst	Kansas State	24	EJNP	PHD	90	N Carol	8-90
Bund, Barbara	SLect	MIT	3	IZ	PHD		Harvard	
Bungum, John	Assoc	Gustavus Ado	37		PHD	77	Nebraska	1979
Bunke, Harvey C.	Prof	Indiana	4	L	PHD	51	Illinois	1967
Bunker, Douglas	Assoc	SUNY-Buffalo	2	F	PHD	60	Harvard	9-67
Bunn, Derek W.	C-Pr	London Bus	7	V	PHD		London	
Buntz, C. Gregory	Prof	Pacific	12	AD	PHD	73	Ohio St	7-78
Buntzman, Gabriel F.	Assoc	W Kentucky	13	CDI	PHD	83	N Carol	1983
Buono, Anthony F.	C-Pr	Bentley	24	FHL	PHD	81	Boston C	1979
Burack, Elmer	Prof	Ill-Chicago	25	NEOI	PHD	64	Northwes	7-78
Burbridge, John J. Jr.	Assoc	Loyola-Maryl	9	Z	PHD		Lehigh	1985
Burch-Konda, Regina	Prof	CS-Fresno	25	EN	PHD		Colorado	1993
Burd, Stephen D.	C-Ac	New Mexico	9	Z	PHD	83	Purdue	1984
Burda, Michael	Assoc	INSEAD			PHD		Harvard	
Burden, Charles Albert	Prof	Georgia St	28	ELY	DBA	70	Geo St	1970
Burdetsky, Ben	Prof	George Wash	5	N	PHD	68	American	1962
Burdick, Richard K.	Prof	Arizona St			PHD		Tx A&M	1976
Bures, Allen L.	C-Pr	Radford	21	EY	PHD	80	Nebraska	8-81
Burgar, Paul	Asst	Georgia Col	37	HIP	PHD	80	Memphis	1990
Burgelman, Robert A.	Assoc	Stanford	3	I	PHD	80	Columbia	1981
Burgess, Thomas F.	Assoc	Univ Leeds	97	ZU	MBA	81	Bradford	1990
Burgess, Thornton W.	Inst	USAF Academy	1	I	MBA		Oklahoma	
Burgoyne, J. G.	Prof	U Lancaster	25	NOP	PHD		Manchest	
Burgress, Gregg M.					PHD	88	Fla St	
Burke, Antaro H.	Assoc	St Thomas-TX	25	EFHP	PHD	62	Boston	8-91
Burke, C. M.	SLect	North Wales	1	A	MA			9-88
Burke, Donald R.	Assoc	Villanova	15	IN	PHD	70	Penn	1972
Burke, Ronald J.	Prof	York Univ	2	EGR	PHD	66	Michigan	
Burke, William A.	C	Stonehill	38		MBA		NYU	1982
Burkhardt, Marlene E.	Asst	Pennsylvania	2	EH	PHD	90	Penn St	7-90
Anheuser-Busch Term Professor of Management								
Burkhardt, Peter H.	Assoc	Western St	12		JD	65	Minn	1989
Burnetas, Apostolos N.	Asst	Case Western			PHD	93	Rutgers	1994
Burnett, Derek	Assoc	Loras	27	AV	ABD		Newcastl	1984
Burnett, Jennifer G.	Asst	Alabama-Birm	25	EN	PHD	93	Florida	1993
Burnett, P.	PLect	Humberside						
Burnett, Walter M.	Assoc	Tulane	13	BIL	PHD	65	Iowa	1968
Burnette, Charles	Inst	Cen Florida	12		MBA	77	NW Mo St	1977

Name	Rank	Institution			Degree		School	Year
Burnham, James	Prof	Duquesne	38		PHD		Wash U	1990
Burnham, Kent T.	Prof	Eastern Wash	9	Z	PHD	71	Iowa	1967
Burns, Lawton R.	Asst	Arizona	2	CH	PHD	81	Chicago	1984
Burns, O. Maxie Jr.	Assoc	Geo Southern	79	UZ	PHD	87	Geo St	1983
Burns, R. N.	Prof	Queen's Univ	7	UV	PHD	70	Waterloo	1981
Burritt, Roger L.	SLect	Australian N		MF	MPHL	75	Oxon	1989
Burrows, William	SLect	U Washington	9	Z	MBA	72	U Wash	1979
Burrus, Robert	Inst	Alabama A&M						
Burton, Frederick N.	SLect	Manches Inst	8	W	BSC		Hull	9-69
Burton, Gene E.	Retir	CS-Fresno	23	1994	PHD		North Tx	1979
Burton, Jonathan S.	Prof	Drexel		U	PHD	77	Tx Tech	1971
Burton, Richard M.	Prof	Duke	28	HIY	DBA	67	Illinois	1970
Burton, Samuel A.	Asst	Lees-McRae	56					
Burton, Von	Asst	Athens State	7	V	DS		SE Inst	1986
Burwell, Timothy H.	Assoc	Appalach St	7	UV	PHD		Clemson	1986
Bury, Harry	Prof	Baldwin-Wal	2	N	PHD		Case Wes	
Busch, Edgar T.	Prof	W Kentucky	13	DI	PHD	70	Arkansas	1979
Busch, Frank M.	Assoc	Louisiana Te	18	JSTY	PHD	66	Indiana	1966
Busenitz, Lowell	Asst	Houston	35	IST	PHD	92	Tx A&M	9-92
Busey, Barbara H.	Assoc	Frostburg St			MBA		Frostbur	8-88
Bush, Bobby	Prof	Freed Hardem	25	ENPQ	EDD	77	Miss St	8-76
Bush, Chandler M.	Retir	N Car-Charl		1994	PHD		Tx-Arlin	1985
Bush-Bacelis, Jean	Asst	E Michigan			PHD	93	Wayne St	1984
Bushardt, Step	C-Pr	So Miss	2	EH	DBA	81	Miss St	1980
Bussard, David T.	Assoc	Susquehanna	3	I	PHD	91	Penn	1978
Butler, G. Robert	Prof	Olivet	6		MBA	56	Chicago	1992
Butler, Grady	Assoc	Jacksonvl St	45	NQ	DBA	82	Oklahoma	1990
Butler, John F	Assoc	U Washington	25		PHD	85	NYU	1965
Butler, John K.	Prof	Clemson	2	EH	DBA	77	Florida	1977
Butler, Mark C.	Prof	San Diego St	28	EFGY	PHD	77	Tx Chr	1981
Butler, Roosevelt D.	Assoc	Trenton St			PHD		US Intl	
Butler, Thomas	Prof	F Dick-Madis			PHD			
Butt, Philip A.	Read	Univ Bath	8	Y	DPH			
Butterfield, D. Anthony	C-Pr	Massachusett	2	ER	PHD	68	Michigan	1972
Buttle, F. A.	SFell	Manchest Bus			PHD		UMUT	1992
Buttner, E. Holly	Asst	N Car-Greens	23	TGR	PHD	86	N Carol	8-85
Butts, Hector	Asst	Morris Brown			MA	84	E Anglia	1992
Butz, Clarence	Asst	Azusa Pacif	14	BE	MBA		Claremont	9-89
Buxey, Geoff M.	SLect	Deakin Univ	7	U	PHD	82	Reading	1984
Buzby, Bruce K.	Asst	Connecticut	97	UZ	PHD	60	Indiana	9-87
Byars, Lloyd	Prof	Clark Atlant	35	IQ	PHD	70	Geo St	
Bycio, Peter	Asst	Xavier	15	EN	PHD	86	Bowl Gr	1987
Byers, C. Randall	C-Ac	Idaho	97	Z	PHD	73	Minn	1973
Bygrave, William D.	Assoc	Babson			PHD		Oxford	
Byles, Charles M.	Asst	Virg Comm	38	CIY	DBA	86	Kent St	1990
Byniem, Karen	Asst	Dallas Bapt	9		PHD		Tx A&M	1994
Bynum, Karen	Asst	Dallas Bapt	9		PHD		Tx A&M	1994
Byrd, John T. III	Dean	Bellarmine			PHD		Ohio St	1982
Byrd, Kimble A.	Assoc	Rowan Col NJ	45	JKLN	JD	76	Penn	1984
Byrd, Steve	Inst	SE Missouri	56	S	MS	75	St Marys	1985
Byrd, Terry A.	Assoc	Auburn	9	Z	PHD	88	S Carol	9-92
Byrne, Francis	Fell	Manchest Bus			BA		Liverpol	1993
Byrnes, Joseph	Prof	Bentley	5	NQ	PHD	74	Northwes	1980
Byron, William SJ	Prof	Georgetown	4	JL	PHD	69	Maryland	1993
Cabell, David W.	Asst	McNeese St			DBA		Kent St	
Cabelly, Alan	Assoc	Portland St	5	N	PHD	80	U Wash	1980
Caccamise, Richard	Asst	St Peters			EDD		Temple	1990
Cachon, Jean-Charles	Assoc	Laurentian	36	PRST	MA	77	Sherbroo	7-83
Cadden, David	Assoc	Quinnipiac	37		PHD		CUNY	
Cadot, Oliver	Asst	INSEAD			PHD		Princeton	
Caggiano, Diane P.	Asst	Fitchburg St	2	EHLR	MBA		Babson	1983
Cagney-Watts, H.	Lect	Humberside	2					
Cahill, Patrick Joseph Sr.	Asst	Marymount			MBA		Duquesne	1970
Cahn, E. S.	Prof	Pace-Westch	7		PHD	80	Columbia	1985
Cahoon, Allan	Prof	Univ Calgary	25	EFNR	PHD	74	Syracuse	1974
Caiden, Naomi J.	Retir	CS-San Bern	1	1994	PHD	78	S Calif	1981
Caillouet, Aaron	Asst	Nicholls St	3	I	DBA	87	Nova	1973
Cain, Fred	Assoc	Troy St	26	ENST	PHD	74	LSU	1974
Cain, Jean A.	Inst	Canisius			BS		SUNY-Buf	
Cain, Rita	Assoc	Mo-Kansas Ct	4	JK	JD	83	Kansas	1987
Calas, Marta	Assoc	Massachusett	28	ERBY	PHD	87	Mass	1986
Calderon, Carmen	Assoc	P Rico-Mayag	7		MS		P Rico	8-58
Caldwell, Dan	Lect	Napier Univ	13	ABI	DMS			1973
Caldwell, David F.	Prof	Santa Clara			PHD	78	UCLA	1978
Caldwell, T.	SLect	Humberside	7					
Calero, Thomas M.	Assoc	Illinois Tch	5	N	PHD	68	Northwes	1968
Calhoun, Kenneth J.	Asst	Slippery Roc	13	D	PHD		Pitt	8-87
Calingo, Luis	Prof	CS-Fresno	3	I	PHD		Pitt	1983
Calista, Donald J.	Assoc	Marist	12	AH	EDD		Sarasota	1977
Callahan, J.	Assoc	Carleton Un			PHD		Toronto	

Name	Rank	Institution			Degree		School	Year
Callahan, Robert E.	Assoc	Seattle	25	EN	PHD		Case Wes	
Callahan, Thomas J.	Asst	Mich-Dearbor	23	HIN	PHD	90	Mich St	1987
Callan, Victor J.	Prof	Queensland	2	F	PHD	79	Aust Nat	1990
Callarman, Thomas E.	Assoc	Arizona St	7	U	PHD		Purdue	1980
Callarman, William G.	Assoc	Cen Florida	32	EFI	PHD	72	Ariz St	1972
Calton, Jerry	Asst	Hawaii-Hilo	3		PHD			
Calvasina, Eugene	H-Pr	Auburn-Montg	37	U	PHD	74	Miss	1984
Calvasina, Gerald E.	Asst	N Car-Charl			PHD		Miss	1982
Calvert, John R.	SLect	Loughborough	9	Z	PHD		Loughbor	
Cambridge, Charles	Prof	CS-Chico			PHD		Minn	1978
Cambronero, Alfredo	Asst	Fisk	78	UVY	PHD		Vanderbt	1992
Camburn, Art	Assoc	Buena Vista	23	EHIL	PHD	88	Florida	8-91
Camealy, John B.	Retir	Xavier	23	EHN	PHD	65	U Wash	1975
Camerer, Colin F.	Prof	Chicago	37	IUVY	PHD	81	Chicago	7-85
Cameron, David		Strathclyde			PHD			
Cameron, Elizabeth A.	Asst	Alma			MBA		Saginaw	1988
Cameron, Gary	Assoc	Washburn			PHD	79	Nebraska	1982
Cameron, Kim S.	Prof	Michigan	5	Q	PHD	78	Yale	1984
Cameron, R. A.	Assoc	Lakehead U	25	EFP	MBA		Toronto	1-76
Camgemi, Robert	Prof	Pace			PHD	72	NYU	
Camillus, John C.	Prof	Pittsburgh	3		DBA	72	Harvard	
Donald Beall Chair in Strategic Management								
Cammock, P. A.	Lect	Canterbury	12	E	PHD	91	Canterbu	1983
Camp, Richaurd	Prof	E Michigan	2		MA		Wayne St	1979
Camp, Sue	Prof	Gardner-Webb	1	DR	EDD	87	Tenn	1975
Campagna, Anthony F.	Assoc	Ohio State	5	Q	PHD	71	UCLA	1970
Campbell, Constance	Asst	Geo Southern	25	ENXG	PHD	92	Fla St	1-92
Campbell, Gerard M.	Assoc	Connecticut	79	UZ	PHD	88	Indiana	9-88
Campbell, John	Lect	Griffith Un	79	VXZ	BCOM		Hons	1-88
Campbell, Kitty	Asst	SE Okla St	51	NS	MAS		SE Okla	8-93
Campbell, Mary Ellen	Prof	Montana	48	CDZ	MA	69	Illinios	1973
Campbell, Nigel C. G.	SLect	Manchest Bus	38	IW	PHD		Manchest	1985
Campbell, Oscar S.	Asst	Athens State	9	Z	MBA		Alabama	1978
Campbell, Rita A.	Assoc	USAF Academy	5	NR	PHD		Colorado	
Campbell, Terry L.		Intl Mgt Dev	9	Z	DBA		Indiana	
Campbell-Hunt, Colin	SLect	Victoria NZ	13	I	PHD		York	5-74
Campion, Michael A.	Prof	Purdue	2	E	PHD	82	N Car St	1986
Canals, Jordi	Assoc	Univ Navarra	3	IY	PHD		Barcelon	3-87
Canavan, Martin J.	Assoc	Skidmore	16		MS		SUNY-Alb	1979
Canavan, Thomas		Lg Isl-Brook						
Cannella, Albert A. Jr.	Asst	Texas A&M		ITY	PHD	89	Columbia	1989
Cannon, James	Inst	Lycoming			MS			1992
Cant, A. G.	Lect	W Australia			MIR		W Austra	
Cantagalli, David			7	U	PHD	87	N Carol	
Cantrell, Joyce	Lect	N Car-Greens	9	Z	MBA		NC-Green	1993
Cantrell, R. Stephen	Assoc	Clemson	7	UV	PHD	82	N Car St	1980
Canty, Ann L.	Asst	Mississippi	2	RS	PHD	85	Miss	1990
Capela, John	Asst	NY Inst Tech	18		MBA			
Capen, Margaret M.	Assoc	East Carol		X	PHD		S Carol	8-81
Caporaletti, Louis	Asst	Cameron			ABD		Miss	
Cappel, Samuel	H-Ac	SE Louisiana	23	EHIK	DBA	90	Memphis	8-91
Cappelli, Peter	Prof	Pennsylvania	5	QN	DPHI	83	Oxford	7-85
Co-Director Center for Human Resources								
Capps, Charles	Asst	Sam Houston			DBA	88	La Tech	1988
Caproni, Paula J.	Asst	Michigan	3	E	PHD	90	Yale	
Carayannopoulos, Peter	Asst	Mich-Flint	1		PHD			
Carbonell, Dora	Asst	Lg Isl-Brook			EDD		Columbia	
Carceller, Araceli	Asst	St Marys-Cnd	2	EN	PHD	83	Madrid	1990
Carcia, Carlos	Asst	Univ Navarra	3	I	PHD		MIT	6-87
Card, Mike	Asst	South Dakota	32	IH	PHD	92	Ohio St	1992
Cardona, Pablo	Asst	Univ Navarra	2	E	MBA		Navarra	6-90
Cardy, Robert L.	Prof	Arizona St	5	N	PHD	82	Virginia	1988
Carew, Anthony B.	SLect	Manches Inst	5	Q	PHD		Sussex	6-76
Carey, Bernard	DSLec	Macquarie Un						
Carey, Jane M.	Assoc	Ariz St-West	9	ZR	PHD	84	Miss	1988
Carey, Justin	C	St Johns			PHD	51	Columbia	1951
Carey, Thomas A.	Assoc	W Michigan	36	IS	EDD	75	W Mich	1974
Carini, Gary	Asst	Baylor			PHD		Penn	1991
Carleton, Joseph	Asst	Marymount			MA		Catholic	1987
Carlson, Patricia	Asst	Suffolk	9	Z	PHD	92	Minn	1992
Carlson, Rodger	Prof	Morehead St	7	U	PHD	71	Claremont	1983
Carmel, Erran	Asst	American U	9	Z	PHD	91	Arizona	1991
Carmichael, Donna	Lect	U Queensland	1		PHD	94	York	1994
Carnahan, George R.	Prof	No Michigan			PHD	67	Ohio St	1987
Carney, M.	Assoc	Concordia U						
Carpano, Claudio	Asst	N Car-Charl			PHD	91	S Carol	1990
Carpenter, Gerald E.	Asst	Pfeiffer	12		MBA	76	Appal St	8-84
Carpenter, James B.	C-Pr	Georgia Col	57	ENU	PHD	69	Purdue	1987
Carpenter, John M.	Prof	Corpus Chris	16		PHD		Tx A&M	
Carpenter, Wallace R.	Assoc	Gardner-Webb	93	ZIL	EDS	80	W Carol	1964

Name	Rank	School	#	Code	Degree	Yr	School2	Year
Carper, William	Prof	Geo Southern	3	I	PHD	79	Va Tech	1987
Carr, Amelia	Inst	Tuskegee						
Carr, Christopher H. C.	SFell	Manchest Bus	38	IWZ	PHD		Warwick	1991
Carr, Houston H.	Prof	Auburn	9	Z	PHD	84	Texas	6-89
Alumni Professor								
Carr, James W.	Asst	West Georgia	5	N	PHD	82	Geogia	6-79
Carr, Mary	Inst	USAF Academy	3	I	MBA		WrightSt	
Carr, Rececca	Inst	Arkansas St	7	V	MS	86	Illinois	1986
Carr, T. Franklin	Asst	Morehouse			MBA		NYU	1983
Carr-Ruffino, Norma J.	Prof	San Fran St	14	EGR	PHD	72	North Tx	1973
Carraher, Shawn	Assoc	CS-Chico			PHD		Oklahoma	1994
Carraway, Robert L.	Assoc	Virg-Grad	7	V	PHD		Purdue	1985
Carrell, Michael R.	Dean	Neb-Omaha	15	CNPQ	DBA	76	Kentucky	1992
Carrera, Maria-Cecilla	Asst	Northeastern			PHD		Car Mel	
Carriher, Susan	Lect	N Car-Charl			PHD		N Car St	
Carroll, Archie B.	Prof	Georgia	34	IJL	DBA	72	Fla St	1972
Robert W. Scherer Chair of Management & Corporate Public Affairs								
Carroll, Frank	Dean	J.F. Kennedy	3	I	MBA		St Marys	1-85
Carroll, Glenn E.	Prof	Wilfrid Laur	2	E	MBA		Western	1960
Carroll, Glenn R.	Prof	Cal-Berkeley	25	EHOP	PHD		Stanford	1982
Paul J. Cortese Professor of Management								
Carroll, John S.	Prof	MIT	2	H	PHD			
Carroll, Lawrence B.	Asst	Elmhurst			MBA		Roosevel	1974
Carroll, Owen T.	Assoc	SUNY-Stony B	79	VZ	PHD	68	Cornell	1967
Carroll, Stephen J. Jr.	Prof	Maryland	25	E	PHD	64	Minn	1964
Carroll, Steven	Asst	Arizona St			PHD		Oregon	1985
Carruthers, Neil	Fell	Manchest Bus			MDA		Manchest	1994
Carson, John	Prof	George Wash	9	Z	PHD	76	Lehigh	
Carson, Kerry	Asst	SW Louisiana	21	BCEP	PHD	91	LSU	1992
Carson, Paula	Asst	SW Louisiana	5	NPE	PHD	92	LSU	1991
Carson, Scott	Dean	St Marys-Cdn	34	TU	PHD	80	London	1993
Carstenson, Larry	Asst	Neb-Kearney	34	IK	JD		Nebraska	1991
Carter, Harrison	Prof	Geo Southern	79	VZ	PHD	74	Georgia	1975
Carter, J. Alvin	C	Catawba			MBA		Geo St	
Carter, John	Prof	Pace	7		PHD	75	Columbia	
Carter, Lavon	Assoc	Harding			ABD		Memphis	
Carter, Nancy	Assoc	Marquette	3	HIT	PHD	81	Nebraska	1987
Carter, Phillip L.	Dean$	Michigan St	7	U	DBA	70	Indiana	1970
Caruth, Donald L.	Prof	East Txs St	35	P	PHD	70	North Tx	1982
Carvalho, Gerry	Assoc	Ohio Univ	3		PHD	68	Michigan	
Cascio, Wayne	Prof	Colo-Denver	5	NPQ	PHD	72	Rochest	1981
Case, Randolph H.	Asst	Boston Coll	3	IT	PHD	93	Penn	9-93
Case, Susan S.	Asst	Case Western	2	E	PHD		SUNY-Buf	1989
Case, Thomas L.	Prof	Geo Southern	19	ZEF	PHD	82	Georgia	1981
Casey, Anthony	Asst	Dayton	7	U	MS	75	Dayton	1969
Casey, Catherine	Lect	U Auckland	58	HLQY	PLH	93	Rochest	5-93
Casey, Jeff	Asst	SUNY-Stony B	25	E	PHD	86	Wiscon	1986
Cashman, James F.	Prof	Alabama	12	DEY	PHD	75	Illinois	1984
Cass, Kimberly	Asst	Marquette	9	Z	PHD	88	Arizona	1989
Casse, Pierre	Prof	Intl Mgt Dev	2	E	PHD		Lille	
Casseres-Gomes, Benjamin	Assoc	Harvard	4	L				
Cassidy, R. G. R.	Assoc	Queen's Univ	17	AV	PHD	71	Dalhousi	1974
Castaldi, Richard M.	Prof	San Fran St	13	ITYM	PHD	82	Va Tech	1988
Castaneda, Maria	Asst	SUNY-Albany	25	NEX	PHD	88	Wiscon	1991
Castellano, John	Prof	Suffolk			PHD		SUNY-Buf	
Castleberry, Stephen B.	Prof	Minn-Duluth			PHD	83	Alabama	1993
Castro, Barry	Prof	Grand Valley			PHD		NYU	1973
Catalanello, Ralph F.	C-Ac	No Illinois	38	EF	PHD	71	Wiscon	1975
Catanese, Margaret	Assoc	DePauw			MBA	78	Mich St	8-79
Cates, Tommy A.	Assoc	Tenn-Martin	36	D	DBA	83	Memphis	9-74
Catron, Bayard	Prof	George Wash	1	A	PHD	75	Berkeley	
Cattaneo, R. J.	Assoc	Univ Windsor	25	ENPY	PHD		Michigan	1980
Caudill, C. Dale	Inst	Morehead St	15	C	MBA	80	Morehead	1983
Caufield, Clyde	Deces	Air Force In	25	1993	PHD			
Cavaleri, Steven	Assoc	Central Conn	23	HUPZ	PHD	88	Renssel	1980
Cavalle, Carlos	Dean	Univ Navarra	3	I	PHD		ETSII	O-58
Cavana, R. Y. (Bob)	SLect	Victoria NZ	37	IVX	PHD		Bradford	1-90
Cavanaugh, J. Michael	Asst	Fairfield	23	DHI	PHD	91	Mass	1990
Cave, John E. Jr.	Dean	Fort Lewis	23	EI	PHD	67	Minn	1990
Caves, Richard E.	Prof	Harvard	4	L				
George Gund Professor of Economics and Business Administration								
Cawsey, Tupper F.	Prof	Wilfrid Laur	2	E	PHD		Western	1972
Cawthon, David L.	C-Pr	Okla City	23	E	EDD		Okla St	8-88
Cech, Paula-Ann	Asst	Northwestern	3	I	PHD	89	Arizona	
Cecil, Earl	Prof	Missouri	5	N	PHD	67	W Virg	1967
Cemery, Alan	Lect	Napier Univ	17	CUV	MBA			1991
Certo, Samuel C.	Prof	Rollins	23		PHD	73	Ohio U	1986
Chachere, Greg	Asst	NE Louisisna	25	EJNQ	PHD	89	Tx A&M	1988
Chacko, Thomas I.	Prof	Iowa State	51	EN	PHD	77	Iowa	1980
Chadbourne, Bruce	Prof	Embry-Riddle			EDD	85	Fla Atl	1973

Name	Rank	Institution			Degree		School	Year
Chadburn, D.	SLect	Humberside	3					
Chadwick, W. F.	Assoc	Univ Regina	35	GINY	MSC		Col	
Chadwin, Mark L.	Prof	Old Dominion						
Chaganti, Radha	Assoc	Rider			PHD		SUNY-Buf	1986
Chaison, Gary N.	Prof	Clark	5	Q	PHD	72	SUNY-Buf	
Chait, Herschel N.	Assoc	Indiana St	15	N	PHD		Indiana	8-81
Chakraborty, Kishore	Asst	Babson			DED		Harvard	
Chakravarthy, Balaji S.	Assoc	Minnesota	3	I	DBA	78	Harvard	1986
Chakravarty, S. P.	SLect	North Wales	13	DI	PHD			8-78
Chamard, John	Prof	St Marys-Cnd	36	RS	MBA	66	Harvard	1974
Chamberlain, Howard E.	Assoc	Texas A&M		IT	PHD	73	U Wash	1970
Chamberlin, Daniel P.	Assoc	Regent	23	EI	MBA	57	Harvard	1985
Chamberlin, William	Assoc	Embry-Riddle			MBA	69	Stetson	1979
Chambers, Brian	Lect	Wayne State	34	IT	PHD	91	Michigan	1990
Chambers, David J.	Prof	London Bus	78	YUV	PHD		Car Mel	
Chambers, Robert J.	VAsst	Emory	7	U	PHD		Purdue	
Chammah, Albert M.	Assoc	Texas	28	EY	PHD	69	Michigan	1969
Champion, Donald L.	Assoc	Radford	7	UVX	DBA	79	Fla St	8-82
Champion, John M.	Prof	Florida	34	EIJN	PHD	58	Purdue	1964
Champlin, Frederic	Asst	Ramapo	5	NQ	PHD	82	Minn	1990
Champoux, Joseph E.	Prof	New Mexico		N	PHD	74	Ca-Irvine	1973
Chan, Andrew	Lect	City Poly HK	52	BHN	MBA	91	HongKong	3-92
Chan, H. L.	Lect	City Poly HK	34	ISTY	MBA	79	HongKong	8-87
Chan, Marjorie	Assoc	CS-Stanislau	38	Y	PHD	81	UCLA	9-90
Chan, Peng S.	Assoc	CS-Fullerton	3	ISY	PHD	86	Texas	8-89
Chand, Suresh	Prof	Purdue	7	U	PHD	79	Car Mel	1979
Chandapass, Vasana			9	Z	PHD	68	N Carol	
Chandler, Gaylen N.	Asst	Utah State	56	NTS	PHD	90	Utah	9-93
Chandler, Pamela Sue	Asst	Mary Hrdn-By	14		MBA	79	SW Texas	1987
Chandler, Tim	Asst	Louisiana St	5	QL	PHD	90	Illinois	8-90
Chandler, William D.	Asst	So Colorado	34	ZI	PHD		Arkansas	1982
Chandler, William G.	Prof	Tarleton St	17	PQVX	PHD	72	North Tx	1973
Chandra, P.	Asst	McGill Univ	7		PHD		Penn	1988
Chandra, Satish	Assoc	Louisville	9	USYZ	PHD	75	Cinn	7-78
Chandrasekaran, R.	Prof	Texas-Dallas	7	V				
Chaney, Courtland	Inst	Louisiana St	5	N	PHD	80	LSU	8-83
Chaney, John S.	C-Pr	CS-San Bern	3	I	PHD	71	Texas	1972
Chang, Chan S.	Prof	Lander	18	YO	PHD	74	American	1974
Chang, Chung-Chau	Assoc	Nat Taiwan U	10	I	PHD	74	Nat Chen	1983
Chang, Hong-Chang	C-Pr	Nat Taiwan U	7	U	PHD	78	Penn	1969
Chang, Tung-Lung	Asst	NJ Inst Tech	8	Y	PHD	90	Geo Wash	1990
Chang, Wei-Chien	Prof	No Illinois		V	PHD	71	Wiscon	1971
Chang, Yih-Long	Assoc	Georgia Tech	7	UV	PHD	85	Texas	1989
Chang, Yu Sang	Prof	Boston Univ	78	UY	DBA		Wash U	
Chang, Yu-Chi	Assoc	Notre Dame	7	V	PHD	72	Wiscon	1971
Changanti, Raj	Assoc	Temple			PHD	78	SUNY-Buf	1981
Chanin, Michael N.	Prof	CUNY-Baruch	3	I	PHD		CUNY	1980
Chanlat, Alain	Prof	HEC-Montreal	12	BFY	DBA		Geo Wash	
Chanlat, Jean-Francois	Assoc	HEC-Montreal	25	CHNR	PHD		Montreal	
Chao, Chiang-Nan	Asst	St Johns			PHD	89	Ariz St	
Chao, Chieh-Chien	Prof	Nat Taiwan U	1		PHD	73	Nat Taiw	1969
Chao, Georgia T.	Assoc	Michigan St	5	O	PHD	82	Penn St	9-85
Chaouch, B.	Asst	Univ Windsor	79	UVWZ	PHD		Waterloo	1985
Chapagne, Paul J.	Assoc	Old Dominion			PHD	77	Mass	
Chapel, William B.	Lect	Mich Tech	6	&T	MS	90	Mi Tech	1985
Chapman, Stephen N.	Asst	N Carol St	73	UWI	PHD	86	Mich St	1992
Charalambedies, Leo C.	Asst	Hartford	3	I	PHD	78	S Carol	
Charkey, Barbara	Assoc	Keene State			MBA		Mass	1987
Charnov, Bruce H.	Assoc	Hofstra	12	KR	PHD	76	US Intl	9-80
Chartres, John A.	C-Pr	Univ Leeds	1	B	PHD	73	Oxford	1969
Chastain, Clark E.	Prof	Mich-Flint	3	E	PHD	58	Michigan	1968
Chatman, Jennifer	Asst	Cal-Berkeley	2	E	PHD	87	Berkeley	
Chatov, Robert	Assoc	SUNY-Buffalo	4	JKL	PHD	73	Berkeley	1972
Chatterjee, Anindya	Asst	Slippery Roc			ABD		Temple	8-92
Chatterjee, Kalyan	Prof	Penn State	7	V	DBA		Harvard	
Chatterjee, Samir	Asst	Georgia St	9	Z	PHD		Cen Fla	
Chatterjee, Sangit	Prof	Northeastern			PHD		NYU	
Chatterjee, Sayan	Assoc	Case Western			DBA		Michigan	
Chatterjee, Subimal	Asst	SUNY-Stony B	17	&V	PHD	93	Pitt	1993
Chatterji, Manas	Prof	SUNY-Bingham	1	C	PHD	63	Penn	1969
Chattopadhyay, A.	Assoc	McGill Univ	3		PHD		Florida	1986
Chaturvedi, Alok	Assoc	Purdue	9	Z	PHD	89	Wiscon	1988
Chaubey, Manmohan	C	Ind-Penna	56	NSTI	PHD	82	Iowa	1985
Chaudhry, Peggy	Asst	Villanova	8	Y	PHD	92	Wiscon	1991
Chaudhry, Sohail	Assoc	Villanova	7	UVW	PHD	85	Columbia	1991
Chauny, Fabien	Adj	HEC-Montreal	7		PHD		EcolePol	
Chausse, Raymond	Prof	HEC-Montreal	16	DS	LSC		HEC-Mont	
Checkland, P. B.	Prof	U Lancaster	13	AEIZ	MA		Oxford	
Cheek, B. R.	H-SLe	U Newcastle	9	Z	MACS			
Cheek, Robert E.	Assoc	Saginaw Vall	32	IF	EDD	70	Wayne St	1984

Name	Rank	Institution			Degree		School	
Christensen, Clayton	Asst	Harvard						
Christensen, H. Kurt	Assoc	Northwestern	3	I	PHD	77	Columbia	
Christensen, Sandra L.	Asst	Eastern Wash	48	LKY	PHD	89	U Wash	1990
Christensen-Szalanski, Jay	Prof	Iowa	79	V	PHD	78	U Wash	1986
Christianson, Charles	Asst	Luther	13	DI	MBA	75	S Dakota	1988
Christie, C. Charles Jr.	Prof	CS-San Bern	1	A	PHD	74	S Calif	1972
Christie, M.	STut	U Newcastle	1	AL	MAEC		New Eng	
Christoph, Rick	Assoc	Jms Madison	3	I	PHD	85	Clemson	9-92
Christopherson, Reid	Inst	St Ambrose	19	AZ	MBA	90	St Ambro	1990
Christy, David P.	Assoc	Penn State	7	V	PHD		Georgia	
Chu, Chao	Assoc	Iowa State	7	UZ	PHD	84	Penn St	1986
Chu, Hung M.	Prof	West Chester			PHD		LSU	1976
Chu, Priscilla P.	Lect	City Poly HK	14	FILR	MSC	86	HongKong	8-86
Chung, An-Min	Emer	Drexel			PHD	53	Penn	1957
Chung, Hyung-Min	Asst	Texas A&M		Z	PHD	89	UCLA	1989
Chung, Joseph	Prof	Illinois Tch			PHD	64	Wayne St	1964
Chung, Kae H.	C-Pr	Old Dominion			PHD	68	LSU	
Chung, Peter Y.	Assoc	Cal-Riversid						
Chung, Q.	Asst	LaSalle	9	Z	PHD		Renssel	1993
Church, John	Prof	Laurentian	7	VZ	PHD	78	W Ontar	7-74
Church, Nancy	Assoc	SUNY-Plattsb	56	RSYL	PHD		Concordi	1977
Churchill, Geoffrey	Prof	Georgia St	7	V	PHD	66	N Carol	
Cianni, Mary	Asst	Susquehanna	5	NR	PHD	86	Penn St	1982
Cicic, Muris	SLect	U Wollongong			PHD		Sarajevo	7-91
Clair, Judith	Asst	Boston Coll	1	EMR	PHD	93	USC	9-93
Clamp, Carl	DisLe	So Carolina						
Clapham, Stephen	Asst	Drake	32	IFH	PHD	93	Indiana	1990
Clapper, James M.	Assoc	Wake Fr-MBA			PHD		Mass	
Clarey, Richard J.	Assoc	So Maine	6	ST	PHD	68	Cornell	1979
Clark, Albert	Asst	Southern	45	KLJQ	JD	75	Southern	1975
Clark, Catherine	Asst	Rio Grande	2	EFHN	PHD	90	Tenn	9-90
Clark, Donald W.	Assoc	Carson-Newm	73	DIVX	MBA		Memphis	1981
Clark, George	Assoc	Florida A&M	29		PHD		Illinois	
Clark, J. Dana	Asst	Appalach St	1	HW	PHD		Va Tech	1991
Clark, Kim B.	Prof	Harvard	7	U				
Harry E. Figgle, Jr. Professor of Business Administration								
Clark, Marian F.	Asst	New Mex St	23	CI	PHD	83	Ariz St	1983
Clark, Robert L.	Prof	N Carol St	5	NQ	PHD	74	Duke	1975
Clark, Sharon C.	Lect	Tx Christian	9	Z	PHD	88	Tx-Arlin	1984
Clark, Thomas B.	Prof	Georgia St	7	UZL	PHD		Geo St	1978
Clark, Thomas D.	Prof	Xavier	12	DES	PHD	76	Indiana	1981
Clark, Thomas D. Jr.	C-Pr	Florida St	97	ZVX	DBA	77	Fla St	8-84
Clark, W.	Asst	SW Baptist	36		MBA		SMSU	1991
Clarke, Barbara A.	Lect	Loughborough			BA		Open	
Clarke, K.	Lect	Univ Bath	3	I	MSC			
Clarke, K. Michael	Prof	CS-San Bern	1	A	PHD	75	Georgia	1976
Clarke, Louise	Asst	Saskatchewan	25		PHD	92	York	1991
Clarke, Richard L.	Asst	Clemson	1	A	PHD	88	Texas	1988
Clarke, Roger	Read	Australian N	9	ILYZ	MCOM	75	NS Wales	1984
Clarke, Ruth	Asst	Suffolk			PHD		Mass	
Clarke, Sandra		Strathclyde	9	Z				
Clawson, James G.	Assoc	Virg-Grad	5	O	DBA		Harvard	1981
Cleary, Michael J.	Prof	Wright State	7	V	PHD	71	Nebraska	1971
Cleek, Margaret A.	Assoc	CS-Sacrament	25	EHNO	PHD	81	Wayne St	1990
Clegg, J. L.	Lect	Univ Bath	8	Y	PHD			
Clelland, Iain	Asst	Tennessee	43	MIZ	PHD	93	S Calif	8-93
Clement, Ronald W.	Prof	Murray State	25	EFHP	PHD	78	Mich St	1982
Clements, Christine	Asst	Wis-Whitewat	2	EFHR	PHD	90	Arkansas	1990
Clemons, Eric K.	Assoc	Pennsylvania	39	IYZ	PHD	76	Cornell	1976
Cleveland, Gary	Prof	Montana	37	IUX	PHD	86	Minn	1985
Clifford, James	Assoc	New York U	9	Z	PHD	82	SUNY-SBr	
Clifton, Thomas	Asst	LeMoyne	5	NQ	PHD	90	Minn	1990
Cline, Philip L.	H	Wash & Lee	79	Z	PHD	75	Okla St	1975
Clinebell, Sharon	C-Ac	No Colorado	25		DBA	88	S Illin	
Clingerman, Debra	Asst	Calif U-Penn	15	N	MBA		W Virg	1984
Clinton, James W.	Prof	No Colorado	43		PHD	73	St Louis	
Clinton, Roy	Assoc	NE Louisiana	7	UVW	DBA	88	S Illin	1986
Close, Jay G.	Assoc	Kentucky St	35	ZO	DBA		US Intl	1984
Close, M. John	Assoc	Wis-Eau Clar		E	PHD		LSU	1975
Clott, Christopher	Assoc	St Xavier	81	Y	MBA		St Xavie	1989
Clouse, Van G. H.	Assoc	Louisville	36	ISTZ	PHD	86	Clemson	8-86
Cnyinda, Chris	Asst	Alabama A&M						
Coakley, Lori	Asst	Bryant	2	ENY	PHD	93	Mass	8-93
Coates, David S.	Lect	Loughborough	7	V	PHD		Newcastl	
Coates, Norman	Prof	Rhode Island	38	IYH	PHD	67	Cornell	1971
Cobb, Anthony T.	Assoc	Virg Tech	2		PHD	77	Ca-Irvine	1978
Cobb, Richard	Asst	Jacksonvl St	37	ZUV	PHD	90	Alabama	1975
Cochran, Charles	Adj	Southeastern			PHD		Tufts	
Cochran, Daniel S.	Prof	Miss State	12	EG	PHD	78	Arkansas	1980
Cochran, Philip L.	Assoc	Penn State	4	JLM	PHD		Wash	

Name	Rank	Institution		Code	Degree		School	Year
Cockburn, Iain	Asst	British Colu	31	IA	PHD	90	Harvard	1989
Coco, Malcolm	Asst	Abilene Chr			PHD		Nova	1990
Coe, L. Charlene	Prof	CS-Fresno	7	U	MBA		CS-Fresn	1988
Coes, Donald V.	Prof	New Mexico	8	V	PHD	78	Princeton	
Coff, Russell W.	Asst	Wash Univ	23	IH	PHD	93	UCLA	1993
Coffey, Robert E.	C-Pr$	So Calif	2	EFH	PHD		Illinois	1963
Coffin, Mark	Asst	East Carol		U	PHD		Va Tech	8-92
Cogger, Kenneth O.	Prof	Kansas	7	V	PHD	71	Michigan	1971
Cohen, Allan R.	Dean	Babson			DBA	67	Harvard	
Cohen, Cynthia	Prof	South Fla	5	QKNR	PHD	80	Geo St	1982
Cohen, Deborah	VAsst	Georgetown	2	EFH	PHD	92	Columbia	1993
Cohen, Debra	Assoc	George Wash	5	N	PHD	87	Ohio St	
Cohen, Isaac	Assoc	San Jose St	41	LBQY	PHD	81	Ca-Davis	1985
Cohen, Mark A.	Assoc	Vanderbilt	4	KLM	PHD	85	Car Mel	9-86
Cohen, Morris A.	C-Pr	Pennsylvania			PHD	74	Northwes	1974
Matsushita Professor of Manufacturing and Logistics								
Cohen, Susan	Assoc	Illinois	7	V	PHD	77	Northwes	1986
Coker, Morgan B.	Retir	Fran Marion			PHD	71	S Carol	
Coker, Robert C.	Prof	Chris Newpor			PHD		Illinois	1977
Colapietro, Vito	Asst	Wm Jewell	24	Q	MA	71	Conn	1992
Colbjornsen, Tom	Prof	Norwegian			PHD			
Colburn, Tracy W.	Asst	USAF Academy	3	I	MBA		FIT	
Cole, George S.	Prof	Shippensburg			PHD		Mich St	
Cole, S.	Asst	Lakehead U	25	DFNR	MA		Waterloo	7-88
Colella, Adrienne	Asst	Rutgers-N Br		ENR	PHD	89	Ohio St	1989
Coleman, B. Jay	Asst	North Fla	7	UVW	PHD	88	Clemson	1988
Coleman, Bruce P.	Assoc	Michigan St	3	U	DBA	67	Indiana	9-65
Coleman, Charles J.	Prof	Rutgers-Camd			PHD			
Coleman, Daniel F.	Assoc	New Brunswic	2	ENY	PHD		SUNY-Buf	1986
Coleman, Jeremy J.	Prof	Fort Lewis	37	IUV	DBA	74	Geo Wash	1983
Coleman, Joseph W.	Assoc	Wright State	7	VZ	PHD	82	Ariz St	1988
Coleman, Lucretia	Prof	Georgia Col	25	ENR	EED	76	Tenn	1977
Coleman, Walter J.	Asst	Fla Southern			MBA		Nova	1988
Colivas, Kynthia	Lect	Mt St Mary's			JD		Santa Cl	
Coll, Joan	C-Ac	Seton Hall			PHD	81	Fordham	
Collett, Nick J.	Fell	Manchest Bus	4	SZ	BA		London	1988
Colley, John L. Jr.	Prof	Virg-Grad	7	U	DBA	68	S Calif	1967
Almand R. Coleman Professor of Business Administration								
Collier, David A.	Assoc	Ohio State			PHD	78	Ohio St	1986
Collier, Millicient	Asst	Chicago St	52	E	MS			
Collins, James	Asst	Alaska-Fairb	3	I	PHD	91	Texas	1991
Collins, James	Inst	So Methodist			MSIE	65	So Meth	
Collins, Judy	Asst	Ark-Ltl Rock			PHD	91	Iowa	1991
Collins, Paul	Asst	U Washington	2		PHD	86	Rutgers	1990
Collins, Robert S.		Intl Mgt Dev	72	U	DBA		Indiana	
Collins, Stephanie J.	Asst	Northeastern			PHD		Wis-Milw	
Collins, Verne	Prof	Shenandoah			EDD		Michigan	1958
Collins, William H. Jr.	Prof	East Carol		V	PHD		S Illin	1970
Collis, David J.	Assoc	Harvard	4	L				
Collis, John W.	Prof	St Ambrose	24	HK	PHD	85	Iowa	1984
Collom, F. D.	Assoc	Queen's Univ	5	PQ	MBA	67	Queen's	1963
Collopy, Fred	Asst	Case Western			PHD	90	Penn	7-90
Colon, Jose F.	Prof	P Rico-Mayag	7		MS	70	Stevens	7-68
Colon, Marta	Assoc	P Rico-Mayag	5		MBA	80	U Miami	8-77
Coltrin, Sally Ann	Prof	North Fla	25	EHN	PHD		Missouri	
Colville, I. G.	Lect	Univ Bath	1	A	PHD			
Comer, Debra R.	Asst	Hofstra	25	EGR	PHD	86	Yale	9-87
Comish, C. Ray	Assoc	McNeese St			DBA		La Tech	
Compeau, D.	Asst	Carleton Un	9	Z	PHD		W Ontar	
Comte, Thomas E.	Dean	No Kentucky		I	PHD	78	Missouri	7-91
Concoran, Jeffrey	Asst	Nichols Col			MBA		Nichols	
Concordia, Louis R.	Prof	Frostburg St			PHD		N Colo	
Condit, Donald F.	Assoc	Lawrence Tec	37		MBA	62	Michigan	1985
Cone, Randolph E.	Prof	New Orleans	21		PHD	71	LSU	8-76
Congden, Steven W.	Asst	Ithaca	3	I	PHD	91	Mass	8-90
Conger, Jay Allen	Assoc	McGill Univ	2		PHD		Harvard	1985
Congram, Carole	Assoc	Bentley	7	UW	PHD	69	Wiscon	1990
Conley, James H.	Prof	E Michigan	1		PHD	69	Mich St	1969
Conlin, George	Asst	Savannah St	14	EK	JD	78	JMarshal	1979
Conlon, Donald E.	Assoc	Delaware			PHD	88	Illinois	1988
Conlon, Edward J.	C-Pr	Notre Dame	2	EH	PHD	78	Car Mel	1992
Conn, Jennie	Asst	Clark Atlant			JD		Geotown	1984
Connelley, Debra	Asst	SUNY-Buffalo			PHD	92	Cornell	0-94
Connelly, Francis J.	Dean	CUNY-Baruch	7	V	DBA	72	Indiana	1972
Conner, Kathleen R.	Asst	Michigan	3	I	PHD	86	UCLA	1991
Connerley, Mary	Asst	Virg Tech	5		PHD	93	Iowa	1993
Connole, Robert	Prof	Montana	3	DI	PHD	68	Iowa	1969
Connolly, Terry	Prof	Arizona	2	EHX	PHD	72	Northwes	1983
Connor, Patrick E.	Prof	Willamette	2	EFGH	PHD	70	U Wash	1982
Conrad, Robert B.	Prof	N Car-Charl			PHD		N Carol	1970

Name	Rank	School			Degree		School	
Conrad, Robert B.			7	U	PHD	68	N Carol	
Conrad, Simon A.	Lect	Manches Inst	79	U	PHD		Manchest	9-72
Conry, Edward J.	Assoc	Colo-Denver	4	J	JD		Ca-Davis	
Considine, Caroline	Asst	Simmons	6	T	MBAM	83	Boston C	
Constable, Gordon K.	Assoc	Wright State	7	U	PHD	72	Purdue	1971
Constas, Kimon	Prof	Fayetteville			PHD			
Conti, Robert	Asst	Bryant	71	DUY	PHD	90	Lehigh	8-91
Contractor, Farok	Prof	Rutgers-Newk	8	Y	PHD		Penn	1980
Conway, B.	Dean	London Guild	59	NY	PHD			1-91
Conway, H. Allan	Assoc	Univ Calgary	13	ID	DBA	83	Harvard	1986
Conway, Richard W.	Prof	Cornell	9	Z	PHD		Cornell	7-84

Emerson Electric Company Professor of Manufacturing Management

Name	Rank	School			Degree		School	
Cooil, Bruce K.	Assoc	Vanderbilt	7	UVXW	PHD	82	Penn	9-82
Cook, Charlie T.	Asst	Livingston	23	GP	ABD	93	Alabama	9-92
Cook, Clifford G.	C-Ac	Ohio Wesley	9	Z	MBA		Drexel	1984
Cook, Curtis	Prof	San Jose St	32	EFHI	DBA	74	S Calif	1982
Cook, Deborah Smith	Assoc	Baltimore	38	IWSN	DBA	82	Indiana	8-89
Cook, Donald L.	Deces	Arkansas	6		PHD	74	Arkansas	1979
Cook, Gas	Fell	Manchest Bus			PHD		Manchest	1992
Cook, Jack	Asst	SUNY-Geneseo	79	UZ	PHD	93	Wash St	9-93
Cook, James S.	Lect	Northeastern	3		AB		Brown	4-87
Cook, Ronald	Asst	Rider	16	ST	PHD	93	Syracuse	1993
Cook, Roy Allen	Asst	Fort Lewis	23	BINS	DBA	89	Miss St	1989
Cook, Suzanne	Assoc	Arizona St	25	GKNR	DBA	73	Tx Tech	1974
Cook, Wade D.	Prof	York Univ	7	V	PHD		Dalhouis	
Cooke, Donna K.	Asst	Fla Atlantic	25	EN	PHD	89	Mia	8-88
Cooke, Robert	Assoc	Ill-Chicago	25	E	PHD	73	Northwes	9-81
Cool, Karel	Assoc	INSEAD	3	I	PHD	85	Purdue	1-85
Cooley, John W.	Prof	Roosevelt			PHD	76	Okla St	1992
Cooley, William	Prof	Jackson St			DBA		Miss St	1984
Coombs, Garth	Asst	Ohio Univ	12		PHD	94	Colorado	
Coombs, Roderick W.	SLect	Manches Inst	79	D	PHD		Manchest	9-79
Coop, Lind	Asst	Azusa Pacif	13	IZ	MBA		National	9-89
Cooper, Arnold C.	Prof	Purdue	3	T	DBA	62	Harvard	1963
Cooper, Cary L.	Prof	Manches Inst	2	G	PHD		Leeds	1975
Cooper, Christine L.	Asst	U Manitoba	25	EQ	PHD	90	Ohio St	1990
Cooper, Clarence A.	Assoc	Suffolk			MPA		Harvard	
Cooper, Colin	Adj	Southeastern			PHD		Maryland	
Cooper, Elizabeth	Assoc	Rhode Island	25	EFNX	PHD	85	Akron	1985
Cooper, J.	Lect	Victoria NZ	13	IDT	MBA		Victoria	
Cooper, James	Assoc	Neb-Kearney	6	ST	PHD	81	Michigan	1992
Cooper, Joseph E.	Asst	Dartmouth			PHD	92	Harvard	1993
Cooper, Juett	Inst	Marshall	3	I	ABD		Kentucky	1993
Cooper, Ken	Prof	Ohio Northrn	3	IJ	PHD	84	Minn	6-86
Cooper, R. C.	Read	U Lancaster	25	EH	PHD		Liverpoo	
Cooper, Randolph B.	Assoc	Houston	9	Z	PHD	83	UCLA	8-90
Cooper, Robin	Prof	Claremont Gr	9	ZDUY	DBA		Harvard	1992
Cooper, Ronald L.	Assoc	Biola	7	V	PHD		Berkeley	1994
Cooper, W. Douglas	C-Ac	N Car-Charl			PHD		N Car St	1985
Cooper, W. H.	Assoc	Queen's Univ	2	EHFX	PHD	78	Toronto	1976
Cooper, William W.	Prof	Texas	37	IUVX	DSC	70	Ohio St	1980
Cooperrider, David L.	Assoc	Case Western	2	E	PHD		Case Wes	
Cooprider, Jay	Asst	Texas	9	Z	PHD	90	MIT	1990
Cope, Rachelle F.	Asst	SE Louisiana		ZI	ABD			
Coppock, James Allen	Assoc	Carson-Newm	23	EFNP	MS		Tenn	1962
Corbett, Lawrie M.	SLect	Victoria NZ	7	U	MBA		Cranfield	1-85
Corcoran, Wayne A.	Prof	Virgin Islan	7	UV	PHD	66	SUNY-Buf	1990
Cordeiro, William	Asst	CS-L Angeles	12	LY	PHD	90	Claremont	1990
Cordero, Rene	Asst	NJ Inst Tech	75	UNE	PHD	85	Rutgers	1990
Cordery, J. C.	Assoc	W Australia			PHD		Sheffiel	
Cordon, Carlos		Intl Mgt Dev	7	UV	PHD		Insead	
Corey, Sharon	Asst	Mercer-Atlan	97	Z	ABD		Florida	1992
Corman, Joel	Prof	Suffolk			PHD	73	Penn	
Corman, Lawrence S.	Assoc	Fort Lewis	19	DZ	PHD	89	North Tx	1982
Cormany, C. D. (Rip)	Lect	S F Austin	78	Y	MBA	83	Lindenwo	1984
Corney, William J.	Prof	Nev-L Vegas	78	UVYZ	PHD	76	Ariz St	1976
Cornuejols, Gerard P.	Prof	Carnegie Mel	7	V	PHD	78	Cornell	1978
Cornwell, Larry	Prof	Bradley	9	Z	PHD	72	Mo-Rolla	1980
Cort, Stanton G.	Assoc	Case Western	86	YI	DBA	72	Harvard	
Cosgrove, William J.	Prof	CS-Pomona	73	UVI	PHD	84	Nebraska	1989
Cosier, Richard A.	Dean	Oklahoma		Mgt	PHD	76	Iowa	1-93

Fred E. Brown Professor; email: rjc@cbadeans.uoknor.edu

Name	Rank	School			Degree		School	
Cossick, Kathy L.	Asst	Houston	9	Z	PHD	92	Fla St	8-91
Costello, Daniel E.	Dean	Baltimore		Comm	PHD	68	Mich St	6-90
Costello, Mary F.	Lect	Northeastern	4		JD		Boston	1-85
Costigan, Robert	Asst	St John Fish	25		PHD		Missouri	
Costley, Dan L.	Prof	New Mex St	25	EFPD	PHD	64	Mich St	1972
Cote, Daniel	Assoc	HEC-Montreal	23	I	PHD		LSU	
Cote, Marcel	Prof	HEC-Montreal	15	CIY	MBA		Chicago	
Cotham, James C. III	Prof	Belmont	34		DBA	67	Indiana	1986

Name	Rank	Institution	No	Code	Degree	Yr	University	Year
Cotlar, Morton	Prof	Hawaii-Manoa			PHD	69	Georgia	
Cottam, Angela	Lect	Napier Univ	38	IY	BSC			1990
Cotterman, William W.	Prof	Georgia St	9	Z	PHD		Geo St	
Cottle, Richard	Prof	So Oregon St	4	K	JD	70	Washburn	1982
Cotton, Chester C.	Prof	CS-Chico			PHD	74	Oregon	1972
Cotton, G. B.	Assoc	Laurentian	8		MBIM		Bath	
Cotton, John L.	Assoc	Marquette	2	E	PHD	79	Iowa	1987
Cottrell, Thomas	Asst	Univ Calgary	3	I	ABD		Berkeley	1993
Cottrill, Melville T.	Assoc	So Conn St	36	KLS	PHD	91	Conn	1990
Couch, Darryl V.	Lect	Florida St	9	Z	MA	62	Fla St	8-85
Couch, Peter D.	Prof	Illinois St	5		PHD	65	Wiscon	1970
Couch, T. Grantham	Assoc	Western St	3		PHD	92	Fla St	1992
Couchman, Paul	SLect	U Wollongong			PHD			4-93
Couger, J. Daniel	Prof	Colorado Spr	9	Z	DBA	64	Colorado	5-65
Distinguished Professor of Management Science								
Coughlan, Paul	Asst	London Bus	7	U	PHD		W Ontari	
Coulter, Mary K.	Assoc	SW Missouri	52	QN	PHD	84	Arkansas	1983
Courtney, James F. Jr.	Prof	Texas A&M		Z	PHD	74	Texas	1986
Tenneco Professorship in Business Administration								
Cousins, P. D.	Lect	Univ Bath	7	W	MBA			
Covin, Jeffrey	C-Ac	Georgia Tech	13	IT	PHD	85	Pitt	1986
Covin, Teresa J.	C-Ac	Kennesaw St	25	FNR	PHD	87	Pitt	1987
Cowan, David S.	Assoc	Miami U-Ohio	2	EFG	PHD	84	Kansas	8-88
Cowden, Anne C.	Prof	CS-Sacrament	25	EPR	DPA	80	S Calif	1979
Cox, Charles J.	Lect	Manches Inst	2	E	BA		Bristol	1966
Cox, James F. III	Prof	Georgia	7	U	PHD	75	Clemson	1983
Cox, Joe Allen	Prof	Baylor	5	N	PHD		Okla St	1977
Cox, John Lew	C-Pr	West Florida	79	TUY	PHD	70	Ariz St	1978
Cox, Larry	Lect	Nebraska	6	ST	MA	90	Nebraska	8-90
Cox, Myron K.	C-Pr	Wright State	7	V	DSC	64	London	1969
Cox, Taylor Jr.	Assoc	Michigan	3	E	PHD	81	Arizona	1988
Coye, Ray W.	C-Ac	DePaul			PHD		Oregon	
Coyne, John	Assoc	George Wash	9	Z	PHD	70	Lehigh	
Cozzolino, John	Assoc	Pace-Westch	7		PHD	67	MIT	1989
Craft, James A.	Prof	Pittsburgh	5		PHD	68	Berkeley	1972
Craft, Robert	Prof	Georgia Col	7	HL	DBA	77	Indiana	1988
Cragg, Wesley A.	Prof	York Univ	4	J	PHD		Oxford	
Cragin, John P.	Prof	Okla Baptist	38	DITY	PHD			8-90
Cragun, John R.	H-Pr	Utah State	25	EPN	PHD	66	Purdue	1966
Craig, Jerry W.	Assoc	Citadel	4	K	JD		NC Cen	
Craig, Ronald G.	D-Ac	Wilfrid Laur	79	SUZ	PHD		Waterloo	1979
Craig, Russell J.	H-Pr	Australian N	14	ABCL	PHD	89	N'cle	1991
Crain, Charles R.	C-Pr	Miami U-Ohio	37	U	PHD	71	Missouri	8-71
Crandall, Richard E.	Assoc	Appalach St	7	UV	PHD	93	S Carol	1985
Crant, J. Michael	Asst	Notre Dame	12	EFH	PHD	90	N Carol	1990
Crant, Mike			3	I	PHD	90	N Carol	
Crary, Marcy	Assoc	Bentley	2	ER	PHD	82	Case Wes	1981
Craven, Thomas	Asst	York of PA	5		MBA		Penn St	1982
Crawford, Alice M.	Adj	Naval Postgr	25	DEFP	MA	73	S Dgo St	4-88
Crawford, John B.	Prof	CS-Pomona	9	Z	PHD	86	CA-Irvin	1984
Crawford, Marian C.	Prof	Ark-Ltl Rock			PHD		Miss	1981
Crawford, Pam	Adj	Montana St	12		MSHR	86	Gold Gt	9-88
Crawford, R.	Prof	Concordia U						
Cray, D.	Assoc	Carleton Un	8	Y	PHD		Wiscon	
Credille, Ronda	Asst	SW Baptist	16		MBA		Drury	1990
Creed, W. E. Douglas	Asst	Boston Coll	2	HJ	PHD	94	Berkeley	9-94
Creighton, Walter H.	Asst	NW St of La			PHD		Colo St	
Crew, James	Assoc	Meredith	23	EI	PHD		N Car St	1990
Crews, Kenneth D.	Assoc	San Jose St	4	KJ	PHD	90	UCLA	1990
Cribbin, James	Retir	St Johns		1993	PHD	51	Fordham	
Crim, John W.	Retir	Columbus	25	1991	PHD	75	Geo St	1977
Crino, Michael D.	Prof	Clemson	2	EH	PHD	78	Florida	1984
Crittenden, William F.	Assoc	Northeastern	13	I	PHD		Arkansas	9-84
Crocitto, Madeline	Asst	SUNY Old Wes	25	EFNR	PHD	89	CUNY	1988
Crocker, Kevin	Asst	Athabasca Un	91		MBA	82	Windsor	1986
Crocker, O. L.	Prof	Univ Windsor	25	EFNR	PHD		U Wash	198-
Crockett, Henry D.	Asst	Portland St	9	Z	PHD	90	Tx-Arlin	1989
Croll, Robert F.	Prof	Cen Michigan	7	U	DBA	69	Indiana	1970
Crook, Connie	Asst	N Car-Charl	9	Z	PHD	92	S Carol	
Crook, Leo V.	Prof	Delta State	57	QV	DBA	78	Miss St	8-79
Crooker, Karen	Asst	Wis-Milwauke	2	HE	ABD	94	Indiana	1994
Crookes, J. G.	SLect	U Lancaster	7	UVZ	MSC		Birmingh	
Cross, Jeffrey	Assoc	St Peters			DBA		Nova	1985
Crossland, Philip	Assoc	Mo-Kansas Ct	3	I	PHD	87	Nebraska	1988
Croteau, Barbara A.	C-As	N Adams St			MBA		Providen	
Crouch, Agd	Prof	Bond Univ	23	FI	PHD	82	NS Wales	1989
Crouch, Henry L.	C-Pr	Pittsburg St	78	SUVY	PHD	77	S Carol	1975
Crouchly, Robert	Lect	London Econ	79	VXZ	PHD			1991
Crow, Steve M.	Asst	New Orleans	53	NE	PHD	89	North Tx	8-89
Crown, Deborah F.	Asst	Alabama	24	EJX	PHD	90	Colorado	1990

Name	Rank	Institution			Degree		School	
Crowner, Robert P.	Assoc	E Michigan	3		MS		Butler	1976
Crumpacker, Martha	Assoc	Washburn		Mgt	DBA	80	La Tech	1977
Cuba, Richard	Prof	Baltimore	16	BDHR	DBA	71	Geo Wash	9-70
Cuff, Robert D.	Prof	York Univ	1	AB	PHD		Princeton	
Culbert, Samuel A.	Prof	UCLA	5	N	PHD	66	UCLA	1969
Culbertson, John	Inst	Seattle	23	IE	DBA		Harvard	
Cullen, Dallas M.	Assoc	Univ Alberta	2	R	PHD	68	Ohio St	1970
Cullen, John	Prof	Wash State						
Cullen, Thoms	Prof	Cornell	23	EIY	PHD	82	Cornell	8-85
Culnan, Mary J.	Assoc	Georgetown	9	ZJLI	PHD	80	UCLA	1988
Culpan, Oya	Asst	Penn St-Harr	4	LR	PHD	74	Hacettep	1984
Culpan, Refik	Assoc	Penn St-Harr	8	Y	PHD	73	NYU	1981
Cumbo, James	C	Emory Henry	12	EHJS	PHD	81	Va Tech	1975
Cummings, Larry L.	Prof	Minnesota	2	EH	DBA	64	Indiana	1984
Cummings, S.	Lect	Victoria NZ			BA		Victoria	
Cummings, Thomas G.	Prof	So Calif	2	EFH	PHD		UCLA	1976
Cunningham, Bernard J.	Asst	Dallas	3		PHD	81	Tx-Dallas	8-81
Cunningham, Craig	Assoc	Athabasca Un	91		BCOM	76	Alberta	1979
Cunningham, M. H.	Inst	Queen's Univ	4	J	ABD	91	Tx A&M	1991
Curl, Steven S.	Asst	CS-Pomona	9	Z	MS	88	Claremont	1990
Curley, Kathleen Foley	Assoc	Northeastern			DBA		Harvard	
Curmody, Seth	Prof	David Lipsc	79	VZ	PHD		Missouri	9-85
Curran, A. Ranger	Prof	Keene State			DBA	77	Georgia	1982
Curran, Kent E.	C-Ac	N Car-Charl			DBA		LSU	1984
Curran, Terence P.	C-Pr	Siena Coll	34	M	PHD		SUNY-Alb	9-88
Current, John R.	Assoc	Ohio State	7	V	PHD	82	J Hopkin	1982
Currie, D.		Humberside	2					
Currie, Elliott	Lect	Wilfrid Laur	3	I	MBA		McMaster	1992
Curtis, Ellen Foster	Assoc	Mass-Lowell	3	IJ	DBA	79	Indiana	
Cusack, Gerald P.	Asst	St Johns			PHD	76	NYU	
Cusson, Rene	Agreg	HEC-Montreal	7		CES		Paris	
Custin, Richard E.	C	Carthage	49		JD	84	Drake	9-90
Cusumano, Michael A.	Asst	MIT	3	I	PHD			
Mitsubishi Career Development Assistant Professor of Management								
Cuthbertson, Harry	Asst	Rowan Col NJ	14		MBA	87	LaSalle	1982
Cutright, Ken	Assoc	Ohio Univ	8		PHD	90	W Virg	
Czander, William	Assoc	Manhattan	25	EOR	PHD	75	NYU	1981
D'Amico, Robert J.	Asst	USAF Academy	3	I	MGA		Maryland	
D'Aveni, Richard	Assoc	Dartmouth			PHD	87	Columbia	1988
D'Souza, Kelwyn	Assoc	Hampton	7	Uvxz	PHD		S Fla	1991
D'Souza, Patricia V.	Prof	CS-San Bern	9	Z	PHD	85	Ohio St	1986
Daboval, Jeanne	Inst	McNeese St						
Dacey, Raymond	Prof	Idaho	87	VY	PHD	70	Purdue	1984
Dacin, M. Tina	Asst	Texas A&M		HI	PHD	93	Toronto	1992
Dada, Macqbool	Assoc	Purdue	7	U	PHD	84	MIT	1992
Dadzie, Evelyn	Asst	Morehouse			MBA			
Daellenbach, H. G.	Prof	Canterbury	7	V	PHD		Berkeley	1970
Daellenbach, Urs	Asst	Univ Calgary	3	I	PHD	93	Purdue	1992
Daft, Richard L.	Prof	Vanderbilt	12	DEF	PHD	74	Chicago	9-89
Dagwell, Ron	SLect	Griffith Un	13	AELP	MFM		Queens	2-82
Dahan, Simon	Agreg	HEC-Montreal	7		DEA		Paris	
Dahl, James G.	Asst	Millikin	2	EG	MS		St Louis	
Dahl, Joan G.	Assoc	CS-Northrdge	25	AFNQ	PHD	86	U Wash	1986
Dailey, John G.	Asst	St Edwards	14	JL	MBA	78	Geo Wash	1991
Dailey, Mike	Asst	Midwest St	25	ENST	DBA	78	La Tech	9-92
Dailey, Richard T.	Prof	Montana	46	IJSY	PHD	68	Penn St	1981
Dailey, Robert	Prof	Drake	12	EFCN	DBA	77	Colorado	1989
Daily, Bonnie	Asst	New Mex St	79	UVZ	PHD	91	Missouri	1991
Daily, Catherine M.	Asst	Ohio State	3	I	PHD	91	Indiana	1992
Daily, James M.	Retir	Wright State	5	NO	DBA	64	Colorado	1972
Daines, David	Assoc	Utah State	4	JK	JD	55	Utah	9-67
Daines, Robert H.	Prof	Brigham Yg	3	I	PHD	66	Indiana	1959
Dakin, S. R.	SLect	Canterbury	2	EF	PHD	73	Toronto	1973
Dalal, Nikunj	Asst	Oklahoma St	9	Z	PHD	90	Tx Tech	8-90
Dale, Barrie G.	SLect	Manches Inst	7	T	PHD		Nottingh	1981
Dale, Cheryl F.	Asst	Delta State	17	UVW	ABD	91	Alabama	8-92
Dale, Leon A.	Retir	CS-Pomona		1991	PHD	49	Wiscon	1969
Dalrymple, Gerald	Inst	Nicholls St	12		MBA	65	Loyola	1979
Dalton, Dan R.	Prof	Indiana	5	Q	PHD	79	Ca-Irvine	1979
Dalton, Robert	C-As	Russell Sage	34	IJ	MBA		Syracuse	1984
Daly, James	Prof	Youngstown	15		MBA	72	Akron	9-72
Daly, Joseph P.	Asst	Appalach St	2	E	PHD		Northwes	1989
Damanpour, Fariborz	Assoc	Rutgers-Newk	12	DHI	PHD	83	Penn	1985
Damewood, Earl	Assoc	Marshall	7	V	PHD	81	W Virg	
Dana, James	Assoc	Northwestern	3	I	PHD	88	MIT	
Danak, Jagdish T.	Assoc	E Michigan	1		PHD	70	Oklahoma	1969
Dandridge, Thomas C.	Assoc	SUNY-Albany	64	STL	PHD	75	UCLA	1975
Danehower, V. Carol	Asst	Memphis	25	EN	DBA	87	Kentucky	1987
Dangerfield, Byron	Dean	Idaho	79	UVXZ	PHD	85	U Wash	1981
Daniel, Cornelia	Asst	Westfield St			PHD		Mass	1990

Name	Rank	School			Degree		Institution	Year
Daniel, Hugh Jr.	Assoc	David Lipsc	7	VU	PHD		Miss	9-86
Daniels, John D.	Prof	Indiana	8	Y	PHD	69	Michigan	1987
Daniels, John P.	Prof	W Illinois			PHD	76	LSU	1976
Daniels, Rhonda	Asst	Univ Sydney		L	BSC		NS Wales	1991
Danielson, Lee E.	Emer	Michigan	5	N	PHD	56	Michigan	1955
Dannenbring, David G.	C-Pr	CUNY-Baruch	7	U	PHD		Columbia	1973
Danos, Barbara	Inst	SE Louisiana	48	JKLY	JD	73	N Carol	8-85
Dansereau, Fred E. Jr.	Assoc	SUNY-Buffalo	2	EH	PHD	72	Illinios	9-73
Darcy, Louise	Lect	Texas A&M		V	MS	74	Tx A&M	1980
Darden, Clifford E.	Assoc	Pepper-L Ang			DBA	82	Harvard	1984
Darling, N.	Asst	Mt St Vincen	25	EFNP	MBA	89	Dalhoise	1989
Darling, Paul		Southeastern			PHD			
Darroch, James L.	Assoc	York Univ	3	I	PHD		York	
Darrow, Arthur L.	Assoc	Bowling Gr	2	FH	PHD	82	Iowa	1980
Darrow, Orien	Asst	Minot St			PHD		Denver	1987
Darrow, William P.	Assoc	Towson State	37		PHD	80	Penn St	1984
Das, Chandra	Prof	No Iowa			PHD	71	Case Wes	1-86
Das, Hari	Prof	St Marys-Cnd	25	HFN	PHD	79	Brit Col	1978
Das, Krishna K.	Prof	Morris Brown			DCS	56	Harvard	
Das, T. K.	Assoc	CUNY-Baruch	3	I	PHD		UCLA	1984
Daser, Sayeste					PHD	75	N Carol	
Dasgupta, Aniruddha	Asst	Penn State	7	V	PHD		Princeton	
Dass, Parshotam	Asst	Arkansas	32	IH	PHD	93	Mich St	1992
Dastmalchian, Ali M.	Prof	Victoria Can	2	EFH	PHD	81	Wales	7-91
Dastoli, Anthony	Asst	Youngstown	37		MBA	64	Pitt	9-69
Dasu, Sriram	Asst	UCLA	7	U	PHD	88	MIT	1988
Datta, Deepka K.	Assoc	Kansas	3	I	PHD		Pitt	1986
Daughety, Andy	Prof	Iowa	7	U	PHD	72	Case Wes	1981
Daumer, Claudia	Assoc	CS-Chico			PHD		Ariz St	1983
Davalos, Sergio	Asst	Portland	9	Z	PHD	92	Arizona	1991
Dave, Dinesh S.	Prof	Appalach St	7	UVZ	PHD		Gujarat	1988
Davenport, Sally J	Lect	Victoria NZ	13	DSMI	PHD	86	Victoria	1-91
Davenport, Thomas		Boston Univ	9	Z	PHD		Harvard	
Davey, Anne	Asst	NE St-Okla	7	UV	PHD	93	Tx A&M	1993
David, Fred R.	Prof	Fran Marion	3	I	PHD	81	S Carol	8-88
TranSouth Professor of Strategic Management								
David, Pierre	Asst	Baldwin-Wal	7	UV	MBA		Pitt	
Davidson, Anthony R.	Asst	Hofstra	79	UVZ	MBA	85	Baruch	9-93
Davidson, Frederick	Prof	Mary Wash	76	PTVF	PHD		Pitt	
Davidson, Marilyn J.	SLec	Manches Inst	2	EX	PHD		Manchest	9-84
Davidson, Martin N.	Asst	Dartmouth			PHD	88	Stanford	1992
Davidson, Naomi Berger	Assoc	CS-Northrdge	45	JKNQ	PHD	81	UCLA	1983
Davidson, Stephen M.	Assoc	Boston Univ	1	C	PHD		Chicago	
Davidson, William	Assoc	So Calif	8	Y	DBA		Harvard	9-86
Davies, G. J.	Prof	Manchest Bus			PHD		London	1992
Davies, John	C-SLe	Victoria NZ	37	HIUV	MA		Lancast	5-80
Davies, Karen	AcAs	U Lethbridge	6	T	MBA	86	Alberta	1988
Davies, Robert	Asst	London Bus	13	DEIY	PHD		Warwick	1991
Davies, Stuart	Assoc	Univ Leeds	13	AI	PHD	82	LSE	1993
Davig, William A.	Assoc	E Kentucky	36	ST	PHD	74	Northwes	1984
Davis, Ann	Assoc	Univ Leeds	2	EF	BSC	85	Nottingh	1990
Davis, Anne	Asst	St Thomas-TX	25	ENY	PHD	90	Ohio St	1992
Davis, Bernard	Dean	Morehead St	76	RTQ	PHD	67	Kentucky	1978
Davis, Bobby	Assoc	Florida A&M	25		PHD		Wiscon	
Davis, Carl	Inst	Savannah St	79	UZ	MBA	80	Sav St	1983
Davis, Dale A.	Assoc	Mich-Flint	13	AYZ	PHD	78	Michigan	9-72
Davis, Dale N.	Prof	E New Mexico		BEFH	DBA	80	Geo St	1982
Davis, Daniel	Asst	Rowan Col NJ	9		MBA	84	Drexel	1984
Davis, Ed	Prof	Macquarie Un						
Davis, Edward	C-Pr	Clark Atlant			PHD		N Car St	
Davis, Edward W.	Prof	Virg-Grad	7	U	PHD	67	Yale	1978
Oliver Wight Professor of Business Administration								
Davis, Elaine	Assoc	St Cloud St	21	EF	PHD	92	Nebraska	1990
Davis, Elizabeth	C-As	St Joseph	23	EIJY	PHD	84	Penn	1988
Davis, Frank S.	Prof	Bloomsburg	9	Z	PHD		Pitt	
Davis, Frederick G.	Prof	Hawaii Pacf	9	Z	PHD	68	Mich St	8-91
Davis, George C.	Inst	Jacksonvl St	45	NJ	MBA	80	W N Eng	1981
Davis, Harry L.	Prof	Chicago			PHD	70	Northwes	1963
Roger L. & Rachel M. Goetz Professor of Creative Management								
Davis, J. Bradley	Lect	Brock Univ	1		MBA		York	1986
Davis, J. Jackson	Asst	St Marys-Txs			PHD	71	Tx Tech	
Davis, J. Steven	Assoc	Clemson	9	Z	PHD	84	Ga Tech	1985
Davis, James	Asst	Notre Dame	13		PHD	91	Iowa	1991
Davis, James	Assoc	So Miss	36	FIST	ABD	61	LSU	1965
Davis, K. Roscoe	Prof	Georgia	7	VW	PHD		North Tx	1972
Davis, K. Shannon	Asst	N Carol St	52	NOPF	PHD	92	Maryland	1992
Davis, Kermit R.	Assoc	Auburn	32	EN	PHD	77	Georgia	9-79
Davis, Mark	Assoc	Bentley	7	UV	DBA	86	Boston U	1986
Davis, Mark Alan	Assoc	Kentucky	5	NEC	PHD	84	Va Tech	1987
Davis, Peter S.	Assoc	Memphis	3	I	PHD	88	S Carol	1989

Name	Rank	Institution	#		Degree	Yr	School	Yr
Davis, Robert A.	Assoc	Texas A&M		U	PHD	82	S Carol	1982
Davis, Samuel G.	Assoc	Penn State	7	V	PHD		Syracuse	
Davis, Sidney M.	Asst	Nebraska	9	VXZ	PHD	89	Indiana	8-89
Davis, Tammy J.	C-Ac$	Indiana St	21	NO	PHD		Georgia	8-90
Davis, Thomas	Lect	Dayton	79		MS	70	Air FIT	1990
Davis, Tim R. V.	Prof	Cleveland St	15	DN	PHD		Nebraska	1979
Davis-Blake, Alison	Assoc	Texas	25	EHNO	PHD	86	Stanford	1990
Davison, Edwin	Asst	Cen St-Ohio	46	KLST	JD		Wiscon	4-86
Davy, Jeanette	Asst	Wright State	5	N	PHD	86	Arizona	1992
Dawson, John E.	Prof	Naval Postgr	13	ABI	PHD	71	Syracuse	1966
Dawson, Julie	Asst	Carthage			MA		Wiscon	1993
Day, Diana L.	Asst	Pennsylvania	3	I	PHD	86	Columbia	7-85
Ehrenkranz/Greenwall Term Assistant Professor of Management								
Day, John	C-Pr	Ohio Univ			PHD		Ohio U	
Day, Nancy	Asst	Mo-Kansas Ct	5	NQ	PHD	87	Kansas	1990
Day, William A.	Prof	Ohio Univ	13		DBA	67	Harvard	1965
Dayal, Sahab	Prof	Cs-Norhtrdge	58	NQY	PHD	73	Cornell	1989
Daymont, Thomas	Assoc	Temple			PHD		Wiscon	
De Leon, Corinna T.	SLect	City Poly HK	28	DEJP	PHD		UK	3-90
De Lodzia, George	Prof	Rhode Island	24	EFH	PHD	69	Syracuse	1970
De Rooij, A. H.	Prof	Univ Limburg	18	YD	MS	58	Delft	1990
De Temple, J.	Prof	McGill Univ	1		DES		LPasteur	1985
De, Mitali	Assoc	Wilfrid Laur	7	V	PHD		Waterloo	1988
De, Prabuddha	Prof	Dayton	9	UVZ	PHD	79	Car Mel	1987
Standard Register-Sherman Distinguished Professor								
Dean, Burton V.	C-Pr	San Jose St	7	U	PHD	52	Illinois	1985
Dean, James W.	Assoc	Cincinnati						
Dean, Roger A.	Prof	Wash & Lee	25	JKNO	PHD	81	Mich St	1984
Dean, Thomas	Asst	Tennessee	36	IT	ABD		Colorado	8-91
Deane, John	Lect	Deakin-Burwo	13	BF	MED		Liverpoo	
Deane, Richard H.	C-Pr	Georgia St	7	U	PHD	71	Purdue	1981
Deans, Candace	Asst	Wake Forest	9	YZ	PHD	89	S Carol	9-89
Dearden, Marlin	Prof	Quinnipiac	2	CEF	PHD		Yale	
DeBauche, Susan D.	Asst	SW Baptist	79		EDD		Arkansas	1985
Debnath, Sukumar C.	Asst	Prairie View	23	EHIN	DBA	89	Miss St	1987
Debusk, Susan	Asst	St Louis			PHD		Texas	1992
DeCastro, Julio O.	Asst	Colorado			PHD	90	S Carol	1989
DeCastro, Sister Ida	Assoc	St Rose	25		MSBA	70	Notre Dm	1973
DeCenzo, David A.	Prof	Towson State	15		PHD	81	W Virg	1986
Dechant, Kathleen	Asst	Connecticut	3	I	PHD	82	Columbia	1988
Deckard, Noble	C-Pr	Mary Hrdn-By	23		PHD		U Wash	1990
Decker, C. Richard	Prof	Millikin	3	I	EDD	68	Indiana	1974
Decker, Philip	Assoc	Hartford	5	N	PHD	79	Ohio St	
Decker, Wayne H.	C-Pr	Salisbury St	27	EJO	PHD	72	Pitt	8-86
Deckop, John	Assoc	Temple			PHD		Minn	
DeCroix, Greg	Asst	U Washington	7	V	PHD	91	Stanford	1991
Dedee, J. Kim	Asst	Wis-Oshkosh	3	I	PHD	85	Arkansas	1987
Deeks, John	Assoc	U Auckland	45	LQT	MA	64	Cambridg	9-72
Deeney, John	Asst	Delaware St			MBA			1972
Dees, J. Gregory	Assoc	Harvard	1					
DeFillipi, Robert	Asst	Suffolk			ABD		Yale	
Defrank, Richard	Assoc	Houston	26	ETYG	PHD	80	Rochest	8-89
DeGenaro, Guy J.	Prof	Virg Comm	2	E	PHD	71	Florida	1970
DeGennaro, Louis A.	Prof	Lawrence Tec	4		JD			1975
DeGeus, Arie	VFel	London Bus	38	IY	MBA		Rotterdm	
DeGouvea, Raul	Assoc	New Mexico	8	Y	PHD	88	Illinois	
DeHaemer, Michael	C-Ac	Loyola-Maryl	9	Z	PHD		Renssel	
Dehler, Gordon	Asst	Dayton	2	EH	PHD	90	Cinn	8-88
Deile, Andrew J.	Assoc	Mercer-Macon	23	HI	PHD	74	Illinios	1986
Deitzer, Bernard A.	Retir	Akron	38	IHOY	PHD	67	Ohio St	1-67
Dejoie, Roy	Asst	Oklahoma	9	Z	PHD	91	Tx A&M	8-92
deJong, Piet	Prof	British Colu	7	V	PHD	75	LaTrobe	1982
Del Pilar, R.	Asst	McGill Univ	7		PHD		Cornell	1989
Delacroix, Jacques	Prof	Santa Clara			PHD	74	Stanford	1983
Delaney, John P.	Retir	Alfred	1	1993	MA		Iowa St	1985
Delaney, John T.	Prof	Iowa	45	Q	PHD	83	Illinois	1989
Delaney, Michael M.	Assoc	St Joseph	9	YZ	PHD	76	Penn	1992
DeLaTorre, Jose'	Prof	UCLA	3	I	DBA	71	Harvard	1987
Delbecq, Andre L.	Prof	Santa Clara			DBA	63	Indiana	1979
Delery, John	Asst	Arkansas	25	En	PHD	92	Tx A&M	1992
Deligonul, Seyda	Prof	St John Fish	18		PHD		Haccette	
Dell'Omo, Gregory G.	Assoc	St Joseph	25	NPQ	PHD	87	Wiscon	1991
Dellana, Scott	Asst	East Carol		U	PHD		Mo-Rolla	8-93
DeLone, William	Assoc	American U	9	SZ	PHD	83	UCLA	1986
DeLoughy, Sara T.	C-Ac	Western Conn	7	V	PHD		New Sch	
Delquie, Philippe	Asst	Texas	7	UV	PHD	89	MIT	1989
Delurgio, Stephen A.	Assoc	Mo-Kansas Ct	7	U	PHD		St Louis	1976
DeMatta, Renato	Asst	Iowa	7	U	PHD	89	Penn	1990
Demers, Christiane	Asst	HEC-Montreal	2	I	PHD		HEC-Mont	
DeMeuse, Kenneth P.	Assoc	Wis-Eau Clar		EFP	PHD		Tenn	1990

Name	Rank	School			Degree			
Demmy, W. Steven	Prof	Wright State	7	V	PHD	71	Ohio St	1975
Dempsey, Richard	Prof	Detroit Merc			PHD	58	Wiscon	1958
Den Hertog, Friso	Prof	Univ Limburg			PHD	75	Delft	1985
Denbo, Susan	Asst	Rider	4	JKLM	JD	77	Villanov	1989
Denison, Barbara B.	Asst	Wright State	7	Z	MBA	74	Dayton	1976
Denison, Daniel R.	Assoc	Michigan	2	E	PHD	82	Michigan	1983
Dennard, Lou	Assoc	So Nazarane	23		EDD	81	Okla St	1991
Dennehy, Robert F.	C-Pr	Pace-Westch	2		PHD		NYU	1978
Dennis, Alan R.	Asst	Georgia	9	DZ	PHD	91	Arizona	1991
DeNoble, Alex F.	Prof	San Diego St	36	IT	PHD	83	Va Tech	1983
Dent, Anne	Asst	Bryant	8	YI	PHD	91	Nice	8-92
Dent-Crews, Marie	Asst	Georgia Col	13	CI	PHD	91	Georgia	1991
Denton, James	Asst	W Virginia	7	V				1991
Denton, Keith	Prof	SW Missouri	7	U	PHD	82	S Illin	1984
Denzler, Dave	Assoc	San Jose St	73	U	DBA	67	Wash U	1987
Deokar, Vijay D.	Assoc	CS-Pomona	9	Z	PHD	68	CSU-LA	1989
deRaadt, J. D. R.	Assoc	Idaho State	9	Z	PHD	86	LaTrobe	1987
Derakhshan, Foad	Prof	CS-San Bern	83	YI	PHD	79	LSU	1985
Deresky, Helen	Prof	SUNY-Plattsb	38	IY	PHD	84	Concordi	1983
Dermer, Jerry	Prof	York Univ	3	I	PHD		Illinios	
Derr, C. Brooklyn	Prof	Utah	2	EFHO	EDD	71	Harvard	1978
Dery, Richard	Asst	HEC-Montreal	12	HV	PHD		Laval	
Desa, D.		Humberside	2					
Desai, Harsha B.	C-Pr	Loyola-Maryl	36	IST	PHD	70	Penn St	1982
Desai, Kiran J.	Assoc	Mid Tenn St	7	U	PHD	72	Penn St	1972
Desalvia, Donald N.	Prof	Syracuse	3	F	PHD	65	Syracuse	1065
Deschamps, Isabelle	Assoc	HEC-Montreal	78	TUV	MBA		Montreal	
Desforges, Jean-Guy	Assoc	HEC-Montreal	13	IX	PHD		Pitt	
Deshmukh, Abhijit	Asst	SUNY-Stony B	17	UV	PHD	93	Purdue	1993
Deshpande, Rohit	Prof	Dartmouth			PHD	79	Pitt	1986
Deshpande, Satish	Assoc	W Michigan	5	NPQS	PHD	90	Iowa	1990
Desilva, Dharma	Prof	Wichita St	84	LYS	PHD	66	Indiana	9-79
DesJardins, Robert			7	V	PHD	65	N Carol	
Desman, Robert	Assoc	Kennesaw St	48	BDH	PHD	83	Ariz St	1987
DeSouza, Glenn	VProf	Mass-Boston	3	I	PHD	76	Fordham	1989
Desrosiers, Jacques	Prof	HEC-Montreal			PHD		Montreal	
Dess, Gregory G.	Prof	Tx-Arlington	3	I	PHD	80	U Wash	1987
Dessler, Gary	C-Pr	Fla Internat		END	PHD	73	CUNY	1971
DeSunctis, Geraldine	Prof	Duke	9	Z	PHD	82	Tx Tech	1994
Deszca, Gene	Assoc	Wilfrid Laur	5	E	PHD		York	1980
Dethy, Ray	Prof	Central Conn	13	AI	PHD	63	Ohio St	1973
DeVader, Christy L.	Assoc	Loyola-Maryl	1	En	PHD		Akron	1987
Devience, Alexander	Assoc	DePaul			JD		Loyola	
Devinatz, Victor	Asst	Illinois St	5		PHD		Minn	1990
DeVito, Raffaele	Assoc	Emporia St	13	Y	EDD	82	Northeas	8-82
DeVivo, Rosemarie	Assoc	Quinnipiac	12		PHD		Minn	
Devoe, Robert	Retir	CS-Long Bch	7	IUVZ	MBA	59	UCLA	1968
DeVogt, John Frederick	Prof	Wash & Lee	47	JUV	PHD	66	N Carol	1962
Dewan, Rajiv	Asst	Rochester	9	Z	PHD	86	Rochest	1994
Dewan, Shashi	Assoc	Winona State			PHD		India	1988
Dewar, Robert D.	Assoc	Northwestern	2	E	PHD	76	Wiscon	1974
Dewasthali, Arun	Assoc	Wake Forest	7	UV	PHD		Delaware	9-75
Dewe, P. J.	Prof	Massey Univ	25	EG	PHD	84	London	1980
Dewhirst, H. Dudley	Prof	Tennessee	23	DEIH	PHD	69	Texas	6-69
Dewhurst, Frank W.	Lect	Manches Inst	7	U	MSC		Manchest	9-80
DeWitt, Calvin	Asst	E New Mexico	79	UVZ	PHD	93	Houston	1987
DeWitt, Rocki-Lee	Asst	Penn State	3	BIN	ABD		Columbia	1989
Dexter, Albert	Assoc	British Colu	9	Z	PHD	70	Columbia	1971
Dexter, Carolyn R.	Prof	Penn St-Harr	2	ERY	PHD	67	Columbia	1969
DeZoort, Frank	Prof	Stetson	78	HUY	PHD		Georgia	1973
Dhar, Vasant	Assoc	New York U	9	Z	PHD	84	Pitt	
Dhiman, Satinder	Asst	Woodbury	1	H	MBA		W Coast	9-92
Dhir, Krishna S.	Dir	Penn St-Harr	3	IV	PHD	75	Colorado	1991
Diaby, Moustopha	Assoc	Connecticut	7	U	PHD	87	SUNY-Buf	9-94
DiBacco, Tom	Prof	American U	4	BL	PHD	65	American	1965
DiBattisa, Ronald	Assoc	Bryant	25	EJN	PHD	79	Ariz St	1-85
Dibble, Richard	Assoc	NY Inst Tech	15		PHD			
DiBella, Anthony J.	VAsst	Boston Coll	1	EHFV	PHD	92	MIT	9-92
Dick, James	Asst	Jamestown	34	IJKN	MBA	88	Moorhead	1984
Dick, Richard J.	Asst	Missouri Wes		NW	MA		N Colo	1985
Dickie, Robert B.	Assoc	Boston Univ	4	K	JD		Yale	
Dickson, Dale L.	Prof	Mesa State	16	S	EDD		N Colo	1969
Dickson, Warren L.	Asst	Ithaca	9	Z	ABD	91	Oklahoma	8-90
Diddams, Margaret	Asst	Seattle Pac	57	NOPQ	PHD	94	NYU	9-93
Diehl, Pidge L.	Prof	St Thomas-FL	27	FGPX	EDD			1983
Diehr, George E.	Prof	CS-S Marcos	7	V	PHD	69	UCLA	1990
Dienesch, Richard M.	Asst	Loyola-Chicg	25	EUN	PHD	87	Ga Tech	8-88
Dierickx, Ingemar	Assoc	INSEAD	3	I	PHD	85	Harvard	9-85
Diersing, Robert J.	Assoc	Tx A&M-Kings	9	Z	PHD	91	Tx A&M	1990
Dietert, Judy	Lect	SW Texas St	6	S	MBA	80	SW Tx St	1984

Name	Rank	Institution			Degree		School	
Donnelly, Robert S.	Prof	Frostburg St	5	OP	EDD	77	Mass	8-76
Donohue, Karen L.	Lect	Pennsylvania			MS		Northwes	1992
Dopp, John A.	Prof	San Fran St	12	EHDF	DA	78	Lehigh	1979
Doran, George	SLect	Arizona St	6		PHD			
Dorf, Richard C.	Prof	Cal-Davis	1	D	PHD		Navy Pos	
Dorfman, Peter W.	Prof	New Mex St	52	ENY	PHD	72	Maryland	1978

  Robert O. Anderson Distinguished Professor

Name	Rank	Institution			Degree		School	
Dorrian, Anne M.	Asst	Ohio Wesley	3		MBA	82	Ohio St	1992
Dorris, James	Prof	Mass-Dartmou			PHD	75	S Illin	1983
Dorsett, Dovalee	Assoc	Baylor		V	PHD		So Meth	1987
Dorsett, Herman W.	Assoc	Fla Internat		EN	EDD	69	Columbia	1972
Dorweiler, Vernon P.	Assoc	Mich Tech	34	IKMY	PHD	59	Iowa	1985
Dory, John	Assoc	Pace	3		DBA		Harvard	
Dosier, Lloyd N.	Assoc	Geo Southern	5	NQ	MBA	66	Geo St	1968
DosSantos, Brain	Assoc	Louisville	9	Z	PHD	82	Case Wes	8-93
Dossett, Dennis L.	Assoc	Mo-St Louis	25	EN	PHD	78	U Wash	1982
Dotan, Amihud	Assoc	Tel Aviv Un		FM	PHD	77	Cornell	1978
Doty, D. Harold	Asst	Arkansas	32	IH	PHD	90	Texas	1990
Doubell, Jennifer		New So Wales						
Doucet, Rene	Assoc	HEC-Montreal	45	KQY	LLM		Montreal	1971
Dougherty, Deborah Jane	Asst	McGill Univ	3		PHD	87	MIT	1987
Dougherty, Thomas W.	Prof	Missouri	25	EN	PHD	81	Houston	1979
Douglas, John	Prof	Miami U-Ohio	1	Y	PHD	60	Cornell	8-73
Douglas, Max E.	Prof	Indiana St	26	S	EDD		Indiana	8-68
Dove, Duane	C-Pr	Sonoma State	5	QH	PHD	71	Fla St	9-86
Dow, Fred	Prof	US Intl	8	Y	PHD		Yale	1978
Dowd, James J. Jr.	Asst	Virginia	2	E	DBA	87	Harvard	
Dowling, J. B.	Assoc	Queen's Univ	4	LM	PHD	78	Stanford	1979
Dowling, Michael J.	Assoc	Georgia	36	ITY	PHD	88	Texas	1988
Dowling, Robert	Prof	CS-Dominguez	6	S	DBA	77	S Calif	1973
Dowling, Tom	Inst	Oregon State	2	E				
Downey, H. Kirk	Dean	Tx Christian	38	E	PHD	74	Penn St	1983
Downie, Bryan M.	D-Pr	Queen's Univ	5	Q	PHD	70	Chicago	1968
Downing, Charles E.	Asst	Boston Coll	97	ZV	PHD	94	Northwes	9-94
Downs, Brian	Inst	So Methodist			PHD	91	Cinn	
Downs, Larry	Asst	Nichols Col			MBA		Mich St	
Doyle, J. R.	Lect	Univ Bath	9	Z	DPHL			
Doyle, Richard B.	Assoc	Naval Postgr	1	A	PHD	84	U Wash	1-90
Doyle, Stephen X.	Assoc	Iona	2	EFHN	DBA	76	Harvard	1990
Doz, Yves L.	Prof	INSEAD	8	YI	DBA	76	Harvard	9-80
Drago, William	Asst	Wis-Whitewat	3	HILM	PHD	90	Arkansas	1990
Dragseth, Deborah M.	Asst	Dickinson St	13		MBA	89	S Dakota	9-89
Draguo, John	Inst	Ball State	17		MBA		Indiana	1988
Drake, Bruce H.	Assoc	Portland	2	H	PHD	76	U Wash	1987
Draman, Rexford	Asst	Alabama-Birm	73	U	ABD		Georgia	1994
Dranove, David	Assoc	Northwestern	17	CU	PHD	83	Stanford	
Drazin, Robert	Assoc	Emory	2	H	PHD	82	Penn	1988
Drebes, Charles B.	Prof	St Louis			DSC	69	Wash U	
Dreher, George F.	Prof	Indiana	5	N	PHD	77	Houston	1987
Drehmer, David E.	Assoc	DePaul			PHD		Ill Tech	
Dreifus, Suzanne	Assoc	Detroit Merc			JD	86	Detroit	1986
Drennan, Judy	Lect	Deakin-Burwo	12	SZ	MED		Melbourn	
Drewry, L. Aubrey	Prof	Birminghm So	8	LY	PHD	60	Virginia	1977
Drexel, Cynthia	Prof	Western St	79		PHD	90	Brig Yg	1982
Drexler, John A. Jr.	Assoc	Oregon State	2	E	PHD	75	Michigan	1980
Drinka, Dennis E.	Lect	Tx-S Antonio						
Driver, Michael J.	Prof	So Calif	2	EFH	PHD		Princeton	1968
Driver, Russell W.	Prof	Oklahoma	25	&ENK	PHD	79	Georgia	1-79
Drosen, James W.	Assoc	No Michigan			PHD	83	Northwes	
Drost, Donald A.	Assoc	CS-San Bern	35	IN	PHD	84	Va Tech	1987
Drucker, Peter F.	Prof	Claremont Gr	12		DRJU		Frankfur	1971

  Clarke Professor of Social Science & Management

Name	Rank	Institution			Degree		School	
Drummond, Graeme	Lect	Napier Univ	37	IYZ	MBA			1985
Drury, D.	Prof	McGill Univ	1		PHD		Northwes	1976
Dry, Eddie	Lect	New Mexico			PHD	75	Tx A&M	
Dsouza, Derrick	Asst	North Texas	38	ISUY	PHD	90	Geo St	1989
Duan, J. C.	Assoc	McGill Univ	1		PHD		Madison	1986
Duarte, Neville	Asst	Auburn-Montg	2	E	PHD	88	Florida	1989
Dubois, Cathy L. Z.	Asst	Kent State			PHD		Minn	1992
Dubose, Phillip B.	Assoc	Jms Madison	12	E	PHD	83	N Carol	9-83
Dubrin, Andrew J.	Prof	Rochest Tech			PHD	60	Mich St	1970
Duchan, Alan I.	C-Ac	Canisius	9	Z	PHD	72	Wiscon	1973
Duchon, Dennis J.	Asst	Tx-S Antonio						
Duckworth, Douglas	Prof	Univ Leeds	2	EF	PHD	76	Leeds	1971
Dudycha, Arthur	Prof	Wis-Parkside	7	V	PHD	67	Ohio St	8-77
Duff, A.	Assoc	McGill Univ	1		MA		Cantab	1968
Duff, Thomas B.	Dean	Minn-Duluth	9	Z	PHD	76	Minn	1974
Duffy, Carol	Asst	Murdoch Univ	5	N	MSC		Manchest	1991
Duffy, Charles	Assoc	Iona	25	EQYI	EDD	80	Columbia	1972
Duffy, Jack F.	Assoc	Dalhousie U	2	E	PHD		Iowa St	

Name	Rank	School			Degree		University	
Duffy, Jo Ann	Asst	Sam Houston			PHD	87	Texas	1988
Dufner, Donna	Asst	Polytechnic			PHD		Rutgers	
Dufour, Yvon	Lect	HEC-Montreal	35	CDI	PHD		Worwick	
Dugal, Sanjiv	Asst	Rhode Island	34	IYJ	PHD	91	Mass	1989
Dugan, Sloane	Assoc	Univ Calgary	25	FOP	PHD	81	Syracuse	1980
Dugas, J.	Lect	U Newcastle	59	FNP	MED		Middlese	
Duguay, Cluade R.	Assoc	HEC-Montreal	7	UVX	MPH		Yale	
Duhon, David	Assoc	So Miss	36	ISTY	PHD	81	LSU	1988
Duke, Robert	Assoc	Univ Leeds	39	I	MBA	85	Bradford	1987
Dukerich, Janet M.	Assoc	Texas	2	EHJ	PHD	85	Minn	1989
Dukes, Thomas A.	C-Pr	Longwood	18	EY	DBA	83	La Tech	1990
Dulek, Ronald E.	H-Pr	Alabama		JMY&	PHD	77	Purdue	1977
Dulz, Thomas H.	Assoc	Frostburg St	7	U	PHD		Mich St	8-90
Dumler, Michael P.	Prof	Illinois St	32		PHD		Kentucky	1982
Dumond, Ellen	Assoc	CS-Fullerton	17	U	PHD	86	Indiana	2-91
Dumstorf, Theodore A.	Inst	East Tenn St	1		MA	51	Louisvil	1985
Dunbar, Roger	Assoc	New York U			PHD	70	Cornell	
Duncan, Robert B.	Prof	Northwestern	3	I	PHD	71	Yale	1970
J. L. Kellogg Distinguished Professor of Strategy & Organization Behavior								
Duncan, W. Jack	Prof	Alabama-Birm	3	CI	PHD	69	LSU	
Dunegan, Kenneth J.	Assoc	Cleveland St	2	EF	PHD		Cinn	1987
Dunford, R.	Prof	Victoria NZ	23	EFHI	PHD		Aust Nat	2-94
Dungam, Heather	Assoc	Centenary			MBA		Rutgers	1-84
Dunham, Randall	Prof	Wisconsin	25	EGNX	PHD	75	Illinois	1975
Dunikoski, Robert H.	Assoc	Dallas	9	Z	PHD	84	Tx Tech	8-85
Dunlevy, John K.	Inst	USAF Academy	3	I	MBA		RPI	
Dunn, Craig P.	Asst	San Diego St	4	LM	PHD	92	Indiana	1991
Dunn, J. Paul	Dean	NE Louisiana	6	IST	PHD	70	Arkansas	1968
Distinguished Professor of Entrepreneurship & Small Business								
Dunn, Steven	Asst	Idaho State		UW	PHD	92	Penn St	1993
Dunn, Thomas W.	VProf	Boston Coll	36	BIST	DBA	68	Harvard	9-63
Dunne, James	C-Pr	Dayton	79	VZ	PHD	73	Illinois	1982
Dunning, John	Prof	Rutgers-Newk	8	Y	PHD		SHampton	1988
Dunning, Kenneth A.	Prof	Akron	79	UVZ	PHD	72	Pitt	9-73
Dunphy, Steve	Asst	NE Illinois	36	IY	PHD		Indiana	9-91
Duplaga, Ed	Asst	Bowling Gr	7	U	PHD	90	Iowa	1992
Dupuis, Jean-Pierre	Asst	HEC-Montreal	25	FM	MSC		Montreal	
Durand, L.	Lect	Laurentian	5		MBA		Sher	
Durgee, Jeffrey F.	Assoc	Rensselaer			PHD		Pitt	1982
Durlabhji, Subhash	Asst	NW St of La			PHD		Mich St	
Durnin, Ellen	Asst	So Conn St	25	EQR	ABD	92	CUNY	1990
Durrani, M. A.		Southeastern			MBA			
Durrett, Virginia	Asst	McNeese St						
Dusseau, David t.	VInst	Oregon	28	EY	PHD	92	Oregon	1992
Dustman, Jack	Prof	No Arizona	5	NQ	DBA	70	S Calif	
Dutt, James S.	C-Ac	Bloomsburg	9	Z	PHD		Penn St	
Dutta, Soumitra	Asst	INSEAD	9	Z	PHD	89	Berkeley	9-89
Dutton, Jane E.	C-Pr	Michigan	2	E	PHD	83	Northwes	1989
Dutton, John C.	Assoc	N Carol St	8	Y	PHD	78	Duke	1989
Dutton, John M.	Prof	New York U			MBA	57	Harvard	
Dutton, Richard E.	Prof	South Fla	28	YE	PHD	63	LSU	1963
Duval, Margaret	Asst	Wichita St	36	TCEF	ABD		Texas	9-94
Duxbury, L.	Asst	Carleton Un	9	Z	PHD		Waterloo	
Dwinell, Merlene		Carroll						
Dworkin, James B.	C-Pr	Purdue	2	Q	PHD	77	Minn	1976
Dwyer, Deborah J.	Asst	Toledo	2		PHD		Nebraska	1989
Dwyer, Hubert	Prof	Pace	7		PHD	71	NYU	
Dyas, Gareth P.	C-Ac	INSEAD	3	I	DBA	72	Harvard	1-73
Dyck, Bruno	Asst	U Manitoba	12	EH	PHD		Alberta	1990
Dyck, Harold	Assoc	CS-San Bern	7	U	PHD	82	Purdue	1989
Dyer, Gibb	C-Ac	Brigham Yg	26	STOE	PHD	84	MIT	1984
Dyer, James S.	Prof	Texas	7	UV	PHD	69	Texas	1978
Dyer, Jeffrey H.	Asst	Pennsylvania	38	YI	PHD	93	UCLA	7-93
Stanley Goldstein Term Assistant Professor of Management								
Dyer, L.	Assoc	Concordia U						
Dyke, L.	Lect	Carleton Un	2	E	PHD		Queens	
Dyson, David	Prof	Oral Roberts	38	IY	PHD	88	Arkansas	8-85
Eager, Wendy M.	Asst	Eastern Wash	52	NPE	PHD	90	Penn St	1989
Eagle, Bruce	Assoc	St Cloud St			ABD		Georgia	1993
Earl, Michael J.	Prof	London Bus	39	ZYI	MSC		Warwick	1991
Andersen Consulting Professor of Information Management								
Earl, Ronald	Assoc	Sam Houston			PHD	78	Tx A&M	1971
Earley, P. Christopher	Asoc	Calif-Irvine	2	E	PHD	84	Illinios	1992
Earnshaw, Jill M.	Lect	Manches Inst	5	K	BLAW			1991
Easley, Eddie	Prof	Wake Forest			PHD		Iowa St	9-84
Eason, Thomas	Prof	Savannah St	6		PHD	68	Miss	1979
Easterby-Smith, M. P. V.	SLect	U Lancaster	25	NOPY	PHD		Durham	
Eastman, Kenneth K.	Asst	Oklahoma St	2	E	PHD	89	Nebraska	8-89
Eastman, Wayne	Asst	Rutgers-Newk	8	Y	JD		Harvard	1991
Eastwood, Karen	Asst	Niagara						

Name	Rank	School			Degree		University	
Fekula, Michael J.	Asst	USAF Academy	2	I	ABD		Penn St	
Felan, Joe E. III	Asst	Bucknell	7	V	ABD		S Carol	9-93
Felch, Robert I.					DBA	78	Fla St	
Feldberg, Meyer	Dean	Columbia	28	EY	PHD	69	Capetown	1989
Feldman, Daniel Charles	Prof	So Carolina			PHD	76	Yale	8-89
Feldman, Howard D.	Assoc	Portland			PHD	76	Geo St	1991
Feldman, Steven P.	Assoc	Case Western	3		PHD		Penn	
Feldman, Wallace	Prof	SUNY-Plattsb	38	SY	DBA	73	Harvard	1986
Feldstein, Paul J.	Prof	Calif-Irvine			PHD	61	Chicago	1987
Feltes, Patricia E.	Asst	SW Missouri	3	Y	PHD	88	Nebraska	1988
Fenton, Howard	Asst	St Scholasti			MBA		Geo Maso	1989
Fenton, James W. Jr.	Dean$	Fran Marion	56	N	PHD	81	Iowa	1-89
Forrest Williams Professor of Entrepreneuship & Human Resources								
Fenwick, Graham D.	Lect	Canterbury	14	L	PHD	84	Canterbu	1990
Ferdows, Kasra	Prof	Georgetown	7	UYI	PHD	72	Wiscon	1990
Ference, Tom	Prof	Columbia	35	IO	PHD	67	Car Mel	1966
Ferguson, R. Wayne	Prof	St Marys-Txs			PHD	72	North Tx	
Myra Stafford Pryor Professor of Free Enterprise								
Ferguson, Wade	Prof	W Kentucky	7	V	PHD	77	Ohio St	1985
Ferguson, William	Assoc	Central Conn	38	ISY	DPS	87	Pace	1980
Ferk, Dyanne	Asst	Sangamon St	12	EFN	MBA		S Illin	1993
Fernald, Lloyd W.	Assoc	Cen Florida	25	DEF	DBA	81	Geo Wash	1983
Fernandez, Eugenia	Asst	Butler	9	Z	PHD	88	Purdue	1990
Fernandez, Lucyann	Assoc	P Rico-Mayag	9		MS	80	Tx A&M	1-81
Fernandez, Pablo	Assoc	Univ Navarra	7	V	PHD		Harvard	4-85
Ferner, Jack D.	Lect	Wake Fr-MBA	3	I	MBA	55	Harvard	1971
Fernie, June M.	SLect	Napier Univ	17	CUVX	PHD			1989
Ferratt, Thomas	Prof	Dayton	9	PZ	PHD	74	Ohio St	1986
Ferris, Mark	Asst	St Louis			PHD		Illinois	
Ferris, William P.	Prof	W New Eng	5	N	PHD		Rensshela	1981
Ferry, Diane	Assoc	Delaware			PHD	78	Penn	1979
Fesmire, Walker	Prof	Mich-Flint	1	A	PHD	82	Miss	1982
Fethke, Gary C.	Prof	Iowa	7	U	PHD	68	Iowa	1975
Fichman, Mark	Assoc	Carnegie Mel	2	E	PHD	82	Michigan	1980
Fidrych, Robert	Assoc	Wis-Plattev	4	J	LLM	79	Mo-KC	1980
Fiebelkorn, George	Prof	Marymount			PHD		Geo St	1986
Fiedler, Anne M.	Asst	Barry	13	EN	PHD	93	Fla Intl	9-94
Fiegener, Mark	Asst	Oregon State	3	I	PHD	90	Penn	1990
Field, Richard	Prof	Univ Alberta	2	E	PHD	81	Toronto	1985
Fields, Mitchell	Assoc	Univ Windsor	25	EFNP	PHD	83	Wayne St	1985
Fields, W. Calvin III	Asst	W Illinois			PHD	86	Tx-Dallas	1986
Fiet, James O.	Asst	Clemson			PHD		Tx A&M	1992
Figler, Robert A.	Assoc	Akron	5	QNH	PHD	84	W Virg	9-85
Fildes, R.	Prof	U Lancaster	71	UVZ	PHD		Calif	
Filemon, Campo-Flores	Prof	CS-Long Bch	6	JRTY	PHD	68	UCLA	1972
Filion, Louis Jacques	Assoc	HEC-Montreal			PHD		Lancastr	
Filley, Alan C.	Prof	Wisconsin	26	EHST	PHD	62	Ohio St	
Finch, Byron J.	Assoc	Miami U-Ohio	7	U	PHD	86	Georgia	8-86
Findley, Hank	Asst	Troy St	25	ENQU	ABD	93	Auburn	1992
Fine, Charles H.	Assoc	MIT	7	U	PHD			
Fine, M. A.	Asst	Lakehead U	9	Z	MBA		Boston C	1-82
Fineman, S.	Read	Univ Bath	2	EFG	PHD			
Fink, Dieter	Lect	Australian N	9	Z	DCOM	91	S Africa	1994
Fink, Laurence	Asst	George Mason	52	N	PHD	90	Purdue	1988
Fink, Ross L.	Asst	Bradley	7	UV	PHD	89	Alabama	1991
Fink, Stephen L.	Prof	New Hampshir	2	E	PHD	59	West Res	1968
Finkelstein, Sydney	Assoc	Dartmouth	3	IQ	PHD	88	Columbia	1994
Finlay, A.	Lect	U Newcastle	45	KLY	BLS		Macquari	
Finlay, Paul N.	Prof	Loughborough	7	V	PHD		Nottingh	
Finley, Lawrence K.	Prof	W Kentucky	36	ST	PHD	71	Ohio St	1977
Finney, Bartlett	Assoc	Emporia St	25		PHD	80	Kan St	8-79
Fiol, C. Marlene	Asst	Colo-Denver	23	HIT	PHD	86	Illinois	1991
Fiore, Mike	Assoc	Lg Isl-Post			PHD		NYU	
Fiorito, Jack T.	Prof	Florida St	57	QHN	PHD	80	Illinois	8-90
Firenze, Louis J.	D-Pr	Northwood	35	BDEN	PHD	82	Mich St	1974
Fischer, Arthur K.	Assoc	Pittsburg St	25	CEHN	PHD	84	Missouri	1988
Fischer, Gregory	Prof	Duke	2	CEI	PHD	72	Michigan	1990
Fischer, Marla	Prof	Western Conn	7	X	PHD		Conn	
Fischl, Louis	Retir	San Jose St	4	K	JD	66	Santa Cl	1956
Fish, Bob	Asst	Detroit Merc			MA	82	Wayne St	1986
Fish, Lynn	Asst	Canisius	7	UV	PHD	93	SUNY-Buf	1993
Fisher, Cynthia D.	Assoc	Bond Univ	25	ENY	PHD	78	Purdue	8-90
Fisher, Dalmar	Assoc	Boston Coll	23	EFO	DBA	68	Harvard	9-68
Fisher, Harry E.	Assoc	Teikyo Mary	52	DN	MBA	86	Illinois	8-87
Fisher, Marshall L.	Prof	Pennsylvania			PHD	70	MIT	1975
Stephen J. Heyman Professor								
Fisher, Phil	Dean	So Indiana	23	IH	PHD	79	Stanford	1991
Fisher, R.		Mt St Vincen	29	FBVZ	PHD	92	Bath	1984
Fisher, Warren W.	Assoc	S F Austin	7	UV	PHD	83	Texas	1990
Fisher, William J.	Retir	East Tenn St	1	1993	EDD	63	Colorado	1966

Name	Rank	School			Deg		Univ	Year
Fitch, H. Gordon	Prof	Kansas	3	L	PHD	69	Purdue	1967
Fitzgerald, Elizabeth	Asst	Kennesaw St	2	F	PHD	92	Syracuse	1992
Fitzgerald, Patricia	Prof	St Marys-Cnd	23	EIX	PHD	74	N Colo	1976
Fitzgibbons, Dale E.	Asst	Illinois St	2		PHD		Illinois	1988
Fitzpatarick, Kathy E.	C-Pr	Appalach St	7	UV	PHD		Clemson	1983
Fitzpatrick, Richard C.	Assoc	Manhattan	24	NL	PHD	84	SUNY-Alb	1984
Fitzpatrick, William	Asst	Villanova	32	EHIZ	PHD	86	Maryland	1983
Fitzsimmons, James A.	Prof	Texas	7	UV	PHD	70	UCLA	1971
Fladmoe-Lindquist, Karin	Asst	Utah	86	YI	PHD	90	Minn	1990
Flamholtz, Eric G.	Prof	UCLA	5	N	PHD	69	Michigan	1973
Flanagan, David	Asst	W Michigan	38	IY	PHD	92	Indiana	1992
Flanagan, John	SLect	U Wollongong			BSC		NS Wales	8-88
Flanagan, Michael	Asst	Illinois Tch						1993
Flanagan, Michael F.	Prof	CS-Bakersf	25	EHNX	PHD			1986
Flannery, William T.	Assoc	Tx-S Antonio			PHD	74	Houston	
Flatt, Robert	Adj	Rice	7	U	MBA	73	Harvard	1988
Flax, Stanley	Asst	St Thomas-FL	38		MBA			1986
Fleck, Robert A. Jr.	Prof	Columbus	9	Z	PHD	71	Illinois	1986
Foundation Distinguished Professor								
Fleenor, C. Patrick	C-Pr	Seattle	23	IY	PHD	75	U Wash	1973
Fleidner, Eugene	Asst	Texas A&M		U	DBA	89	Indiana	1988
Fleisher, Craig	Assoc	Wilfrid Laur	34	I	PHD		Pitt	1993
Fleming, Maureen J.	Prof	Montana	25	YEFN	PHD	69	S Illin	1971
Fleming, Robert	Dean$	Rowan Col NJ	39	IJNZ	EDD	86	Temple	1989
Fleming, Robert F.	Inst	Delta State	13	I	MBA	87	S Miss	8-92
Fletcher, K.	Prof	Strathclyde	3		PHD			
Flor, N.	Asst	Carnegie Mel	9	Z	PHD		San Dgo	1994
Flores, Benito E.	Prof	Texas A&M		U	PHD	69	Houston	1984
Flores, Luis G.	Assoc	No Illinois	38	IY	PHD		Tx Tech	
Florey, Randall	C-Ac	Tx-Brownsvil		Mktg	PHD	82	North Tx	1992
Florkowski, Gary W.	Asst	Pittsburgh	5		PHD		Syracuse	
Flowers, A. Dale	Assoc	Case Western			DBA	72	Indiana	
Floyd, Barry D.	Assoc	Cal Poly-SLO	9	Z	PHD	82	Michigan	1990
Floyd, Steve	Asst	Alabama-Hunt	9	Z	PHD		Georgia	1984
Floyd, Steven W.	Assoc	Connecticut	3	I	PHD	81	Colorado	1986
Flueck, John	Visit	Nev-L Vegas			PHD		Chicago	1992
Flynn, Barbara B.	Assoc	Iowa State	7	U	DBA	84	Indiana	1987
Flynn, David M.	Assoc	Hofstra	34	YIT	PHD	79	Mass	9-87
Flynn, E. James	Assoc	Iowa State	31	I	PHD	85	Indiana	1987
Flynn, J.		Humberside	7					
Flynn, Warren R.	Prof	So Alabama	23	EFGI	PHD	73	Colorado	1988
Foegen, George	Assoc	Metro State	16	DSZ	DBA	71	Geo Wash	1986
Foegen, Joseph H.	Prof	Winona State			PHD		Wiscon	1958
Fogel, Daniel	Prof	Pittsburgh	2		PHD		Wiscon	
Fogel, Robert W.	Prof	Chicago	4	JL	PHD	63	JHopkins	1963
Charles R. Walgreen Professor of American Institutions								
Fogel, Walter A.	Retir	UCLA	5	1994	PHD	62	MIT	1962
Fogg, Dana T.	Inst	Tampa	15	NQ	MS	75	Columbia	1989
Fogliasso, Christine	Assoc	Pittsburg St	4	JKLR	JD	79	Kansas	1984
Fok, Vincent S. C.	ALect	City Poly HK	36	ISTY	MBA	91	HongKong	2-93
Fok, Wing M.	C-Ac	Loyola-N Orl	6	UV	DBA	91	Geo St	1988
Fok, Yee Man L.	Asst	New Orleans	2	Z	BSC	86	Hong Kon	8-89
Folk, Hugh	C-Pr	Hawaii-Manoa			PHD	60	Duke	
Folta, Timothy	Asst	Kentucky	36	IST	PHD	94	Purdue	1994
Fombrun, Charles	Prof	New York U			PHD	80	Columbia	
Fondas, Nanette	Asst	Cal-Riversid	25	EQ	DBA		Harvard	
Fong, Duncan	Assoc	Penn State	7	V	PHD		Purdue	
Font, Vicente	Prof	Univ Navarra	7	V	PHD		Barcelon	O-76
Fontrodona, Juan	Asst	Univ Navarra	2	H	MBA		Navarra	6-90
Foo, Suan Tong	Asst	Marquette	7	UV	PHD	90	Wiscon	1990
Forbes, J. Benjamin	Prof	John Carroll			PHD		Akron	1975
Forbes, Jessie L.	Assoc	Montevallo	2		MBE		Monteval	1981
Forbes, Paul	Asst	Seton Hall			BS	49	Fordham	
Ford, Cameron M.	Asst	Rutgers-Newk	23	DEI	PHD	90	Penn St	1989
Ford, David L. Jr.	Prof	Texas-Dallas	2	E	PHD	72	Wiscon	1975
Ford, F. Nelson	Asst	Auburn	9	Z	PHD	82	Alabama	9-82
Ford, Gerald	Assoc	CS-Long Bch	36	DJKS	DBA	76	S Calif	1969
Ford, I. D.	Prof	Univ Bath	6	St	PHD			
Ford, Jeffrey D.	Assoc	Ohio State	2	EH	PHD	75	Ohio St	1983
Ford, John P.	Assoc	Eastern Wash	9	ZV	MS	65	Wash St	1970
Ford, Kenneth C.	Asst	St Paul's	9	Z	MBA			1991
Ford, Mark	Inst	MidAmer Naz	56	NS	JD			1991
Ford, Roger H.	Assoc	Jms Madison	36	ST	PHD	86	Syracuse	9-85
Ford, Terrell F.	Prof	So Alabama	23	IH	PHD	69	Miss	1970
Forintos, Bruce M.	Assoc	No Iowa			PHD	87	Michigan	2-93
Forker, J. J.	Lect	Univ Bristol	78	L	MS	74		1976
Forker, Laura B.	Asst	Boston Univ			PHD		Ariz St	1994
Forker, Laura B.	Asst	Michigan St	7	W	PHD	93	Arizona	8-92
Forman, Ernest	Prof	George Wash	7	V	DSC	75	Geo Wash	
Forman, Janis S.	Adj	UCLA	1	&	PHD	80	Rutgers	1982

Name	Rank	School			Degree		University	Year
Formisano, Roger A.			7	V	PHD	76	N Carol	
Forough, Abbas	Assoc	So Indiana	9	Z	PHD	90	Indiana	1983
Forrest, A.	Assoc	Univ Windsor	25	PNQR	PHD		Warwick	1986
Forsaith, David M.	LectB	Flinders Un	6	ST	MSC	75	London	7-90
Forsgren, Roderick A.	Prof	Maine			DBA	65	Colorado	1965
Forst, Frank	Assoc	Loyola-Chicg			PHD		Illinois	1986
Fortado, Bruce	Asst	North Fla	5	NQ	PHD	86	Case Wes	1986
Fortenberry, Ed	C	Central Okla			EDD	70	Oklahoma	8-62
Fortman, Marvin	Assoc	Arizona						
Fossum, John A.	Prof	Minnesota	5	N	PHD	75	Mich St	
Foster, Howard	Asst$	Clayton St	2		MBA		Geo St	1989
Foster, Howard G.	Prof	SUNY-Buffalo	5	Q	PHD	69	Cornell	9-69
Foster, Jerry	Assoc	Colorado	7	W	PHD	73	Syrcuse	1973
Foster, K. Dale	Asst	Memorial Un	79	VZ	PHD	94	Dalhousi	1989
Foster, Lawrence W.	Prof	Alabama	38	IY	PHD	73	Texas	1984
Fotopoulos, Stergios	Assoc	Wash State			PHD		Liverpol	
Fottler, Myron D.	Prof	Alabama-Birm	15		PHD	70	Columbia	1970
Foulkes, Fred K.	C-Pr	Boston Univ	5	N	DBA		Harvard	
Fountain, Gwen	Asst	Butler	1	A	PHD	72	Michigan	1986
Fountain, Patrick	Inst	East Central	1		MS	88		1988
Fournier, Bruce	Assoc	Wilfrid Laur	2	EH	PHD		York	1978
Fowler, Aubrey	Assoc	Youngstown	57	NQP	PHD	84	Geo St	9-91
Fowler, George C.	Assoc	Texas A&M		Z	PHD	76	Tx A&M	1979
Fowler, Karen L.	Assoc	No Colorado	3		PHD	85	Nebraska	
Fowler, Oscar S.	H-Ac	Tennessee	78	U	PHD	72	Georgia	9-71
Fowlkes, Melinda J.	Asst	Longwood	12	D	MBA	90	Va Comm	1976
Fox, Douglas M.	Prof	Western Conn	14	AFLJ	PHD		Columbia	1978
Fox, Isaac	Asst	Wash State						
Fox, Jeremy B.	Assoc	Appalach St	5	NQ	PHD		Va Tech	1988
Fox, Marianne	Lect	Butler	9	Z	MBA	81	Indiana	1988
Fox, Marilyn	Asst	Mankato St			PHD	90	Nebraska	1990
Fox, S.	Lect	U Lancaster	25	NOP	PHD		Manchest	
Fox, William	Inst	New York U			MBA			
Fox, William M.	Retir	Florida	25	EFNP	PHD	54	Ohio St	1954
Fox-Wolfgramm, Susan	Asst	San Fran St	23	AHIT	PHD	91	Tx Tech	1991
Fraguas, Rafael	Asst	Univ Navarra	3	I	MBA		Navarra	6-82
Frame, David	Prof	George Wash	9	Z	PHD			
Francesco, Anne Marie	Assoc	Pace	82	YERN	PHD	77	Ohio St	6-90
Francis, G. James	Prof	Colorado St	23	EFHI	PHD	71	Nebraska	1970
Francis, Helen	Lect	Napier Univ	5	FNPQ	BSC			1989
Frand, Jason L.	Asst	UCLA	9	Z	PHD	76	UCLA	1979
Frank, Ellen J.	Prof	So Conn St	52	NRX	PHD	73	Purdue	1983
Frank, Jonathan	Assoc	Suffolk	9	Z	PHD	78	Strathcl	1983
Frank, Murray	Assoc	British Colu	31	IL	PHD	86	Queen's	1988
Franke, Richard H.	Prof	Loyola-Maryl	38	IY	PHD	74	Rochest	1984
Frankenberger, John	Asst	Georgia Col	17	GN	PHD	90	North Tx	1986
Frankenstein, J.	Assoc	Un Hong Kong	38	IY	PHD			1-91
Frankforter, Steven A.	Asst	Ind-So Bend	3		PHD	90	U Wash	8-91
Frankl, Razelle	Assoc	Rowan Col NJ	25	FHR	PHD	84	Bryn Maw	1983
Franklin, Carter L. II	Prof	Houston Bapt	78	UVYZ	PHD	68	Purdue	1974
Franklin, Geralyn M.	C-Ac	S F Austin	52	NQRS	PHD	89	North Tx	1988
Franklin, M.	Assoc	Concordia U						
Franot, Frieda	Prof	British Colu	7	V	PHD	74	Texas	1975
Franz, Charles	Assoc	Missouri	9	Z	PHD	79	Nebraska	1985
Franz, Lori S.	Prof	Missouri	7	V	PHD	80	Nebraska	1985
Franz, Ranoal	Asst	Seattle Pac	24	HEFD	PHD	91	Stanford	9-91
Frary, Paul E.	H-Pr	Muhlenberg	15		PHD		Arkansas	9-90
Frase, Donald W.	Assoc	SUNY-Buffalo	31	IUD	MBA	64	SUNY-Buf	9-88
Fraser, Michele	Inst	Univ Calgary	25	EN	PHD	82	Minn	1990
Fraser, N.	Assoc	Un Waterloo	7	V	PHD	83	Waterloo	1983
Frasier, David W.	Assoc	Houghton	18	YJ	ABD		Nova	1979
Frayne, Colette	Assoc	Cal Poly-SLO	25	ENPY	PHD	86	U Wash	1992
Fredenberger, William B.	Asst	Valdosta St	9	Z	PHD	90	Georgia	1988
Fredendall, Lawrence	Asst	Clemson	7	UV	PHD	90	Michigan	1990
Frederick, Elizabeth	Assoc	Metro State	25	EJNQ	PHD	85	Maryland	1987
Frederickson, E. Wayne	Lect	Tx-El Paso	3	I	PHD	70	Baylor	1994
Frederikson, Peter C.	Prof	Naval Postgr	78	VY	PHD	74	Wash St	1974
Fredrickson, James W.	Assoc	Texas	3	IH	PHD	80	U Wash	1990
Fredriksen, Tor	Assoc	Norwegian			ABD			
Freed, Gerry	Prof	U Wollongong	38	DIY	BSC	58	Manchest	O-91
Freed, Ned	Prof	Portland	7	U	PHD	78	Colorado	
Freed, Rusty	Asst	Tarleton St	25	NS	MBA		Tarleton	1993
Freedman, Richard D.	Prof	New York U			PHD	67	NYU	
Freedman, Sara M.	Prof	Houston	2	ER	PHD	76	N Carol	8-76
Freedman, Stuart	Prof	Mass-Lowell	2	E	PHD	77	Cornell	
Freeland, James R.	Prof	Virg-Grad	7	UVX	PHD	73	Ga Tech	1979
Sponsors Professor of Business Adm								
Freeley, James	Assoc	Lg Isl-Post			PHD		Fordham	
Freeman, Eldridge T. Jr.	Assoc	Chicago St			PHD		Cal Coas	1973
Freeman, Everette	Asst	Case Western	5		EDD	83	Rutgers	1992

Freeman, James	Assoc	Kentucky	4	K	LLM	81	Harvard	1984
Freeman, James M	Lect	Manches Inst	7	U	PHD		Salford	9-81
Freeman, Mark	Inst	Tuskegee						
Freeman, R. Edward	Prof	Virg-Grad	3	IJ	PHD		Wash U	1986

Elis and Signe Olsson Professor of Business Administration

Freeman, Raoul J.	C	CS-Dominguez	9	Z	PHD		MIT	1984
Freeman, Sarah	Asst	Wis-Milwauke	2	H	PHD	92	Michigan	1992
Fremgen, Bonnie	Dean$	St Xavier	12	CE	PHD	88	Illinois	1993
French, J. Lawrence	Assoc	Virg Tech	6		PHD	76	Mass	1990
Frendewey, Jim O.	Asst	Mich Tech	7	UVPH	PHD	83	Colorado	1989
Freund, Robert M.	Prof	MIT	7	V	PHD	83	Stanford	

Elisha Gray II Career Development Associate Professor of Management Science

Frew, David R.	Prof	Gannon	2	EG	PHD		Kent St	
Frew, Michael	Assoc	Okla City	12	O	ABD		Oklahoma	8-82
Frey, Harold K.	Assoc	Bloomsburg	9	Z	MS		Elmira	
Frey, Len	Asst	Nicholls St						
Frey, Merle E.	Prof	Rockhurst	32	EFHI	PHD	77	NYU	1981
Frey, Sherwood C.	Prof	Virg-Grad	7	V	PHD		Hopkins	1979

Ethyl Corp. Professor of Business Administration

Friday, Earnest	Asst	Fla Internat		EIF	PHD	80	U Miami	1972
Frideger, Marcia	Asst	Shippensburg			MA	81	Birg Yg	
Fried, Theodore	Assoc	NY Inst Tech	7		MA			
Fried, Vance H.	Assoc	Oklahoma St	3	IT	JD	76	Michigan	1-87
Fried, Yitzhak	Assoc	Wayne State	5	EGN	PHD	85	Illinois	1985
Friedman, Avraham	Assoc	Hebrew Univ			PHD		Chicago	
Friedman, Hershey H.	Prof	CUNY-Brookly	14	L	PHD			1986
Friedman, Raymond A.	Asst	Harvard	25	EN				
Friel, Terri	Asst	E Kentucky	7	UV	PHD	92	So Meth	1991
Frierson, James G.	Prof	East Tenn St	4	KLN	JD	65	Arkansas	1973
Friesen, P.	Prof	McGill Univ	7		PHD		Stanford	1974
Froelich, Karen	Asst	N Dakota St	23	HI	ABD		Minn	1990
Frohlich, Norm	Prof	U Manitoba	14	LA	PHD	71	Princeton	1979
Fronmueller, Michael	Asst	Boise State	3	I	PHD	91	Wash St	1990
Frost, James	Asst	Idaho State	9	Z	ABD		FSU	1993
Frost, Peter J.	Prof	British Colu	2	EL	PHD	73	Minn	1975
Frost, Taggart Ford	Assoc	No Iowa			PHD	81	Brig Yg	8-78
Fry, Elaine Hobbs	Prof	Nicholls St	45	NKJL	DBA	78	Miss St	1978
Fry, Fred L.	C-Pr	Bradley	26	TS	PHD	72	Okla St	1976
Fry, Ronald	Assoc	Case Western	2	E	PHD		MIT	
Frye, Crissie M.	Inst	No Iowa			MBA	89	N Iowa	8-89
Frye, Randy L.	C-Pr	St Fran-Penn	5		MBA	80	Ind-PA	1980
Fryxell, Gerald E.	Assoc	Tennessee	34	ILX	PHD	86	Indiana	9-86
Fucaloro, Anthony	Dean$	Claremont			PHD	69	Arizona	1974
Fuerst, William Lee	Assoc	Texas A&M		Z	PHD	79	Tx Tech	1979
Fujishige, Satoru	Prof	Univ Tsukuba	7	V	DENG	75	Kyota	8-79
Fukami, Cynthia	C-Ac	Denver	2	E	PHD		Northwes	9-83
Fulford, Mark	Asst	Cornell	25	ENP	PHD	92	Indiana	9-91
Fulks, L. Gerald	H-Pr	David Lipsc	18	BISY	DA		Mid Tenn	9-78
Fuller, Donald E.	LectB	Flinders Un	37	AS	PHD	84	Adelaide	1991
Fuller, Floyd	Assoc	Lees-McRae						
Fuller, Frances	Assoc	Ohio Univ	2					
Fuller, J. D.	C-Ac	Un Waterloo	7	V	PHD	80	Brit Col	1979
Fuller, Jack A.	Prof	W Virginia	7	V	PHD	72	Arkansas	1985
Fuller, Lee	Assoc	Gannon	45	Q	JD		Clev St	
Fuller, Mark A.	Asst	Baylor		Z	PHD		Arizona	1992
Fuller, Sally	Asst	U Washington	25		ABD		Wiscon	1992
Fuller, Stephen	Prof	Ohio Univ	12					
Fullerton, Gordon	Asst	Mt Allison U	23		MBA	88	Dalhousi	7-88
Fullop, Liz	Assoc	U Wollongong			PHD		NS Wales	7-94
Fulmer, Robert	Prof	Wm & Mary	3	EI	PHD	65	UCLA	1991

W. Brooks George Professor of Business Administration

Fulmer, William E.	Prof	Clarion	75	NQU	MBA	76	Clarion	8-76
Fulmer, William E.	Dean$	George Mason	3	I	PHD	74	Penn	1993
Fulton, Paul	Dean	No Carolina	4	JKL				1-94
Fults, Gail J.	Prof	CS-Humboldt	12	FU	PHD	85	Claremont	1986
Furniss, Jerry	Assoc	Montana	5	KP	JD	80	Idaho	1987
Fusilier, Marcelline R.	Assoc	NW St of La			PHD		Purdue	
Gabarro, John J.	Prof	Harvard	25	EN				

The UPS Foundation Professor of Human Resources

Gabel, H. Landis	C-Pr	INSEAD	4		PHD	77	Penn	9-82
Gabriel, Albert H.	C-Pr	SW Okla St	5	M	PHD	65	Mich St	1956
Gabriel, Y.	Lect	Univ Bath	2	E	PHD			
Gaddis, Paul O.	Prof	Texas-Dallas	3	I	MS	61	MIT	1979
Gaddis, Richard	Asst	So Nazarane	14		EDD	84	Arkansas	1992
Gaertner, Karen Newman	Assoc	Georgetown	2	EOHJ	PHD	78	Chicago	1984
Gagnon, Roger	Assoc	Wake Fr-MBA	7	UV	PHD	82	Cinn	1988
Gaimon, Cheryl	Prof	Georgia Tech	7	UV	PHD	81	Car Mel	1988
Gaines, Jeannie	Asst	South Fla	52	EHN	PHD	84	Florida	1989
Gaither, Norman	Retir	Texas A&M			PHD	74	Oklahoma	1979
Gaitley, Normandic J. SSJ	Inst	St Joseph	12	ECLR	ABD		Drexel	1994

Name	Rank	School			Degree	Yr	School2	Yr2
Gal-Or, Esther	Prof	Pittsburgh			PHD	80	Northwes	
Galai, Dan	Prof	Hebrew Univ			PHD		Chicago	
Galante, Joseph	Asst	Marywood		K	JD		Cooley	
Galaskiewicz, Joseph	Prof	Minnesota	2	H	PHD	76	Chicago	1976
Galbraith, Craig	Assoc	N Car-Wilmin	36	DITU	PHD	81	Purdue	8-92
Gale, Jeffrey	Prof	Loyola Marym	13	ILY	PHD	76	UCLA	1985
Gales, Lawrence M.	Assoc	Cincinnati	2	E	PHD	87	N Carol	
Gallagher, Charles	Prof	Barry	79	UVZ	DBA	71	Fla St	9-85
Gallagher, Daniel G.	H	Jms Madison	5	NQ	PHD	77	Illinois	9-87
Gallagher, Francis J.	Prof	Bloomsburg	5		MBA	71	Temple	1-72
Gallagher, Michael C.	Prof	Idaho State		E	PHD	75	Tx A&M	1987
Gallagher, Tom	Prof	Alaska SE	24	DJM	PHD	77	Michigan	1991
Galle, William P. Jr.	Prof	New Orleans	21	E	PHD	72	Arkansas	8-85
Galletta, Dennis	Assoc	Pittsburgh	9		PHD		Minn	
Gallo, Miguel Angel	Prof	Univ Navarra	3	I	PHD		ETSII	2-66
Galloway, Rex F.	C-Pr	W Kentucky	13	DI	DBA	70	Miss St	1991
Galloway, Robert D.	Lect	Tx-S Antonio						
Gallupe, R. B.	Assoc	Queen's Univ	9	ZF	PHD	85	Minn	1986
Galvin, Thomas M.	Assoc	No Illinois		U	PHD		Ill Tech	
Gambhir, Dinesh	Asst	F Dick-Madis			PHD		Polytech	
Gander, Mary J.	Prof	Winona State			PHD		Wiscon	1987
Gandhi, Bodapati	Prof	P Rico-Mayag	7		PHD	83	Tx A&M	7-87
Gandhi, Prem P.	Dean	SUNY-Plattsb		Econ	PHD	73	New Scho	9-66
Gandhi, Srinivas	Inst	P Rico-Mayag	7		MPP	91	Harvard	7-88
Ganitsky, Joseph	Prof	Loyola-N Orl			PHD	74	Harvard	
Ganjavi, Ozhand	D-Ac	Laurentian	7	Mgt	PHD	84	W Ontar	7-79
Gannon, Martin J.	Prof	Maryland	23	Y	PHD	69	Columbia	1969
Ganster, Daniel C.	Prof	Arkansas	25	ENG	PHD	78	Purdue	1990
Raymond F. Orr Chair in General Management								
Gantt, Garnewell	Prof	Idaho State		K	DJ	72	Texas	1987
Ganzach, Yoav	Lect	Hebrew Univ			PHD		Columbia	
Gao, Li-Lian	Asst	Hofstra	79	UVZ	PHD	88	Indiana	9-88
Gappa, Joseph A.	Prof	San Fran St	7	VY	PHD	76	Utah	1984
Gara, Kim	Inst	Azusa Pacif	25	EN	MED		Cent St	9-90
Garaventa, Eugene	Assoc	CUNY-Stn Isl	12	AEL	PHD		NYU	1980
Garber, Samuel B.	Asst	DePaul			JD		Illinois	
Garcha, Bikramjit Singh	Prof	Georgia St	7	V	PHD		Ohio St	
Garcia, Joseph E.	Prof	Western Wash	28	EFA	PHD	83	Utah	9-85
Garcia, Thomas	Adj	Southeastern			PHD		Mass	
Gardener, E. P. M.	C-Pr	North Wales	13	DHI	PHD			9-75
Gardiner, Lorraine	Assoc	Auburn	7	UV	PHD	89	Georgia	3-88
Gardiner, Stanley	Asst	Auburn	7	U	PHD	87	Georgia	9-87
Gardner, Donald G.	C-Pr	Colorado Spr	5	NE	PHD	81	Purdue	1-81
Gardner, Everette S. Jr.	C-Pr	Houston	7	U	PHD	78	N Carol	1-87
Gardner, James H.	Prof	Utah	38	IY	PHD	51	Harvard	
Gardner, Margaret	SLect	Griffith Un	5	ANPR	PHD		Sydney	7-82
Gardner, Richard M.	Lect	W Virginia	2	E	MBA	69	W Virg	1989
Gardner, Susan	Prof	CS-Chico						
Gardner, William L.	Asst	Mississippi	12	EP	PHD	84	Fla St	1989
Garfinkle, Robert S.	Prof	Connecticut	79	UZ	PHD	68	J Hopkin	
Gargeya, Vidyaranya	Asst	N Car-Greens	7	U	PHD	91	Geo St	1993
Gargiulo, Martin	Asst	INSEAD	2	EH	PHD	92	Columbia	9-92
Garland, Howard	C-Pr	Delaware			PHD	72	Cornell	
Garland, John S.	Assoc	Kansas	8	Y	DBA		Indiana	1980
Garmat, John	H-Pr	Southeastern			MBA		Conn	
Garnand, John J.	Inst	Colorado			PHD	76	Colorado	1984
Garrett, Suzanne		J.F. Kennedy	7	VR	MBA		JFKenned	9-88
Garris, John M.	Assoc	N Car-Wilmin	7	V	PHD		Clemson	
Garrity, Edward J.	Asst	Canisius	9	Z	PHD	85	Pitt	1990
Garsombke, Diane J.	Assoc	Wis-Superior	23		PHD	83	Tenn	1991
Garstka, Stanley J.	Prof	Yale	1	IS	PHD	70	Car Mel	1978
Gartner, William B.	Assoc	Georgetown	6	T	PHD	82	U Wash	1989
Garud, Raghu	Asst	New York U			MBA			
Garvin, David A.	Prof	Harvard	7	U	PHD			
Robert & Jane Cizik Professor of Business Administration								
Gassmann, Horand I.	Assoc	Dalhousie U	7	V	PHD		Brit Col	
Gaston, Kevin C.	Fell	Manchest Bus	25	F	PHD		Manchest	1988
Gaston, Terry L.	Assoc	So Oregon St	26	EFNS	DBA	83	Geo Wash	1984
Gates, Bruce L.	Prof	Willamette	37	ISTV	PHD	71	Pitt	1974
Gatewood, Robert D.	C-Ac	Georgia	5	NP	PHD	71	Purdue	1971
Gatewood, Wallace C.	Asst	Morgan State			PHD	75	Illinois	
Gatlin, Kerry P.	C-Pr	No Alabama			PHD	82	Oklahoma	1980
Gattiker, Urs	Assoc	U Lethbridge	2	DEHO	PHD	85	Claremont	1985
Gauch, Ronald	Asst	Marist	17	AV	PHD		NYU	1990
Gauss, Marianne S.	Asst	LaSalle	7	V	MBA		LaSalle	1987
Gavish, Bezalel	Prof	Vanderbilt	9	Z	DSC	75	Technion	9-88
Gedajlovic, Eric R.	Asst	Rutgers-N Br		IY	PHD	93	Concordi	1993
Geddes, Deanna	Asst	Temple			PHD		Purdue	
Gee, Michele	Asst	Wis-Parkside	3	I	PHD	94	WI-Milwa	7-94
Geeding, Daniel W.	Dean	Xavier		Mgt	PHD	72	Cinn	1969

Name	Rank	School			Deg		Inst	Year
Gehani, Ramesh		Rochest Tech			PHD	81	Tokoy In	1990
Geib, Peter	Prof	Moorhead St	83	YI	PHD		Michigan	1982
Geis, George T.	Adj	UCLA	96	ZT	PHD	77	S Calif	1985
Geisel, Martin S.	Dean	Vanderbilt	7	V	PHD	70	Chicago	7-87
Geiser, Leonard	Prof	Goshen	36	IS	MBA		Chicago	8-81
Geisler, Eliezer	Prof	Wis-Whitewat	1	DITZ	PHD	79	Northwes	1988
Geisler, Jerry L.	Dean	Metro State	3		PHD	75	Missouri	9-93
Geiss, Gunther	Prof	Adelphi	91	ZD	PHD	64	Poly-Brk	1972
Geistauts, George A.	Prof	Alaska-Ancho	38	IY	PHD	70	Renssel	1974
Geletkanycz, Marta	Asst	Penn State	3	I	ABD		Columbia	1992
Gellatly, Ian	Asst	U Lethbridge	25	EN	PHD	91	W Ontar	1993
Gellerman, Saul W.	Prof	Dallas	2	E	PHD	56	Penn	8-84
Gely, Rafael	Asst	Texas A&M		QK	PHD	91	Illinois	1990
Gemoets, Leopoldo A.	Asst	Tx-El Paso	9	Z	PHD	83	xan Luci	1987
Gent, Michael J.	Assoc	Canisius	25	EPQ	PHD	78	Tx Chr	1978
Gentry, Paul	Inst	Sam Houston			MBA	69	N Carol	1982
Geoffrion, Arthur M.	Prof	UCLA	7	V	PHD	65	Stanford	1965
Georgantzas, Nicholas C.	Assoc	Fordham	37	IU	PHD		CUNY	1987
George, Edward	Prof	Texas	7	V	PHD	81	Stanford	1992
George, Jennifer M.	Assoc	Texas A&M		E	PHD	87	New York	1987
George, Joey	Assoc	Florida St	9	Z	PHD	86	Ca-Irvine	8-93
George, John	C	Liberty			PHD			
George, John A.	H-SLe	Canterbury	7	V	PHD	80	Canterbu	1968
Gephart, Robert P.	Prof	Univ Alberta	23	HI	PHD	79	Brit Col	1978
Geranios, John W.	C	Mt St Mary's			PHD		S Calif	
Gerbing, David	Assoc	Portland St	7	V	PHD	79	Mich St	1987
Gerchak, Y.	Assoc	Un Waterloo	7	V	PHD	80	Brit Col	1982
Gerhart, Paul F.	Assoc	Case Western	51	QN	PHD		Chicago	1977
Gerin-Lajoie, Jean	Assoc	HEC-Montreal	5	Q	PHD		McGill	1984
Geringer, Michael	Assoc	Cal Poly-SLO	38	ILTY	PHD	86	U Wash	1992
Gerlach, Michael L.	Assoc	British Colu	28	Y	PHD	87	Yale	1993
Gerloff, Edward A.	Prof	Tx-Arlington	2	H	PHD	71	Texas	1970
Gerrity, Thomas P.	Dean	Pennsylvania		ZI	PHD	70	MIT	1990
Reliance Professor of Management & Private Enterprise								
Gershon, Mark	C-Pr	Temple	7	UVY	PHD	81	Arizona	1983
Gersick, Connie J. G.	Assoc	UCLA	5	N	PHD	85	Yale	1984
Gersony, Neal	Asst	New Haven	36	ITY	PHD		Renssel	9-93
Gerstenfeld, Arthur	Prof	Worcester Pl	6	DST	PHD	67	MIT	9-76
Gertner, Robert	Assoc	Chicago			PHD	86	MIT	1986
Gerwin, D.	Prof	Carleton Un	7	U	PHD		Car Mel	
Getz, Kathleen	Asst	American U	48	JLY	PHD	91	Pitt	1991
Geurin, Virginia S.	Prof	N Car-Charl			PHD		Arkansas	1972
Ghadar, Fariborz	Prof	George Wash	8	Y	DBA	75	Harvard	
Gharrity, Norman J.	Prof	Ohio Wesley	8	Y	PHD		J Hopkin	1962
Ghauvmi, Firooz	Asst	Cen St-Ohio	7	UV	MBA		Dayton	9-83
Ghemawat, Pankaj	Prof	Harvard	4	L	PHD		Harvard	
Ghez, Gilbert R.	Prof	Roosevelt			PHD		Columbia	
Ghiaseddin, Nasir	Assoc	Notre Dame	9	Z	PHD		Purdue	1982
Ghoreishi, Minoo	Assoc	Millersville	23	REPY	PHD	87	Arkansas	1988
Ghorpade, Jaisingh V.	Prof	San Diego St	5	N	PHD	68	UCLA	1965
Ghosh, Soumen	Assoc	Michigan St	7	UV	PHD	87	Ohio St	8-86
Ghosh, Stanley	Prof	Hawaii Pacif	14	BL	PHD	50	Indiana	8-82
Ghoshal, Sumantra	Prof	INSEAD	38	IY	DBA	86	Harvard	9-85
Giacalone, Robert A.	Assoc	Richmond	24	EJNY	PHD	84	SUNY-Alb	1988
Giacobbe, Jane	Asst	Massachusett	5	NOE	PHD	86	Cornell	1989
Giallourakis, Michael	Assoc	Miss State	1	&Y	PHD	75	Indiana	1982
Giamartino, Gary A.	Dean	Wilkes	28	YTE	PHD	79	Vanderbt	7-93
Giannantonio, Cristina	Asst	Notre Dame	15	NOPR	PHD	88	Maryland	1988
Giauque, William C.	Prof	Brigham Yg	7	U	DBA	77	Harvard	1977
Gibbs, Manton	Prof	Ind-Penna	37	ISUY	PHD	75	Mich St	1989
Gibbs, Michael J.	Asst	Harvard	25	EN				
Gibson, C. Kendrick	Prof	Hope	35	INT	PHD	78	Arkansas	1986
Gibson, Dana	Asst	Txs Woman's	9	Z	PHD	84	Texas	1993
Gibson, Donald	Prof	Tx A&M-Kings		Mktg	PHD	84	Memphis	1988
Gibson, Donald	Assoc	Macquarie Un						
Gibson, James L.	Prof	Kentucky	21	HD	PHD	62	Kentucky	1966
Gibson, Linda	Asst	Pacific Luth	25	ENOR	PHD	89	Missouri	1989
Gibson, Michael	Assoc	Auburn	9	Z	DBA	84	Kentucky	9-88
Gibson, Peter	Assoc	Bond Univ	37	I	PHD	84	Leichstr	1994
Gibson, T.		Humberside	2					
Gieger, Joseph J.	Prof	Idaho	36	SIAB	EDD	77	Colorado	1988
Giermanski, Jim	Assoc	Tx A&M Intl	58	Y	DA		U Miami	1989
Gifford, Blair	Asst	Colo-Denver						
Gilad, Benjamin	Assoc	Rutgers-Newk	8	Y	PHD	82	NYU	1981
Gilbert, Daniel R.	Assoc	Bucknell	43	IJ	PHD	87	Minn	9-87
Gilbert, James P.	Assoc	Georgia	7	UW	PHD	84	Nebraska	1984
Gilbert, Joseph	Asst	Nev-L Vegas	23	HIJ	PHD	91	S Calif	1990
Gilbert, Kenneth C.	Assoc	Tennessee	79	UV	PHD	76	Tenn	9-80
Gilbert, Ronald	Assoc	Fla Internat		EFHP	PHD	73	S Calif	1977
Gilbert, Stephen	Asst	Case Western			PHD	91	MIT	1991

Name	Rank	School			Degree		University	
Gilbert, Xavier		Intl Mgt Dev	3	I	DBA		Harvard	
Gilbertson, Dai W.	SLect	Victoria NZ	56	DFNT	PHD		Victoria	5-73
Gilbertson, Deb K.	Lect	Victoria NZ	16	DRST	BAGC		Lincoln	9-91
Gilbertson, Diana L.	Prof	CS-Fresno	3	I	PHD		North Tx	1988
Gilchrist, Neil	Assoc	NE Missouri	23	IS	PHD	91	Nebraska	1984
Giles, William F.	Prof	Auburn	52	EN	PHD	74	Tenn	9-74
Gill, Roger	Prof	Strathclyde	2	E				
Gillard, Sharlett	Assoc	So Indiana	9	Z	EDD	78	North Tx	1986
Gillen, Dennis	Assoc	Syracuse	3	I	PHD	81	Maryland	1980
Gillenwater, Edward L.	Asst	Mississippi	7	UV	PHD	88	Kentucky	1989
Gillian, Allen	Asst	South Dakota	5	EN	PHD	92	Illinois	1993
Gillies, James M.	Prof	York Univ	1	A	PHD		Indiana	
Gillis, Marlyn	Assoc	Simmons			MBA	75	Babson	1975
Gillo, Diane	Prof	Wis-Stev Pt	25	JLOR	EDD	82	Michigan	8-83
Gilmore, Carol	Prof	Maine		Q	PHD	79	Mass	1977
Gilmore, Harold L.	Prof	Mass-Dartmou			PHD	70	Syracuse	1987
Gilmore, J. Barry	Assoc	Memphis	36	IT	PHD	71	Oklahoma	1971
Gilmour, Peter	Prof	Macquarie Un						
Gilroy, Faith D.	Prof	Loyola-Maryl	2	R	PHD		St Louis	
Gilroy, Thomas P.	Assoc	Iowa	5	Q	MILR	58	Cornell	1980
Gilson, Clive H. J.	Assoc	St Fran Xav	52	Q	PHD	83	Warwick	1984
Gimeno, F. Javier	Asst	Texas A&M		IT	PHD	93	Purdue	1993
Ginn, Martin E.	Assoc	Illinois Tch			PHD	83	Northwes	1983
Ginsberg, Ari	Assoc	New York U			PHD	85	Pitt	
Ginter, Peter M.	Prof	Alabama-Birm	3	CI	PHD	77	North Tx	1987
Ginzberg, Michael J.	C-Pr	Case Western	9	Z	PHD	75	MIT	9-85
Ginzel, Linda	SLect	Chicago	2	E	PHD	89	Princeton	1992
Gioia, Dennis A.	Prof	Penn State	2	EF	DBA	79	Fla St	
Giordano, Daniel	Lect	F Dick-Ruthe			MA		Manhatan	
Giovanni, Mary	Assoc	NE Missouri	59	RZ	PHD	80	Missouri	1975
Giridharan, P.	Asst	Carnegie Mel	9	Z	PHD		Rochest	1990
Girling, Robert K.	Prof	Sonoma State	28	Y	PHD	74	Stanford	9-76
Gist, Marilyn	Assoc	U Washington	57	EPX	PHD	85	Maryland	1987
Gittell, Ross	Assoc	New Hampshir	4	J	PHD	89	Harvard	1991
Gitter, Robert J.	Prof	Ohio Wesley	5	OQ	PHD	78	Wiscon	1976
Givens, Norma	Prof	Ft Valley St	35		EED	77	Georgia	8-79
Givoly, Dan	C-Ac	Tel Aviv Un		F	PHD	75	New York	1976
Gladwin, Thomas N.	Prof	New York U	8	Y	PHD	75	Michigan	
Glaister, Keith W.	Assoc	Univ Leeds	3	IY	MA	77	Lancaste	1990
Glaser, Stanley	Assoc	Macquarie Un						
Glasgow, Douglas K.	Lect	Texas A&M		KL	JD	79	Miami	1980
Glaskowsky, Nicholas A. Jr.	Prof	U Miami	37	BIUK	PHD	60	Stanford	1974
Glassman, Alan M.	Prof	CS-Northrdge	12	DEPQ	PHD	70	SUNY-Buf	1971
Glen, Roy	Assoc	Boise State	2	EGD	PHD	78	Case Wes	1982
Glen, William	SLect	Griffith Un	6	ST	PHD			7-89
Glenn, James R. Jr.	Prof	San Fran St	24	EHJL	PHD	75	Stanford	1983
Glew, Richard J.	C-As	Lakehead U	9	Z	MBA	88	Queens	8-89
Glick, William H.	Assoc	Texas	2	EHX	PHD	81	Berkeley	1981
Glidden, Priscilla	VAsoc	Bentley	2	F	PHD	83	MIT	1990
Glover, Fred W.	Prof	Colorado	7	VX	PHD	65	Car Mel	1970
US West Chair in System Science & Information Systems								
Glover, Gerald	Prof	Hawaii Pacif	25	EFN	PHD	81	Florida	1-89
Glynn, Joseph	Assoc	Canisius	7	UV	PHD	77	Ohio St	1978
Glynn, Mary Ann	Assoc	Emory	2	E	PHD	88	Columbia	1993
Gnanadesikan, Mrudulla	Prof	F Dick-Madis			PHD		Purdue	
Gnepa, Tahi J.	Asst	CS-Stanislau	85		PHD	89	Wiscon	9-90
Goad, Bill	Assoc	Okla Chr	9		EDD	86	Okla St	8-82
Goad, Susan	Inst	No Illinois		V				
Gobeli, David	Prof	Oregon State	1	D	PHD	82	Minn	1982
Godard, John	Assoc	U Manitoba	25	Q	PHD	89	Cornell	1991
Godbee, Graham	Lect	Macquarie Un						
Goddard, John	Lect	North Wales	7	V	MSC			1-93
Goddard, Robert D. III	Assoc	Appalach St	28	EPY	PHD	81	S Carol	1978
Godin, Victor B.	Assoc	Northeastern			DBA		Harvard	
Godiwalla, Yezdi	Prof	Wis-Whitewat	1	CILY	PHD	77	Oklah St	1977
Godkin, R. Lynn	C-Pr	Lamar			PHD	81	North Tx	1981
Goeller, Thomas	Asst	St Johns			DBA	89	Miss St	
Goelz, Paul C.	Prof	St Marys-Txs			PHD	54	Northwes	1946
Goes, Paulo	Asst	Connecticut	79	UZ	PHD	91	Rochest	9-90
Goff, Wayne	Deces	Texas-Tyler	7	U	PHD	72	North Tx	1979
Goffee, Rob E.	Assoc	London Bus	2	RTOF	PHD		Kent	
Goffin, J.	Prof	McGill Univ	7		PHD		Berkeley	1976
Goitein, Bernard	Prof	Bradley	4	MX	PHD	82	Michigan	1981
Gold, Barry A.	Assoc	Pace	5		PHD	78	Columbia	
Gold, Bela	Prof	Claremont Gr	37	IUVY	PHD		Columbia	1983
Fletcher Jones Professor of Technology & Management								
Gold, Sonia	Prof	Claremont Gr	13	DDIJ	PHD		Pitt	1983
Goldberg, Alan	Assoc	CS-Hayward	7	V	PHD	77	Mass	1979
Goldberg, Henry	Assoc	NJ Inst Tech	7	U	PHD	76	Cornell	1990
Goldberg, Ilene	Asst	Rider			JD		Temple	

Name	Rank	School			Degree		University	
Goldberg, Michael A.	Dean	British Colu		Y	PHD	68	Berkeley	1968
Goldberg, Robert	Lect	Northeastern	3		MBA		Boston	9-89
Goldberg, Robert I.	Assoc	St Fran-NY	16		MA		Columbia	
Goldberg, Steve	Asst	New Haven	63	STI	PHD		Mass	
Golden, Brian R.	Asst	Texas	3	IH	PHD	89	Northwes	1989
Golden, Peggy A.	Asst	Fla Atlantic			PHD	89	Kentucky	9-91
Golden-Biddle, Karen A.	Asst	Emory	5	N	PHD	88	Case Wes	1988
Goldfarb, Jay	Assoc	Virgin Islan	36	ST	MBA			1990
Goldhar, Joel	Prof	Illinois Tch			PHD	71	Geo Wash	1983
Goldin, Elizabeth C.	Asst	Morehouse			MA		Boston C	1983
Golding, D.	Read	Humberside	2					
Golding, J.	PLect	Humberside	2					
Goldman, Arieh	Assoc	Hebrew Univ			PHD		Berkeley	
Goldner, Bernard B.	Deces	LaSalle			PHD			1949
Goldsmith, Art	Assoc	Mass-Boston	3	I	PHD	81	Cornell	1980
Goldstein, David	Asst	Boston Univ	9	Z	PHD		MIT	
Goldstein, Jeffrey	Asst	Adelphi	21	EFHD	PHD	80	Temple	1989
Goldstein, Joel	Assoc	Western Conn	7	Z	PHD		Poly NY	1986
Goldstein, Robert	Assoc	British Colu	9	Z	DBA	74	Harvard	
Goldsten, Joseph	Prof	Wash & Lee	1		PHD	74	Ohio St	1972
Goldsworthy, Ashley W.	Dean	Bond Univ			MSC	80	Griffith	1991
Golen, Richard F.	C-Ac	Mass-Dartmou			JD	83	Suffolk	1984
Golhar, Damodar Y.	C-Pr	W Michigan	7	UV	PHD	83	Michigan	1984
Golin, Myron	Retir	Widener		1993	MBA	52	Ohio St	
Goll, Irene	Asst	Scranton	35	Q	PHD	87	Temple	1988
Goltz, Sonia M.	Asst	Notre Dame	12	EFHR	PHD	87	Purdue	1987
Gomersall, Nicholas	Asst	Luther	47	LVM	PHD	90	Cornell	1991
Gomes, Glen	Prof	CS-Chico			PHD		S Calif	1985
Gomez, Sandalio	Assoc	Univ Navarra	5	N			Complute	8-65
Gomez-Llera, German	Asst	Univ Navarra	5	N	PHD		Politecn	5-82
Gomez-Mejia, Luis	C-Pr	Arizona St	5	N	PHD	81	Minn	1989
Gomolka, Eugene G.	Prof	Robt Morris	4	I	PHD	74	SUNY-Buf	9-93
Gomori, Peter	C-Ac	St Fran-NY			PHD		CUNY	
Gonzalez, Candida	Assoc	P Rico-Mayag	53		MBA	83	Loyola	8-83
Gonzalez, Juan J.	Asst	Tx-S Antonio			PHD	83	S Carol	
Gonzalez, Manolete	Asst	Oregon State	3	I	PHD	85	S Calif	1985
Good, Delmar	C-Pr	Goshen	14	LJ	PHD		Illinois	2-67
Good, Walter	H-Pr	U Manitoba	6	St	PHD	69	Michigan	1970
Goodenow, Mark	Assoc	SW State	1					
Goodfellow, Reginald A.	Prof	CS-Sacrament	25	EN	PHD	73	Bowl Gr	1976
Gooding, Carl W.	Dean	Geo Southern	7	UV	PHD	76	Georgia	1986
Gooding, Richard	Asst	Arizona St	34	EHI	PHD		Michigan	1988
Goodman, John B.	Assoc	Harvard	4	L				
Goodman, John F. B.	C-Pr	Manches Inst	5	Q	PHD		Nottingh	1975
Goodman, Jordan	Lect	Manches Inst	5	B	PHD		London	9-90
Goodman, Paul	Prof	Carnegie Mel	5	P	PHD	66	Cornell	1966
Goodman, Richard A.	Assoc	UCLA	3	I	DBA	66	Wash U	1966
Goodman, Robert	Asst	Wisconsin	34	HIJS	PHD	88	Minn	1991
Goodman, Stephen	Assoc	Cen Florida	7	UWV	PHD	72	Penn St	1984
Goodrick, Elizabeth	Asst	SUNY-Buffalo	2	EHR	DBA	91	Illinios	1991
Goodson, Jane R.	Assoc	Auburn-Montg	2	E	PHD	86	Alabama	1985
Goodstein, Jerry	Asst	Wash State			PHD			
Goodwin, Chester	Asst	Fayetteville			PHD			
Goodwin, James C. Jr.	Prof	Richmond	73	IJU	PHD	74	N Carol	8-76
Goodwin, Vicki	Asst	North Texas	2	E	PHD	91	Tx-Arlin	1991
Goose, Jack N.	C-Pr	Mars Hill	34		DBA	74	Miss St	1964
Gopal, Abhijit	Asst	Univ Calgary	9	Z	PHD	91	Georgia	1990
Gopal, Ram	Asst	Connecticut			PHD	93	SUNY-Buf	
Gopalan, Suresh	Asst	West Txs A&M	23		DBA		La Tech	1990
Gopinath, C.	Asst	Delaware			PHD	90	Mass	1990
Gordon, David	Assoc	Dallas	72		DENG	69	Oklahoma	8-69
Gordon, Gene	Assoc	Bloomsburg	9	Z	EDD		Mass	
Gordon, J. R. M.	Prof	Queen's Univ	37	IU	PHD	66	MIT	1975

Alcan Chair in Management and Technology

Name	Rank	School			Degree		University	
Gordon, Judith	Assoc	Boston Coll	25	EOSR	PHD	77	MIT	9-77
Gordon, Ken	H-Ac	Colorado	78	UVMY	PHD	73	Northwes	1977
Gordon, Milton	Retir	CS-Northrdge	25		PHD	52	Wiscon	1959
Gordon, Paul	Retir	St Johns		1993	PHD	58	Syracuse	
Gordon, Roy H.	SpAst	Hofstra	13	IY	MME	54	Polytech	2-84
Gore, George J.	Prof	Cincinnati	3	I	PHD	61	Michigan	1959
Gorman, Kevin J.	Asst	N Car-Charl			MBA		Cal St	1988
Goroff, Iza	Assoc	Wis-Whitewat	9	UVWZ	PHD	68	Penn	1977
Gorski, Barbara	Lect	St Thomas-MN						
Gosenpud, Jerry	Prof	Wis-Whitewat	1	EI	PHD	74	Case Wes	1980
Goslin, Lewis	Prof	Portland St	3	DTI	PHD	64	U Wash	1968
Gosselin, Alain	Assoc	HEC-Montreal	5	EV	PHD		Maryland	1981
Gotcher, J. William	Prof	CS-Hayward	7	U	PHD	72	Berkeley	1968
Gottfredson, Michael R.	Prof	Arizona	4	LK	PHD	76	SUNY-Alb	1985
Gotting, David A.	Lect	Manches Inst	5	L	BA		Strathcl	9-71
Gottschalk, Donald	Asst	Carthage	5		BS		Marquett	1990

Gough, Newell	Asst	Boise State	36	IT	PHD	90	Utah	1989
Goul, K. Michael	Assoc	Arizona St			PHD		Oregon	1985
Gould, Sam	Dean	Dayton	2	EH	PHD	75	Mich St	1985
Goulet, Lynda L.	Inst	No Iowa			MBA	77	N Iowa	1-78
Goulet, Peter G.	Prof	No Iowa			PHD	70	Ohio St	1974
Govekar, Michele	Asst	Penn St-Erie	38	I	PHD	93	Minn	1993
Govindarajan, Vijay	Prof	Dartmouth			DBA	78	Harvard	1986
Gowan, Jack A. Jr.	Assoc	N Car-Wilmin	9	Z	PHD		Clemson	
Gowan, Mary	Asst	Tx-El Paso	5	N		92	Georgia	1992
Gowen, Charles R.	Assoc	No Illinois	3	I	PHD		Ohio St	
Goyette, Herve	Agreg	HEC-Montreal	9	Z	CPHL		UCLA	
Grabowski, Martha	Asst	LeMoyne	9	Z	PHD	87	RPI	1989
Grace, James L. Jr.	Prof	New Hamp Col	48	K	EDD		Penn	
Grady, Susan	Assoc	Massachusett	4	K	JD	77	W Nw Eng	1978
Graef, David	Lect	Ariz St-West	14	LJC	PHD	71	Ariz St	1988
Graeff, Claude	Prof	Illinois St	23		PHD		Illinois	1977
Graen, George B.	Prof	Cincinnati	2	F	PHD	76	U Wash	
Graetz, Fiona	Lect	Deakin-Burwo	1	D	GRAD		Camberra	
Graf, David K.	Dean	No Illinois		Z	PHD		N Dakota	
Graf, Lee A.	Prof	Illinois St	25		PHD		Miss St	1976
Graham, Brian	Lect	British Colu	7		MBA	84	Brit Col	1984
Graham, Carol	Inst	W Kentucky	15	N	ABD	94	Vanderbt	1992
Graham, Gail	Lect	U Wollongong	82	WJE	PHD	90	Melbourn	2-90
Graham, Gerald H.	Dean	Wichita St	12	EPNT	PHD	67	LSU	9-67
Graham, Gerald H. Jr.	Asst	Loras	37	DTUV	MBA	87	Wichita	1987
Graham, Harry E.	Prof	Cleveland St	5	QK	PHD		Wiscon	1978
Graham, Jill W.	Asst	Loyola-Chicg	2	E	PHD	83	Northwes	
Graham, Jim	Assoc	Univ Calgary	6	ST	PHD	78	W Ontari	1976
Graham-Moore, Brian E.	Prof	Texas	25	EN	PHD	70	Wash U	1972
Gramm, Cynthia L.	Assoc	Alabama-Hunt	45	QKN	PHD	83	Illinois	1990
Grandes, Maria Jusus	Asst	Univ Navarra	7	V	MBA		Navarra	N-84
Grandfield, Raymond J.	C-Pr	Delaware St			EDD			1968
Granger, Mary	Assoc	George Wash	9	Z				
Granger, Sue C.	Prof	Jacksonvl St	12	D	EDD	76	Arkansas	1969
Granito, James	Assoc	Youngstown	4	J	JD	63	Chicago	1-83
Granot, Daniel	Prof	British Colu	7	V	PHD	74	Texas	1978
Grant, Charles T.	Asst	USAF Academy	3	I	PHD		Fla St	
Grant, John H.	Prof	Pittsburgh	3		DBA	72	Harvard	
Robert Kirby Chair in Strategic Management								
Grant, Robert	Asst	Carthage			MBA		Marquett	1990
Grant, Robert	VProf	Georgetown	36	IT	PHD	83	London	1993
Grant, Stephen	Prof	N Adams St			PHD		Clark	
Gratton, Lynda C.	Asst	London Bus	2	NOEF	PHD		Liverpoo	
Graubard, Leon S.	Assoc	Worcester Pl	37	IY	ABD	67	Brown	9-69
Graves, Glenn W.	Retir	UCLA	7	1994	PHD	63	Michigan	1966
Graves, Laura M.	Asst	Clark	2	EFG	PHD	82	Conn	
Graves, Robert L.	Prof	Chicago	7	UV	PHD	52	Harvard	1958
Graves, Samual B.	Assoc	Boston Coll	7	VU	DBA	85	Geo Wash	9-86
Gray, Barbara	Prof	Penn State	2	HLMY	PHD		Case Wes	1979
Gray, Daniel H.	VProf	Babson			PHD		MIT	
Gray, David A.	Assoc	Tx-Arlington	5	QN	PHD	74	Mass	1973
Gray, Edmund R.	Prof	Loyola Marym	14	BIL	PHD	66	UCLA	1986
Gray, George R.	Assoc	Virg Comm	5	NQ	PHD	75	Alabama	1977
Gray, Irwin	Prof	NY Inst Tech	73		PHD			
Gray, Jerry L.	D-Pr	U Manitoba	2	EH	PHD	70	S Carol	1970
Gray, Kenneth	Assoc	Jackson St			PHD		Walden	1992
Gray, Michael	Lect	Ohio Univ	4		JD	75	Wiscon	
Gray, Paul	Prof	Claremont Gr	9	ZIV	PHD		Stanford	1982
Gray, Ralph		DePauw			PHD			
Gray, Sam	Asst	Richmond		VY	PHD	93	Tx A&M	1993
Gray, Van D.	Assoc	Baylor	7	U	PHD		North Tx	1986
Grayson, James	Asst	Augusta	79	UV	PHD	90	North Tx	1992
Greatorex, David	Prof	U Wollongong			BA		Sydney	4-90
Greatorex, Michael	Lect	Manches Inst	7	U	BCOM		Birmingh	9-69
Greckel, Fay E.	Dean	Indiana SE		R	PHD	69	Indiana	1967
Green, Bill	Assoc	N Car-Ashvil	27	&W	PHD	85	North Tx	8-92
Green, Brian	Asst	Mich-Dearbor						
Green, Carolyn W.	Asst	Houston	9	Z	PHD	93	Houston	9-93
Green, Forrest B.	Prof	Radford	7	ZUV	PHD	82	Va Tech	8-87
Green, Joseph G.	Prof	York Univ	1	I	PHD		Indiana	
Green, Kenneth	Lect	Manches Inst	7	M	PHD		Manchest	9-88
Green, R. Earl	Retir	Georgia Tech	13	1994	DBA	52	Indiana	1957
Green, R. H.	Lect	Univ Bath	79	UZ	PHD			
Green, Ronald F.	Asst	East Tenn St	37	IVY	PHD	86	Clemson	1986
Green, Stephen	Prof	Purdue	2	E	PHD	76	U Wash	1987
Green, Steve G.	Assoc	USAF Academy	7	W	PHD			
Green, Susan	Lect	Univ Bristol	2	HI	PHD			1988
Greenbaum, Howard	Emer	Hofstra	2	DEX	PHD	52	Columbia	9-77
Greenberg, Betsy S.	Asst	Texas	7	V	PHD	85	Berkeley	1986
Greenberg, Ellen	Asst	Mass-Boston	2	E	PHD	85	Columbia	1983

Name	Rank	School			Deg			
Greenberg, Jerald	Prof	Ohio State	2	EJN	PHD	75	Wayne St	1981
Greenberger, David B.	Assoc	Ohio State	2	E	PHD	81	Wiscon	1982
Greenberger, Martin	Prof	UCLA	9	Z	PHD	58	Harvard	1982
Greene, Frederick D.	Assoc	Manhattan	36	IST	PHD	74	SUNY-Buf	1974
Greene, G. Robert	Assoc	Old Dominion			PHD	83	Geo St	
Greene, Myron T.	Prof	Georgia St	9	Z	PHD		Geo St	
Greene, Patricia	Asst	Rutgers-Newk	6	TSH	PHD	93	Texas	1993
Greene, Walter E.	Assoc	Tx-Pan Amer			PHD		Arkansas	1976
Greenfeld, Susan T.	Prof	CS-San Bern	3	I	DBA	78	S Calif	1987
Greenfield, Patricia	Assoc	Massachusett	5	QN	PHD	86	Cornell	1986
Greenhalgh, Leonard	Prof	Dartmouth			PHD	79	Cornell	1978
Greenhaus, Jeffrey	Prof	Drexel	2	EGOR	PHD	70	NYU	1981
Greening, Daniel W.	Asst	Missouri	3	I	PHD	91	Penn St	1991
Greenlaw, James A.	Inst	NE Louisiana	57	N	MS	67	AFIT	1984
Greenlaw, Paul S.	Prof	Penn State	5	AKNQ	PHD	55	Syracuse	1960
Greensted, Chris	Dir	Strathclyde	7	V				
Greenwood, Ronald	Prof	GMI	12	BEIL	PHD	71	Oklahoma	1983
F. James McDonald Professor of Industrial Management								
Greenwood, Royston	C	Univ Alberta	23	HIS	PHD	76	Birm UK	1982
Greer, Charles R.	Prof	Tx Christian	15	NQ	PHD	75	Kansas	1988
Greer, William	Asst	St Marys-Cnd	12	CEJL	MBA	75	Boston	1990
Gregersen, Hal B.	Asst	Brigham Yg	28	FINY	PHD	89	Berkeley	1992
Gregoria, Gary	Asst	St Scholasti			MBA		Mich St	1982
Gregory, Ann	Assoc	Memorial Un	38		PHD	76	Columbia	1982
Gregory, D.	SLect	Humberside	2					
Gregory, Karl	Prof	Oakland	36	IST	PHD	62	Michigan	1968
Grehu, Joyce	Prof	Minn-Duluth			PHD	79	Minn	
Greiner, Larry	Prof	So Calif	2	EFH	DBA		Harvard	1973
Greinke, Andrew	Lect	Australian N	4	JKL	BCOM	90	Aust Nat	1992
Greller, Martin	Assoc	Wyoming	12	H	PHD		Yale	8-91
Gresov, Christopher G.	Assoc	Emory	6	H	PHD	88	Columbia	1993
Greve, Avent	Assoc	Norwegian			DREC			
Greville, Mary Rose		Intl Mgt Dev	2	E	MPHI		Kent	
Grey, Christopher	Assoc	Univ Leeds	25	EO	PHD	92	Manchest	1993
Gribbin, S.		Humberside	3					
Grider, Douglas T. Jr.	Assoc	Cen Arkansas	25	EFI	PHD	72	Geo St	8-90
Grier, Wilson C.	Asst	Morehead St	65	RXIQ	EDD	83	Kentucky	1983
Griesinger, Donald W.	Prof	Claremont Gr	12	DEFH	PHD		Ca-SnBar	1982
Griffieth, Roger	Prof	Georgia St						
Griffin, Abbie	Assoc	Chicago	71	U	PHD	89	MIT	1989
Griffin, Adelaide	Prof	Txs Woman's	23	HE	PHD	79	North Tx	1979
Griffin, Barry	Assoc	Fayetteville			PHD			
Griffin, Charlene J.	Assoc	Aquinas	23	EHIZ	ABD		Mich St	1980
Griffin, Kenneth M.	C-Pr	Cen Arkansas	9	Z	DBA		La Tech	
Griffin, Ricky W.	Prof	Texas A&M		EN	PHD	78	Houston	1981
Lawrence E. Fouraker Professor of Business Administration								
Griffin, Waylon D.	Prof	Tx-Prm Basin			PHD	72	Texas	
Griffith, Terri L.	Asst	Arizona	25	EZN	PHD	88	Car Mel	1989
Griffith, Tom	Assoc	Fort Hays St	3	U	PHD	79	Indiana	1992
Griffth, Miriam	Lect	Indiana SE	5	O	MED	76	Louisvil	1991
Grigg, Trevor J.	H-Pr	Queensland	3	IA	PHD	81	Queensld	1983
Griggs, F. Keith	C-Pr	Gardner-Webb	68	SY	EDD	86	Va Tech	1965
Griggs, Jack	Dean	Abilene Chr		Mgt	PHD	71	Texas	1-91
Grigsby, David W.	Prof	Clemson	3	I	PHD	77	N Carol	1980
Grill, George P.	Prof	N Car-Greens	9	Z	EDD		N Dakota	1963
Grimble, M.		Humberside	2					
Grimes, Andrew J.	Prof	Kentucky	2	H	PHD	64	Minn	1967
Grimm S.J., Robert B.	Assoc	Seattle	45	JNOD	PHD		Colorado	
Grimmett, David	Asst	Austin Peay	7	UV	PHD		St Louis	1983
Grimso, Oddleif	Assoc	Norwegian			MAGA			
Groenevelt, Henri	Assoc	Rochester	7	U	PHD		Columbia	
Groom, Steve	Lect	David Lipsc	4	K	JD		Tenn	9-89
Grosse, Robert E.	Prof	U Miami	8	Y	PHD	77	N Carol	1980
Grossman, Amy	Assoc	Pine Manor	9	TS	MBA		Northeas	1981
Grossman, Jack H.	Assoc	DePaul			PHD		Loyola	
Grossman, Robert	Assoc	Marist	4	KL	LLM		NYU	1984
Grousbeck, H. Irving	Lect	Stanford	6	ST	MBA	60	Harvard	1985
Grout, John	Asst	So Methodist			PHD	92	Penn St	
Grove, Ralph F. Jr.	VInst	Louisville	9	Z	MS	74	Louisvil	9-93
Grover, Richard A.	Assoc	So Maine	2	EFC	PHD	84	Ohio St	1988
Grover, Steven L.	Asst	Indiana	4	J	PHD	89	Columbia	1988
Growney, Wallace	Prof	Susquehanna	9	Z	PHD	70	Oklahoma	1965
Grual, Jordi	Assoc	Univ Navarra	7	VY	PHD		Berkeley	3-87
Grub, Phillip	Retir	George Wash	8	1994	DBA	64	Geo Wash	
Grubbs, M. Ray	Assoc	Millsaps	35	IN	PHD	87	Miss	1986
Grude, Jan K.	C-As	Dalhousie U	2	E	PHD		London	
Gruenfeld, Deb	Asst	Northwestern			PHD	93	Illinois	1993
Grunewald, Donald	Prof	Iona	2	EIL	DBA	62	Harvard	1986
Gryskiewicz, Nur	Asst	N Car-Greens	25	NPRY	PHD	79	London	1-86
Grzeda, M.	Asst	Laurentian	5		PHD			

Name	Rank	School			Degree		Institution	
Guan, Jian	Asst	Louisville	9	Z	PHD	92	Louisvil	9-86
Guder, Faruk	Assoc	Loyola-Chicg			PHD		Wiscon	1983
Gudmundson, Donald	Asst	Wis-Oshkosh	32	IHJS	ABD		Kentucky	1991
Guerard, Jean-Claude	Prof	HEC-Montreal	7		MSTA		N Carol	
Gueutal, Hal G.	C-Ac	SUNY-Albany	59	NZVR	PHD	80	Purdue	1985
Guffey, W. Robert	Asst	Elon			PHD	92	Va Tech	1992
Guglielmino, Paul	Asst	Fla Atlantic	89	NPZY	EDD	78	Georgia	1978
Guhde, Lynn	Assoc	Slippery Roc			PHD		Kent St	8-92
Guignard-Spielberg, Monique	Prof	Pennsylvania			DOCT	80	DeLille	1972
Guild, P.	Assoc	Un Waterloo	36	DITX	PHD	78	Oxford	1990
Guiler, Jeffrey	Asst	Robt Morris	5	BNQ	MBA	87	Ind-PA	9-90
Guillen, Mauro		MIT	3	I				
Guinan, Patricia J.	Asst	Boston Univ	9	Z	PHD		Indiana	
Guisinger, Stephen E.	Prof	Texas-Dallas	9	Y	PHD	70	Harvard	1976
Gulati, Ranjay	Asst	Northwestern			PHD	93	Harvard	1993
Gulati, Umest C.	Prof	East Carol		Y	PHD		Virginia	9-67
Gulbro, Robert	Assoc	Jacksonvl St	36	SL	DBA	91	Miss St	1983
Gulezian, Allen K.	Prof	Central Wash			PHD	71	Oregon	1973
Gullett, C. Ray	Prof	Texas-Tyler	5	Q	PHD	70	LSU	1978
Gulliford, Richard	Assoc	Univ Leeds	2	EF	MSC	86	UWIST	1989
Gulve, Salil	Inst	Frostburg St			MS		Conn St	8-88
Gunawardane, Gamini	Prof	CS-Fullerton	37	UV	PHD	77	Chicago	8-82
Gundersen, David E.	Asst	S F Austin	59	NPZE	PHD	92	Miss	1992
Gunderson, Harvey S.	Prof	Wis-Eau Clar		UVW	PHD		Wiscon	1974
Gundry, Lisa K.	Asst	DePaul			PHD		Northwes	
Gunn, L.	Prof	Strathclyde	3	I	PHD			
Gunn, Patricia	Assoc	Ohio Univ	4		JD	74	Boston C	
Gunter, Sevket I.	Asst	Temple	7	UVW	PHD	87	Syracuse	1988
Gupta, Anil	Prof	Maryland	38	IY	PHD	80	Harvard	1986
Gupta, Ashis	Assoc	Univ Calgary	38	IY	PHD	78	Boston	1978
Gupta, Diwakar	Assoc	McMaster Un	17	UV	PHD		Waterloo	
Gupta, Jatinder N. D.	C-Pr	Ball State	7		PHD		Tx Tech	1985
Gupta, Mahesh C.	Asst	Louisville	78	UVY	PHD	90	Louisvil	8-90
Gupta, Nina	Assoc	Arkansas	2	E	PHD	75	Michigan	1984
Gupta, Omprakash K.	Assoc	Indiana NW	7	UVW	PHD	80	Purdue	1990
Gupta, Raj	Assoc	Memorial Un	7		PHD	74	Rochest	1975
Gupta, Rakesh C.	Asst	Adelphi	27	IUV	MBA	75	CUNY-Bar	1978
Gupta, Uma	Asst	East Carol		Z	PHD	91	Cen Fla	8-93
Gupta, Vandna	Asst	F Dick-Ruthe			MS		Carleton	
Gupta, Yash P.	Dean	Colo-Denver	79	IUVZ	PHD	76	Bradford	1992
Gurbaxani, Vijay	Assoc	Calif-Irvine	9	Z	PHD	87	Rochest	1985
Gurdon, Michael A.	Assoc	Vermont	25	QTDY	PHD	79	Cornell	1980
Gutek, Barbara A.	H-Pr	Arizona	2	EXR	PHD	75	Michigan	1989
Guth, William D.	Prof	New York U	6	T	DBA	60	Harvard	
Harold Price Professor of Mgt; Director Center for Entrepreneurial Studies								
Guthrie, James P.	Asst	Kansas	5	N	PHD		Maryland	1988
Gutierrez, Genaro J.	Asst	Texas	7	UV	PHD	88	Stanford	1988
Gutknecht, John	Assoc	Geo Southern	37	I	MBA	65	LSU	1986
Gutman, Gregory	Prof	Adelphi	26	EFT	MBA	66	Penn	1967
Gutteridge, Thomas G.	Dean	Connecticut	5	QNO	PHD	71	Purdue	9-92
Guy, Baylor	Inst	Ark-Monticel						
Guydosh, Ray	C	SUNY-Plattsb	57	QUV	PHD	74	Carnegie	1976
Guzell, Stanley	Prof	Youngstown	58		PHD	80	Pitt	9-79
Gwinnett, E. Anne	Lect	Manches Inst	79	U	PHD		Manchest	9-84
Ha, Albert	Asst	Yale	7	UV	PHD	92	Stanford	1992
Ha, Daesung	Asst	Marshall	7	V	PHD	91	Penn St	1991
Haase, Milton R.	Inst	Georgia St	9	Z	BS		Hofstra	
Haberland, Chris	Asst$	Clayton St	1		MBA		Geo St	1989
Habib, Mohammed	Asst	Temple						
Hacker, James O.	Asst	Winthrop	1	C	MBA		San Fran	1990
Hackett, Rick D.	C-Ac	McMaster Un	5	NE	PHD	85	Bowl Gr	
Hackman, J. Richard	Prof	Harvard	25	EN				
Cahners-Rabb Professor of Social & Organizational Psychology								
Haessler, Robert W.	Assoc	Michigan	7	U	PHD	68	Michigan	1975
Hafey, L.	Lect	U Newcastle	45	KLQ	DIPL		BAB	
Hafrey, Leigh	Lect	Harvard	1	&				
Hafsi, Taieb	Prof	HEC-Montreal	13	AFI	DBA		Harvard	
Haga, William	Adj	Naval Postgr	92	ZVXH	PHD	72	Illinois	4-88
Hagel, Pauline	Lect	Deakin-Burwo	12	DR	MBA		Deakin	
Hagmann, Constanza	Asst	Kansas State	9	Z	PHD	88	Kan St	9-76
Hahn, Chan K.	Prof	Bowling Gr	7	UW	PHD	70	Ohio St	1970
Hahn, F. James	Prof	Western St	4		JD	66	Wiscon	1969
Hahn, William	Assoc	Savannah St	26	EGQ	PHD	80	Geo St	1982
Haile, Semere	Asst	Grambling St	58	Y	PHD	81	Cinn	1987
Hailey, William A.	Prof	Millsaps	79	UVZ	DBA	78	Kentucky	1987
Haine, James	C-Pr	Wis-Stev Pt	49	ZKJ	JD	75	Indiana	8-76
Haines, David	Retir	Eastern Conn			PHD		Conn	1970
Haines, G.	Prof	Carleton Un			PHD		Car Tech	
Haiven, Larry	Assoc	Saskatchewan	25	NQ	PHD	89	Warwick	1988
Halal, William	Prof	George Wash	1	D				

Name	Title	Institution			Degree		School	Year
Halati, Abolhassan	Prof	CS-Pomona	7	UVM	PHD	85	S Calif	1986
Halatin, Theodore J.	Prof	SW Texas St	4	JLS	PHD	73	Tx Tech	1976
Halberg, Richard A.	C-Ac	Houghton	46	SJ	MBA	76	Akron	1975
Hale, A.	Asst	McGill Univ	3		PHD		Texas	1992
Hale, John F.	Prof	Fort Lewis	25	EGNO	PHD	63	Car Mel	1970
Haley, David	Asst	S Col 7th Dy	7	V	MBA	89	Tenn Tec	1989
Halfhill, Susan M.	Prof	CS-Fresno	2	EH	PHD		Bradford	1982
Halkyard, Edwin M.	DisLe	So Carolina						
Hall, Douglas T.	Prof	Boston Univ	25	EFG	PHD		MIT	
Hall, Ernest H. Jr.	Asst	So Indiana	36	I	PHD	88	Miss	1992
Hall, Francine	Assoc	New Hampshir	2	EFQ	PHD	75	Toronto	1980
Hall, Frank D.	Assoc	Ark-Ltl Rock			PHD		Arkansas	
Hall, Graham C.	Lect	Manchest Bus	3	IRS	MSC		City	1981
Hall, H. John	Asst	Florida	13	IJLT	PHD	89	Georgia	1989
Hall, James C.	Assoc	Pace	25	PE	PHD		Chicago	5-79
Hall, James L.	C-Pr	Santa Clara			PHD	71	U Wash	1970
Hall, Katherine H.	LectB	Flinders Un	84	KL	LLB	88	Adelaide	1990
Hall, Nicholas G.	Assoc	Ohio State	7	V	PHD		Berkeley	
Hall, Phillip D.	Asst	Nebraska	38	IY	PHD	88	Nebraska	1987
Hall, Richard	Assoc	Grand Valley			PHD		Cinn	1983
Hall, Roger	Prof	U Manitoba	12	EH	PHD	73	U Wash	1970
Hall, W. Clayton	Assoc	Illinois Tch			PHD	64	Illinois	1966
Hallam, Stephen F.	Dean	Mich-Flint	9	Z	PHD	73	Iowa	
Hallaq, John	Prof	Idaho	8	YL	PHD	72	U Wash	1970
Halliday, Michael	Assoc	Macquarie Un						
Halliday, Robert M.	Asst	Quinnipiac	2	FHO	MA	69	Fairfiel	1074
Hallock, Daniel	Asst	St Edwards			PHD	92	Tenn	1993
Halpern, David	Assoc	Iona	5	QE	PHD	79	NYU	1985
Halpern, Larry	Lect	Boston Coll	36	JT	MBA	58	Columbia	9-90
Halpin, Arthur L.	Asst	Beaver	36	IL	ABD		Drexel	9-84
Hambrick, Donald	Prof	Columbia	23	HI	PHD	79	Penn St	1979
Hamburger, Charles	Prof	CS-Long Bch	24	EOLI	PHD	65	S Calif	1965
Hamel, Gary	Assoc	London Bus	3	I	PHD		Michigan	1983
Hames, David S.	Assoc	Nev-L Vegas	5	NQ	PHD	85	N Carol	1989
Hamilton, Charles	Asst	Illinois Tch			PHD		Illinois	1991
Hamilton, Diane M.	C	Rowan Col NJ	97	Z	PHD	94	Temple	1983
Hamilton, Harold C.	Assoc	Montevallo	3		DBA		La Tech	1981
Hamilton, Harold T.	Asst	Bellevue	6		MBA	64		8-81
Hamilton, James	Asst	SW Louisiana	42	JLME	PHD	72	Emory	1990
Hamilton, James W.	Asst	West Chester			MBA		Northeas	1989
Hamilton, Leonora	Asst	P Rico-Mayag	3		MA	78	Monterre	1-79
Hamilton, R. T.	Prof	Canterbury	36	IS	PHD	82	London	1983
Hamilton, Robert D. III	Asst	Temple			PHD	81	Northwes	1981
Hamilton, William C.	Prof	Columbus	7	V	DBA		La Tech	1973
Hamilton, William F.	Prof	Pennsylvania	36	DIT	PHD	67	London	7-67
Landau Professor of Management and Technology; Director, Mgt & Tech Program								
Hamington, Maurice	Asst	Mt St Mary's			PHD		S Calif	
Hammock, Gordon L.	H-Ac	Mary Baldwin	18	EN	MS		Pace	1987
Hammond, Don H.	Asst	New Orleans	2	DT	PHD	89	Fla St	8-89
Hammond, Janice H.	Assoc	Harvard	7	U				
Hammons, Charles B.	Assoc	Dallas	9	ZVX	PHD	79	Rice	8-92
Hampson, Jane	Lect	Illinois Tch						1993
Hampton, David R.	Prof	San Diego St	2	E	PHD	64	Columbia	1964
Han, Bernie	Asst	Wash State						
Han, Pyung	Assoc	NE Missouri	28	EY	EDD	75	S Calif	1980
Han, S. Bruce	Asst	Merrimack		U	MBA		Michigan	
Han, Sang J.	Asst	Alabama A&M			MBA		Alab A&M	
Hancock, P. Daniel	Lect	Wis-Whitewat	7		MBA	72	Wis-Milw	1980
Hancock, Terence	Assoc	Louisville	79	UVXZ	PHD	87	Indiana	1-87
Hand, Barry M.	Asst	Indiana St	31	I	ABD		Kentucky	8-91
Hand, Herbert H.	Retir	So Carolina		1994	PHD	69	Penn St	
Hand, Michael L.	Prof	Willamette	79	VZ	PHD	78	Iowa St	1979
Hand, R. J.	Deces	Queen's Univ	3	5-91	MBA	51	Chicago	1951
Handfield, Robert B.	Asst	Michigan St	7	W	PHD	90	N Carol	8-92
Handfield, Roger	Assoc	HEC-Montreal	79	UVXZ	MS		Cornell	
Handford, S. B.	Assoc	Lakehead U	25	EHNP	MBA		Alberta	7-87
Handler, Wendy C.	Asst	Babson			DBA		Boston U	
Handley, W. Bruce	Prof	Weber State			PHD	72	Ariz St	1971
Handy, Charles B.	VProf	London Bus	52	OLJA	MS		MIT	
Hanebury, Jean M.	Asst	Salisbury St	54	INOP	PHD	90	Geo St	8-88
Haney, Reginald A.	Prof	Wilfrid Laur	4	K	LLM		Osgoode	1974
Hanks, Steven	Asst	Utah State	63	IST	PHD	90	Utah	9-88
Hanks, Sue	Asst	So Colorado	1	&	EDD		Arkansas	1992
Hanlon, Susan C.	Assoc	Akron	12	DFE	DBA	82	Memphis	1-90
Hanna, Mark D.	Asst	Miami U-Ohio	7	U	PHD	89	Clemson	8-89
Hanna, Robert W.	Prof	CS-Northrdge	23	EFP	PHD	75	UCLA	1975
Hannah, Gregg		Nichols Col						
Hannan, John	Adj	Rice	48	KY	BA	75	Rice	1990
Hannon, John	Asst	Purdue	2	N	PHD	91	Cornell	1991
Hannum, M. K.			2	E	PHD	79	N Carol	

Name	Rank	School	#	Code	Deg	Yr	School2	Year
Hansen, Eric	Asst	CS-Long Bch	6	DTIY	PHD	89	Tenn	1989
Hansen, Gary	Prof	Utah State	5	Q	PHD	71	Cornell	9-67
Hansen, Gary S.	Assoc	U Washington	3	DISY	PHD	87	Michigan	1984
Hansen, Pierre	Prof	HEC-Montreal	7		PHD		Bruxelle	
Hansen, Richard C.	Dean	Ferris State	3		PHD	71	Wiscon	1983
Hansen, Robert	Prof	Dartmouth			PHD	84	UCLA	1983
Hansen, Theodore L.	C	Salem State	5	N	MBA		Stanford	
Hanson, Cynthia	Asst	Greensboro			PHD	93	Maryland	1993
Hanson, E. Mark	Prof	Cal-Riversid	25	EQ	PHD		New Mex	1970
Hanson, Lady A.	Assoc	CS-Pomona	2	EF	PHD	78	Clarmont	1986
Hanson, Lee	Asst	CS-San Bern	3	I	PHD	92	Ca-Irvine	1991
Hanson, Roberta	Assoc	Metro State	54	JLPR	DBA	79	Colorado	1987
Haour, Georges		Intl Mgt Dev	5	Q	PHD		Toronto	
Harari, Oren	Prof	San Francisc			PHD'	78	Calif	1977
Hardaker, J. B.	C-Pr	U New Englan			PHD		New Engl	
Harder, Joseph W.	Asst	Pennsylvania	25	ENQ	PHD	89	Stanford	7-89
Anheuser-Busch Term Assistant Professor								
Hardgrave, William	Retir	George Wash	7	V	DEG	62	J Hopkin	
Hardin, Russell	Asst	Gardner-Webb	67		ABD		Miss	1985
Hardin, William F.			7	U	PHD	66	N Carol	
Harding, Edward	Inst	Plymouth St			MBA	77	Dartmout	
Hardway, Donald E.	Asst	St Louis			PHD		Houston	
Hardy, Cynthia	Assoc	McGill Univ	3		PHD		Calif	1981
Hardy, Virginia L.	Lect	U Lancaster	25	NOP	MSC		UMIST	
Harel Giasson, Francine	Assoc	HEC-Montreal	12	EOR	PHD		HEC-Mont	
Harford, Michael	C $	Morehead St	54	JL	JD	81	Wake For	1983
Hargareaves-Heald, Brooke	Asst	Mass-Lowell	5	QN	JD	74	Northeas	
Hargis, Edyth	Inst	South Fla	25	EN	MS	80	S Fla	1980
Hargrove, C. LaFaye	H	So Car-Aiken	25	EFPR	PHD		Geo Col	1987
Hariharan, Sam	Asst	So Calif	3	I	PHD		Michigan	9-90
Harker, Michael	Lect	Griffith Un	38	IPT	MA			2-90
Harker, Patrick T.	Prof	Pennsylvania			PHD	83	Penn	1984
UPS Trnsportation Professor for the Private Sector								
Harland, Lynn	Asst	Neb-Omaha			PHD	91	Iowa	1989
Harling, Kenneth F.	Assoc	Wilfrid Laur	3	I	PHD		Purdue	1989
Harlow, Howard R.	Prof	Georgia Col	38	IL	PHD	73	Nebraska	1984
Harmon, Joel I.	Asst	F Dick-Madis	12	DEZ	PHD		SUNY-Alb	1993
Harmon, Michael	Prof	George Wash	1	A	PHD	68	S Calif	
Harms, Craig G.	Assoc	North Fla	7	UV	PHD		Ohio St	
Harp, Robert M.	Inst	Miami U-Ohio	1	L	MA	62	Naval Po	8-79
Harpell, John L. Jr.	Assoc	W Virginia	7	V	DBA	74	Geo St	1967
Harper, Earl	Prof	Grand Valley			PHD		Tx Tech	1971
Harper, Steve	Prof	N Car-Wilmin	36	DIST	PHD	75	Ariz St	1976
Harrick, Edward J.	Prof	S Ill-Edward	5	NQ	PHD	74	St Louis	1974
Harrigan, Kathryn	Prof	Columbia	23	EI	DBA	79	Harvard	1981
Harriman, Ann S.	Prof	CS-Sacrament	25	ENR	DPA	80	S Calif	1973
Harrington, Kermith	Asst	Syracuse	2	H	PHD	91	Tx A&M	1990
Harrington, Thomas			7	U	PHD	79	N Carol	
Harris, Albert L.	Assoc	Appalach St	9	Z	PHD		Geo St	1989
Harris, Alma F.	Prof	Weber State			PHD	73	Purdue	1973
Harris, C. Ruth	Asst	Wilfrid Laur	7	UV	PHD		Waterloo	1986
Harris, Christine		Bournemouth			MSC			
Harris, Claudia	Assoc	N Carol Cen	24	ELRY	PHD	84	Utah	9-92
Harris, D. J.	Lect	Univ Bath	7	U	MSC			
Harris, Dawn	Asst	Loyola-Chicg			PHD		Northwes	
Harris, George	Asst	Chicago St			MBA		Roosevlt	1986
Harris, Harry G.	Prof	CS-Fresno	23	BEIY	PHD		Harvard	1980
Harris, James R.	Asst	N Carol A&T	5		PHD	90	Fla St	8-90
Harris, John	Assoc	WI-Green Bay	12	EFGQ	PHD	81	Kentucky	1978
Harris, Kimberly H.	Asst	Wm Jewel	79	U	MBA	78	Kansas	1986
Harris, Michael M.	Assoc	Mo-St Louis	5	N	PHD	84	Ill-Chic	1988
Harris, O. Jeff Jr.	Prof	NE Louisiana	2	EN	PHD	66	Texas	1986
Harris, R. Scott	Assoc	Mont St-Bill		Econ	PHD	85	Calif	1988
Harris, Reuben T.	Prof	Naval Postgr	23	FHIY	PHD	75	Stanford	7-78
Harris, Robert G.	Assoc	Cal-Berkeley	43	IL	PHD		Berkeley	1977
Harris, Roy D.	Retir	Texas	7	1994	PHD	65	UCLA	1965
Harris, Sidney E.	Dean	Claremont Gr	17	DUVY	PHD		Cornell	1987
Harris, Stanley	Assoc	Auburn	52	EN	PHD	88	Michigan	9-86
Harris, Stanley F.	Assoc	Lawrence Tec	2		PHD			1968
Harris, Thomas M.	Assoc	Ball State	9		DBA		Colorado	1978
Harris, Walter	Asst	Southern	13	GI	MBA	69	Atlanta	1973
Harris, William	Assoc	Loyola-Maryl	7	V	DSC		J Hopkin	
Harris, William	Retir	Shippensburg		1991	MBA		American	
Harrison, Allison W.	Asst	Miss State	5	N	PHD	93	Clemson	1993
Harrison, Benjamin	Asst	Salisbury St	7	UV	PHD	90	Geo St	8-88
Harrison, Cliff	C-Pr	Concordia C	15	JN	EDD		Fairl Di	1986
Harrison, David A.	Assoc	Tx-Arlington	2	ENX	PHD		Illinois	1989
Harrison, Edward	C-Pr	So Alabama	25	FNPQ	PHD	75	North Tx	1974
Harrison, Frank	Prof	San Fran St	1		PHD	70	U Wash	1984

Name	Rank	School	#	Code	Degree	Yr	DegSchool	Year
Harrison, J. Michael	Prof	Stanford	7	U	PHD	70	Stanford	1970
Gregor C. Peterson Professor of Operations Management								
Harrison, J. Richard	Assoc	Texas-Dallas	2	E	PHD	86	Stanford	1985
Harrison, Jeffrey S.	Assoc	Cen Florida	3	I	PHD	85	Utah	1993
Harrison, Kline	Asst	Wake Forest	25	EHNP	PHD	87	Maryland	9-90
Harrison, Mernoy			7	U	PHD	88	N Carol	
Harrison, Terry P.	Assoc	Penn State	7	V	PHD		Tenn	
Harshman, Ellen	Asst	St Louis			PHD		St Louis	1993
Hart, Maxine Barton	Prof	Baylor		Z	EDD		Houston	1971
Hart, Pamela M.	Lect	East Carol	56		MBA	86	E Carol	8-86
Hart, Sandra Hile	Dean$	Txs Wesleyan			PHD	84	Tx A&M	1985
Hart, Stuart L.	Asst	Michigan	3	IMH	PHD	83	Michigan	1986
Hart, William S.	Assoc	Mid Tenn St	35	IQ	PHD	69	Florida	1986
Hartenian, Linda	Asst	Wis-Oshkosh	5	NQX	PHD	91	Kentucky	1990
Hartley, Lorraine	AsDn	Franklin	12	EFGH	DBA	92	Nova	1-94
Hartley, Mark F.	Asst	Charleston			DBA		La Tech	1985
Hartley, Nell T.	H-Ac	Robt Morris	21	DEH	PHD	80	Vanderbt	9-81
Hartley, William B.	Assoc	SUNY-Fredon	53	NI	PHD		Wiscon	1977
Hartman, E. Alan	Prof	Wis-Oshkosh	26	ENOT	PHD	72	Mich St	1976
Hartman, Ed	Assoc	Rutgers-Newk			PHD		Princeto	1984
Hartman, Jim Jr.	Asst	Gardner-Webb	73	UP	ABD		Clemson	1983
Hartman, Karen	Asst	Ferris State	8		JD	79	Michigan	1993
Hartman, Richard I.	Prof	Bradley	2	NR	DBA	61	Indiana	1961
Hartman, Sandra J.	Prof	New Orleans	12	E	PHD	85	LSU	8-81
Hartman, Stephen	Assoc	NY Inst Tech	12		PHD			
Hartvigsen, David	Assoc	Notre Dame	7		PHD	85	Car Mel	1993
Hartviksen, K.	Assoc	Lakehead U	6	T	MDA		York	
Hartwick, J.	Assoc	McGill Univ	2		PHD		Illinois	1980
Hartzel, John E.	Retir	Bloomsburg	9	Z	MCD		Lehigh	
Harven, Jeraline	Prof	Savannah St	17	P	EDD	64	Indiana	1975
Harvey, Brian	Prof	Manchest Bus	14	CM	PHD		Nottingh	1992
Harvey, Carol	Assoc	Assumption	25	LRHF	EDD	91	Mass	1990
Harvey, Cheryl A.	Asst	Wilfrid Laur	2	E	PHD		Western	1988
Harvey, Christine		Bournemouth	7	V	MSC		Brunel	9-71
Harvey, Donald	Prof	CS-Bakersf	31	S	PHD			1991
Harvey, Jerry	Prof	George Wash	2	H	PHD	63	Texas	
Harvey, Michael G.	Prof	Oklahoma	38	ISTY	PHD	76	Arizona	8-92
Puterbaugh Chair of American Free Enterprise								
Harvey, Santhi	Asst	Cen St-Ohio	12	Z	MBA		WrightSt	9-89
Harvey, Steve	Asst	Bishop's Un	25	NPQ	PHD		Guelph	1994
Hasan, Naila		Southeastern			MBA			
Hasan, Syed M. Jameel	Prof	Eastern Wash	28	EYL	ABD	64	S Carol	1969
Hashemi, Ali	Prof	Calif U-Penn	2	E	PHD		Northwes	1982
Hasnas, John	Asst	Georgetown	4	JKL	PHD	88	Duke	1991
Haspeslagh, Philippe	Assoc	INSEAD	3	I	DBA	83	Harvard	9-79
Hassan, M. Zia	Dean	Illinois Tch	7	V	PHD	65	Ill Tech	1960
Hassanein, Saad	Prof	Marymount			PHD		Catholic	1988
Hassell, Barbara L.	Asst	North Texas	25	ENC	PHD	91	Fla St	8-89
Hassell, Eloise M.	Lect	N Car-Greens	4	JK	JD	83	Wake For	9-89
Hastings, Barbara	Assoc	SC-Spartanbu	25	EFIN	PHD	77	North Tx	1985
Haswell, Stephen	Lect	Australian N	8	Y	MEC	90	Aust Nat	1986
Hatch, Mary Jo	Assoc	San Diego St	2	EH	PHD	85	Stanford	1987
Hatcher, Jerome M.	Assoc	La St-Shreve	7	U	PHD		Arkansas	8-85
Hatchett, Paul	Asst	Ft Valley St	4		JD	93	Widner	9-92
Hatfield John	Prof	Cen Florida	12	E	PHD	76	Purdue	1990
Hatfield, Donald	Asst	Virg Tech	3		PHD	93	UCLA	1993
Hatfield, Louise	Assoc	Shippenburg			MBA			
Hatten, Kenneth J.	Assoc	Boston Univ	3	I	PHD		Purdue	
Hattersley, Michael	Lect	Harvard	1	&				
Hatton, Lindle	Assoc	CS-Sacrament	36	HIT	PHD	88	Kentucky	1990
Hauck, Vern E.	Prof	Alaska-Ancho	53	QNI	PHD	74	Iowa	1975
Haug, Peter	Assoc	Western Wash	78	UY	PHD	78	U Wash	9-86
Haugen, Dyan	Assoc	St Cloud St	7	UV	PHD	93	Minn	1991
Haugland, Sven	Assoc	Norwegian			DREC			
Haukedal, Wiley	Assoc	Norwegian			DREC			
Haunschild, Pamela	Asst	Wisconsin		EH	PHD	92	Car Mel	1992
Hauser, John R.	Prof	MIT			SCD	75	MIT	
Hauser, Richard D. Jr.	Asst	East Carol		Z	PHD	91	Fla St	8-90
Hauserman, Nancy R.	Assoc	Iowa	4	K	JD	76	Iowa	7-83
Hausman, Warren H.	Prof	Stanford	6	UM	PHD	66	MIT	1977
Haverly, Frederick S.	Assoc	Western St	13		MBA	66	Syracuse	1977
Havird, Lloyd B.	Inst	Hampton	58		MBA		Gold Gt	8-82
Hawang, Mark I.	Asst	Tx-Pan Amer	9	Z	PHD		Texas	1990
Hawes, Beth	Asst	Keene State			EDD		Mass	1987
Hawk, David	Prof	NJ Inst Tech	82	YE	PHD	79	Penn	1981
Hawk, Stephen R.	Assoc	Wis-Parkside	9	Z	PHD	87	Wiscon	8-93
Hawk, Thomas F.	C-Ac	Frostburg St	3	FI	PHD	91	Pitt	8-72
Hawkes, James S.	Asst	Charleston			PHD		Clemson	1977
Haworth, Nigel	Assoc	U Auckland	58	QY	PHD	82	Liverpol	5-88

Name	Rank	School			Degree		University	Year
Hax, Arnoldo C.	Prof	MIT	3	I	PHD	67	Berkeley	1972
Alfred P. Sloan Professor of Management								
Hay, Michael	Asst	London Bus	36	SI	PHD		York	1986
Hayajneh, Abdalla	Asst	Grambling St	23	ENRY	PHD	90	North Tx	1990
Haydel, Belmont F.	Assoc	Rider	38	IY	PHD	83	North Tx	1979
Hayes, John	Prof	Univ Leeds	2	EF	PHD	70	Leeds	1965
Hayes, Robert H.	Prof	Harvard	7	U				
Philip Caldwell Professor of Business Administration								
Hayes, Thomas L.	Asst	John Carroll			MA		J Carrol	1969
Hayford, Stephen L.	Assoc	Wake Fr-MBA	54	NJ	JD	87	Indiana	1990
Hayne, Stephen	Asst	Univ Calgary	9	Z	PHD	90	Arizona	1990
Haynes, Ray M.	Assoc	Cal Poly-SLO	7	U	PHD	88	Ariz St	1989
Haynes, Ulric	Dean	Hofstra	34		JD		Yale	9-91
Haywood, Dale	Prof	Northwood	3	I	PHD		Texas	1970
Haywood, Helen	SLect	Bournemouth	8		BA			7-90
Hayya, Jack S.	Prof	Penn State	7	V	PHD		UCLA	
Hazel, Delores	Asst	Albany State			MBA		Valdosta	
Hazen, Mary Ann	Asst	Detroit Merc			PHD	84	Case Wes	1989
Hazen, Samuel E.	Asst	Tarleton St	5	NOPQ	DBA	88	La Tech	1988
He, Xin	Asst	So Carol St	7	U	PHD			1991
Heacock, Marian V.	Prof	Alabama-Birm	4	JL	PHD	67	Alabama	1967
Head, Keith	Asst	British Colu	81	YA	PHD	91	MIT	1991
Head, Thomas C.	Asst	DePaul			PHD		Tx A&M	
Heady, Ron	Asst	SW Louisiana	7	UVX	PHD	69	MIT	1989
Healy, Howard T.	Asst	Marquette	4		MBA	54	Harvard	1947
Hearn, W. Mark	Asst	Jacksonvl St	28	EY	PHD	92	Arkansas	1989
Heath, F. R. (Chip)	Asst	Chicago	2	EHN	PHD	90	Stanford	1990
Heau, Dominique	Prof	INSEAD	3		DBA	76	Harvard	7-73
Heaver, Trevor D.	Prof	British Colu			PHD	66	Indiana	1960
Heavisides, Alan	Lect	Napier Univ	5	O	BSC			1983
Hebert, Frederic J.	Asst	East Carol	36	IT	DBA	90	La Tech	8-90
Hebert, John E.	Prof	Akron	79	UVZ	PHD	75	Purdue	9-80
Hebert, L.	Asst	Concordia U						
Hebron, Arthur E.	H-Pr	Hardin-Simm	15	ELNQ	PHD	73	Missouri	1979
Hechler, Hans	Adj	Southeastern			MA		American	
Hechler, Peter	Prof	CS-L Angeles	1	N	PHD	73	Case Wes	1973
Heckert, Richard J.	Asst	Millersville	59	EFMP	MA	76	St Franc	1979
Heckmann, Irvin	Emer	Ill-Chicago		1991	PHD	54	Wiscon	6-68
Hedegard, James M.	Prof	Roosevelt	2	F	PHD		Michigan	
Hedin, Scott R.	Asst	Gonzaga	7	U	PHD	93	S Carol	
Hedrick, Travis	Assoc	Quinnipiac	5	BQ	PHD		Brown	
Hefni, Omar	Lect	CS-Fullerton			PHD			
Hegarty, W. Harvey	Prof	Indiana	3	I	PHD	72	N Carol	1974
Hegde, Gajanan G.	Assoc	Pittsburgh	7		PHD		Rochest	
Hegedus, David M.	Assoc	Wis-Oshkosh	62	TE	PHD	81	MIT	1985
Hegglund, Robert K.	Dean	Angelo State		Mgt	PHD	72	Arkansas	1972
Heijden, Kees Van Der	Prof	Strathclyde	3	I				
Heimann, Beverly	Assoc	Ashland		IE	DBA		Kent St	1991
Heimarck, Theodore	Prof	Concordia C	1	C	JD			
Heimovics, Richard D.	Prof	Mo-Kansas Ct	2	E	PHD		Kansas	1973
Heine, R. Peter Jr.	Assoc	Stetson	25	CINE	DBA		Memphis	1987
Heineke, Janelle	Asst	Boston Univ	71	CU	DBA		Boston U	
Heintz, Timothy	Assoc	Marquette	9	Z	DBA	72	Indiana	1972
Heinz, Kristel	Asst	Aquinas	16	DOSR	MM	80	Aquinas	1991
Heizer, Jay	Prof	Tx Lutheran	7	UV	PHD	69	Ariz St	1988
Hejazi, Sassan	Asst	Beaver	97	UZ	MBA		LaSalle	9-89
Helberg, Patricia	Asst	St Thomas-MN						
Helburn, Isadore B.	Retir	Texas	25	1994	PHD	66	Wiscon	1968
Helfat, Constance E.	Asst	Pennsylvania	3	I	PHD	85	Yale	7-91
Charter Banks/Jerry E. Finger Term Assistant Professor of Management								
Helfgott, Roy	Prof	NJ Inst Tech	5	N	PHD	68	New Sch	1957
Distinguished Professor								
Heller, Vic	Assoc	Tx-S Antonio						
Hellriegel, Don	Prof	Texas A&M		IEH	PHD	69	U Wash	1975
Bennett Chair in of Business Administration								
Helmer, Ted	Prof	No Arizona	13	C	PHD	69	Pitt	
Helms, Marilyn M.	Assoc	Tenn-Chattan	3	I	DBA	87	Memphis	1987
UC Foundation Associate Professor								
Helsen, Kristiaan	Asst	Chicago			PHD	90	Penn	1990
Helsing, J. Eric	C-Pr	Wm Jewell			JD		Rutgers	1988
A. Major & Dorthy Hull Chair of Communication Business & Leadership								
Heltne, Mari	Assoc	Luther	9	Z	PHD	88	Arizona	1975
Hemaida, Ramadan	Assoc	So Indiana	7	V	PHD	90	St Louis	1988
Hemmasi, Masoud	Prof	Illinois St	32		PHD		LSU	1983
Henderson, Caroline M.	Adj	Dartmouth			DBA	83	Harvard	1984
Henderson, Iain	Lect	Napier Univ	25	FNPQ	MBA			1991
Henderson, Jeffrey W.	SFell	Manchest Bus	23	EHI	PHD		Warick	1990
Henderson, John C.	Prof	Boston Univ	9	Z	PHD		Texas	
Henderson, Rebecca M.	Asst	MIT	3	I	PHD			
Henderson, Ross	Retir	U Manitoba	37	1994	PHD	75	W Ontar	1968

Name	Rank	School		Code	Degree		University	Year
Hendrickson, Lorraine	Prof	E Michigan	2		PHD		Michigan	1981
Hendrix, William H.	H-Pr	Clemson	2	CEGX	PHD	74	Purdue	1982
Hendry, Linda C.	Lect	U Lancaster	7	UVZ	PHD		Lancaste	
Heneman, Herbert	C-Pr	Wisconsin	5	ENQX	PHD	70	Wiscon	1970
Heneman, Robert L.	Assoc	Ohio State	5	N	PHD	84	Mich St	1984
Hennart, Jean-Francois	Assoc	Illinois	8	Y	PHD	77	Maryland	1990
Hennessey, Harry W. Jr.	Assoc	Hawaii-Hilo	25	EIN	PHD	80	Georgia	8-90
Henning, Dale	Retir	U Washington	2		PHD	54	Illinois	1955
Henninger, Edward	Inst	Lycoming			MS			1988
Henricks, Tom	Asst	Kansas State	38	EHIX	PHD	91	Nebraska	8-90
Henry, John	Asst	Geo Southern	29	EZV	PHD	92	Fla St	8-91
Henry, John F.	C-Pr	Georgia SW	57		PHD		Alabama	
Henshall, Joy L.	Prof	Tenn Tech	1	EFO	PHD	71	North Tx	1975
Hensher, David	D-Pr	Univ Sydney	17	LVX	PHD	90	NS Wales	1990
Henson, Joyce M.	Asst	St Peters			PHD		Fordham	1982
Heppard, Kurt A.	Asst	USAF Academy	3	I	MBA		UCLA	
Herbert, R.	SLect	Humberside	7					
Herbert, Theodore T.	Prof	Rollins	23		DBA	71	Geo St	1985
Hercus, Terry	Prof	U Manitoba	5	N	MBA	55	Toronto	1967
Herd, Ann M.	Assoc	Marymount	2	E	PHD		Tenn	1992
Herden, Richard P.	Assoc	Louisville	12	EF	PHD	79	Pitt	1978
Hergert, Michael L.	C-Pr	San Diego St	38	IY	PHD	83	Harvard	1985
Herman, Ellen D.	Lect	Harvard	1	&				
Herman, Robert D.	Prof	Mo-Kansas Ct	2	E	PHD		Cornell	1972
Herman, Susan	Asst	Keene State			EDD	91	Massachu	1987
Hermon, Mary E.	Prof	E Michigan	1		PHD		Michigan	1977
Herndon, Neil	Lect	City Poly HK			PHD			
Herniter, Bruce	Asst	Hartford	9	Z	PHD	90	Arizona	
Herold, David M.	Prof	Georgia Tech	2	EFN	PHD	74	Yale	1973
Heroux, Lise	Asst	SUNY-Plattsb	8	Y	PHD	87	Concordi	1980
Herreid, Todd J.		Minot St						
Herring, Donald	Prof	SUNY-Oswego	5	FHNG				
Herring, Robert A. III	Asst	Radford	25	EFN	PHD	87	Fla St	8-91
Herrmann, John F.	C-Pr	CS-Long Bch	17	IU	DBA	77	S Calif	1980
Herron, Lanny	Asst	Baltimore	36	SDIJ	PHD	90	S Carol	9-89
Herschel, Richard	Asst	N Car-Greens	9	Z	PHD		Indiana	1991
Hershauer, James C.	Prof	Arizona St			DBA		Indiana	1969
Hershey, Gerald L.	H-Pr	N Car-Greens	9	Z	PHD		Indiana	1976
Hershey, John C.	Prof	Pennsylvania			PHD	70	Stanford	1976
Senior Fellow, Leonard Davis Institute of Health Economics								
Herz, Paul	Assoc	Western St	7		ABD	93	Utah St	1987
Herzberg, Frederick I.	Prof	Utah	52	HEF	PHD	50	Pitt	1972
Heshizer, Brian P.	Assoc	Cleveland St	35	PQ	PHD	79	Wiscon	1979
Heskett, James L.	Prof	Harvard	7	U				
The UPS Foundation Professor of Business Logistics								
Hess, Carl	Prof	Marymount			PHD		Michigan	1984
Hess, George L.	Prof	Loyola Marym	16	STU	DBA	74	Ariz St	1975
Hess, Peter W.	Prof	W New Eng	2	E	EDD		Mass	1980
Hess, Sidney W.	Prof	Drexel	37	JVUX	PHD	60	Case Wes	1987
Hessel, Marek P.	Assoc	Fordham	7	UV	PHD		NYU	1980
Hester, James L.	H-Pr	Louisiana Te	36	INST	PHD	65	Arkansas	1966
Hesterly, William S.	Asst	Utah	21	HNI	PHD	89	UCLA	1988
Hetherington, Barrie	Tutor	Manchest Bus	9	YZ	MBCS			1974
Hetzner, Candace	Assoc	Rutgers-Newk	8	Y	PHD		Chicago	1989
Hewitt, Charles	Adj	Rice	7	U	PHD	56	Michigan	1987
Hewitt, Eileen B.	Asst	Scranton	2	ER	MA	76	Hartford	1982
Heyl, Jeff	Asst	DePaul			PHD		Ariz St	
Heyliger, Wilton	C	Morris Brown			PHD	81	Indiana	
Hiatt, Stephen R.	Prof	Catawba	15		PHD	83	Ariz St	1987
Hickey, John	Asst	Hampton	4	JKLM	JD		Geo Wash	8-87
Hickey, Kristin	SrTch	Bond Univ	3	I	MBA	92	Bond	1992
Hickman, Charles C.	Lect	CS-Northrdge	23	DEIO	ABD		Ohio St	1991
Hickman, William	Assoc	Utica	38	ISTY	MBA			1985
Hicks, Harry E.	Prof	Butler	4	J	JD	79	Indiana	1974
Hicks, Richard	Asst	Nev-L Vegas	9	Z	PHD	91	Texas	1991
Hiemstra, Kathleen	VAsst	John Carroll			PHD		Pitt	1990
Higa, Kunihiko	Asst	Georgia Tech	9	Z	PHD	88	Arizona	1989
Higdon, Leo I. Jr.	Dean	Virg-Grad			MBA	72	Chicago	1993
Charles C. Abbott Professor of Business Administration								
Higgins, David P.	Assoc	Dallas	3	I	PHD	79	Texas	5-86
Higgins, James	Prof	Rollins	23		PHD	74	Geo St	1980
Higginson, Thomas J.	Prof	Mass-Darthmo			EDD	79	Boston U	1963
Hightower, Ross	Asst	Kansas State	9	Z	PHD	91	Geo St	8-91
Hilgert, Raymond L.	Prof	Wash Univ	45	JNQ	DBA	63	Wash U	1964
Hill, Alexander	Assoc	Seattle Pac	14	KJA	JD	80	U Wash	9-79
Joseph C. Hope Professor of Leadership and Ethics								
Hill, Andrew	Asst	Clark Atlant			PHD			
Hill, Charles W. L.	Assoc	U Washington	3		PHD	83	Manchest	1988
Hill, Constance	Lect	U Wollongong			MBA		UTS	7-90
Hill, John	Prof	Alabama	8	IY	PHD	80	Georgia	1985

Name	Rank	School			Degree		Institution	Year
Hill, Joseph A.	Prof	East Carol	82	YEIT	PHD	66	Florida	8-65
Hill, Lawrence	Prof	CS-L Angeles	7	U	PHD	68	S Calif	1969
Hill, Linda	Assoc	Harvard	25	EN				
Hill, Malcolm R.	Read	Loughborough	7	U	PHD		Birmingh	
Hill, Marvin F. Jr.	Prof	No Illinois	45	Q	PHD		Iowa	
Hill, Raymond	Prof	E Michigan	25		PHD	70	Purdue	1989
Hill, Robert	Asst	Houston	36	ITDH	PHD	86	Tx A&M	8-90
Hill, Terry	Prof	London Bus	7	U	MSC		Manchest	
Hill, Timothy R.	Asst	Hawaii-Manoa	7	B	PHD	88	Indiana	
Hill, Valdemar	Assoc	Virgin Islan	36	AFPQ	MBA			1978
Hillard, John	Assoc	Univ Leeds	5	NQ	BA	67	Durham	1972
Hilldrup, David J.	Assoc	Laurentian	7		MBA		Hawaii	
Hiller, Tammy	Asst	Bucknell	25	EN	ABD		N Carol	9-94
Hilliard, Richard Lee	Asst	Nichols Col			MBA		Trinity	
Hillier, Mark	Asst	U Washington			PHD	94	Stanford	1993
Hillmer, Steven C	Prof	Kansas	7	V	PHD		Wiscon	1977
Hills, Stephen M.	Assoc	Ohio State	5	Q	PHD	75	Wiscon	1977
Hillsman, Rovena L.	Prof	CS-Sacrament	2	E	EDD	78	Ariz St	1978
Hilton, Chadwick	Asst	Alabama		EJ&	PHD	83	Tenn	1986
Hindle, A.	SLect	U Lancaster	47	AUVZ	PHD		Nottingh	
Hindman, Hugh D.	Assoc	Appalach St	5	NQ	PHD		Ohio St	1988
Hines, D. Spencer	Asst	Hawaii Pacif	23	HIL	MBA	82	Pepperdi	1-89
Hines, Kenneth	Asst	Txs Southern	26	ES	MBA			
Hinings, C. Bob	Prof	Univ Alberta	23	HI	BA	60	Leeds	1982
Hinings, P. H.	Asst	East Anglia	3	I	FCA			1979
Hinkin, Timothy	Asst	Cornell	15	OB	PHD	85	Florida	1992
Hinkson, Diana W.	Lect	SW Texas St	1	D	MBA	77	Tarleton	1985
Hinsey, Joseph IV	Prof	Harvard	1					
Class of 1957 Professor of Business Administration								
Hinson, Thomas D.	Asst	Miami U-Ohio	3	I	PHD	91	Georgia	8-89
Hinthorne, Thomas D.	Assoc	Mont St-Bill	3		PHD	72	Oregon	1993
Hinton, Bernard L.	Prof	CS-S Marcos	2	E	PHD	66	Stanford	1989
Hipkin, I. B.	Fell	Manchest Bus	7	UV	MA		Capetown	1994
Hipp, Clayton	Assoc	Wake Forest	4	JKL	JD		S Carol	9-91
Hiraga, Ryuta	Asst	Hitotsubashi	5	U	MC	90	Hitotsub	1993
Hirsch, Paul M.	Prof	Northwestern			PHD	73	Michigan	1989
James L. Allen Distinguished Professor of Strategy & Organization Behavior								
Hirschheim, Rudolf A.	Prof	Houston	9	Z	PHD	85	London	9-88
Hiseh, Ching-Cha	Prof	Nat Taiwan U	9	Z	PHD	88	Nat ChiT	1975
Hisker, William J.	Prof	St Vincent	23		PHD		Pitt	1974
Hisrich, Robert D.	Prof	Case Western			PHD	71	Cinn	
Hitt, Michael A.	Prof	Texas A&M		ITY	PHD	74	Colorado	1985
Paul M. and Rosalie Robertson Chair in Business Administration								
Hivner, Walter	Assoc	Colorado St			PHD	71	Calif	1993
Ho, Daniel	H-Pr	Southeastern			PHD			
Ho, David C.	Prof	Oklahoma St	7	UV	PHD	85	Mich St	1983
Ho, Hsien-Chan	Prof	Nat Taiwan U	8	Y	PHD	85	Texas	1986
Ho, Johnny C.	Asst	NE Missouri	79	UV	PHD	91	Ga Tech	1991
Hoadley, Ellen D.	Asst	Loyola-Maryl	9	Z	PHD		Indiana	
Hobbs, C.	Asst	Carleton Un	79	VZ	PENG		Ontario	
Hobbs, Jon R.	Assoc	Wright State	7	Z	PHD	72	Stanford	1977
Hobson, Charles J.	Assoc	Indiana NW	12	CE	PHD	81	Purdue	1981
Hobson, R. H.		SUNY-Plattsb	7	UV	MBA	63	Fair Dic	1976
Hocevar, Susan Page	Adj	Naval Postgr	12	DEFL	PHD	89	S Calif	9-90
Hochbaum, Dorit S.	Prof	Cal-Berkeley	7	V	PHD		Penn	1981
Hochner, Arthur	Assoc	Temple			PHD		Harvard	
Hochwarter, Wayne	Asst	Miss State	5	N	PHD	93	Fla St	1-94
Hockemeyer, Sherrill	Assoc	Ind-Purdue	4	L	MS	67	Ind St	8-67
Hocking, Ralph T.	Prof	Shippensburg	7	V	DBA	72	Kent St	1972
Hockstra, Dale J.	Prof	Evansville	7	UV	PHD	74	Stanford	1976
Hodge, B. J.	Prof	Florida St		I	PHD	61	LSU	8-67
Hodge, John	Prof	Grand Valley			EDD		W Mich	1977
Hodge, Kay	Asst	Neb-Kearney	35	NQI	PHD	88	Nebraska	1984
Hodges, DeWayne		Tx-Pan Amer	79	VZ	PHD			
Hodges, Michael	SLect	London Econ	73	IKY	PHD		Penn	1988
Hodges, Peter B.	VLect	Mass-Dartmou			MBA	76	Northeas	1982
Hodgetts, James C.	Prof	Memphis	5	N	PHD	54	N Dakoka	1965
Hodgetts, Richard M.	Prof	Fla Internat		IEB	PHD	68	Oklahoma	1976
Hodgkinson, L.	Lect	North Wales	9	ZM	PHD			9-87
Hodgson, Allan	SLect	Australian N	37	HILV	MEC	88	NE	1989
Hodgson, Vivien E.	Lect	U Lancaster	25	NOP	PHD		Surrey	
Hoefer, Peter	Prof	Pace	7	F	PHD		Baruch	
Hofer, Charles W.	Prof	Georgia	36	IST	DBA	69	Harvard	1981
UGA Regents Professor								
Hoffer, Durward	Prof	NE Illinios	21	FH	PHD		Northwes	9-79
Hoffman, Alan	Assoc	Bentley	23	HI	DBA	82	Indiana	1987
Hoffman, D. Lynn	Assoc	No Colorado	56		PHD	81	Iowa	
Hoffman, James J.	Assoc	Florida St	3	IY	PHD	88	Nebraska	6-88
Hoffman, L. Richard	Prof	Rutgers-Newk	2	ENS	PHD	57	Michigan	
Hoffman, Richard C. IV	Assoc	Salisbury St	38	IY	PHD	83	Indiana	9-93

Name	Rank	Institution			Degree		School	Year
Hoffmann, Terry	Lect	Deakin-Burwo	5	OP	BA		LaTrobe	
Hoffmann, Walter	Asst	Cedarville	65	QN	MBA	73	SUNY	1990
Hoffner, Vernon	Prof	Lawrence Tec			PHD			1987
Hofmann, Lewis A.	C-As	Trenton St			DBA		Intl Grd	1979
Hofstede, Geert	Prof	Univ Limburg	28	ERXY	PHD	67	Groninge	1985
Hogan, Eileen A.	Asst	Valdosta St	2	EH	PHD	83	Berkeley	1993
Hogan, K.	Asst	McGill Univ	8		PHD		Arizona	1990
Hogarth, Robin M.	Prof	Chicago	2	E	PHD	72	Chicago	1979
Wallace W. Booth Professor of Behavior Sci; Deputy Dean for MBA Programs								
Hogg, C.	SLect	Humberside	2					
Hoggatt, Austin C.	Retir	Cal Berkeley	89	1991	PHD	57	Minn	1957
Hogler, Raymond Lewis	Prof	Colorado St	45	BKQ	PHD	72	Colorado	1989
Hogue, J. P.	Assoc	HEC-Montreal						
Hogue, Jack T.	Assoc	N Car-Charl			PHD		Georgia	1984
Hoh, Andrew K.	Assoc	Creighton	13	EFI	PHD	76	Minn	8-76
Hohma, Nitin	Asst	Harvard	25	EN				
Holden, Alison	Assoc	Deakin-Burwo	12	AZ	EMD		Melbourn	
Holden, Ellsworth	Asst	Ohio Univ			MA		Harvard	
Holland, Christopher P.	Lect	Manchest Bus		YZ	BSC		Warwick	1993
Holland, Phyllis G.	Assoc	Valdosta St	3	IS	PHD	81	Georgia	1987
Hollenbeck, John R.	Prof	Michigan St	2	E	PHD	84	New York	9-84
Hollerman, Leon	Prof	Claremont Gr	8	LY	PHD		Berkeley	1990
Holley, William H.	Prof	Auburn	5	Q	PHD	70	Alabama	9-69
Lowder Professor								
Holliday, A. J.	Asst	Wash & Lee	4	KL	JD	76	IL Tech	1976
Hollier, Gerald	Asst	Tx-Brownsvil			MBA	86	Pan Am-B	1982
Hollier, Robert H	Prof	Manches Inst	7	T	PHD		Birmingh	1977
Hollingsworth, John	Inst	St Johns			MBA		Wheeling	
Hollis, Harry	Assoc	Belmont			PHD		Vanderbt	1975
Hollmann, Robert W.	Prof	Montana	51	NP	PHD	73	U Wash	1980
Holloman, Charles R.	Retir	Augusta	2	E	PHD	65	U Wash	1973
Hollon, Charles J.	C-Pr	Shippensburg			PHD	74	Syracuse	1974
Holloway, Charles A.	Prof	Stanford	47	UVX	PHD	69	UCLA	1968
Herbert Hoover Professor of Public and Private Management								
Holloway, Madison	Asst	Metro State	25	DGNQ	PHD	77	Colorado	1990
Holloway, William L.	Assoc	No Kentucky	34	I	EDD	78	Cinn	8-76
Holman, Pat	Inst	Mont St-Bill	1		MS	82	Utah	1992
Holmberg, Stevan R.	C-Pr	American U	36	IST	DBA	71	Indiana	1977
Holmes, A. Richard	Prof	Simon Fraser	7	QVX	PHD	60	Indiana	1966
Holmes, Barbara	Asst	Evansville	25	ENO	PHD	88	LSU	1988
Holmes, Juanita	Prof	NE St-Okla	2	E	EDD	77	Arkansas	
Holmes, Judy	Asst	Furman	9	Z	PHD	88	Clemson	1990
Holmes, Robert E.	Dean	Jms Madison	31	I	PHD	71	Arkansas	9-83
Holmgreen, John	Lect	Tx-S Antonio						
Holoviak, Stephen J.	Prof	Shippensburg			PHD		West Va	
Holsinger, Alden	Inst	CUNY-Baruch	4	Y	MS		Lehigh	
Holt, David H.	Prof	Jms Madison	16	ST	PHD	78	Strathcl	9-81
Holt, Joseph	Inst	Fayetteville			MBA			
Holthausen, Duncan M.	Prof	N Carol St	7	V	PHD	74	Northwes	1976
Hom, Peter	Prof	Arizona St	25	EN	PHD		Illinois	1984
Hommel, M.	Asst	Univ Windsor	25	ENOR	MBA		Windsor	1993
Honey, W. C.	Assoc	Lakehead U	19	BCDZ	MBA		Oregon	7-69
Hong, Min-Chow	Assoc	Nat Taiwan U	3	IMHT	PHD	89	Illinois	1990
Hong, Shugang	Asst	Georgia St	9	Z	PHD		Conn	
Honts, Arlen K.	Asst	Gardner-Webb	25	EQN	ABD		Vanderbt	1993
Hood, Jacqueline	Asst	New Mexico		N	PHD	89	Colorado	
Hoogerwerf, Richard	Asst	Marian			MS	77	Butler	1988
Hooijberg, Robert	Asst	Rutgers-Newk	2	E	PHD	92	Michigan	1993
Hooker, John	Prof	Carnegie Mel	7	V	PHD		Vanderbt	1984
Hooper, Donald B.	Prof	Jacksonvil U	23	EIY	PHD	68	Ohio St	1976
Hooper, Paul	SLect	Univ Sydney	17	VNX	MS		Tasmania	1991
Hooper, Vince	Lect	Australian N	8	Y	BAHO	90	UofP UK	1994
Hoops, Linda	Prof	Moorhead St	1		PHD		SUNY-Buf	1980
Hoover, Harwood Jr.	Prof	Aquinas	48	IJXY	PHD	84	Mich St	1978
Hope, Jon W.	Assoc	Rockhurst	39	IEDZ	PHD	86	Kansas	1983
Hopeman, Richard J.	Assoc	Villanova	39	HIZ	PHD	62	U Wash	1979
Hopkins, Byron K.	Inst	Georgia St	9	Z	MBA		Geo St	
Hopkins, David M.	Assoc	Denver	8	Y	PHD		Syracuse	9-79
Hopkins, Duane L.	C-As	Fla Southern		Mktg	MBA		Harvard	1982
Hopkins, Harold D.	Assoc	Temple			PHD	83	Penn St	1982
Hopkins, Willie E.	Assoc	Colorado St	3	IJNY	PHD	84	Colorado	1983
Hopley, Robert	VLect	Massachusett	63		MBA		Mass	
Hoppel, Charles J.	Assoc	Bloomsburg	9	Z	PHD		Syracuse	
Hora, Stephen C.	Prof	Hawaii-Hilo	7	V	PHD	73	S Calif	1986
Hormozi, Amir M.	Asst	Oakland	7	U	PHD	87	Houston	1986
Horn, Kevin H.	Prof	North Fla	7	U	PHD		Penn St	
Hornaday, Robert W.					PHD	84	Fla St	
Horner, Katherine	AcLec	U Wollongong			MCOM			6-93
Horniman, Alexander B.	Prof	Virg-Grad	2	E	DBA	68	Harvard	1968
Hornsby, C. R.	SLect	Humberside						

Name	Rank	Institution			Degree		School	Year
Hornsby, Jeffrey S.	Assoc	Ball State	2		PHD		Auburn	1987
Horowitz, Ira	Prof	Florida			PHD	59	MIT	1972
Horton, Gerald T.	Lect	Georgia	36	IJS	AB	56	Harvard	1987
Horton, Howard	Asst	Mary Hrdn-By	1		MBA	75	SW Texas	
Horton, Ray	Prof	Columbia	15	AQ	PHD	71	Columbia	1970
Horton, Veronica	Asst	Mid Tenn St	3	I	PHD	92	Ohio St	1992
Horvath, Dezso J.	Dean	York Univ	3	IY	PHD		UMEA	
Horwitz, Lawrence H.	Adj	Cincinnati						
Hoskisson, Robert E.	Assoc	Texas A&M		ITY	PHD	82	Ca-Irvine	1983
Hosmer, LaRue Tone	Prof	Michigan	46	IJT	DBA	71	Harvard	1971
Hossein, Jamshidi	Asst	Alabama A&M						
Hosseini, Jamshid	Asst	Marquette	7	V	PHD	87	Port St	1987
Hostager, Todd J.	Assoc	Wis-Eau Clar		EI	PHD		Minn	1988
Hotaka, Ryosuke	C-Pr$	Univ Tsukuba	19	Z	DR			3-78
Hotard, Daniel G.	Assoc	SE Louisiana	7	UV	PHD	76	Miss St	1985
Hott, David D.	Assoc	Longwood	7	JUVX	PHD	77	Lehigh	1991
Hottenstein, Michael	Assoc	Penn State	7	V	PHD		Indiana	
Houck, John W.	Prof	Notre Dame	4	KL	LLM	63	Harvard	1957
Hough, Michael	Prof	U Wollongong			BA		Macquari	1-89
Hough, Robbin R.	Prof	Oakland	97	ZV	PHD	62	MIT	1962
Houghton, Edward L.	Prof	So Oregon St	1	B	EDD		Oreg St	1980
Houghton, Jeff	Inst	David Lipsc	25	EL	MBA		W Virg	9-93
Houghton, Keith A.	Dean	Un Melbourne						
Houghton, Susan	Asst	Georgia St			PHD	93	N Carol	1993
House, Robert J.	Prof	Pennsylvania	2	EH	PHD	60	Ohio St	7-88
Joseph Frank Bernstein Professor of Organizational Studies								
Houser, Henry	Retir	Auburn-Montg	35	N	PHD	77	St Louis	1978
Houston, Nancy P.	Inst	Slippery Roc	91	YX	EDD	85	Nova	1975
Houts, Lisa	Prof	CS-Fresno	27	EU	MBA		CS-Fresn	1990
Hovaizi, Fraidoon	Asst	N Adams St						
Hovey, David H. Jr.	Dean	West Georgia	1	T	PHD	78	LSU	8-84
Hovey, Donald	Prof	Youngstown	2		PHD	62	Colorado	9-70
Howard, Cecil G.	Assoc	Howard	3	I	PHD			
Howard, Geoffrey	Assoc	Kent State			DBA		Kent St	1984
Howard, Jack	Asst	Lamar		Mgt	PHD	92	Illinois	9-92
Howard, Michelle E.	Inst	Shenandoah			MA		G Mason	1992
Howard, Ronald A.	Prof	Stanford	37	IVXU	SCD	58	MIT	1965
Howe, Robert C.	Assoc	St Marys-Txs	7	V	MBA	64	Tx Chr	
Howell, Gordon C.	Assoc	Georgia St	9	Z	PHD		Geo St	
Howell, John	Adj	Southeastern			PHD		Columbia	
Howell, Jon P.	Prof	New Mex St	2	ENY	PHD	73	Ca-Irvine	1978
Howell, Robert A.	Prof	New York U			DBA	66	Harvard	
Howes, Mary E.	C-Pr	Governors St			PHD	81	Kansas	
Howorka, Gary V.	Asst	Tx-S Antonio	9	Z	ABD		Arizona	8-93
Howson, H.	Assoc	McGill Univ	9		PHD		Syracuse	1968
Hoyer, Denise Tanguay	Prof	E Michigan	3		PHD		Michigan	1986
Hoyt, Brian	Asst	Teikyo Mary	37	CI	MBA	85	Bryant	8-91
Hoyt, Daniel R.	Prof	Arkansas St	5	NPQ	PHD	76	Nebraska	1976
Hoyt, Elizabeth R.	Asst	Wm Jewel	32	IE	MBA	79	Wiscon	1981
Hrebiniak, Lawrence G.	Assoc	Pennsylvania	23	I	PHD	71	SUNY-Buf	7-76
Hruska, James	Asst	Neb Wesleyan	9		MS	76	Nebraska	1984
Hsee, Christopher K.	Asst	Chicago			PHD	93	Yale	1993
Hsu, L. F.	Assoc	CUNY-Baruch	7	U	PHD		Case Wes	1987
Hsu, Margaretha M.	Assoc	Shippensburg	7	V	PHD		Va Tech	
Hsu, Mu-Lan	Prof	Nat Taiwan U	25	EFHD	PHD	78	Ohio St	1986
Hsu, Yuan-Hsi	Assoc	East Carol		V	PHD		LSU	1980
Huang, Chung-Hsing	Assoc	Nat Taiwan U	79	VZU	PHD	87	Texas	1987
Huang, Jun-Ying	Prof	Nat Taiwan U	7	IV	PHD	74	Iowa	1978
Huang, Zhimin	Asst	Adelphi	97	ZUVX	PHD	91	Texas	1991
Hubbard, Charles	C	Clayton St			PHD	70	Arkansas	1989
Hubberstey, Chris	Lect	Wilfrid Laur	3	I	MBA		Wilfrid	1992
Huber, George P.	Prof	Texas	2	EHI	PHD	66	Purdue	1983
Huber, Vandra L.	Assoc	U Washington	5		PHD	82	Indiana	1987
Hudson, Donald R.	Assoc	U Miami	13	I	PHD	74	Geo St	1974
Hudson, Roger	Assoc	Wis-Parkside	3	I	PHD	90	Minn	8-91
Hudson, Thomas	Asst	Neb Wesleyan	31		PHD	91	Nebraska	1989
Huete, Luis Maria	Assoc	Univ Navarra	7	U	PHD		Boston	6-82
Huettman, Elizabeth	Lect	Cornell	1	D	PHD	90	Purdue	8-86
Huff, Anne	Prof	Colorado	3	IX	PHD	74	Northwes	1991
Huffman, Brian	Inst	Wis-Rvr Fall			MS			
Huffmire, Donald W.	Assoc	Connecticut	3	I	DBA	71	Geo St	1971
Hufft, Edward M.	Asst	Indiana SE	3	I	DBA	91	Kentucky	1990
Huggins, Lawrence P.	Prof	Manhattan	12	HIU	PHD	72	Penn	1979
Hughes, Ann J.	Retir	Georgia St	7	1994	DBA		Geo St	
Hughes, Carlyle D.	Prof	Univ of D C	13	I	PHD	66	U Wash	1974
Hughes, Geoffrey	Lect	U Lethbridge	38	IY	MBA	82	Cty Lond	1989
Hughes, Paula Ann	Prof	Dallas	52	QG	PHD	78	North Tx	8-79
Hughes, R. Eugene	Prof	East Carol	25	EFNP	DBA	75	Kentucky	8-85
Hughes, Stephen G.	Lect	U Auckland	58	QYE	MA	85	Warwick	7-91
Hughs, Richard	Dean	SUNY-Albany	3	IT	PHD	62	Purdue	1991

Inkson, Kerr	H-Pr	U Auckland	12	EO	PHD	80	Otago	9-80
Inman, J. W.	Asst	West Georgia	1		MBA	72	Geo Wash	9-91
Inman, Ray Anthony	Asst	Louisiana Te	7	UV	DBA	88	Memphis	1989
Insley, Robert	Asst	North Texas	1	D	EDD	88	N Illino	1988
Inveiss, Uldis E.	Prof	Carroll			MBA		Wiscon	1963
Ireland, R. Duane	Prof	Baylor	63	IT	PHD		Tx Tech	1983

Associate Dean, Curtis Hankamer Professor of Entrepreuneurship

Ireland, Timothy C.	Prof	Oklahoma St	7	UV	PHD	78	Okla St	1981
Irving, Richard H.	Assoc	York Univ	9	Z	PHD		Waterloo	
Irwin, Charles D.	C-Pr	Corpus Chris	34		EDD		Oklahmoa	
Irwin, Douglas A.	Asst	Chicago	8	Y	PHD	88	Columbia	1991
Irwin, W. Graham	Inst	Miami U-Ohio	13	I	MBA	81	Miami U	1-82
Isaac, Akkanad M.	Prof	Governors St	9	Z	PHD	69	Lehigh	
Isaak, Robert A.	Prof	Pace-Westch	8		PHD	71	NYU	1977
Isabella, Lynn A.	Assoc	Virg-Grad	2	E	DBA		Boston	1990
Isakowitz, Tomas	Asst	New York U	9	Z	PHD	89	Penn	
Isenman, Albert W.	Assoc	Northwestern	13	IJ	PHD	82	Northwes	
IsHak, Samir	Prof	Grand Valley			PHD		Indiana	1968
Isshiki, Koichiro R.	Prof	CS-Pomona	9	Z	PHD	71	UCLA	1971
Ito, J. K.	Assoc	Univ Regina	23	EHIN	PHD		Wash	
Ivancevich, John M.	Dean	Houston	25	GCEN	DBA	68	Maryland	1974
Ives, Blake	C-Pr	So Methodist			PHD	78	Minn	
Ives, Jane	Asst	Mass-Boston	6	T	PHD	85	London	1989
Iyama, Toshikazu			7	U	PHD	84	N Carol	
Iyengar, Jagannathan	Assoc	Jackson St			PHD		Geo St	1993
Iyer, Ananth V.	Assoc	Chicago	7	UV	PHD	87	Ga Tech	1987
Iyogun, Paul O.	Assoc	Wilfrid Laur	7	V	PHD		Brit Col	1987
Izumi, Hiroaki	Lect	City Poly HK	28	EFHY	PHD	92	Tx Tech	9-90
Jackman, Thomas	Asst	Neb Wesleyan	18		MBA	86	DePaul	1991
Jackofsky, Ellen F.	Assoc	So Methodist			PHD	82	Texas	1982
Jackson, Conrad N.	Assoc	Alabama-Hunt	25	EFP	PHD	81	Purdue	1989
Jackson, Don	Assoc	Abilene Chr			DBA		Geo Wash	1987
Jackson, Gary	C-Pr$	Houston-Down						
Jackson, Giles A.	Asst	Shenandoah			PHD		Va Techf	1992
Jackson, Janice J.	C-Ac	Virginia St	31	DER	DBA	90	Memphis	9-92
Jackson, Joe	Assoc	Alabama A&M			MBA		Alab A&M	
Jackson, John H.	Prof	Wyoming	51	NPS	DBA		Colorado	8-73
Jackson, LaMarr	Asst	St John Fish	4		JD		Buffalo	
Jackson, Mary	Asst	London Bus	7	V	MA		Oxford	
Jackson, R. L.	Asst	Queen's Univ	5	Q	MBA	71	Queen's	1974
Jackson, W. Burke	Assoc	Brigham Yg	3	I	PHD	78	Stanford	1973
Jackson, William	Asst	So Oregon St	79	DVZ	PHD	73	N Colo	1991
Jackson, William T.	Asst	S F Austin	36	DIST	DBA	91	Memphis	1991
Jacob, Ronald	Inst	NE St-Okla	6	S	MBA	71	Tulsa	1989
Jacobs, David	Assoc	American U	45	LQ	PHD		Cornell	1986
Jacobs, George W.	Assoc	Mid Tenn St	2	EH	PHD	79	Georgia	1979
Jacobs, Karen L.	Lect	S F Austin	12	JGD	MBA	88	S F Aust	1988
Jacobs, Kathleen C.	C-Pr	Wesley	12		EDD	87	Temple	1988
Jacobs, Larry W.	Assoc	No Illinois		U	PHD	89	Fla St	
Jacobs, Lester	Assoc	Wyoming			PHD			
Jacobs, Mavis	Asst	Athabasca Un	91		MBA	91	Alberta	1988
Jacobs, Neil W.	Prof	No Arizona	2	IZ	PHD	78	Santa Cl	
Jacobs, Raymond A.	Assoc	Ashland		UV	PHD	85	N Carol	9-90
Jacobs, Sheila M.	Asst	Oakland	9	Z	PHD	87	Ariz St	1987
Jacobsen, Lowell R. Jr.	Assoc	Wm Jewel	36	T	PHD	86	Edinburg	1981
Jacobson, Carol	Asst	Arizona St	38	CILY	PHD	88	Minn	1988
Jacobson, Carolyn	Assoc	Marymount	9	Z	PHD		Ohio U	1992
Jacobson, Jeffrey	Asst	Morris Brown			MTX	84	Geo St	1992
Jacobson, Robert	Asst	St Ambrose	74	V	MA	79	Webster	1991
Jacobson, Russell E.	C-Pr	Wis-Whitewat	7	JUV	PHD	76	Mass	1976
Jacobson, Sarah	Asst	N Dakota St	25	EN	ABD		Mass	1991
Jacoby, Sanford M.	Prof	UCLA			PHD	81	Berkeley	1980
Jaeger, A.	Assoc	McGill Univ	2		PHD		Stanford	1978
Jagannathan, Raj	Prof	Iowa	7	U	PHD	69	Car Mel	1975
Jagiello, Kevin G.	Fell	Manchest Bus	3	FIZ	DPBA		Manchest	1987
Jago, Arthur G.	C-Pr	Missouri	2	E	PHD	77	Yale	1994
Jaikumar, Ramchandran	Prof	Harvard	7	U				
Jaillet, Patrick	Assoc	Texas	7	UV	PHD	85	MIT	1991
Jain, Anjani	Asst	Pennsylvania			PHD	87	UCLA	1986

Atlantic Richfield Foundation Term Assistant Professor

Jain, Bharat	Asst	Towson State	79		PHD	92	Penn St	1992
Jain, Harish C.	Prof	McMaster Un	5	NQ	PHD		Wiscon	
Jain, Virod K.	Asst	Tx Christian	3	I	PHD	94	Maryland	1994
Jalife, Paloma	Asst	SUNY-Oswego	38	DIUY	MBA	88	Syracuse	1990
Jamal, A. M. M.	Asst	SE Louisiana	79	UVZ	PHD	79	Tx A&M	1986
Jamal, M.	Prof	Concordia U						
Jambekar, Anil B.	Prof	Mich Tech	7	UV	PHD	71	U Wash	1971
James, Dean F.	Assoc	Embry-Riddle	9		MS	71	UCLA	1981
James, John H.	Assoc	Florida	23	IJ	DBA	61	Indiana	1961

Name	Rank	School			Degree		School	Year
James, Lawrence R.	Prof	Tennessee	25	ENX	PHD	70	Utah	8-88
Pilot Oil Chair								
Jameson, Daphne	Asst	Cornell	18	YD	PHD	79	Illinois	8078
Jamil, Mamnoon	Asst	Rutgers-Camd			PHD			
Janaro, Ralph E.	Assoc	Clarkson	7	V	DBA	82	Fla St	
Janisch, Glenn		Bellevue						
Jankovich, Jackie	Asst	Colorado St	15	P&	MS	80	Kan St	1987
Jankovich, Leslie	Prof	San Jose St	38	YIJT	DSC	72	Brussels	1979
Jankovich, William S.	Prof	Carthage	8		MBA		Marquett	1977
Jankowski, David J.	Asst	CS-S Marcos	9	Z	PHD	94	Arizona	1992
Jankowski, Jan	Assoc	Savannah St	4	K	JD	74	Emory	1979
Jansen, Erik	Asst	Utah	52	EFHO	PHD	87	S Calif	1988
Janz, Tom	Assoc	Univ Calgary	5	NP	PHD	76	Minn	1982
Jarrell, Donald W.	Assoc	Drexel	5	HRPL	PHD	58	Penn	1958
Jarvenpaa, Sirkka L.	Asst	Texas	9	Z	PHD	86	Minn	1986
Jauch, Lawrence R.	Prof	NE Louisiana	3	I	PHD	73	Missouri	1987
Biedenharn Professor								
Javian, Setrak	Assoc	So Conn St	26	EFST	PHD	74	Case Wes	1991
Javidan, Mansour	C-Pr	Univ Calgary	3	I	PHD	83	Minn	1990
Jaw, Yi-Long	Assoc	Nat Taiwan U	38	YI	PHD	87	Ohio St	1987
Jawahar, Jim	Asst	SW Okla St			PHD	93	Okla St	1994
Jayaraman, L.	Assoc	Montclair St	37	ILUV	PHD			1988
Jeanquart, Sandy Ann	Asst	Murray State	25	ENOQ	DBA	91	S Illin	1991
Jedel, Michael Jay	Prof	Georgia St	5	NQ	DBA	72	Harvard	1971
Jedlicka, Allen D.	Prof	No Iowa			PHD	73	Northwes	9-73
Jeffery, Arthur	Inst	So Alabama	79	UV	MDA	90	Kansas	1991
Jeffries, Carol J.	Asst	N Car-Charl			PHD		Tx-Arlin	1989
Jehn, Karen	Asst	Pennsylvania	2	E	PHD	92	Northwes	7-92
May Dept Stores Term Asstistant Professor of Management								
Jehn, Karen	Asst	Wisconsin	24	EHJ	PHD	93	Northwes	1994
Jelassi, Tawfik	C-Ac	INSEAD	9	Z	PHD	85	NYU	1-89
Jemison, David B.	C-Pr	Texas	3	IHY	PHD	78	U Wash	1988
Jenicke, Lawrence	Prof	Cen Michigan	7	U	PHD	67	Mich St	1977
Jenkins, G. Douglas Jr.	Assoc	Arkansas	2	EN	PHD	77	Michigan	1984
Jenkins, M.		Humberside	2					
Jenkins, Sarah	Lect	Australian N	3	BEFI	GRDI	90	CU	1993
Jenner, Paul F.	Asst	Missouri Wes		SY	MA		Drury	1986
Jenner, Richard A.	Prof	San Fran St	6		PHD	64	Colorado	1984
Jenner, Stephen	Prof	CS-Dominguez	3	Y	PHD		Sussez	1991
Jennings, Daniel F.	Assoc	Baylor	32	HI	PHD		Tx A&M	1984
Mrs. W.A. (Agnes) Mays Professor of Entrepreneurship & Strategic Mgt								
Jennings, Kenneth M.	Prof	North Fla	5	NQ	PHD	73	Illinois	1973
Jennings, P. Devereaux	Assoc	British Colu	2	HN	PHD	89	Stanford	1988
Jennings, Sandra	Assoc	Central Okla			PHD	84	Oklahoma	1988
Jensen, Eunice	Assoc	Loyola-Chicg			DBA		Harvard	
Jensen, Michael C.	Prof	Harvard	25	EN				
Edsel Bryant Ford Professor of Business Administation								
Jensen, Ronald L.	Prof	Emory	9	Z	DBA	64	Wash U	
Jenster, Per V.		Intl Mgt Dev	3	I	PHD		Pitt	
Jenzarli, Ali	Asst	Tampa	7	UV	ABD	93	Kansas	1993
Jerden, Jonathan	Lect	Butler	19	AZ	MBA	90	Butler	1986
Jermakowicz, Walter	Prof	So Indiana	18	IS	PHD	74	Warsaw T	1985
Jermier, John M.	Prof	South Fla	2	EH	PHD	79	Ohio St	1983
Jernigan, I. Edward	Asst	N Car-Charl			DBA		Memphis	1989
Jerome, William T.	Prof	Fla Internat		E	DSC	52	Harvard	1963
Distinguished University Professor								
Jerrell, Lee	Retir	San Jose St	32	1994	PHD	78	Stanford	1984
Jesaitis, Patrick	Prof	Mo-Kansas Ct	2	E	DBA	69	Harvard	1968
Jessen, Diane	Asst	Marist			PHD		Renssel	1994
Jessup, Leonard	Assoc	CS-S Marcos	9	Z	PHD	89	Arizona	1990
Jewkes, E.	Assoc	Un Waterloo	7	UV	PHD	88	Waterloo	1988
Jex, C. F.	Lect	U Lancaster	7	UVZ	MSC		London	
Jha, Shelly	Asst	Wilfrid Laur	7	U	PHD		Iowa	1990
Jiang, James J.	Asst	Grand Valley			PHD	92	Cinn	1994
Jiang, William Y.	Assoc	San Jose St	5	NQY	PHD	92	Columbia	1991
Jick, Todd D.	Assoc	Harvard	25	EN				
Jih, W. J. Kenny	Assoc	Tenn-Chattan	9	Z	PHD	85	North Tx	1988
Jin, Gregory		Western Conn						
Joachimsthaler, Erich A.	Assoc	Univ Navarra	7	V	PHD		Kansas	1-89
Job, Tony	Asst	CUNY-Baruch	3	IS	PHD		Claremont	1993
Jobin, Marie-Helene	Asst	HEC-Montreal			PHD		Quebec	
Jogkelar, Prafulla	Prof	LaSalle	7	U	PHD		Penn	1972
Johannesson, Russell E.	Assoc	Temple			PHD		Bowl Gr	
Johns, G.	Prof	Concordia U					Calif	
Johns, J. G.	Assoc	Univ Regina	36	IST	MBA			
Johns, Roger	Asst	E New Mexico	4	JKL	LLM	88	Boston	1988
Johns, T. Reid	Assoc	Clarion	79	UVW	PHD	92	Fla St	8-92
Johnson, Avis L.	Assoc	Akron	25	ERF	PHD	86	Nebraska	1-84
Johnson, B. Cooper	Asst	Delta State	57	ENUV	ABD	90	Miss	8-83
Johnson, Bernard A.	Assoc	Missouri So			MBA	72	C Mo St	1974

Name	Rank	School	No.	Codes	Deg	Yr	University	Year
Johnson, Bradley	Asst	Montana			PHD	89	St Louis	1992
Johnson, Bruce H.	C-Ac	Gustavus Ado	28		PHD	79	Houston	1986
Johnson, Charles H.					DBA	74	Fla St	
Johnson, Dale A.	Assoc	Wis-Eau Clar	9	Z	PHD		Wi-Milwa	1987
Johnson, David G.	SLect	Loughborough	7	V	BSC		Leeds	
Johnson, David W.	Inst	St Paul's	69	SZ	ABD			1989
Johnson, Dewey E.	Prof	CS-Fresno	62	SEI	PHD		Minn	1977
Johnson, Donald	Prof	Carthage	72		MBA		Mich St	1970
Johnson, Donald W.	Assoc	Lynchburg	52	NQ	MA	67	Geo Wash	7-75
Johnson, E. K.	Lect	U Auckland	25	ENP	PHD	90	Tulane	9-92
Johnson, Edward A.	Prof	North Fla	25		PHD	68	Mich St	1989
Johnson, George A.	Prof	Idaho State		U	PHD	70	Oregon	1973
Johnson, George C.	Prof	Sonoma State	7	UV	PHD	72	Berkeley	9-73
Johnson, Grace F.	Asst	Marietta	9	Z	MACC	88	So Fla	1989
Johnson, Guy	Inst	Morris Brown			MTX		CAU	1992
Johnson, J. Lynn	Assoc	North Texas	12	EJ	PHD	76	Arkansas	1979
Johnson, James	Adj	No Carolina	4	J	PHD	80	Mich St	1992
E. Maynard Adams Professor								
Johnson, James W.	Retir	Furman	13	1994	MBA	56	Emory	1957
Johnson, Julius	Asst	Mo-St Louis	34		PHD	91	Geo Wash	1991
Johnson, Karl	Prof	Mo-Kansas Ct	1	AD	PHD	70	Oregon	1972
Johnson, Les	Prof	Univ Sydney	3	I	PHD		Conn	1992
Johnson, M. Eric	Asst	Vanderbilt	7	UVWX	PHD	91	Stanford	9-91
Johnson, Madeline	Assoc	Houston-Down						
Johnson, Mark A.	Assoc	Idaho State		N	PHD	88	Iowa	1987
Johnson, Nancy Brown	Assoc	Kentucky	5	QNR	PHD	87	Kansas	1986
Johnson, Pam	Assoc	CS-Chico			PHD		Wiscon	1984
Johnson, Pamela	Asst	Miami U-Ohio	1	EH	PHD	93	Case Wes	8-93
Johnson, Paul R.	Assoc	Am Grad Intl	68	TSY	PHD	68	Stanford	8-82
Johnson, R.	Assoc	Iowa State	5	N	PHD	86	Bowl Gr	1992
Johnson, Richard	Prof	Siena Coll	14		EDD		SUNY-Alb	
Johnson, Richard A.	Asst	Missouri	3	I	PHD	92	Tx A&M	1991
Johnson, Rob	Assoc	London Bus	6	T	MBA		Virginia	1990
Johnson, Robin	Asst	Virg-Grad	2	E	PHD	94	Harvard	1994
Johnson, Roy	Asst	Appalach St	34	IJLQ	PHD	91	N Carol	1989
Johnson, Sharon	Asst	Worcester Pl	7	UV	PHD	89	Cornell	7-88
Johnson, Sharon G.	C-Ac	Cedarville	3	I	DBA	78	Fla St	1993
Johnson, Stanley	Assoc	St Thomas-MN						
Johnson, Thomas	Prof	CS-Fullerton	25	EN	PHD	72	Illinois	8-81
Johnson, Victoria	Assoc	Mercer-Atlan	14	ACNO	DPA		Georgia	1986
Johnson, Walter II	Inst	Fayetteville			MBA			
Johnston, David A.	Assoc	York Univ	7	U	PHD		W Ontari	
Johnston, Van R.	Prof	Denver	2	L	PHD		S Calif	9-76
Johnston, Wallace R.	Assoc	Virg Comm	1	EFHN	DBA	72	Geo Wash	1971
Johnstone, David J.	Asst	Univ Sydney	17	VXY	PHD		Sydney	6-89
Joiner, Harry	Prof	Athens State	8	AY	PHD		Kentucky	1970
Joiner, W. Carl	Dean	Mercer-Atlan	16	CDT	PHD	78	Alabama	1974
Jolly, Geraldine	Asst	Barton	5		MA		Cen Mich	1988
Jolly, James P.	Assoc	Idaho State		N	PHD	85	Tx-Dallas	1988
Jolly, Vijay K.		Intl Mgt Dev	8	Y	PHD		Harvard	
Jolt, Harvey	Asst	Adelphi	12	CAE	PHD	74	NYU	1988
Joly, Allain	Asst	HEC-Montreal	13	IY	PHD		SaoPaulo	
Jones, Bryce	Prof	NE Missouri	4	JKL	PHD	79	Wiscon	1977
Jones, Candace	Asst	Boston Coll	2	HO	PHD	93	Utah	9-94
Jones, Carol Larson	Assoc	CS-Pomona	1	Z	EDD	80	N Colo	1987
Jones, Charlie C.	Asst	East Central	34	INKQ	JD	86	Oklahoma	8-86
Jones, Christopher V.	Assoc	Simon Fraser	79	UVZ	PHD	85	Cornell	1990
Jones, Coy A.	Prof	Memphis	25	EFN	PHD	82	Oklahoma	1981
Jones, D. R.	Lect	North Wales	5	PQ	PHD			9-85
Jones, Douglas E.	Assoc	Jacksonvil U	15	KLNQ	EDD	86	Florida	1980
Jones, Ellis	Prof	Gustavus Ado	9	Z	EDD	65	N Dakota	1958
Jones, Foard	Asst	Cen Florida	23	EFHI	PHD	90	Georgia	1991
Jones, Gareth L.	Asst	London Bus	25	FHOR	PHD		Kent	
Jones, Gareth R.	Assoc	Texas A&M		HI	PHD	78	Lancaste	1982
Jones, Gerald L.	C-Pr	CS-Fresno	7	U	DBA		Colorado	1979
Jones, Gwen	Asst	Bowling Gr			PHD	92	SUNY-Alb	1993
Jones, Halsey R. Jr.	Prof	Cen Florida	21	EF	PHD		Penn St	1982
Jones, Hester B.	Inst	St Paul's	1	D	ABD			1985
Jones, Jack W.	Assoc	Tx Christian	13		PHD	77	North Tx	1973
Jones, Kathleen	Lect	North Dakota	15		MBA	88	N Dakota	8-88
Jones, Lawrence	Asst	St Louis			PHD		St Louis	
Jones, Lawrence R.	Prof	Naval Postgr	34	AIL	PHD	77	Berkeley	9-87
Jones, M.		Humberside						
Jones, Marilyn S.	Assoc	Winthrop	7	UV	PHD		Va Tech	1989
Jones, Mary	Asst	MidAmer Naz	41	L&				
Jones, Mary C.	Asst	Miss State	6	UVX	PHD	90	Oklahoma	1990
Jones, Max B.	Retir	Old Dominion		1992	PHD	61	N Carol	
Jones, Philip C.	Prof	Iowa	7	U	PHD	77	Brekeley	1994
Jones, Raymond M.	Asst	Loyola-Maryl	3	IY	PHD		Maryland	1990

Name	Rank	Institution			Degree		School	Year
Jones, Robert	SLect	U Wollongong			PHD			2-94
Jones, Rosina	PLect	Humberside	3					
Jones, Thomas E.	Assoc	So Oregon St	15	FJL	MBA	64	Santa Cl	1965
Jones, Thomas M.	Prof	U Washington	4	JLK	PHD	77	Berkeley	1977
Jones, Thomas O.	SLect	Harvard						
Jones, Thomas O. Jr.	C-Pr	Greensboro			DBA	72	Geo Wash	1986
Fred L. Proctor Sr. Professor								
Jones, William A. Jr.	Prof	Georgia St	13	HIL	DPA	72	Georgia	1981
Joplin, Janice	Asst	S Ill-Edward	2	E	ABD		Tx-Arlin	1994
Jordan, David A.	Assoc	Geneva	75	UX	MBA	85	Gold Gt	1980
Jordan, Eleanor W.	Assoc	Texas	9	Z	PHD	78	Texas	1977
Jordan, Paul C.	Prof	Alaska-Ancho	7	UV	PHD	81	N Car St	1984
Jordan, Williabeth	Inst	Fla Internat		E	MPA	78	Fla Intl	1979
Jorgensen, J.	Assoc	McGill Univ	3		PHD		McGill	1980
Jorjani, Soheila	Asst	CS-S Marcos	7	U	PHD	88	Ca-Irvine	1-92
Jose, Anita	Asst	SE Okla St		JY	MBA	93	Dallas	8-93
Joseph, Jacob	Asst	Alaska-Fairb	5	N	ABD			1990
Joseph, Marks	Adj	Southeastern			PHD		Mich St	
Joshi, Mahesh P.	Inst	St Joseph	38	EIY	ABD		Temple	1994
Jourden, Forest	Asst	Illinois	2	EFH	PHD	91	Stanford	1991
Joyce, William F.	Prof	Dartmouth			PHD	77	Penn St	1983
Joyner, Betty C.	Prof	Corpus Chris	25		DBA		La Tech	
Jozsa, Frank P. Jr.	Assoc	Pfeiffer	18		PHD	77	Geo St	7-91
Jubb, Peter	SLect	Australian N	12	AJY	MA	73	Oxon	1975
Judge, William Q.	Asst	Tennessee	34	ILJ	PHD	89	N Carol	8-89
Judy, Richard B.	Prof	Wis-Stev Pt	3	ST	PHD	84	Indiana	1-85
Juett, Samuel	Asst	Moroor Atlan	48	AEJN	ABD		Georgia	1989
Julian, Scott	Inst	Southern			ABD	94	LSU	1993
Jun, Minjoon	Asst	New Mex St	37	IUVW	PHD	89	Geo St	1988
Jung, Jeong-Duk	Asst	Wis-Eau Clar	9	Z	DBA	93	Miss St	1991
Juris, Hervey A.	Prof	Northwestern	5	NPQ	PHD	67	Chicago	1970
Jurkus, Anthony F.	Prof	Louisiana Te	38	HINY	PHD	74	Geo St	1975
Justis, Robert T.	Prof	Louisiana St		IST	DBA	72	Indiana	8-86
Juul, Kenneth A.	Asst	Shepherd	17	BX	MS		Auburn	1975
Kabaliswaran, M.	Asst	CUNY-Baruch	2	H	PHD		NYU	1991
Kabis, Zeinhom M.	Prof	St Ambrose	79	VZ	PHD	68	Illinois	1973
Kaciak, Eugene	Assoc	Brock Univ	79	UVZ	DECO		Warsaw	1989
Kacmar, Miki	Asst	Florida St	25	EN	PHD	90	Tx A&M	8-92
Kadipasaogul, Sukran	Asst	Houston	7	U	PHD	93	Clemson	9-93
Kaehler, Richard C.	Prof	Pepper-L Ang	3	I	PHD	60	S Calif	1975
Kagerer, Rudolph L.	Retir	Georgia	56	6-93	PHD	71	Tenn	1971
Kahai, Surinder	Asst	SUNY-Bingham	9	Z	PHD	91	Michigan	1991
Kahalas, Harvey	Dean	Mass-Lowell		Mgt	PHD	71	Mass	
Kahn, Ben Abraham	Assoc	N Adams St						
Kahn, Beverly	Assoc	Suffolk	9	Z	PHD	79	Michigan	1985
Kahn, William A.	Asst	Boston Univ	2	EH	PHD		Yale	
Kahng, Anthony	Assoc	NJ Inst Tech	5	N	JSD	64	NYU Law	1981
Kainen, Timm	Prof	Mass-Lowell	2	EH	PHD	79	Mass	
Kaiser, Kate	Assoc	Marquette	9	Z	PHD	79	Pitt	1988
Kaitz, Edward	Prof	Marymount	38	IY	DBA		Harvard	1987
Kakalis, Sal	Prof	CS-Long Bch	13	HI	PHD	85	Arizona	1986
Kalina, Megan	Inst	Wis-Rvr Fall			MS			
Kalinowski, Jon G.	C-Pr	Mankato St			PHD	87	Iowa	1984
Kaliski, John	Asst	Mankato St			PHD	92	Iowa	1993
Kalla, M. Sami	Retir	Western Conn	7	1993	PHD		American	
Kalleberg, Arne L.	Prof	No Carolina	2	EFHQ	PHD	75	Wiscon	1992
Kalman, Elias	Inst	CUNY-Baruch	1	B	MBA	62	Baruch	1965
Kaloki, Philip K.	Inst	Dallas Bapt	18		ABD		Dal Bapt	1991
Kaman, Vicki	Assoc	Colorado St	5	NPRE	PHD	80	Colo St	1981
Kamath, Rajan R.	Asst	Cincinnati						
Kambil, Ajit	Asst	New York U	9	Z	PHD	92	MIT	
Kamel, Magdi N.	Asst	Naval Postgr	9	Z	PHD	88	Penn	8-88
Kamm, Judith	Assoc	Bentley	23	DT	DBA	80	Harvard	1979
Kampfner, Roberto A.	Adj	Mich-Dearbor	97	HUVZ	PHD	81	Michigan	1987
Kandunias, Chris	LectA	Flinders Un	1	S	BCOM	92	Adelaid	3-92
Kane, Jeffrey S.	Assoc	N Car-Greens	25	NVXA	PHD	77	Michigan	8-90
Kane, Kathy	Assoc	San Francisc	12	DERY	PHD	92	Clarmont	1991
Kane, Kimberly F.	Asst	Wake Fr-MBA	25	EN	PHD	90	Indiana	1990
Kane, William D.	Assoc	W Carolina	23	DEH	PHD	77	Cornell	8-76
Kanekoa, S. Meilani	Assoc	Hawaii Pacif	8	Y	PHD	86	U Miami	1-90
Kanet, Jack	Prof	Clemson	7	UV	PHD	79	Penn St	1986
Kang, Keebom	Adj	Naval Postgr	79	UZV	PHD	84	Purdue	7-88
Kangas, J. Eugene	H	GMI	17	DIUY	PHD	65	Cinn	1990
Kanter, Rosabeth M.	Prof	Harvard	1					
Class of 1960 Professor of Business Administration								
Kanungo, R. N.	Prof	McGill Univ	2		PHD		McGill	1969
Kao, D.	Asst	Univ Windsor	79	UVWZ	PHD		McMaster	1990
Kao, John J.	Assoc	Harvard	25	EN				
Kaparthi, Shashidhar	Asst	No Iowa			PHD	92	SUNY-Buf	8-92
Kapelner, David I.	Assoc	Merrimack			JD		Suffolk	

Name	Rank	School			Degree			
Kaplan, Edward H.	Assoc	Yale	7	V	PHD	84	MIT	1989
Kaplan, Eileen	Assoc	Montclair St	25	NOPR	PHD		Rutgers	1981
Kappenberger, John	Asst	Mesa State	12	E&	PHD		Colorado	1992
Karagozoglu, Necmi	Prof	CS-Sacrament	23	HIT	PHD	84	Oregon	1984
Karake, Zeinab	Assoc	Catholic		FHIT	PHD			1989
Karambayya, Rekha	Asst	York Univ	5	N	PHD		Northwes	
Karant, Yasha	Assoc	CS-San Bern	9	Z	PHD	81	Berkeley	1989
Karathanos, Demetrius	Prof	SE Missouri	7	VX	PHD	75	N Colo	1979
Karcher, Beverly J.	Asst	Creighton	4	JL	PHD	91	Nebraska	8-90
Kargar, Javad	Asst	N Carol Cen	36	IS	PHD	81	Clarmont	9-90
Karim, Ahmad R.	C-Ac	Ind-Purdue	35	QN	PHD	81	Iowa	8-85
Karlins, Marvin	Prof	South Fla	12	E	PHD	66	Princeton	1974
Karnani, Aneel G.	C-Ac	Michigan	38	IY	PHD	81	Harvard	1980
Karney, Dennis F.	Prof	Kansas	7	V	PHD		Illinois	1984
Karns, Lanny	C-Pr	SUNY Oswego	37	DIJV	PHD	78	Syracuse	1976
Karp, Robert	Prof	Jackson St			EDD		Illinois	1985
Karpak, Birsen	Prof	Youngstown	7	UV	DBA	72	Istanbul	9-85
Karppinen, Richard T.	Assoc	Calvin			ABD		Pitt	1987
Karren, Ronald J.	Assoc	Massachusett	5	NO	PHD	78	Maryland	1982
Karsten, Margaret	Asst	Wis-Plattev	5	N	MBA	81	Wiscon	1981
Karsten, Rex A.	Asst	No Iowa			PHD	94	Nebraska	8-94
Kartchner, Allen	Prof	Utah State	7	UV	PHD	68	Utah	9-67
Kartchner, Eugene	Prof	Utah State	7	UV	PHD	65	U Wash	9-65
Kartha, C. P.	Prof	Mich-Flint	7	UVX	PHD	73	Wiscon	7-79
Karuppan, Corinne	Asst	SW Missouri	7	UV	PHD	90	Nebraska	1991
Kasarda, John D.	Prof	No Carolina	3	WHM	PHD	71	N Carol	1976
Kash, Toby J.	Prof	Pittsburg St	28	LTYI	PHD	78	Mich St	1982
Kashani, Kamran		Intl Mgt Dev	38	IY	DBA		Harvard	
Kashlak, Roger	Asst	Loyola-Maryl	83	Y	ABD	93	Temple	1993
Kashyap, Anil	Assoc	Chicago	8	Y	PHD	89	MIT	1991
Kasiraj, Jothi	Lect	Texas A&M		V	MA	68	New Mex	1985
Kasle, Jill	Assoc	George Wash	1	A	JD	72	Boston	
Kasou, Chickery J.	Asst	Worcester Pl		S	PHD	91	Syracuse	7-90
Kasperson, Conrad J.	Prof	Frank & Mars	23	HY	PHD	76	Renessla	7-76
Kassarjian, J. Barkev	Prof	Babson	3	I	DBA	67	Harvard	
Kassem, Sami M.	Prof	Toledo	25		PHD		NYU	1967
Kassicieh, Suleiman	Prof	New Mexico	9	ZUV	PHD	78	Iowa	1980
Kassner, Marcia	Assoc	North Dakota	12	OP	PHD	85	Illinois	8-84
Kasuganti, Ram	C-Pr	Youngstown	37	IUVX	DBA	76	Kent St	9-77
Kataoka, Hiroshi	Dean	Hitotsubashi						
Katerberg, Ralph Jr.	Assoc	Cincinnati	2	H	PHD	78	Illinois	
Kathuria, Narinder			7	U	PHD	88	N Carol	
Katsenelinboigen, Aron	Prof	Pennsylvania			DSE	66	Moscow	1977
Katsioloudes, Marios I.	Assoc	SC-Coastal	3	I	PHD	90	Penn	1990
Katz, Jerome A.	Assoc	St Louis			PHD		Michigan	
Katz, Joseph L.	Assoc	Georgia St	7	V	PHD		LSU	
Katz, Louis	Prof	Youngstown	4		JD	74	Clevelan	9-77
Katz, Lucy V.	Assoc	Fairfield	45	KLR	JD	68	New York	1983
Katz, Marsha	Prof	Governors St			PHD	78	Mich St	
Katz, Norman	Lect	Cornell	1	E	EDD	85	Harvard	8-92
Katz, Ralph	Prof	Northeastern	2	D	PHD		Penn	9-82
Kauffman, Nancy	Asst	N Car-Ashvil	5	NQ	PHD	89	North Tx	8-88
Kauffman, Robert J.	Assoc	New York U	9	Z	PHD	88	Car Mel	
Kaufman, Allen	C-Ac	New Hampshir	3	I	PHD	80	Rutgers	1983
Kaufman, Charles	Prof	South Dakota	25	AENF	DBA	65	Indiana	1961
Kaufman, Gordan M.	Prof	MIT	7	U	DBA			
Kaufman, Harold G.	Prof	Polytechnic			PHD		NYU	
Kaupins, Gundars	Assoc	Boise State	5	PY	PHD	86	Iowa	1986
Kavan, C. Bruce	Asst	North Fla	9	ZUV	PHD	91	Georgia	1991
Kavanagh, Michael J.	Prof	St Johns			PHD	61	Fordham	
Kavanagh, Michael J.	Prof	SUNY-Albany	52	NXEF	PHD	69	Iowa St	1982
Kawatra, Rakesh	Asst	Mankato St			PHD	91	Iowa	1990
Kazanjian, Robert K.	Assoc	Emory	3	I	PHD	83	Penn	1988
Kazmier, Leonard J.	Prof	Arizona St			PHD		Ohio St	1965
Keane, John G.	Dean	Notre Dame	3	I	PHD	65	Pitt	1989
Keane, Michael	Assoc	Minnesota	57	QV	PHD	90	Brown	
Kearney, William J.	Retir	Cincinnati	5	1994	PHD	65	Mich St	1965
Keating, Robert	Assoc	N Car-Wilmin	38	DIY	DBA	87	Kent St	1985
Keaton, Paul	Assoc	Wis-La Cross			PHD	78	Minn	
Keats, Barbara W.	Assoc	Arizona St	3	I	PHD		Okla St	1984
Keaveny, Timothy J.	C-Pr	Marquette	5	NQ	PHD	71	Minn	1986
Keck, Sara	Assoc	Pace	3	F	PHD	90	Columbia	9-93
Kedia, Banwari L.	Prof	Memphis	38	IY	PHD	76	Case Wes	1988
Kee, James	Assoc	George Wash	1	A	JD	69	New York	
Keef, Kimberlee M.			13	CI	PHD	87	N Carol	1987
Keefe, Michael	Asst	U Manitoba	9	Z	ABD	92	North Tx	1991
Keefe, Thomas	Asst	Indiana SE	25	ENQ	PHD	89	SUNY-Buf	1989
Keefer, Donald L.	Assoc	Arizona St			PHD		Michigan	1987
Keeffe, Michael J.	Assoc	SW Texas St	3	I	PHD	86	Arkansas	1986
Keegan, Charles	Assoc	Montana						

Name	Rank	School			Degree		School 2	Date
Keels, J. Kay	Asst	Louisiana St	3	I	PHD	89	S Carol	1-89
Keenan, J. Michael	Prof	W Michigan	12	NORZ	PHD	65	Ohio St	1968
Keesal, N.	Assoc	McGill Univ	3		MBA		Harvard	1984
Kefalas, Asterios G.	Prof	Georgia	89	IMYZ	PHD	71	Iowa	1971
Keifer, Mary	Assoc	Ohio Univ	4		JD	71	Virginia	
Keil, Mark	Asst	Georgia St	9	Z	PHD		Harvard	
Keim, Gerald D.	Prof	Texas A&M		LYK	PHD	75	Va Tech	1974
Keim, Robert T.	Assoc	Arizona St	9	Z	PHD		Pitt	1979
Kekre, Sunder	Assoc	Carnegie Mel	7	U	PHD		Rochest	1984
Kelada, Joseph	Prof	HEC-Montreal	27	EFUV	MBA		McGill	
Keleman, Ken S.	Prof	Western Wash	25	EPZ	PHD	76	Utah	9-77
Keliiliki, Dale K.	Asst	Brighm Yg-HI	7	V	MS	71	Brig Yg	9-72
Kelleher, N.	Asst	Mt St Vincen	38	BKY	MBA	82	Dalhousi	1986
Keller, Christopher M.	Asst	Naval Postgr	79	VZ	PHD	91	Indiana	1991
Keller, Gerald	Prof	Wilfrid Laur	7	V	PHD		Windsor	1974
Keller, John E.	Adj	Naval Postgr	13	APVE	BA	57	Harvard	9-90
Keller, L. Robin	Assoc	Calif-Irvine	7	UV	PHD	82	UCLA	1989
Keller, Robert	Prof	Houston	28	HDYE	PHD	72	Penn St	8-72
Keller, Thomas	Assoc	Arizona St	39	DIUZ	EDD		Toledo	1980
Keller, Tiffany	Asst	Arkansas St	25	EF	PHD	94	SUNY-Buf	1994
Kellerman, Marcus E.	Asst	New Mex High	19	DUVZ	MBB	68	New Mex	1992
Kelley, C. Aaron	Dean	Ohio Univ	3	IFES	PHD	79	North Tx	8-93
Kelley, Donald E.	Prof	Fran Marion	2	E	PHD	78	S Carol	8-81
Kelley, Lane	Prof	Hawaii-Manoa			PHD	70	North Tx	
Kelley, Patricia C.	Asst	Western Wash	43	IJLM	DBA	88	Boston U	1990
Kellie, J.		Humberside	2					
Kellogg, Calvin	C-Pr	Ark-Ltl Rock	25	NE	PHD	85	Arkansas	1991
Kellogg, Diane	Assoc	Bentley	2	ER	EDD	79	Harvard	1980
Kellogg, Stephen	Asst	SUNY-Buffalo	4	K	JD	66	SUNY-Buf	8-89
Kelly, David L.			7	U	PHD	76	N Carol	
Kelly, Eileen P.	C-Ac	Ithaca	54	QJB	PHD	82	Cinn	8-93
Kelly, Gary	SLect	Australian N		AEHL	MEC	87	NE	1987
Kelly, Horace	Lect	Wake Forest	46	ILST	BA		Baylor	9-87
Kelly, J.	Prof	Concordia U						
Kelly, James	Asst	Colorado	7	UVWX	PHD	90	Maryland	1990
Kelly, James A.					DBA	74	Fla St	
Kelly, James M.	Dean	St Cloud St	3	I	DBA	67	Colorado	1987
Kelson, David	Asst	Ferris State	8		MIM		Amr Grad	1990
Kemelgor, Bruce H.	Assoc	Louisville	26	EFST	PHD	72	Illinois	1979
Kemerer, Chris F.	Assoc	MIT	9	Z	PHD			
Douglas Drane Career Development Assistant Professor of Management Science								
Kemery, Edward	Assoc	Baltimore	25	EGVN	PHD	83	Auburn	8-87
Kemmerer, Barbara	Asst	E Illinois		EQ	PHD		Nebraska	1990
Kemp, B. Wayne	Prof	Tenn-Martin	3	I	DBA	72	Miss St	9-71
Kemp, Robert	Prof	Drake	38	JTY	PHD	79	Ariz St	1982
Kemper, John	Prof	No Arizona	3	EI	PHD	67	U Wash	
Kendall, Elizabeth	Prof	N Adams St			MLS		Mass	
Kendall, Julie E.	Assoc	Rutgers-Camd			PHD			
Kendall, Kenneth L.	Prof	Rutgers-Camd			PHD			
Kende, Michael	Asst	INSEAD			PHD		MIT	
Kenneally, Teresa	Prof	Marymount			PHD		Iowa St	1981
Kennedy, Bryan	Asst	Athens State	2	ENP	EDD		Vanderbt	1987
Kennedy, Charles R. Jr.	Assoc	Wake Fr-MBA	38	IY	PHD	80	Texas	1989
Kennedy, Frederic			7	U	PHD	74	N Carol	
Kennedy, Miles H.	Assoc	Case Western			PHD	71	London	7-69
Kennedy, Patricia	Prof	Norwich	15		EDD			
Kennedy, Robert	Assoc	St Thomas-MN						
Kenney, John R.	Assoc	Salem State	4		JD		Boston C	
Kenney, Raymond	Retir	St Johns		1991	PHD			
Kent, Daniel	Inst	No Kentucky	15		MBA	86	Cinn	8-87
Kent, David	Prof	Plymouth St			JD	71	Boston	
Kent, Robert W.	Lect	Harvard	1	&				
Kent, Russell L.	Assoc	Geo Southern	25	EN	PHD	91	Fla St	1990
Kenz, Marc	Asst	Chicago			PHD	92	Penn	1991
Keon, Tom	Prof	Fla Atlantic	32	HIS	PHD		MSU	8-90
Keppler, Mark J.	Prof	CS-Fresno	45	NJK	JD		Wiscon	1987
Kerfoot, Deborah	Assoc	Univ Leeds	24	NP	PHD	92	Manchest	1993
Kernan, Mary C.	Assoc	Delaware			PHD	85	Akron	1989
Kerns, Richard L.	Prof	East Carol		Z	PHD		Virginia	1975
Kerr, Daryl L.	Asst	N Car-Charl			PHD		Fla St	1988
Kerr, Jeffrey L.	Assoc	U Miami	38	IN	PHD	77	Penn St	1989
Kersten, G.	Assoc	Carleton Un	7	V	PHD		Warsaw	
Kerzner, Harold	Prof	Baldwin-Wal	3	UX	PHD		Illinois	
Kesner, Idalene F.	Assoc	No Carolina	3	ILE	PHD	83	Indiana	1983
Ketcham, Allen	Prof	Tx A&M-Kings	6	DUV	PHD	82	Arizona	1983
Ketcham, Emily M.	Lect	Baylor		Z	MBA		Baylor	1991
Ketchen, David	Asst	Louisiana St	3	I	PHD	94	Penn St	8-93
Ketelhohn, Werner		Intl Mgt Dev	35	IQ	PHD		LSU	
Kets De Vries, Manfred F. R.	Prof	INSEAD	26	ET	DBA	70	Harvard	1-85
Khairullah, Zahid Y.	Prof	St Bonaventu	79	UVZ	PHD		SUNY-Buf	1976

Name	Rank	School			Degree		University	
Khalid, Amin		Southeastern			FCMA			
Khalil, Mohamed	Prof	US Intl	8		PHD		UCLA	1972
Khan, Andy	Prof	Athabasca Un	4	K	MA	71	Keele	1986
Khan, Rauf-Ur	Prof	CS-L Angeles	18	Y	DBA	71	S Calif	1968
Khandekar, Rajendra	C-Ac	Metro State	32	IHES	PHD	83	Kansas	8-89
Khelfaoui, Salah	Asst	Manhattan	7					
Khojasteh, Mak	Asst	Winston-Sal			DBA		US Intl	
Khouja, Moutaz	Asst	N Car-Charl						
Khumawala, Basheer A.	Prof	Houston	7	U	PHD	70	Purdue	9-78
Khurana, Anil	Asst	Boston Univ					Michigan	
Kiang, Melody	Asst	Arizona St	9	Z				
Kibbey, Richard	Asst	Pacific Luth	9	LVYZ	PHD	93	Port St	1988
Kidd, Callum	Assoc	Univ Leeds	79	UZ	MSC	92	Salford	1993
Kidney, James A.	C-Ac	So Conn St	38	ITY	PHD	86	UCLA	1989
Kidwell, Roland	Asst	La St-Shreve	3	I	PHD	94	LSU	8-93
Kiebala, Susan	C-As	Olivet	18		MBA	77	W Mich	1989
Kieff, Allene	Assoc	Aquinas	25	DENP	MA	71	Sam Hou	1986
Kieff, Gary	Asst	Aquinas	12	BDH	MED	73	Houston	1987
Kiehl, Sandra	Assoc	Linfield	3		PHD	88	Port St	1988
Kiel, Geoffrey C.	Prof	Queensland	31	I	PHD	77	NS Wales	1977
Kienast, Philip	Assoc	U Washington	25		PHD	72	Mich St	1970
Kiesner, W. Frederick	Prof	Loyola Marym	16	ST	PHD	84	Claremont	1977
Kiggundu, M.	Assoc	Carleton Un	28	EY	PHD		Toronto	
Kilbourne, Lynda M.	Asst	Texas A&M			NE	PHD	90	Texas	1990
Kilbourne, William	Prof	Sam Houston			PHD	73	Houston	1982
Kilburn, David		Bournemouth	8	Y	MBA			
Kilgore, Jeffrey	Assoc	Norwich	36		JD			
Kilgour, John G.	Prof	CS-Hayward	5	Q	PHD	72	Cornell	1972
Killingsworth, Brenda Lou	Assoc	East Carol		Z	PHD	87	S Carol	1987
Kilmann, Ralph H.	Prof	Pittsburgh	2		PHD	72	UCLA	
George H. Love Chair in Orgnization & Management								
Kilpatrick, John A.	Prof	Idaho State		IY	PHD	78	Iowa	1977
Kim, Bonn Oh	Asst	Nebraska	9	Z	PHD	90	Minn	8-89
Kim, Chong W.	C-Pr	Marshall	2	H	PHD	76	Ohio St	1976
Kim, DaeSoo	Asst	Marquette	7	U	PHD	91	Indiana	1991
Kim, Duck Shin	Assoc	Guam	28	YE	PHD	77	Geo St	1989
Kim, Eonsoo	Assoc	CS-Fullerton			PHD			1994
Kim, Eyong	Asst	Mankato St			PHD	90	Nebraska	1990
Kim, Gyu Chan	Assoc	No Illinois		U	PHD		Nebraska	
Kim, Ihlyung	VAsst	Wash Univ	7	UVW	ABD		UCLA	1994
Kim, Jay	Assoc	Ohio State	2	E	PHD	75	Mich St	1980
Kim, Jay S.	Asst	Boston Univ	37	IUY	PHD		Ohio St	
Kim, Jin	Asst	Chicago St			MBA		Fordham	1989
Kim, Juho	Prof	Miss Vall St			PHD		Oklahoma	1973
Kim, Ken I.	Assoc	Toledo	23		DBA		Indiana	1985
Kim, Michael W.	Asst	Cal-Riversid	9	Z	PHD		Stanford	1990
Kim, Seung-Lae	Asst	Drexel		UV	PHD	90	Penn St	1989
Kim, Yongeom	Asst	F Dick-Madis			PHD		NYU	
Kim, Young Hwa	Assoc	Clark Atlant			PHD		Geo St	
Kim, Young J.	Prof	Wis-Rvr Fall	23		PHD		Oklahoma	9-64
Kim, Young-Gul	Asst	Pittsburgh	9		PHD		Minn	
Kim, Youngjin	Inst	F Dick-Ruthe			MS		NJ Tech	
Kimberly, John R.	Prof	Pennsylvania	2	DHX	PHD	70	Cornell	7-82
Henry Bower Professor of Entrepreneurial Studies								
Kimbrough, Steven Orla	Assoc	Pennsylvania			PHD	82	Wiscon	1984
Kimes, Sheryl	Asst	Cornell	7	UV	PHD	87	Texas	8-88
Kimzey, Bruce	C-Pr	Brighm Yg-HI	1		PHD	70	Wash St	1989
Kinard, Jerry L.	C-Ac	W Carolina		Mgt	DBA	71	Miss St	8-94
Kindsers, Kjell R.	Assoc	Minn-Duluth			PHD	73	Minn	1980
Kindt, John	Prof	Illinois	4	KY	JD		Georgia	1978
Kiner, Susan	Lect	Cornell	1	&D	ABD		Illinois	8-88
King, Albert S.	Prof	No Illinois	35	HIP	DBA	69	Tx Tech	1975
King, Andrew	Asst	New York U			PHD	93	MIT	
King, Barry	Assoc	Butler	79	UZ	PHD	79	Indiana	1991
King, Ian	Asst	Univ Essex	23	DFP	PHD	90		1990
King, Jeanne	Assoc	CS-San Bern	36	EHS	PHD	92	Claremont	1990
King, Jonathan	Assoc	Oregon State	4	J	PHD	80	U Wash	1980
King, M.	Prof	Loughborough	7	V	DPHL		Oxford	
King, Mary	Assoc	Alaska SE	13	DM	PHD	83	U Wash	1993
King, Paula	Assoc	St Cloud St	34	AFN	PHD	89	Minn	1990
King, Ruth C.	Asst	Pittsburgh	9		PHD		Texas	
King, Stan	Retir	E Kentucky	1	1991	DBA	73	Miss St	1973
King, Stephen	Assoc	Univ Leeds	79	UZ	MPHI	92	Bradford	1994
King, Stephen C.	Assoc	Keene State			PHD		Kentucky	1986
King, Wesley C.	Assoc	Miami U-Ohio	2	EFH	PHD	88	Georgia	8-87
King, William	Assoc	Fort Hays St	2	E	PHD		Colo St	1987
King, William R.	Prof	Pittsburgh	9		PHD	64	Case Wes	1967
University Professor								
King-Miller, Elaine	Assoc	Colorado St	15	HJNY	PHD	80	Michigan	1990
Kingsman, B. G.	Prof	U Lancaster	7	UVZ	PHD		Lancaste	

Name	Rank	Institution			Degree		School	Year
Kini, Ranjan B.	Asst	Indiana NW	79	UVZ	PHD	85	Tx Tech	1990
Kinicki, Angelo J.	Assoc	Arizona St	25	EGNX	DBA		Kent St	1982
Kinley, David	Assoc	Benedict Col						
Kinnear, Terry L.	Assoc	W Carolina	12	EFH	DBA	81	Kent St	8-79
Kinney, Susan T.	Asst	Wake Fr-MBA	19	&Z	PHD		Georgia	
Kinnie, N. J.	Lect	Univ Bath	5	QN	PHD			
Kinnunen, Raymond M.	Assoc	Northeastern	3	I	DBA		LSU	9-74
Kinory, Shimshon	Assoc	Jersey City	7		PHD		Sc SocRs	
Kinslinger, Howard J.	Assoc	Bloomsburg	15		PHD		Purdue	8-82
Kirby, Daria	Lect	Pittsburgh	2		ABD		Michigan	
Kirchhoff, Bruce	Prof	NJ Inst Tech	3	I	PHD	71	Utah	1992
Kirchmajer, L.	Lect	U Wollongong	63	TSDI	MBA	88	U Wollon	2-91
Kirchmeyer, Catherine	Asst	Wayne State	25	EN	PHD	88	York	1992
Kirk, Carey H.	Asst	No Iowa			PHD	72	Vanderbt	8-83
Kirk, Delaney	Assoc	Drake	57	JKSR	PHD	88	North Tx	1989
Kirk, F.	Assoc	Carleton Un	38	IY	PHD		N Carol	
Kirk, George E.	Retir	Wright State	34	DI	JD	73	W Virg	1979
Kirkham, Kate	Assoc	Brigham Yg	12	RNE	PHD	77	Union	1978
Kirkland, B. R.	Assoc	Tarleton St	18	BE	EDD	78	E Tx St	1979
Kirklin, W. Wayne	Assoc	Heidelberg	14	Y	MS	61	NYU	1978
Kirkpatrick, Shelley	Asst	American U	25	NE	PHD	92	Maryland	1993
Kirkpatrick, Thomas	Prof	Montana	13	INSX	PHD	67	Ohio St	1967
Kirkwood, Craig W.	Prof	Arizona St			PHD		MIT	1983
Kirsch, Laurie	Lect	Pittsburgh	9		ABD		Minn	
Kisfalvi, Veronika	Lect	HEC-Montreal	5	E	MBA		HEC-Mont	
Kishimoto, Kazuo	Assoc	Univ Tsukuba	7	V	DENG	80	Tokyo	1-87
Kittel, Phyllis	Dean	Ill Benedict						
Klu, Hong	Lect	Manchest Bus			PHD		Warwick	1992
Kivikink, Ron	Asst	Laurentian	71		MBA	84	Laurenti	7-82
Kizior, Ronald J.	Asst	Loyola-Chicg			PHD		Not Dame	1969
Klaas, Brian S.	Asst	So Carolina			PHD	87	Wiscon	
Klafehn, Keith A.	Prof	Akron	7	VCU	DBA	73	Kent St	9-70
Klapstein, Raymond E.	Assoc	Dalhousie U	3	I	LLM		Osgoode	
Klasson, Charles	Prof	Iowa	3	FI	PHD	60	Indiana	9-75
Klastorin, Theodore D.	C-Pr	U Washington	7	U	PHD	73	Texas	1974
Klatt, Lawrence A.	Prof	Fla Atlantic	56	NST	PHD	57	Missouri	1972
Klaudt, William J.	C-Ac	Jamestown	68	STY	MED	64	Black Hl	1967
Klayman, Joshua	Prof	Chicago			PHD	82	Minn	1980
Kleiman, Lawrence S.	Prof	Tenn-Chattan	5	NPL	PHD	78	Tenn	1979
Klein, David	Asst	Boston Univ	9	Z	PHD		Penn	
Klein, Deiter	Assoc	Worcester Pl	14	C&U	PHD	73	Berkeley	9-79
Klein, Esther	Inst	CUNY-Stn Isl	79	LSVZ	ABD		CUNY	1990
Klein, Gerald D.	Assoc	Rider	12	DELN	PHD	77	Case Wes	1977
Klein, Harold E.	Assoc	Temple			PHD	73	Columbia	1975
Klein, Heinz K.	Assoc	SUNY-Bingham	9	Z	DBA	68	Munich	1984
Klein, Howard	Assoc	Ohio State	5	P	PHD	87	Mich St	1987
Klein, Johnathan I.	Asst	CS-Northrdge	21	EHXF	PHD	87	S Calif	1991
Klein, Ronald D.	Prof	Columbus	9	Z	PHD		Geo St	1974
Klein, Stuart M.	Prof	Cleveland St	23	UV	PHD	63	Cornell	1972
Klein, Walter	Retir	St Fran-Penn		1991	MA			
Klein, Walter H.	Retir	Boston Coll	34	IL	PHD	54	Pitt	9-69
Kleindorfer, George B.	C-Pr	Penn State	7	V	PHD		Car Mel	
Kleindorfer, Paul R.	Prof	Pennsylvania			PHD	70	Car Mel	1973
Universal Furniture Professor								
Kleiner, Brian	Prof	CS-Fullerton	2	E	PHD	77	UCLA	8-77
Kleingartner, Archie	Prof	UCLA	5	N	PHD	65	Wiscon	1964
Kleinman, David C.	SLect	Chicago	3	I	PHD	77	Chicago	1971
Kleinstein, Arnold	Prof	NY Inst Tech	79		PHD			
Kleisath, Stephen	Assoc	Wis-Plattev	25	E	DBA		Nova	1980
Klekamp, Robert C.	Prof	Xavier	27	DU	PHD	77	Cinn	1963
Kletke, Marilyn G.	Prof	Oklahoma St	9	Z	PHD	81	Okla St	9-81
Klich, Nancy R.	Asst	N Car-Charl			PHD		Florida	
Klimberg, Ronald K.	Asst	Boston Univ	71	UVX	PHD		J Hopkin	
Kline, Max E.	Asst	York of PA	3	I	MS		Loyola C	1982
Kline, Robert S.	Prof	Winthrop	12	P	EDD	70	Pitt	1970
Klingler, James W.	Asst	Villanova	15	ENOR	PHD	85	Temple	1979
Klingman, Darwin D.	Deces	Texas		1991	PHD	69	Texas	
The Hugh Ray Cullen Centennnial Chair in Business Adm								
Klingsmith, Phil C.	C-Pr	Western St	4		JD	79	Calif We	1980
Kliorys, Constantine	Assoc	Gannon	7	V	PHD		Kent St	
Klocke, Ronald A.	Prof	Mankato St			PHD	73	Wash St	1966
Klosky, J. Michael	C-Pr	CS-Pomona	9	Z	PHD	75	Clemson	1989
Klotz, Dorothy	Asst	Fordham	7	UV	PHD		Penn St	1990
Kluger, Avraham	Lect	Hebrew Univ			PHD		Stevens	
Klugman, Ellen	Lect	Mt St Mary's			JD		UCLA	
Klumpes, Paul	Lect	Australian N	4	KY	MCOM	90	NS Wales	1990
Kmetz, John L.	Assoc	Delaware			DBA	75	Maryland	1977
Knabe, Rudy	Assoc	Embry-Riddle			MBA	76	Mid Tenn	1976
Knapp, Robert W.	Prof	Colorado Spr	3	T	PHD		Michigan	8-67
Knappp, Jeff	Inst	NW Missouri			MBA	91	NW Mo St	1992

Name	Rank	School			Degree		University	
Knight, John E.	Prof	Tenn-Martin	7	V	PHD	71	Ga Tech	9-71
Knight, Kenneth E.	Dean	Seattle Pac	36	DITZ	PHD	63	Carnegie	9-89
Knight, Tom	Assoc	British Colu	5	Q	PHD	82	Cornell	1982
Knights, David	Read	Manches Inst	45	H	PHD		Manchest	7-71
Knights, Ronald	Assoc	Metro State	25	DEFH	PHD	76	New Mex	1982
Knipes, Bradford	Asst	Westfield St			PHD		Mass	1988
Knippen, Jay T.	Assoc	South Fla	13	PI	DBA	70	Fla St	1970
Knod, Edward M. Jr.	Prof	W Illinois			PHD	74	Nebraska	1974
Knode, Steve	Prof	Marymount			PHD		Syracuse	1985
Knopp, Jacky Jr.	Retir	Canisius	4	1994	PHD	65	SUNY-Buf	1967
Knotts, Rose	Asst	North Texas	3	IRY	PHD	72	Tx A&M	1982
Knotts, Ulysses S. Jr.	Prof	Geo Southern	37	CIU	PHD	71	Nebraska	1977
Knouse, Stephen	Prof	SW Louisiana	25	EJN	PHD	77	Ohio St	1986
Knowles, Joel B.	Prof	CS-Sacrament	37	IUV	PHD	76	Oregon	1980
Knowles, Thomas	Assoc	Illinois Tch			PHD	70	Chicago	1969
Knowlton, Stuart L.	Assoc	Cen Michigan	35		PHD	50	MIT	1980
Knox, John E.	Assoc	CS-Pomona	7	VZ	PHD	89	Colorado	1989
Knudson, Harry	Prof	U Washington	36		PHD	58	Harvard	1961
Knutson, Jerry L.	Dean	St Martin's			MBA	83	Puget Sd	
Ko, Anthony C. K.	Lect	City Poly HK	16	HINY	MBA	85	HongKong	8-88
Ko, Kwangsoo	Assoc	Guam	79	VZ	PHD	90	Purdue	1991
Koberg, Christine S.	Assoc	Colorado			PHD	81	Oregon	1982
Kobrin, Stephen J.	Prof	Pennsylvania	8	YI	PHD	75	Michigan	7-87
William H. Worster Professor of Multinational Mgt;Director Wurster Center								
Kobu, Bulent	Assoc	Mass-Dartmou			PHD	71	Istanbul	1987
Koch, Douglass V.	Assoc	Lawrence Tec	5		MBA	70	Nevada	1980
Koch, Harold	Assoc	Bellarmine			PHD		Clev St	
Koch, James L.	Dean	Santa Clara		Mgt	PHD	72	UCLA	1990
Koch, Marianne J.	Asst	Oregon	5	N	PHD	88	Columbia	1988
Kochan, Thomas A.	Prof	MIT	5	NQ	PHD			
George Maverick Bunker Professor of Management								
Kochenash, Tony	Prof	Wayne St Col	23	AEN	PHD	73	Colo St	1990
Kochenberger, Gary	Prof	Colo-Denver	7	U	PHD	69	Colorado	1989
Koehler, Cortus T.	Prof	CS-Sacrament	2	E	PHD	72	Claremont	1973
Koehler, Gary J.	Prof	Florida	9	Z	PHD	73	Purdue	1987
on leave to Purdue University								
Koehler, J. W.	Assoc	South Fla	26	F	DED	68	Penn St	1985
Koehn, Nancy F.	Asst	Harvard	4	L				
Koen, Clifford M.	Assoc	New Orleans	5		JD	84	Memphis	8-86
Koenigsberg, Ernest	Retir	Cal Berkeley	7	1991	PHD		Iowa St	1971
Koerner, Richard	Lect	U Queensland	3	I	PHD	93	QueensIn	1992
Kogut, Bruce M.	Assoc	Pennsylvania	8	Y	PHD	83	MIT	7-83
Koh, Chang	Asst	N Car-Greens	9	Z	PHD		Georgia	1990
Kohl, John	C-Pr	Nev-L Vegas	45	JLNR	PHD	82	Penn St	1988
Kohls, John	Assoc	Gonzaga	42	JL	PHD	83	U Wash	9-80
Kohn, Johnathan W.	Prof	Shippensburg	7	V	PHD		NY Univ	
Kohn, Thomas O.	Asst	Boston Univ	31	IDY	DBA		Harvard	
Kohut, Gary F.	Assoc	N Car-Charl			PHD		S Illin	1983
Kolb, Darl	Lect	U Auckland	21	FPXY	PHD	91	Cornell	1-92
Kolb, David A.	Prof	Case Western	2	E	PHD		Harvard	
Kolb, Harry	Assoc	Southern Ark			MS		Arkansas	1983
Kolchin, Michael G.	Prof	Lehigh			DBA	80	Indiana	1979
Kolenko, Tom	Assoc	Kennesaw St	15	EFNO	PHD	86	Wiscon	1990
Koller, Albert M.					DBA	74	Fla St	
Komatsu, Akira	Prof	Hitotsubashi	4	L	MC	72	Hitotsub	1992
Kondrasuk, John N.	Assoc	Portland			PHD	72	Minn	1975
Konecny, Ron	Asst	Neb-Kearney	7	UV	PHD		Nebraska	1988
Konoylis, Nickolas	Prof	Bentley	7	UV	PHD	74	Syracuse	1973
Konrad, Alison M.	Assoc	Temple			PHD		Claremnt	
Konsynski, Benn	C-Pr	Emory	9	Z	PHD		Purdue	
George S. Craft Professor of Business Administration								
Koop, Rebecca B.	Asst	Wright State	9	Z	PHD	94	Cinn	1992
Koot, Ronald S.	Prof	Penn State	7	V	PHD		Oregon	
Kooti, Ghanbar	Assoc	Albany State			PHD		Mich St	
Kopelman, Richard E.	Prof	CUNY-Baruch	1	A	PHD	74	Harvard	1974
Kopf, Jerry	Assoc	Radford	36	IST	PHD	89	Akansas	8-92
Kopp, Daniel G.	Assoc	SW Missouri	3	I	PHD	77	Va Tech	1981
Kopp, Lori	Inst	Tuskegee						
Korf, Fred	Prof	US Intl			PHD		Columbia	1973
Korman, Abraham K.	Prof	CUNY-Baruch	2	Psy	PHD		Minn	1962
Korn, Willard M.	Prof	Wis-Eau Clar	9	Z	EDD	68	N Colo	1968
Kornbluth, Jonathan	Prof	Hebrew Univ			PHD		Imperial	
Korsgaard, M. Audrey	Asst	So Carolina			PHD	90	NYU	
Kortanek, Ken	C-Pr	Iowa	7	V	PHD	64	Northwes	1986
Korukonda, A. Rao	C-Pr	St Bonaventu	2		PHD		Tx Tech	1986
Kory, Delores	Asst	St Thomas-FL	12		DPA			1984
Kosnik, Rita	Assoc	Trinity	13	DKIL	PHD	86	Northwes	9-83
Kossack, Edgar	Prof	Fla Atlantic			PHD		Georgia	1977
Kotamraju, P.	Assoc	St Scholasti			PHD			1991
Kotha, Suresh	Asst	New York U			PHD	88	Rensséla	

Name	Rank	School			Degree		University	
Kotter, John P.	Prof	Harvard	25	EN				
Konosuke Matsushita Professor of Leadership								
Kottermann, Jeffrey	C-Pr	Salisbury St			PHD	84	Arizona	8-94
Kottukapalli, Joseph A.	Asst	Dallas	8		PHD	66	Montreal	8-87
Koushik, Murlidhar V.	Asst	U Washington	9	Z	MBA	72	Calcutta	1986
Kouskoulas, Barbara	Asst	Lawrence Tec			PHD			1993
Kouvelis, Panagiotis	Assoc	Duke	7	UV	PHD	88	Stanford	1992
Kovach, Barbara E.	Prof	Rutgers-N Br		EO	PHD	73	Maryland	1984
Kovach, Kenneth	Prof	George Mason	5	QNBP	PHD	75	Maryland	1975
Kovner, Tony	Prof	New York-Gr	12		PHD			
Kovoor, Sarah	Asst	Colo-Denver	24	EFGM	PHD	91	S Calif	1991
Kowalczyk, Stan J.	Prof	San Fran St	34	IL	PHD	76	Berkeley	1973
Koys, Daniel J.	Assoc	DePaul			PHD		Cornell	
Koyuncu, Ibrahim		Southeastern			PHD		Toronto	
Koza, Mitchell P.	Asst	INSEAD	23	IY	PHD	85	Chicago	1-89
Kozan, Kamil	Prof	St John Fish	12		PHD		UCLA	
Koziara, Karen S.	Prof	Temple			PHD		Wiscon	
Koziell, John	Assoc	Merrimack			MBA		Conn	
Kozmetsky, George	Prof	Texas	38	DITY	DCS	57	Harvard	1966
Kpo, Wolanyo	Prof	Chicago St	5	N	PHD		Ill Tech	1985
Kraay, David	Asst	Purdue	9	Z	ABD	91	Penn	1991
Krachenberg, A. Richard	Emer	Mich-Dearbor	23	HIY	PHD	63	Michigan	1968
Kraemer, Kenneth L.	Prof	Calif-Irvine	9	AEYZ	PHD	67	S Calif	1967
Krafka, Frank	Prof	St Edwards	27	UV	PHD	81	Texas	1978
Kraft, George	Assoc	Illinois Tch			PHD		Case Wes	1968
Kraft, Kenneth L.	Assoc	Tampa	23	HIT	DBA	82	Maryland	1991
Krajewski, LeRoy J.	Prof	Ohio State	7	U	PHD	69	Wiscon	1969
Krajewski, Lorraine	Assoc	La St-Shreve	81	D	PHD		Ariz St	8-83
Kram, Kathy E.	Asst	Boston Univ	2	EFGH	PHD		Yale	
Kramer, Gerald H.	Assoc	NW Missouri			PHD		Iowa	1988
Kramer, Roderick M.	Assoc	Stanford	2	E	PHD	85	UCLA	1985
Krasnostein, John	Assoc	Murdoch Univ	38	IY	MBA		Notre Dm	1990
Kratzec, Thomas	Assoc	Roosevelt	7	U				
Kraut, A.	Prof	CUNY-Baruch	5	N	PHD		Michigan	1965
Kraut, Robert	Prof	Carnegie Mel	9	Z	PHD		Yale	1993
Krefting, Linda A.	Assoc	Texas Tech	5	N	PHD	74	Minn	1981
Kreitner, Robert	SLect	Arizona St			PHD			
Krejcar, Barbara	Lect	Deakin-Burwo	1	D	MED		Monash	
Krell, Terence	Assoc	W Illinois			PHD	84	UCLA	1984
Kress, Guenther G.	Prof	CS-San Bern	1	A	PHD	72	Ca-Davis	1987
Kretovich, Duncan J.	Asst	Mich-Flint	1		PHD	85	Mich St	1988
Krickx, Guido A.	Asst	Pennsylvania	34	IDHB	PHD	88	UCLA	7-87
Kriebel, Charles H.	Prof	Carnegie Mel	79	VZ	PHD	64	MIT	1964
Krigline, Alan G.	Prof	Akron	73	IDY	PHD	77	Geo St	9-73
Krilowicz, Thomas J.	Asst	Georgia Col	45	GJP	DBA	75	Florida	1988
Krishnakumar, P.	Prof	Slippery Roc			PHD	74	Florida	8-74
Krishnamoorthy, M.	Assoc	US Intl	7		PHD		Manchest	1989
Krishnan, Hema	Asst	Xavier	34	ILRY	PHD	93	Tenn	1993
Krishnan, K. S.	Assoc	Wayne State	7	UV	PHD	71	Penn	1981
Krishnan, Rama	Prof	Youngstown	3		PHD	67	American	9-69
Krishnan, Vish	Asst	Texas	7	UV	PHD	93	MIT	1993
Kritzberg, Joan H.	Prof	CS-San Bern	4	K	JD	84	Brig Yg	1987
Kroder, Stanley L.	Asst	Dallas	3		MS	59	Case Wes	5-89
Kroeber, Donald W.	Prof	Radford	79	UVZ	PHD	76	Georgia	8-85
Kroeck, K. Galen	Assoc	Fla Internat		NEX	PHD	82	Akron	1982
Kroll, Mark J.	Dean$	Texas-Tyler	3	I	DBA	87	Miss St	5-87
Kroll, Yoram	Assoc	Hebrew Univ			PHD		Hebrew	
Kropf, Roger	Assoc	New York-Gr	12		PHD			
Kropp, Dean	Prof	Wash Univ	7	UVW	PHD	77	Stanford	1986
Dan Broida Professor of Operations & Manufacturing Management								
Kroszner, Randall S.	Asst	Chicago			PHD	90	Harvard	1990
Krueger, Dale	Asst	Missouri Wes		EFH	PHD		Mo-KC	1984
Krueger, David	Assoc	Baldwin-Wal	4	J	PHD		Chicago	
Krueger, David	Asst	Okla City	3	I	ABD		Purdue	8-92
Krug, Jeffrey	Asst	Memphis	38	IY	PHD	93	Indiana	1994
Kruger, Evonne J.	Asst	LaSalle	3	I	PHD		Temple	1991
Krzystofiak, Frank J.	Assoc	SUNY-Buffalo	5	NP	PHD	78	Minn	1977
Kubes, Z. Jan.		Intl Mgt Dev	35	IN	MBAA		Harvard	
Kubiak, Wieslaw	Assoc	Memorial Un	7		PHD	86	Warsaw	1990
Kuehl, Charles R.	Assoc	Mo-St Louis	36	IS	PHD	71	Iowa	1971
Kuei, Chu-Hua	Asst	Monmouth	79	UZ	PHD	90	CUNY	9-90
Kuffel, Thomas	Assoc	Wis-La Cross			PHD	79	Iowa	
Kuhn, Arthur J.	Assoc	San Fran St	23	BHI	PHD	72	Berkeley	1987
Kuhn, David G.	Assoc	Florida St	23	EFI	PHD	71	Penn St	1971
Kuhn, James	Prof	Columbia	45	JQ	PHD	54	Yale	1955
Kuilboer, Jean-Pierre	Asst	Salisbury St	9	Z	PHD	92	Tx-Arlin	8-91
Kuiper, Shirley	Assoc	So Carolina			EDD	79	Indiana	
Kujawa, Duane A.	Prof	U Miami	38	Y	PHD	70	Michigan	1980
Kuklah, Hooshang	C-Pr	N Carol Cen	38	EGIY	DPA	74	SUNY-Alb	9-80
Kulick, George	Asst	LeMoyne	7	V	PHD	88	Syracuse	1989

Name	Rank	School			Degree		Institution	
Kulik, Carol T.	Assoc	Illinois	2	EFH	PHD	87	Illinois	1990
Kulisch, William A.	Assoc	Pacific	25	DENP	PHD	76	Colorado	8-81
Kulkarni, Uday R.	Asst	Arizona St			MBA		India In	
Kulzick, Raymond S.	Asst	St Thomas-FL	39	IZS	DBA			1977
Kumar, A.	Asst	Montclair St					Va Tech	1988
Kumar, Akhil	Asst	Cornell	9	Z	PHD		Berkeley	7-88
Kumar, Ashok	Asst	Grand Valley			PHD	90	Purdue	1992
Kumar, Kuldeep	Assoc	Georgia St	9	Z	PHD		McMaster	
Kumar, Rachna	Asst	Texas	9	Z	PHD	93	NYU	1993
Kumar, U.	Assoc	Carleton Un	9	Z	PHD		Kanpur	
Kumar, V.	Assoc	Carleton Un	7	U	PHD		Manitoba	
Kunkel, Scott W.	Asst	San Diego	32	IT	PHD	91	Georgia	1992
Kunreuther, Howard	Prof	Pennsylvania			PHD	65	MIT	1972
Meshulam Riklis Professor in Practice of Creative Management								
Kuntz, Ed	Prof	SE Missouri	38	I	DBA	78	Tx Tech	1977
Kuo, Cheng-Kun	Assoc	Nat Taiwan U	1	Y	PHD	86	Texas	1989
Kuo, Chin	Asst	Eastern Wash	9	ZV	PHD	88	Ariz St	1989
Kuo, Ching-Chung	Asst	Penn St-Harr	7	U	PHD	89	Northwes	1989
Kupsh, Joyce	Prof	CS-Pomona	94	ZJ	EDD	75	Ariz St	1978
Kuratko, Donald F.	Prof	Ball State	6		DBA		Nova	1983
Kurke, Lance B.	C-Ac	Duquesne	23		PHD		Cornell	1989
Kurland, Nancy	Asst	So Calif	4	JLKM	PHD		Pitt	1993
Kurtulus, Ibrahim S.			7	U	PHD	78	N Carol	
Kusewitt, John B.	Assoc	Dallas	17		PHD	79	Tx-Arlin	8-81
Kushell, Elliot	Prof	CS-Fullerton	2	E	PHD	78	Hawaii	8-77
Kusunoki, Takeshi	Asst	Hitotsubashi	7	I	MC	89	Hitotsub	1992
Kuzdrall, Paul J.	Prof	Akron	79	UZV	PHD	77	St Louis	9-85
Kuzmicki, Jana	Asst	Indiana SE	3	I	PHD	93	Alabama	1993
Kuzmits, Frank E.	Prof	Louisville	5	NOP	PHD	75	Geo St	8-78
Kwak, NoKyoon	Prof	St Louis			PHD	64	S Calif	1985
Kwon, Ik-Whan	C-Pr	St Louis			PHD	68	Georgia	1968
Kwon, O. Yul	Prof	Univ Regina	18	ALY	PHD		McMaster	
Kwon, Tae Hyong			9	Z	PHD	87	N Carol	
Kwong, Kwok Keung	Prof	CS-L Angeles	67	U	PHD	86	Geo St	1986
Kyj, Myroslaw J.	Assoc	Widener			PHD		Temple	
Kyle, William Jr.	Adj	Montana St	48		MSSC	91	Maccau	9-89
Kyryluk, Robert	C-Ac	Bemidji St		NR	MBA		Mankato	1978
Kyungdoo, Nam	Asst	Tx-Perm Bas			PHD		North Tx	
LaBarre, James E.	Prof	Wis-Eau Clar	9	Z	PHD	72	N Dakota	1970
LaBarre, Richard E.	Assoc	Ferris State	6		MBA		Central	1978
Labig, Chalmer E.	Assoc	Oklahoma St	5	NQP	PHD	84	Texas	1984
Labovitz, George H.	Prof	Boston Univ	21	ECFH	PHD		Ohio St	
Lachman, Judith A.	Assoc	MIT			PHD			
Lacho, Kenneth J.	Prof	New Orleans	27		DBA	69	Wash U	8-64
LaCivita, Charles J.	Assoc	Naval Postgr	78	VY	PHD	81	Ca-SnBar	1985
Lacy, Gywynette	C	Howard	5	N	PHD			
Lacy, Joyce	Inst	Widener			MBA			
Lad, Larry	Assoc	Butler	3	I	DBA	85	Boston	1991
Ladd, Robert T.	Assoc	Tennessee	25	ENX	PHD	80	Georgia	9-80
Lado, Augustine A.	Asst	Cleveland St	3	I	PHD		Memphis	1992
Laessig, Robert E.	Prof	Drexel	37	MAVU	PHD	71	Cornell	1970
LaFarge, Vicki	Asst	Bentley	2	E	PHD	88	Yale	1987
Laffin, Martin J.	SLect	Univ Sydney	12	AEH	PHD		Bradford	1989
LaFollette, William R.	Prof	Ball State	1		DBA	73	Indiana	1977
LaForge, R. Lawrence	Prof	Clemson	7	UV	PHD	76	Georgia	1984
Lafreniere, Ginette	Lect	Laurentian	48	DEJR	MA	87	Sherbroo	7-90
Laguna, Manuel	Asst	Colorado	7	UVWX	PHD	90	Texas	1991
Lahiff, James M.	Assoc	Georgia	15	DEP	PHD	69	Penn St	1972
Lahr, Leland A.	Prof	Lawrence Tec	37		PHD	81	Mich St	1964
Lai, Andrew W.	Assoc	Wright State	7	V	PHD	74	Ohio St	1967
Lai, Vincent	Asst	Alabama-Hunt	9	Z	PHD		Texas	1993
Laing, James D.	Prof	Pennsylvania			PHD	67	Stanford	1976
Laing, Susan	Lect	Napier Univ	38	IY	BA			1989
Laker, Dennis R.	Assoc	Widener			PHD		Illinois	
Lalonde, Robert J.	Assoc	Chicago	5	QP	PHD	85	Princeton	1985
Lam, Long W.	Asst	Houston-C Lk	14		PHD		Oregon	9-94
Lam, S. S.	Asst	Un Hong Kong	79	VUZ	MSC			9-89
Lamar, Bruce W.	SLect	Canterbury	7	UV	PHD		MIT	1991
Lamb, Mary Lou	Assoc	Savannah St	17	P	EDD	69	Indiana	1979
Lamb, Robert	Prof	New York U			PHD		LondonEc	
Lambert, John D.	Prof	Virg Comm	7	EU	PHD	73	Michigan	1955
Lambert, R.	SLect	W Australia			PHD		Witwater	
Lambrinos, James	Assoc	Union			PHD	79	Rutgers	1979
Lamm, Felicity A.	STut	U Auckland	54	QMKC	MPHI	89	Auckland	1-91
Lamming, R. C.	Prof	Univ Bath	7	W				
IPS Professor of Purchasing and Supply Management								
Lamond, David	Lect	Macquarie Un						
Lamont, Bruce T.	Assoc	Florida St	3	HIJY	PHD	89	N Carol	8-89
Lamont, Lawrence Michael Jr.	Prof	Wash & Lee	1	DIX	PHD	69	Michigan	1974
Lampel, Joseph	Asst	New York U			MS			

Name	Rank	Institution		Code	Degree		University	Year
Lancaster, Lilly	Assoc	SC-Spartanbu	71	UVDH	PHD	86	Mass	
Land, Frank P.	Assoc	N Car-Greens	48	JYNL	JD	66	Colorado	8-79
Landau, Jacqueline C.	Assoc	Suffolk			PHD		Cornell	
Lande, R.	Assoc	Concordia U						
Landel, Robert D.	Prof	Virg-Grad	3	U	PHD	70	Ga Tech	1969
Henry E. McWane Professor of Business Administration								
Landeros, Robert	Asst	W Michigan	73	UOZ	PHD	88	Mich St	1989
Landis, Brook I.	Assoc	York of PA	5		PHD		Cornell	1977
Landrum, Fred	VProf	Fla Atlantic			MBA		Fla Atl	1974
Landry, Elaine	Asst	Babson			EDM		Harvard	
Landry, Sylvain	Asst	HEC-Montreal			PHD		Montreal	
Landskroner, Yoram	Assoc	Hebrew Univ			PHD		Penn	
Landson, Barry	Assoc	Marymount			PHD		Syracuse	1985
Landstrom, Ronald L.	Assoc	Neb-Kearney	24	EFGN	MBA	59	Denver	1958
Lane, George	Prof	Univ Calgary	34	ILM	PHD	69	U Wash	1974
Lane, Larry	Asst	American U			PHD			
Lane, Michael S.	Deces	W Virginia	3	1991	PHD	83	Memphis	1983
Lane, Peggy	Asst	Bradley	9	Z	PHD	92	Arkansas	1991
Lane, Richard O.D.	Lect	Queensland	7	V	PHD	66	Lancast	1974
Laneyrie, Frances	AcLec	U Wollongong			BA			D-90
Lang, Dorothy	Assoc	CUNY-Stn Isl	15	EGOV	PHD		CUNY	1988
Lang, James R.	Prof	Virg Tech	6		PHD	76	Mass	1990
Charles O. Strickler Professor of Entrepreneurial Studies								
Lang, William	Lect	CS-Fullerton						
Langer, Manfred		Southeastern			PHD		Enlargen	
Langford, Hal	Asst	SW Louisiana	76	STUV	PHD	86	Geo St	1981
Langford, Joe	Asst	U Washington	9	Z	PHD	87	Rochest	1987
Langford, Margaret	Prof	St Marys-Txs			PHD	92	Houston	
Langlois, Catherine	Asst	Georgetown	73	DIJY	PHD	83	Berkeley	1991
Langowitz, Nan S.	Asst	Babson			DBA	86	Harvard	
Langton, Nancy	Asst	British Colu	2	HER	PHD	84	Stanford	1988
Lanier, Michael T.	Asst	Murray State	37	DIUW	DBA	91	S Illin	1990
Lank, Alden G.		Intl Mgt Dev	56	NS	DBA		Harvard	
Lanser, Kris	Asst	St Xavier	23	EFI	PHD		Miss	
Lansing, Paul	Prof	Illinois	4	KY	JD	71	Illinois	1990
Lant, Theresa K.	Asst	New York U			PHD	87	Stanford	
Lapierre, Laurent	Assoc	HEC-Montreal	25	D	PHD		McGill	
LaPorte, Arthur J. Jr.	Prof	Salem State	1		MBA		Arizona	
Laporte, Gilbert	Prof	HEC-Montreal	7		PHD		London	
Laroche, Evans A.	Retir	Clemson			PHD	71	S Carol	
Larracuente, Maria	Inst	P Rico-Mayag	9		MS	91	Akron	8-87
Larrick, Richard P.	Asst	Chicago	2	E	PHD	91	Michigan	1993
Larsen, Allen F.	Assoc	Fla Southern			PHC		Indiana	1982
Larsen, John E.	Asst	Florida St	7	UV	PHD	89	Texas	8-91
Larson, Andrea	Asst	Virg-Grad	6	TR	PHD		Harvard	1988
Larson, Erik	Assoc	Oregon State	2	E	PHD	82	SUNY-Buf	1980
Larson, Frederick A.	Lect	Texas A&M		KL	JD	78	S Calif	1989
Larson, John A.	Prof	Mich-Flint	43	LJ	PHD	56	Northwes	1976
Larson, Lars Erik	Assoc	Wis-Whitewat	1	ABHL	PHD	66	Cornell	1982
Larson, Lars L.	C	Grand Valley			PHD	71	Illinois	1994
Larson, Mark D.	C-Ac	Bloomsburg	5		PHD		Ohio St	8-91
Larson, Paul	Asst	Montana	36	ISTD	PHD	84	Utah	1985
Larsson, Stig O.	Assoc	Dalhousie U	7	V	PHD		Brit Col	
Larwood, Laurie G.	Prof	Nevada-Reno	23	ERJI	PHD	74	Tulane	1990
Lasdon, Leon S.	Prof	Texas	7	UV	PHD	64	Case Wes	1977
David Bruton Jr. Centennial Chair in Business Decision Support Systems								
Lash, Lewis W.	Dean$	Barry	13	IN	DBA	81	Nova	9-87
Lasher, Harry J.	Prof	Kennesaw St	15	DFNP	PHD	70	Syracuse	1984
Lasker, Jos	Asst	Univ Limburg	25	EFHN	MA	90	Nijmegen	1991
Lasserre, Phillippe	Prof	INSEAD	3	I	PHD	75	Texas	5-75
Lataif, Louis E.	Dean	Boston Univ		Mgt	MBA		Harvard	9-91
Latham, Donald	Assoc	N Car-Wilmin	23	EI	PHD	78	Arkansas	1988
Latham, Jefferson M.	Assoc	Adelphi	79	VZ	PHD	75	Hofstra	1978
Latona, Joseph C.	Prof	Akron	36	IST	DBA	70	Kent St	9-71
LaTour, Robert	Agreg	HEC-Montreal	7	EGNP	CES		Paris	
Latzko, David	Asst	Wilkes	57	Q	PHD		Maryland	9-93
Lau, Agnes T. W.	Lect	City Poly HK	25	DFOP	MSC	88	UK	3-92
Lau, Hon-Shiang	Prof	Oklahoma St	7	V	PHD	73	N Carol	1984
Regents Professor								
Lau, Pinky M. M.	Lect	City Poly HK	14	ELP	MA	85	Lancast	9-88
Laudon, Kenneth C.	Prof	New York U	9	Z	PHD	72	Stanford	
Lauer, Joachim A.	Prof	No Illinois		Z	PHD		Ill Tech	
Lauer, Thomas M.	Assoc	Oakland	9	Z	PHD	86	Indiana	1985
Laughlin, John	C-Ac	So Oregon St	15	AFN	PHD	90	S Calif	1984
Laurent, Andre	Prof	INSEAD	28	EY	DOCT	68	Paris	8-72
LaVan, Helen N.	Prof	DePaul			PHD		Loyola	
Lavanty, Donald	Prof	Marymount			JD		Geo Wash	1979
Lavengood, Lawrence G.	Prof	Northwestern	4	JKL	PHD	53	Chicago	
Lavoie, Dina	Assoc	HEC-Montreal						
Lawler, Edward	Prof	So Calif	2	EFH	PHD		Berkeley	1978

Name	Rank	Inst			Deg		Grad	
Lawless, Michael W.	Assoc	Colorado			PHD	80	UCLA	1982
Lawrence, Ann	Lect	Deakin-Burwo	35	DR	BED		Monash	
Lawrence, Anne T.	Assoc	San Jose St	25	HNQL	PHD	85	Berkeley	1-88
Lawrence, Barbara S.	Assoc	UCLA	3	I	PHD	83	MIT	1983
Lawrence, Clark	Adj	Cincinnati						
Lawrence, John	Asst	Idaho	7	UD	PHD	93	Penn St	1993
Lawrence, Kenneth	Prof	NJ Inst Tech	7	U	EDD	79	Rutgers	1992
Lawrence, Peter A.	Prof	Loughborough	8	Y	MA		Essex	
Lawrence, Stephen R.	Asst	Colorado	78	UIMY	PHD	88	Car Mel	1993
Lawrence, W. Fred	Dean	North Dakota		Mgt	PHD	80	Geo St	8-76
Lawrenson, D.	Asst	East Anglia	2	EH	PHD			1991
Lawson, James W.	Asst	St Peters			DBA	88	Nova	9-88
Lawson, Marian B.	Asst	No Kentucky	34	EH	PHD	89	Minn	1-90
Lawson, Michael E.	Assoc	Boston Univ	9	Z	PHD		Iowa	
Lawson, W.	Assoc	Carleton Un			PHD		York	
Lawton, Stephen J.	Assoc	Oregon State	8	Y	MBA	75	Cornell	1980
Layton, Roger	Dean	New So Wales						
Lazarus, Harold	Prof	Hofstra	2	EFP	PHD	63	Columbia	9-61
Mel Weitz Distinguished Professor								
Lea, John	Lect	Arizona St			MBA			
Leach, Evan	Asst	West Chester						
Leader, Alan H.	Dean	So Conn St			DBA	63	Indiana	
Leader, Gerald C.	Assoc	Boston Univ	2	EFGH	DBA		Harvard	
Leake, Richard	Assoc	Luther	56	NS	ABD	75	Ohio U	1975
Leana, Carrie R.	Assoc	Pittsburgh	2		PHD		Houston	
Leap, Terry	Prof	Clemson	2	EH	PHD	78	Iowa	1985
Leatherwood, Marya	Assoc	Sangamon St	12	EF	PHD		Iowa	1991
Leavitt, Harold J.	Prof	Stanford	2	E	PHD	49	MIT	1966
Walter Kenneth Kilpatrick Prof of Organizational Behavior & Psy, Emeritus								
Leavy, Richard L.	Prof	Ohio Wesley	2	FL	PHD		Mass	1980
LeBlanc, Audrey	C-Ac$	Southern	4	JK	JD	58	Southern	1962
Leblanc, Larry J.	Prof	Vanderbilt	7	VUWX	PHD	73	Northwes	9-80
LeBlanc, Louis Anthony	Prof	Ark-Ltl Rock			PHD		Tx A&M	1990
Leblebici, Huseyin	Prof	Illinois	2	EFH	PHD	75	Illinois	1982
Lebrasseur, Roland	Lect	Laurentian	25		MBA		McGill	1-85
Lebsack, Richard	Prof	Neb-Kearney	19	DENZ	PHD	76	N Colo	1976
Lebsack, Sandra	Lect	Neb-Kearney	7	VX	MAC		Mankato	1977
Leck, Johanne	Prof	HEC-Montreal	5	NR	PHD		McGill	1991
Leclerc, France	Asst	MIT	7	V	PHD	91	Cornell	
Lederer, Albert L.	C-Pr	Oakland	9	Z	PHD	83	Ohio St	1989
Lederer, Phillip J.	Assoc	Rochester	7	U	PHD		Northwes	
Ledgerwood, Donna E.	Assoc	North Texas	45	KMNQ	PHD	80	Oklahoma	1978
Ledolter, Johannes	Prof	Iowa	7	V	PHD	75	Wisconsi	1978
LeDuc, Robert W.	Lect	Stanford	2	E	PHD	75	Stanford	1988
Ledvinka, James D.	Prof	Georgia	52	NQ	PHD	69	Michigan	1970
Lee, Chng-Kuei	C-Pr	Nat Taiwan U	25	NEPQ	PHD	65	Pitt	1981
Lee, Choong	Assoc	Pittsburg St	7	UVZ	PHD	88	Iowa St	1989
Lee, Choong	Asst	Salisbury St	9	Z	PHD	93	S Carol	
Lee, Cynthia K.	Assoc	Northeastern	25	EG	PHD		Maryland	9-87
Lee, Daniel	Prof	Tx-Pan Amer	9	Z	PHD		Florida	1977
Lee, David	Assoc	Dayton	13	BI	PHD	72	Purdue	8-82
Lee, Denis	Prof	Suffolk	9	Z	PHD	80	MIT	1989
Lee, Huei	Asst	Lamar			PHD	91	Geo St	1991
Lee, I.	Asst	Carleton Un	3	I	PHD		Carleton	
Lee, J. Finley	Prof	No Carolina	4	Z	PHD	65	Penn	1970
Julian Price Professor								
Lee, James A.	Retir	Ohio Univ			DBA	68	Harvard	1969
Lee, James B.	Prof	Montana St	3		PHD	74	Arizona	9-87
Lee, Jenny S. Y.	Lect	City Poly HK	19	PZ	MBA	80	St Louis	8-87
Lee, Jonathan	Asst	Fayetteville			ABD			
Lee, Jooh	Assoc	Rowan Col NJ	7	IUY	PHD	88	Miss	1988
Lee, M.	Lect	U Lancaster	25	NPY	PHD			
Lee, Mary Dean	Assoc	McGill Univ	2		PHD		Yale	1982
Lee, Michael B.	Asst	Georgia St	5	NQ	PHD	88	Minn	1991
Lee, Nag	Assoc	NY Inst Tech	97		PHD			
Lee, Patrick S.	Asst	LaSalle	7	U	PHD		Car Mel	1989
Lee, Raymond	Asst	U Manitoba	25	Jne	PHD	89	Wayne St	1991
Lee, Sang M.	C-Pr	Nebraska	79	DPUV	PHD	68	Georgia	1975
University Eminent Scholar								
Lee, Soonchul	Asst	Boston Univ	9	Z	PHD		MIT	
Lee, Terry Nels	Assoc	Brigham Yg	7	U	PHD	73	U Wash	1970
Lee, Thomas W.	Assoc	U Washington	25	NQ	PHD	84	Oregon	1983
Lee, Tien-Sheng	Assoc	Utah	7	U	PHD	82	Missouri	1985
Lee, Tsun-Siou	Assoc	Nat Taiwan U	1		PHD	88	Berkeley	1988
Lee, William B.			7	U	PHD	73	N Carol	
Lee, Won J.	Retir	Marquette	7	1994	PHD	89	Indiana	1989
Lee, Wonsick	Asst	Penn St-Erie	25	EH	PHD	90	SUNY-Buf	1990
Lee, Yoon R.	Asst	Hofstra	79	UVZ	PHD	86	Kansas	9-87
Leeper, Jeffrey C.	Asst	LaSierra	5		MAC	89	Auburn	9-89
Lees, C.	Lect	W Australia			PHD		Monash	

Name	Rank	School			Degree		University	Year
Lees, S.	Lect	U Lancaster	25	EHIP	PHD		London	
Leese, David	Prof	Mt St Mary's			PHD		Brandeis	
Legault, Richard D.	Prof	Mass-Dartmou			PHD	79	Boston U	1973
Legge, Karen	Prof	U Lancaster	25	EHN	DSAS		Oxford	
Lehman, Carol	Assoc	Miss State	1	&	EDD	84	Arkansas	1984
Lehman, John A.	Prof	Alaska-Fairb	9	Z	PHD	82	Michigan	1987
Lehrman, William G.	Asst	Virg Tech	2		PHD	89	Princeton	1987
Lei, David	Asst	So Methodist			PHD	85	Columbia	1990
Leidecker, Joel K.	Assoc	Santa Clara			PHD	69	U Wash	1968
Leidner, Dorothy E.	Asst	Baylor		Z	PHD		Texas	1992
Leif, Doug		Bemidji St	9	Z				
Leifer, Richard P.	Assoc	Rensselaer	92	EZ	PHD		Wiscon	
Leigh, William E.	Assoc	Cen Florida	97	Z	PHD	84	Cinn	1987
Leitheiser, Robert	Assoc	Wis-Whitewat	9	EHXZ	PHD	88	Minnesot	1991
Lelon, Tom		Nichols Col						
Lemak, David	Asst	Wash State						
Lemanski, Daniel V.	Inst	No Illinois			MBA		N Illin	
LeMaster, Jane	Asst	Tx A&M Intl	28	HY	ABD		North Tx	1992
LeMay, Richard P.	Assoc	Rensselaer			PHD		Iowa	1970
Lemelin, Maurice	Dir	HEC-Montreal	5	QN	PHD		UCLA	1969
Lemke, Dwight	Asst	Wis-Oshkosh	34	IJ	ABD		Iowa	1991
LeMoult, William D.	Asst	Pace-Westch	5		JD	62	Fordham	1984
Lenard, Melanie L.	Assoc	Boston Univ	7	UVX	SCD		Columbia	
Lengel, Robert	Assoc	Tx-S Antonio						
Lengnick-Hall, Cynthia	Prof	Wichita St	32	HINT	PHD	81	Texas	9-90
Lengnick-Hall, Mark	Assoc	Wichita St	25	ENPR	PHD	88	Purdue	9-90
Lenn, D. Jeffrey	Assoc	George Wash	4	J	PHD	81	Boston C	
Lentz, Christine	Assoc	Rider	18	YR	PHD	81	Northwes	1984
Lenway, Stephanie A.	Assoc	Minnesota	4	LY	PHD	82	Berkeley	1984
Lenz, R. Thomas	Prof	Indiana	3	I	DBA	78	Indiana	1977
Leonard, Edwin C. Jr.	Prof	Ind-Purdue	24	EJNP	PHD	70	Purdue	8-66
Leonard, Jonathan S.	Assoc	Cal-Berkeley	25	EQ	PHD		Harvard	1982
Harold Furst Associate Professor of Management Philosophy and Values								
Leonard, Joseph W.	Asst	Miami U-Ohio	38	IY	PHD	83	Arkansas	8-82
Leonard, Kevin	Assoc	Wilfrid Laur	7	V	PHD		Concordi	1990
Leonard, Marion S.	Prof	Frostburg St	1	&	MBA		Drexel	8-78
Leonard-Barton, Dorothy	Assoc	Harvard	7	U				
Leone, Robert A.	Prof	Boston Univ	7	U	PHD		Yale	
Leong, Foo Weng	Lect	City Poly HK	81	INPY	MBA	84	Okla St	9-89
Leontiades, Milton	Dean	Rutgers-Camd		Mgt	PHD	66	American	1974
Lepak, Gregory	Assoc	LeMoyne	7	VX	PHD	85	SUNY-Alb	1987
Lerch, Javier	Assoc	Carnegie Mel	9	Z	PHD		Michigan	1986
Lerman, Paul	Dean	F Dick-Madis			PHD	74	NYU	
Lerme, Catherine S.	Asst	Boston Coll	7	UV	PHD	91	Massachu	9-91
Lermer, George	Dean	U Lethbridge	1	AK	PHD		McGill	1981
Lerner, Linda D.	Asst	Tenn Tech	23	IR	PHD	91	Tenn	1991
Lesko, John	VAsst	Bentley	24	ER	PHD	92	Boston C	1994
Lessard, Donald R.	Prof	MIT	3	I	PHD	70	Stanford	1974
Lester, Rick A.	Prof	No Alabama			PHD	85	Miss	1984
Lester, Wanda	Asst	Florida A&M			ABD		Fla St	8-92
Lethbridge, David G.	Prof	Deakin Univ	13	I	MSC		London	1979
Letourneau, Richard H.	Assoc	Belhaven	1	D	PHD	70	Okla St	1993
Leu, Yow-Yuk (Jack)	Asst	CS-S Marcos	7	U	PHD	91	Va Tech	1991
Leuser, David	Assoc	Plymouth St			PHD	79	N Hamp	
Lev, Benjamin	Prof	Mich-Dearbor	7	UV	PHD	70	Case Wes	9-90
Levanoni, Eli	Assoc	Brock Univ	25	EFGH	PHD		Toronto	1979
Levary, Reuven R.	Prof	St Louis			PHD		Case Wes	
Levejhagej, Michael J.	Assoc	Cal Poly-SLO	38	IYT	PHD	93	Illinois	1994
Lever, Jacqueline	Asst	Albright	36	IST	PHD	82	Pitt	9-90
Levesque, Christian	Asst	HEC-Montreal	5	Q	PHD		Quebec	1993
Levesque, Delmas	Assoc	HEC-Montreal	25	EFQ	MA		Montreal	
Levin, Richard I.	Prof	No Carolina	36	LISU	PHD	59	N Carol	1959
Phillip Hettleman Professor								
Levine, David	Asst	Cal-Berkeley	25	EQ	PHD		Harvard	
Levine, Mark	Prof	CS-Chico			PHD		UCLA	1978
Levine, Marvin J.	Prof	Maryland	5	Q	PHD	64	Wiscon	1967
Levinthal, Daniel A.	Assoc	Pennsylvania	3	IHD	PHD	85	Stanford	7-85
May Department Stores Term Associate Professor								
Levitt, Barbara	Asst	Santa Clara			PHD	88	Stanford	1990
Levsen, Virginia	Asst	SC-Coastal	25	HZ	PHD	92	Wash	1992
Levy, Haim	Prof	Hebrew Univ			PHD		Hebrew	
Levy, Steven M.	Prof	CS-San Bern	3	E	PHD	78	Geo Wash	1983
Lewandowski, Mark	Inst	Oral Roberts	1	H	MBA	92	Oral Rob	8-92
Lewicki, Roy	Prof	Ohio State	3	I	PHD	74	Wiscon	1974
Lewin, Arie Y.	Prof	Duke	4	HJ	PHD	68	Car Mel	1974
Lewin, David	Prof	UCLA	5	N	PHD	71	UCLA	1990
Lewis, Alfred	Asst	SUNY-Bingham	3	I	PHD	89	US Intl	1989
Lewis, Edward	Prof	Belmont	97	Z	PHD	78	SUNY	1982
Lewis, Holly S.	Asst	Penn State	7	V	PHD	89	S Carol	
Lewis, John W. III	Assoc	Boston Coll	25	GFNT	PHD	70	Case Wes	9-70

Name	Rank	School			Degree		University	
Lewis, Kathryn	Prof	CS-Chico			PHD		Ariz St	1978
Lewis, Neil R.	LectC	Flinders Un	12	HTZI	MBA	87	Montash	7-91
Lewis, P. J.	Lect	U Lancaster	9	IZ	PHD		Lancast	
Lewis, Pamela	C-Ac	Cen Florida	38	ITY	PHD	88	Tenn	1986
Lewis, Phillip V.	Dean	Azusa Pacif	34	IJ	EDD	70	Houston	9-92
Lewis, R. Dean	Prof	Sam Houston			PHD	72	Arkansas	1987
Lewis, Ralph	Prof	CS-Long Bch	12	EOP	PHD	74	UCLA	1972
Lewis, Suanne M.	Asst	Frostburg St	12	&E	EDD		W Virg	8-93
Lewthwaite, Barbara Jayne	Assoc	Centenary	25	EPR	MBA		St Johns	8-87
Li, Cheng	Asst	CS-L Angeles	7	U	PHD	89	Indiana	1988
Li, Chung-Lun	Asst	Wash Univ	7	UVW	ENGD	90	Columbia	1990
Li, Eldon	Assoc	Cal Poly-SLO	9	Z	PHD	81	Tx Tech	1982
Li, Lode	Assoc	Yale	7	UV	PHD	84	Northwes	1988
Li, Mingfang	Asst	CS-Northrdge	23	DHIX	PHD	90	Va Tech	1990
Li, S.	Asst	McGill Univ	7		PHD		Texas	1991
Li, Susan	Asst	Adelphi	97	ZUVX	PHD	92	Texas	1992
Liang, Diane Wei	Asst	Minnesota	2	EH	PHD	94	Car Mel	1994
Liang, Neng	Asst	Loyola-Maryl	8	Y	PHD		Indiana	1990
Liao, Jun-Yuan	Assoc	Nat Taiwan U	8	Y	MS	68	Nat Taiw	1971
Libby, Barbara	Prof	Niagara						
Liberatore, Matthew	C-Pr	Villanova	7	DUVZ	PHD	76	Penn	1983
Licata, Betty Jo	Dean	Gannon	5	NP	PHD		Renssel	
Lichtman, Robert Jay	Assoc	Cen Michigan	25	EN	PHD	77	LSU	1983
Licker, Paul	C-Pr	Univ Calgary	9	Z	PHD	77	Penn	1981
Liddell, William W.	Prof	Brock Univ	12	EFHE	PHD		Penn St	1981
Liddell, Wingham	Prof	Sonoma State	23	EH	PHD	69	Berkeley	9-71
Liden, Robert C.	Assoc	Ill-Chicago	25	EN	PHD	81	Cinn	8-91
Lieb, Robert C.	Prof	Northeastern			DBA		Maryland	9-70
Lieber, Zvi	Assoc	Tel Aviv Un		M	PHD	71	Chicago	1975
Lieberman, Herman	Asst	St Peters			MS		Michigan	1978
Lieberman, Marvin B.	Assoc	UCLA	3	I	PHD	82	Harvard	1990
Liebeskind, Julia	Asst	So Calif	3	I	PHD		UCLA	1991
Liebowitz, Jay	Assoc	Duquesne			PHD		Tenn	1984
Liebowitz, Jay	Prof	George Wash	9	Z	DSC	85	Geo Wash	
Liedtka, Jeanne	Assoc	Virg-Grad	3	I	DBA		Boston	1989
Lientz, Bennet P.	Prof	UCLA	9	Z	PHD	68	U Wash	1974
Liesz, Thomas J.	Assoc	Western St	16		PHD	89	Idaho	1990
Lifton, Donald E.	Assoc	Ithaca	32	ADE	PHD	88	Cornell	8-82
Ligon, Helen H.	Prof	Baylor		Z	PHD		Tx A&M	1958
Lilien, Gary L.	Prof	Penn State	7	V	DES		Columbia	
Research Professor of Management Science								
Lim, Yet Mee	Asst	Alabama St	2		PHD	93	Alabama	8-91
Limerick, David	Prof	Griffith Un	23	DEFI	PHD		Witwatnd	7-79
Lin, Binshan	Assoc	La St-Shreve	79	VZ	PHD		LSU	8-88
Lin, Frank	Asst	CS-San Bern	9	Z	PHD	92	SUNY-Buf	1992
Lin, Lianlian	Asst	CS-Pomona	8	Y	PHD	92	Texas	1992
Lin, Neng-Pai	Assoc	Nat Taiwan U	79	UZ	PHD	89	Ohio St	1989
Lin, Tsong-Ming	Prof	Nat Taiwan U	17	U	PHD	77	Clemson	1980
Lin, Winston T.	Assoc	SUNY-Buffalo	7	V	PHD	76	Northwes	9-75
Linamen, Larry H.	Dean	Dallas Bapt	26		EDD		Ball St	1991
Lincoln, James R.	Prof	Cal-Berkeley	25	EQ	PHD		Wiscon	1988
Lind, Mary R.	Assoc	N Carol A&T	9	Z	PHD	88	N Carol	8-86
Lind, Robert C.	Prof	Cornell	1	A	PHD	66	Stanford	8-74
Lindamood, Robert	Lect	Mass-Boston	4	JH	PHD	75	Ohio St	1987
Lindberg, Lynne R.	STut	U Auckland	25		MA	89		1-91
Lindemann, Bonnie	Assoc	St Ambrose	25	EN	PHD	93	Iowa	1993
Lindman, Frank	Asst	St Xavier	7	UV	PHD		Arizona	1988
Lindsay, Alice J.	Lect	N Car-Charl			MS		Winthrop	1988
Lindsay, William M.	Prof	No Kentucky	17	DU	PHD	75	Geo St	8-72
Lindsley, William B.	Assoc	Belmont	3	I	PHD	87	MIT	1993
Lindstrom, Grant L.	Asst	Wyoming	31	IST	PHD		Utah	8-90
Ling, Cyril	Prof	Ill Weselyan	34	IJLN	DBA		Indiana	9-90
Telling Chair of Business Administration								
Lingaraj, Bangalore P.	Prof	Ind-Purdue	7	W	PHD	73	Pitt	8-83
Linowes, Richard	Asst	American U	23	IYT	DBA		Harvard	1986
Linstead, Stephen	Prof	U Wollongong			PHD		Sheffiel	9-94
Lipman-Blumen, Jean	Prof	Claremont Gr	12	ADEF	PHD		Harvard	
Bradshaw Professor of Public Policy & Organizational Behavior								
Lipp, Astrid	Asst	Clemson	9	Z	PHD	84	Georgia	1989
Lippman, Steven A.	Prof	UCLA	7	V	PHD	68	Stanford	1967
Lirtzman, S.	Prof	CUNY-Baruch	2	E	PHD		Columbia	1973
Litecky, Charles R.	Prof	Miss State	9	XZ	PHD	74	Minnesot	1991
Litherland, David	Asst	St Marys-Txs						
Litschert, Robert J.	Prof	Virg Tech	3		DBA	66	Colorado	1965
Litt, Benjamin	Prof	Lehigh			PHD	70	NYU	1970
Litteral, Lewis A.	C-Ac	Richmond	7	UV	PHD	82	Clemson	1982
Little, Beverly L.	Asst	W Carolina	25	EFN	PHD	93	Va Tech	8-93
Little, John D. C.	Prof	MIT	7	V	PHD	55	MIT	
Little, Lillian O.	Assoc	Salem State	2		PHD		Syracuse	
Lituchy, T.	Asst	Concordia U						

Litvak, Isaiah A. (Al)	Prof	York Univ	8	Y	PHD		Columbia	
Litzinger, William D.	Retir	Tx-S Antonio		1993	DBA	63	S Calif	1973
Liu, Ben S.	Asst	Illinois			PHD		SUNY-Buf	
Liu, Christina	Assoc	Nat Taiwan U	8	Y	PHD	86	Chicago	1990
Liu, Lai	Asst	Norfolk St	9	Z	PHD		Miss St	7-90
Liu, You Jen	Adj	Southeastern			MBA			
Liuzzo, Anthony L.	Assoc	Wilkes	45	KQ	PHD		NYU	9-90
Livesay, Corinne	Asst	Liberty	5		MBA		Oakland	8-86
Livesay, Robin R.	Dean	Indianapolis			PHD		Ohio St	1978
Livesey, Sharon M.	Lect	Harvard	1	&				
Livingstone, Linda	Asst	Baylor	25	EN	PHD		Okla St	1991
Lloyd-Williams, J.	Tutor	North Wales	3	I	MPHL			4-91
Royal Insurance Tutorial Fellow								
Lloyd-Williams, M.	Lect	North Wales	13	DI	MA			9-90
Lo, Amber	Asst	Millersville	79	IVYZ	ABD	91	Tx A&M	1993
Lobel, Sharon A.	Assoc	Seattle	25	ENOR	PHD	84	Harvard	8-91
Lobert, Beata	Asst	Lg Isl-Post			PHD		Baruch	
Lobuts, John	Prof	George Wash	2	E	EDD	70	Geo Wash	
Lobutz, John	Prof	George Wash	2	E				
Loch, Karen D.	Assoc	Georgia St	7	V	PHD		Nebraska	
Lockamy, Archie	Asst	Florida A&M	7	U	PHD	91	Georgia	1993
Lockard, Nick A.	C-Ac	Tx Lutheran	15	EQ	MBA		Trinity	1980
Locke, Edwin A.	C-Pr	Maryland	2	E	PHD	64	Cornell	1967
Locke, Karen	Asst	Wm & Mary	1	EF	PHD	89	Case Wes	1989
Locke, Richard M.	Asst	MIT	5	Q	PHD			
I.R.I. Careeer Development Assistant Professor of Mgt & Political Science								
Lockett, A. Geoffrey	Prof	Manchest Bus	79	TUY	MSC		Manchest	1984
Lockwood, Chris	Asst	No Arizona	13	IN	PHD	91	Ariz Ot	
Lockwood, Diane	Assoc	Seattle	0	Z	PHD		U Wash	
Loeser, Norma M.	Retir	George Wash	5	N	DBA	71	Geo Wash	
Loowenberg, J. Joseph	Prof	Temple			DBA		Harvard	
Loftin, William E.	Prof	Jacksonvl St	12		DBA	72	Miss St	1978
Loftus, Barbara S.	Asst	Wilkes	6	DRT	PHD		Syracuse	9-91
Logan, James W. Jr.	Asst	New Orleans	13	I	PHD	90	LSU	8-88
Logan, John E.	Assoc	So Carolina			PHD	69	Columbia	
Logozzo, Richard	Asst	Central Conn	25	EHN	PHD	89	Mass	1989
Logsdon, Jeanne M.	C-As	New Mexico	4	JL	PHD	83	Berkeley	
Lohmann, David	Prof	Hawaii Pacif	79	BHN	PHD	73	Ariz St	8-86
Lohse, Gerald	Asst	Pennsylvania			PHD	91	Michigan	1991
Nelson Peltz Term Assistant Professor								
Lombardo, Gary A.	Assoc	So Maine	3	IY	PHD	86	Oregon	1987
Lomi, Alessandro	PostD	London Bus	2	F	PHD		Cornell	
London, Anne	Asst	Hartford	2	E	PHD	91	Case Wes	
London, Manuel	Prof	SUNY-Stony B	25	ENOP	PHD	74	Ohio St	1989
Lonergan, Janis	C	Augustana IL	38		PHD	78	S Illin	9-76
Long, Albert W.	Prof	Delta State	28	EIY	DBA	83	US Intl	8-83
Long, David K.	Dean	Ithaca	2	E	PHD	74	Kent	8-73
Long, Esther	Asst	West Florida	12	NO	PHD	92	Tenn	1991
Long, Hugh W.	Assoc	Tulane	4	AK	PHD	74	Stanford	1969
Long, James	Inst	SW Okla St	1	S	MBA	88	Utah	1992
Long, Rebecca	Asst	Louisiana Te	23	ONIQ	PHD	92	LSU	1992
Long, Richard J.	Prof	Saskatchewan	2	DFNH	PHD	77	Cornell	1977
Long, Stephen F.	Asst	Univ Regina	25	FHNP	MBA		Dalhousi	
Longenecker, Clinton O.	Assoc	Toledo	25		PHD		Penn St	1978
Longshore, John	Assoc	Embry-Riddle			PHD	88	Nova	1992
Loo, Bob	Assoc	U Lethbridge	25	EGNP	PHD	78	Calgary	1989
Loomba, Arvinder P.S.	Asst	No Iowa			PHD	93	USC	8-93
Loomba, Narendra P.	Prof	CUNY-Baruch	1	B	PHD	59	Wiscon	1968
Lopes, Lola	Prof	Iowa	2	E	PHD	74	Ca-SnDgo	1990
Pomerantz Professor								
Lopez-Molina, Radames	Prof	P Rico-Mayag	9		MBA	71	Inter Am	7-69
Loque, Dennis E.	Prof	Dartmouth			PHD	71	Cornell	1974
Lorange, Peter	Pres	Intl Mgt Dev	3	I	DBA	72	Harvard	1979
Lorbiecki, Anna	Lect	U Lancaster	25	NOP	MAP		Lancaste	
Lorentz, Richard D.	Assoc	Wis-Eau Clar		STI	PHD		N Colo	1971
Lorentz, Royce A.	Assoc	Slippery Roc	79	UTRS	ABD		Colorado	8-75
Lorenzi, Peter	Dean	Cen Arkansas	23	EFI	PHD	78	Penn St	6-92
Lorsch, Jay W.	Prof	Harvard	25	En				
Louis E. Kirstein Professor of Human Relations; Senior Associate Dean								
Loseby, Paul	Asst	Lyndon State		OB	DPS	90	Pace	1992
Losik, Robert	Assoc	New Hamp Col	23	I	EDD		Vanderbt	
Lotfi, Vahid	Assoc	Mich-Flint	7	UV	PHD	81	SUNY-Buf	8-90
Lott Jr., John R.	Asst	Pennsylvania			PHD	84	UCLA	1991
Carl D. Covitz Term Assistant Professor								
Lou, Cheri	Lect	U Washington	9	Z	MBA	84	Wyoming	1990
Lou, Sheldon	Prof	CS-S Marcos	7	U	PHD	85	MIT	1993
Loucks, John	Asst	St Edwards			PHD			1993
Loucks, Kenneth E.	Prof	Brock Univ	13	IST	PHD		Western	1986
Loughman, Thomas P.	Asst	Columbus	1	E	PHD		Auburn	1975
Louis, Meryl R.	Assoc	Boston Univ	2	E	PHD		UCLA	

Name	Rank	Institution			Degree		School	
Loulou, R.	Prof	McGill Univ	7		PHD		Berkeley	1970
Loutzenhiser, Janice	Assoc	CS-San Bern	4	K	JD	75	Virginia	1976
Love, C. Ernest	Prof	Simon Fraser	37	IUVX	PHD	75	London	1977
Love, Kevin G.	Prof	Cen Michigan	25	EFNP	PHD	79	S Fla	1979
Love, Robert F.	Prof	McMaster Un	17	UV	PHD		Stanford	
Love, Thomas E.	Asst	Case Western			PHD	94	Penn	1994
Lovejoy, William	Prof	Michigan	7	U	PHD	83	Delaware	1994
Loveland, John P.	Prof	New Mex St	23	EIJM	PHD	70	Ariz St	1972
Lovell, Joseph B.	Lect	CS-San Bern	62	SE	MBA	66	Creighto	1981
Lovell, Ross	Prof	Sam Houston			PHD	62	Texas	1972
Loveman, Gary W.	Asst	Harvard	25	EN				
Low, George	Lect	U Lethbridge			ABD			1988
Low, Murray	Asst	Columbia	6	ST	PHD	90	Penn	1990
Low, William T.	Lect	Napier Univ	25	EFNP	MPHI			1983
Lowe, Calvin	Prof	Utah State	6	S	EDD	63	Utah	9-62
Lowe, Tim	Prof	Iowa	7	U	PHD	73	Northwes	1989
Lower, Robert	Inst	Minot St			MA		Cen Mich	1986
Lownes, Millicent G.	Assoc	Tenn State			PHD			
Lowry, Wally		Sonoma State						
Lowy, Ronald	C-Ac	Eastern Conn			PHD		Kent St	1989
Lubatkin, Michael	Assoc	Connecticut	3	I	DBA	82	Tenn	1982
Lucas, Ann F.	Prof	F Dick-Madis	2		PHD		Fordham	
Lucas, Henry C. Jr.	Prof	New York U	9	Z	PHD	70	MIT	
Research Professor								
Lucas, Robert	Prof	Metro State	67	STUW	DBA	71	Colorado	1976
Lucas, Robert G.	Assoc	York Univ	5	Q	PHD		Cornell	
Lucchesi, Carol Y.	Assoc	Wittenberg	2	NR	PHD	83	Georgia	1983
Lucchesi, Ronald P.	Asst	Wittenberg	7	UV	ABD		Georgia	1983
Lucchetti, Lynn	Adj	Southeastern			MA		San Fran	
Luce, Thomas G.	Prof	Ohio Univ			PHD		Purdue	
Lucero, Margaret A.	Asst	Wyoming	52	NOE	PHD		Houston	8-90
Luchsinger, V. P.	Prof	Baltimore	38	DISW	PHD	62	Tx Tech	8-81
Ludwick, Mark H.	Asst	Mich-Flint	52	NPF	PHD	87	Wayne St	9-91
Ludwig, Dean C.	Asst	Toledo	4		PHD		Penn	1988
Luebbe, Richard L.	Assoc	Miami U-Ohio	7	U	PHD	85	Nebraska	8-84
Luechauer, David L.	Asst	Butler	2	EF	PHD	90	Cinn	1992
Luke, Cheryl M.	Retir	So Carolina		1994	PHD	67	Indiana	
Lumley, Jane	Lect	Cornell	1	D	MA	76	Penn St	1979
Lummus, Rhonda	Asst	Cen Missouri	7	UW	PHD	92	Iowa	1992
Lumpkin, Joan B.	Inst	Wright State	9	Z	MBA	76	Dayton	1991
Lund, Mark	Prof	Luther	48	LY	PHD	75	Iowa St	1978
Lundberg, Craig	Prof	Cornell	2	EF	PHD	66	Cornell	1-87
Blanchard Professor of Human Resources Management								
Lundberg, Olof H. Jr.	C-Pr	New Orleans	32	IH	PHD	71	Penn St	8-71
Lunde, Harold I.	Prof	Bowling Gr	3	I	PHD	66	Minn	1980
Lunden, John H.	Assoc	Ferris State	3		MBA		Michigan	1980
Lundin, Jean	Assoc	Lk Superior	23	EIJL	PHD		Wiscon	9-91
Lundquist, Ronald W.	C-Pr	CS-Stanislau	2	HBK	PHD	72	Oregon	9-87
Lunn, Robert O.			2	E	PHD	82	N Carol	
Lust, John	Asst	Illinois St	51		PHD		Kentucky	1989
Luthans, Fred	Prof	Nebraska	28	EGLY	PHD	65	Iowa	1967
George Holmes Professor								
Luthar, Harsh	Asst	Bryant	5	EN	PHD	93	Va Tech	8-93
Luthar, Vipan K.	Inst	St Paul's	23	FIY	MBA			1989
Lutz, Raymond	Prof	Texas-Dallas	7	U				
Lutz, Richard C.	Retir	Akron	5	NPQ	PHD	72	Tx Tech	1-73
Luxmore, Stephen	Asst	St John Fish	38		PHD		Toronto	
Luytjes, Jan B.	Prof	Fla Internat		TY	PHD	62	Penn	1971
Luzadis, Rebecca A.	Asst	Miami U-Ohio	5	NX	PHD	86	Cornell	8-89
Lye, A. R.	ALect	Canterbury	8	Y	MBA	81	Iowa	1994
Lyew, Peter A.	Asst	Pace-Westch	7		DBA	85	La Tech	1981
Lyles, Carole	Asst	Loyola-Maryl	2	EN	ABD	94	Geo Wash	1993
Lyles, Marjorie A.	Assoc	Indiana	8	Y	PHD	77	Pitt	1990
Lyman, Steve	Asst	Mid Tenn St	7	U	PHD	93	Mich St	1994
Lynch, Brian	Asst	Wis-La Cross		Z	PHD		SUNY-Buf	
Lynch, Dan	Asst	Mont St-Bill	1		MPA	77	Boulder	1989
Lynch, James E.	Prof	Univ Leeds	3	I	PHD	82	Bradford	1991
Lynch, Jeanne M.	Assoc	Rensselaer	3	I	DBA		Harvard	
Wellington Professor								
Lynch, Larry A.	C-Pr	Roanoke Col	3		PHD	87	Va Tech	1978
Lynch, Lisa	Assoc	MIT	5	QN	PHD			
Lynch, Robert D.	Prof	Rowan Col NJ	37	I	PHD	55	Car Mel	1973
Lynch, Robert G.	Assoc	Dallas	13	BI	MBA	66	Ohio St	6-66
Lyne, George E. Jr.	C-Ac	Appalach St	23	EHI	PHD	74	N Carol	1973
Lyne, S. R.	Lect	Univ Bristol	2	HI	PHD	90	Bristol	1980
Lynn, Billy G.	Assoc	Teikyo Mary	46	TM	PHD	91	Illinois	8-87
Lynn, Leonard H.	Assoc	Case Western	8	Y	PHD		Michigan	
Lynn, Marc P.	Asst	John Carroll			PHD		Clev St	1987
Lynn, Monty L.	Assoc	Abilene Chr	2	BEHQ	PHD	85	Brig Yg	1985
Lyons, Patrick	Assoc	St Johns			PHD	73	Adelphi	

Name	Rank	School			Deg		Grad School	Year
Lyons, Paul R.	Prof	Frostburg St	2	EK	PHD		Florida	8-84
Lyons, Thomas F.	Prof	Mich-Dearbor	12	EFHP	PHD	67	Michigan	1974
Lytle, Donald E.	SInst	Oregon	1		MBA	76	Oregon	1976
Lytle, Richard	Asst	Abilene Chr			ABD		Ariz St	1991
Ma, Hao	Asst	Bryant	18	IN	PHD	94	Texas	8-94
Maakestad, William	Assoc	W Illinois			JD	77	Valparai	1977
Maanavi, Noureddin	Prof	Norfolk St	37	U	PHD	76	Penn	1983
Maasarani, Aly	Prof	St Johns			PHD	62	Texas	
Mabin, Vicky J.	SLect	Victoria NZ	7	RUVW	PHD		Lancaste	5-91
MacAvoy, Paul W.	Dean	Yale	31	I	PHD	60	Yale	1991
MacAvoy, Thomas C.	Prof	Virg-Grad	3	U	PHD		Cinn	1969
Paul M. Hammaker Professor of Business Administration								
MacColl, Michael	Assoc	San Fran St	23	HIY	PHD	92	Toronto	1989
MacCrimmon, K. R.	Prof	British Colu	3	I	PHD	65	UCLA	1970
MacDonald, Diane	Assoc	Pacific Luth	4	KLPS	JD	80	J Marsh	1987
Macdonald, Ian H.	Prof	York Univ	1	A	PHD		Oxford	
Macdonald, Jean L	Prof	Norwich	16		PHD			
MacDuffie, John Paul	Asst	Pennsylvania	2	EJ	PHD	90	MIT	7-90
Roger Stone Term Assistant Professor of Management								
Macey, William	Assoc	NE Illinios	52	E	PHD		Loyala	5-82
MacHaffie, Fraser G.	C-Ac	Marietta	7	U	MBA	82	Clev St	1982
Maciariello, Joseph	Prof	Claremont Gr	13	DI	PHD	72	NYU	1979
Horton Professor of Business Administration								
Mack, John E.	Prof	Salem State	1		PHD		St Louis	
Mack, Rhonda	C-Pr	Charleston			PHD	83	Georgia	1994
MacKay, Jane M.	C-Ac	Tx Christian	9	Z	PHD	87	Texas	1986
MacKenzie, Kenneth D.	Prof	Kansas	2	EH	PHD	64	Berkeley	1972
Mackey, Gerald	SrRes	Georgia Tech	39	IZ	PHD	00	Geo St	1979
MacKinnon, Richard	SLoot	MIT	9	Z				
MacKinnon, Ronald J.	Prof	St Fran Xav	9	Z	PHD		Okla St	1961
MacLean, Leonard	Prof	Dalhousie U	9	Z	PHD		Dalhousi	1975
MacLeod, Kenneth R.	Asst	East Carol		V	PHD	90	S Carol	1989
MacMillan, Ian C.	Prof	Pennsylvania	36	IT	DBA	75	S Africa	7-86
George W. Taylor Professor of Entrepreneurinal Studies;Dir Sol C Snider Er								
MacMillan, Ronnie		Strathclyde	7	U				
Macomber, James Howard	Assoc	Tenn-Chattan	7	UVX	DBA	79	Kent St	1978
Macpherson, Neil C.	SLect	Napier Univ	38	IY	MSC			1971
MacQueen, James B.	Prof	UCLA	7	V	PHD	58	Oregon	1962
Macy, Barry A.	Prof	Texas Tech	23	XIFH	PHD	75	Ohio St	1980
Macy, Granger	Asst	Missouri	3	I	PHD	91	Indiana	1990
Madan, Manohar	Assoc	Wis-Whitewat	7	UVWZ	PHD	88	Tenn	1989
Madansky, Albert	Prof	Chicago	7	V	PHD	58	Chicago	1974
Madden, Lynne K.	Asst	Aurora			MBA	84	N Illin	1984
Madden, Regan B.	Assoc	Ark-Ltl Rock			PHD		Va Tech	
Maddox, Ann	Inst	Angelo State			MBA		Tx Tech	
Maddox, E. Nicholas	Assoc	Stetson	24	EFGJ	PHD		Fla St	1985
Maddox, Robert C.	Assoc	Tennessee	18	Y	PHD	68	Texas	9-72
Madey, Gregory	Assoc	Kent State			PHD		Case Wes	1984
Madhok, Anoop	Asst	Utah	38	IY	PHD	93	McGill	1993
Madigan, Robert M.	Assoc	Virg Tech	5		PHD	82	Mich St	1980
Madison, Dan	Assoc	CS-Long Bch	13	IBH	PHD	81	Irvine	1983
Madison, William J.	Inst	Miami U-Ohio	15	L	MPA	74	Cinn	1-87
Madkins, Jerry B.	Asst	Tarleton St	45	JLQO	DMIN	80	SBTS	1989
Madnick, Stuart E.	Prof	MIT	9	Z	PHD	72	MIT	
Leaders for Manufacturing Professor of Mgt Sci & John Norris Maguire Prof								
Madu, Christian	Prof	Pace	7	F	PHD		Baruch	
Madura, Jeffrey	Prof	Ill Benedict			MBA	72	Northwes	1971
Maes, Jeanne	Asst	So Alabama	12	DEFT	PHD	94	S Miss	1994
Maestas, Ronald W.		New Mex High	24	Z	EDD			1972
Maffei, Mary Jo	Asst	Miami U-Ohio	7	U	PHD	91	Cinn	1-91
Mafi, Shirine	Asst	Otterbein	7	U	MBA	78	Marshall	1987
Magazine, M. J.	Prof	Un Waterloo	7	UV	PHD	69	Florida	1975
Magee-Egan, Pauline	Assoc	St Johns			PHD	63	Fordham	
Magenau, John M.	Dir	Penn St-Erie	25	EQ	PHD	88	SUNY-Buf	1985
Maggard, Michael	C-Pr	Northeastern			PHD		UCLA	
Magill, Sharon L.	Asst	Louisville	32	HIYZ	PHD	92	Indiana	8-92
Magjuka, Richard J.	Asst	Indiana	2	H	PHD	86	Chicago	1988
Magnan, Gregory	Asst	Seattle	7	U	ABD		Mich St	
Magnanti, Thomas L.	Prof	MIT	7	UV	PHD	72	Stanford	
George Eastman Professor of Management Science								
Magnusen, Karl O.	Assoc	Fla Internat		QH	PHD	70	Wiscon	1974
Mahaffey, Thomas R.	Asst	Siena Coll	18		MBA		Chicago	9-86
Maher, Karen	Asst	Mo-St Louis	25	EN	PHD	91	Akron	1991
Maher, Larry	Asst	SUNY-Oswego	25	EFNP				
Maher, P. Michael	Dean	Univ Calgary		Mgt	PHD	70	Northwes	
Mahesh, Sathiadev	Prof	New Orleans	79	Z	PHD	84	Purdue	8-84
Maheshwari, Sharad	Asst	Hampton		UVZX	PHD		S Fla	8-91
Mahmood, Mo Adam	Assoc	Tx-El Paso	9	Z	PHD	82	Tx Tech	1987
Mahmoodi, Farzad	Asst	Clarkson	1		PHD		Minn	
Mahmoud, Mohamed	Assoc	Athabasca Un	79	UV	PHD	79	Penn	1991

Name	Rank	School			Degree		Institution	Year
Mahmoud, Watad	Asst	Monmouth	9	Z	PHD	91	NYU	9-94
Mahon, John F.	Assoc	Boston Univ	1	DH	DBA		Boston	
Mahoney, Darrell	Prof	Deakin-Burwo	38	I	MADM		Monash	
Mahoney, Frank	VProf	Houston Bapt						
Mahoney, J. J.	Retir	Citadel	65		MS		Ga Tech	
Mahoney, Joan	Asst	So Calif	2	E	PHD		SUNY-Buf	1-92
Mahoney, Joseph	Asst	Illinois	3	I	PHD	88	Penn	1988
Mahoney, Thomas A.	Prof	Vanderbilt	5	NOPQ	PHD	56	Minn	9-82
Mai-Dalton, Renate R.	Assoc	Kansas	2	E	PHD		U Wash	1979
Maidique, Modesto A.	Prof	Fla Internat		TD	PHD	70	MIT	
Maier, Ernest L.	Prof	Lawrence Tec	1		MBA	61	Detroit	1972
Mainiero, Lisa A.	Assoc	Fairfield	23	FGEI	PHD	83	Yale	1983
Mainstone, Lawrence	Prof	Valparaiso	17	EFV	PHD		Mich St	1991
Maitland, Ian H.	Assoc	Minnesota	4	LJ	PHD	79	Columbia	1979
Major, Don	Asst	Florida A&M	83		ABD		Miami	
Majthay, Antael	Assoc	Florida			PHD	61	Szeged	1972
Majumdar, S. K.	Asst	Michigan			PHD	90	Minn	1990
Mak, L. F. Brenda	Asst	Dalhousie U	9	Z	PHD		Northwes	
Mak, Simon K. M.	Lect	City Poly HK	38	ILY	MBA	84	Cty P HK	8-88
Makens, James C.	Assoc	Wake Fr-MBA	8	Y	PHD		Mich St	
Makhija, Indra	Asst	Illinois Tch			PHD		Chicago	1986
Makhija, Mona	Asst	Pittsburgh	8		PHD		Wiscon	
Makhlouf, Hany H.	C-Pr	Univ of D C	15	IY	PHD	70	American	1971
Makin, Peter J.	Lect	Manches Inst	2	E	PHD		Bradford	7-81
Maksymiw, W.	SLect	Humberside	2					
Maldonado, Leo	Asst	Tx-Brownsvil			MBA	84	Pan Am-B	1973
Malekzadeh, Ali R.	Assoc	Ariz St-West	23	IHTY	PHD	82	Utah	1987
Malik, Kavindra	Asst	Cornell	7	V	PHD		Penn	7-88
Malik, S. Dolly	Asst	SUNY-Geneseo	35	EN	PHD	89	Mich St	9-88
Malik, Zafar	Prof	Governors St			PHD		Renessel	
Mallette, Paul	Asst	Colorado St	3	DIL	PHD	88	Nebraska	1988
Malley, John Corbin	Assoc	Cen Arkansas	9	Z	DBA		Fla St	
Malliaris, Mary	Asst	Loyola-Chicg			PHD		Chicago	1990
Mallick, Debasish N.	Asst	Boston Coll	7	UV	PHD	93	Texas	9-93
Mallinger, Mark A.	Prof	Pepper-Malib	2	EFGP	PHD	80	S Calif	1980
Mallory, Elgin	Asst	Mesa State	17		PHD		Colo St	1990
Mallory, G.	Asst	Carleton Un			PHD		Brandon	
Malnight, Thomas W.	Asst	Pennsylvania	83	YI	DBA	92	Harvard	7-92
Roger Stone Assistant Professor of Management								
Malo, Marie-Claire	Assoc	HEC-Montreal	5	Q	D.3		Paris	
Malone, Elizabeth Anne	Asst	Mt St Mary's			MA		UCLA	
Malone, Paul B. III	Assoc	George Wash	5	N	DBA	73	Geo Wash	
Malone, Stewart C.	Assoc	Virginia			PHD		Temple	
Malone, Thomas W.	Prof	MIT	9	Z	PHD			
Patrick J. McGovern Professor of Information Systems								
Maloney, Kevin J.	Assoc	Dartmouth			PHD	83	U Wash	1983
Mamaghani, Farrokh	Assoc	St John Fish	7		DSD		Geo Wash	
Mamer, John W.	C-Ac	UCLA	7	V	PHD	82	Berkeley	1981
Mandell, Myra P.	Prof	CS-Northrdge	12	ADHL	PHD	81	S Calif	1980
Mandry, Gordon D.	Lect	Manchest Bus	3	IZ	MA		Oxford	1976
Mang, Paul	Asst	Texas	3	I	PHD	93	Harvard	1993
Mangaliso, Mzamo	Asst	Massachusett	34	YI	PHD	88	Mass	1989
Mangel, Robert	Asst	Temple			PHD		Penn	
Mangham, I. L.	H-Pr	Univ Bath	2	E	PHD			
Mangos, Nicholas C.	LectB	Flinders Un	34	DJ	MBA	85	Adelaide	7-90
Mangum, Garth	Prof	Utah	5	NQ	PHD	60	Harvard	1968
Mangum, Stephen	C-Ac	Ohio State	5	NQ	PHD	84	Geo Wash	1983
Mangum, Wiley	Assoc	Pace	37	EOUV	PHD	85	Fordham	1980
Manheim, Marvin L.	Prof	Northwestern	39	IZ	PHD	64	MIT	
William A. Patterson Distinguished Professor of Transportation								
Manjulika, Koshal	Prof	Ohio Univ	7	U	PHD	64	Patna	
Mankelow, G.	Lect	U Newcastle	46	DT	BCOM		NS Wales	
Manley, Douglas	Adj	SUNY-Fredon	35					
Mann, Athol W.	Dean	Victoria NZ						
Mann, Phillip	Inst	Fla Internat		T	EDD	67	Virginia	1991
Mann, Richard A.	Prof	No Carolina	4	JKL	JD	73	Yale	1974
Mann, Thomas	Asst	No Illinois		V	PHD		Iowa St	1973
Manning, Michael R.	Assoc	New Mex St	25	EFN	PHD	79	Purdue	1989
Manning, William A.	Prof	Portland St	97	Z	PHD	70	Oregon	1969
Mannino, Michael V.	Asst	U Washington	9	Z	PHD	83	Arizona	1991
Mannix, Elizabeth A.	Assoc	Chicago	2	E	PHD	89	Chicago	1989
Manns, Curtis	Assoc	Virgin Islan	7	DT	PHD			1989
Mannweiler, Richard A.	Dean	Millikin			MSIR		Purdue	1979
Manocha, Dineshnandini	Assoc	Slippery Roc	79	UT	DBA	86	Kent St	8-86
Manoochehri, Ghasem H.	Prof	CS-Fullerton	7	U	PHD	78	LSU	8-81
Manson, Daniel P.	Assoc	CS-Pomona	9	Z	MSBA	85	CS-Pomon	1992
Mansour, Ali	C-Pr	W Virginia	7	V	PHD	78	Georgia	1978
Mansur, Iqbal	Assoc	Widener			PHD		Cinn	
Manton, Edgar J.					DBA	71	Fla St	
Manz, Charles	Assoc	Arizona St	25	EGNP	PHD	81	Penn St	1988

Name	Rank	Institution			Degree		School	Year
Maranto, Cheryl L.	Asst	Marquette	5	NQ	PHD	82	Mich St	1989
Marcelle, Earl	Asst	Southern	16	ENST	MBA	70	Texas	1980
March, Douglas	Assoc	W Illinois			JD	73	Illinois	1973
March, James G.	Prof	Stanford	2	H	PHD	53	Copenhag	
Fred H. Merrill Professor of Managment								
Marchand, Don		Intl Mgt Dev			PHD		UCLA	
Marchant, A.	SLect	Humberside	3					
Marchewka, Jack	Asst	No Illinois			PHD		Geo St	1994
Marchington, Michael P.	SLect	Manches Inst	5	N	PHD		Manchest	1-86
Marcolin, Barbara	Asst	Univ Calgary	9	Z	PHD	93	Western	1993
Marcus, Alfred A.	Prof	Minnesota	4	IJ	PHD	77	Harvard	1984
Mardfin, Ward	Assoc	Hawaii Pacif	17	STVY	PHD	79	Hi-Manoa	8-93
Marer, Paul	Prof	Indiana	8	Y	PHD	68	Penn	1967
Margenthaler, C. Robert	Prof	Loyola-Maryl	9	Z	PHD	72	Illinois	1981
Margulies, Newton	Prof	Calif-Irvine	2	E	PHD	65	UCLA	1969
Margulis, Stephen	Prof	Grand Valley			PHD		Minn	1986
Marin, Daniel B.	Prof	Louisiana St	4	L	PHD	72	Iowa	8-84
Marino, Kenneth E.	Prof	San Diego St	3	I	PHD	78	Mass	1986
Marinoni, Ann	Prof	Lk Superior	23	DEJP	PHD		Mich St	9-76
Marion, Frank M.	Assoc	Christian Br			DBA		Memphis	
Markell, Steve	Assoc	Bloomsburg	23		PHD		N Carol	8-90
Marker, Michael	Asst	Jacksonvl St	12	JM	PHD	84	Alabama	1978
Markham, Frank B.	Asst	Radford	23	I	ABD		La Tech	8-91
Markham, In	Asst	N Car-Wilmin	7	V	PHD		Va Tech	
Markham, Stephen K.	Asst	N Carol St	23	EDHI	PHD	93	Purdue	1992
Markham, Steve E.	Prof	Virg Tech	2		PHD	78	SUNY-Buf	1978
Markides, Costas	Asst	London Bus	38	DIY	DBA		Harvard	1990
Markovich, Michael		Ly Isl-Brook						
Markowitz, H. M.	VProf	London Bus	7	V	PHD		Chicago	
Markowitz, James R.	Assoc	Ithaca	5	Q	JD	70	Yale	8-73
Marks, Joseph	Adj	Southeastern			MADM		SEastern	
Markulis, Peter	Assoc	SUNY-Geneseo	39	IZ	PHD	80	SUNY-Buf	9-81
Markus, M. Lynne	Assoc	Claremont Gr	9	Z&X	PHD	79	Case Wes	1992
Marlow, Edward K.	Prof	E Illinois		E	PHD	75	Illinois	1984
Marmor, Theodore R.	Prof	Yale	1	A	PHD	66	Harvard	1979
Marquardt, John D.	Assoc	Mich-Flint	1	A	PHD	75	Illinois	1980
Marschak, Thomas A.	Prof	Cal-Berkeley	7	V	PHD		Stanford	1959
Marsden, James R.	H-Prof	Connecticut			PHD	70	Purdue	8-93
Marsden, Richard	Asst	Athabasca Un	5	Q	PHD	94	Warwick	1983
Marsh, Michael	Asst	Shippensburg	7	V	PHD		Ohio St	
Marsh, Paul R.	Prof	London Bus	1		PHD		London	
Marshall, A. R.	Retir	McGill Univ	1	8-93	MBA		Wiscon	1955
Marshall, Brenda S.	Asst	Cleveland St	1	C	PHD		Michigan	1991
Marshall, Dianne L.	Inst	Alaska-Fairb	9	Z	MBA	86	Alaska	1987
Marshall, J.	SLect	Univ Bath	2	E	PHD			
Marshall, Jennings B.	Assoc	Samford			PHD		Kentucky	1986
Marshall, Kimball P.	Assoc	Jackson St		DILZ	PHD	75	Florida	9-92
Marshall, Louise	Assoc	Marymount			PHD		Maryland	1976
Marshall, Paul S.	Assoc	Widener			PHD		Bath	
Marshall, Thomas E.	Asst	Auburn	9	Z	PHD	91	North Tx	9-91
Martell, Kathryn	Asst	S Ill-Edward	38	INY	PHD	89	Maryland	8-91
Martello, Bill	Asst	Univ Calgary	3	1	ABD		Pitt	1993
Martin, Christopher	C	La St-Shreve	25	E	PHD	87	Ga Tech	1-88
Martin, Clarence	Assoc	Ohio Univ	7		PHD	79	Car Mel	
Martin, David C.	Prof	American U	25	N	PHD	84	Maryland	1981
Martin, Gene	Assoc	Clarkson	7		PHD		Wash U	
Martin, Harry J.	C-Ac	Cleveland St	12	FEN	PHD		S Illin	1980
Martin, James E.	Prof	Wayne State	5	NQ	PHD	73	Wash	1976
Martin, Joanne	Assoc	Stanford	2	E	PHD	77	Harvard	1977
Martin, Michael J. C.	C-Pr	Dalhousie U	7	U	PHD		Sheffiel	
Martin, Miles	Prof	SUNY-Plattsb	38	IY	PHD		Case	1982
Martin, R. Kipp	Prof	Chicago	37	IV	PHD	80	Cinn	1980
Martin, Raymond L.	Assoc	Cen Florida	7	U	PHD	68	American	1971
Martin, Robert G.	Assoc	NE Louisiana	36	IST	PHD	84	Texas	1983
Martin, Roger	Asst	Keene State			MBA		Hartford	1986
Martin, Roger G.	Assoc	HEC-Montreal	5	Q	MA		Montreal	1978
Martin, Thomas	C-Pr	Neb-Omaha	12	EFH	PHD	77	Iowa	1989
Martin, William B.	Assoc	Tx-El Paso			PHD	72	North Tx	1975
Martin, William R. D.	C-Pr	Mich-Dearbor	12	EIPS	MBA	58	Chicago	1976
Martinec Ponte, Cindy	Asst	W Virginia	3	I	PHD	88	SUNY	1988
Martinez, Eduardo	Asst	Univ Navarra	7	V	PHD		Barcelon	9-60
Martinez, Zaida L.	Prof	St Marys-Txs			PHD	87	S Carol	
Martinko, Mark J.	Prof	Florida St	2	EX	PHD	77	Nebraska	9-78
Martinsons, Maris G.	Lect	City Poly HK	39	ITYV	MBA	84	Toronto	8-88
Marvasti, Frank	C-Ac	Redlands	79	VZ	PHD			
Marx, Don	Prof	Alaska-Ancho	7	V	PHD	74	Houston	1981
Marx, Robert D.	Assoc	Massachusett	2	EP	PHD	71	Illinois	1982
Mascarenhas, Briance	Prof	Rutgers-Camd	8	Y	PHD	80	Berkeley	
Maser, Steven M.	Prof	Willamette	14	AJKL	PHD	75	Rochest	1978
Masifern, Esteban	Assoc	Univ Navarra	3	I			ETSII	7-60

Name	Rank	University			Degree			
Mason, E. Sharon	Lect	Brock Univ	25	EFLZ	PHD		Toronto	1991
Mason, Ida	Prof	CS-Pomona	9	Z	PHD	84	Ariz St	1980
Mason, Jim R.	Assoc	Univ Regina	36	IST	PHD		Wash	
Mason, Mark	Assoc	Yale	8	Y	PHD	88	Harvard	1990
Mason, Phyllis	Asst	Seton Hall			PHD	86	Columbia	
Mason, R.	SLect	Humberside	7					
Mason, Richard O.	Prof	So Methodist			PHD	68	Calif	
Mason, Robert H.	Prof	Case Western			PHD	73	Ga Tech	9-87
Mason, Robert H.	Retir	UCLA		1991	PHD	67	Stanford	1966
Mason, Thomas	Assoc	St Thomas-MN						
Massarik, Fred	Prof	UCLA	5	N	PHD	57	UCLA	1950
Massengill, Douglas	Assoc	Loyola-Chicg			PHD		Tenn	
Massetti, Brenda	Asst	St Johns			PHD	91	Fla St	
Masters, Marick F.	Assoc	Pittsburgh	5		PHD		Illinois	
Masters, Neil	Lect	U Wollongong	79	RUTA	MSC	77	U Wollon	7-83
Masters, Robert	C-Pr	Fort Hays St			PHD	75	Purdue	1980
Masuda, Yasushi	Asst	Cal-Riversid	9	Z	PHD		Rochest	1987
Matejka, J. Kenneth	Prof	Duquesne	23		PHD		Arkansas	1987
Matherly, Timothy A.	Assoc	Florida St	34	DEI	DBA	83	Indiana	9-80
Mathews, Clive M. H.	LectB	Flinders Un	19	Z	MBS	90	Massey	1990
Mathieson, Kieran	Asst	Oakland	9	Z	PHD	87	Indiana	1991
Mathieu, Richard	Asst	N Car-Wilmin	9	Z	PHD		Virginia	
Mathis, Robert L.	Prof	Neb-Omaha			DBA	72	Colorado	1974
Mathison, David L.	C-Pr	Loyola Marym	48	ELYR	PHD	78	Bowl Gr	1983
Mathur, Kamlesh	Assoc	Case Western			PHD	80	Case Wes	
Mathys, Nicholas J.	Prof	DePaul			PHD		Ill Tech	
Matika, Lawrence	Assoc	Lawrence Tec			PHD			1994
Matsuo, Hirofumi	Assoc	Texas	7	UV	PHD	84	MIT	1984
Matsuura, Nanshi	Prof	San Francisc	78	JMQY	PHD	78	Inidana	1981
Matta, Khalil F.	Assoc	Notre Dame	79	UZ	PHD	82	Notre Dm	1982
Mattei, Michael D.	Inst	Bellarmine			MBA		Indiana	
Matteson, Michael	C-Pr	Houston	2	GE	PHD	69	Houston	8-68
Matthews, Charles H.	Asst	Cincinnati						
Matthews, William H.	Asst	Intl Mgt Dev	13	DI	PHD		MIT	
Mattox, Charles	Asst	St Marys-Txs						
Maulden, Hoyt	Assoc	Embry-Riddle			MBA	68	Geo Wash	1980
Maule, John	Assoc	Univ Leeds	2	EG	PHD	76	Dundee	1991
Maurer, John	Prof	Wayne State	26	UTS	PHD	67	Mich St	1965
Mauriel, John J.	Assoc	Minnesota	3	ADP	DBA	64	Harvard	1965
Mawhinney, Thomas	C-Pr	Detroit Merc			PHD	76	Ohio St	1987
May, Douglas	Assoc	Appalach St	9	Z	PHD		N Colo	1982
May, Douglas	Asst	Nebraska	2	E	PHD	92	Illinois	8-89
May, Jerrold H.	Prof	Pittsburgh	7		PHD		Yale	
Mayer, Donald O.	Asst	Oakland	4	KJ	LLM	85	Geotown	8-90
Mayer, Lawrence S.	Prof	Arizona St			PHD		Ohio St	1983
Mayer, Robert W.	Asst	Mesa State	1	OP	MBA		N Colo	1987
Mayer, Roger C.	Asst	Notre Dame	25	EFHN	PHD	89	Purdue	1988
Mayes, Bronston T.	Prof	CS-Fullerton	2	EF	PHD	88	Irvine	8-84
Mayfield, Jacqueline R.	Asst	Radford	12	DE	PHD	93	Alabama	8-92
Mayo, G.	STut	U Newcastle	52	EFNQ	BCOM			
Mazen, A. Magid	Assoc	Suffolk			PHD		Purdue	
Mazerolle, Maurice	Asst	Wilfrid Laur		Q	PHD		Toronto	1990
Mazumdar, S.	Asst	McGill Univ	1		PHD		Dallas	1990
Mazursky, David	SLect	Hebrew Univ			PHD		NYU	
Mazzola, Joseph B.	C-Ac	Duke			PHD		Car Mel	
McAdams, Tony N.	Prof	No Iowa			JD	69	Iowa	6-82
McAfee, R. Bruce	Prof	Old Dominion			PHD	79	Wayne St	
McAlister, M. Khris	C-As	Alabama-Birm	91	Z	PHD	76	Iowa	1975
McAllister, Dan	Assoc	Nev-L Vegas	23	EFIP	PHD	78	U Wash	1982
McArthur, Angeline	Assoc	Wis-Parkside	2	EH	PHD	88	Oregon	8-88
McAulay, L.	Lect	Univ Bath	9	Z	MSC			
McBeth, James M.	Asst	NE Louisiana	12	EN	DBA	84	La Tech	1969
McBride, Duane	Prof	Andrews	1	C	PHD		Kentucky	1986
McCabe, Brendan	Asst	British Colu	7	V	PHD	89	Amsterda	1989
McCabe, Donald L.	Assoc	Rutgers-Newk	34	HIJ	PHD	85	New York	1988
McCabe, Douglas M.	Prof	Georgetown	52	QNE	PHD	77	Cornell	1976
McCabe, Jim	AsDn	St Xavier	69	TZ	MBA		Gov St	1981
McCaffery, Jerry L.	Prof	Naval Postgr	13	ADIJ	PHD	72	Wiscon	8084
McCahon, Cynthia S.	Assoc	Kansas State	7	UV	PHD	87	Knsas St	1-91
McCain, Barbara	Asst	Okla City	1	R	PHD		Oklahoma	8-89
McCain, Wayne	Assoc	Athens State	7	V	PHD		Alabama	1993
McCall, Brian	Asst	Minnesota	57	QV	PHD	88	Princeton	
McCallister, Linda	Dean	Chris Newpor	28	EOPY	PHD	81	Purdue	1993
McCambridge, James A.	Asst	Colorado St	1	EFNA	PHD	76	Colo St	1982
McCann, Joseph E.	Dean	Pacific Luth	13	DINS	PHD	80	Penn	1992
McCanna, Walter F.		Rochest Tech			PHD	69	Wiscon	1982
McCarrey, Leon	Prof	Utah State	31	DH	PHD	63	Oregon	9-82
McCart, Christina D.	Asst	Roanoke Col	79	Z	PHD			1990
McCarthy, Anne M.	Asst	Indiana	6	ST	PHD	92	Purdue	1990
McCarthy, Daniel J.	Prof	Northeastern	3	IY	DBA		Harvard	9-62

Name	Rank	School			Degree		Institution	Year
McCarthy, John J.	Assoc	W Illinois			JD	68	Illinois	1968
McCarthy, Michael A.	Asst	Slippery Roc			ABD		Pitt	1-93
McCarthy, Terry E.	SLect	Deakin Univ	25	NQ	MA	80	Melbourn	1982
McCartney, William W.	C-Pr	Geo Southern	23	EIZ	PHD		LSU	8-91
McCarty, Donald	Asst	Pitts-Johnst	23		MA		USC	1989
McCaul, Harriette S.	Dean	N Dakota St	25	EN	PHD	86	Nebraska	1983
McClain, John O.	Prof	Cornell	7	V	PHD	70	Yale	2-70
McClanahan, Anne H.	Prof	Ohio Univ			PHD		Ohio U	
McClean, Ronald J.	Asst	York Univ	9	Z	PHD		Waterloo	
McClellan, Hassell H.	Assoc	Boston Coll	83	IY	DBA	78	Harvard	9-84
McClellan, Robie	Assoc	Elon	51		EDD	79	NC-Green	1980
McClelland, Douglas	Asst	Montana St	4		JD	71	Berkeley	9-78
McClelland, Marilyn K.					PHD	84	N Carol	
McClendon, John	Asst	Temple			PHD	89	S Carol	
McClive, Marthe A.	Asst	Frostburg St	25	FN	PHD		USC	8-89
McClurg, Timothy	Asst	Geo Southern	7	U	PHD	93	Purdue	1993
McClymont, Trevor L.	Assoc	LaSierra			DBA	88	Intl Grd	7-91
McColl-Kennedy, Janet	SLect	Queensland	1	R	PHD	86	Queensld	1985
McCollom, Marion	Asst	Boston Univ	2	EFG	PHD		Yale	
McCollum, James K.	Prof	Alabama-Hunt	25	BHQN	PHD	79	Va Tech	1984
McConnell, D.	Lect	U Lancaster	59	NOP	PHD		Surrey	
McConnell, Renee V.	ClAc	Utah	2	ED	PHD	88	Utah	1988
McCormick, Beverly	Assoc	Morehead St	4	ML	JD	83	Louisvil	1985
McCormick, Lis	Lect	Napier Univ	25	EFNP	MA			1990
McCormick, Micheal B.	H-Pr	Jacksonvl St	27	EF	PHD	75	Missouri	1984
McCormick, Thomas	Assoc	British Colu	7	V	PHD	83	Stanford	1989
McCoy, Elaine	SLect	Criffith Un	38	AIKL	PHD			9-89
McCoy, Walter D.	Assoc	Mich Tech	5	Q	PHD	80	Texas	1989
McCracken, Melody J.	Asst	Appalach St	7	UV	PHD		Geo St	1989
McCrae, Ralph S.	Inst	Tx-El Paso	9	Z	MS	86	Drake U	1988
McCraken, Gail K.	Asst	Mich-Dearbor	4	JK	JD	83	Wayne St	1987
McCraw, Thomas K.	Prof	Harvard	4	L				
Isidor Straus Professor of Business History; Chairmam Executive Education								
McCray, John	Asst	Tx-S Antonio						
McCuddy, Michael K.	Prof	Valparaiso	25	EF	PHD	77	Purdue	1983
McCullough, Charles	Dean	Midwest St		Mktg	PHD		Tx Tech	
McCutchen, William Jr.	Asst	CUNY-Baruch	1	A	PHD		Indiana	1988
McCutcheon, James R.	Asst	Wilfrid Laur	3	I	MBA		McMaster	1974
McDaniel, J. R.	Asst	Suffolk			PHD		Mass	
McDaniel, James	Asst	Winona State			PHD		Tx Tech	1989
McDaniel, Larry	Asst	Alabama A&M			MBA		Sanford	
McDaniel, Reuben R.	Prof	Texas	3	IACH	EDD	71	Indiana	1972
McDermed, Ann	Assoc	N Carol St	7	QV	PHD	83	N Car St	1983
McDermott, Christopher	Asst	Rensselaer	3	I	PHD		N Carol	1994
McDevitt, William J.	Asst	St Joseph	4	KLQ	JD	75	Villanov	1987
McDonald, George	Lect	Tx-S Antonio						
McDonald, James Michael	Prof	Geo Southern	32	EDF	PHD	76	Georgia	1987
McDonald, Paul	SLect	Victoria NZ	25	PHDE	PHD		W Ontari	8-91
McDonald, Tracy	Prof	CS-Chico			PHD		Ohio St	1983
McDonnell, John F.	Prof	CS-San Bern	7	U	PHD	74	Claremont	1969
McDonough, Edward F. III	Assoc	Northeastern	2	D	PHD		Mass	9-79
McDonough, John J.	Prof	UCLA	2	E	DBA	69	Harvard	1968
McDougall, Patricia P.	Assoc	Georgia Tech	3	IR	PHD	87	S Carol	1991
McElroy, James C.	C-Pr	Iowa State	21	EN	PHD	79	Okla St	1979
McElroy, Jerome L.	Prof	St Marys-Ind	8	M	PHD	71	Colorado	8-82
McEnery, Jean	Prof	E Michigan	2		PHD		Wayne St	1980
McEnrue, Mary Pat	Prof	CS-L Angeles	1	RE	PHD	80	Wayne St	1981
McEvoy, Glenn	Prof	Utah State	52	EPN	DBA	85	Colorado	9-85
McEvoy, Sharlene A.	Asst	Fairfield	34	JLKI	PHD	85	UCLA	1986
McFadden, Fred R.	Prof	Colorado Spr	9	Z	PHD	68	Stanford	8-70
McFadden, John	Asst	Loyola-Maryl	3		MSA		Geo Wash	
McFadden, Kathleen	Asst	No Illinois			PHD		Texas	1993
McFarland, C. K.	Prof	Arkansas St	5	NQ	PHD	65	Arizona	1971
McFarland, James W.	Dean	Tulane	78	IY	PHD	71	Tx A&M	1988
McFarland, Tom	Asst	Jacksonvl U	23	EHI	PHD	88	Florida	1990
McFarlane, Dale D.	Retir	Oregon State	7	1994	DBA	66	Indiana	1965
McFarlin, Dean B.	Assoc	Marquette	2	E	PHD	86	SUNY-Buf	1986
McFarlin, Thomas	Asst	Westfield St			MBA		W New En	1978
McFetridge, Peter R.	SLect	City Poly HK			PHD			8-85
McFillen, James	Prof	Bowling Gr	25	E	DBA	76	Indiana	1983
McGahan, Anita M.	Asst	Harvard	4	L				
McGahey, Stanley	Inst	Guam	1	X	MS	82	W Illin	1993
McGaugh, Jack D.	Lect	Mich-Flint	23	PS	PHD	74	US Intl	9-85
McGaughey, Ron	Assoc	Ark Tech	79	UZ	PHD	91	Auburn	
McGee, Charles H.	Assoc	West Chester			PHD		Northwes	1987
McGee, Gail W.	Assoc	Alabama-Birm	2	E	PHD	83	Alabama	1983
McGee, Jeff	Asst	Neb-Omaha			PHD	92	Georgia	1992
McGee, Victor E.	Prof	Dartmouth			PHD	62	Princeton	1969
McGill, John	Asst	Trenton St			PHD			1992
McGill, Michael E.	C-Pr	So Methodist			PHD	71	S Calif	1971

Name	Rank	School			Degree			
McGinty, Robert L.	Prof	Eastern Wash	35	NIP	PHD	79	Denver	1980
McGivern, F.		Humberside	2					
McGlashan, Robert	Prof	Houston-C Lk	3	I	PHD	68	Texas	8-74
McGlone, Teresa	Assoc	E Kentucky	7	U	DBA	90	Kentucky	1989
McGough, Philip	Prof	Sonoma State	4	KL	PHD	72	Berkeley	9-88
McGoun, Elton G.	Assoc	Bucknell	8	Y	PHD	87	Indiana	9-87
McGowan, Richard A.	Assoc	Scranton	4	L	PHD	88	Boston U	1993
McGowan, Robert P.	Assoc	Denver	3	I	PHD		Syracuse	9-83
McGowen, Raymond D.	Asst	St Johns			PHD	70	St Johns	
McGrath, John	Inst	Pitts-Johnst	13		MA		Northwes	1994
McGrath, Leanne C.	Prof	So Car-Aiken	13	CQ	PHD	83	S Carol	1989
McGrath, Roger R. Jr.					PHD	83	Fla St	
McGrath, T. J.	Assoc	SUNY-Plattsb	7	UVW	PHD	71	Okla St	1980
McGraw, Van C.	Prof	NE Louisiana	1	EN	PHD	66	LSU	1959
McGuire, J.	Assoc	Concordia U						
McGuire, Sharon	Assoc	Athabasca Un	2	EFHJ	PHD	88	Alberta	1979
McHenry, William K.	Assoc	Georgetown	9	YZ	PHD	85	Arizona	1985
McIlnay, Dennis	Assoc	St Fran-Penn	2		MBA			
McInerney, Marjorie L.	Assoc	Marshall	4	RQ	PHD	83	Ohio St	1983
McIntire, Harold B.	Asst	Mesa State	1		MBA		E Nw Mex	1987
McIntosh, Barbara R.	Assoc	Vermont	25	ENY	PHD	79	Purdue	1984
McIntosh, Ellen	Lect	British Colu	4	K	LLM	91	Alberta	1987
McIntosh, Nancy J.	Assoc	South Fla	21	EH	PHD	84	Florida	1984
McInturff, Patrick S. Jr.	Prof	CS-San Bern	4	K	PHD	79	Ca-River	1978
McIntyre, John R.	Assoc	Georgia Tech	8	Y	PHD	81	Georgia	1981
McKay, Kenneth N.	Asst	Memorial Un	9	UZ	PHD	92	Waterloo	1992
McKay, R. Ross	SLect	North Wales	5	QS	MA			6-79
McKeage, R. L.	Asst	Scranton	2	E	EDD	91	Temple	1974
McKechnie, Graeme H.	Assoc	York Univ	5	Q	PHD		Wiscon	
McKee, Gaile H.	Asst	Roanoke Col	52	NG	PHD		Va Tech	1986
McKeen, Carol A.	Assoc	Queen's Univ		R	MBA	76	Queen's	1982
McKeen, J. D.	Assoc	Queen's Univ	9	Z	PHD	81	Minn	1973
McKellar, James	Prof	York Univ	1	A	MSC		Penn	
McKelvey, William W.	Prof	UCLA	3	I	PHD	67	MIT	1967
McKemey Dale	Assoc	Fort Hays St	2	H	PHD		Indiana	1990
McKendall, Marie A.	Asst	Grand Valley			PHD	90	Mich St	1988
McKendrick, David	Asst	Texas-Dallas		Y				
McKenna, Brian	Asst	St Xavier	4	K	JD		J Marsha	1989
McKenna, David R.	Lect	Boston Coll	7	VU	MBA	70	Boston C	9-84
McKenna, Dorothy		Lg Isl-Brook						
McKenna, Ian	Assoc	U Lethbridge	54	QR	LLM		Dundee	1985
McKenna, Jack	Prof	CS-Chico			PHD		Irvine	1977
McKenna, Thomas J.	Asst	Lawrence Tec	14		LLM	60	Wayne St	1986
McKenney, William A.	Asst	Mississippi	7	UV	PHD	87	Tenn	1990
McKenry, Carl E. B.	Prof	U Miami	56	YTNK	LLM	65	NYU	1956
McKenzie, R. Kenneth	Assoc	Txs Wesleyan			MBA	66	North Tx	1967
McKenzie, Richard B.	Prof	Calif-Irvine			PHD	72	Va Tech	1991
McKenzie, Roger I.	Asst	Brighm Yg-HI	38	BILY	MBA	67	Harvard	8-82
McKeown, Patrick G.	Prof	Georgia	79	VZ	PHD	73	N Carol	1976
McKern, Bruce	Prof	Carnegie Mel	8	Y	PHD		Harvard	1993
McKersie, Robert B.	Prof	MIT	5	Q	DBA			
Leaders for Manufacturing Professor								
McKinley, William	Assoc	So Illinios	28	HIW	PHD	83	Columbia	8-90
McKinney, Earl Jr.	Assoc	USAF Academy	9	Z	PHD		Texas	
McKinney, Richard	Assoc	S Ill-Edward	2	DEF	PHD	69	St Louis	1966
McKinney, T. Charles	Prof	Howard	2	E	PHD			
McKinnon, Richard A.		Boston Univ			MBA		Harvard	
McKirdy, J. G. M.	Asst	Queen's Univ	67	ST	MSC	66	Car Mel	1966
McKnew, Mark	Prof	Clemson	7	UV	PHD	78	MIT	1978
McKnight, Mel	Assoc	No Arizona	2	M	PHD	79	UCLA	
McLachlan, Jeffrey E.	Dean	Napier Univ	3	I	BA			1975
McLachlin, Ron	Asst	U Manitoba	7	U	PHD	92	Ontario	1993
McLain, David	Asst	Virginia St	21	MH	PHD	91	Wiscon	9-93
McLaren, R. I.	Prof	Univ Regina	14	ABHL	PHD		Pitt	
McLaughlin, Frank S.	Prof	North Fla	7	UV	PHD	67	Florida	1971
McLaughlin, Josetta	Asst	Radford	34	IJL	PHD	93	Va Tech	8-91
McLaughlin, Marilou	Dean	New Haven	36	D	PHD		Wisconsi	9-77
McLean Parks, Judi	Asst	Minnesota	2	EFHN	PHD	90	Iowa	
McLean, Ephraim R. III	Prof	Georgia St	9	Z	PHD		MIT	
George E. Smith Eminent Scholar Chair in Computer Information Systems								
McLeay, S. J.	Prof	North Wales	1	D	PHD			1-88
TBS Professor of Treasury								
McLennan, W. Roy	SLect	Victoria NZ	25	EFNO	MA		Auckland	7-75
McLeod, Michael E.	Assoc	East Carol		Z	PHD		Georgia	8-82
McLeod, Poppy L.	Assoc	Iowa	2	E	PHD	85	Harvard	1992
McLeod, Randall J.	D-As	Harding			JD	74	Memphis	
McLeod, Raymond Gregg Jr.	Assoc	Texas A&M		Z	DBA	75	Colorado	1980
McLimore, Fred	Assoc	Ill-Chicago	45	NLJG	PHD	71	Purdue	1-81
McMahon, Anne	Prof	Youngstown	13	REF	PHD	70	Mich St	9-83
McMahon, Richard G. P.	Assoc	Flinders Un	6	ST	MBA	80	Adelaide	1978

Name	Rank	School			Degree		University	
McMahon, Timothy	Prof	Houston	28	EFHY	DBA	72	Kentucky	8-72
McMasters, Alan W.	Prof	Naval Postgr	7	VU	PHD	66	Berkeley	9-65
McMeen, Albert		Lg Isl-Brook						
McMillan, Charles J.	Assoc	York Univ	8	Y	PHD	75	Bradford	1974
McMillin, John G.	C-Pr	Northwest C	38	IY	PHD	74	U Wash	1991
McMinn, Nathan E.	Asst	Montevallo	9		MBA		W Carol	1978
McMullan, Ed	Prof	Univ Calgary	6	T	PHD	75	Brit Col	1973
McMullen, Ronald	Assoc	Quinnipiac	25	FHNP	EDD		Mass	
McNally, Joyce E.	Prof	Aquinas	12	BDHR	DBA	87	Intl Gr	1982
McNally, Mary	Asst	Mont St-Bill	12		PHD	91	Chicago	1987
McNally, Vincent	Asst	St Joseph	1	AGMP	PHD	79	Temple	1976
McNamara, Brian	Prof	CS-Bakersf	69	CPSZ	PHD			1986
McNamara, Daniel	Assoc	St Thomas-MN						
McNary, George W.	Asst	Creighton	4	K	JD	80	Creightn	8-83
McNay, William Rose	Prof	Mercer-Atlan	35	IN	PHD		Penn	1981
McNeely, Bonnie	Asst	Murray State	25	DEGR	PHD	91	S Carol	1987
McNeil, Ronald	Dean	Mass-Dartmou	2	DFP	PHD	82	Memphis	9-92
McNeill, John D.	Asst	Miami U-Ohio	23	EFI	DBA	79	Kentucky	8-75
McNichols, Charles W.	Prof	Radford	9	Z	PHD	73	Stanford	8-90
Holder of Dalton Chair								
McNickle, Donald	SLect	Canterbury	7	V	PHD	74	Auckland	1977
McNitt, Lawrence L.			7	V	PHD	69	N Carol	
McPhillips, David	Assoc	British Colu	54	QK	LLM	79	Brit Col	1975
McQuillen, Charles	Asst	Embry-Riddle			PHD	69	Florida	1993
McRae, Lissa	Assoc	Bishop's Un	12	E	MBA		St Marys	1987
McRostie, Clair	Prof	Gustavus Ado	38		PHD	64	Wiscon	1957
McWatters, C.	Asst	McGill Univ	1		PHD		Queens	1993
McWilliam, Davo	VLect	Mich-Dearbor						
McWilliams, Abagail	Asst	Ariz St-West	34	IK	PHD	87	Ohio St	1993
McWilliams, Donald B.	Assoc	Txs Wesleyan			PHD	74	North Tx	1982
McWilliams, John	SLect	Deakin Univ	2	EF	PHD	82	Manchest	1990
McWilliams, Thomas P.	Assoc	Ariz St-West	7	UV	PHD	79	Stanford	1990
Mead, R.	Lect	W Australia			MBA		W Austra	
Meadows, Jack E. Jr.	Assoc	Henderson St			MBA		Arkansas	
Meadows, Robert	Assoc	Morehead St	72	EP	DBA	81	Kent St	1982
Mealiea, Laird W.	Assoc	Dalhousie U	2	E	PHD		Mass	
Mears, Peter M.	Prof	Louisville	4	AU	DBA	72	Miss St	8-71
Mechling, George W.	Assoc	W Carolina	17	UVX	PHD	85	Nebraska	8-92
Medcof, John W.	Asst	McMaster Un	2	E	PHD	84	Toronto	
Medina, Maria	Inst	P Rico-Mayag	7		MS	92	P Rico	8-92
Medlin, Bobby	Dean	Ark-Monticel			DBA	93	La Tech	
Medlin, Dawn	Lect	Appalach St	9	Z	MA		Appal St	1988
Medsker, Gina J.	Asst	U Miami	25	ENY	PHD	93	Purdue	1993
Meek, Christopher B.	Assoc	Brigham Yg	59	YQBL	PHD	83	Cornell	1984
Meek, Gary E.	H-Pr	Akron	7	VUX	PHD	70	Case Wes	9-71
Megley, John E.	Prof	Christian Br			PHD	70	Memphis	
Meglino, Bruce M.	Prof	So Carolina	25	ENHX	PHD	75	Mass	8-73
Mehrez, Abraham	Prof	Kent State			PHD		J Hopkin	1977
Mehta, Kamlesh	Asst	St Marys-Txs			DBA	90	US Intl	
Meindl, James R.	Prof	SUNY-Buffalo	2	EHJ	PHD	81	Waterloo	9-81
Meiners, Arthur	Assoc	Marymount	14	JUBD	DBA		Geo Wash	1988
Meinhart, Wayne A.	H-Pr	Oklahoma St	32	H	PHD	64	Illinois	1962
Meisel, Steven Ian	Asst	LaSalle	2	E	PHD		Temple	1981
Meisenhelter, Christopher M.	Asst	York of PA	14	JL	MBA		Baltimor	1987
Meisenhelter, Mary	Asst	York of PA	5		MBA		Baltimor	1985
Meiser, Charles	Assoc	Lk Superior	67	DTUV	ABD		Purdue	9-68
Melan, Eugene H.	Prof	Marist	37	UV	MS		Union C	1988
Melcher, Arlyn J.	C-Pr	So Illinois	23	DHYW	PHD	64	Chicago	8-89
Melcher, Bonita	Assoc	Baldwin-Wal		I	DBA	83	Kent St	1991
Meldman, Jeffrey A.	SLect	MIT	9	Z	PHD			
Mele, Domenec	Assoc	Univ Navarra	4	J	PHD		Politecn	D-85
Meleka, Agia H.	Deces	CS-Northrdge	38	IKSY	PHD	79	S Calif	1982
Melese, Francois	Assoc	Naval Postgr	78	VY	PHD	82	Catholic	6-87
Meli, John T.	Prof	Widener			PHD	71	Penn	
Mellon, Elizabeth O.	Asst	London Bus	25	AF	MBA		London	
Melnyk, Steven A.	Prof	Michigan St	7	U	PHD	80	W Ontar	9-80
Meloche, Gaston	Assoc	HEC-Montreal	48	Y	DES		Ottawa	
Melrose, John E.	Prof	Wis-Eau Clar	9	Z	EDD	74	Montana	1970
Meltzer, Yale	Asst	CUNY-Stn Isl	78	VYUZ	MBA		NYU	1979
Mena, Manuel	Prof	SUNY-Oswego	28	FPY	PHD	75	Cornell	1974
Menard, Kirk	Asst	Russell Sage	52	NP	MBA		SUNY-Buf	1990
Mendelow, Aubrey L.	Assoc	Kent State	23	HI	PHD		S Africa	1982
Mendelson, Haim	Prof	Stanford	9	Z	PHD	79	Rochest	1989
James Irvin Miller Professor of Information Systems								
Mendenhall, J. Stanley	Assoc	Mont St-Bill	63		PHD	75	Wiscon	1986
Mendenhall, Mark E.	Assoc	Tenn-Chattan	28	EX	PHD	83	Brig Yg	1989
Frierson Chair of Excellence								
Mendenhall, Terry L.	Dean	Pittsburg St	56	NSTY	PHD	81	Kans St	1964
Mendleson, Jack L.	Assoc	Radford	25	NPQ	DBA	67	Mich St	8-91
Mendoza, Gaston	Assoc	F Dick-Ruthe	7	V	PHD		Temple	

Name	Rank	School			Degree		University	
Menger, Richard	Prof	St Marys-Txs			PHD	92	Tx A&M	
Menneck, G.	Asst	East Carol		Z	PHD		Indiana	8-93
Mensah, Samuel	Asst	Mich-Flint	1		PHD		Toronto	1991
Mensz, Pawel	Assoc	New Haven	7	UV	PHD		Polish A	
Mento, Anthony J.	Prof	Loyola-Maryl	2	E	PHD		Maryland	1984
Mentzer, Marc S.	Asst	Saskatchewan	2	HN	PHD	86	Indiana	1989
Merah, Ajay	Asst	W Virginia			PHD		Mass	1992
Mercer, A.	Prof	U Lancaster	73	AUVZ	PHD		London	
Merchant, John E.	Prof	CS-Sacrament	36	BIST	PHD	73	Denver	1983
Meredith, John W.	Prof	Mary Hrdn-By	78	UVYZ	PHD	75	North Tx	1-88
Meredith, Mary	Assoc	SW Louisiana	79	VRZ	DBA	81	Indiana	1983
Meredith, Paul	Assoc	SW Louisiana	39	DIR	DBA	81	Indiana	1983
Merenda, Michael	Assoc	New Hampshir	3	I	PHD	78	Mass	1977
Mericle, Mary F.			2	E	PHD	77	N Carol	
Meridith, Deborah J.	Lect	British Colu	4	K	LLM	87	Brit Col	1980
Mernlees, W.	Asst	U Newcastle	23	DIS	PHD		Toronto	
Merolla, C. R.	SpAst	Hofstra	13	AI	MBA	62	NYU	9-89
Merrell, Ronald D.	Prof	St Marys-Txs			PHD	75	Oklahoma	
Merrifield, D. Bruce	VProf	Pennsylvania	36	ADIT	PHD	50	Chicago	7-89
Walter C. Bladstrom Visiting Executive Professor of Management								
Merrill, Craig	Asst	Brigham Yg						
Merriman, A. M.	Lect	Univ Bristol	2	J	BA	56		1969
Mersha, Tigineh	Assoc	Baltimore	78	TW	PHD	82	Cinn	8-84
Merten, Alan G.	Dean	Cornell	9	Z	PHD	70	Wiscon	8-89
The Anne & Elmer Lindseth Dean								
Meshulach, Avraham	D	Hebrew Univ			DBA		Harvard	
Messick, David	Prof	Northwestern			PHD	65	N Carol	1991
Alice and Morris Kaplan Professor of Ethics & Decision in Management								
Messick, Judith	Assoc	Northwestern			PHD	82	Ca-SnBar	1992
Meszaros, Jacqueline	Asst	Temple			PHD	88	Penn	1991
Metcalfe, Brian	Assoc	Brock Univ	8	Y	PHD		Queens	1981
Methe, David T.	Asst	Michigan	3	IY	PHD	85	Ca-Irvine	1991
Metheny, William	Asst	Mont St-Bill	75		PHD	90	North Tx	1990
Metters, Richard D.	Asst	Vanderbilt	7	UVWX	PHD	93	N Carol	9-93
Meusborn, Mike M.	Retir	Neb-Kearney	67	1993	MBA	46	Harvard	1974
Meyer, Alan D.	Prof	Oregon	2	HE	PHD	78	Berkeley	1984
E. E. & J. W. Cone Professor of Management								
Meyer, Bradley	Asst	Drake	7	JUV	PHD	89	Iowa St	1989
Meyer, David G.	Assoc	Akron	5	QDN	PHD	86	Michigan	8-89
Meyer, G. Dale	C-Pr	Colorado			PHD	70	Iowa	1970
Meyer, Harry	Inst	St Johns			MIE		NYU	
Meyer, Jan	Asst	St Thomas-MN						
Meyer, Jennifer	Asst	Nebraska	79	V	PHD	89	Stanford	8-88
Meyer, Marc H.	Assoc	Northeastern	6	TZ	PHD		MIT	9-86
Patrick F. & Helen C. Walsh Research Professor								
Meyer, Marshall W.	Prof	Pennsylvania	2	HA	PHD	67	Chicago	7-87
Anheuser-Busch Professor of Management								
Meyer, Stuart	Assoc	Northwestern	6	ST	PHD	62	Princeton	
Meyers, Bruce	Assoc	W Illinois			DBA	73	Wash U	1973
Meyers, Martin	Assoc	Wis-Stev Pt	81	YD	MS	79	DePaul	8-86
Meyerson, Debra E.	Asst	Michigan	2	E	PHD	89	Stanford	
Mezias, Stephen	Asst	New York U	2	E	PHD		Stanford	
Mian, Sarfraz	Asst	SUNY Oswego	36	ISTD	PHD	91	Geo Wash	1992
Miano, Edward	Asst	N Adams St			MBA		Pace	
Miccio, Ralph	Assoc	Rensselaer	4	K	JD		Albany L	
Miceli, Marcia P.	Prof	Ohio State	5	N	DBA	82	Indiana	1981
Michael, James	Asst	Wagner	25	EH	PHD		SUNY-Alb	9-92
Michael, Thomas A.	Assoc	Rowan Col NJ	23	EFIO	PHD	73	Drexel	1972
Michaels, Charles E. Jr.	Assoc	South Fla	25	NE	PHD	83	S Fla	1984
Michaelsen, Larry K.	Prof	Oklahoma	23	EGD	PHD	73	Michigan	1974
David Ross Boyd Professor								
Michalowski, W.	Assoc	Carleton Un			PHD		Warsaw	
Michel, John	Inst	Notre Dame	3		ABD		Columbia	1993
Michlitsch, Joseph	Asst	S Ill-Edward	23	IH	PHD	80	Minn	1979
Middaugh, J. Kendall II	Assoc	Wake Fr-MBA	3	I	PHD	81	Ohio St	1987
Middlebrook, Bill	Prof	SW Texas St	3	I	PHD	80	North Tx	1983
Middlemist, Dennis	Prof	Colorado St	12	EJN	PHD	73	U Wash	1981
Middleton, Karen	Asst	Okla City	2	E	PHD		Houston	8-93
Middleton, Ken	Dean	SW Baptist	52		PHD			1991
Miesing, Paul	Assoc	SUNY-Albany	34	IL	DBA	77	Colorado	1979
Might, Robert J.			7	U	PHD	81	N Carol	
Mighty, E. Joy	Asst	New Brunswic	2	E	PHD		York	1992
Migliore, R. Henry	Prof	NE St-Okla	3	I	PHD	75	Arkansas	1987
Miguel, Mabel	Inst	No Carolina	25	EN	PHD	93	N Carol	
Mikan, Kurt W.	Assoc	Montevallo	6		PHD		Alabama	1980
Milbourn, Eugene	Prof	Baltimore	23	EFI	PHD		North Tx	8-75
Miles, Edward W.	Asst	Georgia St	2	EX	PHD	88	Georgia	1989
Miles, Grant	Asst	Wilfrid Laur	3	I	PHD		Penn St	1993
Miles, Raymond E.	Retir	Cal-Berkeley	3	1993	PHD	63	Stanford	1963

Miles, Robert H.	C-Pr	Emory	2	HI	PHD	74	N Carol	1987
Isaac Stiles Hopkins Professor of Organization & Management								
Miles, Wilford G.	Assoc	Hartford	3	I	PHD	68	Arkansas	
Militello, Jack	Assoc	St Thomas-MN						
Miljus, Robert	Assoc	South Fla	23	NQ	PHD	83	Wiscon	1991
Millen, Robert A.	Prof	Northeastern			PHD		UCLA	
Miller, Alan A.	Inst	Angelo State			MBA		AngeloSt	
Miller, Alan N.	Prof	Nev-L Vegas	23	INE	PHD	81	CUNY	1978
Miller, Alex	Assoc	Tennessee	36	ITX	PHD	83	Wash	9-84
Miller, Ben	Retir	St Johns		1991	PHD	59	NYU	1959
Miller, C. Chet	Asst	Baylor	23	EHI	PHD		Texas	1989
Miller, Charles	Assoc	Marymount			MBA		Geo Wash	1985
Miller, Christine	Asst	Tenn Tech	2	EY	PHD	93	Houston	1993
Miller, D.	Assoc	McGill Univ	3		PHD		McGill	1978
Miller, D.	Lect	U Newcastle	25	EFNR	MBA		SAInstTe	
Miller, Donald	Prof	Emporia St	35		EDD	72	Okla St	8-66
Miller, Edwar	Inst	CS-Stanislau			PHD		Gold Gt	9-90
Miller, Edwin L.	Prof	Michigan			PHD	64	Berkeley	1964
Miller, Gary J.	Prof	Wash Univ	2	AHIL	PHD	76	Texas	1986
Ruben C. Taylor Jr., & Anne Carpenter Taylor Professor of Political Econ								
Miller, Holmes		Muhlenberg	79		PHD		Northwes	9-91
Miller, Howard	Prof	Mankato St			PHD	81	Illinois	1986
Miller, J.	Lect	U Newcastle	14	AKL	LLB		Sydney	
Miller, J. G.	Prof	Boston Univ	7	UY	PHD		Purdue	
Miller, Janis	Asst	Clemson	7	UV	PHD	90	Missouri	1990
Miller, John A.	Prof	Bucknell	2	GH	PHD	74	Rochest	9-78
Miller, Keith T.	Assoc	Quinnipiac	5	Q	PHD		Arizona	
Miller, Kent	Asst	Purdue	3	I	PHD	91	Minn	1991
Miller, Lois S.	C	Hampton	9	PYZ	EDD		N Illin	9-64
Miller, Louis	Prof	Tenn State			PHD	60	Rochest	1973
Miller, Lynn E.	Prof	LaSalle	2	E	PHD		N Illin	1981
Miller, Marianne	Asst	Virg Comm	25	EHNR	PHD	92	Oregon	1993
Miller, Otis	Prof	Wm Jewell	37	U	PHD	62	Missouri	1978
Miller, P.	Asst	Univ Windsor	79	UVWZ	MBA		Toronto	1977
Miller, Paddy	Assoc	Univ Navarra	2	F	DBA		Navarra	5-84
Miller, Pamela	Inst	Southern			ABD	94	LSU	1993
Miller, Patricia A.	Asst	Rockhurst	42	ERLM	PHD	83	Texas	1984
Miller, Peggy	Lect	Ohio Univ	12		PHD	87	Ohio U	
Miller, Phillip E.	Asst	East Tenn St	7	U	PHD	85	N Carol	1994
Miller, Ralph A.	Asst	Regent			MA		Regent	
Miller, Ralph H.	C-Pr	CS-Pomona	7	VX	PHD	79	Claremont	1979
Miller, Richard U.	Prof	Wisconsin	5	NQ	PHD	66	Cornell	1971
Miller, Robert J.	Assoc	No Michigan			PHD	78	U Wash	1978
Miller, Ronald L.	C-Pr	Oregon State	5	Q	PHD	69	Penn	1987
Miller, Stephen H.	Prof	CS-Hayward	25	E	PHD	69	Purdue	1971
Miller, Thomas R.	C-Pr	Memphis	12	BN	PHD	72	Ohio St	1971
Miller, Tim R.	Assoc	Sangamon St	12	AEF	PHD		Utah	1987
Miller, Van V.	Asst	Dayton	38	Y	PHD	81	New Mex	1988
Miller, William F.	Prof	Stanford	3	I	PHD	56	Purdue	1965
Milligan, Glenn W.	Prof	Ohio State	7	V	PHD	78	Ohio St	1979
Milligan, Patricia Mayer	Assoc	Baylor		Z	PHD		North Tx	1983
Milliken, Frances	Assoc	New York U			PHD	85	CUNY	
Milliman, John F.	Asst	Colorado Spr	5	N	PHD	92	S Calif	1092
Milller, Daniel J.	Asst	Central Conn	23	ABFH	ABD		Texas	1991
Mills, D. Quinn	Prof	Harvard	25	EN				
Alfred J. Weatherhead Jr. Professor of Business Administration								
Mills, Larry	C-Pr	So Nazarane	23		PHD	78	Oklahoma	1969
Mills, Lawrence L.	Asst	Chris Newpor			MBA		Ohio St	1984
Mills, Peter K.	Assoc	Indiana	2	H	PHD	80	Ca-Irvine	1989
Mills, R. Bryant	C-Pr	CS-Dominguez	5	N	PHD	72	Iowa	1983
Mills, R. Lavelle	Prof	Tarleton St	2	EHP	PHD	81	North Tx	1979
Milman, Claudio	Asst	W Michigan	38	IY	PHD	92	Ohio St	1992
Milosevic, Dragan	Inst	Oregon State						
Milsom, B.	SLect	Humberside	2					
Miltenburg, John G.	C-Pr	McMaster Un	17	UV	PHD		Waterloo	
Milter, Richard G.	Assoc	Ohio Univ	29		PHD	86	SUNY-Alb	
Milthorpe, Frank		Univ Sydney		VNXZ	BSC		Macquari	1990
Milton, Charles R.	Retir	So Carolina		7-93	PHD	60	N Carol	
Milutinovich, Jugoslav V.	Assoc	Temple	7	UYZ	PHD	70	NYU	1969
Min, Byung K.	C-Ac	Montclair St	59	EHNZ	PHD		Penn St	1973
Mindak, William	Prof	Tulane			PHD	54	Illinois	1978
Miner, Anne S.	Assoc	Wisconsin	23	HI	PHD	85	Stanford	1985
Miner, John B.	Prof	SUNY-Buffalo	26	ENPT	PHD	55	Princeton	9-87
Miner, Rick	Prof	St Marys-Cnd	25	EFN	PHD	76	Minn	1976
Miners, Ian	Asst	New Mexico		N	PHD	84	Mich St	
Minghe, Sun	Asst	Tx-S Antonio						
Mingo, Dan	Asst	Athens State	9	UZ	MS		Arkansas	1981
Minifie, Janet R.	Assoc	SW Texas St	7	U	PHD	83	S Carol	1988
Minks, L. C.	C-Pr	Brescia			EDD	80	N Colo	1988
Minter, Robert L.	Dean	No Iowa			PHD	69	Purdue	1990

Name	Rank	Institution			Degree		School	Year
Minton, John W.	Assoc	Appalach St	25	EFJP	PHD	88	Duke	1993
Mintzberg, Henry	Prof	McGill Univ	3		PHD		MIT	1968
Mintzberg, Henry	VProf	London Bus	23	HIO	PHD		MIT	
Mirchandani, Prakash	Asst	Pittsburgh	7		PHD		MIT	
Mireault, Paul	Agreg	HEC-Montreal	9	Z	PHD		MIT	
Mishina, Kazahiro	Asst	Harvard	7	U				
Mishra, Aneil	Asst	Penn State	25	EFP	PHD	92	Michigan	1992
Mishra, Jitendra M. (Jim)	Prof	Grand Valley			PHD		Lucknow	1972
Miskin, Val	Asst	Wash State						
Missick, Judith	Assoc	Georgia St			PHD	82	Ca-SnBar	1992
Missirian, Agnes	Prof	Bentley	38	IY	PHD	80	Mass	1980
Mitcham, Don	Prof	So Car-Aiken	12	SI	PHD		E Tenn	1975
Mitchell, Alfred Cameron	Assoc	Houston	9	Z	PHD	72	Texas	1972
Mitchell, Daniel J. B.	Prof	UCLA	5	N	PHD	68	MIT	1968
Mitchell, Donna	Asst	La St-Shreve	79	Z	DBA		La St Sh	1987
Mitchell, George	C	SW State	79	UZ	ABD			
Mitchell, Rex C.	Prof	CS-Northrdge	23	EFI	PHD	69	UCLA	1982
Mitchell, Robert B.	Prof	Ark-Ltl Rock			DBA		La Tech	1989
Mitchell, Terence R.	Prof	U Washington	5	BFHN	PHD	69	Illinois	1969
Mitchell, Victoria	Asst	N Carol St	93	ZI	PHD	93	Fla St	1993
Mitchell, William G.	Assoc	Michigan	3	IY	PHD	88	Berkeley	1988
Mitnick, Barry M.	Assoc	Pittsburgh	3		PHD		Penn	
Mitra, Amit	Prof	Auburn	7	UV	PHD	77	Clemson	9-79
Mitra, Atul	Asst	Arkansas Col	25	EN	DBA		Arkansas	1991
Mitroff, Ian	Prof	So Calif	3	GI	PHD		Berkeley	1980
Mitton, Daryl G.	Retir	San Diego St	6	T	PHD	53	Minn	1966
Mixon, Herman	C-Pr	Alabama A&M			JD		Alabama	
Miyataki, Glenn K.	Assoc	Hawaii-Manoa			DBA	77	Colorado	
Mize, Jan Lee	Assoc	Georgia St	9	Z	PHD		Geo St	
Moag, Joseph S.	C-Pr	Northwestern			PHD	64	Northwes	1960
Moberg, Dennis J.	Prof	Santa Clara			DBA	74	S Calif	1975
Mobilia, Pam	Asst	CUNY-Brookly	5	P	PHD			1991
Moch, Michael K.	C-Pr	Michigan St	3	H	PHD	73	Cornell	8-84
Mockler, Robert J.	Prof	St Johns			PHD	61	Columbia	1963
Modianos, Doan	Prof	Bradley	1	U	PHD	73	Tx Tech	1981
Moeeni, Farhad	Asst	Arkansas St	7	UV	ABD	91	Arizona	1991
Moesel, Douglas	Inst	Lehigh			MS		Oklahoma	1993
Moffett, Dave	Lect	Neb-Kearney	9	Z	MBA		Nebraska	1989
Mogg, Melanie	Asst	St Scholasti			MBA		Minn	1988
Moghaddam, John M.	Prof	CS-Fresno	7	U	PHD		North Tx	1979
Mohaghegh, Saeed	Assoc	Assumption	79		MA	86	Clark	1982
Mohamed, Zubair	Asst	W Kentucky	7	U	PHD	91	Kentucky	1989
Mohammadi, Hamid	Assoc	St Xavier	7	UV	PHD		Ill Tech	1988
Mohan, R.	Asst	CUNY-Baruch	7	U	PHD		Ohio St	1991
Mohanty, Bidhu B.	Assoc	Norfolk St		U	PHD		Case Wes	7-92
Moily, Jaya	Assoc	Baltimore	78	TWY	PHD	82	Wiscon	8-89
Moinzadeh, Kamran	Prof	U Washington	7	U	PHD	84	Stanford	1984
Moison, G. Lawrence	Asst	Shepherd	26	SD	MS		Southeas	1989
Molander, Earl A.	Prof	Portland St	4	L	PHD	72	Berkeley	1975
Mollenkopf, Douglas	Inst	SW Texas St	2	F	MBA	77	SW Texas	1984
Molloy, James F. Jr.	C-Ac	Northeastern	68	STY	PHD		MIT	9-81
Molloy, Stephen	Asst	Canisius	36	IH	PHD	90	Indiana	1990
Molstad, Clark	Prof	CS-San Bern	35	EQ	PHD	89	UCLA	1984
Molyneux, P.	SLect	North Wales	13	DI	MA			9-86
Molz, Ferdinand L.	Prof	Millersville	36	AT	PHD	68	Catholic	1970
Molz, R.	Assoc	Concordia U			PHD		Northeas	
Momen, Abdul	Asst	Merrimack			PHD		Northeas	
Monahan, George	Assoc	Illinois	7	UV	PHD	77	Northwes	1986
Monat, Jonathan S.	Prof	CS-Long Bch	2	ENOQ	PHD	72	Minn	1978
Monczka, Robert M.	Prof	Michigan St	7	W	PHD	70	Mich St	1974
NAPM Professor								
Mondejar, Reuben	Lect	City Poly Hk	14	BHLY	PHD	89	Navarre	9-89
Monden, Yasuhiro	Prof	Univ Tsukuba	37	UI	PHD			3-83
Mondino, Guillermo	Asst	Chicago			PHD	91	Yale	1991
Mondy, Judy B.	Asst	McNeese St			MS		La Tech	
Mone, Mark A.	Asst	Wis-Milwauke	2	H	PHD	88	Wash St	
Monroe, Carolyn	Lect	Baylor		VZ	MBA		Baylor	1983
Monroe, Kent	H-Pr	Illinois			PHD	68	Illinois	1991
Monson, Terry D.	Dean	Mich Tech	8	YP	PHD	72	Minn	1977
Montagno, Ray V.	Prof	Ball State	2		PHD		Purdue	1980
Montague, Richard A.	Prof	Western Conn	9	Z	PHD		Columbia	1985
Montana, Patrick J.	Prof	Hofstra	25	AOP	PHD	66	NYU	9-80
Montanari, John R.	Prof	CS-S Marcos	3	I	DBA	76	Colorado	1-91
Montazemi, Ali R.	Assoc	McMaster Un	9	Z	PHD		Waterloo	
Monteverde, Kirk A.	Asst	St Joseph	39	FIVZ	PHD	81	Stanford	1992
Montgomery, Cynthia A.	Prof	Harvard	4	L				
Montgomery, David	Prof	Stanford						
Sebastian S. Kresge Professor of Marketing Strategy								
Montgomery, Kathleen	Asst	Cal-Riversid	25	EQ	PHD		NYU	1990
Moody, Janette W.	Asst	Citadel	9	Z	ABD		S Fla	

Name	Rank	School			Degree		Institution	Year
Mookerjee, V.	Asst	U Washington	9	Z	PHD	91	Purdue	1991
Moon, I. Doug	Prof	Mich-Flint	7	UV	PHD	76	Va Tech	9-89
Mooney, Marta W.	Assoc	Fordham	2	EH	PHD		UCLA	1976
Moor, R. Carl	Prof	Fla Atlantic	83		PHD	71	Geo St	1971
Moorcroft, Christina	Assoc	Luther	15	CR	MBA	85	Wi-LaCro	1978
Moore, Carl C.	Dean	So Alabama	7	FDJ	PHD	71	Alabama	1973
Moore, Daniel		Plymouth St						
Moore, Dorothy Perrin	Prof	Citadel	25	ENR	PHD	81	S Carol	
Moore, Gary	H-Pr	SUNY-Geneseo	45	KQ	PHD	74	Nebraska	9-74
Moore, Herff L. Jr.	Assoc	Cen Arkansas	25	ENP	PHD	80	Tx-Arlin	8-85
Moore, J. B.	Assoc	Un Waterloo	79	UZV	PHD	71	Waterloo	1971
Moore, James S.	Assoc	Ind-Purdue	97	VZ	PHD	74	Purdue	8-80
Moore, Jeffrey H.	Lect	Stanford	9	Z	PHD	73	Berkeley	1972
Moore, Keith	Inst	Morehead St	74	JU	MBA	91	Morehead	1991
Moore, Kris K.	Prof	Baylor		V	PHD	74	Tx A&M	1970
Moore, Larry F.	Assoc	British Colu	2	NYE	DBA	65	Colorado	1965
Moore, Lynda L.	Assoc	Simmons	2	R	EDD	83	Mass	
Moore, Molly	Assoc	Moorhead St	9	Z	PHD		N Dakota	1975
Moore, Peter G.	VProf	London Bus	7	V	PHD		London	
Moore, Richard	Assoc	Cornell	9	Z	MBA	70	Cornell	1970
Moore, Robert	Prof	Nev-L Vegas	38	LOY	PHD	77	Claremont	1971
Moore, Roy N.	Dean	Delta State	15	Q	PHD	71	Alabama	8-88
Moore, W. Kent	Assoc	Valdosta St	7	PZ	PHD	75	Texas	1971
Moore, William L.	Prof	CS-Hayward	25	Q	PHD	79	Berkeley	1975
Moore, Willie M.	C-As	Drake	52	QN	PHD	87	Ohio St	1987
Moores, Brian	Retir	Manchest Bus	79	1994	PHD		John Hop	
Moorhead, Gregory	Assoc	Arizona St	12	FFH	PHD	79	Houston	1978
Moorman, Robert H.	Asst	W Virginia	2	E	PHD	90	Indiana	1990
Moran, Thomas M.	Lect	Prairie View	38	KLY	MBA	51	Michigan	1990
Morand, David	Asst	Penn St-Harr	5	Q	PHD	91	Cornell	1990
More, Elizabeth	D-Pr	Macquarie Un						
Moreau, A.	Asst	McGill Univ	1		PHD		Iowa	1986
Morecroft, John	Assoc	London Bus	39	IY	PHD		MIT	1986
Moreno, Abel	Asst	N Dakota St	78	U	PHD	90	N Dak St	1989
Morey, Nancy	Assoc	W Illinois			PHD	86	Nebraska	1986
Morey, Russell W.	Prof	W Illinois			PHD	73	Nebraska	1973
Morgan, A.	Prof	Univ Windsor	36	ISTU	PHD		American	1969
Morgan, Catherine L.	Prof	Jacksonvil U	7	SVUE	PHD	75	S Carol	1975
Morgan, Cyril P. Jr.	Prof	Wash State		Mgt	PHD		Case Wes	
Morgan, David T.	Asst	St Ambrose	27	EU	MS	76	Fla Inst	1992
Morgan, E. J.	SLect	Univ Bath	3	I	MA			
Morgan, G. D.	Lect	Manchest Bus	2	EG	MA		Cambridg	1992
Morgan, Gareth	Prof	York Univ	2	H	PHD		Lancast	
Morgan, Ivor P.	VProf	Babson			DBA	80	Harvard	
Morgan, James	C-Pr	CS-Chico			JD		Ca-Davis	1983
Morgan, Sandra	Asst	Hartford	2	EF	PHD	83	MIT	
Moriarty, James	Assoc	N Adams St			MBA		Am Intl	
Morin, Estelle M.	Lect	HEC-Montreal	12	EN	PHD		Montreal	
Moritz, Thomas	Asst	Hardin-Simm						
Morone, Joseph	Dean	Rensselaer	3	I	PHD		Yale	1988
Morouney, Kim	Lect	Wilfrid Laur	2	EHR	PHD		Alberta	1993
Morrell, J. B.	Lect	North Wales	23	FI	BA			9-75
Morrice, Douglas	Asst	Texas	7	V	PHD	90	Cornell	1990
Morris, Brenda K.	Lect	Baylor		Z	MBA		Baylor	1989
Morris, James H.	Prof	Naval Postgr	2	EFH	PHD	76	Oregon	1982
Morris, Joella W.	Asst	SE Louisiana			MBA			
Morris, John S.	Assoc	Idaho	73	UV	PHD	88	Oklahoma	1973
Morris, Rebecca	Asst	Neb-Omaha			PHD	88	Nebraska	1983
Morris, Sara A.	Asst	Old Dominion			PHD	87	Texas	
Morris, Tim J.	Asst	London Bus	52	QF	PHD		London	
Morris, Tom	Asst	San Diego	38	IY	PHD	89	Denver	1988
Morrison, Allen	Assoc	Am Grad Intl			PHD	89	S Carol	
Morrison, Beth	Inst	E New Mexico	89	DRYZ	MBA	90	E N Mex	1992
Morrison, Edward J.	Prof	Colorado			DBA	59	Indiana	1959
Morrison, Elizabeth	Asst	New York U			PHD	91	Northwes	
Morrison, Joline	Asst	Iowa	9	Z	PHD	92	Arizona	1992
Morrison, Mike	Asst	Iowa	9	Z	PHD	92	Arizona	1992
Morrison, R.	Prof	McGill Univ	3		MA		Oxon	1962
Morrow, Ira	Assoc	Pace	25		PHD		NYU	
Morrow, Paula C.	Prof	Iowa State	2	EON	PHD	78	Iowa St	1978
Morse, Gail	Inst	St Fran-NY	25		MBA		Baruch	
Morse, Kenneth	Asst	SUNY-Geneseo	8	Y	PHD	91	Denver	9-91
Morton, Jack	Prof	Montana	4	K	JD	71	Montana	1971
Morton, James R.	Prof	Pfeiffer	31	IV	DBA	74	S Calif	5-89
Morton, Thomas	Prof	Carnegie Mel	7	U	PHD		Chicago	1969
Mosca, Joseph	Assoc	Monmouth	13	DFNI	DED	83	NYU	9-87
Moschella, Paul	Assoc	Hartford	3	I	PHD	73	Mass	
Moscoso, Pedro F.	Asst	Catawba	15	NPS	MS	68	N Carol	1984
Moser, K.	Asst	Iowa State	9	Z	PHD	91	Ariz St	1991
Moser, Martin	Assoc	Mass-Lowell	32	JF	PHD	83	Mass	

Name	Rank	Institution			Degree		School	
Moser, Steven B.	Asst	North Dakota	25	ENS	PHD	90	Cinn	8-90
Moses, Michael A.	Assoc	New York U			PHD	67	Northwes	
Moshe, Leshno	Lect	Hebrew Univ			PHD		Tel Aviv	
Mosheiov, Gur	Lect	Hebrew Univ			PHD		Columbia	
Mosier, Charles T.	Assoc	Clarkson	7	V	PHD	83	N Carol	
Moskowitz, Herbert	Prof	Purdue	7	V	PHD	70	UCLA	1970
Mosley, Donald C.	Prof	So Alabama	23	EFGH	PHD	65	Alabama	1973
Moss, Martha	Asst	NW Missouri			MSED		Missouri	1958
Moss, Sherry E.	Asst	Fla Internat		HE	PHD	91	Fla St	1990
Mossholder, Kevin	Prof	Louisiana St	2	NO	PHD	78	Tenn	8-91
Motamedi, Kurt K.	Prof	Pepper-L Ang			PHD	74	UCLA	1982
Mote, John R.	Assoc	Texas	7	UV	PHD	79	Texas	1985
Moten, Sebrena	Asst	Tuskegee						
Motiwalla, Luvai	Asst	Hartford	9	Z	PHD	89	Arizona	
Motowidlo, Stephan J.	Assoc	Florida	25	EGNR	PHD	76	Minn	
Mottilla, Donna T.	Prof	Shippensburg	7	V	DBA		Kent St	
Mottola, Louis F.	Assoc	New Haven	79	VZ	PHD	72	N Colo	
Motwani, J. D.	Asst	Grand Valley			PHD	90	North Tx	1990
Mount, Daniel	Asst	US Intl			MBA		Mich St	1991
Mount, Michael K.	Prof	Iowa	5	N	PHD	77	Iowa St	1986
Moursi, Mahmoud A.	Prof	Cen Michigan	3	I	PHD	70	NYU	1970
Mousa, Haidar		Chicago St	9		PHD		Ill Tech	1992
Moussa, Faten	Asst	SUNY-Plattsb	38	IY	PHD		CUNY-Bar	1989
Moussavi, Farzad	Assoc	No Iowa			PHD	85	Arkansas	8-85
Mowday, Richard T.	Prof	Oregon	2	EH	PHD	75	Ca-Irvine	1977
Gerald B. Bashaw Professor of Management								
Mowery, David	Assoc	Cal-Berkeley	38	YD	PHD		Stanford	1989
Moxon, Richard	Assoc	U Washington	38	IY	DBA	73	Harvard	1976
Muchinsky, Paul	Prof	N Car-Greens	25	EFN	PHD	73	Purdue	1993
Bryan Distinguished Professor of Business								
Muczyk, Jan P.	Prof	Cleveland St	25	EFQ	DBA		Maryland	1973
Mudie, Peter	Lect	Napier Univ	38	IY	MED			1973
Mudrack, Peter	Asst	Wayne State	24	EL	ABD	91	Toronto	1990
Mueller, Leslie C.	Prof	Central Wash			DBA	78	S Calif	1979
Muhs, Bill	Assoc	Montana St	3		PHD	76	Tx Tech	9-82
Muiderman, Anthony	Assoc	Hope	16		MBA	77	Grd Vall	1977
Muir, Nan	Asst	Houston-C Lk	38	IYHD	PHD		Tx-Arlin	8-90
Mukherjee, Pracheta	Asst	Slippery Roc	23	EHWX	PHD		Kansas	1989
Mukhopadyyay, Tridas	Assoc	Carnegie Mel	9	Z	PHD		Michigan	1986
Mukhtar, S. M.	Fell	Manchest Bus	6	ST	MPHI		London	1993
Mulder, Maria	Asst	Univ Limburg	25	RPT	MA	80	Leiden	1986
Mulford, Oliver J.	Prof	Mankato St			EDD	71	Illinois	1962
Mulkowsky, G.	Asst	CUNY-Baruch	1	A	PHD		NYU	1977
Mullen, Michael R.			3	I	PHD	88	N Carol	
Mullen, Robert	Asst	So Conn St	79	UZ	SCD	92	NewHaven	1992
Mullen, Thomas	Adj	New York U			PHD	86	NYU	
Mullen, Tom		Strathclyde	7	U				
Muller, Helen Juliette	C-Pr	New Mexico		N	PHD	82	S Calif	
Mullery, Colleen	Asst	CS-Humboldt	34	IK	PHD	91	Port St	1986
Mulligan, Thomas M.	Assoc	Brock Univ	49	JZ	PHD		Northwes	1987
Mullin, Ralph F.	Assoc	Cen Missouri	3	HJ	PHD	87	Florida	1986
Mullins, James E.	Prof	St Ambrose	79	UZ	MA	65	Marquett	1969
Mullins, Terry W.	Dean	Evansville	2	E	PHD	78	Houston	1993
Mulvey, C.	Prof	W Australia			PHD			
Mulvey, Paul W.	Asst	Connecticut	5	N	PHD	91	Ohio St	1991
Mumford, Larry G.	Assoc	Lawrence Tec	19		MBA	77	Wayne St	1983
Munchus, George M.	Prof	Alabama-Birm	5	NQ	PHD	76	North Tx	1976
Mundie, John	Prof	U Manitoba	13	I	PHD	66	Stanford	1955
Munn, Joseph R.	Asst	Baylor	7	U	PHD		Tx A&M	1988
Munoz-Seca, Beatriz	Asst	Univ Navarra	7	V	PHD		Navarra	1-90
Munro, David	Assoc	Wis-Whitewat	9	JVZ	PHD	88	Wis-Milw	1989
Munro, Malcolm	Prof	Univ Calgary	9	Z	PHD	75	Minn	1974
Munshi, Jamal	Assoc	Sonoma State	9	Z	PHD	91	Arkansas	2-91
Munter, Mary F.	Adj	Dartmouth			MA	75	Stanford	1983
Murata, Kazuhiko	Prof	Hitotsubashi	5	U	DC	78	Hitotsub	1973
Murch, Ron	Inst	Univ Calgary	9	Z	MBA		Calgary	1985
Murchison, Richard L.	Assoc	Wesley	15		MAS	66	Delaware	1988
Murchland, Bernard	Prof	Ohio Wesley	4	J	PHD		SUNY Buf	1967
Murdick, Robert G.	Prof	Fla Atlantic	3	I	PHD	72	Florida	9-68
Murgatroyd, Stephen	Prof	Athabasca Un	2	EUH	PHD	87	Open	1986
Murkison, Eugene C.	Assoc	Geo Southern	15	QENP	PHD	86	Missouri	1984
Murnighan, J. Keith	Prof	British Colu	2	EFHX	PHD	74	Purdue	1993
Murphy, Anne P.	Asst	West Chester			MBA		Penn	1989
Murphy, Charles	Prof	Howard	3	I	PHD			
Murphy, David	Lect	Manches Inst	45	L	PHD		Manchest	9-74
Murphy, David C.	Assoc	Boston Coll	73	UVI	DBA	70	Indiana	1970
Murphy, Frederic	Prof	Temple	7	AUV	PHD	71	Yale	1982
Murphy, Jerry	Assoc	Portland St	7	UZ	ABD	70	Wash St	
Murphy, Kathleen M.	Assoc	St Bonaventu	24		PHD		Denver	1986
Murphy, Kevin J.	Assoc	Harvard	25	EN				

Name	Rank	University			Degree		School	Year
Murphy, Kevin M.	Prof	Chicago	37	IV	PHD	86	Chicago	1976
Murphy, Peter		Victoria Can	12	AD	PHD		Ohio St	7-91
Murphy, Terence M.	Asst	Plymouth St			MBA	69	Suffolk	
Murray, Alan	Assoc	Am Grad Intl			PHD			
Murray, Edwin A. Jr.	Assoc	Boston Univ	38	IY	DBA		Harvard	
Murray, Ian E.	Lect	Napier Univ	17	BU	BA			1978
Murray, Michael A.	Prof	DePaul			JD		Illinois	
Murray, Patricia	Inst	Virg Union			MBA			1991
Murray, Peter W.	Dean	Chaminade	13		MBA		Penn	1966
Murray, Robert B.	Inst	Brigham Yg						
Murray, Thomas	Prof	NJ Inst Tech	9	Z	PHD	73	Mass	1992
Murray, Vernon	Asst	Marist			PHD		Alabama	1993
Murray, Victor V.	Prof	York Univ	5	N	FHD		Cornell	
Murray, William	Prof	Chaminade	13		EDD		S Calif	1982
Murrell, Audrey J.	Asst	Pittsburgh	2		PHD		Delaware	
Murrell, Kenneth L.	Prof	West Florida	28	FHW	DBA	77	Geo Wash	1982
Murrmann, Kent F.	Assoc	Virg Tech	5		PHD	79	Mich St	1978
Murry, William D.	Asst	SUNY-Bingham		EFHN	PHD	93	Va Tech	1994
Murtagh, Bruce	Prof	Macquarie Un						
Murtagh, T.		Humberside	7					
Murtha, Thomas	Assoc	Minnesota	3	LY	PHD	89	NYU	1994
Muscat, Eugene	Prof	San Francisc	79	VZ	EDD	74	S Calif	1973
Muse, Andrew	Asst	Hampton	3	I	JD		Lincoln	1-91
Musgrave, W. F.	D-Pr	U New Englan			PHD		Sydney	
Mussa, Michael		Chicago			PHD	74	Chicago	1976
William H. Abbott Professor of International Business; on leave								
Mueton, Donald	Asst	Elizabethtwn	23	EQ	BIM	77	Thunderb	9-77
Muthuchidambaram, S.	Prof	Univ Regina	45	JKLQ	PHD		Wiscon	
Muzyka, Daniel	Asst	INSEAD	6	TI	DBA	89	Harvard	9-90
Myers, Donald W.	Prof	Virg Comm	5	FNPQ	DBA	72	Geo St	1982
Myers, Elwin	Assoc	Corpus Chris	1		PHD		Ariz St	
Myers, James	Prof	Hardin-Simm	25	DENP	PHD	84	North Tx	1981
Myers, James H.	Prof	Claremont Gr	1	D	PHD		S Calif	
Myers, Robert C.	Assoc	Louisville	7	UV	MS	64	Richmond	1966
Myles, Keith	Asst	Rockhurst	83	YISE	PHD	90	Kansas	1989
Mylonadis, Yiorgas	Asst	Pennsylvania	34	IM	PHD	93	MIT	7-92
Douglas Vickers Lecturer in Management								
Myrna, Peter	Asst	Illinois Tch						1993
Naadimuthu, G.	C-Pr	F Dick-Ruthe			PHD		KSU	
Nadim, Abbas	C-Pr	New Haven	36	DIT	PHD		Penn	
Naffziger, Douglas W.	Assoc	Ball State	6		DBA		Colorado	1990
Nag, Barin N.	Assoc	Towson State	79		PHD	86	Maryland	1987
Nagarajan, S.	Asst	McGill Univ	1		PHD		Northwes	1988
Nagy, Thomas	Assoc	George Wash	9	Z	PHD	74	Texas	
Nahavandi, Afsaneh	Assoc	Ariz St-West	25	EIST	PHD	83	Utah	1988
Nair, Suresh K.	Assoc	Connecticut	79	UZ	PHD	89	Northwes	9-88
Nakhai, Behnam	Prof	Millersville	78	UWY	PHD	82	Claremnt	1987
Nale, Robert D.	Prof	SC-Coastal	5	E	PHD	84	Miss	1985
Nalebuff, Barry	Prof	Yale	1	IV	DPHL	83	Oxford	1989
Nambimadom, Ramakrishnan	Asst	Case Western			PHD	94	Rochest	1993
Namiki, Nobuaki	Prof	CS-Sacrament	38	IY	PHD	84	Tx-Dallas	1984
Namit, Kal	Assoc	Winston-Sal	7	U	PHD	78	Wiscon	
Nandakumar, P.	Asst	Duke			PHD		Car Mel	
Nangia, Madan M.	Assoc	So Conn St	15	BEIN	PHD	73	NYU	1986
Napier, Nancy K.	Prof	Boise State	38	IY	PHD	81	Ohio St	1986
Narapareddy, V.	Asst	Denver	8	Y	PHD	87	Illinois	9-93
Narasimhan, Ram	Prof	Michigan St	7	UV	PHD	76	Minn	9-77
Narayanan, V. K.	Prof	Kansas	3	I	PHD		Pitt	1978
Nash, Allen	Asst	Murdoch Univ	39	IZ	MBA		W Aust	1989
Nash, Bernard A.	Asst	Dallas	8		PHD	80	North Tx	8-90
Nasierowski, Wojciech	Assoc	New Brunswic	83	Y	PHD		Warsaw	1990
Nasif, Ercan	Asst	Tx-Pan Amer	1	EH	PHD	88	North Tx	1988
Nath, Raghu	Assoc	Pittsburgh	2		PHD		MIT	
Natiello, Thomas A.	Prof	U Miami	23	CDHI	PHD	66	Mich St	1966
Naude, Peter	Lect	Manchest Bus	7	IUZ	MSC		Sussex	1990
Naughton, Anthony J.	SLect	U Wollongong	78	Y	MBA	80	Bradford	2-87
Naughton, Thomas J.	Assoc	Wayne State	24	EGOT	PHD	82	SUNY-Buf	1980
Nault, Barrie	Asst	Calif-Irvine	9	Z	PHD	90	Brit Col	1994
Naumes, Williams	Assoc	New Hampshir	3	I	PHD	71	Stanford	1989
Nauss, Robert M.	Dean	Mo-St Louis			PHD		UCLA	
Navarro, Peter	Assoc	Calif-Irvine	5	JL	PHD	86	Harvard	1988
Nayyar, Praveen	Asst	New York U			PHD	88	Michigan	
Neal, Derrick J.	Lect	Canterbury	3		PHD	80	Canterbu	1987
Neal, Judith A.	Assoc	New Haven	54	FJR	PHD		Yale	
Neal, Rodney D.	Prof	Ark-Ltl Rock			PHD	72	Northwes	1970
Neal, William G.	Dean	Brighm Yg-HI	9	Z	EDD	77	Va Tech	1984
Neale, M. A.	Prof	Northwestern	2	E	PHD	82	Texas	1987
J. L. & Helen Kellogg Distinguished Prof of Dispute Resolution & Organization								
Near, Janet P.	C-Pr	Indiana	4	L	PHD	77	SUNY-Buf	1979
Neck, Christopher P.	Asst	Virg Tech	1		PHD	93	Arizona	1994

Anheuser-Busch Term Assistant Professor of Management

Name	Rank	School			Degree		PhD School	Year
Ottemann, Robert L.	Assoc	Neb-Omaha			PHD	74	Nebraska	1973
Ottensmeyer, Edward J.	Asst	Clark	43	IJ	PHD	83	Indiana	
Ouchi, William G.	Prof	UCLA	3	I	PHD	72	Chicago	1979
Ouellet, Roch	Agreg	HEC-Montreal	7		PHD		Montreal	
Ouimet, Gerard	Asst	HEC-Montreal	17	DEJR	PHD		Montreal	
Oum, Tae	Prof	British Colu		Y	PHD	79	Brit Col	1983
Overby, John D.	Assoc	Tenn-Martin	25	EHN	DBA	85	La Tech	9-81
Overmeer, Willem	Asst	INSEAD	3	I	PHD	89	MIT	9-90
Overstreet, James S.					DBA	80	Fla St	
Overton, Craig	Prof	Rhode Island	5	QN	PHD	71	Mass	1969
Oviatt, Benjamin M.	Asst	Georgia St	3	HIQ	PHD	85	S Carol	1988
Owen, Crystal	Assoc	Wright State	2	EFN	PHD	87	Ohio St	1989
Owens, Bob R.	Dean	Louisiana Te	3	IT	PHD	65	Arkansas	1965
Owens, Ernest	Lect	St Thomas-MN						
Owens, Eugene	Prof	Western Wash	15	DFNQ	PHD	70	UCLA	1975
Owens, Heidi	Asst	Portland St	9	Z	PHD	92	Ariz St	1992
Owens, James	Assoc	CS-Chico	4	L	JD		Western	1979
Owens, Stephen D.	Assoc	W Carolina	58	NQY	PHD	81	North Tx	8-81
Ozatalay, Savas	H-Pr	Widener			PHD		Northwes	
Ozbekhan, Hasan	Emer	Pennsylvania	8		PHD	45	London	7-71
Ozelli, Tunc	Assoc	NY Inst Tech	61		PHD			
Ozernoy, Vladimir M.	Prof	CS-Hayward	7	V	PHD	75	Moscow	1983
Ozgur, Ceyhun	Asst	Valparaiso	7	UV	PHD	90	Kent St	1988
Ozkarahan, Irem	Assoc	Bloomsburg	7		PHD		ASU	8-92
Ozmun, Jon	C-Pr	No Arizona	73	IU	PHD	75	Oklahoma	
Pablo, Amy	Assoc	Univ Calgary	2	IH	PHD	91	Texas	1991
Pabon, Jaime	Assoc	P Rico-Mayag	3		MBA	83	Tx A&M	8-83
Pace, Larry	Assoc	La St-Shreve	2	FH	PHD	77	Georgia	8-90
Pace, R. Wayne	Prof	Brigham Yg	25	&GPX	PHD	60	Purdue	1978
Pack, Howard	Prof	Pennsylvania						
Pack, Janet Rothenberg	C-Pr	Pennsylvania			PHD	65	Berkeley	1970
Packwood, Gary	Assoc	Baldwin-Wal	34	MC	MBA		Bald Wal	
Paden, David L.	Prof	West Chester			DBA		Indiana	1988
Padgett, Jerry H.	Dean	Winthrop	13	IP	PHD	68	Purdue	1970
Padgett, Margaret	Asst	Butler	2	E	PHD	88	Mich St	1989
Padgett, Thomas A.	Prof	West Georgia	7	UZ	DBA	75	Fla St	9-82
Paetzold, Ramona L.	Asst	Texas A&M		XR	DBA	79	Indiana	1990
Pagano, Anthony	Assoc	Ill-Chicago	34	ILN	PHD	78	Penn St	9-78
Pagano, LeRoy	Prof	St Johns			PHD	74	American	
Page, Alfred N. Distinguished Professor								
Page, David A.	Dean	Wm & Mary	8	Y	PHD	64	Chicago	1990
Page, Diana	Assoc	Robt Morris	3	AIX	PHD	65	Harvard	9-85
Paik, Youngsun	Asst	West Florida	12	DNX	EDD	86	Fla St	1988
Paine, Lynn	Asst	Loyola Marym	4	L	PHD	91	U Washin	1991
Painter, Sidney G.	Assoc	Harvard						
Paisley, Clyde A.	Inst	Cen Arkansas	9	Z	BBA		Arkansas	
Pal, Surenda	Assoc	Morris Brown			MBA	69	Calif St	1981
Palaniswami, Shanthakumar	Assoc	Widener			PHD		Penn	
Palencia, Luis Enrique	Prof	Cen Michigan	7	UV	PHD	85	IIT	1984
Palich, Leslie	Asst	Univ Navarra	7	V	MBA		Navarra	9-72
Palmer, David	Asst	Baylor	38	I	PHD		Ariz St	1991
Palmer, David D.	SLect	Santa Clara			PHD	83	Calif	1980
Palmer, Donald A.	Asst	Connecticut			PHD	75	SUNY-Buf	1976
Palmer, Gill	Assoc	Cal-Davis	2	FH	PHD		SUNY-SBr	
Palmer, Kermit G.	H-Pr	U Wollongong			PHD		City UK	1-92
Palmer, Timothy	Prof	Eastern Wash	9	Z	EDD	67	S Carol	1968
Palmer, Todd	Asst	Louisiana St	3	I	PHD	94	Ariz St	8-94
Pan, William S. V.	Asst	Penn St-Erie	43	IK	PHD	94	Georgia	1994
Panda, Dandeson	Prof	New Haven	7	VX	PHD		Columbia	
Pandit, N. R.	Asst	Delaware St			PHD			1989
Pang, Mary Y. N.	Lect	Manchest Bus			MSC		Manchest	1991
Panico, Victor G.	Lect	City Poly HK			PHD			
Panicucci, Richard	Prof	CS-Fresno	2	EH	EDD	71	Ariz St	1970
Panko, Raymond R.	Prof	F Dick-Teane			MBA		Fairl Di	
Pankoff, Lyn D.	Prof	Hawaii-Manoa	7	B	PHD	75	Stanford	
Pant, Narayan	Dean$	Wash Univ			PHD	67	Chicago	1967
Paolillo, Joseph G. P.	Asst	Univ Alberta	3	HI	PHD	91	NYU	1991
Papadopoulos, Nick	C-Pr	Mississippi	3	HI	PHD	77	Oregon	1986
Papageorge, Andrew J.	Assoc	Carleton Un	8	Y	DBA		Athens	
Paper, Lawrence N.	Retir	CS-Stanislau	18	EY	PHD	67	UCLA	9-85
Pappalardo, John	Assoc	Robt Morris	4	KL	JD	71	Duquesne	9-67
Paradice, David B.	Asst	Keene State			PHD		Va Comm	1990
Paradise-Tornow, Carol	Asst	Texas A&M		Z	PHD	86	Tx Tech	1986
Paranilam, Margaret A.	Asst	N Car-Greens	23	IDFN	PHD	86	Minn	8-93
Parasuraman, Saroj	Assoc	Loyola-N Orl	15	NP	PHD	67	Nebraska	1970
Parayre, Roch	Prof	Drexel	2	EG	PHD	77	SUNY Buf	1983
Pardoe, Kevin	Asst	So Methodist			PHD	91	Brit Col	1990
Pare, Guy	Dean	Humberside	7					
Parent, Regis	Assoc	HEC-Montreal	9	Z	MSC		Montreal	
	Agreg	HEC-Montreal	7	UVX	MSC		N Ariz	

Name	Rank	Institution	#	Code	Deg	Yr	University	Year
Parham, James	Lect	Pittsburgh	3		ABD		Michigan	
Parhizgar, Kamal D.	Assoc	Tx A&M Intl	12	E	PHD		Northwes	1992
Pariseau, Susan E.	Assoc	Merrimack		U	PHD	94	Mass	
Park, Daewoo	Asst	Xavier	23	DEFY	PHD	92	Tx A&M	1992
Park, Jaesun	Assoc	North Dakota	7	DUV	PHD	85	Northwes	8-84
Park, Jinsop	Asst	Dallas Bapt	1		PHD		Berkeley	1993
Park, June	Asst	Iowa	9	Z	PHD	88	Ohio	1989
Park, Paul	Assoc	Illinois St	7		PHD		Oregon	1988
Park, Seung Ho	Asst	Rutgers-N Br		IY	PHD	92	Oregon	1992
Park, Taeho	Assoc	San Jose St	7	U	PHD	87	Wiscon	1988
Park, Yoon	Prof	George Wash	8	Y	DBA	70	Harvard	
Parke, E. Lauck	Assoc	Vermont	13	DJY	PHD	76	Mass	1977
Parker, Barbara	Asst	Seattle	38	IY	PHD	89	Colorado	8-91
Parker, Drew C.	Assoc	Simon Fraser	9	DZ	PHD	86	W Ontari	1984
Parker, George G. C.	Prof	Stanford			PHD	67	Stanford	1973
Parker, Gerald E.	Prof	St Louis			PHD	72	St Louis	1972
Parker, Lee D.	H-Pr	Flinders Un	13	ABIJ	PHD	83	Montash	5-88
Parkhe, Arvind	Asst	Indiana			PHD	89	Temple	1989
Parkinson, David	Asst	Univ Alberta	38	HY			Penn	1993
Parkman, Allen M.	Prof	New Mexico			PHD	73	UCLA	
Parks, Don M.	Asst	Wyoming	36	IHTY	PHD		Tx A&M	8-88
Parks, George M.	Deces	Pace		1991	PHD	63	Calif	
Parks, Michael S.	Assoc	Houston	9	Z	PHD	73	Georgia	1973
Parkum, Kurt	Assoc	Penn St-Harr	1	D	PHD	69	Wiscon	1981
Parlar, Mahmut	Prof	McMaster Un	71	UV	PHD		Waterloo	
Parnell, John	Asst	Mid Tenn St	38	IY	DBA	92	Memphis	1992
Parrish, Leo	Prof	Geo Southern	7	IJV	PHD	74	Ga Tech	1990
Parry, Linda	Asst	Minn-Duluth	24	HIRL	PHD	90	SUNY-Alb	1983
Parry, Thomas	Dean	U Wollongong			PHD			4-94
Parsa, Farmarz	Asst	West Georgia	7	U	PHD	86	Geo St	9-86
Parsinia, Alex	Assoc	Pepper-L Ang			PHD	76	LSU	1982
Parson, Gary I.	Asst	Central Wash			ABD	69	Wiscon	1975
Parsons, Charles K.	Prof	Georgia Tech	2	ENP	PHD	80	Illinois	1979
Parsons, Henry	C-Ac	So Maine	7	UV	PHD	83	Oregon	1974
Parsons, Jeffrey	Asst	Memorial Un	9	Z	PHD	92	Brit Col	1993
Parsons, Robert	Assoc	Northeastern					Boston C	
Parthasarthy, Raghavan	Asst	Seton Hall			PHD	91	CUNY	
Partovi, Fariborz Y.	Asst	Drexel	7	UV	PHD	88	Penn	1988
Partridge, Dane M.	Asst	So Indiana	5	Q	PHD	91	Cornell	1993
Partridge, Scott H.	Prof	CS-Hayward	34	I	DBA	70	Harvard	1970
Pascal, Laurie	C-Ac	Pine Manor	34	IE	MBA		Northwes	1982
David & Barbara Gray Professor of Management								
Paschke, Paul Edward	Assoc	Oregon State	7	V	DBA	70	Indiana	1969
Pasin, Federico	Asst	HEC-Montreal			PHD		Paris	
Pasis, Harvey	Assoc	Athabasca Un	1	AI	MA	70	McMaster	1981
Pasmore, William A.	Prof	Case Western	2	E	PHD		Purdue	
Pastin, Mark J.	Prof	Arizona St	4	J	PHD	73	Harvard	1980
Pastore, Joseph Jr.	Prof	Pace-Westch			PHD	69	St Louis	1976
Patankar, Jay G.	Prof	Akron	7	VXU	PHD	78	Clemson	9-78
Pate, Larry	Prof	Utah	2	E	PHD			1993
Patel, Ranjna K.	C-Ac	Bethune-Cook			DBA		Kent St	1985
Pati, Gopal C.	Prof	Indiana NW	45	FLN	PHD	70	Ill Tech	1972
Pati, Niranjan	Asst	Wis-La Cross			PHD		Nowthwes	
Patinka, Paul J.	Inst	Colo-Denver			PHD	59	Purdue	
Patrick, Floyd A.	Prof	E Michigan	5		PHD	62	Iowa	1970
Patrick, Hugh	Prof	Columbia	8	Y	PHD	60	Michigan	1984
Patrone, Ferdinand	Prof	Metro State	13	IST	PHD	71	Syracuse	1975
Patten, Thomas H.	Prof	CS-Pomona	5	KQ	PHD	59	Cornell	1984
Patterson, Cheryl	Asst	Furman	23	EHUI	PHD	87	Clemson	1984
Patterson, Dennis	Asst	Notre Dame	13	I	PHD	92	Illinois	1990
Patterson, Gary D.	Asst	CS-San Bern	4	K	JD	83	Wstrn St	1987
Patterson, J. Wayne	Assoc	Clemson	7	UV	PHD	77	Arkansas	1982
Patterson, Mike C.	Prof	Midwest St	7	UVQ	PHD	78	North Tx	9-78
Patterson, Paul	Assoc	U Wollongong			PHD		Wollongo	1-89
Patton, Donald J.	Assoc	Dalhousie U	8	Y	DBA		Indiana	
Patuwo, B. Eddy	Asst	Kent State			PHD		Va Tech	1988
Patz, Alan L.	Assoc	So Calif	3	I	PHD	67	Car Mel	1972
Patzig, William	Assoc	Jms Madison	13	IE	PHD	73	Texas	9-80
Pauchant, Thierry C.	Asst	HEC-Montreal	23	DFM	PHD		S Calif	
Paul, Allison A.	Asst	St Joseph	23	ENPR	PHD	91	Temple	1990
Paul, H.	SLect	Canterbury	7	Y	DENG	75	Asian Te	1987
Paul, R. H.	Prof	Laurentian	2		PHD		London	
Paul, Robert J.	Prof	Kansas State	25	ENPR	PHD	66	Arkansas	9-78
Paulas, John		Lg Isl-Brook						
Pauley, Robert	Lect	SC-Spartanbu	43	JIST	MBA	65	Howard	1985
Paulson, Albert	Asst	Rensselaer						
Paulson, C. Richard	Prof	Mankato St			PHD	73	Florida	1968
Paulson, Dan	Deces	U Lethbridge	97	1994	PHD	89	Brit Col	1983
Paulson, Kathy	Asst	SUNY-Stony B	15	PQ	MS	91	Purdue	1993
Paulson, Steven K.	Prof	North Fla	24	EHLX	PHD		Iowa St	

Name	Rank	Institution			Degree			
Pavelchak, Mark	Asst	Redlands	27	EX	PHD			
Pavelle, James R.	Inst	Hawaii Pacif	35	ANIL	MBA	91	HI Pacif	6-91
Pavett, Cynthia	Prof	San Diego	28	CGY	PHD	78	Utah	1978
Pawar, Sheelwant B.	Prof	Idaho State		Q	PHD	67	Utah	1967
Pawle, Laura	Inst	P Rico-Mayag	5		MS	88	Mass	1-90
Paxton, Ian	Lect	Napier Univ	71	BIV	MBA			1977
Paxton, John	Assoc	Wayne St Col	79	VX	PHD	88	Nebraska	1992
Payne, Dinah M.	Asst	New Orleans	5	KJ	JD	87	Loyola	8-88
Payne, John W.	C-Pr	Duke	27	EVZ	PHD	73	Ca-Irvine	1977
Payne, Stephen L.	Prof	E Illinois		JL	PHD		Ariz St	1989
Paz, Armando	Lect	Mt St Mary's			PHD		US Intrl	
Peach, Brian	Asst	West Florida	23	EI	PHD	92	Oklahoma	1991
Peach, David A.	Prof	Cal Poly-SLO	5	NQ	DBA	69	Harvard	1987
Peacock, Andrew C.	Assoc	Dalhousie U	9	Z	PHD		W Ontari	
Peacock, Peter R.	Assoc	Wake Fr-MBA	9	Z	PHD		Chicago	
Peake, Lloyd	Asst	CS-San Bern	3	E	JD	74	Southwes	1990
Pearce, C. Glenn	Assoc	Virg Comm	12	&EP	PHD	74	Geo St	1975
Pearce, James W.	Asst	W Carolina	27	IKUV	JD	73	S Carol	8-91
Pearce, John A. II	Prof	George Mason	3	IT	PHD	76	Penn St	1986
Pearce, Jone L.	Assoc	Calif-Irvine	25	ENY	PHD	78	Yale	1979
Pearce, Thomas	Assoc	Moorhead St	25	NEQ	PHD		U Wash	1988
Pearce, Wayne E.	Inst	Brigham Yg						
Pearlson, Keri	Asst	Texas	9	Z	PHD	92	Harvard	1992
Pearman, Alan D.	Prof	Univ Leeds	7	VU	PHD	78	Leeds	1971
Pearson, Alan W.	Dean	Manchest Bus	12	DIOS	BSC		London	1970
Pearson, Andrall	Prof	Harvard						
Pearson, Cecil	Assoc	Murdoch Univ	2	EFHU	PHD		W Aust	1992
Pearson, Christine	Asst	No Carolina	25	EN	PHD	88	S Calif	1993
Pearson, John M.	Asst	Kansas State	9	SYZ	DBA	91	Miss St	8-89
Pearson, Rodney	Assoc	Miss State	9	Z	DBA	84	Harvard	1987
Pecenka, Joseph O.	Reitr	No Illinois			PHD	67	Illinois	1967
Pedler, Michael	Lect	Australian N	9	AISZ	MEC	93	NE	1993
Peek, Stephen	Assoc	Utica	27	FUVW	MBA			1987
Peery, Newman S.	Prof	Pacific	46	JLTI	PHD	74	U Wash	8-82
Peffers, Kenneth G.	Asst	Rutgers-Camd			PHD			
Pegels, C. Carl	Prof	SUNY-Buffalo	37	IUY	PHD	66	Purdue	9-66
Pegnetter, Richard	Prof	Colorado St	5	Q	PHD	71	Cornell	1986
Peirce, Ellen R.	Assoc	No Carolina	4	JKLQ	JD	76	Duke	1980
Pekar, Peter P.	Prof	CS-Pomona	3	IL	PHD	74	Ill Tech	1991
Pelc, Karol I.	Prof	Mich Tech	78	DIY	PHD	68	Poland	1985
Pelechette, Joy V.	Asst	So Indiana	12	E	PHD	91	S Illin	1991
Peles, Yoram	Prof	Hebrew Univ			PHD			
Pelled, Lisa	Asst	So Calif	2	E	PHD		Stanford	1993
Pelletier, Monique A.		San Fran St	23	HI	PHD	77	Ill St	1986
Pellissier, James M.	Asst	Loyola-Chicg			PHD		Northwes	1990
Pena, Leticia	Asst	Wis-La Cross			ABD		Harvard	
Penalva, Fernando	Asst	Univ Navarra	7	V			Politecn	9-92
Penbera, Joseph John	Prof	CS-Fresno	28	EY	PHD	70	American	8-85
Pendegraft, Norman	Assoc	Idaho	79	VZ	PHD	78	UCLA	1983
Pender, Albert R.	Assoc	No Illinois	1	D	PHD	67	N Dakota	
Pendleton, Barbara A.	Assoc	Mars Hill	15		EDD	76	Va Tech	1988
Pendse, Shripad G.	Prof	St Marys-Cnd	23	DEIH	PHD	73	Stanford	1966
Penfield, Robert	Assoc	Missouri	5	Q	PHD	66	Cornell	1972
Penlesky, Richard	Assoc	Bowling Gr	7	U	DBA	83	Indiana	1990
Penley, Larry E.	Dean	Arizona St	25	Mgt	PHD	76	Georgia	1985
Penn, William M.	Prof	Belhaven	7	J	PHD	81	Duke	1981
Pennings, Hans	Prof	Univ Limburg	32	IXY	PHD	73	Michigan	1987
Pennings, Johannes M.	Assoc	Pennsylvania	23	HD	PHD	73	Michigan	7-83
Pentland, Brian T.	Asst	UCLA	9	Z	PHD	91	MIT	1992
Penwell, Larry W.	Asst	Mary Wash	25	FEGP	PHD		Cinn	
Peper, Merle J.	Assoc	Wilkes	12	BHIY	PHD		LSU	9-89
Perdue, John	Assoc	Ferris State	5		MBA		Detroit	1983
Peregoy, Richard P.	Assoc	Dallas	13	I	DPS	78	Pace	8-91
Perería, Fernando	Prof	Univ Navarra	7	H	PHD		ETSICCP	9-58
Perez, Jorge	Asst	N Carol A&T	9	Z	ABD		Fla St	1-93
Perez, Juan Antonio	Prof	Univ Navarra	2	E	DBA		Harvard	O-61
Peridis, Theodoros	Assoc	York Univ	3	I	PHD		NYU	
Perkins, Carlton	Asst	Txs Southern	46	JKLT	JD		Tx South	1978
Perkins, Charles A.	Dean	Missouri Wes		UW	PHD		Geo Wash	1991
Perkins, Nichelle	Asst	W Virginia			JD		Iowa	1992
Perlaki, Ivan	VProf	East Tenn St	25	EFHN	PHD	76	Czechosl	1988
Perles, Benjamin M.	Prof	Suffolk			PHD		Boston U	
Perlmutter, Howard V.	Prof	Pennsylvania	8	PHD	PHD	52	Kansas	7-68
Permenter, Vivian	Assoc	Tx-Brownsvil			MS	70	Oklahoma	1974
Peroff, Nicholas	Assoc	Mo-Kansas Ct	1	AD	PHD	77	Wiscon	1974
Perotti, James	Prof	Ohio Univ			PHD		Duquesne	
Perotti, Valerie	Assoc	Ohio Univ	12		PHD	87	Ohio U	
Perrewe, Pamela L.	C-Ac	Florida St	25	EGNR	PHD	85	Nebraska	1-84
Perry, Charles E.	Dean	Dallas			CPH	72	Michigan	5-93
Perry, Charles R.	Assoc	Pennsylvania	5	NQ	PHD	68	Chicago	7-68

Name	Rank	School			Degree		Institution	Date
Pilcher, M.	SLect	U Washington		ZUV	PHD	85	Ga Tech	1987
Pillai, Rajnandini K.	Asst	U Miami	2	E	PHD	93	SUNY-Buf	1993
Pilon, Pierre-Paul	Agreg	HEC-Montreal	9	Z	MPH		Yale	
Pin, Jose Ramon	Asst	Univ Navarra	2	V	PHD		Pontific	D-86
Pinckney, Richard P.	Prof	Lander	79	V	PHD	75	Clemson	1980
Pincus, Laura	Asst	DePaul			JD		Chicago	
Pinder, Craig C.	Prof	British Colu	2	EN	PHD	75	Cornell	1975
Pinder, Jonathan P.	Asst	Wake Fr-MBA	7	UV	PHD	89	Carolina	1990
Pineda, Rodley C.	Asst	Tenn Tech	38	IY	PHD	93	Tx Tech	1993
Pinkley, Robin L.	Asst	So Methodist			PHD	88	N Carol	1989
Pinkney, Willie	Asst	Tuskegee						
Pinkston, T. S.	Asst	Oklahoma	38	IJ	PHD	91	Georgia	8-91
Pinkus, Charles E.	Prof	CS-Pomona	71	UVA	DSC	71	Geo Wash	1980
Pinsonneault, Alain	Agreg	HEC-Montreal	9	Z	PHD		Ca-Irvine	
Pinter, Janos		Dalhousie U	9	Z	PHD	82	MoscowSt	
Pinto, Jeffrey K.	Asst	Maine			PHD	86	Pitt	1988
Pinto, Jeffrey K.	Asst	Penn St-Erie	2	H	PHD	86	Pitt	1994
Pinto, Peter	Prof	Bowling Gr	7	U	PHD	75	N Carol	1976
Piore, Michael J.	Prof	MIT	5	NQ	PHD			
Piper, William	Prof	No Georgia			PHD	93	Am Londn	1985
Piramuthu, Selwyn	Asst	Florida			PHD	92	Illinois	1991
Pirkle, Kipling M.	Assoc	Wash & Lee	36	IST	PHD	85	Clemson	1989
Pisano, Gary P.	Asst	Harvard	7	U	PHD			
Pitcher Johnston, Patricia	Lect	HEC-Montreal	1	I	PHD		McGill	
Pitsiladis, P. E.	Assoc	Concordia U						
Pitt, D.	Dean	Strathclyde	2	E				
Pitt, M. R.	Lect	Univ Bath	3	I	MSC			
Pittenger, Khushwant K.	Assoc	Ashland		&ERY	PHD		Cinncinn	9-87
Pittman, Paul	Asst	Indiana SE	7	UV	PHD	93	Georgia	1993
Pitts, Barbara M. C.	Lect	McMaster Un	2	EFNP	MBA		McMaster	
Pitts, Michael W.	Assoc	Virg Comm	36	CIS	DBA	84	Tenn	1981
Pitts, Robert A.	Prof	Gettysburg	23	YI	PHD	72	Harvard	1986
Pizzolato, Nelio D.			7	U	PHD	77	N Carol	
Pizzolatto, Allayne	C-Ac	Nicholls St	24	EJLN	PHD	88	LSU	1981
Plane, Donald	Prof	Rollins	7	V	DBA	65	Indiana	1984
Planisek, R. J.	Retir	Grand Valley		1994	PHD		Kent St	1985
Plante, Robert	Prof	Purdue	7	V	PHD	80	Georgia	1980
Plaschka, Gerhard	Asst	DePaul			PHD		Viennna	
Plater, Michael	Lect	Florida	36	IT	PHD	93	Wm&Mary	1993
Platt, Marjorie	Assoc	Northeastern			PHD		Michigan	
Platt, Richard G.	Asst	West Florida	97	UY	PHD	72	North Tx	1991
Plenert, Gerhard J.	Assoc	Brigham Yg	7	U	PHD	89	Co-Mines	1990
Plovnick, Mark S.	Dean	Pacific	21	EFQ	PHD	75	MIT	3-89
Plumlee, E. Leroy	Prof	Western Wash	41	JLMF	PHD	71	Tx Tech	9-76
Poag, Lois A.	Prof	Univ of D C	2	GR	PHD	81	Howard	1986
Poblador, N. S.	SLect	City Poly HK	2	H	PHD	72	Penn	9-89
Podell, Lawrence	Prof	SUNY Old Wes	48	JLMY	PHD	54	Cornell	1992
Podlesnik, Richard A.	Prof	Fort Lewis	17	SU	PHD	77	Northwes	1979
Podsakoff, Philip M.	Prof	Indiana	5	N	DBA	80	Indiana	1982
Pogue, Danny H.	Assoc	N Carol A&T	5		PHD	73	Ohio St	1-73
Pohl, Stuart M.	Asst	St Bonaventu	5		JD		SUNY-Buf	1987
Pohlen, Michael F.	Assoc	Delaware		U	PHD	67	Ohio St	1973
Poitevent, Joe	Retir	Texas A&M		1994	MS	83	Tx A&M	1982
Pokryfka, Richard T.	Prof	Citadel	79	VZ	PHD		Pitt	
Polak, George G.	Assoc	Wright State	7	V	PHD	83	Car Mel	1988
Pollard, Carol	Asst	Univ Calgary	9	Z	ABD		Pitt	1991
Pollard, Hinda	Prof	Bryant	5	NQ	JD	64	Berkeley	8-79
Pollay, Richard W.	Prof	British Colu	4		PHD	70	Chicago	1970
Polley, Doug	Assoc	St Cloud St	3	IJ	PHD	91	Minn	1991
Pollock, Eugenia	Inst	East Tenn St	4		JD	77	Tennesse	1988
Polonsky, M. J.	Lect	U Newcastle	8	MY	MA		Temple	
Polson, Houston H.	C-As	Bellevue	47	K	JD	89	Creighto	8-85
Polster, Eleanor	Inst	Fla Internat		E	MBA	81	Fla Intl	1981
Polzer, Jeffrey	Asst	Texas	2	E	PHD	94	Northwes	1994
Polzin, Paul	Prof	Montana	7	V	PHD	68	Mich St	1968
Pommerenka, Pamela	Asst	Michigan St	5	O	PHD		Stanford	8-94
Pomnichowski, Alex S.	Prof	Ferris State	5		PHD		Mich St	1967
Pompian, Richard O.	VAsst	SW Texas St	1	D	PHD	92	Texas	1993
Ponak, Allen	C-Pr	Univ Calgary	5	Q	PHD	77	Wiscon	1982
Ponce-De-Leon, Jesus	Asst	So Illinois	38	ITYW	PHD	89	Indiana	
Ponder, Eunice	Prof	Fisk	26	REN	PHD		S Carol	1993
Pons, Jose Maria	Asst	Univ Navarra	7	V			Automona	O-83
Ponthieu, Louis	Asst	North Texas	36	ST	PHD	68	Arkansas	1988
Pool, Steven W.	Asst	Ashland		ST	ABD		Akron	9-86
Poole, Peter	Assoc	Lehigh			PHD	86	Penn St	1988
Poole, Rob	Asst	Cen Missouri	7	UVW	ABD		Texas	1993
Pooley, John M.	Asst	Eastern Wash	7	UVX	PHD	89	Penn St	1989
Poon, Wai K.	SLect	Chinese HK	25	EFNP	PHD	76	Toronto	8-91
Poorsoltan, Keramat	C-Ac	Frostburg St			PHD	77	Georgia	8-86

Name	Rank	Institution			Degree		School	
Poorvu, William J.	Prof	Harvard	1					
MBA Class of 1961 Adjunct Professor in Entrepreneurship								
Pope, James A.	Dean	Shippensburg	7	V	PHD	78	N Carol	
Pope, John L.	Prof	Embry-Riddle	25		PHD	75	Berkeley	1981
Pope, Terry	Assoc	Abilene Chr			PHD	69	So Meth	1992
Popejoy, Steven	Asst	Cen Missouri	5	KQ	ABD		Iowa	1993
Popken, Douglas	VAsst	Dayton	7	UV	PHD	88	Berkeley	1991
Poplin, Toby L.	Assoc	Pfeiffer	1		MA	68	Appal St	8-76
Popper, Edward T.	Dean	Aurora			DBA	78	Harvard	1991
Poppo, Laura	Asst	Wash Univ	32	I	PHD	91	Penn	1991
Porao, Joseph F.	Assoc	Illinois	2	DEFH	PHD	79	Rochest	1978
Porras, Jerry I.	Prof	Stanford	2	EH	PHD	74	UCLA	1972
Fred H. Merrill Professor of Organizational Behavior and Change								
Portaro, Ron M.	Prof	Toledo	1		JD		Toledo	1982
Porter, Brian	Assoc	Calvin			PHD	94	Indiana	1994
Porter, David O.	Dean	Alaska-Fairb	1		PHD	70	Syracuse	1994
Porter, Donald E.	Assoc	North Dakota	36	T	PHD	61	Stanford	8-82
Porter, Gayle	Asst	Rutgers-Camd			PHD			
Porter, James L.	Assoc	New Mexico	4	K	JD	75	Temple	
Porter, Lyman W.	Prof	Calif-Irvine	25	EPY	PHD	56	Yale	1967
Porter, Michael E.	Prof	Harvard	4	L	PHD	73	Harvard	
C. Roland Christensen Professor of Business Administration								
Porterfield, Donald	Deces	Tx-S Antonio						
Porth, Stephen J.	Asst	St Joseph	38	EIY	PHD	88	Temple	1984
Portwood, James	Assoc	Temple			PHD		Michigan	
Posner, Barry Z.	Prof	Santa Clara			PHD	79	Mass	1976
Post, Frederick R.	Asst	Toledo			JD		Toledo	1988
Post, James E.	Prof	Boston Univ	34	ILM	PHD	75	SUNY-Buf	1974
Postlewaite, Andrew	Prof	Pennsylvania						
Postrel, Steven R.	Asst	UCLA	3	I	PHD	88	MIT	1986
Potash, Sidney	Prof	Marietta	25	EHN	PHD	73	SUNY	1974
Pouder, Richard W.	Asst	Clemson	3	I	PHD	93	Conn	1993
Poulos, Mark S.	Assoc	St Edwards	36	IS	PHD	84	Texas	1985
Poulson, Christian F.	Asst	CS-Pomona	2	EF	PHD	89	Yale	1991
Pounds, William F.	Prof	MIT	3	I	PHD	62	Case Wes	1961
Poutinen, Jay	Assoc	Wis-Stev Pt	1	D	MBA	68	Michigan	8-82
Powell, Catherine	Asst	Tuskegee						
Powell, Gary N.	Prof	Connecticut	2	E	PHD	74	Mass	1976
Powell, J. Don	Prof	North Texas	3	ILM	PHD	77	LSU	1977
Powell, Michael	SLect	U Auckland	21	HBL	PHD	82	Chicago	1-89
Powell, Sandra	Asst	Weber State			PHD	93	Utah	
Powell, Stephen G.	Assoc	Dartmouth			PHD	83	Stanford	1987
Powell, Steven R.	Assoc	CS-Pomona	93	IVZ	PHD	73	S Calif	1990
Powell, Thomas	Assoc	Bryant	3	ITN	PHD	89	NYU	6-91
Power, Daniel J.	H-Pr	No Iowa	3	I	PHD	82	Wiscon	8-89
Power, Sally J.	Prof	St Thomas-MN						
Powers, Kathleen J.	Assoc	Willamette	52	JNPQ	PHD	86	Florida	8-89
Poyner, Catherine	Inst	NE Missouri	9	Z	MBA	90	LSU	1990
Pozzebon, Sylvana	Asst	HEC-Montreal	15	NQ	MS		Cornell	1990
Prabhaker, Paul	Asst	Illinois Tch			PHD			1992
Pradas, Antonio	Inst	Fla Internat		Y	MS	70	MIT	1991
Pragman, Claudia	Asst	Mankato St			PHD	93	Nebraska	1991
Prahalad, C. K.	Prof	Michigan	38	IY	DBA	75	Harvard	1978
Prasad, Durga	Assoc	So Conn St	48	JKL	JSD	82	Yale	1982
Prasad, Jayesh	Asst	Dayton	9	Z	ABD		Pitt	1990
Prasad, Jyoti	Assoc	E Illinios		I	PHD			1989
Prasad, Pushkala	Assoc	Univ Calgary	28	EH	PHD	92	Mass	1993
Prasad, S. B.	Prof	Cen Michigan	38	IY	PHD	63	Wiscon	1981
Prasad, Srinivas	Assoc	George Wash	9	Z				
Prater, George L.	Assoc	U Washington	9	Z	PHD	63	Stanford	1965
Pratt, Joseph	Prof	Houston	48	BILY	PHD	81	J Hopkin	8-86
Preble, John F.	Assoc	Delaware			PHD	81	Mass	1982
Preece, Stephen	Asst	Wilfrid Laur	38	IY				
Pregel, Gert	Asst	Univ Navarra	7	V	MBA		Navarra	6-87
Preiser-Houy, Larisa	Asst	CS-Pomona	9	Z	MBA	90	Claremont	1992
Preismeyer, Richard	C	St Marys-Txs			PHD	84	Arkansas	
Prelec, Drazen	Assoc	MIT	7	V	PHD	83	Harvard	
Premeaux, Shane	Prof	McNeese St			PHD		Arkansas	
Premeaux, Sonya A.	Inst	McNeese St			MBA		McNeese	
Premkumar, G.	Asst	Iowa State	9	Z	PHD	89	Pitt	1989
Prendergast, Canice	Asst	Chicago			PHD	89	Yale	1990
Prenting, Theodore O.	Prof	Marist	53	QU	MBA		Chicago	1968
Prescott, Jean	SLect	Bournemouth	52	ON	MSC		Salford	9-71
Prescott, John	Assoc	Pittsburgh	3		PHD		Penn St	
Pressley, Trezzie A.	Dean	East Txs St		Mgt	PHD	66	Arkansas	1965
Preston, Anne E.	Assoc	SUNY-Stony B	5	OR	PHD	83	Harvard	1986
Preston, Diane	Lect	Loughborough	5	N	BA		Lancast	
Preston, Paul	Assoc	Tx-S Antonio			DBA	72	Colorado	
Prestwich, Thomas L.			2	E	PHD	80	N Carol	
Presutti, William D. Jr.	Assoc	Duquesne	17		PHD		Carn Mel	1985

Name	Rank	Institution			Degree		School	Year
Prewitt, Lena B.	Prof	Alabama	45	GNR	EDD	61	Indiana	1975
Pribyl, Frank J.	Prof	Western St	8		PHD	76	North Tx	1967
Price, Courtney	Prof	Metro State	65	TCDN	DPA	81	Colorado	1982
Price, Kenneth H.	Assoc	Tx-Arlington	2	E	PHD	73	Mich St	1973
Price, R. Leon	Assoc	Oklahoma	9	Z	DBA	78	Oklahoma	9-79
Priem, Richard L.	Asst	Tx-Arlington	3	I	PHD	90	Tx-Arlin	1990
Prieve, E. Arthur	Prof	Wisconsin	1		DBA	65	Geo Wash	
Prince, J. B.	Assoc	Concordia U						
Prince, M.	Asst	Univ Windsor	36	ISTU	PHD		Bradford	1986
Pringle, Charles D.	Prof	Jms Madison	12	EI	PHD	76	Kentucky	9-86
Pritchett, Jeannette	Asst	Missouri Wes		V	MA		Mo-KC	1991
Probasco, Preston	Prof	San Jose St	21	EFGJ	PHD	69	Wiscon	1967
Procelli, M.	Lect	SUNY-Stony B	5	NQ	MBA	53	Hofstra	1985
Prochaska, Nancy	Asst	Kennesaw St	1		MBA			1989
Proe, John D.	Prof	Shenandoah			PHD		Iowa	1990
Prokop, Jacek	Asst	Northwestern	78	UY	PHD		Va Tech	1990
Proudfoot, Susan	Dir	London Guild	3	I	MBA			4-93
Prout, Howard W.	Assoc	Brock Univ	7	UW	PHD		Western	1984
Provan, Keith G.	Prof	Kentucky	2	HCA	PHD	78	SUNY-Buf	1985
Provost, Michel	Assoc	HEC-Montreal	1	AFJM	MBA		HEC-Mont	
Pruchansky, Neal R.	C-Ac	Keene State			Mgt		Mass	1985
Prussia, Gregory	Asst	Seattle	5	N	PHD		Ariz St	
Psenicka, Clement	Prof	Youngstown	7	EUVX	DBA	76	Kent St	9-77
Ptaszynski, James G.	Lect	Wake Fr-MBA	2	F	PHD	89	N Carol	1985
Puffer, Sheila M.	Asst	Northeastern	25	YE	PHD		Berkeley	9-88
Pugh, Robert	Assoc	Fran Marion	7	U	PHD	75	American	8-90
Puia, George	Asst	Tampa	46	IST	PHD	93	Kansas	1992
Puig, Maria	Inst	P Rico-Mayag	9		MS	92	Wiscon	1-92
Pulhamus, Aaron	Lect	NJ Inst Tech	5	N	EDD	84	Rutgers	1984
Pulich, Marcia	Assoc	Wis-Whitewat	5	NPQ	PHD	79	North Tx	1980
Pullin, James	Inst	Cen Florida	7		MBA	77	NW Mo St	1987
Punnett, B. J.	Assoc	Univ Windsor	28	EJNY	PHD		NYU	1985
Purao, Sandeep	Asst	Georgia St	9	Z	PHD		Wi-Milwa	
Purvis, Russel	Asst	Cen Florida	9	Z	PHD	94	Fla St	1994
Puryear, A.	Prof	CUNY-Baruch	7	V	PHD		Columbia	1970
Pustay, Michael W.	Prof	Texas A&M		LYK	PHD	73	Yale	1980
Puterman, Martin	Prof	British Colu	7	V	PHD	71	Stanford	1974
Putt, Allen D.	Prof	CS-Sacrament	2	E	PHD	75	Kansas	1976
Pyatt, R.	Asst	Un Hong Kong	13	I	MSC			9-90
Pye, A.	Lect	Univ Bath	2	F	PHD			
Pyke, David M.	Assoc	Dartmouth			PHD	87	Penn	1987
Qiu, Man Ying	Asst	Longwood	78	UVXY	PHD	93	Clemson	1994
Quaglieri, Phillip	Assoc	Mass-Boston	5	N	PHD	82	Stevens	1983
Qualls, William J.	Asst	MIT	3	I	DBA	82	Indiana	
Quarstein, Vernon A.	Asst	Old Dominion			PHD	87	Va Comm	
Quaye, Ago	Asst	Norfolk St		Z	PHD	90	S Carol	7-92
Queyranne, Maurice	Prof	British Colu	7	V	PHD	77	Grenoble	1983
Quick, James C.	Prof	Tx-Arlington	2	GE	PHD	77	Houston	1977
Quick, Larry	Prof	Ill Benedict			PHD	84	Northwes	1984
Quigley, John V.	Assoc	East Tenn St	9	Z	PHD	79	Geo St	1984
Quinlan, Michael	Assoc	Griffith Un	5	Q	PHD		Sydney U	1-81
Quinn, Dennis P.	Assoc	Georgetown	48	LYQK	PHD	84	Columbia	1984
Quinn, Michel Thomas	Prof	CS-Long Bch	2	EOPN	PHD	67	Ohio St	1970
Quinn, Robert E.	Prof	Michigan	2	E	PHD	75	Cinn	1988
Quirk, Thomas	Assoc	Webster	1		PHD	67	Stanford	1987
Rabin, Bonnie R.	Asst	Ithaca	5	N	PHD	87	Cornell	8-89
Rabinowitz, Samuel	Assoc	Rutgers-Camd			PHD			
Rachel, Frank M.	Prof	North Texas	25	FNPE	DBA	62	Illinios	1962
Rackow, Paul	Assoc	Fordham	7	UV	PHD		NYU	1973
Radford, Russell	Asst	U Manitoba	7	U	DBA	86	Harvard	1990
Radhakrishnan, Ramaswamy	Prof	Illinois St	7		PHD		Car Mel	
Radnor, Michael	Prof	Northwestern	2	E	PHD	64	Northwes	1964
Radosevich, Raymond	Prof	New Mexico	3	I	PHD	69	Carnegie	
Radovilsky, Zinovy	Assoc	CS-Hayward	7	UVWX	PHD	84	Moscow	1991
Raedels, Alan R.	Prof	Portland St	7	UW	PHD	77	Purdue	1980
Raelin, Joseph A.	Prof	Boston Coll	24	ELNP	PHD	77	SUNY-Buf	8-76
Rafaeli, Anat	SLect	Hebrew Univ			PHD		Ohio	
Rafaeli, Sheizaf	SLect	Hebrew Univ			PHD		Stanford	
Raffaele, Gary C.	Assoc	Tx-S Antonio			DBA	73	Harvard	
Raffield, William	Asst	St Thomas-MN						
Rafii, Farshad	Assoc	Babson			DBA		Harvard	
Ragan, James W.	Asst	Georgia St	5	ENQ	PHD	88	Houston	1988
Ragatz, Gary L.	Assoc	Michigan St	7	U	PHD	85	Indiana	9-84
Raghavan, Srikant	Asst	Lawrence Tec	7		PHD	78	Houston	1987
Raghunathan, Sankaran P.	Asst	Rutgers-Newk	8	Y	PHD		Temple	1991
Ragins, Belle Rose	Asst	Marquette	25	EOR	PHD	87	Tenn	1987
Rahali, Boubekeur	Asst	Mich Tech	7	UV	PHD	84	Oklahoma	1989
Rahim, M. Afzalur	Prof	W Kentucky	2	EFH	PHD	76	Pitt	1983
Rahman, M. Shakil-Ur	Asst	Frostburg St			PHD	89	Iowa St	8-89
Rahnema, Ahmad	Asst	Univ Navarra	7	V	DBA		Navarra	6-91

Name	Rank	School		Code	Deg		Inst	Year
Raho, Louis E.	Assoc	Louisville	9	ZJM	PHD	80	Fla St	8-79
Rai, Arun	Asst	So Illinios	79	DUTY	PHD	90	Kent St	8-90
Raia, Anthony P.	Retir	UCLA	5	1991	PHD	63	UCLA	1969
Rainer, R. Kelly Jr.	Assoc	Auburn	9	Z	PHD	81	Georgia	9-88
Rainey, Bessye C.	Prof	St Paul's	9	Z	EDD			1969
Raiszadeh, Mohammad E.	Prof	Tenn-Chattan	7	UVW	PHD	82	LSU	1981
Rajagopalan, Nandini	Asst	So Calif	3	I	PHD		Pitt	9-88
Rajagopalan, Srinivasan	Asst	SUNY-Buffalo	3	IU	DBA	91	Columbia	1990
Rajan, G. S.	Assoc	Concordia U						
Rajan, Roby	Assoc	Wis-Parkside	7	VU	PHD	83	Va Tech	8-84
Rakestraw, Thomas L.	Assoc	Youngstown	29	EX	PHD		Purdue	9-83
Rakich, Jonathon S.	Prof	Akron	3	CIL	PHD	70	St Louis	9-72
Rallo, Joseph C.	H-Pr	Ferris State	8		PHD	80	Syracuse	1992
Ralser, Thomas	Asst	Mesa State	1		MS		Utah	1987
Ralston, David A.	Assoc	Connecticut	2	E	DBA	81	Fla St	1981
Ramadurai, K. S.	Asst	St Fran Xav	7	V	PHD		W Ontar	1989
Ramakrishna, Hindupur	Assoc	Salisbury St	79	Z	PHD	83	Geo St	8-92
Ramalingam, Panchatcharam	Prof	CS-Pomona	7	UVW	PHD	73	Oregon	1970
Ramamurti, Ravi	Assoc	Northeastern	3	YI	DBA		Harvard	9-81
Raman, Narayan	Asst	Illinois	7	UV	PHD	88	Michigan	1987
Ramana, Sheela	Asst	Idaho State	6	Z	PHD	91	Kan St	1991
Ramanathan, Jayaram	Asst	Oklahoma St	9	Z	ABD		Pitt	1-91
Ramanujam, Vasudevan	Assoc	Case Western	3	I	PHD		Pitt	
Ramaprasad, Arkalgud	Prof	So Illinois	39	IHY	PHD	80	Pitt	8-80
Ramarapu, Nariender	Asst	Tenn-Martin	79	UVZ	DBA	93	Memphis	8-93
Ramaswamy, Kannan	Asst	Fla Internat		I	PHD	90	Va Tech	1990
Ramdas, Kamalini	Asst	Texas	7	UV	PHD	94	Penn	1994
Rameau, Claude	Dean	INSEAD	7		MBA	62	INSEAD	9-67
Ramenofsky, Samuel D.	C-Ac	Loyola-Chicg			PHD		Oklahoma	1973
Ramesh, Ramaswamy	Assoc	SUNY-Buffalo	79	UZV	PHD	85	SUNY-Buf	9-84
Ramey, Judith	Asst	Univ of D C	1	A	MPA	72	Pitt	1973
Ramirez, R.	Asst	Iowa State	9	Z	PHD	87	Tx A&M	1991
Ramnarayanan, Renu	Asst	Ball State	7		PHD		Miss	1991
Ramser, Charles R.	Prof	Midwest St	25	ENST	PHD	69	North Tx	9-69
Ramsey, Gerald D.	Assoc	Indiana SE	1		PHD	75	Purdue	1980
Ramsey, Jackson Eugene	Prof	Jms Madison	3	I	PHD	75	SUNY-Buf	9-73
Ramsey, Patricia P.	Prof	Fordham	7	UV	PHD		Hofstra	1981
Ramsey, V. Jean	Prof	Txs Southern	23	R	PHD	90	Michigan	1979
Ramsoomair, H. Franklin	Asst	Wilfrid Laur	2	P	PHD		Toronto	1989
Ramsower, Reagan Mays	Prof	Baylor		Z	PHD		Minn	1976
Rana, Dharam	Assoc	Jackson St			PHD		Georgia	1980
Rand, G. K.	SLect	U Lancaster	7	UVYZ	BSC		Liverpoo	
Rand, James	Exec	Seattle Pac	57	NOPU	PHD	76	Cal West	9-93
Rand, Shirley M.	Asst	St Vincent	45		JD		Missouri	1987
Randall, Cindy House	Asst	Geo Southern	79	ZV	MBA	81	Memphis	1982
Randall, Donna	C-Pr	Wash State			PHD			
Randall, Linda	Asst	Rhode Island	38	YI	PHD	93	Mass	1993
Randolph, Janice	Lect	Mt St Mary's			MBA		Florida	
Randolph, W. Alan	Prof	Baltimore	28	DEFW	PHD	75	Mass	8-88
Rands, Gordon	Asst	Penn State	4	JLM	ABD		Minn	1992
Rangan, U. Srinivasa	Asst	Babson			DBA	88	Harvard	
Rao, H. Rhagav	Asst	SUNY-Buffalo	9	Z	PHD	87	Purdue	8-87
Rao, M. V. Hayagreeva	Asst	Emory	2	H	PHD	89	Case Wes	1989
Rao, Uday	Asst	Carnegie Mel	7	U	PHD		Cornell	1994
Rao, V. Srinivasan	Asst	British Colu	9	Z	PHD	90	Texas	1990
Rapoport, Amnon	Prof	Arizona	7	V	PHD	65	N Carol	1965
Rappa, Michael A.	Asst	MIT			PHD			
Rappaport, Jack M.	Asst	LaSalle	7	U	MS		NYU	1979
Rappell, J. C.	SLect	U Newcastle	25	EFNS	MBA		NSWIT	
Rarick, Charles A.	Prof	Transylvania			PHD		St Louis	1986
Rasberry, Robert W.	Asst	So Methodist			PHD	77	Kansas	1974
Rasch, Sara B.	Assoc	Winona State			PHD		Kansas	1988
Rasheed, Abdul	Assoc	Tx-Arlington	3	IN	PHD	88	Pitt	1988
Rasheed, Howard	VInst	West Florida	67	RS	MBA		W Fla	1990
Rasher, Arthur A.	Assoc	Tulsa	9	Z	PHD	82	Mich St	1988
Rasmussen, Erling	SLect	U Auckland	51	QNPA	PHD	86	Florente	3-93
Rasmussen, Ken A.	Asst	Univ Regina	12	AHJL	PHD		Toronto	
Rasmussen, Raymond	Prof	Univ Alberta	2	EM	PHD	70	Berkeley	1970
Rasnake, Lee R.	Inst	Radford	7	U	MBA	90	Va Tech	8-80
Raspen, Richard G.	C-Ac	Wilkes	12	&EJL	PHD		Penn	7-67
Rastetter, Arthur L.					PHD	85	Fla St	
Rath, G. Norris	C-Pr	Shepherd	35	EOQ	MS		W Virg	1963
Rathburn, Jude	Asst	N Car-Greens	23	HIJY	ABD		Ariz St	8-93
Rattner, Laurie	Asst	New Mexico	9	ZU	PHD	90	Rensssela	1992
Rausch, Bernard	Lect	Illinois Tch						1986
Raveh, Adi	SLect	Hebrew Univ			PHD		Hebrew	
Raver, Daniel H.	Asst	Geneva	13	I	MBA	85	Pitt	1980
Ravichandran, R.	Asst	Ball State	9		PHD		Indiana	1988
Ravinder, H. V.	Assoc	New Mexico	7	UV	PHD	86	Texas	1986
Ravlin, Elizabeth C.	Assoc	So Carolina			PHD	86	Car Mel	

Name	Rank	School	No.	Code	Degree	Yr	Institution	Yr
Ray, Dennis F.	Retir	Miss State	12	6-93	PHD	66	Florida	
Ray, G. H.	Lect	Univ Bath			PHD			
Ray, Howard N.	Prof	Valdosta St	9	Z	PHD	86	North Tx	1986
Ray, J. B. Jr.	C-Pr	Florida		BLaw	JD	63	Florida	1962
Ray, John W.	Assoc	Appalach St	36	STI	PHD	82	S Carol	1980
Raymond, Bruce	Asst	Montana St	7		PHD	87	Utah	8-90
Raynis, Susan A.	Asst	Clarkson	5		PHD		Colo St	
Raynolds, Peter	Prof	No Arizona	2	ED	PHD	69	UCLA	
Raza, M. Ali	Prof	CS-Sacrament	2	ENQ	PHD	62	Oregon	1968
Razavi, Mehdi B.	Assoc	Hampton	7	DIUV	PHD		Nebraska	8-89
Read, E. G.	SLect	Canterbury	7	V	PHD	79	Canterbu	1985
Read, Raymond L.	Prof	Baylor	2	EH	PHD	69	Texas	1974
Ready, Kathryn J.	Assoc	Wis-Eau Clar		QRNY	PHD		Iowa	1988
Reardon, Kathleen	Assoc	So Calif	1	D	PHD		Mass	1990
Reason, P. W.	SLect	Univ Bath	2	E	PHD			
Reavley, Martha	Asst	Univ Windsor	25	AENR	PHD	92	Wayne St	1986
Reber, Robert A.	Assoc	W Kentucky	15	NPQ	PHD	82	LSU	1982
Rebitzer, James B.	Asst	MIT	35	IN	PHD			
Rebstack, Susan	Asst	Geo Southern	79	Z	ABD		Okla St	1994
Rechner, Paula	Assoc	Houston	34	ILRJ	PHD	86	Indiana	8-90
Redding, S. G.	Prof	Un Hong Kong	23	EIN	PHD			9-82
Reddy, Mohan	Assoc	Case Western	4	L	PHD		Case Wes	
Reddy, Sabine	Asst	Wayne State			PHD	94	Illinois	1994
Reddy, Surender C.	Assoc	Saginaw Vall	78	UVXY	PHD	91	Case Wes	1989
Redel, Charles	Assoc	Wis-La Cross			JD		Wiscon	
Redlack, Austin R.	Assoc	Memorial Un	7	V	PHD	73	Warford	1969
Redmer, Timothy	Prof	Regent			PHD	88	Va Comm	1982
Redpath, Lindsay	Asst	Athabasca Un	2	EFH	PHD	92	Alberta	1992
Redwood, Anthony L.	Prof	Kansas	5	N	PHD		Illinois	1972
Reece, James S.	Prof	Michigan	3	I	DBA	70	Harvard	1975
Reed, Diana	Assoc	Drake	15	EHYR	PHD	77	Wiscon	1981
Reed, John H.	Prof	Clarion	73	AUV	PHD	72	American	8-71
Reed, M. I.	Lect	U Lancaster	25	EHP	PHD		Wales	
Reed, Marlene M.	Assoc	Samford			DBA		La Tech	1981
Reed, Patricia D.	Lect	CS-San Bern	3	E	MA	86	CS-SnBer	1988
Reed, Paul	Assoc	Sam Houston			DBA	82	Miss St	1983
Reed, Richard	Assoc	Wash State						
Reeder, A. John	Assoc	Appalach St	38	HIY	PHD		SUNY-Buf	1979
Reeder, Robert	Prof	SW Okla St	78	QS	PHD	81	Arizona	1982
Reely, Robert H. Jr.	Prof	Harding			EDD	76	Auburn	
Reeves, Carol A.	Asst	Arkansas	36	IT	PHD	88	Georgia	1990
Reeves, E. Thomas	Asst	St Marys-Txs	79	UVZ	PHD			1992
Reeves-Ellington, Richard	Lect	SUNY-Bingham	3	I	PHD	79	City Col	1991
Refenes, Paul	Assoc	London Bus						
Reger, Rhonda Kay	Asst	Arizona St	3	I	PHD	88	Illinois	1988
Regibeau, Pierre	Asst	Northwestern	78	UY	PHD	87	Berkeley	
Rehbein, Kathleen	Asst	Marquette	48	JL	PHD	85	Wash U	1987
Rehder, Robert R.	Prof	New Mexico		N	PHD	61	Stanford	
Rehfuss, John A.	Prof	CS-Sacrament	24	EL	DPA	65	S Calif	1978
Reich, Blaize Horner	Asst	Simon Fraser	93	FHIZ	ABD	93	Brit Col	1991
Reichers, Arnon E.	Assoc	Ohio State	2	E	PHD	83	Mich St	1982
Reichman, Deborah	Adj	Montana St	4		JD	83	Texas	9-88
Reid, D. M.	Asst	Un Hong Kong	3	IX	PHD			1-90
Reid, Margaret A.	Assoc	Univ Leeds	5	P	MA	76	Leeds	1989
Reid, Richard A.	Prof	New Mexico	7	UV	PHD	70	Ohio St	1971
Reif, William	Prof	Arizona St			PHD	66	Iowa	1970
Reigle, Pam	Inst	Ball State	15		MBA		Ball St	1986
Reilley, Bernard James	Prof	Widener			PHD		Geo St	
Reilly, Anne	Asst	Loyola-Chicg			PHD		Northwes	
Reimann, Bernard C.	Prof	Cleveland St	23	DH	DBA	72	Kent St	1976
Reinganum, Jennifer	Prof	Iowa	7	V	PHD	79	Northwes	1987
Reinhardt, Forest L.	Asst	Harvard	4	L				
Reinsch, N. L. Jr.	Prof	Abilene Chr	15	JND	PHD	73	Kansas	1984
on leave to Georgetown								
Reis, Dayr	Assoc	Wis-La Cross			PHD		Mich St	
Reiser, Mark	Assoc	Arizona St			PHD		Chicago	1988
Reisman, Arnold	Prof	Case Western			PHD	63	UCLA	
Reitman, Frieda	Prof	Pace-Westch	4		PHD		NYU	1982
Reitman, Walter	Prof	Rensselaer						
Reitsch, Arthur G.	Prof	Eastern Wash	3	IV	PHD	73	Oregon	1969
Reitz, Frank	Asst	N Carol Cen	25	BQS	ABD		Duke	9-89
Reitz, Joe	Prof	Kansas	2	VJ	PHD		MIT	1988
Relf, William B.	Prof	CS-Pomona	6	ST	PHD	71	Clarmont	1976
Remaley, William	Prof	Susquehanna			PHD	71	NYU	1973
Remus, William E.	Prof	Hawaii-Manoa	7	B	PHD	74	Mich St	
Renard, Monika	Asst	W Virginia	2	E				1991
Renart, Lluis G.	Asst	Univ Navarra	7	V	MBA		Chicago	9-81
Render, Barry	Prof	Rollins	79	UVZ	PHD	75	Cinn	1989
Harwood Chair Professor								
Renn, Robert W.	Asst	Memphis	12	EN	PHD	89	Geo St	1989

Name	Rank	Institution			Degree		University	
Reno, Sam C.	Prof	Neb-Kearney	34	IJL	EDD	72	Nebraska	1967
Repack, William	Asst	Robt Morris	56	PS	MS	74	Loyola	8-86
Repede, John	Asst	N Car-Charl						
Replogle, Steven	Prof	Arkansas St	7	UV	PHD	71	Arkansas	1970
Resnick, Paul	Asst	MIT	9	Z	PHD	92	MIT	
Restuccia, Joseph D.	Assoc	Boston Univ	17	CU	DPH		Berkeley	
Reutzel, Edward T.	Assoc	Penn State	7	V	PHD		Penn St	
Reve, Torger	Prof	Norwegian			PHD			
Revuelta, John	Lect	Napier Univ	38	IY	BA			1990
Reyes, Mario	Assoc	Idaho	8	Y	PHD	87	Arkansas	1985
Reyniers, Diane	Lect	London Econ	7	V	PHD		London	
Reynolds, John E.	H-Pr	Tenn State			PHD	72	Okla St	1961
Reynolds, P. M.	SLect	U Lancaster	25	NOP	PHD		Durham	
Reynolds, Paul	Prof	Marquette	6	T	PHD	69	Stanford	1990
Reza, Ernesto M.	Assoc	CS-San Bern	3	E	PHD	93	Michigan	1987
Rhee, Wansoo T.	Prof	Ohio State	7	V	PHD	79	Kent St	1981
Rhee, Yinsog	Assoc	St Cloud St	5	NQ	PHD	85	Minn	1988
Rhoads, Gary	Assoc	Brigham Yg						
Rhodes, James T.	Assoc	Christian Br			MBA		Memphis	
Rhodes, Rhonda L.	Prof	CS-Pomona	93	ZI	PHD	83	Ariz St	1985
Rhodes, Susan R.	Assoc	Syracuse	5	NE	PHD	78	Oregon	1978
Rhyne, Larry C.	Assoc	San Diego St	3	I	PHD	81	Northwes	1987
Ribbens, Barbara	Assoc	St Cloud St			ABD		Conn	1993
Ribera, Jaume	Prof	Univ Navarra	7	V	PHD		Politecn	9-82
Ribordy, A.	Asst	Laurentian	1		MBA		Laurentn	
Ricart, Joan Enric	Prof	Univ Navarra	3	I	PHD		Politecn	9-84
Rice, Charles A.	Inst	Colo-Denver			MBA	75	Denvor	
Rice, George H.	Retir	Toxas A&M			JD		Toledo	
Rice, Horace	Prof	Alabama A&M			JD		Toledo	
Rice, John J.	Asst	Hampton	4	KM	JD	73	Marsh-Wy	8-73
Richard, Donald W.	Prof	Tenn State			PHD			
Richard, Sandra	Assoc	Tx A&M Intl	38	Y	PHD		Texas	1981
Richards, Clinton	Assoc	Nev-L Vegas	23	EJNP	PHD	78	Kansas	1977
Richards, Swannie	Retir	Savannah St	1	1994	MS	58	NC Cent	1980
Richardson, Gary	Lect	Sam Houston			PHD	70	North Tx	1987
Richardson, James A.	Inst	Angelo State			MBA		AngeloSt	
Richardson, John D.			2	E	PHD	67	N Carol	
Richardson, P. R.	Prof	Queen's Univ	13	DI	PHD	75	Western	1977
Richardson, Peter E.	Assoc	SW Missouri	2	CG	PHD	79	Houston	1979
Richardson, Woody	Asst	Alabama-Birm	3	JI	PHD	86	Arkansas	1987
Richins, H.	SLect	U Newcastle	4	DLS	MBA		Oregon	
Richman, Eugene	Prof	Nev-L Vegas	17	DIUY	PHD	50	NYU	1989
Rickards, Tudor	SLect	Manchest Bus	2	DEFZ	PHD		Wales	1980
Ricker, H. O.	Assoc	Univ Regina	79	UVZ	PHD		Waterloo	
Rickman, Charles	Asst	Central Okla			PHD	90	Oklahoma	1989
Ricks, Betty R.	Retir	Old Dominion		1992	EDD	75	Va Tech	
Rico, Leonard	Emer	Pennsylvania	5	1994	PHD	61	MIT	7-67
Riddle, Emma Jane	Assoc	Winthrop	7	UZYS	PHD		S Carol	1988
Rider, Caroline V.	Assoc	Marist	45	K	JD		New York	1984
Ridgley, Diane	Lect	Neb-Kearney	9	Z	MBA	92	Nebraska	1992
Ridgley, Jerry	Assoc	Neb-Kearney	13	ES	PHD	77	Denver	1984
Ridley, Dennis	Asst	Florida A&M	7				Clemson	
Riecken, W. Glen	C-Pr	East Tenn St			PHD	79	Va Tech	1982
Rieger, F.	Assoc	Univ Windsor	38	HISY	PHD		McGill	1984
Riera, Juan	Prof	P Rico-Mayag	4		LLB	63	P Rico	8-67
Ries, John	Asst	British Colu	81	YA	PHD	90	Michigan	1990
Rifai, Ahmed K.	Prof	No Illinois		V	PHD	70	Syracuse	1970
Rifkin, Willy	Lect	U Wollongong			PHD		Stanford	9-94
Rigby, Elaine	Lect	Australian N	1	AE	MED	89	Sydney	1992
Rigby, Paul	Prof	Penn State	7	V	PHD		Texas	
Riggs, Walter E.	Assoc	Georgia St	7	U	PHD	81	S Carol	1985
Riley, M. J.	Retir	Kansas State		5-91				
Rimler, George W.	Prof	Virg Comm	67	STU	DBA	69	Geo St	1970
Rinefort, Foster C.	Assoc	E Illinios	1		PHD		Tx A&M	1981
Ring, Peter	Prof	Loyola Marym	34	IJN	PHD		Irvine	1990
Ringer, Richard	Asst	Illinois St	12		PHD	93	Colorado	1993
Ringuest, Jeffrey L.	C-Pr	Boston Coll	7	VU	PHD	81	Clemson	9-86
Rinne, Heikki	C	Brigham Yg			PHD			
Rishel, Tracy D.	Asst	Susquehanna	3	I	PHD	91	Penn St	1988
Risker, D. Christopher	Asst	Webster	1	CA	PHD	92	Colorado	1991
Ritchie, J. Bonner	Prof	Brigham Yg	12	HYQ	PHD	68	Berkeley	1973
Ritchken, Peter	Prof	Case Western			PHD	81	Case Wes	
Ritz, Zvi	Assoc	Illinois	7	V	PHD	81	Northwes	1979
Rivard, Suzanne	Prof	HEC-Montreal	9		PHD		W Ontar	
Rivera, C. Julio	Asst	Alabama-Birm	9	Z	DBA	92	S Miss	1988
Rivera, Fernando	Assoc	P Rico-Mayag	9		MS	75	Penn St	7-68
Rivera, Joan	Asst	West Txs A&M	12		PHD		Tx Tech	1993
Riverola, Josep	Prof	Univ Navarra	7	U	PHD		ETSII	9-64
Rizzo, John R.	Prof	W Michigan	25	EGFP	PHD	64	Ohio St	1969
Roach, Dave	Assoc	Ark Tech	67	ENF	PHD	91	Arkansas	8-83

Name	Rank	School			Degree		Institution	Year
Roach, Ed D.	VProf	SW Texas St	3	I	PHD		Texas	1993
Roach, William L.	Prof	Washburn			PHD	73	Michigan	1983
Robak, Nicholas J.	Prof	St Joseph	9	PSXZ	PHD	72	Penn	1972
Robbins, D. Keith	Asst	George Mason	31	ITLF	PHD	89	S Carol	1987
Robbins, M.	Lect	SUNY-Stony B	3	I	MBA	80	Harvard	1988
Robbins, Shelley R.	Asst	Wis-Milwauke	32	IH	PHD	89	Northwes	
Robbins, Stephanie S.	Assoc	N Car-Charl			PHD		LSU	1981
Robbins, Stephen R.	Retir	San Diego St	2	1993	PHD	71	Arizona	1979
Robbins, Tina	Asst	Clemson	2	EH	PHD	91	S Carol	1990
Robbins, W. David	Retir	Richmond	3	Y	PHD	53	Ohio St	1959
Roberson, Jessie	Assoc	Ohio Univ	4		JD	80	Michigan	
Roberson, Loriann	Assoc	Arizona St	5		PHD			
Roberson, Michael T.	Prof	E Kentucky	5	NPQ	PHD	86	Tenn	1987
Roberts, Barry S.	Prof	No Carolina	4	JKL	LLM	76	Harvard	1976
Roberts, Benjamin	Assoc	Naval Postgr	25	EFMP	PHD	77	Penn St	9-85
Roberts, C. Richard	Assoc	Tulsa	9	Z	PHD	78	Minn	1976
Roberts, Donald	Prof	Illinois	7	UV	PHD	59	Stanford	1959
Roberts, Edward B.	Prof	MIT			PHD			
David Sarnoff Professor of Management of Technology								
Roberts, Gary B.	Assoc	Kennesaw St	36	BIST	PHD	82	Geo St	1985
Roberts, Hilary J.	Fell	Manchest Bus	29	EFHY	PHD		Manchest	1988
Roberts, Karlene A.	Prof	Cal Berkeley	25	EQY	PHD	67	Berkeley	1968
Roberts, Lloyd	Prof	Miss College			PHD	74	Miss	1983
Roberts, Michael J.	Asst	Harvard	1					
Roberts, Nancy C.	Assoc	Naval Postgr	32	DFIH	PHD	83	Stanford	1-86
Roberts, Ralph M.	Prof	West Florida	34	BI	PHD	69	Alabama	1969
Roberts, Wayne	Assoc	Alaska SE	16	DS	PHD	89	Ariz St	1975
Robertson, Bruce D.	Asst	Lock Haven	83	YI	MAS		Illinois	9-90
Robertson, Helen	STut	Deakin Univ	25	EFN	BA	75	Monash	1989
Robertson, Ivan T.	Prof	Manches Inst	2	E	PHD			9-90
Robertson, Leon	Prof	Mo-Kansas Ct	3	I	PHD	68	Geo St	1990
Robertson-Sanders, Pat	Assoc	Howard	1	E	PHD			
Robichaux, Barry	Asst	Houston	9	Z	PHD	90	Georgia	8-90
Robinson, Alan	Exec	Simmons	38	Y	MBA	60	Columbia	
Robinson, Bettye	Assoc	Jackson St			EDD		Miss St	1992
Robinson, Don R.	Assoc	Illinois St	7		PHD		La St	
Robinson, E. Powell	Asst	Texas A&M		U	PHD	85	Texas	1992
Robinson, James	Prof	Univ Calgary	13	DI	PHD	65	Ohio St	1967
Robinson, Jerald F.	Prof	Virg Tech	5		PHD	73	Illinois	1970
Robinson, John W. Jr.	Inst	USAF Academy	1	I	MBA		RPI	
Robinson, Laura	Asst	SUNY-Stony B	46	LJ	PHD	93	Columbia	1993
Robinson, Lawrence W.	Assoc	Cornell	7	U				
Robinson, Marion	Asst	So Carol St	9	Z	PHD			1988
Robinson, O.	Read	Univ Bath	5	N	PHD			
Robinson, Patricia	Prof	Fayetteville			PHD			
Robinson, Peter	Assoc	Univ Calgary	6	ST	PHD		Brig Yg	1992
Robinson, Richard	Prof	So Carolina						
Robinson, Robert J.	Asst	Harvard	25	EN				
Robinson, Robert K.	Asst	Mississippi	35	NQ	PHD	88	North Tx	1990
Robinson, Sandra	Asst	New York U			PHD	92	Northwes	
Robinson, William N.	Asst	Georgia St	9	Z	PHD		Oreg St	
Robles, Fernando	Assoc	George Wash	8	Y	PHD	79	Penn St	
Robson, Bill	Assoc	Bishop's Un	12	DH	MBA		McMaster	1982
Robson, R. Thayne	Prof	Utah	5	Q	ABD		Cornell	1967
Robson, Ross	Assoc	Utah State	45	N	PHD	73	Maryland	9-79
Rocha, Joseph R.	Assoc	LaSierra	12	ACEK	PHD	75	Claremont	7-83
Rochlin, Robert		Lg Isl-Brook						
Rock, Marie	VInst	Bentley	23	I	MBA	86	Bentley	1990
Rockart, John F.	SLect	MIT	9	Z	PHD	68	MIT	1966
Rocke, David M.	Prof	Cal-Davis	79	VXZ	PHD		Illinois	
Rockford, Linda	Asst	Northwestern	3	HI	PHD	88	Berkeley	
Rockett, Katharine	Asst	Minn-Duluth			PHD	89	Minn	1993
Rockmore, B. Wayne	Asst	East Tenn St	53	NQI	PHD	91	Georgia	1990
Roderick, Joan C.	Assoc	SW Texas St	1	DY	EDD	85	Okla St	1985
Roderick, Roger	Dean	Arkansas St	24	EGJO	PHD	70	Illinois	1993
Rodgers, William	Assoc	San Francisc	3	I	MBA	52	S Calif	1990
Rodrigues, Carl A.	Assoc	Montclair St	18	EHY	DPA		Nova	1982
Rodriguez, Andres	Asst	Chicago			ABD	94	Stanford	1994
Rodriguez, Jose Maria	Prof	Univ Navarra	2	EN	DBA		Navarra	3-61
Rodriguez, Julissa	Inst	P Rico-Mayag	3		MBA	91	Loyola	1-92
Rodriguez, Leonardo	Prof	Fla Internat		ES	DBA	75	Fla St	1973
Roe, C. William	H-Pr	SW Louisiana	25	ENOR	DBA	76	Miss St	1990
Roebuck, Deborah M.	Assoc	Kennesaw St	1	DEFP	PHD	90	Geo St	1984
Roegiers, Charles	Prof	South Dakota	2	EP	PHD	72	Kansas	1980
Roehl, Thomas	Asst	Illinois	8	Y	PHD		Wash	1992
Roels, Shirley	C-Ac	Calvin			PHD	93	Mich St	1979
Roering, William D.	Assoc	Butler	3	I	PHD	89	Minn	1993
Roffey, Bet H.	LectB	Flinders Un	35	AFIP	MBA	90	RMIT	1991
Rogalski, Richard J.	Prof	Dartmouth			PHD	74	Michigan	1976
Roger, Craig	Asst	Nicholls St	97	Z	MBA	77	NcholSt	1971

Name	Rank	School	#	Code	Deg	#	School2	Year
Rosser, Leonard	Prof	Memphis	26	St	DBA	70	Miss St	1967
Rossi, Thomas	D-Ac	Utica	15	BHIN	MBA			1979
Rossin, Donald F.	Asst	Mich-Dearbor	7	TU	PHD	85	UCLA	1994
Rossy, Gerard L.	C-Ac	CS-Northrdge	34	DIMP	PHD	79	UCLA	1977
Roszkowski, Mark	Assoc	Illinois	4	KL	JD	75	Illinois	1975
Roth, Allan	Prof	Rutgers-Newk	8	Y	JD		Harvard	1969
Roth, Kevin J.	Assoc	Clarion	36	I	ABD		Pitt	8-90
Roth, Larry	Assoc	St Cloud St	51	NPQ	PHD	71	Tulane	1990
Roth, Phillip L.	Assoc	Clemson	2	EH	PHD	88	Houston	1991
Roth, Roberta M.	Asst	No Iowa			PHD	90	Iowa	8-80
Rothberg, Helen	Asst	Rutgers-Newk	23	EIA	PHD	90	Baruch	1989
Rothermel, Mary Anne	Assoc	Akron	7	VXP	PHD	81	Ohio St	9-84
Rothman, Miriam	Assoc	San Diego	25	NQY	PHD	84	U Wash	1984
Rothstein, H.	Assoc	CUNY-Baruch	5	P	PHD		Maryland	1980
Rothstein, Steven Maze	Adj	Boston Univ	83	YI	MBA		Northeas	
Rotondi, Thomas	Assoc	Marquette	3	I	DBA	72	Colorado	1973
Rotter, Naomi	Prof	NJ Inst Tech	52	NE	PHD	74	NYU	1974
Roukis, George S.	Prof	Hofstra	5	KQY	PHD	73	NYU	9-78
Roure, Juan	Prof	Univ Navarra	7	V	PHD		Stanford	7-81
Rouse, Joanne	Prof	No Illinois			MS		N Illin	
Rousseau, Denise M.	Prof	Northwestern	2	E	PHD	77	Berkeley	1981
Rovelstad, James	C	Wis-Parkside		Mktg	PHD	70	Michigan	8-82
Rovenpor, Janet	Asst	Manhattan	34	DI				
Rowan, Richard L.	Prof	Pennsylvania	5	NQY	PHD	61	N Carol	7-61
Rowe, Mary P.	Adj	MIT	5	QN				
Rowland, Sam E.	Lect	Texas A&M		St	JD	69	So Meth	1985
Rowley, Daniel James	Assoc	No Colorado	23		PHD	87	Colorado	
Rowney, J. I. A.	Prof	Univ Calgary	25	FNR	PHD	75	Calgary	1978
Roy, Asim	Assoc	Arizona St			PHD		Texas	1983
Roy, J. Adams	Prof	McMaster Un	5	Q	PHD	73	Wiscon	
Roy, Melvin	Prof	Appalach St	9	Z	PHD		N Colo	1973
Roy, Prober	Assoc	Mo-Kansas Ct	7	V	PHD		Cinn	1983
Roy, Sam	Assoc	Moorhead St	97	VZ	MBA		LSU	1978
Roychoudhury, Buddhadev	Asst	Mankato St			PHD	91	Indiana	1990
Royksund, Conrad	Prof	Luther	49	LZ	PHD	70	Chicago	1969
Rozell, Elizabeth	Asst	Missouri So			PHD	93	Miss	1992
Rozelle, James P.	Retir	Georgia St	9	1992	PHD		Geo St	
Rubenfeld, Stephen A.	Prof	Minn-Duluth	5	NOPQ	PHD	77	Wiscon	1973
Rubenson, George	Assoc	Salisbury St	35	INT	PHD	89	Maryland	8-87
Rubery, Jill C.	Lect	Manches Inst	5	Q	PHD		Cambridg	8-89
Rubin, Beth	Asst	U Manitoba	25	AQR	PHD	90	Michigan	1990
Rubin, Paul A.	Assoc	Michigan St	7	V	PHD	80	Mich St	1-80
Ruble, Thomas L.	Assoc	Rider	12	E	PHD	73	UCLA	1981
Ruch, Richard S.	Dean	Rider	32	DFNQ	PHD	76	Rennesl	1982
Ruch, William A.	Prof	Arizona St	7	U	DBA		Indiana	1968
Ruchs, Andy	Prof	Samford	7	U				
Rucker, William A. III	Asst	Ark-Pine Blf			MS		US Naval	
Rude, Dale E.	Assoc	Houston	2	EX	PHD	84	Iowa	8-93
Rudell, LaVerne	C-Pr	Neb Wesleyan	45		PHD	82	Nebraska	1971
Rudin, Joel	Asst	St Louis			PHD		Cornell	
Rudolf, Uwe	Prof	Luther	18	DY	MBA	78	S Calif	1971
Rue, Leslie W.	Prof	Georgia St	13	I	PHD	73	Geo St	1974
Ruefli, Timothy W.	Prof	Texas	3	IV	PHD	69	Car Mel	1968
Rueschhoff, M. Susan	Assoc	No Iowa			PHD	86	Nebraska	8-85
Rugimbona, R.	STut	U Newcastle	8	Y	MBA			
Ruhe, John A.	Assoc	St Marys-Ind	34	J	PHD	73	Florida	8-78
Ruhleder, Karen	Asst	Worcester Pl	9	Z	PHD	91	Ca-Irvine	8-92
Ruhnka, John C.	Prof	Colo-Denver			LLM	91	Cambridg	
Ruhnke, Henry O.	Asst	St Johns			MBA	64	Baruch	
Rumelt, Richard P.	Prof	UCLA	3	I	DBA	72	Harvard	1976
Rummel, Jeff	Assoc	Duke			PHD		Rochest	
Rundle, Jaclyn	Asst	East Central	23	EFHJ	PHD	92	Utah	8-93
Ruocco, Joseph	Assoc	Adelphi	52	NPEF	PHD	62	Fordham	1981
Rush, Michael C.	Prof	Tennessee	25	ENP	PHD	78	Akron	9-78
Rusinko, Cathy	Asst	Villanova	32	IFH	PHD	92	Penn St	1991
Russ, Gail	Asst	Illinois St	32		PHD		Tx A&M	1990
Russell, C. W. Jr.	C-Ac	Carson-Newm	45	KNPQ	JD		Tenn	1991
Russell, Craig	Assoc	Louisiana St	5	PN	PHD	82	Iowa	8-91
Russell, Gregory R.	Asst	Geo Southern	7	U	PHD	93	S Carol	1992
Russell, James W.	Assoc	Pace	37	IVY	PHD	86	New York	1-76
Russell, John R.	Prof	Boston Univ	34	ILQ	DBA		Harvard	
Russell, Joyce E. A.	Assoc	Tennessee	25	ENP	PHD	82	Akron	9-82
Russell, Randy	Assoc	Univ Calgary	7	U	PHD		Ohio St	1993
Russell, Robert	Asst	Emory Henry	37	IU	MBA	84	Virginia	1984
Russell, Robert		Stonehill	16		MBA		Boston U	1987
Russell, Robert A.	Prof	Tulsa	7	UV	PHD	72	Texas	1973
Russell, Robert D.	Asst	Penn St-Harr	6	ST	PHD	90	Pitt	1991
Russo, Joseph A.	Prof	Pace			PHD	93	Rutgers	
Russo, Michael V.	Asst	Oregon	34	IL	PHD	89	Berkeley	1989
Russo, Nancy	Asst	No Illinois		Z				

Name	Rank	School	#	Codes	Degree	#	Grad School	Year
Rutenberg, D. P.	Prof	Queen's Univ	38	IY	PHD	67	Berkeley	1977
Ruthstrom, Carl R.	Assoc	Houston-Down	67	SUVW	PHD	86	Texas	9-90
Rutland, John	Asst	U Lethbridge	31	IML	PHD		Wash	1990
Rutsohn, Phil	Prof	Augusta	14	ACK	DPH	76	Texas	1976
Ruud, William N.	Dean	Boise State	21		PHD		Nebraska	9-93
Ryan CSV, Leo V.	Prof	DePaul			PHD		St Louis	
Ryan, Allan	Asst	Univ Alberta	43	HI			Cornell	1993
Ryan, Grace Ann	Asst	Ind-Penna	23	DEFH	PHD	82	Pitt	1981
Ryan, John	Assoc	Ind-Penna	12	EZ	PHD	92	Pitt	1987
Ryan, John	SLect	Napier Univ	3	IY	MBA			1976
Ryan, Lori V.	Asst	Georgia	34	HIJL	PHD	94	Wash	1994
Ryan, Mike	Asst	North Texas	3	ILM	PHD	85	Tx-Dallas	1991
Ryan, William	Assoc	Fla Atlantic	23	HIY	DBA	66	Indiana	8-67
Ryba, Walter G. Jr.	Assoc	Fairfield	43	JILY	JD	75	Conn	1982
Rydl, Les		Tx-Pan Amer	79	VZ	PHD			
Ryeson, James	Assoc	Marymount			MBA		Clarkson	1982
Ryland, Elisabeth K.	Prof	CS-San Bern	3	E	PHD	86	N Carol	1986
Rynes, Sara	Prof	Iowa	5	N	PHD	81	Wiscon	1990
Ryu, Young	Asst	Texas-Dallas	7	V				
Saad, Germaine	Assoc	Widener			PHD		Penn	
Saaty, Thomas L.	Prof	Pittsburgh	7		PHD	53	Yale	
University Professor								
Saba, Alexandra	Asst	Woodbury	23	E	PHD	81	Stanford	4-93
Sabavala, Darius	Assoc	Polytechnic			PHD		Columbia	
Sabo, R. Richard	Prof	CS-Pomona	5	N	MBA	65	San Jose	1967
Sabria, Frederic	Asst	Univ Navarra	7	V	PHD		ETSICCP	6-87
Sacchetti, G.	Asst	Lakehead U	9	Z	MBA	93	Queens	
Sacino, Joseph J.	Asst	Marist	34	EIL	EDD		Seton I II	1988
Sack, Allen	Prof	New Haven	1	BD	PHD		Penn St	
Sackett, Paul	Prof	Minnesota	5	NP	PHD	79	Ohio St	
Sadan, Simcha	Assoc	Tel Aviv Un		F	PHD	72	Berkeley	1974
Sadd, William C.	Asst	Assumption	34	IL	MBA	63	Dartmout	1986
Saddoris, Jane Weston	Inst	West Chester			MA		Villanov	1971
Sadoughi, Mohammad	Assoc	Delaware St			EDD			1990
Saenz, Francisco R.	Adj	Southeastern			PHD		Columbia	
Safayeni, F.	Assoc	Un Waterloo	2	EH	PHD	79	Victoria	1980
Safizadeh, Hossein M.	Asst	Boston Coll	7	UV	PHD	80	Okla St	9-89
Sagafi-Nejad, Tagi	Prof	Loyola-Maryl	8	Y	PHD		Penn	1985
Sage, Earl R.	Assoc	N Car-Charl			PHD	73	Ohio St	1973
Sager, Thomas W.	Assoc	Texas	7	V	PHD	73	Iowa	1979
Saha, Sudhir K.	Prof	Memorial Un	25		PHD	72	Brit Col	1980
Sahlman, William A.	Prof	Harvard	1					
Dimitri V. Arbeloff MBA Class of 1955 Professor of Business Administration								
Sakamoto, Shiori	Prof	CS-Pomona	5	N	DBA	75	S Calif	1972
Saker, James M.	Lect	Loughborough	3	I	MSC		Warwick	
Saks, A.	Asst	Concordia U						
Saladin, Brooke	Assoc	Wake Fr-MBA	7	U	PHD	80	Ohio St	1983
Salam, Ahmad W.	Prof	Widener			PHD	68	Illinois	
Salama, Ibrahim M.	Assoc	So Carol St	2	E	MS	65	Colo St	1973
Salameh, Tamer	Asst	US Intl	9	Z	DBA		US Intl	1989
Salamone, Joseph F.	Assoc	SUNY-Buffalo	5	NQ	MBA	73	SUNY-Buf	9-81
Salancik, Gerald R.	H-Pr	Ill-Chicago	2	BECH	PHD	71	Yale	8-93
Salazar, Ron	Asst	Idaho State		I	PHD	90	Texas	1993
Salchenberger, Linda M.	Assoc	Loyola-Chicg			PHD		Northwes	1985
Salegna, Gary	Asst	Illinois St	7		PHD		Tx Tech	1991
Saleh, S. D.	Prof	Un Waterloo	25	DEYH	PHD	63	Case Wes	1967
Sales, Carol A.	Assoc	Brock Univ	25	EFGH	PHD		Waterloo	1979
Salimian, Fatollah	Asst	Salisbury St	7	UV	ABD		Kent St	8-82
Salinas, Teresita S.	Assoc	Washburn			PHD	80	Kansas	1982
Salipante, Paul F. Jr.	C-Pr	Case Western	5	QNY	PHD	75	Chicago	1975
Salisbury, Tiina	Lect	McMaster Un	17	UV	MBA		McMaster	
Salk, Jane E.	Asst	Duke	8	EH	PHD		MIT	1991
Salkin, Harvey	Prof	Case Western			PHD	69	Renssela	1969
Saloner, Garth	Prof	Stanford	3	I				
Robert A. Magowan Professor of Economics and Strategic Management								
Salorio, Eugene M.	Asst	Georgetown	83	YIL	PHD	91	Harvard	9-89
Salstrom, Roger	Assoc	San Jose St	7	UV	PHD	89	Berkeley	1989
Salter, Malcolm S.	Prof	Harvard	1					
MBA Class of 1952 Professor of Business Administration								
Saltzman, Gregory M.	Assoc	Albion		QN	PHD	82	Wiscon	1986
Saluja, Madan	Prof	Lk Superior	15	KNQR	PHD		Minn	9-69
Salvate, James M.	Prof	CS-Pomona	73	UWI	PHD	70	Columbia	1985
Samaras, John	Prof	Central Okla			PHD	82	Oklahoma	1975
Sambamurthy, V.	Asst	Florida St	9	Z	PHD	89	Minn	8-89
Sambharya, Rakesh	Asst	Rutgers-Camd			PHD			
Sample, Travis	Prof	Shenandoah			DPA		USC	1987
Sampler, Jeff	Asst	London Bus	9	ZDIH	PHD			1990
Sampson, Nancy S.	Prof	Denver	1	Z	DBA	71	Oklahoma	1-72
Sampson, Scott	Asst	Florida St	7	U	DBA		Virginia	8-93
Samuel, Phillips	Assoc	Shenandoah			PHD		Houston	1993

Name	Rank	Institution			Degree		Degree Inst	Year
Samuelson, Susan S.	Asst	Boston Univ	4	K	JD		Harvard	
Sanchez, Pedro	Prof	George Wash	7	V				
Sanchez, Ronald	Asst	Illinois	3	I	PHD	91	MIT	1991
Sanchez, Victoria D.	Asst	E New Mexico	52	ENR	PHD	86	Ariz St	1972
Sanchez-Runde, Carlos	Asst	Univ Navarra	5	N	MBA		Navarra	6-90
Sandberg, Mark E.	Assoc	Rider	2	P	PHD	71	Cornell	1970
Sandberg, William R.	Assoc	So Carolina			PHD	84	Georgia	
Sandbothe, Richard	Asst	SUNY-Bingham	7	UVX	PHD	86	Car Mel	1989
Sandelands, Lance E.	Assoc	Michigan	2	E	PHD	82	Penn	1989
Sanders, Charles	Asst	Dillard						
Sanders, Eddie Jr.	C-Ac	Chicago St	5	N	PHD		Cal Coas	1973
Sanders, G. Lawrence	Assoc	SUNY-Buffalo	9	Z	PHD	83	Tx Tech	1983
Sanders, Martha	Asst	Wichita St	25	EFNP	PHD	91	Ohio St	9-91
Sanders, Nada R.	Asst	Wright State	7	U	PHD	86	Ohio St	1988
Sanders, Patricia	Dean$	Siena Coll	28	FY	PHD		Conn	9-93
Sanderson, Susan	Assoc	Rensselaer	8	Y	PHD		Pitt	
Sandver, Marcus H.	Prof	Ohio State	5	Q	PHD	76	Wiscon	1976
Sankar, Chetan	Assoc	Auburn	9	Z	PHD	81	Penn	9-89
Sankar, Yassin	Prof	Dalhousie U			PHD		JHopkins	
Sankaran, Sam	Prof	Univ Regina	47	LUVX	DBA		Indiana	
Sankowsky, Daniel A.	C-Ac	Suffolk			PHD		Berkeley	
Santana-Melgoza, Carmen	Asst	New Mex St	24	EIR	PHD	90	Ariz St	1984
Santoma, Javier	Assoc	Univ Navarra	7	V	PHD		Penn	7-81
Sanyal, Rajib	Assoc	Trenton St			PHD		Geo St	
Sappington, Sidney	Asst	York of PA	4	K	JD		Balitmor	
Sara, Tejinder	C-Pr	Tuskegee			PHD	74	Mass	9-73
Sarachek, Bernard	Prof	Mo-Kansas Ct	8	Y	PHD	62	Illinois	1970
Saraph, Jayant	Prof	St Cloud St	73	UV	PHD	87	Minn	1985
Sarathy, Ravi	Prof	Northeastern	8	IZY	PHD		Michigan	9-80
Sargent, George	Assoc	Wis-Whitewat	9	DZ	PHD	75	Mich St	1987
Sarig, Oded	Assoc	Tel Aviv Un		F	PHD	83	Berkeley	1987
Sarigollu, E.	Asst	McGill Univ	3		PHD		Penn	1988
Sarin, Rakesh K.	Prof	UCLA	7	U	PHD	75	UCLA	1979
Sarnat, Marshall	Prof	Hebrew Univ			PHD		Northwes	
Sass, Robert	Prof	Saskatchewan	5	QC	MS	67	Cornell	1982
Sassalos, Susan	Asst	Cal-Riversid						
Sasser, W. Earl Jr.	Prof	Harvard	7	U				
The UPS Foundation Professor of Service Management								
Sathe, Vijay	Prof	Claremont Gr	12	DEFH	PHD		Ohio St	1987
Sato, Ryo	Asst	Univ Tsukuba	9	Z	PHD	89	Toyko In	4-88
Satterlee, Brian	C-Ac	Warner So	14	EIJN	EDD	91	Nova	1992
Satterwaite, Mark A.	Prof	Northwestern	37	IUV	PHD	73	Wiscon	
Earl Dean Howard Professor of Managerial Economics								
Satzinger, John W.	Asst	Georgia	9	Z	PHD	91	Claremont	1991
Sauer, Robert	Prof	Wis-Whitewat	5	ENQY	PHD	69	Wiscon	1965
Sauer, William	Prof	Susquehanna	6		PHD	75	Minn	1989
Sauers, Dale G.	Prof	York of PA	7	UV	MBA		Houston	1978
Sauers, Daniel A.					PHD	86	Fla St	
Sauget, Clyde	Assoc	Guam	81	Z	PHD	77	Gold Gt	1993
Saunders, David M.	Assoc	McGill Univ	2		PHD		W Ont	1986
Saunders, Homer L.	Deces	Cen Arkansas	63	3-93	PHD	77	Arkansas	8-67
Sauter, Fred	Asst	Susquehanna	4		MBA	67	Columbia	1967
Savage, Grant T.	Assoc	Texas Tech	12	CEI	PHD	84	Ohio St	1983
Savas, E. S.	Prof	CUNY-Baruch	1	A	PHD		Columbia	1960
Savino, David M.	Assoc	Ohio Northrn	52	QNE	MBA	79	Young St	6-86
Sawaya, William J.	Assoc	Brigham Yg	7	U	PHD	71	Arizona	1978
Sawhney, Shiv	C	Quinnipiac	13	BDI	PHD		NYU	
Sawyer, Granville	H-Ac	Norfolk St		T	PHD		Tenn	7-92
Sawyer, John E.	Asst	Delaware			PHD	87	Illinois	1991
Saxberg, Borje	Prof	U Washington	26	DHTY	PHD	58	Illinois	1957
Saxena, Narain D.	Retir	Kentucky St	7	5-94	DBA	73	Kent St	1989
Saxton, Todd	Asst	Louisville	38	ITY	BA	85	Virginia	8-94
Saydam, Cem A.	Assoc	N Car-Charl			PHD		Clemson	1986
Sayeed, Lutfus	Asst	W Virginia	9	Z				1991
Sayles, Leonard	Reitr	Columbia	2	E	PHD	50	MIT	1956
Scalberg, Ernest	Dean	Fordham		EU	PHD		UCLA	1994
Scales, Cinda	Asst	Shepherd	4	K	LLD		Maryland	1984
Scaletta, Phillip J.	Prof	Purdue	4	K	JD	50	Iowa	1966
Scamehorn, Richard	Lect	Ohio Univ	38		MBA	67	Indiana	
Scamell, Richard W.	Prof	Houston	9	Z	PHD	72	Texas	1972
Scandura, Terri A.	Assoc	U Miami	28	EOYR	PHD	88	Cinn	1990
Scanlan, Bert K.	Prof	Oklahoma	12	DEX	PHD	64	Nebraska	6-69
David Ross Boyd Professor								
Scarborough, David	Asst	Tx-Perm Bas			ABD		North Tx	
Scarborough, Jack W.	Assoc	Barry	38	IYE	PHD	88	Maryland	8-89
Scarpello, Vida	Prof	Georgia St	25	EFIN	PHD	80	Minn	1992
Schachter, Hindy L.	Prof	NJ Inst Tech	92	ZE	PHD	79	Columbia	1979
Schaefer, Norbert V.	Prof	New Brunswic	34	ILTY	PHD	78	Berkeley	1976
Schaefer, Susan	Prof	CS-Hayward	52	NX	PHD	73	Stanford	1970
Schaefer, Thomas E.	Prof	Tx-Prm Basin			PHD	63	Geotown	

Name	Rank	Institution			Degree		School	Year
Schroeder, Dean	Assoc	Valparaiso	3	IU	PHD	85	Minn	1990
Schroeder, Hal	Assoc	U Lethbridge	34	IL	PHD	81	S Calif	1981
Schroeder, Machelle	Asst	Wis-Plattev	5	N	MBA		Wi-White	1990
Schuh, Allen J.	Prof	CS-Hayward	2	E	PHD	73	Ohio St	1971
Schuler, Douglas	Asst	Rice	4	K	PHD	91	Minn	1991
Schuler, Randall S.	Prof	New York U			PHD	73	Mich St	
Research Professor								
Schulman, Martin	Assoc	SUNY-Bingham	1	A	PHD	83	Fla St	1986
Schulte Jr., William D.	Dir	George Mason	16	IDTY	MS	86	LSU	1988
Schultz, Carl R.	Prof	New Mexico	7	UV	PHD	79	N Carol	1981
Schultz, Marian C.	Assoc	West Florida	12	CEGO	PHD	82	S Calif	1989
Schultz, Todd A.	Assoc	Augusta	79	UVZ	PHD	87	J Hopkin	1987
Schulz, Martin	Asst	U Washington	27	JH	ABD		Stanford	9-93
Schulz, Robert	Prof	Univ Calgary	36	IT	PHD	71	Ohio St	1973
Schulz, William	Asst	Ogelthorpe	36	TIYD	PHD	93	Georgia	8-92
Schulze, W.	Asst	Connecticut		I	PHD	94	Colorado	1994
Schumann, Paul	Assoc	Mankato St			PHD	83	Cornell	1987
Schuster, Fred E.	Prof	Fla Atlantic	25	NEFL	DBA	69	Harvard	1969
Schuster, Michael	Prof	Syracuse	5	N	PHD	79	Syracuse	1980
Schuster, Stephan D.	Retir	CS-Northrdge	25	EFGP	PHD	66	Texas	1982
Schuttler, Robert	Inst	Marian			MBA	80	Evansvil	
Schwab, Bernhard	Prof	British Colu	7	IV	PHD	67	UCLA	1968
Schwab, Donald P.	Prof	Wisconsin		ENQX	PHD	68	Minn	
Schwab, Robert	Prof	Andrews	2	E	PHD		Oregon	1993
Schwallie, Ed	Inst	Oregon State	7	U				
Schwartz, Howard S.	Prof	Oakland	2	HJ	PHD	80	Cornell	1978
Schwartz, Jules J.	Prof	Boston Univ	37	IVX	DBA		Harvard	
Schwartz, Ned S.	C-Ac	W New Eng	3	I	JD		Emory	1979
Schwartz, Robert H.	Assoc	Toledo	2		PHD		Michigan	1988
Schwartz, Ronald D.	Assoc	Wilkes	79	UVXZ	PHD		Akron	9-90
Schwartz, Stanley J.	Assoc	Rider	15	Q	EDD		Temple	1978
Schwartz, Theodore M.	Prof	Iona	2	EF	PHD	65	New York	1963
Schwarz, Joshua L.	Assoc	Miami U-Ohio	5	KL	PHD	85	Cornell	8-89
Schwarz, Leroy	Prof	Purdue	7	U	PHD	71	Chicago	1977
Schwarz, Samuel	Assoc	CUNY-Stn Isl	7	UV	PHD		Columbia	1986
Schwarze, John	Assoc	Warner So	5	UZ	MBA	74	St Franc	1989
Schwarzkopf, A. B.	D-Ac	Oklahoma	97	ZVU	PHD	68	Virginia	9-70
Schweiger, David M.	Prof	So Carolina			DBA	80	Maryland	
Schweitzer, Maurice E.	Asst	U Miami	17	CVX	PHD	93	Penn	1994
Schweitzer, Paul J.	Prof	Rochester	7	U	SCD		MIT	
Schweizer, Jason	Assoc	Am Grad Intl	52	NEY	PHD	79	Nebraska	
Schweizer, Timothy	Assoc	Luther	25	EQ	PHD	88	Arkansas	1987
Schwenk, Charles R.	Prof	Indiana	3	I	DBA	80	Indiana	1986
Schwering, Randolph	Asst	Rockhurst	91	APZF	PHD	87	Kansas	1989
Schwind, Hermann F.	Prof	St Marys-Cnd	58	NW	PHD	79	Brit Col	1976
Schwochau, Susan	Asst	Iowa	5	Q	PHD	86	Illinois	1990
Schwoerer, Catherine	Assoc	Kansas	2	EO	PHD	90	N Carol	1989
Sciarrino, Alfred	Asst	SUNY-Geneseo	4	K	LLM	84	Wiscon	9-90
Scifres, Elton L.	Asst	S F Austin	32	I	PHD	94	LSU	1993
Scinta, Kate	Lect	Indiana SE	1	&	MA	80	Boston C	1993
Scott Morton, Michael S.	Prof	MIT	3	I	DBA	67	Harvard	1966
Jay W. Forrester Professor of Management								
Scott, C. Richard	Assoc	Metro State	35	YIN	DBA	88	La Tech	1991
Scott, Carlton H.	Prof	Calif-Irvine	7	UV	PHD	71	NS Wales	1982
Scott, Charlotte H.	Prof	Virginia			LLD		Alleghen	
University Professor								
Scott, Clyde J.	Assoc	Alabama	5	AN	PHD	82	Minn	1981
Scott, Cuthbert L. III	Assoc	Indiana NW	23	FHI	PHD	75	Oregon	1982
Scott, Frederick C.	Assoc	Boston Univ	36	LT	MBA		Harvard	
Scott, George M.	Prof	Connecticut	79	UZ	DBA	68	U Wash	9-81
Scott, K. Dow	Assoc	Virg Tech	5		PHD	79	Mich St	1979
Scott, Philip	Lect	U Wollongong			MBA		Georgia	1-92
Scott, Richard C.	Dean	Baylor	6	Mgt	DBA	68	Indiana	1968
Scott, Robert A.	Assoc	Alabama-Birm	1	A	PHD	78	Geo St	1976
Scott, Robert L.	C-Pr	Benedict Col		Mgt	EDD		S Carol	
Scott, Timothy	Prof	Mankato St			PHD	74	Minn	1974
Scott, W. Richard	Prof	Stanford	2	EFGH	PHD	61	Chicago	1960
Scott, Walter D.	Prof	Northwestern	18	DY	MS	58	Columbia	
Scott, William C.	Prof	Indiana St	13	I	PHD		Iowa	8-77
Scott, William E. Jr.	Reitr	Indiana	2	H	PHD	63	Purdue	
Scott, William G.	Prof	U Washington	12	ABH	DBA	57	Indiana	1966
Scotti, Dennis J.	Prof	F Dick-Madis	1		PHD		Temple	
Scoville, James	Prof	Minnesota	5	Q	PHD	65	Harvard	
Scow, Roger	Lect	SW Texas St	6	S	MBA	83	SW Tx St	1983
Scriven, Jolene D.	Assoc	No Illinois	1	D	EDD		N Illin	
Scudder, Gary D.	Prof	Vanderbilt	7	UVWX	PHD	81	Stanford	9-90
Scully, Judity	Asst	Florida	25	ENQ	PHD	94	Maryland	1994
Scully, Maureen		MIT	5	QN				
Sealey, C. W.	Prof	McGill Univ	1		PHD		Georgia	
Sealy, Hyacinth	Lect	Morgan State						1980

Name	Rank	School			Degree		Institution	Year
Seaman, John W. Jr.	Assoc	Baylor		V	PHD		Tx-Dallas	1989
Randall W. & Sandra Ferguson Professor of Information Systems								
Seaman, Samuel L.	Assoc	Baylor		V	PHD		Florida	1987
Seaquist, Gwen	Assoc	Ithaca	4		JD	78	Miss	8-79
Searle, Frank R.					DBA	74	Fla St	
Sears, Paul	Assoc	Baldwin-Wal	6	ST	PHD		Case Wes	
Seawright, Kristie	Asst	Brigham Yg	73	UIVL	PHD	93	Utah	1993
Seay, Robert M.	Asst	East Txs St	27	U	DBA	85	La Tech	1982
Sebastian, Richard J.	Prof	St Cloud St	2	GE	PHD	74	Wiscon	1983
Sebora, Terrence C.	Asst	Nebraska	3	I	PHD	92	N Carol	8-89
Seeger, John	Prof	Bentley	34	I	DBA	78	Harvard	1982
Seeley, Robert D.	Assoc	Wilkes	5	Q	PHD		Maryland	9-89
Seely, Doug	AcAs	U Lethbridge	9		BED		Lethbrid	1988
Seers, Anson	Assoc	Alabama	2	E	PHD	81	Cinn	1980
Segall, Maurice	SLect	MIT	3	I				
Segar, James	Assoc	S Col 7th Dy	15	ABI	MA	68	Cen Mich	1994
Segarra, Jose Antonio	Asst	Univ Navarra	7	V	MBA		Navarra	9-80
Segars, Albert H.	Asst	Boston Coll	93	ZI	PHD	94	S Carol	9-94
Segev, Arie	Assoc	Cal-Berkeley	9	Z	PHD		Rochest	1983
Segovis, James	Asst	Bryant	2	EGH	PHD	90	Texas	8-92
Segrist, Cheryl A.			2	E	PHD	81	N Carol	
Segui, Miguel	Asst	P Rico-Mayag	7		MBA	92	Catholic	6-86
Seguin, Francine	D-Pr	HEC-Montreal	12	H	PHD		Harvard	
Sehadri, Srivatsa	Asst	Neb-Kearney	87	XYVI	PHD	93	Arkansas	1993
Seibert, Scott	Asst	Notre Dame	15		PHD	93	Cornell	1991
Seidmann, Abraham	Assoc	Rochester	97	ZU	PHD		Tx Tech	
Seila, Andrew F.	Assoc	Georgia	7	V	PHD		N Carol	
Seldin, Peter	Prof	Pace-Westch	2		PHD	74	Fordham	1979
Distinguished Professor			7	U	PHD	69	N Carol	
Seleim, Mohammed	Asst	Alabama St	5	N	PHD		Georgia	8-91
Self, Robin	Prof	LaSierra	8	Y	PHD	64	American	7-84
Selivanoff, George A.	Assoc	Alaska-Ancho	61	ST	MBA	77	Alaska	1981
Selk, Gary	Inst	Prairie View	25	EHNY	ABD	89	Tx A&M	1986
Selladurai, Raja S.	Prof	Youngstown	23	EIN	PHD		Kent St	9-84
Sellaro, Louise	Prof	Belmont	72	U	PHD	76	Vanderbt	1976
Sellick, Jay P.	Assoc	American U	7	UV	DSCI	69	Geo Wash	1976
Selman, Victor	Prof	LaSalle	2	E	PHD		Pitt	1976
Seltzer, Joseph	C-Ac	West Chester			PHD		Paris	1986
Selvanathan, Rani G.	SLect	Griffith Un	7	VY	PHD	89	W.A.	8-89
Selvanathan, Saroja	C	Jackson St		N	PHD		Wayne St	1981
Semko, Elizabeth A.	VAsst	NJ Inst Tech	9	Z	PHD	90	Calcutta	1992
Sen, Anup	Assoc	Texas A&M		Z	PHD	79	Penn St	1986
Sen, Arun	Prof	St John Fish	79		PHD		Rutgers	
Sen, Asim	Asst	Towson State	79		PHD		Alabama	1992
Sen, Babita	Assoc	Fordham	13	DEI	PHD		Northwes	1986
Sen, Falguni K.	Assoc	Concordia U			PHD			
Sen, J.	Prof	N Carol A&T	7		DBA	80	Tx Tech	8-92
Sen, Tapan								
Sena, James	Prof	Cal Poly-SLO	9	Z	DBA	72	Kentucky	1987
Sendall, Patricia	Asst	Merrimack		ZOR	MBA		St Joe	1990
Sendry, Jeanett	Inst	W Illinois			PHD	77	UCLA	1977
Sengupta, Kishore	Asst	Naval Postgr	9	VX	PHD	90	Case Wes	9-89
Senn, James A.	Prof	Georgia St	9	Z	PHD		Minn	
Senn, Robert	Prof	Shippensburg			JD		Syracuse	
Sepehri, Mohamad	Assoc	Jacksonvil U	38	DIYZ	PHD	82	Indiana	1989
Sepic, F. Thomas	Prof	Pacific Luth	25	EFNP	PHD	79	U Wash	1979
Serafin, Louise	Asst	Calif U-Penn	5	FHI	ABD		Pitt	1989
Serapio, Manuel	Asst	Colo-Denver	28	HY	PHD	88	Illinois	1989
Serey, Timothy T.	Prof	No Kentucky	28	EY	PHD	81	Cinn	8-80
Seshan, Venkatachalam	Assoc	Pepper-Malib	38	ILMY	PHD	65	Lehigh	1986
Seth, Anju	Asst	Houston	38	IYXL	PHD	88	Michigan	8-87
Sethi, S. Prakash	Prof	CUNY-Baruch	8	Z	PHD		Columbia	1968
Sethi, Vijay	Assoc	Oklahoma	9	Z	PHD	88	Pitt	9-91
Sethia, Nirmal K.	Prof	CS-Pomona	9	Y	PHD	80	IndianIn	1991
Sethuraman, Kannan	Asst	Michigan	7	U	PHD	93	Penn	1992
Seward, James M.	Assoc	Dartmouth			PHD	87	Wiscon	1987
Seward, Samuel	Prof	Sonoma State	7	UV	DBA	76	Colorado	9-89
Sewell, Graham	SLect	U Wollongong	7	Y	PHD		Wales	9-94
Sexton, Don	Prof	Ohio State	3	IT	PHD	72	Ohio St	1986
Sexton, Thomas R.	Assoc	SUNY-Stony B	7	CV	PHD	79	SUNY-SBr	1979
Sexton, William P.	Prof	Notre Dame	12	EF	PHD	66	Ohio St	
Sexty, Robert	Prof	Memorial Un	43		PHD	74	Colorado	1968
Seybolt, Patricia	ResAc	Utah	5	QNP	PHD	86	Utah	1988
Seydel, John F.	Asst	Mississippi	7	UV	PHD	90	Tx A&M	1990
Seyfarth, Robert	Prof	Lock Haven	25	UIN	EDD		Nev-Reno	9-81
Seyfert, Jeff	Asst	So Nazarane	25		MBA	89	Tulsa	1990
Seymour, William E.	Asst	SUNY-Albany	3	IP	MBA	58	Cornell	1958
Shaaban, Farouk	Prof	Governors St			PHD	72	Illinois	
Shackelford, James	Assoc	Fisk	7	UVX	PHD		Vanderbt	1992

Name	Rank	School			Degree			
Shafa, Hossein	Prof	Okla City	8	Y	PHD		Texas	8-88
Shafai, Yaghoub	Assoc	Dalhousie U	2	E	PHD		Mich St	1980
Shafer, Scott M.	Asst	U Miami	79	IUVZ	PHD	89	Cinn	1988
Shaffer, Brian	Asst	Kentucky	3	L	PHD	92	Calif	1991
Shaffer, Paul	Dean	Cen Missouri	35	Mgt	PHD	74	Oklahoma	1986
Shaft, Teresa M.	Asst	Tulsa	9	Z	PHD	92	Penn St	1990
Shah, A.	Lect	Univ Bristol	3	I	PPD	93	LSE	1992
Shah, Amit J.	Asst	Frostburg St			DBA		US Intl	8-89
Shah, Pri P.	Asst	Minnesota	2	E	PHD	94	Northwes	1994
Shah, Umanglal G.	Asst	Albany State			MA		Houston	
Shahabuddin, Syed	Prof	Cen Michigan	7	U	PHD	76	Missouri	1980
Shailer, Gregory	SLect	Australian N	14	ESIL	MCOM	85	Newcastl	1990
Shambu, Girish	Asst	Canisius	7	UV	PHD	93	SUNY-Buf	1989
Shamsie, Jamal	Asst	New York U			PHD	92	McGill	
Shanabruch, Chuck	Asst	St Xavier	3	IJ	PHD		Chicago	1988
Shane, Barry	Assoc	Oregon State	3	I	PHD	73	Mass	1972
Shane, Guy S.	Assoc	Air Force In	25	ENXZ	PHD		Geo Wash	N-81
Shane, Hugh	C-Pr	W Illinois			PHD	77	Iowa	1977
Shane, Scott	Asst	Georgia Tech	3	I				
Shaner, Michael C.	Assoc	St Louis			PHD	74	S Carol	
Shang, Shiou-Chen	Asst	Pittsburgh	7		PHD		Texas	
Shani, A. B. (Rami)	H-Pr	Cal Poly-SLO	2	EFH	PHD	81	Case Wes	1981
Shank, John K.	Prof	Dartmouth			PHD	69	Ohio St	1984
Shank, Michael			3	I	PHD	92	N Carol	
Shanker, Murali	Asst	Kent State			PHD		Minn	1990
Shanley, Mark T.	Assoc	Northwestern	32	IE	PHD	86	Penn	1991
Shanthikumar, J. George	Prof	Cal-Berkeley	7	U	PHD		Toronto	1984
Shapiro, Debra L.	Assoc	No Carolina	2	E	PHD	86	Northwes	1986
Shapiro, Harris J.	Prof	CUNY-Baruch	1	A	PHD	73	CUNY	1973
Shapiro, Helen	Asst	Harvard	4	L				
Shapiro, Jeremy F.	Prof	MIT	7	UV	PHD			
Shapiro, Perry	Prof	Cal-Santa Br			PHD	68	Berkeley	1987
Shapiro, Roy D.	Prof	Harvard	7	U				
Shapiro, Zur	Prof	New York U			PHD	76	Rochest	
Sharbrough, William C.	Assoc	Citadel	52	E&	PHD		LSU	
Sharda, Ramesh	Prof	Oklahoma St	7	V	PHD	81	Wiscon	9-80
Sharfman, Mark P.	Asst	Oklahoma	38	IJY	PHD	85	Arizona	8-90
Sharif-Zadeh, Mansour	Asst	CS-Pomona	3	I	PHD	79	North Tx	1988
Sharkey, C. B.	Assoc	Loyola-Maryl	7		PHD		JHopkins	
Sharkey, Thomas W.	Assoc	Toledo	38		PHD		Indiana	1984
Sharma, Anurag	Asst	Massachusett	3	I	PHD	93	N Carol	1993
Sharma, Sat Pal	Asst	Morris Brown			MBA	67	Atlanta	1968
Sharpin, Arthur	Prof	McNeese St			PHD		LSU	
Distinguished Professor of Management								
Shaver, Myles	Inst	New York U			ABD		Michigan	
Shaw, D. E.	Prof	Univ Regina	34	ILZ	PHD		Saskatch	
Shaw, James B.	Assoc	Bond Univ	58	ENY	PHD	78	Purdue	8-90
Shaw, Karyll	Asst	Villanova	21	EHNO	PHD	84	Maryland	1990
Shaw, Kathryn	Assoc	Carnegie Mel	5	Q	PHD	81	Harvard	1981
Shaw, Michael	Assoc	Illinois	79	VZ	PHD	84	Purdue	1984
Shayo, Conrad	Lect	CS-San Bern	9	Z	PHD	94	Claremont	1994
Shearer, Robert	Assoc	So Alabama	45	JKNQ	JD	81	Stetson	1986
Sheehan, Michael J.	Lect	Griffith Un	25	FJNP	MSC	92	Griffith	2-91
Sheehan, Thomas		Southeastern			PHD			
Sheehy, William J.	Assoc	Lawrence Tec	4		LLM	72	NYU	1984
Shelby, Annette	Prof	Georgetown	1	BD	PHD	73	LSU	1980
Sheldon, Peter	Lect	Griffith Un	5	BQ	PHD	89	Wollong	2-91
Shell, L. Wayne	Prof	Nicholls St	79	UZ	PHD	77	LSU	1971
Shelley, Charles J.	Asst	Suffolk			PHD		Mass	
Shelton, Deanna	Asst	Cheyney	12	E	MPA	68	American	1977
Shelton, Lois	Asst	Ill-Chicago		I	PHD	85	Harvard	8-93
Shenas, D.	Assoc	Laurentian	5		PHD		NTS	
Shenkar, Oded	Assoc	Hawaii-Manoa			PHD	81	Columbia	
Shenoy, Prakash	Prof	Kansas	7	U	PHD		Cornell	1978
Shepard, Jon M.	H-Pr	Virg Tech	4		PHD	68	Michigan	1989
Shepherd, Dean	SrTch	Bond Univ	36	IT	MBA	92	Bond	1992
Shepherd, Jennifer	Lect	Napier Univ	5	NPQ	BCOM			1989
Shepparat, Barie	SLect	Deakin-Burwo	14		MA		Monash	
Sheppard, Blair	Prof	Duke	23	EQ	PHD	80	Illinois	1986
Sheppard, Sallie	Prof	Texas A&M		Z	PHD	77	Pitt	1992
Sheppeck, Michael	Asst	St Thomas-MN						
Sherany,	Prof	No Michigan			PHD			
Sherer, Peter D.	Assoc	Pennsylvania	5	NQEP	PHD	85	Wiscon	7-89
N. Richard Kalikow Term Associate Professor of Management								
Sherer, Susan A.	Assoc	Lehigh			PHD	88	Penn	1987
Sheridan, Donald P.	Assoc	Dalhousie U	9	Z	PHD		Alberta	
Sherman, Herbert	Asst	Marist	34	EIL	PHD		Union	1988
Sherman, Hugh D.	C-As	York of PA	38		PHD		Temple	1985
Sherman, J. Daniel	C-Pr	Alabama-Hunt	12	DEHX	PHD	81	Alabama	1981
Sherman, Kimbrough	Assoc	Loyola-Maryl	7	V	PHD		Maryland	1975

Name	Title	School	#	Code	Degree	Yr	University	Date
Sherman, Mark R.	Asst	Houston-C Lk	45	KNQY	PHD		NS Wales	8-89
Sherman, Rodney	Assoc	Cen Missouri	56	LE	PHD	72	Geo St	1986
Sherr, Lawrence A.	Prof	Kansas	7	U	PHD	66	Michigan	1965
Sherry, John E. H.	Prof	Cornell	4	JK	JD	69	Columbia	7-72
Sheth, Kishor	Asst	Delaware St			MBA			1971
Shetty, Bala	Assoc	Texas A&M	V		PHD	85	So Meth	1985
Shetty, Y. K.	Prof	Utah State	31	I	PHD	67	UCLA	1967
Sheu, Chwen	Asst	Kansas State	7	UVWY	PHD	90	Ohio St	8-90
Shiba, Shoji	Prof	Univ Tsukuba	57	PU	DECO	74	Tokyo	4-76
Shibakawa, Rinya	Prof	Hitotsubashi	8	I	DE	80	Hitotsub	1990
Shiel, Christine		Bournemouth	25	NYR	BA			1990
Shiffler, Ronald E.	C-Pr	Louisville	7	VOP	PHD	80	Florida	7-82
Shihadeh, Emile	Prof	St Norbert	23	EINY	PHD	65	Cornell	1985
Shilbury, David	SLect	Deakin-Burwo	13	ID	MSC		Mass	
Shilliff, Karl A.	Prof	Akron	13	IUS	PHD	71	Penn St	9-67
Shim, Jung P.	Prof	Miss State	79	VXZ	PHD	83	Nebraska	1983
Shim, Sung J.	Asst	Montclair St		RPI	ABD		Renssela	1993
Shim, Won	Asst	Boise State	28	EY	PHD	91	Oregon	1991
Shimazaki, Hiroshi (Tanaka)	Prof	U Lethbridge	8	Y	PHD	75	S Fraser	1976
Shimko, Barbara	Assoc	Widener			PHD		Wash	
Shimshak, Daniel	Prof	Mass-Boston	7	V	PHD	76	CUNY	1978
Shin, Dooyoung	Assoc	Mankato St			PHD	87	Iowa	1987
Shipley, Margaret F.	Asst	Houston-Down	27	UVS	PHD	86	Pitt	9-86
Shipper, Frank M.	Prof	Salisbury St	23	EFIL	PHD	78	Utah	8-91
Shirakawa, Hiroshi	Asst	Univ Tsukuba	7	V	DENG	89	Toyko In	1-92
Shirland, Larry E.	Dean$	Vermont	7	U	PHD	72	Oreg St	1976
Shirley, Britt M.	C-Ac	Tampa	7	UV	PHD	88	Alabama	1992
Shirley, Gordon V.	Asst	UCLA	7	U	DBA	87	Harvard	1987
Shively, Robert W.	Prof	Wake Fr-MBA	2	E	PHD	72	Cornell	1970
Shively, Thomas S.	Asst	Texas	7	V	PHD	86	Chicago	1986
Shlager, Julian M.	Assoc	Plymouth St			PHD	72	Boston	
Shockney, Thomas D.	C-Pr	Ashland		ABCH	PHD	71	Ohio St	9-64
Shoemaker, Craig	Asst	St Ambrose	17	DU	MBA	83	Keller	1992
Shogan, Andrew W.	C-Ac$	Cal-Berkeley	7	V	PHD		Stanford	1974
Shonesy, Linda B.	Asst	Athens State	3	I	EDD		Alabama	1985
Shooshtari, Nader	Prof	Montana			PHD	83	Ariz St	1991
Shore, Harvey H.	Assoc	Connecticut	5	N	DBA	66	Harvard	1966
Shore, Lynn M.	Assoc	Georgia St	25	EN	PHD	85	Colo St	1986
Shore, Ted H.	Asst	Kennesaw St	25	EN	PHD	85	Colo St	1986
Short, Daniel G.	Dean	Kansas State			PHD	77	Michigan	6-92
Short, Jim	Asst	London Bus	93	ZIHX	PHD		MIT	
Shortell, Stephen M.	Prof	Northwestern			PHD	72	Chicago	1982
A.C. Buehler Professor of Hospital & Health Services Management								
Shorter, Jack D.	Asst	Tx A&M-Kings	9	Z	EDD	84	Okla St	1993
Shoukat, Michael M.	Asst	Air Force In	9	IZ	PHD		Mo-Rolla	9-92
Shovlain, Ray	Prof	St Ambrose	19	AZ	MBA	80	St Ambro	1982
Showalter, Michael J.	Prof	Florida St	7	U	PHD	76	Ohio St	8-81
Shrader, Charles B.	Assoc	Iowa State	34	IHLJ	PHD	84	Indiana	1984
Shrage, Harvey M.	Assoc	W New Eng	5	QK	JD		Northeas	1988
Shreve, Richard R.	Assoc	Indiana NW	39	IZ	PHD	78	Ill Tech	1991
Shriberg, Arthur	Assoc	Xavier	23	DEGS	EDD	72	Columbia	1982
Shrivastava, Paul	Prof	Bucknell	34	IM	PHD	81	Pitt	9-89
Shrode, William A.	Prof	Florida St	97	ZV	DBA	68	Oregon	9-69
Shropshire, William O.	Prof	Ogelthorpe		Econ	PHD	63	Duke	1979
Calloway Professor								
Shub, Allen	Assoc	NE Illinios	26	EP	PHD		Loyola	9-85
Shubert, Janelle J.	VProf	London Bus	24	LFI	PHD		Michigan	
Shukla, Pradip K.	Assoc	Chapman		IEY	PHD		UCLA	1985
Shulman, Arthur D.	Read	Queensland	25	QF	PHD	69	SUNY-Buf	1990
Shuman, Jeffrey	Assoc	Bentley	36	T	PHD	72	Renssel	1982
Shurden, Michael C.	Asst	Lander	7	UV	DBA	87	La Tech	1987
Shwartz, Michael	C-Ac	Boston Univ	17	CU	PHD		Michigan	
Shyam, Manjula	Lect	Carnegie Mel	8	Y	PHD	75	Pitt	1988
Sibary, Scott	Prof	CS-Chico			JD		Berkeley	1983
Sibley, Stan	C	Wis-Oshkosh			PHD	72	Mich St	1972
Siciliano, Julie	Asst	W New Eng	3	I	PHD		Mass	1990
Sick, Todd	Assoc	INSEAD	25	EF	PHD7	78	Cornell	9-92
Sickmeier, Marie	Asst	U Manitoba	25	QE	PHD	89	Ohio St	1991
Siddarth, Sivaramakrishnan	Asst	British Colu	7		PHD	92	UCLA	1992
Siebers, Larry	Inst	Utah State	15	IN	PHD			9-93
Siegall, Marc	Assoc	CS-Chico			PHD		Northwes	1986
Siegel, Abraham J.	Prof	MIT	5	NQ	PHD	61	Berkeley	
Howard W. Johnson Professor of Management								
Siegel, Andrew F.	Prof	U Washington	7	V	PHD	77	Stanford	1983
Siegel, Donald	Asst	SUNY-Stony B	34	IL	PHD	88	Columbia	1990
Siegel, Rachel	Asst	Lyndon State			MPPM		Yale	1990
Siegel, Sidney R.	Assoc	Drexel	27	EFHU	PHD	72	Drexel	
Siehl, Caren Joy	Assoc	Am Grad Intl	38	IYH	PHD	84	Stanford	
Siferd, Sue P.	Asst	Arizona St	7	U	PHD		Ohio St	1989
Sightler, Kevin	Asst	Kennesaw St	25	ENVX	PHD			1990

Name	Rank	School			Degree		University	Year
Sikula, Andrew	Prof	CS-Chico			PHD		Mich St	1980
Silber, Harriet	Assoc	Lg Isl-Brook			MBA		Lg Islnd	
Sillah, Marion	Assoc	Morehouse			PHD		S Carol	1987
Silve, N.	Lect	W Australia			BCOM		W Austra	
Silver, Edward	Prof	Univ Calgary	7	UVX	PHD	63	MIT	1981
Silver, Mark S.	Asst	New York U	9	Z	PHD	86	Penn	
Silver, Milton	H-Pr	Drexel	12	FDPT	PHD	62	Columbia	1965
Silver, William	Asst	Denver	5	N	PHD		Nebraska	9-90
Silverblatt, Ronnie	Assoc	Fla Internat		QN	PHD	82	Geo St	1983
Silverman, Fred	Prof	Pace	7		PHD	74	Columbia	
Silverman, Murray I.	Prof	San Fran St	3	I	PHD	72	Stanford	1986
Silvers, Robert C.	Asst	Central Wash			PHD	92	Stanford	1993
Silvester, Katherine	Asst	Rensselaer						
Sim, A. B.	Assoc	U Wollongong	38	IY	PHD	75	UCLA	O-87
Simendinger, Earl A.	V	Tampa	12	ACE	PHD	81	Case Wes	1994
Simerly, Roy L.	Asst	East Carol	13	IJ	PHD	90	Va Tech	8-90
Simis, Peter	Dean$	CS-Fresno		InSy	DBA	78	Ariz St	8-70
Simko, Gene	Assoc	Monmouth	3	I	PHD	91	CUNY	9-79
Simmonds, Paul G.	Assoc	Old Dominion	38	ISY	PHD	87	Temple	1992
Simmons, Franklin B.	Assoc	Akron	36	IJK	PHD	81	Cinn	1-82
Simmons, Laurette P.	Assoc	Loyola-Maryl	9	Z	PHD		North Tx	
Simmons, LeRoy	Prof	Loyola-Maryl	7	V	PHD		Tenn	
Simmons, Susan A.	Prof	Citadel	7	UVX	PHD	76	Miss	
Simmons, Yvonne M.	Asst	Virg Union			MS			
Simon, Alice E.	Assoc	Ohio Wesley	5	Q	PHD		Ohio St	1985
Simon, Bernard	Asst	St Edwards	25	EPUX	MBA	76	St Edwar	1991
Simon, D. S.	Read	Humberside						
Simon, John T.	Asst	Notre Dame	7	UV	PHD	89	Northwes	1989
Simonetti, Jack L.	Prof	Toledo	25		DBA	72	Kent St	1972
Simons, Robert	Assoc	Harvard						
Simpson, Bertrand Jr.	Asst	No Illinois	4	K	JD		Wiscon	
Simpson, Douglas B.	Prof	CS-Fresno	2	EH	PHD	71	U Wash	1971
Simpson, Leo R.	Prof	Eastern Wash	67	STU	DBA	75	Colorado	1977
Sims, D. B. P.	SLect	Univ Bath	2	F	PHD			
Sims, Dale B.	Asst	Dallas Bapt	9		MS		Houst Bp	1990
Sims, Henry P.	Prof	Maryland	2	E	PHD	71	Mich St	1989
Sims, Ronald R.	Prof	Wm & Mary	2	EFH	PHD	81	Case Wes	1986
Sina, Reza	Asst	Laurentian	38		PHD	87	Grenoble	7-88
Sineath, William Palmer III					PHD	82	S Carol	
Singer, A. E.	SLect	Canterbury	34	IJL	PHD	93	Canterbu	1984
Singer, Joe	Prof	Mo-Kansas Ct	6	ST	PHD	71	Arkansas	1975
Singer, Marc G.	Prof	Mid Tenn St	25	ENQ	PHD	73	Tenn	1990
Singh, Harbir	Assoc	Pennsylvania	38	IYD	PHD	84	Michigan	7-84
Singh, Jang	Assoc	Univ Windsor	14	JKLY	PHD		Toronto	1986
Singh, Jitendra V.	Assoc	Pennsylvania	34	BIKY	PHD	83	Stanford	7-87
Singh, Medini R.	Assoc	Dartmouth			PHD	89	Car Mel	1994
Singh, R.	Lect	U Lancaster	25	EQ	PHD		Leeds	
Singh, Ranjit	Prof	Clark Atlant			PHD		S Illin	
Singh, Sanjay K.	Asst	Alabama-Birm	9	Z	PHD	93	Georiga	1993
Singhal, Kalyan	Prof	Baltimore	7	T	PHD	72	Kent St	9-83
Singhal, Vinod	Asst	Georgia Tech	7	U	PHD	88	Rochest	1989
Singleton, Timothy	Prof	No Georgia			PHD	89	Geo St	
Sinha, Atish	Asst	Dayton	9	Z	PHD	93	Pitt	1991
Sinha, Deepak	Asst	Purdue	3	I	PHD	90	MIT	1990
Sinha, Diptendu	Assoc	Notre Dame	7	UV	PHD	85	Wiscon	1985
Sinicropi, Anthony V.	Retir	Iowa	4	Q	PHD	68	Iowa	1963
Sink, Clay V.	C-Pr	Rhode Island	16	PSE&	PHD	68	Ohio St	1969
Sinkiewicz, Anthony T.	Assoc	Winona State			DBA		US Intl	1987
Sipior, Janice C.	Asst	Villanova	9	Z	PHD	88	SUNY-Buf	1990
Sirbu, Marvin A.	Prof	Carnegie Mel	9	ZL	SCD	73	MIT	1985
Sirdeshmulch, Deepak	Asst	Case Western			PHD		Ohio St	1994
Sirotnik, Barbara	Prof	CS-San Bern	7	V	PHD	80	Ca-River	1980
Sirower, Mark	Asst	New York U			PHD	93	Columbia	
Sisak, James	Lect	Wis-Whitewat	7	EUW	MBA	78	Wis-Whit	1981
Sison, Alejo Jose	Asst	Univ Navarra	4	J	PHD		Navarra	9-92
Sjoblom, Leif		Intl Mgt Dev	9	Z	PHD		Stanford	
Skalbeck, Bruce	Assoc	St Cloud St	7	UV	PHD	75	N Colo	1977
Skelton, Bonnie M.	Inst	Radford	9	Z	MS	86	Radford	8-89
Skinker, Harry J.	SLect	Mary Wash	13		MBA		Alabama	
Skipton, Michael D.	Assoc	Memorial Un	13	DIPT	PHD	74	Warwick	4-85
Skivington, Kristen D.	Asst	Mich-Flint	2	H	PHD	87	Tx A&M	8-86
Skorin-Kapov, Darko	Asst	SUNY-Stony B	79	VZ	PHD	89	Brit Col	1989
Skorin-Kapov, Jadranka	Assoc	SUNY-Stony B	79	VZ	PHD	87	Brit Col	1988
Slade, Stephen	Asst	New York U	9	Z	PHD	91	Yale	
Slagle, Michelle L.	Assoc	So Alabama	23	DFIL	DPA	83	Geo Wash	1986
Slatter, Stuart St. P.	Assoc	London Bus	36	IS	PHD		London	1972
Slattery, Jeff	Asst	NE St-Okla	3	I	PHD	93	Arkansas	1993
Slauson, Mike	Asst	Mesa State	1	OP	MBA		S Colo	1990
Sleeper, Brad	Asst	Boise State			JD	76	Minn	1994
Sleeth, Randall G.	Assoc	Virg Comm	2	DE	PHD	77	Mass	1975

Slevin, Dennis P.	Prof	Pittsburgh	2		PHD	69	Stanford
Sligo, F. X.	Assoc	Massey Univ	25	EZN	PHD	87	Massey	1980
Sloan, B. R.	Assoc	So Nazarane	79		PHD	91	Oklahoma	1980
Sloan, Carla L.	Inst	Liberty	1		MS		Twsn St	8-84
Sloane, Arthur A.	Prof	Delaware			DBA	63	Harvard	1966
Sloane, Carl S.	Prof	Harvard	1					
Slocomb, Thomas	Asst	Chapman		EFT	PHD		Missouri	1991
Slocum, John W.	Prof	So Methodist			PHD	67	U Wash	1979
Slotnick, Susan	Asst	SUNY-Stony B	79	UVZ	PHD	93	Car Mel	1993
Slusher, E. Allen	Prof	Missouri	29	HZ	PHD	73	Iowa	1975
Sluti, Donald	Asst	Neb-Kearney	17	UW	PHD	92	N Zealan	1992
Small, Charles	Assoc	Abilene Chr			PHD	78	Tx A&M	1977
Small, Michael	Asst	East Tenn St	7	UV	PHD	93	Cleve St	1994
Smart, Dennis	Asst	Neb-Omaha			PHD	93	Tx A&M	1993
Smart, John P.	C-Pr	Deakin-Burwo	35	EN	MBA	68	Melbourn	
Smayling, Miles	Prof	Mankato St			PHD	87	Minn	1982
Smedlay, Stanley	Prof	Gardner-Webb	23	ELY	PHD	80	Penn St	1981
Smelcer, John	Asst	American U	9	Z	PHD		Michigan	1989
Smelewicz, Jean	Adj	Nichols Col						
Smeltz, Wayne J.	Assoc	Rider			PHD		Houston	1979
Smiles, Ronald	Prof	Dallas Bapt	13		PHD		Tx-Arlin	1987
Smiley, Barry A.	D-Pr	NW St of La			DBA	75	La Tech	
Smiley, Tex	Retir	Intl Mgt Dev	5	N	MSC		Kan St	
Smilor, Raymond W.	Prof	Mo-Kansas Ct	6	ST	PHD	78	Texas	1992
Smircich, Linda	Prof	Massachusett	2	ERBJ	PHD	78	Syracuse	1982
Smith, Albert C. Jr.	Assoc	Radford	25	GN	EDD	81	Va Tech	8-80
Smith, Allen E.	Asst	East Tenn St	79	UZ	PHD	00	S Carol	1987
Smith, Anne	Asst	McGill Univ	3		PHD	93	N Carol	1992
Smith, Brien N.	Asst	Ball State	5		PHD		Auburn	1989
Smith, Brock	Asst	Victoria Can	1	X	ABD		W Ontar	7-91
Smith, Bud	Asst	No Alabama			MBA	72	Harvard	1977
Smith, C. A. P.	Asst	Montana	9	Z	PHD	90	Arizona	1990
Smith, Charles H.	Assoc	Hofstra	23	DHJ	PHD	85	Syracuse	7-86
Smith, Chuck	Asst	Niagara						
Smith, Clayton G.	Assoc	Okla City	3	I	PHD		Purdue	8-93
Smith, Clifton	Asst	Boston Univ	6	ST	MBA		Dartmout	
Smith, D.	H	Liverpool JM	5	GHIL	MBA			1990
Smith, Dayle	Assoc	San Francisc	25	GP	PHD	86	S Calif	1993
Smith, Faye L.	Asst	Oklahoma St	3	I	PHD	89	Iowa	8-89
Smith, Fred	Inst	W Illinois			MBA	87	W Illin	1987
Smith, Garry D.	C-Pr	Miss State	3	I	DBA	76	La Tech	1980
Smith, Gary R.	Prof	Brighm Yg-HI	34	BEJT	EDD	70	Idaho	8-84
Smith, George	Asst	St Scholasti			MBA		CorpusCh	1986
Smith, Gordon	Asst	So Methodist			PHD	91	Car Mel	
Smith, Gwendolyn N.	Asst	La St-Shreve	1	D	MS		E Tx St	8-78
Smith, H. Jeff	Asst	Georgetown	93	ZIJL	DBA	90	Harvard	1991
Smith, Hanson H.	Asst	W Carolina	17	UV	MBA	75	W Carol	8-75
Smith, Howard L.	Prof	New Mexico	3	IL	PHD	76	U Wash	
Smith, J. G.	Prof	McGill Univ	3		PHD		Ohio St	1973
Smith, J. Michael	SLect	Manches Inst	2	E	PHD		Liverpol	1976
Smith, J. R.	Asst	Jackson St			DBA		Tenn	1971
Smith, James	Asst	Northern St	3	AHE	DPA	92	Alabama	8-91
Smith, James	Lect	Tx-Pan Amer	9	Z	MBA			
Smith, James O. Jr.	Assoc	East Carol	25	FER	PHD	80	Miss	8-78
Smith, Jan	Prof	Ohio Wesley	28	EHY	PHD		Princeton	1977
Smith, Jerald R.	Asst	Fla Atlantic	38	FTY	PHD	78	Louisvil	9-91
Smith, Jonathan E.	Assoc	John Carroll			PHD		Georgia	1985
Smith, Ken G.	Prof	Maryland	36	IT	PHD	83	Washingt	1983
Smith, Kenneth	Asst	Syracuse	3	I	PHD	90	Maryland	1990
Smith, Larry	Inst	Geo Southern	9	Z	MBA	81	So Meth	1989
Smith, Mark	Assoc	SW Louisiana	3	IZT	MBA	77	Howard	1985
Smith, Nariida	SLect	Univ Sydney	79	VXZ	PHD	72	Monash	1990
Smith, Patricia L.	Asst	Berry	56	LNSR	PHD			8-90
Smith, Peggy C.	Assoc	Tulsa	25	DENR	PHD	79	Oklahoma	1982
Smith, Peter	Adj	Southeastern			PHD		Penn St	
Smith, Raymond D.	Asst	Towson State	13		PHD	88	Maryland	1990
Smith, Robert	Assoc	Okla Chr	15		ABD			
Smith, Robert	Retir	CS-Long Bch	23	IMZ	PHD	77	Irvine	1966
Smith, Robert D.	Prof	Kent State			PHD	66	Penn St	1966
Smith, Ronald	Prof	CUNY-Hunter			DBA		Louisian	
Smith, Scott	Prof	Brigham Yg	8	Y	PHD	79	Penn St	1981
Smith, Solomon	D-Pr	Fisk	37	UVY	PHD		S Illin	1988
Smith, Spencer	Prof	Illinois Tch			PHD	58	Columbia	1966
Smith, Stephanie C.	Asst	Lander	35	ID	DBA	88	Memphis	1986
Smith, Steve	Asst	NE Missouri	4	JKL	JD	85	Texas	1986
Smith, Stuart	Asst	Purdue	7	V	PHD	90	Texas	1991
Smith, Susan Kay	Assoc	Cen Michigan	15	NQ	PHD	86	Mich St	1981
Smith, Teresa L.	Asst	N Car-Charl			PHD		Va Tech	1989
Smith, Virgil O	Assoc	Biola	39	IZ	ABD		Tx Tech	1994
Smith, Wanda J.	Asst	Syracuse	25	CEFR	PHD	91	N Carol	

Name	Rank	School			Degree		School	Year
Specter, Christine	Assoc	Fla Internat		VM	DBA	86	Geo Wash	1986
Spector, Bert A.	Assoc	Northeastern	25	EFN	PHD		Missouri	9-86
Spector, Yishay	Lect	Hebrew Univ			PHD		Tel Aviv	
Spelman, Duncan	Assoc	Bentley	2	ER	PHD	80	Case Wes	1981
Spencer, Barbara	Prof	British Colu	83	YA	PHD	79	Car Mel	1985
Spencer, Barbara A.	Assoc	Miss State	23	HIR	PHD	85	Va Tech	1987
Spencer, Bruce	Assoc	Athabasca Un	5	Q	MA	76	Warwick	1990
Spencer, Daniel G.	Assoc	Kansas	2	E	PHD		Orgeon	1979
Spencer, Michael S.	Asst	No Iowa			PHD	92	Georgia	8-92
Spender, J.C.	Prof	Rutgers-Newk	23	BHIT	PHD	80	Manchest	1991
Spero, Stuart	Asst	Neb Wesleyan	12		MBA	85	Nebraska	1990
Sphicas, Georghios P.	Prof	CUNY-Baruch	7	X	PHD	73	Columbia	1973
Spiegel, Ruth	Inst	Lg Isl-Post			MBA		Long Isl	
Spiegelglas, Stephen	Emer	Manhattan	48	MY	PHD	54	Wiscon	1978
Spier, Kathryn	Assoc	Northwestern	34	IK	PHD	89	MIT	
Spier, Leo	Prof	San Fran St		IJLY	PHD	62	U Wash	1980
Spillane, Lynda	Lect	Macquarie Un						
Spillane, Robert	Prof	Macquarie Un						
Spiller, Lisa D.	Asst	Chris Newpor			PHD	90	Missouri	1991
Spillman, Robert D.	Asst	Radford	9	Z	PHD	83	Ohio St	8-84
Spinetto, Richard D.	Assoc	Colorado	7	UVX	PHD	71	Cornell	1971
Spirer, Herbert F.	Emer	Connecticut	79	UZ	PHD	70	NYU	
Spirer, Janet	Prof	Marymount	13	INPZ	PHD		Ohio St	1984
Spirn, Steve	Prof	Toledo			PHD	73	Toledo	1973
Spiro, George	Prof	Massachusett	4	KJQ	JD	74	Syracuse	1981
Spiro, Michael	Prof	Pittsburgh			PHD	65	MIT	
Spital, Frank C.	Assoc	Northeastern	23	D	PHD		MIT	9-70
Spraggins, H. Barry	Assoc	Nevada-Reno	7	UV	PHD	76	Minerto	1987
Sprague, David	C-Pr	Cen Michigan	7	U	PHD	75	Iowa	1990
Sprague, Ralph H.	Prof	Hawaii-Manoa	7	B	DBA	64	Indiana	
Spreitzer, Gretchen	Asst	So Calif	2	E	PHD		Michigan	1992
Springer, Donald M.	Assoc	Portland	9	Z	PHD	74	Colo St	1975
Springer, Mark	Assoc	Western Wash	7	UX	PHD	88	Vanderbt	9-87
Spritzer, Allan D.	Dean	East Tenn St		Mgt	PHD	71	Cornell	1981
Sprotzer, Ira B.	C-Ac	Rider	4	K	JD		Boston C	1979
Sproull, Lee S.	C-Pr	Boston Univ	29	ZEH	PHD		Stanford	
Sproull, Natalie	Prof	W Illinois			PHD	69	Mich St	1969
Spruce, William	Lect	Tx-S Antonio						
Spulber, Daniel	Prof	Northwestern	37	IV	PHD	79	Northwes	
Thomas G. Ayers Professor of Energy Resource Management								
Sridhar, B. S.	Asst	Wis-Oshkosh	23	EHJY	PHD	87	Ohio St	1989
Sridhar, Sandhya	Asst	WI-Green Bay	25	EFHN	PHD	88	Ohio St	1989
Sridharan, V.	Assoc	Clemson	7	UV	PHD	87	Iowa	1987
Srikanth, Rajan	Asst	Cal-Berkeley	9	Z	PHD		NYU	1990
Srinivas, K. M.	Prof	Univ Regina	25	EFNP	PHD		UCLA	
Srinivas, Shanthi	Asst	CS-Pomona	7	V	PHD	79	Penn St	1987
Srinivasan, Ashok	Asst	Purdue	7	U	PHD	89	Car Mel	1989
Srinivasan, M. M.	Assoc	Tennessee	79	UVZ	PHD	85	Northwes	8-92
Srinivasan, Padmini	Assoc	Iowa	9	Z	PHD	85	Syracuse	1989
Srinivasan, S.	Assoc	Louisville	9	Z	PHD	81	Pitt	8-87
Sriram, Ramaier	Asst	Ind-Purdue	97	VZ	PHD	90	Tenn	8-91
Srivastava, Alok	Assoc	Georgia St	7	V	PHD		Clemson	
Srivastava, Baharatendu	Asst	Marquette	7	UV	PHD	92	Wash St	1992
Srivastava, Sureshma	C-Ac	Alaska-Ancho			PHD	88	Maryland	1987
Srivastva, Suresh	Prof	Case Western	2	E	PHD	60	Michigan	1970
St-Onge, Sylvie	Asst	HEC-Montreal	15	N	PHD		Toronto	1985
St. John, Anne	Asst	Marymount			JD		Geo Wash	1991
St. John, August		Lg Isl-Brook						
St. John, Caron H.	Asst	Clemson	3	I	PHD	88	Geo St	1988
St. John, William	SLect	Rensselaer			PHD		Renssela	1990
St. Louis, Robert D.	Assoc	Arizona St			PHD		Purdue	1982
St. Onge, John	Assoc	Eastern Conn			MBA		Harvard	1980
Staber, Udo H.	Prof	New Brunswic	2	H	PHD		C'Nell	1985
Stack, Robert T.	H	Hawaii-Hilo	6	S	PHD	78	Mich St	1984
Stafford, Edward F.	Prof	Alabama-Hunt	7	UV	PHD		Penn St	1984
Stage, H. Daniel	Prof	Loyola Marym	12	DY	DBA	75	S Calif	1973
Stahl, Michael	Prof	Tennessee	3	EHI	PHD	75	Renssel	8-89
Stair, Ralph M. Jr.	Prof	Florida St	97	ZV	PHD	74	Oregon	9-78
Staley, Tom	Prof	San Fran St	1	K	PHD	74	Texas	1975
Stalnaker, Armand C.	Retir	Wash Univ	3	I	PHD	51	Ohio St	
Stam, Antonie	Assoc	Georgia	79	VZ	PHD	86	Kansas	1986
Stamm, Carol Lee	Prof	W Michigan	7	UV	PHD	74	Wiscon	1981
Stamm, John H.	Prof	Babson			DBA	69	Harvard	
Stanbury, William	Prof	British Colu	13	AIL	PHD	72	Berkeley	1970
Stander, Norman E.	Assoc	Rider	2	E	PHD	60	Ohio St	1970
Stanford, Donald M.	Adj	No Carolina	4	K				
Stanford, Jane	C-Ac	Tx A&M-Kings	38	HIYE	PHD	92	North Tx	1990
Stanford, Melvin J.	Prof	Mankato St			PHD	68	Illinois	1982
Stanger, Anthony M. J.	LectB	Flinders Un	6	ST	BCOM	85	Tasmania	2-89
Stanley, Sande Richards	Asst	NW Missouri			ABD		S Illin	1991

Name	Rank	School			Degree		Institution	
Stanton, Erwin S.	Prof	St Johns			PHD	58	Columbia	
Stanton, H. T.	Assoc	Barton	2		EDD		N Carol	1976
Stanton, Roger	Prof	CS-Long Bch	13	AIL	DBA	76	S Calif	1966
Stapleton, Richard J.	Prof	Geo Southern	36	STI	PHD	69	Tx Tech	1970
Star, Harold	Asst	Gettysburg	34	I	PHD		Concordi	1989
Starbuck, William H.	Prof	New York U			PHD	64	Car Mel	
ITT Professor Of Creative Management; Director of Doctoral Program								
Starke, Frederick A.	H-Pr	U Manitoba	12	EH	PHD	74	Ohio St	1968
Starkey, Paul L.	Asst	Delta State	25	EJP	MBA	85	Miss	8-86
Starling, G.	Prof	Houston-C Lk	4	AHL	PHD		Texas	8-74
Starner, John W.	Asst	Tx-El Paso	9	Z	PHD	76	New Mex	1990
Starr, G. W.	SLect	U Newcastle	14	AIL	PHD		West VA	
Staruck, James E.	Asst	DePaul			JD		Chi-Kent	
Staudohar, Paul	Prof	CS-Hayward	5	Q	PHD	69	S Calif	1969
Staughton, R. V. W.	Lect	Univ Bath	7	U	MIPR			
Staw, Barry M.	C-Pr	Cal-Berkeley	25	EQI	PHD		Northwes	1980
Lorrinae Tyson Mitchell Professor in Leadership and Communication								
Stawicki, Robert	Asst	F Dick-Madis			PHD		Rutgers	
Stead, Jean Garner	Assoc	East Tenn St	3	IM	PHD	83	LSU	1982
Stead, W. Edward	Prof	East Tenn St	3	EFMP	PHD	76	LSU	1982
Stearns, Timothy M.	Asst	Marquette	3	HIT	DBA	83	Indiana	1988
Stebbins, Michael W.	Prof	Cal Poly-SLO	2	EFH	PHD	73	Berkeley	1982
Stecke, Kathryn E.	Assoc	Michigan	7	U	PHD	81	Purdue	1981
Steckler, Mel	Asst	Samford	7	U				
Steckler, Nicole	Asst	Oregon	2	E	PHD	90	Harvard	1990
Stedham, Yvonne	C-As	Nevada-Reno	52	NE	PHD	90	Kansas	1988
Steel, Robert P.	Prof	Air Force In	25	EFHN	PHD		Tenn	6-81
Steele, Joe L.	Prof	Tx Christian	13	V	PHD	68	Texas	1965
Steele, Thaddeus	Asst	Alabama A&M						
Steele, Thomas	Prof	Montana			PHD	74	Penn St	1987
Steelquist, John A.	Prof	Chaminade	13		PHD		Tx A&M	1984
Steen, Jack E.	Assoc	Florida St	5	Q	PHD	65	Alabama	1964
Steenberg, Laurence	Asst	Evansville	36	IJ	MBA	70	Chicago	1989
Steers, Richard M.	Prof	Oregon	2	HEY	PHD	73	Ca-Irvine	1975
Kazumitsu Shiome Professor of Management								
Steffans, Paul	Lect	U Queensland	3	I	PHD	94	Monash	1994
Steffen, Hans	Prof	S Ill-Edward	28	Y	PHD	60	Nebraska	1969
Steffy, Brian D.	Assoc	Frank & Mars	23	NC	PHD	84	Georgia	7-88
Steidinger, Gene L.	Asst	Loras	25	N	MBA	85	Wiscon	1989
Steidlmeier, Paul	Assoc	SUNY-Bingham	34	IJL	PHD	75	Stanford	1987
Steier, Lloyd	Asst	Univ Alberta	36	S	PHD	85	Alberta	1991
Steiger, David	Asst	Car-Greens	9	Z	PHD		Okla St	1993
Stein, Herman	Assoc	Bellarmine	7	U	PHD		Columbia	
Stein, William E.	Assoc	Texas A&M		V	PHD	75	N Carol	1982
Steinbaugh, Robert P.	Retir	Indiana St	28	1991	PHD	57	Ohio St	8-57
Steinberg, C.	Retir	McGill Univ	5		PHD		Col	1976
Steinberg, Geoffrey	Asst	Kent State			PHD		Penn	1991
Steiner, George	Prof	McMaster Un	17	UV	PHD		Waterloo	
Steiner, John F.	C-Pr	CS-L Angeles	4	L	PHD	73	Arizona	1973
Steinke, Gerhard	Assoc	Seattle Pac	49	JLZ	PHD	92	Passau	9-92
Steirert, Alfred	Asst	Lamar			MBA	59	Florida	9-66
Stelzer, Leigh	Assoc	Seton Hall			PHD	71	Michigan	
Stembridge, Allen	C-Pr	Andrews	28	PDE	EDD		Andrews	1988
Stengrevics, John M.	Lect	Babson			DBA		Harvard	
Stephan, Eric	Prof	Brigham Yg	25	G&N	PHD	66	Utah	1968
Stephens, Carroll	Asst	Virg Tech	2		PHD	93	Duke	1993
Stephens, Charlotte	Asst	Columbus	79	Z	PHD		Auburn	1990
Stephens, David B.	Dean	Utah State	35	IQ	PHD	75	Texas	6-87
Stephens, Elvis C.	Prof	North Texas	5	NQ	DBA	66	Indiana	1963
Stephens, Gregory K.	Asst	Tx Christian	28	EY	PHD	92	Ca-Irvine	1991
Stephens, Robert L.	Assoc	Georgia SW	56	US	PHD		Miss St	
Stephens, Ron	C-Pr	Cen Missouri	51	NR	EDD	76	Missouri	1972
Stephenson, Harriet B.	Prof	Seattle	26	IS	PHD	66	U Wash	1967
Stephenson, Karen A.	Asst	UCLA	5	N	PHD	90	Harvard	1990
Stepina, Lee P.	Assoc	Florida St	25	EN	PHD	81	Illinois	8-81
Stepp, Randy	Assoc	Shippensburg			PHD		Georgia	
Sterkel-Powell, Karen	Asst	Colorado St	15	NPR&	PHD	87	N Colo	1976
Sterling, Charles	Asst	Chapman		NPO	PHD		Ohio St	1992
Sterman, John	Assoc	MIT	9	Z	PHD			
Stern, George A. Jr.	Lect	CUNY-Stn Isl	25	DEFP	MBA		Pace	1968
Stern, Joseph	Asst	Jersey City	8		PHD		NYU	
Stern, Louis W.	Assoc	CUNY-Baruch	9	Z	PHD	70	Lehigh	1970
Stern, Paul G.	VProf	Pennsylvania			PHD		Manchest	7-93
Stern, Stephen	Adj	Southeastern			MBA		Penn	
Sterngold, Arthur	Asst	Lycoming			PHD			
Sterrett, Charles R.	Prof	Frostburg St			PHD		American	
Steuer, Ralph E.	Prof	Georgia	7	V	PHD	73	N Carol	
Stevens, C. Wanda	Assoc	Cameron	9	Z	PHD	87	Oklahoma	1981
Stevens, Cindy	Asst	Maryland	5	N	PHD	91	Wash	1990
Stevens, Dixon	Assoc	St Rose	3	FIDE	PHD	76	SUNY-Alb	1978

Name	Rank	School	#	Code	Deg	Yr	Inst	Year
Stevens, Flumo Y.	Assoc	Lawrence Tec	78		PHD	74	Nebraska	1987
Stevens, George E.	Dean	Oakland	45	NJLR	DBA	79	Kent St	1-91
Stevens, John E.	Prof	Lehigh			PHD	75	Cinn	1975
Stevens, Kathy	Assoc	Merrimack		Z	PHD	80	Purdue	1987
Stevens, Michael	Asst	Tx-El Paso	2	E	PHD	93	Purdue	1993
Stevens, William F.	Assoc	Guilford	2	E	PHD	77	Mich St	1982
Stevens, William R.	Asst	Missouri So			PHD	85	Arkansas	1988
Stevenson, Charlease	C-Pr	Savannah St	12	AEL	DPA	91	Georgia	1973
Stevenson, Howard H.	Prof	Harvard	1		DBA	69	Harvard	1971
Sarofim-Rock Professor Business Administration								
Stevenson, Lois	Assoc	St Marys-Cdn	36	ST	MPH	90	Bath	1992
Stevenson, William B.	Assoc	Boston Coll	2	EHX	PHD	80	Calif	9-88
Stewart, Alex	Asst	Texas Tech	38	ITY	PHD	87	York U	1990
Stewart, Alice C.	Lect	Pittsburgh	3		PHD	90	N Carol	
Stewart, Carol	Inst	Univ Calgary	38	IY	MBA		Lancastr	1982
Stewart, Greg L.	Asst	Vanderbilt	5	NOPQ	PHD	93	Arizona	9-93
Stewart, James E.	Assoc	Merrimack			MBA		Gold Gt	
Stewart, Jean C.	SLect	Napier Univ	5	O	BSC			1973
Stewart, Kim A.	Asst	Denver	3	I	PHD		Houston	9-89
Stewart, Morag I.	Asst	Eastern Wash	9	ZY	PHD	88	Ariz St	1988
Stewart, Roosevelt	Assoc	Alabama A&M			MBA		Atlanta	
Stewart, S. E. A.	C-Ac	Un Hong Kong	18	M	MA			1-83
Stewart, Walter T. Jr.	Prof	CS-San Bern	9	Z	PHD	84	Ohio	1984
Stewart, Wayne	Lect	Sam Houston			MBA	88	W Carol	1993
Stewart, William	Dean	No Alabama			PHD	77	Miss	1960
Stewart-Belle, Sue	Asst	Illinois St	52		PHD	92	Houston	1991
Stickney, Clyde P.	Prof	Dartmouth			DBA	70	Fla St	1977
Stickney, Frank A.	Prof	Wright State	3	EFG	PHD	60	Ohio St	1069
Stiles, Curt	Prof	CS-Bakersf	3		PHD			1988
Still, Thomas W.					DBA	74	Fla St	
Stillwell, C. Dean	Asst	Dayton	25	ENO	PHDA	93	Geo Tech	8-90
Stimpert, J. Larry	Asst	Michigan St	3	M	PHD	91	Illinois	9-91
Stinson, Joel P.			7	U	PHD	76	N Carol	
Stinson, John E.	Prof	Ohio Univ	23		PHD	70	Ohio St	1964
Stobaugh, Robert B.	Prof	Harvard	7	U				
Charles E. Wilson Professor of Business Administration								
Stobie, David H.	Head	Napier Univ	49	JLW	MSC			1975
Stochaj, John	Prof	NJ Inst Tech	9	Z	PHD	63	NYU	1963
Stockman, John W.	Prof	CS-Sacrament	25	ENP	PHD	69	U Wash	1970
Stockport, G.	Lect	Victoria NZ	36	ISTY	PHD		Cranfield	7093
Stodt, Martha	Adj	No Carolina	2	EC				
Stoeberl, Phillip A.	Prof	St Louis			PHD	72	St Louis	
Stoever, William	Prof	Seton Hall			PHD	78	NYU	
Endowed Chair								
Stohr, Edward	C-Pr	New York U			PHD	73	Berkeley	
Stokes, George	Adj	Southeastern			MA		NC Cen	
Stokes, S. Lynne	Assoc	Texas	7	V	PHD	79	N Carol	1985
Stoller, Martin	Asst	Northwestern			PHD	89	Northwes	1991
Storms, James T.					DBA	73	Fla St	
Stone, Dianna L.	Assoc	SUNY-Albany	25	NEJ	PHD	81	Purdue	1990
Stone, Herbert	Prof	CS-Long Bch	13	IOV	DBA	65	UCLA	1958
Stone, Melissa M.	Asst	Boston Univ	2	E	PHD		Yale	
Stone, Richard G.	Assoc	Elizabethtwn	37	IU	PHD	88	Temple	9-87
Stone, Robert W.	Assoc	Geo Southern	79	ZV	PHD	83	Purdue	1983
Stone, Ron	Inst	Jms Madison	13	IE	PHD	90	Nova	9-93
Stone, Thomas H.	Prof	Oklahoma St	5	NQ	PHD	69	Minn	1-89
Stone, Wayne E.	Asst	Air Force In	23	EHIZ	DBA		S Illin	8-90
Stonebraker, Peter W.	Assoc	NE Illinios	7	U	PHD		Ariz St	9-90
Stoner, Charles R.	Prof	Bradley	23	EGTR	DBA	79	Fla St	1980
Stoner, James A. F.	Prof	Fordham	2	EH	PHD	67	MIT	1975
Stoops, David L.	Asst	Northwest C	56	T	MBA	91	Phoenix	1993
Stopford, John M.	C-Pr	London Bus	38	YI	DBA		Harvard	1971
Storbeck, James E.	Assoc	Ohio State	7	V	PHD	80	Texas	1980
Storey, Jerry	Prof	Weber State			PHD	72	Utah	1971
Storey, John	SLect	Loughborough	5	N	PHD		Lancast	
Storey, Ronald G.	Dean	New Brunswic	2	E	PHD	74	Mich St	1989
Storey, Veda	Asst	Rochester	9	Z	PHD		Brit Col	
Stork, Diana	C-Ac	Hartford	2	EH	PHD	88	Columbia	
Story, Jonathan	Prof	INSEAD	8	Y	PHD	73	J Hopkin	7-74
Stough, Stanley	C-Pr	SE Missouri	13	IY	PHD	83	Arkansas	1987
Stout, Suzanne K.	Asst	Texas-Dallas		E	PHD	91	Stanford	
Stover, Dana L.	Asst	Idaho	25	REHD	PHD	90	Wash St	1990
Strach, Lauren K.	Asst	St Marys-Ind	15	R	PHD	90	Mich St	8-89
Straley, William	Assoc	Ogelthorpe	78	UXAT	PHD	79	Auburn	8-90
Strand, Larry	Dean$	Biola	3	I	MBA		S Calif	1986
Strang, Daniel	Prof	SUNY-Geneseo	7	V	PHD	75	Cornell	9-72
Strang, Roger	Dean	Quinnipiac	3	ISY	DBA		Harvard	
Strasser, Sandra	Asst	Valparaiso	7	VU	PHD	90	Colorado	1990
Stratton, William E.	C-Pr	Idaho State		EH	PHD	74	Case Wes	1974
Stratton-Devine, Kay	Assoc	Univ Alberta	5	NQ	PHD	88	Wash St	1988

Name	Rank	School			Degree		Institution	
Straub, Detmar W. Jr.	Assoc	Georgia St	9	Z	PHD		Indiana	
Straub, Paul	VAsst	Northwestern			PHD	93	Illinois	1993
Strauch, A. Bruce	Assoc	Citadel	4	KJ	JD		N Carol	
Straus, Susan	Asst	Carnegie Mel	52	E	PHD	92	Illinois	1991
Strausbaugh, Rolland L.	Assoc	Purdue	4	K	JD	63	Indiana	1970
Strauss, George	Retir	Cal Berkeley	25	1993	PHD		Northwes	1980
Strauss, Harold	Prof	U Miami	28	BNOP	PHD	52	Geneva	1968
Strauss, Judy P.	Prof	Augustana IL	23		PHD	93	Iowa	9-93
Strauss, Todd	Asst	Yale	7	V	PHD	92	Berkeley	1992
Strebel, Paul		Intl Mgt Dev	38	IY	PHD		Princeton	
Streeter, Victor J.	Assoc	Mich-Dearbor	9	Z	PHD	69	Michigan	1963
Streever, Donald C.	Prof	Pace-Westch	3		PHD	57	Illinois	1981
Strempek, R. Barth	Asst	Elon	39	Y	DBA	89	Miss St	1994
Strickland, A. J. (Lonnie)	Prof	Alabama	3	I	PHD	69	Geo St	1982
Strickland, Ben	Inst	Morris Brown			MBA	76	CAU	1992
Strickland, Donald E.	C-Ac	S Ill-Edward	2	EFH	PHD	77	Tulane	1985
Strickland, Ted	Asst	Louisville	9	Z	PHD	89	Arizona	8-89
Strigel, Stephen	Inst	USAF Academy	1	I	MS		Arkansas	
Strong, Charles R.	Prof	Tx-Pan Amer	5	Q	PHD	73	Alabama	1972
Strong, Diane	Asst	Boston Univ	9	Z	PHD		Car Mel	
Strong, Kelly	Asst	Illinois St	34		PHD	92	Colorado	1992
Strosberg, Martin	D-Ac	Union			PHD	77	Syracuse	
Stross, Randall	Prof	San Jose St	84	Y	PHD	82	Stanford	1986
Strouble, Dennis D.	Asst	Dallas	94	ZKN	PHD	84	Tx Tech	5-92
Stuart, Robert W.	Lect	Northeastern	6	TO	PHD		Renssela	9-87
Stuck, James Michael	Asst	Valparaiso	38	IYZ	PHD	81	Claremont	1987
Stucke, Harry	Assoc	Lg Isl-Brook			MBA		New York	
Stuk, Stephen P.	Asst	Emory	7	U	PHD		Ga Tech	
Stulberg, Joseph	C-Ac	Wayne State	45	KQ	PHD	75	Rochest	1989
Stumpf, Robert V.	Prof	CS-Pomona	9	Z	PHD	75	Claremont	1968
Stumpf, Stephen A.	Prof	Tampa	25	EF	PHD	78	NYU	1993
Stylianou, Anthony C.	Asst	N Car-Charl			PHD		Kent St	1990
Suaraez, Jose Luis	Prof	Univ Navarra	7	V	DBA		Navarra	7-82
Subbanarasimha, P. N.	Asst	Drexel	3	IT	PHD	90	NYU	1989
Subramanian, Ram	Asst	Grand Valley			PHD	90	North Tx	1990
Subramanian, S. K.	Prof	NJ Inst Tech	8	Y	PHD	60	Bingham	1993
Distinguished Professor								
Subramanian, Vankat	Asst	Wis-Parkside	9	Z	PHD	90	Kent St	8-87
Succari, Owais R.	Assoc	DePaul			PHD		Louvain	
Suchan, James	Assoc	Naval Postgr	12	DEZ	PHD	80	Illinois	1-86
Suchon, Kathleen	Asst	Mass-Lowell	3	IN	PHD	90	SUNY-Alb	
Sugumaran, Vijay	Asst	LeMoyne	9	Z	PHD	93	G Mason	1993
Suh, Myung W.	Asst	Naval Postgr	9	VZU	PHD	90	Rochest	1-89
Suh, Yung-Ho	Asst	Wis-Eau Clar	9	Z	PHD	91	Syracuse	1991
Suits, Martin	Retir	Houston-Down	15	1993	MA	55	Michigan	9-74
Sulek, Joanne M.	Asst	N Carol A&T	7		PHD	89	N Carol	8-86
Sullenberger, A. Gale	Dean	Bradley	9	Z	PHD	71	Oklahoma	6-86
Sullivan, Brian	Assoc	W Kentucky	4	K	JD	72	Kentucky	1976
Sullivan, Dale B.	Prof	Toledo	2		DBA		Kent St	1973
Sullivan, Daniel	Asst	Delaware			PHD	88	S Carol	1993
Sullivan, Gary L.	C-Pr	Tx-El Paso		Mktg	PHD	78	Florida	1985
Betty M. MacGuire Professor of Business Administration								
Sullivan, George	Assoc	S Ill-Edward	4	KL	JD	71	Seton Hl	1987
Sullivan, James	Asst	Alabama A&M						
Sullivan, Jay	Asst	US Intl			PHD		US Intl	1992
Sullivan, John	Prof	San Fran St	5	NQ	PHD	78	Florida	1978
Sullivan, Kathryn	Asst	Westfield St			PHD		Mass	1992
Sullivan, Patrick H.	Assoc	US Intl			DBA	72	Fla St	1987
Sullivan, Sherry	Assoc	Bowling Gr			PHD	88	Ohio St	1933
Sullivan, Terence	Retir	Manchest Bus	5	1994	BA		Leeds	1986
Sumita, Ushio	Assoc	Rochester	79	UZ	PHD		Rochest	
Summers, David F.	Inst	West Txs A&M	13	EI	MBA		West Tx	1985
Summers, Michael R.	Prof	Pepper-Malib	7	UV	PHD	78	Illinois	1980
Summers, Russell	C-Ac	St Marys-Cnd	25	ENX	PHD	87	Waterloo	1987
Summers, Timothy P.	Assoc	Clemson	2	EH	PHD	86	S Carol	1987
Summiel, Laverne S.	Asst	St Paul's	9	Z	MBA			1973
Sundaram, Anant K.	Assoc	Dartmouth			PHD	87	Yale	1986
Sundarraj, R. P.	Asst	Clark	9	Z	PHD	90	Tenn	
Sundberg, Ronald E.	Prof	Suffolk			EDD		Boston U	
Sunder, Shyam	Prof	Carnegie Mel	89	YZ	PHD	74	Car Mel	1988
Richard M. Cyert Professor of Management & Economics								
Sunduramurthy, C.	Asst	Kentucky	3	I	PHD	92	Illinois	1991
Sung, Simona	Asst	St Rose	7	V	PHD	90	Renssela	1990
Suntrup, Edward	Assoc	Ill-Chicago	85	QNKY	PHD	75	Minn	9-76
Superina, Susan C.	LectA	Flinders Un	69	ZST	BEC	79	Adelaide	1988
Superville, Claude	Asst	Valdosta St	7	UVWX	ABD	93	Alabama	1993
Suphi, Djan		Southeastern			MBA		Boston U	
Suran, Jerome	SLect	Cal-Davis			BSEE		Columbia	
Suresh, Nallan C.	Assoc	SUNY-Buffalo	7	U	PHD	82	Cinn	1986
Susbauer, Jeffery C.	Assoc	Cleveland St	36	STI	PHD		Texas	1970

Susman, Gerald I.	C-Pr	Penn State	3	DFU	PHD	68	UCLA	1969
Susmann, Philip	Assoc	Norwich	79		MBA			
Sussman, Lyle	Prof	Louisville	2	EF	PHD	73	Purdue	1973
Sussna, Edward	Prof	Pittsburgh	8		PHD		Illinois	
Sutcliffe, Kathleen	Asst	Minnesota	2	EH	PHD	91	Texas	1991
Sutherland, David	Assoc	Ohio Univ			PHD		Kansas	
Sutherland, Lee	Asst	Suffolk			EDD		Nova	
Sutija, George	Assoc	Fla Internat		Y	MBA	61	Columbia	1973
Sutton, Charlotte D.	Assoc	Auburn	15	EN	PHD	86	Tx A&M	9-86
Sutton, Cynthia	Asst	Ind-So Bend			PHD	93	Ariz St	8-92
Sutton, Robert	C-Ac$	Wis-Eau Clai		Mktg	PHD	84	Iowa	8-80
Sutton, Tim	VProf	Univ Navarra	7	V	PHD		U Wash	7-89
Suyderhould, Jack P.	Assoc	Hawaii-Manoa	7	B	PHD	78	Purdue	
Suzuki, Shinichi	Prof	Univ Tsukuba	5	NP	MPOL			4-92
Svaan, Eric	Asst	Michigan		U	PHD	93	Car Mel	1991
Svanoe, Atlee	Lect	Wis-Whitewat	9	Z	MBA	72	Wis-Whit	1972
Swain, Donald	Adj	Southeastern			PHD		Stanford	
Swamidass, Paul M.	Assoc	Auburn	7	U	PHD	83	U Wash	6-92
Swaminathan, Anand	Asst	Michigan	3	IH	PHD	91	Berkeley	1991
Swanda, John R. Jr.	D-Pr	Ind-So Bend	24	EJ	PHD	68	Illinois	9-68
Swangard, Randy	AdjIn	Oregon	6		MBA	71	Wash	1987
Swanson, Carl L.	Assoc	North Texas	3	IKL	PHD	82	Tx-Dallas	1982
Swanson, David M.	Assoc	Clemson	8	Y	PHD	72	N Carol	1970
Swanson, E. Burton	Prof	UCLA	9	Z	PHD	71	Berkeley	1974
Swanson, James	Assoc	Embry-Riddle	9	Z	PHD	70	Fla St	1986
Swanson, Larry	Asst	Montana	37	LVMX	PHD	80	Nebraska	1988
Swanson, Laura	Asst	S Ill-Edward	7	U	ABD		Purdue	1994
Swari, Ifschak	Prof	Tel Aviv Un		F	PHD	78	Rochest	1989
Swartz, Louis B.	Asst	Robt Morris	1	JK	JD	09	Duquesne	9-83
Swartz, Rose Ann	Prof	Ferris State	2		PHD		Mich St	1978
Swartzmeyer, Elmer G.	Asst	Georgia St	9	Z	PHD		Geo St	
Swearingen, Eugene	Dean	Oral Roberts	46	TJ	PHD	55	Stanford	8-82
Sweeney, Paul	Asst	Marquette	27	EY	PHD	83	Pitt	1987
Sweeney, Paul E.	Asst	Michigan	7	U	PHD	88	Michigan	1987
Swenseth, Scott	Asst	Nebraska	7	UVX	PHD	88	Tx A&M	8-87
Swenson, David		St Scholasti			PHD			1992
Swenson, H. Raymond	H-Pr	Butler	79	UZ	PHD	63	Chicago	1961
Swenson, James K.	Prof	Moorhead St	2	EH	PHD	71	N Dakota	1972
Swersey, Arthur J.	Prof	Yale	7	UV	DENG	72	Columbia	1976
Swiercz, Paul M.	Prof	George Wash	5	N	PHD	84	Virg St	
Swim, Keith D. Jr.	Lect	Texas A&M			JD	80	Tx Tech	1989
Swindley, David	Lect	Bournemouth	34	IJL	MSC			1-91
Swinehart, Kerry D.	Asst	East Tenn St	7	U	PHD	89	Georgia	1990
Swinth, Robert L.	Assoc	Montana St	4		PHD	64	Stanford	9-79
Sylla, Cheickna	Assoc	NJ Inst Tech	79	UZ	PHD	83	SUNY-Buf	1989
Symes, Christopher S.	LectA	Flinders Un	4	KS	LLB	89	Adelaide	3-93
Symons, Ian R.	SLect	Deakin-Warrn	12	DG	MBA	85	Deakin	1991
Symons, Richard	Assoc	Ashland		UV	DBA		Tenn	1992
Sype, Gail E.	Asst	Saginaw Vall	28	EHY	PHD	93	Mich St	1990
Sypolt, Linda T.	Asst	W Virginia	4	K	JD	75	W Virg	1975
Szabat, Kathryn A.	Asst	LaSalle	3	I	PHD		Penn	1981
Szabo-White, Marta					PHD	92	Fla St	
Szajna, Bernadette A.	Asst	Tx Christian	9	Z	PHD	90	Houston	1990
Szecsy, Richard E.	Prof	St Marys-Txs			PHD	73	Illinois	
Szewczak, Edward J.	Assoc	Canisius	9	Z	PHD	88	SUNY-Buf	1988
Szilagyi, Andrew	Prof	Houston	36	DEIT	PHD	73	Indiana	8-73
Sztager, George	Asst	St Ambrose	17	DU	MBA	79	Iowa	1993
Taber, Thomas D.	Prof	SUNY-Albany	25	EN	PHD	72	Illinios	1979
Tabibzadeh, Kambiz	Asst	E Kentucky	7	ZQ	PHD	85	Houston	1985
Tabor, Charles Dwight Jr.	C-Pr	Georgia St			PHD		Geo St	
Tabor, Patty	Inst	Southern Ark			MBA		La Tech	1988
Tacker, Tom	Assoc	Embry-Riddle			PHD	87	N Carol	1988
Tadikamalla, Pandu R.	Assoc	Pittsburgh	7		PHD		Iowa	
Tadisina, Suresh	Asst	So Illinios	79	UVTY	PHD	87	Cinn	8-86
Taggart, William M.	Prof	Fla Internat		DGZ	PHD	71	Penn	1972
Taghaboni, Fataneh	Asst	Mich-Flint	7	UV	PHD	89	Purdue	9-90
Tahir, Mohammad	Lect	Australian N	7	VY	MSC	82	Aust Nat	1990
Tajima, Moriyuki	Prof	Hitotsubashi	2	U	DC	74	Hitotsub	1961
Takayanagi, Satoru	Prof	Univ Tsukuba	23	HI	MECO	59	Tokyo	4-79
Takemura, Kazuhisa	Asst	Univ Tsukuba	1	EHX	MART	85		4-92
Tala, Jasmine	Asst	Tx-Brownsvil			PHD	93	Syracuse	1993
Talbot, F. Brian	C-Pr	Michigan	7	U	PHD	76	Penn St	1977
Talbot, Irwin N.	Assoc	St Peters		ESTH	PHD		NYU	9-79
Talbot, Jean	Adj	HEC-Montreal	9		PHD		Montpell	
Talbot, Reginald J.	Lect	Manches Inst	2	E	BSC		London	9-76
Tallent, Dwaine	C-Pr	St Cloud St	36	IS	PHD	70	Nebraska	1979
Tallman, Stephen	Assoc	Utah	38	YI	PHD	88	UCLA	1990
Tallon, William J.	C-As	No Illinois			PHD		Iowa	1987
Talmor, Eli	Assoc	Tel Aviv Un		M	PHD	81	N Carol	1983
Tam, S. K. W.	Asst	Un Hong Kong	26	HT	MSC			1-85

Name	Rank	School			Degree			Year
Tama, Joseph M.	Asst	Notre Dame	7		PHD	90	Car Mel	1991
Tamaschke, Rick U.	Read	Queensland	78	Y	PHD		Queensld	1989
Tamura, Hirokuni	Prof	U Washington	7	V	PHD	67	Michigan	1967
Tan, Chinteck		Cumberland			MBA	88	Tenn Tec	1988
Tan, Doreen S. K.	Lect	City Poly HK	25	ENPQ	MSC	78	London	1-91
Tan, J. Justin	Asst	CS-S Marcos			PHD	93	Va Tech	9-94
Tan, L. H.	Asst	McGill Univ	8		PHD		Harvard	1993
Tang, Foh-Tsrang	Prof	Nat Taiwan U	3	I	PHD	75	Penn	1975
Tang, Jen	Assoc	Purdue	7	V	PHD	82	Bowl Gr	1991
Tang, Ming-Je	Assoc	Illinois	3	IY	PHD	85	MIT	1985
Tang, Siu S. (Christopher)	Assoc	UCLA	7	V	PHD	85	Yale	1985
Tang, Thomas	Assoc	Mid Tenn St	25	EFN	PHD	81	Case Wes	1983
Tang, Y. Edwin	Asst	N Carol St	13	DIV	PHD	89	Tx-Dall	1988
Tangedahl, Lee	Prof	Montana	79	V	PHD	76	Colorado	1976
Tannenbaum, Scott I.	Assoc	SUNY-Albany	5	NPZ	PHD	86	Old Dom	1985
Tanner, Ian R.	Lect	Manchest Bus	23	EFHT	BSC		Aston	1982
Tanner, John	Prof	SW Louisiana	7	ZRO	PHD	73	Arkansas	1990
Tansik, David M.	Assoc	Arizona	23	EHN	PHD	69	Northwes	1970
Tansky, Judith	Asst	Jms Madison	52	NP	PHD	91	Ohio St	9-92
Tanton, Morgan	Lect	U Lancaster	25	NOPR	CTED		Lancaste	
Tao, I. H. H.	Asst	Un Hong Kong	9	Z	MSC			9-83
Tapia, Daniel	Asst	St Thomas-FL	48		LLM			1985
Tapies, Josep	Prof	Univ Navarra	7	V	PHD		Politecn	9-82
Tapp, Carol	Inst	Savannah St	17	PV	MED	83	Armst St	1983
Targett, D.	Prof	Univ Bath	9	Z	PHD			
ICL Professor of Information Systems								
Tarimcilar, M. Murat	Asst	Suffolk			PHD		LSU	
Tarjan, John	Prof	CS-Bakersf	29	HZ	PHD			1986
Tarnoff, Karen	Asst	East Tenn St	5	N	PHD	94	Va Tech	1994
Tarnutzer, Sharon	Inst	Utah State	12	DE	MBA	86	Utah St	9-90
Tarwater, Ben B.	Assoc	Ark-Ltl Rock			PHD	72	Missouri	
Tatum, James C.	Prof	Henderson St			DBA	76	Miss St	
Taube, Larry R.	Assoc	N Car-Greens	7	U	PHD	84	N Carol	1982
Taucher, George		Intl Mgt Dev	3	I	DR		Lausanne	
Tavakoli, Assad	Prof	Fayetteville			PHD	76	England	1983
Tavakolian, Hamid	Assoc	CS-Fullerton	9	Z	PHD	87	Geo St	8-89
Tavana, Madjid	C-As	LaSalle	9	Z	MBA		LaSalle	1984
Taylor, A. J.	Assoc	Queen's Univ	7	UV	PHD	76	Stanford	1977
Taylor, Frank	Assoc	Tx A&M-Kings	7	UV	PHD	79	Houston	1979
Taylor, Gregory	Assoc	Winston-Sal						
Taylor, John N.	Prof	Alaska-Fairb	5	N	DBA	76	Utah	1982
Taylor, Keith	Read	City Poly HK	2	EFHO	PHD	75	Melbourn	1-91
Taylor, Lary	Assoc	Pacific Unio	8	Y	MBA		Maryland	1978
Taylor, Lewis A. III	C-Pr	North Texas	23	EFIX	DBA	84	India U	1992
Taylor, M. Susan	Assoc	Maryland	5	FNO	PHD	78	Purdue	1983
Taylor, Marilyn L.	Prof	Kansas	3	I	DBA		Harvard	1977
Taylor, Mary S.	Asst	Portland St	85	YN	PHD	89	U Wash	1990
Taylor, Michael B.	Prof	Marietta	48	BJY	PHD	76	Harvard	9-77
Taylor, Natalie T.	Assoc	Babson			DBA		Harvard	
Taylor, Priscilla			2	E	PHD	80	N Carol	
Taylor, Richard W.	Assoc	Akron	7	VUX	PHD	83	Ga Tech	8-89
Taylor, Robert E.			2	E	PHD	74	N Carol	
Taylor, Robert R.	Assoc	Memphis	2	EP	PHD	79	LSU	1983
Taylor, Ronald	Prof	Metro State	4	JKL	JD	75		1980
Taylor, Ronald	Prof	Rice	23	EI	PHD	70	Minn	1983
Chaired Professor								
Taylor, Samuel G.	Prof	Wyoming	7	UVW	PHD		Ariz St	8-78
Taylor, Shannon	Asst	Montana St	92		PHD	76	Colorado	9-79
Taylor, Sherrie	Inst	Txs Woman's	56	NST	MBA	86	Tx Woman	1993
Taylor, Stephen	Assoc	Miss State	5	NP	PHD	85	Va Tech	1987
Taylor, Stuart	Assoc	F Dick-Madis	15	NTM	DBA		Indiana	1992
Taylor, W.	Assoc	Concordia U						
Taylor, Wagiha A.	Prof	Wilkes	8	Y	PHD		Clark	6-69
Taylor, William	Lect	City Poly HK	58	MQUY	MA	86	UK	1-93
Tayur, Sridhar	Assoc	Carnegie Mel	7	U	PHD		Cornell	1991
Te'eni, Dov	Asst	Case Western			PHD	86	Tel Aviv	7-86
Teagarden, Linda	Asst	Virg Tech	3		PHD	92	Colorado	1994
Teagarden, Mary	Assoc	San Diego St	83	YI	PHD	89	S Calif	1986
Teague, Lavette C. Jr.	Prof	CS-Pomona	9	ZJ	PHD	68	MIT	1980
Teal, Steven L.	Inst	Air Force In	9	IZ	ABD		Car Mel	9-92
Teece, David	Prof	Cal-Berkeley	38	IY	PHD		Penn	1984
Teeter, Shirley L.	Assoc	CS-Northrdge	13	EGIN	PHD	75	UCLA	1969
Teeven, Kevin	Prof	Bradley	4	K	JD	71	Illinois	1974
Tegarden, David P.	Asst	CS-San Bern	9	Z	PHD	91	Colorado	1993
Tehran, Minoo	Assoc	Bloomsburg	38		PHD		Ariz St	8-90
Teich, Jeffrey E.	Asst	New Mex St	79	VXZ	PHD	91	SUNY-Buf	1990
Teisberg, Elizabeth Olmsted	Asst	Harvard	4	L				
Teitelbaum, Israel	Prof	Lg Isl-Brook			PHD	69	NYU	
Teitlebaum, A. D.	Prof	McGill Univ	7		PHD		McGill	1968
Telias, Moises G.					DBA	80	Fla St	

Name	Rank	School			Degree		University	
Tellier, Richard D.	Prof	CS-Fresno	7	U	DBA	73	Fla St	1973
Telly, Charles S.	Prof	SUNY-Fredon	13	BI	PHD		U Wash	1985
Templer, Andrew	Prof	Univ Windsor	25	NOPQ	PHD	80	Witwater	1984
Temponi, Cecilia	Asst	SW Texas St	7	U	PHD	92	Tx-Arlin	1990
Teplensky, Jill D.	Asst	Case Western	3	ICD	PHD	90	Penn	1991
Tepper, Bennett J.	Asst	Kentucky	2	E	PHD	91	U Miami	1990
Terborg, James R.	Prof	Oregon	2	E	PHD	75	Purdue	1980
Carolyn S. Chambers Professor of Management								
Terpstra, David E.	Prof	Mississippi	5	NP	PHD	78	Tenn	1990
Tersine, Michele G.	Inst	Oklahoma	7	U	MBA	79	Old Dom	8-80
Tersine, Richard J.	Prof	Oklahoma	7	UV	DBA	69	Fla St	8-80
Baldwin Professor								
Tesch, Frederick F.	Prof	Western Conn	25	FINP	PHD		Cinn	1976
Testerman, Jack	Asst	SE Okla St			PHD	70	Texas	8-86
Testerman, Ward D.	Prof	CS-Pomona	9	Z	DBA	75	S Calif	1971
Thachenkary, Cherian S.	Assoc	Georgia St	7	V	PHD		Waterloo	
Thacker, James	Prof	Univ Windsor	25	NOPQ	PHD	84	Wayne St	1982
Thacker, Rebecca A.	Asst	Ohio Univ	5	KNQ	PHD	87	Tx A&M	
Thakur, Lakshman S.	Assoc	Connecticut	79	UZ	SCD	71	Columbia	9-87
Thakur, Manab N.	Prof	CS-Fresno	3	I	PHD		Brunel	1988
Thaler, Richard H.	Prof	Cornell	2	H	PHD	74	Rochest	7-78
Henrietta Johnson Louis Professor of Management								
Thalmann, Gerald	C-Ac	Teikyo Mary	18	CY	MBA		Wi-White	8-87
Tham, Alex K. S.	ALect	City Poly HK	37	IPSY	MBA	92	UK	9-92
Thamer, Theresa	Asst	Embry-Riddle			MBA	81	Geo St	1990
Thamhain, Hans	Assoc	Bentley	1	D	PHD	72	Syracuse	1986
Thanheiser, Heinz T.	Prof	INSEAD	3	I	DBA	72	Harvard	1-72
Thavikulwat, Precha	Assoc	Towson State	37		PHD	78	Minn	1988
Theeke, Herman	Asst	Con Michigan	15	Q	PHD	00	Minn	1989
Theis, Ann	Asst	Adrian	17	IUZ	MBA	86	Michigan	8-89
Theroux, James	VAsst	Massachusett	16		EDD		Mass	1990
Theye, Larry D.	Prof	Neb-Kearney	25	E	PHD	77	Nebraska	1977
Thibault, Christopher	Asst	Norwich	9		MBA			
Thibodeaux, Mary S.	Assoc	North Texas	76	HIYR	PHD	76	North Tx	1976
Thiel, Glenn R.	Asst	Robt Morris	57	NPQW	MBA	77	Duquesne	9-83
Thiemann, Bernard F.	Prof	Bellarmine			JD		Louisvil	
Thierauf, Robert J.	Prof	Xavier			PHD	66	Ohio St	1965
Thies, Clifford F.	Prof	Shenandoah			PHD		Boston C	1992
Durell Professor of Money, Banking & Finance								
Thoenig, Jean-Claude	Prof	INSEAD	2	H	LIC	63	Geneve	9-78
Thomas, Alan B.	Lect	Manchest Bus	25	EHZ	PHD		Open	1984
Thomas, Anisya	Asst	Fla Internat		I	PHD	90	Va Tech	1990
Thomas, D. Roland	D-Ac	Carleton Un		Mgt	PHD		Imperial	
Thomas, Dave	Prof	St Cloud St	36	ST	PHD	79	Nebraska	1980
Thomas, David A.	Asst	Harvard	25	EN	PHD			
Thomas, Dwight	Prof	Athabasca Un	6	STY	DBA	75	Colorado	1980
Thomas, Gail Fann	Assoc	Naval Postgr	12	EFHT	EDD	86	Ariz St	6-86
Thomas, Graham	SLect	Napier Univ	7	UV	MENG			1980
Thomas, Howard	Dean	Illinois	3	IX	PHD	70	Edinburg	1981
Thomas, James B.	Assoc	Penn State	23	HI	PHD		Texas	1987
Thomas, Joe G.	Prof	Mid Tenn St	31	I	PHD	83	Texas	1989
Thomas, John M.	Assoc	SUNY-Buffalo	48	EKY	PHD	60	MIT	9-68
Thomas, Johnny	Asst	LaSierra	16	ST	MBA	88	Loma Lin	9-89
Thomas, Kenneth W.	Prof	Naval Postgr	12	EG	PHD	71	Purdue	1-87
Thomas, L. Joseph	Prof	Cornell	7	UV	PHD	68	Yale	9-67
Nicholas H. Noyes Professor of Manufacturing								
Thomas, Lacy Glenn	Assoc	Emory	3	I	PHD	79	Duke	1991
Thomas, Louis A.	Asst	Pennsylvania	3	I	PHD	91	Harvard	7-92
Whitney M. Young, Jr. Term Assistant Professor of Management								
Thomas, Lula	Asst	Southern	15	GSK	MED	71	Southern	1972
Thomas, Mark J.	Assoc	Brock Univ	25	ENH	PHD		New York	1983
Thomas, Otis A.	Dean	Morgan State		QMth	PHD	71	American	1972
Thomas, Robert J.	Assoc	MIT	5	N	PHD			
Leaders for Manufactuirng Associate Professor								
Thomas, Sebastian	Asst	St Fran-Penn			MBA			
Thomas, Steve L.	Asst	SW Missouri	52	QN	PHD	89	Kansas	1990
Thomas, Tom E.	Asst	U Washington	2		PHD	88	Berkeley	1988
Thomason, T.	Asst	McGill Univ	5		PHD		Cornell	1988
Thomassin, Singh Daniele	Asst	York Univ	79	Z	PHD		Case Wes	
Thommas, Maureen		Bemidji St	9	Z				
Thomopoulos, Nick	Prof	Illinois Tch	7	V	PHD	66	Ill Tech	1968
Thompson, A.	Asst	Mt St Vincen	79	UTRZ	MBA	82	Dalhousi	1986
Thompson, C.		Humberside	3					
Thompson, Cynthia A.	Asst	CUNY-Baruch	5	N	PHD		Tenn	1985
Thompson, Denise	Asst	Tuskegee						
Thompson, Duane E.	Prof	Iowa	5	N	PHD	69	Iowa	1965
Thompson, G. Fred	Prof	Willamette	14	ABJL	PHD	72	Claremont	1986
Grace and Elmer Goudy Professor of Public Management and Policy Analysis								
Thompson, Gary M.	Assoc	Utah	7	UX	PHD	88	Fla St	1987
Thompson, J.		Humberside	2					

Name	Rank	School			Degree		School	Year
Thompson, John	Asst	Loyola-Maryl	2		MBA		Temple	
Thompson, John Clair	Assoc	Connecticut	3	I	PHD	61	Illinois	1966
Thompson, Judith K.	Asst	New Mexico	4	JL	PHD	87	Berkeley	
Thompson, Kenneth R.	Assoc	DePaul			PHD		Nebraska	
Thompson, Lloyd	Prof	Warner So	20	UVWZ	EDD	77	N Colo	1993
Thompson, Mark	Prof	British Colu	5	QY	PHD	66	Cornell	1971
Thompson, Mark	AcAs	U Lethbridge	9		BMGT	92	Lethbrid	1992
Thompson, Mary	AcAs	U Lethbridge	25		ABD		Calgary	1992
Thompson, Michael	Asst	Wake Forest	4	JK	JD		N Carol	1-91
Thompson, Pamela L.	Asst	Catawba			MBA		Jms Mad	
Thompson, Patrick	Asst	Florida			PHD	84	Wiscon	1989
Thompson, William J.	Prof	Dallas Bapt	79		PHD		Geo St	1991
Thoms, Margaret	Asst	Penn St-Erie	25	EN	PHD	94	Ohio St	1994
Thomsen, Wayne	Asst	Nev-L Vegas	9	JPZ	PHD	86	Colo St	1987
Thomson, Jim S.	SLect	Napier Univ	79	VZ	BSC			1973
Thomson, John R.	Lect	Napier Univ	38	IY	MBA			1990
Thorn, Ron	Assoc	Tx-Pan Amer	7	U	PHD	73	Tx Tech	1988
Thornberry, Neal E.	Assoc	Babson			PHD		Bowl Gr	
Thorne, John R.	Prof	Carnegie Mel	6	T	MSIA	52	Car Mel	
David T. & Lindsay J. Morgenthaler Professor of Enterpreneurship								
Thorne, Neil	Assoc	No Alabama			DBA	92	Memphis	1993
Thornthwaite, Louise	Lect	Griffith Un	5	BQ	PHD	91	Sydney	7-90
Thornton, Billy	Prof	Colorado St	27	HUZ	PHD	72	Tx A&M	1981
Thornton, Carl L.	Prof	GMI	25	EHNP	PHD	74	Akron	1989
Thornton, Jack W. Jr.	Prof	East Carol		Z	PHD		Missouri	1968
Thornton, Nelson L. Jr.	Prof	Sam Houston			PHD	73	North Tx	1970
Thorp, Cary D.	Assoc	Nebraska	5	N	PHD	70	Missouri	9-70
Throop, Gary	Asst	Clarkson			PHD		Mass	
Thumin, Frederick J.	Prof	Mo-St Louis	25	EN	PHD	57	Wash U	1966
Thwaites, Desmond	Assoc	Univ Leeds	3	DI	PHD	90	Bradford	1989
Tibrewala, Raj	Prof	NY Inst Tech	73		PHD			
Tichy, Noel M.	Prof	Michigan	2	E	PHD	72	Columbia	1980
Tierney, Pam	Asst	Portland St	2	EQ	PHD	92	Cinn	1992
Till, Lee	Lect	SW Texas St	5	N	MS	67	Chicago	1987
Tillery, Kenneth R.	Assoc	Mid Tenn St	38	IY	PHD	85	Georgia	1988
Tilles, Seymour	Lect	Northeastern	3	I	DBA		Harvard	9-87
Tillman, Gerald J.	Assoc	Appalach St	9	Z	PHD		Georgia	1985
Tilt, Carol A.	LectA	Flinders Un	1	M	DACC	91	Flinders	3-93
Tilton, Rita	Visit	Nev-L Vegas	4	GR	PHD	67	Minn	1987
Timmins, Sherman A.	Prof	Toledo	2		PHD		Penn St	1976
Timmons, Jeffry A.	Prof	Babson			DBA		Harvard	
Frederic C. Hamilton Professor for Free Enterprise								
Timpany, Gordon A.	Asst	No Iowa			MA	67	Minn	9-67
Timperley, Stuart R.	Assoc	London Bus	23	FHIO	PHD		Liverpoo	
Tindall, Robert M.	Assoc	Arizona	38	IYT	PHD	81	London	1963
Tinney, Cathie	C	Tx-Perm Bas			PHD	81	Minn	
Tirney, Thomas	Asst	Temple			PHD	71	Penn	1989
Tirtiroglu, Ercan	Assoc	Mass-Dartmou			PHD	75	Florida	1992
Tirupati, Devanath	Assoc	Texas	7	UV	PHD	87	MIT	1986
Tischler, Len	Asst	Scranton	23	ED	PHD	90	Maryland	1990
Tisone, Albert Sr.	Adj	Southeastern			DBA		Geo Wash	
Titus, George J.	Assoc	Temple			PHD	77	Penn	1977
Todd, Jerry	C-Pr	St Marys-Txs			PHD	68	Wiscon	
Charles E. Cheever Professor of Risk Management								
Todd, John T.	Prof	Arkansas	26	EST	DBA	72	Harvard	1972
Todd, P.	Lect	W Australia			MIR		W Austra	
Todd, P.A.	Asst	Queen's Univ	9	Z	PHD	88	Brit Col	1989
Todd, Wayne	Asst	Baltimore	37	DIUX	BA	76	Emory	8-90
Todor, William D.	Assoc	Ohio State	2	E	PHD	79	Ca-Irvine	1979
Toelle, Richard A.	Asst	Idaho	7	UVW	PHD	86	Oklahoma	1986
Toftoy, Charles	Assoc	George Wash	6	S	DBA	85	Nova	
Toh, Rex	Prof	Seattle	7	X	PHD		Minn	
Tolchin, Susan	Prof	George Wash	1	A	PHD	68	New York	
Tolliver, James	Prof	New Brunswic	2	E	PHD	77	Ohio St	1981
Tolner, Thera	Asst	Univ Limburg	23	IEFH	MA	90	Utrecht	1990
Toma, Al	Inst	SW Louisiana	81	YST	MBA	70	American	1983
Tombak, Mihkel	Asst	British Colu	73	UI	PHD	88	Penn	1991
Tombaugh, Jay R.	Assoc	Houston-C Lk	24	DE	PHD		Bowl Gr	8-84
Tomkiewicz, Joseph M.	C-Pr	East Carol	25	EFNR	PHD	78	Temple	8-81
Tomkins, C. R.	Prof	Univ Bath	1	A	MSC			
Tomlin, Sharyn	Inst	Angelo State			ABD		North Tx	
Tomlinson, William	Assoc	British Colu	8	Y	PHD	68	MIT	1970
Tomlinson, William H.	Assoc	North Fla	35	INY	PHD	74	American	1972
Tompkins, Donald	Assoc	Slippery Roc	25	EW	PHD		Ohio St	8-82
Tong, Vincent	Asst	Bridgeport	2	EFH	PHD	91	Yale	9-93
Tonn, Joan C.	Assoc	Mass-Boston	2	E	PHD	73	Michigan	1975
Tonnesen, Edwin	Assoc	Bowling Gr	32	I	PHD	70	Syracuse	1971
Toombs, Leslie A.	C-As	Texas-Tyler	3	I	DBA	89	La Tech	1989
Tootoonchi, Ahmad	Asst	Frostburg St			PHD		US Intl	8-89

Name	Rank	School			Degree		University	
Topel, Robert H.	Prof	Chicago			PHD	80	UCLA	1983
Isidore Brown & Gladys J. Brown Professor of Urban & Labor Economics								
Topkis, Donald M.	Prof	Cal-Davis	9	Z	PHD		Stanford	
Topping, Sharon	Asst	So Miss	13	I	PHD		Al-Birm	1990
Torabinejad, Majid	Inst	Alabama A&M	7	V				
Torbert, William R.	Prof	Boston Coll	2	DEF	PHD	71	Yale	9-78
Torello, Robert	Asst	New Haven	7	V	MBA		SCSU	
Toren, Nina	Assoc	Hebrew Univ			PHD		Columbia	
Torkzadeh, G.	C-Pr	Tx-El Paso	9	ZV	PHD	83	Lanc UK	1993
Toro, Juan Manuel de	Asst	Univ Navarra	7	V	MBA		Navarra	6-88
Torrence, Nancy	Asst	Liberty	2		MBA		Lynchbur	8-88
Torrence, William D.	Emer	Nebraska	5	Q	PHD	62	Nebraska	1957
Happold Professor								
Torres, David	Assoc	Ill-Chicago	24	HQTS	PHD	83	Northwes	1-91
Torres, Maximilian B.	Asst	Univ Navarra	4	J	PHD		Harvard	9-92
Torrington, Derek P.	Prof	Manches Inst	5	N	MPHI		CNAA	6-90
Tosi, Henry L. Jr.	Prof	Florida	12	E	PHD	64	Ohio St	1978
McGriff Professor								
Toulson, P. K.	Assoc	Massey Univ	25	EN	PHD	91	Massey	1985
Tourk, Khairy	Assoc	Illinois Tch			PHD	71	Calif	1971
Towell, Elizabeth	Asst	No Illinois			PHD		Wiscon	1993
Tower, Burk	Assoc	Wis-Oshkosh	6	T	DBA	73	Kentucky	
Tower, John E.	Assoc	Oakland	9	Z	PHD	68	SUNY-Buf	1968
Townley, Barbara	Assoc	Univ Alberta	5	NR	PHD	82	LSE UK	1990
Townsend, James B.	H-Pr	Kansas State	3	AIKY	DBA	76	Geo Wash	9-77
Toyne, Brian	Prof	St Marys-Txs			PHD	75	Geo St	
Tracy, Kay	Asst	Gettysburg	2		PHD	92	Maryland	1990
Tracy, Lane N.	Prof	Ohio Univ	25		PHD	71	U Wash	
Trainham, W. Emory	Retir	Ashland		IJKL				
Tran, Alfred	Lect	Australian N	4		MSS	88	HongKong	1991
Traub, Rodney	Asst	Iowa	7	U	PHD	94	Purdue	1993
Trauth, Eileen M.	Assoc	Northeastern			PHD		Pitt	
Traxler, Ralph	Prof	Savannah St	13	BI	PHD	53	Chicago	1982
Traynor, William	Retir	CS-Long Bch	2	EPON	PHD	72	Brig Yg	1973
Treble, J. G.	Prof	North Wales	5	NPQ	PHD			9-91
Treleven, Mark D.	Assoc	John Carroll			PHD	82	N Carol	1989
James S. Reid Professor								
Tremblay, Benoit	Assoc	HEC-Montreal			DEA		Aix-Mars	1989
Tremblay, Michel	Asst	HEC-Montreal	3	O	MS		Va Comm	
Trenchard, Wm. H.	Assoc	Catawba			PHD	93	Mich St	1993
Trent, Robert J.	Assoc	Lehigh			PHD	93	Mich St	1993
Tretheway, Michael	Assoc	British Colu		Y	PHD	81	Wiscon	1983
Tretter, Marietta J.	Assoc	Texas A&M		V	PHD	73	Wiscon	1981
Trevino, Len J.	Asst	U Miami	83	IY	PHD	91	Indiana	1990
Trevino, Melanie	Assoc	Tx-El Paso	3	IY	DBA	87	Geo Wash	1987
Trewatha, Robert L.	Prof	SW Missouri	38	YN	PHD	63	Arkansas	1968
Trick, Michael	Assoc	Carnegie Mel	7	V	PHD		Ga Tech	1988
Tricker, R. I.	Prof	Un Hong Kong	23	IJFD	PHD			9-86
Trigg, Marie	Lect	Deakin-Burwo	38	DR	MBA		Monash	
Tripp, Tom	Asst	Wash State						
Trnavskis, Boris	Assoc	Embry-Riddle	37		PHD	74	Calgary	1986
Trofi, Vincent C.	C	Providence						
Tromley, Cheryl L.	Asst	Fairfield	24	EFLH	PHD	84	Yale	1987
Trostel, Al	Prof	St Thomas-MN						
Trostle, Randolph	C-Ac	Elizabethtwn			PHD	83	Lehigh	9-72
Trotter, Richard	Assoc	Baltimore	45	KLNQ	PHD	70	Penn	9-79
Troutt, Marvin	Prof	So Illinios	79	UTY	PHD	75	Ill-Chic	6-80
Trower, Jonathan	Asst	Baylor		Z	PHD		Minn	1983
Troxell, Joseph R.	Assoc	LaSalle	9	Z	PHD		Rutgers	1971
Troyer, Michael D.	Assoc	WI-Green Bay	34	DIJT	PHD	75	Duke	1971
Trueblood, Robert	Assoc	Alabama-Hunt	9	Z	PHD		Va Tech	1991
Truex, Duane P. III	Asst	Georgia St	9	Z	PHD		SUNY-Bin	
Truitt, J. Frederick	Prof	Willamette	8	Y	DBA	69	Indiana	1991
Helen Simpson Jackson Professor of International Management								
Trumble, Robert R.	Prof	Virg Comm	3	IQ	PHD	71	Minn	1988
Truscott, William G.	Dean	McMaster Un	17	UV	DBA	73	Indiana	7-69
Tryfos, Peter	Prof	York Univ	7	V	PHD		Berkeley	
Tsai, Yann-Ching	Assoc	Nat Taiwan U	7	V	PHD	90	UCLA	1990
Tschirgi, Harvey D.	Retir	Ohio Univ		1994	PHD	60	UCLA	
Tschoegl, Adrian	VAsso	Pennsylvania	8	Y	PHD	80	MIT	7-93
Tse, David	Assoc	British Colu	8	Y	PHD	84	Berkeley	1984
Tse, Olivia K. M.	Lect	City Poly HK	35	INGY	MBA		HongKong	9-87
Tseng, C. S.	Lect	City Poly HK	38	DIY	MSC	70	London	1-89
Tseng, Fan-Tsong	Assoc	Alabama-Hunt	7	UV	PHD		Texas	1984
Tsengg, S. C.	Prof	Catawba			PHD		Oklahoma	
Tso, P. S.	Asst	Un Hong Kong	17		PHD			4-79
Tsolakides, Jordan A.	Prof	Governors St			PHD	68	Mich St	
Tsui, Anne	Assoc	Calif-Irvine	25	EHNR	PHD	81	UCLA	1988
Tu, Howard	Asst	Memphis	38	IY	PHD	88	Mass	1988
Tubbs, Stewart L.	Dean	E Michigan	2	E	PHD	69	Kansas	1986

Name	Rank	School	No	Codes	Deg	Yr	Institution	Range
Tucci, Louis	Asst	Widener			PHD			
Tucker, Bernard	Prof	Tenn State			PHD			
Tucker, Dean	C-Ac	Ogelthrope	13	IM	PHD	79	Mich St	1-88
Rikard Chaired Professor								
Tucker, Ken A.	Prof	Queensland	8	Y	PHD		London	1986
Tucker, Mary L.	Asst	Colorado St	21	E&				
Tuckman, Howard P.	Dean	Virg Comm		Econ	PHD	70	Wiscon	1993
Tuggle, Francis D. (Doug)	Dean	American U	23	IZ	PHD	71	Car Mel	1990
Tulett, David M.	Asst	Memorial Un	7	V	PHD	86	Queen's	1985
Tullar, William L.	Assoc	N Car-Greens	25	EHNY	PHD	75	Rochest	8-73
Tullous, Raydel	Asst	Tx-S Antonio						
Tully, Lindsay B.	SLect	Napier Univ	17	CUV	MSC			1980
Tully, Paul F.	Prof	CS-Sacrament	37	HIUV	PHD	80	Houston	1983
Tunc, Enar A.	Assoc	Ball State	7		PHD		Clemson	1987
Tunwall, Craig A.	Asst	Ithaca	53	IN	PHD	91	Iowa	8-89
Turban, Daniel B.	Asst	Missouri	52	NE	PHD	89	Houston	1989
Turk, Thomas	Assoc	Chapman		IN	PHD		Ca-Irvine	1992
Turner, Betty	C-As	Guilford	4	K	JD		Vanderbt	1991
Turner, Charles F. III	Asst	Geo Southern	79	Z	PHD		Georgia	1989
Turner, Gregory	Asst	Livingston	48		ABD	93	Miss St	1-94
Turner, J. Scott	Prof	Oklahoma St	7	V	PHD	70	So Meth	1982
Turner, John H.	Prof	Montclair St	2	EFH	PHD	72	CUNY	1972
Turner, Jon A.	Assoc	New York U	9	Z	PHD	80	Columbia	
Turner, Marlene E.	Assoc	San Jose St	21	E	PHD	88	Car Mel	1987
Turnipseed, David L. Jr.	Asst	Ind-Purdue	23	EYV	PHD	87	Alabama	8-92
Turnquist, Philip	Assoc	Troy St	31	IUV	DBA	86	Miss St	1990
Turoff, Murray	Prof	NJ Inst Tech	9	Z	PHD	65	Brandeis	1973
Turpin, Dominique V.		Intl Mgt Dev	83	YI	PHD		Sophia	
Tushman, Michael	Prof	Columbia	19	DFZ	PHD	76	MIT	1975
Tustin, Charles O.	Asst	Fort Lewis	17	JUV	PHD	92	Ariz St	1986
Tuzhilin, Alexander	Asst	New York U	9	Z	PHD	89	NYU	
Twark, Richard D.	Assoc	Penn State	7	V	PHD		Penn St	
Twombly, John	Asst	Illinois Tch			PHD		Chicago	1992
Twomey, Dan	Prof	F Dick-Madis	56	NTM	DBA		Kent St	1987
Twotress, Kaylynn	VProf	Miami U-Ohio	8	Y	MS	88	Drake	1-92
Tychsen, Norman E.	Assoc	Aquinas	3	I	MBA	67	Chicago	1974
Tyler, Beverly Baker	Asst	Indiana	3	I	PHD	92	Tx A&M	1991
Tyler, Richard F.	C-As	Fairfield	15	EQP	MBA	66	New York	1977
Tymon, Walter G.	Asst	Villanova	23	EFHI	PHD	88	Temple	1990
Tyran, Craig	Asst	Wash State			PHD			
Tyre, Marcie J.	Asst	MIT			PHD			
Tyree, L. Mark	Prof	Shenandoah			EDD		Wm&Mary	1987
Tyson, Laura	Prof	Cal-Berkeley	48	Y	PHD		MIT	1978
Tzur, Michal	Asst	Pennsylvania			PHD	92	Columbia	1991
Anheuser-Busch Lecturer								
Ubelhoer, Jane	Assoc	Marymount			PHD		Missouri	1992
Udayagiri, Naren D.	Asst	Pennsylvania	38	I	PHD	92	Minn	7-92
John Sculley Lecturer in Management								
Udeh, Igwe	H	Grambling St	38	SYTH	PHD	87	St Louis	1989
Udoka, Sylanus	Asst	N Carol A&T	5		PHD		Okla St	8-92
Ugboro, Isaiah O.	Asst	N Carol A&T	3		PHD		North Tx	1-89
Uhl-Bien, Mary	Asst	Alaska-Ancho	2	EFH	PHD	91	Cinn	1991
Ulferts, Gregory W.	Dean	Detroit Merc	7	U	DBA	75	La Tech	1983
Ullman, Joseph C.	Prof	So Carolina			PHD	65	Chicago	
Ullmann, Arieh A.	Assoc	SUNY-Bingham	3	I	PHD	76	St Gall	1982
Ullmann, Steven G.	Prof	U Miami	14	CDJL	PHD	80	Michigan	1979
Ullrich, Robert A.	Dean	Clark	2	EH	DBA	68	Wash U	7-88
Ulrich, David O.	Adj	Michigan	2	E	PHD	82	UCLA	1982
Ulrich, Karl T.	Assoc	MIT	7	U	SCD			
Ford International Career Development Associate Professor								
Umanath, N. S.	Assoc	Tulsa	9	Z	PHD	87	Houston	1993
Umble, M. Michael	Prof	Baylor	7	U	PHD		LSU	1977
Umpleby, Stuart	Assoc	George Wash	2	H				
Underhill, George	Prof	NE St-Okla	3	I	PHD	84	Arkansas	1985
Underwood, Jim D.	Assoc	Dallas Bapt	31		DBA		US Intl	1989
Ungson, Gerardo R.	Assoc	Oregon	3	IY	PHD	78	Penn St	
Unwalla, Darab B.	C-Pr	Fla Atlantic	32	STL	PHD	57	Bombay	1969
Upchurch, Leo	Assoc	Tuskegee						
Upton, David M.	Asst	Harvard	7	U				
Upton, Nancy	Asst	Baylor	6	T	PHD		Baylor	1983
Ben H. Williams Professor in Entrepreneurship								
Urban, Glen L.	Dean	MIT			PHD		Northwes	
Dai-Ichi Kangyo Bank Professor of Management								
Urban, Timothy L.	C-Ac	Tulsa	7	UV	PHD	87	Tx-Arlin	1987
Uretsky, Myron	Prof	New York U	9	Z	PHD	65	Ohio St	
Ursacki, Terry	Assoc	Univ Calgary	8	Y	PHD	91	Brit Col	1990
Uselding, Paul J.	Dean	Ill-Chicago		DecS	PHD	70	Northwes	1992
Usher, John	Asst	Univ Alberta	23	HI	PHD	90	Toronto	1988
Utecht, Kathleen	Assoc	Cen Michigan	12	EN	PHD	85	Mich St	1980
Utecht, Ronald	Prof	Tx Lutheran	12	E	PHD	70	Ariz St	1985

Name	Pos	Institution			Deg		School	Year
Utterback, Jim	Prof	MIT						
Uyeno, Dean H.	Assoc	British Colu	7	UV	PHD	71	Northwes	1971
Uyterhoeven, Hugo E. R.	Prof	Harvard	1					
Timken Professor of Business Administration								
Uzumeri, Mustafa V.	Asst	Auburn	73	U	PHD	91	Renssela	9-91
Uzzi, Brian	Asst	Northwestern			PHD	93	SUNY-SBr	1993
V Iterson, Ad	Asst	Univ Limburg	42	BHLT	MA	79	Amsterda	1986
V Witteloostuijn, Arjen	Assoc	Univ Limburg	23	EHIY	PHD	86	Masstric	1990
Vachani, Sushil	Asst	Boston Univ	38	IY	DBA		Harvard	
Vaden, Richard	Prof	Ind-Kokomo	25	AEFP	PHD	70	Tx Tech	1992
Vaghefi, M. Reza	Prof	North Fla	38	IY	PHD		Mich St	
Vaicys, Remigijus	Asst	Grambling St	27	N	DBA	90	La Tech	1981
Vaidyanathers, Rajiv	Asst	Minn-Duluth			PHD	93	Wash St	1993
Vaill, Peter	Prof	George Wash	2	E	DBA	64	Harvard	
Vaishnavi, Vijay K.	Prof	Georgia St	9	Z	PHD		Indian T	
Vakharia, Asoo	Asst	Florida			PHD	87	Wiscon	1994
Valas, John	Prof	Ferris State	2		MA		Michigan	1982
Valdez, Jude	Adj	Tx-S Antonio						
Valenzi, Enzo R.	Prof	Fla Internat		NEV	PHD	70	Bowl Gr	1975
Valero, Antonio	Prof	Univ Navarra	3	I	PHD		EEIIT	9-58
Valle, Awilda	Asst	P Rico-Mayag	9		MS	81	Purdue	1-90
Valor, Josep	Prof	Univ Navarra	4	Z	PHD		MIT	9-85
Van Der Heyden, Ludo	Dean	INSEAD	7	V	PHD	79	Yale	9-88
VanAckere, Ann	Assoc	London Bus	7	V	PHD		Stanford	
VanAuken, Philip Mark	Prof	Baylor	3	I	PHD		Tx Tech	1978
VanBuer, Michael	Asst	Loyola-Chicg			PHD		Northwes	1991
Vanbuskirk, William	Assoc	LaSalle	2	E	PHD		Case Wes	1987
VanCamp, Karen	Asst	Northwestern			ABD		Northwes	1990
Vance, Charles M.	Prof	Loyola Marym	25	FNO	PHD	81	Syracuse	1985
Vance, Susan M.	C-Ac	St Marys-Ind			JD		Cooley	
VandeGuchte, Peter	Prof	Calvin			EDD	73	W Mich	1991
Vandenberg, Robert J.	Assoc	Georgia	25	EFHX	PHD	82	Georgia	1993
Vandenbosch, Betty	Asst	Case Western			PHD	93	W Ontar	7-93
Vandermerwe, Andre'		Intl Mgt Dev	83	YI	DCOM		Stellenb	
Vandermerwe, Sandra		Intl Mgt Dev	38	IY	DBA		Stellenb	
Vanderwerf, Pieter	Asst	Boston Univ	59	QZ	PHD		MIT	
VanDeVen, Andrew H.	Prof	Minnesota	2	DH	PHD	72	Wiscon	1983
VanDyne, Linn	Asst	Michigan St	2	E	PHD	93	Minn	8-93
VanEaton, Charles	C-Pr	Hillsdale		Econ	PHD	74	Tulane	1978
Vanecek, Frank T.	H	Norwich	9		DBA			
VanEynde, Donald F.	Assoc	Trinity	12	EFP	PHD	84	Columbia	1-84
VanFleet, David	Prof	Ariz St-West	12	EBHP	PHD	69	Tenn	1989
VanGelderen, Cynthia G.	C	Aquinas	3	I	MBA	84	W Mich	1980
VanGigch, John P.	Emer	CS-Sacrament	37	IUVX	PHD	68	Oreg St	1968
VanHook, Barry	Assoc	Arizona St	63	ST	EDD	76	N Illin	1976
VanHorn, Richard	Prof	Oklahoma						
VanHuss, Susie H.	Dean$	So Carolina			PHD	69	Indiana	
VanLoo, Fran	C-Ac	Cal-Berkeley	1	A	PHD		Berkeley	1981
VanMaanen, John E.	Prof	MIT	2	H	PHD			
Edwin H. Schell Professor of Organizational Studies								
VanOver, David	Asst	Idaho	9	Z	PHD	88	Houston	1991
Vanover, Donald	Prof	Sangamon St	13	IE	PHD		S Illin	1981
VanScotter, James R.		Air Force In	25	EHNZ			Florida	9-94
VanSell, Mary P.	Assoc	Oakland	2	RG	PHD	81	Iowa	1985
VanSpeybroeck, James O.	Prof	St Ambrose	79	VZ	MS	80	W Illin	1983
VanTassel, John E.	Retir	Boston Coll	3	IUP	PHD	57	Havard	9-56
VanVoorhis, Kenneth	Prof	South Fla	36	STI	DBA	71	LSU	1970
VanWright, Evelyn D.	Prof	Ark-Pine Blf			EDD		Columbia	
Varanelli, Andrew Jr.	C-Pr	Pace	37	IUV	DED	71	Rutgers	1968
Varano, Michael	Assoc	Villanova	79	ZV	PHD	71	Penn	1968
Varca, Philip E.	Assoc	Wyoming	52	EGKY	PHD		LSU	8-89
Vardaman, Betsy	Lect	Baylor			MA		Baylor	1981
Vardhau, Harsh	Prof	Rio Grande	38	IY	MBA	78	Ohio St	9-85
Vardi, Yoav	Assoc	Cleveland St	23	EH	PHD		Cornell	1989
Vargas, Gustavo	Assoc	CS-Fullerton	7	U	PHD	77	Penn St	8-86
Vargas, Vince	Asst	Emory						
Vargus, Luis G.	Assoc	Pittsburgh	7		PHD		Penn	
Varin, Dennis L.	Prof	So Oregon St	37	IV	PHD	75	Oreg St	1970
Varlow, P.	SLect	Humberside						
Varney, G. H.	Prof	Bowling Gr	2	F	PHD	71	Case Wes	1970
Varzandeh, Javad	Prof	CS-San Bern	7	U	PHD	81	Oklah St	1987
Vasigh, Bijan	Assoc	Embry-Riddle	7		PHD	84	SUNY	1990
Vass, P.	Lect	Univ Bath	1	A	MSC			
Vassallo, Helen	H	Worcester Pl	12	DEFG	PHD	67	Clark	8-82
Vassar, John	Prof	La St-Shreve	35	CN	PHD	81	North Tx	8-80
Vaughan, Jerry	D	Franklin	23	EFHI	MBA		Capital	
Vaughan, Mary Jo	Asst	Mercer-Macon	25	ENP	ABD		Florida	1993
Vaughan, Thomas		West Chester						
Vaughan, Thomas P.	Asst	St Joseph	79	CUVW	PHD	81	Michigan	1994
Vaughn, Randal L.	Assoc	Baylor		Z	PHD		Tx-Arlin	1982

Name	Rank	School			Deg			Year
Vaughn, William	Prof	Tx-Brownsvil			PHD	72	North Tx	1975
Vaught, Bobby C.	Prof	SW Missouri	52	QN	PHD	79	North Tx	1979
Vazquez-Dodero, Juan Carlos	Prof	Univ Navarra	4	V	DBA		Navarra	8-69
Vazzana, Gary	Asst	Cen Missouri	3	LZ	PHD	87	Missouri	1990
Vd Grinten, P.M.E.M.	Prof	Univ Limburg	23	DIY	PHD	62	Eindhove	1991
Vecchio, Robert P.	Prof	Notre Dame	12	EFH	PHD		Illinois	1976
Franklin D. Schurz Professor of Management								
Veglahn, Peter A.	Prof	Jms Madison	5	QN	PHD	74	Iowa	9-83
Vegso, Raymond W.	Prof	Canisius	34	LY	PHD	75	Cinn	1970
Veiga, John F.	H-Pr	Connecticut	2	E	DBA	71	Kent St	1972
Velasquez, Manuel G.	Prof	Santa Clara			PHD	75	Calif	
Velez, Jorge I.	Prof	P Rico-Mayag	78		PHD	78	Florida	8-72
Velilla, Manuel	Prof	Univ Navarra	7	V	DBA		Navarra	7-71
Velthouse, Betty A.	Asst	Mich-Flint	28	EJY	PHD	90	Pitt	9-88
Venezia, Itzhak	Assoc	Hebrew Univ			PHD		Berkeley	
Venkataraman, Ramanathan	Asst	DePaul			PHD		Ill Tech	
Venkataraman, S.	Asst	Pennsylvania	63	ITSD	PHD	89	Minn	7-89
Paul M. Yeakel Term Assistant Professor of Management								
Venkateswarlu, P.	Lect	Canterbury	7	UV	PHD	83	IITBomba	1991
Venkatraman, N.	Assoc	Boston Univ	39	IZ	PHD		Pitt	
Venne, Rosemary	Asst	Saskatchewan	25	NO	PHD	93	Toronto	1991
Venta, Enrique R.	Prof	Loyola-Chicg			PHD		Northwes	1979
Venuto, Peter	Prof	Bloomsburg	12		PHD		Santa Cl	8-80
Veral, E.	Asst	CUNY-Baruch	1	B	PHD		Clemson	1986
Verderber, Kathleen S.	Assoc	No Kentucky	27	ER	PHD	84	Cinn	8-82
Verdin, Paul	Asst	INSEAD	3	I	PHD	89	Harvard	9-91
Verdini, William A.	Assoc	Arizona St			DBA		Kent St	1976
Verma, Harish	Assoc	Wayne State	7	U	PHD	70	Mich St	1970
Verney, Thomas P.	Prof	Shippensburg			PHD		Bowl Gr	
Vernon, Alex	Asst	Missouri So			MBA	88	Miss	
Vernon-Wortzel, Heidi	Prof	Northeastern	8	Y	PHD		Boston U	9-80
Verser, Gertrude	Assoc	W Michigan	32	TSNP	DBA	78	Harvard	1985
Vertinsky, Ilan	Prof	British Colu	38	AIVY	PHD	68	Berkeley	1970
Veryzer, Robert	Asst	Rensselaer			PHD		Florida	1993
Vesper, Karl	Prof	U Washington	36		PHD		Stanford	1988
Vessal, Ahmad	Lect	Mt St Mary's			PHD		Clark	
Vessey, Iris	Assoc	Penn State	9	Z	PHD		Queensld	
Vest, Carl	Prof	Marymount			PHD		American	1976
Vest, Jusanne	Asst	So Miss	25	NOQR	PHD	89	Va Tech	1989
Vest, Michael	Assoc	So Miss	52	ENQ	PHD	88	Va Tech	1989
Vibhakar, Ashzin	Dean	Ark-Ltl Rock		Fnce	PHD		Arkansas	
Vician, Chelley	Asst	Mich Tech	9	Z	PHD	94	Minn	1994
Vickery, Shawnee K.	Assoc	Michigan St	7	UV	PHD	83	S Carol	1-84
Vickroy, Ronald	C-Ac	Pitts-Johnst	12		MS	80	Car Mel	1985
Vickson, R. G.	Prof	Un Waterloo		UV	PHD	69	MIT	1973
Vicmas, Robert	Prof	Tx A&M Intl			PHD			1994
Victor, Bart Irwin	Assoc	No Carolina	34	HEJD	PHD	85	N Carol	1988
Victor, David A.	Assoc	E Michigan	1		PHD		Michigan	1985
Vidal, Robert	Adj	Cincinnati						
Vietor, Richard H. K.	Prof	Harvard	4	L				
Vigen, James W.	Prof	CS-Bakersf	7	SUV	PHD	65	Ohio St	1971
Vijayalakshmi, Viji B.	Asst	Loyola-Chicg			PHD		IIM	1992
Vijayaraman, Bindiganavale S	Assoc	Akron	9	ZUV	PHD	87	Geo St	8-89
Vila, Joaquim	Asst	Univ Navarra	3	I	PHD		Penn	9-90
Villanova, Peter	Asst	Appalach St	25	NEX	PHD		Va Tech	1993
Villarreal, John J.	Prof	CS-Hayward	3	I	PHD	72	CUNY	1971
Villere, Maurice F.	Prof	New Orleans	2	NE	PHD	71	Illinois	8-71
Vincelette, Joyce P.	Prof	Trenton St			DBA		Indiana	
Vincent, Vern		Tx-Pan Amer	7	V	PHD			
Vinson, Earl	Prof	Grambling St	15	Q	PHD		U Wash	1977
Vinton, Karen	Prof	Montana St	26		PHD	83	Utah	1-83
Vinze, Ajay	Asst	Texas A&M		Z	PHD	88	Arizona	1988
Virgo, John M.	Prof	S Ill-Edward	45	LQY	PHD	72	Claremont	1974
Vistad, Jeffrey S.	Lect	North Dakota	17		MBA	91	N Dakota	8-90
Visudtibhan, Kanoknart	Asst	George Wash	8	Y	PHD	88	Penn	
Vittetoe, Jerry	Prof	NE Missouri	9	Z	EDD	73	N Illin	1966
Vitton, John J.	Assoc	North Dakota	35	IN	PHD	82	Nebraska	8-86
Vlahos, George	Prof	Dayton	7	VYZ	PHD	74	N Colo	1978
Vlahos, Kiriakos	Asst	London Bus	7	V	PHD		London	
Vlahovich, Vladimir	Assoc	Widener			PHD		Penn	
Vogel, David J.	Prof	Cal-Berkeley	38	IY	PHD	74	Princeton	1974
Vogel, Joseph P.	Prof	St Ambrose	79	VZ	MA	60	Arizona	1989
Vogt, Karl	Prof	Bowling Gr	23	I	PHD	61	Syracuse	1967
Vohra, Rakesh V.	Assoc	Ohio State	7	V	PHD	85	Maryland	1985
Voich, Dan Jr.	Prof	Florida St	38	IBLY	PHD	65	Illinois	1964
Volard, Sam	Asst	Hampton	8		PHD		Queensln	8-91
Volkema, Roger	Assoc	American U	2	EIZ	PHD		Wiscon	1987
Vollmann, Thomas E.		Intl Mgt Dev	7	UV	PHD		UCLA	
Vollrath, David A.	Assoc	Ind-So Bend	24	EJ	PHD	84	Illinoia	8-88
Volonino, Linda A.	Asst	Canisius	9	Z	PHD	88	SUNY-Buf	1987

Volz, William H.	Dean	Wayne State	4	JK	MBA	78	Harvard	1978
Von der Embse, Thomas J.	Dean	Ind-Kokomo	34	FIJP	PHD	68	Ohio St	1990
Von der Mehden, Fred	Prof	Rice	8	Y	PHD	57	Berkeley	1980
Chaired Professor								
vonHippel, Eric A.	Prof	MIT			PHD			
VonPagenhart, Robert	Prof	Naval Postgr	38	AIYF	PHD	71	Stanford	7-67
VonStroh, Gordon E.	Prof	Denver	3	O	PHD	67	Oklahoma	9-67
Vora, Jay	Prof	St Cloud St	38	UY	PHD	69	Renssela	1978
Voss, Chris	Prof	London Bus	7	UI	PHD		London	
Voth, Richard	Dean	Pacific Unio	32	IE	PHD	73	Ariz St	1968
Voyer, John J.	Assoc	So Maine	3	I	PHD	86	Mass	1987
Vozikis, George S.	Prof	Citadel	38	IET	PHD		Georgia	
Vrancken, Robert	Assoc	Grand Valley			MBA	84	Notre Dm	1982
Vredenburgh, Donald	Prof	CUNY-Baruch	2	E	PHD		SUNY-Buf	
Vroom, Victor H.	Prof	Yale	1	EFH	PHD	58	Michigan	1972
Vrooman, David M.	Prof	Wittenberg	3	B	PHD	75	Northwes	1974
Wabe, J. S.	Lect	Univ Bath	8	Y	DPH			
Wachspress, David	Assoc	NY Inst Tech			PHD			
Wachter, Renee	Asst	Ball State	9		PHD		Indiana	1993
Wacker, J.	Prof	Iowa State	7	U	PHD	75	Wayne St	1983
Waddock, Sandra A.	Assoc	Boston Coll	43	LMHI	DBA	85	Boston U	9-86
Wade, David	Asst	No Illinois	4	K	JD		Iowa	
Wade, James	Asst	Illinois	2	EFH	PHD	92	Berkeley	1992
Wadsworth, Richard B.	Assoc	Tx-S Antonio			PHD	69	Arizona	1973
Wafa, Marvin	Assoc	So Indiana	7	U	PHD	86	Clemson	1986
Wagar, Terry H.	Assoc	St Marys-Cnd	45	KNQ	PHD	91	Va Tech	1985
Wageman, Ruth	Asst	Columbia	2	E	PHD	92	Harvard	1992
Wagley, Robert E.	Assoc	Wright State	34	AIJ	EDD	74	Cinn	1972
Wagman, George	Assoc	Tx A&M-Kings	25	CGNS	PHD	84	Ix A&M	1984
Wagner, Gerald E.	Prof	CS-Pomona	9	OZ	EDD	73	UCLA	1966
Wagner, Jennifer	Assoc	Roosevelt	9	Z	PHD		Northwes	
Wagner, John A. III	Assoc	Michigan St	2	H	PHD	82	Illinois	9-81
Wagner, Richard	Asst	Wis-Whitewat	5	FNPQ	PHD	90	Indiana	1990
Wagner, Samuel	Prof	Frank & Mars	27	B	PHD	71	Penn	7-82
Clair R. McCullough Professor of Business Administration								
Wagner, William	Asst	Villanova	9	ZY	PHD	92	Kentucky	1991
Wahba, Mahammed	Assoc	Hofstra	1	EI	PHD	80	Penn St	9-81
Wahlers, James	Asst	Georgia Col	57	NQU	PHD	93	Georgia	1989
Waikar, Avinash	Assoc	SE Louisiana	7	UV	PHD	84	Oklahoma	8-91
Waissi, Gary	Asst	Mich-Dearbor	7	V	PHD	85	Michigan	1986
Walbank, W. Martin	Lect	Manches Inst	7	T	MSC		London	1-75
Walck, Christa L.	Assoc	Mich Tech	28	EFYR	PHD	80	Harvard	1986
Waldman, D.	Assoc	Concordia U						
Waldman, Joel A.	Asst	Robt Morris	4	K	JD	74	U Miami	9-81
Waldman, Joseph M.	Prof	Indiana	6	S	DBA	66	Indiana	1963
Waldo, Robert D.	Dean	Puget Sound			PHD	72	Claremnt	1974
Waldorf, Larry	Assoc	Boise State	2		PHD	71	Colo St	1970
Waldron, Darryl G.	Prof	Trinity	38	IY	PHD	75	Miss	8-80
Walizer, Ottis		Minot St						
Walker, Burley	Assoc	Tx-Arlington	7	U	MBA	60	Oklahoma	1960
Walker, G. P.	Lect	U Newcastle	36	ST	MBA			
Walker, George H.	Asst	Sam Houston			PHD	67	Texas	1990
Walker, Gordon	Assoc	So Methodist	3	HIX	PHD	82	Penn	1993
Walker, Ian R. S.	Lect	Napier Univ	38	IY	BA			1988
Walker, James	Assoc	Moorhead St	63	IS	PHD		North Tx	1989
Walker, John	Assoc	US Intl			DBA		US Intl	1985
Walker, Larry R.	Prof	Cleveland St	1	C	PHD		Temple	1988
Walker, Ronald J.	Prof	Cedarville	7	V	DBA	86	Kent St	1978
Walker, William F. Jr.	Prof	F Dick-Madis			PHD		Rutgers	
Wall, James A. Jr.	Prof	Missouri	2	E	PHD	72	N Carol	1978
Wall, Jerry L.	Prof	NE Louisiana	5	I	PHD	74	Missouri	1983
Wall, Kent D.	Prof	Naval Postgr	79	VZ	PHD	71	Minn	8-85
Wallace, Clarence S.	Adj	Southeastern			MA		Dist Col	
Wallace, John	Assoc	Marshall	6	ST	PHD	68	Florida	1968
Wallace, Mary	SLect	Napier Univ	5	NPQR	BA			1986
Wallace, William D.	Asst	St Martin	24		PHD		U Wash	
Waller, D.	Lect	U Newcastle	8	Y	MCOM		NS Wales	
Waller, Matthew	Asst	W Michigan			PHD	93	Penn St	1993
Waller, Robert J.	Prof	No Iowa			DBA	68	Indiana	9-68
Walley, Paul	Lect	Loughborough	7	X	MBA		Warwick	
Wallin, Jerry	Prof	SW Louisiana	26	ENT	PHD	74	Nebraska	1986
Wallman, Kenneth		Houston-Down	68	QSTY	MBA	70	New Eng	9-76
Wally, Stefan	Asst	Maryland	23	HI	PHD	91	New York	1990
Walsh, David	Asst	Miami U-Ohio	25	EQ	PHD	91	Cornell	8-91
Walsh, J. T.	Asst	Capital			MBA		Ohio St	1987
Walsh, James P.	Assoc	Michigan		E	PHD	85	Northwes	1991
Walsh, Janet	Assoc	Univ Leeds	5	QR	PHD	89	Warwick	1991
Walsh, John E. Jr.	Prof	Wash Univ	83	YI	DBA	60	Harvard	
Walsh, Lynn	Asst	SUNY Old Wes	16	LSTR	PHD	80	NYU	1987
Walsh, Malcomb		Southeastern			PHD		Bradford	

Name	Rank	School			Degree			Year
Walsh, Paul K.	SLect	Univ Sydney	79	UV	PHD		NewCastl	7-91
Walsh, Vivien M.	SLect	Manches Inst	7	T	PHD		Manchest	8-84
Walsh, William	Asst	Ill Weselyan	15	NQ	PHD		Indiana	9-90
Walter, Gordon A.	Assoc	British Colu	2	EJH	PHD	71	Berkeley	1970
Walter, Ingo	Prof	INSEAD	8	Y	PHD	66	NYU	9-88
Walters, James E.	Prof	Ball State	7		DBA		Kent St	1976
Walters, Kenneth D.	Dean	New Mexico		Mgt	PHD	72	Berkeley	1990
Waltman, John L.	Prof	E Michigan	1		PHD		Texas	1985
Walton, Alice	Asst	Detroit Merc			PHD	88	Iowa St	1990
Walton, E. J.	SLect	W Australia			PHD		London	
Walton, H. Charles	Assoc	Gettysburg	9	Z	PHD	81	Fla St	1989
Walton, Richard E.	Prof	Harvard	25	EN				
Wallace Brett Donham Professor of Business Administration								
Walton, Spring	Asst	Gettysburg	4	K	JD	90	Maryland	1990
Walton, Steve	Asst	N Carol A&T			PHD		N Carol	1993
Walz, Diane	Asst	Tx-S Antonio	9	Z	PHD			
Wand, Yair	Assoc	British Colu	9	Z	DSC	77	Israelln	1986
Wang, Chiang	Prof	CS-Sacrament	37	HIUX	PHD	79	Iowa	1984
Wang, Chih-Kang	Prof	Nat Taiwan U		I	PHD	78	Tx A&M	1979
Wang, J.	Asst	Montclair St					Temple	1992
Wang, Jia	Prof	CS-Fresno	3	I	PHD	91	Tenn	1991
Wang, JinChang	Asst	Missouri Wes		ZUV	PHD		Ga Tech	1990
Wang, Min-Chiang	Prof	Wash State			PHD		Wiscon	
Wang, Ruth	Prof	CS-Sacrament	78	UVY	PHD	79	Iowa	1984
Wang, Y. Richard	Assoc	MIT	9	Z	PHD			
Wang, Yijiang	Asst	Minnesota	2	HE	PHD	91	Harvard	
Wang, Zhaobo	Asst	F Dick-Ruthe			PHD		Rutgers	
Wankel, Charles	Assoc	St Johns			PHD	89	NYU	
Wanna, John	SLect	Griffith Un	14	AL	PHD		Adelaide	1-85
Wanous, John P.	Prof	Ohio State	2	E	PHD	72	Yale	1983
Wansink, Brian C.	Asst	Dartmouth			ABD		Stanford	1990
Warbelow, Art	Asst	Alaska-Fairb	9	Z	PHD	91	Harvard	1990
Warburton, Arthur R.	Assoc	Simon Fraser	79	VZ	PHD	81	Brit Col	1987
Ward, Ed	Assoc	St Cloud St	25	EJNS	PHD	86	Nebraska	1990
Ward, Edna C.	Prof	Winthrop	12	NP	EDD		Tenn	1975
Ward, James	Assoc	Purdue	7	U	PHD	80	Car Mel	1981
Ward, John L.	Prof	Loyola-Chicg			PHD	73	Stanford	
Ward, Peter T.	Asst	Ohio State	7	U	PHD	88	Boston U	1988
Ward, R. J.	Assoc	Bowling Gr	35	IN	DBA	72	Colorado	1969
Ward, Richard J.	Prof	Mass-Dartmou			PHD	58	Michigan	1974
Ward, Richard T.	Prof	Hawaii Pacif	57	BHN	EDD	86	S Calif	8-86
Ward, William A.	Prof	Susquehanna	3	I	PHD	70	Colorado	1986
Alan Warehime Distinguished Professor								
Wardell, Don G.	VAsst	Utah	7	VU	PHD	90	Purdue	1992
Ware, Fred A.	Prof	Valdosta St	68	PY	PHD	74	Geo St	1971
Waring, Craig W.	Asst	West Florida	79	TUVY	PHD	92	Fla St	1988
Waring, Goeffry	Asst	Emory	3	I	PHD	93	UCLA	1993
Warlick, Steven	Assoc	Mo-St Louis	34		PHD	79	U Wash	1990
Warner, Daniel	Assoc	Western Wash	4	KM	JD	75	U Wash	9-84
Warner, Ricky	Inst	Miss Vall St			MBA		Atlanta	1988
Warnock, Charles F.					DBA	68	Fla St	
Warnock, Stuart	Asst	So Colorado	73	IUV	PHD		North Tx	1994
Warren, Bruce W.	C-Pr	Simmons			JD	76	Suffolk	
Warren, E. Kirby	C-Pr	Columbia	35	FIN	PHD	61	Columbia	1961
Warren, Helen L.	Retir	F Dick-Madis		1993	MA		Columbia	
Warren, Kim	Asst	London Bus	31		MBA		London	1991
Warrick, Donald D.	Prof	Colorado Spr	2	EFGH	DBA	72	S Calif	1-71
Warrick, Walter	Retir	Drake	37	DIUV	PHD	64	Purdue	1970
Warton, Robert	Asst	Minn-Duluth	23	DHIY	PHD	88	Rutgers	1979
Washburn, Paul V.	Prof	CS-L Angeles	12	EIC	PHD	74	Ohio St	1974
Washbush, John	Asst	Wis-Whitewat	1	BEHI	PHD	75	Marquett	1989
Washington, Charles	Assoc	Benedict Col						
Wasil, Ed	Assoc	American U	7	V	PHD		Maryland	1985
Waters, Donald	Assoc	Univ Calgary	7	UVX	PHD	86	Strathcl	1987
Waters, Elmer	Retir	Montclair St	34	1994	PHD	73	CUNY	1972
Waters, Gail R.	Prof	CS-Pomona	16	BITY	PHD	82	Arkansas	1992
Waters, Harry Jr.	Prof	CS-Hayward	2	EP	PHD	86	Oregon	1986
Waters, W. G. II	Assoc	British Colu			PHD	69	Wiscon	1969
Watford, Louise	Asst	Bournemouth	12	NH	BA	87		1990
Wathen, Samuel	Asst	SC-Coastal	7	U	PHD	88	Minn	1993
Watkins, Donna	Assoc	So Colorado	6	S	PHD		New Mex	1988
Watkins, Thomas L.	Prof	Denver	5	Q	PHD	71	Cinn	9-74
Watson, Carol D.	Assoc	Rider	12	ER	PHD		Columbia	1989
Watson, Charles E.	Prof	Miami U-Ohio	23	LP	PHD	70	Illinios	8-74
Watson, Collin	Prof	Utah	7	V	PHD	76	Utah	1981
Watson, Hugh J.	Prof	Georgia	9	Z	DBA	69	Fla St	1970
C. Herman & Mary Virginia Terry Chair of Business Administration								
Watson, J.	SLect	Humberside	7					
Watson, John G.	Prof	St Bonaventu	23		PHD		St Louis	1975
Watson, Kathleen	Assoc	CS-S Marcos	2	3	PHD	78	Utah	1-92

Name	Rank	School			Deg		Institution	Year
Watson, Mary Anne	Asst	Tampa	28	ELY	PHD	88	S Carol	1986
Watson, Richard T.	Assoc	Georgia	9	DZ	PHD	87	Minn	1989
Watson, Warren E.	Assoc	North Texas	2	EFGH	PHD	74	Chicago	1983
Watts, Charles A.	Assoc	Bowling Gr	7	UW	DBA	87	Indiana	1987
Watts, James Brian	Assoc	CS-San Bern	1	A	PHD		Vanderbt	1989
Watts, Larry R.	Assoc	S F Austin	36	ISTE	PHD	87	Ariz St	1987
Watts, Robert T.	Assoc	Idaho State	9	Z	PHD	71	New Mex	1978
Watzke, Gerard E.	Assoc	Tulane	28	IY	PHD	72	Stanford	1977
Wayland, Robert	Asst	E Illinois		NQI			North Tx	1991
Wayman, Shari	Asst	SE Louisiana			MBA			
Wayne, Sandra L.	Assoc	Ill-Chicago	5	NE	PHD	87	Tx A&M	9-87
Wea, Chi-Lin	Prof	Nat Taiwan U	8	Y	PHD	81	Paris U	1987
Weatherford, Larry		Wyoming	7	UVW	ABD		Virginia	8-91
Weatherford, Philip A.	Assoc	Embry-Riddle	31		EDD	83	Fla Atl	1973
Weathersby, Rita	Assoc	New Hampshir	2	EFQ	DED	77	Harvard	1978
Weaver, Amy B.	Lect	Appalach St	9	Z	MBA		Appal St	1991
Weaver, Charles N.	Prof	St Marys-Txs	27	IVX	PHD	67	Texas	1965
Emil C. E. Jurica Professor of Quantitative Management								
Weaver, Gary	Asst	Delaware			PHD	94	Penn St	1994
Weaver, H. Bruce	Prof	Lycoming			JD			
Weaver, K. Mark	Assoc	Alabama	68	LSTY	PHD	74	LSU	1976
Weaver, Robert B.	H-Ac	Air Force In			PHD		Renssela	7-90
Weavil, Linda	Prof	Elon	1		EDD	85	NC-Green	1973
Webb, Eugene J.	Prof	Stanford	2	E	PHD	56	Chicago	1968
Lane Professor of Organizational Behavior								
Webb, Ian R.	Asst	Connecticut	79	UZ	PHD	89	MIT	9-89
Webb, Natalie J.	Asst	Naval Postgr	7	UV	PHD	92	Duke	1992
Webber, Douglas	Asst	INSEAD	8	Y	PHD	85	Essex	1-91
Webber, Russ A.	C-Pr	Pennsylvania	26	EOPR	PHD	66	Columbia	7-64
Weber, Bruce W.	Asst	New York U	9	Z	PHD	92	Penn	
Weber, C. Edward	Prof	Wis-Milwauke	3	IJ	PHD	58	Princeton	1966
Weber, Elke U.	Assoc	Chicago			PHD	84	Harvard	1988
Weber, Eric	Asst	Univ Navarra	7	V	MBA		Navarra	6-87
Weber, James F.	Retir	Marquette	4		1994	PHD	88	Pitt	1988
Weber, Leonard	Prof	Detroit Merc			PHD	74	McMaster	
Weber, Myron	Assoc	Univ Calgary	25	NQ	PHD	86	Minn	1975
Weber, R. Jack	Assoc	Virg-Grad	5	P	PHD		Berkeley	1972
Weber, W.	Assoc	Carleton Un	5	N	PHD		Car Mel	
Weber, Warren C.	Prof	CS-Pomona	5	NP	EDD	69	Ariz St	1969
Weber, Yaakov	Lect	Hebrew Univ			PHD		S Carol	
Webster, Frederick E.	Prof	Dartmouth			PHD	64	Stanford	1965
Webster, Jane	Assoc	Un Waterloo	25	O	PHD	89	New York	1994
Webster, Neville	Assoc	Andrews	8		DBA		U of SA	1990
Webster, William F.	VAsst	North Fla	37	UV	PHD		Texas	1993
Wedding, Donald K.	Assoc	Toledo			JD		American	1968
Wedley, William C.	Prof	Simon Fraser	67	SUVY	PHD	71	Columbia	1986
Wee, Warren	Prof	Hawaii Pacif	7	X	PHD	82	U Wash	8-88
Weeks, Benjamin	D-Ac	St Xavier	34	JLD	PHD		Miss	1986
Weeks, James K.	Dean	N Car-Greens	7	U	PHD	74	S Carol	1976
Wegman, Jerry	Assoc	Idaho	4	K	JD	70	Columbia	1977
Wehrell, Roger	Assoc	Mt Allison U	26	T	PHD	82	Ottawa	7-83
Wehrs, William E.	Assoc	Wis-La Cross			PHD	72	Purdue	1972
Wehrung, Donald A.	Prof	British Colu	37	IV	PHD	75	Stanford	1974
Wei, Che-Yung	Assoc	Notre Dame	7	UV	PHD	87	Tx A&M	1987
Weible, Ray	Asst	Marshall	9	Z	DBA	93	Miss St	1993
Weick, Karl E.	Prof	Michigan	2	E	PHD	62	Ohio St	1988
Rensis Likert College Professor of Org Behavior & Psychology								
Weida, Nancy C.	Assoc	Bucknell	7	U	PHD	88	Delaware	9-87
Weidenaar, Dennis J.	Dean	Purdue	1	Mgt	PHD	69	Purdue	1966
Weigelt, Keith	Assoc	Pennsylvania	3	I	PHD	86	Northwes	7-88
Weigle, Jerry	Prof	Shippensburg						
Weihrich, Heinz	Prof	San Francisc			PHD	73	UCLA	1980
Weikle, Roger D.	Prof	Winthrop	52	NQ	PHD	85	S Carol	1982
Weil, D. Wallace	Prof	Wis-Eau Clar		I	PHD		Wilmette	1971
Weil, Jeffrey	Assoc	Manhattan	57	NOPQ	PHD	80	CUNY	1980
Weiler, B.	SLect	U Newcastle	4	DLS	PHD		Victoria	
Wein, Lawrence M.	Prof	MIT	7	U	PHD			
Weinberg, Charles B.	Prof	British Colu	7		PHD	70	Columbia	1979
Weinbrenner, David	Dean	Drake	1	A	PHD	73	Colorado	1979
Weindling, Ralph E.	H-Pr	Polytechnic			MBA		Harvard	
Weiner, Harry	Assoc	SUNY-Stony B	1	ABLJ	MS	70	MIT	1973
Weiner, Joan	Assoc	Drexel	42	DEFJ	PHD	81	Penn	1981
Weingart, Laurie R.	Asst	Carnegie Mel	25	EQ	PHD	89	Northwes	1989
Weininger, Michael	SLect	City Poly HK	38	YIB	PHD	90	Texas	9-91
Weinroth, Jay	C-Ac	Kent State			PHD		Union	1976
Weinstein, Alan G.	Prof	Canisius	26	STE	PHD	69	Wayne St	1976
Weinstein, Arnold K.	Dean	Adelphi	81	YD	PHD	73	Columbia	1992
Weinstein, Larry	Inst	Wright State	7	Uz	MS	88	GMI	1993
Weintraub, Joseph R.	Assoc	Babson			PHD	73	Bowl Gr	
Weintraub, Rick	Asst	Dallas Bapt	7		MS		SnDgo St	1992

Name	Rank	School		Codes	Degree		Institution	
Weinzimmer, Larry	Asst	Bradley	3	IT	PHD	93	Wiscon	1993
Weisbord, Ellyn S.	Assoc	Pace-Westch			PHD	90	NYU	1993
Weisenfeld, Batia	Inst	New York U			ABD		Columbia	
Weiss, Elliott N.	Assoc	Virg-Grad	7	U	PHD		Penn	1987
Weiss, Howard	Prof	Temple	7	UVW	PHD	75	Northwes	1976
Weiss, Janet A.	Prof	Michigan	2	E	PHD	77	Harvard	1983
Weiss, Joseph	Assoc	Bentley	24	HJY	PHD	84	Wiscon	1982
Weiss, Richard M.	Assoc	Delaware			PHD	81	Cornell	1980
Weiss, Stephen E.	Assoc	York Univ	38	IY	PHD	85	Penn	
Weissenberg, Peter	Prof	Rutgers-Camd			PHD			
Weitzel, William	Prof	Oklahoma	25	EHNP	PHD	66	Wayne St	8-78
Weitzman, Ronald A.	Assoc	Naval Postgr	72	EPJ	PHD	59	Princeton	9-71
Welch, Ben D,	SLect	Texas A&M		EN	PHD	90	Tx A&M	1990
Welch, Jane	Lect	Tx-S Antonio						
Welch, O. James	Asst	St Marys-Txs	79	UVZ	ABD			1993
Weldon, Elizabeth	Assoc	Indiana	2	E	PHD	82	Ohio St	1991
Weldy, Teresa	Inst	So Alabama	12	DFH	MBA	92	S Alab	
Welke, Richard J.	C-Pr	Georgia St	9	Z	PHD		SUNY-Buf	
Weller, James C.	Asst	Cen Arkansas	9	V	PHD		W Tx St	
Wells, Charles	Prof	Dayton	7	UV	PHD	82	Cinn	1984
Wells, Connie E.	Asst	Georgia St	9	Z	PHD		Minn	
Wells, Deborah L.	Asst	Creighton	5	NR	PHD	87	Iowa St	8-87
Wells, Louis T. Jr.	Prof	Harvard	4	L				
Herbert F. Johnson Professor of International Business Management								
Wells, Murray C.	Dean	Univ Sydney	9	B	PHD		Sydney	1972
Wells, Robert A.	Assoc	Geo Southern	79	ZV	EDD	73	Georgia	1975
Wells, Stuart Jay	Prof	San Jose St	13	DFIT	PHD	74	Stanford	1976
Wells, William	Assoc	George Wash	8	Y				
Welsch, Harold P.	Prof	DePaul			PHD	75	Northwes	
Welsch, Roy E.	Prof	MIT	7	X	PHD	69	Stanford	
Leaders for Manufacturing Professor								
Welsh, Dianne	Asst	Eastern Wash	25	ENQP	PHD	88	Nebraska	1988
Welsh, M. Ann	Assoc	Cincinnati	2	F	PHD	82	Missouri	
Welty, William	Prof	Pace	3		PHD		NYU	
Wendell, Richard E.	Prof	Pittsburgh	7		PHD		Northwes	
Wendt, Ann C.	Assoc	Wright State	5	QNR	PHD	87	Utah	1988
Wendt, Steve	Lect	Nev-L Vegas	69	TUR	MBA	87	Nev-LV	1985
Weng, James C. M.	Assoc	Nat Taiwan U	8	DIVY	PHD	90	Mich St	1990
Wenger, Michael S.	Assoc	USAF Academy	3	I	PHD		Oxford	
Werbel, James D.	Assoc	Louisiana St	2	ENO	PHD	80	Northwes	8-84
Werhane, Patricia	C-Pr	Virg-Grad	4	J	PHD	69	Northwes	1993
Ruffin Professor of Business Administration								
Werner, Jon	Asst	So Carolina			PHD	92	Mich St	
Werner, Steve	Asst	Houston	58	NQY	PHD	93	Florida	9-93
Wernerfelt, Birger	Prof	MIT	7	V	DBA	77	Harvard	
Wersun, Alec		Strathclyde	8	Y				
Wertheim, Edward G.	Assoc	Northeastern	25	N	PHD		Yeshiva	9-77
Werther, William B.	Prof	U Miami	35	INOP	PHD	71	Florida	1985
Wesman, Elizabeth	Assoc	Syracuse	5	NQR	PHD	82	Cornell	1981
Wesolowski, Mark	Asst	Miami U-Ohio	25	EN	PHD	91	Auburn	1-90
Wesolowsky, George O.	Prof	McMaster Un	17	UV	PHD		Wiscon	
Wesson, Thomas	Asst	York Univ	1	A	PHD		Harvard	
West, Charles	Retir	N Car-Wilmin	12	DI	PHD	78	Louisvll	1981
West, Clifford T.	Asst	Akron	31	ILD	ABD	89	Indiana	8-90
West, E.	Prof	Univ Windsor	79	UVWY	PHD		Iowa St	1983
West, Ellen L.	Asst	Portland St	2	EP	PHD	81	Oreg St	1986
West, Jude P.	Assoc	Iowa	5	GNQ	PHD	69	Iowa	1965
West, Judy F.	Prof	Tenn-Chattan	1	D	PHD	76	Geo St	1981
West, Larry	Asst	Florida St	97	ZV	PHD	91	Tx A&M	8-90
Westacott, George H.	Assoc	SUNY-Bingham	8	Y	PHD	70	Cornell	1971
Westbrook, Roy K.	Asst	London Bus	7	UZ	ABD		London	
Westby, Kenneth L.	Asst	North Dakota	35		MS	67	Geo Wash	8-77
Westley, F.	Assoc	McGill Univ	3		PHD		McGill	1983
Westney, D. Eleanor	Prof	MIT	35	IN	PHD			
Weston, Rae	Prof	Macquarie Un			PHD			
Westwood, John B.	SLect	Manchest Bus	37	ITU	PHD		Manchest	1981
Wetmore, Charles H.	Retir	CS-Fresno	2	E	DBA	70	Ariz St	1970
Wetzel, Kurt	H-Pr	Saskatchewan	5	DQ	PHD	78	Illinois	1976
Weymann, Elizabeth (Betsy)	Assoc	Loyola-N Orl	2	GHE	PHD	87	Tulane	1979
Whalen, Thomas H.	Prof	Georgia St	7	V	PHD		Mich St	
Whaley, Gary	Asst	Norfolk St	24	EJ	PHD	83	SUNY	7-84
Whaley, George	Prof	San Jose St	52	NEPV	PHD	74	Colorado	1979
Wharton, Robert M.	C-Pr	Fordham	7	UV	PHD		Temple	1981
Wharton, T. J.	Assoc	Oakland	7	UV	PHD	85	Minn	1990
Whatley, Arthur A.	Prof	New Mex St	58	FNPY	PHD	71	North Tx	1970
Wheat, Jerry	C-Pr	Indiana SE	48	JY	DBA	73	Indiana	1977
Wheatley, Walter J.	Assoc	West Florida	39	DIV	PHD	85	Fla St	1985
Wheelen, Thomas L.	Prof	South Fla	3	I	DBA	69	Geo Wash	1983
Wheeler, Hoyt	Prof	So Carolina			PHD	74	Wiscon	
Wheeler, Kenneth	Assoc	Tx-Arlington	5	N	PHD	78	Minn	1979

Name	Rank	School			Degree		School	
Wheeler, Patricia A.	Asst	Siena Coll	1	DIST	PHD	90	Renssel	9-91
Wheelwright, Steven C.	Prof	Harvard	7	U				
MBA Class of 1949 Professor of Business Administration								
Whelan, Frank E.	Prof	So Conn St	79	UVZ	EDD	75	Nova	1979
Whinston, Andrew	Prof	Texas	9	Z	PHD	62	Car Mel	1989
Whippple, David R.	C-Pr	Naval Postgr	7	D	PHD	71	Kansas	8-71
Whisler, William D.	Prof	CS-Hayward	7	V	PHD	65	Berkeley	1972
Whitaker, A.	Lect	U Lancaster	52	EHNQ	DCOM		Birmingh	
Whitcomb, Laura	Asst	CS-L Angeles	34	ILY	PHD	91	Indiana	1989
White, B. Joseph	Dean	Michigan	2	E	PHD	75	Michigan	1987
White, Charles	Prof	Hardin-Simm						
White, Charles Stephen	Prof	Tenn-Chattan	21	EH	DBA	81	Arizona	1981
UC Foundation Professor								
White, Charles W.	Assoc	GMI	39	IJVZ	PHD	71	Tx A&M	1989
White, Clarence D.	Prof	Radford	12	E	PHD	82	Ohio St	8-82
White, Daniel L.	Inst	Drexel	35	GT	MBA	69	Mich St	1979
White, Donald	Inst	Grambling St	7		MBA	87	Gramblin	1989
White, Donald D.	H-Pr	Arkansas	2	EHG	PHD	71	Nebraska	1971
White, Ellen E.	Asst	New Orleans	9		PHD	85	Fla St	6-85
White, Greg	Assoc	So Illinios	7	UT	PHD	76	Cinn	8-78
White, Harold C.	Retir	Arizona St	25	5-93	PHD	66	Florida	1966
White, Judith	Asst	Loyola Marym	2	R	PHD	92	Case Wes	1992
White, Lesley	Lect	U Wollongong			MCOM		NS Wales	3-93
White, Louis P.	Prof	Houston-C Lk	12	EF	PHD		S Fla	8-76
White, Margaret A.	Assoc	Oklahoma St	23	I	PHD	89	Tx A&M	8-86
White, Marion	Asst	Jms Madison	18	EY	PHD	90	Houston	9-90
White, Max	Inst	SW Okla St	9	Z	MBA	83	Southwes	1983
White, Michael C.	Prof	Louisiana Te	23	EHIM	PHD	78	Georgia	1991
White, Norman H.	Assoc	New York U	9	Z	PHD	74	NYU	
White, Randy	Assoc	Auburn-Montg	3	I	PHD	78	Arkansas	1900
White, Richard	Asst	North Texas	37	IU	PHD	90	Ariz St	1990
White, Sally Blount	Asst	Chicago			PHD	92	Northwes	1992
White, Sam E.	Prof	Portland St	3	I	PHD	76	U Wash	1983
White, Sandra	Inst	NW Missouri			MBA	89	NW Mo St	1989
White, Scott A.	C-Ac	Wis-Plattev	4	J	JD	79	Creighto	1980
White, Sharon	Asst	N Carol A&T	9	Z	ABD		Fla St	8-92
White, Susan C.	Inst	NW St of La			PHD		Tx A&M	8-94
on sabbatical leave to Texas A&M University								
White, Thomas	Assoc	Rider	4	JR	PHD	74	Columbia	1989
Whitehead, Carlton J.	C-Pr	Texas Tech	28	HYC	PHD	64	LSU	1965
Whitehead, J. David	C-Ac	Brock Univ	25	Q	PHD		Western	1987
Whitehead, Jo	Asst	London Bus	3	I	MBA		Harvard	
Whitehouse, Frank Jr.	Assoc	Lynchburg	27	EGL	ABD	87		7-80
Whitely, William T.	Prof	Oklahoma	25	OY	PHD	76	Minn	8-80
Whitener, Ellen M.	C-Ac	Virginia			PHD		Mich St	
Whitlark, David B.	Asst	Brigham Yg	7	U	PHD	88	Virginia	1989
on leave to Virginia								
Whitley, Richard D.	Prof	Manchest Bus	28	HLW	PHD		Penn	1977
Whitlock, David	C-As	SE Okla St	61	TPS	MAS	85	SE OK St	8-85
Whitlow, Mike	C-As	Southern Ark		Mgt	MBA		Centenry	1989
Whitman, Fred T.	SLect	Mary Wash	13		MBA		Alabama	
Whitman, J. D.	Asst	Un Hong Kong	9	Z	MSC			9-86
Whitman, Katherine	Assoc	Mt St Mary's			MA		UCLA	
Whitmore, A.	Prof	McGill Univ	7		PHD		Minn	1969
Whitney, Gary	Assoc	San Diego	3	EI	PHD	76	U Wash	1980
Whitney, John	Prof	Columbia	23	HI	AB	48	Tulsa	1987
Whitney, L. Keith	Assoc	Pepper-Malib	4	K	JD	77	Tx Tech	1990
Whitt, Darnell	Assoc	Naval Postgr	13	IY	PHD	77	JHopkins	1988
Whitt, Jerry D.	Prof	Millsaps	84	YL	PHD	73	Arkansas	1980
Whitten, Betty J.	Prof	Georgia	7	V	PHD		Georgia	
Whitty, Michael	Prof	Detroit Merc			PHD	69	Syracuse	1967
Wholihan, John T.	Dean	Loyola Marym	13	Mgt	PHD	73	American	1984
Wichern, Dean W.	Prof	Texas A&M		V	PHD	69	Wiscon	1984
John E. Pearson Professorship in Business Administration								
Wickham, Wm. T.	C-Pr	Heidelberg	15	EN	PHD	56	Case Wes	1977
Wicks, Andrew	Asst	U Washington	4	J	PHD	92	Virginia	1992
Widgery, Robin N.	Prof	Mich-Flint	2	EF	PHD	71	Mich St	7-88
Wiebe, Frank A.	Assoc	Mississippi	26	ET	PHD	75	Kansas	1978
Wiener, Yoash	Prof	Cleveland St	5	NP	PHD	69	Ohio St	1975
Wiersema, Margarethe F.	Asst	Calif-Irvine	3	I	PHD	85	Michigan	1987
Wiesner, W.	Asst	McMaster Un	5	NE	PHD	88	Waterloo	
Wiest, Jerome	Prof	Utah	7	V	PHD	63	Car Mel	1958
Wieters, C. David	C-Ac$	New Mex St	7	UVW	PHD	76	Ariz St	1985
Wiggins, Bynetta M.	Asst	Virg Union			MED			
Wilder, Kathy H.	C-As	Delta State	13	FIXZ	ABD	94	Memphis	8-91
Wiletzky, Les	Inst	Hawaii Pacif	15	AFNP	MPA	78	Penn St	8-91
Wiley, C. Jeffrey	Asst	Fla Southern			MBA		Indiana	1976
Wiley, Carolyn	Assoc	Tenn-Chattan	51	NE	PHD	82	UCLA	1990
Wiley, Donna	Prof	CS-Hayward	5	NPR	PHD	83	Tenn	1983
Wilhelm, Paul G.	Asst	Tx-El Paso	53	NPQ	PHD	82	Iowa	1988

Name	Rank	Institution			Degree		Institution	
Wilkens, Paul L.	Prof	Florida St	23	BP	PHD	71	Ohio St	1970
Wilkerson, Mary Lynn	Inst	NW St of La			MBA		Northwes	
Wilkie, Pat	Assoc	Mass-Boston	2	E	PHD	73	Wayne St	1973
Wilkins, Alan L.	Prof	Brigham Yg	13	DEIP	PHD	79	Stanford	1978
Wilkins, Allison M.	VAsst	Utah	7	U	PHD	93		1993
Wilkins, C. Joseph	Assoc	Sangamon St	13	IY	MA		S Illin	1978
Wilkins, Henry T.	Retir	Shippensburg			1991		Temple	
Wilkins, Susan J.	Prof	CS-Pomona	9	Z	PHD	85	Nebraska	1985
Wilkinson, Adrian J.	Lect	Manches Inst	5	N	PHD		Durham	9-91
Wilkinson, Edward	Retir	Houston-Down	18	1993	ED	80	Nova	9-69
Wilkinson, Harry	VProf	Rice	23	AEI	DBA	60	Harvard	1990
Wilkinson, R. Stanley Jr.	Asst	Appalach St	9	Z	MA		Appal St	1975
Wilkinson, Robert E.					DBA	74	Fla St	
Willard, Gary	Asst	Illinois	36	IT	PHD	82	Purdue	1991
Willes, J. A.	Prof	Queen's Univ	4	K	LLM	67	Osgoode	1970
Willey, Susan	Assoc	Wis-La Cross			JD		Indiana	
William, R. Don	Assoc	Abilene Chr			PHD		Tx A&M	1992
Williams CSC, Oliver F.	Assoc	Notre Dame	4	KLM	PHD		Vanderbt	
Williams, A. J.	Prof	U Newcastle	36	GIST	PHD		W Austra	
Williams, Anderson	Prof	Morehouse			PHD		Geo St	1982
Williams, Art	Assoc	Mo-Kansas Ct	1	AC	PHD	81	Cornell	1989
Williams, Charles M.	Prof	Georgia St	9	Z	PHD		Texas	
Williams, Charles R.	Assoc	Tx Christian	12	EN	PHD	90	Mich St	1991
Williams, D. Ervin	Prof	Georgia St	6	ST	PHD	65	Ohio St	1968
Williams, David	H	Bournemouth			MSC			1980
Williams, Edgar	Prof	Norfolk St	3	I	PHD	76	Utah	7-84
Williams, Edward E.	C-Pr	Cheyney		Mgt	PHD		Drexel	1972
Williams, Fred E.	Dean	Bowling Gr	7	MgtS	PHD	70	Purdue	1990
Williams, Fredrik P.	Prof	North Texas	7	U	PHD	68	Texas	1968
Williams, James D.	C-Ac	Virgin Islan	8	YST	DBA			1988
Williams, Jane Gray	Lect	Baylor		VZ	MSED	70	Baylor	1972
Williams, Jeffrey	Prof	Carnegie Mel	3	I	PHD		Michigan	1977
Williams, Jennifer	Asst	So Indiana	9	Z	PHD	94	S Illin	1992
Williams, John G.	Inst	NW St of La			JD		Tulane	
Williams, Karen	Asst	Tx-S Antonio	9	Z	PHD	92	Fla St	8-92
Williams, Larry	Assoc	Purdue	2	E	PHD	88	Indiana	1987
Williams, Margaret	Asst	Purdue	2	N	PHD	89	Indiana	1989
Williams, Patrick	Prof	San Jose St	21	F	PHD	66	UCLA	1964
Williams, Ralph W.	Prof	SW Missouri	21	Y	PHD	66	Oregon	1980
Williams, Robert	Asst	No Alabama			PHD	93	Fla St	1993
Williams, Steven C.	SLect	Queensland	8	R	PHD	88	Queensln	1989
Williams, William Lee	Prof	Millikin	7	ZU	EDD		Illin St	
Williamson, J. Peter	Prof	Dartmouth			DBA	61	Harvard	1961
Williamson, Oliver	Prof	Cal-Berkeley	34	I	PHD		Minn	1989
Williamson, Peter J.	Asst	London Bus	38	YI	PHD		Harvard	1987
Williamson, Stan	Asst	NE Louisiana	23	EJ	PHD	90	North Tx	1990
Williamson, Steven A.	Assoc	North Fla	12	EFHP	DBA		Memphis	
Willis, David	Inst	Freed Hardem	35	IP	MA	87	Webster	8-93
Willis, Donald E.	Asst	Dallas Bapt	7		MDS		Geo St	1978
Willis, G. W. Ketchel	C-Pr	Baylor		Z	PHD	77	Tx A&M	1983
Willis, Geoff	Asst	Seattle	7	V	PHD		Tx Tech	
Willis, Harry W. Jr.	Asst	LaSierra	3	I	MBA	68	Geo St	7-84
Willis, J. Clay	Asst	Okla Baptist	18	DHNP	MBA			8-86
Willis, Raymond E.	Prof	Minnesota	3	BDI	PHD	61	MIT	1959
Willis, T. Hillman	Assoc	Louisiana Te	71	ISUV	PHD	72	LSU	1979
Willman, Edward	Assoc	Tx A&M Intl	7	V	PHD		North Tx	1971
Willman, Paul W.	Prof	London Bus	52	OZN	DPHL		Oxford	
Willmott, Hugh C.	SLect	Manches Inst	5	H	PHD		Mancehst	9-88
Willoughby, Floyd G.	Assoc	Oakland	3	I	PHD	84	Mich St	1983
Willoughby, K.	Lect	W Australia			PHD		Murdoch	
Wilmer, Jack	Lect	Baylor			MBA		Baylor	1977
Wilmer, James A.	Inst	No Kentucky	17		MBA	62	Xavier	8-90
Wilson, B.	SLect	U Lancaster	1	AEIZ	PHD		Nottingh	
Wilson, Brent D.	Assoc	Brigham Yg	3	I	PHD	79	Harvard	1982
Wilson, Carol	Assoc	Moorhead St	1		PHD		Missouri	1988
Wilson, Donald O.	Asst	Rochest Tech			PHD	88	Calif	1987
Wilson, Dwayne	Dean	Freed Hardem	36	IST	PHD	91	Miss	8-75
Wilson, E. Walter	Assoc	Georgia	67	SU	PHD	74	Georgia	1964
Wilson, Elaine	Lect	Napier Univ	5	O	MA			1975
Wilson, Glenn T.	Prof	Mid Tenn St	7	U	PHD	65	Penn	1989
Wilson, H. Thomas	Prof	York Univ	4	JR	PHD		Rutgers	
Wilson, Haldon D. Jr.	C-As	St Martin's	35		MBA		Puget So	
Wilson, Jack W.	H-Pr	N Carol St	7	V	PHD	66	Oklahoma	1965
Wilson, James M.	Assoc	Tx-Pan Amer	1		PHD	71	Arkansas	1971
Wilson, James Q.	Prof	UCLA	3	I	PHD	59	Chicago	1984
Wilson, Jeffrey R.	Assoc	Arizona St			PHD		Iowa St	1985
Wilson, John M.	SLect	Loughborough	7	V	DPHL		Sussex	
Wilson, Katherine	Assoc	Embry-Riddle			MBA	77	Stetson	1984
Wilson, Keathen A.	Inst	St Paul's	7	UW	MA			1984
Wilson, Leslie K.	Asst	No Iowa			PHD	92	Iowa	8-87

Name	Rank	School			Degree			
Wilson, Marie	Assoc	U Auckland	52	EFNP	PHD	90	Arizona	7-91
Wilson, Mary C.	Asst	Cleveland St	5	NPR	PHD		Tenn	1991
Wilson, Mary E.	Asst	Georgia SW	15	DIN	PHD		Alabama	
Wilson, Rick L.	Asst	Oklahoma St	9	Z	PHD	90	Nebraska	8-90
Wilson, Robert	Assoc	CS-San Bern	9	Z	PHD	77	Ca-River	1991
Wilson, Ronald	Adj	Southeastern			MBA		SEastern	
Wilson, Samuel M.	Retir	Temple		1993	PHD	55	Penn	1948
Wilson, Shirley	Asst	Bryant	2	E	PHD	92	Case Wes	8-92
Wilson-Ward, J. S.	Lect	Univ Bath	4	K	BBA			
Wilterding, Jim	Prof	Boise State	5	P	PHD	70	Tx Tech	1976
Wimbush, James	Asst	Indiana	5	N	PHD	91	Va Tech	1991
Wimmergren, Lyle E.	Assoc	Worcester Pl	13	IST	MBA	57	Penn	9-69
Windsor, Oliver Duane	Prof	Rice	34	AIJL	PHD	78	Harvard	1977
Chaired Professor								
Wines, William A.	C-Pr	Boise State	4	JK	JD	74	Michigan	1985
Winfield, Fairlee	Prof	No Arizona	18	RY	PHD	78	New Mex	
Winfrey, Frank	Asst	Kent State	23	HI	PHD	91	S Carol	1990
Wing, Kevin	Asst	Georgia Tech	7	U				
Winick, Mara	Asst	Redlands	15	EKNQ	PHD			
Winn, Joan	Asst	Denver	3	I	PHD		Georgia	9-88
Winne, Donald W.	Assoc	Nevada-Reno	4	JKL	LLD			
Winslow, Erik K.	C-Pr	George Wash	5	N	PHD	67	Case Wes	
Winston, Bruce	Asst	Regent	57	UVN	MBA		Regent	1991
Winston, Rudy	Adj	Nichols Col						
Wint, Alvin	Asst	Northeastern	18	YI	DBA		Harvard	9-88
Winter, Frederick W.	Dean	SUNY-Buffalo		Mgt	PHD	72	Purdue	5-94
Winter, George M.	Dean	Athabasca Un		I	PHD	62	Iowa	1993
Winter, Sidney G.	Prof	Pennsylvania	3	I	PHD	64	Yale	7-93
Deloitte and Touche Porfessor of Management								
Winterscheid, Beverly	Assoc	Baldwin-Wal	8		PHD		Case Wes	
Wirth, Itzhak	Assoc	St Johns			PHD	76	Berkeley	
Wirtz, Philip	Prof	George Wash	7	V	PHD	83	Geo Wash	
Wisdom, Barry L.	C-Pr$	SW Missouri	27	E	PHD	81	Arkansas	1987
Wiseman, Robert	Asst	Arizona St	23	I	ABD			1991
Wiseman, Timothy	Asst	Warner So	2	K	JD	85	Illinois	1992
Wisner, Joel	Asst	Nev-L Vegas	7		PHD	91	Ariz St	1991
Withane, S.	Prof	Univ Windsor	23	FHNY	PHD		SUNY	1987
Withey, Michael J.	Assoc	Memorial Un	2		PHD	86	Queen's	1984
Withycombe, Richard	Prof	Montana	7	UV	PHD	72	Oregon	1972
Witt, Robert E.	Dean	Texas		Mktg	PHD	68	Penn	9-68
Centennial Chair in Business Education Leadership								
Witte, Robert	Prof	Wis-Stev Pt	52	EH	PHD	67	Wiscon	8-87
Wittig-Berman, Ursula	Assoc	Iona	2	EHI	PHD	85	CUNY	1985
Wittmer, Dennis	Asst	Denver	1	J	PHD		Syracuse	9-91
Witwer, Keith L.	C-As	Minot St			MBA		Michigan	1982
Wlaker, Moses	C-Pr$	Fayetteville			PHD	83	Iowa	1987
Wofford, Jerry C.	Prof	Tx-Arlington	2	E	PHD	62	Baylor	1966
Woiceshyn, Jaana	Assoc	Univ Calgary	34	IJ	PHD	88	Penn	1987
Wokutch, Richard E.	Prof	Virg Tech	4		PHD	77	Pitt	1977
Wolanin, Robert	Assoc	Youngstown	12		MA	60	Pitt	9-67
Wolek, Francis W.	Prof	Villanova	27	DI	DBA	67	Harvard	1983
Wolf, Gerrit	Prof	SUNY-Stony B	26	ESTX	PHD	67	Cornell	1985
Wolfe, Donald M.	Prof	Case Western	2	E	PHD	60	Michigan	1963
Wolfe, Douglas	Assoc	So Miss	23	DEFH	PHD	69	Case Wes	1980
Wolfe, Helen W.	Asst	Teikyo Post			MBA			
Wolfe, Joseph A.	Prof	Tulsa	38	IP	PHD	71	NYU	6-78
Wolfe, Michael	Asst	W Virginia	9	Z	PHD	88	Texas	1989
Wolfe, Michael N.	Assoc	Houston-C Lk	53	NQI	PHD		Mass	8-74
Wolfe, Richard A.	Asst	Univ Alberta	23	D	PHD	89	Michigan	1988
Wolff, James	Asst	Wichita St	32	HIY	ABD		Wash St	9-94
Wolfmeyer, Pamela	Prof	Winona State			MA		Wiscon	1969
Wolnizer, Peter W.	Dean	Deakin Univ			PHD	86	Sydney	1989
Woltemade, Uwe J.	Prof	Ohio Wesley	4	J	PHD		Texas	1965
Wolters, Roger	Assoc	Auburn	5	Q	PHD	81	Illinios	9-80
Womack, Kent L.	Asst	Dartmouth			PHD	94	Cornell	1994
Wonder, Bruce D.	C-Ac	Western Wash	5	NOEL	PHD	71	Wash	9-81
Wondoloski, Edward	Prof	Bentley	1	AE	MBA	65	Northeas	1962
Wong, Bo	Assoc	Youngstown	9	Z	PHD	90	Miss St	9-89
Wong, D. W. S.	Asst	Un Hong Kong	1		MBA			9-76
Wong, G. Y. Y.	Asst	Un Hong Kong	12	EF	MBA			1-81
Wong, Helen	ALect	City Poly HK	25	EHPQ	BA	89	London	9-92
Wong, Kenman L.	Asst	Biola	49	JZ	ABD		S Calif	1989
Wong, M. Y.	Asst	Un Hong Kong	37	IUV	PHD			3-92
Wong, May M. L.	Lect	City Poly HK	25	EN	MSC	85	Tokyo	9-89
Wong, Ralph L. K.	ALect	City Poly HK	25	NO	MA	85	Hull	9-90
Wong, Yim Yu	Asst	Indiana St	13	I	PHD		Nebraska	8-91
Woo, Carolyn Y.	Prof	Purdue	3	I	PHD	79	Purdue	1981
Woo, Carson	Asst	British Colu	9	Z	PHD	88	Toronto	1987
Wood, Cynthia	Asst	Longwood	12	EFH	PHD	75	Virginia	1992
Wood, D. Robley	Prof	Virg Comm	3	DI	DBA	77	Tenn	1979

Name	Rank	Institution			Degree		University	
Wood, Donald A.	Prof	Indiana	5	N	PHD	68	Purdue	1968
Wood, Donna J.	Assoc	Pittsburgh	3		PHD		Vanderbt	
Wood, Douglas	Assoc	Univ Leeds	7	V	MA	60	Combridg	1977
Wood, Erma	Asst	Ark-Ltl Rock			EDD		Arkansas	
Wood, Jack D.		Intl Mgt Dev	2	E	PHD		Yale	
Wood, Jack M.	D-Ac	Univ Sydney	25	DEFN	PHD		Alberta	1990
Wood, James	Asst	Ark Tech	9	Z	MBA	83	Houst Bp	8-92
Wood, R.	Prof	W Australia			PHD		Wash	
Wood, Steven D.	Prof	Arizona St			PHD		Wiscon	1973
Wood, William C.	Asst	No Iowa			PHD	84	Virginia	8-87
Woodhouse, Robert	Assoc	St Thomas-MN						
Woodin, Norman J.	Dean	Tri State			EDD		WMU	1984
Woodman, Richard W.	C-Pr	Texas A&M		FED	PHD	78	Purdue	1978
Clayton Professor of Business Administration								
Woodruff, Charles K.	Assoc	Winthrop	23	EI	PHD		Geo St	1980
Woodruff, David L.	Asst	Cal-Davis	7	U	PHD		Northwes	
Woods, Douglas W.	Prof	Worcester Pl	1		PHD	70	MIT	9-70
Woodward, Bill			2	E	PHD	89	N Carol	
Woodworth, Robert	Assoc	U Washington	5		PHD	64	Northwes	1966
Woodworth, Warner	Prof	Brigham Yg	48	FJLS	PHD	74	Michigan	1976
Woody, James R.	H-Pr	USAF Academy	3	I	PHD	81	Virginia	7-78
Wooldridge, William	Assoc	Massachusett	34	I	DBA	84	Colorado	1985
Woolley, John T.	VAsso	Georgetown	34	IJ	PHD	80	Wiscon	1992
Woolley, Virginia	Inst	Ohio Univ	1		MA	61	Wiscon	
Wooten, Kevin C.	Asst	Houston-C Lk	52	JPNO	PHD		Tulane	9-92
Wooton, L. Michael	Assoc	So Methodist			PHD	72	S Calif	1972
Worden, Jack	Assoc	Napier Univ	25	ENPT	MA			1985
Worley, Joel K.	Assoc	NW St of La			PHD		Va Tech	
Wormley, Wayne M.	Asst	Drexel	25	EHNO	PHD	78	Stanford	1984
Wormuth, Frank	Asst	Scranton	4	K	JD	72	Duquesne	1979
Worrell, Dan L.	C	Tx-Arlington	34	IJL	PHD	78	LSU	1993
Worrell, Malcolm	Lect	NJ Inst Tech	9	Z	MBA	66	Mich St	1990
Worthington, D. J.	Lect	U Lancaster	74	AUVZ	PHD		Reading	
Wortman, Max S.	Prof	Iowa State	6	IT	PHD	62	Minn	
Pioneer Chair of Agricultural Business								
Woudstra, Andrew	Prof	Athabasca Un	91	Z	MBA	78	W Ontar	1981
Wozniak, Douglas R.	Assoc	Ferris State	2		MBA		Bowl Gr	1978
Woznick, Jan	Assoc	Lawrence Tec			PHD			1993
Wray, Barry	Asst	N Car-Wilmin	7	V	PHD		Va Tech	
Wrege, Charles	Retir	Rutgers-N Br		1991	PHD	61	NYU	1961
Wren, Daniel A.	Prof	Oklahoma	13	BI	PHD	64	Illinois	1973
David Ross Boyd Prof; McCasland Prof of Am Free Entrpr; Curator Bass Collectn								
Wright, Alan	Asst	Henderson St			ABD		Memphis	
Wright, Charles	Retir	Tarleton St	36	IST	PHD	65	Texas	1985
Wright, David	Inst	SW Okla St	1	E	MBA	90	Texas-PB	1992
Wright, George	Asst	Loyola-Maryl	9	Z	DBA		Geo Wash	
Wright, George		Strathclyde	7	V				
Wright, Gordon P.	Prof	Purdue	7	V	PHD	67	Case Wes	1970
Wright, J. Ward	Prof	E Kentucky	45	KLJ	DPA	78	S Calif	1983
Wright, Judy	Prof	Sonoma State			PHD	73	Indiana	9-73
Wright, Lorna L.	Asst	Queen's Univ	8	IMY	PHD	90	Western	1986
Wright, M. B.	Lect	U Lancaster	74	AUVZ	MSC		Oxford	
Wright, Marie		Western Conn						
Wright, Patrick M.	Asst	Texas A&M		NE	PHD	88	Mich St	1989
Wright, Penny L.	Prof	San Diego St	2	EH	PHD	80	Ca-Irvine	1972
Wright, Peter	Prof	Memphis	38	IY	PHD	75	LSU	1988
Wright, R.	Prof	McGill Univ	8		DBA		Indiana	
Wright, Robert G.	Prof	Pepper-L Ang			DBA	67	S Calif	1976
Julian A. Virtue Distinguished Fellowship								
Wright, Ronald	Assoc	LeMoyne	7	UV	PHD	76	Kentucky	1977
Wright, Thomas	Asst	Nevada-Reno	25	EGHN	PHD		Berkeley	1990
Wright, V. E.	Assoc	U New Englan	13	I	PHD		New Engl	1975
Wrigley, C.	Asst	McGill Univ	9		PHD		Brit Col	1989
Wu, Ching-Sung	Assoc	Nat Taiwan U	38	DITY	PHD	88	UCLA	1990
Wu, D.	Assoc	St Marys-Cal	2	EHR	PHD	80	Wright I	1981
Wu, Hui-Lin	C-Pr	Nat Taiwan U	5	Q	PHD	84	Nat Taiw	1990
Wu, Terry Y. S.	Assoc	Univ Regina	14	A	PHD		Manitoba	
Wunsch, Daniel R.	C-Ac	No Illinois	1	D	PHD		UCLA	
Wurst, John C.	Asst	Emory	7	V	PHD		Georgia	
Wyatt, Thomas	Lect	City Poly HK			PHD			
Wybo, M.	Asst	McGill Univ	9		PHD		Minn	1992
Wyman, John	Lect	Florida	3	I	DPS	89	Pace	1988
Wynekoop, Judy	Asst	Tx-S Antonio	9	Z	PHD			
Wynn, Pamela	Assoc	Bloomsburg	46		PHD		Tx-Arlin	8-89
Wyplosz, Charles	Prof	INSEAD			PHD		Harvard	
Wyse, Rodney E.	Retir	Cen St-Ohio	25	8-94	PHD	72	Ohio St	9-67
Wyvill, Maribeth	Asst	Marymount	5	NP	MA		Marymoun	1987
Xu, Li D.	Asst	Wright State	7	Z	PHD	86	Port St	1988
Xu, Susan H.	Assoc	Penn State	7	V	PHD		Rennsela	
Xue, Jue	Asst	Clark	7	U	PHD	91	Car Mel	

Name	Rank	Institution			Degree		School	
Xydias, Maira	LectA	Flinders Un	1	D	BCOM	92	Adelaide	3-93
Yacoub, Ignatius I.	Dean	LaSierra	25	EHN	PHD	76	Claremont	7-84
Yager, William F.	Assoc	Pacific Luth	35	IY	PHD	91	Oregon	1987
Yagiz, Omer			7	U	PHD	73	N Carol	
Yago, Glenn	Assoc	SUNY-Stony B	3	HI	PHD	80	Wiscon	1980
Yahalom, Raphel	Lect	Hebrew Univ			PHD		Cambridg	
Yahr, Michael A.	Asst	Robt Morris	12	BEDY	MBA	75	Pitt	9-87
Yalovsky, M.	Assoc	McGill Univ	9		PHD		McGill	1974
Yamamoto, Yoshitsugu	Prof	Univ Tsukuba	7	UV	DENG	78	Keio	9-80
Yammarino, Francis	Assoc	SUNY-Bingham	2	EFH	PHD	83	SUNY-Buf	1986
Yan, Aimin	Asst	Boston Univ			PHD	93	Penn St	
Yaney, Joseph P.	Prof	No Illinois	25	EQ	PHD	69	Michigan	
Yang, Chau-Jan	Prof	Nat Taiwan U	1	L	MBA	68	Rockches	1963
Yang, Chung-Sen	Prof	Nat Taiwan U	4	K	JSD	72	NYU	1989
Yang, Jiagin	Asst	North Dakota	7	UV	PHD	90	Geo St	8-90
Yang, Ping	Asst	Texas-Dallas	7	Z				
Yang, Zhuang	Asst	Fordham	25	EINY	PHD		Columbia	1990
Yannopoulos, P. Peter	Assoc	Brock Univ	7	U	PHD		Toronto	1983
Yanouzas, John N.	Prof	Connecticut	2	E	PHD	63	Penn St	1970
Yanowitz, Richard B.	Lect	Harvard	1	&				
Yantis, Betty	Prof	Nev-L Vegas	34	DI	PHD	72	Arkansas	1975
Yao, Dennis A.	Assoc	Pennsylvania	34	AIL	PHD	84	Stanford	7-83
Yasai, Masoud	Assoc	Wis-Milwauke	3	I	PHD	79	Cty Lond	1981
Yasin, Mahmoud M.	Asst	East Tenn St	79	UVXY	PHD	86	Clemson	1988
Yates, George	Asst	N Car-Ashvil	5	I	PHD	91	North Tx	8-91
Yates, Jere E.	C-Pr	Pepper-Malib	14	GJLP	PHD	68	Boston	1969
Yates, JoAnne	Asst	MIT			PHD			
Yates, Valerie	Asst	CS-L Angeles	45	N	PHD	92	Tx A&M	1990
Yauger, Charles	Asst	Arkansas St	32	EI	PHD	90	Miss	1977
Yavitz, Boris	Retir	Columbia	3	I	PHD	64	Columbia	1964
Yballe, Leodones	Asst	Norfolk St	24	EJ	PHD	91	Case Wes	7-90
Ye, Yinyu	Prof	Iowa	7	V	PHD	87	Stanford	1988
Yeargain, John W.	Prof	SE Louisiana	48	JKQY	JD	76	Loyola	8-79
Yearout, Robert D.	Asst	N Car-Ashvil	7	MUV	PHD	87	Kan St	8-87
Yeh, Hsiaw-Chan	Prof	Nat Taiwan U	7	V	PHD	83	Calif RS	1984
Yehle, Arthur L.	Prof	Georgia Col	6	FNS	PHD	67	U Miami	1984
Yen, Ching-Chang	Assoc	Nat Taiwan U	4	K	PHD	80	Michigan	1990
Yen, Vincent C.	Assoc	Wright State	9	Z	PHD	75	Ohio St	1980
Yen, Yueh-Chu	Assoc	Nat Taiwan U	7	V	BS	69	Nat Taiw	1969
Yeomans, J. Scott	Asst	York Univ	79	UZ	PHD		McMaster	
Yermish, Ira	Asst	St Joseph	79	ISUZ	PHD	75	Penn	1984
Yeung, Arthur	Assoc	San Fran St	2	HINY	PHD	90	Michigan	1992
Yeung, Jack K. W.	ALect	City Poly HK	1	DSZ	MSC	88	London	1990
Yilmaz, Mustafa R.	Assoc	Northeastern			PHD		JHopkins	
Yin, Jason ZS	Asst	Seton Hall			PHD	89	New York	
Yoffie, David B.	Prof	Harvard	4	L				
Yoo, S. M.	Asst	McGill Univ	8		PHD		Columbia	1993
Yoon, K. Paul	Prof	F Dick-Madis			PHD		KSU	
Yoon, Shinil	Asst	Kentucky St	93	UZ	DBA		Miss St	1993
Yoos, Charles J. II	Prof	USAF Academy	3	I	DBA		Colorado	
York, Kenneth M.	C-Ac	Oakland	52	N	PHD	86	Bowl Gr	1986
Yorks, Lyle	Prof	Eastern Conn			ABD		Columbia	1978
Yoshino, Michael Y.	C-Pr	Harvard	25	EN				
Herman C. Krannert Professor of Business Administration								
Yoshise, Akiko	Asst	Univ Tsukuba	7	V	DENG	90	Tokyo In	4-91
Yost, Edward B.	Assoc	Ohio Univ	25		PHD	87	Ohio St	
Yost, S. William	Adj	UCLA	3	I	DBA	68	Harvard	1990
Young, Carol E.	Assoc	Georgia St	9	Z	PHD		Ohio St	
Young, Clifford	C-Pr	CS-San Bern	1	A	DPA	88	S Calif	1989
Young, Corinne	Asst	Tampa	38	Y	PHD	93	Tulane	1993
Young, Dean Max	Prof	Baylor			PHD		Tx-Dallas	1980
Ben H. Williams Professor of Information Systems								
Young, Debbie	Prof	CS-Fresno	2	EF	MBA		Pitt St	1989
Young, Earl C.	Assoc	DePaul			PHD		Northwes	
Young, Greggry S.	Asst	N Carol St	36	IZYS	PHD	93	Maryland	1993
Young, J.	Asst	Mt St Vincen	25	POEF	MBA	83	Saint Ms	1987
Young, Jerald W.	Assoc	Florida	12	DEFP	PHD	74	Yale	1974
Young, John E.	Assoc	New Mexico	6	T	PHD	80	Kansas	
Young, Marilyn	Prof	Texas-Tyler	2	S	PHD	74	Arkansas	1974
Young, R. Kent	Assoc	St Fran Xav	2	O	PHD	68	Toronto	1976
Young, Richard O.	Lect	Carnegie Mel	3	&	PHD	89	Car Mel	1985
Young, Roslyn	Asst	Jersey City	4		JD		Brooklyn	
Young, Saul	Assoc	Dayton	7	UV	PHD	75	Stanford	1983
Young, Scott	C-Ac	Utah	7	UX	PHD	87	Geo St	1987
Youngblood, Stuart A.	Prof	Tx Christian			PHD	78	Purdue	1981
Neeley Professor								
Youngdahl, William	Asst	Ariz St-West	7	UW	PHD	92	S Calif	1992
Yourstone, Steven	Asst	New Mexico	7	U	PHD	88	U Wash	1987
Youssef, Mohamed A.	Asst	Ithaca	7	UI	PHD	91	CUNY	8-91
Yrle, Augusta C.	Assoc	New Orleans	59	BC	EDD	78	New Orl	8-72

Zuboff, Shoshana	Prof	Harvard	25	EN				
Zuckerman, Dror	Prof	Hebrew Univ			PHD		Cornell	
Zulian, Flora	SLect	Deakin-Burwo	19	Z	BCOM		Melbourn	
Zurada, Jozef	Asst	Louisville	9	Z	MS	73	Gdansk	5-87
Zurenko, John	C-Pr	Eastern Wash						
Zvi, Covaliu	Prof	George Wash	7	V				
Zviran, Moshe	Asst	Naval Postgr	9	Z	PHD	88	Tel Aviv	8-88
Zwerling, H.	Asst	McGill Univ	5		PHD		Wiscon	1988
Zydiak, James Lee	Assoc	Loyola-Chicg			PHD		Northwes	1988

NOTES

NOTES

NOTES

NOTES

NOTES

NOTES

NOTES

NOTES

NOTES

NOTES

NOTES